CONTRACT LAW

Selected Source Materials
Annotated

2020 EXPANDED Edition

STEVEN J. BURTON
John F. Murray Professor of Law Emeritus
University of Iowa

MELVIN A. EISENBERG
Jesse H. Choper Professor of Law Emeritus
University of California at Berkeley

The publisher is not engaged in rendering legal or other professional advice, and this publication is not a substitute for the advice of an attorney. If you require legal or other expert advice, you should seek the services of a competent attorney or other professional.

© 2019 LEG, Inc. d/b/a West Academic
© 2020 LEG, Inc. d/b/a West Academic
    444 Cedar Street, Suite 700
    St. Paul, MN 55101
    1-877-888-1330

Printed in the United States of America

ISBN: 978-1-64708-076-1

[No claim of copyright is made for official U.S. government statutes, rules or regulations.]

EDITORS' INTRODUCTION

Until the Twentieth Century, there were very few statutes governing contracts. Instead, judges made contract law through the common law process—on a case-by-case basis, bound by precedents. Today, much of contract law continues to be common law, but it is subject to many statutes, which are enacted by Congress and signed by the President or enacted by a state legislature and signed by a governor. There are four main drawbacks to the common law process insofar as contract law goes. First, judges normally are bound to follow precedent, which ties the law to the past. Consequently, the common law tends to change slowly. Second, because the common law is a matter of state law, the common law tends not to be uniform across different states. This diversity hampers transactions between parties in different states by making the law less predictable and contracting more costly. Third, courts cannot take the initiative to revise the common law; they can decide only the legal issues that litigating parties present to them. Fourth, also because courts only decide cases, they generally are not supposed to make laws by announcing new, broadly applicable rules. The common law consequently evolves on a piecemeal basis, by contrast with legislation. For these reasons, the common law can become outdated as contracting practices evolve. This, too, hampers transacting, makes contracting more costly, and also may fail to provide redress for new kinds of unfairness.

Several developments in the Twentieth Century led to the enactment of a number of important statutes and some landmark common law cases. Contracting between parties in different states increased. Mainly to promote greater uniformity, for example, the National Conference of Commissioners on Uniform State Laws (now called the "Uniform Law Commission") began proposing uniform laws for enactment by the states. The Uniform Commercial Code ("UCC") is among the most successful of their proposals. Upon enactment, it supplants the common law of contracts in a number of ways, including the law governing the sale of goods. Moreover, the American Law Institute ("ALI") developed and published the Restatement of Contracts (1932) and the Restatement (Second) of Contracts (1981). They state, and comment on, the common law in an effort to promote the law's uniformity, clarity, fairness, and relevance to current practices. Though the ALI is a private, non-profit organization that does not have the power to make law, both have been very influential with many courts. In addition, some contracts, such as those between merchants and consumers or employers and employees, were seen to be susceptible to unfairness. Several statutes and restatements, as well as a few landmark cases, responded with new laws and doctrines to correct for imbalances in the contracting process, contract terms, or both. Further, new technologies changed the contracting process in many ways, as by introducing contracting over the Internet. Statutes, restatements, and cases responded, again with new law. Finally, the globalization of the economy led to a burst of contracting across national borders. These contracts were governed by the laws of different nations, many of which differ fundamentally because they emerged from differing legal traditions. The lack of uniformity globally posed problems analogous to those that increased the costs of contracting between parties in different states of the United States. Several international conventions, and the UNIDROIT Principles of International Commercial Contracts, seek to ease these problems.

Contract law has changed considerably since the turn of the Twentieth Century. It will change more in the Twenty-First Century as change accelerates. This book includes legal documents that reflect the changes that already have occurred and several that may be harbingers of the future.

TABLE OF CONTENTS

Editors' Introduction		III
Tables of Comparison		VII
I.	Uniform Commercial Code Article 1, Article 2, Article 3 (excerpts), Article 9 (excerpts)	1
II.	Restatement (Second) of Contracts	131
III.	Restatement (Third) of Employment Law (excerpts) (2015)	641
IV.	Restatement (Third) of Restitution and Unjust Enrichment	645
V.	Electronic Contracting	649
	Uniform Electronic Transactions Act	650
	Electronic Signatures in Global and National Commerce Act	667
	American Law Institute Principles of the Law of Software Contracts	672
VI.	International Contract Law	689
	United Nations Convention on Contracts for the International Sale of Goods (1980)	690
	United Nations Convention on the Use of Electronic Communications in International Contracts	712
	The UNIDROIT Principles of International Commercial Contracts	717
	The Principles of European Contract Law	748
	European Community Council Directive 93/13/EEC of 5 April 1993 on Unfair Terms in Consumer Contracts	784
	Directive 2005/29/EC of the European Parliament and of the Council of 11 May 2005	789
	Directive 2011/83/EU of the European Parliament and of the Council of 25 October 2011	798
	Standard Contracts Law 5743–1982 (Israel)	806
VII.	Miscellaneous Statutes, Directives, and Administrative Regulations	809
	Magnuson-Moss Warranty Act	810
	Federal Trade Commission, Trade Regulation Rules: Rule Concerning Cooling-Off Period for Sales Made at Homes or at Certain Other Locations (1995)	820
	Federal Trade Commission, Trade Regulation Rules: Retail Food Store Advertising and Marketing Practices	824
	Federal Trade Commission, Trade Regulation Rules: Preservation of Consumers' Claims and Defenses	825
	Consumer Review Fairness Act of 2016	827
	Postal Reorganization Act: Mailing of Unordered Merchandise	831
	Bankruptcy Code	832
	Uniform Consumer Credit Code	834
	Truth in Lending: Regulation Z	836
VIII.	Sample Contracts	849
	American Institute of Architects Sample Form Contracts	850

TABLES OF COMPARISON BETWEEN UCC, C.I.S.G., UNIDROIT PRINCIPLES, AND RESTATEMENT (SECOND) OF CONTRACTS

Table 1

U.C.C.	C.I.S.G.	UNIDROIT Principles
General Provisions		
§ 1–101		
§ 1–102		Preamble
§ 1–103(a)	Art. 7	Arts. 1, 6
§ 1–103(b)	Art. 7(2)	
§ 1–104		
§ 1–105		
§ 1–106		
§ 1–107		
§ 1–201		
§ 1–201(b)(46)	Art. 13	
§ 1–202	Art. 24	Art. 1.9
§ 1–203		
§ 1–204		
§ 1–205		
§ 1–206		
§ 1–301	Art. 1(1)	
§ 1–302	Art. 6	Art. 1.4
§ 1–303	Art. 9	Art. 1.8
§ 1–304	Art. 7(1)	Art. 1.7
§ 1–305	Arts. 5, 74	
§ 1–306		
§ 1–307		
§ 1–308		
§ 1–309		
§ 1–310		
Sales		
§ 2–101		
§ 2–102	Arts. 1, 2, 3, 4	
§ 2–103		
§ 2–104		
§ 2–105		
§ 2–106		
§ 2–106(3)–(4)	Art. 81	
§ 2–106(4)		Arts. 7.3.1, 7.3.5

TABLES OF COMPARISON

U.C.C.	C.I.S.G.	UNIDROIT Principles
§ 2–107		
§ 2–201	Art. 11	Art. 1.2
§ 2–202	Art. 11	Arts. 1.2, 2.17
§ 2–203		Art. 1.7
§ 2–204	Art. 23	Arts. 2.1, 2.2
§ 2–204(3)		Art. 2.14
§ 2–205	Art. 16(2)	Art. 2.4(2)
§ 2–206		Art. 2.6
§ 2–206(1)(a)		Art. 18(1)
§ 2–206(1)(b)–(c)		Art. 18(3)
§ 2–207	Art. 19	Arts. 2.11, 2.12, 2.22
§ 2–208	Art. 8	Art. 4.3
§ 2–209	Art. 29	Art. 2.18
§ 2–210		
§ 2–301	Arts. 30, 53, 54, 59	
§ 2–302		
§ 2–303		
§ 2–304		
§ 2–305		
§ 2–305(1)	Art. 55	Art. 5.7
§ 2–306		
§ 2–307		Arts. 6.1.2, 6.1.4
§ 2–308	Art. 31	Arts. 1.10, 6.1.6
§ 2–309(1)	Art. 33	Art. 6.1.1
§ 2–310	Arts. 57, 58	
§ 2–311	Arts. 60, 65	
§ 2–312	Arts. 41–43	
§ 2–313		
§ 2–314	Arts. 35, 36, 66	
§ 2–315		
§ 2–316		
§ 2–317		
§ 2–318		
§ 2–319	Art. 32	
§ 2–320	Art. 32	
§ 2–321		
§ 2–322		
§ 2–323		
§ 2–324		
§ 2–325		
§ 2–326		
§ 2–327		

TABLES OF COMPARISON

U.C.C.	C.I.S.G.	UNIDROIT Principles
§ 2–328	Art. 2(b)	
§ 2–401		
§ 2–402		
§ 2–403		Art. 3.3(2)
§ 2–501		
§ 2–502		
§ 2–503		
§ 2–504		
§ 2–505		
§ 2–506		
§ 2–507		
§ 2–508	Arts. 37, 48	Art. 7.1.4
§ 2–509	Arts. 67, 68, 69	
§ 2–510	Art. 36	
§ 2–511		Art. 6.1.7
§ 2–512		
§ 2–513	Art. 38	
§ 2–514	Art. 34	
§ 2–515		
§ 2–601	Art. 45	
§ 2–602	Arts. 39, 49(2)	
§ 2–603	Arts. 85, 86, 88	
§ 2–604	Art. 87	
§ 2–605		
§ 2–606		
§ 2–607		
§ 2–608		
§ 2–609	Arts. 71–72	Art. 7.3.4
§ 2–610	Arts. 71–72	Art. 7.3.3
§ 2–611	Art. 73	
§ 2–612		
§ 2–613		
§ 2–614		
§ 2–615	Art. 79	Art. 7.1.7
§ 2–616		
§ 2–701		
§ 2–702		
§ 2–703	Art. 61	
§ 2–704		
§ 2–705		
§ 2–706		Art. 7.4.5
§ 2–707		

TABLES OF COMPARISON

U.C.C.	C.I.S.G.	UNIDROIT Principles
§ 2–708	Arts. 74, 77	Art. 7.4
§ 2–709	Art. 62	Art. 7.2.1
§ 2–710		Art. 7.4.2
§ 2–711		
§ 2–712	Art. 75	Art. 7.4.5
§ 2–713	Art. 74	Art. 7.4.6
§ 2–714	Art. 74	
§ 2–715		Arts. 7.4.2, 7.4.4
§ 2–716	Art. 46(1)–(2)	Arts. 7.2.1, 7.2.2
§ 2–717	Art. 50	
§ 2–718		Arts. 7.4.13, 7.3.6
§ 2–719		
§ 2–720		
§ 2–721		
§ 2–722		
§ 2–723	Art. 76	Art. 7.4.6(2)
§ 2–724		
§ 2–725		

Table 2

U.C.C.	Restatement (Second) of Contracts	UNIDROIT Principles
	§ 1	Art. 1.3
	§§ 7, 85	Arts. 3.12–3.16
	§ 12	Art. 3.1
	§ 17	Art. 3.2
§ 2–204	§§ 19, 22	Art. 2.1
§ 2–204	§ 24	Art. 2.2
	§§ 26–27; cf. § 205	
	§ 27	Art. 2.13
§ 2–204(3)	§§ 33–34, 204	Art. 2.14
	§§ 35, 36(1)(c), 42, 43, 46	Arts. 2.3(2), 2.4(1)
	§§ 36(1)(b), 41	Arts. 2.7–2.8
	§§ 38, 40 Art.	Art. 2.5, 2.10
§ 2–207	§§ 39, 59	Art. 2.11(1)
§ 2–206	§§ 50, 53, 54–56, 69	Art. 2.6(1)
§ 2–206	§ 54	Art. 2.6(3)
§ 2–207	§ 61	Art. 2.11(2)
§ 1–207	§§ 63, 66–70	Arts. 1.9(2)–(3), 2.6(2)
§ 2–206	§§ 63, 66–70	Art. 2.6(2)
	§§ 63, 66–67, 70	Art. 2.9
	§§ 64–65	Art. 1.9(1)

TABLES OF COMPARISON

U.C.C.	Restatement (Second) of Contracts	UNIDROIT Principles
	§ 77	Art. 7.1.6
§ 2–201	Chapter 5 (§§ 110–150)	Art. 1.2
§ 2–209	§§ 148–150	Art. 2.18
	§ 151	Art. 3.4
	§§ 152–154, 201	Art. 3.5
	§ 152(2)	Art. 3.7
	§ 154(c)	Art. 3.6
	§§ 159–164	Art. 3.8
	§ 164	Art. 3.11
	§§ 175–176	Art. 3.9
	§ 177, § 79 (see Comment e)	Art. 3.10
§ 2–208	§§ 202–203	Arts. 4.1–4.4
	§ 202(1)	Art. 5.2(a)
	§§ 202(4)–(5), 222, 223	Art. 5.2(b)
	§ 203(d)	Art. 2.21
§§ 2–203, 1–102(3)	§ 205	Art. 1.7
	§ 203(a)	Art. 4.5
	§ 204	Art. 4.8
§ 2–305(1)	§ 204	Art. 5.7
	§ 205	Art. 5.2(c)–(d)
	§ 205	Art. 5.3
	§ 206	Art. 4.6
§ 2–202	§§ 209–210, 212–215	Art. 2.17
	§ 211(1)–(2)	Art. 2.19
	§ 211(3)	Art. 2.20
§ 2–207	§ 216	Art. 2.12
§ 1–303	§§ 219–223	Art. 1.8
	§ 230(2)(a)	Art. 7.1.2
§ 2–309(1)	§§ 233–234	Art. 6.1.1
§ 2–307	§ 233	Art. 6.1.2
§ 2–307	§ 234	Art. 6.1.4
	§ 235(2)	Art. 7.1.1
	§ 238	Art. 7.1.3
§ 2–106(4)	§ 241	Art. 7.3.1
	§ 240	Art. 6.1.3
§ 2–508	§ 241(d)	Art. 7.1.4
	§§ 241(d), 242	Art. 7.1.5
§ 2–610	§ 250	Art. 7.3.3
§ 2–609	§ 251	Art. 7.3.4
	§§ 261, 264	Art. 6.1.17
	§§ 261, 265–266	Arts. 6.2.1–6.2.2
§ 2–615	§§ 261–271	Art. 7.1.7

TABLES OF COMPARISON

U.C.C.	Restatement (Second) of Contracts	UNIDROIT Principles
	§ 266	Art. 3.3(1)
	§§ 267–268	Art. 6.2.3
§ 2–716(1)–(2)	§ 345(b)–(c)	Arts. 7.2.2–7.2.3
	§ 346	Art. 7.4.1
§ 2–708 (2), § 2–715	§ 347	Art. 7.4.2(1)
	§ 350	Arts. 7.4.7–7.4.8
§ 2–715	§ 351	Art. 7.4.4
	§ 352	Art. 7.4.3
§ 2–715	§§ 353, 355	Art. 7.4.2(2)
	§ 356	Art. 7.4.13
§ 2–718(2)	§§ 370–377	Art. 7.3.6
	§ 376	Art. 3.17

CONTRACT LAW

Selected Source Materials
Annotated
2020 EXPANDED Edition

PART I

UNIFORM COMMERCIAL CODE ARTICLE 1, ARTICLE 2, ARTICLE 3 (EXCERPTS), ARTICLE 9 (EXCERPTS)

UNIFORM COMMERCIAL CODE

[The National Conference of Commissioners on Uniform State Laws (now called the "Uniform Law Commission") and the American Law Institute ("ALI") initially proposed the Uniform Commercial Code ("UCC") in 1952. Upon enactment by a state, the UCC supplants the state's common law when that common law conflicts with the statute.

[In recent years, the Uniform Law Commission and the ALI have proposed various revisions and amendments to the UCC, many of which have been widely enacted by the states. The UCC now consists of ten main "Articles" on such topics as sales of goods, leases of goods, bank deposits and collections, funds transfers, letters of credit, and secured transactions. For a basic course in contracts, the most important Articles are Article 1, which contains general provisions that apply to any transaction governed by any other Article, and Article 2, which contains rules and standards that apply to transactions in goods. As of May 1, 2012, the version of Article 1 below had been enacted by 41 states, and Article 2 had been enacted by 49 states. Parts of Article 3, concerning commercial paper, and Article 9, concerning secured transactions, are also important. Accordingly, Part I of this pamphlet contains the entirety of Articles 1 and 2, and excerpts from Articles 3 and 9. In addition, Part II contains excerpts from an earlier version of Article 9, because though all 50 states have enacted a revision of Article 9, most of the cases addressing the relevant issues were decided before the revised version was proposed.

[Note that UCC § 1–201 contains a number of definitions that establish the meanings of many terms used in the statute. Sections 2–103 to 2–106 contain more definitions, which establish the meanings of many terms used in Article 2. When a statute defines a term, for the purposes of interpreting and applying that statute the term has the meaning as defined, not any other meaning. Note also that many of the Official Comments to specific sections include "definitional cross references" to definitions of terms used in that section but defined in another. In principle, this statute, like others, should be interpreted in accordance with these definitions as well, so as to further its purposes.]

ARTICLE 1

GENERAL PROVISIONS

In 2018 Congress enacted the National Residential Mortgage Note Repository Act. Subsequently, several Articles of the UCC, including Article 1, were amended to accommodate the Act. Although Article 1 generally governs contracts, the Act and the amendments, which are very complex, essentially concern property law and the law of secured transactions. Accordingly, the amendments have for the most part been elided from Article 1 as it appears in this book. The elisions are indicated by ellipses of three dots.

PART 1. GENERAL PROVISIONS

Sec.
- 1–101. Short Titles.
- 1–102. Scope of Article.
- 1–103. Construction of [Uniform Commercial Code] to Promote Its Purposes and Policies; Applicability of Supplemental Principles of Law.
- 1–104. Construction Against Implied Repeal.
- 1–105. Severability.
- 1–106. Use of Singular and Plural; Gender.
- 1–107. Section Captions.
- 1–108. Relation to Electronic Signatures in Global and National Commerce Act.

PART 2. GENERAL DEFINITIONS AND PRINCIPLES OF INTERPRETATION

- 1–201. General Definitions.
- 1–202. Notice; Knowledge.
- 1–203. Lease Distinguished From Security Interest.
- 1–204. Value.
- 1–205. Reasonable Time; Seasonableness.
- 1–206. Presumptions.

PART 3. TERRITORIAL APPLICABILITY AND GENERAL RULES

- 1–301. Territorial Applicability; Parties' Power to Choose Applicable Law [as amended in 2008].
- 1–302. Variation by Agreement.
- 1–303. Course of Performance, Course of Dealing, and Usage of Trade.
- 1–304. Obligation of Good Faith.
- 1–305. Remedies to Be Liberally Administered.
- 1–306. Waiver or Renunciation of Claim or Right After Breach.
- 1–307. Prima Facie Evidence by Third-Party Documents.
- 1–308. Performance or Acceptance Under Reservation of Rights.
- 1–309. Option to Accelerate at Will.
- 1–310. Subordinated Obligations.

PART 1

GENERAL PROVISIONS

§ 1–101. Short Titles.

(a) This [Act] may be cited as the Uniform Commercial Code.

(b) This article may be cited as Uniform Commercial Code—General Provisions.

§ 1–102. Scope of Article.

This article applies to a transaction to the extent that it is governed by another article of [the Uniform Commercial Code].

§ 1–103. Construction of [Uniform Commercial Code] to Promote Its Purposes and Policies; Applicability of Supplemental Principles of Law.

(a) [The Uniform Commercial Code] must be liberally construed and applied to promote its underlying purposes and policies, which are:

(1) to simplify, clarify, and modernize the law governing commercial transactions;

(2) to permit the continued expansion of commercial practices through custom, usage, and agreement of the parties, and

(3) to make uniform the law among the various jurisdictions.

(b) Unless displaced by the particular provisions of [the Uniform Commercial Code], the principles of law and equity, including the law merchant and the law relative to capacity to contract, principal and agent, estoppel, fraud, misrepresentation, duress, coercion, mistake, bankruptcy, and other validating or invalidating cause supplement its provisions.

§ 1–104. Construction Against Implied Repeal.

[The Uniform Commercial Code] being a general act intended as a unified coverage of its subject matter, no part of it shall be deemed to be impliedly repealed by subsequent legislation if such construction can reasonably be avoided.

§ 1–105. Severability.

If any provision or clause of [the Uniform Commercial Code] or its application to any person or circumstance is held invalid, the invalidity does not affect other provisions or applications of [the Uniform Commercial Code] which can be given effect without the invalid provision or application, and to this end the provisions of [the Uniform Commercial Code] are severable.

§ 1–106. Use of Singular and Plural; Gender.

In [the Uniform Commercial Code], unless the statutory context otherwise requires:

(1) words in the singular number include the plural, and those in the plural include the singular; and

(2) words of any gender also refer to any other gender.

§ 1–107. Section Captions.

Section captions are part of [the Uniform Commercial Code].

§ 1–108. Relation to Electronic Signatures in Global and National Commerce Act.

This [Act] modifies, limits, and supersedes the federal Electronic Signatures in Global and National Commerce Act, (15 U.S.C. Section 7001, et. seq.) but does not modify, limit, or supersede Section 101(c) of that act (15 U.S.C. Section 7001(c)) or authorize electronic delivery of any of the notices described in Section 103 (b) of that act (15 U.S.C. Section 103(b)).

PART 2

GENERAL DEFINITIONS AND PRINCIPLES OF INTERPRETATION

§ 1–201. General Definitions.

(a) Unless the context otherwise requires, words or phrases defined in this section, or in the additional definitions contained in other articles of [the Uniform Commercial Code] that apply to particular articles or parts thereof, have the meanings stated.

(b) Subject to definitions contained in other [articles] of [the Uniform Commercial Code] that apply to particular [articles] or [parts] thereof:

(1) "Action", in the sense of a judicial proceeding, includes recoupment, counterclaim, set-off, suit in equity, and any other proceeding in which rights are determined.

(2) "Aggrieved party" means a party entitled to pursue a remedy.

(3) "Agreement", as distinguished from "contract", means the bargain of the parties in fact, as found in their language or inferred from other circumstances, including course of performance, course of dealing, or usage of trade as provided in Section 1–303.

(4) "Bank" means a person engaged in the business of banking and includes a savings bank, savings and loan association, credit union, and trust company.

(5) "Bearer" means a person in control of a negotiable electronic document of title or a person in possession of a negotiable instrument, negotiable tangible document of title or certificated security that is payable to bearer or indorsed in blank.

(6) "Bill of lading" means a document evidencing the receipt of goods for shipment issued by a person engaged in the business of transporting or forwarding goods.

(7) "Branch" includes a separately incorporated foreign branch of a bank.

(8) "Burden of establishing" a fact means the burden of persuading the trier of fact that the existence of the fact is more probable than its nonexistence.

(9) "Buyer in ordinary course of business" means a person that buys goods in good faith, without knowledge that the sale violates the rights of another person in the goods, and in the ordinary course from a person, other than a pawnbroker, in the business of selling goods of that kind. A person buys goods in the ordinary course if the sale to the person comports with the usual or customary practices in the kind of business in which the seller is engaged or with the seller's own usual or customary practices. A person that sells oil, gas, or other minerals at the wellhead or minehead is a person in the business of selling goods of that kind. A buyer in ordinary course of business may buy for cash, by exchange of other property, or on secured or unsecured credit, and may acquire goods or documents of title under a preexisting contract for sale. Only a buyer that takes possession of the goods or has a right to recover the goods from the seller under Article 2 may be a buyer in ordinary course of business. "Buyer in ordinary course of business" does not include a person that acquires goods in a transfer in bulk or as security for or in total or partial satisfaction of a money debt.

(10) "Conspicuous", with reference to a term, means so written, displayed, or presented that a reasonable person against which it is to operate ought to have noticed it. Whether a term is "conspicuous" or not is a decision for the court. Conspicuous terms include the following:

(A) a heading in capitals equal to or greater in size than the surrounding text, or in contrasting type, font, or color to the surrounding text of the same or lesser size; and

(B) language in the body of a record or display in larger type than the surrounding text, or in contrasting type, font, or color to the surrounding text of the same size, or set off from surrounding text of the same size by symbols or other marks that call attention to the language.

(11) "Consumer" means an individual who enters into a transaction primarily for personal, family, or household purposes

(12) "Contract", as distinguished from "agreement", means the total legal obligation that results from the parties' agreement as determined by [the Uniform Commercial Code] as supplemented by any other applicable laws.

(13) "Creditor" includes a general creditor, a secured creditor, a lien creditor, and any representative of creditors, including an assignee for the benefit of creditors, a trustee in bankruptcy, a receiver in equity, and an executor or administrator of an insolvent debtor's or assignor's estate.

(14) "Defendant" includes a person in the position of defendant in a counterclaim, cross-claim, or third-party claim.

(15) "Delivery", with respect to an instrument, document of title, or chattel paper, means voluntary transfer of possession.

(16) "Document of title" includes bill of lading, dock warrant, dock receipt, warehouse receipt or order for the delivery of goods, and also any other document which in the regular course of business or financing is treated as adequately evidencing that the person in possession of it is entitled to receive, hold, and dispose of the document and the goods it covers. To be a document of title, a document must purport to be issued by or addressed to a bailee and purport to cover goods in the bailee's possession which are either identified or are fungible portions of an identified mass.

(17) "Fault" means a default, breach, or wrongful act or omission.

(18) "Fungible goods" means:

(A) goods of which any unit, by nature or usage of trade, is the equivalent of any other like unit; or

(B) goods that by agreement are treated as equivalent.

(19) "Genuine" means free of forgery or counterfeiting.

(20) "Good faith," except as otherwise provided in Article 5, means honesty in fact and the observance of reasonable commercial standards of fair dealing.

(21) "Holder" means, with respect to:

(A) a negotiable instrument other than an electronic mortgage note, the person in possession if the negotiable instrument is payable either to bearer or to an identified person that is the person in possession;

(B) a negotiable tangible document of title, the person in possession if the goods are deliverable either to bearer or to the order of the person in possession;

(C) a negotiable electronic document of title, the person in control. . . .

(22) "Insolvency proceeding" includes an assignment for the benefit of creditors or other proceeding intended to liquidate or rehabilitate the estate of the person involved.

(23) "Insolvent" means:

(A) having generally ceased to pay debts in the ordinary course of business other than as a result of bona fide dispute;

(B) being unable to pay debts as they become due; or

(C) being insolvent within the meaning of federal bankruptcy law.

(24) "Money" means a medium of exchange currently authorized or adopted by a domestic or foreign government. The term includes a monetary unit of account established by an intergovernmental organization or by agreement between two or more countries.

(25) "Organization" means a person other than an individual.

(26) "Party", as distinguished from "third party", means a person that has engaged in a transaction or made an agreement subject to [the Uniform Commercial Code].

(27) "Person" means an individual, corporation, business trust, estate, trust, partnership, limited liability company, association, joint venture, government, governmental subdivision, agency, or instrumentality, public corporation, or any other legal or commercial entity.

(28) "Present value" means the amount as of a date certain of one or more sums payable in the future, discounted to the date certain by use of either an interest rate specified by the parties if that rate is not manifestly unreasonable at the time the transaction is entered into or, if an interest rate is not so specified, a commercially reasonable rate that takes into account the facts and circumstances at the time the transaction is entered into.

(29) "Purchase" means taking by sale, lease, discount, negotiation, mortgage, pledge, lien, security interest, issue or reissue, gift, or any other voluntary transaction creating an interest in property.

(30) "Purchaser" means a person that takes by purchase.

(31) "Record" means information that is inscribed on a tangible medium or that is stored in an electronic or other medium and is retrievable in perceivable form.

(32) "Remedy" means any remedial right to which an aggrieved party is entitled with or without resort to a tribunal.

(33) "Representative" means a person empowered to act for another, including an agent, an officer of a corporation or association, and a trustee, executor, or administrator of an estate.

(34) "Right" includes remedy.

(35) "Security interest" means an interest in personal property or fixtures which secures payment or performance of an obligation. "Security interest" includes any interest of a consignor and a buyer of accounts, chattel paper, a payment intangible, or a promissory note in a transaction that is subject to Article 9. "Security interest" does not include the special property interest of a buyer of goods on identification of those goods to a contract for sale under Section 2–401, but a buyer may also acquire a "security interest" by complying with Article 9. Except as otherwise provided in Section 2–505, the right of a seller or lessor of goods under Article 2 or 2A to retain or acquire possession of the goods is not a "security interest", but a seller or lessor may also acquire a "security interest" by complying with Article 9. The retention or reservation of title by a seller of goods notwithstanding shipment or delivery to the buyer under Section 2–401 is limited in effect to a reservation of a "security interest." Whether a transaction in the form of a lease creates a "security interest" is determined. pursuant to Section 1–203.

(36) "Send" in connection with a writing, record, or notice means:

(A) to deposit in the mail or deliver for transmission by any other usual means of communication with postage or cost of transmission provided for and properly addressed and, in the case of an instrument, to an address specified thereon or otherwise agreed, or if there be none to any address reasonable under the circumstances; or

(B) in any other way to cause to be received any record or notice within the time it would have arrived if properly sent.

(37) "Signed" includes using any symbol executed or adopted with present intention to adopt or accept a writing.

(38) "State" means a State of the United States, the District of Columbia, Puerto Rico, the United States Virgin Islands, or any territory or insular possession subject to the jurisdiction of the United States.

(39) "Surety" includes a guarantor or other secondary obligor.

(40) "Term" means a portion of an agreement that relates to a particular matter.

(41) "Unauthorized signature" means a signature made without actual, implied, or apparent authority. The term includes a forgery.

(42) "Warehouse receipt" means a receipt issued by a person engaged in the business of storing goods for hire.

(43) "Writing" includes printing, typewriting, or any other intentional reduction to tangible form. "Written" has a corresponding meaning. . . .

Official Comments

. . .

10. "Conspicuous." Derived from former Section 1–201(10). This definition states the general standard that to be conspicuous a term ought to be noticed by a reasonable person. Whether a term is conspicuous is an issue for the court. Subparagraphs (A) and (B) set out several methods for making a term conspicuous. Requiring that a term be conspicuous blends a notice function (the term ought to be noticed) and a planning function (giving guidance to the party relying on the term regarding how that result can be achieved). Although these paragraphs indicate some of the methods for making a term attention-calling, the test is whether attention can reasonably be expected to be called to it. The statutory language should not be construed to permit a result that is inconsistent with that test. . . .

20. "Good faith." Former Section 1–201(19) defined "good faith" simply as honesty in fact; the definition contained no element of commercial reasonableness. Initially, that definition applied throughout the Code with only one exception. Former Section 2–103(1)(b) provided that "in this Article . . . good faith in the case of a merchant means honesty in fact and the observance of reasonable commercial standards of fair dealing in the trade." This alternative definition was limited in applicability in three ways. First, it applied only to transactions within the scope of Article 2. Second, it applied only to merchants. Third, strictly construed it applied only to uses of the phrase "good faith" in Article 2; thus, so construed it would not define "good faith" for its most important use—the obligation of good faith imposed by former Section 1–203.

Over time, however, amendments to the Uniform Commercial Code brought the Article 2 merchant concept of good faith (subjective honesty and objective commercial reasonableness) into other Articles. First, Article 2A explicitly incorporated the Article 2 standard. See Section 2A–103(7). Then, other Articles broadened the applicability of that standard by adopting it for all parties rather than just for merchants. See, e.g., Sections 3–103(a)(4), 4A–105(a)(6), 8–102(a)(10), and 9–102(a)(43). All of these definitions are comprised of two elements—honesty in fact and the observance of reasonable commercial standards of fair dealing. Only revised Article 5 defines "good faith" solely in terms of subjective honesty, and only Article 6 and Article 7 are without definitions of good faith. (It should be noted that, while revised Article 6 did not define good faith, Comment 2 to revised Section 6–102 states that "this Article adopts the definition of 'good faith' in Article 1 in all cases, even when the buyer is a merchant.") Given these developments, it is appropriate to move the broader definition of "good faith" to Article 1—of course, this definition is subject to the applicability of the narrower definition in revised Article 5. . . .

§ 1–202. Notice; Knowledge.

(a) Subject to subsection (f), a person has "notice" of a fact if the person:

(1) has actual knowledge of it;

(2) has received a notice or notification of it; or

(3) from all the facts and circumstances known to the person at the time in question, has reason to know that it exists.

(b) "Knowledge" means actual knowledge. "Knows" has a corresponding meaning.

(c) "Discover", "learn", or words of similar import refer to knowledge rather than to reason to know.

(d) A person "notifies" or "gives" a notice or notification to another person by taking such steps as may be reasonably required to inform the other person in ordinary course, whether or not the other person actually comes to know of it.

(e) Subject to subsection (f), a person "receives" a notice or notification when:

(1) it comes to that person's attention; or

(2) it is duly delivered in a form reasonable under the circumstances at the place of business through which the contract was made or at another location held out by that person as the place for receipt of such communications.

(f) Notice, knowledge, or a notice or notification received by an organization is effective for a particular transaction from the time it is brought to the attention of the individual conducting that transaction and, in any event, from the time it would have been brought to the individual's attention if the organization had exercised due diligence. An organization exercises due diligence if it maintains reasonable routines for communicating significant information to the person conducting the transaction and there is reasonable compliance with the routines. Due diligence does not require an individual acting for the organization to communicate information unless the communication is part of the individual's regular duties or the individual has reason to know of the transaction and that the transaction would be materially affected by the information.

§ 1–203. Lease Distinguished From Security Interest.

(a) Whether a transaction in the form of a lease creates a lease or security interest is determined by the facts of each case.

(b) A transaction in the form of a lease creates a security interest if the consideration that the lessee is to pay the lessor for the right to possession and use of the goods is an obligation for the term of the lease and is not subject to go termination by the lessee, and:

(1) the original term of the lease is equal to or greater than the remaining economic life of the goods;

(2) the lessee is bound to renew the lease for the remaining economic life of the goods or is bound to become the owner of the goods;

(3) the lessee has an option to renew the lease for the remaining economic life of the goods for no additional consideration or for nominal additional consideration upon compliance with the lease agreement; or

(4) the lessee has an option to become the owner of the goods for no additional consideration or for nominal additional consideration upon compliance with the lease agreement.

(c) A transaction in the form of a lease does not create a security interest merely because:

(1) the present value of the consideration the lessee is obligated to pay the lessor for the right to possession and use of the goods is substantially equal to or is greater than the fair market value of the goods at the time the lease is entered into;

(2) the lessee assumes risk of loss of the goods;

(3) the lessee agrees to pay, with respect to the goods, taxes, insurance, filing, recording, or registration fees, or service or maintenance costs;

(4) the lessee has an option to renew the lease or to become the owner of the goods;

(5) the lessee has an option to renew the lease for a fixed rent that is equal to or greater than the reasonably predictable fair market rent for the use of the goods for the term of the renewal at the time the option is to be performed; or

(6) the lessee has an option to become the owner of the goods for a fixed price that is equal to or greater than the reasonably predictable fair market value of the goods at the time the option is to be performed.

(d) Additional consideration is nominal if it is less than the lessee's reasonably predictable cost of performing under the lease agreement if the option is not exercised. Additional consideration is not nominal if

(1) when the option to renew the lease is granted to the lessee, the rent is stated to be the fair market rent for the use of the goods for the term of the renewal determined at the time the option is to be performed; or

(2) when the option to become the owner of the goods is granted to the lessee, the price is stated to be the fair market value of the goods determined at the time the option is to be performed.

(e) The "remaining economic life of the goods" and "reasonably predictable" fair market rent, fair market value, or cost of performing under the lease agreement must be determined with reference to the facts and circumstances at the time the transaction is entered into.

§ 1–204. Value.

Except as otherwise provided in Articles 3, 4, [and] 5, [and 6], a person gives value for rights if the person acquires them:

(1) in return for a binding commitment to extend credit or for the extension of immediately available credit, whether or not drawn upon and whether or not a charge-back is provided for in the event of difficulties in collection;

(2) as security for, or in total or partial satisfaction of, a preexisting claim;

(3) by accepting delivery under a preexisting contract for purchase; or

(4) in return for any consideration sufficient to support a simple contract.

§ 1–205. Reasonable Time; Seasonableness.

(a) Whether a time for taking an action required by [the Uniform Commercial Code] is reasonable depends on the nature, purpose, and circumstances of the action.

(b) An action is taken seasonably if it is taken at or within the time agreed or, if no time is agreed, at or within a reasonable time.

§ 1-206. Presumptions.

Whenever [the Uniform Commercial Code] creates a "presumption" with respect to a fact, or provides that a fact is "presumed," the trier of fact must find the existence of the fact unless and until evidence is introduced that supports a finding of its nonexistence.

Legislative Note: Former Section 1-206, a Statute of Frauds for sales of "kinds of personal property not otherwise covered," has been deleted, The other articles of the Uniform Commercial Code make individual determinations as to requirements for memorializing transactions within their scope, so that the primary effect of former Section 1-206 was to impose a writing requirement on sales transactions not otherwise governed by the UCC. Deletion of former Section 1-206 does not constitute a recommendation to legislatures as to whether such sales transactions should be covered by a Statute of Frauds; rather, it reflects a determination that there is no need for uniform commercial law to resolve that issue.

PART 3

TERRITORIAL APPLICABILITY AND GENERAL RULES

§ 1-301. Territorial Applicability; Parties' Power to Choose Applicable Law [as amended in 2008].

(a) Except as otherwise provided in this section, when a transaction bears a reasonable relation to this state and also to another state or nation the parties may agree that the law either of this state or of such other state or nation shall govern their rights and duties.

(b) In the absence of an agreement effective under subsection (a), and except as provided in subsection (c), [the Uniform Commercial Code] applies to transactions bearing an appropriate relation to this state.

(c) If one of the following provisions of [the Uniform Commercial Code] specifies the applicable law, that provision governs and a contrary agreement is effective only to the extent permitted by the law so specified:

    (1) Section 2-402.

. . .

§ 1-302. Variation by Agreement.

(a) Except as otherwise provided in subsection (b) or elsewhere in [the Uniform Commercial Code], the effect of provisions of [the Uniform Commercial Code] may be varied by agreement.

(b) The obligations of good faith, diligence, reasonableness, and care prescribed by [the Uniform Commercial Code] may not be disclaimed by agreement. The parties, by agreement, may determine the standards by which the performance of those obligations is to be measured if those standards are not manifestly unreasonable. Whenever [the Uniform Commercial Code] requires an action to be taken within a reasonable time, a time that is not manifestly unreasonable may be fixed by agreement.

(c) The presence in certain provisions of [the Uniform Commercial Code] of the phrase "unless otherwise agreed", or words of similar import, does not imply that the effect of other provisions may not be varied by agreement under this section.

Official Comments

...

1. Subsection (a) states affirmatively at the outset that freedom of contract is a principle of the Uniform Commercial Code: "the effect" of its provisions may be varied by "agreement." The meaning, of the statute itself must be found in its text, including its definitions, and in appropriate extrinsic aids; it cannot be varied by agreement. But the Uniform Commercial Code seeks to avoid the type of interference with evolutionary growth found in pre-Code cases such as Manhattan Co. v. Morgan, 242 N.Y. 38, 150 N.E. 594 (1926). Thus, private parties cannot make an instrument negotiable within the meaning of Article 3 except as provided in Section 3–104; nor can they change the meaning of such terms as "bona fide purchaser," "holder in due course," or "due negotiation," as used in the Uniform Commercial Code. But an agreement can change the legal consequences that would otherwise flow from the provisions of the Commercial Code. "Agreement" here includes the effect given to course of dealing, usage of trade and course of performance by Sections 1–201 and 1–303; the effect of an agreement on the rights of third parties is left to specific provisions of the Uniform Commercial Code and to supplementary principles applicable under Section 1–103. The rights of third parties under Section 9–317 when a security interest is unperfected, for example, cannot be destroyed by a clause in the security agreement.

This principle of freedom of contract is subject to specific exceptions found elsewhere in the Uniform Commercial Code and to the general exception stated here. The specific exceptions vary in explicitness: the statute of frauds found in Section 2–201, for example, does not explicitly preclude oral waiver of the requirement of a writing, but a fair reading denies enforcement to such a waiver as part of the "contract" made unenforceable; Section 9–602, on the other hand, is a quite explicit limitation on freedom of contract. Under the exception for "the obligations of good faith, diligence, reasonableness and care prescribed by [the Uniform Commercial Code]," provisions of the Uniform Commercial Code prescribing such obligations are not to be disclaimed. However, the section also recognizes the prevailing practice of having agreements set forth standards by which due diligence is measured and explicitly provides that, in the absence of a showing that the standards manifestly are unreasonable, the agreement controls. In this connection, Section 1–303 incorporating into the agreement prior course of dealing and usages of trade is of particular importance.

Subsection (b) also recognizes that nothing is stronger evidence of a reasonable time than the fixing of such time by a fair agreement between the parties. However, provision is made for disregarding a clause which whether by inadvertence or overreaching fixes a time so unreasonable that it amounts to eliminating all remedy under the contract. The parties are not required to fix the most reasonable time but may fix any time which is not obviously unfair as judged by the time of contracting.

2. An agreement that varies the effect of provisions of the Uniform Commercial Code may do so by stating the rules that will govern, in lieu of the provisions varied. Alternatively, the parties may vary the affect of such provisions by stating that their relationship will be governed by recognized bodies of rules or principles applicable to commercial transactions. Such bodies of rules or principles may include, for example, those that are promulgated by intergovernmental authorities such as UNCITRAL or UNIDROIT (see, e.g., UNIDROIT Principles of International Commercial Contracts), or non-legal codes such as trade codes.

3. Subsection (c) is intended to make it clear that, as a matter of drafting phrases such as "unless otherwise agreed" have been used to avoid controversy as to whether the subject matter of a particular section does or does not fall within the exceptions to subsection (b), but absence of such words contains no negative implication since under subsection (b) the general and residual rule is that the effect of all provisions of the Uniform Commercial Code may be varied by agreement.

§ 1–303. Course of Performance, Course of Dealing, and Usage of Trade.

(a) A "course of performance" is a sequence of conduct between the parties to a particular transaction that exists if

(1) the agreement of the parties with respect to the transaction involves repeated occasions for performance by a party; and

(2) the other party, with knowledge of the nature of the performance and opportunity for objection to it, accepts the performance or acquiesces in it without objection.

(b) A "course of dealing" is a sequence of conduct concerning previous transactions between the parties to a particular transaction that is fairly to be regarded as establishing a common basis of understanding for interpreting their expressions and other conduct.

(c) A "usage of trade" is any practice or method of dealing having such regularity of observance in a place, vocation, or trade as to justify an expectation that it will be observed with respect to the transaction in question. The existence and scope of such a usage must be proved as facts. If it is established that such a usage is embodied in a trade code or similar record, the interpretation of the record is a question of law.

(d) A course of performance or course of dealing between the parties or usage of trade in the vocation or trade in which they are engaged or of which they are or should be aware is relevant in ascertaining, the meaning of the parties' agreement, may give particular meaning to specific terms of the agreement, and may supplement or qualify the terms of the agreement. A usage of trade applicable in the place in which part of the performance under the agreement is to occur may be so utilized as to that part of the performance.

(e) Except as otherwise provided in subsection (f), the express terms of an agreement and any applicable course of performance, course of dealing, or usage of trade must be construed whenever reasonable as consistent with each other. If such a construction is unreasonable:

(1) express terms prevail over course of performance, course of dealing, and usage of trade;

(2) course of performance prevails over course of dealing and usage of trade; and

(3) course of dealing prevails over usage of trade.

(f) Subject to Section 2–209, a course of performance is relevant to show a waiver or modification of any term inconsistent with the course of performance.

(g) Evidence of a relevant usage of trade offered by one party is not admissible unless that party has given the other party notice that the court finds sufficient to prevent unfair surprise to the other party.

Official Comment

. . .

Changes from former law. This section integrates the "course of performance" concept from Articles 2 and 2A into the principles of former Section 1–205, which deals with course of dealing and usage of trade. In so doing, the section slightly modifies the articulation of the course of performance rules to fit more comfortably with the approach and structure of former Section 1–205. There are also slight modifications to be more consistent with the definition of "agreement" in former Section 1–201(3). . . .

1. The Uniform Commercial Code rejects both the "lay-dictionary" and the "conveyancer's" reading of a commercial agreement. Instead the meaning of the agreement of the parties is to be determined by the language used by them and by their action, read and interpreted in the light of commercial practices and other surrounding circumstances. The measure and background for interpretation are set by the commercial context, which may explain and supplement even the language of a formal or final writing.

2. "Course of dealing," as defined in subsection (b), is restricted, literally, to a sequence of conduct between the parties previous to the agreement. A sequence of conduct after or under the agreement, however, is a "course of performance." "Course of dealing" may enter the agreement either by explicit provisions of the agreement or by tacit recognition.

3. The Uniform Commercial Code deals with "usage of trade" as a factor in reaching the commercial meaning of the agreement that the parties have made. The language used is to be interpreted as meaning what it may fairly be expected to mean to parties involved in the particular commercial transaction in a given locality or in a given vocation or trade. By adopting in this context the term "usage of trade," the

Uniform Commercial Code expresses its intent to reject those cases which see evidence of "custom" as representing an effort to displace or negate "established rules of law." A distinction is to be drawn between mandatory rules of law such as the Statute of Frauds provisions of Article. 2 on Sales whose very office is to control and restrict the actions of the parties, and which cannot be abrogated by agreement, or by a usage of trade, and those rules of law (such as those in Part 3 of Article 2 on Sales) which fill in points which the parties have not considered and in fact agreed upon. The latter rules hold "unless otherwise agree" but yield to the contrary agreement of the parties. Part of the agreement of the parties to which such rules yield is to be sought for in the usages of trade which furnish the background and give particular meaning to the language used, and are the framework of common understanding controlling any general rules of law which hold only when there is no such understanding.

4. A usage of trade under subsection (c) must have the "regularity of observance" specified. The ancient English tests for "custom" are abandoned in this connection. Therefore, it is not required that a usage of trade be "ancient or immemorial," "universal," or the like. Under the requirement of subsection (c) full recognition is thus available for new usages and for usages currently observed by the great majority of decent dealers, even though dissidents ready to cut corners do not agree. There is room also for proper recognition of usage agreed upon by merchants in trade codes.

5. The policies of the Uniform Commercial Code controlling explicit unconscionable contracts and clauses (Sections 1–304, 2–302) apply to implicit clauses that rest on usage of trade and carry forward the policy underlying the ancient requirement that a custom or usage must be "reasonable." However, the emphasis is shifted. The very fact of commercial acceptance makes out a *prima facie* case that the usage is reasonable, and the burden is no longer on the usage to establish itself as being reasonable. But the anciently established policing of usage by the courts is continued to the extent necessary to cope with the situation arising if an unconscionable or dishonest practice should become standard.

6. Subsection (d), giving the prescribed effect to usages "of which the parties are or should be aware," reinforces the provision of subsection (c) requiring not universality but only the described "regularity of observance" of the practice or method. This subsection also reinforces the point of subsection (c) that such usages may be either general to [a] trade or particular to a special branch of trade.

7. Although the definition of "agreement" in Section 1–201 includes the elements of course of performance, course of dealing, and usage of trade, the fact that express reference is made in some sections to those elements is not to be construed as carrying a contrary intent or implication elsewhere. Compare Section 1–302(c).

8. In cases of a well established line of usage varying from the general rules of the Uniform Commercial Code where the precise amount of the variation has not been worked out into a single standard, the party relying on the usage is entitled, in any event, to the minimum variation demonstrated. The whole is not to be disregarded because no particular line of detail has been established. In case a dominant pattern has been fairly evidenced, the party relying on the usage is entitled under this section to go to the trier of fact on the question of whether such dominant pattern has been incorporated into the agreement.

9. Subsection (g) is intended to insure that this Act's liberal recognition of the needs of commerce in-regard to usage of trade shall not be made into an instrument of abuse.

§ 1–304. Obligation of Good Faith.

Every contract or duty within [the Uniform Commercial Code] imposes an obligation of good faith in its performance and enforcement.

Official Comment

. . .

1. This section sets forth a basic principle running throughout the Uniform Commercial Code. The principle is that in commercial transactions good faith is required in the performance and enforcement of all agreements or duties. While this duty is explicitly stated in some provisions of the Uniform Commercial Code, the applicability of the duty is broader than merely these situations and applies generally, as stated in this section, to the performance or enforcement of every contract or duty within this Act. It is further

implemented by Section 1-303 on course of dealing course of performance, and usage of trade. This section does not support an independent cause of action for failure to perform or enforce in good faith. Rather, this section means that a failure to perform or enforce, in good faith, a specific duty or obligation under the contract, constitutes a breach of that contract or makes unavailable, under the particular circumstances, a remedial right or power. This distinction makes it clear that the doctrine of good faith merely directs a court towards interpreting contracts within the commercial context in which they are created, performed, and enforced, and does not create a separate duty of fairness and reasonableness which can be independently breached.

2. "Performance and enforcement" of contracts and duties within the Uniform Commercial Code include the exercise of rights created by the Uniform Commercial Code.

§ 1–305. Remedies to Be Liberally Administered.

(a) The remedies provided by [the Uniform Commercial Code] must be liberally administered to the end that the aggrieved party maybe put in as good a position as if the other party had fully performed but neither-consequential or special damages nor penal damages may be had except as specifically provided in [the Uniform Commercial Code] or by other rule of law.

(b) Any right or obligation declared by [the Uniform Commercial Code] is enforceable by action unless the provision declaring it specifies a different and limited effect.

§ 1–306. Waiver or Renunciation of Claim or Right After Breach.

A claim or right arising out of an alleged breach may be discharged in whole or in part without consideration by agreement of the aggrieved party in an authenticated record.

§ 1–307. Prima Facie Evidence by Third-Party Documents.

A document in due form purporting to be a bill of lading, policy or certificate of insurance, official weigher's or inspector's certificate, consular invoice, or any other document authorized or required by the contract to be issued by a third party is prima facie evidence of its own authenticity and genuineness and of the facts stated in the document by the third party.

§ 1–308. Performance or Acceptance Under Reservation of Rights.

(a) A party that with explicit reservation of rights performs or promises performance or assents to performance in a manner demanded or offered by the other party does not thereby prejudice the rights reserved. Such words as "without prejudice," "under protest," or the like are sufficient.

(b) Subsection (a) does not apply to an accord and satisfaction.

Official Comment

1. This section provides machinery for the continuation of performance along the lines contemplated by the contract despite a pending dispute, by adopting the mercantile device of going ahead with delivery, acceptance, or payment "without prejudice," "under protest," "under reserve," "with reservation of all our rights," and the like. All of these phrases completely reserve all rights within the meaning of this section. The section therefore contemplates that limited as well as general reservations and acceptance by a party may be made "subject to satisfaction of our purchaser," "subject to acceptance by our customers," or the like. . . .

3. Subsection (b) states that this section does not apply to an accord and satisfaction. Section 3–311 governs if an accord and satisfaction is attempted by tender of a negotiable instrument as stated in that section. If Section 3–311 does not apply, the issue of whether an accord and satisfaction has been effected is determined by the law of contract. Whether or not Section 3–311 applies, this section has no application to an accord and satisfaction.

§ 1–309. Option to Accelerate at Will.

A term providing that one party or that party's successor in interest may accelerate payment or performance or require collateral or additional collateral "at will" or when the party "deems itself insecure," or words of similar import, means that the party has power to do so only if that party in good faith believes that the prospect of payment or performance is impaired. The burden of establishing lack of good faith is on the party against which the power has been exercised.

§ 1–310. Subordinated Obligations.

An obligation may be issued as subordinated to performance of another obligation of the person obligated, or a creditor may subordinate its right to performance of an obligation by agreement with either the person obligated or another creditor of the person obligated. Subordination does not create a security interest as against either the common debtor or a subordinated creditor.

ARTICLE 2

SALES

PART I. SHORT TITLE, GENERAL CONSTRUCTION AND SUBJECT MATTER

Sec.
- 2–101. Short Title.
- 2–102. Scope; Certain Security and Other Transactions Excluded From This Article.
- 2–103. Definitions and Index of Definitions.
- 2–104. Definitions: "Merchant"; "Between Merchants"; "Financing Agency".
- 2–105. Definitions: Transferability; "Goods"; "Future" Goods; "Lot"; "Commercial Unit".
- 2–106. Definitions: "Contract"; "Agreement"; "Contract for Sale"; "Sale"; "Present Sale"; "Conforming" to Contract; "Termination"; "Cancellation".
- 2–107. Goods to Be Severed From Realty: Recording.

PART II. FORM, FORMATION AND READJUSTMENT OF CONTRACT

- 2–201. Formal Requirements; Statute of Frauds.
- 2–202. Final Written Expression: Parol or Extrinsic Evidence.
- 2–203. Seals Inoperative.
- 2–204. Formation in General.
- 2–205. Firm Offers.
- 2–206. Offer and Acceptance in Formation of Contract.
- 2–207. Additional Terms in Acceptance or Confirmation.
- 2–208. Course of Performance or Practical Construction.
- 2–209. Modification, Rescission and Waiver.
- 2–210. Delegation of Performance; Assignment of Rights.

PART III. GENERAL OBLIGATION AND CONSTRUCTION OF CONTRACT

- 2–301. General Obligations of Parties.
- 2–302. Unconscionable Contract or Clause.
- 2–303. Allocation or Division of Risks.
- 2–304. Price Payable in Money, Goods, Realty, or Otherwise.
- 2–305. Open Price Term.
- 2–306. Output, Requirements and Exclusive Dealings.
- 2–307. Delivery in Single Lot or Several Lots.
- 2–308. Absence of Specified Place for Delivery.
- 2–309. Absence of Specific Time Provisions; Notice of Termination.
- 2–310. Open Time for Payment or Running of Credit; Authority to Ship Under Reservation.
- 2–311. Options and Cooperation Respecting Performance.
- 2–312. Warranty of Title and Against Infringement; Buyer's Obligation Against Infringement.
- 2–313. Express Warranties by Affirmation, Promise, Description, Sample.
- 2–314. Implied Warranty: Merchantability; Usage of Trade.
- 2–315. Implied Warranty: Fitness for Particular Purpose.
- 2–316. Exclusion or Modification of Warranties.
- 2–317. Cumulation and Conflict of Warranties Express or Implied.
- 2–318. Third Party Beneficiaries of Warranties Express or Implied.
- 2–319. F.O.B. and F.A.S. Terms.
- 2–320. C.I.F. and C. & F. Terms.
- 2–321. C.I.F. or C. & F.: "Net Landed Weights"; "Payment on Arrival"; Warranty of Condition on Arrival.

2–322.	Delivery "Ex-ship".
2–323.	Form of Bill of Lading Required in Overseas Shipment; "Overseas".
2–324.	"No Arrival, No Sale" Term.
2–325.	"Letter of Credit" Term; "Confirmed Credit".
2–326.	Sale on Approval and Sale or Return; Rights of Creditors.
2–327.	Special Incidents of Sale on Approval and Sale or Return.
2–328.	Sale by Auction.

PART IV. TITLE, CREDITORS AND GOOD FAITH PURCHASERS

2–401.	Passing of Title; Reservation for Security; Limited Application of This Section.
2–402.	Rights of Seller's Creditors Against Sold Goods.
2–403.	Power to Transfer; Good Faith Purchase of Goods; "Entrusting".

PART V. PERFORMANCE

2–501.	Insurable Interest in Goods; Manner of Identification of Goods.
2–502.	Buyer's Right to Goods on Seller's Repudiation, Failure to Deliver, or Insolvency.
2–503.	Manner of Seller's Tender of Delivery.
2–504.	Shipment by Seller.
2–505.	Seller's Shipment Under Reservation.
2–506.	Rights of Financing Agency.
2–507.	Effect of Seller's Tender; Delivery on Condition.
2–508.	Cure by Seller of Improper Tender or Delivery; Replacement.
2–509.	Risk of Loss in the Absence of Breach.
2–510.	Effect of Breach on Risk of Loss.
2–511.	Tender of Payment by Buyer; Payment by Check.
2–512.	Payment by Buyer Before Inspection.
2–513.	Buyer's Right to Inspection of Goods.
2–514.	When Documents Deliverable on Acceptance; When on Payment.
2–515.	Preserving Evidence of Goods in Dispute.

PART VI. BREACH, REPUDIATION AND EXCUSE

2–601.	Buyer's Rights on Improper Delivery.
2–602.	Manner and Effect of Rightful Rejection.
2–603.	Merchant Buyer's Duties as to Rightfully Rejected Goods.
2–604.	Buyer's Options as to Salvage of Rightfully Rejected Goods.
2–605.	Waiver of Buyer's Objections by Failure to Particularize.
2–606.	What Constitutes Acceptance of Goods.
2–607.	Effect of Acceptance; Notice of Breach; Burden of Establishing Breach After Acceptance; Notice of Claim or Litigation to Person Answerable Over.
2–608.	Revocation of Acceptance in Whole or in Part.
2–609.	Right to Adequate Assurance of Performance.
2–610.	Anticipatory Repudiation.
2–611.	Retraction of Anticipatory Repudiation.
2–612.	"Installment Contract"; Breach.
2–613.	Casualty to Identified Goods.
2–614.	Substituted Performance.
2–615.	Excuse by Failure of Presupposed Conditions.
2–616.	Procedure on Notice Claiming Excuse.

PART VII. REMEDIES

- 2–701. Remedies for Breach of Collateral Contracts Not Impaired.
- 2–702. Seller's Remedies on Discovery of Buyer's Insolvency.
- 2–703. Seller's Remedies in General.
- 2–704. Seller's Right to Identify Goods to the Contract Notwithstanding Breach or to Salvage Unfinished Goods.
- 2–705. Seller's Stoppage of Delivery in Transit or Otherwise.
- 2–706. Seller's Resale Including Contract for Resale.
- 2–707. "Person in the Position of a Seller".
- 2–708. Seller's Damages for Non-Acceptance or Repudiation.
- 2–709. Action for the Price.
- 2–710. Seller's Incidental Damages.
- 2–711. Buyer's Remedies in General; Buyer's Security Interest in Rejected Goods.
- 2–712. "Cover"; Buyer's Procurement of Substitute Goods.
- 2–713. Buyer's Damages for Non-Delivery or Repudiation.
- 2–714. Buyer's Damages for Breach in Regard to Accepted Goods.
- 2–715. Buyer's Incidental and Consequential Damages.
- 2–716. Buyer's Right to Specific Performance or Replevin.
- 2–717. Deduction of Damages From the Price.
- 2–718. Liquidation or Limitation of Damages; Deposits.
- 2–719. Contractual Modification or Limitation of Remedy.
- 2–720. Effect of "Cancellation" or "Rescission" on Claims for Antecedent Breach.
- 2–721. Remedies for Fraud.
- 2–722. Who Can Sue Third Parties for Injury to Goods.
- 2–723. Proof of Market Price: Time and Place.
- 2–724. Admissibility of Market Quotations.
- 2–725. Statute of Limitations in Contracts for Sale.

PART I

SHORT TITLE, GENERAL CONSTRUCTION AND SUBJECT MATTER

§ 2–101. Short Title.

This Article shall be known and may be cited as Uniform Commercial Code—Sales.

Official Comment

This Article is a complete revision and modernization of the Uniform Sales Act which was promulgated by the National Conference of Commissioners on Uniform State Laws in 1906 and has been adopted in [49] states and the District of Columbia.

The coverage of the present Article is much more extensive than that of the old Sales Act and extends to the various bodies of case law which have been developed both outside of and under the latter.

The arrangement of the present Article is in terms of contract for sale and the various steps of its performance. The legal consequences are stated as following directly from the contract and action taken under it without resorting to the idea of when property or title passed or was to pass as being the determining factor. The purpose is to avoid making practical issues between practical men turn upon the location of an intangible something, the passing of which no man can prove by evidence and to substitute for such abstractions proof of words and actions of a tangible character.

§ 2–102. Scope; Certain Security and Other Transactions Excluded From This Article.

Unless the context otherwise requires, this Article applies to transactions in goods; it does not apply to any transaction which although in the form of an unconditional contract to sell or present sale is intended to operate only as a security transaction nor does this Article impair or repeal any statute regulating sales to consumers, farmers or other specified classes of buyers.

Official Comment

. . .

Definitional Cross References:

"Contract". Section 1–201.

"Contract for sale". Section 2–106.

"Present sale". Section 2–106.

"Sale". Section 2–106.

§ 2–103. Definitions and Index of Definitions.

(1) In this Article unless the context otherwise requires

    (a) "Buyer" means a person who buys or contracts to buy goods.

    (b) "Good faith" in the case of a merchant means honesty in fact and the observance of reasonable commercial standards of fair dealing in the trade.

    (c) "Receipt" of goods means taking physical possession of them.

    (d) "Seller" means a person who sells or contracts to sell goods.

(2) Other definitions applying to this Article or to specified Parts thereof, and the sections in which they appear are:

"Acceptance". Section 2–606.

"Banker's credit". Section 2–325.

"Between merchants". Section 2–104.

"Cancellation". Section 2–106(4).

"Commercial unit". Section 2–105.

"Confirmed credit". Section 2–325.

"Conforming to contract". Section 2–106.

"Contract for sale". Section 2–106.

"Cover". Section 2–712.

"Entrusting". Section 2–403.

"Financing agency". Section 2–104.

"Future goods". Section 2–105.

"Goods". Section 2–105.

"Identification". Section 2–501.

"Installment contract". Section 2–612.

"Letter of Credit". Section 2–325.

| Art. 2 | SALES | § 2–104 |

"Lot". Section 2–105.

"Merchant". Section 2–104.

"Overseas". Section 2–323.

"Person in position of seller". Section 2–707.

"Present sale". Section 2–106.

"Sale". Section 2–106.

"Sale on approval". Section 2–326.

"Sale or return". Section 2–326.

"Termination". Section 2–106.

(3) The following definitions in other Articles apply to this Article:

"Check". Section 3–104.

"Consignee". Section 7–102.

"Consignor". Section 7–102.

"Consumer goods". Section 9–102.

"Dishonor". Section 3–502.

"Draft". Section 3–104.

(4) In addition Article 1 contains general definitions and principles of construction and interpretation applicable throughout this Article.

As amended in 1994.

Official Comment

. . .

Definitional Cross Reference:

"Person". Section 1–201.

§ 2–104. Definitions: "Merchant"; "Between Merchants"; "Financing Agency".

(1) "Merchant" means a person who deals in goods of the kind or otherwise by his occupation holds himself out as having knowledge or skill peculiar to the practices or goods involved in the transaction or to whom such knowledge or skill may be attributed by his employment of an agent or broker or other intermediary who by his occupation holds himself out as having such knowledge or skill.

(2) "Financing agency" means a bank, finance company or other person who in the ordinary course of business makes advances against goods or documents of title or who by arrangement with either the seller or the buyer intervenes in ordinary course to make or collect payment due or claimed under the contract for sale, as by purchasing or paying the seller's draft or making advances against it or by merely taking it for collection whether or not documents of title accompany the draft. "Financing agency" includes also a bank or other person who similarly intervenes between persons who are in the position of seller and buyer in respect to the goods (Section 2–707).

(3) "Between merchants" means in any transaction with respect to which both parties are chargeable with the knowledge or skill of merchants.

Official Comment

. . .

Purposes:

1. This Article assumes that transactions between professionals in a given field require special and clear rules which may not apply to a casual or inexperienced seller or buyer. It thus adopts a policy of expressly stating rules applicable "between merchants" and "as against a merchant", wherever they are needed instead of making them depend upon the circumstances of each case as in the statutes cited above. . . .

2. The term "merchant" as defined here roots in the "law merchant" concept of a professional in business. The professional status under the definition may be based upon specialized knowledge as to the goods, specialized knowledge as to business practices, or specialized knowledge as to both and which kind of specialized knowledge may be sufficient to establish the merchant status is indicated by the nature of the provisions.

The special provisions as to merchants appear only in this Article and they are of three kinds. Sections 2–201(2), 2–205, 2–207 and 2–209 dealing with the statute of frauds, firm offers, confirmatory memoranda and modification rest on normal business practices which are or ought to be typical of and familiar to any person in business. For purposes of these sections almost every person in business would, therefore, be deemed to be a "merchant" under the language "who . . . by his occupation holds himself out as having knowledge or skill peculiar to the practices . . . involved in the transaction . . . " since the practices involved in the transaction are non-specialized business practices such as answering mail. In this type of provision, banks or even universities, for example, well may be "merchants." But even these sections only apply to a merchant in his mercantile capacity; a lawyer or bank president buying fishing tackle for his own use is not a merchant.

On the other hand, in Section 2–314 on the warranty of merchantability, such warranty is implied only "if the seller is a merchant with respect to goods of that kind." Obviously this qualification restricts the implied warranty to a much smaller group than everyone who is engaged in business and requires a professional status as to particular kinds of goods. The exception in Section 2–402(2) for retention of possession by a merchant-seller falls in the same class; as does Section 2–403(2) on entrusting of possession to a merchant "who deals in goods of that kind".

A third group of sections includes 2–103(1)(b), which provides that in the case of a merchant "good faith" includes observance of reasonable commercial standards of fair dealing in the trade; 2–327(1)(c), 2–603 and 2–605, dealing with responsibilities of merchant buyers to follow seller's instructions, etc.; 2–509 on risk of loss, and 2–609 on adequate assurance of performance. This group of sections applies to persons who are merchants under either the "practices" or the "goods" aspect of the definition of merchant. . . .

Definitional Cross References:

"Bank". Section 1–201.

"Buyer". Section 2–103.

"Contract for sale". Section 2–106.

"Document of title". Section 1–201.

"Draft". Section 3–104.

"Goods". Section 2–105.

"Person". Section 1–201.

"Purchase". Section 1–201.

"Seller". Section 2–103.

§ 2–105. Definitions: Transferability; "Goods"; "Future" Goods; "Lot"; "Commercial Unit".

(1) "Goods" means all things (including specially manufactured goods) which are movable at the time of identification to the contract for sale other than the money in which the price is to be paid, investment securities (Article 8) and things in action. "Goods" also includes the unborn young of animals and growing crops and other identified things attached to realty as described in the section on goods to be severed from realty (Section 2–107).

(2) Goods must be both existing and identified before any interest in them can pass. Goods which are not both existing and identified are "future" goods. A purported present sale of future goods or of any interest therein operates as a contract to sell.

(3) There may be a sale of a part interest in existing identified goods.

(4) An undivided share in an identified bulk of fungible goods is sufficiently identified to be sold although the quantity of the bulk is not determined. Any agreed proportion of such a bulk or any quantity thereof agreed upon by number, weight or other measure may to the extent of the seller's interest in the bulk be sold to the buyer who then becomes an owner in common.

(5) "Lot" means a parcel or a single article which is the subject matter of a separate sale or delivery, whether or not it is sufficient to perform the contract.

(6) "Commercial unit" means such a unit of goods as by commercial usage is a single whole for purposes of sale and division of which materially impairs its character or value on the market or in use. A commercial unit may be a single article (as a machine) or a set of articles (as a suite of furniture or an assortment of sizes) or a quantity (as a bale, gross, or carload) or any other unit treated in use or in the relevant market as a single whole.

Official Comment

. . .

Purposes of Changes and New Matter:

1. Subsection (1) on "goods": The phraseology of the prior uniform statutory provision has been changed so that:

The definition of goods is based on the concept of movability and the term "chattels personal" is not used. It is not intended to deal with things which are not fairly identifiable as movables before the contract is performed.

Growing crops are included within the definition of goods since they are frequently intended for sale. The concept of "industrial" growing crops has been abandoned, for under modern practices fruit, perennial hay, nursery stock and the like must be brought within the scope of this Article. The young of animals are also included expressly in this definition since they, too, are frequently intended for sale and may be contracted for before birth. The period of gestation of domestic animals is such that the provisions of the section on identification can apply as in the case of crops to be planted. The reason of this definition also leads to the inclusion of a wool crop or the like as "goods" subject to identification under this Article.

The exclusion of "money in which the price is to be paid" from the definition of goods does not mean that foreign currency which is included in the definition of money may not be the subject matter of a sales transaction. Goods is intended to cover the sale of money when money is being treated as a commodity but not to include it when money is the medium of payment.

As to contracts to sell timber, minerals, or structures to be removed from the land Section 2–107(1) (Goods to be severed from realty: recording) controls.

The use of the word "fixtures" is avoided in view of the diversity of definitions of that term. This Article in including within its scope "things attached to realty" adds the further test that they must be capable of severance without material harm thereto. As between the parties any identified things which fall within that definition becomes "goods" upon the making of the contract for sale.

"Investment securities" are expressly excluded from the coverage of this Article. It is not intended by this exclusion, however, to prevent the application of a particular section of this Article by analogy to securities (as was done with the Original Sales Act in Agar v. Orda, 264 N.Y. 248, 190 N.E. 479, 99 A.L.R. 269 (1934)) when the reason of that section makes such application sensible and the situation involved is not covered by the Article of this Act dealing specifically with such securities (Article 8). . . .

Definitional Cross References:

"Buyer". Section 2–103.

"Contract". Section 1–201.

"Contract for sale". Section 2–106.

"Fungible". Section 1–201.

"Money". Section 1–201.

"Present sale". Section 2–106.

"Sale". Section 2–106.

"Seller". Section 2–103.

§ 2–106. Definitions: "Contract"; "Agreement"; "Contract for Sale"; "Sale"; "Present Sale"; "Conforming" to Contract; "Termination"; "Cancellation".

(1) In this Article unless the context otherwise requires "contract" and "agreement" are limited to those relating to the present or future sale of goods. "Contract for sale" includes both a present sale of goods and a contract to sell goods at a future time. A "sale" consists in the passing of title from the seller to the buyer for a price (Section 2–401). A "present sale" means a sale which is accomplished by the making of the contract.

(2) Goods or conduct including any part of a performance are "conforming" or conform to the contract when they are in accordance with the obligations under the contract.

(3) "Termination" occurs when either party pursuant to a power created by agreement or law puts an end to the contract otherwise than for its breach. On "termination" all obligations which are still executory on both sides are discharged but any right based on prior breach or performance survives.

(4) "Cancellation" occurs when either party puts an end to the contract for breach by the other and its effect is the same as that of "termination" except that the cancelling party also retains any remedy for breach of the whole contract or any unperformed balance.

Official Comment

. . .

Purposes of Changes and New Matter:

1. Subsection (1): "Contract for sale" is used as a general concept throughout this Article, but the rights of the parties do not vary according to whether the transaction is a present sale or a contract to sell unless the Article expressly so provides.

2. Subsection (2): It is in general intended to continue the policy of requiring exact performance by the seller of his obligations as a condition to his right to require acceptance. However, the seller is in part safeguarded against surprise as a result of sudden technicality on the buyer's part by the provisions of Section 2–508 on seller's cure of improper tender or delivery. Moreover usage of trade frequently permits commercial leeways in performance and the language of the agreement itself must be read in the light of

such custom or usage and also, prior course of dealing, and in a long term contract, the course of performance.

3. Subsections (3) and (4): These subsections are intended to make clear the distinction carried forward throughout this Article between termination and cancellation.

. . .

Definitional Cross References:

"Agreement". Section 1–201.

"Buyer". Section 2–103.

"Contract". Section 1–201.

"Goods". Section 2–105.

"Party". Section 1–201.

"Remedy". Section 1–201.

"Rights". Section 1–201.

"Seller". Section 2–103.

§ 2–107. Goods to Be Severed From Realty: Recording.

(1) A contract for the sale of minerals or the like (including oil and gas) or a structure or its materials to be removed from realty is a contract for the sale of goods within this Article if they are to be severed by the seller but until severance a purported present sale thereof which is not effective as a transfer of an interest in land is effective only as a contract to sell.

(2) A contract for the sale apart from the land of growing crops or other things attached to realty and capable of severance without material harm thereto but not described in subsection (1) or of timber to be cut is a contract for the sale of goods within this Article whether the subject matter is to be severed by the buyer or by the seller even though it forms part of the realty at the time of contracting, and the parties can by identification effect a present sale before severance.

(3) The provisions of this section are subject to any third party rights provided by the law relating to realty records, and the contract for sale may be executed and recorded as a document transferring an interest in land and shall then constitute notice to third parties of the buyer's rights under the contract for sale.

Official Comment

. . .

Definitional Cross References:

"Buyer". Section 2–103.

"Contract". Section 1–201.

"Contract for sale". Section 2–106.

"Goods". Section 2–105.

"Party". Section 1–201.

"Present sale". Section 2–106.

"Rights". Section 1–201.

"Seller". Section 2–103.

PART II

FORM, FORMATION AND READJUSTMENT OF CONTRACT

§ 2–201. Formal Requirements; Statute of Frauds.

(1) Except as otherwise provided in this section a contract for the sale of goods for the price of $500 or more is not enforceable by way of action or defense unless there is some writing sufficient to indicate that a contract for sale has been made between the parties and signed by the party against whom enforcement is sought or by his authorized agent or broker. A writing is not insufficient because it omits or incorrectly states a term agreed upon but the contract is not enforceable under this paragraph beyond the quantity of goods shown in such writing.

(2) Between merchants if within a reasonable time a writing in confirmation of the contract and sufficient against the sender is received and the party receiving it has reason to know its contents, it satisfies the requirements of subsection (1) against such party unless written notice of objection to its contents is given within 10 days after it is received.

(3) A contract which does not satisfy the requirements of subsection (1) but which is valid in other respects is enforceable

(a) if the goods are to be specially manufactured for the buyer and are not suitable for sale to others in the ordinary course of the seller's business and the seller, before notice of repudiation is received and under circumstances which reasonably indicate that the goods are for the buyer, has made either a substantial beginning of their manufacture or commitments for their procurement; or

(b) if the party against whom enforcement is sought admits in his pleading, testimony or otherwise in court that a contract for sale was made, but the contract is not enforceable under this provision beyond the quantity of goods admitted; or

(c) with respect to goods for which payment has been made and accepted or which have been received and accepted (Sec. 2–606).

Official Comment

. . .

Purposes of Changes: The changed phraseology of this section is intended to make it clear that:

1. The required writing need not contain all the material terms of the contract and such material terms as are stated need not be precisely stated. All that is required is that the writing afford a basis for believing that the offered oral evidence rests on a real transaction. It may be written in lead pencil on a scratch pad. It need not indicate which party is the buyer and which the seller. The only term which must appear is the quantity term which need not be accurately stated but recovery is limited to the amount stated. The price, time and place of payment or delivery, the general quality of the goods, or any particular warranties may all be omitted.

Special emphasis must be placed on the permissibility of omitting the price term in view of the insistence of some courts on the express inclusion of this term even where the parties have contracted on the basis of a published price list. In many valid contracts for sale the parties do not mention the price in express terms, the buyer being bound to pay and the seller to accept a reasonable price which the trier of the fact may well be trusted to determine. Again, frequently the price is not mentioned since the parties have based their agreement on a price list or catalogue known to both of them and this list serves as an efficient safeguard against perjury. Finally, "market" prices and valuations that are current in the vicinity constitute a similar check. Thus if the price is not stated in the memorandum it can normally be supplied without danger of fraud. Of course if the "price" consists of goods rather than money the quantity of goods must be stated.

Art. 2   SALES   § 2–201

Only three definite and invariable requirements as to the memorandum are made by this subsection. First, it must evidence a contract for the sale of goods; second, it must be "signed", a word which includes any authentication which identifies the party to be charged; and third, it must specify a quantity.

2. "Partial performance" as a substitute for the required memorandum can validate the contract only for the goods which have been accepted or for which payment has been made and accepted.

Receipt and acceptance either of goods or of the price constitutes an unambiguous overt admission by both parties that a contract actually exists. If the court can make a just apportionment, therefore, the agreed price of any goods actually delivered can be recovered without a writing or, if the price has been paid, the seller can be forced to deliver an apportionable part of the goods. The overt actions of the parties make admissible evidence of the other terms of the contract necessary to a just apportionment. This is true even though the actions of the parties are not in themselves inconsistent with a different transaction such as a consignment for resale or a mere loan of money.

Part performance by the buyer requires the delivery of something by him that is accepted by the seller as such performance. Thus, part payment may be made by money or check, accepted by the seller. If the agreed price consists of goods or services, then they must also have been delivered and accepted.

3. Between merchants, failure to answer a written confirmation of a contract within ten days of receipt is tantamount to a writing under subsection (2) and is sufficient against both parties under subsection (1). The only effect, however, is to take away from the party who fails to answer the defense of the Statute of Frauds; the burden of persuading the trier of fact that a contract was in fact made orally prior to the written confirmation is unaffected. Compare the effect of a failure to reply under Section 2–207.

4. Failure to satisfy the requirements of this section does not render the contract void for all purposes, but merely prevents it from being judicially enforced in favor of a party to the contract. For example, a buyer who takes possession of goods as provided in an oral contract which the seller has not meanwhile repudiated, is not a trespasser. Nor would the Statute of Frauds provisions of this section be a defense to a third person who wrongfully induces a party to refuse to perform an oral contract, even though the injured party cannot maintain an action for damages against the party so refusing to perform.

5. The requirement of "signing" is discussed in the comment to Section 1–201.

6. It is not necessary that the writing be delivered to anybody. It need not be signed or authenticated by both parties but it is, of course, not sufficient against one who has not signed it. Prior to a dispute no one can determine which party's signing of the memorandum may be necessary but from the time of contracting each party should be aware that to him it is signing by the other which is important.

7. If the making of a contract is admitted in court, either in a written pleading, by stipulation or by oral statement before the court, no additional writing is necessary for protection against fraud. Under this section it is no longer possible to admit the contract in court and still treat the Statute as a defense. However, the contract is not thus conclusively established. The admission so made by a party is itself evidential against him of the truth of the facts so admitted and of nothing more; as against the other party, it is not evidential at all.

. . .

Definitional Cross References:

"Action". Section 1–201.

"Between merchants". Section 2–104.

"Buyer". Section 2–103.

"Contract". Section 1–201.

"Contract for sale". Section 2–106.

"Goods". Section 2–105.

"Notice". Section 1–201.

"Party". Section 1–201.

"Reasonable time". Section 1–204.

"Sale". Section 2–106.

"Seller". Section 2–103.

§ 2–202. Final Written Expression: Parol or Extrinsic Evidence.

Terms with respect to which the confirmatory memoranda of the parties agree or which are otherwise set forth in a writing intended by the parties as a final expression of their agreement with respect to such terms as are included therein may not be contradicted by evidence of any prior agreement or of a contemporaneous oral agreement but may be explained or supplemented

(a) by course of performance, course of dealing, or usage of trade (Section 1–303); and

(b) by evidence of consistent additional terms unless the court finds the writing to have been intended also as a complete and exclusive statement of the terms of the agreement.

Official Comment

. . .

Purposes:

1. This section definitely rejects:

    (a) Any assumption that because a writing has been worked out which is final on some matters, it is to be taken as including all the matters agreed upon;

    (b) The premise that the language used has the meaning attributable to such language by rules of construction existing in the law rather than the meaning which arises out of the commercial context in which it was used; and

    (c) The requirement that a condition precedent to the admissibility of the type of evidence specified in paragraph (a) is an original determination by the court that the language used is ambiguous.

2. Paragraph (a) makes admissible evidence of course of dealing, usage of trade and course of performance to explain or supplement the terms of any writing stating the agreement of the parties in order that the true understanding of the parties as to the agreement may be reached. Such writings are to be read on the assumption that the course of prior dealings between the parties and the usages of trade were taken for granted when the document was phrased. Unless carefully negated they have become an element of the meaning of the words used. Similarly, the course of actual performance by the parties is considered the best indication of what they intended the writing to mean.

3. Under paragraph (b) consistent additional terms, not reduced to writing, may be proved unless the court finds that the writing was intended by both parties as a complete and exclusive statement of all the terms. If the additional terms are such that, if agreed upon, they would certainly have been included in the document in the view of the court, then evidence of their alleged making must be kept from the trier of fact.

. . .

Definitional Cross References:

"Agreed" and "agreement". Section 1–201.

"Course of dealing". Section 1–303.

"Course of performance". Section 1–303.

"Party". Section 1–201.

"Term". Section 1–201.

"Usage of trade". Section 1–205.

"Written" and "writing". Section 1–201.

§ 2–203. Seals Inoperative.

The affixing of a seal to a writing evidencing a contract for sale or an offer to buy or sell goods does not constitute the writing a sealed instrument and the law with respect to sealed instruments does not apply to such a contract or offer.

Official Comment

. . .

Definitional Cross References:

"Contract for sale". Section 2–106.

"Goods". Section 2–105.

"Writing". Section 1–201.

§ 2–204. Formation in General.

(1) A contract for sale of goods may be made in any manner sufficient to show agreement, including conduct by both parties which recognizes the existence of such a contract.

(2) An agreement sufficient to constitute a contract for sale may be found even though the moment of its making is undetermined.

(3) Even though one or more terms are left open a contract for sale does not fail for indefiniteness if the parties have intended to make a contract and there is a reasonably certain basis for giving an appropriate remedy.

Official Comment

. . .

Purposes of Changes:

Subsection (1) continues without change the basic policy of recognizing any manner of expression of agreement, oral, written or otherwise. The legal effect of such an agreement is, of course, qualified by other provisions of this Article.

Under subsection (1) appropriate conduct by the parties may be sufficient to establish an agreement. Subsection (2) is directed primarily to the situation where the interchanged correspondence does not disclose the exact point at which the deal was closed, but the actions of the parties indicate that a binding obligation has been undertaken.

Subsection (3) states the principle as to "open terms" underlying later sections of the Article. If the parties intend to enter into a binding agreement, this subsection recognizes that agreement as valid in law, despite missing terms, if there is any reasonably certain basis for granting a remedy. The test is not certainty as to what the parties were to do nor as to the exact amount of damages due the plaintiff. Nor is the fact that one or more terms are left to be agreed upon enough of itself to defeat an otherwise adequate agreement. Rather, commercial standards on the point of "indefiniteness" are intended to be applied, this Act making provision elsewhere for missing terms needed for performance, open price, remedies and the like.

The more terms the parties leave open, the less likely it is that they have intended to conclude a binding agreement, but their actions may be frequently conclusive on the matter despite the omissions.

. . .

Definitional Cross References:

"Agreement". Section 1–201.

"Contract". Section 1–201.

"Contract for sale". Section 2–106.

"Goods". Section 2–105.

"Party". Section 1–201.

"Remedy". Section 1–201.

"Term". Section 1–201.

§ 2–205. Firm Offers.

An offer by a merchant to buy or sell goods in a signed writing which by its terms gives assurance that it will be held open is not revocable, for lack of consideration, during the time stated or if no time is stated for a reasonable time, but in no event may such period of irrevocability exceed three months; but any such term of assurance on a form supplied by the offeree must be separately signed by the offeror.

Official Comment

. . .

Purposes of Changes:

1. This section is intended to modify the former rule which required that "firm offers" be sustained by consideration in order to bind, and to require instead that they must merely be characterized as such and expressed in signed writings.

2. The primary purpose of this section is to give effect to the deliberate intention of a merchant to make a current firm offer binding. The deliberation is shown in the case of an individualized document by the merchant's signature to the offer, and in the case of an offer included on a form supplied by the other party to the transaction by the separate signing of the particular clause which contains the offer. "Signed" here also includes authentication but the reasonableness of the authentication herein allowed must be determined in the light of the purpose of the section. The circumstances surrounding the signing may justify something less than a formal signature or initialing but typically the kind of authentication involved here would consist of a minimum of initialing of the clause involved. . . . However, despite settled courses of dealing or usages of the trade whereby firm offers are made by oral communication and relied upon without more evidence, such offers remain revocable under this Article since authentication by a writing is the essence of this section. . . .

Definitional Cross References:

"Goods". Section 2–105.

"Merchant". Section 2–104.

"Signed". Section 1–201.

"Writing". Section 1–201.

§ 2–206. Offer and Acceptance in Formation of Contract.

(1) Unless otherwise unambiguously indicated by the language or circumstances

(a) an offer to make a contract shall be construed as inviting acceptance in any manner and by any medium reasonable in the circumstances;

(b) an order or other offer to buy goods for prompt or current shipment shall be construed as inviting acceptance either by a prompt promise to ship or by the prompt or current shipment of conforming or non-conforming goods, but such a shipment of non-conforming goods does not constitute an acceptance if the seller seasonably notifies the buyer that the shipment is offered only as an accommodation to the buyer.

(2) Where the beginning of a requested performance is a reasonable mode of acceptance an offeror who is not notified of acceptance within a reasonable time may treat the offer as having lapsed before acceptance.

Official Comment

. . .

Purposes of Changes: To make it clear that:

1. Any reasonable manner of acceptance is intended to be regarded as available unless the offeror has made quite clear that it will not be acceptable. Former technical rules as to acceptance, such as requiring that telegraphic offers be accepted by telegraphed acceptance, etc., are rejected and a criterion that the acceptance be "in any manner and by any medium reasonable under the circumstances," is substituted. This section is intended to remain flexible and its applicability to be enlarged as new media of communication develop or as the more time-saving present day media come into general use.

2. Either shipment or a prompt promise to ship is made a proper means of acceptance of an offer looking to current shipment. In accordance with ordinary commercial understanding the section interprets an order looking to current shipment as allowing acceptance either by actual shipment or by a prompt promise to ship and rejects the artificial theory that only a single mode of acceptance is normally envisaged by an offer. . . .

3. The beginning of performance by an offeree can be effective as acceptance so as to bind the offeror only if followed within a reasonable time by notice to the offeror. Such a beginning of performance must unambiguously express the offeree's intention to engage himself. For the protection of both parties it is essential that notice follow in due course to constitute acceptance. Nothing in this section however bars the possibility that under the common law performance begun may have an intermediate effect of temporarily barring revocation of the offer, or at the offeror's option, final effect in constituting acceptance. . . .

Definitional Cross References:

"Buyer". Section 2–103.

"Conforming". Section 2–106.

"Contract". Section 1–201.

"Goods". Section 2–105.

"Notifies". Section 1–201.

"Reasonable time". Section 1–204.

§ 2–207. Additional Terms in Acceptance or Confirmation.

(1) A definite and seasonable expression of acceptance or a written confirmation which is sent within a reasonable time operates as an acceptance even though it states terms additional to or different from those offered or agreed upon, unless acceptance is expressly made conditional on assent to the additional or different terms.

(2) The additional terms are to be construed as proposals for addition to the contract. Between merchants such terms become part of the contract unless:

(a) the offer expressly limits acceptance to the terms of the offer;

(b) they materially alter it; or

(c) notification of objection to them has already been given or is given within a reasonable time after notice of them is received.

(3) Conduct by both parties which recognizes the existence of a contract is sufficient to establish a contract for sale although the writings of the parties do not otherwise establish a contract. In such case the terms of the particular contract consist of those terms on which the writings of the parties agree, together with any supplementary terms incorporated under any other provisions of this Act.

Official Comment

. . .

Purposes of Changes:

1. This section is intended to deal with two typical situations. The one is the written confirmation, where an agreement has been reached either orally or by informal correspondence between the parties and is followed by one or both of the parties sending formal memoranda embodying the terms so far as agreed upon and adding terms not discussed. The other situation is offer and acceptance, in which a wire or letter expressed and intended as an acceptance or the closing of an agreement adds further minor suggestions or proposals such as "ship by Tuesday," "rush," "ship draft against bill of lading inspection allowed," or the like. A frequent example of the second situation is the exchange of printed purchase order and acceptance (sometimes called "acknowledgment") forms. Because the forms are oriented to the thinking of the respective drafting parties, the terms contained in them often do not correspond. Often the seller's form contains terms different from or additional to those set forth in the buyer's form. Nevertheless, the parties proceed with the transaction. [Comment 1 was amended in 1966.]

2. Under this Article a proposed deal which in commercial understanding has in fact been closed is recognized as a contract. Therefore, any additional matter contained in the confirmation or in the acceptance falls within subsection (2) and must be regarded as a proposal for an added term unless the acceptance is made conditional on the acceptance of the additional or different terms. [Comment 2 was amended in 1966.]

3. Whether or not additional or different terms will become part of the agreement depends upon the provisions of subsection (2). If they are such as materially to alter the original bargain, they will not be included unless expressly agreed to by the other party. If, however, they are terms which would not so change the bargain they will be incorporated unless notice of objection to them has already been given or is given within a reasonable time.

4. Examples of typical clauses which would normally "materially alter" the contract and so result in surprise or hardship if incorporated without express awareness by the other party are: a clause negating such standard warranties as that of merchantability or fitness for a particular purpose in circumstances in which either warranty normally attaches; a clause requiring a guaranty of 90% or 100% deliveries in a case such as a contract by cannery, where the usage of the trade allows greater quantity leeways; a clause reserving to the seller the power to cancel upon the buyer's failure to meet any invoice when due; a clause requiring that complaints be made in a time materially shorter than customary or reasonable.

5. Examples of clauses which involve no element of unreasonable surprise and which therefore are to be incorporated in the contract unless notice of objection is seasonably given are: a clause setting forth and perhaps enlarging slightly upon the seller's exemption due to supervening causes beyond his control, similar to those covered by the provision of this Article on merchant's excuse by failure of presupposed conditions or a clause fixing in advance any reasonable formula of proration under such circumstances; a clause fixing a reasonable time for complaints within customary limits, or in the case of a purchase for sub-sale, providing for inspection by the sub-purchaser; a clause providing for interest on overdue invoices or fixing the seller's standard credit terms where they are within the range of trade practice and do not limit any credit bargained for; a clause limiting the right of rejection for defects which fall within the customary trade tolerances for acceptance "with adjustment" or otherwise limiting remedy in a reasonable manner (see Sections 2–718 and 2–719).

6. If no answer is received within a reasonable time after additional terms are proposed, it is both fair and commercially sound to assume that their inclusion has been assented to. Where clauses on confirming forms sent by both parties conflict each party must be assumed to object to a clause of the other conflicting with one on the confirmation sent by himself. As a result the requirement that there be notice of objection which is found in subsection (2) is satisfied and the conflicting terms do not become a part of the contract. The contract then consists of the terms originally expressly agreed to, terms on which the

confirmations agree, and terms supplied by this Act, including subsection (2). The written confirmation is also subject to Section 2–201. Under that section a failure to respond permits enforcement of a prior oral agreement; under this section a failure to respond permits additional terms to become part of the agreement. [Comment 6 was amended in 1966.]

7. In many cases, as where goods are shipped, accepted and paid for before any dispute arises, there is no question whether a contract has been made. In such cases, where the writings of the parties do not establish a contract, it is not necessary to determine which act or document constituted the offer and which the acceptance. See Section 2–204. The only question is what terms are included in the contract, and subsection (3) furnishes the governing rule. [Comment 7 was added in 1966.]

. . .

Definitional Cross References:

"Between merchants". Section 2–104.

"Contract". Section 1–201.

"Notification". Section 1–201.

"Reasonable time". Section 1–204.

"Seasonably". Section 1–204.

"Send". Section 1–201.

"Term". Section 1–201.

"Written". Section 1–201.

§ 2–208. Course of Performance or Practical Construction.

(1) Where the contract for sale involves repeated occasions for performance by either party with knowledge of the nature of the performance and opportunity for objection to it by the other, any course of performance accepted or acquiesced in without objection shall be relevant to determine the meaning of the agreement.

(2) The express terms of the agreement and any such course of performance, as well as any course of dealing and usage of trade, shall be construed whenever reasonable as consistent with each other; but when such construction is unreasonable, express terms shall control course of performance and course of performance shall control both course of dealing and usage of trade (Section 1–205).

(3) Subject to the provisions of the next section on modification and waiver, such course of performance shall be relevant to show a waiver of modification of any term inconsistent with such course of performance.

§ 2–209. Modification, Rescission and Waiver.

(1) An agreement modifying a contract within this Article needs no consideration to be binding.

(2) A signed agreement which excludes modification or rescission except by a signed writing cannot be otherwise modified or rescinded, but except as between merchants such a requirement on a form supplied by the merchant must be separately signed by the other party.

(3) The requirements of the statute of frauds section of this Article (Section 2–201) must be satisfied if the contract as modified is within its provisions.

(4) Although an attempt at modification or rescission does not satisfy the requirements of subsection (2) or (3) it can operate as a waiver.

(5) A party who has made a waiver affecting an executory portion of the contract may retract the waiver by reasonable notification received by the other party that strict performance will be

required of any term waived, unless the retraction would be unjust in view of a material change of position in reliance on the waiver.

Official Comment

...

Purposes of Changes and New Matter:

1. This section seeks to protect and make effective all necessary and desirable modifications of sales contracts without regard to the technicalities which at present hamper such adjustments.

2. Subsection (1) provides that an agreement modifying a sales contract needs no consideration to be binding.

However, modifications made thereunder must meet the test of good faith imposed by this Act. The effective use of bad faith to escape performance on the original contract terms is barred, and the extortion of a "modification" without legitimate commercial reason is ineffective as a violation of the duty of good faith. Nor can a mere technical consideration support a modification made in bad faith.

The test of "good faith" between merchants or as against merchants includes "observance of reasonable commercial standards of fair dealing in the trade" (Section 2–103), and may in some situations require an objectively demonstrable reason for seeking a modification. But such matters as a market shift which makes performance come to involve a loss may provide such a reason even though there is no such unforeseen difficulty as would make out a legal excuse from performance under Sections 2–615 and 2–616.

...

Definitional Cross References:

"Agreement". Section 1–201.

"Between merchants". Section 2–104.

"Contract". Section 1–201.

"Notification". Section 1–201.

"Signed". Section 1–201.

"Term". Section 1–201.

"Writing". Section 1–201.

§ 2–210. Delegation of Performance; Assignment of Rights.

(1) A party may perform his duty through a delegate unless otherwise agreed or unless the other party has a substantial interest in having his original promisor perform or control the acts required by the contract. No delegation of performance relieves the party delegating of any duty to perform or any liability for breach.

(2) Except as otherwise provided in Section 9–406, unless otherwise agreed, all rights of either seller or buyer can be assigned except where the assignment would materially change the duty of the other party, or increase materially the burden or risk imposed on him by his contract, or impair materially his chance of obtaining return performance. A right to damages for breach of the whole contract or a right arising out of the assignor's due performance of his entire obligation can be assigned despite agreement otherwise.

(3) The creation, attachment, perfection, or enforcement of a security interest in the seller's interest under a contract is not a transfer that materially changes the duty of or increases materially the burden or risk imposed on the buyer or impairs materially the buyer's chance of obtaining return performance within the purview of subsection (2) unless, and then only to the extent that, enforcement actually results in a delegation of material performance of the seller. Even in that event, the creation, attachment, perfection, and enforcement of the security interest remain effective, but (i) the seller is

liable to the buyer for damages caused by the delegation to the extent that the damages could not reasonably be prevented by the buyer, and (ii) a court having jurisdiction may grant other appropriate relief, including cancellation of the contract for sale or an injunction against enforcement of the security interest or consummation of the enforcement.

(4) Unless the circumstances indicate the contrary a prohibition of assignment of "the contract" is to be construed as barring only the delegation to the assignee of the assignor's performance.

(5) An assignment of "the contract" or of "all my rights under the contract" or an assignment in similar general terms is an assignment of rights and unless the language or the circumstances (as in an assignment for security) indicate the contrary, it is a delegation of performance of the duties of the assignor and its acceptance by the assignee constitutes a promise by him to perform those duties. This promise is enforceable by either the assignor or the other party to the original contract.

(6) The other party may treat any assignment which delegates performance as creating reasonable grounds for insecurity and may without prejudice to his rights against the assignor demand assurances from the assignee (Section 2–609).

Official Comment

. . .

Purposes:

1. Generally, this section recognizes both delegation of performance and assignability as normal and permissible incidents of a contract for the sale of goods. . . .

3. Under subsection (2) rights which are no longer executory such as a right to damages for breach may be assigned although the agreement prohibits assignment. In such cases no question of delegation of any performance is involved. Subsection (2) is subject to Section 9–406, which makes rights to payment for goods sold ("accounts"), whether or not earned, freely alienable notwithstanding a contrary agreement or rule of law.

4. The nature of the contract or the circumstances of the case, however, may bar assignment of the contract even where delegation of performance is not involved. This Article and this section are intended to clarify this problem, particularly in cases dealing with output requirement and exclusive dealing contracts. In the first place the section on requirements and exclusive dealing removes from the construction of the original contract most of the "personal discretion" element by substituting the reasonably objective standard of good faith operation of the plant or business to be supplied. Secondly, the section on insecurity and assurances, which is specifically referred to in subsection (6) of this section, frees the other party from the doubts and uncertainty which may afflict him under an assignment of the character in question by permitting him to demand adequate assurance of due performance without which he may suspend his own performance. Subsection (6) is not in any way intended to limit the effect of the section on insecurity and assurances and the word "performance" includes the giving of orders under a requirements contract. Of course, in any case where a material personal discretion is sought to be transferred, effective assignment is barred by subsection (2). . . .

. . .

Definitional Cross References:

"Agreement". Section 1–201.

"Buyer". Section 2–103.

"Contract". Section 1–201.

"Party". Section 1–201.

"Rights". Section 1–201.

"Seller". Section 2–103.

"Term". Section 1–201.

PART III

GENERAL OBLIGATION AND CONSTRUCTION OF CONTRACT

§ 2–301. General Obligations of Parties.

The obligation of the seller is to transfer and deliver and that of the buyer is to accept and pay in accordance with the contract.

Official Comment

Definitional Cross References:

"Buyer". Section 2–103.

"Contract". Section 1–201.

"Party". Section 1–201.

"Seller". Section 2–103.

§ 2–302. Unconscionable Contract or Clause.

(1) If the court as a matter of law finds the contract or any clause of the contract to have been unconscionable at the time it was made the court may refuse to enforce the contract, or it may enforce the remainder of the contract without the unconscionable clause, or it may so limit the application of any unconscionable clause as to avoid any unconscionable result.

(2) When it is claimed or appears to the court that the contract or any clause thereof may be unconscionable the parties shall be afforded a reasonable opportunity to present evidence as to its commercial setting, purpose and effect to aid the court in making the determination.

Official Comment

. . .

1. This section is intended to make it possible for the courts to police explicitly against the contracts or clauses which they find to be unconscionable. In the past such policing has been accomplished by adverse construction of language, by manipulation of the rules of offer and acceptance or by determinations that the clause is contrary to public policy or to the dominant purpose of the contract. This section is intended to allow the court to pass directly on the unconscionability of the contract or particular clause therein and to make a conclusion of law as to its unconscionability. The basic test is whether, in the light of the general commercial background and the commercial needs of the particular trade or case, the clauses involved are so one-sided as to be unconscionable under the circumstances existing at the time of the making of the contract. Subsection (2) makes it clear that it is proper for the court to hear evidence upon these questions. The principle is one of the prevention of oppression and unfair surprise (Cf. Campbell Soup Co. v. Wentz, 172 F.2d 80, 3d Cir. 1948) and not of disturbance of allocation of risks because of superior bargaining power. The underlying basis of this section is illustrated by the results in cases such as the following:

Kansas City Wholesale Grocery Co. v. Weber Packing Corporation, 93 Utah 414, 73 P.2d 1272 (1937), where a clause limiting time for complaints was held inapplicable to latent defects in a shipment of catsup which could be discovered only by microscopic analysis; Hardy v. General Motors Acceptance Corporation, 38 Ga.App. 463, 144 S.E. 327 (1928), holding that a disclaimer of warranty clause applied only to express warranties, thus letting in a fair implied warranty; Andrews Bros. v. Singer & Co. (1934 CA) 1 K.B. 17, holding that where a car with substantial mileage was delivered instead of a "new" car, a disclaimer of warranties, including those "implied," left unaffected an "express obligation" on the description, even though the Sale of Goods Act called such an implied warranty; New Prague Flouring Mill Co. v. G. A. Spears, 194 Iowa 417, 189 N.W. 815 (1922), holding that a clause permitting the seller, upon the buyer's failure to supply shipping instructions, to cancel, ship, or allow delivery date to be indefinitely postponed 30 days at a time by the inaction, does not indefinitely postpone the date of measuring damages for the buyer's breach, to the seller's advantage; and Kansas Flour Mills Co. v. Dirks, 100 Kan. 376, 164 P. 273 (1917), where under a similar clause in a rising market the court permitted the buyer to measure his damages for non-delivery at the end of only one 30 day postponement; Green v. Arcos, Ltd. (1931 CA) 47 T.L.R. 336, where a blanket clause prohibiting rejection of shipments by the buyer was restricted to apply to shipments where discrepancies represented merely mercantile variations; Meyer v. Packard Cleveland Motor Co., 106 Ohio St. 328, 140 N.E. 118 (1922), in which the court held that a "waiver" of all agreements not specified did not preclude implied warranty of fitness of a rebuilt dump truck for ordinary use as a dump truck; Austin Co. v. J. H. Tillman Co., 104 Or. 541, 209 P. 131 (1922), where a clause limiting the buyer's remedy to return was held to be applicable only if the seller had delivered a machine needed for a construction job which reasonably met the contract description; Bekkevold v. Potts, 173 Minn. 87, 216 N.W. 790, 59 A.L.R. 1164 (1927), refusing to allow warranty of fitness for purpose imposed by law to be negated by clause excluding all warranties "made" by the seller; Robert A. Munroe & Co. v. Meyer (1930) 2 K.B. 312, holding that the warranty of description overrides a clause reading "with all faults and defects" where adulterated meat not up to the contract description was delivered.

2. Under this section the court, in its discretion, may refuse to enforce the contract as a whole if it is permeated by the unconscionability, or it may strike any single clause or group of clauses which are so tainted or which are contrary to the essential purpose of the agreement, or it may simply limit unconscionable clauses so as to avoid unconscionable results.

3. The present section is addressed to the court, and the decision is to be made by it. The commercial evidence referred to in subsection (2) is for the court's consideration, not the jury's. Only the agreement which results from the court's action on these matters is to be submitted to the general triers of the facts.

Definitional Cross Reference:

"Contract". Section 1–201.

§ 2–303. Allocation or Division of Risks.

Where this Article allocates a risk or a burden as between the parties "unless otherwise agreed", the agreement may not only shift the allocation but may also divide the risk or burden.

Official Comment

. . .

Definitional Cross References:

"Party". Section 1–201.

"Agreement". Section 1–201.

§ 2–304. Price Payable in Money, Goods, Realty, or Otherwise.

(1) The price can be made payable in money or otherwise. If it is payable in whole or in part in goods each party is a seller of the goods which he is to transfer.

(2) Even though all or part of the price is payable in an interest in realty the transfer of the goods and the seller's obligations with reference to them are subject to this Article, but not the transfer of the interest in realty or the transferor's obligations in connection therewith.

Official Comment

. . .

Definitional Cross References:

"Goods". Section 2–105.

"Money". Section 1–201.

"Party". Section 1–201.

"Seller". Section 2–103.

§ 2–305. Open Price Term.

(1) The parties if they so intend can conclude a contract for sale even though the price is not settled. In such a case the price is a reasonable price at the time for delivery if

(a) nothing is said as to price; or

(b) the price is left to be agreed by the parties and they fail to agree; or

(c) the price is to be fixed in terms of some agreed market or other standard as set or recorded by a third person or agency and it is not so set or recorded.

(2) A price to be fixed by the seller or by the buyer means a price for him to fix in good faith.

(3) When a price left to be fixed otherwise than by agreement of the parties fails to be fixed through fault of one party the other may at his option treat the contract as cancelled or himself fix a reasonable price.

(4) Where, however, the parties intend not to be bound unless the price be fixed or agreed and it is not fixed or agreed there is no contract. In such a case the buyer must return any goods already received or if unable so to do must pay their reasonable value at the time of delivery and the seller must return any portion of the price paid on account.

Official Comment

. . .

Purposes of Changes:

1. This section applies when the price term is left open on the making of an agreement which is nevertheless intended by the parties to be a binding agreement. This Article rejects in these instances the formula that "an agreement to agree is unenforceable" if the case falls within subsection (1) of this section, and rejects also defeating such agreements on the ground of "indefiniteness". Instead this Article recognizes the dominant intention of the parties to have the deal continue to be binding upon both. As to future performance, since this Article recognizes remedies such as cover (Section 2–712), resale (Section 2–706) and specific performance (Section 2–716) which go beyond any mere arithmetic as between contract price and market price, there is usually a "reasonably certain basis for granting an appropriate remedy for breach" so that the contract need not fail for indefiniteness.

2. Under some circumstances the postponement of agreement on price will mean that no deal has really been concluded, and this is made express in the preamble of subsection (1) ("The parties *if they so intend*") and in subsection (4). Whether or not this is so is, in most cases, a question to be determined by the trier of fact.

3. Subsection (2), dealing with the situation where the price is to be fixed by one party rejects the uncommercial idea that an agreement that the seller may fix the price means that he may fix any price he may wish by the express qualification that the price so fixed must be fixed in good faith. Good faith includes observance of reasonable commercial standards of fair dealing in the trade if the party is a merchant. (Section 2–103). But in the normal case a "posted price" or a future seller's or buyer's "given price," "price in effect," "market price," or the like satisfies the good faith requirement.

4. The section recognizes that there may be cases in which a particular person's judgment is not chosen merely as a barometer or index of a fair price but is an essential condition to the parties' intent to make any contract at all. For example, the case where a known and trusted expert is to "value" a particular painting for which there is no market standard differs sharply from the situation where a named expert is to determine the grade of cotton, and the difference would support a finding that in the one the parties did not intend to make a binding agreement if that expert were unavailable whereas in the other they did so intend. Other circumstances would of course affect the validity of such a finding.

5. Under subsection (3), wrongful interference by one party with any agreed machinery for price fixing in the contract may be treated by the other party as a repudiation justifying cancellation, or merely as a failure to take cooperative action thus shifting to the aggrieved party the reasonable leeway in fixing the price.

6. Throughout the entire section, the purpose is to give effect to the agreement which has been made. That effect, however, is always conditioned by the requirement of good faith action which is made an inherent part of all contracts within this Act. (Section 1–203).

. . .

Definitional Cross References:

"Agreement". Section 1–201.

"Burden of establishing". Section 1–201.

"Buyer". Section 2–103.

"Cancellation". Section 2–106.

"Contract". Section 1–201.

"Contract for sale". Section 2–106.

"Fault". Section 1–201.

"Goods". Section 2–105.

"Party". Section 1–201.

"Receipt of goods". Section 2–103.

"Seller". Section 2–103.

"Term". Section 1–201.

§ 2–306. Output, Requirements and Exclusive Dealings.

(1) A term which measures the quantity by the output of the seller or the requirements of the buyer means such actual output or requirements as may occur in good faith, except that no quantity unreasonably disproportionate to any stated estimate or in the absence of a stated estimate to any normal or otherwise comparable prior output or requirements may be tendered or demanded.

(2) A lawful agreement by either the seller or the buyer for exclusive dealing in the kind of goods concerned imposes unless otherwise agreed an obligation by the seller to use best efforts to supply the goods and by the buyer to use best efforts to promote their sale.

Official Comment

. . .

Purposes:

1. Subsection (1) of this section, in regard to output and requirements, applies to this specific problem the general approach of this Act which requires the reading of commercial background and intent into the language of any agreement and demands good faith in the performance of that agreement. It applies to such contracts of nonproducing establishments such as dealers or distributors as well as to manufacturing concerns.

2. Under this Article, a contract for output or requirements is not too indefinite since it is held to mean the actual good faith output or requirements of the particular party. Nor does such a contract lack mutuality of obligation since, under this section, the party who will determine quantity is required to operate his plant or conduct his business in good faith and according to commercial standards of fair dealing in the trade so that his output or requirements will approximate a reasonably foreseeable figure. Reasonable elasticity in the requirements is expressly envisaged by this section and good faith variations from prior

requirements are permitted even when the variation may be such as to result in discontinuance. A shut-down by a requirements buyer for lack of orders might be permissible when a shut-down merely to curtail losses would not. The essential test is whether the party is acting in good faith. Similarly, a sudden expansion of the plant by which requirements are to be measured would not be included within the scope of the contract as made but normal expansion undertaken in good faith would be within the scope of this section. One of the factors in an expansion situation would be whether the market price had risen greatly in a case in which the requirements contract contained a fixed price. Reasonable variation of an extreme sort is exemplified in Southwest Natural Gas Co. v. Oklahoma Portland Cement Co., 102 F.2d 630 (C.C.A.10, 1939). . . .

3. If an estimate of output or requirements is included in the agreement, no quantity unreasonably disproportionate to it may be tendered or demanded. Any minimum or maximum set by the agreement shows a clear limit on the intended elasticity. In similar fashion, the agreed estimate is to be regarded as a center around which the parties intend the variation to occur. . . .

5. Subsection (2), on exclusive dealing, makes explicit the commercial rule embodied in this Act under which the parties to such contracts are held to have impliedly, even when not expressly, bound themselves to use reasonable diligence as well as good faith in their performance of the contract. Under such contracts the exclusive agent is required, although no express commitment has been made, to use reasonable effort and due diligence in the expansion of the market or the promotion of the product, as the case may be. The principal is expected under such a contract to refrain from supplying any other dealer or agent within the exclusive territory. An exclusive dealing agreement brings into play all of the good faith aspects of the output and requirement problems of subsection (1). It also raises questions of insecurity and right to adequate assurance under this Article.

. . .

Definitional Cross References:

"Agreement". Section 1–201.

"Buyer". Section 2–103.

"Contract for sale". Section 2–106.

"Good faith". Section 1–201.

"Goods". Section 2–105.

"Party". Section 1–201.

"Term". Section 1–201.

"Seller". Section 2–103.

§ 2–307. Delivery in Single Lot or Several Lots.

Unless otherwise agreed all goods called for by a contract for sale must be tendered in a single delivery and payment is due only on such tender but where the circumstances give either party the right to make or demand delivery in lots the price if it can be apportioned may be demanded for each lot.

Official Comment

. . .

Definitional Cross References:

"Contract for sale". Section 2–106.

"Goods". Section 2–105.

"Lot". Section 2–105.

"Party". Section 1–201.

§ 2–308. Absence of Specified Place for Delivery.

Unless otherwise agreed

(a) the place for delivery of goods is the seller's place of business or if he has none his residence; but

(b) in a contract for sale of identified goods which to the knowledge of the parties at the time of contracting are in some other place, that place is the place for their delivery; and

(c) documents of title may be delivered through customary banking channels.

Official Comment

. . .

Purposes of Change:

. . .

4. The rules of this section apply only "unless otherwise agreed." The surrounding circumstances, usage of trade, course of dealing and course of performance, as well as the express language of the parties, may constitute an "otherwise agreement".

. . .

Definitional Cross References:

"Contract for sale". Section 2–106.

"Delivery". Section 1–201.

"Document of title". Section 1–201.

"Goods". Section 2–105.

"Party". Section 1–201.

"Seller". Section 2–103.

§ 2–309. Absence of Specific Time Provisions; Notice of Termination.

(1) The time for shipment or delivery or any other action under a contract if not provided in this Article or agreed upon shall be a reasonable time.

(2) Where the contract provides for successive performances but is indefinite in duration it is valid for a reasonable time but unless otherwise agreed may be terminated at any time by either party.

(3) Termination of a contract by one party except on the happening of an agreed event requires that reasonable notification be received by the other party and an agreement dispensing with notification is invalid if its operation would be unconscionable.

Official Comment

. . .

Purposes of Changes and New Matter:

1. Subsection (1) requires that all actions taken under a sales contract must be taken within a reasonable time where no time has been agreed upon. The reasonable time under this provision turns on the criteria as to "reasonable time" and on good faith and commercial standards set forth in Sections 1–203, 1–204 and 2–103. It thus depends upon what constitutes acceptable commercial conduct in view of the nature, purpose and circumstances of the action to be taken. Agreement as to a definite time, however, may be found in a term implied from the contractual circumstances, usage of trade or course of dealing or

performance as well as in an express term. Such cases fall outside of this subsection since in them the time for action is "agreed" by usage.

. . .

Definitional Cross References:

"Agreement". Section 1–201.

"Contract". Section 1–201.

"Notification". Section 1–201.

"Party". Section 1–201.

"Reasonable time". Section 1–204.

"Termination". Section 2–106.

§ 2–310. Open Time for Payment or Running of Credit; Authority to Ship Under Reservation.

Unless otherwise agreed

(a) payment is due at the time and place at which the buyer is to receive the goods even though the place of shipment is the place of delivery; and

(b) if the seller is authorized to send the goods he may ship them under reservation, and may tender the documents of title, but the buyer may inspect the goods after their arrival before payment is due unless such inspection is inconsistent with the terms of the contract (Section 2–513); and

(c) if delivery is authorized and made by way of documents of title otherwise than by subsection (b) then payment is due at the time and place at which the buyer is to receive the documents regardless of where the goods are to be received; and

(d) where the seller is required or authorized to ship the goods on credit the credit period runs from the time of shipment but post-dating the invoice or delaying its dispatch will correspondingly delay the starting of the credit period.

Official Comment

. . .

Definitional Cross References:

"Buyer". Section 2–103.

"Delivery". Section 1–201.

"Document of title". Section 1–201.

"Goods". Section 2–105.

"Receipt of goods". Section 2–103.

"Seller". Section 2–103.

"Send". Section 1–201.

"Term". Section 1–201.

§ 2–311. Options and Cooperation Respecting Performance.

(1) An agreement for sale which is otherwise sufficiently definite (subsection (3) of Section 2–204) to be a contract is not made invalid by the fact that it leaves particulars of performance to be

specified by one of the parties. Any such specification must be made in good faith and within limits set by commercial reasonableness.

(2) Unless otherwise agreed specifications relating to assortment of the goods are at the buyer's option and except as otherwise provided in subsections (1)(c) and (3) of Section 2–319 specifications or arrangements relating to shipment are at the seller's option.

(3) Where such specification would materially affect the other party's performance but is not seasonably made or where one party's cooperation is necessary to the agreed performance of the other but is not seasonably forthcoming, the other party in addition to all other remedies

(a) is excused for any resulting delay in his own performance; and

(b) may also either proceed to perform in any reasonable manner or after the time for a material part of his own performance treat the failure to specify or to cooperate as a breach by failure to deliver or accept the goods.

Official Comment

. . .

Purposes:

1. Subsection (1) permits the parties to leave certain detailed particulars of performance to be filled in by either of them without running the risk of having the contract invalidated for indefiniteness. The party to whom the agreement gives power to specify the missing details is required to exercise good faith and to act in accordance with commercial standards so that there is no surprise and the range of permissible variation is limited by what is commercially reasonable. The "agreement" which permits one party so to specify may be found as well in a course of dealing, usage of trade, or implication from circumstances as in explicit language used by the parties. . . .

3. Subsection (3) applies when the exercise of an option or cooperation by one party is necessary to or materially affects the other party's performance, but it is not seasonably forthcoming; the subsection relieves the other party from the necessity for performance or excuses his delay in performance as the case may be. The contract-keeping party may at his option under this subsection proceed to perform in any commercially reasonable manner rather than wait. In addition to the special remedies provided, this subsection also reserves "all other remedies". The remedy of particular importance in this connection is that provided for insecurity. Request may also be made pursuant to the obligation of good faith for a reasonable indication of the time and manner of performance for which a party is to hold himself ready. . . .

. . .

Definitional Cross References:

"Agreement". Section 1–201.

"Buyer". Section 2–103.

"Contract for sale". Section 2–106.

"Goods". Section 2–105.

"Party". Section 1–201.

"Remedy". Section 1–201.

"Seasonably". Section 1–204.

"Seller". Section 2–103.

§ 2–312. Warranty of Title and Against Infringement; Buyer's Obligation Against Infringement.

(1) Subject to subsection (2) there is in a contract for sale a warranty by the seller that

§ 2-313 UNIFORM COMMERCIAL CODE Pt. I

(a) the title conveyed shall be good, and its transfer rightful; and

(b) the goods shall be delivered free from any security interest or other lien or encumbrance of which the buyer at the time of contracting has no knowledge.

(2) A warranty under subsection (1) will be excluded or modified only by specific language or by circumstances which give the buyer reason to know that the person selling does not claim title in himself or that he is purporting to sell only such right or title as he or a third person may have.

(3) Unless otherwise agreed a seller who is a merchant regularly dealing in goods of the kind warrants that the goods shall be delivered free of the rightful claim of any third person by way of infringement or the like but a buyer who furnishes specifications to the seller must hold the seller harmless against any such claim which arises out of compliance with the specifications.

Official Comment

. . .

Definitional Cross References:

"Buyer". Section 2–103.

"Contract for sale". Section 2–106.

"Goods". Section 2–105.

"Person". Section 1–201.

"Right". Section 1–201.

"Seller". Section 2–103.

§ 2-313. Express Warranties by Affirmation, Promise, Description, Sample.

(1) Express warranties by the seller are created as follows:

(a) Any affirmation of fact or promise made by the seller to the buyer which relates to the goods and becomes part of the basis of the bargain creates an express warranty that the goods shall conform to the affirmation or promise.

(b) Any description of the goods which is made part of the basis of the bargain creates an express warranty that the goods shall conform to the description.

(c) Any sample or model which is made part of the basis of the bargain creates an express warranty that the whole of the goods shall conform to the sample or model.

(2) It is not necessary to the creation of an express warranty that the seller use formal words such as "warrant" or "guarantee" or that he have a specific intention to make a warranty, but an affirmation merely of the value of the goods or a statement purporting to be merely the seller's opinion or commendation of the goods does not create a warranty.

Official Comment

. . .

Purposes of Changes: To consolidate and systematize basic principles with the result that:

1. "Express" warranties rest on "dickered" aspects of the individual bargain, and go so clearly to the essence of that bargain that words of disclaimer in a form are repugnant to the basic dickered terms. "Implied" warranties rest so clearly on a common factual situation or set of conditions that no particular language or action is necessary to evidence them and they will arise in such a situation unless unmistakably negated. . . .

2. Although this section is limited in its scope and direct purpose to warranties made by the seller to the buyer as part of a contract for sale, the warranty sections of this Article are not designed in any way

to disturb those lines of case law growth which have recognized that warranties need not be confined either to sales contracts or to the direct parties to such a contract. They may arise in other appropriate circumstances such as in the case of bailments for hire, whether such bailment is itself the main contract or is merely a supplying of containers under a contract for the sale of their contents. . . .

3. The present section deals with affirmations of fact by the seller, descriptions of the goods or exhibitions of samples, exactly as any other part of a negotiation which ends in a contract is dealt with. No specific intention to make a warranty is necessary if any of these factors is made part of the basis of the bargain. In actual practice affirmations of fact made by the seller about the goods during a bargain are regarded as part of the description of those goods; hence no particular reliance on such statements need be shown in order to weave them into the fabric of the agreement. Rather, any fact which is to take such affirmations, once made, out of the agreement requires clear affirmative proof. The issue normally is one of fact.

4. In view of the principle that the whole purpose of the law of warranty is to determine what it is that the seller has in essence agreed to sell, the policy is adopted of those cases which refuse except in unusual circumstances to recognize a material deletion of the seller's obligation. Thus, a contract is normally a contract for a sale of something describable and described. A clause generally disclaiming "all warranties, express or implied" cannot reduce the seller's obligation with respect to such description and therefore cannot be given literal effect under Section 2–316.

This is not intended to mean that the parties, if they consciously desire, cannot make their own bargain as they wish. But in determining what they have agreed upon good faith is a factor and consideration should be given to the fact that the probability is small that a real price is intended to be exchanged for a pseudo-obligation.

5. Paragraph (1)(b) makes specific some of the principles set forth above when a description of the goods is given by the seller.

A description need not be by words. Technical specifications, blueprints and the like can afford more exact description than mere language and if made part of the basis of the bargain goods must conform with them. Past deliveries may set the description of quality, either expressly or impliedly by course of dealing. Of course, all descriptions by merchants must be read against the applicable trade usages with the general rules as to merchantability resolving any doubts.

6. The basic situation as to statements affecting the true essence of the bargain is no different when a sample or model is involved in the transaction. This section includes both a "sample" actually drawn from the bulk of goods which is the subject matter of the sale, and a "model" which is offered for inspection when the subject matter is not at hand and which has not been drawn from the bulk of the goods.

Although the underlying principles are unchanged, the facts are often ambiguous when something is shown as illustrative, rather than as a straight sample. In general, the presumption is that any sample or model just as any affirmation of fact is intended to become a basis of the bargain. But there is no escape from the question of fact. When the seller exhibits a sample purporting to be drawn from an existing bulk, good faith of course requires that the sample be fairly drawn. But in mercantile experience the mere exhibition of a "sample" does not of itself show whether it is merely intended to "suggest" or to "be" the character of the subject-matter of the contract. The question is whether the seller has so acted with reference to the sample as to make him responsible that the whole shall have at least the values shown by it. The circumstances aid in answering this question. If the sample has been drawn from an existing bulk, it must be regarded as describing values of the goods contracted for unless it is accompanied by an unmistakable denial of such responsibility. If, on the other hand, a model of merchandise not on hand is offered, the mercantile presumption that it has become a literal description of the subject matter is not so strong, and particularly so if modification on the buyer's initiative impairs any feature of the model.

7. The precise time when words of description or affirmation are made or samples are shown is not material. The sole question is whether the language or samples or models are fairly to be regarded as part of the contract. If language is used after the closing of the deal (as when the buyer when taking delivery asks and receives an additional assurance), the warranty becomes a modification, and need not be supported by consideration if it is otherwise reasonable and in order (Section 2–209).

8. Concerning affirmations of value or a seller's opinion or commendation under subsection (2), the basic question remains the same: What statements of the seller have in the circumstances and in objective judgment become part of the basis of the bargain? As indicated above, all of the statements of the seller do so unless good reason is shown to the contrary. The provisions of subsection (2) are included, however, since common experience discloses that some statements or predictions cannot fairly be viewed as entering into the bargain. Even as to false statements of value, however, the possibility is left open that a remedy may be provided by the law relating to fraud or misrepresentation.

. . .

Definitional Cross References:

"Buyer". Section 2–103.

"Conforming". Section 2–106.

"Goods". Section 2–105.

"Seller". Section 2–103.

§ 2–314. Implied Warranty: Merchantability; Usage of Trade.

(1) Unless excluded or modified (Section 2–316), a warranty that the goods shall be merchantable is implied in a contract for their sale if the seller is a merchant with respect to goods of that kind. Under this section the serving for value of food or drink to be consumed either on the premises or elsewhere is a sale.

(2) Goods to be merchantable must be at least such as

(a) pass without objection in the trade under the contract description; and

(b) in the case of fungible goods, are of fair average quality within the description; and

(c) are fit for the ordinary purposes for which such goods are used; and

(d) run, within the variations permitted by the agreement, of even kind, quality and quantity within each unit and among all units involved; and

(e) are adequately contained, packaged, and labeled as the agreement may require; and

(f) conform to the promise or affirmations of fact made on the container or label if any.

(3) Unless excluded or modified (Section 2–316) other implied warranties may arise from course of dealing or usage of trade.

Official Comment

. . .

Purposes of Changes:

This section, drawn in view of the steadily developing case law on the subject, is intended to make it clear that:

1. The seller's obligation applies to present sales as well as to contracts to sell subject to the effects of any examination of specific goods. (Subsection (2) of Section 2–316). Also, the warranty of merchantability applies to sales for use as well as to sales for resale.

2. The question when the warranty is imposed turns basically on the meaning of the terms of the agreement as recognized in the trade. Goods delivered under an agreement made by a merchant in a given line of trade must be of a quality comparable to that generally acceptable in that line of trade under the description or other designation of the goods used in the agreement.

3. A specific designation of goods by the buyer does not exclude the seller's obligation that they be fit for the general purposes appropriate to such goods. A contract for the sale of second-hand goods, however, involves only such obligation as is appropriate to such goods for that is their contract description. A person

making an isolated sale of goods is not a "merchant" within the meaning of the full scope of this section and, thus, no warranty of merchantability would apply. His knowledge of any defects not apparent on inspection would, however, without need for express agreement and in keeping with the underlying reason of the present section and the provisions on good faith, impose an obligation that known material but hidden defects be fully disclosed.

4. Although a seller may not be a "merchant" as to the goods in question, if he states generally that they are "guaranteed" the provisions of this section may furnish a guide to the content of the resulting express warranty. This has particular significance in the case of second-hand sales, and has further significance in limiting the effect of fine-print disclaimer clauses where their effect would be inconsistent with large-print assertions of "guarantee." . . .

6. Subsection (2) does not purport to exhaust the meaning of "merchantable" nor to negate any of its attributes not specifically mentioned in the text of the statute, but arising by usage of trade or through case law. The language used is "must be at least such as . . .," and the intention is to leave open other possible attributes of merchantability.

7. Paragraphs (a) and (b) of subsection (2) are to be read together. Both refer, as indicated above, to the standards of that line of the trade which fits the transaction and the seller's business. "Fair average" is a term directly appropriate to agricultural bulk products and means goods centering around the middle belt of quality, not the least or the worst that can be understood in the particular trade by the designation, but such as can pass "without objection." Of course a fair percentage of the least is permissible but the goods are not "fair average" if they are all of the least or worst quality possible under the description. In cases of doubt as to what quality is intended, the price at which a merchant closes a contract is an excellent index of the nature and scope of his obligation under the present section.

8. Fitness for the ordinary purposes for which goods of the type are used is a fundamental concept of the present section and is covered in paragraph (c). As stated above, merchantability is also a part of the obligation owing to the purchaser for use. Correspondingly, protection, under this aspect of the warranty, of the person buying for resale to the ultimate consumer is equally necessary, and merchantable goods must therefore be "honestly" resalable in the normal course of business because they are what they purport to be. . . .

12. Subsection (3) is to make explicit that usage of trade and course of dealing can create warranties and that they are implied rather than express warranties and thus subject to exclusion or modification under Section 2–316. A typical instance would be the obligation to provide pedigree papers to evidence conformity of the animal to the contract in the case of a pedigreed dog or blooded bull. . . .

. . .

Definitional Cross References:

"Agreement". Section 1–201.

"Contract". Section 1–201.

"Contract for sale". Section 2–106.

"Goods". Section 2–105.

"Merchant". Section 2–104.

"Seller". Section 2–103.

§ 2–315. Implied Warranty: Fitness for Particular Purpose.

Where the seller at the time of contracting has reason to know any particular purpose for which the goods are required and that the buyer is relying on the seller's skill or judgment to select or furnish suitable goods, there is unless excluded or modified under the next section an implied warranty that the goods shall be fit for such purpose.

Official Comment

. . .

Purposes of Changes:

1. Whether or not this warranty arises in any individual case is basically a question of fact to be determined by the circumstances of the contracting. Under this section the buyer need not bring home to the seller actual knowledge of the particular purpose for which the goods are intended or of his reliance on the seller's skill and judgment, if the circumstances are such that the seller has reason to realize the purpose intended or that the reliance exists. The buyer, of course, must actually be relying on the seller.

2. A "particular purpose" differs from the ordinary purpose for which the goods are used in that it envisages a specific use by the buyer which is peculiar to the nature of his business whereas the ordinary purposes for which goods are used are those envisaged in the concept of merchantability and go to uses which are customarily made of the goods in question. For example, shoes are generally used for the purpose of walking upon ordinary ground, but a seller may know that a particular pair was selected to be used for climbing mountains.

A contract may of course include both a warranty of merchantability and one of fitness for a particular purpose.

The provisions of this Article on the cumulation and conflict of express and implied warranties must be considered on the question of inconsistency between or among warranties. In such a case any question of fact as to which warranty was intended by the parties to apply must be resolved in favor of the warranty of fitness for particular purpose as against all other warranties except where the buyer has taken upon himself the responsibility of furnishing the technical specifications. . . .

4. . . . Although normally the [implied warranty of fitness for a particular purpose] will arise only where the seller is a merchant with the appropriate "skill or judgment," it can arise as to non-merchants where this is justified by the particular circumstances.

5. . . . Under the present section the existence of a patent or other trade name and the designation of the article by that name, or indeed in any other definite manner, is only one of the facts to be considered on the question of whether the buyer actually relied on the seller, but it is not of itself decisive of the issue. If the buyer himself is insisting on a particular brand he is not relying on the seller's skill and judgment and so no warranty results. But the mere fact that the article purchased has a particular patent or trade name is not sufficient to indicate nonreliance if the article has been recommended by the seller as adequate for the buyer's purposes.

. . .

Definitional Cross References:

"Buyer". Section 2–103.

"Goods". Section 2–105.

"Seller". Section 2–103.

§ 2–316. Exclusion or Modification of Warranties.

(1) Words or conduct relevant to the creation of an express warranty and words or conduct tending to negate or limit warranty shall be construed wherever reasonable as consistent with each other; but subject to the provisions of this Article on parol or extrinsic evidence (Section 2–202) negation or limitation is inoperative to the extent that such construction is unreasonable.

(2) Subject to subsection (3), to exclude or modify the implied warranty of merchantability or any part of it the language must mention merchantability and in case of a writing must be conspicuous, and to exclude or modify any implied warranty of fitness the exclusion must be by a writing and conspicuous. Language to exclude all implied warranties of fitness is sufficient if it states, for example, that "There are no warranties which extend beyond the description on the face hereof."

(3) Notwithstanding subsection (2)

(a) unless the circumstances indicate otherwise, all implied warranties are excluded by expressions like "as is", "with all faults" or other language which in common understanding calls the buyer's attention to the exclusion of warranties and makes plain that there is no implied warranty; and

(b) when the buyer before entering into the contract has examined the goods or the sample or model as fully as he desired or has refused to examine the goods there is no implied warranty with regard to defects which an examination ought in the circumstances to have revealed to him; and

(c) an implied warranty can also be excluded or modified by course of dealing or course of performance or usage of trade.

(4) Remedies for breach of warranty can be limited in accordance with the provisions of this Article on liquidation or limitation of damages and on contractual modification of remedy (Sections 2–718 and 2–719).

Official Comment

. . .

1. This section is designed principally to deal with those frequent clauses in sales contracts which seek to exclude "all warranties, express or implied." It seeks to protect a buyer from unexpected and unbargained language of disclaimer by denying effect to such language when inconsistent with language of express warranty and permitting the exclusion of implied warranties only by conspicuous language or other circumstances which protect the buyer from surprise.

2. . . . This Article treats the limitation or avoidance of consequential damages as a matter of limiting remedies for breach, separate from the matter of creation of liability under a warranty. If no warranty exists, there is of course no problem of limiting remedies for breach of warranty. Under subsection (4) the question of limitation of remedy is governed by the sections referred to rather than by this section. . . .

7. Paragraph (a) of subsection (3) deals with general terms such as "as is," "as they stand," "with all faults," and the like. Such terms in ordinary commercial usage are understood to mean that the buyer takes the entire risk as to the quality of the goods involved. The terms covered by paragraph (a) are in fact merely a particularization of paragraph (c) which provides for exclusion or modification of implied warranties by usage of trade.

. . .

Definitional Cross References:

"Agreement". Section 1–201.

"Buyer". Section 2–103.

"Contract". Section 1–201.

"Course of dealing". Section 1–205.

"Goods". Section 2–105.

"Remedy". Section 1–201.

"Seller". Section 2–103.

"Usage of trade". Section 1–205.

§ 2–317. Cumulation and Conflict of Warranties Express or Implied.

Warranties whether express or implied shall be construed as consistent with each other and as cumulative, but if such construction is unreasonable the intention of the parties shall determine which warranty is dominant. In ascertaining that intention the following rules apply:

(a) Exact or technical specifications displace an inconsistent sample or model or general language of description.

(b) A sample from an existing bulk displaces inconsistent general language of description.

(c) Express warranties displace inconsistent implied warranties other than an implied warranty of fitness for a particular purpose.

Official Comment

. . .

Purposes of Changes:

1. The present section rests on the basic policy of this Article that no warranty is created except by some conduct (either affirmative action or failure to disclose) on the part of the seller. Therefore, all warranties are made cumulative unless this construction of the contract is impossible or unreasonable. . . .

2. The rules of this section are designed to aid in determining the intention of the parties as to which of inconsistent warranties which have arisen from the circumstances of their transaction shall prevail. These rules of intention are to be applied only where factors making for an equitable estoppel of the seller do not exist and where he has in perfect good faith made warranties which later turn out to be inconsistent. To the extent that the seller has led the buyer to believe that all of the warranties can be performed, he is estopped from setting up any essential inconsistency as a defense.

. . .

Definitional Cross Reference:

"Party". Section 1–201.

§ 2–318. Third Party Beneficiaries of Warranties Express or Implied.

Note: *If this Act is introduced in the Congress of the United States this section should be omitted. (States to select one alternative.)*

Alternative A

A seller's warranty whether express or implied extends to any natural person who is in the family or household of his buyer or who is a guest in his home if it is reasonable to expect that such person may use, consume or be affected by the goods and who is injured in person by breach of the warranty. A seller may not exclude or limit the operation of this section.

Alternative B

A seller's warranty whether express or implied extends to any natural person who may reasonably be expected to use, consume or be affected by the goods and who is injured in person by breach of the warranty. A seller may not exclude or limit the operation of this section.

Alternative C

A seller's warranty whether express or implied extends to any person who may reasonably be expected to use, consume or be affected by the goods and who is injured by breach of the warranty. A seller may not exclude or limit the operation of this section with respect to injury to the person of an individual to whom the warranty extends.

As amended in 1966.

Official Comment

. . .

Definitional Cross References:

"Buyer". Section 2–103.

"Goods". Section 2–105.

"Seller". Section 2–103.

§ 2–319. F.O.B. and F.A.S. Terms.

(1) Unless otherwise agreed the term F.O.B. (which means "free on board") at a named place, even though used only in connection with the stated price, is a delivery term under which

  (a) when the term is F.O.B. the place of shipment, the seller must at that place ship the goods in the manner provided in this Article (Section 2–504) and bear the expense and risk of putting them into the possession of the carrier; or

  (b) when the term is F.O.B. the place of destination, the seller must at his own expense and risk transport the goods to that place and there tender delivery of them in the manner provided in this Article (Section 2–503);

  (c) when under either (a) or (b) the term is also F.O.B. vessel, car or other vehicle, the seller must in addition at his own expense and risk load the goods on board. If the term is F.O.B. vessel the buyer must name the vessel and in an appropriate case the seller must comply with the provisions of this Article on the form of bill of lading (Section 2–323).

(2) Unless otherwise agreed the term F.A.S. vessel (which means "free alongside") at a named port, even though used only in connection with the stated price, is a delivery term under which the seller must

  (a) at his own expense and risk deliver the goods alongside the vessel in the manner usual in that port or on a dock designated and provided by the buyer; and

  (b) obtain and tender a receipt for the goods in exchange for which the carrier is under a duty to issue a bill of lading.

(3) Unless otherwise agreed in any case falling within subsection (1)(a) or (c) or subsection (2) the buyer must seasonably give any needed instructions for making delivery, including when the term is F.A.S. or F.O.B. the loading berth of the vessel and in an appropriate case its name and sailing date. The seller may treat the failure of needed instructions as a failure of cooperation under this Article (Section 2–311). He may also at his option move the goods in any reasonable manner preparatory to delivery or shipment.

(4) Under the term F.O.B. vessel or F.A.S. unless otherwise agreed the buyer must make payment against tender of the required documents and the seller may not tender nor the buyer demand delivery of the goods in substitution for the documents.

Official Comment

. . .

Definitional Cross References:

"Agreed". Section 1–201.

"Bill of lading". Section 1–201.

"Buyer". Section 2–103.

"Goods". Section 2–105.

"Seasonably". Section 1–204.

"Seller". Section 2–103.

"Term". Section 1–201.

§ 2–320. C.I.F. and C. & F. Terms.

(1) The term C.I.F. means that the price includes in a lump sum the cost of the goods and the insurance and freight to the named destination. The term C. & F. or C.F. means that the price so includes cost and freight to the named destination.

(2) Unless otherwise agreed and even though used only in connection with the stated price and destination, the term C.I.F. destination or its equivalent requires the seller at his own expense and risk to

(a) put the goods into the possession of a carrier at the port for shipment and obtain a negotiable bill or bills of lading covering the entire transportation to the named destination; and

(b) load the goods and obtain a receipt from the carrier (which may be contained in the bill of lading) showing that the freight has been paid or provided for; and

(c) obtain a policy or certificate of insurance, including any war risk insurance, of a kind and on terms then current at the port of shipment in the usual amount, in the currency of the contract, shown to cover the same goods covered by the bill of lading and providing for payment of loss to the order of the buyer or for the account of whom it may concern; but the seller may add to the price the amount of the premium for any such war risk insurance; and

(d) prepare an invoice of the goods and procure any other documents required to effect shipment or to comply with the contract; and

(e) forward and tender with commercial promptness all the documents in due form and with any indorsement necessary to perfect the buyer's rights.

(3) Unless otherwise agreed the term C. & F. or its equivalent has the same effect and imposes upon the seller the same obligations and risks as a C.I.F. term except the obligation as to insurance.

(4) Under the term C.I.F. or C. & F. unless otherwise agreed the buyer must make payment against tender of the required documents and the seller may not tender nor the buyer demand delivery of the goods in substitution for the documents.

Official Comment

. . .

Definitional Cross References:

"Bill of lading". Section 1–201.

"Buyer". Section 2–103.

"Contract". Section 1–201.

"Goods". Section 2–105.

"Rights". Section 1–201.

"Seller". Section 2–103.

"Term". Section 1–201.

§ 2–321. C.I.F. or C. & F.: "Net Landed Weights"; "Payment on Arrival"; Warranty of Condition on Arrival.

Under a contract containing a term C.I.F. or C. & F.

(1) Where the price is based on or is to be adjusted according to "net landed weights", "delivered weights", "out turn" quantity or quality or the like, unless otherwise agreed the seller must reasonably estimate the price. The payment due on tender of the documents called for by the contract is the

amount so estimated, but after final adjustment of the price a settlement must be made with commercial promptness.

(2) An agreement described in subsection (1) or any warranty of quality or condition of the goods on arrival places upon the seller the risk of ordinary deterioration, shrinkage and the like in transportation but has no effect on the place or time of identification to the contract for sale or delivery or on the passing of the risk of loss.

(3) Unless otherwise agreed where the contract provides for payment on or after arrival of the goods the seller must before payment allow such preliminary inspection as is feasible; but if the goods are lost delivery of the documents and payment are due when the goods should have arrived.

Official Comment

. . .

Definitional Cross References:

"Agreement". Section 1–201.

"Contract". Section 1–201.

"Delivery". Section 1–201.

"Goods". Section 2–105.

"Seller". Section 2–103.

"Term". Section 1–201.

§ 2–322. Delivery "Ex-ship".

(1) Unless otherwise agreed a term for delivery of goods "ex-ship" (which means from the carrying vessel) or in equivalent language is not restricted to a particular ship and requires delivery from a ship which has reached a place at the named port of destination where goods of the kind are usually discharged.

(2) Under such a term unless otherwise agreed

(a) the seller must discharge all liens arising out of the carriage and furnish the buyer with a direction which puts the carrier under a duty to deliver the goods; and

(b) the risk of loss does not pass to the buyer until the goods leave the ship's tackle or are otherwise properly unloaded.

Official Comment

. . .

Definitional Cross References:

"Buyer". Section 2–103.

"Goods". Section 2–105.

"Seller". Section 2–103.

"Term". Section 1–201.

§ 2–323. Form of Bill of Lading Required in Overseas Shipment; "Overseas".

(1) Where the contract contemplates overseas shipment and contains a term C.I.F. or C. & F. or F.O.B. vessel, the seller unless otherwise agreed must obtain a negotiable bill of lading stating that the goods have been loaded in board or, in the case of a term C.I.F. or C. & F., received for shipment.

(2) Where in a case within subsection (1) a bill of lading has been issued in a set of parts, unless otherwise agreed if the documents are not to be sent from abroad the buyer may demand tender of the

full set; otherwise only one part of the bill of lading need be tendered. Even if the agreement expressly requires a full set

(a) due tender of a single part is acceptable within the provisions of this Article on cure of improper delivery (subsection (1) of Section 2–508); and

(b) even though the full set is demanded, if the documents are sent from abroad the person tendering an incomplete set may nevertheless require payment upon furnishing an indemnity which the buyer in good faith deems adequate.

(3) A shipment by water or by air or a contract contemplating such shipment is "overseas" insofar as by usage of trade or agreement it is subject to the commercial, financing or shipping practices characteristic of international deep water commerce.

Official Comment

. . .

Definitional Cross References:

"Bill of lading". Section 1–201.

"Buyer". Section 2–103.

"Contract". Section 1–201.

"Delivery". Section 1–201.

"Financing agency". Section 2–104.

"Person". Section 1–201.

"Seller". Section 2–103.

"Send". Section 1–201.

"Term". Section 1–201.

§ 2–324. "No Arrival, No Sale" Term.

Under a term "no arrival, no sale" or terms of like meaning, unless otherwise agreed,

(a) the seller must properly ship conforming goods and if they arrive by any means he must tender them on arrival but he assumes no obligation that the goods will arrive unless he has caused the non-arrival; and

(b) where without fault of the seller the goods are in part lost or have so deteriorated as no longer to conform to the contract or arrive after the contract time, the buyer may proceed as if there had been casualty to identified goods (Section 2–613).

Official Comment

. . .

Definitional Cross References:

"Buyer". Section 2–103.

"Conforming". Section 2–106.

"Contract". Section 1–201.

"Fault". Section 1–201.

"Goods". Section 2–105.

"Sale". Section 2–106.

"Seller". Section 2–103.

"Term". Section 1–201.

§ 2–325. "Letter of Credit" Term; "Confirmed Credit".

(1) Failure of the buyer seasonably to furnish an agreed letter of credit is a breach of the contract for sale.

(2) The delivery to seller of a proper letter of credit suspends the buyer's obligation to pay. If the letter of credit is dishonored, the seller may on seasonable notification to the buyer require payment directly from him.

(3) Unless otherwise agreed the term "letter of credit" or "banker's credit" in a contract for sale means an irrevocable credit issued by a financing agency of good repute and, where the shipment is overseas, of good international repute. The term "confirmed credit" means that the credit must also carry the direct obligation of such an agency which does business in the seller's financial market.

Official Comment

. . .

Definitional Cross References:

"Buyer". Section 2–103.

"Contract for sale". Section 2–106.

"Draft". Section 3–104.

"Financing agency". Section 2–104.

"Notifies". Section 1–201.

"Overseas". Section 2–323.

"Purchaser". Section 1–201.

"Seasonably". Section 1–204.

"Seller". Section 2–103.

"Term". Section 1–201.

§ 2–326. Sale on Approval and Sale or Return; Rights of Creditors.

(1) Unless otherwise agreed, if delivered goods may be returned by the buyer even though they conform to the contract, the transaction is

(a) a "sale on approval" if the goods are delivered primarily for use, and

(b) a "sale or return" if the goods are delivered primarily for resale.

(2) Goods held on approval are not subject to the claims of the buyer's creditors until acceptance; goods held on sale or return are subject to such claims while in the buyer's possession.

(3) Any "or return" term of a contract for sale is to be treated as a separate contract for sale within the statute of frauds section of this Article (Section 2–201) and as contradicting the sale aspect of the contract within the provisions of this Article on parol or extrinsic evidence (Section 2–202).

Official Comment

1. Both a "sale on approval" and a "sale or return" should be distinguished from other types of transactions with which they frequently have been confused. A "sale" on approval, "sometimes also called a sale 'on trial' or 'on satisfaction,' deals with a contract under which the seller undertakes a risk in order to satisfy its prospective buyer with the appearance or performance of the goods that are sold." The goods are

delivered to the proposed purchaser but they remain the property of the seller until the buyer accepts them. The price has already been agreed. The buyer's willingness to receive and test the goods is the consideration for the seller's engagement to deliver and sell. A "sale or return," on the other hand, typically is a sale to a merchant whose unwillingness to buy is overcome by the seller's engagement to take back the goods (or any commercial unit of goods) in lieu of payment if they fail to be resold. A sale or return is a present sale of goods which may be undone at the buyer's option. Accordingly, subsection (2) provides that goods delivered on approval are not subject to the prospective buyer's creditors until acceptance, and goods delivered in a sale or return are subject to the buyer's creditors while in the buyer's possession.

These two transactions are so strongly delineated in practice and in general understanding that every presumption runs against a delivery to a consumer being a "sale or return" and against a delivery to a merchant for resale being a "sale on approval."

2. The right to return goods for failure to conform to the contract of sale does not make the transaction a "sale on approval" or "sale or return" and has nothing to do with this section or Section 2–327. This section is not concerned with remedies for breach of contract. It deals instead with a power given by the contract to turn back the goods even though they are wholly as warranted. This section nevertheless presupposes that a contract for sale is contemplated by the parties, although that contract may be of the particular character that this section addresses (i.e., a sale on approval or a sale or return).

If a buyer's obligation as a buyer is conditioned not on its personal approval but on the article's passing a described objective test, the risk of loss by casualty pending the test is properly the seller's and proper return is at its expense. On the point of "satisfaction" as meaning "reasonable satisfaction" when an industrial machine is involved, this Article takes no position. . . .

§ 2–327. Special Incidents of Sale on Approval and Sale or Return.

(1) Under a sale on approval unless otherwise agreed

(a) although the goods are identified to the contract the risk of loss and the title do not pass to the buyer until acceptance; and

(b) use of the goods consistent with the purpose of trial is not acceptance but failure seasonably to notify the seller of election to return the goods is acceptance, and if the goods conform to the contract acceptance of any part is acceptance of the whole; and

(c) after due notification of election to return, the return is at the seller's risk and expense but a merchant buyer must follow any reasonable instructions.

(2) Under a sale or return unless otherwise agreed

(a) the option to return extends to the whole or any commercial unit of the goods while in substantially their original condition, but must be exercised seasonably; and

(b) the return is at the buyer's risk and expense.

Official Comment

. . .

Definitional Cross References:

"Agreed". Section 1–201.

"Buyer". Section 2–103.

"Commercial unit". Section 2–105.

"Conform". Section 2–106.

"Contract". Section 1–201.

"Goods". Section 2–105.

"Merchant". Section 2–104.

Art. 2 SALES § 2–328

"Notifies". Section 1–201.

"Notification". Section 1–201.

"Sale on approval". Section 2–326.

"Sale or return". Section 2–326.

"Seasonably". Section 1–204.

"Seller". Section 2–103.

§ 2–328. Sale by Auction.

(1) In a sale by auction if goods are put up in lots each lot is the subject of a separate sale.

(2) A sale by auction is complete when the auctioneer so announces by the fall of the hammer or in other customary manner. Where a bid is made while the hammer is falling in acceptance of a prior bid the auctioneer may in his discretion reopen the bidding or declare the goods sold under the bid on which the hammer was falling.

(3) Such a sale is with reserve unless the goods are in explicit terms put up without reserve. In an auction with reserve the auctioneer may withdraw the goods at any time until he announces completion of the sale. In an auction without reserve, after the auctioneer calls for bids on an article or lot, that article or lot cannot be withdrawn unless no bid is made within a reasonable time. In either case a bidder may retract his bid until the auctioneer's announcement of completion of the sale, but a bidder's retraction does not revive any previous bid.

(4) If the auctioneer knowingly receives a bid on the seller's behalf or the seller makes or procures such a bid, and notice has not been given that liberty for such bidding is reserved, the buyer may at his option avoid the sale or take the goods at the price of the last good faith bid prior to the completion of the sale. This subsection shall not apply to any bid at a forced sale.

Official Comment

. . .

Definitional Cross References:

"Buyer". Section 2–103.

"Good faith". Section 1–201.

"Goods". Section 2–105.

"Lot". Section 2–105.

"Notice". Section 1–201.

"Sale". Section 2–106.

"Seller". Section 2–103.

PART IV

TITLE, CREDITORS AND GOOD FAITH PURCHASERS

§ 2–401. Passing of Title; Reservation for Security; Limited Application of This Section.

Each provision of this Article with regard to the rights, obligations and remedies of the seller, the buyer, purchasers or other third parties applies irrespective of title to the goods except where the

§ 2–401

provision refers to such title. Insofar as situations are not covered by the other provisions of this Article and matters concerning title become material the following rules apply:

(1) Title to goods cannot pass under a contract for sale prior to their identification to the contract (Section 2–501), and unless otherwise explicitly agreed the buyer acquires by their identification a special property as limited by this Act. Any retention or reservation by the seller of the title (property) in goods shipped or delivered to the buyer is limited in effect to a reservation of a security interest. Subject to these provisions and to the provisions of the Article on Secured Transactions (Article 9), title to goods passes from the seller to the buyer in any manner and on any conditions explicitly agreed on by the parties.

(2) Unless otherwise explicitly agreed title passes to the buyer at the time and place at which the seller completes his performance with reference to the physical delivery of the goods, despite any reservation of a security interest and even though a document of title is to be delivered at a different time or place; and in particular and despite any reservation of a security interest by the bill of lading

(a) if the contract requires or authorizes the seller to send the goods to the buyer but does not require him to deliver them at destination, title passes to the buyer at the time and place of shipment; but

(b) if the contract requires delivery at destination, title passes on tender there.

(3) Unless otherwise explicitly agreed where delivery is to be made without moving the goods,

(a) if the seller is to deliver a document of title, title passes at the time when and the place where he delivers such documents; or

(b) if the goods are at the time of contracting already identified and no documents are to be delivered, title passes at the time and place of contracting.

(4) A rejection or other refusal by the buyer to receive or retain the goods, whether or not justified, or a justified revocation of acceptance revests title to the goods in the seller. Such revesting occurs by operation of law and is not a "sale".

Official Comment

. . .

Definitional Cross References:

"Agreement". Section 1–201.

"Bill of lading". Section 1–201.

"Buyer". Section 2–103.

"Contract". Section 1–201.

"Contract for sale". Section 2–106.

"Delivery". Section 1–201.

"Document of title". Section 1–201.

"Good faith". Section 2–103.

"Goods". Section 2–105.

"Party". Section 1–201.

"Purchaser". Section 1–201.

"Receipt" of goods. Section 2–103.

"Remedy". Section 1–201.

"Rights". Section 1–201.

"Sale". Section 2–106.

"Security interest". Section 1–201.

"Seller". Section 2–103.

"Send". Section 1–201.

§ 2–402. Rights of Seller's Creditors Against Sold Goods.

(1) Except as provided in subsections (2) and (3), rights of unsecured creditors of the seller with respect to goods which have been identified to a contract for sale are subject to the buyer's rights to recover the goods under this Article (Sections 2–502 and 2–716).

(2) A creditor of the seller may treat a sale or an identification of goods to a contract for sale as void if as against him a retention of possession by the seller is fraudulent under any rule of law of the state where the goods are situated, except that retention of possession in good faith and current course of trade by a merchant-seller for a commercially reasonable time after a sale or identification is not fraudulent.

(3) Nothing in this Article shall be deemed to impair the rights of creditors of the seller

(a) under the provisions of the Article on Secured Transactions (Article 9); or

(b) where identification to the contract or delivery is made not in current course of trade but in satisfaction of or as security for a pre-existing claim for money, security or the like and is made under circumstances which under any rule of law of the state where the goods are situated would apart from this Article constitute the transaction a fraudulent transfer or voidable preference.

Official Comment

. . .

Definitional Cross References:

"Contract for sale". Section 2–106.

"Creditor". Section 1–201.

"Good faith". Section 2–103.

"Goods". Section 2–105.

"Merchant". Section 2–104.

"Money". Section 1–201.

"Reasonable time". Section 1–204.

"Rights". Section 1–201.

"Sale". Section 2–106.

"Seller". Section 2–103.

§ 2–403. Power to Transfer; Good Faith Purchase of Goods; "Entrusting".

(1) A purchaser of goods acquires all title which his transferor had or had power to transfer except that a purchaser of a limited interest acquires rights only to the extent of the interest purchased. A person with voidable title has power to transfer a good title to a good faith purchaser for value. When goods have been delivered under a transaction of purchase the purchaser has such power even though

(a) the transferor was deceived as to the identity of the purchaser, or

(b) the delivery was in exchange for a check which is later dishonored, or

(c) it was agreed that the transaction was to be a "cash sale", or

(d) the delivery was procured through fraud punishable as larcenous under the criminal law.

(2) Any entrusting of possession of goods to a merchant who deals in goods of that kind gives him power to transfer all rights of the entruster to a buyer in ordinary course of business.

(3) "Entrusting" includes any delivery and any acquiescence in retention of possession regardless of any condition expressed between the parties to the delivery or acquiescence and regardless of whether the procurement of the entrusting or the possessor's disposition of the goods have been such as to be larcenous under the criminal law. . . .

Official Comment

. . .

Definitional Cross References:

"Buyer in ordinary course of business". Section 1–201.

"Good faith". Sections 1–201 and 2–103.

"Goods". Section 2–105.

"Person". Section 1–201.

"Purchaser". Section 1–201.

"Signed". Section 1–201.

"Term". Section 1–201.

"Value". Section 1–201.

PART V

PERFORMANCE

§ 2–501. Insurable Interest in Goods; Manner of Identification of Goods.

(1) The buyer obtains a special property and an insurable interest in goods by identification of existing goods as goods to which the contract refers even though the goods so identified are non-conforming and he has an option to return or reject them. Such identification can be made at any time and in any manner explicitly agreed to by the parties. In the absence of explicit agreement identification occurs

(a) when the contract is made if it is for the sale of goods already existing and identified;

(b) if the contract is for the sale of future goods other than those described in paragraph (c), when goods are shipped, marked or otherwise designated by the seller as goods to which the contract refers;

(c) when the crops are planted or otherwise become growing crops or the young are conceived if the contract is for the sale of unborn young to be born within twelve months after contracting or for the sale of crops to be harvested within twelve months or the next normal harvest season after contracting whichever is longer.

(2) The seller retains an insurable interest in goods so long as title to or any security interest in the goods remains in him and where the identification is by the seller alone he may until default or insolvency or notification to the buyer that the identification is final substitute other goods for those identified.

(3) Nothing in this section impairs any insurable interest recognized under any other statute or rule of law.

Official Comment

. . .

Purposes:

1. The present section deals with the manner of identifying goods to the contract so that an insurable interest in the buyer and the rights set forth in the next section will accrue. Generally speaking, identification may be made in any manner "explicitly agreed to" by the parties. The rules of paragraphs (a), (b) and (c) apply only in the absence of such "explicit agreement".

2. In the ordinary case identification of particular existing goods as goods to which the contract refers is unambiguous and may occur in one of many ways. It is possible, however, for the identification to be tentative or contingent. In view of the limited effect given to identification by this Article, the general policy is to resolve all doubts in favor of identification. . . .

Definitional Cross References:

"Agreement". Section 1–201.

"Contract". Section 1–201.

"Contract for sale". Section 2–106.

"Future goods". Section 2–105.

"Goods". Section 2–105.

"Notification". Section 1–201.

"Party". Section 1–201.

"Sale". Section 2–106.

"Security interest". Section 1–201.

"Seller". Section 2–103.

§ 2–502. Buyer's Right to Goods on Seller's Repudiation, Failure to Deliver, or Insolvency.

(1) Subject to subsections (2) and (3) and even though the goods have not been shipped a buyer who has paid a part or all of the price of goods in which he has a special property under the provisions of the immediately preceding section may on making and keeping good a tender of any unpaid portion of their price recover them from the seller if:

(a) in the case of goods bought for personal, family, or household purposes, the seller repudiates or fails to deliver as required by the contract; or

(b) in all cases, the seller becomes insolvent within ten days after receipt of the first installment on their price.

(2) The buyer's right to recover the goods under subsection (1)(a) vests upon acquisition of a special property, even if the seller had not then repudiated or failed to deliver.

(3) If the identification creating his special property has been made by the buyer he acquires the right to recover the goods only if they conform to the contract for sale.

§ 2–503. Manner of Seller's Tender of Delivery.

(1) Tender of delivery requires that the seller put and hold conforming goods at the buyer's disposition and give the buyer any notification reasonably necessary to enable him to take delivery.

The manner, time and place for tender are determined by the agreement and this Article, and in particular

(a) tender must be at a reasonable hour, and if it is of goods they must be kept available for the period reasonably necessary to enable the buyer to take possession; but

(b) unless otherwise agreed the buyer must furnish facilities reasonably suited to the receipt of the goods.

(2) Where the case is within the next section respecting shipment tender requires that the seller comply with its provisions.

(3) Where the seller is required to deliver at a particular destination tender requires that he comply with subsection (1) and also in any appropriate case tender documents as described in subsections (4) and (5) of this section.

(4) Where goods are in the possession of a bailee and are to be delivered without being moved

(a) tender requires that the seller either tender a negotiable document of title covering such goods or procure acknowledgment by the bailee of the buyer's right to possession of the goods; but

(b) tender to the buyer of a non-negotiable document of title or of a written direction to the bailee to deliver is sufficient tender unless the buyer seasonably objects, and receipt by the bailee of notification of the buyer's rights fixes those rights as against the bailee and all third persons; but risk of loss of the goods and of any failure by the bailee to honor the non-negotiable document of title or to obey the direction remains on the seller until the buyer has had a reasonable time to present the document or direction, and a refusal by the bailee to honor the document or to obey the direction defeats the tender.

(5) Where the contract requires the seller to deliver documents

(a) he must tender all such documents in correct form, except as provided in this Article with respect to bills of lading in a set (subsection (2) of Section 2–323); and

(b) tender through customary banking channels is sufficient and dishonor of a draft accompanying the documents constitutes non-acceptance or rejection.

Official Comment

. . .

Purposes of Changes:

1. The major general rules governing the manner of proper or due tender of delivery are gathered in this section. The term "tender" is used in this Article in two different senses. In one sense it refers to "due tender" which contemplates an offer coupled with a present ability to fulfill all the conditions resting on the tendering party and must be followed by actual performance if the other party shows himself ready to proceed. Unless the context unmistakably indicates otherwise this is the meaning of "tender" in this Article and the occasional addition of the word "due" is only for clarity and emphasis. At other times it is used to refer to an offer of goods or documents under a contract as if in fulfillment of its conditions even though there is a defect when measured against the contract obligation. Used in either sense, however, "tender" connotes such performance by the tendering party as puts the other party in default if he fails to proceed in some manner.

. . .

Definitional Cross References:

"Agreement". Section 1–201.

"Bill of lading". Section 1–201.

"Buyer". Section 2–103.

"Conforming". Section 2–106.

"Contract". Section 1–201.

"Delivery". Section 1–201.

"Dishonor". Section 3–508.

"Document of title". Section 1–201.

"Draft". Section 3–104.

"Goods". Section 2–105.

"Notification". Section 1–201.

"Reasonable time". Section 1–204.

"Receipt" of goods. Section 2–103.

"Rights". Section 1–201.

"Seasonably". Section 1–204.

"Seller". Section 2–103.

"Written". Section 1–201.

§ 2–504. Shipment by Seller.

Where the seller is required or authorized to send the goods to the buyer and the contract does not require him to deliver them at a particular destination, then unless otherwise agreed he must

(a) put the goods in the possession of such a carrier and make such a contract for their transportation as may be reasonable having regard to the nature of the goods and other circumstances of the case; and

(b) obtain and promptly deliver or tender in due form any document necessary to enable the buyer to obtain possession of the goods or otherwise required by the agreement or by usage of trade; and

(c) promptly notify the buyer of the shipment.

Failure to notify the buyer under paragraph (c) or to make a proper contract under paragraph (a) is a ground for rejection only if material delay or loss ensues.

Official Comment

. . .

Definitional Cross References:

"Agreement". Section 1–201.

"Buyer". Section 2–103.

"Contract". Section 1–201.

"Delivery". Section 1–201.

"Goods". Section 2–105.

"Notifies". Section 1–201.

"Seller". Section 2–103.

"Send". Section 1–201.

"Usage of trade". Section 1–205.

§ 2–505. Seller's Shipment Under Reservation.

(1) Where the seller has identified goods to the contract by or before shipment:

(a) his procurement of a negotiable bill of lading to his own order or otherwise reserves in him a security interest in the goods. His procurement of the bill to the order of a financing agency or of the buyer indicates in addition only the seller's expectation of transferring that interest to the person named.

(b) a non-negotiable bill of lading to himself or his nominee reserves possession of the goods as security but except in a case of conditional delivery (subsection (2) of Section 2–507) a non-negotiable bill of lading naming the buyer as consignee reserves no security interest even though the seller retains possession of the bill of lading.

(2) When shipment by the seller with reservation of a security interest is in violation of the contract for sale it constitutes an improper contract for transportation within the preceding section but impairs neither the rights given to the buyer by shipment and identification of the goods to the contract nor the seller's powers as a holder of a negotiable document.

Official Comment

. . .

Definitional Cross References:

"Bill of lading". Section 1–201.

"Buyer". Section 2–103.

"Consignee". Section 7–102.

"Contract". Section 1–201.

"Contract for sale". Section 2–106.

"Delivery". Section 1–201.

"Financing agency". Section 2–104.

"Goods". Section 2–105.

"Holder". Section 1–201.

"Person". Section 1–201.

"Security interest". Section 1–201.

"Seller". Section 2–103.

§ 2–506. Rights of Financing Agency.

(1) A financing agency by paying or purchasing for value a draft which relates to a shipment of goods acquires to the extent of the payment or purchase and in addition to its own rights under the draft and any document of title securing it any rights of the shipper in the goods including the right to stop delivery and the shipper's right to have the draft honored by the buyer.

(2) The right to reimbursement of a financing agency which has in good faith honored or purchased the draft under commitment to or authority from the buyer is not impaired by subsequent discovery of defects with reference to any relevant document which was apparently regular on its face.

Official Comment

. . .

Definitional Cross References:

"Buyer". Section 2–103.

"Document of title". Section 1–201.

"Draft". Section 3–104.

"Financing agency". Section 2–104.

"Good faith". Section 2–103.

"Goods". Section 2–105.

"Honor". Section 1–201.

"Purchase". Section 1–201.

"Rights". Section 1–201.

"Value". Section 1–201.

§ 2–507. Effect of Seller's Tender; Delivery on Condition.

(1) Tender of delivery is a condition to the buyer's duty to accept the goods and, unless otherwise agreed, to his duty to pay for them. Tender entitles the seller to acceptance of the goods and to payment according to the contract.

(2) Where payment is due and demanded on the delivery to the buyer of goods or documents of title, his right as against the seller to retain or dispose of them is conditional upon his making the payment due.

Official Comment

. . .

Definitional Cross References:

"Buyer". Section 2–103.

"Contract". Section 1–201.

"Delivery". Section 1–201.

"Document of title". Section 1–201.

"Goods". Section 2–105.

"Rights". Section 1–201.

"Seller". Section 2–103.

§ 2–508. Cure by Seller of Improper Tender or Delivery; Replacement.

(1) Where any tender or delivery by the seller is rejected because non-conforming and the time for performance has not yet expired, the seller may seasonably notify the buyer of his intention to cure and may then within the contract time make a conforming delivery.

(2) Where the buyer rejects a non-conforming tender which the seller had reasonable grounds to believe would be acceptable with or without money allowance the seller may if he seasonably notifies the buyer have a further reasonable time to substitute a conforming tender.

Official Comment

. . .

Purposes:

1. Subsection (1) permits a seller who has made a non-conforming tender in any case to make a conforming delivery within the contract time upon seasonable notification to the buyer. It applies even where the seller has taken back the non-conforming goods and refunded the purchase price. He may still make a good tender within the contract period. The closer, however, it is to the contract date, the greater is the necessity for extreme promptness on the seller's part in notifying of his intention to cure, if such notification is to be "seasonable" under this subsection.

The rule of this subsection, moreover, is qualified by its underlying reasons. Thus if, after contracting for June delivery, a buyer later makes known to the seller his need for shipment early in the month and the seller ships accordingly, the "contract time" has been cut down by the supervening modification and the time for cure of tender must be referred to this modified time term.

2. Subsection (2) seeks to avoid injustice to the seller by reason of a surprise rejection by the buyer. However, the seller is not protected unless he had "reasonable grounds to believe" that the tender would be acceptable. Such reasonable grounds can lie in prior course of dealing, course of performance or usage of trade as well as in the particular circumstances surrounding the making of the contract. The seller is charged with commercial knowledge of any factors in a particular sales situation which require him to comply strictly with his obligations under the contract as, for example, strict conformity of documents in an overseas shipment or the sale of precision parts or chemicals for use in manufacture. Further, if the buyer gives notice either implicitly, as by a prior course of dealing involving rigorous inspections, or expressly, as by the deliberate inclusion of a "no replacement" clause in the contract, the seller is to be held to rigid compliance. If the clause appears in a "form" contract evidence that it is out of line with trade usage or the prior course of dealing and was not called to the seller's attention may be sufficient to show that the seller had reasonable grounds to believe that the tender would be acceptable.

3. The words "a further reasonable time to substitute a conforming tender" are intended as words of limitation to protect the buyer. What is a "reasonable time" depends upon the attending circumstances. Compare Section 2–511 on the comparable case of a seller's surprise demand for legal tender.

4. Existing trade usages permitting variations without rejection but with price allowance enter into the agreement itself as contractual limitations of remedy and are not covered by this section.

. . .

Definitional Cross References:

"Buyer". Section 2–103.

"Conforming". Section 2–106.

"Contract". Section 1–201.

"Money". Section 1–201.

"Notifies". Section 1–201.

"Reasonable time". Section 1–204.

"Seasonably". Section 1–204.

"Seller". Section 2–103.

§ 2–509. Risk of Loss in the Absence of Breach.

(1) Where the contract requires or authorizes the seller to ship the goods by carrier

(a) if it does not require him to deliver them at a particular destination, the risk of loss passes to the buyer when the goods are duly delivered to the carrier even though the shipment is under reservation (Section 2–505); but

(b) if it does require him to deliver them at a particular destination and the goods are there duly tendered while in the possession of the carrier, the risk of loss passes to the buyer when the goods are there duly so tendered as to enable the buyer to take delivery.

(2) Where the goods are held by a bailee to be delivered without being moved, the risk of loss passes to the buyer

(a) on his receipt of a negotiable document of title covering the goods; or

(b) on acknowledgment by the bailee of the buyer's right to possession of the goods; or

(c) after his receipt of a non-negotiable document of title or other written direction to deliver, as provided in subsection (4)(b) of Section 2–503.

(3) In any case not within subsection (1) or (2), the risk of loss passes to the buyer on his receipt of the goods if the seller is a merchant; otherwise the risk passes to the buyer on tender of delivery.

(4) The provisions of this section are subject to contrary agreement of the parties and to the provisions of this Article on sale on approval (Section 2–327) and on effect of breach on risk of loss (Section 2–510).

Official Comment

. . .

1. The underlying theory of these sections on risk of loss is the adoption of the contractual approach rather than an arbitrary shifting of the risk with the "property" in the goods. The scope of the present section, therefore, is limited strictly to those cases where there has been no breach by the seller. Where for any reason his delivery or tender fails to conform to the contract, the present section does not apply and the situation is governed by the provisions on effect of breach on risk of loss. . . .

. . .

Definitional Cross References:

"Agreement". Section 1–201.

"Buyer". Section 2–103.

"Contract". Section 1–201.

"Delivery". Section 1–201.

"Document of title". Section 1–201.

"Goods". Section 2–105.

"Merchant". Section 2–104.

"Party". Section 1–201.

"Receipt" of goods. Section 2–103.

"Sale on approval". Section 2–326.

"Seller". Section 2–103.

§ 2–510. Effect of Breach on Risk of Loss.

(1) Where a tender or delivery of goods so fails to conform to the contract as to give a right of rejection the risk of their loss remains on the seller until cure or acceptance.

(2) Where the buyer rightfully revokes acceptance he may to the extent of any deficiency in his effective insurance coverage treat the risk of loss as having rested on the seller from the beginning.

(3) Where the buyer as to conforming goods already identified to the contract for sale repudiates or is otherwise in breach before risk of their loss has passed to him, the seller may to the extent of any deficiency in his effective insurance coverage treat the risk of loss as resting on the buyer for a commercially reasonable time.

Official Comment

. . .

Definitional Cross References:

"Buyer". Section 2–103.

"Conform". Section 2–106.

"Contract for sale". Section 2–106.

"Goods". Section 2–105.

"Seller". Section 2–103.

§ 2–511. Tender of Payment by Buyer; Payment by Check.

(1) Unless otherwise agreed tender of payment is a condition to the seller's duty to tender and complete any delivery.

(2) Tender of payment is sufficient when made by any means or in any manner current in the ordinary course of business unless the seller demands payment in legal tender and gives any extension of time reasonably necessary to procure it.

(3) Subject to the provisions of this Act on the effect of an instrument on an obligation (Section 3–310), payment by check is conditional and is defeated as between the parties by dishonor of the check on due presentment.

As amended in 1994.

Official Comment

. . .

Definitional Cross References:

"Buyer". Section 2–103.

"Check". Section 3–104.

"Dishonor". Section 3–508.

"Party". Section 1–201.

"Reasonable time". Section 1–204.

"Seller". Section 2–103.

§ 2–512. Payment by Buyer Before Inspection.

(1) Where the contract requires payment before inspection non-conformity of the goods does not excuse the buyer from so making payment unless

(a) the non-conformity appears without inspection; or

(b) despite tender of the required documents the circumstances would justify injunction against honor under the provisions of this Act (Section 5–114).

(2) Payment pursuant to subsection (1) does not constitute an acceptance of goods or impair the buyer's right to inspect or any of his remedies.

Official Comment

. . .

Definitional Cross References:

"Buyer". Section 2–103.

"Conform". Section 2–106.

"Contract". Section 1–201.

"Financing agency". Section 2–104.

"Goods". Section 2–105.

"Remedy". Section 1–201.

"Rights". Section 1–201.

§ 2–513. Buyer's Right to Inspection of Goods.

(1) Unless otherwise agreed and subject to subsection (3), where goods are tendered or delivered or identified to the contract for sale, the buyer has a right before payment or acceptance to inspect them at any reasonable place and time and in any reasonable manner. When the seller is required or authorized to send the goods to the buyer, the inspection may be after their arrival.

(2) Expenses of inspection must be borne by the buyer but may be recovered from the seller if the goods do not conform and are rejected.

(3) Unless otherwise agreed and subject to the provisions of this Article on C.I.F. contracts (subsection (3) of Section 2–321), the buyer is not entitled to inspect the goods before payment of the price when the contract provides

(a) for delivery "C.O.D." or on other like terms; or

(b) for payment against documents of title, except where such payment is due only after the goods are to become available for inspection.

(4) A place or method of inspection fixed by the parties is presumed to be exclusive but unless otherwise expressly agreed it does not postpone identification or shift the place for delivery or for passing the risk of loss. If compliance becomes impossible, inspection shall be as provided in this section unless the place or method fixed was clearly intended as an indispensable condition failure of which avoids the contract.

Official Comment

. . .

Definitional Cross References:

"Buyer". Section 2–103.

"Conform". Section 2–106.

"Contract". Section 1–201.

"Contract for sale". Section 2–106.

"Document of title". Section 1–201.

"Goods". Section 2–105.

"Party". Section 1–201.

"Presumed". Section 1–201.

"Reasonable time". Section 1–204.

"Rights". Section 1–201.

"Seller". Section 2–103.

§ 2–514. When Documents Deliverable on Acceptance; When on Payment.

Unless otherwise agreed documents against which a draft is drawn are to be delivered to the drawee on acceptance of the draft if it is payable more than three days after presentment; otherwise, only on payment.

Official Comment

. . .

Definitional Cross References:

"Delivery". Section 1–201.

"Draft". Section 3–104.

§ 2–515. Preserving Evidence of Goods in Dispute.

In furtherance of the adjustment of any claim or dispute

(a) either party on reasonable notification to the other and for the purpose of ascertaining the facts and preserving evidence has the right to inspect, test and sample the goods including such of them as may be in the possession or control of the other; and

(b) the parties may agree to a third party inspection or survey to determine the conformity or condition of the goods and may agree that the findings shall be binding upon them in any subsequent litigation or adjustment.

Official Comment

. . .

Definitional Cross References:

"Conform". Section 2–106.

"Goods". Section 2–105.

"Notification". Section 1–201.

"Party". Section 1–201.

PART VI

BREACH, REPUDIATION AND EXCUSE

§ 2–601. Buyer's Rights on Improper Delivery.

Subject to the provisions of this Article on breach in installment contracts (Section 2–612) and unless otherwise agreed under the sections on contractual limitations of remedy (Sections 2–718 and 2–719), if the goods or the tender of delivery fail in any respect to conform to the contract, the buyer may

(a) reject the whole; or

(b) accept the whole; or

(c) accept any commercial unit or units and reject the rest.

Official Comment

. . .

Purposes of Changes: To make it clear that:

    1. A buyer accepting a non-conforming tender is not penalized by the loss of any remedy otherwise open to him. This policy extends to cover and regulate the acceptance of a part of any lot improperly tendered in any case where the price can reasonably be apportioned. Partial acceptance is permitted whether the part of the goods accepted conforms or not. The only limitation on partial acceptance is that good faith and commercial reasonableness must be used to avoid undue impairment of the value of the remaining portion of the goods. This is the reason for the insistence on the "commercial unit" in paragraph (c). In this respect, the test is not only what unit has been the basis of contract, but whether the partial acceptance produces so materially adverse an effect on the remainder as to constitute bad faith.

    2. Acceptance made with the knowledge of the other party is final. An original refusal to accept may be withdrawn by a later acceptance if the seller has indicated that he is holding the tender open. However, if the buyer attempts to accept, either in whole or in part, after his original rejection has caused the seller to arrange for other disposition of the goods, the buyer must answer for any ensuing damage since the next section provides that any exercise of ownership after rejection is wrongful as against the seller. Further, he is liable even though the seller may choose to treat his action as acceptance rather than conversion, since the damage flows from the misleading notice. Such arrangements for resale or other disposition of the goods by the seller must be viewed as within the normal contemplation of a buyer who has given notice of rejection. However, the buyer's attempts in good faith to dispose of defective goods where the seller has failed to give instructions within a reasonable time are not to be regarded as an acceptance.

. . .

Definitional Cross References:

    "Buyer". Section 2–103.

    "Commercial unit". Section 2–105.

    "Conform". Section 2–106.

    "Contract". Section 1–201.

    "Goods". Section 2–105.

    "Installment contract". Section 2–612.

    "Rights". Section 1–201.

§ 2–602. Manner and Effect of Rightful Rejection.

    (1) Rejection of goods must be within a reasonable time after their delivery or tender. It is ineffective unless the buyer seasonably notifies the seller.

    (2) Subject to the provisions of the two following sections on rejected goods (Sections 2–603 and 2–604),

    (a) after rejection any exercise of ownership by the buyer with respect to any commercial unit is wrongful as against the seller; and

    (b) if the buyer has before rejection taken physical possession of goods in which he does not have a security interest under the provisions of this Article (subsection (3) of Section 2–711), he is under a duty after rejection to hold them with reasonable care at the seller's disposition for a time sufficient to permit the seller to remove them; but

    (c) the buyer has no further obligations with regard to goods rightfully rejected.

    (3) The seller's rights with respect to goods wrongfully rejected are governed by the provisions of this Article on Seller's remedies in general (Section 2–703).

Official Comment

...

Purposes of Changes: To make it clear that:

1. A tender or delivery of goods made pursuant to a contract of sale, even though wholly non-conforming, requires affirmative action by the buyer to avoid acceptance. Under subsection (1), therefore, the buyer is given a reasonable time to notify the seller of his rejection, but without such seasonable notification his rejection is ineffective. The sections of this Article dealing with inspection of goods must be read in connection with the buyer's reasonable time for action under this subsection. Contract provisions limiting the time for rejection fall within the rule of the section on "Time" and are effective if the time set gives the buyer a reasonable time for discovery of defects. What constitutes a due "notifying" of rejection by the buyer to the seller is defined in Section 1–201.

2. Subsection (2) lays down the normal duties of the buyer upon rejection, which flow from the relationship of the parties. Beyond his duty to hold the goods with reasonable care for the buyer's [seller's] disposition, this section continues the policy of . . . generally relieving the buyer from any duties with respect to them, except when the circumstances impose the limited obligation of salvage upon him under the next section.

3. The present section applies only to rightful rejection by the buyer. If the seller has made a tender which in all respects conforms to the contract, the buyer has a positive duty to accept and his failure to do so constitutes a "wrongful rejection" which gives the seller immediate remedies for breach. Subsection (3) is included here to emphasize the sharp distinction between the rejection of an improper tender and the non-acceptance which is a breach by the buyer.

4. The provisions of this section are to be appropriately limited or modified when a negotiation is in process.

...

Definitional Cross References:

"Buyer". Section 2–103.

"Commercial unit". Section 2–105.

"Goods". Section 2–105.

"Merchant". Section 2–104.

"Notifies". Section 1–201.

"Reasonable time". Section 1–204.

"Remedy". Section 1–201.

"Rights". Section 1–201.

"Seasonably". Section 1–204.

"Security interest". Section 1–201.

"Seller". Section 2–103.

§ 2–603. Merchant Buyer's Duties as to Rightfully Rejected Goods.

(1) Subject to any security interest in the buyer (subsection (3) of Section 2–711), when the seller has no agent or place of business at the market of rejection a merchant buyer is under a duty after rejection of goods in his possession or control to follow any reasonable instructions received from the seller with respect to the goods and in the absence of such instructions to make reasonable efforts to sell them for the seller's account if they are perishable or threaten to decline in value speedily. Instructions are not reasonable if on demand indemnity for expenses is not forthcoming.

Art. 2   SALES   § 2–604

(2) When the buyer sells goods under subsection (1), he is entitled to reimbursement from the seller or out of the proceeds for reasonable expenses of caring for and selling them, and if the expenses include no selling commission then to such commission as is usual in the trade or if there is none to a reasonable sum not exceeding ten per cent on the gross proceeds.

(3) In complying with this section the buyer is held only to good faith and good faith conduct hereunder is neither acceptance nor conversion nor the basis of an action for damages.

Official Comment

. . .

Purposes:

1. This section recognizes the duty imposed upon the merchant buyer by good faith and commercial practice to follow any reasonable instructions of the seller as to reshipping, storing, delivery to a third party, reselling or the like. Subsection (1) goes further and extends the duty to include the making of reasonable efforts to effect a salvage sale where the value of the goods is threatened and the seller's instructions do not arrive in time to prevent serious loss.

2. The limitations on the buyer's duty to resell under subsection (1) are to be liberally construed. The buyer's duty to resell under this section arises from commercial necessity and thus is present only when the seller has "no agent or place of business at the market of rejection". . . .

4. Since this section makes the resale of perishable goods an affirmative duty in contrast to a mere right to sell as under the case law, subsection (3) makes it clear that the buyer is liable only for the exercise of good faith in determining whether the value of the goods is sufficiently threatened to justify a quick resale or whether he has waited a sufficient length of time for instructions, or what a reasonable means and place of resale is.

5. A buyer who fails to make a salvage sale when his duty to do so under this section has arisen is subject to damages pursuant to the section on liberal administration of remedies.

. . .

Definitional Cross References:

"Buyer". Section 2–103.

"Good faith". Section 1–201.

"Goods". Section 2–105.

"Merchant". Section 2–104.

"Security interest". Section 1–201.

"Seller". Section 2–103.

§ 2–604. Buyer's Options as to Salvage of Rightfully Rejected Goods.

Subject to the provisions of the immediately preceding section on perishables if the seller gives no instructions within a reasonable time after notification of rejection the buyer may store the rejected goods for the seller's account or reship them to him or resell them for the seller's account with reimbursement as provided in the preceding section. Such action is not acceptance or conversion.

Official Comment

. . .

Purposes:

The basic purpose of this section is twofold: on the one hand it aims at reducing the stake in dispute and on the other at avoiding the pinning of a technical "acceptance" on a buyer who has taken steps towards realization on or preservation of the goods in good faith. This section is essentially a salvage section and the buyer's right to act under it is conditioned upon (1) non-conformity of the goods, (2) due notification of rejection to the seller under the section on manner of rejection, and (3) the absence of any instructions from the seller which the merchant-buyer has a duty to follow under the preceding section.

This section is designed to accord all reasonable leeway to a rightfully rejecting buyer acting in good faith. The listing of what the buyer may do in the absence of instructions from the seller is intended to be not exhaustive but merely illustrative. This is not a "merchant's" section and the options are pure options given to merchant and nonmerchant buyers alike. The merchant-buyer, however, may in some instances be under a duty rather than an option to resell under the provisions of the preceding section.

. . .

Definitional Cross References:

"Buyer". Section 2–103.

"Notification". Section 1–201.

"Reasonable time". Section 1–204.

"Seller". Section 2–103.

§ 2–605. Waiver of Buyer's Objections by Failure to Particularize.

(1) The buyer's failure to state in connection with rejection a particular defect which is ascertainable by reasonable inspection precludes him from relying on the unstated defect to justify rejection or to establish breach

  (a) where the seller could have cured it if stated seasonably; or

  (b) between merchants when the seller has after rejection made a request in writing for a full and final written statement of all defects on which the buyer proposes to rely.

(2) Payment against documents made without reservation of rights precludes recovery of the payment for defects apparent on the face of the documents.

Official Comment

. . .

Purposes:

1. The present section rests upon a policy of permitting the buyer to give a quick and informal notice of defects in a tender without penalizing him for omissions in his statement, while at the same time protecting a seller who is reasonably misled by the buyer's failure to state curable defects.

2. Where the defect in a tender is one which could have been cured by the seller, a buyer who merely rejects the delivery without stating his objections to it is probably acting in commercial bad faith and seeking to get out of a deal which has become unprofitable. Subsection (1)(a), following the general policy of this Article which looks to preserving the deal wherever possible, therefore insists that the seller's right to correct his tender in such circumstances be protected.

3. When the time for cure is past, subsection (1)(b) makes it plain that a seller is entitled upon request to a final statement of objections upon which he can rely. What is needed is that he make clear to the buyer exactly what is being sought. A formal demand under paragraph (b) will be sufficient in the case of a merchant-buyer.

4. Subsection (2) applies to the particular case of documents the same principle which the section on effects of acceptance applies to the case of goods. . . .

. . .

Definitional Cross References:

"Between merchants". Section 2–104.

"Buyer". Section 2–103.

"Seasonably". Section 1–204.

"Seller". Section 2–103.

"Writing" and "written". Section 1–201.

§ 2–606. What Constitutes Acceptance of Goods.

(1) Acceptance of goods occurs when the buyer

(a) after a reasonable opportunity to inspect the goods signifies to the seller that the goods are conforming or that he will take or retain them in spite of their non-conformity; or

(b) fails to make an effective rejection (subsection (1) of Section 2–602), but such acceptance does not occur until the buyer has had a reasonable opportunity to inspect them; or

(c) does any act inconsistent with the seller's ownership; but if such act is wrongful as against the seller it is an acceptance only if ratified by him.

(2) Acceptance of a part of any commercial unit is acceptance of that entire unit.

Official Comment

. . .

Purposes of Changes and New Matter: To make it clear that:

1. Under this Article "acceptance" as applied to goods means that the buyer, pursuant to the contract, takes particular goods which have been appropriated to the contract as his own, whether or not he is obligated to do so, and whether he does so by words, action, or silence when it is time to speak. If the goods conform to the contract, acceptance amounts only to the performance by the buyer of one part of his legal obligation.

2. Under this Article acceptance of goods is always acceptance of identified goods which have been appropriated to the contract or are appropriated by the contract. There is no provision for "acceptance of title" apart from acceptance in general, since acceptance of title is not material under this Article to the detailed rights and duties of the parties. (See Section 2–401). The refinements of the older law between acceptance of goods and of title become unnecessary in view of the provisions of the sections on effect and revocation of acceptance, on effects of identification and on risk of loss, and those sections which free the seller's and buyer's remedies from the complications and confusions caused by the question of whether title has or has not passed to the buyer before breach. . . .

Definitional Cross References:

"Buyer". Section 2–103.

"Commercial unit". Section 2–105.

"Goods". Section 2–105.

"Seller". Section 2–103.

§ 2–607. Effect of Acceptance; Notice of Breach; Burden of Establishing Breach After Acceptance; Notice of Claim or Litigation to Person Answerable Over.

(1) The buyer must pay at the contract rate for any goods accepted.

(2) Acceptance of goods by the buyer precludes rejection of the goods accepted and if made with knowledge of a non-conformity cannot be revoked because of it unless the acceptance was on the reasonable assumption that the non-conformity would be seasonably cured but acceptance does not of itself impair any other remedy provided by this Article for non-conformity.

§ 2–607

(3) Where a tender has been accepted

(a) the buyer must within a reasonable time after he discovers or should have discovered any breach notify the seller of breach or be barred from any remedy; and

(b) if the claim is one for infringement or the like (subsection (3) of Section 2–312) and the buyer is sued as a result of such a breach he must so notify the seller within a reasonable time after he receives notice of the litigation or be barred from any remedy over for liability established by the litigation.

(4) The burden is on the buyer to establish any breach with respect to the goods accepted.

(5) Where the buyer is sued for breach of a warranty or other obligation for which his seller is answerable over

(a) he may give his seller written notice of the litigation. If the notice states that the seller may come in and defend and that if the seller does not do so he will be bound in any action against him by his buyer by any determination of fact common to the two litigations, then unless the seller after seasonable receipt of the notice does come in and defend he is so bound.

(b) if the claim is one for infringement or the like (subsection (3) of Section 2–312) the original seller may demand in writing that his buyer turn over to him control of the litigation including settlement or else be barred from any remedy over and if he also agrees to bear all expense and to satisfy any adverse judgment, then unless the buyer after seasonable receipt of the demand does turn over control the buyer is so barred.

(6) The provisions of subsections (3), (4) and (5) apply to any obligation of a buyer to hold the seller harmless against infringement or the like (subsection (3) of Section 2–312).

Official Comment

. . .

Purposes of Changes: To continue the prior basic policies with respect to acceptance of goods while making a number of minor though material changes in the interest of simplicity and commercial convenience so that: . . .

4. The time of notification [under subsection (3)(a)] is to be determined by applying commercial standards to a merchant buyer. "A reasonable time" for notification from a retail consumer is to be judged by different standards so that in his case it will be extended, for the rule of requiring notification is designed to defeat commercial bad faith, not to deprive a good faith consumer of his remedy.

The content of the notification need merely be sufficient to let the seller know that the transaction is still troublesome and must be watched. There is no reason to require that the notification which saves the buyer's rights under this section must include a clear statement of all the objections that will be relied on by the buyer, as under the section covering statements of defects upon rejection (Section 2–605). Nor is there reason for requiring the notification to be a claim for damages or of any threatened litigation or other resort to a remedy. The notification which saves the buyer's rights under this Article need only be such as informs the seller that the transaction is claimed to involve a breach, and thus opens the way for normal settlement through negotiation.

. . .

Definitional Cross References:

"Burden of establishing". Section 1–201.

"Buyer". Section 2–103.

"Conform". Section 2–106.

"Contract". Section 1–201.

"Goods". Section 2–105.

"Notifies". Section 1–201.

"Reasonable time". Section 1–204.

"Remedy". Section 1–201.

"Seasonably". Section 1–204.

§ 2–608. Revocation of Acceptance in Whole or in Part.

(1) The buyer may revoke his acceptance of a lot or commercial unit whose non-conformity substantially impairs its value to him if he has accepted it

    (a) on the reasonable assumption that its non-conformity would be cured and it has not been seasonably cured; or

    (b) without discovery of such non-conformity if his acceptance was reasonably induced either by the difficulty of discovery before acceptance or by the seller's assurances.

(2) Revocation of acceptance must occur within a reasonable time after the buyer discovers or should have discovered the ground for it and before any substantial change in condition of the goods which is not caused by their own defects. It is not effective until the buyer notifies the seller of it.

(3) A buyer who so revokes has the same rights and duties with regard to the goods involved as if he had rejected them.

Official Comment

. . .

Purposes of Changes: To make it clear that:

    1. Although the prior basic policy is continued, the buyer is no longer required to elect between revocation of acceptance and recovery of damages for breach. Both are now available to him. The non-alternative character of the two remedies is stressed by the terms used in the present section. The section no longer speaks of "rescission," a term capable of ambiguous application either to transfer of title to the goods or to the contract of sale and susceptible also of confusion with cancellation for cause of an executed or executory portion of the contract. The remedy under this section is instead referred to simply as "revocation of acceptance" of goods tendered under a contract for sale and involves no suggestion of "election" of any sort.

    2. Revocation of acceptance is possible only where the non-conformity substantially impairs the value of the goods to the buyer. For this purpose the test is not what the seller had reason to know at the time of contracting; the question is whether the non-conformity is such as will in fact cause a substantial impairment of value to the buyer though the seller had no advance knowledge as to the buyer's particular circumstances.

    3. "Assurances" by the seller under paragraph (b) of subsection (1) can rest as well in the circumstances or in the contract as in explicit language used at the time of delivery. The reason for recognizing such assurances is that they induce the buyer to delay discovery. These are the only assurances involved in paragraph (b). Explicit assurances may be made either in good faith or bad faith. In either case any remedy accorded by this Article is available to the buyer under the section on remedies for fraud.

. . .

Definitional Cross References:

"Buyer". Section 2–103.

"Commercial unit". Section 2–105.

"Conform". Section 2–106.

"Goods". Section 2–105.

"Lot". Section 2–105.

"Notifies". Section 1–201.

"Reasonable time". Section 1–204.

"Rights". Section 1–201.

"Seasonably". Section 1–204.

"Seller". Section 2–103.

§ 2–609. Right to Adequate Assurance of Performance.

(1) A contract for sale imposes an obligation on each party that the other's expectation of receiving due performance will not be impaired. When reasonable grounds for insecurity arise with respect to the performance of either party the other may in writing demand adequate assurance of due performance and until he receives such assurance may if commercially reasonable suspend any performance for which he has not already received the agreed return.

(2) Between merchants the reasonableness of grounds for insecurity and the adequacy of any assurance offered shall be determined according to commercial standards.

(3) Acceptance of any improper delivery or payment does not prejudice the aggrieved party's right to demand adequate assurance of future performance.

(4) After receipt of a justified demand failure to provide within a reasonable time not exceeding thirty days such assurance of due performance as is adequate under the circumstances of the particular case is a repudiation of the contract.

Official Comment

. . .

Purposes:

1. The section rests on the recognition of the fact that the essential purpose of a contract between commercial men is actual performance and they do not bargain merely for a promise, or for a promise plus the right to win a lawsuit and that a continuing sense of reliance and security that the promised performance will be forthcoming when due, is an important feature of the bargain. If either the willingness or the ability of a party to perform declines materially between the time of contracting and the time for performance, the other party is threatened with the loss of a substantial part of what he has bargained for. A seller needs protection not merely against having to deliver on credit to a shaky buyer, but also against having to procure and manufacture the goods, perhaps turning down other customers. Once he has been given reason to believe that the buyer's performance has become uncertain, it is an undue hardship to force him to continue his own performance. Similarly, a buyer who believes that the seller's deliveries have become uncertain cannot safely wait for the due date of performance when he has been buying to assure himself of materials for his current manufacturing or to replenish his stock of merchandise.

2. Three measures have been adopted to meet the needs of commercial men in such situations. First, the aggrieved party is permitted to suspend his own performance and any preparation therefor, with excuse for any resulting necessary delay, until the situation has been clarified. "Suspend performance" under this section means to hold up performance pending the outcome of the demand, and includes also the holding up of any preparatory action. . . .

Secondly, the aggrieved party is given the right to require adequate assurance that the other party's performance will be duly forthcoming. This principle is reflected in the familiar clauses permitting the seller to curtail deliveries if the buyer's credit becomes impaired, which when held within the limits of reasonableness and good faith actually express no more than the fair business meaning of any commercial contract.

Third, and finally, this section provides the means by which the aggrieved party may treat the contract as broken if his reasonable grounds for insecurity are not cleared up within a reasonable time. This is the principle underlying the law of anticipatory breach, whether by way of defective part performance or by repudiation. The present section merges these three principles of law and commercial practice into a single theory of general application to all sales agreements looking to future performance.

3. Subsection (2) of the present section requires that "reasonable" grounds and "adequate" assurance as used in subsection (1) be defined by commercial rather than legal standards. The express reference to commercial standards carries no connotation that the obligation of good faith is not equally applicable here.

Under commercial standards and in accord with commercial practice, a ground for insecurity need not arise from or be directly related to the contract in question. The law as to "dependence" or "independence" of promises within a single contract does not control the application of the present section.

Thus a buyer who falls behind in "his account" with the seller, even though the items involved have to do with separate and legally distinct contracts, impairs the seller's expectation of due performance. Again, under the same test, a buyer who requires precision parts which he intends to use immediately upon delivery, may have reasonable grounds for insecurity if he discovers that his seller is making defective deliveries of such parts to other buyers with similar needs. . . .

The nature of the sales contract enters also into the question of reasonableness. For example, a report from an apparently trustworthy source that the seller had shipped defective goods or was planning to ship them would normally give the buyer reasonable grounds for insecurity. But when the buyer has assumed the risk of payment before inspection of the goods, as in a sales contract on C.I.F. or similar cash against documents terms, that risk is not to be evaded by a demand for assurance. Therefore no ground for insecurity would exist under this section unless the report went to a ground which would excuse payment by the buyer.

4. What constitutes "adequate" assurance of due performance is subject to the same test of factual conditions. For example, where the buyer can make use of a defective delivery, a mere promise by a seller of good repute that he is giving the matter his attention and that the defect will not be repeated, is normally sufficient. Under the same circumstances, however, a similar statement by a known corner-cutter might well be considered insufficient without the posting of a guaranty or, if so demanded by the buyer, a speedy replacement of the delivery involved. By the same token where a delivery has defects, even though easily curable, which interfere with easy use by the buyer, no verbal assurance can be deemed adequate which is not accompanied by replacement, repair, money-allowance, or other commercially reasonable cure. . . .

The entire foregoing discussion as to adequacy of assurance by way of explanation is subject to qualification when repeated occasions for the application of this section arise. This Act recognizes that repeated delinquencies must be viewed as cumulative. On the other hand, commercial sense also requires that if repeated claims for assurance are made under this section, the basis for these claims must be increasingly obvious.

5. A failure to provide adequate assurance of performance and thereby to re-establish the security of expectation, results in a breach only "by repudiation" under subsection (4). Therefore, the possibility is continued of retraction of the repudiation under the section dealing with that problem, unless the aggrieved party has acted on the breach in some manner.

The thirty day limit on the time to provide assurance is laid down to free the question of reasonable time from uncertainty in later litigation.

6. Clauses seeking to give the protected party exceedingly wide powers to cancel or readjust the contract when ground for insecurity arises must be read against the fact that good faith is a part of the obligation of the contract and not subject to modification by agreement and includes, in the case of a merchant, the reasonable observance of commercial standards of fair dealing in the trade. Such clauses can thus be effective to enlarge the protection given by the present section to a certain extent, to fix the reasonable time within which requested assurance must be given, or to define adequacy of the assurance in any commercially reasonable fashion. But any clause seeking to set up arbitrary standards for action is ineffective under this Article.

. . .

Definitional Cross References:

"Aggrieved party". Section 1–201.

"Between merchants". Section 2–104.

"Contract". Section 1–201.

"Contract for sale". Section 2–106.

"Party". Section 1–201.

"Reasonable time". Section 1–204.

"Rights". Section 1–201.

"Writing". Section 1–201.

§ 2–610. Anticipatory Repudiation.

When either party repudiates the contract with respect to a performance not yet due the loss of which will substantially impair the value of the contract to the other, the aggrieved party may

    (a) for a commercially reasonable time await performance by the repudiating party; or

    (b) resort to any remedy for breach (Section 2–703 or Section 2–711), even though he has notified the repudiating party that he would await the latter's performance and has urged retraction; and

    (c) in either case suspend his own performance or proceed in accordance with the provisions of this Article on the seller's right to identify goods to the contract notwithstanding breach or to salvage unfinished goods (Section 2–704).

Official Comment

. . .

Purposes: To make it clear that:

    1. With the problem of insecurity taken care of by the preceding section and with provision being made in this Article as to the effect of a defective delivery under an installment contract, anticipatory repudiation centers upon an overt communication of intention or an action which renders performance impossible or demonstrates a clear determination not to continue with performance.

Under the present section when such a repudiation substantially impairs the value of the contract, the aggrieved party may at any time resort to his remedies for breach, or he may suspend his own performance while he negotiates with, or awaits performance by, the other party. But if he awaits performance beyond a commercially reasonable time he cannot recover resulting damages which he should have avoided.

    2. It is not necessary for repudiation that performance be made literally and utterly impossible. Repudiation can result from action which reasonably indicates a rejection of the continuing obligation. And, a repudiation automatically results under the preceding section on insecurity when a party fails to provide adequate assurance of due future performance within thirty days after a justifiable demand therefor has been made. Under the language of this section, a demand by one or both parties for more than the contract calls for in the way of counter-performance is not in itself a repudiation nor does it invalidate a plain expression of desire for future performance. However, when under a fair reading it amounts to a statement of intention not to perform except on conditions which go beyond the contract, it becomes a repudiation.

    3. The test chosen to justify an aggrieved party's action under this section is the same as that in the section on breach in installment contracts—namely the substantial value of the contract. . . .

. . .

Definitional Cross References:

"Aggrieved party". Section 1–201.

"Contract". Section 1–201.

"Party". Section 1–201.

"Remedy". Section 1–201.

§ 2–611. Retraction of Anticipatory Repudiation.

(1) Until the repudiating party's next performance is due he can retract his repudiation unless the aggrieved party has since the repudiation cancelled or materially changed his position or otherwise indicated that he considers the repudiation final.

(2) Retraction may be by any method which clearly indicates to the aggrieved party that the repudiating party intends to perform, but must include any assurance justifiably demanded under the provisions of this Article (Section 2–609).

(3) Retraction reinstates the repudiating party's rights under the contract with due excuse and allowance to the aggrieved party for any delay occasioned by the repudiation.

Official Comment

. . .

Purposes: To make it clear that: . . .

2. Under subsection (2) an effective retraction must be accompanied by any assurances demanded under the section dealing with right to adequate assurance. A repudiation is of course sufficient to give reasonable ground for insecurity and to warrant a request for assurance as an essential condition of the retraction. However, after a timely and unambiguous expression of retraction, a reasonable time for the assurance to be worked out should be allowed by the aggrieved party before cancellation.

. . .

Definitional Cross References:

"Aggrieved party". Section 1–201.

"Cancellation". Section 2–106.

"Contract". Section 1–201.

"Party". Section 1–201.

"Rights". Section 1–201.

§ 2–612. "Installment Contract"; Breach.

(1) An "installment contract" is one which requires or authorizes the delivery of goods in separate lots to be separately accepted, even though the contract contains a clause "each delivery is a separate contract" or its equivalent.

(2) The buyer may reject any installment which is non-conforming if the non-conformity substantially impairs the value of that installment and cannot be cured or if the non-conformity is a defect in the required documents; but if the non-conformity does not fall within subsection (3) and the seller gives adequate assurance of its cure the buyer must accept that installment.

(3) Whenever non-conformity or default with respect to one or more installments substantially impairs the value of the whole contract there is a breach of the whole. But the aggrieved party reinstates the contract if he accepts a non-conforming installment without seasonably notifying of cancellation or if he brings an action with respect only to past installments or demands performance as to future installments.

Official Comment

. . .

§ 2–612

Purposes of Changes:

. . .

3. This Article rejects any approach which gives clauses such as "each delivery is a separate contract" their legalistically literal effect. Such contracts nonetheless call for installment deliveries. Even where a clause speaks of "a separate contract for all purposes", a commercial reading of the language under the section on good faith and commercial standards requires that the singleness of the document and the negotiation, together with the sense of the situation, prevail over any uncommercial and legalistic interpretation.

4. One of the requirements for rejection under subsection (2) is non-conformity substantially impairing the value of the installment in question. However, an installment agreement may require accurate conformity in quality as a condition to the right to acceptance if the need for such conformity is made clear either by express provision or by the circumstances. In such a case the effect of the agreement is to define explicitly what amounts to substantial impairment of value impossible to cure. A clause requiring accurate compliance as a condition to the right to acceptance must, however, have some basis in reason, must avoid imposing hardship by surprise and is subject to waiver or to displacement by practical construction.

Substantial impairment of the value of an installment can turn not only on the quality of the goods but also on such factors as time, quantity, assortment, and the like. It must be judged in terms of the normal or specifically known purposes of the contract. . . .

5. Under subsection (2) an installment delivery must be accepted if the non-conformity is curable and the seller gives adequate assurance of cure. Cure of non-conformity of an installment in the first instance can usually be afforded by an allowance against the price, or in the case of reasonable discrepancies in quantity either by a further delivery or a partial rejection. This Article requires reasonable action by a buyer in regard to discrepant delivery and good faith requires that the buyer make any reasonable minor outlay of time or money necessary to cure an overshipment by severing out an acceptable percentage thereof. The seller must take over a cure which involves any material burden; the buyer's obligation reaches only to cooperation. Adequate assurance for purposes of subsection (2) is measured by the same standards as under the section on right to adequate assurance of performance.

6. Subsection (3) is designed to further the continuance of the contract in the absence of an overt cancellation. The question arising when an action is brought as to a single installment only is resolved by making such action waive the right to cancellation. This involves merely a defect in one or more installments, as contrasted with the situation where there is a true repudiation within the section on anticipatory repudiation. Whether the non-conformity in any given installment justifies cancellation as to the future depends, not on whether such non-conformity indicates an intent or likelihood that the future deliveries will also be defective, but whether the non-conformity substantially impairs the value of the whole contract. If only the seller's security in regard to future installments is impaired, he has the right to demand adequate assurances of proper future performance but has not an immediate right to cancel the entire contract. It is clear under this Article, however, that defects in prior installments are cumulative in effect, so that acceptance does not wash out the defect "waived." Prior policy is continued, putting the rule as to buyer's default on the same footing as that in regard to seller's default. . . .

. . .

Definitional Cross References:

"Action". Section 1–201.

"Aggrieved party". Section 1–201.

"Buyer". Section 2–103.

"Cancellation". Section 2–106.

"Conform". Section 2–106.

"Contract". Section 1–201.

"Lot". Section 2–105.

"Notifies". Section 1–201.

"Seasonably". Section 1–204.

"Seller". Section 2–103.

§ 2–613. Casualty to Identified Goods.

Where the contract requires for its performance goods identified when the contract is made, and the goods suffer casualty without fault of either party before the risk of loss passes to the buyer, or in a proper case under a "no arrival, no sale" term (Section 2–324) then

(a) if the loss is total the contract is avoided; and

(b) if the loss is partial or the goods have so deteriorated as no longer to conform to the contract the buyer may nevertheless demand inspection and at his option either treat the contract as avoided or accept the goods with due allowance from the contract price for the deterioration or the deficiency in quantity but without further right against the seller.

Official Comment

. . .

Definitional Cross References:

"Buyer". Section 2–103.

"Conform". Section 2–106.

"Contract". Section 1–201.

"Fault". Section 1–201.

"Goods". Section 2–105.

"Party". Section 1–201.

"Rights". Section 1–201.

"Seller". Section 2–103.

§ 2–614. Substituted Performance.

(1) Where without fault of either party the agreed berthing, loading, or unloading facilities fail or an agreed type of carrier becomes unavailable or the agreed manner of delivery otherwise becomes commercially impracticable but a commercially reasonable substitute is available, such substitute performance must be tendered and accepted.

(2) If the agreed means or manner of payment fails because of domestic or foreign governmental regulation, the seller may withhold or stop delivery unless the buyer provides a means or manner of payment which is commercially a substantial equivalent. If delivery has already been taken, payment by the means or in the manner provided by the regulation discharges the buyer's obligation unless the regulation is discriminatory, oppressive or predatory.

Official Comment

. . .

Purposes:

1. Subsection (1) requires the tender of a commercially reasonable substituted performance where agreed to facilities have failed or become commercially impracticable. Under this Article, in the absence of specific agreement, the normal or usual facilities enter into the agreement either through the circumstances, usage of trade or prior course of dealing.

This section appears between Section 2–613 on casualty to identified goods and the next section on excuse by failure of presupposed conditions, both of which deal with excuse and complete avoidance of the contract where the occurrence or non-occurrence of a contingency which was a basic assumption of the contract makes the expected performance impossible. The distinction between the present section and those sections lies in whether the failure or impossibility of performance arises in connection with an incidental matter or goes to the very heart of the agreement. The differing lines of solution are contrasted in a comparison of International Paper Co. v. Rockefeller, 161 App.Div. 180, 146 N.Y.S. 371 (1914) and Meyer v. Sullivan, 40 Cal.App. 723, 181 P. 847 (1919). In the former case a contract for the sale of spruce to be cut from a particular tract of land was involved. When a fire destroyed the trees growing on that tract the seller was held excused since performance was impossible. In the latter case the contract called for delivery of wheat "f.o.b. Kosmos Steamer at Seattle." The war led to cancellation of that line's sailing schedule after space had been duly engaged and the buyer was held entitled to demand substituted delivery at the warehouse on the line's loading dock. Under this Article, of course, the seller would also be entitled, had the market gone the other way, to make a substituted tender in that manner.

There must, however, be a true commercial impracticability to excuse the agreed to performance and justify a substituted performance. When this is the case a reasonable substituted performance tendered by either party should excuse him from strict compliance with contract terms which do not go to the essence of the agreement.

. . .

Definitional Cross References:

"Buyer". Section 2–103.

"Fault". Section 1–201.

"Party". Section 1–201.

"Seller". Section 2–103.

§ 2–615. Excuse by Failure of Presupposed Conditions.

Except so far as a seller may have assumed a greater obligation and subject to the preceding section on substituted performance:

(a) Delay in delivery or non-delivery in whole or in part by a seller who complies with paragraphs (b) and (c) is not a breach of his duty under a contract for sale if performance as agreed has been made impracticable by the occurrence of a contingency the non-occurrence of which was a basic assumption on which the contract was made or by compliance in good faith with any applicable foreign or domestic governmental regulation or order whether or not it later proves to be invalid.

(b) Where the causes mentioned in paragraph (a) affect only a part of the seller's capacity to perform, he must allocate production and deliveries among his customers but may at his option include regular customers not then under contract as well as his own requirements for further manufacture. He may so allocate in any manner which is fair and reasonable.

(c) The seller must notify the buyer seasonably that there will be delay or non-delivery and, when allocation is required under paragraph (b), of the estimated quota thus made available for the buyer.

Official Comment

. . .

Purposes:

. . .

2. The present section deliberately refrains from any effort at an exhaustive expression of contingencies and is to be interpreted in all cases sought to be brought within its scope in terms of its underlying reason and purpose.

3. The first test for excuse under this Article in terms of basic assumption is a familiar one. The additional test of commercial impracticability (as contrasted with "impossibility," "frustration of performance" or "frustration of the venture") has been adopted in order to call attention to the commercial character of the criterion chosen by this Article.

4. Increased cost alone does not excuse performance unless the rise in cost is due to some unforeseen contingency which alters the essential nature of the performance. Neither is a rise or a collapse in the market in itself a justification, for that is exactly the type of business risk which business contracts made at fixed prices are intended to cover. But a severe shortage of raw materials or of supplies due to a contingency such as war, embargo, local crop failure, unforeseen shutdown of major sources of supply or the like, which either causes a marked increase in cost or altogether prevents the seller from securing supplies necessary to his performance, is within the contemplation of this section. . . .

5. Where a particular source of supply is exclusive under the agreement and fails through casualty, the present section applies rather than the provision on destruction or deterioration of specific goods. The same holds true where a particular source of supply is shown by the circumstances to have been contemplated or assumed by the parties at the time of contracting. (See Davis Co. v. Hoffmann-LaRoche Chemical Works, 178 App.Div. 855, 166 N.Y.S. 179 (1917) and International Paper Co. v. Rockefeller, 161 App.Div. 180, 146 N.Y.S. 371 (1914).) There is no excuse under this section, however, unless the seller has employed all due measures to assure himself that his source will not fail. (See Canadian Industrial Alcohol Co., Ltd., v. Dunbar Molasses Co., 258 N.Y. 194, 179 N.E. 383, 80 A.L.R. 1173 (1932) and Washington Mfg. Co. v. Midland Lumber Co., 113 Wash. 593, 194 P. 777 (1921).)

In the case of failure of production by an agreed source for causes beyond the seller's control, the seller should, if possible, be excused since production by an agreed source is without more a basic assumption of the contract. Such excuse should not result in relieving the defaulting supplier from liability nor in dropping into the seller's lap an unearned bonus of damages over. The flexible adjustment machinery of this Article provides the solution under the provision on the obligation of good faith. A condition to his making good the claim of excuse is the turning over to the buyer of his rights against the defaulting source of supply to the extent of the buyer's contract in relation to which excuse is being claimed.

6. In situations in which neither sense nor justice is served by either answer when the issue is posed in flat terms of "excuse" or "no excuse," adjustment under the various provisions of this Article is necessary, especially the sections on good faith, on insecurity and assurance and on the reading of all provisions in the light of their purposes, and the general policy of this Act to use equitable principles in furtherance of commercial standards and good faith.

7. The failure of conditions which go to convenience or collateral values rather than to the commercial practicability of the main performance does not amount to a complete excuse. However, good faith and the reason of the present section and of the preceding one may properly be held to justify and even to require any needed delay involved in a good faith inquiry seeking a readjustment of the contract terms to meet the new conditions.

8. The provisions of this section are made subject to assumption of greater liability by agreement and such agreement is to be found not only in the expressed terms of the contract but in the circumstances surrounding the contracting, in trade usage and the like. Thus the exemptions of this section do not apply when the contingency in question is sufficiently foreshadowed at the time of contracting to be included among the business risks which are fairly to be regarded as part of the dickered terms, either consciously or as a matter of reasonable, commercial interpretation from the circumstances. . . .

9. The case of a farmer who has contracted to sell crops to be grown on designated land may be regarded as falling either within the section on casualty to identified goods or this section, and he may be excused, when there is a failure of the specific crop, either on the basis of the destruction of identified goods or because of the failure of a basic assumption of the contract.

Exemption of the buyer in the case of a "requirements" contract is covered by the "Output and Requirements" section both as to assumption and allocation of the relevant risks. But when a contract by a manufacturer to buy fuel or raw material makes no specific reference to a particular venture and no such reference may be drawn from the circumstances, commercial understanding views it as a general deal in the general market and not conditioned on any assumption of the continuing operation of the buyer's plant. Even when notice is given by the buyer that the supplies are needed to fill a specific contract of a normal commercial kind, commercial understanding does not see such a supply contract as conditioned on the continuance of the buyer's further contract for outlet. On the other hand, where the buyer's contract is in reasonable commercial understanding conditioned on a definite and specific venture or assumption as, for instance, a war procurement subcontract known to be based on a prime contract which is subject to termination, or a supply contract for a particular construction venture, the reason of the present section may well apply and entitle the buyer to the exemption.

10. Following its basic policy of using commercial practicability as a test for excuse, this section recognizes as of equal significance either a foreign or domestic regulation and disregards any technical distinctions between "law," "regulation," "order" and the like. Nor does it make the present action of the seller depend upon the eventual judicial determination of the legality of the particular governmental action. The seller's good faith belief in the validity of the regulation is the test under this Article and the best evidence of his good faith is the general commercial acceptance of the regulation. However, governmental interference cannot excuse unless it truly "supervenes" in such a manner as to be beyond the seller's assumption of risk. And any action by the party claiming excuse which causes or colludes in inducing the governmental action preventing his performance would be in breach of good faith and would destroy his exemption.

11. An excused seller must fulfill his contract to the extent which the supervening contingency permits, and if the situation is such that his customers are generally affected he must take account of all in supplying one. Subsections (a) and (b), therefore, explicitly permit in any proration a fair and reasonable attention to the needs of regular customers who are probably relying on spot orders for supplies. Customers at different stages of the manufacturing process may be fairly treated by including the seller's manufacturing requirements. A fortiori, the seller may also take account of contracts later in date than the one in question. The fact that such spot orders may be closed at an advanced price causes no difficulty, since any allocation which exceeds normal past requirements will not be reasonable. However, good faith requires, when prices have advanced, that the seller exercise real care in making his allocations, and in case of doubt his contract customers should be favored and supplies prorated evenly among them regardless of price. Save for the extra care thus required by changes in the market, this section seeks to leave every reasonable business leeway to the seller.

. . .

Definitional Cross References:

"Between merchants". Section 2–104.

"Buyer". Section 2–103.

"Contract". Section 1–201.

"Contract for sale". Section 2–106.

"Good faith". Section 1–201.

"Merchant". Section 2–104.

"Notifies". Section 1–201.

"Seasonably". Section 1–201.

"Seller". Section 2–103.

§ 2–616. Procedure on Notice Claiming Excuse.

(1) Where the buyer receives notification of a material or indefinite delay or an allocation justified under the preceding section he may by written notification to the seller as to any delivery concerned, and where the prospective deficiency substantially impairs the value of the whole contract

under the provisions of this Article relating to breach of installment contracts (Section 2–612), then also as to the whole,

(a) terminate and thereby discharge any unexecuted portion of the contract; or

(b) modify the contract by agreeing to take his available quota in substitution.

(2) If after receipt of such notification from the seller the buyer fails so to modify the contract within a reasonable time not exceeding thirty days the contract lapses with respect to any deliveries affected.

(3) The provisions of this section may not be negated by agreement except in so far as the seller has assumed a greater obligation under the preceding section.

Official Comment

. . .

Definitional Cross References:

"Buyer". Section 2–103.

"Contract". Section 1–201.

"Installment contract". Section 2–612.

"Notification". Section 1–201.

"Reasonable time". Section 1–204.

"Seller". Section 2–103.

"Termination". Section 2–106.

"Written". Section 1–201.

PART VII

REMEDIES

§ 2–701. Remedies for Breach of Collateral Contracts Not Impaired.

Remedies for breach of any obligation or promise collateral or ancillary to a contract for sale are not impaired by the provisions of this Article.

Official Comment

. . .

Definitional Cross References:

"Contract for sale". Section 2–106.

"Remedy". Section 1–201.

§ 2–702. Seller's Remedies on Discovery of Buyer's Insolvency.

(1) Where the seller discovers the buyer to be insolvent he may refuse delivery except for cash including payment for all goods theretofore delivered under the contract, and stop delivery under this Article (Section 2–705).

(2) Where the seller discovers that the buyer has received goods on credit while insolvent he may reclaim the goods upon demand made within ten days after the receipt, but if misrepresentation of solvency has been made to the particular seller in writing within three months before delivery the ten day limitation does not apply. Except as provided in this subsection the seller may not base a right

to reclaim goods on the buyer's fraudulent or innocent misrepresentation of solvency or of intent to pay.

(3) The seller's right to reclaim under subsection (2) is subject to the rights of a buyer in ordinary course or other good faith purchaser under this Article (Section 2–403). Successful reclamation of goods excludes all other remedies with respect to them.

As amended in 1966.

Official Comment

. . .

Definitional Cross References:

"Buyer". Section 2–103.

"Buyer in ordinary course of business". Section 1–201.

"Contract". Section 1–201.

"Good faith". Section 1–201.

"Goods". Section 2–105.

"Insolvent". Section 1–201.

"Person". Section 1–201.

"Purchaser". Section 1–201.

"Receipt" of goods. Section 2–103.

"Remedy". Section 1–201.

"Rights". Section 1–201.

"Seller". Section 2–103.

"Writing". Section 1–201.

§ 2–703. Seller's Remedies in General.

Where the buyer wrongfully rejects or revokes acceptance of goods or fails to make a payment due on or before delivery or repudiates with respect to a part or the whole, then with respect to any goods directly affected and, if the breach is of the whole contract (Section 2–612), then also with respect to the whole undelivered balance, the aggrieved seller may

(a) withhold delivery of such goods;

(b) stop delivery by any bailee as hereafter provided (Section 2–705);

(c) proceed under the next section respecting goods still unidentified to the contract;

(d) resell and recover damages as hereafter provided (Section 2–706);

(e) recover damages for non-acceptance (Section 2–708) or in a proper case the price (Section 2–709);

(f) cancel.

Official Comment

. . .

Purposes:

1. This section is an index section which gathers together in one convenient place all of the various remedies open to a seller for any breach by the buyer. This Article rejects any doctrine of election of remedy

as a fundamental policy and thus the remedies are essentially cumulative in nature and include all of the available remedies for breach. Whether the pursuit of one remedy bars another depends entirely on the facts of the individual case. . . .

4. It should also be noted that this Act requires its remedies to be liberally administered and provides that any right or obligation which it declares is enforceable by action unless a different effect is specifically prescribed (Section 1–106).

. . .

Definitional Cross References:

"Aggrieved party". Section 1–201.

"Buyer". Section 2–103.

"Cancellation". Section 2–106.

"Contract". Section 1–201.

"Goods". Section 2–105.

"Remedy". Section 1–201.

"Seller". Section 2–103.

§ 2–704. Seller's Right to Identify Goods to the Contract Notwithstanding Breach or to Salvage Unfinished Goods.

(1) An aggrieved seller under the preceding section may

(a) identify to the contract conforming goods not already identified if at the time he learned of the breach they are in his possession or control;

(b) treat as the subject of resale goods which have demonstrably been intended for the particular contract even though those goods are unfinished.

(2) Where the goods are unfinished an aggrieved seller may in the exercise of reasonable commercial judgment for the purposes of avoiding loss and of effective realization either complete the manufacture and wholly identify the goods to the contract or cease manufacture and resell for scrap or salvage value or proceed in any other reasonable manner.

Official Comment

. . .

Purposes of Changes:

1. This section gives an aggrieved seller the right at the time of breach to identify to the contract any conforming finished goods, regardless of their resalability, and to use reasonable judgment as to completing unfinished goods. It thus makes the goods available for resale under the resale section, the seller's primary remedy, and in the special case in which resale is not practicable, allows the action for the price which would then be necessary to give the seller the value of his contract.

2. Under this Article the seller is given express power to complete manufacture or procurement of goods for the contract unless the exercise of reasonable commercial judgment as to the facts as they appear at the time he learns of the breach makes it clear that such action will result in a material increase in damages. The burden is on the buyer to show the commercially unreasonable nature of the seller's action in completing manufacture.

. . .

Definitional Cross References:

"Aggrieved party". Section 1–201.

"Conforming". Section 2–106.

"Contract". Section 1–201.

"Delivery". Section 2–103.

"Goods". Section 2–105.

"Rights". Section 1–201.

"Seller". Section 2–103.

§ 2–705. Seller's Stoppage of Delivery in Transit or Otherwise.

(1) The seller may stop delivery of goods in the possession of a carrier or other bailee when he discovers the buyer to be insolvent (Section 2–702) and may stop delivery of carload, truckload, planeload or larger shipments of express or freight when the buyer repudiates or fails to make a payment due before delivery or if for any other reason the seller has a right to withhold or reclaim the goods.

(2) As against such buyer the seller may stop delivery until

(a) receipt of the goods by the buyer; or

(b) acknowledgment to the buyer by any bailee of the goods except a carrier that the bailee holds the goods for the buyer; or

(c) such acknowledgment to the buyer by a carrier by reshipment or as warehouseman; or

(d) negotiation to the buyer of any negotiable document of title covering the goods.

(3)(a) To stop delivery the seller must so notify as to enable the bailee by reasonable diligence to prevent delivery of the goods.

(b) After such notification the bailee must hold and deliver the goods according to the directions of the seller but the seller is liable to the bailee for any ensuing charges or damages.

(c) If a negotiable document of title has been issued for goods the bailee is not obliged to obey a notification to stop until surrender of the document.

(d) A carrier who has issued a non-negotiable bill of lading is not obliged to obey a notification to stop received from a person other than the consignor.

Official Comment

. . .

Definitional Cross References:

"Buyer". Section 2–103.

"Contract for sale". Section 2–106.

"Document of title". Section 1–201.

"Goods". Section 2–105.

"Insolvent". Section 1–201.

"Notification". Section 1–201.

"Receipt" of goods. Section 2–103.

"Rights". Section 1–201.

"Seller". Section 2–103.

§ 2–706. Seller's Resale Including Contract for Resale.

(1) Under the conditions stated in Section 2–703 on seller's remedies, the seller may resell the goods concerned or the undelivered balance thereof. Where the resale is made in good faith and in a commercially reasonable manner the seller may recover the difference between the resale price and the contract price together with any incidental damages allowed under the provisions of this Article (Section 2–710), but less expenses saved in consequence of the buyer's breach.

(2) Except as otherwise provided in subsection (3) or unless otherwise agreed resale may be at public or private sale including sale by way of one or more contracts to sell or of identification to an existing contract of the seller. Sale may be as a unit or in parcels and at any time and place and on any terms but every aspect of the sale including the method, manner, time, place and terms must be commercially reasonable. The resale must be reasonably identified as referring to the broken contract, but it is not necessary that the goods be in existence or that any or all of them have been identified to the contract before the breach.

(3) Where the resale is at private sale the seller must give the buyer reasonable notification of his intention to resell.

(4) Where the resale is at public sale

(a) only identified goods can be sold except where there is a recognized market for a public sale of futures in goods of the kind; and

(b) it must be made at a usual place or market for public sale if one is reasonably available and except in the case of goods which are perishable or threaten to decline in value speedily the seller must give the buyer reasonable notice of the time and place of the resale; and

(c) if the goods are not to be within the view of those attending the sale the notification of sale must state the place where the goods are located and provide for their reasonable inspection by prospective bidders; and

(d) the seller may buy.

(5) A purchaser who buys in good faith at a resale takes the goods free of any rights of the original buyer even though the seller fails to comply with one or more of the requirements of this section.

(6) The seller is not accountable to the buyer for any profit made on any resale. A person in the position of a seller (Section 2–707) or a buyer who has rightfully rejected or justifiably revoked acceptance must account for any excess over the amount of his security interest, as hereinafter defined (subsection (3) of Section 2–711).

Official Comment

. . .

Purposes of Changes: To simplify the prior statutory provision and to make it clear that: . . .

2. In order to recover the damages prescribed in subsection (1) the seller must act "in good faith and in a commercially reasonable manner" in making the resale. . . . Failure to act properly under this section deprives the seller of the measure of damages here provided and relegates him to that provided in Section 2–708. . . .

3. If the seller complies with the prescribed standard of duty in making the resale, he may recover from the buyer the damages provided for in subsection (1). Evidence of market or current prices at any particular time or place is relevant only on the question of whether the seller acted in a commercially reasonable manner in making the resale. . . .

4. Subsection (2) frees the remedy of resale from legalistic restrictions and enables the seller to resell in accordance with reasonable commercial practices so as to realize as high a price as possible in the circumstances. By "public" sale is meant a sale by auction. A "private" sale may be effected by solicitation

and negotiation conducted either directly or through a broker. In choosing between a public and private sale the character of the goods must be considered and relevant trade practices and usages must be observed.

. . .

Definitional Cross References:

"Buyer". Section 2–103.

"Contract". Section 1–201.

"Contract for sale". Section 2–106.

"Good faith". Section 2–103.

"Goods". Section 2–105.

"Merchant". Section 2–104.

"Notification". Section 1–201.

"Person in position of seller". Section 2–707.

"Purchase". Section 1–201.

"Rights". Section 1–201.

"Sale". Section 2–106.

"Security interest". Section 1–201.

"Seller". Section 2–103.

§ 2–707. "Person in the Position of a Seller".

(1) A "person in the position of a seller" includes as against a principal an agent who has paid or become responsible for the price of goods on behalf of his principal or anyone who otherwise holds a security interest or other right in goods similar to that of a seller.

(2) A person in the position of a seller may as provided in this Article withhold or stop delivery (Section 2–705) and resell (Section 2–706) and recover incidental damages (Section 2–710).

Official Comment

. . .

Definitional Cross References:

"Consignee". Section 7–102.

"Consignor". Section 7–102.

"Goods". Section 2–105.

"Security interest". Section 1–201.

"Seller". Section 2–103.

§ 2–708. Seller's Damages for Non-Acceptance or Repudiation.

(1) Subject to subsection (2) and to the provisions of this Article with respect to proof of market price (Section 2–723), the measure of damages for non-acceptance or repudiation by the buyer is the difference between the market price at the time and place for tender and the unpaid contract price together with any incidental damages provided in this Article (Section 2–710), but less expenses saved in consequence of the buyer's breach.

(2) If the measure of damages provided in subsection (1) is inadequate to put the seller in as good a position as performance would have done then the measure of damages is the profit (including

reasonable overhead) which the seller would have made from full performance by the buyer, together with any incidental damages provided in this Article (Section 2–710), due allowance for costs reasonably incurred and due credit for payments or proceeds of resale.

Official Comment

...

Purposes of Changes: To make it clear that: ...

2. The provision of this section permitting recovery of expected profit including reasonable overhead where the standard measure of damages is inadequate, together with the new requirement that price actions may be sustained only where resale is impractical, are designed to eliminate the unfair and economically wasteful results arising under the older law when fixed price articles were involved. This section permits the recovery of lost profits in all appropriate cases, which would include all standard priced goods. The normal measure there would be list price less cost to the dealer or list price less manufacturing cost to the manufacturer. It is not necessary to a recovery of "profit" to show a history of earnings, especially if a new venture is involved.

...

Definitional Cross References:

"Buyer". Section 2–103.

"Contract". Section 1–201.

"Seller". Section 2–103.

§ 2–709. Action for the Price.

(1) When the buyer fails to pay the price as it becomes due the seller may recover, together with any incidental damages under the next section, the price

   (a) of goods accepted or of conforming goods lost or damaged within a commercially reasonable time after risk of their loss has passed to the buyer; and

   (b) of goods identified to the contract if the seller is unable after reasonable effort to resell them at a reasonable price or the circumstances reasonably indicate that such effort will be unavailing.

(2) Where the seller sues for the price he must hold for the buyer any goods which have been identified to the contract and are still in his control except that if resale becomes possible he may resell them at any time prior to the collection of the judgment. The net proceeds of any such resale must be credited to the buyer and payment of the judgment entitles him to any goods not resold.

(3) After the buyer has wrongfully rejected or revoked acceptance of the goods or has failed to make a payment due or has repudiated (Section 2–610), a seller who is held not entitled to the price under this section shall nevertheless be awarded damages for non-acceptance under the preceding section.

Official Comment

...

Purposes of Changes: To make it clear that: ...

2. The action for the price is now generally limited to those cases where resale of the goods is impracticable except where the buyer has accepted the goods or where they have been destroyed after risk of loss has passed to the buyer. ...

6. This section is intended to be exhaustive in its enumeration of cases where an action for the price lies.

Definitional Cross References:

"Action". Section 1–201.

"Buyer". Section 2–103.

"Conforming". Section 2–106.

"Contract". Section 1–201.

"Goods". Section 2–105.

"Seller". Section 2–103.

§ 2–710. Seller's Incidental Damages.

Incidental damages to an aggrieved seller include any commercially reasonable charges, expenses or commissions incurred in stopping delivery, in the transportation, care and custody of goods after the buyer's breach, in connection with return or resale of the goods or otherwise resulting from the breach.

Official Comment

. . .

Definitional Cross References:

"Aggrieved party". Section 1–201.

"Buyer". Section 2–103.

"Goods". Section 2–105.

"Seller". Section 2–103.

§ 2–711. Buyer's Remedies in General; Buyer's Security Interest in Rejected Goods.

(1) Where the seller fails to make delivery or repudiates or the buyer rightfully rejects or justifiably revokes acceptance then with respect to any goods involved, and with respect to the whole if the breach goes to the whole contract (Section 2–612), the buyer may cancel and whether or not he has done so may in addition to recovering so much of the price as has been paid

(a) "cover" and have damages under the next section as to all the goods affected whether or not they have been identified to the contract; or

(b) recover damages for non-delivery as provided in this Article (Section 2–713).

(2) Where the seller fails to deliver or repudiates the buyer may also

(a) if the goods have been identified recover them as provided in this Article (Section 2–502); or

(b) in a proper case obtain specific performance or replevy the goods as provided in this Article (Section 2–716).

(3) On rightful rejection or justifiable revocation of acceptance a buyer has a security interest in goods in his possession or control for any payments made on their price and any expenses reasonably incurred in their inspection, receipt, transportation, care and custody and may hold such goods and resell them in like manner as an aggrieved seller (Section 2–706).

Official Comment

. . .

Art. 2   SALES   § 2–712

Purposes of Changes:

    1. To index in this section the buyer's remedies, subsection (1) covering those remedies permitting the recovery of money damages, and subsection (2) covering those which permit reaching the goods themselves. The remedies listed here are those available to a buyer who has not accepted the goods or who has justifiably revoked his acceptance. The remedies available to a buyer with regard to goods finally accepted appear in [§ 2–714] dealing with breach in regard to accepted goods. . . .

    3. It should also be noted that this Act requires its remedies to be liberally administered and provides that any right or obligation which it declares is enforceable by action unless a different effect is specifically prescribed (Section 1–106).

. . .

Definitional Cross References:

    "Aggrieved party". Section 1–201.

    "Buyer". Section 2–103.

    "Cancellation". Section 2–106.

    "Contract". Section 1–201.

    "Cover". Section 2–712.

    "Goods". Section 2–105.

    "Notifies". Section 1–201.

    "Receipt" of goods. Section 2–103.

    "Remedy". Section 1–201.

    "Security interest". Section 1–201.

    "Seller". Section 2–103.

§ 2–712. "Cover"; Buyer's Procurement of Substitute Goods.

    (1) After a breach within the preceding section the buyer may "cover" by making in good faith and without unreasonable delay any reasonable purchase of or contract to purchase goods in substitution for those due from the seller.

    (2) The buyer may recover from the seller as damages the difference between the cost of cover and the contract price together with any incidental or consequential damages as hereinafter defined (Section 2–715), but less expenses saved in consequence of the seller's breach.

    (3) Failure of the buyer to effect cover within this section does not bar him from any other remedy.

Official Comment

. . .

Purposes:

    1. This section provides the buyer with a remedy aimed at enabling him to obtain the goods he needs thus meeting his essential need. This remedy is the buyer's equivalent of the seller's right to resell.

    2. The definition of "cover" under subsection (1) envisages a series of contracts or sales, as well as a single contract or sale; goods not identical with those involved but commercially usable as reasonable substitutes under the circumstances of the particular case; and contracts on credit or delivery terms differing from the contract in breach, but again reasonable under the circumstances. The test of proper cover is whether at the time and place the buyer acted in good faith and in a reasonable manner, and it is immaterial that hindsight may later prove that the method of cover used was not the cheapest or most effective.

§ 2–713   UNIFORM COMMERCIAL CODE   Pt. I

The requirement that the buyer must cover "without unreasonable delay" is not intended to limit the time necessary for him to look around and decide as to how he may best effect cover. The test here is similar to that generally used in this Article as to reasonable time and seasonable action.

3. Subsection (3) expresses the policy that cover is not a mandatory remedy for the buyer. The buyer is always free to choose between cover and damages for non-delivery under the next section.

However, this subsection must be read in conjunction with the section which limits the recovery of consequential damages to such as could not have been obviated by cover. . . .

4. This section does not limit cover to merchants, in the first instance. It is the vital and important remedy for the consumer buyer as well. Both are free to use cover: the domestic or non-merchant consumer is required only to act in normal good faith while the merchant buyer must also observe all reasonable commercial standards of fair dealing in the trade, since this falls within the definition of good faith on his part.

. . .

Definitional Cross References:

"Buyer". Section 2–103.

"Contract". Section 1–201.

"Good faith". Section 2–103.

"Goods". Section 2–105.

"Purchase". Section 1–201.

"Remedy". Section 1–201.

"Seller". Section 2–103.

§ 2–713. Buyer's Damages for Non-Delivery or Repudiation.

(1) Subject to the provisions of this Article with respect to proof of market price (Section 2–723), the measure of damages for non-delivery or repudiation by the seller is the difference between the market price at the time when the buyer learned of the breach and the contract price together with any incidental and consequential damages provided in this Article (Section 2–715), but less expenses saved in consequence of the seller's breach.

(2) Market price is to be determined as of the place for tender or, in cases of rejection after arrival or revocation of acceptance, as of the place of arrival.

Official Comment

. . .

Purposes of Changes: To clarify the former rule so that:

1. The general baseline adopted in this section uses as a yardstick the market in which the buyer would have obtained cover had he sought that relief. So the place for measuring damages is the place of tender (or the place of arrival if the goods are rejected or their acceptance is revoked after reaching their destination) and the crucial time is the time at which the buyer learns of the breach.

2. The market or current price to be used in comparison with the contract price under this section is the price for goods of the same kind and in the same branch of trade. . . .

5. The present section provides a remedy which is completely alternative to cover under the preceding section and applies only when and to the extent that the buyer has not covered.

. . .

Definitional Cross References:

"Buyer". Section 2–103.

"Contract". Section 1–201.

"Seller". Section 2–103.

§ 2–714. Buyer's Damages for Breach in Regard to Accepted Goods.

(1) Where the buyer has accepted goods and given notification (subsection (3) of Section 2–607) he may recover as damages for any non-conformity of tender the loss resulting in the ordinary course of events from the seller's breach as determined in any manner which is reasonable.

(2) The measure of damages for breach of warranty is the difference at the time and place of acceptance between the value of the goods accepted and the value they would have had if they had been as warranted, unless special circumstances show proximate damages of a different amount.

(3) In a proper case any incidental and consequential damages under the next section may also be recovered.

Official Comment

. . .

Definitional Cross References:

"Buyer". Section 2–103.

"Conform". Section 2–106.

"Goods". Section 1–201.

"Notification". Section 1–201.

"Seller". Section 2–103.

§ 2–715. Buyer's Incidental and Consequential Damages.

(1) Incidental damages resulting from the seller's breach include expenses reasonably incurred in inspection, receipt, transportation and care and custody of goods rightfully rejected, any commercially reasonable charges, expenses or commissions in connection with effecting cover and any other reasonable expense incident to the delay or other breach.

(2) Consequential damages resulting from the seller's breach include

(a) any loss resulting from general or particular requirements and needs of which the seller at the time of contracting had reason to know and which could not reasonably be prevented by cover or otherwise; and

(b) injury to person or property proximately resulting from any breach of warranty.

Official Comment

. . .

Purposes of Changes and New Matter:

1. Subsection (1) is intended to provide reimbursement for the buyer who incurs reasonable expenses in connection with the handling of rightfully rejected goods or goods whose acceptance may be justifiably revoked, or in connection with effecting cover where the breach of the contract lies in non-conformity or non-delivery of the goods. The incidental damages listed are not intended to be exhaustive but are merely illustrative of the typical kinds of incidental damage.

2. Subsection (2) operates to allow the buyer, in an appropriate case, any consequential damages which are the result of the seller's breach. The "tacit agreement" test for the recovery of consequential damages is rejected. Although the older rule at common law which made the seller liable for all consequential damages of which he had "reason to know" in advance is followed, the liberality of that rule

is modified by refusing to permit recovery unless the buyer could not reasonably have prevented the loss by cover or otherwise. Subparagraph (2) carries forward the provisions of the prior uniform statutory provision as to consequential damages resulting from breach of warranty, but modifies the rule by requiring first that the buyer attempt to minimize his damages in good faith, either by cover or otherwise.

3. In the absence of excuse under the section on merchant's excuse by failure of presupposed conditions, the seller is liable for consequential damages in all cases where he had reason to know of the buyer's general or particular requirements at the time of contracting. It is not necessary that there be a conscious acceptance of an insurer's liability on the seller's part, nor is his obligation for consequential damages limited to cases in which he fails to use due effort in good faith.

Particular needs of the buyer must generally be made known to the seller while general needs must rarely be made known to charge the seller with knowledge.

Any seller who does not wish to take the risk of consequential damages has available the section on contractual limitation of remedy.

4. The burden of proving the extent of loss incurred by way of consequential damage is on the buyer, but the section on liberal administration of remedies rejects any doctrine of certainty which requires almost mathematical precision in the proof of loss. Loss may be determined in any manner which is reasonable under the circumstances.

5. Subsection (2)(b) states the usual rule as to breach of warranty, allowing recovery for injuries "proximately" resulting from the breach. Where the injury involved follows the use of goods without discovery of the defect causing the damage, the question of "proximate" cause turns on whether it was reasonable for the buyer to use the goods without such inspection as would have revealed the defects. If it was not reasonable for him to do so, or if he did in fact discover the defect prior to his use, the injury would not proximately result from the breach of warranty. . . .

. . .

Definitional Cross References:

"Cover". Section 2–712.

"Goods". Section 1–201.

"Person". Section 1–201.

"Receipt" of goods. Section 2–103.

"Seller". Section 2–103.

§ 2–716. Buyer's Right to Specific Performance or Replevin.

(1) Specific performance may be decreed where the goods are unique or in other proper circumstances.

(2) The decree for specific performance may include such terms and conditions as to payment of the price, damages, or other relief as the court may deem just.

(3) The buyer has a right of replevin for goods identified to the contract if after reasonable effort he is unable to effect cover for such goods or the circumstances reasonably indicate that such effort will be unavailing or if the goods have been shipped under reservation and satisfaction of the security interest in them has been made or tendered. In the case of goods bought for personal, family, or household purposes, the buyer's right of replevin vests upon acquisition of a special property, even if the seller had not then repudiated or failed to deliver.

Official Comment

. . .

Purposes of Changes: To make it clear that:

    1. The present section continues in general prior policy as to specific performance and injunction against breach. However, without intending to impair in any way the exercise of the court's sound discretion in the matter, this Article seeks to further a more liberal attitude than some courts have shown in connection with the specific performance of contracts of sale.

    2. In view of this Article's emphasis on the commercial feasibility of replacement, a new concept of what are "unique" goods is introduced under this section. Specific performance is no longer limited to goods which are already specific or ascertained at the time of contracting. The test of uniqueness under this section must be made in terms of the total situation which characterizes the contract. Output and requirements contracts involving a particular or peculiarly available source or market present today the typical commercial specific performance situation, as contrasted with contracts for the sale of heirlooms or priceless works of art which were usually involved in the older cases. However, uniqueness is not the sole basis of the remedy under this section for the relief may also be granted "in other proper circumstances" and inability to cover is strong evidence of "other proper circumstances".

    3. The legal remedy of replevin is given to the buyer in cases in which cover is reasonably unavailable and goods have been identified to the contract. This is in addition to the buyer's right to recover identified goods under Section 2–502. For consumer goods, the buyer's right to replevin vests upon the buyer's acquisition of a special property, which occurs upon identification of the goods to the contract. See Section 2–501. Inasmuch as a secured party normally acquires no greater rights in its collateral that its debtor had or had power to convey, see Section 2–403(1) (first sentence), a buyer who acquires a right of replevin under subsection (3) will take free of a security interest created by the seller if it attaches to the goods after the goods have been identified to the contract. The buyer will take free, even if the buyer does not buy in ordinary course and even if the security interest is perfected. Of course, to the extent that the buyer pays the price after the security interest attaches, the payments will constitute proceeds of the security interest.

    4. This section is intended to give the buyer rights to the goods comparable to the seller's rights to the price. . . .

    . . .

Definitional Cross References:

    "Buyer". Section 2–103.

    "Goods". Section 1–201.

    "Rights". Section 1–201.

§ 2–717. Deduction of Damages From the Price.

The buyer on notifying the seller of his intention to do so may deduct all or any part of the damages resulting from any breach of the contract from any part of the price still due under the same contract.

Official Comment

    . . .

Purposes:

    1. This section permits the buyer to deduct from the price damages resulting from any breach by the seller and does not limit the relief to cases of breach of warranty as did the prior uniform statutory provision. To bring this provision into application the breach involved must be of the same contract under which the price in question is claimed to have been earned.

    2. The buyer, however, must give notice of his intention to withhold all or part of the price if he wishes to avoid a default within the meaning of the section on insecurity and right to assurances. In conformity with the general policies of this Article, no formality of notice is required and any language which reasonably indicates the buyer's reason for holding up his payment is sufficient.

Definitional Cross References:

"Buyer". Section 2–103.

"Notifies". Section 1–201.

§ 2–718. Liquidation or Limitation of Damages; Deposits.

(1) Damages for breach by either party may be liquidated in the agreement but only at an amount which is reasonable in the light of the anticipated or actual harm caused by the breach, the difficulties of proof of loss, and the inconvenience or nonfeasibility of otherwise obtaining an adequate remedy. A term fixing unreasonably large liquidated damages is void as a penalty.

(2) Where the seller justifiably withholds delivery of goods because of the buyer's breach, the buyer is entitled to restitution of any amount by which the sum of his payments exceeds

   (a) the amount to which the seller is entitled by virtue of terms liquidating the seller's damages in accordance with subsection (1), or

   (b) in the absence of such terms, twenty per cent of the value of the total performance for which the buyer is obligated under the contract or $500, whichever is smaller.

(3) The buyer's right to restitution under subsection (2) is subject to offset to the extent that the seller establishes

   (a) a right to recover damages under the provisions of this Article other than subsection (1), and

   (b) the amount or value of any benefits received by the buyer directly or indirectly by reason of the contract.

(4) Where a seller has received payment in goods their reasonable value or the proceeds of their resale shall be treated as payments for the purposes of subsection (2); but if the seller has notice of the buyer's breach before reselling goods received in part performance, his resale is subject to the conditions laid down in this Article on resale by an aggrieved seller (Section 2–706).

Official Comment

. . .

Purposes:

1. Under subsection (1) liquidated damage clauses are allowed where the amount involved is reasonable in the light of the circumstances of the case. The subsection sets forth explicitly the elements to be considered in determining the reasonableness of a liquidated damage clause. A term fixing unreasonably large liquidated damages is expressly made void as a penalty. An unreasonably small amount would be subject to similar criticism and might be stricken under the section on unconscionable contracts or clauses.

2. Subsection (2) refuses to recognize a forfeiture unless the amount of the payment so forfeited represents a reasonable liquidation of damages as determined under subsection (1). A special exception is made in the case of small amounts (20% of the price or $500, whichever is smaller) deposited as security. No distinction is made between cases in which the payment is to be applied on the price and those in which it is intended as security for performance. Subsection (2) is applicable to any deposit or down or part payment. In the case of a deposit or [trade] in of goods resold before the breach, the amount actually received on the resale is to be viewed as the deposit rather than the amount allowed the buyer for the trade in. However, if the seller knows of the breach prior to the resale of the goods [traded] in, he must make reasonable efforts to realize their true value, and this is assured by requiring him to comply with the conditions laid down in the section on resale by an aggrieved seller.

Definitional Cross References:

"Aggrieved party". Section 1–201.

"Agreement". Section 1–201.

"Buyer". Section 2–103.

"Goods". Section 2–105.

"Notice". Section 1–201.

"Party". Section 1–201.

"Remedy". Section 1–201.

"Seller". Section 2–103.

"Term". Section 1–201.

§ 2–719. Contractual Modification or Limitation of Remedy.

(1) Subject to the provisions of subsections (2) and (3) of this section and of the preceding section on liquidation and limitation of damages,

(a) the agreement may provide for remedies in addition to or in substitution for those provided in this Article and may limit or alter the measure of damages recoverable under this Article, as by limiting the buyer's remedies to return of the goods and repayment of the price or to repair and replacement of non-conforming goods or parts; and

(b) resort to a remedy as provided is optional unless the remedy is expressly agreed to be exclusive, in which case it is the sole remedy.

(2) Where circumstances cause an exclusive or limited remedy to fail of its essential purpose, remedy may be had as provided in this Act.

(3) Consequential damages may be limited or excluded unless the limitation or exclusion is unconscionable. Limitation of consequential damages for injury to the person in the case of consumer goods is prima facie unconscionable but limitation of damages where the loss is commercial is not.

Official Comment

. . .

Purposes:

1. Under this section parties are left free to shape their remedies to their particular requirements and reasonable agreements limiting or modifying remedies are to be given effect.

However, it is of the very essence of a sales contract that at least minimum adequate remedies be available. If the parties intend to conclude a contract for sale within this Article they must accept the legal consequence that there be at least a fair quantum of remedy for breach of the obligations or duties outlined in the contract. Thus any clause purporting to modify or limit the remedial provisions of this Article in an unconscionable manner is subject to deletion and in that event the remedies made available by this Article are applicable as if the stricken clause had never existed. Similarly, under subsection (2), where an apparently fair and reasonable clause because of circumstances fails in its purpose or operates to deprive either party of the substantial value of the bargain, it must give way to the general remedy provisions of this Article.

2. Subsection (1)(b) creates a presumption that clauses prescribing remedies are cumulative rather than exclusive. If the parties intend the term to describe the sole remedy under the contract, this must be clearly expressed.

3. Subsection (3) recognizes the validity of clauses limiting or excluding consequential damages but makes it clear that they may not operate in an unconscionable manner. Actually such terms are merely an allocation of unknown or undeterminable risks. The seller in all cases is free to disclaim warranties in the manner provided in Section 2–316.

. . .

Definitional Cross References:

> "Agreement". Section 1–201.
>
> "Buyer". Section 2–103.
>
> "Conforming". Section 2–106.
>
> "Contract". Section 1–201.
>
> "Goods". Section 2–105.
>
> "Remedy". Section 1–201.
>
> "Seller". Section 2–103.

§ 2–720. Effect of "Cancellation" or "Rescission" on Claims for Antecedent Breach.

Unless the contrary intention clearly appears, expressions of "cancellation" or "rescission" of the contract or the like shall not be construed as a renunciation or discharge of any claim in damages for an antecedent breach.

Official Comment

. . .

Definitional Cross References:

> "Cancellation". Section 2–106.
>
> "Contract". Section 1–201.

§ 2–721. Remedies for Fraud.

Remedies for material misrepresentation or fraud include all remedies available under this Article for non-fraudulent breach. Neither rescission or a claim for rescission of the contract for sale nor rejection or return of the goods shall bar or be deemed inconsistent with a claim for damages or other remedy.

Official Comment

. . .

Definitional Cross References:

> "Contract for sale". Section 2–106.
>
> "Goods". Section 1–201.
>
> "Remedy". Section 1–201.

§ 2–722. Who Can Sue Third Parties for Injury to Goods.

Where a third party so deals with goods which have been identified to a contract for sale as to cause actionable injury to a party to that contract

(a) a right of action against the third party is in either party to the contract for sale who has title to or a security interest or a special property or an insurable interest in the goods; and if the goods have been destroyed or converted a right of action is also in the party who either bore the risk of loss under the contract for sale or has since the injury assumed that risk as against the other;

(b) if at the time of the injury the party plaintiff did not bear the risk of loss as against the other party to the contract for sale and there is no arrangement between them for disposition of the recovery, his suit or settlement is, subject to his own interest, as a fiduciary for the other party to the contract;

(c) either party may with the consent of the other sue for the benefit of whom it may concern.

Official Comment

. . .

Definitional Cross References:

"Action". Section 1–201.

"Buyer". Section 2–103.

"Contract for sale". Section 2–106.

"Goods". Section 2–105.

"Party". Section 1–201.

"Rights". Section 1–201.

"Security interest". Section 1–201.

§ 2–723. Proof of Market Price: Time and Place.

(1) If an action based on anticipatory repudiation comes to trial before the time for performance with respect to some or all of the goods, any damages based on market price (Section 2–708 or Section 2–713) shall be determined according to the price of such goods prevailing at the time when the aggrieved party learned of the repudiation.

(2) If evidence of a price prevailing at the times or places described in this Article is not readily available the price prevailing within any reasonable time before or after the time described or at any other place which in commercial judgment or under usage of trade would serve as a reasonable substitute for the one described may be used, making any proper allowance for the cost of transporting the goods to or from such other place.

(3) Evidence of a relevant price prevailing at a time or place other than the one described in this Article offered by one party is not admissible unless and until he has given the other party such notice as the court finds sufficient to prevent unfair surprise.

Official Comment

. . .

Purposes: To eliminate the most obvious difficulties arising in connection with the determination of market price, when that is stipulated as a measure of damages by some provision of this Article. Where the appropriate market price is not readily available the court is here granted reasonable leeway in receiving evidence of prices current in other comparable markets or at other times comparable to the one in question. In accordance with the general principle of this Article against surprise, however, a party intending to offer evidence of such a substitute price must give suitable notice to the other party.

This section is not intended to exclude the use of any other reasonable method of determining market price or of measuring damages if the circumstances of the case make this necessary.

Definitional Cross References:

"Action". Section 1–201.

"Aggrieved party". Section 1–201.

"Goods". Section 2–105.

"Notifies". Section 1–201.

"Party". Section 1–201.

"Reasonable time". Section 1–204.

"Usage of trade". Section 1–205.

§ 2–724. Admissibility of Market Quotations.

Whenever the prevailing price or value of any goods regularly bought and sold in any established commodity market is in issue, reports in official publications or trade journals or in newspapers or periodicals of general circulation published as the reports of such market shall be admissible in evidence. The circumstances of the preparation of such a report may be shown to affect its weight but not its admissibility.

Official Comment

. . .

Definitional Cross Reference:

"Goods". Section 2–105.

§ 2–725. Statute of Limitations in Contracts for Sale.

(1) An action for breach of any contract for sale must be commenced within four years after the cause of action has accrued. By the original agreement the parties may reduce the period of limitation to not less than one year but may not extend it.

(2) A cause of action accrues when the breach occurs, regardless of the aggrieved party's lack of knowledge of the breach. A breach of warranty occurs when tender of delivery is made, except that where a warranty explicitly extends to future performance of the goods and discovery of the breach must await the time of such performance the cause of action accrues when the breach is or should have been discovered.

(3) Where an action commenced within the time limited by subsection (1) is so terminated as to leave available a remedy by another action for the same breach such other action may be commenced after the expiration of the time limited and within six months after the termination of the first action unless the termination resulted from voluntary discontinuance or from dismissal for failure or neglect to prosecute.

(4) This section does not alter the law on tolling of the statute of limitations nor does it apply to causes of action which have accrued before this Act becomes effective.

Official Comment

. . .

Definitional Cross References:

"Action". Section 1–201.

"Aggrieved party". Section 1–201.

"Agreement". Section 1–201.

"Contract for sale". Section 2–106.

"Goods". Section 2–105.

"Party". Section 1–201.

"Remedy". Section 1–201.

"Term". Section 1–201.
"Termination". Section 2–106.

ARTICLE 3

COMMERCIAL PAPER

(Excerpts)

PART I. SHORT TITLE, FORM AND INTERPRETATION

Sec.
3–103. Definitions.
3–104. Negotiable Instrument.
3–106. Unconditional Promise or Order.
3–201. Negotiation.
3–302. Holder in Due Course.
3–303. Value and Consideration.
3–305. Defenses and Claims in Recoupment.
3–311. Accord and Satisfaction by Use of Instrument.

PART I

SHORT TITLE, FORM AND INTERPRETATION

§ 3–103. Definitions.

(a) In this Article

. . .

(4) "Good faith" means honesty in fact and the observance of reasonable commercial standards of fair dealing. . . .

§ 3–104. Negotiable Instrument.

(a) Except as otherwise provided in subsections (c) and (d), "negotiable instrument" means:

(1) an unconditional promise or order to pay a fixed amount of money, with or without interest or other charges described in the promise or order, if it:

(A) is payable to bearer or to order at the time it is issued or first comes into possession of a holder;

(B) is payable on demand or at a definite time; and

(C) does not state any other undertaking or instruction by the person promising or ordering payment to do any act in addition to the payment of money, but the promise or order may contain (i) an undertaking or power to give, maintain, or protect collateral to secure payment, (ii) an authorization or power to the holder to confess judgment or realize on or dispose of collateral, or (iii) a waiver of the benefit of any law intended for the advantage or protection of an obligor. . . .

(b) "Instrument" means a negotiable instrument.

(c) An order that meets all of the requirements of subsection (a), except paragraph (1), and otherwise falls within the definition of "check" in subsection (f) is a negotiable instrument and a check.

(d) A promise or order other than a check is not an instrument if, at the time it is issued or first comes into possession of a holder, it contains a conspicuous statement, however expressed, to the effect that the promise or order is not negotiable or is not an instrument governed by this Article. . . .

§ 3–106. Unconditional Promise or Order.

(a) Except as provided in this section, for the purposes of Section 3–104(a), a promise or order is unconditional unless it states (i) an express condition to payment, (ii) that the promise or order is subject to or governed by another writing, or (iii) that rights or obligations with respect to the promise or order are stated in another writing. A reference to another writing does not of itself make the promise or order conditional.

(b) A promise or order is not made conditional (i) by a reference to another writing for a statement of rights with respect to collateral, prepayment, or acceleration, or (ii) because payment is limited to resort to a particular fund or source.

(c) If a promise or order requires, as a condition to payment, a countersignature by a person whose specimen signature appears on the promise or order, the condition does not make the promise or order conditional for the purposes of Section 3–104(a). If the person whose specimen signature appears on an instrument fails to countersign the instrument, the failure to countersign is a defense to the obligation of the issuer, but the failure does not prevent a transferee of the instrument from becoming a holder of the instrument.

(d) If a promise or order at the time it is issued or first comes into possession of a holder contains a statement, required by applicable statutory or administrative law, to the effect that the rights of a holder or transferee are subject to claims or defenses that the issuer could assert against the original payee, the promise or order is not thereby made conditional for the purposes of Section 3–104(a); but if the promise or order is an instrument, there cannot be a holder in due course of the instrument.

§ 3–201. Negotiation.

(a) "Negotiation" means, with respect to an instrument other than an electronic mortgage note, a transfer of possession, whether voluntary or involuntary, of the instrument by a person other than the issuer to a person that thereby becomes its holder. . . .

(b) This subsection does not apply to an electronic mortgage note. Except for negotiation by a remitter, if an instrument is payable to an identified person, negotiation requires transfer of possession of the instrument and its indorsement by the holder. If an instrument is payable to bearer, it may be negotiated by transfer of possession alone.

(c) "Negotiation" means, with respect to an electronic mortgage note, a registered transfer of the electronic mortgage note to a person that, by the registered transfer, . . . becomes its holder. . . .

§ 3–302. Holder in Due Course.

(a) Subject to subsection (c) and Section 3–106(d), "holder in due course" means the holder of an instrument if:

(1) the instrument when issued or negotiated to the holder does not bear such apparent evidence of forgery or alteration or is not otherwise so irregular or incomplete as to call into question its authenticity; and

(2) the holder took the instrument (i) for value, (ii) in good faith, (iii) without notice that the instrument is overdue or has been dishonored or that there is an uncured default with respect to payment of another instrument issued as part of the same series, (iv) without notice that the instrument contains an unauthorized signature or has been altered, (v) without notice of any claim to the instrument described in Section 3–306, and (vi) without notice that any party has a defense or claim in recoupment described in Section 3–305(a).

(b) Notice of discharge of a party, other than discharge in an insolvency proceeding, is not notice of a defense under subsection (a), but discharge is effective against a person who became a holder in due course with notice of the discharge. Public filing or recording of a document does not of itself constitute notice of a defense, claim in recoupment, or claim to the instrument. . . .

(c) Except to the extent a transferor or predecessor in interest has rights as a holder in due course, a person does not acquire rights of a holder in due course of an instrument taken (i) by legal process or by purchase in an execution, bankruptcy, or creditor's sale or similar proceeding, (ii) by purchase as part of a bulk transaction not in ordinary course of business of the transferor, or (iii) as the successor in interest to an estate or other organization.

(d) If, under Section 3–303(a)(1), the promise of performance that is the consideration for an instrument has been partially performed, the holder may assert rights as a holder in due course of the instrument only to the fraction of the amount payable under the instrument equal to the value of the partial performance divided by the value of the promised performance.

(e) If (i) the person entitled to enforce an instrument has only a security interest in the instrument and (ii) the person obliged to pay the instrument has a defense, claim in recoupment, or claim to the instrument that may be asserted against the person who granted the security interest, the person entitled to enforce the instrument may assert rights as a holder in due course only to an amount payable under the instrument which, at the time of enforcement of the instrument, does not exceed the amount of the unpaid obligation secured.

(f) To be effective, notice must be received at a time and in a manner that gives a reasonable opportunity to act on it.

(g) This section is subject to any law limiting status as a holder in due course in particular classes of transactions. . . .

§ 3–303. Value and Consideration.

(a) An instrument is issued or transferred for value if:

(1) the instrument is issued or transferred for a promise of performance, to the extent the promise has been performed;

(2) the transferee acquires a security interest or other lien in the instrument other than a lien obtained by judicial proceeding;

(3) the instrument is issued or transferred as payment of, or as security for, an antecedent claim against any person, whether or not the claim is due;

(4) the instrument is issued or transferred in exchange for a negotiable instrument; or

(5) the instrument is issued or transferred in exchange for the incurring of an irrevocable obligation to a third party by the person taking the instrument.

(b) "Consideration" means any consideration sufficient to support a simple contract. The drawer or maker of an instrument has a defense if the instrument is issued without consideration. If an instrument is issued for a promise of performance, the issuer has a defense to the extent performance of the promise is due and the promise has not been performed. If an instrument is issued for value as stated in subsection (a), the instrument is also issued for consideration.

§ 3–305. Defenses and Claims in Recoupment.

(a) Except as stated in subsection (b), the right to enforce the obligation of a party to pay an instrument is subject to the following:

(1) a defense of the obligor based on (i) infancy of the obligor to the extent it is a defense to a simple contract, (ii) duress, lack of legal capacity, or illegality of the transaction which, under

other law, nullifies the obligation of the obligor, (iii) fraud that induced the obligor to sign the instrument with neither knowledge nor reasonable opportunity to learn of its character or its essential terms, or (iv) discharge of the obligor in insolvency proceedings;

(2) a defense of the obligor stated in another section of this Article or a defense of the obligor that would be available if the person entitled to enforce the instrument were enforcing a right to payment under a simple contract; and

(3) a claim in recoupment of the obligor against the original payee of the instrument if the claim arose from the transaction that gave rise to the instrument; but the claim of the obligor may be asserted against a transferee of the instrument only to reduce the amount owing on the instrument at the time the action is brought.

(b) The right of a holder in due course to enforce the obligation of a party to pay the instrument is subject to defenses of the obligor stated in subsection (a)(1), but is not subject to defenses of the obligor stated in subsection (a)(2) or claims in recoupment stated in subsection (a)(3) against a person other than the holder.

(c) Except as stated in subsection (d), in an action to enforce the obligation of a party to pay the instrument, the obligor may not assert against the person entitled to enforce the instrument a defense, claim in recoupment, or claim to the instrument (Section 3–306) of another person, but the other person's claim to the instrument may be asserted by the obligor if the other person is joined in the action and personally asserts the claim against the person entitled to enforce the instrument. An obligor is not obliged to pay the instrument if the person seeking enforcement of the instrument does not have rights of a holder in due course and the obligor proves that the instrument is a lost or stolen instrument.

(d) In an action to enforce the obligation of an accommodation party to pay an instrument, the accommodation party may assert against the person entitled to enforce the instrument any defense or claim in recoupment under subsection (a) that the accommodated party could assert against the person entitled to enforce the instrument, except the defenses of discharge in insolvency proceedings, infancy, and lack of legal capacity.

§ 3–311. Accord and Satisfaction by Use of Instrument.

(a) If a person against whom a claim is asserted proves that (i) that person in good faith tendered an instrument to the claimant as full satisfaction of the claim, (ii) the amount of the claim was unliquidated or subject to a bona fide dispute, and (iii) the claimant obtained payment of the instrument, the following subsections apply.

(b) Unless subsection (c) applies, the claim is discharged if the person against whom the claim is asserted proves that the instrument or an accompanying written communication contained a conspicuous statement to the effect that the instrument was tendered as full satisfaction of the claim.

(c) Subject to subsection (d), a claim is not discharged under subsection (b) if either of the following applies:

(1) The claimant, if an organization, proves that (i) within a reasonable time before the tender, the claimant sent a conspicuous statement to the person against whom the claim is asserted that communications concerning disputed debts, including an instrument tendered as full satisfaction of a debt, are to be sent to a designated person, office, or place, and (ii) the instrument or accompanying communication was not received by that designated person, office, or place.

(2) The claimant, whether or not an organization, proves that within 90 days after payment of the instrument, the claimant tendered repayment of the amount of the instrument to the person against whom the claim is asserted. This paragraph does not apply if the claimant is an organization that sent a statement complying with paragraph (1)(i).

(d) A claim is discharged if the person against whom the claim is asserted proves that within a reasonable time before collection of the instrument was initiated, the claimant, or an agent of the claimant having direct responsibility with respect to the disputed obligation, knew that the instrument was tendered in full satisfaction of the claim.

Official Comment

. . .

3. As part of the revision of Article 3, Section 1–207 has been amended to add subsection (2) stating that Section 1–207 "does not apply to an accord and satisfaction." Because of that amendment and revised Article 3, Section 3–311 governs full satisfaction checks. Section 3–311 follows the common law rule with some minor variations to reflect modern business conditions. . . .

4. Subsection (a) states three requirements for application of Section 3–311. "Good faith" in subsection (a)(i) is defined in Section 3–103(a)(4) as not only honesty in fact, but the observance of reasonable commercial standards of fair dealing. The meaning of "fair dealing" will depend upon the facts in the particular case. For example, suppose an insurer tenders a check in settlement of a claim for personal injury in an accident clearly covered by the insurance policy. The claimant is necessitous and the amount of the check is very small in relationship to the extent of the injury and the amount recoverable under the policy. If the trier of fact determines that the insurer was taking unfair advantage of the claimant, an accord and satisfaction would not result from payment of the check because of the absence of good faith by the insurer in making the tender. Another example of lack of good faith is found in the practice of some business debtors in routinely printing full satisfaction language on their check stocks so that all or a large part of the debts of the debtor are paid by checks bearing the full satisfaction language, whether or not there is any dispute with the creditor. Under such a practice the claimant cannot be sure whether a tender in full satisfaction is or is not being made. Use of a check on which full satisfaction language was affixed routinely pursuant to such a business practice may prevent an accord and satisfaction on the ground that the check was not tendered in good faith under subsection (a)(i).

Section 3–311 does not apply to cases in which the debt is a liquidated amount and not subject to a bona fide dispute. Subsection (a)(ii). Other law applies to cases in which a debtor is seeking discharge of such a debt by paying less than the amount owed. For the purpose of subsection (a)(iii) obtaining acceptance of a check is considered to be obtaining payment of the check. . . .

5. Subsection (c)(1) is a limitation on subsection (b) in cases in which the claimant is an organization. It is designed to protect the claimant against inadvertent accord and satisfaction. If the claimant is an organization payment of the check might be obtained without notice to the personnel of the organization concerned with the disputed claim. Some business organizations have claims against very large numbers of customers. Examples are department stores, public utilities and the like. These claims are normally paid by checks sent by customers to a designated office at which clerks employed by the claimant or a bank acting for the claimant process the checks and record the amounts paid. If the processing office is not designed to deal with communications extraneous to recording the amount of the check and the account number of the customer, payment of a full satisfaction check can easily be obtained without knowledge by the claimant of the existence of the full satisfaction statement. This is particularly true if the statement is written on the reverse side of the check in the area in which indorsements are usually written. Normally, the clerks of the claimant have no reason to look at the reverse side of checks. Indorsement by the claimant normally is done by mechanical means or there may be no indorsement at all. . . . Subsection (c)(1) allows the claimant to protect itself by advising customers by a conspicuous statement that communications regarding disputed debts must be sent to a particular person, office, or place. The statement must be given to the customer within a reasonable time before the tender is made. This requirement is designed to assure that the customer has reasonable notice that the full satisfaction check must be sent to a particular place. The reasonable time requirement could be satisfied by a notice on the billing statement sent to the customer. If the full satisfaction check is sent to the designated destination and the check is paid, the claim is discharged. If the claimant proves that the check was not received at the designated destination the claim is not discharged unless subsection (d) applies.

6. Subsection (c)(2) is also designed to prevent inadvertent accord and satisfaction. It can be used by a claimant other than an organization or by a claimant as an alternative to subsection (c)(1). Some organizations may be reluctant to use subsection (c)(1) because it may result in confusion of customers that

causes checks to be routinely sent to the special designated person, office, or place. Thus, much of the benefit of rapid processing of checks may be lost. An organization that chooses not to send a notice complying with subsection (c)(1)(i) may prevent an inadvertent accord and satisfaction by complying with subsection (c)(2). If the claimant discovers that it has obtained payment of a full satisfaction check, it may prevent an accord and satisfaction if, within 90 days of the payment of the check, the claimant tenders repayment of the amount of the check to the person against whom the claim is asserted.

    7.   Subsection (c) is subject to subsection (d). If a person against whom a claim is asserted proves that the claimant obtained payment of a check known to have been tendered in full satisfaction of the claim by "the claimant or an agent of the claimant having direct responsibility with respect to the disputed obligation," the claim is discharged even if (i) the check was not sent to the person, office, or place required by a notice complying with subsection (c)(1), or (ii) the claimant tendered repayment of the amount of the check in compliance with subsection (c)(2). . . .

ARTICLE 9

SECURED TRANSACTIONS*

(2000)

PART 1. GENERAL PROVISIONS

[SUBPART 1. SHORT TITLE, DEFINITIONS, AND GENERAL CONCEPTS]

Sec.
9–101. Short Title.
9–102. Definitions and Index of Definitions.

[SUBPART 2. APPLICABILITY OF ARTICLE]

9–109. Scope.

PART 2. EFFECTIVENESS OF SECURITY AGREEMENT; ATTACHMENT OF SECURITY INTEREST; RIGHTS OF PARTIES TO SECURITY AGREEMENT

[SUBPART 2. EFFECTIVENESS AND ATTACHMENT]

9–201. General Validity of Security Agreement.
9–203. Attachment and Enforceability of Security Interest; Proceeds; Supporting Obligations; Formal Requisites.
9–204. After-Acquired Property; Future Advances.

PART 3. PERFECTION AND PRIORITY

[SUBPART 2. PERFECTION]

9–308. When Security Interest or Agricultural Lien is Perfected; Continuity of Perfection.
9–309. Security Interest Perfected Upon Attachment.
9–310. When Filing Required to Perfect Security Interest or Agricultural Lien; Security Interests and Agricultural Liens to Which Filing Provisions Do Not Apply.
9–312. Perfection of Security Interests in Chattel Paper, Deposit Accounts, Documents, Goods Covered by Documents, Instruments, Investment Property, Letter-of-Credit Rights, and Money; Perfection by Permissive Filing; Temporary Perfection Without Filing or Transfer of Possession.
9–313. When Possession by or Delivery to Secured Party Perfects Security Interest Without Filing.

[SUBPART 3. PRIORITY]

9–317. Interests That Take Priority Over or Take Free of Security Interest or Agricultural Lien.
9–322. Priorities Among Conflicting Security Interests in and Agricultural Liens on Same Collateral.
9–323. Future Advances.
9–324. Priority of Purchase-Money Security Interests.
9–325. Priority of Security Interests in Transferred Collateral.

---

* Article 9 has been adopted by all 50 states in its 2000 version, excerpts from which are set forth here. In 2010, however, the Uniform Law Commission adopted some amendments. The states are expected to enact these amendments within a few years and the version of Article 9 set forth in this pamphlet includes those amendments. Most of the cases decided under Article 9 were decided under a pre-2000 version of the Article. For this reason, Part II of this pamphlet contains excerpts from that version.

PART 4. RIGHTS OF THIRD PARTIES

9–403. Agreement Not to Assert Defenses Against Assignee.
9–404. Rights Acquired by Assignee; Claims and Defenses Against Assignee.
9–405. Modification of Assigned Contract.
9–406. Discharge of Account Debtor; Notification of Assignment; Identification and Proof of Assignment; Restrictions on Assignment of Accounts, Chattel Paper, Payment Intangibles, and Promissory Notes Ineffective.

PART 1

GENERAL PROVISION

[SUBPART 1. SHORT TITLE, DEFINITIONS, AND GENERAL CONCEPTS]

§ 9–101. Short Title.

This article may be cited as Uniform Commercial Code—Secured Transactions.

§ 9–102. Definitions and Index of Definitions.

(a) **[Article 9 definitions.]** In this article:

(1) "Accession" means goods that are physically united with other goods in such a manner that the identity of the original goods is not lost.

(2) "Account", except as used in "account for", means a right to payment of a monetary obligation, whether or not earned by performance, (i) for property that has been or is to be sold, leased, licensed, assigned, or otherwise disposed of, (ii) for services rendered or to be rendered, (iii) for a policy of insurance issued or to be issued, (iv) for a secondary obligation incurred or to be incurred, (v) for energy provided or to be provided, (vi) for the use or hire of a vessel under a charter or other contract, (vii) arising out of the use of a credit or charge card or information contained on or for use with the card, or (viii) as winnings in a lottery or other game of chance operated or sponsored by a state, governmental unit of a state, or person licensed or authorized to operate the game by a state or governmental unit of a state. The term includes health-care-insurance receivables. The term does not include (i) rights to payment evidenced by chattel paper . . . or an instrument, (ii) commercial tort claims, (iii) deposit accounts, (iv) investment property, (v) letter-of-credit rights or letters of credit, or (vi) rights to payment for money or funds advanced or sold, other than rights arising out of the use of a credit or charge card or information contained on or for use with the card.

(3) "Account debtor" means a person obligated on an account, chattel paper, or general intangible. The term does not include persons obligated to pay a negotiable instrument, even if the instrument constitutes part of chattel paper. . . .

(7) "Authenticate" means:

(A) to sign; or

(B) with present intent to adopt or accept a record, to attach to or logically associate with the record an electronic sound, symbol, or process. . . .

(11) "Chattel paper" means a record or records that evidence both a monetary obligation and a security interest in specific goods, a security interest in specific goods and software used in the goods, a lease of specific goods, or a lease of specific goods and license of software used in the

goods. In this paragraph, "monetary obligation" means a monetary obligation secured by the goods or owed under a lease of the goods and includes a monetary obligation with respect to software used in the goods. The term chattel paper does not include (i) charters or other contracts involving the use or hire of a vessel, [or] (ii) records that evidence a right to payment arising out of the use of a credit or charge card or information contained on or for use with the card.... If a transaction is evidenced by records that include an instrument or series of instruments, the group of records taken together constitutes chattel paper.

(12) "Collateral" means the property subject to a security interest or agricultural lien. The term includes:

(A) proceeds to which a security interest attaches;

(B) accounts, chattel paper, payment intangibles, and promissory notes that have been sold; and

(C) goods that are the subject of a consignment.

(13) "Commercial tort claim" means a claim arising in tort with respect to which:

(A) the claimant is an organization; or

(B) the claimant is an individual and the claim:

(i) arose in the course of the claimant's business or profession; and

(ii) does not include damages arising out of personal injury to or the death of an individual.

(14) "Commodity account" means an account maintained by a commodity intermediary in which a commodity contract is carried for a commodity customer....

(15) "Commodity contract" means a commodity futures contract, an option on a commodity futures contract, a commodity option, or another contract if the contract or option is:

(A) traded on or subject to the rules of a board of trade that has been designated as a contract market for such a contract pursuant to federal commodities laws; or

(B) traded on a foreign commodity board of trade, exchange, or market, and is carried on the books of a commodity intermediary for a commodity customer....

(22) "Consumer debtor" means a debtor in a consumer transaction.

(23) "Consumer goods" means goods that are used or bought for use primarily for personal, family, or household purposes.

(24) "Consumer-goods transaction" means a consumer transaction in which:

(A) an individual incurs an obligation primarily for personal, family, or household purposes; and

(B) a security interest in consumer goods secures the obligation.

(25) "Consumer obligor" means an obligor who is an individual and who incurred the obligation as part of a transaction entered into primarily for personal, family, or household purposes.

(26) "Consumer transaction" means a transaction in which (i) an individual incurs an obligation primarily for personal, family, or household purposes, (ii) a security interest secures the obligation, and (iii) the collateral is held or acquired primarily for personal, family, or household purposes. The term includes consumer-goods transactions....

(29) "Deposit account" means a demand, time, savings, passbook, or similar account maintained with a bank. The term does not include investment property or accounts evidenced by an instrument.

(30) "Document" means a document of title or a receipt of the type described in § 7–201(2).

(31) "Electronic chattel paper" means chattel paper evidenced by a record or records consisting of information stored in an electronic medium.

(32) "Encumbrance" means a right, other than an ownership interest, in real property. The term includes mortgages and other liens on real property. . . .

(37) "Filing office" means an office designated in § 9–501 as the place to file a financing statement. . . .

(39) "Financing statement" means a record or records composed of an initial financing statement and any filed record relating to the initial financing statement. . . .

(42) "General intangible" means any personal property, including things in action, other than accounts, chattel paper, commercial tort claims, deposit accounts, documents, goods, instruments, investment property, letter-of-credit rights, letters of credit, money, and oil, gas, or other minerals before extraction. The term includes payment intangibles and software.

(43) [Reserved.]

(44) "Goods" means all things that are movable when a security interest attaches. The term includes (i) fixtures, (ii) standing timber that is to be cut and removed under a conveyance or contract for sale, (iii) the unborn young of animals, (iv) crops grown, growing, or to be grown, even if the crops are produced on trees, vines, or bushes, and (v) manufactured homes. The term also includes a computer program embedded in goods and any supporting information provided in connection with a transaction relating to the program if (i) the program is associated with the goods in such a manner that it customarily is considered part of the goods, or (ii) by becoming the owner of the goods, a person acquires a right to use the program in connection with the goods. The term does not include a computer program embedded in goods that consist solely of the medium in which the program is embedded. The term also does not include accounts, chattel paper, commercial tort claims, deposit accounts, documents, general intangibles, instruments, investment property, letter-of-credit rights, letters of credit, money, or oil, gas, or other minerals before extraction. . . .

(46) "Health-care-insurance receivable" means an interest in or claim under a policy of insurance, which is a right to payment of a monetary obligation for health-care goods or services provided.

(47) "Instrument" means a negotiable instrument, other than an electronic mortgage note, or any other writing that evidences a right to the payment of a monetary obligation, is not itself a security agreement or lease, and is of a type that in ordinary course of business is transferred by delivery with any necessary endorsement or assignment. The term does not include (i) investment property, (ii) letters of credit, or (iii) writings that evidence a right to payment arising out of the use of a credit or charge card or information contained on or for use with the card.

(48) "Inventory" means goods, other than farm products, which:

(A) are leased by a person as lessor;

(B) are held by a person for sale or lease or to be furnished under a contract of service;

(C) are furnished by a person under a contract of service; or

(D) consist of raw materials, work in process, or materials used or consumed in a business.

(49) "Investment property" means a security, whether certificated or uncertificated, security entitlement, securities account, commodity contract, or commodity account. . . .

(51) "Letter-of-credit right" means a right to payment or performance under a letter of credit, whether or not the beneficiary has demanded or is at the time entitled to demand payment

or performance. The term does not include the right of a beneficiary to demand payment or performance under a letter of credit.

(52) "Lien creditor" means:

(A) a creditor that has acquired a lien on the property involved by attachment, levy, or the like;

(B) an assignee for benefit of creditors from the time of assignment;

(C) a trustee in bankruptcy from the date of the filing of the petition; or

(D) a receiver in equity from the time of appointment. . . .

(56) "New debtor" means a person that becomes bound as debtor under § 9–203(d) by a security agreement previously entered into by another person.

(57) "New value" means (i) money, (ii) money's worth in property, services, or new credit, or (iii) release by a transferee of an interest in property previously transferred to the transferee. The term does not include an obligation substituted for another obligation. . . .

(59) "Obligor" means a person that, with respect to an obligation secured by a security interest in or an agricultural lien on the collateral, (i) owes payment or other performance of the obligation, (ii) has provided property other than the collateral to secure payment or other performance of the obligation, or (iii) is otherwise accountable in whole or in part for payment or other performance of the obligation. The term does not include issuers or nominated persons under a letter of credit.

(60) "Original debtor" means a person that, as debtor, entered into a security agreement to which a new debtor has become bound under § 9–203(d).

(61) "Payment intangible" means a general intangible under which the account debtor's principal obligation is a monetary obligation. . . .

(62) "Person related to", with respect to an individual, means:

(A) the spouse of the individual;

(B) a brother, brother-in-law, sister, or sister-in-law of the individual;

(C) an ancestor or lineal descendant of the individual or the individual's spouse; or

(D) any other relative, by blood or marriage, of the individual or the individual's spouse who shares the same home with the individual. . . .

(63) "Person related to", with respect to an organization, means:

(A) a person directly or indirectly controlling, controlled by, or under common control with the organization;

(B) an officer or director of, or a person performing similar functions with respect to, the organization;

(C) an officer or director of, or a person performing similar functions with respect to, a person described in subparagraph (A);

(D) the spouse of an individual described in subparagraph (A), (B), or (C); or

(E) an individual who is related by blood or marriage to an individual described in subparagraph (A), (B), (C), or (D) and shares the same home with the individual. . . .

(65) "Promissory note" means an instrument that evidences a promise to pay a monetary obligation, does not evidence an order to pay, and does not contain an acknowledgment by a bank that the bank has received for deposit a sum of money or funds. . . .

(70) "Record", except as used in "for record", "of record", "record or legal title", and "record owner", means information that is inscribed on a tangible medium or which is stored in an electronic or other medium and is retrievable in perceivable form. . . .

(73) "Secured party" means:

(A) a person in whose favor a security interest is created or provided for under a security agreement, whether or not any obligation to be secured is outstanding;

(B) a person that holds an agricultural lien;

(C) a consignor;

(D) a person to which accounts, chattel paper, payment intangibles, or promissory notes have been sold;

(E) a trustee, indenture trustee, agent, collateral agent, or other representative in whose favor a security interest or agricultural lien is created or provided for; or

(F) a person that holds a security interest arising under § 2–401, 2–505, 2–711(3), 2A–508(5), 4–210, or 5–118.

(74) "Security agreement" means an agreement that creates or provides for a security interest.

(75) "Send", in connection with a record or notification, means:

(A) to deposit in the mail, deliver for transmission, or transmit by any other usual means of communication, with postage or cost of transmission provided for, addressed to any address reasonable under the circumstances; or

(B) to cause the record or notification to be received within the time that it would have been received if properly sent under subparagraph (A). . . .

(c) **[Article 1 definitions and principles.]** Article 1 contains general definitions and principles of construction and interpretation applicable throughout this article.

[SUBPART 2. APPLICABILITY OF ARTICLE]

§ 9–109. Scope.

(a) **[General scope of article.]** Except as otherwise provided in subsection (c) and (d), this article applies to:

(1) a transaction, regardless of its form, that creates a security interest in personal property or fixtures by contract;

(2) an agricultural lien;

(3) a sale of accounts, chattel paper, payment intangibles, or promissory notes. . . .

(5) a security interest arising under § 2–401, 2–505, 2–711(3), or 2A–508(5), as provided in § 9–110; and

(6) a security interest arising under § 4–210 or 5–118. . . .

(d) **[Inapplicability of article.]** This article does not apply to:

(1) a landlord's lien, other than an agriculture lien;

(2) a lien, other than an agriculture lien, given by statute or other rule of law for services or materials, but Section 9–333 applies with respect to priority of the lien;

(3) an assignment of a claim for wages, salary, or other compensation of an employee;

(4) a sale of accounts, chattel paper, payment intangibles, or promissory notes as part of a sale of the business out of which they arose;

(5) an assignment of accounts, chattel paper, payment intangibles, or promissory notes which is for the purpose of collection only;

(6) an assignment of a right to payment under a contract to an assignee that is also obligated to perform under the contract;

(7) an assignment of a single account, payment intangible, or promissory note to an assignee in full or partial satisfaction of a preexisting indebtedness; . . .

(9) an assignment of a right represented by a judgment, other than a judgment taken on a right to payment that was collateral; . . .

(12) an assignment of a claim arising in tort, other than a commercial tort claim, but Sections 9–315 and 9–322 apply with respect to proceeds and priorities in proceeds. . . .

PART 2

EFFECTIVENESS OF SECURITY AGREEMENT; ATTACHMENT OF SECURITY INTEREST; RIGHTS OF PARTIES TO SECURITY AGREEMENT

[SUBPART 2. EFFECTIVENESS AND ATTACHMENT]

§ 9–201. General Validity of Security Agreement.

(a) **[General effectiveness.]** Except as otherwise provided in [the Uniform Commercial Code], a security agreement is effective according to its terms between the parties, against purchasers of the collateral, and against creditors. . . .

§ 9–203. Attachment and Enforceability of Security Interest; Proceeds; Supporting Obligations; Formal Requisites.

(a) **[Attachment.]** A security interest attaches to collateral when it becomes enforceable against the debtor with respect to the collateral, unless an agreement expressly postpones the time of attachment.

(b) **[Enforceability.]** Except as otherwise provided in subsections (c) through (j), a security interest is enforceable against the debtor and third parties with respect to the collateral only if:

(1) value has been given;

(2) the debtor has rights in the collateral or the power to transfer rights in the collateral to a secured party; and

(3) one of the following conditions is met:

(A) the debtor has authenticated a security agreement that provides a description of the collateral and, if the security interest covers timber to be cut, a description of the land concerned;

(B) the collateral is not a certificated security and is in the possession of the secured party under § 9–313 pursuant to the debtor's security agreement;

(C) the collateral is a certificated security in registered form and the security certificate has been delivered to the secured party under § 8–301 pursuant to the debtor's security agreement; or

(D) the collateral is deposit accounts, electronic chattel paper, investment property, or letter-of-credit rights, . . . and the secured party has control under § 9–104, 9–105, 9–106, or 9–107 pursuant to the debtor's security agreement. . . .

(e) **[Effect of new debtor becoming bound.]** If a new debtor becomes bound as debtor by a security agreement entered into by another person:

(1) the agreement satisfies subsection (b)(3) with respect to existing or after-acquired property of the new debtor to the extent the property is described in the agreement; and

(2) another agreement is not necessary to make a security interest in the property enforceable.

(f) **[Proceeds and supporting obligations.]** The attachment of a security interest in collateral gives the secured party the rights to proceeds provided by § 9–315 and is also attachment of a security interest in a supporting obligation for the collateral.

(g) **[Lien securing right to payment.]** The attachment of a security interest in a right to payment or performance secured by a security interest or other lien on personal or real property is also attachment of a security interest in the security interest, mortgage, or other lien. . . .

§ 9–204. After-Acquired Property; Future Advances.

(a) **[After-acquired collateral.]** Except as otherwise provided in subsection (b), a security agreement may create or provide for a security interest in after-acquired collateral.

(b) **[When after-acquired property clause not effective.]** A security interest does not attach under a term constituting an after-acquired property clause to:

(1) consumer goods, other than an accession when given as additional security, unless the debtor acquires rights in them within 10 days after the secured party gives value; or

(2) a commercial tort claim.

(c) **[Future advances and other value.]** A security agreement may provide that collateral secures, or that accounts, chattel paper, payment intangibles, or promissory notes are sold in connection with, future advances or other value, whether or not the advances or value are given pursuant to commitment.

PART 3

PERFECTION AND PRIORITY

[SUBPART 2. PERFECTION]

§ 9–308. When Security Interest or Agricultural Lien is Perfected; Continuity of Perfection.

(a) **[Perfection of security interest.]** Except as otherwise provided in this section and § 9–309, a security interest is perfected if it has attached and all of the applicable requirements for perfection in § 9–310 through 9–316 have been satisfied. A security interest is perfected when it attaches if the applicable requirements are satisfied before the security interest attaches.

(b) **[Perfection of agricultural lien.]** An agricultural lien is perfected if it has become effective and all of the applicable requirements for perfection in § 9–310 have been satisfied. An agricultural lien is perfected when it becomes effective if the applicable requirements are satisfied before the agricultural lien becomes effective.

(c) **[Continuous perfection; perfection by different methods.]** A security interest or agricultural lien is perfected continuously if it is originally perfected by one method under this article and is later perfected by another method under this article, without an intermediate period when it was unperfected.

(d) **[Supporting obligation.]** Perfection of a security interest in collateral also perfects a security interest in a supporting obligation for the collateral.

(e) **[Lien securing right to payment.]** Perfection of a security interest in a right to payment or performance also perfects a security interest in a security interest, mortgage, or other lien on personal or real property securing the right.

(f) **[Security entitlement carried in securities account.]** Perfection of a security interest in a securities account also perfects a security interest in the security entitlements carried in the securities account.

(g) **[Commodity contract carried in commodity account.]** Perfection of a security interest in a commodity account also perfects a security interest in the commodity contracts carried in the commodity account. . . .

§ 9–309. Security Interest Perfected Upon Attachment.

The following security interests are perfected when they attach:

(1) a purchase-money security interest in consumer goods, except as otherwise provided in § 9–311(b) with respect to consumer goods that are subject to a statute or treaty described in § 9–311(a);

(2) an assignment of accounts or payment intangibles which does not by itself or in conjunction with other assignments to the same assignee transfer a significant part of the assignor's outstanding accounts or payment intangibles;

(3) a sale of a payment intangible;

(4) a sale of a promissory note. . . .

(12) an assignment for the benefit of all creditors of the transferor and subsequent transfers by the assignee thereunder; and

(13) a security interest created by an assignment of a beneficial interest in a decedent's estate.

§ 9–310. When Filing Required to Perfect Security Interest or Agricultural Lien; Security Interests and Agricultural Liens to Which Filing Provisions Do Not Apply.

(a) **[General rule: perfection by filing.]** Except as otherwise provided in subsection (b) and § 9–312(b), a financing statement must be filed to perfect all security interests and agricultural liens.

(b) **[Exceptions: filing not necessary.]** The filing of a financing statement is not necessary to perfect a security interest:

(1) that is perfected under § 9–308(d), (e), (f), or (g);

(2) that is perfected under § 9–309 when it attaches;

(3) in property subject to a statute, regulation, or treaty described in § 9–311(a);

(4) in goods in possession of a bailee which is perfected under § 9–312(d)(1) or (2);

(5) in certificated securities, documents, goods, or instruments which is perfected without filing or possession under § 9–312(e), (f), (g), or (h);

(6) in collateral in the secured party's possession under § 9–313;

(7) in a certificated security which is perfected by delivery of the security certificate to the secured party under § 9–313;

(8) in deposit accounts, electronic chattel paper, investment property, or letter-of-credit rights which is perfected by control under § 9–314;

(9) in proceeds which is perfected under § 9–315; or

(10) that is perfected under § 9–316.

(c) **[Assignment of perfected security interest.]** If a secured party assigns a perfected security interest or agricultural lien, a filing under this article is not required to continue the perfected status of the security interest against creditors of and transferees from the original debtor.

§ 9–312. Perfection of Security Interests in Chattel Paper, Deposit Accounts, Documents, Goods Covered by Documents, Instruments, Investment Property, Letter-of-Credit Rights, and Money; Perfection by Permissive Filing; Temporary Perfection Without Filing or Transfer of Possession.

(a) **[Perfection by filing permitted.]** A security interest in chattel paper, negotiable documents, instruments, or investment property may be perfected by filing.

(b) **[Control or possession of certain collateral.]** Except as otherwise provided in § 9–315(c) and (d) for proceeds:

(1) a security interest in a deposit account may be perfected only by control under § 9–314;

(2) and except as otherwise provided in § 9–308(d), a security interest in a letter-of-credit right may be perfected only by control under § 9–314; and

(3) a security interest in money may be perfected only by the secured party's taking possession under § 9–313.

(c) **[Goods covered by negotiable document.]** While goods are in the possession of a bailee that has issued a negotiable document covering the goods:

(1) a security interest in the goods may be perfected by perfecting a security interest in the document; and

(2) a security interest perfected in the document has priority over any security interest that becomes perfected in the goods by another method during that time.

(d) **[Goods covered by nonnegotiable document.]** While goods are in the possession of a bailee that has issued a nonnegotiable document covering the goods, a security interest in the goods may be perfected by:

(1) issuance of a document in the name of the secured party;

(2) the bailee's receipt of notification of the secured party's interest; or

(3) filing as to the goods. . . .

§ 9–313. When Possession by or Delivery to Secured Party Perfects Security Interest Without Filing.

(a) **[Perfection by possession or delivery.]** Except as otherwise provided in subsection (b), a secured party may perfect a security interest in negotiable documents, goods, instruments . . ., money, or tangible chattel paper by taking possession of the collateral. A secured party may perfect a security interest in certificated securities by taking delivery of the certificated securities under § 8–301.

(b) **[Goods covered by certificate of title.]** With respect to goods covered by a certificate of title issued by this State, a secured party may perfect a security interest in the goods by taking possession of the goods only in the circumstances described in § 9–316(d).

(c) **[Collateral in possession of person other than debtor.]** With respect to collateral other than certificated securities and goods covered by a document, a secured party takes possession of collateral in the possession of a person other than the debtor, the secured party, or a lessee of the collateral from the debtor in the ordinary course of the debtor's business, when:

(1) the person in possession authenticates a record acknowledging that it holds possession of the collateral for the secured party's benefit; or

(2) the person takes possession of the collateral after having authenticated a record acknowledging that it will hold possession of collateral for the secured party's benefit.

(d) **[Time of perfection by possession; continuation of perfection.]** If perfection of a security interest depends upon possession of the collateral by a secured party, perfection occurs no earlier than the time the secured party takes possession and continues only while the secured party retains possession. . . .

(e) **[Time of perfection by delivery; continuation of perfection.]** A security interest in a certificated security in registered form is perfected by delivery when delivery of the certificated security occurs under § 8–301 and remains perfected by delivery until the debtor obtains possession of the security certificate. . . .

[SUBPART 3. PRIORITY]

§ 9–317. Interests That Take Priority Over or Take Free of Security Interest or Agricultural Lien.

(a) **[Conflicting security interests and rights of lien creditors.]** A security interest or agricultural lien is subordinate to the rights of:

(1) a person entitled to priority under § 9–322; and

(2) except as otherwise provided in subsection (e), a person that becomes a lien creditor before the earlier of the time the security interest or agricultural lien is perfected or a financing statement covering the collateral is filed.

(b) **[Buyers that receive delivery.]** Except as otherwise provided in subsection (e), a buyer, other than a secured party, of tangible chattel paper, documents, goods, instruments, or a certificated security takes free of a security interest or agricultural lien if the buyer gives value and receives delivery of the collateral without knowledge of the security interest or agricultural lien and before it is perfected.

(c) **[Lessees that receive delivery.]** Except as otherwise provided in subsection (e), a lessee of goods takes free of a security interest or agricultural lien if the lessee gives value and receives delivery of the collateral without knowledge of the security interest or agricultural lien and before it is perfected.

(d) **[Licensees and buyers of certain collateral.]** A licensee of a general intangible or a buyer, other than a secured party, of collateral other than tangible chattel paper, tangible documents, goods, instruments, or a certificated security takes free of a security interest if the licensee or buyer gives value without knowledge of the security interest and before it is perfected.

(e) **[Purchase-money security interest.]** Except as otherwise provided in sections 9–320 and 9–321, if a person files a financing statement with respect to a purchase-money security interest before or within 20 days after the debtor receives delivery of the collateral, the security interest takes priority over the rights of a buyer, lessee, or lien creditor which arise between the time the security interest attaches and the time of filing.

§ 9–322. Priorities Among Conflicting Security Interests in and Agricultural Liens on Same Collateral.

(a) **[General priority rules.]** Except as otherwise provided in this section, priority among conflicting security interests and agricultural liens in the same collateral is determined according to the following rules:

(1) Conflicting perfected security interests and agricultural liens rank according to priority in time of filing or perfection. Priority dates from the earlier of the time a filing covering the collateral is first made or the security interest or agricultural lien is first perfected, if there is no period thereafter when there is neither filing nor perfection.

(2) A perfected security interest or agricultural lien has priority over a conflicting unperfected security interest or agricultural lien.

(3) The first security interest or agricultural lien to attach or become effective has priority if conflicting security interests and agricultural liens are unperfected.

(b) **[Time of perfection: proceeds [and] supporting obligations. . . .]** For the purposes of subsection (a)(1):

(1) the time of filing or perfection as to a security interest in collateral is also the time of filing or perfection as to a security interest in proceeds; . . .

(2) the time of filing or perfection as to a security interest in collateral supported by a supporting obligation is also the time of filing or perfection as to a security interest in the supporting obligation. . . .

(c) **[Special priority rules: proceeds and supporting obligations.]** Except as otherwise provided in subsection (f), a security interest in collateral which qualifies for priority over a conflicting security interest under § 9–327, 9–328, 9–329, 9–330, or 9–331 also has priority over a conflicting security interest in:

(1) any supporting obligation for the collateral; and

(2) proceeds of the collateral if:

(A) the security interest in proceeds is perfected;

(B) the proceeds are cash proceeds or of the same type as the collateral; and

(C) in the case of proceeds that are proceeds of proceeds, all intervening proceeds are cash proceeds, proceeds of the same type as the collateral, or an account relating to the collateral. . . .

(d) **[First-to-file priority rule for certain collateral.]** Subject to subsection (e) and except as otherwise provided in subsection (f), if a security interest in chattel paper, deposit accounts, negotiable documents, instruments, investment property, or letter-of-credit rights is perfected by a method other than filing, conflicting perfected security interests in proceeds of the collateral rank according to priority in time of filing.

(e) **[Applicability of subsection (d).]** Subsection (d) applies only if the proceeds of the collateral are not cash proceeds, chattel paper, negotiable documents, instruments, investment property, or letter-of-credit rights.

§ 9–323. Future Advances.

(a) **[When priority based on time of advance.]** Except as otherwise provided in subsection (c), for purposes of determining the priority of a perfected security interest under § 9–322(a)(1), perfection of the security interest dates from the time an advance is made to the extent that the security interest secures an advance that:

    (1) is made while the security interest is perfected only:

        (A) under § 9–309 when it attaches; or

        (B) temporarily under § 9–312(e), (f), or (g); and

    (2) is not made pursuant to a commitment entered into before or while the security interest is perfected by a method other than under § 9–309 or 9–312(e), (f), or (g).

(b) **[Lien creditor.]** Except as otherwise provided in subsection (c), a security interest is subordinate to the rights of a person that becomes a lien creditor to the extent that the security interest secures an advance made more than 45 days after the person becomes a lien creditor unless the advance is made:

    (1) without knowledge of the lien; or

    (2) pursuant to a commitment entered into without knowledge of the lien.

(c) **[Buyer of receivables.]** Subsections (a) and (b) do not apply to a security interest held by a secured party that is a buyer of accounts, chattel paper, payment intangibles, or promissory notes or a consignor.

(d) **[Buyer of goods.]** Except as otherwise provided in subsection (e), a buyer of goods other than a buyer in ordinary course of business takes free of a security interest to the extent that it secures advances made after the earlier of:

    (1) the time the secured party acquires knowledge of the buyer's purchase; or

    (2) 45 days after the purchase.

(e) **[Advances made pursuant to commitment: priority of buyer of goods.]** Subsection (d) does not apply if the advance is made pursuant to a commitment entered into without knowledge of the buyer's purchase and before the expiration of the 45-day period.

(f) **[Lessee of goods.]** Except as otherwise provided in subsection (g), a lessee of goods, other than a lessee in ordinary course of business, takes the leasehold interest free of a security interest to the extent that it secures advances made after the earlier of:

    (1) the time the secured party acquires knowledge of the lease; or

    (2) 45 days after the lease contract becomes enforceable.

(g) **[Advances made pursuant to commitment: priority of lessee of goods.]** Subsection (f) does not apply if the advance is made pursuant to a commitment entered into without knowledge of the lease and before the expiration of the 45-day period.

§ 9–324. Priority of Purchase-Money Security Interests.

(a) **[General rule: purchase-money priority.]** Except as otherwise provided in subsection (g), a perfected purchase-money security interest in goods other than inventory or livestock has priority over a conflicting security interest in the same goods, and, except as otherwise provided in § 9–327, a perfected security interest in its identifiable proceeds also has priority, if the purchase-money security interest is perfected when the debtor receives possession of the collateral or within 20 days thereafter.

(b) **[Inventory purchase-money priority.]** Subject to subsection (c) and except as otherwise provided in subsection (g), a perfected purchase-money security interest in inventory has priority over a conflicting security interest in the same inventory, has priority over a conflicting security interest in chattel paper or an instrument constituting proceeds of the inventory and in proceeds of the chattel paper, if so provided in § 9–330, and, except as otherwise provided in § 9–327, also has priority in identifiable cash proceeds of the inventory to the extent the identifiable cash proceeds are received on or before the delivery of the inventory to a buyer, if:

(1) the purchase-money security interest is perfected when the debtor receives possession of the inventory;

(2) the purchase-money secured party sends an authenticated notification to the holder of the conflicting security interest;

(3) the holder of the conflicting security interest receives the notification within five years before the debtor receives possession of the inventory; and

(4) the notification states that the person sending the notification has or expects to acquire a purchase-money security interest in inventory of the debtor and describes the inventory.

(c) **[Holders of conflicting inventory security interests to be notified.]** Subsections (b)(2) through (4) apply only if the holder of the conflicting security interest had filed a financing statement covering the same types of inventory:

(1) if the purchase-money security interest is perfected by filing, before the date of the filing; or

(2) if the purchase-money security interest is temporarily perfected without filing or possession under § 9–312(f), before the beginning of the 20-day period thereunder.

(d) **[Livestock purchase-money priority.]** Subject to subsection (e) and except as otherwise provided in subsection (g), a perfected purchase-money security interest in livestock that are farm products has priority over a conflicting security interest in the same livestock, and, except as otherwise provided in § 9–327, a perfected security interest in their identifiable proceeds and identifiable products in their unmanufactured states also has priority, if:

(1) the purchase-money security interest is perfected when the debtor receives possession of the livestock;

(2) the purchase-money secured party sends an authenticated notification to the holder of the conflicting security interest;

(3) the holder of the conflicting security interest receives the notification within six months before the debtor receives possession of the livestock; and

(4) the notification states that the person sending the notification has or expects to acquire a purchase-money security interest in livestock of the debtor and describes the livestock.

(e) **[Holders of conflicting livestock security interests to be notified.]** Subsections (d)(2) through (4) apply only if the holder of the conflicting security interest had filed a financing statement covering the same types of livestock:

(1) if the purchase-money security interest is perfected by filing, before the date of the filing; or

(2) if the purchase-money security interest is temporarily perfected without filing or possession under § 9–312(f), before the beginning of the 20-day period thereunder.

(f) **[Software purchase-money priority.]** Except as otherwise provided in subsection (g), a perfected purchase-money security interest in software has priority over a conflicting security interest in the same collateral, and, except as otherwise provided in § 9–327, a perfected security interest in its identifiable proceeds also has priority, to the extent that the purchase-money security interest in the goods in which the software was acquired for use has priority in the goods and proceeds of the goods under this section.

(g) **[Conflicting purchase-money security interests.]** If more than one security interest qualifies for priority in the same collateral under subsection (a), (b), (d), or (f):

(1) a security interest securing an obligation incurred as all or part of the price of the collateral has priority over a security interest securing an obligation incurred for value given to enable the debtor to acquire rights in or the use of collateral; and

(2) in all other cases, § 9–322(a) applies to the qualifying security interests.

§ 9–325. Priority of Security Interests in Transferred Collateral.

(a) **[Subordination of security interest in transferred collateral.]** Except as otherwise provided in subsection (b), a security interest created by a debtor is subordinate to a security interest in the same collateral created by another person if:

(1) the debtor acquired the collateral subject to the security interest created by the other person;

(2) the security interest created by the other person was perfected when the debtor acquired the collateral; and

(3) there is no period thereafter when the security interest is unperfected.

(b) **[Limitation of subsection (a) subordination.]** Subsection (a) subordinates a security interest only if the security interest:

(1) otherwise would have priority solely under § 9–322(a) or 9–324; or

(2) arose solely under § 2–711(3) or 2A–508(5).

PART 4

RIGHTS OF THIRD PARTIES

§ 9–403. Agreement Not to Assert Defenses Against Assignee.

(a) **["Value."]** In this section, "value" has the meaning provided in § 3–303(a).

(b) **[Agreement not to assert claim or defense.]** Except as otherwise provided in this section, an agreement between an account debtor and an assignor not to assert against an assignee any claim or defense that the account debtor may have against the assignor is enforceable by an assignee that takes an assignment:

(1) for value;

(2) in good faith;

(3) without notice of a claim of a property or possessory right to the property assigned; and

(4) without notice of a defense or claim in recoupment of the type that may be asserted against a person entitled to enforce a negotiable instrument under § 3–305(a).

(c) **[When subsection (b) not applicable.]** Subsection (b) does not apply to defenses of a type that may be asserted against a holder in due course of a negotiable instrument under § 3–305(b).

(d) **[Omission of required statement in consumer transaction.]** In a consumer transaction, if a record evidences the account debtor's obligation, law other than this article requires that the record include a statement to the effect that the rights of an assignee are subject to claims or defenses that the account debtor could assert against the original obligee, and the record does not include such a statement:

(1) the record has the same effect as if the record included such a statement; and

(2) the account debtor may assert against an assignee those claims and defenses that would have been available if the record included such a statement.

(e) **[Rule for individual under other law.]** This section is subject to law other than this article which establishes a different rule for an account debtor who is an individual and who incurred the obligation primarily for personal, family, or household purposes.

(f) **[Other law not displaced.]** Except as otherwise provided in subsection (d), this section does not displace law other than this article which gives effect to an agreement by an account debtor not to assert a claim or defense against an assignee.

§ 9–404. Rights Acquired by Assignee; Claims and Defenses Against Assignee.

(a) **[Assignee's rights subject to terms, claims, and defenses; exceptions.]** Unless an account debtor has made an enforceable agreement not to assert defenses or claims, and subject to subsections (b) through (e), the rights of an assignee are subject to:

(1) all terms of the agreement between the account debtor and assignor and any defense or claim in recoupment arising from the transaction that gave rise to the contract; and

(2) any other defense or claim of the account debtor against the assignor which accrues before the account debtor receives a notification of the assignment authenticated by the assignor or the assignee.

(b) **[Account debtor's claim reduces amount owed to assignee.]** Subject to subsection (c) and except as otherwise provided in subsection (d), the claim of an account debtor against an assignor may be asserted against an assignee under subsection (a) only to reduce the amount the account debtor owes.

(c) **[Rule for individual under other law.]** This section is subject to law other than this article which establishes a different rule for an account debtor who is an individual and who incurred the obligation primarily for personal, family, or household purposes.

(d) **[Omission of required statement in consumer transaction.]** In a consumer transaction, if a record evidences the account debtor's obligation, law other than this article requires that the record include a statement to the effect that the account debtor's recovery against an assignee with respect to claims and defenses against the assignor may not exceed amounts paid by the account debtor under the record, and the record does not include such a statement, the extent to which a claim of an account debtor against the assignor may be asserted against an assignee is determined as if the record included such a statement.

(e) **[Inapplicability to health-care-insurance receivable.]** This section does not apply to an assignment of a health-care-insurance receivable.

§ 9–405. Modification of Assigned Contract.

(a) **[Effect of modification on assignee.]** A modification of or substitution for an assigned contract is effective against an assignee if made in good faith. The assignee acquires corresponding rights under the modified or substituted contract. The assignment may provide that the modification or substitution is a breach of contract by the assignor. This subsection is subject to subsections (b) through (d).

(b) **[Applicability of subsection (a).]** Subsection (a) applies to the extent that:

(1) the right to payment or a part thereof under an assigned contract has not been fully earned by performance; or

(2) the right to payment or a part thereof has been fully earned by performance and the account debtor has not received notification of the assignment under § 9–406(a).

(c) **[Rule for individual under other law.]** This section is subject to law other than this article which establishes a different rule for an account debtor who is an individual and who incurred the obligation primarily for personal, family, or household purposes.

(d) **[Inapplicability to health-care-insurance receivable.]** This section does not apply to an assignment of a health-care-insurance receivable.

§ 9–406. Discharge of Account Debtor; Notification of Assignment; Identification and Proof of Assignment; Restrictions on Assignment of Accounts, Chattel Paper, Payment Intangibles, and Promissory Notes Ineffective.

(a) **[Discharge of account debtor; effect of notification.]** Subject to subsections (b) through (i), an account debtor on an account, chattel paper, or a payment intangible may discharge its obligation by paying the assignor until, but not after, the account debtor receives a notification, authenticated by the assignor or the assignee, that the amount due or to become due has been assigned and that payment is to be made to the assignee. After receipt of the notification, the account debtor may discharge its obligation by paying the assignee and may not discharge the obligation by paying the assignor.

(b) **[When notification ineffective.]** Subject to subsection (h), notification is ineffective under subsection (a):

(1) if it does not reasonably identify the rights assigned;

(2) to the extent that an agreement between an account debtor and a seller of a payment intangible limits the account debtor's duty to pay a person other than the seller and the limitation is effective under law other than this article; or

(3) at the option of an account debtor, if the notification notifies the account debtor to make less than the full amount of any installment or other periodic payment to the assignee, even if:

(A) only a portion of the account, chattel paper, or general intangible has been assigned to that assignee;

(B) a portion has been assigned to another assignee; or

(C) the account debtor knows that the assignment to that assignee is limited.

(c) **[Proof of assignment.]** Subject to subsection (h), if requested by the account debtor, an assignee shall seasonably furnish reasonable proof that the assignment has been made. Unless the assignee complies, the account debtor may discharge its obligation by paying the assignor, even if the account debtor has received a notification under subsection (a).

(d) **[Term restricting assignment generally ineffective.]** Except as otherwise provided in subsection (e) and sections 2A–303 and 9–407, and subject to subsection (h), a term in an agreement between an account debtor and an assignor or in . . . a promissory note is ineffective to the extent that it:

(1) prohibits, restricts, or requires the consent of the account debtor or person obligated on . . . the promissory note to the assignment or transfer of, or the creation, attachment, perfection, or enforcement of a security interest in, the account, chattel paper, payment intangible, or promissory note; or

(2) provides that the assignment or transfer or the creation, attachment, perfection, or enforcement of the security interest may give rise to a default, breach, right of recoupment, claim, defense, termination, right of termination, or remedy under the account, chattel paper, payment intangible, or promissory note.

(e) **[Inapplicability of subsection (d) to certain sales.]** Subsection (d) does not apply to the sale of a payment intangible or promissory note, other than a sale pursuant to a disposition under Section 9–610 or an acceptance of collateral under Section 9–620.

(f) **[Legal restrictions on assignment generally ineffective.]** Except as otherwise provided in sections 2A–303 and 9–407 and subject to subsections (h) and (i), a rule of law, statute, or regulation that prohibits, restricts, or requires the consent of a government, governmental body or official, or account debtor to the assignment or transfer of, or creation of a security interest in, an account or chattel paper is ineffective to the extent that the rule of law, statute, or regulation:

   (1) prohibits, restricts, or requires the consent of the government, governmental body or official, or account debtor to the assignment or transfer of, or the creation, attachment, perfection, or enforcement of a security interest in the account or chattel paper; or

   (2) provides that the assignment or transfer or the creation, attachment, perfection, or enforcement of the security interest may give rise to a default, breach, right of recoupment, claim, defense, termination, right of termination, or remedy under the account or chattel paper.

(g) **[Subsection (b)(3) not waivable.]** Subject to subsection (h), an account debtor may not waive or vary its option under subsection (b)(3).

(h) **[Rule for individual under other law.]** This section is subject to law other than this article which establishes a different rule for an account debtor who is an individual and who incurred the obligation primarily for personal, family, or household purposes.

(i) **[Inapplicability to health-care-insurance receivable.]** This section does not apply to an assignment of a health-care-insurance receivable.

(j) **[Section prevails over specified inconsistent law.]** This section prevails over any inconsistent provisions of the following statutes, rules, and regulations: [List here any statutes, rules, and regulations containing provisions inconsistent with this section.] . . . .

PART II
RESTATEMENT (SECOND) OF CONTRACTS

RESTATEMENT (SECOND) OF CONTRACTS*

(1981)

[The American Law Institute (ALI) is a private, but publicly oriented, organization composed of lawyers, judges, and legal academics. Its objective is to promote the clarification and simplification of the law and its better adaptation to social needs. It has sought to achieve this objective in part by preparing "Restatements" of various branches of the common law, including Contracts. The Restatements consist of statements of legal rules and standards (the "black letter law"), comments that explain each rule or standard and illustrate its application, and reporter's notes that refer to the main precedents and scholarly works upon which the rules, standards, comments, and illustrations were based. The ALI, however, has no law-making power. Its Restatements are only persuasive authorities—not binding authorities—until a court adopts one or more provisions as common law in the relevant jurisdiction. Nonetheless, many of the Restatements, especially the Restatement [First] of Contracts (1932) and much of the Restatement (Second) of Contracts (1981), have been highly influential in the courts. But the Restatements, convenient though they are, are not substitutes for the statutes and precedents that constitute the law in the relevant jurisdiction.

[The theory of the Restatements has changed somewhat over time. The introduction to the Restatement [First] of Contracts stated that "The function of the Institute is to state clearly and precisely in the light of the [courts'] decisions the principles and rules of the common law." The present theory is that the ALI "should feel obliged in [its] deliberations to give weight to all of the considerations that the courts, under a proper view of the judicial function, deem it right to weigh in theirs." Wechsler, *The Course of the Restatements*, 55 A.B.A.J. 147, 156 (1969).

[The complete Restatement (Second) of Contracts takes up three large volumes. This pamphlet contains the sections and comments, and a few illustrations, that should be most helpful to students in a basic course in contracts. Note that the Restatement (Second)'s rules and standards are stated as though they applied to all contracts. This is a bit misleading. When the Uniform Commercial Code ("UCC") or another statute applies, the rules of the statute override any inconsistent common law rules as the ALI restates them or otherwise. It is important to bear this in mind, especially when the transaction in question involves goods and, therefore, Article 2 of the UCC applies. In addition, the ALI has published several new Restatements, in final or draft form, whose subject matters partially overlap that of the Restatement (Second) of Contracts, including the Restatement (Third) of Employment Law (2015), the Restatement (Third) of Restitution and Unjust Enrichment (2011), and the ALI Principles of the Law of Software Contracts (2010). Parts IV and V of this pamphlet contain relevant excerpts from these documents.]

---

* Copyright © 1981 by the American Law Institute. Reproduced with permission.

Pt. II RESTATEMENT (SECOND) OF CONTRACTS

CHAPTER 1. MEANING OF TERMS

Sec.
1. Contract Defined.
2. Promise; Promisor; Promisee; Beneficiary.
3. Agreement Defined; Bargain Defined.
4. How a Promise May Be Made.
5. Terms of Promise, Agreement, or Contract.
6. Formal Contracts.
7. Voidable Contracts.
8. Unenforceable Contracts.

CHAPTER 2. FORMATION OF CONTRACTS—PARTIES AND CAPACITY

9. Parties Required.
10. Multiple Promisors and Promisees of the Same Performance.
11. When a Person May Be Both Promisor and Promisee.
12. Capacity to Contract.
13. Persons Affected by Guardianship.
14. Infants.
15. Mental Illness or Defect.
16. Intoxicated Persons.

CHAPTER 3. FORMATION OF CONTRACTS—MUTUAL ASSENT

TOPIC 1. IN GENERAL

17. Requirement of a Bargain.

TOPIC 2. MANIFESTATION OF ASSENT IN GENERAL

18. Manifestation of Mutual Assent.
19. Conduct as Manifestation of Assent.
20. Effect of Misunderstanding.
21. Intention to Be Legally Bound.
22. Mode of Assent: Offer and Acceptance.
23. Necessity That Manifestations Have Reference to Each Other.

TOPIC 3. MAKING OF OFFERS

24. Offer Defined.
25. Option Contracts.
26. Preliminary Negotiations.
27. Existence of Contract Where Written Memorial Is Contemplated.
28. Auctions.
29. To Whom an Offer Is Addressed.
30. Form of Acceptance Invited.
31. Offer Proposing a Single Contract or a Number of Contracts.
32. Invitation of Promise or Performance.
33. Certainty.
34. Certainty and Choice of Terms; Effect of Performance or Reliance.

TOPIC 4. DURATION OF THE OFFEREE'S POWER OF ACCEPTANCE

35. The Offeree's Power of Acceptance.
36. Methods of Termination of the Power of Acceptance.

37. Termination of Power of Acceptance Under Option Contract.
38. Rejection.
39. Counter-Offers.
40. Time When Rejection or Counter-Offer Terminates the Power of Acceptance.
41. Lapse of Time.
42. Revocation by Communication From Offeror Received by Offeree.
43. Indirect Communication of Revocation.
44. Effect of Deposit on Revocability of Offer.
45. Option Contract Created by Part Performance or Tender.
46. Revocation of General Offer.
47. Revocation of Divisible Offer.
48. Death or Incapacity of Offeror or Offeree.
49. Effect of Delay in Communication of Offer.

TOPIC 5. ACCEPTANCE OF OFFERS

50. Acceptance of Offer Defined; Acceptance by Performance; Acceptance by Promise.
51. Effect of Part Performance Without Knowledge of Offer.
52. Who May Accept an Offer.
53. Acceptance by Performance; Manifestation of Intention Not to Accept.
54. Acceptance by Performance; Necessity of Notification to Offeror.
55. Acceptance of Non-Promissory Offers.
56. Acceptance by Promise; Necessity of Notification to Offeror.
57. Effect of Equivocal Acceptance.
58. Necessity of Acceptance Complying With Terms of Offer.
59. Purported Acceptance Which Adds Qualifications.
60. Acceptance of Offer Which States Place, Time or Manner of Acceptance.
61. Acceptance Which Requests Change of Terms.
62. Effect of Performance by Offeree Where Offer Invites Either Performance or Promise.
63. Time When Acceptance Takes Effect.
64. Acceptance by Telephone or Teletype.
65. Reasonableness of Medium of Acceptance.
66. Acceptance Must Be Properly Dispatched.
67. Effect of Receipt of Acceptance Improperly Dispatched.
68. What Constitutes Receipt of Revocation, Rejection, or Acceptance.
69. Acceptance by Silence or Exercise of Dominion.
70. Effect of Receipt by Offeror of a Late or Otherwise Defective Acceptance.

CHAPTER 4. FORMATION OF CONTRACTS—CONSIDERATION

TOPIC 1. THE REQUIREMENT OF CONSIDERATION

71. Requirement of Exchange; Types of Exchange.
72. Exchange of Promise for Performance.
73. Performance of Legal Duty.
74. Settlement of Claims.
75. Exchange of Promise for Promise.
76. Conditional Promise.
77. Illusory and Alternative Promises.
78. Voidable and Unenforceable Promises.
79. Adequacy of Consideration; Mutuality of Obligation.
80. Multiple Exchanges.
81. Consideration as Motive or Inducing Cause.

Pt. II **RESTATEMENT (SECOND) OF CONTRACTS**

TOPIC 2. CONTRACTS WITHOUT CONSIDERATION

82. Promise to Pay Indebtedness; Effect on the Statute of Limitations.
83. Promise to Pay Indebtedness Discharged in Bankruptcy.
84. Promise to Perform a Duty in Spite of Non-Occurrence of a Condition.
85. Promise to Perform a Voidable Duty.
86. Promise for Benefit Received.
87. Option Contract.
88. Guaranty.
89. Modification of Executory Contract.
90. Promise Reasonably Inducing Action or Forbearance.
91. Effect of Promises Enumerated in §§ 82–90 When Conditional.
92. To Whom Promises Enumerated in §§ 82–85 Must Be Made.
93. Promises Enumerated in §§ 82–85 Made in Ignorance of Facts.
94. Stipulations.
95. Requirements for Sealed Contract or Written Contract or Instrument.
96. What Constitutes a Seal.

TOPIC 3. CONTRACTS UNDER SEAL; WRITING AS A STATUTORY SUBSTITUTE FOR THE SEAL

97. When a Promise Is Sealed.
98. Adoption of a Seal by Delivery.
99. Adoption of the Same Seal by Several Parties.
100. Recital of Sealing or Delivery.
101. Delivery.
102. Unconditional Delivery.
103. Delivery in Escrow; Conditional Delivery to the Promisee.
104. Acceptance or Disclaimer by the Promisee.
105. Acceptance Where Return Promise Is Contemplated.
106. What Amounts to Acceptance of Instrument.
107. Creation of Unsealed Contract by Acceptance by Promisee.
108. Requirement of Naming or Describing Promisor and Promisee.
109. Enforcement of a Sealed Contract by Promisee Who Does Not Sign or Seal It.

CHAPTER 5. THE STATUTE OF FRAUDS

110. Classes of Contracts Covered.

TOPIC 1. THE EXECUTOR-ADMINISTRATOR PROVISION

111. Contract of Executor or Administrator.

TOPIC 2. THE SURETYSHIP PROVISION

112. Requirement of Suretyship.
113. Promises of the Same Performance for the Same Consideration.
114. Independent Duty of Promisor.
115. Novation.
116. Main Purpose; Advantage to Surety.
117. Promise to Sign a Written Contract of Suretyship.
118. Promise to Indemnify a Surety.
119. Assumption of Duty by Another.
120. Obligations on Negotiable Instruments.
121. Contract of Assignor or Factor.

122. Contract to Buy a Right From the Obligee.
123. Contract to Discharge the Promisee's Duty.

TOPIC 3. THE MARRIAGE PROVISION

124. Contract Made Upon Consideration of Marriage.

TOPIC 4. THE LAND CONTRACT PROVISION

125. Contract to Transfer, Buy, or Pay for an Interest in Land.
126. Contract to Procure Transfer or to Act as Agent.
127. Interest in Land.
128. Boundary and Partition Agreements.
129. Action in Reliance; Specific Performance.

TOPIC 5. THE ONE-YEAR PROVISION

130. Contract Not to Be Performed Within a Year.

TOPIC 6. SATISFACTION OF THE STATUTE BY A MEMORANDUM

131. General Requisites of a Memorandum.
132. Several Writings.
133. Memorandum Not Made as Such.
134. Signature.
135. Who Must Sign.
136. Time of Memorandum.
137. Loss or Destruction of a Memorandum.

TOPIC 7. CONSEQUENCES OF NON-COMPLIANCE

138. Unenforceability.
139. Enforcement by Virtue of Action in Reliance.
140. Defense of Failure to Perform.
141. Action for Value of Performance Under Unenforceable Contract.
142. Tort Liability for Acts Under Unenforceable Contract.
143. Unenforceable Contract as Evidence.
144. Effect of Unenforceable Contract as to Third Parties.
145. Effect of Full Performance.
146. Rights of Competing Transferees of Property.
147. Contract Containing Multiple Promises.
148. Rescission by Oral Agreement.
149. Oral Modification.
150. Reliance on Oral Modification.

CHAPTER 6. MISTAKE

151. Mistake Defined.
152. When Mistake of Both Parties Makes a Contract Voidable.
153. When Mistake of One Party Makes a Contract Voidable.
154. When a Party Bears the Risk of a Mistake.
155. When Mistake of Both Parties as to Written Expression Justifies Reformation.
156. Mistake as to Contract Within the Statute of Frauds.
157. Effect of Fault of Party Seeking Relief.
158. Relief Including Restitution.

RESTATEMENT (SECOND) OF CONTRACTS

CHAPTER 7. MISREPRESENTATION, DURESS AND UNDUE INFLUENCE

TOPIC 1. MISREPRESENTATION

159. Misrepresentation Defined.
160. When Action Is Equivalent to an Assertion (Concealment).
161. When Non-Disclosure Is Equivalent to an Assertion.
162. When a Misrepresentation Is Fraudulent or Material.
163. When a Misrepresentation Prevents Formation of a Contract.
164. When a Misrepresentation Makes a Contract Voidable.
165. Cure by Change of Circumstances.
166. When a Misrepresentation as to a Writing Justifies Reformation.
167. When a Misrepresentation Is an Inducing Cause.
168. Reliance on Assertions of Opinion.
169. When Reliance on an Assertion of Opinion Is Not Justified.
170. Reliance on Assertions as to Matters of Law.
171. When Reliance on an Assertion of Intention Is Not Justified.
172. When Fault Makes Reliance Unjustified.
173. When Abuse of a Fiduciary Relation Makes a Contract Voidable.

TOPIC 2. DURESS AND UNDUE INFLUENCE

174. When Duress by Physical Compulsion Prevents Formation of a Contract.
175. When Duress by Threat Makes a Contract Voidable.
176. When a Threat Is Improper.
177. When Undue Influence Makes a Contract Voidable.

CHAPTER 8. UNENFORCEABILITY ON GROUNDS OF PUBLIC POLICY

TOPIC 1. UNENFORCEABILITY IN GENERAL

178. When a Term Is Unenforceable on Grounds of Public Policy.
179. Bases of Public Policies Against Enforcement.
180. Effect of Excusable Ignorance.
181. Effect of Failure to Comply With Licensing or Similar Requirement.
182. Effect of Performance if Intended Use Is Improper.
183. When Agreement Is Enforceable as to Agreed Equivalents.
184. When Rest of Agreement Is Enforceable.
185. Excuse of a Condition on Grounds of Public Policy.

TOPIC 2. RESTRAINT OF TRADE

186. Promise in Restraint of Trade.
187. Non-Ancillary Restraints on Competition.
188. Ancillary Restraints on Competition.

TOPIC 3. IMPAIRMENT OF FAMILY RELATIONS

189. Promise in Restraint of Marriage.
190. Promise Detrimental to Marital Relationship.
191. Promise Affecting Custody.

TOPIC 4. INTERFERENCE WITH OTHER PROTECTED INTERESTS

192. Promise Involving Commission of a Tort.
193. Promise Inducing Violation of Fiduciary Duty.

RESTATEMENT (SECOND) OF CONTRACTS

194. Promise Interfering With Contract With Another.
195. Term Exempting From Liability for Harm Caused Intentionally, Recklessly or Negligently.
196. Term Exempting From Consequences of Misrepresentation.

TOPIC 5. RESTITUTION

197. Restitution Generally Unavailable.
198. Restitution in Favor of Party Who Is Excusably Ignorant or Is Not Equally in the Wrong.
199. Restitution Where Party Withdraws or Situation Is Contrary to Public Interest.

CHAPTER 9. THE SCOPE OF CONTRACTUAL OBLIGATIONS

TOPIC 1. THE MEANING OF AGREEMENTS

200. Interpretation of Promise or Agreement.
201. Whose Meaning Prevails.
202. Rules in Aid of Interpretation.
203. Standards of Preference in Interpretation.
204. Supplying an Omitted Essential Term.

TOPIC 2. CONSIDERATIONS OF FAIRNESS AND THE PUBLIC INTEREST

205. Duty of Good Faith and Fair Dealing.
206. Interpretation Against the Draftsman.
207. Interpretation Favoring the Public.
208. Unconscionable Contract or Term.

TOPIC 3. EFFECT OF ADOPTION OF A WRITING

209. Integrated Agreements.
210. Completely and Partially Integrated Agreements.
211. Standardized Agreements.
212. Interpretation of Integrated Agreement.
213. Effect of Integrated Agreement on Prior Agreements (Parol Evidence Rule).
214. Evidence of Prior or Contemporaneous Agreements and Negotiations.
215. Contradiction of Integrated Terms.
216. Consistent Additional Terms.
217. Integrated Agreement Subject to Oral Requirement of a Condition.
218. Untrue Recitals; Evidence of Consideration.

TOPIC 4. SCOPE AS AFFECTED BY USAGE

219. Usage.
220. Usage Relevant to Interpretation.
221. Usage Supplementing an Agreement.
222. Usage of Trade.
223. Course of Dealing.

TOPIC 5. CONDITIONS AND SIMILAR EVENTS

224. Condition Defined.
225. Effects of the Non-Occurrence of a Condition.
226. How an Event May Be Made a Condition.
227. Standards of Preference With Regard to Conditions.
228. Satisfaction of the Obligor as a Condition.
229. Excuse of a Condition to Avoid Forfeiture.

Pt. II   **RESTATEMENT (SECOND) OF CONTRACTS**

CHAPTER 10. PERFORMANCE AND NON-PERFORMANCE

TOPIC 1. PERFORMANCES TO BE EXCHANGED UNDER AN EXCHANGE OF PROMISES

230. Event That Terminates a Duty.
231. Criterion for Determining When Performances Are to Be Exchanged Under an Exchange of Promises.
232. When It Is Presumed That Performances Are to Be Exchanged Under an Exchange of Promises.
233. Performance at One Time or in Installments.
234. Order of Performances.

TOPIC 2. EFFECT OF PERFORMANCE AND NON-PERFORMANCE

235. Effect of Performance as Discharge and of Non-Performance as Breach.
236. Claims for Damages for Total and for Partial Breach.
237. Effect on Other Party's Duties of a Failure to Render Performance.
238. Effect on Other Party's Duties of a Failure to Offer Performance.
239. Effect on Other Party's Duties of a Failure Justified by Non-Occurrence of a Condition.
240. Part Performances as Agreed Equivalents.
241. Circumstances Significant in Determining Whether a Failure Is Material.
242. Circumstances Significant in Determining When Remaining Duties Are Discharged.
243. Effect of a Breach by Non-Performance as Giving Rise to a Claim for Damages for Total Breach.
244. Effect of Subsequent Events on Duty to Pay Damages.
245. Effect of a Breach by Non-Performance as Excusing the Non-Occurrence of a Condition.
246. Effect of Acceptance as Excusing the Non-Occurrence of a Condition.
247. Effect of Acceptance of Part Performance as Excusing the Subsequent Non-Occurrence of a Condition.
248. Effect of Insufficient Reason for Rejection as Excusing the Non-Occurrence of a Condition.
249. When Payment Other Than by Legal Tender Is Sufficient.

TOPIC 3. EFFECT OF PROSPECTIVE NON-PERFORMANCE

250. When a Statement or an Act Is a Repudiation.
251. When a Failure to Give Assurance May Be Treated as a Repudiation.
252. Effect of Insolvency.
253. Effect of a Repudiation as a Breach and on Other Party's Duties.
254. Effect of Subsequent Events on Duty to Pay Damages.
255. Effect of a Repudiation as Excusing the Non-Occurrence of a Condition.
256. Nullification of Repudiation or Basis for Repudiation.
257. Effect of Urging Performance in Spite of Repudiation.

TOPIC 4. APPLICATION OF PERFORMANCES

258. Obligor's Direction of Application.
259. Creditor's Application.
260. Application of Payments Where Neither Party Exercises His Power.

CHAPTER 11. IMPRACTICABILITY OF PERFORMANCE AND FRUSTRATION OF PURPOSE

261. Discharge by Supervening Impracticability.
262. Death or Incapacity of Person Necessary for Performance.
263. Destruction, Deterioration or Failure to Come Into Existence of Thing Necessary for Performance.
264. Prevention by Governmental Regulation or Order.
265. Discharge by Supervening Frustration.
266. Existing Impracticability or Frustration.

267. Effect on Other Party's Duties of a Failure Justified by Impracticability or Frustration.
268. Effect on Other Party's Duties of a Prospective Failure Justified by Impracticability or Frustration.
269. Temporary Impracticability or Frustration.
270. Partial Impracticability.
271. Impracticability as Excuse for Non-Occurrence of a Condition.
272. Relief Including Restitution.

CHAPTER 12. DISCHARGE BY ASSENT OR ALTERATION

TOPIC 1. THE REQUIREMENT OF CONSIDERATION

273. Requirement of Consideration or a Substitute.
274. Cancellation, Destruction or Surrender of a Writing.
275. Assent to Discharge Duty of Return Performance.
276. Assent to Discharge Duty to Transfer Property.
277. Renunciation.
278. Substituted Performance.
279. Substituted Contract.
280. Novation.
281. Accord and Satisfaction.

TOPIC 2. SUBSTITUTED PERFORMANCE, SUBSTITUTED CONTRACT, ACCORD AND ACCOUNT STATED

282. Account Stated.

TOPIC 3. AGREEMENT OF RESCISSION, RELEASE AND CONTRACT NOT TO SUE

283. Agreement of Rescission.
284. Release.
285. Contract Not to Sue.

TOPIC 4. ALTERATION

286. Alteration of Writing.
287. Assent to or Forgiveness of Alteration.

CHAPTER 13. JOINT AND SEVERAL PROMISORS AND PROMISEES

TOPIC 1. JOINT AND SEVERAL PROMISORS

288. Promises of the Same Performance.
289. Joint, Several, and Joint and Several Promisors of the Same Performance.
290. Compulsory Joinder of Joint Promisors.
291. Judgment in an Action Against Co-Promisors.
292. Effect of Judgment for or Against Co-Promisors.
293. Effect of Performance or Satisfaction on Co-Promisors.
294. Effect of Discharge on Co-Promisors.
295. Effect of Contract Not to Sue; Reservation of Rights.
296. Survivorship of Joint Duties.

TOPIC 2. JOINT AND SEVERAL PROMISEES

297. Obligees of the Same Promised Performance.
298. Compulsory Joinder of Joint Obligees.
299. Discharge by or Tender to One Joint Obligee.
300. Effect of Violation of Duty to a Co-Obligee.

Pt. II   RESTATEMENT (SECOND) OF CONTRACTS

301. Survivorship of Joint Rights.

CHAPTER 14. CONTRACT BENEFICIARIES

302. Intended and Incidental Beneficiaries.
303. Conditional Promises; Promises Under Seal.
304. Creation of Duty to Beneficiary.
305. Overlapping Duties to Beneficiary and Promisee.
306. Disclaimer by a Beneficiary.
307. Remedy of Specific Performance.
308. Identification of Beneficiaries.
309. Defenses Against the Beneficiary.
310. Remedies of the Beneficiary of a Promise to Pay the Promisee's Debt; Reimbursement of Promisee.
311. Variation of a Duty to a Beneficiary.
312. Mistake as to Duty to Beneficiary.
313. Government Contracts.
314. Suretyship Defenses.
315. Effect of a Promise of Incidental Benefit.

CHAPTER 15. ASSIGNMENT AND DELEGATION

316. Scope of This Chapter.

TOPIC 1. WHAT CAN BE ASSIGNED OR DELEGATED

317. Assignment of a Right.
318. Delegation of Performance of Duty.
319. Delegation of Performance of Condition.
320. Assignment of Conditional Rights.
321. Assignment of Future Rights.
322. Contractual Prohibition of Assignment.
323. Obligor's Assent to Assignment or Delegation.

TOPIC 2. MODE OF ASSIGNMENT OR DELEGATION

324. Mode of Assignment in General.
325. Order as Assignment.
326. Partial Assignment.
327. Acceptance or Disclaimer by the Assignee.
328. Interpretation of Words of Assignment; Effect of Acceptance of Assignment.
329. Repudiation by Assignor and Novation With Assignee.
330. Contracts to Assign in the Future, or to Transfer Proceeds to Be Received.

TOPIC 3. EFFECT BETWEEN ASSIGNOR AND ASSIGNEE

331. Partially Effective Assignments.
332. Revocability of Gratuitous Assignments.
333. Warranties of an Assignor.

TOPIC 4. EFFECT ON THE OBLIGOR'S DUTY

334. Variation of Obligor's Duty by Assignment.
335. Assignment by a Joint Obligee.
336. Defenses Against an Assignee.
337. Elimination of Defenses by Subsequent Events.
338. Discharge of an Obligor After Assignment.

339. Protection of Obligor in Cases of Adverse Claims.

TOPIC 5. PRIORITIES BETWEEN ASSIGNEE AND ADVERSE CLAIMANTS

340. Effect of Assignment on Priority and Security.
341. Creditors of an Assignor.
342. Successive Assignees From the Same Assignor.
343. Latent Equities.

CHAPTER 16. REMEDIES

TOPIC 1. IN GENERAL

344. Purposes of Remedies.
345. Judicial Remedies Available.

TOPIC 2. ENFORCEMENT BY AWARD OF DAMAGES

346. Availability of Damages.
347. Measure of Damages in General.
348. Alternatives to Loss in Value of Performance.
349. Damages Based on Reliance Interest.
350. Avoidability as a Limitation on Damages.
351. Unforeseeability and Related Limitations on Damages.
352. Uncertainty as a Limitation on Damages.
353. Loss Due to Emotional Disturbance.
354. Interest as Damages.
355. Punitive Damages.
356. Liquidated Damages and Penalties.

TOPIC 3. ENFORCEMENT BY SPECIFIC PERFORMANCE AND INJUNCTION

357. Availability of Specific Performance and Injunction.
358. Form of Order and Other Relief.
359. Effect of Adequacy of Damages.
360. Factors Affecting Adequacy of Damages.
361. Effect of Provision for Liquidated Damages.
362. Effect of Uncertainty of Terms.
363. Effect of Insecurity as to the Agreed Exchange.
364. Effect of Unfairness.
365. Effect of Public Policy.
366. Effect of Difficulty in Enforcement or Supervision.
367. Contracts for Personal Service or Supervision.
368. Effect of Power of Termination.
369. Effect of Breach by Party Seeking Relief.

TOPIC 4. RESTITUTION

370. Requirement That Benefit Be Conferred.
371. Measure of Restitution Interest.
372. Specific Restitution.
373. Restitution When Other Party Is in Breach.
374. Restitution in Favor of Party in Breach.
375. Restitution When Contract Is Within Statute of Frauds.
376. Restitution When Contract Is Voidable.

377. Restitution in Cases of Impracticability, Frustration, Non-Occurrence of Condition or Disclaimer by Beneficiary.

TOPIC 5. PRECLUSION BY ELECTION AND AFFIRMANCE

378. Election Among Remedies.
379. Election to Treat Duties of Performance Under Aleatory Contract as Discharged.
380. Loss of Power of Avoidance by Affirmance.
381. Loss of Power of Avoidance by Delay.
382. Loss of Power to Affirm by Prior Avoidance.
383. Avoidance in Part.
384. Requirement That Party Seeking Restitution Return Benefit.
385. Effect of Power of Avoidance on Duty of Performance or on Duty Arising Out of Breach.

CHAPTER 1

MEANING OF TERMS

§ 1. Contract Defined.

A contract is a promise or a set of promises for the breach of which the law gives a remedy, or the performance of which the law in some way recognizes as a duty.

Comment

a. Other meanings. The word "contract" is often used with meanings different from that given here. It is sometimes used as a synonym for "agreement" or "bargain." It may refer to legally ineffective agreements, or to wholly executed transactions such as conveyances; it may refer indifferently to the acts of the parties, to a document which evidences those acts, or to the resulting legal relations. In a statute the word may be given still other meanings by context or explicit definition. As is indicated in the Introductory Note to the Restatement of this Subject, definition in terms of "promise" excludes wholly executed transactions in which no promises are made; such a definition also excludes analogous obligations imposed by law rather than by virtue of a promise.

b. Act and resulting legal relations. As the term is used in the Restatement of this Subject, "contract," like "promise," denotes the act or acts of promising. But, unlike the term "promise," "contract" applies only to those acts which have legal effect as stated in the definition given. Thus the word "contract" is commonly and quite properly also used to refer to the resulting legal obligation, or to the entire resulting complex of legal relations. Compare Uniform Commercial Code § 1–201(11), defining "contract" in terms of "the total legal obligation which results from the parties' agreement."

c. Set of promises. A contract may consist of a single promise by one person to another, or of mutual promises by two persons to one another; or there may be, indeed, any number of persons or any number of promises. One person may make several promises to one person or to several persons, or several persons may join in making promises to one or more persons. To constitute a "set," promises need not be made simultaneously; it is enough that several promises are regarded by the parties as constituting a single contract, or are so related in subject matter and performance that they may be considered and enforced together by a court.

d. Operative acts other than promise. The definition does not attempt to state what acts are essential to create a legal duty to perform a promise. In many situations other acts in addition to the making of a promise are essential, and the formation of the contract is not completed until those acts take place. For example, an act may be done as the consideration for a contract (see § 71), and may be essential to the creation of a legal duty to perform the promise (see § 17). Similarly, delivery is required for the formation of a contract under seal (see § 95). Such acts are not part of the promise, and are not specifically included in the brief definition of contract adopted here.

e. Remedies. The legal remedies available when a promise is broken are of various kinds. Direct remedies of damages, restitution and specific performance are the subject of Chapter 16. Whether or not such direct remedies are available, the law may recognize the existence of legal duty in some other way such as recognizing or denying a right, privilege or power created or terminated by the promise.

Illustration

1. A orally agrees to sell land to B; B orally agrees to buy the land and pays $1000 to A. The agreement is unenforceable under the Statute of Frauds. B's right to restitution of the $1000, however, is governed by the same rules as if the agreement were enforceable. B has a right to recover the $1000 paid if A refuses to convey the land, but not if A is ready and willing to convey. See § 140 and the provisions on restitution in § 375. By virtue of this indirect recognition of the duty to convey, the agreement is a contract.

f. Varieties of contracts. The term contract is generic. As commonly used, and as here defined, it includes varieties described as voidable, unenforceable, formal, informal, express, implied (see Comment a to § 4), unilateral, bilateral. In these varieties neither the operative acts of the parties nor the resulting relations are identical.

g. "Binding promise." A promise which is a contract is said to be "binding." As the term "contract" is defined, a statement that a promise is binding does not necessarily mean that any particular remedy is available in the event of breach, or indeed that any remedy is available. Because of the limitations inherent in stating or illustrating rules for the legal relations resulting from promises, it frequently becomes necessary to indicate that a legal duty to perform arises from the facts stated, assuming the absence of other facts. In order to avoid the connotation that the duty stated exists under all circumstances, the word "binding" or a statement that the promisor is "bound" is used to indicate that the duty arises if the promisor has full capacity, if there is no illegality or fraud in the transaction, if the duty has not been discharged, an

§ 2. Promise; Promisor; Promisee; Beneficiary.

(1) A promise is a manifestation of intention to act or refrain from acting in a specified way, so made as to justify a promisee in understanding that a commitment has been made.

(2) The person manifesting the intention is the promisor.

(3) The person to whom the manifestation is addressed is the promisee.

(4) Where performance will benefit a person other than the promisee, that person is a beneficiary.

Comment

a. Acts and resulting relations. "Promise" as used in the Restatement of this Subject denotes the act of the promisor. If by virtue of other operative facts there is a legal duty to perform, the promise is a contract; but the word "promise" is not limited to acts having legal effect. Like "contract," however, the word "promise" is commonly and quite properly also used to refer to the complex of human relations which results from the promisor's words or acts of assurance, including the justified expectations of the promisee and any moral or legal duty which arises to make good the assurance by performance. The performance may be specified either in terms describing the action of the promisor or in terms of the result which that action or inaction is to bring about.

b. Manifestation of intention. Many contract disputes arise because different people attach different meanings to the same words and conduct. The phrase "manifestation of intention" adopts an external or objective standard for interpreting conduct; it means the external expression of intention as distinguished from undisclosed intention. A promisor manifests an intention if he believes or has reason to believe that the promisee will infer that intention from his words or conduct. Rules governing cases where the promisee could reasonably draw more than one inference as to the promisor's intention are stated in connection with the acceptance of offers (see §§ 19 and 20), and the scope of contractual obligations (see §§ 201, 219).

c. Promise of action by third person; guaranty. Words are often used which in terms promise action or inaction by a third person, or which promise a result obtainable only by such action. Such words are commonly understood as a promise of conduct by the promisor which will be sufficient to bring about the action or inaction or result, or to answer for harm caused by failure. An example is a guaranty that a third person will perform his promise. Such words constitute a promise as here defined only if they justify a promisee in an expectation of some action or inaction on the part of the promisor.

d. Promise of event beyond human control; warranty. Words which in terms promise that an event not within human control will occur may be interpreted to include a promise to answer for harm caused by the failure of the event to occur. An example is a warranty of an existing or past fact, such as a warranty that a horse is sound, or that a ship arrived in a foreign port some days previously. Such promises are often made when the parties are ignorant of the actual facts regarding which they bargain, and may be dealt with as if the warrantor could cause the fact to be as he asserted. It is then immaterial that the actual condition of affairs may be irrevocably fixed before the promise is made.

Words of warranty, like other conduct, must be interpreted in the light of the circumstances and the reasonable expectations of the parties. In an insurance contract, a "warranty" by the insured is usually not a promise at all; it may be merely a representation of fact, or, more commonly, the fact warranted is a condition of the insurer's duty to pay (see § 225(3)). In the sale of goods, on the other hand, a similar warranty normally also includes a promise to answer for damages (see Uniform Commercial Code § 2–715).

Illustration

1. A, the builder of a house, or the inventor of the material used in part of its construction, says to B, the owner of the house, "I warrant that this house will never burn down." This includes a promise to pay for harm if the house should burn down.

Illustration

2. A, by a charter-party, undertakes that the "good ship Dove," having sailed from Marseilles a week ago for New York, shall take on a cargo for B on her arrival in New York. The statement of the quality of the ship and the statement of her time of sailing from Marseilles include promises to pay for harm if the statement is untrue.

e. Illusory promises; mere statements of intention. Words of promise which by their terms make performance entirely optional with the "promisor" whatever may happen, or whatever course of conduct in other respects he may pursue, do not constitute a promise. Although such words are often referred to as forming an illusory promise, they do not fall within the present definition of promise. They may not even manifest any intention on the part of the promisor. Even if a present intention is manifested, the reservation of an option to change that intention means that there can be no promisee who is justified in an expectation of performance.

On the other hand, a promise may be made even though no duty of performance can arise unless some event occurs (see §§ 224, 225(1)). Such a conditional promise is no less a promise because there is small likelihood that any duty of performance will arise, as in the case of a promise to insure against fire a thoroughly fireproof building. There may be a promise in such a case even though the duty to perform depends on a state of mind of the promisor other than his own unfettered wish (see § 228), or on an event within the promisor's control.

Illustration

3. A says to B, "I will employ you for a year at a salary of $5,000 if I go into business." This is a promise, even though it is wholly optional with A to go into business or not.

f. Opinions and predictions. A promise must be distinguished from a statement of opinion or a mere prediction of future events. The distinction is not usually difficult in the case of an informal gratuitous opinion, since there is often no manifestation of intention to act or refrain from acting or to bring about a result, no expectation of performance and no consideration. The problem is frequently presented, however, whether words of a seller of goods amount to a warranty. Under Uniform Commercial Code § 2–313(2) a statement purporting to be merely the seller's opinion does not create a warranty, but the buyer's reliance on the seller's skill and judgment may create an implied warranty that the goods are fit for a particular purpose under Uniform Commercial Code § 2–315. In any case where an expert opinion is paid for, there is likely to be an implied promise that the expert will act with reasonable care and skill.

A promise often refers to future events which are predicted or assumed rather than promised. Thus a promise to render personal service at a particular future time commonly rests on an assumption that the promisor will be alive and well at that time; a promise to paint a building may similarly rest on an assumption that the building will be in existence. Such cases are the subject of Chapter 11. The promisor may of course promise to answer for harm caused by the failure of the future event to occur; if he does not, such a failure may discharge any duty of performance.

Illustration

4. A, on seeing a house of thoroughly fireproof construction, says to B, the owner, "This house will never burn down." This is not a promise but merely an opinion or prediction. If A had been paid for his opinion as an expert, there might be an implied promise that he would employ reasonable care and skill in forming and giving his opinion.

g. Promisee and beneficiary. The word promisee is used repeatedly in discussion of the law of contracts, and it cannot be avoided here. In common usage the promisee is the person to whom the promise is made; as promise is defined here, the promisee might be the person to whom the manifestation of the promisor's intention is communicated. In many situations, however, a promise is complete and binding before the communication is received (see, for example, §§ 63 and 104(1)). To cover such cases, the promisee is defined here as the addressee. As to agents or purported agents of the addressee, see § 52 Comment c.

In the usual situation the promisee also bears other relations to the promisor, and the word promisee is sometimes used to refer to one or more of those relations. Thus, in the simple case of a loan of money, the lender is not only the addressee of the promise but also the person to whom performance is to be rendered, the person who will receive economic benefit, the person who furnished the consideration, and the person to whom the legal duty of the promisor runs. As the word promisee is here defined, none of these relations is essential.

Contractual rights of persons not parties to the contract are the subject of Chapter 14. The promisor and promisee are the "parties" to a promise; a third person who will benefit from performance is a "beneficiary." A beneficiary may or may not have a legal right to performance; like "promisee", the term is neutral with respect to rights and duties. A person who is entitled under the terms of a letter of credit to draw or demand payment is commonly called a beneficiary, but such a person is ordinarily a promisee under the present definition. See Uniform Commercial Code § 5–103.

§ 3. Agreement Defined; Bargain Defined.

An agreement is a manifestation of mutual assent on the part of two or more persons. A bargain is an agreement to exchange promises or to exchange a promise for a performance or to exchange performances.

Comment

a. Agreement distinguished from bargain. Agreement has in some respects a wider meaning than contract, bargain or promise. On the other hand, there are contracts which do not require agreement. See, e.g., §§ 82–90, 94, 104. The word "agreement" contains no implication that legal consequences are or are not produced. It applies to transactions executed on one or both sides, and also to those that are wholly executory. The word contains no implication of mental agreement. Such agreement usually but not always exists where the parties manifest assent to a transaction.

b. Manifestation of assent. Manifestation of assent may be made by words or by any other conduct (see § 19). Even silence in some circumstances is such a manifestation (see § 69). Compare the definition of "agreement" in Uniform Commercial Code § 1–201(3).

c. Bargain distinguished from agreement. Bargain has a narrower meaning than agreement, since it is applicable only to a particular class of agreements. It includes agreements which are not contracts, such as transactions where one party makes a promise and the other gives something in exchange which is not consideration, or transactions where what would otherwise be a contract is invalidated by illegality. As here defined, it includes completely executed transactions, such as exchanges of goods (barters) or of services, or sales where goods have been transferred and the price paid for them, although such transactions are not within the scope of this Restatement unless a promise is made.

d. Offer. A bargain is ordinarily made by an offer by one party and an acceptance by the other party or parties, the offer specifying the two subjects of exchange to which the offeror is manifesting assent (see §§ 22 and 24).

e. Contract distinguished from bargain. A contract is not necessarily a bargain. Thus, a promise to make a gift, if made under seal, may be a contract (see § 95), but it is not a bargain. Other contracts which are not bargains are the subject of §§ 82–94. Such contracts do not require manifestations of mutual assent in the form of offer and acceptance.

§ 4. How a Promise May Be Made.

A promise may be stated in words either oral or written, or may be inferred wholly or partly from conduct.

Comment:

a. Express and implied contracts. Contracts are often spoken of as express or implied. The distinction involves, however, no difference in legal effect, but lies merely in the mode of manifesting assent. Just as assent may be manifested by words or other conduct, sometimes including silence, so intention to make a promise may be manifested in language or by implication from other circumstances, including course of dealing or usage of trade or course of performance. See Uniform Commercial Code § 1–201(3), defining "agreement."

Illustration

1. A telephones to his grocer, "Send me a ten-pound bag of flour." The grocer sends it. A has thereby promised to pay the grocer's current price therefor.

Illustration

2. A, on passing a market, where he has an account, sees a box of apples marked "25 cts. each." A picks up an apple, holds it up so that a clerk of the establishment sees the act. The clerk nods, and A passes on. A has promised to pay twenty-five cents for the apple.

b. Quasi-contracts. Implied contracts are different from quasi-contracts, although in some cases the line between the two is indistinct. See Comment a to § 19. Quasi-contracts have often been called implied contracts or contracts implied in law; but, unlike true contracts, quasi-contracts are not based on the apparent intention of the parties to undertake the performances in question, nor are they promises. They are obligations created by law for reasons of justice. Such obligations were ordinarily enforced at common law in the same form of action (assumpsit) that was appropriate to true contracts, and some confusion with reference to the nature of quasi-contracts has been caused thereby. They are dealt with in the Restatement of Restitution. See also §§ 141, 158, 197–99, 272, 370–77.

Illustration

3. A's wife, B, separates from A for justifiable cause, and, in order to secure necessary clothing and supplies, buys them from C and charges their cost to A. A is bound to pay for them, though he has directed C not to furnish his wife with such supplies; but A's duty is quasi-contractual, not contractual. See Restatement of Restitution § 113.

§ 5. Terms of Promise, Agreement, or Contract.

(1) A term of a promise or agreement is that portion of the intention or assent manifested which relates to a particular matter.

(2) A term of a contract is that portion of the legal relations resulting from the promise or set of promises which relates to a particular matter, whether or not the parties manifest an intention to create those relations.

Comment:

a. Agreed terms. The terms of a promise or agreement are those expressed in the language of the parties or implied in fact from other conduct. Both language and conduct are to be understood in the light of the circumstances, including course of dealing or usage of trade or course of performance. See Comment a to § 4. If a promise is binding, a term of the promise becomes a term of the contract unless it is rendered inoperative by some rule of law.

b. Contract terms supplied by law. Much contract law consists of rules which may be varied by agreement of the parties. Such rules are sometimes stated in terms of presumed intention, and they may be thought of as implied terms of an agreement. They often rest, however, on considerations of public policy rather than on manifestation of the intention of the parties. In the Restatement of this Subject, such rules are stated in terms of the operative facts which make them applicable.

c. Statutory contract terms. Statutes providing for contract terms vary in the extent to which they follow the terminology used here, and in the extent to which they permit variation by agreement. Under Uniform Commercial Code § 1–102(3), for example, the effect of provisions of the Code may be freely varied by agreement, with limited exceptions; at the other extreme are statutes or administrative regulations prescribing standard forms of such documents as insurance policies or bills of lading. Transactions entered into under statutes providing either optional or required terms commonly contain promises within the present definition, but they may also produce obligations which do not rest upon any manifestation of the intention of the obligor.

Such statutory obligations are beyond the scope of the Restatement of this Subject. The statutes are sometimes written in terms of presumed intention, and they are sometimes properly interpreted as imposing the same legal consequences as if one of the parties to a contract had made a promise in the prescribed terms. If so, rules stated here may be applicable.

Illustration

1. A contracts to sell B a described automobile. Both parties sign a printed contract form on which the description is typed and which contains the printed words, "Seller hereby excludes all warranties, express or implied." Under Uniform Commercial Code § 2–316 the quoted words do not exclude an implied warranty of merchantability, and under § 2–314 A warrants that the automobile is fit to drive. Under § 2–714 the warranty has the effect of a promise to pay for harm if the warranty is broken.

§ 6. Formal Contracts.

The following types of contracts are subject in some respects to special rules that depend on their formal characteristics and differ from those governing contracts in general:

    (a) Contracts under seal,

    (b) Recognizances,

    (c) Negotiable instruments and documents,

    (d) Letters of credit.

Comment

a. "Formal contracts." The contracts referred to in this Section are sometimes referred to as "formal contracts," and other contracts may then be called "informal" or "simple" contracts. This usage is avoided in this Restatement because contracts other than those enumerated are also subject to formal requirements. Thus statutes modeled on the English Statute of Frauds make certain classes of contracts unenforceable unless evidenced by a writing; rules developed under such statutes are stated in Chapter 5. Similarly, Uniform Commercial Code § 9–201 gives effect to a "security agreement" according to its terms, with exceptions which include the specification of formal requisites in § 9–203. Except for contracts under seal, the special rules governing the contracts enumerated in this Section are not stated in the Restatement of this Subject. Many of the rules here stated as applicable to contracts in general also have application to these special types of contract. See, for example, Uniform Commercial Code § 1–103.

b. Contracts under seal. The rules governing the formation of sealed contracts are stated in Chapter 4, and peculiar incidents attached to such contracts after formation are referred to where appropriate. In many States the legal effect of seals has been modified or abolished by statute. Under Uniform Commercial Code § 2–203, contracts or offers to buy or sell goods are not contracts under seal even though a seal is affixed. Under Uniform Commercial Code § 3–113, a negotiable instrument under seal is nevertheless subject to Article 3 of the Code, including the rule of § 3–408 that want or failure of consideration is a defense.

c. Recognizances. A recognizance is an acknowledgment in court by the recognizor that he is bound to make a certain payment unless a specified condition is performed. They are in use chiefly to secure, first, the attendance in court at a future day of the recognizor, or, second, the prosecution of an action, or, third, the payment of bail.

d. Negotiable instruments. Negotiable instruments are such drafts, certificates of deposit, and promissory notes as are payable to bearer or to the order of a specified person, and such bonds, certificates of shares of stock, and other investment securities as are in bearer or registered form. In every State they are subject either to Article 3 or Article 8 of the Uniform Commercial Code or to the older statutes, the Uniform Negotiable Instruments Law and the Uniform Stock Transfer Act.

e. Negotiable documents. Negotiable documents are such warehouse receipts, bills of lading, and other documents of title as run to bearer or to the order of a named person, or, where recognized in overseas trade, to a named person or assigns. Warehouse receipts are subject in every State either to Article 7 of the Uniform Commercial Code or to the Uniform Warehouse Receipts Act. Interstate and export bills of lading are subject to the Federal Bills of Lading Act; import and local bills are subject in most States to Article 7 of the Uniform Commercial Code or to the Uniform Bills of Lading Act.

f. Letters of credit. A letter of credit is a promise to honor drafts or other demands for payment which is within the scope of Article 5 of the Uniform Commercial Code. The Code defines that scope, prescribes formal requirements, provides that no consideration is necessary to establish a letter of credit, and partially codifies the governing law. The governing law is closely related to the law of negotiable instruments; it has been developed from the law merchant and influenced by Section 135 of the Uniform Negotiable Instruments Law and by statutes and usages relating to banking. The Uniform Commercial Code makes no radical change in the law developed by judicial decision.

§ 7. Voidable Contracts.

A voidable contract is one where one or more parties have the power, by a manifestation of election to do so, to avoid the legal relations created by the contract, or by ratification of the contract to extinguish the power of avoidance.

Comment

a. "Void contracts." A promise for breach of which the law neither gives a remedy nor otherwise recognizes a duty of performance by the promisor is often called a void contract. Under § 1, however, such a promise is not a contract at all; it is the "promise" or "agreement" that is void of legal effect. If the term "contract" were defined to refer to the acts of the parties without regard to their legal effect, a contract could without inconsistency be referred to as "void."

b. Grounds of avoidance. Typical instances of voidable contracts are those where one party was an infant, or where the contract was induced by fraud, mistake, or duress, or where breach of a warranty or other promise justifies the aggrieved party in putting an end to the contract. Usually the power to avoid is confined to one party to the contract, but where, for instance, both parties are infants, or where both parties enter into a contract under a mutual mistake, the contract may be voidable by either one of the parties. Avoidance is often referred to as "disaffirmance."

c. Consequences of avoidance. The legal relations that exist after avoidance vary with the circumstances. In some cases the party who avoids the contract is entitled to be restored to a position as good as that which he occupied immediately before the formation of the contract; in other cases the parties may be left in the same condition as at the time of the avoidance. In many cases the power of avoidance exists only if the original situation of the parties can be and is restored at least substantially; but this is not necessarily the case. An infant, for instance, in many jurisdictions is allowed to avoid his contract without this qualification, so that when the infant exercises his power the parties frequently are left in a very different situation from that which existed when the contract was made. See § 14; Restatement of Restitution § 62. As to breach of contract, see Chapters 10 and 16 of this Restatement; as to mistake, misrepresentation, duress and undue influence, see Chapters 6 and 7.

Illustration

1. A, an infant, sells and delivers his watch to B, an adult, in return for B's promise to pay $20. There is a contract whereby B becomes owner of the watch and is under an enforceable duty to pay $20 to A. But A has the power to extinguish his own right to the money and B's duty to pay it and, as against B, to revest in himself the ownership of the watch.

d. Promptness of election. Voidable contracts differ with respect to the requirement that the avoiding party manifest his election promptly. In some cases the power of avoidance may be lost by unreasonable delay in returning benefits received or in manifesting the election to avoid. In other cases, particularly where the contract is entirely executory on both sides, no manifestation of intention is necessary until an action is brought against the party having the power of avoidance.

Illustration

2. A, by fraud, induces B to make a promise to pay A money in consideration of goods delivered by A to B. There is a contract, but the fraudulent representations of A give B a power to avoid by tendering back to A within a reasonable time the goods received from him.

Illustration

3. A, an infant, makes an agreement with B, an adult, the infant promising to pay money and the adult promising to deliver a chattel. This is enforceable against B, but not against A. If A has not previously avoided, he will have the power of ratification upon attaining his majority.

e. Power of ratification. The propriety of calling a transaction a voidable contract rests primarily on the traditional view that the transaction is valid and has its usual legal consequences until the power of avoidance is exercised. Where each party has a power of avoidance, there is no legal duty of performance; but the term voidable contract is appropriate if ratification by one of the parties would terminate his power of avoidance and make the contract enforceable against him. See § 85. Moreover, action may be necessary in order to prevent the contract from producing the ordinary legal consequences of a contract; often such action in order to be effectual must be taken promptly.

Illustration

4. A, by fraud, induces B to promise to pay for certain advice which A gives. This promise creates no duty in B, but is not wholly void, because it can be validated by B after he learns the facts.

§ 8. Unenforceable Contracts.

An unenforceable contract is one for the breach of which neither the remedy of damages nor the remedy of specific performance is available, but which is recognized in some other way as creating a duty of performance, though there has been no ratification.

Comment

a. Distinction between "voidable" and "unenforceable." Just as a contract may be voidable by one party or by either party, so it may be enforceable by one and not by the other or it may be unenforceable by either. Similarly, one party to an unenforceable contract may have a power to make the contract enforceable by all the usual remedies, and both voidable and unenforceable contracts may have collateral consequences. Voidable contracts might be defined as one type of unenforceable contract. As defined here, however, the term unenforceable contract refers to rules under which the duty of performance does not depend solely on the election of one party. In the transactions here classified as unenforceable, some legal consequences other than the creation of a power of ratification follow without further action by either party.

Illustration

1. A, an infant, orally accepts a written offer signed by B, an adult, to sell a tract of land. A's promise is voidable by him because of his infancy and unenforceable under the Statute of Frauds. Upon attaining his majority, A delivers to B a signed writing stating the terms of the contract and manifesting an election to avoid it. Under § 133, the Statute of Frauds no longer prevents enforcement; but the contract is avoided.

Illustration

2. A is indebted to B, but the statute of limitations has barred a direct remedy. A has the power to make direct remedies available or to make a new contract without consideration by making a new promise or part payment of the debt (see § 82). Even without such further acts, legal consequences may flow from the barred debt. If the creditor has security, he may have a right to apply it towards payment of the debt.

b. Types of unenforceable contracts. Some contracts are unenforceable because they arise out of illegal bargains which are neither wholly void nor voidable. See Comments b-d to § 178; §§ 183–84; Comment b to § 197. Others are unenforceable because of laws relating primarily to remedies, such as the Statute of Frauds (see Chapter 5) or Statute of Limitations.

Illustration

3. A agrees to sell specific goods to B, and B agrees to buy them. A has previously contracted to sell the same goods to C, as B knows. The bargain between A and B is unenforceable on grounds of public policy (§ 194), and neither party can enforce it while executory. But if either party performs his promise, he can recover what he has transferred or its value. The return promise, though unenforceable, is given legal effect as showing that the performance was not gratuitous, and is therefore a contract.

Illustration

4. A makes an oral purchase of goods from B for an agreed price of $500. There is no delivery or part payment, and the bargain is unenforceable under the Statute of Frauds. A insures the goods as owner. The insurer cannot defeat a claim under the policy on the ground that A did not own the goods, although A would have had no direct remedy against B for failure to deliver.

c. Government contracts. Contracts with a government or governmental agency are sometimes unenforceable under remnants of the historic English tradition that the sovereign is immune from suit. Yet the legal consequences of such a contract show that what is promised by the government is due as of right and not as a favor. Thus, a claim against the government arising out of the contract may pass to the executor or trustee in bankruptcy of the claimant. Sometimes such a claim, though not enforceable by action, may be asserted defensively in an action by the government.

Increasingly, governments have enacted statutes giving general consent to actions on contracts. Contracts enforceable by judicial proceedings under such statutes fall outside the present definition of unenforceable contracts, even though the action may be brought only in a special court, or relief may be limited to money damages, or execution cannot be levied on a money judgment. The critical element is not compulsion by physical force, but the availability of judicial machinery to make a final determination of legal obligation. Thus, where the only direct remedy is by legislative approval of a private bill or by unreviewable administrative action, the contract is within the present definition of unenforceable contracts.

The question whether a contract is enforceable by direct legal proceedings is quite different from the question whether the legal right will be converted into money or its equivalent. The latter question may depend on whether there is a regular practice of making appropriations to pay judgments, or, as in cases of private obligors, on the solvency of the government against whom the judgment is rendered. There is sometimes more assurance of payment under an unenforceable contract than under a judgment.

Illustration

5. A, an American citizen, holds notes issued by B, a foreign government. Because of the sovereign immunity of B, the notes are not enforceable against B in the courts of the United States. In an action by B against A on an unrelated claim, however, A may use the notes as an offset to reduce the amount of B's recovery.

Illustration

6. A, an American citizen, has a contract with the United States government, and after a breach by the government obtains a judgment for damages in the United States Court of Claims. Under the tax laws, money receivable under the contract is taxable as accrued income when there is a reasonable expectancy that the right will be converted into money. The income accrues in the year in which the time for appellate review of the judgment expires, even though Congress does not appropriate money to pay the judgment until the following year.

CHAPTER 2

FORMATION OF CONTRACTS— PARTIES AND CAPACITY

§ 9. Parties Required.

There must be at least two parties to a contract, a promisor and a promisee, but there may be any greater number.

Comment:

a. Promise to oneself. In one sense a person can make a promise to himself, but the law does not provide remedies for breach of such promises. This rule, which is implicit in the definition of "promise" in § 2, has been thought to be a rule of substantive law independent of mere procedural requirements. But it is unlikely to have practical significance unless some other person becomes involved, and in such cases it is an unreliable basis for prediction of legal consequences. Thus a contract may be formed in which the same person is one of several on one side of a bargain, and either alone or with others a party on the other side. See § 11. Again, where one party to a contract becomes both obligor and obligee and there are no other parties to the contract, the contract is not necessarily deprived of all legal consequences. See the provisions on discharge in Chapter 12; compare Uniform Commercial Code §§ 3–208, 3–601.

b. Different capacities. One person may have different capacities, as for instance as trustee, as executor, as partner, and as individual. If he purports to make a promise in one capacity to himself in another capacity, there may be legal consequences. He cannot make a contract by his own undisclosed mental processes; a contract requires a manifestation of intention. Even if his intention is manifested by execution of a formal document or by other conduct, it may not be technically accurate to say that in one capacity he holds a claim against himself in another capacity, but that may be substantially the effect of his acts. Thus if a trust company holds a sum of money in trust, and in accordance with the terms of the trust deposits the money in its banking department, it is under substantially the same duties to the beneficiaries as if it held a claim against a third person in trust. See Restatement, Second, Trusts § 87; compare Restatement, Second, Agency § 24. Such self-dealing by a fiduciary may involve a breach of duty to a beneficiary or principal. See Restatement, Second, Trusts § 170; Restatement, Second, Agency § 387.

c. Multiple parties. Under § 1 a contract may be a "set of promises", and there may be multiple promisors and multiple promisees in one set.

Illustration

1. A, B, C and D enter into a written contract by which A makes certain promises to B, other promises to C, and other promises to D. In return B, C and D promise a single performance to A, or each promises A a separate performance. In either case there is a contract, and numerous variations may be made from this illustration in regard to the number of parties and the various promises which they may make.

§ 10. Multiple Promisors and Promisees of the Same Performance.

(1) Where there are more promisors than one in a contract, some or all of them may promise the same performance, whether or not there are also promises of separate performances.

(2) Where there are more promisees than one in a contract, a promise may be made to some or all of them as a unit, whether or not the same or another performance is separately promised to one or more of them.

Comment

a. Procedural limitations at common law. Historically it was said that there could be only two sides to an action at law, that of the plaintiff and that of the defendant. There might be more than one person on each side, but it was necessary that all the parties joined as plaintiffs assert a common right and that all the persons joined as defendants be charged with a common duty. In equity, however, there has never been a requirement that the parties to a suit must consist of merely two units, one seeking to enforce a right against the other. On the contrary, any number of parties having diverse and conflicting legal relations could be dealt with under equity procedure; and the same thing is true where under modern statutes or rules of court legal and equitable procedures have been merged in a single form of action. The extent to which remnants of common-law procedure survive in the United States is beyond the scope of the Restatement of this Subject.

b. Multiple promises; suretyship. As a matter of substantive law, an indefinite number of persons may contract with one another, and there may be three or more individuals or groups, each with distinct rights and duties. Promises may be made by individuals or by groups acting together, and they may be made to individuals or to groups acting together.

Rules governing multiple promises of the same performance are stated in Chapter 13. Where promises of the same performance are made by two or more promisors, there is necessarily a relation of suretyship among the promisors. Thus, if there are two promisors, either one is the principal obligor and the other his surety, or each is a principal obligor as to a part and a surety as to the balance. Rules of suretyship are stated in the Restatement of Security; in general they are beyond the scope of the Restatement of this Subject.

Illustration

1. A promises to convey a tract of land to his three sons, B, C and D. In return B and C promise to build and maintain a home for A; D promises to live with A and to support and care for him; B, C and D promise that A will receive $200 a year. As to the home, B is the principal obligor for his share and C for his; B is C's surety for C's share and C is B's surety for B's share. Similarly, as to the $200, each is principal as to a third and surety for each of the others. D alone is bound to furnish care and support.

§ 11. When a Person May Be Both Promisor and Promisee.

A contract may be formed between two or more persons acting as a unit and one or more but fewer than all of these persons, acting either singly or with other persons.

Comment

a. The Section is applicable to contracts in general, including the types enumerated in § 6. It does not touch upon the rightfulness of making such contracts. Self-dealing may render a contract voidable. As to persons acting in more than one capacity, see Comment b to § 9.

Illustrations

1. A becomes a member of an unincorporated society, and by so doing promises to pay dues to the society. He is bound by a contract.

2. A, a trustee of an estate jointly with B, enters into a written agreement by which he individually promises to buy and A and B as trustees promise to sell a piece of land belonging to the trust. This is a contract; and, though it is voidable by the beneficiaries if made without either their consent or the authority of a court, it is enforceable unless the beneficiaries elect to avoid it.

b. Historically contracts falling within the terms of this Section were said not to be enforceable at common law, but this difficulty could be obviated by resort to a court of equity. The extent to which this procedural distinction survives in the United States is beyond the scope of the Restatement of this Subject.

§ 12. Capacity to Contract.

(1) No one can be bound by contract who has not legal capacity to incur at least voidable contractual duties. Capacity to contract may be partial and its existence in respect of a particular transaction may depend upon the nature of the transaction or upon other circumstances.

(2) A natural person who manifests assent to a transaction has full legal capacity to incur contractual duties thereby unless he is

  (a) under guardianship, or

  (b) an infant, or

  (c) mentally ill or defective, or

  (d) intoxicated.

Comment

a. Total and partial incapacity. Capacity, as here used, means the legal power which a normal person would have under the same circumstances. See Restatement, Second, Agency § 20; Restatement, Second, Trusts § 18. Incapacity may be total, as in cases where extreme physical or mental disability prevents manifestation of assent to the transaction, or in cases of mental illness after a guardian has been appointed. Often, however, lack of capacity merely renders contracts voidable. See § 7. Incapacity sometimes relates only to particular types of transactions; on the other hand, persons whose capacity is limited in most circumstances may be bound by particular types of transactions. In cases of partial disability, the law of mistake or of misrepresentation, duress and undue influence may be relevant. See Chapters 6 and 7, particularly §§ 153, 157, 161(d), 163, 164, 167, 169(c) and 177, Comment b to § 172 and Comment c to § 175.

b. Types of incapacity. Historically, the principal categories of natural persons having no capacity or limited capacity to contract were married women, infants, and insane persons. Those formerly referred to as insane are included in the more modern phrase "mentally ill," and mentally defective persons are treated similarly. Statutes sometimes authorize the appointment of guardians for habitual drunkards, narcotics addicts, spendthrifts, aged persons or convicts as in cases of mental illness. Even without the appointment of a guardian, civil powers of convicts may be suspended in whole or in part during imprisonment; and American Indians are for some purposes treated as wards of the United States government. The contractual powers of convicts and Indians are beyond the scope of the Restatement of this Subject. As to convicts, see Model Penal Code § 306.5.

c. Inability to manifest assent. In order to incur a contractual duty, a party must make a promise, manifesting his intention; in most cases he must manifest assent to a bargain. See §§ 2, 17, 18. The conduct of a party is not effective as a manifestation of his assent unless he intends to engage in the conduct. See § 19. Hence if physical disability prevents a person from acting, or if mental disability is so extreme that he cannot form the necessary intent, there is no contract. Similarly, even if he intends to engage in the conduct, there is no contract if the other party knows or has reason to know that he does not intend the resulting appearance of assent. See § 20. In such cases it is proper to say that incapacity prevents the formation of a contract.

d. Married women. At common law a married woman had no capacity to incur contractual duties, although courts of equity recognized a limited power with respect to property conveyed to her separate use. Modern statutes in most States have given married women full power to contract, and they are therefore omitted from the list in subsection (2) of persons who may not have full capacity. In some States, however, capacity is still denied with respect to particular types of contracts, such as contracts between husband and wife, contracts of suretyship, contracts for the sale of real property, or contracts relating to the management of community property.

e. Artificial persons. The contractual powers of artificial persons such as corporations and governmental agencies are beyond the scope of the Restatement of this Subject. The tendency of modern legislation is to restrict the assertion of the defense of ultra vires by business corporations, and in effect to give them full capacity; what was once lack of capacity then resembles lack of authority as used in the law of agency. See Model Business Corporation Act § 6 (1961). Where partnerships or unincorporated associations have no power to contract as such, contracts made in their names bind the members instead. Compare Restatement, Second, Agency § 20; Restatement, Second, Trusts §§ 97, 98.

f. Necessaries. Persons having no capacity or limited capacity to contract are often liable for necessaries furnished to them or to their wives or children. Though often treated as contractual, such liabilities are quasi-contractual: the liability is measured by the value of the necessaries rather than by the terms of the promise. The rules governing such liabilities are beyond the scope of the Restatement of this Subject. See Restatement of Restitution §§ 62, 112–17, 139.

§ 13. Persons Affected by Guardianship.

A person has no capacity to incur contractual duties if his property is under guardianship by reason of an adjudication of mental illness or defect.

Comment:

a. Rationale. The reason for appointing a guardian of property is to preserve the property from being squandered or improvidently used. The guardianship proceedings are treated as giving public notice of the ward's incapacity and establish his status with respect to transactions during guardianship even though the other party to a particular transaction may have no knowledge or reason to know of the guardianship: the guardian is not required to give personal notice to all persons who may deal with the ward. The control of the ward's property is vested in the guardian, subject to court supervision; that control and supervision are not to be impaired or avoided by proof that the ward has regained his reason or has had a lucid interval, unless the guardianship is terminated or abandoned.

The rules governing contracts made by a guardian are beyond the scope of the Restatement of this Subject. A contract purporting not to bind the guardian personally but to bind the ward's estate raises problems much like those raised by a similar contract made by a trustee. See Restatement, Second, Trusts §§ 262, 263, 271. But the powers of guardians are usually defined by statute, and are ordinarily much narrower than those of trustees.

b. Non-contractual obligations. Property under guardianship may be reached in some circumstances to redress the torts of the ward or to satisfy his quasi-contractual obligations. See Restatement of Restitution § 139. The guardian is not required, in order to defend the ward against contractual liability arising out of a transaction during guardianship, to restore the other party to his original position, since such a requirement might force the guardian to use other property to replace property dissipated by the ward. Compare Restatement of Restitution § 62. But the other party may be able to reclaim the consideration received by the ward if it can be found. In some cases, as where necessaries have been furnished, the other party, to avoid unjust enrichment, may recover the fair value of the consideration received by the ward. See Comment f to § 12.

Illustration

1. A, under guardianship by reason of mental illness, buys an old car from B for $300, giving a promissory note for that amount. A subsequently abandons the car. A is not liable on the note. B may reclaim the car or, if the car is found to be a necessary, has a claim for having furnished it to A.

c. Types of guardianship. The rule of this Section had its origin in cases of insanity. It does not apply to cases where a person is committed or voluntarily admitted to an asylum or hospital without the appointment of a guardian, or where a guardian of the person only is appointed. In such cases the adjudication may have evidentiary value under § 15, but there may be a voidable contract notwithstanding mental illness or defect. Nor does the rule apply to infants: parents are natural guardians of the person but not the property of an infant, and the appointment of a guardian of the infant's property does not prevent the infant from affirming his contract when he becomes of age.

Unless a statute provides otherwise, the rule governing insane persons applies also to persons under guardianship by reason of mental illness or defect or as habitual drunkards, narcotics addicts, spendthrifts, aged persons or convicts. In some states it makes no difference that the guardian is known as a committee, conservator, or curator, or by some other title, but in others, conservatorship is a less drastic procedure not conclusive and sometimes not even probative on the issue of incompetency. Where a statute authorizes the appointment of a guardian on the voluntary application of the ward-to-be without any adjudication of disability, the ward may retain some capacity to contract, subject to subsequent judicial approval, either where the guardian consents or where the guardian's control of the property is not impaired.

Illustration

2. Shortly after commitment to a hospital for the insane and while still confined, A conveys land to B, taking back a purchase-money mortgage. Subsequently C is appointed guardian of A's property. On A's behalf, C ratifies the conveyance and sues to enforce the mortgage by foreclosure. B has no defense: since A was not under guardianship, the conveyance and mortgage were voidable, not void. See § 15.

d. Termination of guardianship. When the reason for guardianship ceases, the guardianship should ordinarily be terminated by judicial decree. But when the ward recovers from mental illness, for example, the guardianship is sometimes abandoned without any formality. In such cases, if the guardian dies or is removed and no successor is appointed, the guardianship is no longer conclusive of contractual incapacity, and the same may be true in other cases if the ward resumes full control of his property without interference over a substantial period of time.

§ 14. Infants.

Unless a statute provides otherwise, a natural person has the capacity to incur only voidable contractual duties until the beginning of the day before the person's eighteenth birthday.

Comment

a. Who are infants. The common law fixed the age of twenty-one as the age at which both men and women achieve full capacity to contract, and the rule that the critical moment is the beginning of the preceding day was established on the ground that the law disregards fractions of a day. In almost every State these rules have been changed by statute. It appears that 49 States have lowered the age of majority, either generally or for contract capacity, to less than twenty-one; usually, the age is eighteen. See the table in the Reporter's Note to this Comment. The birthday rather than the preceding day is the date of majority in some States; in some both men and women have full capacity upon marriage.

b. Obligations which are not voidable. Infants' contracts were at one time classified as void, voidable or valid, but the modern rule in the absence of statute is that they are voidable by the infant. See § 7. Compare Restatement, Second, Agency § 20. An infant may be bound by obligations imposed by law independently of contract, such as tort and quasi-contractual obligations. See Comment f to § 12, Restatement of Restitution § 139. In addition, certain contracts are held binding, ordinarily by statute, such as recognizances for appearance in court or contracts made with judicial approval. Modern statutes also sometimes deny the power of disaffirmance as to such transactions as withdrawal of bank deposits or payment of life insurance premiums.

c. Restoration of consideration. An infant need not take any action to disaffirm his contracts until he comes of age. If sued upon the contract, he may defend on the ground of infancy without returning the consideration received. His disaffirmance revests in the other party the title to any property received by the infant under the contract. If the consideration received by the infant has been dissipated by him, the other party is without remedy unless the infant ratifies the contract after coming of age or is under some non-contractual obligation. But some states, by statute or decision, have restricted the power of disaffirmance, either generally or under particular circumstances, by requiring restoration of the consideration received. Where the infant seeks to enforce the contract, the conditions of the other party's promise must be fulfilled. The problems arising when an infant seeks to disaffirm a conveyance or executed contract are beyond the scope of the Restatement of this Subject, whether the disaffirmance is attempted before or after he comes of age. As to what constitutes ratification, see § 85.

§ 15. Mental Illness or Defect.

(1) A person incurs only voidable contractual duties by entering into a transaction if by reason of mental illness or defect

 (a) he is unable to understand in a reasonable manner the nature and consequences of the transaction, or

(b) he is unable to act in a reasonable manner in relation to the transaction and the other party has reason to know of his condition.

(2) Where the contract is made on fair terms and the other party is without knowledge of the mental illness or defect, the power of avoidance under Subsection (1) terminates to the extent that the contract has been so performed in whole or in part or the circumstances have so changed that avoidance would be unjust. In such a case a court may grant relief as justice requires.

Comment

a. Rationale. A contract made by a person who is mentally incompetent requires the reconciliation of two conflicting policies: the protection of justifiable expectations and of the security of transactions, and the protection of persons unable to protect themselves against imposition. Each policy has sometimes prevailed to a greater extent than is stated in this Section. At one extreme, it has been said that a lunatic has no capacity to contract because he has no mind; this view has given way to a better understanding of mental phenomena and to the doctrine that contractual obligation depends on manifestation of assent rather than on mental assent. See §§ 2, 19. At the other extreme, it has been asserted that mental incompetency has no effect on a contract unless other grounds of avoidance are present, such as fraud, undue influence, or gross inadequacy of consideration; it is now widely believed that such a rule gives inadequate protection to the incompetent and his family, particularly where the contract is entirely executory.

b. The standard of competency. It is now recognized that there is a wide variety of types and degrees of mental incompetency. Among them are congenital deficiencies in intelligence, the mental deterioration of old age, the effects of brain damage caused by accident or organic disease, and mental illnesses evidenced by such symptoms as delusions, hallucinations, delirium, confusion and depression. Where no guardian has been appointed, there is full contractual capacity in any case unless the mental illness or defect has affected the particular transaction: a person may be able to understand almost nothing, or only simple or routine transactions, or he may be incompetent only with respect to a particular type of transaction. Even though understanding is complete, he may lack the ability to control his acts in the way that the normal individual can and does control them; in such cases the inability makes the contract voidable only if the other party has reason to know of his condition. Where a person has some understanding of a particular transaction which is affected by mental illness or defect, the controlling consideration is whether the transaction in its result is one which a reasonably competent person might have made.

Illustration

1. A, a school teacher, is a member of a retirement plan and has elected a lower monthly benefit in order to provide a benefit to her husband if she dies first. At age 60 she suffers a "nervous breakdown," takes a leave of absence, and is treated for cerebral arteriosclerosis. When the leave expires she applies for retirement, revokes her previous election, and elects a larger annuity with no death benefit. In view of her reduced life expectancy, the change is foolhardy, and there are no other circumstances to explain the change. She fully understands the plan, but by reason of mental illness is unable to make a decision based on the prospect of her dying before her husband. The officers of the plan have reason to know of her condition. Two months after the changed election she dies. The change of election is voidable.

c. Proof of incompetency. Where there has been no previous adjudication of incompetency, the burden of proof is on the party asserting incompetency. Proof of irrational or unintelligent behavior is essential; almost any conduct of the person may be relevant, as may lay and expert opinions and prior and subsequent adjudications of incompetency. Age, bodily infirmity or disease, use of alcohol or drugs, and illiteracy may bolster other evidence of incompetency. Other facts have significance when there is mental illness or defect but some understanding: absence of independent advice, confidential or fiduciary relationship, undue influence, fraud, or secrecy; in such cases the critical fact often is departure from the normal pattern of similar transactions, and particularly inadequacy of consideration.

d. Operative effect of incompetency. Where no guardian has been appointed, the effect on executory contracts of incompetency by reason of mental illness or defect is very much like that of infancy. Regardless of the other party's knowledge or good faith and regardless of the fairness of the terms, the incompetent person on regaining full capacity may affirm or disaffirm the contract, or the power to affirm or disaffirm may be exercised on his behalf by his guardian or after his death by his personal representative. There may, however, be related obligations imposed by law independently of contract which cannot be disaffirmed. See Comment f to § 12, Comment b to § 14. And if the other party did not know of the incompetency at the time of contracting he cannot be compelled to perform unless the contract is effectively affirmed.

Illustration

2. A, an incompetent not under guardianship, contracts to sell land to B, who does not know of the incompetency. A continues to be incompetent. On discovering the incompetency, B may refuse to perform until a guardian is appointed, and if none is appointed within a reasonable time may obtain a decree canceling the contract.

e. Effect of performance. Where the contract has been performed in whole or in part, avoidance is permitted only on equitable terms. In the traditional action at law, the doing of equity by or on behalf of the incompetent was accomplished by a tender before suit, but in equity or under modern merged procedure it is provided for in the decree. Any benefits still retained by the incompetent must be restored or paid for, and restitution must be made for any necessaries furnished under the contract. See Comment f to § 12. If the other party knew of the incompetency at the time of contracting, or if he took unfair advantage of the incompetent, consideration not received by the incompetent or dissipated without benefit to him need not be restored.

Illustrations

3. A, an incompetent not under guardianship, contracts to buy land for a fair price from B, who does not know of the incompetency. Shortly after transfer of title to A and part payment by A, A dies. A's personal representative may recover A's part payment on reconveying the land to B.

4. The facts being otherwise as stated in Illustration 3, C, with knowledge of A's incompetency, renders legal services to A in the transaction; after learning of A's incompetency, B pays $500 to C pursuant to the contract. A's personal representative need not reimburse B for the payment.

f. When avoidance is inequitable. If the contract is made on fair terms and the other party has no reason to know of the incompetency, performance in whole or in part may so change the situation that the parties cannot be restored to their previous positions or may otherwise render avoidance inequitable. The contract then ceases to be voidable. Where the other party, though acting in good faith, had reason to know of the incompetency at the time of contracting or performance, or where the equities can be partially adjusted by the decree, the court may grant or deny relief as the situation requires. Factors to be taken into account in such cases include not only benefits conferred and received on both sides but also the extent to which avoidance will benefit the incompetent and the extent to which others who will benefit from avoidance had opportunities to prevent the situation from arising.

Illustrations

5. A, an incompetent spouse not under guardianship, mortgages land on fair terms to B, a bank which has no knowledge or reason to know of the incompetency, for a loan of $2,000. At A's request the money is paid to the other spouse, C, who absconds with it. The contract is not voidable.

6. A, a congenital imbecile not under guardianship, has an interest in unimproved land which is contingent on his surviving his father B. A joins B and C, a cousin, in leasing the land on fair terms for 25 years to D, who has no reason to know of the incompetency. Subsequently A assigns his interest in the rent to C in return for C's agreement to support A for life, which C duly performs. Five years later A joins B and C in an outright sale of the land to D. On B's death avoidance of the sale of A's interest may be equitable if D can be assured of repayment of the price and of retaining improvements made by him after the sale; avoidance of the lease would be inequitable.

7. A, an incompetent not under guardianship, lives on a homestead with his mother B and brother C. A also holds a mortgage on a second tract of land owned by C. To prevent foreclosure of a mortgage on the homestead, A, B and C join in borrowing money from D on a mortgage of both tracts on fair terms. D acts in good faith but has reason to know of A's incompetency. A dies, leaving B his sole heir. The mortgage to D is not voidable for the benefit of B.

§ 16. Intoxicated Persons.

A person incurs only voidable contractual duties by entering into a transaction if the other party has reason to know that by reason of intoxication

    (a) he is unable to understand in a reasonable manner the nature and consequences of the transaction, or

    (b) he is unable to act in a reasonable manner in relation to the transaction.

Comment

a. Rationale. Compulsive alcoholism may be a form of mental illness; and when a guardian is appointed for the property of a habitual drunkard, his transactions are treated like those of a person under guardianship by reason of mental illness. See §§ 13, 15. If drunkenness is so extreme as to prevent any manifestation of assent, there is no capacity to contract. See §§ 2, 12, 19. It would be possible to treat voluntary intoxication as a temporary mental disorder in all cases, but voluntary intoxication not accompanied by any other disability has been thought less excusable than mental illness. Compare Model Penal Code § 2.08 and Comment. Hence a contract made by an intoxicated person is enforceable by the other party even though entirely executory, unless the other person has reason to know that the intoxicated person lacks capacity. Elements of overreaching or other unfair advantage may be relevant on the issues of competency, of the other party's reason to know, and of the appropriate remedy.... Use of drugs may raise similar problems.

b. What contracts are voidable. The standard of competency in intoxication cases is the same as that in cases of mental illness. If the intoxication is so extreme as to prevent any manifestation of assent, there is no contract. Otherwise the other party is affected only by intoxication of which he has reason to know. A contract made by a person who is so drunk he does not know what he is doing is voidable if the other party has reason to know of the intoxication. Where there is some understanding of the transaction despite intoxication, avoidance depends on a showing that the other party induced the drunkenness or that the consideration was inadequate or that the transaction departed from the normal pattern of similar transactions; if the particular transaction in its result is one which a reasonably competent person might have made, it cannot be avoided even though entirely executory.

Illustrations

1. A, while in a state of extreme intoxication, signs and mails a written offer on fair terms to B, who has no reason to know of the intoxication. B accepts the offer. A has no right to avoid the contract.

2. A is ill and confined to his bed. B, knowing that the illness is incurable, plies A with intoxicating liquor for a week and then purports to treat him by rubbing him with oil. While intoxicated, A executes by mark a contract to sell land to B for a grossly inadequate consideration. Six days later A dies. A's heirs may avoid the contract.

3. A has been drinking heavily. B, who has also been drinking, meets A, offers to buy A's farm for $50,000, a fair price, and offers A a drink which A accepts. In drunken exhilaration A, as a joke, writes out and signs a memorandum of agreement to sell, gets his wife to sign it, and delivers it to B, who understands the transaction as a serious one. A's intoxication is no defense to B's suit for specific performance.

c. Ratification and avoidance. Where a contract is voidable on the ground of intoxication, the rules as to ratification and avoidance are much the same as in cases of misrepresentation. See Chapter 7. On becoming sober, the intoxicated person must act promptly to disaffirm and must offer to restore consideration received. Such an offer may be excused, however, if the consideration has been dissipated during the period of drunkenness.

Illustration

4. A buys a barber shop from B for $650. Shortly afterward, A, helplessly drunk and evidently not aware of what he is doing, sells the shop back to B for $200. On recovering his senses, A cannot

remember the transaction and cannot find out what happened to the $200. On prompt disaffirmance, A may recover the shop without repaying the $200.

CHAPTER 3

FORMATION OF CONTRACTS—MUTUAL ASSENT

TOPIC 1. IN GENERAL

§ 17. Requirement of a Bargain.

(1) Except as stated in Subsection (2), the formation of a contract requires a bargain in which there is a manifestation of mutual assent to the exchange and a consideration.

(2) Whether or not there is a bargain a contract may be formed under special rules applicable to formal contracts or under the rules stated in §§ 82–94.

Comment

a. Formal contracts. The types of contracts listed in § 6 are not necessarily subject to the requirements of manifestation of assent and consideration. Where contracts under seal still have their common-law effect, neither manifestation of assent by the promisee nor consideration is essential. See §§ 95, 104(1). Under Uniform Commercial Code § 3–408, a negotiable instrument may be binding without consideration in some cases. Under Uniform Commercial Code §§ 5–105, 5–106, neither manifestation of assent by the customer or the beneficiary nor consideration is necessary to the establishment of a letter of credit.

b. Bargains. Contracts of types enumerated in § 6 can be used in many of the transactions essential to civilized life: e.g., sale or lease of land, goods, or intangible property; the rendering of services for hire; the lending of money. But in modern times less formal contracts are far more important. The typical contract is a bargain, and is binding without regard to form. The governing principle in the typical case is that bargains are enforceable unless some other principle conflicts. This chapter and the next deal with the two essential elements of a bargain: agreement and exchange.

c. "Meeting of the minds." The element of agreement is sometimes referred to as a "meeting of the minds." The parties to most contracts give actual as well as apparent assent, but it is clear that a mental reservation of a party to a bargain does not impair the obligation he purports to undertake. The phrase used here, therefore, is "manifestation of mutual assent," as in the definition of "agreement" in § 3. . . . Topics 2–5, §§ 18–70, explain this requirement.

d. "Sufficient consideration." The element of exchange is embodied in the concept of consideration. In some cases a promise is not binding for want of consideration, despite the presence of an element of exchange. "Consideration" has sometimes been used to refer to the element of exchange, without regard to whether it is sufficient to make an informal promise legally binding; the consideration which satisfies the legal requirement has then been called "sufficient consideration." As the term "consideration" is used here, however, it refers to an element of exchange which is legally sufficient, and the word "sufficient" would therefore be redundant. The requirement of consideration is the subject of §§ 71–81.

Illustration

1. A owes B $50. In exchange for A's payment of the debt B makes a promise. Under the rule stated in § 73, B's promise is without consideration.

e. Informal contract without bargain. There are numerous atypical cases where informal promises are binding though not made as part of a bargain. In such cases it is often said that there is consideration by virtue of reliance on the promise or by virtue of some circumstance, such as a "past consideration," which does not involve the element of exchange. In this Restatement, however, "consideration" is used only to refer to the element of exchange, and contracts not involving that element are described as promises binding without consideration. There is no requirement of agreement for such contracts. They are the subject of §§ 82–94.

TOPIC 2. MANIFESTATION OF ASSENT IN GENERAL

§ 18. Manifestation of Mutual Assent.

Manifestation of mutual assent to an exchange requires that each party either make a promise or begin or render a performance.

Comment

a. Manifestation of assent. Assent to the formation of an informal contract is operative only to the extent that it is manifested. Compare § 3 and Comment b to § 2. As to the manifestation of assent by conduct other than words, see §§ 4 and 19. Rules for cases where one party could reasonably draw more than one inference as to the intention of another are stated in the following sections, in connection with the scope of contractual obligations (see §§ 201, 219), and in connection with mistake (see § 151–58).

b. Assent by promise or performance. Where a bargain has been fully performed on one side, there is commonly no need to determine the moment of making of the contract or whether the performing party made a promise before he performed. Those issues ordinarily become important only when a dispute arises at an earlier stage. In the typical case such a dispute involves an exchange of promises before any performance takes place; there is an offer containing a promise and made binding by an acceptance containing a return promise. Section 50. The beginning or tender of performance may operate as such a return promise under § 63. In less common cases, acceptance may be made by a performance under § 54, and the beginning of performance may have an intermediate effect of making the offer irrevocable under § 45.

c. Sham or jest. Where all the parties to what would otherwise be a bargain manifest an intention that the transaction is not to be taken seriously, there is no such manifestation of assent to the exchange as is required by this Section. In some cases the setting makes it clear that there is no contract, as where a business transaction is simulated on a stage during a dramatic performance. In other cases, there may be doubt as to whether there is a joke, or one of the parties may take the joke seriously. If one party is deceived and has no reason to know of the joke the law takes the joker at his word. Even if the deceived party had reason to know of the joke, there may be a claim for fraud or unjust enrichment by virtue of the promise made. Where the parties to a sham transaction intend to deceive third parties, considerations of public policy may sometimes preclude a defense of sham. . . .

§ 19. Conduct as Manifestation of Assent.

(1) The manifestation of assent may be made wholly or partly by written or spoken words or by other acts or by failure to act.

(2) The conduct of a party is not effective as a manifestation of his assent unless he intends to engage in the conduct and knows or has reason to know that the other party may infer from his conduct that he assents.

(3) The conduct of a party may manifest assent even though he does not in fact assent. In such cases a resulting contract may be voidable because of fraud, duress, mistake, or other invalidating cause.

Comment

a. Conduct other than words. Words are not the only medium of expression. Conduct may often convey as clearly as words a promise or an assent to a proposed promise. See Comment a to § 4 and Illustrations. Where no particular requirement of form is made by the law a condition of the validity or enforceability of a contract, there is no distinction in the effect of the promise whether it is expressed in writing, or orally, or in acts, or partly in one of these ways and partly in others. Purely negative conduct is sometimes, though not usually, a sufficient manifestation of assent. See § 69.

Like words, non-verbal conduct often has different meanings to different people. Indeed, the meaning of conduct not used as a conventional symbol is more uncertain and more dependent on its setting than are words. A wide variety of elements of the total situation may be relevant to the interpretation of such conduct. The problem is illustrated in cases of claims against a decedent's estate for services rendered. In such cases the line between a contractual claim based on agreement and a quasi-contractual claim based on unjust enrichment is often indistinct; on either basis a major question may be whether the services were rendered gratuitously, and the circumstances are often critical.

Illustration

1. A lives in B's home and renders services to B over a period of years, and after B's death claims the value of the services. By statute A is incompetent to testify to transactions with B, and there is no evidence of a verbal promise. Among the factors relevant to a determination whether the services were gratuitous are the following: a request by B that A render the services, the relation between A and B, the value of the services to B, the alternatives foregone and hardship suffered by A, the financial circumstances of the parties, the relation between B and his legatees or distributees, and their connection with A's services.

b. *"Reason to know."* A person has reason to know a fact, present or future, if he has information from which a person of ordinary intelligence would infer that the fact in question does or will exist. A person of superior intelligence has reason to know a fact if he has information from which a person of his intelligence would draw the inference. There is also reason to know if the inference would be that there is such a substantial chance of the existence of the fact that, if exercising reasonable care with reference to the matter in question, the person would predicate his action upon the assumption of its possible existence.

Reason to know is to be distinguished from knowledge and from "should know." Knowledge means conscious belief in the truth of a fact; reason to know need not be conscious. "Should know" imports a duty to others to ascertain facts; the words "reason to know" are used both where the actor has a duty to another and where he would not be acting adequately in the protection of his own interests were he not acting with reference to the facts which he has reason to know. . . . Uniform Commercial Code § 1–201(25).

c. *Responsibility for unintended appearance of assent.* A "manifestation" of assent is not a mere appearance; the party must in some way be responsible for the appearance. There must be conduct and a conscious will to engage in that conduct. Thus, when a party is used as a mere mechanical instrument, his apparent assent does not affect his contractual relations. See the rules on duress in §§ 174–77. This is true even though the other party reasonably believes that the assent is genuine.

Similarly, even though the intentional conduct of a party creates an appearance of assent on his part, he is not responsible for that appearance unless he knows or has reason to know that his conduct may cause the other party to understand that he assents. In effect there must be either intentional or negligent creation of an appearance of assent. Compare § 20 and the rules on mistake, misrepresentation, duress and undue influence in Chapters 6 and 7. The other party must also manifest assent, but no further change of position on his part is necessary to the formation of a bargain. Change of position may of course be relevant to the existence of a power of avoidance, but the law must take account of the fact that in a society largely founded on credit bargains will be relied on in subtle ways, difficult or incapable of proof.

Illustrations

2. A offers to sell B his library at a stated price, forgetting that his favorite Shakespeare, which he did not intend to sell, is in the library. B accepts the offer. There is a contract including the Shakespeare, unless B knows or has reason to know of A's temporary forgetfulness. Whether the contract is voidable for mistake depends on the rules stated in Chapter 6.

3. A writes an offer to B, which he encloses in an envelope, addresses and stamps. Shortly afterwards, he decides not to send the offer, but by mistake he deposits it in the mail. It is delivered to B, who accepts the offer. There is a contract unless B knows or has reason to know of A's error. Whether the contract is voidable for mistake is governed by the rules stated in Chapter 6.

d. *Voidable manifestations distinguished.* Actual mental assent is not essential to the formation of an informal contract enforceable as a bargain. This is made clear by the definitions of "bargain" and "agreement" in terms of "manifestation" of mutual assent. See §§ 3, 17, 18; compare Comment b to § 2. But the fact that apparent assent is not genuine may have legal significance in rendering the contract voidable or unenforceable for mistake, misrepresentation, duress, or undue influence. See Chapters 6 and 7. In such cases it is often necessary to inquire whether the power of avoidance has been exercised with sufficient promptness, or whether the other party has so changed his position that avoidance would be inequitable.

Where there is no manifestation of mutual assent, on the other hand, the contractual relations of the parties are not affected, and such inquiries are unnecessary.

§ 20. Effect of Misunderstanding.

(1) There is no manifestation of mutual assent to an exchange if the parties attach materially different meanings to their manifestations and

    (a) neither party knows or has reason to know the meaning attached by the other; or

    (b) each party knows or each party has reason to know the meaning attached by the other.

(2) The manifestations of the parties are operative in accordance with the meaning attached to them by one of the parties if

    (a) that party does not know of any different meaning attached by the other, and the other knows the meaning attached by the first party; or

    (b) that party has no reason to know of any different meaning attached by the other, and the other has reason to know the meaning attached by the first party.

Comment

a. Scope. Subsection (1) states the implications of the rule of § 19(2) as to the meaning of "manifestation of mutual assent" in cases of mistake in the expression of assent. The subject-matter of this Section is more fully treated in Chapter 9 on the scope of contractual obligations. Rules are stated here only for two-party transactions; multi-party transactions are more complex, but are governed by the same principles. As to the meaning of "reason to know," see Comment b to § 19.

b. The need for interpretation. The meaning given to words or other conduct depends to a varying extent on the context and on the prior experience of the parties. Almost never are all the connotations of a bargain exactly identical for both parties; it is enough that there is a core of common meaning sufficient to determine their performances with reasonable certainty or to give a reasonably certain basis for an appropriate legal remedy. See § 33. But material differences of meaning are a standard cause of contract disputes, and the decision of such disputes necessarily requires interpretation of the language and other conduct of the parties in the light of the circumstances.

c. Interpretation and agreement. There is a problem of interpretation in determining whether a contract has been made as well as in determining what obligations a contract imposes. Where one party makes a precise and detailed offer and the other accepts it, or where both parties sign the same written agreement, there may be an "integrated" agreement (see § 209) and the problem is then one of interpreting the offer or written agreement. In other cases agreement may be found in a jumble of letters, telegrams, acts and spoken words. In either type of case, the parties may have different understandings, intentions and meanings. Even though the parties manifest mutual assent to the same words of agreement, there may be no contract because of a material difference of understanding as to the terms of the exchange. Where there is no integration, the parties may also differ as to whether there was an offer of any kind, or whether there was an acceptance. Rules of interpretation governing various situations are stated in Chapter 9 on the scope of contractual obligations; those rules are applicable in the determination of what each party "knows or has reason to know."

d. Error in expression. The basic principle governing material misunderstanding is stated in Subsection (1): no contract is formed if neither party is at fault or if both parties are equally at fault. Subsection (2) deals with cases where both parties are not equally at fault. If one party knows the other's meaning and manifests assent intending to insist on a different meaning, he may be guilty of misrepresentation. Whether or not there is such misrepresentation as would give the other party a power of avoidance, there is a contract under Subsection (2) (a), and the mere negligence of the other party is immaterial. See § 166 as to reformation of a written contract in such a case. Under Subsection (2) (b) a party may be bound by a merely negligent manifestation of assent, if the other party is not negligent. The question whether such a contract is voidable for mistake is dealt with in §§ 151–58.

Illustrations

1. A offers to sell B goods shipped from Bombay ex steamer "Peerless". B accepts. There are two steamers of the name "Peerless", sailing from Bombay at materially different times. If both parties intend the same Peerless, there is a contract, and it is immaterial whether they know or have reason to know that two ships are named Peerless.

2. The facts being otherwise as stated in Illustration 1, A means Peerless No. 1 and B means Peerless No. 2. If neither A nor B knows or has reason to know that they mean different ships, or if they both know or if they both have reason to know, there is no contract.

3. The facts being otherwise as stated in Illustration 1, A knows that B means Peerless No. 2 and B does not know that there are two ships named Peerless. There is a contract for the sale of the goods from Peerless No. 2, and it is immaterial whether B has reason to know that A means Peerless No. 1. If A makes the contract with the undisclosed intention of not performing it, it is voidable by B for misrepresentation (see §§ 159–64). Conversely, if B knows that A means Peerless No. 1 and A does not know that there are two ships named Peerless, there is a contract for the sale of the goods from Peerless No. 1, and it is immaterial whether A has reason to know that B means Peerless No. 2, but the contract may be voidable by A for misrepresentation.

4. The facts being otherwise as stated in Illustration 1, neither party knows that there are two ships Peerless. A has reason to know that B means Peerless No. 2 and B has no reason to know that A means Peerless No. 1. There is a contract for the sale of goods from Peerless No. 2. In the converse case, where B has reason to know and A does not, there is a contract for sale from Peerless No. 1. In either case the question whether the contract is voidable for mistake is governed by the rules stated in §§ 151–58.

5. A says to B, "I offer to sell you my horse for $100." B, knowing that A intends to offer to sell his cow for that price, not his horse, and that the word "horse" is a slip of the tongue, replies, "I accept." The price is a fair one for either the horse or the cow. There is a contract for the sale of the cow and not of the horse. If B makes the contract with the undisclosed intention of not performing it, it is voidable by A for misrepresentation. See §§ 159–64.

§ 21. Intention to Be Legally Bound.

Neither real nor apparent intention that a promise be legally binding is essential to the formation of a contract, but a manifestation of intention that a promise shall not affect legal relations may prevent the formation of a contract.

Comment

a. Intent to be legally bound. Most persons are now aware of the existence of courts and rules of law and of the fact that some promises are binding. The parties to a transaction often have a reasonably accurate understanding of the applicable law, and an intention to affect legal relations. Such facts may be important in interpreting their manifestations of intention and in determining legal consequences, but they are not essential to the formation of a contract. The parties are often quite mistaken about particular rules of law, but such mistakes do not necessarily deprive their acts of legal effect.

Illustrations

1. A draws a check for $300 payable to B and delivers it to B in return for an old silver watch worth about $15. Both A and B understand the transaction as a frolic and a banter, but each believes that he would be legally bound if the other dishonestly so asserted. There is no contract.

2. A orally promises to sell B a book in return for B's promise to pay $5. A and B both think such promises are not binding unless in writing. Nevertheless there is a contract, unless one of them intends not to be legally bound and the other knows or has reason to know of that intention.

b. Agreement not to be legally bound. Parties to what would otherwise be a bargain and a contract sometimes agree that their legal relations are not to be affected. In the absence of any invalidating cause, such a term is respected by the law like any other term, but such an agreement may present difficult questions of interpretation: it may mean that no bargain has been reached, or that a particular manifestation of intention is not a promise; it may reserve a power to revoke or terminate a promise under certain circumstances but not others. In a written document prepared by one party it may raise a question of misrepresentation or mistake or overreaching; to avoid such questions it may be read against the party who prepared it.

The parties to such an agreement may intend to deny legal effect to their subsequent acts. But where a bargain has been fully or partly performed on one side, a failure to perform on the other side may result in unjust enrichment, and the term may then be unenforceable as a provision for a penalty or forfeiture. See §§ 185, 229, 356. In other cases the term may be unenforceable as against public policy because it unreasonably limits recourse to the courts or as unconscionably limiting the remedies for breach of contract. See §§ 178–79, 208; Uniform Commercial Code §§ 2–302, 2–719 and Comment 1.

Illustrations

3. A, an employer, issues to B, an employee, a "certificate of benefit", promising stated sums increasing yearly, payable to a named beneficiary if B dies while still in A's employ. The certificate provides that it "constitutes no contract" and "confers no legal right." The quoted language may be read as reserving a power of revocation only until B dies.

4. A and B, two business corporations, have a contract by which B is the exclusive distributor in a certain territory of goods made by A. By a detailed written agreement they agree to continue the distributorship for three years. The writing provides that it is not to be a legal agreement or subject to legal jurisdiction in the law courts. The written agreement may be read and given effect to terminate the prior contract and to prevent any legal duty arising from the making of the agreement or from the acceptance of orders under it; but it does not excuse B from paying for goods delivered under it.

c. Social engagements and domestic arrangements. In some situations the normal understanding is that no legal obligation arises, and some unusual manifestation of intention is necessary to create a contract. Traditional examples are social engagements and agreements within a family group. See §§ 189–91. Where the family relation is not close, valuable services rendered in the home may make binding an express or implied promise to pay for the services; but even in such cases it would often be understood that there is no legal obligation while the agreement is entirely executory on both sides. See Comment a to § 19, Comment b to § 32.

Illustrations

5. A invites his friend B to dinner in his home, and B accepts. There is no contract. If A promised B a fee for attending and entertaining other guests, and B did so, there would be a contract to pay the fee.

6. A, a husband, is living in harmony with his wife, B. Before A leaves on a trip, A and B assess B's financial needs and agree that A will remit a fixed sum per month to support her. There is no contract.

§ 22. Mode of Assent: Offer and Acceptance.

(1) The manifestation of mutual assent to an exchange ordinarily takes the form of an offer or proposal by one party followed by an acceptance by the other party or parties.

(2) A manifestation of mutual assent may be made even though neither offer nor acceptance can be identified and even though the moment of formation cannot be determined.

Comment:

a. The usual practice. Subsection (1) states the usual practice in the making of bargains. One party ordinarily first announces what he will do and what he requires in exchange, and the other then agrees. Where there are more than two parties, the second party to agree may be regarded as accepting the offer made by the first party and as making a similar offer to subsequent parties, and so on. It is theoretically possible for a third person to state a suggested contract to the parties and for them to say simultaneously that they assent. Or two parties may sign separate duplicates of the same agreement, each manifesting assent whether the other signs before or after him. Compare Illustration 5 to § 23.

    b. Assent by course of conduct. Problems of offer and acceptance are important primarily in cases where advance commitment serves to shift a risk from one party to the other, as in sales of goods which are subject to rapid price fluctuations, in sales of land, and in insurance contracts. Controversies as to whether and when the commitment is made are less likely to be important even in such cases once performance is well under way. Offer and acceptance become still less important after there have been repeated occasions for performance by one party where the other knows the nature of the performance and has an opportunity for objection to it. See Uniform Commercial Code § 2–208 (1); compare Comment a to § 19. In such cases it is unnecessary to determine the moment of making of the contract, or which party made the offer and which the acceptance. Thus, Uniform Commercial Code §§ 2–204 and 2–207(3), relating to contracts for the sale of goods, provide that conduct by both parties which recognizes the existence of a contract is sufficient to establish it although the writings of the parties do not otherwise establish a contract. The principle has also been applied in non-sales contexts.

Illustration

    1. A, a general contractor preparing a bid on a government construction contract, receives a bid by a proposed subcontractor, B, in a given amount. A names B as a subcontractor in A's bid, but after A receives the government contract, A unsuccessfully asks B to reduce its bid, and also unsuccessfully seeks permission from the Government to replace B as a subcontractor.

    Pursuant to A's instructions, B proceeds with the work, but refuses to accept a work order from A which recites that A is still seeking permission to replace B. No new work order is issued. A does issue "change orders" using B's bid as the base "contract amount." B completes the job, but A refuses to pay the full amount, contending that B is entitled only to restitutionary damages because there never was a contract. There is an enforceable contract based upon A's assent to B's bid, as manifested by A's conduct, and B is entitled to the amount it bid, as modified by the change orders.

§ 23. Necessity That Manifestations Have Reference to Each Other.

It is essential to a bargain that each party manifest assent with reference to the manifestation of the other.

Comment

    a. Mutuality of assent. Two manifestations of willingness to make a bargain, though having the same terms, do not constitute a bargain unless each is made with reference to the other. Ordinarily one party, by making an offer, assents in advance; the other, upon learning of the offer, assents by accepting it and thereby forms the contract. The offer may be communicated directly or through an agent; but information received by one party that another is willing to enter into a bargain is not necessarily an offer. The test is whether the offer is so made as to justify the accepting party in a belief that the offer is made to him.

Illustration

    1. A advertises in a large New York newspaper that he will pay a specified reward to anyone who will give him certain information within one year. B sees a copy of this advertisement in a Tokyo newspaper, correctly translated into Japanese, and sends A the information within the year. There is a contract.

    b. Unintended appearance of mutual assent. Either the offeror or the offeree may be bound by an unintended appearance of assent created by his intentional conduct. See § 19. The mutual reference required by this Section is ordinarily intended by both parties to a contract, but if one party believes that there is such reference and the other knows that his conduct creates that appearance, the requirement is satisfied. Similarly, if one party believes that there is such reference and has no reason to know that the other has a different understanding, the requirement is satisfied if the other has reason to know that his conduct creates the unintended appearance. Section 20. Thus where an offer is contained in a writing either the offeror or the offeree may, without reading the writing, manifest assent to it and bind himself without knowing its terms. Again, where goods are sent by a seller as an offer to a buyer, the buyer, without examining them or knowing precisely what they are or that a bargain is proposed, can bind himself by accepting the goods. So in many cases usages of business or of local exchanges are annexed as terms to an offer, and an offeror or offeree who should be aware of those terms may be bound in accordance with them if he manifests assent. See §§ 219–23; Uniform Commercial Code §§ 1–205, 2–104.

c. Unknown offers of rewards. Obligations arising from unintended manifestations of assent by an offeree are imposed in order to protect the offeror in justifiable reliance on the offeree's promise. If the offer clearly contemplates no commitment by the offeree, so that no binding return promise can be made and justifiable reliance by the offeror is impossible, this reason disappears. Thus if a general offer of reward to anyone who does a certain act or achieves a certain result is treated as contemplating a bargain, the only expectations to be fulfilled are those of the offeree, and he may have none unless he knows of the offer.

Such an offer is commonly interpreted as intended to induce action by people who know of the reward. A person who acts without such knowledge is then not within the terms of the offer, even though he intends to accept any offer which may be outstanding and thus does not act gratuitously. Standing offers of rewards made by governmental bodies, however, may be regarded as intended to create a climate in which people do certain acts in the hope of earning unknown rewards. Theoretically, an act so done might create a bargain, but recovery of the reward can be justified just as well by treating the offer as a promise binding without mutual assent or consideration or as creating a non-contractual obligation.

Illustrations

2. A advertises that he will give a specified reward for certain information, or writes B a similar proposal. B gives the information in ignorance of the advertisement, or without having received the letter. There is no contract enforceable as a bargain.

3. A city ordinance provides that a standing reward of $1000 will be paid for information leading to the arrest and conviction of anyone guilty of arson within the city limits. A furnishes such information. A is entitled to the reward whether or not he knew of the reward or was motivated by hope of reward.

d. Cross offers. Cases have occurred in which identical offers have crossed in the mails. Such an event is unusual, and the ordinary offer does not manifest assent to the formation of a contract in this way. Hence, neither offer accepts the other, and there is no contract unless one of the parties accepts the offer he has received. This is a matter of interpretation; theoretically, just as the offeror may assent in advance to an acceptance, so each of two offerors could assent in advance to a cross-offer. Such assent is rare, but it may be inferred where both parties think a contract has already been made. The use of a cross-offer to assist in the interpretation of a previous offer should be distinguished.

Illustrations

4. A sends B an offer through the mail to sell A's horse for $500. While this offer is in the mail, B, in ignorance thereof, mails to A an offer to pay $500 for the horse. There is no contract.

5. After negotiations through a broker, A writes B a letter purporting to confirm a contract for the sale of cloth. A's letter crosses in the mail a similar letter from B, which differs as to quantity and time of payment. A replies insisting on the quantity stated in his first letter but otherwise agreeing; B replies insisting on the time of payment stated in his first letter but otherwise agreeing. The two replies cross in the mail. There is a contract.

6. A offers by letter to sell goods to B, stating no definite time limit for acceptance. B accepts by letter after what might or might not be more than a reasonable time. The acceptance crosses a letter from A stating that he has not heard from B and that A's offer will terminate if B does not reply by return mail. There is a contract.

e. Acceptance of unknown terms. An offeree, knowing that an offer has been made to him, need not know all its terms. Knowing that an offer has been made, he can accept without investigation of the exact terms, either intentionally or by words or conduct creating an unintended appearance of intention to accept. The governing principles are the same as those for unrecognized offers, explained in Comment b.

Illustration

7. A sends to B an offer to sell a specified lot for $5,000, also stating terms as to time of payment, mortgage security, taxes and insurance. B is so anxious to buy the lot that, without reading any of these additional terms, he sends to A an unconditional acceptance. There is a contract on the terms stated in A's offer.

TOPIC 3. MAKING OF OFFERS

§ 24. Offer Defined.

An offer is the manifestation of willingness to enter into a bargain, so made as to justify another person in understanding that his assent to that bargain is invited and will conclude it.

Comment

a. Offer as promise. An offer may propose an executed sale or barter rather than a contract, or it may propose the exchange of a promise for a performance or an exchange of promises, or it may propose two or more such transactions in combination or in the alternative. In the normal case of an offer of an exchange of promises, or in the case of an offer of a promise for an act, the offer itself is a promise, revocable until accepted. There may also be an offer of a performance, to be exchanged either for a return promise (§ 55) or for a return performance; in such cases the offer is not necessarily a promise, but there are often warranties or other incidental promises.

Illustration

1. A says to B, "That book you are holding is yours if you promise to pay me $5 for it." This is an offer empowering B, by making the requested promise, to make himself owner of the book and thus complete A's performance. In that event there is also an implied warranty of title made by A. See Uniform Commercial Code §§ 2–312, 2–401.

b. Proposal of contingent gift. A proposal of a gift is not an offer within the present definition; there must be an element of exchange. Whether or not a proposal is a promise, it is not an offer unless it specifies a promise or performance by the offeree as the price or consideration to be given by him. It is not enough that there is a promise performable on a certain contingency.

Illustration

2. A promises B $100 if B goes to college. If the circumstances give B reason to know that A is not undertaking to pay B to go to college but is promising a gratuity, there is no offer.

c. Offer as contract. A promise made by the offeror as part of his offer may itself be a contract. Such a contract is commonly called an "option". See § 25.

§ 25. Option Contracts.

An option contract is a promise which meets the requirements for the formation of a contract and limits the promisor's power to revoke an offer.

Comment

a. "Option." A promise which constitutes an option contract may be contained in the offer itself, or it may be made separately in a collateral offer to keep the main offer open. Such promises are commonly called "options." But the word "option" is also often used for any continuing offer, even though revocable, and indeed is sometimes used to refer to any power to make a choice. To avoid ambiguity the phrase "option contract" is used in this Restatement.

Illustrations

1. A promises B under seal or in return for $100 paid or promised by B that A will sell B 100 shares of stock in a specified corporation for $5,000 at any time within thirty days that B selects. There is an option contract under which B has an option.

2. A offers to sell B Blackacre for $5,000 at any time within thirty days. Subsequently A promises under seal or in return for $100 paid or promised by B that the offer will not be revoked. There is an option contract under which B has an option.

b. The need for irrevocable offers. To provide the offeree with a dependable basis for decision whether or not to accept, the rule in many legal systems is that an offer is irrevocable unless it provides otherwise. The common-law rule, on the other hand, resting on the requirement of consideration, permits the revocation of offers even though stated to be firm. See Comment a to § 42. The offeree's need for a dependable basis for decision is met in part by the common-law rule that mailed acceptance prevents revocation. See § 63. Where more is needed, the option contract is available.

c. Types of option contracts. The traditional common-law devices for making an offer irrevocable are the giving of consideration and the affixing of a seal. The requirement of consideration may be met in any of the ways permitted by the rules stated in §§ 71–81: payment of money or some other performance by the offeree is effective, as is a promise of such performance; one option may furnish consideration for another, and a single consideration may support both a present contract and a future option. Compare Illustration 3 to § 47; see § 45 as to the beginning or tender of performance.

The option under seal is the traditional mode of making an offer irrevocable without consideration. Cf. § 95. In some cases a negotiable instrument or a letter of credit may operate as an offer binding without consideration. See Uniform Commercial Code §§ 3–408, 5–105, 5–106. Offers may also be irrevocable by statute or by virtue of reliance by the offeree or other circumstances bringing into play one of the rules stated in §§ 82–94. See, especially, § 87.

d. Effect of option contract. The principal legal consequence of an option contract is that stated in this Section: it limits the promisor's power to revoke an offer. The termination of the offeree's power of acceptance is subject to the requirements for discharge of a contractual duty. See § 37. A revocation by the offeror is not of itself effective, and the offer is properly referred to as an irrevocable offer.

§ 26. Preliminary Negotiations.

A manifestation of willingness to enter into a bargain is not an offer if the person to whom it is addressed knows or has reason to know that the person making it does not intend to conclude a bargain until he has made a further manifestation of assent.

Comment

a. Interpretation of proposals for exchange. The rule stated in this Section is a special application of the definition in § 24 and of the principles governing the interpretation of manifestations of assent. See § 20 and Chapter 9. Conduct which resembles an offer may not be so intended either because there is an intent not to affect legal relations (see § 18), or because the actor does not intend to engage in the conduct (see § 19), or because the proposal is not addressed to the recipient or is not received by the addressee (see § 23), or because the proposal contemplates a gift rather than a bargain (see Comment b to § 24). This Section deals rather with the case where the actor intends to make a bargain in the future, but only if he makes some further manifestation of assent. If the addressee of a proposal has reason to know that no offer is intended, there is no offer even though he understands it to be an offer. "Reason to know" depends not only on the words or other conduct, but also on the circumstances, including previous communications of the parties and the usages of their community or line of business.

b. Advertising. Business enterprises commonly secure general publicity for the goods or services they supply or purchase. Advertisements of goods by display, sign, handbill, newspaper, radio or television are not ordinarily intended or understood as offers to sell. The same is true of catalogues, price lists and circulars, even though the terms of suggested bargains may be stated in some detail. It is of course possible to make an offer by an advertisement directed to the general public (see § 29), but there must ordinarily be some language of commitment or some invitation to take action without further communication.

Illustrations

1. A, a clothing merchant, advertises overcoats of a certain kind for sale at $50. This is not an offer, but an invitation to the public to come and purchase. The addition of the words "Out they go Saturday; First Come First Served" might make the advertisement an offer.

2. A advertises that he will pay $5 for every copy of a certain book that may be sent to him. This is an offer, and A is bound to pay $5 for every copy sent while the offer is unrevoked.

c. *Quotation of price.* A "quotation" of price is usually a statement of price per unit of quantity; it may omit the quantity to be sold, time and place of delivery, terms of payment, and other terms. It is sometimes associated with a price list or circular, but the word "quote" is commonly understood as inviting an offer rather than as making one, even when directed to a particular customer. But just as the word "offer" does not necessarily mean that an offer is intended, so the word "quote" may be used in an offer. In determining whether an offer is made relevant factors include the terms of any previous inquiry, the completeness of the terms of the suggested bargain, and the number of persons to whom a communication is addressed.

Illustration

3. A writes to B, "I can quote you flour at $5 a barrel in carload lots." This is not an offer, in view of the word "quote" and incompleteness of the terms. The same words, in response to an inquiry specifying detailed terms, would probably be an offer; and if A added "for immediate acceptance" the intent to make an offer would be unmistakable.

d. *Invitation of bids or other offers.* Even though terms are specified in detail, it is common for one party to request the other to make an offer. The words "Make me an offer" would normally indicate that no offer is being made, and other conduct such as the announcement of an auction may have similar effect. See § 28. A request for bids on a construction project is similar, even though the practice may be to accept the lowest bid conforming to specifications and other requirements. And forms used or statements made by a traveling salesman may make it clear that the customer is making an offer to be accepted at the salesman's home office. See § 69.

Illustration

4. A writes B, "I am eager to sell my house. I would consider $20,000 for it." B promptly answers, "I will buy your house for $20,000 cash." There is no contract. A's letter is a request or suggestion that an offer be made to him. B has made an offer.

§ 27. Existence of Contract Where Written Memorial Is Contemplated.

Manifestations of assent that are in themselves sufficient to conclude a contract will not be prevented from so operating by the fact that the parties also manifest an intention to prepare and adopt a written memorial thereof; but the circumstances may show that the agreements are preliminary negotiations.

Comment

a. Parties who plan to make a final written instrument as the expression of their contract necessarily discuss the proposed terms of the contract before they enter into it and often, before the final writing is made, agree upon all the terms which they plan to incorporate therein. This they may do orally or by exchange of several writings. It is possible thus to make a contract the terms of which include an obligation to execute subsequently a final writing which shall contain certain provisions. If parties have definitely agreed that they will do so, and that the final writing shall contain these provisions and no others, they have then concluded the contract.

b. On the other hand, if either party knows or has reason to know that the other party regards the agreement as incomplete and intends that no obligation shall exist until other terms are assented to or until the whole has been reduced to another written form, the preliminary negotiations and agreements do not constitute a contract.

c. Among the circumstances which may be helpful in determining whether a contract has been concluded are the following: the extent to which express agreement has been reached on all the terms to be included, whether the contract is of a type usually put in writing, whether it needs a formal writing for its full expression, whether it has few or many details, whether the amount involved is large or small, whether it is a common or unusual contract, whether a standard form of contract is widely used in similar transactions, and whether either party takes any action in preparation for performance during the negotiations. Such circumstances may be shown by oral testimony or by correspondence or other preliminary or partially complete writings.

d. Even though a binding contract is made before a contemplated written memorial is prepared and adopted, the subsequent written document may make a binding modification of the terms previously agreed to.

§ 28. Auctions.

(1) At an auction, unless a contrary intention is manifested,

(a) the auctioneer invites offers from successive bidders which he may accept or reject;

(b) when goods are put up without reserve, the auctioneer makes an offer to sell at any price bid by the highest bidder, and after the auctioneer calls for bids the goods cannot be withdrawn unless no bid is made within a reasonable time;

(c) whether or not the auction is without reserve, a bidder may withdraw his bid until the auctioneer's announcement of completion of the sale, but a bidder's retraction does not revive any previous bid.

(2) Unless a contrary intention is manifested, bids at an auction embody terms made known by advertisement, posting or other publication of which bidders are or should be aware, as modified by any announcement made by the auctioneer when the goods are put up.

Comment

a. Manifestation of contrary intention. The rules stated in this Section reflect the usual understanding at an auction sale. Established auctions often have their own customary rules, made known by publication or by announcement at the commencement of the auction. Such rules prevail even though they are contrary to the rules stated here. Compare the phrase, "unless otherwise agreed," explained in the Introductory Note to this Restatement; see Uniform Commercial Code §§ 1–102, 1–205, 2–328. But where an auction is held pursuant to statute or court order, there may be requirements or terms which cannot be varied by private agreement.

b. Auction with reserve. An auction as ordinarily conducted furnishes an illustration of the principle stated in § 26. The auctioneer, by beginning to auction property, does not impliedly say: "I offer to sell this property to which ever of you makes the highest bid," but rather requests that the bidders make offers to him, as indeed he frequently states in his remarks to those before him. Hence, it is understood that he may reject all bids and withdraw the goods from sale until he announces completion of the sale. Similarly, under § 42, a bidder may withdraw his bid at any time before the announcement of completion. See Uniform Commercial Code § 2–328(3).

Illustrations

1. A publishes an advertisement saying that he will sell his household goods at public auction at a specific time and place. This in no way affects his legal relations.

2. A's auctioneer, in Illustration 1, at the specified time and place holds up a chattel and says, "How much am I bid for this?" After each bid is made he urges others to bid higher. Each bidder makes an offer to the auctioneer, but he makes no offer to them.

c. Advertisement for bids. Governmental agencies or private persons often advertise for bids from construction contractors prepared to undertake the building of a building or other structure, or from persons prepared to supply goods or services. It may be customary or required by law that the contract be awarded to the lowest responsible bidder whose bid conforms to published specifications. A bidder in such a case may seek bids from subcontractors for part of the work. The rule in such cases is much like that governing auctions—unless a contrary intention is manifested, the advertisement is not an offer but a request for offers; bidders on both prime contract and subcontract make offers when they submit bids; and all bids may be rejected. As to irrevocable bids, see § 25.

Illustrations

3. A advertises, "I offer my farm Blackacre for sale to the highest cash bidder and undertake to make conveyance to the person submitting the highest bid received at the address below within the next thirty days." This is an offer, and each bid operates as an acceptance creating rights and duties conditional on no higher bid being received within thirty days.

4. The United States Navy Department advertises for bids on a naval station, the bids to be opened on June 6. Several prospective bidders, including A, request B to submit a "quotation" for the electrical work. B submits to A an "estimate", stating "If our estimate used wire us collect prior to June 6 or else same is withdrawn." A sends the requested telegram and submits a bid which turns out to be low on June 6. Whether or not the advertisement reserved the right to reject all bids, the Navy has that right; B has made an offer which A can accept or reject after the Navy awards the contract to him.

d. Auction without reserve. Where an auction is advertised as "without reserve" and the goods are put up without any contrary announcement, or where the auctioneer opens the sale by announcing that the sale will be "without reserve," the normal understanding is that the goods are not to be withdrawn. There is an offer, and it is made irrevocable by Uniform Commercial Code § 2–328(3), unless no bid is made within a reasonable time. See § 25. Nevertheless, unless a contrary intention is manifested, bids can be withdrawn until the auctioneer announces completion of the sale, as in other auctions; and a bid is discharged when a higher bid is made, even though the higher bid is later withdrawn. Uniform Commercial Code § 2–328(3).

Illustration

5. A advertises a sale of his household furniture without reserve. An article is put up for sale without contrary announcement and B is the highest bidder; but A, dissatisfied with the bidding, either accepts a higher fictitious bid from an agent employed for the purpose, or openly withdraws the article from sale. A is bound by contract to sell the article to B. Neither B nor the others attending the auction have legal ground for complaint if A withdraws the remaining furniture from sale before it is actually put up.

e. Published and announced terms. The terms on which goods are to be sold at auction are often made known in advertisements or catalogues or posted at the place where the auction is to be held. When the goods are put up, the auctioneer commonly refers to such terms, and sometimes he announces a modification of the published terms. Ordinarily bidders are or should be aware of terms so published or announced. A bid need not repeat such terms; it is understood as embodying them. Hence the bidder is held to the published or announced terms, even though he may have neglected to read them or may have arrived at the auction after the announcement was made. Theoretically, a bidder could make an offer on terms different from those announced, but bidders seldom or never do so.

§ 29. To Whom an Offer Is Addressed.

(1) The manifested intention of the offeror determines the person or persons in whom is created a power of acceptance.

(2) An offer may create a power of acceptance in a specified person or in one or more of a specified group or class of persons, acting separately or together, or in anyone or everyone who makes a specified promise or renders a specified performance.

Comment

a. Terms of offer control. The rule stated in Subsection (1) is an elaboration of the definition of offer in § 24, and it is to be read in the light of the rules stated in §§ 23 and 26. The offeror is the master of his offer; just as the making of any offer at all can be avoided by appropriate language or other conduct, so the power of acceptance can be narrowly limited. The offeror is bound only in accordance with his manifested assent; he is not bound just because he receives a consideration as good as or better than the one he bargained for. But if he knows or has reason to know that he is creating an appearance of assent, he may be bound by that appearance. These considerations apply to the identity of the offeree or offerees as well as to the mode of manifesting acceptance (see § 30) and the substance of the exchange (see §§ 31, 32, 58).

b. General offers. An offer may create separate powers of acceptance in an unlimited number of persons, and the exercise of the power by one person may or may not extinguish the power of another. Where one acceptor only is to be selected, various methods of selection are possible: for example, "first come, first served" (see Illustration 1 to § 26), the highest bidder (see Illustration 3 to § 28), or the winner of a contest. Who can accept, and how, is determined by interpretation of the offer.

Illustrations

1. A publishes an offer of reward to whoever will give him certain information. There is no indication that A intends to pay more than once. Any person learning of the offer has power to accept (see Comments a and c to § 23), but the giving of the information by one terminates the power of every other person.

2. A, a bank, issues a traveler's letter of credit promising to repay anyone who makes advances to a named beneficiary, up to a certain amount, the amounts advanced to be noted on the letter of credit. This creates a power of acceptance in anyone to whom the letter is presented, but only if the notation is made and only so long as the noted amounts do not exceed the maximum. See Uniform Commercial Code § 5–108.

3. A, the proprietor of a medical preparation, offers $100 to anyone who contracts a certain disease after using the preparation as directed. B, C and D use it as directed. Each has made a contract independent of the others, and is entitled to the $100 if he later contracts the disease.

§ 30. Form of Acceptance Invited.

(1) An offer may invite or require acceptance to be made by an affirmative answer in words, or by performing or refraining from performing specified act, or may empower the offeree to make a selection of terms in his acceptance.

(2) Unless otherwise indicated by the language or the circumstances, an offer invites acceptance in any manner and by any medium reasonable in the circumstances.

Comment

a. Required form. The offeror is the master of his offer. See Comment a to § 29. The form of acceptance is less likely to affect the substance of the bargain than the identity of the offeree, and is often quite immaterial. But the offeror is entitled to insist on a particular mode of manifestation of assent. The terms of the offer may limit acceptance to a particular mode; whether it does so is a matter of interpretation.

Illustration

1. A sends a letter to B stating the terms of a proposed contract. At the end he writes, "You can accept this offer only by signing on the dotted line below my own signature." A replies by telegram, "I accept your offer." There is no contract.

b. Invited form. Insistence on a particular form of acceptance is unusual. Offers often make no express reference to the form of acceptance; sometimes ambiguous language is used. Language referring to a particular mode of acceptance is often intended and understood as suggestion rather than limitation; the suggested mode is then authorized, but other modes are not precluded. In other cases language which in terms refers to the mode of acceptance is intended and understood as referring to some more important aspect of the transaction, such as the time limit for acceptance. See §§ 60, 63.

c. Term supplied in acceptance. An offer may contain a choice of terms, and may invite or require an acceptance making a selection among the terms stated. Or the offer may indicate a term such as quantity to be filled in by the offeree. An acceptance to be effective must comply with the terms of the offer, and those terms or the circumstances may make it plain that the acceptance must specify terms. Section 60. In such cases the offer does not fail for indefiniteness, but no contract is made by an attempted acceptance which does not supply the term as indicated. See § 33. The offer assents in advance to the term chosen or filled in by the offeree.

Illustration

2. A offers to deliver to B at any time during the next 30 days any amount of coal, up to 100 tons, for which B will promise to pay $15 a ton. In order to accept this offer B must specify the amount of coal he desires and must promise to pay $15 a ton for it. An order for 50 tons by B concludes a definite agreement.

d. Form not specified. Interpretation of the offer is necessary in order to determine whether there is any limitation on the mode of acceptance. The meaning given the offer by the offeree controls if it is a meaning of which the offeror knew or had reason to know. See §§ 19, 20. Since limitation is not customary, the offeror has reason to know that the offeree may understand that the offer can be accepted in any reasonable manner, and a contrary intention is not operative unless manifested. See Uniform Commercial Code § 2–206(1).

Illustrations

3. A orally offers to sell and deliver to B 100 tons of coal at $20 a ton payable 30 days after delivery. B replies, "I accept your offer." B has manifested assent in a sufficient form, even though A neither suggested nor required that form.

4. A makes a bid at an auction sale. By the usual custom at auctions, the auctioneer may accept by letting the hammer fall, by saying "Sold", or by any words manifesting acceptance.

e. Reasonable manner. As to acceptance by promise or non-promissory performance, see § 32. Cases where the contract leaves terms to be chosen in the course of performance are the subject of § 34. What manner and medium are reasonable is governed by the rules stated in §§ 60 and 65. Sometimes, though not ordinarily, even silent inaction may be effective as a mode of acceptance. See § 69.

§ 31. Offer Proposing a Single Contract or a Number of Contracts.

An offer may propose the formation of a single contract by a single acceptance or the formation of a number of contracts by successive acceptances from time to time.

Comment

a. Separate contracts. An offer may request several acts or promises as the indivisible exchange for the promise or promises in the offer, or it may request a series of contracts to be made from time to time. Whether several promises create several contracts or are all part of one contract is determined by principles of interpretation stated in Chapter 9.

b. Continuing guaranty. A standard example of a divisible offer is the continuing guaranty, the promise to guarantee performance of such obligations of a specified type as a third party may incur to the offeree from time to time. An offer of suretyship may be directed to one offeree or to many offerees; it may contemplate a single extension of credit by the offeree or many; it may or may not be expressly limited in time or amount. See Restatement of Security §§ 82–88. Where there is a continuing guaranty as to future loans or sales to be made by the offeree and each loan or sale furnishes the sole consideration for the corresponding part of the guaranty, the guaranty is often characterized as an offer for a series of separate contracts.

This characterization, if sound, means that the offer is revocable and revoked by death (see §§ 47, 48), and that a separate acceptance is required for each contract (see § 50 et seq.). Often, however, the characterization is unsound. Thus, where the rule of § 54 is inapplicable because the offer requests a notification, although communication of acceptance is required, a single notice of intention to act is ordinarily sufficient. Again, where the guaranty is under seal or is supported by a consideration, it is more than a mere offer. Even in such cases guaranties are commonly revocable not only where a power of revocation is expressly reserved or fairly implied but also in circumstances where there is no manifested intention to reserve such a power.

Whether the case is one of divisible offer or of reserved power, the power of revocation is reinforced by the considerations underlying limitation of the recovery of damages for avoidable harm and denial of specific performance where return performance is not well secured (see §§ 350, 363). Even if there is no absolute power of revocation, as where a substantial consideration is given at the outset, those considerations may limit relief, once notice of revocation is given, to obligations incurred before the promisee has had a reasonable opportunity to prevent further obligations from arising or to secure a substitute surety. In many States statutes give particular types of sureties a right to apply to the court for relief from future obligations.

c. Sale of goods. The standing offer for the sale or purchase of goods furnishes another example of the divisible offer. Continuing arrangements for the sale of goods may provide terms for contracts made under them even though there is no offer until particular goods are ordered or actually delivered. See Illustration 4 to § 21. Or there may be a divisible standing offer which can be separately accepted with respect to each lot of goods by either a promise or a performance. See Comment c to § 32. Or the continuing arrangement may itself be a binding contract, as in the case of an output or requirements contract. See § 77.

Illustrations

1. A offers B, a railway company, such quantities of certain goods as B's storekeeper may order from time to time during the next twelve months. In the absence of a revocation, each order of B's storekeeper during that period creates a separate contract for the quantity ordered.

2. A offers B to sell and deliver to him during the following year any quantity of goods between 4000 and 6000 pounds in amount, acceptance to specify the total quantity. B must within a reasonable time specify a particular amount of not less than 4000 pounds and not more than 6000 pounds in order to create a contract; and there can be but one acceptance and one contract.

3. A offers B to sell him in monthly installments the coal which B may require in his business during the next six months, not exceeding one hundred tons in any one month. B has an established manufacturing business which has used an average of 75 tons of coal a month for several years. The offer is one for a single contract under which B promises not to buy coal elsewhere during the six months unless he has excess requirements.

§ 32. Invitation of Promise or Performance.

In case of doubt an offer is interpreted as inviting the offeree to accept either by promising to perform what the offer requests or by rendering the performance, as the offeree chooses.

Comment

a. Promise or performance. In the ordinary commercial bargain a party expects to be bound only if the other party either renders the return performance or binds himself to do so either by express words or by part performance or other conduct. Unless the language or the circumstances indicate that one party is to have an option, therefore, the usual offer invites an acceptance which either amounts to performance or constitutes a promise. The act of acceptance may be merely symbolic of assent and promise, or it may also be part or all of the performance bargained for. See §§ 2, 4, 18, 19. In either case notification of the offeror may be necessary. See §§ 54, 56.

The rule of this Section is a particular application of the rule stated in § 30(2). The offeror is often indifferent as to whether acceptance takes the form of words of promise or acts of performance, and his words literally referring to one are often intended and understood to refer to either. Where performance takes time, however, the beginning of performance may constitute a promise to complete it. See § 62.

Illustrations

1. A writes B, "If you will mow my lawn next week, I will pay you $10." B can accept A's offer either by promptly promising to mow the lawn or by mowing it as requested.

2. A says to B: "If you finish that table you are making and deliver it to my house today, I will give you $100 for it." B replies, "I'll do it." There is a contract. B could also accept by delivering the table as requested.

b. Offer limited to acceptance by performance only. Language or circumstances sometimes make it clear that the offeree is not to bind himself in advance of performance. His promise may be worthless to the offeror, or the circumstances may make it unreasonable for the offeror to expect a firm commitment from the offeree. In such cases, the offer does not invite a promissory acceptance, and a promise is ineffective as an acceptance. Examples are found in offers of reward or of prizes in a contest, made to a large number of people but to be accepted by only one. See § 29. Non-commercial arrangements among relatives and friends... and offers which leave important terms to be fixed by the offeree in the course of performance (see §§ 33, 34) provide other examples.

It is a separate question whether the offeree undertakes any responsibility to complete performance once begun, or whether he takes any responsibility for the quality of the performance when completed.

Illustrations

3. A publishes the following offer: "I will pay $50 for the return of my diamond bracelet lost yesterday on State Street." B sees this advertisement and at once sends a letter to A, saying "I accept your offer and will search for this bracelet." There is no acceptance.

4. A writes to B, his nephew aged 16, that if B will refrain from drinking, using tobacco, swearing, and playing cards or billiards for money until he becomes 21 years of age, A will pay B $5,000. B makes a written reply promising so to refrain. There is probably no contract. But if B begins to refrain, A may be bound by an option contract under § 45; and if B refrains until he becomes 21, A is bound to pay him $5,000.

c. Shipment of goods. An order or other offer to buy goods for prompt or current shipment normally invites acceptance either by a prompt promise to ship or by prompt or current shipment. Uniform Commercial Code § 2–206(1)(b). If non-conforming goods are shipped, the shipment may be an acceptance and at the same time a breach. But there is no acceptance if the offeror has reason to know that none is intended, as where the offeree promptly notifies him that non-conforming goods are being shipped and are offered only as an accommodation to him.

Illustrations

5. A mails a written order to B, offering to buy specified machinery on specified terms. The order provides, "Ship at once." B immediately mails a letter to A, saying "I accept your offer and will ship at once." This is a sufficient acceptance to form a contract. See Uniform Commercial Code § 2–206(1).

6. In Illustration 5, instead of mailing a letter of acceptance, B immediately ships the machinery as requested. This is a sufficient acceptance to form a contract. If the machinery is defective, the shipment is both an acceptance forming a contract and a breach of that contract, unless B promptly notifies A that the shipment is offered only as an accommodation to A. See Uniform Commercial Code § 2–206(1).

§ 33. Certainty.

(1) Even though a manifestation of intention is intended to be understood as an offer, it cannot be accepted so as to form a contract unless the terms of the contract are reasonably certain.

(2) The terms of a contract are reasonably certain if they provide a basis for determining the existence of a breach and for giving an appropriate remedy.

(3) The fact that one or more terms of a proposed bargain are left open or uncertain may show that a manifestation of intention is not intended to be understood as an offer or as an acceptance.

Comment

a. Certainty of terms. It is sometimes said that the agreement must be capable of being given an exact meaning and that all the performances to be rendered must be certain. Such statements may be appropriate in determining whether a manifestation of intention is intended to be understood as an offer. But the actions of the parties may show conclusively that they have intended to conclude a binding agreement, even though one or more terms are missing or are left to be agreed upon. In such cases courts endeavor, if possible, to attach a sufficiently definite meaning to the bargain. An offer which appears to be indefinite may be given precision by usage of trade or by course of dealing between the parties. Terms may be supplied by factual implication, and in recurring situations the law often supplies a term in the absence of agreement to the contrary. See § 5, defining "term." Where the parties have intended to conclude a bargain, uncertainty as to incidental or collateral matters is seldom fatal to the existence of the contract. If the essential terms are so uncertain that there is no basis for deciding whether the agreement has been kept or broken, there is no contract. But even in such cases partial performance or other action in reliance on the agreement may reinforce it under § 34.

b. Certainty in basis for remedy. The rule stated in Subsection (2) reflects the fundamental policy that contracts should be made by the parties, not by the courts, and hence that remedies for breach of contract must have a basis in the agreement of the parties. Where the parties have intended to make a contract and there is a reasonably certain basis for granting a remedy, the same policy supports the granting of the remedy. The test is not certainty as to what the parties were to do nor as to the exact amount of damages due to the plaintiff; uncertainty may preclude one remedy without affecting another. See Uniform Commercial Code § 2–204(3) and Comment.

Thus the degree of certainty required may be affected by the dispute which arises and by the remedy sought. Courts decide the disputes before them, not other hypothetical disputes which might have arisen. It is less likely that a reasonably certain term will be supplied by construction as to a matter which has been the subject of controversy between the parties than as to one which is raised only as an afterthought. In some cases greater definiteness may be required for specific performance than for an award of damages; in others the impossibility of accurate assessment of damages may furnish a reason for specific relief. Partial relief may sometimes be granted when uncertainty prevents full-scale enforcement through normal remedies. See §§ 357–62.

Illustrations

1. A agrees to sell and B to buy goods for $2,000, $1,000 in cash and the "balance on installment terms over a period of two years," with a provision for liquidated damages. If it is found that both parties manifested an intent to conclude a binding agreement, the indefiniteness of the quoted language does not prevent the award of the liquidated damages.

2. A agrees to sell and B to buy a specific tract of land for $10,000, $4,000 in cash and $6,000 on mortgage. A agrees to obtain the mortgage loan for B or, if unable to do so, to lend B the amount, but the terms of loan are not stated, although both parties manifest an intent to conclude a binding agreement. The contract is too indefinite to support a decree of specific performance against B, but B may obtain such a decree if he offers to pay the full price in cash.

c. Preliminary negotiations. The rule stated in Subsection (3) is a particular application of the rule stated in § 26 on preliminary negotiations. Incompleteness of terms is one of the principal reasons why advertisements and price quotations are ordinarily not interpreted as offers. Similarly, if the parties to negotiations for sale manifest an intention not to be bound until the price is fixed or agreed, the law gives effect to that intention. Uniform Commercial Code § 2–305(4). The more terms the parties leave open, the less likely it is that they have intended to conclude a binding agreement. See Uniform Commercial Code § 2–204 and Comment.

d. Uncertain time of performance. Valid contracts are often made which do not specify the time for performance. Where the contract calls for a single performance such as the rendering of a service or the delivery of goods, the time for performance is a "reasonable time." Compare § 41 on the time for accepting an offer; see Uniform Commercial Code §§ 1–204, 2–309(1). Payment is due when the service is completed or the goods received. Uniform Commercial Code § 2–310. When the contract calls for successive performances but is indefinite in duration, it is commonly terminable by either party, with or without a requirement of reasonable notice. Uniform Commercial Code §§ 2–309(2), (3).

Illustrations

3. A and B promise that certain performances shall be mutually rendered by them "immediately" or "at once," or "promptly," or "as soon as possible," or "in about one month." All these promises are sufficiently definite to form contracts.

4. A promises B to sell certain goods to him, and B promises to pay a specified price therefor. No time of performance is fixed. The time for delivery and payment is a reasonable time. Uniform Commercial Code §§ 2–309(1), 2–310(a). What is a reasonable time depends on the nature, purpose and circumstances of the action to be taken. Uniform Commercial Code § 1–204(2).

5. A offers to employ B for a stated compensation as long as B is able to do specified work, or as long as a specified business is carried on, and B accepts the terms offered. The length of the engagement is sufficiently definite for the formation of a contract.

6. A promises B to serve B as chauffeur, and B promises to pay him $100 a month. Nothing further is stated as to the duration of the employment. There is at once a contract for one month's service. At the end of the first month, in the absence of revocation, there is a contract for a second month. But circumstances may show that such an agreement merely specifies the rate of compensation for an employment at will.

e. Indefinite price. Where the parties manifest an intention not to be bound unless the amount of money to be paid by one of them is fixed or agreed and it is not fixed or agreed there is no contract. Uniform Commercial Code § 2–305(4). Where they intend to conclude a contract for the sale of goods, however, and the price is not settled, the price is a reasonable price at the time of delivery if (a) nothing is said as to price, or (b) the price is left to be agreed by the parties and they fail to agree, or (c) the price is to be fixed in terms of some agreed market or other standard as set or recorded by a third person or agency and it is not so set or recorded. Uniform Commercial Code § 2–305(1). Or one party may be given power to fix the price within limits set by agreement or custom or good faith. Similar principles apply to contracts for the rendition of service. But substantial damages cannot be recovered unless they can be estimated with reasonable certainty (§ 352), and if the contract is entirely executory and specific performance is not an appropriate remedy, relief may be limited to the recovery of benefits conferred and specific expense incurred in reliance on the contract.

Illustrations

7. A promises to sell and B to buy goods "at cost plus a nice profit." The quoted words strongly indicate that the parties have not yet concluded a bargain.

8. A promises to do a specified piece of work and B promises to pay a price to be thereafter mutually agreed. The provision for future agreement as to price strongly indicates that the parties do not intend to be bound. If they manifest an intent to be bound, the price is a reasonable price at the time for doing the work.

f. Other indefinite terms. Promises may be indefinite in other aspects than time and price. The more important the uncertainty, the stronger the indication is that the parties do not intend to be bound; minor items are more likely to be left to the option of one of the parties or to what is customary or reasonable. Even when the parties intend to enter into a contract, uncertainty may be so great as to frustrate their intention. Thus a promise by A to give B employment, even though consideration is paid for it, does not provide a basis for any remedy if neither the character of the employment nor the compensation therefor is stated. In such cases the consideration paid, or its value, can be recovered. Restatement of Restitution §§ 15, 40, 47, 53.

Illustrations

9. A promises B to execute a conveyance in fee or a lease for a year of specified land and B promises to make specified payments therefor. Although the terms of leases and conveyances vary, the promises are interpreted as providing for documents in the form in common local use, and are sufficiently definite to form contracts.

10. A promises to sell and B to buy all goods of a certain character which B shall need in his business during the ensuing year. The quantity to be sold is sufficiently definite to provide a basis for remedy, since the promises are interpreted to refer to B's actual good-faith requirements. Uniform Commercial Code § 2–306.

11. A promises B to construct a building according to stated plans and specifications, and B promises A to pay $30,000 therefor. It is also provided that the character of the window fastenings shall be subject to further agreement of the parties. Unless a contrary intention is manifested, the indefiniteness of the agreement with reference to this matter will not prevent the formation of a contract.

12. A and B have a settlement of accounts, and A promises to pay B a stated balance, "errors and omissions excepted." A's promise is reasonably certain in the absence of a showing of error or omission, but it may be corrected on such a showing.

§ 34. Certainty and Choice of Terms; Effect of Performance or Reliance.

(1) The terms of a contract may be reasonably certain even though it empowers one or both parties to make a selection of terms in the course of performance.

(2) Part performance under an agreement may remove uncertainty and establish that a contract enforceable as a bargain has been formed.

(3) Action in reliance on an agreement may make a contractual remedy appropriate even though uncertainty is not removed.

Comment

a. Choice in the course of performance. A bargain may be concluded which leaves a choice of terms to be made by one party or the other. If the agreement is otherwise sufficiently definite to be a contract, it is not made invalid by the fact that it leaves particulars of performance to be specified by one of the parties. Uniform Commercial Code § 2–311(1). The more important the choice is, the more it is likely that the parties do not intend to be bound until the choice is made. But even on such matters as subject matter and price, one party is often given a wide choice. If the parties intend to make a contract and there is a reasonably certain basis for granting an appropriate remedy, such alternative terms do not invalidate the contract. See § 33. Often a basis for remedy can be found in the rule of Comment b to § 362, permitting a remedy in accordance with the alternative chosen or in accordance with the alternative that will result in the smallest recovery. In other cases the failure of one party to choose may shift the right to choose to the other party or to an arbitrator or to the court.

Illustrations

1. A promises B to give him any one of a number of specified things which A shall choose, and B promises A to pay a specified price. The agreement is sufficiently definite to be a contract. A method is provided for determining what A is to give; though what he gives is subject to his choice, he must give some one of the things specified.

2. A agrees to sell and B to buy 50,000 pounds of white worsted yarn on a basis which enables the parties to compute 48 prices for 48 styles and sizes. The agreement is sufficiently definite to be a contract. Unless otherwise agreed specifications relating to assortment of the goods are at the buyer's option, but if B does not make a seasonable specification, A may proceed to perform in any reasonable manner. Uniform Commercial Code § 2–311.

b. Unlimited choice; good faith and fair dealing. If one party to an agreement is given an unlimited choice, that party may not be a promisor (see Comment e to § 2), and the contract may fail for want of consideration. See § 79. The other party's promise may be unconscionable and may be wholly or partly illegal. Compare §§ 178, 208; see Uniform Commercial Code § 2–302. These difficulties are commonly avoided, however, by the fact that the choice granted is limited. Just as the power of selection may be given not only by explicit agreement but also by course of dealing or usage of trade or course of performance under the particular agreement or by other implication from circumstances, so limits on the power may be either express or implied. Often the choice made must be reasonable in the circumstances. See § 228; Uniform Commercial Code §§ 2–306, 2–311(1). And in any event discretionary power granted by a commercial contract must be exercised in good faith and in accordance with fair dealing. Uniform Commercial Code §§ 1–203, 2–103(1) (b). A price to be fixed by a seller or buyer of goods, for example, means a price for him to fix in good faith. Uniform Commercial Code § 2–305(2).

Illustration

3. A promises B to do specified work or to transfer certain goods or land and B promises A to make specified payments if the work or property is satisfactory to B in specified respects. These promises are sufficiently definite to form contracts, since B's duty depends not on his mere whim but on his exercise of an honest judgment, or in some cases of a reasonable judgment. See § 228.

c. Subsequent conduct removing uncertainty. Indefiniteness may prevent enforcement of a contract in two different ways: it may mean that a manifestation of intention is not intended to be understood as an offer; or, even though the parties intended to enter into a contract, there may be no sufficient basis for giving an appropriate remedy. See § 33. Subsequent conduct of one or both parties may remove either obstacle or both. Preliminary manifestations may propose terms which are incorporated in a subsequent offer and become part of a contract. See Comment f to § 26. The contract may then be thought of as concluded only at the time of the acceptance of the subsequent offer. Or part performance may give meaning to indefinite terms of an agreement, or may have the effect of eliminating indefinite alternatives by waiver or modification. Uniform Commercial Code § 2–208. In such cases a bargain may be concluded, but it may be impossible to identify offer or acceptance or to determine the moment of formation. See § 22(2). The obstacle of indefiniteness may nevertheless be removed.

d. Reliance and appropriate remedies. The need for a particular remedy may sometimes become apparent as a result of part performance or other action in reliance on an indefinite agreement, even though the original uncertainty remains. The appropriate remedy may be non-contractual. Thus benefits conferred on the other party under an agreement void for indefiniteness may ordinarily be recovered. Restatement of Restitution §§ 15, 40, 47, 53. In some such cases the measure of benefit may appropriately be the value of the plaintiff's performance rather than the economic benefit to the defendant. See Restatement of Restitution § 155 and Caveat; compare § 370 of this Restatement. Where one party has suffered loss because of his reliance on such an agreement, the other party may be subject to liability in tort. See Restatement, Second, Torts § 323, and Caveat; Restatement, Second, Agency § 378.

In many cases, however, reliance makes appropriate a contractual remedy. Thus the agreement may be treated as divisible and recovery for benefits conferred may then be permitted at the promised rate. An express or implied promise may be found to reimburse expenses incurred pursuant to the indefinite agreement. In some cases partial or full enforcement through an award of damages for breach of contract or a decree of specific performance may become appropriate. See § 90. As to detrimental reliance not consisting of the performance of the agreement, compare Comment a to § 129.

Illustrations

4. A says to B: "I will employ you for some time at $10 a day." An acceptance by B either orally or in writing will not create a contract. But if B serves one or more days with A's assent A is bound to pay $10 for each day's service.

5. A agrees to sell and B to buy a specific house and lot for $10,000, mortgage terms to be agreed. At B's request, reinforced by a threat not to perform, A makes certain alterations in the house, which add nothing to its value. B then repudiates the agreement without reference to mortgage terms. A may recover the cost of the alterations. See § 349.

6. A leases land to B for three years, giving B an option to buy the land for $10,000 "on terms to be agreed on." B occupies the land for three years, making extensive improvements, and seeks to exercise the option, offering to pay "either in cash or upon such terms as A may impose." B may obtain a decree of specific performance. See Illustration 2 to § 362.

TOPIC 4. DURATION OF THE OFFEREE'S POWER OF ACCEPTANCE

§ 35. The Offeree's Power of Acceptance.

(1) An offer gives to the offeree a continuing power to complete the manifestation of mutual assent by acceptance of the offer.

(2) A contract cannot be created by acceptance of an offer after the power of acceptance has been terminated in one of the ways listed in § 36.

Comment

a. "Duration of an offer." It is common to speak of the duration "of an offer." But "offer" is defined in § 24 as a manifestation of assent, and the reference here is not to the time occupied by the offeror's conduct but to the duration of its legal operation. Hence this topic speaks of the duration and termination of the offeree's power rather than the duration and termination of the offer.

b. Continuing power. Under Subsection (1) the offeree's power arises when the offeror's manifestation of assent is complete. Since the acceptance must have reference to the offer it is ordinarily necessary that the offeree have knowledge of the offer. See § 23. Once the power arises it continues until terminated. Methods of termination are listed in § 36 and explained in the following sections. There is no requirement that the offer be accompanied by the mental assent of the offeror, or that mental assent which exists at the time of the offer continue until the time of acceptance. See § 19.

c. Creation of contract. Exercise of the power of acceptance concludes an agreement and a bargain, and thus satisfies one of the requirements for formation of an informal contract enforceable as a bargain. See §§ 17, 18. But a contract is not created unless the other requirements are met. Thus there may be no consideration; or impossibility or illegality may prevent any duty of performance from arising.

§ 36. Methods of Termination of the Power of Acceptance.

(1) An offeree's power of acceptance may be terminated by

    (a) rejection or counter-offer by the offeree, or

    (b) lapse of time, or

    (c) revocation by the offeror, or

    (d) death or incapacity of the offeror or offeree.

(2) In addition, an offeree's power of acceptance is terminated by the non-occurrence of any condition of acceptance under the terms of the offer.

Comment

a. Scope. This Section merely lists the methods of termination which are possible. The circumstances under which each method operates are stated in §§ 36–49.

b. Conditions of acceptance. Subsection (2) provides for any condition of acceptance arising under the terms of the offer itself. Compare the definition of "condition" in § 224. A condition of acceptance, like a condition, may be express or implied in fact or constructive. See Comment c to § 226. Thus by common understanding a reward offer can ordinarily be accepted only once; the first acceptance terminates the power of acceptance of other offerees. See Illustration 1 to § 29. Compare the effect on a bid at an auction when a higher bid is made. See § 28(1)(c).

c. Impossibility and illegality. The power of acceptance may be terminated by the death or destruction of a person or thing essential for performance or by supervening legal prohibition. The extent to which such events have the effect of a failure of a condition of acceptance depends on the terms of the offer and on the circumstances. Such events may also prevent a duty of performance from arising from an acceptance if they occur before the offer is made, or may discharge a duty of performance if they occur after acceptance. The effects of such events are therefore stated in Chapters 6–12, which deal with Mistake

(Chapter 6), Misrepresentation, Duress and Undue Influence (Chapter 7), Unenforceability on Grounds of Public Policy (Chapter 8), The Scope of Contractual Obligations (including conditions and similar events) (Chapter 9), Performance and Non-performance (Chapter 10), Impracticability of Performance and Frustration of Purpose (Chapter 11) and Discharge by Assent or Alteration (Chapter 12).

§ 37. Termination of Power of Acceptance Under Option Contract.

Notwithstanding §§ 38–49, the power of acceptance under an option contract is not terminated by rejection or counter-offer, by revocation, or by death or incapacity of the offeror, unless the requirements are met for the discharge of a contractual duty.

Comment

a. Option contracts. An option contract is a promise which meets the requisites of a contract and limits the promisor's power to revoke an offer. See § 25. The power given the offeree by such an option differs from a power to specify particulars of performance after a contract is made, since the offeree under an option contract can choose not to undertake any contractual duties at all. But both types of choice may be given to the same offeree at the same time. See § 34(1).

b. Requirements for discharge. An option contract binds the offeror and gives rise to a duty of performance conditional on the offeree's acceptance exercising the option. The rules governing discharge of contractual duties therefore apply. See Chapter 12; compare Comment c to § 42; § 256 on the nullification of a repudiation.

Illustrations

1. A leases land to B, giving B an option to purchase the land for $10,000 in cash during the term of the lease. Misinterpreting the lease, B attempts to exercise the option by tendering a mortgage for $10,000. A refuses to accept the mortgage. B retains power to exercise the option by a tender conforming to the terms of the lease.

2. A gives B the same option as that stated in Illustration 1. A receives an offer from C to purchase the land and so informs B. B states that he will not exercise the option and A conveys the land to C. B's power to exercise the option is terminated. See §§ 89; 273–85.

§ 38. Rejection.

(1) An offeree's power of acceptance is terminated by his rejection of the offer, unless the offeror has manifested a contrary intention.

(2) A manifestation of intention not to accept an offer is a rejection unless the offeree manifests an intention to take it under further advisement.

Comment

a. The probability of reliance. The legal consequences of a rejection rest on its probable effect on the offeror. An offeror commonly takes steps to prepare for performance in the event that the offer is accepted. If the offeree states in effect that he declines to accept the offer, it is highly probable that the offeror will change his plans in reliance on the statement. The reliance is likely to take such negative forms as failure to prepare or failure to send a notice of revocation, and hence is likely to be difficult or impossible to prove. To protect the offeror in such reliance, the power of acceptance is terminated without proof of reliance. This rule also protects the offeree in accordance with his manifested intention that his subsequent conduct is not to be understood as an acceptance.

Illustrations

1. A makes an offer to B and adds: "This offer will remain open for a week." B rejects the offer the following day, but later in the week purports to accept it. There is no contract unless the offer was itself a contract. B's purported acceptance is itself a new offer.

2. A makes an offer to sell water rights to B, and states, "You may accept this offer by applying to the appropriate authority for a permit to use the water." B rejects the offer, obtains water rights elsewhere, and later applies for the permit contemplated by the offer. There is no contract. Even if A's offer was a binding option, B has not exercised it.

b. Contrary statement of offeror or offeree. The rule of this Section is designed to give effect to the intentions of the parties, and a manifestation of intention on the part of either that the offeree's power of acceptance is to continue is effective. Thus if the offeree states that he rejects the offer for the present but will reconsider it at a future time, there is no basis for a change of position by the offeror in reliance on a rejection, and under Subsection (2) there is no rejection. Similarly a statement in the offer that it will continue in effect despite a rejection is effective, and a similar statement after a rejection makes a new offer.

Where the manifestation of intention of either party is misunderstood by the other, the principles underlying § 20 apply. If the offeror is justified in inferring from the words or conduct of the offeree, interpreted in the light of the offeror's prior words or conduct, that the offeree intends not to accept the offer and not to take it under further advisement, the power of acceptance is terminated. Compare § 39.

§ 39. Counter-Offers.

(1) A counter-offer is an offer made by an offeree to his offeror relating to the same matter as the original offer and proposing a substituted bargain differing from that proposed by the original offer.

(2) An offeree's power of acceptance is terminated by his making of a counter-offer, unless the offeror has manifested a contrary intention or unless the counter-offer manifests a contrary intention of the offeree.

Comment

a. Counter-offer as rejection. It is often said that a counter-offer is a rejection, and it does have the same effect in terminating the offeree's power of acceptance. But in other respects a counter-offer differs from a rejection. A counter-offer must be capable of being accepted; it carries negotiations on rather than breaking them off. The termination of the power of acceptance by a counter-offer merely carries out the usual understanding of bargainers that one proposal is dropped when another is taken under consideration; if alternative proposals are to be under consideration at the same time, warning is expected.

Illustration

1. A offers B to sell him a parcel of land for $5,000, stating that the offer will remain open for thirty days. B replies, "I will pay $4800 for the parcel," and on A's declining that, B writes, within the thirty day period, "I accept your offer to sell for $5,000." There is no contract unless A's offer was [an option supported by consideration], or unless A's reply to the counter-offer manifested an intention to renew his original offer.

b. Qualified acceptance, inquiry or separate offer. A common type of counter-offer is the qualified or conditional acceptance, which purports to accept the original offer but makes acceptance expressly conditional on assent to additional or different terms. See § 59. Such a counter-offer must be distinguished from an unqualified acceptance which is accompanied by a proposal for modification of the agreement or for a separate agreement. A mere inquiry regarding the possibility of different terms, a request for a better offer, or a comment upon the terms of the offer, is ordinarily not a counter-offer. Such responses to an offer may be too tentative or indefinite to be offers of any kind; or they may deal with new matters rather than a substitution for the original offer; or their language may manifest an intention to keep the original offer under consideration.

Illustration

2. A makes the same offer to B as that stated in Illustration 1, and B replies, "Won't you take less?" A answers, "No." An acceptance thereafter by B within the thirty-day period is effective. B's inquiry was not a counter-offer, and A's original offer stands.

c. Contrary statement of offeror or offeree. An offeror may state in his offer that it shall continue for a stated time in any event and that in the meanwhile he will be glad to receive counter-offers. Likewise an offeree may state that he is holding the offer under advisement, but that if the offeror desires to close a bargain at once the offeree makes a specific counter-offer. Such an answer will not extend the time that the original offer remains open, but will not cut that time short. Compare § 38.

Illustration

3. A makes the same offer to B as that stated in Illustration 1. B replies "I am keeping your offer under advisement, but if you wish to close the matter at once I will give you $4800." A does not reply, and within the thirty-day period B accepts the original offer. B's acceptance is effective.

§ 40. Time When Rejection or Counter-Offer Terminates the Power of Acceptance.

Rejection or counter-offer by mail or telegram does not terminate the power of acceptance until received by the offeror, but limits the power so that a letter or telegram of acceptance started after the sending of an otherwise effective rejection or counter-offer is only a counter-offer unless the acceptance is received by the offeror before he receives the rejection or counter-offer.

Comment

a. Receipt essential. A rejection terminates the offeree's power of acceptance because of the probability of reliance by the offeror, and there is no possibility of reliance until the rejection is received. See § 38. Hence the power continues until receipt. The same rule is applied by analogy to a counter-offer, although the reason is somewhat different: a counter-offer cannot be taken under consideration as a substitute proposal until it is received. See § 39. As to when a rejection is received, see § 68; compare Restatement, Second, Agency §§ 268–83, Uniform Commercial Code § 1–201(25) to (27).

b. Subsequent acceptance. Since a rejection or counter-offer is not effective until received, it may until that time be superseded by an acceptance. But the probability remains that the offeror will rely on the rejection or counter-offer if it is received before the acceptance. To protect the offeror in such reliance, the offeree who has dispatched a rejection is deprived of the benefit of the rule that an acceptance may take effect on dispatch (§ 63). The rule of this Section only applies, however, to a rejection or counter-offer which is otherwise effective. A rejection or counter-offer may be denied effect to terminate the power of acceptance if the original offer is itself a contract or if the offeror or offeree manifests an intention that the power continue. See §§ 37–39. Similarly, a purported rejection or counter-offer dispatched after an effective acceptance is in effect a revocation of acceptance, governed by § 63 rather than by this Section.

Illustration

1. A makes B an offer by mail. B immediately after receiving the offer mails a letter of rejection. Within the time permitted by the offer B accepts. This acceptance creates a contract only if received before the rejection, or if the power of acceptance continues under §§ 37–39.

§ 41. Lapse of Time.

(1) An offeree's power of acceptance is terminated at the time specified in the offer, or, if no time is specified, at the end of a reasonable time.

(2) What is a reasonable time is a question of fact, depending on all the circumstances existing when the offer and attempted acceptance are made.

(3) Unless otherwise indicated by the language or the circumstances, and subject to the rule stated in § 49, an offer sent by mail is seasonably accepted if an acceptance is mailed at any time before midnight on the day on which the offer is received.

Comment

a. Specified time. Just as the offer may prescribe the identity of the offeree (§ 29) or the form of acceptance (§ 30), so it may prescribe a time limit for acceptance. Such a limitation must be complied with. See § 60. In cases of misunderstanding, the principles underlying § 20 are applicable. See Chapter 9.

b. Reasonable time. In the absence of a contrary indication, just as acceptance may be made in any manner and by any medium which is reasonable in the circumstances (§ 30), so it may be made at any time which is reasonable in the circumstances. The circumstances to be considered have a wide range: they include the nature of the proposed contract, the purposes of the parties, the course of dealing between them, and any relevant usages of trade. In general, the question is what time would be thought satisfactory to the offeror by a reasonable man in the position of the offeree; but circumstances not known to the offeree may be relevant to show that the time actually taken by the offeree was satisfactory to the offeror. See Illustration 6 to § 23.

c. Time for acceptance by act; rewards. Where the offeree is invited to accept by performing or refraining from performing an act, a reasonable time for so doing is ordinarily a reasonable time for accepting. But the purposes of the offeror, if the offeree knows or has reason to know of them, must also be taken into account. Thus an offer of reward for the capture of the person guilty of a specific crime cannot ordinarily be accepted after the statute of limitations has barred prosecution.

Illustrations

1. A publishes an offer of reward for information leading to the arrest and conviction of the person guilty of a specified murder. B, intending to obtain the reward, gives the requested information a year after the publication of the offer. The acceptance is timely.

2. After a series of incendiary attempts, a city publishes each day for a week an offer of reward for information leading to the arrest and conviction of any person who shall set fire to any building within the city. The responsible city officials serve for one year terms. A fire set three years after the last publication is not within the terms of the offer.

3. A bank posts in its office an offer of reward for information leading to the arrest and conviction of any person who robs any bank which is a member of an association of banks in the same county. After several years the poster is removed. A robbery three years after the removal may be found to be within the terms of the offer.

d. Direct negotiations. Where the parties bargain face to face or over the telephone, the time for acceptance does not ordinarily extend beyond the end of the conversation unless a contrary intention is indicated. A contrary intention may be indicated either by express words or by the circumstances. For example, the delivery of a written offer to the offeree, or an expectation that some action will be taken before acceptance, may indicate that a delayed acceptance is invited.

Illustration

4. While A and B are engaged in conversation, A makes B an offer to which B then makes no reply, but on meeting A again a few hours later B states that he accepts the offer. There is no contract unless the offer or the circumstances indicate that the offer is intended to continue beyond the immediate conversation.

e. Offers made by mail or telegram. Where the parties are at a distance from each other, the normal understanding is that the time for acceptance is extended at least by the normal time for transmission of the offer and for the sending of the offeree's reply. Compare § 49.

Subsection (3) reflects the normal understanding that mail is promptly answered if a reply is mailed at any time on the day of receipt. Compare Uniform Commercial Code §§ 4–301, 4–302, fixing the time for settlement by a bank for demand items. But in the absence of a significant speculative element in the situation, a considerably longer time may be reasonable. The fact that an offer is made by telegram or mailgram may or may not indicate that the time for reply is shorter than it would be if the mail were used. Compare § 65.

Illustration

5. A makes B an offer by mail to sell goods. B receives the offer at the close of business hours and accepts it by letter promptly the next morning. The acceptance is timely.

f. Speculative transactions. The rule that an offer becomes irrevocable when an acceptance is mailed (§§ 42, 63) in effect imposes a risk of commitment on the offeror during the period required for communication of the acceptance, although during that period the offeror has no assurance that the bargain has been concluded. The rule that the power of acceptance is terminated by the lapse of a reasonable time serves to limit this risk. The more significant the risk, the greater is the need for limitation, and hence the shorter is the time which is reasonable.

These considerations have their principal application in the sale of property which may be subject to rapid fluctuation in value, such as commodities, securities or land. The value of such property, however, may be stable for substantial periods of time, particularly in the case of land. Absence of actual fluctuation during the period before acceptance is a factor tending to indicate that acceptance occurred within a reasonable time. Similarly, delay in acceptance of an offer to insure may not be unreasonable if there is no change in the risk or in the applicable insurance rates.

The reasonable time for acceptance in a speculative transaction is brief not only because the offeror does not ordinarily intend to assume an extended risk without compensation but also because he does not intend to give the offeree an extended opportunity for speculation at the offeror's expense. If the offeree makes use for speculative purposes of time allowed for communication, there may be a lack of good faith, and an acceptance may not be timely even though it arrives within the time contemplated by the offeror. Compare Uniform Commercial Code §§ 1–203, 2–103.

Illustrations

6. A sends B an offer by mail to sell a piece of farm land. B does not reply for three days and then mails an acceptance. It is a question of fact under the circumstances of the particular case whether the delay is unreasonable.

7. A sends B a telegraphic offer to sell oil which at the time is subject to rapid fluctuations in price. The offer is received near the close of business hours, and a telegraphic acceptance is sent the next day, after the offeree has learned of a sharp price rise. The acceptance is too late if a fixed price was offered, but may be timely if the price is market price at time of delivery.

8. A sends B an offer by mail to sell at a fixed price corporate stock not listed on an exchange. B waits two days after receiving the offer and then sends a telegraphic acceptance after learning of a sharp rise in the price bid over-the-counter. The acceptance may be too late even though it arrives before a prompt acceptance by mail would have arrived.

§ 42. Revocation by Communication From Offeror Received by Offeree.

An offeree's power of acceptance is terminated when the offeree receives from the offeror a manifestation of an intention not to enter into the proposed contract.

Comment

a. Revocability of offers. Most offers are revocable. Revocability may rest on the express or implied terms of the offer, as in the case of bids at an auction. See § 28. But the ordinary offer is revocable even though it expressly states the contrary, because of the doctrine that an informal agreement is binding as a bargain only if supported by consideration. Inroads have been made on that doctrine by statute and by rules giving effect to nominal consideration and to action in reliance on a promise. Where such rules are applicable, or where the offer is itself a formal contract or an agreement binding as a bargain, the case is governed by § 37 rather than by this Section. See § 25.

Illustration

1. A makes a written offer to B to sell him a piece of land. The offer states that it will remain open for thirty days and is not subject to countermand. The next day A orally informs B that the offer is terminated. B's power of acceptance is terminated unless the offer is a contract under § 25.

b. Necessity that communication be received. An offeror may reserve the power to revoke the offer without notice, and such a reservation will be given effect whether contained in the offer or in a later communication received by the offeree before a contract is created. But such a reservation is unusual; it deprives the offeree of a dependable basis for decision whether to accept and greatly impairs the usefulness of the offer. In the absence of such a reservation, the offeree is justified in relying on the offeror's manifested intention regardless of any undisclosed change in the offeror's state of mind. As to when a revocation is received by the offeree, see § 68; compare Restatement, Second, Agency §§ 268–83, Uniform Commercial Code § 1–201(25) to (27).

c. Purported revocation after acceptance. Once the offeree has exercised his power to create a contract by accepting the offer, a purported revocation is ineffective as such. Where an acceptance by mail is effective on dispatch, for example, it is not deprived of effect by a revocation subsequently received by the offeree. See § 63. But the revocation may have effect, depending on its terms, as a failure of condition discharging the offeree's duty of performance, as a breach by anticipatory repudiation, or as an offer to modify or rescind the contract.

Illustrations

2. A sends B an offer by mail to buy a piece of land for $5000. The next day A sends B a letter stating that unless B has already accepted A revokes the offer and makes a new offer to buy the same land for $4800. B receives A's second letter after he has duly mailed a letter of acceptance, but promptly sells the land to C without further communication with A. The sale is a breach of contract by B.

3. A sends B an offer by mail to buy a piece of land. The next day A sends B a letter stating that A has changed his mind and will not buy the land even if B has already accepted the offer. B receives A's second letter after he has duly mailed a letter of acceptance, but promptly sells the land to C. B's duty of performance is discharged. See Comment a to § 283.

d. What constitutes revocation. The word "revoke" is not essential to a revocation. Any clear manifestation of unwillingness to enter into the proposed bargain is sufficient. Thus a statement that property offered for sale has been otherwise disposed of is a revocation. But equivocal language may not be sufficient.

Illustrations

4. A makes an offer to buy goods from B, and later requests B not to deliver the goods until A is in a better condition to handle them. The request does not revoke the offer.

5. A makes an offer to B, and later says to B, "Well, I don't know if we are ready. We have not decided, we might not want to go through with it." The offer is revoked.

§ 43. Indirect Communication of Revocation.

An offeree's power of acceptance is terminated when the offeror takes definite action inconsistent with an intention to enter into the proposed contract and the offeree acquires reliable information to that effect.

Comment

a. Direct and indirect communication. This Section extends the principle giving effect to a revocation communicated directly by the offeror to the offeree, and is subject to the same qualifications. See § 42. Thus a revocation is ineffective, whether communication is direct or indirect, if the offer is itself a contract, or after the power of acceptance has been duly exercised. On the other hand, no communication at all is necessary for revocation if the offer so provides. Where a revocation is communicated through a person or persons having power to act for the offeror or offeree, the case is governed by § 42, supplemented by the law of agency.

b. Sale of land. The rule of this Section has been applied most frequently to offers for the sale of an interest in land. If the offeror, after making such an offer, sells or contracts to sell the interest to another person than the offeree, his act manifests an intention not to perform in accordance with the offer and creates a probable inability to perform. Compare the rules on vendor's prospective inability in §§ 250–52. Moreover, the other person has title to the land or a right to specific performance prior to any right of the offeree, and interference by the offeree with the rights of the other person may be tortious. See Restatement, Second, Torts §§ 766, 773. An agreement in derogation of those rights may be unenforceable as against public policy. See §§ 192, 194.

Illustration

1. A offers a parcel of land to B at a stated price, and gives B a week in which to consider the proposal. Within the week A contracts to sell the parcel to C, and B is informed of that fact by a tenant of the premises. B nevertheless sends a formal acceptance which is received by A within the week. There is no contract between A and B.

    c. Other transactions. The considerations applicable to offers to sell land are equally applicable to offers to sell other specific property, if the offeror enters into a transaction which confers on a third person rights prior to those of the offeree. But the rule stated is not limited to such cases. Nor is this Section an exhaustive statement of the circumstances under which indirect communication may result in termination of the offeree's power of acceptance. Compare, e.g., §§ 20, 153 on the effect of the offeree's acquisition of knowledge of a misunderstanding or mistake.

Illustration

2. A offers to employ B to replace C, an employee of A who has given A a month's notice of intention to quit. A gives B a week to consider the proposal. C changes his mind and makes a contract with A for continued employment for a year. B asks C about his duties, and C informs B of the new contract. B immediately mails a letter of acceptance to A, which arrives within the week allowed for acceptance. There is no contract between A and B.

    d. Definite action; reliable information. This Section does not apply to cases where the offeror takes no action or takes equivocal action. Thus mere negotiations with a third person, or even a definite offer to a second offeree, may be consistent with an intention on the part of the offeror to honor an acceptance by the original offeree. Even a binding contract with a third person may be expressly subject to any rights arising under the outstanding offer. Moreover, a mere rumor does not terminate the power of acceptance, if the offeree disbelieves it and is reasonable in doing so, even though the rumor is later verified. The basic standard to which the offeree is held is that of a reasonable person acting in good faith.

Illustration

3. A offers to sell B a hundred shares of stock at a fixed price, and states that the offer will not be revoked for a week. Within the week C offers A a higher price for the same stock, and B learns of the higher offer. B's power of acceptance is not terminated, since he is entitled to assume that A will honor his commitment regardless of its legal effect.

§ 44. Effect of Deposit on Revocability of Offer.

An offeror's power of revocation is not limited by the deposit of money or other property to be forfeited in the event of revocation, but the deposit may be forfeited to the extent that it is not a penalty.

Comment

    a. Deposits. Money or other property is often transferred by an offeror to the account of the offeree, and such property may ordinarily be recovered if the offer is not accepted. See Restatement of Restitution § 56. If it is agreed that the property may be forfeited in the event of revocation of the offer, the agreement is subject to the rules governing liquidated damages and penalties. See § 356; Uniform Commercial Code § 2–718. The agreement may be valid as a provision for liquidated damages, or as a provision of security for the payment of actual damages. In either case, the offer is treated as irrevocable for the purpose of determining rights in the deposit, but the offeror's power of revocation is not otherwise impaired. In cases of bids on government contracts, statutes often authorize forfeiture without regard to the distinction between liquidated damages and penalty.

Illustration

1. A offers to buy Blackacre from B for $10,000 and deposits $500 to be forfeited in the event of revocation. A revokes the offer before acceptance, and the market value of the land at the time for conveyance fixed in the offer is $9,000. B's power of acceptance is terminated, but B may retain the $500.

§ 45. Option Contract Created by Part Performance or Tender.

(1) Where an offer invites an offeree to accept by rendering a performance and does not invite a promissory acceptance, an option contract is created when the offeree tenders or begins the invited performance or tenders a beginning of it.

(2) The offeror's duty of performance under any option contract so created is conditional on completion or tender of the invited performance in accordance with the terms of the offer.

Comment

a. Offer limited to acceptance by performance only. This Section is limited to cases where the offer does not invite a promissory acceptance. Such an offer has often been referred to as an "offer for a unilateral contract." Typical illustrations are found in offers of rewards or prizes and in non-commercial arrangements among relatives and friends. See Comment b to § 32. As to analogous cases arising under offers which give the offeree power to accept either by performing or by promising to perform, as he chooses, see §§ 32, 62.

b. Manifestation of contrary intention. The rule of this Section is designed to protect the offeree in justifiable reliance on the offeror's promise, and the rule yields to a manifestation of intention which makes reliance unjustified. A reservation of power to revoke after performance has begun means that as yet there is no promise and no offer.

Illustrations

1. B owes A $5000 payable in installments over a five-year period. A proposes that B discharge the debt by paying $4,500 cash within one month, but reserves the right to refuse any such payment. A has not made an offer. A tender by B in accordance with the proposal is an offer by B.

2. A, an insurance company, issues a bulletin to its agents, entitled "Extra Earnings Agreement," providing for annual bonus payments to the agents varying according to "monthly premiums in force" and "lapse ratio," but reserving the right to change or discontinue the bonus, individually or collectively, with or without notice, at any time before payment. There is no offer or promise.

c. Tender of performance. A proposal to receive a payment of money or a delivery of goods is an offer only if acceptance can be completed without further cooperation by the offeror. If there is an offer, it follows that acceptance must be complete at the latest when performance is tendered. A tender of performance, so bargained for and given in exchange for the offer, ordinarily furnishes consideration and creates a contract. See §§ 17, 71, 72.

This is so whether or not the tender carries with it any incidental promises. See §§ 54, 62. If no commitment is made by the offeree, the contract is an option contract. See § 25.

Illustration

3. A promises B to sell him a specified chattel for $5, stating that B is not to be bound until he pays the money. B tenders $5 within a reasonable time, but A refuses to accept the tender. There is a breach of contract.

d. Beginning to perform. If the invited performance takes time, the invitation to perform necessarily includes an invitation to begin performance. In most such cases the beginning of performance carries with it an express or implied promise to complete performance. See § 62. In the less common case where the offer does not contemplate or invite a promise by the offeree, the beginning of performance nevertheless completes the manifestation of mutual assent and furnishes consideration for an option contract. See § 25. If the beginning of performance requires the cooperation of the offeror, tender of part performance has the same effect. Part performance or tender may also create an option contract in a situation where the offeree is invited to take up the option by making a promise, if the offer invites a preliminary performance before the time for the offeree's final commitment.

Illustrations

4. A offers a reward for the return of lost property. In response to the offer, B searches for the property and finds it. A then notifies B that the offer is revoked. B makes a tender of the property to A conditional on payment of the reward, and A refuses. There is a breach of contract by A.

5. A, a magazine, offers prizes in a subscription contest. At a time when B has submitted the largest number of subscriptions, A cancels the contest. A has broken its contract with B.

6. A writes to her daughter B, living in another state, an offer to leave A's farm to B if B gives up her home and cares for A during A's life, B remaining free to terminate the arrangement at any time. B gives up her home, moves to A's farm, and begins caring for A. A is bound by an option contract.

7. A offers to sell a piece of land to B, and promises that if B incurs expense in employing experts to appraise the property the offer will be irrevocable for 30 days. B hires experts and pays for their transportation to the land. A is bound by an option contract.

8. In January A, an employer, publishes a notice to his employees, promising a stated Christmas bonus to any employee who is continuously in A's employ from January to Christmas. B, an employee hired by the week, reads the notice and continues at work beyond the expiration of the current week. A is bound by an option contract, and if B is continuously in A's employ until Christmas a notice of revocation of the bonus is ineffective.

e. Completion of performance. Where part performance or tender by the offeree creates an option contract, the offeree is not bound to complete performance. The offeror alone is bound, but his duty of performance is conditional on completion of the offeree's performance. If the offeree abandons performance, the offeror's duty to perform never arises. See § 224, defining "condition," and Illustration 4 to that Section. But the condition may be excused, for example, if the offeror prevents performance, waives it, or repudiates. See Comment b to § 225 and §§ 239, 278.

f. Preparations for performance. What is begun or tendered must be part of the actual performance invited in order to preclude revocation under this Section. Beginning preparations, though they may be essential to carrying out the contract or to accepting the offer, is not enough. Preparations to perform may, however, constitute justifiable reliance sufficient to make the offeror's promise binding under § 87(2).

In many cases what is invited depends on what is a reasonable mode of acceptance. See § 30. The distinction between preparing for performance and beginning performance in such cases may turn on many factors: the extent to which the offeree's conduct is clearly referable to the offer, the definite and substantial character of that conduct, and the extent to which it is of actual or prospective benefit to the offeror rather than the offeree, as well as the terms of the communications between the parties, their prior course of dealing, and any relevant usages of trade.

Illustration

9. A makes a written promise to pay $5000 to B, a hospital, "to aid B in its humanitarian work." Relying upon this and other like promises, B proceeds in its humanitarian work, expending large sums of money and incurring large liabilities. Performance by B has begun, and A's offer is irrevocable.

g. Agency contracts. This Section frequently applies to agency arrangements, particularly offers made to real estate brokers. Sometimes there is a return promise by the agent, particularly if there is an agreement for exclusive dealing, since such an agreement normally imposes an obligation on the agent to use best efforts. See Uniform Commercial Code § 2–306(2); compare Restatement, Second, Agency § 378. In other cases the agent does not promise to act, but the principal must compensate him if he does act. The rules governing the principal's duty of compensation are stated in detail in Chapter 14 of the Restatement, Second, Agency, particularly §§ 443–57.

§ 46. Revocation of General Offer.

Where an offer is made by advertisement in a newspaper or other general notification to the public or to a number of persons whose identity is unknown to the offeror, the offeree's power of acceptance is terminated when a notice of termination is given publicity by advertisement or other general notification equal to that given to the offer and no better means of notification is reasonably available.

Comment

a. Revocability. This Section is an extension of the principle giving effect to a communicated revocation, and is subject to the same limitations. See § 42; compare § 43. Theoretically, a general offer may be made irrevocable under §§ 25 and 37 in the same ways as any other offer, but irrevocable offers to a number of unidentified persons are rare except where such documents as letters of credit are issued. See Illustration 2 to § 29. An irrevocable offer, or a revocable offer which has been duly accepted, cannot of course be revoked under this Section. On the other hand, this Section does not exclude revocation under § 42 or § 43 or under a power to revoke expressly reserved in the offer; a published notice of revocation which does not comply with this Section is nonetheless effective as to an offeree who actually learns of it.

b. Available means of notice. The rule of this Section reconciles the principle that an offer is ordinarily revocable with the fact that general publication is not a reliable means of informing offerees of the revocation of an offer. Revocation by a notification not actually received is given effect only where such revocation is provided for in the offer or where the alternative is that the offer is as a practical matter irrevocable. Where a feasible and customary substitute is available which is better calculated to produce actual receipt of notice, newspaper publication is not enough. Even where publication is the only or the best available means of giving notice, it may not be effective immediately. There must be publicity equivalent to that given the offer, including in appropriate cases a reasonable time for equivalent indirect circulation. Compare Illustration 1 to § 23.

Illustrations

1. A, a newspaper, publishes an offer of prizes to the persons who procure the largest number of subscriptions as evidenced by cash or checks received by a specified time. B completes and mails an entry blank giving his name and address, which is received by A. Thereafter, during the contest, A publishes a notice that personal checks will not be counted; B does not see the notice. Unless the original offer provided otherwise, B is not bound by the later notice, since A could have given B personal.

2. The United States Government publishes an offer of reward for the arrest of a named fugitive. Seven months later the President publishes a proclamation revoking the offer, which is given the same publicity as the offer. Five months after the proclamation, A, who has been in Italy continuously and who learned indirectly of the offer but not of the revocation, arrests the fugitive in Italy. There is no contract.

§ 47. Revocation of Divisible Offer.

An offer contemplating a series of independent contracts by separate acceptances may be effectively revoked so as to terminate the power to create future contracts, though one or more of the proposed contracts have already been formed by the offeree's acceptance.

Comment

a. Divisible offers. An offer may propose several contracts, to arise at different times; typical examples are continuing guaranties and standing offers for the sale of goods. See § 31 and Comment. Such an offer is divisible, and the power to make an effective revocation continues pari passu with the continuing power of the offeree to accept. Compare §§ 33–34.

Illustrations

1. A offers to guarantee the payment of all bills of exchange drawn by B and discounted by C. C discounts one such bill. A is bound to pay it. A then notifies C that the guaranty is withdrawn. A is not bound to pay bills subsequently discounted.

2. A offers B to sell him five tons of steel daily, and tenders five tons at once. B accepts the tender. The same amount is furnished daily for a number of days. A then states to B that he revokes

the offer. A contract is formed each day that steel is furnished, but the revocation prevents the formation of any contracts thereafter.

b. Acceptance by beginning performance. Ordinarily an offer invites acceptance in any manner which is reasonable under the circumstances, and rendering a requested performance is often a reasonable mode of acceptance. See §§ 30, 32. Where performance takes time, the beginning of performance may be a reasonable mode of acceptance, and the offer may then become irrevocable, whether or not the offeree's action constitutes a promise to complete performance. See §§ 45, 62. These principles apply to divisible offers, but the beginning of performance of one contract of the contemplated series makes irrevocable only the offer for that one. See § 50.

c. Divisible option contracts. It is possible to make a divisible offer irrevocable, not just as to the contracts already formed by acceptances, but also as to the power to create future contracts. An irrevocable divisible offer is in effect a series of binding option contracts, but all may be made binding by a single consideration or a single formal document.

Illustration

3. A offers to buy from B at the market price 100 tons of steel per month for the next 12 months, promising that in consideration of the delivery of the first installment B is to have an option to sell any or all of the other eleven installments. B delivers the first 100 tons as requested. There is an irrevocable offer to buy the eleven undelivered installments.

§ 48. Death or Incapacity of Offeror or Offeree.

An offeree's power of acceptance is terminated when the offeree or offeror dies or is deprived of legal capacity to enter into the proposed contract.

Comment

a. Death of offeror. The offeror's death terminates the power of the offeree without notice to him. This rule seems to be a relic of the obsolete view that a contract requires a "meeting of minds," and it is out of harmony with the modern doctrine that a manifestation of assent is effective without regard to actual mental assent. See § 19. Some inroads have been made on the rule by statutes and decisions with respect to bank deposits and collections, and by legislation with respect to powers of attorney given by servicemen. See Uniform Commercial Code § 4–405; Restatement, Second, Agency § 120 and Comment a. In the absence of legislation, the rule remains in effect. See also Restatement of Security § 87.

b. Incapacity of offeror. The common types of incapacity and their effects are indicated in the Comment to § 12. The offeror's permanent lack of capacity to enter into a contract terminates the offeree's power of acceptance in the same manner as the offeror's death. Compare Restatement, Second, Agency §§ 122, 133; Restatement of Security § 84. But persons under a disability often have power to enter into voidable contracts. See § 7 and Comment; §§ 12–16.

c. Death or incapacity of offeree. Only the offeree can accept an offer which is not also a contract. See § 52. When the offeree dies or lacks capacity, therefore, acceptance is impossible. Compare Comment b to § 36. By the terms of the offer, however, the personal representative or distributee of the offeree may be made an additional offeree.

d. Option contracts. The rule stated in this Section does not affect option contracts. See § 37. But the death or incapacity of one of the parties may discharge any contractual duty by reason of failure of consideration, frustration, impossibility or failure of condition. See § 36 and Comment

§ 49. Effect of Delay in Communication of Offer.

If communication of an offer to the offeree is delayed, the period within which a contract can be created by acceptance is not thereby extended if the offeree knows or has reason to know of the delay, though it is due to the fault of the offeror; but if the delay is due to the fault of the offeror or to the means of transmission adopted by him, and the offeree neither knows nor has reason to know that there has been delay, a contract can be created by acceptance within the period which would have been permissible if the offer had been dispatched at the time that its arrival seems to indicate.

Illustration

1. A sends B a misdirected offer which is delayed in delivery, as is apparent from the date of the letter or the postmark on the envelope, so that the offeree does not receive the offer until some time later than he would have received it had the direction been correct. The offeree cannot accept the offer unless he can do so within the time which would have been permissible had the offer arrived seasonably.

TOPIC 5. ACCEPTANCE OF OFFERS

§ 50. Acceptance of Offer Defined; Acceptance by Performance; Acceptance by Promise.

(1) Acceptance of an offer is a manifestation of assent to the terms thereof made by the offeree in a manner invited or required by the offer.

(2) Acceptance by performance requires that at least part of what the offer requests be performed or tendered and includes acceptance by a performance which operates as a return promise.

(3) Acceptance by a promise requires that the offeree complete every act essential to the making of the promise.

Comment

a. Mode of acceptance. The acceptance must manifest assent to the same bargain proposed by the offer, and must also comply with the terms of the offer as to the identity of the offeree and the mode of manifesting acceptance. Offers commonly invite acceptance in any reasonable manner, but a particular mode of acceptance may be required. See § 30. In case of doubt, the offeree may choose to accept either by promising or by rendering the requested performance. See § 32.

b. Acceptance by performance. Where the offer requires acceptance by performance and does not invite a return promise, as in the ordinary case of an offer of a reward, a contract can be created only by the offeree's performance. See Comment b to § 32. In such cases the act requested and performed as consideration for the offeror's promise ordinarily also constitutes acceptance; under § 45 the beginning of performance or the tender of part performance of what is requested may both indicate assent and furnish consideration for an option contract. In some other cases the offeree may choose to create a contract either by making a promise or by rendering or tendering performance; in most such cases the beginning of performance or a tender of part performance operates as a promise to render complete performance. See §§ 32, 62. Mere preparation to perform, however, is not acceptance, although in some cases preparation may make the offeror's promise binding under § 87(2).

Illustrations

1. A, who is about to leave on a month's vacation, tells B that A will pay B $50 if B will paint A's porch while A is away. B says he may not have time, and A says B may decide after A leaves. If B begins the painting, there is an acceptance by performance which operates as a promise to complete the job. See §§ 32, 62.

2. In Illustration 1, B also expresses doubt whether he will be able to finish the job, and it is agreed that B may quit at any time but will be paid only if he finishes the job during A's vacation. If B begins the painting, there is an acceptance by performance creating an option contract. See § 45.

c. Acceptance by promise. The typical contract consists of mutual promises and is formed by an acceptance constituting a return promise by the offeree. A promissory acceptance may be explicitly required by the offer, or may be the only type of acceptance which is reasonable under the circumstances, or the offeree may choose to accept by promise an offer which invites acceptance either by promise or by performance. See §§ 30, 32. The promise may be made in words or other symbols of assent, or it may be implied from conduct, other than acts of performance, provided only that it is in a form invited or required by the offer. An act of performance may also operate as a return promise, but the acceptance in such a case is treated as an acceptance by performance rather than an acceptance by promise; thus the requirement of notification is governed by § 54 rather than by § 56. As appears from § 63, acceptance by promise may be effective when a written promise is started on its way, but the offeree must complete the acts necessary on his part to constitute a promise by him. Similarly, in cases where communication to the offeror is unnecessary under § 69, the acts constituting the promise must be complete.

Illustrations

3. A sends to B plans for a summer cottage to be built on A's land in a remote wilderness area, and writes, "If you will undertake to build a cottage in accordance with the enclosed plans, I will pay you $5,000." B cannot accept by beginning or completing performance, since A's letter calls for acceptance by promise. See § 58.

4. A mails a written order to B, offering to buy on specified terms a machine of a type which B regularly sells from stock. The order provides, "Ship at once." B immediately mails a letter of acceptance. This is an acceptance by promise, even though under § 32 B might have accepted by performance.

5. A gives an order to B Company's traveling salesman which provides, "This proposal becomes a contract without further notification when approval by an executive officer of B Company is noted hereon at its home office." The notation of approval is an acceptance by promise. See §§ 56, 69 as to the requirement of notification.

§ 51. Effect of Part Performance Without Knowledge of Offer.

Unless the offeror manifests a contrary intention, an offeree who learns of an offer after he has rendered part of the performance requested by the offer may accept by completing the requested performance.

Comment

a. Performance without knowledge. Where an offer invites a return promise, the offeree may manifest assent and thereby make a return promise even though he does not have actual knowledge of the offer. See § 23 Comment c; § 69. But when an offer contemplates no commitment, as in cases of offers of reward, it is ordinarily essential to the acceptance of the offer that the offeree know of the proposal made. In general, performance completed before the offer comes to the offeree's knowledge does not have reference to the offer, and the terms of the offer are not satisfied by such action. See §§ 23, 71.

b. Completion of performance with knowledge. Where part performance has been rendered by a person ignorant of the existence of an offer, the offer can no longer serve the purpose of inducing that performance. But it can induce the completion of performance. It is commonly intended by the offeror to have that effect and so understood by the offeree. The inference that the offeror so intends is strengthened when the part performance is valueless to him unless completed, or when the offeror knows of the offeree's continuing performance and fails to revoke. In the absence of contrary indications, the law gives effect to the common understanding. But there may be no consideration if the offeree is under a legal duty to the offeror to complete the performance. See § 73.

Illustrations

1. A offers a reward for the apprehension and delivery into police custody of a criminal. Before learning of the reward, B arrests the criminal. After learning of the reward, B delivers the criminal into police custody. B is entitled to the reward.

2. A posts a notice on his bulletin board offering a specified bonus to any employee who remains in A's employment for four months. B, one of the employees, continues to work for one month before learning of the offer. Thereafter, B completes the four-month period of employment. B is entitled to the bonus.

§ 52. Who May Accept an Offer.

An offer can be accepted only by a person whom it invites to furnish the consideration.

Comment

a. Rationale. This Section states a negative fairly implied in § 29. The offeror is the master of his offer, and the power of acceptance rests on his manifested intention. The rule that the power of acceptance is personal to the offeree is applied strictly, even in cases where the offeree after acceptance could assign his rights and delegate performance to the assignee under §§ 317(2) and 318(1). As to death of the offeree, compare § 37 with § 48.

Illustrations

1. A makes an offer to B, who dies after receiving it. His executor, though acting within the permitted time, cannot accept.

2. A offers to guarantee payment for goods delivered to B by C. D cannot accept by delivering goods to B.

b. Identity of the offeree. Just as the person to whom a promise is addressed is the promisee (§ 2), so the person to whom an offer is addressed is the offeree. An offer which is itself a promise may contemplate the furnishing of consideration by a person other than the promisee. See § 71(4). That other person is then the offeree.

In case of misunderstanding as to identity of the offeree, the principles stated in § 20 are applicable. An offeror who knows or has reason to know that he is apparently making an offer to a particular person may be bound by that appearance. But one who knows that he is not the intended offeree cannot take advantage of such an appearance, and one who has reason to know the offeror's meaning can accept only if the offeror in fact knows of the offeree's contrary understanding.

Illustrations

3. A promises B that A will sell and deliver a set of books to B if B's father C will promise to pay $150 for the set. B is the promisee of A's promise; C is the offeree of A's offer. Only C can accept the offer by making the return promise invited by A.

4. A sends B an order for goods. C, from whom A has previously refused to buy such goods, has purchased B's business. Without notifying A of the change of proprietorship, C ships the goods as ordered. Neither B nor C has accepted A's offer.

5. A, in Illustration 4, before using the goods, discovers that they have come from C. A's retention or use of them is an acceptance of an offer from C, and a contract arises.

c. Agency. The rules stated in the Restatement of this Subject are supplemented by the law of agency, and in the absence of contrary statement it is assumed that any necessary act may be performed on behalf of a contracting party by his agent. Thus an offer may be accepted by an agent of the offeree. See Restatement, Second, Agency § 292. Even an acceptance by a purported agent, acting without agency power, may in appropriate cases be ratified by the offeree. See Restatement, Second, Agency §§ 82–104. Ratification must occur, however, before the offeror manifests withdrawal from the transaction and before the termination of the offeree's power of acceptance. See Restatement, Second, Agency § 88.

Under the law of agency, an offeree who purports to act on his own behalf may in fact be acting for an undisclosed principal, and the undisclosed principal may be bound by the contract and may have rights under it. See Restatement, Second, Agency §§ 186 Comment a, 302–10, 372.

§ 53. Acceptance by Performance; Manifestation of Intention Not to Accept.

(1) An offer can be accepted by the rendering of a performance only if the offer invites such an acceptance.

(2) Except as stated in § 69, the rendering of a performance does not constitute an acceptance if within a reasonable time the offeree exercises reasonable diligence to notify the offeror of non-acceptance.

(3) Where an offer of a promise invites acceptance by performance and does not invite a promissory acceptance, the rendering of the invited performance does not constitute an acceptance if before the offeror performs his promise the offeree manifests an intention not to accept.

Comment

a. Invitation of acceptance by performance. Subsection (1) makes explicit with respect to acceptance by performance the offeror's power to control the mode of acceptance. See §§ 30(1), 50(1). In the absence of contrary indication, the question is whether acceptance by performance is reasonable under the circumstances. See § 30(2). Where either acceptance by performance or acceptance by promise is reasonable, the offeree may choose between them. Where no return commitment is invited and the invited performance takes time, the beginning of performance creates an option contract. See § 45. In other cases the beginning of performance may carry with it a promise to complete performance. See § 62.

b. Rejection by the performing offeree. Subsection (2) states the power of the offeree to reject an offer even though he engages in conduct invited by the offer. Compare §§ 38–40. Ordinarily the making of an offer does not limit the offeree's freedom of action or inaction; he may act or forbear without reference to the offer. But if he has reason to know that the offeror may reasonably infer from his conduct that he assents, he runs the risk of being bound by his manifestation of assent. See §§ 19, 20. He may guard against that risk by manifesting an intention not to accept. Although a rejection does not terminate the power of acceptance until received by the offeror (§ 40), reasonable diligence to notify the offeror is sufficient to protect the offeree against an unintended acceptance, except as stated in § 69. Thus Uniform Commercial Code § 2–206(1)(b) provides that a shipment of non-conforming goods in response to an offer to buy is not an acceptance if the seller seasonably notifies the buyer that the shipment is offered only as an accommodation to the buyer. See Illustrations 5 and 6 to § 32. The exceptional cases covered by § 69 involve taking the benefit of offered goods or services, or prior conduct of the offeree justifying the offeror in inferring assent.

c. Rejection or disclaimer where return promise is not contemplated. Where no promise by the offeree is contemplated, there is no problem of justifiable reliance by the offeror. See Comment d to § 23. The offeree's conduct ordinarily constitutes an acceptance in such cases only if he knows of the offer. His rendering of the invited performance with knowledge of the offer is a sufficient manifestation of assent, and inquiry into his motives is unnecessary. But the meaning of non-verbal conduct is even more dependent on its setting than the meaning of words. See Comment a to § 19. The words or conduct of the offeree may show that he acts gratuitously, or otherwise without reference to the offer. There is then no bargain. See § 23. Moreover, as in other cases where it is assumed that a promisee accepts a promise beneficial to him, disclaimer renders the promise inoperative from the beginning. Compare §§ 104, 306. The effect of disclaimer in violation of duty to third persons and the effect of disclaimer on the rights of third persons are beyond the scope of this Restatement. See, e.g., Restatement, Second, Trusts §§ 35, 102.

Illustrations

1. A offers a reward for information leading to the conviction of a criminal. B, a friend of the criminal, knows of the reward and gives the information voluntarily. B is entitled to the reward even though he acts because he thinks he is about to die and wants both to ease his conscience and to revenge himself for a beating received from the criminal.

2. The facts being otherwise as stated in Illustration 1, B is interrogated by the police and threatened with arrest as an accomplice of the criminal. During the interrogation, without any mention of the reward, B is tricked into giving the information to clear himself. B is not entitled to the reward.

3. The facts being otherwise as stated in Illustration 1, B states after giving the information that he does not claim the reward. B is not entitled to the reward.

4. A, an elderly widow apparently in dire poverty, promises B, a distant relative of her deceased husband, that she will pay for board and lodging in B's home. B furnishes board and lodging to A for a year without requesting or receiving any payment, and on A's death states that nothing is due to B. It is a question of fact on all the circumstances whether B has manifested an intention not to seek payment even if A is found to have left a substantial bank account.

§ 54. Acceptance by Performance; Necessity of Notification to Offeror.

(1) Where an offer invites an offeree to accept by rendering a performance, no notification is necessary to make such an acceptance effective unless the offer requests such a notification.

(2) If an offeree who accepts by rendering a performance has reason to know that the offeror has no adequate means of learning of the performance with reasonable promptness and certainty, the contractual duty of the offeror is discharged unless

  (a) the offeree exercises reasonable diligence to notify the offeror of acceptance, or

  (b) the offeror learns of the performance within a reasonable time, or

  (c) the offer indicates that notification of acceptance is not required.

Comment

a. Rationale. In the usual commercial bargain the offeror expects and receives prompt notification of acceptance, and such notification is ordinarily essential to an acceptance by promise. See § 56. But where an offer invites the offeree to accept by rendering a performance, the offeree needs a dependable basis for his decision whether to accept. Compare § 63 and Comment a. When the offeree performs or begins to perform in response to such an offer, there is need for protection of his justifiable reliance. Compare § 45. Those needs are met by giving the performance the effect of temporarily barring revocation of the offer; but ordinarily notification of the offeror must follow in due course. See Uniform Commercial Code § 2–206 Comment 3.

b. Performance operating as return promise. This Section applies only to offers which invite acceptance by performance. Where the offeree is empowered to choose between acceptance by performance and acceptance by promise (see § 32), this Section applies only if he chooses to accept by performance. See § 50(2). In such a case the acceptance often carries with it a return commitment (see § 62), and it is rare that the offer dispenses with notification of such a commitment. Compare §§ 56, 69. Unless the performance will come to the offeror's attention in normal course, it is not likely to be a reasonable mode of acceptance. See § 30. In the exceptional case where acceptance is invited by a performance which will not come promptly to the offeror's attention, Subsection (2) usually requires notification of acceptance. Uniform Commercial Code § 2–206(2) provides that if no notification is sent within a reasonable time in such a case, the offeror may treat the offer as having lapsed before acceptance. Compare § 41.

Illustration

1. A mails a written order to B for goods to be manufactured specially for A, and requests B to begin at once since manufacture will take several weeks. Under § 62 acceptance is complete when B begins, but A's contractual duty is discharged and he may treat the offer as having lapsed before acceptance unless within a reasonable time B sends notification of acceptance or unless the offer or a prior course of dealing indicates that notification is not required.

c. Where no return promise is contemplated. Performance may be invited as an alternative mode of acceptance or as the exclusive mode of acceptance. See §§ 30, 32. Where no return commitment is involved, the only notification of acceptance called for is often that necessarily involved in performance by the offeree, or that which accompanies the offeree's request for performance by the offeror. Performance itself both manifests assent and furnishes consideration. Notification is requisite only where the offeror has no convenient means of ascertaining whether the requisite performance has taken place. Even then, it is not the notification which creates the contract, but lack of notification which ends the duty. Compare § 224. Moreover, the offeror may effectively waive notification either before or after the time when it would otherwise be due. See § 84.

Illustrations

2. A, the proprietor of a medical preparation, offers $100 to anyone who contracts a certain disease after using the preparation as directed. B uses it as directed. B has accepted the offer, and is entitled to the $100 if she later contracts the disease. No notification to A is required until after B has contracted the disease.

3. A, a newspaper, requests B to discontinue distribution of a rival newspaper, and offers to pay B $10 per week as long as B abstains from such distribution. B discontinues the distribution. B has accepted the offer, and no notification to A is required.

d. Notice to guarantor. This Section has an important application in the field of suretyship. See Restatement of Security § 86. An offer to become guarantor for another commonly invites the offeree to accept by advancing money, goods, or services on credit. See Comment b to § 31. Notification is not essential to acceptance of such an offer, and often is not necessary at all. But Subsection (2) may apply to require notification unless the terms of the offer in the circumstances manifest a contrary intention. An offer of guaranty which does not require notification is often called an "absolute guaranty," while an offer requiring notification is referred to as a "mere offer to guarantee." Where an offer of a continuing guaranty requires notification, a single notice of intention to act is ordinarily sufficient, and notice of individual transactions is not required.

In guaranty cases, notification may be dispensed with if the offer uses language of completed contractual assent, or is under seal, or recites a nominal consideration, or contains an express waiver, or provides for termination by notification of revocation. Facts other than the written terms may have the same effect: a request for the offer made by the offeree, the offeror's knowledge of a particular intended credit transaction or participation in it, a prior course of dealing, a prior or subsequent waiver, or a close relationship between the offeror and the principal obligor.

Illustrations

4. A, the president of a corporation, agrees to guarantee payment for goods to be sold to the corporation by B. B sells and delivers the goods. B has accepted A's offer, and no notification of acceptance is necessary.

5. A writes an informal letter to B, a friend in another country, saying, "If you will let my brother C have $100, I will guarantee its repayment." Promptly on receiving the letter, B advances the money to C, but B takes no steps to notify A, and A does not learn of the advance for a year. B cannot enforce the guaranty if C fails to pay the debt.

6. The facts being otherwise as stated in Illustration 5, B receives a letter of revocation from A an hour after advancing the money. B promptly mails a letter notifying A of the advance. The guaranty is binding even though the letter never arrives.

§ 55. Acceptance of Non-Promissory Offers.

Acceptance by promise may create a contract in which the offeror's performance is completed when the offeree's promise is made.

Comment

a. "Reverse unilateral contracts." It is possible to offer a performance without making any promise. Like other offers, a non-promissory offer may require acceptance by performance or acceptance by promise or a combination of the two, or it may leave the mode of acceptance to the offeree's choice. An exchange of performances is not within the definition of "contract" in § 1 and is beyond the scope of the Restatement of this Subject. But where a non-promissory offer is accepted by promise, there is a contract if the requirements other than manifestation of mutual assent are met. Since the contract formed by a performance in response to an offer of a promise such as an offer of reward is often called a "unilateral contract," the type of contract referred to in this Section is sometimes referred to as a "reverse unilateral contract." Contracts so referred to often involve incidental promises by the performing offeror, and in that event the word "unilateral" is not entirely appropriate.

b. Types of non-promissory offers. Most offers are themselves promises. But if the offeror's performance is complete at the moment of acceptance, the element of futurity required by the definition of "promise" in § 2 is lacking. Performance may be thus complete when the offer takes the form of a tender of money or other property; indeed, the acceptance of the offer may then be implied from the fact that the offeree takes the offered benefits, without more. See § 69. In such cases the offeree's manifestation of assent may effect the transfer of property from offeror to offeree which furnishes consideration for the offeree's promise. This element is lacking when services alone are offered, but a contract may nonetheless be formed if the offeree takes the benefit of the services.

Illustrations

1. A applies to B, an insurance company, for a policy of life insurance, and pays the first premium on an understanding that the insurance must be approved at B's home office. B's notification that the approval has been given is an acceptance of A's offer and forms a contract of insurance.

2. A offers to lend B $100 on specified terms and tenders the money to B. B's acceptance of the tender forms a contract on the terms specified.

3. A, the owner of a horse in B's possession, offers to sell the horse to B for $100 payable in thirty days. On B's promise to pay in accordance with the offer, ownership of the horse is transferred to him and there is a contract. Uniform Commercial Code § 2–401(3).

4. A, a real estate broker, without authority from B, the owner of property, obtains from C an offer to purchase the property from B on terms which include the payment of a specified commission by B to A. A then presents C's offer to B. B's acceptance of C's offer also accepts A's offer of services and forms a contract between A and B.

§ 56. Acceptance by Promise; Necessity of Notification to Offeror.

Except as stated in § 69 or where the offer manifests a contrary intention, it is essential to an acceptance by promise either that the offeree exercise reasonable diligence to notify the offeror of acceptance or that the offeror receive the acceptance seasonably.

Comment

a. Necessity of notification. Where the offeree has performed in whole or in part, notification to the offeror is not essential to acceptance, although failure to notify may discharge the offeror's duty of performance. See § 54. Similarly, where the offeror has rendered a performance and the offeree has taken the benefit of that performance, the offeree may be bound without notification to the offeror. See § 69. In such cases the enforcement of the promise rests in part on a change of position in justifiable reliance on a promise, often reinforced by a corresponding benefit received by the promisor. Section 69 also provides for some cases of offers which manifest an intention to dispense with notification. In other cases of the exchange of promises which are entirely executory on both sides, the offeror is entitled to notification of acceptance unless the offer manifests a contrary intention.

Illustrations

1. A gives an order to B Company's traveling salesman for a $2000 machine "to purify water of the character shown by sample to be submitted," shipment to be made in one month. The order provides: "This proposal becomes a contract when approved by an executive officer of B Company at its home office." Notation of such approval on the order is an acceptance by promise without any notification, but A's duty to perform is conditional on reasonable notification to send the sample.

2. A makes written application for life insurance through an agent for B Insurance Company, pays the first premium, and is given a receipt stating that the insurance "shall take effect as of the date of approval of the application" at B's home office. Approval at the home office in accordance with B's usual practice is an acceptance of A's offer even though no steps are taken to notify A.

b. Failure of communication. It is sometimes said that the acceptance must be communicated to the offeror, and when the parties deal face to face communication is ordinarily required. The rule is more accurately stated as one requiring reasonable diligence on the part of the offeree, however, since in cases of misunderstanding acceptance turns on what each party knew or had reason to know. See § 20. In cases of communication by mail or telegram, moreover, an acceptance may be effective on dispatch even though it fails to reach the addressee. See § 63. Failure of diligence becomes immaterial if the offeror receives the acceptance seasonably. See § 67. As to when a written acceptance is received, see § 68. Compare

Restatement, Second, Agency §§ 268–83, Uniform Commercial Code § 1–201(25)-(27). Of course reasonable diligence, or even receipt, is not enough if the terms of the offer require more. See § 58.

§ 57. Effect of Equivocal Acceptance.

Where notification is essential to acceptance by promise, the offeror is not bound by an acceptance in equivocal terms unless he reasonably understands it as an acceptance.

Comment

a. Requirement of notification. Notification of acceptance by promise is required in most circumstances. See § 56. Where notification is dispensed with by the terms of the offer, the offeror cannot complain of the resulting uncertainty of his position. See § 69. In cases of acceptance by performance, the reliance of the offeree or the unjust enrichment of the offeror may justify a legal remedy for breach in spite of uncertainty in the offeror's position. Compare §§ 34, 54. Hence this Section is limited to cases of acceptance by promise in which notification is required.

b. Equivocation. This Section is a particular application of the general principles stated in § 20. Where notification is essential to acceptance by promise, the offeror is entitled to know in clear terms whether the offeree accepts his proposal. It is not enough that the words of a reply justify a probable inference of assent. But the circumstances may make it proper to protect an offeror who acts on such an inference. Or subsequent conduct of one or both parties may bind one to an agreement in accordance with the understanding of the other. Compare § 70.

Illustrations

1. A gives an order for goods to B's traveling salesman, subject to approval by B at his home office. B sends a letter to A stating that the order has been received and will receive B's attention. A promptly sends a letter of revocation to B, which B receives before doing anything further. There is no contract.

2. The facts being otherwise as stated in Illustration 1, A does not revoke, but after two months, when it is too late for A to procure substitute goods, B writes a letter to A stating that "it is necessary to cancel this order." B has broken a contract with A.

3. Pursuant to the terms of a lease from A to B, A writes to B that he is about to sell the premises and that B may have the option to purchase by meeting an offer of $37,000. B replies, "I tender you $37,000 in exercise of my option rights. I demand that I be notified concerning your acceptance or rejection of my offer within ten days." Within ten days, A notifies B that A has decided not to sell. There is no contract.

4. A writes to B offering to extend a lease for two years. B replies, "I accept your offer, but I am assigning my interest to C, and have had a lease drawn up from you to C. C has signed it in duplicate, and when you sign it will be complete. Keep one copy and mail the other to me for C. If this is not satisfactory let me know." A's letter of revocation crosses B's letter in the mail. There is no contract.

§ 58. Necessity of Acceptance Complying With Terms of Offer.

An acceptance must comply with the requirements of the offer as to the promise to be made or the performance to be rendered.

Comment

a. Scope. This rule applies to the substance of the bargain the basic principle that the offeror is the master of his offer. See Comment a to § 29. That principle rests on the concept of private autonomy underlying contract law. It is mitigated by the interpretation of offers, in accordance with common understanding, as inviting acceptance in any reasonable manner unless there is contrary indication. See §§ 20, 30(2), 32. Usage of trade or course of dealing may permit inconsequential variations; or a variation clearly to the offeror's advantage, such as a reduction in the price of ordered goods, may be within the scope of the offer. But even in such cases the offeror is entitled, if he makes his meaning clear, to insist on a prescribed type of acceptance.

Illustrations

1. A offers to sell a book to B for $5 and states that no other acceptance will be honored but the mailing of B's personal check for exactly $5. B personally tenders $5 in legal tender, or mails a personal check for $10. There is no contract.

2. A offers to pay B $100 for plowing Flodden field, and states that acceptance is to be made only by posting a letter before beginning work and before the next Monday noon. Before Monday noon B completes the requested plowing and mails to A a letter stating that the work is complete. There is no contract.

§ 59. Purported Acceptance Which Adds Qualifications.

A reply to an offer which purports to accept it but is conditional on the offeror's assent to terms additional to or different from those offered is not an acceptance but is a counter-offer.

Comment

a. Qualified acceptance. A qualified or conditional acceptance proposes an exchange different from that proposed by the original offeror. Such a proposal is a counter-offer and ordinarily terminates the power of acceptance of the original offeree. See § 39. The effect of the qualification or condition is to deprive the purported acceptance of effect. But a definite and seasonable expression of acceptance is operative despite the statement of additional or different terms if the acceptance is not made to depend on assent to the additional or different terms. See § 61; Uniform Commercial Code § 2–207(1). The additional or different terms are then to be construed as proposals for modification of the contract. See Uniform Commercial Code § 2–207(2). Such proposals may sometimes be accepted by the silence of the original offeror. See § 69.

Illustration

1. A makes an offer to B, and B in terms accepts but adds, "This acceptance is not effective unless prompt acknowledgment is made of receipt of this letter." There is no contract, but a counter-offer.

b. Statement of conditions implied in offer. To accept, the offeree must assent unconditionally to the offer as made, but the fact that the offeree makes a conditional promise is not sufficient to show that his acceptance is conditional. The offer itself may either expressly or by implication propose that the offeree make a conditional promise as his part of the exchange. By assenting to such a proposal the offeree makes a conditional promise, but his acceptance is unconditional. The offeror's promise may also be conditional on the same or a different fact or event.

Illustrations

2. A makes a written offer to sell B a patent in exchange for B's promise to pay $10,000 if B's adviser X approves the purchase. B signs the writing in a space labelled "Accepted:" and returns the writing to A. B has made a conditional promise and an unconditional acceptance. There is a contract, but B's duty to pay the price is conditional on X's approval.

3. A makes a written offer to B to sell him Blackacre. By usage the offer is understood as promising a marketable title. B replies, "I accept your offer if you can convey me a marketable title." There is a contract.

§ 60. Acceptance of Offer Which States Place, Time or Manner of Acceptance.

If an offer prescribes the place, time or manner of acceptance its terms in this respect must be complied with in order to create a contract. If an offer merely suggests a permitted place, time or manner of acceptance, another method of acceptance is not precluded.

Comment

a. Interpretation of offer. If the offeror prescribes the only way in which his offer may be accepted, an acceptance in any other way is a counter-offer. But frequently in regard to the details of methods of acceptance, the offeror's language, if fairly interpreted, amounts merely to a statement of a satisfactory method of acceptance, without positive requirement that this method shall be followed.

Illustrations

1. A mails an offer to B in which A says, "I must receive your acceptance by return mail." An acceptance sent within a reasonable time by any other means, which reaches A as soon as a letter sent by return mail would normally arrive, creates a contract on arrival. As to what is a reasonable time, see Illustration 8 to § 41.

2. A makes an offer to B and adds, "Send your office boy around with an answer to this by twelve o'clock." The offeree comes himself before twelve o'clock and accepts. There is a contract.

3. A offers to sell his land to B on certain terms, also saying: "You must accept this, if at all, in person at my office at ten o'clock tomorrow." B's power is strictly limited to one method of acceptance.

4. A offers to sell his land to B on certain terms, also saying: "You may accept by leaving word at my house." This indicates one operative mode of acceptance; but B's power is not limited to that mode alone. A personal statement to A would serve just as well.

5. A makes an offer to B and adds, "my address is 53 State Street." This is a business address. B sends an acceptance to A's home which A receives promptly. Unless the circumstances indicate that A has made a positive requirement of the place where the acceptance must be sent, there is a contract.

§ 61. Acceptance Which Requests Change of Terms.

An acceptance which requests a change or addition to the terms of the offer is not thereby invalidated unless the acceptance is made to depend on an assent to the changed or added terms.

Comment

a. Interpretation of acceptance. An acceptance must be unequivocal. But the mere inclusion of words requesting a modification of the proposed terms does not prevent a purported acceptance from closing the contract unless, if fairly interpreted, the offeree's assent depends on the offeror's further acquiescence in the modification. See Uniform Commercial Code § 2–207(1).

Illustrations

1. A offers to sell B 100 tons of steel at a certain price. B replies, "I accept your offer. I hope that if you can arrange to deliver the steel in weekly installments of 25 tons you will do so." There is a contract, but A is not bound to deliver in installments.

2. A offers to sell specified hardware to B on stated terms. B replies: "I accept your offer; ship in accordance with your statement. Please send me also one No. 5 hand saw at your list price." The request for the saw is a separate offer, not a counter-offer.

§ 62. Effect of Performance by Offeree Where Offer Invites Either Performance or Promise.

(1) Where an offer invites an offeree to choose between acceptance by promise and acceptance by performance, the tender or beginning of the invited performance or a tender of a beginning of it is an acceptance by performance.

(2) Such an acceptance operates as a promise to render complete performance.

Comment

a. The offeree's power to choose. The offeror normally invites a promise by the offeree for the purpose of obtaining performance of the promise. Full performance fulfills that purpose more directly than the promise invited, and hence constitutes a reasonable mode of acceptance. The offeror can insist on any mode of acceptance, but ordinarily he invites acceptance in any reasonable manner; in case of doubt, an offer is interpreted as inviting the offeree to choose between acceptance by promise and acceptance by performance. See §§ 30, 32, 58.

b. Part performance or tender. Where acceptance by performance is invited and no promise is invited, the beginning of performance or the tender of part performance creates an option contract and renders the offer irrevocable. See §§ 37, 45. Under Subsection (1) of this Section the offer is similarly rendered irrevocable where it invites the offeree to choose between acceptance by promise and acceptance by performance. In both types of cases, if the invited performance takes time, the invitation to perform necessarily includes an invitation to begin performance; if performance requires cooperation by the offeror, there is an offer only if acceptance can be completed by tender of performance. But unless an option contract is contemplated, the offeree is expected to be bound as well as the offeror, and Subsection (2) of this Section states the implication of promise which results from that expectation. See Illustration 5 to § 32. In such standard cases as the shipment of goods in response to an order, the acceptance will come to the offeror's attention in normal course; in other cases, the rule of § 54(2) ordinarily requires prompt notification.

c. Manifestation of contrary intention. The rule of Subsection (1), like the rule of § 45, is designed to protect the offeree in justifiable reliance on the offeror's promise; both rules yield to a manifestation of intention which makes such reliance unjustified. Moreover, in most cases of both types the offeree may prevent the formation of a contract by seasonably notifying the offeror of non-acceptance. Section 53(2). Similarly, the rule of Subsection (2) is designed to preclude the offeree from speculating at the offeror's expense where no option contract is contemplated by the offer (compare § 63), and to protect the offeror in justifiable reliance on the offeree's implied promise; this rule also yields to a manifestation of contrary intention under § 53(2).

d. Preparations for performance. As under § 45, what is begun or tendered must be part of the actual performance invited, rather than preparation for performance, in order to make the rule of this Section applicable. See Comment *f* to § 45. But preparations to perform may bring the case within § 87(2) on justifiable reliance.

Illustrations

1. A, a merchant, mails B, a carpenter in the same city, an offer to employ B to fit up A's office in accordance with A's specifications and B's estimate previously submitted, the work to be completed in two weeks. The offer says, "You may begin at once," and B immediately buys lumber and begins to work on it in his own shop. The next day, before B has sent a notice of acceptance or begun work at A's office or rendered the lumber unfit for other jobs, A revokes the offer. The revocation is timely, since B has not begun to perform.

2. A, a regular customer of B, orders fragile goods from B which B carries in stock and ships in his own trucks. Following his usual practice, B selects the goods ordered, tags them as A's, crates them and loads them on a truck at substantial expense. Performance has begun, and A's offer is irrevocable. See Uniform Commercial Code § 2–206 and Comment 2.

§ 63. Time When Acceptance Takes Effect.

Unless the offer provides otherwise,

(a) an acceptance made in a manner and by a medium invited by an offer is operative and completes the manifestation of mutual assent as soon as put out of the offeree's possession, without regard to whether it ever reaches the offeror; but

(b) an acceptance under an option contract is not operative until received by the offeror.

Comment

a. Rationale. It is often said that an offeror who makes an offer by mail makes the post office his agent to receive the acceptance, or that the mailing of a letter of acceptance puts it irrevocably out of the offeree's control. Under United States postal regulations, however, the sender of a letter has long had the power to stop delivery and reclaim the letter. A better explanation of the rule that the acceptance takes effect on dispatch is that the offeree needs a dependable basis for his decision whether to accept. In many legal systems such a basis is provided by a general rule that an offer is irrevocable unless it provides otherwise. The common law provides such a basis through the rule that a revocation of an offer is ineffective if received after an acceptance has been properly dispatched. See Comment c to § 42. Acceptance by telegram is governed in this respect by the same considerations as acceptance by mail.

Illustration

1. A makes B an offer, inviting acceptance by telegram, and B duly telegraphs an acceptance. A purports to revoke the offer in person or by telephone or telegraph, but the attempted revocation is received by B after the telegram of acceptance is dispatched. There is no effective revocation.

b. Loss or delay in transit. In the interest of simplicity and clarity, the rule has been extended to cases where an acceptance is lost or delayed in the course of transmission. The convenience of the rule is less clear in such cases than in cases of attempted revocation of the offer, however, and the language of the offer is often properly interpreted as making the offeror's duty of performance conditional upon receipt of the acceptance. Indeed, where the receipt of notice is essential to enable the offeror to perform, such a condition is normally implied. See Comment c to § 226.

Illustrations

2. A offers to buy cotton from B, the operator of a cotton gin, B to accept by specifying the number of bales in a telegram sent before 8 p.m. the same day. B duly sends a telegram of acceptance and ships the cotton, but the telegram is not delivered. There is a contract, and A is bound to take and pay for the cotton.

3. A mails to B an offer to lease land, stating, "Telegraph me Yes or No. If I do not hear from you by noon on Friday, I shall conclude No." B duly telegraphs "Yes," but the telegram is not delivered until after noon on Friday. Any contract formed by the telegraphic acceptance is discharged.

4. A offers to buy cattle for B, on an understanding that if B telegraphs "Yes" A will notify B of the amount of money needed and B will supply it. B's "Yes" telegram is duly dispatched but does not arrive within a reasonable time. Any contract formed by the dispatch of the telegram is discharged.

c. Revocation of acceptance. The fact that the offeree has power to reclaim his acceptance from the post office or telegraph company does not prevent the acceptance from taking effect on dispatch. Nor, in the absence of additional circumstances, does the actual recapture of the acceptance deprive it of legal effect, though as a practical matter the offeror cannot assert his rights unless he learns of them. An attempt to revoke the acceptance by an overtaking communication is similarly ineffective, even though the revocation is received before the acceptance is received. After mailing an acceptance of a revocable offer, the offeree is not permitted to speculate at the offeror's expense during the time required for the letter to arrive.

A purported revocation of acceptance may, however, affect the rights of the parties. It may amount to an offer to rescind the contract or to a repudiation of it, or it may bar the offeree by estoppel from enforcing it. In some cases it may be justified as an exercise of a right of stoppage in transit or a demand for assurance of performance. Compare Uniform Commercial Code §§ 2–609, 2–702, 2–705. Or the contract may be voidable for mistake or misrepresentation, §§ 151–54, 164. See particularly the provisions of § 153 on unilateral mistake.

Illustrations

5. A mails to B a note payable by C with instructions to collect the amount of the note and remit by mailing B's own check. At C's request B mails his own check as instructed. Subsequently, at C's request, B recovers his letter and check from the post office. The recovery does not discharge the

contract formed by the mailing of B's check. But if B is a bank, its remittance may be provisional under Uniform Commercial Code § 4–211.

6. The facts being otherwise as stated in Illustration 5, B recovers his letter and check from the post office because he has learned that C is insolvent and cannot reimburse B. B is entitled to rescind the contract for mistake. See §§ 153–54; compare Uniform Commercial Code § 4–212.

7. A mails an offer to B to appoint B A's exclusive distributor in a specified area. B duly mails an acceptance. Thereafter B mails a letter which is received by A before the acceptance is received and which rejects the offer and makes a counter-offer. On receiving the rejection and before receiving the acceptance, A executes a contract appointing C as exclusive distributor instead of B. B is estopped to enforce the contract. Compare § 40.

8. The Government mails to A an offer to pay the amount quoted by him for the manufacture of two sets of ship propellers, and A mails an acceptance. A then discovers that by mistake he has quoted the price for a single set, and so informs the Government by a telegram which arrives before the acceptance. A's mailing the acceptance created a contract. The question whether the contract is voidable for mistake is governed by the rules stated in §§ 153–54.

d. Other types of cases. The question when and where an acceptance takes effect may arise in determining the application of tax and regulatory laws, choice of governing law, venue of litigation, and other issues. Such cases often turn on policies beyond the scope of the Restatement of this Subject. To the extent that the issue is referred to the rule governing private contract disputes, the rules stated in this Section are applicable. Where the issue is what obligation is imposed by a contract, whether those rules apply is ordinarily a matter of interpretation.

Illustrations

9. A mails to B an offer to buy goods, and B mails an acceptance. The application of a new tax statute depends on when title to the goods passes to A, and under Uniform Commercial Code § 2–401(3)(b) title passes at the time of contracting. The time of contracting is the time when B's acceptance is mailed.

10. A offers to insure B's house against fire, the insurance to take effect upon actual payment of the premium, and invites B to reply by mailing his check for a specified amount. B duly mails the check. While B's letter is in transit, the house burns. The loss is within the period of insurance coverage.

e. The offeree's possession. The rule of Subsection (1) gives effect to an acceptance when "put out of the offeree's possession." Its principal application is to the use of mail and telegraph, but it would apply equally to any other similar public service instrumentality, even though the instrumentality may for some purposes be the offeree's agent. See Restatement, Second, Agency § 1. It may also apply to a private messenger service which is independent of the offeree and can be relied on to keep accurate records. But, except where the Government or a telegraph company can make use of its own postal or telegraph facilities, communication by means of the offeree's employee is excluded; the employee's possession is treated as that of the employer.

Illustration

11. A makes B an offer by mail, or messenger, and B promptly sends an acceptance by his own employee. There is no contract until the acceptance is received by the offeror. As to receipt, see § 68.

f. Option contracts. An option contract provides a dependable basis for decision whether to exercise the option, and removes the primary reason for the rule of Subsection (1). Moreover, there is no objection to speculation at the expense of a party who has irrevocably assumed that risk. Option contracts are commonly subject to a definite time limit, and the usual understanding is that the notification that the option has been exercised must be received by the offeror before that time. Whether or not there is such a time limit, in the absence of a contrary provision in the option contract, the offeree takes the risk of loss or delay in the transmission of the acceptance and remains free to revoke the acceptance until it arrives. Similarly, if there is such a mistake on the part of the offeror as justifies the rescission of his unilateral obligation, the right to rescind is not lost merely because a letter of acceptance is posted. See §§ 151–54.

Illustrations

12. A, for consideration, gives B an option to buy property, written notice to be given on or before a specified date. Notice dispatched before but not received until after that date is not effective to exercise the option.

13. A submits a bid to supply goods to the Government, which becomes irrevocable when bids are opened. Within a reasonable time the Government mails a notice of award of the contract to A. Until A receives the notice, there is no contract binding on the Government.

§ 64. Acceptance by Telephone or Teletype.

Acceptance given by telephone or other medium of substantially instantaneous two-way communication is governed by the principles applicable to acceptances where the parties are in the presence of each other.

Comment

a. Rationale. Where the parties are in each other's presence, the offeree can accept without being in doubt as to whether the offeror has attempted to revoke his offer or whether the offeror has received the acceptance. His need of a dependable basis for decision whether to accept is therefore met without the rules stated in § 63. The situation prevents the question from arising whether a revocation of the offer or acceptance can be effective during the period required for communication of the acceptance, and all that remains is the risk of misunderstanding. Where the parties are not in each other's presence, but are able to communicate with each other without any substantial lapse of time, the situation is similar and the governing principles are the same.

b. Failure of communication. Where the parties are in each other's presence, ambiguities and misunderstandings, if perceived by either party, can be cleared up on the spot. The governing rules where a misunderstanding is not corrected are stated in § 20. The risk of failure of telephone, teletype or other similar communication is similar in that ordinarily one or both parties will know or have reason to know of the failure, and the same principles apply. If one party has reason to know of a failure of communication and hence that the other party's understanding may be different from his own, he runs the risk of being held to a manifestation of assent unless he takes immediate steps to clear up any misunderstanding. But if both parties are equally innocent or equally at fault, there is no contract.

Illustrations

1. A makes an offer to B by telephone. The telephone connection is then broken, but B speaks an acceptance in ignorance of the break. A's failure to answer gives B reason to know of the break. There is no contract.

2. A makes an offer to B by teletype. B transmits an acceptance, and A knows that a reply has been transmitted; but a mechanical failure at A's end, unknown to B, prevents A from learning the contents of the reply. There is a contract.

c. Place of contracting. The question where an acceptance takes effect may arise in cases turning on policies beyond the scope of the Restatement of this Subject. Compare Comment d to § 63. To the extent that the issue is referred to the rule governing private contract disputes, the analogy of acceptance by mail or telegram is controlling in cases of contracts made by parties in each other's presence and also in cases of contracts made by telephone or teletype: the contract is created at the place where the acceptor speaks or otherwise completes his manifestation of ass

§ 65. Reasonableness of Medium of Acceptance.

Unless circumstances known to the offeree indicate otherwise, a medium of acceptance is reasonable if it is the one used by the offeror or one customary in similar transactions at the time and place the offer is received.

Comment

a. Significance of use of reasonable medium. Under § 30 an offer invites acceptance by any reasonable medium unless there is contrary indication; under § 63 an acceptance so invited is ordinarily effective upon dispatch. If an unreasonable medium of acceptance is used, on the other hand, the governing rule is that stated in § 67. Thus if an offer is made by mail, an acceptance by mail is ordinarily effective on dispatch. Exception is made by this section if circumstances known to the offeree indicate otherwise, by § 63 if the offer otherwise provides, and by § 30 if the offer or circumstances forbid acceptance by mail regardless of reasonableness.

b. Circumstances relevant to reasonableness. This Section specifies certain circumstances which ordinarily indicate that a particular medium of acceptance is reasonable, but it does not exhaust the circumstances which may be relevant. Among the relevant circumstances not specified in this Section may be the speed and reliability of the medium, a prior course of dealing between the parties, and a usage of trade. See Chapter 9. The concept of reasonableness is flexible, and its applicability may be enlarged as new media develop or existing media become more speedy or reliable or come into more general use. See Comment 1 to Uniform Commercial Code § 2–206.

c. Mail. Acceptance by mail is ordinarily reasonable where the parties are negotiating at a distance, unless there is some special reason for speed such as rapid price fluctuation. Compare § 41. The same is true when the parties are located in the same city, if the offer is in writing, even though it is left with the offeree in person or delivered to his messenger. Even though an offer is transmitted by telephone or telegraph, acceptance by mail may well be reasonable.

Illustration

1. By telegram A in Oklahoma orders two car-loads of potatoes from B in Wisconsin. B wires back an acceptance "if you will give us time to fill." Immediately on receiving B's reply A mails a confirming letter stating "we wish if possible you would ship at once" and giving shipping instructions. A has accepted B's counter-offer by a reasonable medium of acceptance.

d. Telegraph. Acceptance by telegram or mailgram is affected by the same considerations as acceptance by mail. In addition, there is a risk of mistake in transmission which may be provided for by agreement or may be reduced by a practice of confirmation by mail or by use of repeated messages. Notwithstanding that risk, telegraphic communication is now sufficiently reliable that telegraphic acceptance of an offer made by mail is ordinarily reasonable. But a contrary provision in the offer or a course of dealing or usage of trade requiring confirmation by mail is effective. See Comment c to § 221.

§ 66. Acceptance Must Be Properly Dispatched.

An acceptance sent by mail or otherwise from a distance is not operative when dispatched, unless it is properly addressed and such other precautions taken as are ordinarily observed to insure safe transmission of similar messages.

Comment

a. Rationale. Under § 50, acceptance by promise is not effective until the offeree has completed every act essential to the making of the promise. Reasonable diligence to notify is essential under § 56, except as stated in § 69. It follows that, notwithstanding § 63, acceptance by mail or telegram is not effective on dispatch unless the acceptor exercises reasonable diligence to notify the offeror. Compare the rules as to acceptance by performance stated in § 54. This Section specifies what constitutes reasonable diligence: it would be most unusual for an offer to invite acceptance by the sending, for example, of a misdirected letter or telegram.

b. Proper address. The offeree may fulfill the requirement that an acceptance be properly addressed by using a return address indicated in the offer, whether in a letterhead or otherwise. But any other place held out by the offeror as the place for receipt of such communications will do as well. Compare Uniform Commercial Code § 1–201(26). Whether a reply to an offer may properly be sent to a residential address not specified in the negotiations depends on the circumstances. If the acceptance is duly received despite misdirection, the rule of § 67 may apply.

c. Other precautions. The other precautions to be taken depend on what is ordinarily observed to insure safe transmission of similar messages. In cases of acceptance by mail, the postal regulations are ordinarily controlling on such matters as the necessity for prepayment of postage. In unusual circumstances, however, as when the mails are stopped by war, reasonable diligence may require more than compliance with postal regulations. Unless the offeror manifests a contrary intention, an acceptance is not effective on dispatch if the offeree knows or has reason to know that it will not reach the offeror.

§ 67. Effect of Receipt of Acceptance Improperly Dispatched.

Where an acceptance is seasonably dispatched but the offeree uses means of transmission not invited by the offer or fails to exercise reasonable diligence to insure safe transmission, it is treated as operative upon dispatch if received within the time in which a properly dispatched acceptance would normally have arrived.

Comment

a. Improper medium of transmission. Ordinarily an offer invites acceptance by any reasonable medium, and acceptance by such a medium is operative on dispatch. See §§ 30, 63, 65. An acceptance which is not operative on dispatch may be operative on its receipt by the offeror. The rule stated in this Section goes further: once the acceptance reaches the offeror, the means of transmission becomes immaterial. Compare Uniform Commercial Code § 1–201(38). Since the offeror's interest in receiving notification is satisfied, the offeree is not permitted to disavow his own act, and the usual rules are applied to bind both parties at the same instant. Just as if the acceptance had been properly dispatched, a revocation of the offer which crosses the acceptance in the mail, or an overtaking letter revoking the acceptance, is ineffective. Of course the offer may provide for a contrary rule. And the rule is limited to acceptance seasonably dispatched: the offeree is not empowered to use for speculation the time allowed for communication. See Comment f to § 41.

Illustration

1. A makes an offer to B by telegram on Monday, requesting a reply by telegram to be sent no later than Thursday noon. B mails an acceptance on Monday which A receives on Thursday morning. Even if the mail is an unreasonable medium of acceptance under the circumstances, a revocation of the offer by A by telephone on Tuesday, or a revocation of the acceptance by B by telephone, is ineffective.

b. Misdirection and the like. The same rule applies to cases where the offeree uses the wrong address or fails to provide for postage or other cost of transmission. In such cases the offeree takes the risk of loss or delay in transmission. See §§ 63, 66. But it is not uncommon for communications to arrive promptly despite misdirection or the omission of ordinary precautions to insure safe transmission. In such cases the improper dispatch becomes immaterial.

§ 68. What Constitutes Receipt of Revocation, Rejection, or Acceptance.

A written revocation, rejection, or acceptance is received when the writing comes into the possession of the person addressed, or of some person authorized by him to receive it for him, or when it is deposited in some place which he has authorized as the place for this or similar communications to be deposited for him.

Comment

a. Point of receipt. Under § 42, a revocation if sent from a distance must be received in order to be effectual. Under § 63 acceptance from a distance need not be received if started on its way in a method authorized, unless receipt is made a condition of the offer. This, however, may be the case; and though there is no such condition, an acceptance sent by an unauthorized method may, under § 67, create a contract when received by the offeror. What amounts to receipt in all these cases is defined by the present Section, under which a written communication may be received though it is not read or though it does not even reach the hands of the person to whom it is addressed. Compare Uniform Commercial Code § 1–201(26) on when a notification is received, and § 1–201(27) on receipt by an organization.

Illustrations

1. A sends B by mail an offer dated from A's house and states as a condition of the offer that an acceptance must be received within three days. B mails an acceptance which reaches A's house and is delivered to a servant or is deposited in a mail box at the door within three days; but A has been called away from home and does not personally receive the letter for a week. There is a contract.

2. A sends B by mail an offer, but later, desiring to revoke the offer, telegraphs B to that effect. The messenger boy carrying the telegram from the receiving office meets C, B's neighbor, who volunteers to carry the telegram to B, and accordingly is given it by the messenger boy. C forgets to deliver it to B until the following morning. An acceptance by B mailed prior to this time creates a contract.

§ 69. Acceptance by Silence or Exercise of Dominion.

(1) Where an offeree fails to reply to an offer, his silence and inaction operate as an acceptance in the following cases only:

(a) Where an offeree takes the benefit of offered services with reasonable opportunity to reject them and reason to know that they were offered with the expectation of compensation.

(b) Where the offeror has stated or given the offeree reason to understand that assent may be manifested by silence or inaction, and the offeree in remaining silent and inactive intends to accept the offer.

(c) Where because of previous dealings or otherwise, it is reasonable that the offeree should notify the offeror if he does not intend to accept.

(2) An offeree who does any act inconsistent with the offeror's ownership of offered property is bound in accordance with the offered terms unless they are manifestly unreasonable. But if the act is wrongful as against the offeror it is an acceptance only if ratified by him.

Comment

a. Acceptance by silence is exceptional. Ordinarily an offeror does not have power to cause the silence of the offeree to operate as acceptance. See Comment b to § 53. The usual requirement of notification is stated in § 54 on acceptance by performance and § 56 on acceptance by promise. The mere receipt of an unsolicited offer does not impair the offeree's freedom of action or inaction or impose on him any duty to speak. The exceptional cases where silence is acceptance fall into two main classes: those where the offeree silently takes offered benefits, and those where one party relies on the other party's manifestation of intention that silence may operate as acceptance. Even in those cases the contract may be unenforceable under the Statute of Frauds. See Chapter 5.

b. Acceptance of offered services. Services rendered cannot be recovered in specie, and there is in general no right to restitution of the value of services rendered officiously or gratuitously. Even where services are rendered by mistake, the right to restitution is limited. See Restatement of Restitution §§ 40–42, 56. But when the recipient knows or has reason to know that the services are being rendered with an expectation of compensation, and by a word could prevent the mistake, his privilege of inaction gives way; under Subsection (1) (a) he is held to an acceptance if he fails to speak. The resulting duty is not merely a duty to pay fair value, but a duty to pay or perform according to the terms of the offer.

Illustration

1. A gives several lessons on the violin to B's child, intending to give the child a course of twenty lessons, and to charge B the price. B never requested A to give this instruction but silently allows the lessons to be continued to their end, having reason to know A's intention. B is bound to pay the price of the course.

2. A offers by mail to sell to B a horse already in B's possession for $250, saying: "I am so sure that you will accept that you need not trouble to write me. Your silence alone will operate as acceptance." B makes no reply, but he does not intend to accept. There is no contract.

3. The facts being otherwise as stated in Illustration 2, B replies by return mail, saying: "I accept your offer." There is a contract.

4. The facts being otherwise as stated in Illustration 2, B makes no reply and remains inactive with the intention of thereby expressing his acceptance. There is a contract.

d. Prior conduct of the offeree. Explicit statement by the offeree, usage of trade, or a course of dealing between the parties may give the offeror reason to understand that silence will constitute acceptance. In such a situation the offer may tacitly incorporate that understanding, and if the offeree intends to accept the case then falls within Subsection (1) (b). Under Subsection (1) (c) the offeree's silence is acceptance, regardless of his actual intent, unless both parties understand that no acceptance is intended. See § 20.

In a number of recurring situations, statutes have codified the application of these rules. See Uniform Commercial Code § 2–207(2) on additional terms proposed in an acceptance or written confirmation of a contract between merchants for the sale of goods, § 2–327(1) on retention of goods sold on approval, § 4–302 on retention by a bank of commercial paper received for payment or acceptance. In many states by statute or decision an insurance company is under a duty to act without unreasonable delay on insurance applications solicited by its agents; circumstances may be such as to give the applicant reason to understand that he is insured if that duty is not performed, particularly where a premium payment has been made. Compare § 56.

Illustrations

5. A, through salesmen, has frequently solicited orders for goods from B, the orders to be subject to A's personal approval. In every case A has shipped the goods ordered within a week and without other notification to B than billing the goods to him on shipment. A's salesman solicits and receives another order from B. A receives the order and remains silent. B relies on the order and forbears to buy elsewhere for a week. A is bound to fill the order.

6. A has for years insured B's property against fire under annual policies. At the expiration of one policy, in accordance with the usual practice, A sends B a renewal policy and a bill for the premium. B retains the policy for two months and then refuses to pay the premium on demand. B is liable for the premium accrued prior to his rejection.

e. Exercise of dominion. An offeree in possession of offered property commonly has a duty or privilege to hold it for the offeror, or, if storage is inconvenient or hazardous, to return it, sell it for the offeror's account, or otherwise dispose of it. Compare Uniform Commercial Code §§ 2–602 through 2–604, 7–206. But the offeree's privilege to remain silent without accepting does not extend to acts of ownership not assented to by the offeror. Hence exercise of dominion, even though not intended as acceptance under Subsection (1) (b) and not given meaning by prior conduct under Subsection (1) (c), is a sufficient manifestation of assent under Subsection (2). Compare Uniform Commercial Code § 2–606.

Where the exercise of dominion does not comply with the terms of the offer, the offeror is not bound to treat it as an acceptance but may instead pursue his remedies for tortious interference with his property. But the offeree is not ordinarily permitted to avoid contract obligation by asserting that he is a tortfeasor rather than a promisor; at the option of the offeror he may be held to an acceptance despite his manifestation of a contrary intention. Such an obligation may fairly be characterized as quasi-contractual rather than contractual, but its terms are fixed by the offer rather than by the fair value of the property. Compare Restatement of Restitution § 56.

An exception is made where the offered terms are manifestly unreasonable. In such cases the offeror has reason to know that no acceptance is intended, and the offered terms do not serve as an administratively convenient substitute for fair value. Particularly where the offeror seeks to take unconscionable advantage of a mistake made in good faith, no social purpose is served by an award plainly in excess of reasonable value even though the exercise of dominion is tortious.

Illustrations

7. A sends B a one-volume edition of Shakespeare with a letter, saying, "If you wish to buy this book send me $6.50 within one week after receipt hereof, otherwise notify me and I will forward postage for return." B examines the book and without replying makes a gift of it to his wife. B owes A $6.50.

8. The facts being otherwise as stated in Illustration 7, B examines the book and without replying carefully lays it on a shelf to await A's messenger. There is no contract.

9. The facts being otherwise as stated in Illustration 7, B examines the book and uses it or gives it to his wife, writing A at the same time that he has taken the book, but that it is worth only $5 and that he will pay no more. A may at his option treat B as a tort-feasor or as contracting to pay $6.50.

10. Under a claim of right made in error but in good faith, A digs a well on B's unused land and takes water therefrom which has no market value and no value to B, doing no injury to the value of the land. B notifies A that he will charge A $50 a day for every day on which A takes water from his land. Even after it is adjudicated that A's right is nonexistent, A does not accept B's terms by taking water.

§ 70. Effect of Receipt by Offeror of a Late or Otherwise Defective Acceptance.

A late or otherwise defective acceptance may be effective as an offer to the original offeror, but his silence operates as an acceptance in such a case only as stated in § 69.

Comment

a. Counter-offers. A purported acceptance conditional on a change of terms commonly has the effect of a counter-offer. In such cases the original offeror has not ordinarily given the original offeree reason to understand that silence will operate as an acceptance of a counter-offer. Moreover, although an acceptance would not call for a reply, a purported acceptance is not ordinarily a sufficient manifestation of assent to silence as acceptance of the counter-offer. Nor can the original offeror "waive" his right to reject, or at his election regard the counter-offer as an acceptance. But the original offeror may have a duty to speak, for example, if the purported acceptance embodies a plausible but erroneous reading of the original offer. Compare § 20.

Illustration

1. A offers by mail to sell B 100 acres of land "for $15 per acre cash and give you till July 18 to accept." On July 1 A receives from B a purported acceptance not accompanied by the cash. A waits until after July 18 and then notifies B that his acceptance was ineffective because the price was not paid by July 18. There is a contract. Any ambiguity in the quoted language is resolved against A in view of his failure to object to B's interpretation.

b. Late acceptance. Where an offer is subject to a definite time limit, the offeree commonly is in as good a position as the offeror to ascertain whether he has made a timely acceptance. A late acceptance may be an offer which can be accepted by the original offeror, but there is no more reason to treat silence as acceptance than in any other case. But if the original offer lapses only on the expiration of an indefinite reasonable time, the failure of the original offeror to object to an acceptance and his subsequent preparations for performance may be evidence that the acceptance was made within a reasonable time.

Illustration

2. A invites B to make an offer to buy hay in A's barn. On Friday B inspects the hay and mails A an offer which is received the following day. The following Thursday A mails B an acceptance which is received the following day, and B then employs a third party to haul the hay. There is a contract.

CHAPTER 4

FORMATION OF CONTRACTS—CONSIDERATION

TOPIC 1. THE REQUIREMENT OF CONSIDERATION

§ 71. Requirement of Exchange; Types of Exchange.

(1) To constitute consideration, a performance or a return promise must be bargained for.

(2) A performance or return promise is bargained for if it is sought by the promisor in exchange for his promise and is given by the promisee in exchange for that promise.

(3) The performance may consist of

    (a) an act other than a promise, or

    (b) a forbearance, or

    (c) the creation, modification, or destruction of a legal relation.

(4) The performance or return promise may be given to the promisor or to some other person. It may be given by the promisee or by some other person.

Comment

a. Other meanings of "consideration." The word "consideration" has often been used with meanings different from that given here. It is often used merely to express the legal conclusion that a promise is enforceable. Historically, its primary meaning may have been that the conditions were met under which an action of assumpsit would lie. It was also used as the equivalent of the quid pro quo required in an action of debt. A seal, it has been said, "imports a consideration," although the law was clear that no element of bargain was necessary to enforcement of a promise under seal. On the other hand, consideration has sometimes been used to refer to almost any reason asserted for enforcing a promise, even though the reason was insufficient. In this sense we find references to promises "in consideration of love and affection," to "illegal consideration," to "past consideration," and to consideration furnished by reliance on a gratuitous promise.

Consideration has also been used to refer to the element of exchange without regard to legal consequences. Consistent with that usage has been the use of the phrase "sufficient consideration" to express the legal conclusion that one requirement for an enforceable bargain is met. Here § 17 states the element of exchange required for a contract enforceable as a bargain as "a consideration." Thus "consideration" refers to an element of exchange which is sufficient to satisfy the legal requirement; the word "sufficient" would be redundant and is not used.

b. "Bargained for." In the typical bargain, the consideration and the promise bear a reciprocal relation of motive or inducement: the consideration induces the making of the promise and the promise induces the furnishing of the consideration. Here, as in the matter of mutual assent, the law is concerned with the external manifestation rather than the undisclosed mental state: it is enough that one party manifests an intention to induce the other's response and to be induced by it and that the other responds in accordance with the inducement. See § 81; compare §§ 19, 20. But it is not enough that the promise induces the conduct of the promisee or that the conduct of the promisee induces the making of the promise; both elements must be present, or there is no bargain. Moreover, a mere pretense of bargain does not suffice, as where there is a false recital of consideration or where the purported consideration is merely nominal. In such cases there is no consideration and the promise is enforced, if at all, as a promise binding without consideration under §§ 82–94. See Comments b and c to § 87.

Illustrations

1. A offers to buy a book owned by B and to pay B $10 in exchange therefor. B accepts the offer and delivers the book to A. The transfer and delivery of the book constitute a performance and are

consideration for A's promise. See Uniform Commercial Code §§ 2–106, 2–301. This is so even though A at the time he makes the offer secretly intends to pay B $10 whether or not he gets the book, or even though B at the time he accepts secretly intends not to collect the $10.

    2.   A receives a gift from B of a book worth $10. Subsequently A promises to pay B the value of the book. There is no consideration for A's promise. This is so even though B at the time he makes the gift secretly hopes that A will pay him for it. As to the enforcement of such promises, see § 86.

    3.   A promises to make a gift of $10 to B. In reliance on the promise B buys a book from C and promises to pay C $10 for it. There is no consideration for A's promise. As to the enforcement of such promises, see § 90.

    4.   A desires to make a binding promise to give $1000 to his son B. Being advised that a gratuitous promise is not binding, A writes out and signs a false recital that B has sold him a car for $1000 and a promise to pay that amount. There is no consideration for A's promise.

    5.   A desires to make a binding promise to give $1000 to his son B. Being advised that a gratuitous promise is not binding, A offers to buy from B for $1000 a book worth less than $1. B accepts the offer knowing that the purchase of the book is a mere pretense. There is no consideration for A's promise to pay $1000.

    c. *Mixture of bargain and gift.* In most commercial bargains there is a rough equivalence between the value promised and the value received as consideration. But the social functions of bargains include the provision of opportunity for free individual action and exercise of judgment and the fixing of values by private action, either generally or for purposes of the particular transaction. Those functions would be impaired by judicial review of the values so fixed. Ordinarily, therefore, courts do not inquire into the adequacy of consideration, particularly where one or both of the values exchanged are difficult to measure. See § 79. Even where both parties know that a transaction is in part a bargain and in part a gift, the element of bargain may nevertheless furnish consideration for the entire transaction.

    On the other hand, a gift is not ordinarily treated as a bargain, and a promise to make a gift is not made a bargain by the promise of the prospective donee to accept the gift, or by his acceptance of part of it. This may be true even though the terms of gift impose a burden on the donee as well as the donor. See Illustration 2 to § 24. In such cases the distinction between bargain and gift may be a fine one, depending on the motives manifested by the parties. In some cases there may be no bargain so long as the agreement is entirely executory, but performance may furnish consideration or the agreement may become fully or partly enforceable by virtue of the reliance of one party or the unjust enrichment of the other. Compare § 90.

Illustrations

    6.   A offers to buy a book owned by B and to pay B $10 in exchange therefor. B's transfer and delivery of the book are consideration for A's promise even though both parties know that such books regularly sell for $5 and that part of A's motive in making the offer is to make a gift to B. See §§ 79, 81.

    7.   A owns land worth $10,000 which is subject to a mortgage to secure a debt of $5,000. A promises to make a gift of the land to his son B and to pay off the mortgage, and later gives B a deed subject to the mortgage. B's acceptance of the deed is not consideration for A's promise to pay the mortgage debt.

    8.   A and B agree that A will advance $1000 to B as a gratuitous loan. B's promise to accept the loan is not consideration for A's promise to make it. But the loan when made is consideration for B's promise to repay.

    d. *Types of consideration.* Consideration may consist of a performance or of a return promise. Consideration by way of performance may be a specified act of forbearance, or any one of several specified acts or forbearances of which the offeree is given the choice, or such conduct as will produce a specified result. Or either the offeror or the offeree may request as consideration the creation, modification or destruction of a purely intangible legal relation. Not infrequently the consideration bargained for is an act with the added requirement that a certain legal result shall be produced. Consideration by way of return promise requires a promise as defined in § 2. Consideration may consist partly of promise and partly of other acts or forbearances, and the consideration invited may be a performance or a return promise in the alternative. Though a promise is itself an act, it is treated separately from other acts. See § 75.

Illustrations

9. A promises B, his nephew aged 16, that A will pay B $1000 when B becomes 21 if B does not smoke before then. B's forbearance to smoke is a performance and if bargained for is consideration for A's promise.

10. A says to B, the owner of a garage, "I will pay you $100 if you will make my car run properly." The production of this result is consideration for A's promise.

11. A has B's horse in his possession. B writes to A, "If you will promise me $100 for the horse, he is yours." A promptly replies making the requested promise. The property in the horse at once passes to A. The change in ownership is consideration for A's promise.

12. A promises to pay B $1,000 if B will make an offer to C to sell C certain land for $25,000 and will leave the offer open for 24 hours. B makes the requested offer and forbears to revoke it for 24 hours, but C does not accept. The creation of a power of acceptance in C is consideration for A's promise.

13. A mails a written order to B, offering to buy specified machinery on specified terms. The order provides "Ship at once." B's prompt shipment or promise to ship is consideration for A's promise to pay the price. See § 32; Uniform Commercial Code § 2–206(1) (b).

e. Consideration moving from or to a third person. It matters not from whom the consideration moves or to whom it goes. If it is bargained for and given in exchange for the promise, the promise is not gratuitous.

Illustrations

14. A promises B to guarantee payment of a bill of goods if B sells the goods to C. Selling the goods to C is consideration for A's promise.

15. A makes a promissory note payable to B in return for a payment by B to C. The payment is consideration for the note.

16. A, at C's request and in exchange for $1 paid by C, promises B to give him a book. The payment is consideration for A's promise.

17. A promises B to pay B $1, in exchange for C's promise to A to give A a book. The promises are consideration for one another.

18. A promises to pay $1,000 to B, a bank, in exchange for the delivery of a car by C to A's son D. The delivery of the car is consideration for A's promise.

§ 72. Exchange of Promise for Performance.

Except as stated in §§ 73 and 74, any performance which is bargained for is consideration.

Comment

a. Enforcement of bargains. Section 17(1) embodies the principle that bargains are enforceable unless some other principle conflicts. Chapter 3 on Formation of Contracts-Mutual Assent deals with one essential element of a bargain, agreement; this Topic on the Requirement of Consideration deals with the other essential element, exchange. See § 3. The requirement laid down in § 17(1) is that there be a "consideration." Under § 71 "consideration" requires an element of exchange. This Section states the general rule that exchange of performance for promise is an enforceable bargain; Sections 73 and 74 deny enforcement to certain bargains despite the presence of an element of exchange. Sections 75–78 state corresponding rules for the exchange of promise for promise.

b. Substantive bases for enforcement; the half-completed exchange. Bargains are widely believed to be beneficial to the community in the provision of opportunities for freedom of individual action and exercise of judgment and as a means by which productive energy and product are apportioned in the economy. The enforcement of bargains rests in part on the common belief that enforcement enhances that utility. Where one party has performed, there are additional grounds for enforcement. Where, for example, one party has received goods from the other and has broken his promise to pay for them, enforcement of the promise not only encourages the making of socially useful bargains; it also reimburses the seller for a loss incurred in reliance on the promise and prevents the unjust enrichment of the buyer at the seller's expense. Each of these three grounds of enforcement, bargain, reliance and unjust enrichment, has independent force, but the bargain element alone satisfies the requirement of consideration except in the cases covered by §§ 73, 74, 76 and 77. Cases of promises binding by virtue of reliance or unjust enrichment are dealt with in §§ 82–94.

c. Formality. Consideration furnishes a substantive rather than a formal basis for the enforcement of a promise. Many bargains, particularly when fully performed on one side, involve acts in the course of performance which satisfy some or all of the functions of form and thus may be thought of as natural formalities. Four principal functions have been identified which legal formalities in general may serve: the *evidentiary* function, to provide evidence of the existence and terms of the contract; the *cautionary* function, to guard the promisor against ill-considered action; the *deterrent* function, to discourage transactions of doubtful utility; and the *channeling* or signalizing function, to distinguish a particular type of transaction from other types and from tentative or exploratory expressions of intention in the way that coinage distinguishes money from other metal. But formality is not essential to consideration; nor does formality supply consideration where the element of exchange is absent. Rules under which formality makes binding a promise not supported by consideration are stated in §§ 82–94 and in §§ 95–109 on contracts under seal.

d. Unconscionable and illegal bargains. The rule stated in this Section does not require that consideration have an economic value equivalent to that of the promise. See § 79. Nor does the Section require that the consideration or the promise be lawful. The problems raised by unconscionable and illegal bargains are dealt with in § 208 on unconscionability, Chapter 6 on mistake, Chapter 7 on misrepresentation, duress and undue influence, and Chapter 8 on unenforceability on grounds of public policy. In addition, particular types of bargains which are likely to be unconscionable are the subject of §§ 73 and 74.

§ 73. Performance of Legal Duty.

Performance of a legal duty owed to a promisor which is neither doubtful nor the subject of honest dispute is not consideration; but a similar performance is consideration if it differs from what was required by the duty in a way which reflects more than a pretense of bargain.

Comment

a. Rationale. A claim that the performance of a legal duty furnished consideration for a promise often raises a suspicion that the transaction was gratuitous or mistaken or unconscionable. . . . Mistake, misrepresentation, duress, undue influence, or public policy may invalidate the transaction even though there is consideration. See Chapters 6–8. But the rule of this Section renders unnecessary any inquiry into the existence of such an invalidating cause, and denies enforcement to some promises which would otherwise be valid. Because of the likelihood that the promise was obtained by an express or implied threat to withhold performance of a legal duty, the promise does not have the presumptive social utility normally found in a bargain. Enforcement must therefore rest on some substantive or formal basis other than the mere fact of bargain. See Comments b and c to § 72. As to such bases, see Topics 2 and 3, and particularly § 89.

b. Public duties; torts and crimes. A legal duty may be owed to the promisor as a member of the public, as when the promisee is a public official. In such cases there is often no direct sanction available to a member of the public to compel performance of the duty, and the danger of express or implied threats to withhold performance affects public as well as private interests. A bargain by a public official to obtain private advantage for performing his duty is therefore unenforceable as against public policy. See Chapter 8. And under this Section performance of the duty is not consideration for a promise.

Similar reasoning may apply to duties of public utilities, duties of fiduciaries, and in some cases to duties of citizens generally. Thus a bargain to pay a witness for testimony may be unenforceable as against public policy. See §§ 178–80. A bargain induced by an improper threat may be voidable for duress. See §§ 175–76. If the only thing bargained for is forbearance to commit a crime or tort, the bargain may be unenforceable as against public policy. See § 178. The performance of legal duty is not consideration for a promise in any such case if the duty is owed to the promisor. If the legal duty is not owed to the promisor, there is consideration but the violation of public policy or other invalidating cause may remain.

In applying this Section it is first necessary to define the legal duty. The requirement of consideration is satisfied if the duty is doubtful or is the subject of honest dispute, or if the consideration includes a performance in addition to or materially different from the performance of the duty. Whether such facts eliminate duress or violation of public policy or other invalidating cause depends on the circumstances. Ordinarily a mere formality such as the affixing of a seal, though sufficient to render consideration unnecessary, does not cure such defects. In some situations, however, where there is no other invalidating cause but lack of consideration, the bargain may be enforceable by virtue of reliance or unjust enrichment or formality. See §§ 82–109.

Illustrations

1. A offers a reward to whoever produces evidence leading to the arrest and conviction of the murderer of B. C produces such evidence in the performance of his duty as a police officer. C's performance is not consideration for A's promise.

2. In Illustration 1, C's duties as a police officer are limited to crimes committed in a particular State, and while on vacation he gathers evidence as to a crime committed elsewhere. C's performance is consideration for the promise.

3. In a State where contracts between husband and wife are enforced and spouses are under a duty not to leave without just cause, A's wife, B, leaves him without just cause. A promises to pay B $1,000 if she will return. Induced thereby, B returns. Her return is not consideration. Compare §§ 175–77, 190.

c. *Contractual duty to the promisor.* Legal remedies for breach of contract ordinarily involve delay and expense and rarely put the promisee in fully as good a position as voluntary performance. It is therefore often to a promisee's advantage to offer a bonus to a recalcitrant promisor to induce performance without legal proceedings, and an unscrupulous promisor may threaten breach in order to obtain such a bonus. In extreme cases, a bargain for additional compensation under such circumstances may be voidable for duress. See §§ 175–76. And the lack of social utility in such bargains provides what modern justification there is for the rule that performance of a contractual duty is not consideration for a new promise.

But the rule has not been limited to cases where there was a possibility of unfair pressure, and it has been much criticized as resting on scholastic logic. Slight variations of circumstance are commonly held to take a case out of the rule, particularly where the parties have made an equitable adjustment in the course of performance of a continuing contract, or where an impecunious debtor has paid part of his debt in satisfaction of the whole. See §§ 89, 273–77. And in some states the rule has simply been repudiated.

Illustrations

4. A, an architect, agrees with B to superintend a construction project for a fixed fee. During the course of the project, without excuse, A takes away his plans and refuses to continue, and B promises him an extra fee if A will resume work. A's resumption of work is not consideration for B's promise of an extra fee.

5. A files a claim for total disability under an accident insurance policy written by B. Without investigation, discussion or dispute, B pays A the lesser amount which would be payable for partial disability, and A signs a receipt for "full payment" of the claim. The payment is not consideration for A's promise to accept it in full satisfaction of his claim for total disability.

6. A, being insolvent and contemplating bankruptcy, offers B $30 in full settlement of a debt of $100. B dissuades A from going into bankruptcy, accepts the offer, receives the money, and closes the account. A's forbearance to seek a discharge in bankruptcy is consideration for B's promise not to seek further payment.

7. A owes B a liquidated sum. Any payment by A at an earlier time, or in a different medium from that required by the duty, is consideration for B's promise to accept it in full satisfaction if the difference in performance is part of what is requested and given in exchange for the promise.

8. A owes B a matured liquidated debt bearing interest. Mutual promises to extend the debt for a year even at a lower rate of interest are binding. By such an agreement A gives up the right to terminate the running of interest by paying the debt.

d. Contractual duty to third person. The rule that performance of legal duty is not consideration for a promise has often been applied in cases involving a contractual duty owed to a person other than the promisor. In such cases, however, there is less likelihood of economic coercion or other unfair pressure than there is if the duty is owed to the promisee. In some cases consideration can be found in the fact that the promisee gives up his right to propose to the third person the rescission or modification of the contractual duty. But the tendency of the law has been simply to hold that performance of contractual duty can be consideration if the duty is not owed to the promisor. Relief may still be given to the promisor in appropriate cases under the rules governing duress and other invalidating causes.

Illustrations

9. A and B are engaged to be married. In an antenuptial agreement C, A's father, promises B that C will pay an annuity to A, and A and B marry in reliance on the promise. The marriage is consideration for C's promise.

10. A and her husband B are employed as domestic servants of C. B having become ill, C employs A to care for B in the home of A and B. A's care for B is consideration for C's promise to pay wages to A.

11. A contracts with B to install heating units in houses being built by B for C. B becomes insolvent and discontinues work, and C promises to pay A if A completes the installation in accordance with the contract between A and B. A's performance is consideration for C's promise.

12. A is employed to drive B's horse in a race. C owns the dam of B's horse and is entitled to a prize if B's horse wins the race. C promises A a bonus if he wins the race. A's driving in the race is consideration for C's promise, but B may be entitled to the bonus. See Restatement, Second, Agency §§ 313, 388.

e. Voidable and unenforceable duties. The duty referred to in the Section is confined to a duty for which any remedy ordinarily allowed by the law for that kind of duty is still available. One who may at will avoid a legal relation or refrain from any performance without legal consequences, or against whom all remedies appropriate to the enforcement of his duty have become barred, is not under a duty within the meaning of the Section.

Illustrations

13. A, an infant, promises B to pay B $50 for a set of books which A does not need. B delivers the books. A becomes of age and threatens to rescind the bargain, as the law permits him to do. B promises A that if A will pay the $50 as originally agreed, B will give A another book. A, induced thereby, pays the $50. The payment is consideration.

14. A sells goods to B, who becomes indebted therefor in the sum of $100. The Statute of Limitations bars any remedy of A to recover the debt. A promises B that if B will pay the debt, A will give B a specified book. B pays the debt. The payment is consideration.

f. Doubtful, disputed and unliquidated duties. Such duties are not within this Section. They are the subject of § 74.

§ 74. Settlement of Claims.

(1) Forbearance to assert or the surrender of a claim or defense which proves to be invalid is not consideration unless

    (a) the claim or defense is in fact doubtful because of uncertainty as to the facts or the law, or

Ch. 4   FORMATION OF CONTRACTS—CONSIDERATION   § 74

(b) the forbearing or surrendering party believes that the claim or defense may be fairly determined to be valid.

(2) The execution of a written instrument surrendering a claim or defense by one who is under no duty to execute it is consideration if the execution of the written instrument is bargained for even though he is not asserting the claim or defense and believes that no valid claim or defense exists.

Comment

a. Relation to legal-duty rule. Subsection (1) elaborates a limitation on the scope of the legal-duty rule stated in § 73. That limitation is based on the traditional policy of favoring compromises of disputed claims in order to reduce the volume of litigation.

Surrender of an invalid defense commonly means that a legal duty is performed, but in cases of invalid claims Subsection (1) may go beyond the legal-duty rule, since in many situations any legal duty not to litigate unfounded claims is likely to be unenforceable. In any event, the subject of compromise agreements is of sufficient importance to deserve separate treatment. Subsection (2) is clearly beyond the scope of the legal-duty rule, and merely states for greater clarity an application of § 72.

b. Requirement of good faith. The policy favoring compromise of disputed claims is clearest, perhaps, where a claim is surrendered at a time when it is uncertain whether it is valid or not. Even though the invalidity later becomes clear, the bargain is to be judged as it appeared to the parties at the time; if the claim was then doubtful, no inquiry is necessary as to their good faith. Even though the invalidity should have been clear at the time, the settlement of an honest dispute is upheld. But a mere assertion or denial of liability does not make a claim doubtful, and the fact that invalidity is obvious may indicate that it was known. In such cases Subsection (1)(b) requires a showing of good faith.

Illustrations

1. A, a shipowner, has a legal duty to provide maintenance and cure for B, a seaman. B honestly but unreasonably claims that adequate care is not available in a free public hospital and that he is entitled to treatment by a private physician. B's forbearance to press this claim is consideration for A's promise to be responsible for the consequences of any improper treatment in the public hospital.

2. A, knowing that he has no legal basis for complaint, frequently complains to B, his father, that B has made more gifts to B's other children than to A. B promises that if A will cease complaining, B will forgive a debt owed by A to B. A's forbearance to assert his claim of discrimination is not consideration for B's promise.

3. A, knowing that B is a married man, cohabits with him for several years. During that time B promises to marry A as soon as he is divorced. After the cohabitation ceases, A surrenders all her claims on account of the promise to marry in consideration of B's promise to pay her $1000 a month during her life. Under applicable state law A has no valid claim. If it is found that A knew there was no valid claim, there is no consideration for B's promise of payment. Compare §§ 189–90.

c. Unliquidated obligations. An undisputed obligation may be unliquidated, that is, uncertain or disputed in amount. The settlement of such a claim is governed by the same principles as settlement of a claim the existence of which is doubtful or disputed. The payment of any definite sum of money on account of a single claim which is entirely unliquidated is consideration for a return promise. An admission by the obligor that a minimum amount is due does not liquidate the claim even partially unless he is contractually bound to the admission. But payment of less than is admittedly due may in some circumstances tend to show that a partial defense or offset was not asserted in good faith.

Payment of an obligation which is liquidated and undisputed is not consideration for a promise to surrender an unliquidated claim which is wholly distinct. See § 73. Whether in a particular case there is a single unliquidated claim or a combination of separate claims, some liquidated and some not, depends on the circumstances and the agreements of the parties. If there are no circumstances of unfair pressure or economic coercion and a disputed item is closely related to an undisputed item, the two are treated as making up a single unliquidated claim; and payment of the amount admittedly due can be consideration for a promise to surrender the entire claim.

Illustration

4. A, a real estate broker, is entitled to a commission for selling B's land, amounting to five per cent or $1,500. B claims in good faith that he owes only one per cent or $300, and offers to pay that amount in full settlement of the claim for commission. A accepts the offer. The payment is consideration for B's promise to surrender his entire claim.

5. A owes B at least $4,280 on a logging contract. Additional items in the account are unliquidated, and some of them are the subject of honest dispute. A disputes B's right to all above $4,280 on grounds he knows to be untrue, and offers $4,000 in full settlement. A's payment of $4,000 is not consideration for B's promise to surrender his entire claim.

6. A contracts to sell and deliver a lot of goods to B. On delivery B accepts a commercial unit priced at $30 and rejects the rest, priced at $50. See Uniform Commercial Code § 2–601. B claims in good faith but erroneously that the rejected goods are defective. A promises to surrender any claim based on the rejection if B pays the $30. B's payment is consideration for A's promise.

7. A stops payment on a check for $200 drawn on his account in the B bank, but the bank pays the check and charges his account, leaving a balance of $800. There is an honest dispute as to the propriety of the charge, and the bank refuses to pay any part of the $800 until the dispute is settled. To obtain the money, A promises to make no further claim. Payment of the $800 by the bank is not consideration for the promise.

d. Forbearance without surrender. Forbearance to assert a valid claim or a doubtful or honestly-asserted claim may be consideration for a promise, just as surrender of the claim would be. Where the forbearance is temporary and it is contemplated that the claim will be asserted later, there is sometimes a question whether the forbearance is bargained for and given in exchange for the promise. If an offer specifies a return promise to forbear as the requested consideration, forbearance without promise is not an acceptance. Compare § 53. But a promise to forbear may be implied. Compare §§ 32, 62. Whether a promise is consideration depends on the rules stated in §§ 75–78. Forbearance which is not bargained for may in some cases be reliance sufficient to bring § 90 into play.

Illustrations

8. A owes B $120. Without requesting B to forbear suit, C promises B in April that if A does not pay by October 1 C will pay $100. B's forbearance to sue until October is not consideration for C's promise.

9. A owes B a debt secured by mortgage, and B begins foreclosure proceedings. C requests B to forbear and promises to pay the debt. B's forbearance for a reasonable time is consideration for C's promise.

e. Execution of release or quit-claim deed. Subsection (2) provides for the situation where the party who would be subject to a claim or defense, if one existed, wants assurance of its non-existence. Such assurance may be useful, for example, to enable him to obtain credit or to sell property. Although surrender of a non-existent claim by one who knows he has no claim is not consideration for a promise, the execution of an instrument of surrender may be consideration if there is no improper pressure or deception. See § 79. But there is no consideration if the surrendering party is under a duty to execute the instrument, as under Uniform Commercial Code §§ 3–505(1)(d), 9–208, 9–404.

Illustration

10. A owns land and desires to mortgage it. He is informed that his title may be defective by reason of a possible interest in B. B says that he has no claim and has previously given a deed to the land to A's grantor. A promises to pay $50 for a new quit-claim deed. B's execution and delivery of such a deed is consideration for A's promise.

§ 75. Exchange of Promise for Promise.

Except as stated in §§ 76 and 77, a promise which is bargained for is consideration if, but only if, the promised performance would be consideration.

Ch. 4 FORMATION OF CONTRACTS—CONSIDERATION § 75

Comment

a. The executory exchange. In modern times the enforcement of bargains is not limited to those partly completed, but is extended to the wholly executory exchange in which promise is exchanged for promise. In such a case the element of unjust enrichment is not present; the element of reliance, if present at all, is less tangible and direct than in the case of the half-completed exchange. The promise is enforced by virtue of the fact of bargain, without more. Since the principle that bargains are binding is widely understood and is reinforced in many situations by custom and convention, the fact of bargain also tends to satisfy the cautionary and channeling functions of form. Compare Comments b and c to § 72. Evidentiary safeguards, however, are largely left to the Statute of Frauds rather than to the requirement of consideration. . . .

b. Promise and performance. The principle of this Section is that, in determining whether there is consideration, one's word is as good as one's deed but no better. More detailed rules are stated in §§ 76–78 for cases in which the application of this principle has produced problems. Certain cases which have sometimes been thought to be exceptions to the principle are commented upon below.

c. Performance of legal duty and settlement of claims. A promise to perform a legal duty is not consideration for a return promise unless performance would be. Similarly, a promise to surrender a claim or defense or to forbear from asserting it is consideration only if performance would be. Thus a promise of such performance may raise the same questions as the performance would: Is the duty owed to the maker of the return promise? Is the claim or defense known to be invalid? See §§ 73, 74.

Illustrations

1. A promises to pay a debt to B, or to perform an existing contractual duty to B, or to perform his duty as a public official. The legal duty is neither doubtful nor the subject of honest dispute, but A would not have fulfilled the duty but for B's return promise. A's promise is not consideration for B's return promise. Compare § 73.

2. A promises B to surrender or to forbear suit upon a claim either against B or against C. A knows the claim is invalid. A's promise is not consideration for a return promise by B. Compare § 74.

d. "Void" promises. The value of a promise does not necessarily depend upon the availability of a legal remedy for breach, and bargains are often made in consideration of promises which are voidable or unenforceable. Such a promise may be consideration for a return promise. See § 78. But it is sometimes suggested that a promise is not consideration if it is not binding, or if it is "void." The examples used commonly involve total lack of capacity to contract (see §§ 12, 13), indefinite promises (see §§ 33–34), promises lacking consideration, or promises unenforceable as against public policy (see Chapter 8). Such cases are not exceptions to the rule stated in this Section. In some of them there is no promise within the definition in § 2, in others the return promise would not be binding whether the consideration consisted of a promise or of performance, in some the invalidity of the return promise rests on other policies than those embodied in the requirement of consideration.

Illustrations

3. While A's property is under guardianship by reason of an adjudication of mental illness, A makes an agreement with B in which B makes a promise. B's promise is not a contract, whether the consideration consists of a promise by A or performance by A. Compare § 13; Restatement of Restitution § 139.

A promises to forbear suit against B in exchange for B's promise to pay a liquidated and undisputed debt 4. to A. A's promise is not binding because B's promise is not consideration under § 73, but A's promise is nevertheless consideration for B's. Moreover, B's promise would be enforceable without consideration under § 82. On either basis, B's promise is conditional on A's forbearance and can be enforced only if the condition is met.

5. A, a married man, and B, an unmarried woman, make mutual promises to marry. B neither knows nor has reason to know that A is married. B's promise is consideration and B may recover damages from A for breach of his promise though B would have a defense to a similar action by A. See § 180.

225

6. A promises B $100 in return for B's promise to cut timber on land upon which A is a trespasser. B neither knows nor has reason to know that A is not privileged to cut the timber. B's promise is consideration and B may recover damages from A for breach of his promise though B would have a defense to a similar action by A. See Illustration 2 to § 180.

§ 76. Conditional Promise.

(1) A conditional promise is not consideration if the promisor knows at the time of making the promise that the condition cannot occur.

(2) A promise conditional on a performance by the promisor is a promise of alternative performances within § 77 unless occurrence of the condition is also promised.

Comment

a. "Conditional promise." Conditions and similar events are the subject of Topic 5 of Chapter 9. A promise is "conditional" for the purposes of this Section if an event must occur before a duty of immediate performance of the promise arises, and the "condition" is the event which must occur. See § 224. A condition may be provided for by a term of a promise, either in words or by virtue of other conduct or the circumstances, or it may be supplied by law. See § 5.

b. Impossible conditions. Words of conditional promise do not constitute a promise within the definition in § 2 if both promisor and promisee know that the condition cannot occur. If the promisor has such knowledge but the promisee does not, there may be a promise, but the promisee receives only the false appearance of a commitment by the promisor; in such cases the promise is not consideration for a return promise. But if the promisor honestly believes he is making a commitment, the promise may be consideration even though the facts are such that no duty of immediate performance can ever arise. Thus in dealing with promises conditional on past events the law takes the standpoint of the promisor and treats as uncertain that which is uncertain to him. For this purpose, an event is uncertain to a promisor who does not know even though he has reason to know.

Illustrations

1. A promises B to pay him $5,000 if B's ship now at sea has already been lost, knowing that the ship has not been lost. A's promise is illusory and is not consideration for a return promise.

2. The facts being otherwise as stated in Illustration 1, A makes the promise not knowing whether the ship has been lost or not. A's promise is consideration even though A has reason to know that the ship has not been lost.

3. A sells to B a tract of land said to contain 500 acres. Later A and B agree to have the land surveyed; A promises to pay B $16 for each acre of deficiency; B promises to pay A $16 for each acre of excess. A's promise is consideration for B's promise, and B's promise is consideration for A's.

c. Aleatory promises. A party may make an aleatory promise, under which his duty to perform is conditional on the occurrence of a fortuitous event. See §§ 225, 226, 239. Such a promise may be consideration for a return promise.

Illustration

4. A promises to sell and B to buy goods if A's employees do not strike before the time for delivery. The promises are consideration for each other.

5. A promises to convey to B immediately a patent owned by A; B promises to pay A $10,000 when pending litigation is terminated, if the patent is not held invalid. B's promise is consideration for A's promise.

6. A promises B to pay him $5000 if his house burns within a year. This is consideration for a return promise.

d. Conditions within the promisor's control. Words of promise do not constitute a promise if they make performance entirely optional with the purported promisor. See Comment e to § 2. Such words, often referred to as forming an illusory promise, do not constitute consideration for a return promise. See § 77. But a promise may be conditional on an event within the control of the promisor. Such a promise may be consideration if he has also promised that the condition will occur. Similarly, even though he does not promise occurrence of the condition, there may be consideration if forbearance from causing the condition to occur would itself have been consideration if it alone had been bargained for. In such a case, there is in effect a promise in the alternative, and the rules stated in § 77 apply.

Illustrations

7. A promises B to pay him $5000 if A enters a competing business within three years. This is consideration for a return promise, since forbearance to compete would be consideration. See § 77.

8. A promises B that, "subject to purchase" of a certain ship, he will charter it to B, and B promises to accept the charter. A's promise is consideration for B's. A's forbearance to buy the ship could have been consideration for a different promise, such as a promise to pay money. See § 77.

§ 77. Illusory and Alternative Promises.

A promise or apparent promise is not consideration if by its terms the promisor or purported promisor reserves a choice of alternative performances unless

    (a) each of the alternative performances would have been consideration if it alone had been bargained for; or

    (b) one of the alternative performances would have been consideration and there is or appears to the parties to be a substantial possibility that before the promisor exercises his choice events may eliminate the alternatives which would not have been consideration.

Comment

a. Illusory promises. Words of promise which by their terms make performance entirely optional with the "promisor" do not constitute a promise. See Comment e to § 2; compare § 76. In such cases there might theoretically be a bargain to pay for the utterance of the words, but in practice it is performance which is bargained for. Where the apparent assurance of performance is illusory, it is not consideration for a return promise. A different rule applies, however, where performance is optional, not by the terms of the agreement, but by virtue of a rule of law. See § 5 (defining "term"), § 78.

Illustrations

1. A offers to deliver to B at $2 a bushel as many bushels of wheat, not exceeding 5,000, as B may choose to order within the next 30 days. B accepts, agreeing to buy at that price as much as he shall order from A within that time. B's acceptance involves no promise by him, and is not consideration. Compare §§ 31, 34.

2. A promises B to act as B's agent for three years from a future date on certain terms; B agrees that A may so act, but reserves the power to terminate the agreement at any time. B's agreement is not consideration, since it involves no promise by him.

b. Alternative promises. A promise in the alternative may be made because each of the alternative performances is the object of desire to the promisee. Or the promisee may desire one performance only, but the promisor may reserve an alternative which he may deem advantageous. In either type of case the promise is consideration if it cannot be kept without some action or forbearance which would be consideration if it alone were bargained for. But if the promisor has an unfettered choice of alternatives, and one alternative would not have been consideration if separately bargained for, the promise in the alternative is not consideration.

Illustrations

3. A offers to deliver to B at $2 a bushel as many bushels of wheat, not exceeding 5,000, as B may choose to order within the next 30 days, if B will promise to order at least 1,000 bushels within

that time. B accepts. B's promise is consideration since it reserves only a limited option and cannot be performed without doing something which would be consideration if it alone were bargained for.

4. A agrees to sell and B to buy between 400 and 600 tons of fertilizer in installments as ordered by B, A reserving the right to terminate the agreement at any time without notice. B's promise is without consideration.

5. A promises B to act as B's agent for three years on certain terms, starting immediately; B agrees that A may so act, but reserves the power to terminate the agreement on 30 days notice. B's agreement is consideration, since he promises to continue the agency for at least 30 days.

6. A owes B an undisputed debt of $5,000 payable in five years. A makes a subsequent promise that he will either pay $4,000 at the end of the first year or pay the debt at maturity; in return B promises to accept the $4,000, if paid at the end of the first year, in full satisfaction of the debt. A's subsequent promise is not consideration for B's return promise, since the alternative of performing his legal duty is not consideration. See §§ 73, 75.

c. Alternatives not dependent on promisor's free choice. A promise may give the promisee a right to choose one of several stated performances. Or the selection among alternative performances may be left to events not within the control of either party. In such cases the promise, if bargained for, is consideration if any one of the alternatives would have been, unless the promisor knows that all such alternatives are subject to conditions which cannot exist or occur. See § 76(1). Similarly, the promise may be consideration even though a conditional power of choice is left to the promisor. For example, the promisor may reserve an option to terminate only after he has rendered performance which would be consideration, or only in a contingency which may never occur, or only on a condition of forbearance by him which would have been consideration. Compare Comment d to § 76.

Illustration

7. A orders goods from B for shipment within three months, reserving the right to cancel the order before shipment. B has the goods in stock and accepts the order. A's promise to pay for the goods is consideration for B's promise to ship, since B can prevent cancellation by shipping immediately.

d. Implied limitations on promisor's choice. A limitation on the promisor's freedom of choice need not be stated in words. It may be an implicit term of the promise, or it may be supplied by law. Thus a power to terminate a contract for the sale of goods may be subject to a statutory requirement of reasonable notification, and an agreement dispensing with notification may be unconscionable and invalid. See Uniform Commercial Code § 2–309(3). Again, an alternative promise may cease to be alternative when performance of one alternative becomes impossible or unenforceable on grounds of public policy. See §§ 270, 184. If such a contingency is within the contemplation of the parties so that it is part of what is bargained for, the promise is consideration.

Illustrations

8. A promises to sell his output or buy his requirements of a specified type of goods from B on specified terms. A's promise is consideration for a return promise by B. A must operate his plant or conduct his business in good faith and according to commercial standards of fair dealing in the trade so that his output or requirements will approximate a reasonably foreseeable figure. See Comment 2 to Uniform Commercial Code § 2–306.

9. A promises to pay B half of any profits he derives from the sale of goods manufactured by B; in return B promises that A shall have the exclusive right to market such goods. The promises are consideration for each other, since the agreement for exclusive dealing imposes an obligation on A to use best efforts to promote sale of the goods and on B to use best efforts to supply them. See Uniform Commercial Code § 2–306(2).

10. A owes B a matured liquidated debt bearing interest. In an agreement to extend the debt for a year at a lower rate of interest, B reserves the right to accelerate payment "at will," but under Uniform Commercial Code § 1–208, B may accelerate payment only if he in good faith believes that the prospect of payment is impaired. B's surrender of the unconditional right to demand immediate payment is consideration. Compare Illustration 8 to § 73.

11. A is under a contractual duty to deliver to B a described automobile. Because it is doubtful whether such a car will be available at the agreed time, A promises that if he cannot obtain it he will deliver a described substitute; B agrees to accept the substitute if delivered. A's promise is consideration.

§ 78. Voidable and Unenforceable Promises.

The fact that a rule of law renders a promise voidable or unenforceable does not prevent it from being consideration.

Comment

a. Rationale. The value of a promise depends on its terms and on the probability that it will be performed. The value is not necessarily affected adversely by the fact that no legal remedy will be available in the event of breach; the probability of performance may be greater for a voidable or unenforceable promise, or even for a promise which is not binding or is against public policy, than for the judgment or decree of a court. In general the law of contracts leaves to the parties the valuation of a promise in the formation of a bargain. See § 79. The fact that no legal remedy is available for breach of a promise does not prevent it from being a part of a bargain or remove the bargain from the scope of the general principle that bargains are enforceable. See §§ 17, 71. As to "void" promises, see Comment d to § 75.

b. Voidable promises. A contract may be voidable by one party by reason of his incapacity or mistake, or by reason of the fraud, breach or other fault of the other party. See § 7. In many such cases a reservation of a similar power by the terms of the agreement would mean that he had made no promise or that his promise was not consideration for a return promise. See § 77. But where the power of avoidance is given by the law to protect one party from actual or possible imposition, he often regards himself as bound in conscience if not in law. He may in some circumstance lose the power by ratification without consideration. See § 85. Until the power is exercised, it does not prevent enforcement of a return promise.

Illustration

1. A makes a promise in exchange for a return promise by B. The fact that the contract is voidable by A because of his own infancy or because of B's fraud does not prevent A's promise from being consideration for B's promise.

c. Unenforceable promises. A promise may be unenforceable by reason of lack of consideration or public policy, or because of a statute relating to remedies, such as the Statute of Frauds, or because of the traditional immunity of the sovereign from suit. See § 8. In such cases a return promise may or may not be unenforceable on the same or other grounds. But the fact that a promise is unenforceable does not mean that the return promise lacks consideration. See Illustrations 4 6 to § 75.

Illustrations

2. A makes a promise in exchange for a return promise by B. The fact that A's promise is unenforceable under the local Statute of Frauds does not prevent it from being consideration for B's promise.

3. A makes a promise in exchange for a promise by B, a foreign government not subject to suit. The fact that B's promise is unenforceable does not prevent it from being consideration for A's promise.

§ 79. Adequacy of Consideration; Mutuality of Obligation.

If the requirement of consideration is met, there is no additional requirement of

(a) a gain, advantage, or benefit to the promisor or a loss, disadvantage, or detriment to the promisee; or

(b) equivalence in the values exchanged; or

(c) "mutuality of obligation."

Comment

a. Rationale. In such typical bargains as the ordinary sale of goods each party gives up something of economic value, and the values exchanged are often roughly or exactly equivalent by standards independent of the particular bargain. Quite often promise is exchanged for promise, and the promised performances are sometimes divisible into matching parts. See § 31. Hence it has sometimes been said that consideration must consist of a "benefit to the promisor" or a "detriment to the promisee"; it has frequently been claimed that there was no consideration because the economic value given in exchange was much less than that of the promise or the promised performance; "mutuality of obligation" has been said to be essential to a contract. But experience has shown that these are not essential elements of a bargain or of an enforceable contract, and they are negated as requirements by the rules stated in §§ 71–78. This Section makes that negation explicit.

b. Benefit and detriment. Historically, the common law action of debt was said to require a quid pro quo, and that requirement may have led to statements that consideration must be a benefit to the promisor. But contracts were enforced in the common-law action of assumpsit without any such requirement; in actions of assumpsit the emphasis was rather on the harm to the promisee, and detrimental reliance on a promise may still be the basis of contractual relief. See § 90. But reliance is not essential to the formation of a bargain, and remedies for breach have long been given in cases of exchange of promise for promise where neither party has begun to perform. Today when it is said that consideration must involve a detriment to the promisee, the supposed requirement is often qualified by a statement that a "legal detriment" is sufficient even though there is no economic detriment or other actual loss. It is more realistic to say simply that there is no requirement of detriment.

Illustrations

1. A contracts to sell property to B. As a favor to B, who is C's friend, and in consideration of A's performance of the contract, C guarantees that B will pay the agreed price. A's performance is consideration for C's promise. See § 73.

2. A has executed a document in the form of a guaranty which imposes no obligation on A and has no value. B's surrender of the document to A, if bargained for, is consideration for a promise by A to pay $10,000. Compare § 74.

c. Exchange of unequal values. To the extent that the apportionment of productive energy and product in the economy are left to private action, the parties to transactions are free to fix their own valuations. The resolution of disputes often requires a determination of value in the more general sense of market value, and such values are commonly fixed as an approximation based on a multitude of private valuations. But in many situations there is no reliable external standard of value, or the general standard is inappropriate to the precise circumstances of the parties. Valuation is left to private action in part because the parties are thought to be better able than others to evaluate the circumstances of particular transactions. In any event, they are not ordinarily bound to follow the valuations of others.

Ordinarily, therefore, courts do not inquire into the adequacy of consideration. This is particularly so when one or both of the values exchanged are uncertain or difficult to measure. But it is also applied even when it is clear that the transaction is a mixture of bargain and gift. See Comment c to § 71. Gross inadequacy of consideration may be relevant to issues of capacity, fraud and the like, but the requirement of consideration is not a safeguard against imprudent and improvident contracts except in cases where it appears that there is no bargain in fact.

Illustrations

3. A borrows $300 from B to enable A to begin litigation to recover a gold mine through litigation, and promises to repay $10,000 when he recovers the mine. The loan is consideration for the promise.

4. A is pregnant with the illegitimate child of B, a wealthy man. A promises to give the child A's surname and B's given name, and B promises to provide for the support and education of the child and to set up a trust of securities to provide the child with a minimum net income of $100 per week until he reaches the age of 21. The naming of the child is consideration for B's promise.

d. Pretended exchange. Disparity in value, with or without other circumstances, sometimes indicates that the purported consideration was not in fact bargained for but was a mere formality or pretense. Such a sham or "nominal" consideration does not satisfy the requirement of § 71. Promises are enforced in such cases, if at all, either as promises binding without consideration under §§ 82–94 or as promises binding by virtue of their formal characteristics under § 6. See, for example, §§ 95–109 on contracts under seal.

Illustrations

5. In consideration of one cent received, A promises to pay $600 in three yearly installments of $200 each. The one cent is merely nominal and is not consideration for A's promise.

6. A dies leaving no assets and owing $4000 to the B bank. C, A's widow, promises to pay the debt, and B promises to make no claim against A's estate. Without some further showing, B's promise is a mere formality and is not consideration for C's promise.

e. Effects of gross inadequacy. Although the requirement of consideration may be met despite a great difference in the values exchanged, gross inadequacy of consideration may be relevant in the application of other rules. Inadequacy "such as shocks the conscience" is often said to be a "badge of fraud," justifying a denial of specific performance. See § 364(1)(c). Inadequacy may also help to justify rescission or cancellation on the ground of lack of capacity (see §§ 15, 16), mistake, misrepresentation, duress or undue influence (see Chapters 6 and 7). Unequal bargains are also limited by the statutory law of usury, by regulation of the rates of public utilities and some other enterprises, and by special rules developed for the sale of an expectation of inheritance, for contractual penalties and forfeitures (see §§ 229, 356), and for agreements between secured lender and borrower (see Restatement of Security § 55, Uniform Commercial Code § 9–501).

f. Mutuality. The word "mutuality," though often used in connection with the law of Contracts, has no definite meaning. "Mutual assent" as one element of a bargain is the subject of Topic 2 of this Chapter. "Mutuality of remedy" is dealt with in Comment c to § 363. Clause (c) of this Section negates any supposed requirement of "mutuality of obligation." Such a requirement has sometimes been asserted in the form, "Both parties must be bound or neither is bound." That statement is obviously erroneous as applied to an exchange of promise for performance; it is equally inapplicable to contracts governed by §§ 82–94 and to contracts enforceable by virtue of their formal characteristics under § 6. Even in the ordinary case of the exchange of promise for promise, § 78 makes it clear that voidable and unenforceable promises may be consideration. The only requirement of "mutuality of obligation" even in cases of mutual promises is that stated in §§ 76–77.

§ 80. Multiple Exchanges.

(1) There is consideration for a set of promises if what is bargained for and given in exchange would have been consideration for each promise in the set if exchanged for that promise alone.

(2) The fact that part of what is bargained for would not have been consideration if that part alone had been bargained for does not prevent the whole from being consideration.

Comment

a. One consideration for a number of promises. Since consideration is not required to be adequate in value (see § 79), two or more promises may be binding even though made for the price of one. A single performance or return promise may thus furnish consideration for any number of promises. But if the performance or return promise would not be consideration for a single promise, it is not consideration for that promise as part of a set of promises, or for the other promises in the set.

Illustrations

1. A pays B or promises B to pay him $5, not then owed by A, in consideration of which B promises A to give him a book and also promises to surrender a letter. Both of B's promises are supported by consideration.

2. A pays B or promises B to pay him $50 not then owed by A, in exchange for the following promises: a promise by C to dig a well for D, a promise by E to discharge F from a debt of $100 owing by F to E. All the promises are supported by consideration.

b. Several performances or return promises as consideration. In cases within Subsection (2) the promisor has received all he bargained for. The fact that part of it would not have been consideration standing alone does not make enforcement of the bargain unjust to the promisor or contrary to the public interest. The effect of public policy on part of the consideration, however, may invalidate the entire bargain under some circumstances. See §§ 178, 183–85.

Illustration

3. A owes B $5. B promises to give A a book if A will pay the $5 and $1 in addition. A pays the $6. B's promise is binding, although A's payment of the $5 which he owed would not of itself have been consideration.

c. Compositions with creditors. Composition agreements between a debtor and his creditors illustrate Subsection (2). The consideration for which each assenting creditor bargains may be any or all of the following: (1) part payment of the sum due him, (2) the promise of each other creditor to forego a portion of his claim, (3) forbearance or promise of forbearance by the debtor to pay the assenting creditors more than equal proportions, (4) the action of the debtor in securing the assent of the other creditors, (5) the part payments made to the other creditors. The first is not consideration, but each of the others may be consideration. The last two are seldom bargained for in fact, but (2) and (3) are practically always bargained for by implication if not in so many words. Still other considerations may be agreed upon in any case.

Illustration

4. A makes a composition with B, C and D, three of his creditors, whereby each of them promises to accept forty cents on the dollar as full satisfaction, A promising to treat all assenting creditors equally. A's promise and the promises of the other two creditors are consideration for the promise of each creditor, even though there are other non-assenting creditors.

§ 81. Consideration as Motive or Inducing Cause.

(1) The fact that what is bargained for does not of itself induce the making of a promise does not prevent it from being consideration for the promise.

(2) The fact that a promise does not of itself induce a performance or return promise does not prevent the performance or return promise from being consideration for the promise.

Comment

a. "Bargained for." Consideration requires that a performance or return promise be "bargained for" in exchange for a promise; this means that the promisor must manifest an intention to induce the performance or return promise and to be induced by it, and that the promisee must manifest an intention to induce the making of the promise and to be induced by it. See § 71 and Comment b. In most commercial bargains the consideration is the object of the promisor's desire and that desire is a material motive or cause inducing the making of the promise, and the reciprocal desire of the promisee for the making of the promise similarly induces the furnishing of the consideration.

b. Immateriality of motive or cause. This Section makes explicit a limitation on the requirement that consideration be bargained for. Even in the typical commercial bargain, the promisor may have more than one motive, and the person furnishing the consideration need not inquire into the promisor's motives. Unless both parties know that the purported consideration is mere pretense, it is immaterial that the promisor's desire for the consideration is incidental to other objectives and even that the other party knows this to be so. Compare § 79 and Illustrations. Subsection (2) states a similar rule with respect to the motives of the promisee.

TOPIC 2. CONTRACTS WITHOUT CONSIDERATION

§ 82. Promise to Pay Indebtedness; Effect on the Statute of Limitations.

(1) A promise to pay all or part of an antecedent contractual or quasi-contractual indebtedness owed by the promisor is binding if the indebtedness is still enforceable or would be except for the effect of a statute of limitations.

(2) The following facts operate as such a promise unless other facts indicate a different intention:

(a) A voluntary acknowledgment to the obligee, admitting the present existence of the antecedent indebtedness; or

(b) A voluntary transfer of money, a negotiable instrument, or other thing by the obligor to the obligee, made as interest on or part payment of or collateral security for the antecedent indebtedness; or

(c) A statement to the obligee that the statute of limitations will not be pleaded as a defense.

Comment

a. Requirement of a writing. Statutes enacted in most States provide that a promise included in the Section is not binding unless it is in writing and signed by or on behalf of the promisor, except where the promise is inferred from part payment or from the giving of a negotiable instrument or collateral security as stated in Subsection (2) (b). See § 110. In a few States, no writing is required in any case. In a few other States, the rule is more stringent than that generally prevailing and even part payment or giving of security imposes no promissory duty on a debtor unless there is also a signed writing. Most of the statutes requiring a writing are inapplicable to promises supported by consideration or made enforceable by reliance. See § 90.

b. Historical note: types of indebtedness. The rule of Subsection (1) was established in the action of general or indebitatus assumpsit, based on a fictitious promise to pay an antecedent debt. Such an action could be brought on a simple contract debt, and the subsequent promise could be set up by way of replication to a plea of the statute of limitations. The rule was the same whether the new promise was made before or after the statute of limitations had run on the original debt; it was enough that the new promise was made within the statutory period before the bringing of the action. General assumpsit was extended to unliquidated contractual obligations and later to quasi-contractual obligations; it was not available for claims to damages for breach of a promissory bargain not performed on either side or for tort claims not involving unjust enrichment. The word "indebtedness" is intended to carry forward the distinction: a promise to pay damages for a tort or breach of contract may be made binding by consideration or reliance, but it is not within the rule stated in Subsection (1).

General assumpsit was extended to foreign judgments, but it did not lie for debts founded on domestic judgments or on contracts under seal. Some American courts have therefore denied effect to new promises to pay judgment debts or obligations under seal. In England there was no statute of limitations for such obligations until the nineteenth century, and the nineteenth-century statutes expressly gave effect to acknowledgments and part payments. Modern American statutes have changed the setting in which the question of the effect of a new promise arises. Statutes in many States have abrogated some or all of the common-law effects of the seal, and have thus weakened the basis for distinguishing contracts under seal from other contracts. Statutes also commonly make explicit provision for the extension or revival of judgments; such statutes may affect the question whether a new promise to pay a judgment can be the basis of an action.

Illustrations

1. A owes B $100 and the claim is not yet barred by the statute of limitations. A promises B in a signed writing to pay the debt. The promise is binding, and the statute of limitations will not bar the claim for the statutory period after the making of the new promise.

2. A owes B three debts of $500 each. All of the debts are barred by the statute of limitations. A writes to B, "I promise to pay you one of those $500 debts which I owe; the other two I shall not pay." A's promise of $500 is binding.

3. A owes B a debt for some work which B has done but the amount due is in dispute. A writes to B, "I will pay you whatever I owe." The promise is binding during the statutory period of limitation from the time when it was made, and subjects A to a duty to pay whatever amount B can prove was due him.

4. A wrongfully purports to sell B's horse to C, who pays A $100 and takes possession of the horse. A later promises B in a signed writing to pay B either $100 or the value of the horse, or C signs a written promise to pay B the value of the horse. The promise is binding as a promise to pay a quasi-contractual indebtedness. See Restatement of Restitution § 128.

5. A is indebted to B on a judgment, which is barred by a twelve-year statute of limitations, and makes a written promise to B to pay the debt. The subsequent promise does not revive the judgment, but may be the basis of an action.

c. Historical note: requirement and effect of promise. In early cases the effect of a new promise, acknowledgment or part payment was sometimes explained in terms of rebuttal of a presumption of payment raised by the statute of limitations, or in terms of waiver of a statutory defense which the debtor in honesty ought not to assert. Aside from the statute of limitations, a common-law or statutory presumption of payment may arise by lapse of time, and acknowledgment or part payment may rebut such a presumption even though any promise to pay is negated. But in the absence of a contrary statutory provision, the modern rule is that acknowledgment or part payment is effective to extend the running of the statute of limitations only if a new promise is fairly implied. Whatever the form of pleading permitted or required, the claim is based on the new promise and is limited by the terms of the new promise. And the extended or renewed obligation is subject to the statute of limitations and to other rules appropriate to the form and terms of the new promise.

Illustrations

6. A owes B a debt of $500, and writes to B, "I will pay you $400 in full satisfaction if you will so accept it." B does not reply. A's promise is not binding, whether made before or after the debt of $500 was barred by the statute of limitations, because B has not complied with the condition requiring acceptance.

7. A owes B $500, barred by the statute of limitations. A has an invalid claim for $250 against B, and writes B, "I will pay you the $500 I owe you subject to my claim of setoff." A is bound by his new promise to pay only $250.

8. A is indebted to B on a bond under seal, which is barred by a twelve-year statute of limitations, and makes a promise to B in a signed writing not under seal to pay the debt. The statute of limitations for debts under written contracts not under seal is six years. An action on the subsequent promise is subject to the six-year statute.

9. A owes B a debt barred by the statute of limitations, and promises B in a signed writing to pay the debt as soon as he is able to do so. B has no claim on the subsequent promise until A is able to pay, and the statute of limitations runs again from that time.

d. Acknowledgment. An unqualified admission that a debt is owing operates as a promise to pay it for the purposes of the rule stated in Subsection (1). It does not so operate for all purposes. See § 83; Uniform Commercial Code § 3–102(1) (c). The implication of a promise from an acknowledgment may be a survival of the view that the statute of limitations raises a presumption of payment, and in some States an acknowledgment is still said to be effective without any promise to pay. But circumstances indicating an intention not to pay deprive the acknowledgment of effect in most States.

Illustrations

10. A owes B a debt, and lists the debt in a sworn schedule required to be filed in his voluntary bankruptcy proceeding. A's admission that he owes the debt does not impose a new obligation on him, whether the statute of limitations has or has not completely run on the original obligation when the admission is made. See Comment a to § 83.

11. A owes B $500, and writes B, "I admit that I owe you $500, but I am unable to pay it." A's letter imposes no duty upon him.

e. *Part payment and giving of collateral.* Part payment of a debt amounts to an admission that it is owing and thus has the same effect as an acknowledgment, except that most of the statutes requiring a writing expressly preserve the effect previously given to a part payment. See § 110. Payment on account of interest is treated as part payment for this purpose, and the giving of a negotiable instrument or of collateral security has the same effect. There must be a voluntary transfer by the debtor; the creditor's exercise of a power given by law or of a power irrevocably given at a previous time does not operate as a promise by the debtor. See Restatement, Second, Agency §§ 14H, 138–39. Nor does a voluntary transfer so operate if the circumstances indicate that the debtor has no such intention. If the debtor makes a part payment in performance of a promise to pay in installments or on condition, he is bound only in accordance with the promise.

Illustrations

12. A owes B $500 and without comment sends B a check for $300. Absent other facts establishing that the check is referrable to the larger debt, it does not operate as a new promise.

13. A owes B $5,000, secured by a pledge of corporate bonds. On A's default B sells the bonds under a power given by law or by the pledge agreement and applies the proceeds to the debt, leaving a balance of $2000. The part payment does not operate as a new promise by A.

14. A owes B $500 and sends B a post-dated check for $200, stating that it is sent as part payment of the debt. The delivery of the check operates as a new promise to pay the debt, and payment of the check by the drawee bank on the subsequent date shown on the check operates as a second new promise. The bank's authority to pay was revocable, and A could have stopped payment.

15. A owes B a debt of $1000, barred by the statute of limitations. A orally promises to pay the debt in monthly installments of $10, and subsequently pays $5 on account of the first installment. The part payment, though excepted from a statute requiring a writing, binds A only to pay in monthly installments.

f. *Promise not to plead the statute of limitations.* The rule stated in Subsection (2) (c) has no application to promises not to plead the statute made as part of the original contract, but is limited to promises relating to antecedent indebtedness. Nor does it apply to a promise not to plead the statute if the promisor denies any obligation and reserves the right to assert all other defenses; such a promise is not binding unless there is consideration or reliance. But unless the circumstances indicate a contrary intention, a promise not to plead the statute is a promise to pay the debt.

Illustration

16. A owes B $500, and writes B "I cannot pay you now, but I will never set up the statute of limitations against your claim." B delays bringing an action to collect his claim until more than the statutory period from the time of A's promise not to set up the statute has expired. A may then successfully assert the bar of the statute.

g. *New promise by agent, co-debtor or fiduciary.* Despite early English decisions that a joint debtor was bound by a part payment made by his co-debtor, the modern rule by statute or decision is that a new promise binds a debtor only if made by him or by a person having power to bind him under the law of agency. An assignee for creditors or like fiduciary does not ordinarily have power to bind the debtor by a new promise. In the absence of consideration or reliance a fiduciary does not bind himself personally unless he was bound by the original obligation. Whether a fiduciary has power to bind the estate he administers by a new promise depends on the terms of the statute or instrument under which he acts. In many States statutes deny such a power to the executor or administrator of a decedent.

§ 83. Promise to Pay Indebtedness Discharged in Bankruptcy.

An express promise to pay all or part of an indebtedness of the promisor, discharged or dischargeable in bankruptcy proceedings begun before the promise is made, is binding.

Comment

a. Rationale. The early history of the rule of this Section is the same as that of the rule of § 82, relating to the statute of limitations, and the two rules are similar in many respects. But only a few States have enacted statutes requiring the promises described in this Section to be in writing. In modern times discharge in bankruptcy has been thought to reflect a somewhat stronger public policy than the statute of limitations, and a promise implied from acknowledgment or part payment does not revive a debt discharged in bankruptcy. Although in the absence of a statute an oral promise is effective, the courts have insisted on the formality of express promise, denying effect to expressions of expectation or of good intention.

Illustrations

1. A owes B $100 and is about to go into bankruptcy. Immediately before filing his petition he promises B to pay the debt in spite of any discharge that he may get in bankruptcy. The promise is not binding but would have been binding if it had been made after the petition in bankruptcy was filed.

2. A owes B $100, and the debt is discharged in A's bankruptcy. Thereafter A promises in writing to pay the debt "as soon as I sell the mill." Two years later A sells the mill. B can recover the debt from A by an action brought within the period fixed by the statute of limitations after the sale. If the subsequent promise were oral, B would be limited in most States to an action within the statutory period after the original debt became due.

b. Voluntary compositions. The rule of this Section applies to a promise to pay a debt discharged by a composition between a bankrupt and his creditors pursuant to the Bankruptcy Reform Act, but not to a promise to pay a debt discharged without bankruptcy by voluntary action of the creditor such as a composition with creditors or an accord and satisfaction or release by the particular creditor. In the absence of bankruptcy such agreements by the creditor are regarded as discharging the moral as well as the legal obligation to pay. But an express reservation of the debtor's moral obligation may be effective in such a case.

Illustration

3. A owes B $100, and the debt is discharged by a composition among creditors without bankruptcy proceedings, B receiving $45 and expressly reserving A's "moral obligation." A subsequently promises to pay B the balance of $55. The promise is binding.

§ 84. Promise to Perform a Duty in Spite of Non-Occurrence of a Condition.

(1) Except as stated in Subsection (2), a promise to perform all or part of a conditional duty under an antecedent contract in spite of the non-occurrence of the condition is binding, whether the promise is made before or after the time for the condition to occur, unless

    (a) occurrence of the condition was a material part of the agreed exchange for the performance of the duty and the promisee was under no duty that it occur; or

    (b) uncertainty of the occurrence of the condition was an element of the risk assumed by the promisor.

(2) If such a promise is made before the time for the occurrence of the condition has expired and the condition is within the control of the promisee or a beneficiary, the promisor can make his duty again subject to the condition by notifying the promisee or beneficiary of his intention to do so if

    (a) the notification is received while there is still a reasonable time to cause the condition to occur under the antecedent terms or an extension given by the promisor; and

    (b) reinstatement of the requirement of the condition is not unjust because of a material change of position by the promisee or beneficiary; and

    (c) the promise is not binding apart from the rule stated in Subsection (1).

Comment

a. Rationale. Like the rules stated in §§ 82 and 83, the rule of Subsection (1) can be thought of in terms of waiver of a defense not addressed to the merits, and rests in large part on the policies against forfeiture and unjust enrichment. Where the waiver is made before the time for the occurrence of the condition, it may induce non-occurrence of the condition, and enforcement may also rest on reliance or on excuse by prevention or hindrance. See §§ 89, 90. But a waiver made after the original duty has been discharged, though it is sometimes said to "reinstate" the duty, in fact creates a new duty unqualified by the condition.

Conditions are the subject of more detailed treatment in §§ 224–29. In many situations an agreement or a rule of law, in the interest of simplicity and certainty, provides for absolute discharge of the promisor although a discharge to the extent of loss caused by a non-occurrence of condition might seem more equitable. See, e.g., Uniform Commercial Code § 3–502. The likelihood of waiver and the pressure to find waiver or other excuse increase in proportion to the extent and unfairness of the forfeiture involved; in extreme cases the non-occurrence of the condition may be excused without other reason. See § 229.

b. "Waiver" and "estoppel"; mistake. "Waiver" is often inexactly defined as "the voluntary relinquishment of a known right." When the waiver is reinforced by reliance, enforcement is often said to rest on "estoppel." Compare §§ 89, 90. Since the more common definition of estoppel is limited to reliance on a misrepresentation of an existing fact, reliance on a waiver or promise as to the future is sometimes said to create a "promissory estoppel." The common definition of waiver may lead to the incorrect inference that the promisor must know his legal rights and must intend the legal effect of the promise. But under § 93 it is sufficient if he has reason to know the essential facts. And if the waiver is supported by reliance or by consideration, the effect of mistake on the part of the promisor depends on the rules stated in Chapter 6.

c. Conditions material to the exchange or risk. A promise is often conditional on the receipt of some performance regarded as the equivalent of the performance promised, as in the case of an option contract to sell a horse if the promisee pays $500 for him. A promise may also be conditional on a fortuitous event, and the risk or burden assumed by the promisor may depend on the probability that the condition will occur, as in a promise to insure a house against fire. In both types of cases, where a promise to disregard the non-occurrence of the condition materially affects the value received by the promisor or the burden or risk assumed by him, the promise is not binding under Subsection (1). Such a promise may be binding by virtue of reliance or for some other reason. See §§ 89, 90. See also § 246. But a waiver of the price of a horse or of the fire required by an insurance policy is not within this Section.

Illustration

1. In an insurance policy the insurer promises to pay $1000 if the insured is killed on a railroad. The insurer's subsequent promise to pay $1000 even though the insured is not killed on a railroad is not binding under this Section, whether the promise is made before or after the death of the insured.

d. Conditions which may be waived. The rule of Subsection (1) applies primarily to conditions which may be thought of as procedural or technical, or to instances in which the non-occurrence of condition is comparatively minor. Examples are conditions which merely relate to the time or manner of the return performance or provide for the giving of notice or the supplying of proofs. Insurance policies ordinarily contain conditions of notice and proof of loss and of time for suit; and guarantors, indorsers and other sureties may be discharged by an agreement varying the duty of the principal debtor, by failure of diligence in presentment or prosecution, or by failure to give a required notice. In such cases, even though a promise to disregard the non-occurrence of the condition subjects the promisor to a new duty, the new duty is not regarded as significantly different from the old and the promise is binding without consideration, reliance, or formality. See, e.g., Uniform Commercial Code § 3–606, Comment 2.

Illustrations

2. A is surety for B on a debt due C. C makes a contract with B, the principal debtor, extending the time for payment. Thereafter A, with knowledge of that fact, promises C to pay the debt. The promise is binding, and A has no power to retract it.

3. A employs B to build a house, promising to pay therefor $10,000 on the production of a certificate from A's architect, C, stating that the work has been satisfactorily completed. B builds the house but the work is defective in certain trivial particulars. C refuses to give B a certificate. A says to B, "My architect rightfully refuses to give you a certificate but the defects are not serious; I will pay you the full price which I promised." A is bound to do so, and has no power to restore the requirement of the condition.

4. A, an insurance company, insures B's house for $5000 against loss by fire. The insurance policy provides that it shall be payable only if B gives written notification of any loss within thirty days after its occurrence. An insured loss occurs and B gives only oral notification thereof within thirty days. A tells him, either before or after the lapse of thirty days from the loss, that this notification is sufficient. A cannot thereafter rely upon B's failure to give written notification as an excuse for failure to pay for the loss.

e. Form. Adjustments in an on-going transaction commonly take place in a setting which fulfills some of the functions of legal formalities, and the probability of reliance is high. Compare § 89. Even when the requirement of a technical condition is waived after the non-occurrence of that condition, the effect is often to achieve a result which seems fair without regard to waiver. The Statute of Frauds may make unenforceable an oral promise which has not been relied on. See § 150; compare Uniform Commercial Code § 2–209, Comment 4. Otherwise, formal requirements are at a minimum. It is immaterial how the promisor manifests his intention to fulfill the prior duty without the performance of the condition. Words of promise or waiver, though often used, are unnecessary; in many situations non-verbal conduct is enough. A mere acknowledgment of the antecedent duty does not suffice unless there is a manifestation of intention to disregard the condition, and a conditional or partial waiver is effective only according to its terms.

Illustration

5. A, an insurance company, issues to B a policy of automobile liability insurance, under which it is a condition of A's duty to pay that B notify A "as soon as practicable" after an accident. An accident occurs, but B does not notify A as soon as practicable. Without any statement concerning the non-occurrence of the condition, A begins to defend B in an action brought against B as a result of the accident. A's beginning to defend B operates as a promise to pay in spite of the non-occurrence of the condition.

f. Reinstatement after waiver. If the requirement of a condition has been eliminated from a contract by an agreement supported by consideration it cannot be reinstated by unilateral action of the promisor. Nor can it be reinstated if a new unconditional duty has been created by a promise made after the original duty was discharged by non-occurrence of the condition, or if reinstatement would be unjust in view of a change of position by the other party. Compare Uniform Commercial Code § 2–209(5); Restatement of Restitution § 142. But where the requirement of a condition is waived in advance, the promisor may reinstate the requirement by giving notice to the other party before the latter has materially changed his position. Whether delay alone makes reinstatement unjust depends upon the circumstances: in some cases a reasonable extension of time sufficiently protects the other party; in others the extension may be required to be both definite and reasonable; in some no extension can put him in as good a position to perform as before the waiver.

Illustrations

6. In Illustration 4, A can restore the requirement of the condition by notifying B of his intention to do so if there still remains a reasonable time for the occurrence of the condition before the expiration of the thirty-day period, unless such action would be unjust in view of a material change of position by B in reliance on A's waiver. If a reasonable time does not remain, A cannot restore the requirement of the condition by extending the time.

7. A, an insurance company, insures B's house against loss by fire. The insurance policy provides that unless suit is brought on the policy within twelve months after a loss, no recovery can be had. An insured loss occurs and A tells B that it is unnecessary to bring suit within that time. Unless B has so changed his position that it would be unjust to restore the time limitation, A can do so by giving B notice. Thereafter B has a reasonable time to bring suit. In the absence of special circumstances, the reasonable time will expire twelve months after the notice is received.

8. On February 1, A agrees to sell and B to buy land for the price of $10,000, the transfer to be made on March 1. B makes an advance payment of $1,000, and the contract provides that time is of the essence and that if the balance of the price is not paid promptly B's rights are forfeited and A may retain the $1,000. On February 15, A informs B that A will not insist on the March 1 date. In the

absence of special circumstances, A can thereafter restore the requirement of the condition by giving B notice that A will insist on performance within thirty days from the time of the notice.

§ 85. Promise to Perform a Voidable Duty.

Except as stated in § 93, a promise to perform all or part of an antecedent contract of the promisor, previously voidable by him, but not avoided prior to the making of the promise, is binding.

Comment

a. Types of voidable contracts. The rule of this Section may be thought of as implicit in the definition of "voidable contract" in § 7. Such a contract is distinguished from the "unenforceable contract" defined in § 8 by the existence of a power of ratification. The power of avoidance may rest on lack of capacity under the rules stated in §§ 12–16, on mistake, misrepresentation, duress or undue influence under Chapters 6 and 7. In such cases exercise of the power of avoidance discharges the contractual duty and terminates the power of ratification; conversely, exercise of the power of ratification terminates the power of avoidance. See §§ 378–85.

b. Ratification and new promise. This Section relates only to action which constitutes a promise under the definition in § 2. Such a promise may be binding under this Section or because of its formal character or because it is supported by consideration or reliance. Even though it is "binding" under this Section, the new promise may itself be voidable for the same reason as the original promise, or it may be voidable or unenforceable for some other reason. See § 1, Comment g. In particular, a few states require the new promise of a former infant to be in writing and signed. A power of avoidance may also be lost in various other ways: by delay in giving notice, by failure to restore performance received, by exercise of dominion over things received, or by change of circumstances. See, e.g., as to avoidance for misrepresentation, § 164.

Illustrations

1. A is induced by B's fraud to promise $100 in return for a worthless chattel. After discovering the fraud A promises B to pay as agreed. The promise is binding.

2. A, an infant, promises B to pay him $100 in consideration of a bicycle which B transfers to him. The bicycle is worth $60. On coming of age A promises to pay B the sum he originally agreed to pay. He is bound to do so. If instead of such a promise he promises to pay a smaller sum, as $40, he is also bound, but only to that extent.

§ 86. Promise for Benefit Received.

(1) A promise made in recognition of a benefit previously received by the promisor from the promisee is binding to the extent necessary to prevent injustice.

(2) A promise is not binding under Subsection (1)

(a) if the promisee conferred the benefit as a gift or for other reasons the promisor has not been unjustly enriched; or

(b) to the extent that its value is disproportionate to the benefit.

Comment

a. "Past consideration;" "moral obligation." Enforcement of promises to pay for benefit received has sometimes been said to rest on "past consideration" or on the "moral obligation" of the promisor, and there are statutes in such terms in a few states. Those terms are not used here: "past consideration" is inconsistent with the meaning of consideration stated in § 71, and there seems to be no consensus as to what constitutes a "moral obligation." The mere fact of promise has been thought to create a moral obligation, but it is clear that not all promises are enforced. Nor are moral obligations based solely on gratitude or sentiment sufficient of themselves to support a subsequent promise.

Illustrations

1. A gives emergency care to B's adult son while the son is sick and without funds far from home. B subsequently promises to reimburse A for his expenses. The promise is not binding under this Section.

2. A lends money to B, who later dies. B's widow promises to pay the debt. The promise is not binding under this Section.

3. A has immoral relations with B, a woman not his wife, to her injury. A's subsequent promise to reimburse B for her loss is not binding under this Section.

Compare Restatement, Second, Agency § 462 on ratification of the acts of a person who officiously purports to act as an agent. Enforcement of the subsequent promise sometimes makes it unnecessary to decide a difficult question as to the limits on quasi-contractual relief.

Many of the cases governed by the rules stated in §§ 82–85 are within the broader principle stated in this Section. But the broader principle is not so firmly established as those rules, and it may not be applied if there is doubt whether the objections to restitution are fully met by the subsequent promise. Facts such as the definite and substantial character of the benefit received, formality in the making of the promise, part performance of the promise, reliance on the promise or the probability of such reliance may be relevant to show that no imposition results from enforcement.

c. Promise to correct a mistake. One who makes a mistake in the conferring of a benefit is commonly entitled to restitution regardless of any promise. But restitution is often denied to avoid prejudice to the recipient of the benefit. Thus restitution of the value of services or of improvements to land or chattels may require a payment which the recipient cannot afford. See Restatement of Restitution §§ 41, 42. Where a subsequent promise shows that the usual protection is not needed in the particular case, restitution is granted to the extent promised.

Illustrations

4. A is employed by B to repair a vacant house. By mistake A repairs the house next door, which belongs to C. A subsequent promise by C to pay A the value of the repairs is binding.

5. A pays B a debt and gets a signed receipt. Later B obtains a default judgment against A for the amount of the debt, and A pays again. B's subsequent promise to refund the second payment if A has a receipt is binding.

d. Emergency services and necessaries. The law of restitution in the absence of promise severely limits recovery for necessaries furnished to a person under disability and for emergency services. See Restatement of Restitution §§ 113–17, 139. A subsequent promise in such a case may remove doubt as to the reality of the benefit and as to its value, and may negate any danger of imposition or false claim. A positive showing that payment was expected is not then required; an intention to make a gift must be shown to defeat restitution.

Illustrations

6. A finds B's escaped bull and feeds and cares for it. B's subsequent promise to pay reasonable compensation to A is binding.

7. A saves B's life in an emergency and is totally and permanently disabled in so doing. One month later B promises to pay A $15 every two weeks for the rest of A's life, and B makes the payments for 8 years until he dies. The promise is binding.

e. Benefit conferred as a gift. In the absence of mistake or the like, there is no element of unjust enrichment in the receipt of a gift, and the rule of this Section has no application to a promise to pay for a past gift. Similarly, when a debt is discharged by a binding agreement, the transaction is closed even though full payment is not made. But marginal cases arise in which both parties understand that what is in form a gift is intended to be reimbursed indirectly, or in which a subsequent promise to pay is expressly contemplated. See Illustration 3 to § 83. Enforcement of the subsequent promise is proper in some such cases.

Illustrations

8. A submits to B at B's request a plan for advertising products manufactured by B, expecting payment only if the plan is adopted. Because of a change in B's selling arrangements, B rejects the plan without giving it fair consideration. B's subsequent promise to reimburse A's expenses in preparing the plan is binding.

9. A contributes capital to B, an insurance company, on the understanding that B is not liable to reimburse A but that A will be reimbursed through salary and commissions. Later A withdraws from the company and B promises to pay him ten percent of premiums received until he is reimbursed. The promise is binding.

f. Benefit conferred pursuant to contract. By virtue of the policy of enforcing bargains, the enrichment of one party as a result of an unequal exchange is not regarded as unjust, and this Section has no application to a promise to pay or perform more or to accept less than is called for by a pre-existing bargain between the same parties. Compare §§ 79, 89. Similarly, if a third person receives a benefit as a result of the performance of a bargain, this Section does not make binding the subsequent promise of the third person to pay extra compensation to the performing party. But a promise to pay in substitution for the return performance called for by the bargain may be binding under this Section.

Illustration

10. A digs a well on B's land in performance of a bargain with B's tenant C. C is unable to pay as agreed, and B promises to pay A the reasonable value of the well. The promise is binding.

g. Obligation unenforceable under the Statute of Frauds. A promise to pay a debt unenforceable under the Statute of Frauds is very similar to the promises governed by §§ 82–85. But the problem seldom arises. Part performance often renders the Statute inapplicable; if it does not, the contract can be made enforceable by a subsequent memorandum. See § 136. In any event, the Statute does not ordinarily foreclose the remedy of restitution. See § 375. Where the question does arise, the new promise is binding if the policy of the Statute is satisfied.

Illustration

11. By statute an agreement authorizing a real estate broker to sell land for compensation is void unless the agreement or a memorandum thereof is in writing. A, a real estate broker, procures a purchaser for B's land without any written agreement. In the written sale agreement, signed by B, B promises to pay A $200, the usual commission, "for services rendered." The promise is binding.

h. Obligation unenforceable because usurious. If a promise is unenforceable because it is usurious, an agreement in renewal or substitution for it that provides for a payment including the usurious interest is also unenforceable, even though the interest from the date of renewal or substitution is not usurious. However, a promise to pay the original debt with interest that is not usurious in substitution for the usurious interest is enforceable.

i. Partial enforcement. The rules stated in §§ 82–85 refer to promises to perform all or part of an antecedent duty, and do not make enforceable a promise to do more. Similarly, where a benefit received is a liquidated sum of money, a promise is not enforceable under this Section beyond the amount of the benefit. Where the value of the benefit is uncertain, a promise to pay the value is binding and a promise to pay a liquidated sum may serve to fix the amount due if in all the circumstances it is not disproportionate to the benefit. See Illustration 7. A promise which is excessive may sometimes be enforced to the extent of the value of the benefit, and the remedy may be thought of as quasi-contractual rather than contractual. In other cases a promise of disproportionate value may tend to show unfair pressure or other conduct by the promisee such that justice does not require any enforcement of the promise. Compare Comment c to § 72.

Illustrations

12. A, a married woman of sixty, has rendered household services without compensation over a period of years for B, a man of eighty living alone and having no close relatives. B has a net worth of three million dollars and has often assured A that she will be well paid for her services, whose

reasonable value is not in excess of $6,000. B executes and delivers to A a written promise to pay A $25,000 "to be taken from my estate." The promise is binding.

13. The facts being otherwise as stated in Illustration 12, B's promise is made orally and is to leave A his entire estate. A cannot recover more than the reasonable value of her services.

§ 87. Option Contract.

(1) An offer is binding as an option contract if it

   (a) is in writing and signed by the offeror, recites a purported consideration for the making of the offer, and proposes an exchange on fair terms within a reasonable time; or

   (b) is made irrevocable by statute.

(2) An offer which the offeror should reasonably expect to induce action or forbearance of a substantial character on the part of the offeree before acceptance and which does induce such action or forbearance is binding as an option contract to the extent necessary to avoid injustice.

Comment

a. Consideration and form. The traditional common-law devices for making a firm offer or option contract are the giving of consideration and the affixing of a seal. See §§ 25, 95. But the firm offer serves a useful purpose even though no preliminary bargain is made: it is often a necessary step in the making of the main bargain proposed, and it partakes of the natural formalities inherent in business transactions. The erosion of the formality of the seal has made it less and less satisfactory as a universal formality. As literacy has spread, the personal signature has become the natural formality and the seal has become more and more anachronistic. The rules stated in this section reflect the judicial and legislative response to this situation.

b. Nominal consideration. Offers made in consideration of one dollar paid or promised are often irrevocable under Subsection (1)(a). The irrevocability of an offer may be worth much or little to the offeree, and the courts do not ordinarily inquire into the adequacy of the consideration bargained for. See § 79. Hence a comparatively small payment may furnish consideration for the irrevocability of an offer proposing a transaction involving much larger sums. But gross disproportion between the payment and the value of the option commonly indicates that the payment was not in fact bargained for but was a mere formality or pretense. In such a case there is no consideration as that term is defined in § 71.

Nevertheless, such a nominal consideration is regularly held sufficient to support a short-time option proposing an exchange on fair terms. The fact that the option is an appropriate preliminary step in the conclusion of a socially useful transaction provides a sufficient substantive basis for enforcement, and a signed writing taking a form appropriate to a bargain satisfies the desiderata of form. In the absence of statute, however, the bargaining form is essential: a payment of one dollar by each party to the other is so obviously not a bargaining transaction that it does not provide even the form of an exchange.

Illustrations

1. In consideration of twenty-five cents paid by B, A executes and delivers to B a written option agreement giving B the right to buy a piece of land for $100,000 if B gives notice of intention to buy within 120 days. The price and terms of sale are fair. A has made an irrevocable offer.

2. In consideration of one dollar paid by B, A, a widow who owns land worth $25,000 as a farm, gives B a ten-year option to take phosphate rock from the land on paying a royalty of twenty-five cents per ton. As B knows but A does not, the prevailing royalty in such transactions ranges from $1.00 to $1.10 per ton. The offer is not made irrevocable by the one-dollar payment.

c. False recital of nominal consideration. A recital in a written agreement that a stated consideration has been given is evidence of that fact as against a party to the agreement, but such a recital may ordinarily be contradicted by evidence that no such consideration was given or expected. See § 218. In cases within Subsection (1)(a), however, the giving and recital of nominal consideration performs a formal function only. The signed writing has vital significance as a formality, while the ceremonial manual delivery of a dollar or a peppercorn is an inconsequential formality. In view of the dangers of permitting a solemn written agreement to be invalidated by oral testimony which is easily fabricated, therefore, the option agreement is not invalidated by proof that the recited consideration was not in fact given. A fictitious rationalization has sometimes been used for this rule: acceptance of delivery of the written instrument conclusively imports a promise to make good the recital, it is said, and that promise furnishes consideration. Compare § 218. But the sound basis for the rule is that stated above.

Illustration

3. A executes and delivers to B a written agreement "in consideration of one dollar in hand paid" giving B an option to buy described land belonging to A for $15,000, the option to expire at noon six days later. The fact that the dollar is not in fact paid does not prevent the offer from being irrevocable.

d. Statutory firm offers. In many states the seal is no longer an effective substitute for consideration, see Introductory Note to Topic 3 of this Chapter. In addition, Uniform Commercial Code § 2–203 withdraws contracts and offers for the sale of goods from the law of sealed instruments. Statutes have sometimes given effect to a signed writing as a substitute formality, either generally or in cases of offers made in a signed writing and stated to be irrevocable. More common, however, are statutes dealing with particular types of offers. Thus when goods are put up at auction without reserve, an offer is made which is irrevocable under Uniform Commercial Code § 2–328(3). See § 28. Again, when statutes authorize or require that government work be awarded to contractors on the basis of competitive bidding, it may be fairly implied that the public officials in charge may protect the integrity of the competition by refusing to allow a bid to be withdrawn after the bids are opened. A similar implication may be drawn when an offer is required to be submitted to a court for approval. A more general provision for irrevocable offers is found in Uniform Commercial Code § 2–205, giving effect for a reasonable time not exceeding three months to a firm offer to buy or sell goods, made by a merchant in a signed writing.

e. Reliance. Subsection (2) states the application of § 90 to reliance on an unaccepted offer, with qualifications which would not be appropriate in some other types of cases covered by § 90. It is important chiefly in cases of reliance that is not part performance. If the beginning of performance is a reasonable mode of acceptance, it makes the offer fully enforceable under § 45 or § 62; if not, the offeror commonly has no reason to expect part performance before acceptance. But circumstances may be such that the offeree must undergo substantial expense, or undertake substantial commitments, or forego alternatives, in order to put himself in a position to accept by either promise or performance. The offer may be made expressly irrevocable in contemplation of reliance by the offeree. If reliance follows in such cases, justice may require a remedy. Compare Restatement, Second, Torts § 325; Restatement, Second, Agency § 378. But the reliance must be substantial as well as foreseeable.

Full-scale enforcement of the offered contract is not necessarily appropriate in such cases. Restitution of benefits conferred may be enough, or partial or full reimbursement of losses may be proper. Various factors may influence the remedy: the formality of the offer, its commercial or social context, the extent to which the offeree's reliance was understood to be at his own risk, the relative competence and the bargaining position of the parties, the degree of fault on the part of the offeror, the ease and certainty of proof of particular items of damage and the likelihood that unprovable damages have been suffered.

Illustrations

4. A leases a farm to B and later gives B an "option" to buy the farm for $15,500 within five years. With A's approval, B makes permanent improvements in the farm buildings, builds roads, drains and dams, and contours plow land, using his own labor and expending several thousand dollars. Toward the end of the five years, A purports to revoke the option, demanding a higher price. B then gives written notice of acceptance in accordance with the terms of the offer. Specific performance by A may be decreed.

5. A offers to B a "blanket arrangement" to buy "poultry grown by you" at stated prices. As contemplated, B buys 7,000 baby chicks and begins raising them for sale to A as "broilers." Thereafter A purports to revoke the offer. B has the rights of an aggrieved seller under a contract for the sale of 7,000 "broilers."

§ 88   RESTATEMENT (SECOND) OF CONTRACTS   Pt. II

    6. A submits a written offer for paving work to be used by B as a partial basis for B's bid as general contractor on a large building. As A knows, B is required to name his subcontractors in his general bid. B uses A's offer and B's bid is accepted. A's offer is irrevocable until B has had a reasonable opportunity to notify A of the award and B's acceptance of A's offer.

§ 88. Guaranty.

A promise to be surety for the performance of a contractual obligation, made to the obligee, is binding if

    (a) the promise is in writing and signed by the promisor and recites a purported consideration; or

    (b) the promise is made binding by statute; or

    (c) the promisor should reasonably expect the promise to induce action or forbearance of a substantial character on the part of the promisee or a third person, and the promise does induce such action or forbearance.

Comment

a. Rationale. Like option contracts, guaranties are ancillary to bargains, and have some of the same presumptive utility. See §§ 72 and 87 and Comments. A guaranty is commonly supported by the consideration which supports the obligation guaranteed. See § 80. Or it may be binding because it is under seal. But there has been much confusion where a guaranty not under seal is given after the principal obligor has received the consideration for his promise. The elements of a bargain with the guarantor can sometimes be found in such cases, either because the original bargain was not completed until the guaranty was furnished or by virtue of forbearance to pursue the principal debtor. The rules stated in this Section often render the search for such elements unnecessary. Where applicable, the formal requirements of the Statute of Frauds must of course be met. See §§ 112–23.

b. Nominal consideration and recital thereof. A contract of suretyship is aleatory, like familiar forms of insurance, and if the surety is called upon to pay he commonly has recourse against the principal obligor by way of reimbursement or subrogation. See Restatement of Security §§ 104, 141. The amount paid for a guaranty is often only a small fraction of the amount of the principal obligation; indeed, consideration may be furnished by the mere extension of credit to the principal obligor. Hence it would often be difficult to say whether a consideration of one dollar is adequate in amount, and courts do not ordinarily inquire into that question. See § 79. Like § 87 on option contracts, this Section goes further and precludes inquiry into the question whether the consideration recited in a written contract of guaranty was mere formality or pretense, or whether it was in fact given.

Illustration

    1. A executes a written guaranty to B of a debt then due from C. The guaranty is stated to be "in consideration of one dollar paid to me by B, the receipt of which is hereby acknowledged." The guaranty is binding whether the dollar is in fact paid or not.

c. Statutes. A guaranty may be binding by virtue of a seal or a statutory substitute for the seal. Although Uniform Commercial Code § 2–203 withdraws contracts for the sale of goods from the law of sealed instruments, § 2–701 provides that remedies for breach of collateral or ancillary obligations or promises are not impaired. Again, Uniform Commercial Code § 3–113 makes the provisions of the Code relating to commercial paper applicable despite the presence of a seal, but § 3–408 makes consideration unnecessary for an instrument or obligation thereon given in payment of or as security for an antecedent obligation of any kind.

d. Reliance. Paragraph (c) states the application of § 90 to reliance on a guaranty, with modifications appropriate to the particular type of case. Reliance commonly takes the form of an extension of new credit to the principal obligor or of forbearance to pursue him, and often can be found to have been bargained for. Where a written guaranty is executed in a commercial context, such reliance is extremely probable, though mixed motives on the part of the obligee may make specific proof difficult. Whether the guarantor is entitled to notice of the obligee's intention to act in such cases depends on the terms of the guaranty and on the circumstances. See § 54. Even in a non-commercial context, if the reliance is foreseeable and substantial, no further inquiry is necessary as to whether justice requires enforcement.

If the conditions of enforcement are met, the appropriate remedy is enforcement of the guaranty according to its terms. Difficult problems of measurement of the extent of the reliance are thereby avoided, and the guarantor is left to his recourse against the principal obligor.

The effect of repudiation of a guaranty on action taken by the obligee thereafter depends on the divisibility of the guaranty and rules relating to avoidable consequences and assurance of counter-performance. See §§ 31, 255, 350, 363.

Illustrations

2. A owes $10,000 to B, a stockbroker. To prevent sale of A's stock held by B as collateral, C executes a written guaranty to B of A's account. A's father D subsequently executes a written guaranty to C against losses in the account. There are no further transactions in the account, but in reliance on D's guaranty C for two years refrains from liquidating the account, while the stock fluctuates in value. The guaranty is binding.

3. A, an agent to sell books published by B, dies owing B $4,000 and leaves all his property to his widow C. C, desiring to continue the agency, promises in writing to pay the debt. In reliance on the promise B continues the agency for a year and makes no claim against A's estate, which is solvent, until the time for filing claims has expired. C's promise is binding.

4. A draws checks on the B bank, forging the signature of A's father-in-law C as drawer. After the checks are paid and the forgeries discovered C promises B to make good the amount, since C wants no prosecution of A and no publicity about the matter. In reliance on C's promise B forbears for a month to seek evidence of the forgery or to seek recourse against A and solvent indorsers. C's promise is binding. Under Uniform Commercial Code § 3–404(2) the promise is binding without regard to reliance.

5. A owes $10,000 to the B bank. In response to criticism by a bank examiner that there is insufficient collateral for the obligation, C, an officer of the bank, executes a written guaranty of the obligation, and the bank examiner then finds the bank's assets sufficient. Subsequently the bank is found to be insolvent and placed in liquidation. C's guaranty is binding.

§ 89. Modification of Executory Contract.

A promise modifying a duty under a contract not fully performed on either side is binding

(a) if the modification is fair and equitable in view of circumstances not anticipated by the parties when the contract was made; or

(b) to the extent provided by statute; or

(c) to the extent that justice requires enforcement in view of material change of position in reliance on the promise.

Comment

a. Rationale. This Section relates primarily to adjustments in on-going transactions. Like offers and guaranties, such adjustments are ancillary to exchanges and have some of the same presumptive utility. See §§ 72, 87, 88. Indeed, paragraph (a) deals with bargains which are without consideration only because of the rule that performance of a legal duty to the promisor is not consideration. See § 73. This Section is also related to § 84 on waiver of conditions: it may apply to cases in which § 84 is inapplicable because a condition is material to the exchange or risk. As in cases governed by § 84, relation to a bargain tends to satisfy the cautionary and channeling functions of legal formalities. See Comment c to § 72. The Statute of Frauds may prevent enforcement in the absence of reliance. See §§ 149–50. Otherwise formal requirements are at a minimum.

b. Performance of legal duty. The rule of § 73 finds its modern justification in cases of promises made by mistake or induced by unfair pressure. Its application to cases where those elements are absent has been much criticized and is avoided if paragraph (a) of this Section is applicable. The limitation to a modification which is "fair and equitable" goes beyond absence of coercion and requires an objectively demonstrable reason for seeking a modification. Compare Uniform Commercial Code § 2–209 Comment. The reason for modification must rest in circumstances not "anticipated" as part of the context in which the contract was made, but a frustrating event may be unanticipated for this purpose if it was not adequately covered, even though it was foreseen as a remote possibility. When such a reason is present, the relative financial strength of the parties, the formality with which the modification is made, the extent to which it is performed or relied on and other circumstances may be relevant to show or negate imposition or unfair surprise.

The same result called for by paragraph (a) is sometimes reached on the ground that the original contract was "rescinded" by mutual agreement and that new promises were then made which furnished consideration for each other. That theory is rejected here because it is fictitious when the "rescission" and new agreement are simultaneous, and because if logically carried out it might uphold unfair and inequitable modifications.

Illustrations

1. By a written contract A agrees to excavate a cellar for B for a stated price. Solid rock is unexpectedly encountered and A so notifies B. A and B then orally agree that A will remove the rock at a unit price which is reasonable but nine times that used in computing the original price, and A completes the job. B is bound to pay the increased amount.

2. A contracts with B to supply for $300 a laundry chute for a building B has contracted to build for the Government for $150,000. Later A discovers that he made an error as to the type of material to be used and should have bid $1,200. A offers to supply the chute for $1000, eliminating overhead and profit. After ascertaining that other suppliers would charge more, B agrees. The new agreement is binding.

3. A is employed by B as a designer of coats at $90 a week for a year beginning November 1 under a written contract executed September 1. A is offered $115 a week by another employer and so informs B. A and B then agree that A will be paid $100 a week and in October execute a new written contract to that effect, simultaneously tearing up the prior contract. The new contract is binding.

4. A contracts to manufacture and sell to B 2,000 steel roofs for corn cribs at $60. Before A begins manufacture a threat of a nationwide steel strike raises the cost of steel about $10 per roof, and A and B agree orally to increase the price to $70 per roof. A thereafter manufactures and delivers 1700 of the roofs, and B pays for 1,500 of them at the increased price without protest, increasing the selling price of the corn cribs by $10. The new agreement is binding.

5. A contracts to manufacture and sell to B 100,000 castings for lawn mowers at 50 cents each. After partial delivery and after B has contracted to sell a substantial number of lawn mowers at a fixed price, A notifies B that increased metal costs require that the price be increased to 75 cents. Substitute castings are available at 55 cents, but only after several months delay. B protests but is forced to agree to the new price to keep its plant in operation. The modification is not binding.

c. *Statutes.* Uniform Commercial Code § 2–209 dispenses with the requirement of consideration for an agreement modifying a contract for the sale of goods. Under that section the original contract can provide against oral modification, and the requirements of the Statute of Frauds must be met if the contract as modified is within its provisions; but an ineffective modification can operate as a waiver. The Comment indicates that extortion of a modification without legitimate commercial reason is ineffective as a violation of the duty of good faith imposed by the Code. A similar limitation may be applicable under statutes which give effect to a signed writing as a substitute for the seal, or under statutes which give effect to acceptance by the promisee of the modified performance. In some States statutes or constitutional provisions flatly forbid the payment of extra compensation to Government contractors.

d. *Reliance.* Paragraph (c) states the application of § 90 to modification of an executory contract in language adapted from Uniform Commercial Code § 2–209. Even though the promise is not binding when made, it may become binding in whole or in part by reason of action or forbearance by the promisee or third persons in reliance on it. In some cases the result can be viewed as based either on estoppel to contradict a representation of fact or on reliance on a promise. Ordinarily reliance by the promisee is reasonably foreseeable and makes the modification binding with respect to performance by the promisee under it and any return performance owed by the promisor. But as under § 84 the original terms can be reinstated for the future by reasonable notification received by the promisee unless reinstatement would be unjust in view of a change of position on his part. Compare Uniform Commercial Code § 2–209(5).

Illustrations

6. A defaults in payment of a premium on a life insurance policy issued by B, an insurance company. Pursuant to the terms of the policy, B notifies A of the lapse of the policy and undertakes to continue the insurance until a specified future date, but by mistake specifies a date two months later than the insured would be entitled to under the policy. On inquiry by A two years later, B repeats the mistake, offering A an option to take a cash payment. A fails to do so, and dies one month before the specified date. B is bound to pay the insurance.

7. A is the lessee of an apartment house under a 99-year lease from B at a rent of $10,000 per year. Because of war conditions many of the apartments become vacant, and in order to enable A to stay in business B agrees to reduce the rent to $5,000. The reduced rent is paid for five years. The war being over, the apartments are then fully rented, and B notifies A that the full rent called for by the lease must be paid. A is bound to pay the full rent only from a reasonable time after the receipt of the notification.

8. A contracts with B to carry a shipment of fish under refrigeration. During the short first leg of the voyage the refrigeration equipment on the ship breaks down, and A offers either to continue under ventilation or to hold the cargo at the first port for later shipment. B agrees to shipment under ventilation but later changes his mind. A receives notification of the change before he has changed his position. A is bound to ship under refrigeration.

§ 90. Promise Reasonably Inducing Action or Forbearance.

(1) A promise which the promisor should reasonably expect to induce action or forbearance on the part of the promisee or a third person and which does induce such action or forbearance is binding if injustice can be avoided only by enforcement of the promise. The remedy granted for breach may be limited as justice requires.

(2) A charitable subscription or a marriage settlement is binding under Subsection (1) without proof that the promise induced action or forbearance.

Comment

a. Relation to other rules. Obligations and remedies based on reliance are not peculiar to the law of contracts. This Section is often referred to in terms of "promissory estoppel," a phrase suggesting an extension of the doctrine of estoppel. Estoppel prevents a person from showing the truth contrary to a representation of fact made by him after another has relied on the representation. See Restatement, Second, Agency § 8B; Restatement, Second, Torts §§ 872, 894. Reliance is also a significant feature of numerous rules in the law of negligence, deceit and restitution. See, e.g., Restatement, Second, Agency §§ 354, 378; Restatement, Second, Torts §§ 323, 537; Restatement of Restitution § 55. In some cases those rules and this Section overlap; in others they provide analogies useful in determining the extent to which enforcement is necessary to avoid injustice.

It is fairly arguable that the enforcement of informal contracts in the action of assumpsit rested historically on justifiable reliance on a promise. Certainly reliance is one of the main bases for enforcement of the half-completed exchange, and the probability of reliance lends support to the enforcement of the executory exchange. See Comments to §§ 72, 75. This Section thus states a basic principle which often renders inquiry unnecessary as to the precise scope of the policy of enforcing bargains. Sections 87–89 state particular applications of the same principle to promises ancillary to bargains, and it also applies in a wide variety of non-commercial situations. See, e.g., § 94.

Illustration

1. A, knowing that B is going to college, promises B that A will give him $5,000 on completion of his course. B goes to college, and borrows and spends more than $5,000 for college expenses. When he has nearly completed his course, A notifies him of an intention to revoke the promise. A's promise

is binding and B is entitled to payment on completion of the course without regard to whether his performance was "bargained for" under § 71.

b. Character of reliance protected. The principle of this Section is flexible. The promisor is affected only by reliance which he does or should foresee, and enforcement must be necessary to avoid injustice. Satisfaction of the latter requirement may depend on the reasonableness of the promisee's reliance, on its definite and substantial character in relation to the remedy sought, on the formality with which the promise is made, on the extent to which the evidentiary, cautionary, deterrent and channeling functions of form are met by the commercial setting or otherwise, and on the extent to which such other policies as the enforcement of bargains and the prevention of unjust enrichment are relevant. Compare Comment to § 72. The force of particular factors varies in different types of cases: thus reliance need not be of substantial character in charitable subscription cases, but must in cases of firm offers and guaranties. Compare Subsection (2) with §§ 87, 88.

Illustrations

2. A promises B not to foreclose, for a specified time, a mortgage which A holds on B's land. B thereafter makes improvements on the land. A's promise is binding and may be enforced by denial of foreclosure before the time has elapsed.

3. A sues B in a municipal court for damages for personal injuries caused by B's negligence. After the one year statute of limitations has run, B requests A to discontinue the action and start again in the superior court where the action can be consolidated with other actions against B arising out of the same accident. A does so. B's implied promise that no harm to A will result bars B from asserting the statute of limitations as a defense.

4. A has been employed by B for 40 years. B promises to pay A a pension of $200 per month when A retires. A retires and forbears to work elsewhere for several years while B pays the pension. B's promise is binding.

c. Reliance by third persons. If a promise is made to one party for the benefit of another, it is often foreseeable that the beneficiary will rely on the promise. Enforcement of the promise in such cases rests on the same basis and depends on the same factors as in cases of reliance by the promisee. Justifiable reliance by third persons who are not beneficiaries is less likely, but may sometimes reinforce the claim of the promisee or beneficiary.

Illustrations

5. A holds a mortgage on B's land. To enable B to obtain a loan, A promises B in writing to release part of the land from the mortgage upon payment of a stated sum. As A contemplated, C lends money to B on a second mortgage, relying on A's promise. The promise is binding and may be enforced by C.

6. A executes and delivers a promissory note to B, a bank, to give B a false appearance of assets, deceive the banking authorities, and enable the bank to continue to operate. After several years B fails and is taken over by C, a representative of B's creditors. A's note is enforceable by C.

7. A and B, husband and wife, are tenants by the entirety of a tract of land. They make an oral promise to B's niece C to give her the tract. B, C and C's husband expend money in building a house on the tract and C and her husband take possession and live there for several years until B dies. The expenditures by B and by C's husband are treated like those by C in determining whether justice requires enforcement of the promise against A.

d. Partial enforcement. A promise binding under this section is a contract, and full-scale enforcement by normal remedies is often appropriate. But the same factors which bear on whether any relief should be granted also bear on the character and extent of the remedy. In particular, relief may sometimes be limited to restitution or to damages or specific relief measured by the extent of the promisee's reliance rather than by the terms of the promise. See §§ 84, 89; compare Restatement, Second, Torts § 549 on damages for fraud. Unless there is unjust enrichment of the promisor, damages should not put the promisee in a better position than performance of the promise would have put him. See §§ 344, 349. In the case of a promise to make a gift it would rarely be proper to award consequential damages which would place a greater burden on the promisor than performance would have imposed.

Illustrations

8. A applies to B, a distributor of radios manufactured by C, for a "dealer franchise" to sell C's products. Such franchises are revocable at will. B erroneously informs A that C has accepted the application and will soon award the franchise, that A can proceed to employ salesmen and solicit orders, and that A will receive an initial delivery of at least 30 radios. A expends $1,150 in preparing to do business, but does not receive the franchise or any radios. B is liable to A for the $1,150 but not for the lost profit on 30 radios. Compare Restatement, Second, Agency § 329.

9. The facts being otherwise as stated in Illustration 8, B gives A the erroneous information deliberately and with C's approval and requires A to buy the assets of a deceased former dealer and thus discharge C's "moral obligation" to the widow. C is liable to A not only for A's expenses but also for the lost profit on 30 radios.

10. A, who owns and operates a bakery, desires to go into the grocery business. He approaches B, a franchisor of supermarkets. B states to A that for $18,000 B will establish A in a store. B also advises A to move to another town and buy a small grocery to gain experience. A does so. Later B advises A to sell the grocery, which A does, taking a capital loss and foregoing expected profits from the summer tourist trade. B also advises A to sell his bakery to raise capital for the supermarket franchise, saying "Everything is ready to go. Get your money together and we are set." A sells the bakery taking a capital loss on this sale as well. Still later, B tells A that considerably more than an $18,000 investment will be needed, and the negotiations between the parties collapse. At the point of collapse many details of the proposed agreement between the parties are unresolved. The assurances from B to A are promises on which B reasonably should have expected A to rely, and A is entitled to his actual losses on the sales of the bakery and grocery and for his moving and temporary living expenses. Since the proposed agreement was never made, however, A is not entitled to lost profits from the sale of the grocery or to his expectation interest in the proposed franchise from B.

11. A is about to buy a house on a hill. Before buying he obtains a promise from B, who owns adjoining land, that B will not build on a particular portion of his lot, where a building would obstruct the view from the house. A then buys the house in reliance on the promise. B's promise is binding, but will be specifically enforced only so long as A and his successors do not permanently terminate the use of the view.

12. A promises to make a gift of a tract of land to B, his son-in-law. B takes possession and lives on the land for 17 years, making valuable improvements. A then dispossesses B, and specific performance is denied because the proof of the terms of the promise is not sufficiently clear and definite. B is entitled to a lien on the land for the value of the improvements, not exceeding their cost.

e. Gratuitous promises to procure insurance. This Section is to be applied with caution to promises to procure insurance. The appropriate remedy for breach of such a promise makes the promisor an insurer, and thus may result in a liability which is very large in relation to the value of the promised service. Often the promise is properly to be construed merely as a promise to use reasonable efforts to procure the insurance, and reliance by the promisee may be unjustified or may be justified only for a short time. Or it may be doubtful whether he did in fact rely. Such difficulties may be removed if the proof of the promise and the reliance are clear, or if the promise is made with some formality, or if part performance or a commercial setting or a potential benefit to the promisor provide a substitute for formality.

Illustrations

13. A, a bank, lends money to B on the security of a mortgage on B's new home. The mortgage requires B to insure the property. At the closing of the transaction A promises to arrange for the required insurance, and in reliance on the promise B fails to insure. Six months later the property, still uninsured, is destroyed by fire. The promise is binding.

14. A sells an airplane to B, retaining title to secure payment of the price. After the closing A promises to keep the airplane covered by insurance until B can obtain insurance. B could obtain

insurance in three days but makes no effort to do so, and the airplane is destroyed after six days. A is not subject to liability by virtue of the promise.

f. Charitable subscriptions, marriage settlements, and other gifts. One of the functions of the doctrine of consideration is to deny enforcement to a promise to make a gift. Such a promise is ordinarily enforced by virtue of the promisee's reliance only if his conduct is foreseeable and reasonable and involves a definite and substantial change of position which would not have occurred if the promise had not been made. In some cases, however, other policies reinforce the promisee's claim. Thus the promisor might be unjustly enriched if he could reclaim the subject of the promised gift after the promisee has improved it.

Subsection (2) identifies two other classes of cases in which the promisee's claim is similarly reinforced. American courts have traditionally favored charitable subscriptions and marriage settlements, and have found consideration in many cases where the element of exchange was doubtful or nonexistent. Where recovery is rested on reliance in such cases, a probability of reliance is enough, and no effort is made to sort out mixed motives or to consider whether partial enforcement would be appropriate.

Illustrations

15. A promises B $5000, knowing that B desires that sum for the purchase of a parcel of land. Induced thereby, B secures without any payment an option to buy the parcel. A then tells B that he withdraws his promise. A's promise is not binding.

16. A orally promises to give her son B a tract of land to live on. As A intended, B gives up a homestead elsewhere, takes possession of the land, lives there for a year and makes substantial improvements. A's promise is binding.

17. A orally promises to pay B, a university, $100,000 in five annual installments for the purposes of its fund-raising campaign then in progress. The promise is confirmed in writing by A's agent, and two annual installments are paid before A dies. The continuance of the fund-raising campaign by B is sufficient reliance to make the promise binding on A and his estate.

18. A and B are engaged to be married. In anticipation of the marriage A and his father C enter into a formal written agreement by which C promises to leave certain property to A by will. A's subsequent marriage to B is sufficient reliance to make the promise binding on C and his estate.

§ 91. Effect of Promises Enumerated in §§ 82–90 When Conditional.

If a promise within the terms of §§ 82–90 is in terms conditional or performable at a future time the promisor is bound thereby, but performance becomes due only upon the occurrence of the condition or upon the arrival of the specified time.

Illustration

1. A owes B a debt of $60, but B's claim is barred by the statute of limitations. A promises in a signed writing to pay B in satisfaction of the claim $5 monthly for a year. The promise is binding but B's only right is to the payment of $5 at the end of each month.

§ 92. To Whom Promises Enumerated in §§ 82–85 Must Be Made.

The new promise referred to in §§ 82–85 is not binding unless it is made to a person who is then an obligee of the antecedent duty.

Comment

a. Rationale. The promises referred to in §§ 82–85 are binding without mutual assent or consideration. In the absence of consideration or reliance, there is need to distinguish between promises and expressions of expectation or good intention. Even a writing in the form of a promise is not effective if it is not delivered to anyone or is delivered only to the agent of the writer. An informal statement to a third person is likewise ineffective, even though words of promise are used, until there is communication to the promisee or to someone acting on his behalf. But a written promise is made when it is mailed to the promisee.

Compare § 63. And delivery to a third person may have the same effect if no power of revocation is reserved and the promisor manifests an intention that the contents of the writing be communicated to the promisee. Compare §§ 101–03.

Illustrations

1. A holds bonds issued by B, a city, which are overdue as to principal and interest. B's city treasurer writes a letter to B's fiscal agents in another city, acknowledging B's indebtedness on the bonds held by A and instructing the fiscal agents to redeem the bonds to the extent of the fund in their hands. The letter is not binding as a new promise by B to A.

2. A owes $5,000 to his daughter B on a note which B has lost. A signs and mails a letter to C, a bank named as executor in A's will, describing the debt and the note and stating that interest has been paid to date although not credited on the note because of its loss. The letter is binding as a new promise from A to B.

b. Obligees: promisee, beneficiary and surety. The new promise must be made to a person to whom the antecedent duty runs at the time of the new promise. Where the duty was created by a contract for the benefit of a third person, both the original promisee and the beneficiary may be obligees. See §§ 305–06. If there are several obligees of the same duty, a new promise to one may be binding for the benefit of all. A surety of the promisor is an obligee to the extent of any right to exoneration which would exist in the absence of the defenses referred to in §§ 82–85. See Restatement of Security §§ 108, 112.

Illustration

3. A owes B $500 on a negotiable note. C, an indorser of the note, was duly charged at maturity. B's rights against A and C are barred by the statute of limitations. A promises C to pay B the amount of the note. The promise is binding for the benefit of B.

c. Obligees: assignor, assignee and distributee. When an obligation is assigned or transferred by operation of law the assignee or transferee becomes an obligee and a new promise to him is binding.

In some cases the assignor may also be an obligee, as where he retains a beneficial interest after making an assignment as collateral security. In other cases the assignor may act as agent of the assignee. In cases of transfers to a trustee or other representative there may be ambiguity as to who is an obligee, and a new promise to one beneficially interested in the obligation may be binding. Thus after the death of an obligee a new promise to a distributee of his estate may be binding.

Illustrations

4. A, induced by B's fraud, contracts to pay B $100. B assigns to C who knows of the fraud. A with knowledge of the fraud now promises C to pay C $100 as promised originally to B. The promise to C is binding.

5. A owes B $500 on a negotiable promissory note. B's right against A is barred by the statute of limitations. A promises B to pay the note. Subsequently B indorses the note to C. C may recover from A.

6. A is an indorser of a negotiable note which is dishonored by the maker. The holder B fails to give due notification of dishonor to A. Subsequently A promises B to pay the note. B transfers the note to C. C, though ignorant of the promise at the time of the transfer, may recover upon it.

7. A owes his father B a $500 debt barred by the statute of limitations. B dies intestate, and A is appointed administrator. A then promises his sister C to pay the debt. The promise is binding for the benefit of B's estate.

§ 93. Promises Enumerated in §§ 82–85 Made in Ignorance of Facts.

A promise within the terms of §§ 82–85 is not binding unless the promisor knew or had reason to know the essential facts of the previous transaction to which the promise relates, but his knowledge of the legal effect of the facts is immaterial.

Illustrations

1. A secures from B a promise to pay $100 by fraudulently representing that a watch given as consideration for the promise is made of gold. B, knowing the facts but not knowing that A's fraud justifies him in avoiding the transaction, promises to pay the $100. The promise is binding.

2. A, an indorser of a note, did not receive due notification of its dishonor by the maker. Subsequently, in ignorance of the fact that the lack of notification had discharged him, A promises B, the holder of the note, to pay it. The promise is binding.

§ 94. Stipulations.

A promise or agreement with reference to a pending judicial proceeding, made by a party to the proceeding or his attorney, is binding without consideration. By statute or rule of court such an agreement is generally binding only

(a) if it is in writing and signed by the party or attorney, or

(b) if it is made or admitted in the presence of the court, or

(c) to the extent that justice requires enforcement in view of material change of position in reliance on the promise or agreement.

Comment

a. Consideration. Such agreements as are within the rules stated in the Section are called stipulations. Stipulations with respect to matters of form and procedure serve the convenience of the parties to litigation and often serve to simplify and expedite the proceeding. In some cases they are supported by the policy of favoring compromise in order to reduce the volume of litigation. Hence they are favored by the courts and enforced without regard to consideration.

b. Formality. Statutes or rules of court in most jurisdictions require stipulations to be in writing. In some States other formalities, such as filing in court, are also required. Such requirements relieve the courts of the duty to decide unseemly disputes between attorneys whose memories differ as to the terms of the agreement, disputes which would often be highly technical, time-consuming, and collateral to the matter in litigation. But a lawyer must comply with local customs of courtesy and practice unless he gives timely notice of his intent not to comply. American Bar Association, Code of Professional Responsibility, Disciplinary Rule 7–106(c)(5). Thus, it appears that it is dishonorable for an attorney to avoid performance of an agreement fairly made because it is not reduced to writing. Cf. American Bar Association, Former Canons of Professional Ethics 25. Admitted stipulations and stipulations made in open court are enforced without regard to form. And where a stipulation has been acted on, the court will not let a party take unfair advantage of the action he has induced. See § 90.

Illustration

1. A owes a debt to B secured by a mortgage. In foreclosure proceedings A signs and files in court a stipulation waiving service of all papers, relying on B's oral promise to bid the amount of the debt and costs at a sale of the mortgaged premises. At the sale B bids less and a judgment is entered against A for the deficiency. Notwithstanding a rule of court requiring a writing, the court may order a resale on A's application.

§ 95. Requirements for Sealed Contract or Written Contract or Instrument.

(1) In the absence of statute a promise is binding without consideration if

(a) it is in writing and sealed; and

(b) the document containing the promise is delivered; and

(c) the promisor and promisee are named in the document or so described as to be capable of identification when it is delivered.

(2) When a statute provides in effect that a written contract or instrument is binding without consideration or that lack of consideration is an affirmative defense to an action on a written contract or instrument, in order to be subject to the statute a promise must either

    (a) be expressed in a document signed or otherwise assented to by the promisor and delivered; or

    (b) be expressed in a writing or writings to which both promisor and promisee manifest assent.

Comment

a. Rationale. The explanation of these requirements is given in §§ 96–109. The nonexistence of one or more of them does not preclude the formation of a contract binding as a bargain under § 17.

b. "Written." The word "written" and the word "writing" not only in the present Section but throughout the Restatement include printing, typewriting or any other intentional reduction to tangible form. Compare Uniform Commercial Code § 1–201(46). "Written contract" includes contracts under seal, negotiable instruments and documents, and letters of credit. It may also include contracts embodied in more than one document.

c. Signature. A contract under seal is almost invariably signed, but such a contract is possible without signature. Written contracts are also commonly signed, but a written contract may consist of an exchange of correspondence, of a letter written by the promisee and assented to by the promisor without signature, or even of a memorandum or printed document not signed by either party. Statutes relating to written contracts are often expressly limited to contracts signed by one or both parties. See, e.g., Chapter 5. Whether such a limitation is to be implied when not explicit depends on the purpose and context.

d. Delivery. The moment of effectiveness of a contract under seal is defined in terms of "delivery" rather than in terms of offer and acceptance or manifestation of mutual assent. Where a written contract is binding without consideration the same definition is appropriate, and §§ 101–03 on delivery therefore apply to written promises, sealed or unsealed. In such cases the rule of § 104, that no acceptance is necessary, is also applicable.

e. Acceptance of promisee. Contracts under seal often embody all or part of a bargain. It is then ordinarily understood that neither party is bound until both have manifested assent, and the law gives effect to that understanding under the rules stated in §§ 105–07. Where consideration is required by law either for a contract under seal or for a written contract, a manifestation of mutual assent is part of the requirement. See § 71. Section 104 is therefore inapplicable where consideration is required, even though there may be a presumption of consideration; but §§ 105–07 do apply. In such cases, as stated in Subsection (2) of this Section, an unsealed written contract may be formed without delivery of a document.

f. Other rules relating to sealed instruments. As is indicated in the Introductory Note to this Topic, in medieval England the seal had numerous consequences other than that stated in this Section. Although those consequences have been modified by statute and decision, some of them persist to some extent in States which still recognize the seal. See, e.g., Restatement, Second, Agency §§ 151, 191, on the extent to which a principal is bound by an instrument sealed by his agent. Rules with respect to such consequences are stated in appropriate places in this Restatement. See, e.g., § 303 on third party beneficiaries.

§ 96. What Constitutes a Seal.

(1) A seal is a manifestation in tangible and conventional form of an intention that a document be sealed.

(2) A seal may take the form of a piece of wax, a wafer or other substance affixed to the document or of an impression made on the document.

(3) By statute or decision in most States in which the seal retains significance a seal may take the form of a written or printed seal, word, scrawl or other sign.

Comment

a. Historical note. The use of the seal in England seems to have begun after the Norman Conquest, spreading from royalty and a few of the nobility to those of lesser rank. Originally a seal often consisted of wax bearing the imprint of an individualized signet ring, and in the seventeenth century Lord Coke said that wax without impression was not a seal. But in the United States the courts have not required either wax or impression. Impressions directly on the paper were recognized early and are still common for notarial and corporate seals, and gummed wafers have been widely used. In the absence of statute decisions have divided on the effectiveness of the written or printed word "seal," the printed initials "L. S." (locus sigilli, meaning place of the seal), a scrawl made with a pen (often called a "scroll") and a recital of sealing. Most states in which the seal is still recognized now have statutes giving effect to one or more such devices.

b. Extrinsic circumstances. In the early law a contract under seal was treated as a grant rather than a promise, and the document was treated as the obligation rather than as evidence of it. It is still sometimes said that whether a document is under seal is to be determined from the document itself, without recourse to extrinsic circumstances. But a document which bears a seal does not establish its own authenticity. Evidence of extrinsic circumstances may be necessary to show that a promisor affixed or adopted a seal and that the document was delivered. See §§ 98, 102. It may be shown that a seal was accidentally or wrongfully removed, or even, as a ground for equitable relief, that sealing was omitted by accident or mistake. Similarly, where the printed word "seal" or the scrawl of a pen may serve as a seal if so intended, the circumstances may be relevant to the question whether it manifests such an intention.

Illustrations

1. A signs a written promise to B and after his signature attaches a gummed wafer. The document contains no recital that it is sealed. In the absence of circumstances manifesting a contrary intention, it is inferred from A's act that he intended the wafer to serve as a seal.

2. A signs a written promise to B and after his signature adds a dash or wavy line. The document contains no recital that it is sealed. Even though a seal may consist of a pen scrawl, these facts are insufficient to establish a contract under seal.

3. The facts being otherwise as stated in Illustration 2, the document recites that it is under seal. The court may infer that the dash or line is a seal.

TOPIC 3. CONTRACTS UNDER SEAL; WRITING AS A STATUTORY SUBSTITUTE FOR THE SEAL

§ 97. When a Promise Is Sealed.

A written promise is sealed if the promisor affixes or impresses a seal on the document or adopts a seal already thereon.

Comment

a. Scope. The rule stated in this Section is appropriate to the traditional type of seal referred to in § 96(2). Adoption is also appropriate where a written or printed word or sign is recognized as stated in § 96(3). Where so recognized, writing by the promisor has the same effect as the affixing or impressing of the traditional seal.

Illustration

1. A signs a written promise to B. B, without A's knowledge, affixes a wafer after A's signature. Inspection of the document indicates that the wafer is a seal, but as A neither affixed nor adopted it, he is not bound by a promise under seal.

§ 98. Adoption of a Seal by Delivery.

Unless extrinsic circumstances manifest a contrary intention, the delivery of a written promise by the promisor amounts to the adoption of any seal then on the document which has apparent reference to his signature or to the signature of another party to the document.

Comment

a. Adoption. The adoption of a seal may be shown or negated by any relevant evidence as to the intention manifested by the promisor. This Section states the inference to be drawn in a common type of case. Very often the inference is strengthened by a recital of sealing contained in the document. See § 100. Where the promisor manifests a contrary intention, the rules stated in § 20 are applicable.

Illustrations

1. A signs and delivers a written promise to B, his signature being immediately in front of the word "seal," which has been previously printed or written there by another person. Unless A manifests a contrary intention, he thereby adopts the seal and makes a contract under seal.

2. A, B and C sign a written promise in that order, and C affixes a seal after his signature. Thereafter A, B and C deliver the document. It is inferred that A and B adopt the seal. But if the promisee knows or has reason to know that A has a contrary intention, the seal is not adopted by A.

§ 99. Adoption of the Same Seal by Several Parties.

Any number of parties to the same instrument may adopt one seal.

Illustration

1. A, B, C and D sign a subscription paper by which each agrees to pay a sum set opposite his name. There is one seal on the document which recites, "A seal is attached hereto which each of the subscribers adopts." The promise of each of the subscribers is under seal.

§ 100. Recital of Sealing or Delivery.

A recital of the sealing or of the delivery of a written promise is not essential to its validity as a contract under seal and is not conclusive of the fact of sealing or delivery unless a statute makes a recital of sealing the equivalent of a seal.

Comment

a. Recital not required. When the seal consisted of an individualized impression on wax, a recital was unnecessary to show whether sealing was intended, and delivery seems originally not to have been required. The practice is common to recite sealing and delivery, but the recital is not an independent requirement. Recital is sometimes required where a scrawl or other substitute for the more formal seal is recognized, but even in such cases the prevailing view is that the recital is not essential.

b. Recital not conclusive. A recital may give meaning to a manifestation of intention, indicating that a dash or scrawl after a signature is intended as a seal or that a promisor intends to adopt a seal affixed by another party. See §§ 96–99. By statute or decision in some states a recital of sealing is the equivalent of a seal. Otherwise, however, recitals are often false, and their falsity may be shown by any relevant evidence. In particular, a recital of delivery printed on a document commonly indicates only that a party signing the document then intended to deliver it.

§ 101. Delivery.

A written promise, sealed or unsealed, may be delivered by the promisor in escrow, conditionally to the promisee, or unconditionally.

Comment

a. Delivery. This Section states how the requirement of delivery stated in § 95 may be met. Unconditional delivery is the subject of § 102, and conditional delivery to the promisee and delivery in escrow are the subject of § 103.

Illustration

1. A delivers to B a sealed promise naming B or C as promisee. There is a present contract under seal, whether or not the promisee knows of the promise. If the delivery is conditional or in escrow, the contract is conditional.

   b. *Return promise.* A promisor cannot by delivering a document impose on the promisee a duty to perform a return promise stated in the document; there must be a manifestation of assent by the promisee. Whether there is a delivery in such a case and if so whether it is conditional or unconditional depend on the rules stated in §§ 105–07.

§ 102. Unconditional Delivery.

A written promise is delivered unconditionally when the promisor puts it out of his possession and manifests an intention that it is to take effect at once according to its terms.

Comment

   a. *Transfer of possession without delivery.* "Delivery" is often used in the sense of voluntary transfer of possession. See Uniform Commercial Code § 1–201(14). But as it is used in this Section more is required. There is no delivery if the promisor manifests an intention to reserve a power of revocation. Thus manual tradition to the promisor's own servant or agent is not delivery; nor is a transfer of possession for the purpose of inspection or discussion, for use as a sample or model, or merely for safekeeping. But mailing to the promisee is sufficient if the promisor manifests an intention that the promise take immediate effect. Compare § 63.

Illustrations

1. A hands to B a sealed promise by A in which C is named as promisee, and requests B to give the document to C unless B receives contrary instructions from A. There is no delivery and no contract under seal until the document is delivered to C.

2. A signs and seals a written promise to make a gift to B and deposits the document in the mail addressed to B. There has been a delivery, and unless consideration is required the promise is binding even though A dies before B receives the document.

   b. *Retention of possession by promisor.* In England and in some States a manifestation of intention that a document take effect immediately is the equivalent of delivery. Where there is consideration and a manifestation of mutual assent in such circumstances, there may be a contract binding as a bargain. See § 57. Otherwise, however, tradition requires that the promisor put the document out of his possession. But the change of possession need not be permanent; a delivery for the purpose of public recording, for example, may suffice even though the document is then redelivered to the promisor.

Illustrations

3. A signs and seals a written promise to B and deposits the document in the drawer of his own desk, saying to B and to a third person as he does so that he intends the promise to be immediately binding. There has been no delivery.

4. A delivers to B a sealed promise by A in which B is named as promisee. On receiving the document B returns it to A, saying "Please keep it for me." The return does not impair the effectiveness of the delivery.

   c. *Unconditional delivery of conditional promise.* This Section refers to the unconditional delivery of a document. The promise contained in the document may be conditional or unconditional. If the promise is conditional it may create a conditional duty even though it takes immediate effect. See § 224.

§ 103. Delivery in Escrow; Conditional Delivery to the Promisee.

(1) A written promise is delivered in escrow by the promisor when he puts it into the possession of a person other than the promisee without reserving a power of revocation and manifests an intention that the document is to take effect according to its terms upon the occurrence of a stated condition but not otherwise.

(2) A written promise is delivered conditionally to the promisee when the promisor puts it into the possession of the promisee without reserving a power of revocation and manifests an intention that the document is to take effect according to its terms upon the occurrence of a stated condition but not otherwise.

(3) Delivery of a written promise in escrow or its conditional delivery to the promisee has the same effect as unconditional delivery would have if the requirement of the condition were expressed in the writing.

(4) In the absence of a statute modifying the significance of a seal, delivery of a sealed promise in escrow or its conditional delivery to the promisee is irrevocable for the time specified by the promisor for the occurrence of the condition, or, if no time is specified, for a reasonable time.

Comment

a. Escrow. Like "scroll" and "scrawl," the word "escrow" is derived from the Norman-French word for a writing or a written instrument. It has come in practice to refer to a security device: one or both parties to a transaction deposit property or an instrument with a third party until some condition has occurred. The property or instrument may be referred to as "the escrow"; the delivery is said to be "in escrow."

b. Effect of delivery in escrow. Where the owner of property delivers in escrow the property or an instrument of transfer, the title to the property does not pass until the condition has occurred, but the delivery is irrevocable and creates immediate conditional rights in the transferee. Where the owner manifests an intention that the transferee is to hold the property in trust, a trust may be created at the time of the delivery in escrow. See Restatement, Second, Trusts § 32, Comment d. Delivery in escrow of a promise under seal is similarly irrevocable where the seal retains its common-law effect. Thus the delivery creates immediate conditional rights in the promisee, and the device may be used to create an option contract in which the promisee has the option. See §§ 25, 87.

Illustration

1. A delivers to B a sealed promise to pay C $10,000, stating that it is delivered in escrow and is to be delivered to C if C within ten days deposits with B a deed to a parcel of land. In the absence of statute A has made an option contract under seal which cannot be revoked during the ten-day period.

c. Reservation of power of revocation. If the promisor reserves a power to revoke the delivery or if the delivery is made conditional on his own future manifestation of assent, his purported promise is illusory just as it would be if such a term were expressed in the writing. See §§ 2, 76, 77. The person to whom delivery is made is then an agent of the promisor rather than an escrow holder, and there is no contract until either the promisor or his agent acts further. See Restatement, Second, Agency § 14D. Unless there is a manifestation of donative intent or an agreement between promisor and promisee, the entrusting of an instrument to a third person for delivery to the promisee upon the performance of an act by the promisee ordinarily creates a revocable agency rather than an escrow.

d. Conditional delivery to the promisee. A written promise may be delivered to the promisee on terms substantially like those of a delivery in escrow, and the legal effect is substantially the same. But such a transaction is not ordinarily referred to as a delivery in escrow, since it does not afford the security to the promisor of possession by an impartial third person. See § 217 and Comment b to that Section.

Illustration

2. A delivers to B a sealed promise in which B is named as promisee, stating that the document is not to take effect unless B shall first erect a certain fence, and that the fence must be erected by July 1. In the absence of statute A cannot revoke the delivery until B has had the time specified for building the fence.

§ 104. Acceptance or Disclaimer by the Promisee.

(1) Neither acceptance by the promisee nor knowledge by him of the existence of a promise is essential to the formation of a contract by the delivery of a written promise which is binding without consideration.

(2) A promisee who has not manifested assent to a written promise may, within a reasonable time after learning of its existence and terms, render it inoperative by disclaimer.

(3) Acceptance or disclaimer is irrevocable.

Comment

a. Acceptance. It is sometimes said that acceptance of a promise which is beneficial to the promisee is presumed. But the "presumption" cannot be rebutted in the cases governed by the rule stated in Subsection (1), and a more accurate form of statement is that acceptance is unnecessary. Compare §§ 306, 327. Thus a promise under seal to make a gift to a person without capacity to assent by reason of infancy or mental illness is not revoked by the death of the promisor, and may be accepted thereafter. But Subsection (1) is applicable only to promises binding without consideration; where by statute a seal merely raises a presumption of consideration, proof of failure to accept may rebut the presumption.

The promise may of course be explicitly conditional on an acceptance by the promisee, or such a condition may be imposed by the terms of delivery under § 103. Where a return promise is contemplated, such a condition may be implied, or the promisor may manifest an intention to create an option contract pending acceptance by return promise. The rules governing cases where an acceptance is contemplated are stated in §§ 105–07.

Illustration

1. A makes a promise to B under seal, and unconditionally delivers the document to C, an independent third person, as a present contract. It is immediately operative according to its terms and remains so unless B disclaims within a reasonable time after learning of its existence and terms.

b. Disclaimer. An offeree is entitled to reject an offered benefit, whether or not there is a related burden. See § 38. Where no return promise is invited, there is no problem of justifiable reliance by the promisor, and a disclaimer by the promisee is effective in accordance with his manifested intention. See § 53(3). No particular formality is required for disclaimer, and its usual effect is the same as if no promise had been made. But once the promisee has manifested assent, either before or after the making of the promise, disclaimer is effective only if the requirements are met for discharge of a contractual duty. Compare § 37.

Illustration

2. A seals and delivers to B a written promise to C to transfer Blackacre to C, stating at the time that the promise is to be enforceable only when C shall marry X. On learning of the promise either before or after marrying X, C notifies either A or B that he refuses the benefit of the promise. The contract under seal is discharged, and an intervening conveyance by A to D is validated even though D knew of the contract.

§ 105. Acceptance Where Return Promise Is Contemplated.

Where a conveyance or a document containing a promise also purports to contain a return promise by the grantee or promisee, acceptance by the grantee or promisee is essential to create any contractual obligation other than an option contract binding on the grantor or promisor.

Comment

a. Exchange of promises. Where one promise is to be exchanged for another, it is essential that each promisor manifest assent. Compare §§ 17, 50. Moreover, it is ordinarily not contemplated that one promise shall be made without the other. But if consideration is given or is not required and an intention is manifested to create an option contract, one promise may be made irrevocable, the promisee remaining free to accept or reject. See § 25. The intention may be manifested either by the terms of the document or by the terms on which it is delivered.

Illustrations

1. A signs and seals a document containing promises by him and by B and hands it to B for execution. Until B executes it, neither party is bound.

2. A signs and seals a written promise to pay B $30,000 on B's completion of a building and delivers the document to C, instructing C that the promise is to be irrevocable for 30 days and is to be effective thereafter only if within that time B files with C specified written promises and other documents. A is bound by an option contract.

b. Promise by grantee. The same principles apply to a promise by the grantee contained in a conveyance. Compare § 55. The grantee is not bound unless he accepts, and ordinarily the grantor is not bound before the grantee accepts. But if the grantor, either in the conveyance or in the terms on which it is delivered, manifests an intention that the conveyance shall be irrevocable pending acceptance, delivery may have that effect.

Illustration

3. A makes a deed of conveyance of Blackacre to his son B. The deed contains this clause: "This conveyance is subject to a mortgage of $10,000 to D which the said B assumes and agrees to pay." A delivers the deed unconditionally to C to hold on behalf of B. B is subject to no duty to pay the mortgage unless he accepts the deed.

§ 106. What Amounts to Acceptance of Instrument.

Acceptance of a conveyance or of a document containing a promise is a manifestation of assent to the terms thereof made, either before or after delivery, in accordance with any requirements imposed by the grantor or promisor. If the acceptance occurs before delivery and is not binding as an option contract, it is revocable until the moment of delivery.

Comment

a. Manifestation of assent. Acceptance of a promise under seal or a conveyance is the acceptance of an offer if the acceptance is made after delivery. Compare § 50. An acceptance before delivery can be thought of as an offer accepted by the delivery. Compare § 24. In either case the effect of misunderstanding is governed by the principles stated in § 20.

Illustration

1. The facts being otherwise as stated in Illustration 3 to § 105, C hands the deed to B and B takes it without objection. Unless A or C has reason to know that B is ignorant of the clause relating to the mortgage, B is bound by a contract to pay the mortgage debt. The question whether the contract is voidable by reason of such ignorance is governed by the rules stated in Chapters 6 and 7 on mistake, misrepresentation, duress and undue influence.

b. Acceptance before delivery. Like other offers, a manifestation of assent to a promise under seal or conveyance to be delivered in the future is ordinarily revocable. Compare § 42. But such an acceptance in advance may be irrevocable by virtue of a seal or consideration. See § 25. In any event delivery of the instrument terminates the power of revocation.

Illustration

2. A and B agree orally that A shall transfer to B Blackacre, which is subject to a mortgage, that the deed shall contain a promise by B to pay the mortgage debt, and that the deed may be delivered to C on B's behalf. A makes and delivers to C a deed in accordance with the oral agreement. There has been acceptance by B, and though he refuses to take the deed from C, he is bound by a contract to pay the mortgage debt.

§ 107. Creation of Unsealed Contract by Acceptance by Promisee.

Where a grantee or promisee accepts a sealed document which purports to contain a return promise by him, he makes the return promise. But if he does not sign or seal the document his promise is not under seal, and whether it is binding depends on the rules governing unsealed contracts.

Illustration

1. A owes B a liquidated debt of $200. A prepares and signs and seals a writing in duplicate, which states a promise on his part to pay $100 immediately and a promise on B's part to forbear for a year any attempt to collect the remaining $100 on account of the debt. A sends the duplicates to B by mail with a letter saying "If you care to accept my proposition sign these papers and return one to me." B with intent to accept the proposition retains one copy and returns the other with a letter saying "I accept your proposition," but does not sign or seal either writing. His promise to forbear is inoperative for failure to comply with A's offer.

§ 108. Requirement of Naming or Describing Promisor and Promisee.

A promise under seal is not binding without consideration unless both the promisor and the promisee are named in the document or so described as to be capable of identification when it is delivered.

Comment

a. Historical Note. In the common-law courts of medieval England the sealed instrument was treated as almost complete in itself, and evidence of extrinsic circumstances was not permitted even to show that the instrument was voidable for fraud. A different view was taken in equity, and in modern times extrinsic evidence may be relevant to show conditional delivery or for a variety of other purposes.

The rule of this Section is a remnant of the former strictness, and it may not be followed where the law of seals has been changed by statute or decision. Compare Restatement, Second, Agency §§ 151, 191, 296, under which a principal is not a party to a sealed instrument unless he appears in the instrument as a party. Where the seal is not essential to the validity of the contract, it may be treated as superfluous, and a party not named in the writing may then have rights or duties under the rules governing unsealed contracts.

Illustrations

1. A promise under seal purporting to be by "the eldest son of A," is duly sealed and delivered by B under this description without the use of his own name. B is at the time the eldest son of A. The promise is operative as a contract under seal by him. The fact that before the time for performance the eldest living son of A, owing to the death of B, is a different person, does not alter this effect or make the instrument binding upon the survivor.

2. A promise purporting to be made by whoever may be the eldest son of A at the time when performance thereof is due, though sealed and delivered by the son who ultimately turns out to be the eldest at the time of the promised performance, is not his contract under seal.

3. A promise under seal to whoever shall be the wife of A at the time when performance of the promise is due, is not a contract under seal with the person who ultimately fulfills that description, though she is A's wife at the time when the writing is delivered, as well as when performance is due.

4. A gives an option under seal to B. B is acting on behalf of C, but C's name does not appear in the instrument. Within the time limited in the option B accepts by an unsealed writing delivered to A. C is bound by an unsealed contract created by the unsealed acceptance by B.

§ 109. Enforcement of a Sealed Contract by Promisee Who Does Not Sign or Seal It.

The promisee of a promise under seal is not precluded from enforcing it as a sealed contract because he has not signed or sealed the document, unless his doing so was a condition of the delivery, whether or not the document contains a promise by him.

Comment

a. Failure to sign or seal. Other circumstances (as indicated by §§ 105 and 107) than the fact that the promisee has not signed or sealed the document may prevent the promisee from acquiring a right, but the failure to sign or seal does not itself have this effect, unless such an act is made a condition when the document is delivered.

CHAPTER 5

THE STATUTE OF FRAUDS

§ 110. Classes of Contracts Covered.

(1) The following classes of contracts are subject to a statute, commonly called the Statute of Frauds, forbidding enforcement unless there is a written memorandum or an applicable exception:

    (a) a contract of an executor or administrator to answer for a duty of his decedent (the executor-administrator provision);

    (b) a contract to answer for the duty of another (the suretyship provision);

    (c) a contract made upon consideration of marriage (the marriage provision);

    (d) a contract for the sale of an interest in land (the land contract provision);

    (e) a contract that is not to be performed within one year from the making thereof (the one-year provision).

. . .

(5) In many states other classes of contracts are subject to a requirement of a writing.

Comment

a. Classes of contracts. The five classes of contracts listed in Subsection (1) were included in different language in § 4 of the English Statute of Frauds, enacted in 1677. The English Statute was repealed in 1954 except for the suretyship and land contract provisions. Subsections (2) and (3) refer to four separate Statute of Frauds sections found in the Uniform Commercial Code, which displace § 4 of the Uniform Sales Act and § 17 of the English statute. The Code sections are not elaborated in this Restatement. Subsection (4) is a statement of a provision of Lord Tenterden's Act, 1828, which has been widely copied in the United States. As to the extent of enactment of these and other similar statutes, see the Statutory Note preceding this Section. The formal contracts referred to in § 6 of this Restatement are not affected by the Statute of Frauds, but in some cases are subject to separate statutes containing formal requirements.

b. Overlap of classes. The clauses of the English statute apply separately; one contract may be within more than one clause of the statute, and facts which except it from one class may not except it from another. Thus contracts in consideration of marriage or for the sale of land or goods may also be contracts not to be performed within a year, and the statutory requirements in one clause may be satisfied and those of another clause unsatisfied.

Illustration

1. A and B orally agree to marry three years later. The contract is unenforceable because not to be performed within a year, even though it is excepted from the provision for contracts in consideration of marriage.

c. Variations in the statutes. The English Statute of Frauds and many American statutes take the form, "No action shall be brought whereby to charge . . . unless . . . ." In some states non-complying contracts are said to be "void" or "invalid" or "not binding," but in spite of such differences there is much similarity in the interpretation given. Lord Tenterden's Act and statutes modeled on it, however, are generally construed to require the acknowledgment or promise itself to be in writing; under such statutes a subsequent memorandum does not render enforceable a prior oral promise. See § 136.

d. Consequences of non-compliance. The consequences of non-compliance are the subject of Topic 7, §§ 138–47. In general a contract subject to the Statute of Frauds is unenforceable if the requirements of the statute are not satisfied. See § 8. The Statute does not in general bar the remedy of restitution; indeed, recovery of benefits conferred pursuant to an unenforceable contract is a standard remedy. See § 375; Restatement of Restitution § 108. Where there has been part performance or other action in reliance on an unenforceable contract, the effect is in some situations to make the contract fully enforceable, in others to make particular remedies available. See, e.g., § 129. Even though no such rule is applicable, the circumstances may be such that justice requires enforcement of the promise. To the extent that justice so requires, the promise is then enforced by virtue of the doctrine of estoppel or by virtue of reliance on a promise notwithstanding the Statute. See § 139.

TOPIC 1. THE EXECUTOR-ADMINISTRATOR PROVISION

§ 111. Contract of Executor or Administrator.

A contract of an executor or administrator to answer personally for a duty of his decedent is within the Statute of Frauds if a similar contract to answer for the duty of a living person would be within the Statute as a contract to answer for the duty of another.

Comment

a. Analogy to suretyship. The first clause of § 4 of the English Statute of Frauds is treated as a special application of the suretyship provision of the second clause. Where the principal obligor dies before the promise in question is made, the case may not fall precisely within the usual definition of suretyship. See Restatement of Security § 82. But the situation is similar, and similar rules are applied. If there was no obligation before the death of the decedent, the promise is not within this clause. Where the executor or administrator makes a contract on behalf of the estate, the creditor's right against the estate ordinarily depends on the right of the executor or administrator to exoneration. Compare Restatement, Second, Trusts §§ 266–71A.

Illustrations

1. S, executor of D, promises C, a creditor of D at the time of D's death, in consideration of C's promise to forego part of the debt, to guarantee payment of the balance by the estate. S's promise is within the executor provision.

2. S, executor of D, contracts with C for funeral services, or for work and material necessary in closing D's business, promising orally "I guarantee that D's estate will pay you." S's promise is not within the executor provision.

b. Exceptions. The executor provision is subject to the same exceptions as the suretyship provision. See Topic 2, §§ 112–23; Restatement of Security §§ 89–100. Thus the rule relating to novations stated in § 115 and the "main purpose" rule stated in § 116 are similarly applied to promises of executors or administrators.

Illustrations

3. S, executor of D, promises C, a creditor of D at the time of D's death, in consideration of C's promise never to prove his claim against D's estate, to pay the debt. S's promise is not within the executor provision. See § 115.

4. S and C enter into a contract in which S promises that if C will assent to S's appointment as administrator of D's estate, S will pay a debt owing by D's estate to C. S's promise is not within the administrator provision. See § 116.

TOPIC 2. THE SURETYSHIP PROVISION

§ 112. Requirement of Suretyship.

A contract is not within the Statute of Frauds as a contract to answer for the duty of another unless the promisee is an obligee of the other's duty, the promisor is a surety for the other, and the promisee knows or has reason to know of the suretyship relation.

Comment

a. The statutory purpose. In general the primary purpose of the Statute of Frauds is assumed to be evidentiary. See Statutory Note preceding § 110. In the case of suretyship contracts, however, the Statute also serves the cautionary function of guarding the promisor against ill-considered action. The suretyship provision is not limited to important or complex contracts, but is limited to suretyship and to promises made to an obligee of the principal obligation. Such promises serve a useful purpose, and the requirement of consideration is commonly met by the same promise or performance which is consideration for the principal obligation. See Comment to § 72; compare § 88. But the motivation of the surety is often essentially gratuitous, his obligation depends on a contingency which may seem remote at the time of contracting, and natural formalities which often attend an extension of credit are likely not to provide reliable evidence of the existence and terms of the surety's undertaking. Hence the requirement of a writing. Reliance of the kinds usual in suretyship situations—extension of credit or forbearance to pursue the principal obligor—does not render the requirement inapplicable.

b. "Debt, default or miscarriages." The word "duty" is used here as a substitute for the words "debt, default or miscarriages" used in the English statute to describe the principal obligation. Those words and corresponding words in American statutes include all kinds of duties recognized by law, whether or not contractual and whether already incurred or to be incurred in the future. The person owing the duty is called the principal debtor or obligor. The duty may be conditional, voidable or unenforceable; but if there is no duty at all, the Statute does not apply.

Illustrations

1. D commits a tort against C. S promises C orally for consideration to pay C the damages which C has suffered from the tort if D fails to do so. S's promise is within the Statute of Frauds, since D is under a direct duty to C, and S's promise is to perform D's duty if D fails to do so.

2. S promises C orally to guarantee the performance of any duty that D may incur to C within the ensuing year. Relying on this promise, C enters into contracts with D, by which D undertakes within the year to sell materials for a house and to act as supervising architect during its construction. D, without excuse, fails to perform his contract. S's promise is within the Statute of Frauds.

3. D, an infant, obtains goods on credit from C, who is induced to part with them by S's oral guaranty that D will pay the price as agreed. The goods are not necessaries but D is subject to a duty, though it is voidable. S's promise is within the Statute of Frauds.

4. D, an insane person under guardianship, obtains goods on credit from C, who is induced to part with them by S's oral guaranty that D will keep his promise to pay the price. D's promise is void. S's promise is not within the Statute of Frauds.

c. Promisor must be surety. The suretyship provision applies only if there is a principal obligation "of another" than the promisor. The promisor must promise as a surety for the principal obligor. Whether the promisor and the other are surety and principal depends on their contract or relation to each other. The essential elements of the relation are that they are bound for the same performance and that as between them the other rather than the promisor should perform. See Restatement of Security § 82. A promise to be surety for part of the principal obligation is within the Statute, but a promise of a distinct performance is not, even though its purpose is to render more certain the performance of the principal obligation.

Illustrations

5. S obtains goods from C on this oral promise: "Charge them to D, and, if he does not pay for them, I will." S has no authority to charge the goods to D, and D makes no promise to pay for them. S's promise is not within the suretyship provision of the Statute of Frauds, since D is under no duty, and hence is not a principal obligor.

6. In consideration of the delivery of goods by C to D at S's request, S orally promises to pay the price of them. S's promise is not within the Statute of Frauds, since D is under no duty.

7. S induces C to sell goods to D and take D's note for the price by warranting orally or in an unsigned writing that D's note is not voidable on account of infancy. S's warranty is not within the

Statute of Frauds, whether D's promise is or is not voidable, since S does not bind himself for the performance which D has undertaken. S will become liable for such damages as C may suffer if D is an infant and whether D's note is or is not voidable it will not be discharged by S's performance.

8. D contracts with S to build a house for S. C contracts with D to furnish materials for the purpose. D in violation of his contract with C fails to pay C for some of the materials furnished, and C justifiably cancels his contract with D. S orally promises C that if C will continue to furnish D with materials that C had previously agreed to furnish, S will pay the price therefor. C does so. S's promise is not within the Statute of Frauds because D is not bound to pay C for the materials supplied in consideration of S's promise.

d. Promisee must be obligee; "reason to know." The suretyship provision does not apply to a promise unless the promisee is the person to whom the principal obligation is owed, or who is entitled to damages for the default or miscarriage. Moreover, the obligee-promisee must know or have reason to know of the suretyship relation, either from the terms of his contract with the principal or with the surety or from extrinsic facts. As to what constitutes "reason to know," see Comment b to § 19.

Illustrations

9. S, for consideration, orally promises E to pay a debt of E's son D to C, if D fails to pay it at maturity. S's promise is not within the Statute of Frauds because it was made to E, not to the creditor C.

10. D and S severally and unconditionally in an unsigned writing promise C, for consideration inuring to the benefit of both D and S, that C shall be paid the sum of $100 a month for the next six months. D has induced S to make this promise by promising to hold S harmless. If C knows or has reason to know of this contract between D and S, when S makes his promise to C, S's promise is unenforceable. Otherwise S's promise is not within the Statute of Frauds.

11. D induces S to purchase goods from C. Though the purchase is for D's benefit, the goods are delivered by C to S, who afterwards turns them over to D. S orally promises C to pay for them. D, as part of the transaction, guarantees C that S will pay. C neither knows nor has reason to know that S is a surety. Though S is a surety as between himself and D, his promise is not within the Statute of Frauds. D's promise also is not within the Statute, since the duty to pay is in truth his.

§ 113. Promises of the Same Performance for the Same Consideration.

Where promises of the same performance are made by two persons for a consideration which inures to the benefit of only one of them, the promise of the other is within the Statute of Frauds as a contract to answer for the duty of another, whether or not the promise is in terms conditional on default by the one to whose benefit the consideration inures, unless

(a) the other is not a surety for the one to whose benefit the consideration inures; or

(b) the promises are in terms joint and do not create several duties or joint and several duties; or

(c) the promisee neither knows nor has reason to know that the consideration does not inure to the benefit of both promisors.

Comment

a. Rationale. This Section provides for the application of the rule of § 112 to a common situation, and makes an exception for cases of joint duties. Unless a contrary intention is manifested, the fact that promises of the same performance are made by two persons for a consideration which inures to the benefit of only one of them sufficiently shows that the other is a surety. A promisee who has reason to know that the consideration inures to the benefit of only one has sufficient reason to know of the suretyship relation to satisfy the requirement of § 112.

b. Joint obligations. Historically, joint promisors were treated for many purposes as a unit. Hence as against one joint promisor the obligation of his co-promisor was not treated as that "of another" within the Statute of Frauds, even though a suretyship relation in fact existed between them. In modern times the historic rules governing joint obligations have been greatly modified by statute or decision in most states. See Chapter 13. But where the distinction between joint duties and joint and several duties retains significance, the suretyship provision of the Statute of Frauds does not apply to suretyship between joint promisors.

Illustrations

1. D and S jointly and orally promise C to pay C for goods which C knows are to be delivered for the exclusive benefit of D. If S is under no several duty, his promise is not within the Statute of Frauds.

2. The facts being otherwise as stated in Illustration 1, the promise is joint and several. S's promise is within the Statute of Frauds.

3. The facts being otherwise as stated in Illustration 2, C has no reason to know that the goods are not for the benefit of both parties. S's promise is not within the Statute of Frauds.

§ 114. Independent Duty of Promisor.

A contract to perform or otherwise to satisfy all or part of a duty of a third person to the promisee is not within the Statute of Frauds as a contract to answer for the duty of another if, by the terms of the promise when it is made, performance thereof can involve no more than

    (a) the application of funds or property held by the promisor for the purpose, or

    (b) performance of any other duty owing, irrespective of his promise, by the promisor to the promisee, or

    (c) performance of a duty which is either owing, irrespective of his promise, by the promisor to the third person, or which the promisee reasonably believes to be so owing.

Comment

a. Rationale. Where the promisor, if he keeps his promise, will be doing no more than he is bound to do by reason of a duty other than that imposed by the promise, the promise is not within the Statute. Even though the promisor is a surety, he promises to answer for his own obligation as well as that of another and is not within the reason of the Statute. The terms of the promise will commonly refer to the independent duty, but need not do so. The independent duty may exist when the promise is made or may arise subsequently.

b. Application of funds. Subsection (a) deals primarily with cases where the promisor is a trustee and the promisee a beneficiary of the trust, although the trust relationship is not essential. In such cases the promise usually shows by its terms the independent duty and the limitation of the promise. To the extent that the promise goes beyond the duty, the case is not within Subsection (a).

Illustrations

1. D owes C $100 and pays that sum to S in trust to pay it to C. Then or thereafter S orally promises C to pay D's debt. Whether or not C knows of the trust, C acquires an enforceable right against S.

2. D pays $100 to S in trust to apply it to whatever judgment C may recover against D in an action then pending. S orally promises C to pay the judgment in full. C recovers judgment for $125. C has an enforceable right against S for only $100.

c. Other independent duties. Where the promisor merely promises to perform an independent duty owed to the promisee or to the principal obligor, the promise is not within the Statute. In such cases the terms of the promise often do not disclose the independent duty. Where the promisee in good faith believes, when the promise is made, that such a duty is owed by the promisor to his co-obligor, the same rule is applied even though the duty does not in fact exist.

Illustrations

3. S is a member of a partnership. After he retires but before the debts of the partnership are paid, S orally promises C, a partnership creditor, to pay the amount due him. The promise is not within the Statute of Frauds.

4. S, at D's request, orally promises C to guarantee the payment by D to C of the price of any goods sold by C to D, to the extent of the indebtedness S may owe D at the time when C notifies S that D has made default. C thereupon sells goods to D. S's promise is not within the Statute of Frauds.

5. S and D severally promise C to pay for goods to be delivered to D. The goods are really for S and D is the real surety, but S and D lead C to suppose that S is the surety. S's promise is not within the Statute of Frauds; under § 113(c) neither is D's.

§ 115. Novation.

A contract that is itself accepted in satisfaction of a previously existing duty of a third person to the promisee is not within the Statute of Frauds as a contract to answer for the duty of another.

Comment

a. This Section relates to novations. It makes no difference whether the new promisor promises the same performance as that formerly due from the first obligor or a different performance. The promise is not one to answer for another's duty since that other ceases to be under a duty when the new promise becomes binding, and the promisor is not a surety. The case must be distinguished where performance of the new promise—not the promise itself—is to be taken in satisfaction of the old duty.

§ 116. Main Purpose; Advantage to Surety.

A contract that all or part of a duty of a third person to the promisee shall be satisfied is not within the Statute of Frauds as a promise to answer for the duty of another if the consideration for the promise is in fact or apparently desired by the promisor mainly for his own economic advantage, rather than in order to benefit the third person. If, however, the consideration is merely a premium for insurance, the contract is within the Statute.

Comment

a. Rationale. This Section states what is often called the "main purpose" or "leading object" rule. Where the surety-promisor's main purpose is his own pecuniary or business advantage, the gratuitous or sentimental element often present in suretyship is eliminated, the likelihood of disproportion in the values exchanged between promisor and promisee is reduced, and the commercial context commonly provides evidentiary safeguards. Thus there is less need for cautionary or evidentiary formality than in other cases of suretyship. The situation is comparable to a sale or purchase of a third person's obligation, which is also outside the purposes of the suretyship provision of the Statute of Frauds. See §§ 121, 122. Historically, the rule could be reconciled with the words of the Statute on the ground that a promisor who received a bargained-for benefit could be sued in debt or indebitatus assumpsit; hence he promised to pay his own debt rather than the debt "of another", and the promise was not "special" in the sense that special assumpsit was the only appropriate remedy. In modern times, however, the rule is applied in terms of its reason rather than to accord with abandoned procedural categories.

b. Factors affecting application of the rule. The fact that there is consideration for the surety's promise is insufficient to bring the rule into play. Slight and indirect possible advantage to the promisor is similarly insufficient. The expected advantage must be such as to justify the conclusion that his main purpose in making the promise is to advance his own interests. Facts such as the following tend to indicate such a main purpose when there is an expected pecuniary or business advantage: prior default, inability or repudiation of the principal obligor; forbearance of the creditor to enforce a lien on property in which the promisor has an interest or which he intends to use; equivalence between the value of the benefit and the amount promised; lack of participation by the principal obligor in the making of the surety's promise; a larger transaction to which the suretyship is incidental. The benefit may be supplied to the promisor by the promisee, by the principal obligor, or by some other person; if it is substantial and meets the main purpose test it may come indirectly through benefit to the principal obligor.

Illustrations

1. D owes C $1,000. C is about to levy an attachment on D's factory. S, who is a friend of D's desiring to prevent his friend's financial ruin, orally promises C that if C will forbear to take legal proceedings against D for three months S will pay D's debt if D fails to do so. S has no purpose to benefit himself and C has no reason to suppose so. S's promise is not enforceable.

2. D owes C $1,000. C is about to levy an attachment on D's factory. S, who is also a creditor of D's, fearing that the attachment will ruin D's business and thereby destroy his own chance of collecting his claim, orally promises C that if C will forbear to take legal proceedings against D for three months, S will pay D's debt if D fails to do so. S's promise is enforceable.

3. D contracts with S to build a house for S. C contracts with D to furnish materials for the purpose. D, in violation of his contract with C, fails to pay C for some of the materials furnished. C justifiably refuses to furnish further materials. S orally promises C, that if C will continue to furnish D with materials that C had previously agreed to furnish, S will pay the price not only for the materials already furnished but also for the remaining materials if D fails to do so. S's promise is enforceable.

4. C, a bank, discounts negotiable promissory notes of D, a corporation. D becomes financially involved. An official bank examiner threatens to close the bank on account of the impairment of its assets because of the loans to D. S, a substantial shareholder of the bank, in consideration of forbearance by the examiner, orally promises the bank that if D fails to pay the note, he will do so. The promise of S is enforceable.

c. Insurance premiums. The rule of this Section excludes from the main purpose rule contracts of guaranty insurance whether making such contracts is or is not the promisor's regular business. Promises of commercial surety companies are practically always in writing. See Restatement of Security § 82 Comment i, defining "compensated surety." An isolated oral guaranty by an individual is within the reason of the Statute if a small fee is paid for guaranty of a much larger debt.

Illustration

5. In consideration of a premium of $100, S guarantees C in an unsigned writing the fidelity of D, C's employee, during D's term of employment. The guaranty is not enforceable.

§ 117. Promise to Sign a Written Contract of Suretyship.

A promise to sign a written contract as a surety for the performance of a duty owed to the promisee or to sign a negotiable instrument for the accommodation of a person other than the promisee is within the Statute of Frauds.

Comment

a. Scope. The promises covered by the Section are not in terms promises to answer for a duty of another. They are promises to execute written instruments by which the promisor will on signing undertake to answer for such a duty. In substance, however, such promises, if binding, subject the promisor to an action if the performance due from the obligor is not rendered. The Section is applicable whether the promise relates to an existing duty or to one expected to arise in the future.

Illustrations

1. In consideration of a loan by C to D, S orally promises C to execute a written instrument guaranteeing the debt. S's promise is within the Statute.

2. D owes C $1,000. In consideration of C's forbearance to sue D, S orally promises C that S will sign as acceptor for the accommodation of D a draft for $1,000 to be drawn by D. S's promise is within the Statute.

§ 118. Promise to Indemnify a Surety.

A promise to indemnify against liability or loss made to induce the promisee to become a surety is not within the Statute of Frauds as a contract to answer for the duty of another.

Comment

a. Non-surety indemnitor. Where an indemnitor is not a surety, his promise to indemnify is not within the Statute of Frauds. See § 112. For example, a promise to indemnify a surety may be made by the principal obligor or by a person who has assumed the obligation as principal obligor. Or the person assumed to be principal obligor may not be subject to the assumed duty.

Illustrations

1. I promises to indemnify S if he will guarantee I's obligation to C. I's promise is not within the Statute of Frauds. S's promise is.

2. I promises to indemnify S if he will sign an accommodation note to C for I's benefit. I's promise is not within the Statute of Frauds.

3. I promises D to assume his liability to S, and also promises S to indemnify him against loss sustained by S as surety for D's obligation to C. I is now the principal obligor and his promise is not within the Statute of Frauds.

4. Relying on I's promise to indemnify him, S obtains goods from C on S's promise to pay for them if D does not. D comes under no duty to pay for them. I's promise is not within the Statute of Frauds.

b. Indemnitor as surety. The principal obligor has a duty to exonerate or reimburse a surety. See Restatement of Security §§ 104, 112. A promise to indemnify the surety has sometimes been treated as a promise to answer for the default of the principal obligor in the event of his failure to exonerate or reimburse the surety. Such treatment is appropriate when it accords with the understanding of the parties. But commonly the parties treat the promise to indemnify as a promise to a prospective debtor rather than as a promise to a prospective creditor. So viewed, the promise is not within the Statute. See §§ 112, 123. Many such cases are also within the main purpose rule. See § 116. In any event they do not ordinarily present the need for cautionary and evidentiary formalities which the Statute is designed to meet.

Illustrations

5. To induce C, a commercial surety company, to file a bond in an action against D company, S gives C a written guaranty against loss. After judgment against D company, I, a stockholder, orally promises S to indemnify him against loss. Unless I's promise is within the main purpose rule, it is within the Statute of Frauds.

6. I requests S to indorse notes made by I's son D, in order to enable D to obtain credit for use in D's business, and orally promises to indemnify S for any resulting loss. S indorses the notes as requested. Even though for some purposes I is treated as surety for D, I's promise is not within the Statute of Frauds.

§ 119. Assumption of Duty by Another.

A contract not within the Statute of Frauds as a contract to answer for the duty of another when made is not brought within it by a subsequent promise of another person to assume performance of the duty as principal obligor.

Comment

a. Scope. An obligor originally bound as a principal debtor may become a surety by agreement with another who subsequently assumes the duty, but this will not make the original promise subject to the Statute of Frauds. The rule stated in this Section applies, for example, where a partner retires from a partnership and the remaining partners agree to assume all of the partnership obligations. If the obligation on which the retiring partner was originally bound was oral, it does not become unenforceable merely because, as between the retiring partner and the others, the retiring partner becomes a surety.

§ 120. Obligations on Negotiable Instruments.

(1) An obligation on a negotiable instrument or a guaranty written on the instrument is not within the Statute of Frauds.

(2) A promise to pay a negotiable instrument, made by a party to it who has been or may be discharged by the holder's failure or delay in making presentment or giving notice of dishonor or in making protest, is not within the Statute of Frauds.

Comment

a. Uniform Commercial Code. Under Article 3 of the Uniform Commercial Code, the obligation of a party to a negotiable instrument is required to be evidenced by his signature on the instrument. See Uniform Commercial Code §§ 3–104 (maker or drawer), 3–202 (indorser), 3–410 (acceptor). A party who signs in any capacity for the purpose of lending his name to another party is an "accommodation party" and a surety; he is liable in the capacity in which he signs even though the taker knows of the suretyship. See § 3–415. A guaranty written on the instrument is explicitly made enforceable "notwithstanding any statute of frauds," to make clear the nonapplication of any requirement of "a writing which states the consideration for the promise." See § 3–416 and Comment. Section 3–805 extends these rules to certain non-negotiable instruments, and they may also apply to instruments not within the scope of Article 3. See, e.g., § 8–105(1). On the other hand, promises not written on an instrument are left to general contract law and may be subject to the Statute of Frauds. See §§ 1–103, 3–409 on obligation of drawee.

b. Waiver. Subsection (2) deals with promises which are enforced as waivers. Presentment, notice of dishonor, or protest may be waived expressly or by implication, either before or after the instrument is due. See Uniform Commercial Code § 3–511.

§ 121. Contract of Assignor or Factor.

(1) A contract by the assignor of a right that the obligor of the assigned right will perform his duty is not within the Statute of Frauds as a contract to answer for the duty of another.

(2) A contract by an agent with his principal that a purchaser of the principal's goods through the agent will pay their price to the principal is not within the Statute of Frauds as a contract to answer for the duty of another.

Comment

a. Rationale. The promisors referred to in this Section become sureties for the debts of others, but the promises are commonly made in contexts which provide evidence and eliminate the need of cautionary formality. The assignor's promise is ordinarily made for a consideration wholly for his own benefit. See § 116. The selling agent who guarantees customers' accounts is commonly called a "del credere factor"; an important inducement for the promise is his desire to advance his own interest. In addition, the guaranty is likely to be part of a course of business rather than an isolated transaction.

Illustrations

1. S holds a note made by D payable to bearer, and sells and delivers it to C, orally guaranteeing that D will pay the note. S's promise is not within the Statute.

2. S is engaged in selling goods for others on commission. To induce C to employ him, S orally guarantees payment by those to whom he sells C's goods. Later S sells goods for C on credit to D. S's promise is not within the Statute.

§ 122. Contract to Buy a Right From the Obligee.

A contract to purchase a right which the promisee has or may acquire against a third person is not within the Statute of Frauds as a contract to answer for the duty of another.

Comment

a. Contract to buy. Ordinarily a promise to buy a right and a promise to pay the debt of another are quite different transactions. A promise to buy is not within the suretyship provision of the Statute of Frauds, but it may be within other provisions, particularly Uniform Commercial Code §§ 1–206, 8–319, 9–203. See § 110; Statutory Note preceding § 110.

Illustration

1. D owes C $1,000 on open account. S, who specializes in the purchase of slow accounts, orally promises to buy C's right against D for $800 if assignment is made within three months. At the end of three months, C tenders S an assignment of the account. S's promise is not within the suretyship provision of the Statute of Frauds.

b. Suretyship in form of purchase. Where a promise to buy a debt is conditional on the debtor's default and the amount to be paid is the same as if the debt had been guaranteed, the consequences of a contract to purchase and a contract of a surety are the same. The distinction between a contract to buy and a contract of a surety does not lie in the formal difference in the words used but in the reality of the transaction. For the purposes of the Statute of Frauds, the test is whether in all the circumstances the promisor is acquiring a right or protecting a creditor against a default. Compare § 116.

Illustration

2. D corporation owes C $1,000 which is due. S orally promises C that if C will grant D an extension of 60 days, S will purchase the debt at that time if it is not then paid. The circumstances indicate that S is really guaranteeing the account, and the promise is unenforceable.

§ 123. Contract to Discharge the Promisee's Duty.

A contract to discharge a duty owed by the promisee to a third person is not within the Statute of Frauds as a contract to answer for the duty of another.

Comment

a. Rationale. In most jurisdictions the promise described in this Section gives the creditor as beneficiary a direct right against the promisor without destroying his right against the original debtor. The promise is not within the Statute of Frauds, however, because the Statute is designed to require written evidence only in the case where the promise is made to the creditor. See § 112. In contrast to the language of the Statute, the contract here considered is one to answer for the default of the promisee, not for the default "of another," that is of a third person.

Illustration

1. D owes C $100. S orally promises D that S will discharge the debt, or promises to lend D money with which to pay it. In either case, S's promise is not within the Statute of Frauds.

TOPIC 3. THE MARRIAGE PROVISION

§ 124. Contract Made Upon Consideration of Marriage.

A promise for which all or part of the consideration is either marriage or a promise to marry is within the Statute of Frauds, except in the case of an agreement which consists only of mutual promises of two persons to marry each other.

Comment

a. Engagement to marry. Mutual promises to marry were within the words of the English statute, but were not within the statutory purpose and were soon excluded by judicial interpretation. A number of American statutes explicitly except such promises from the marriage provision. They may, however, fall within the one-year provision. Statutes in many states bar actions for breach of a promise to marry.

b. Marriage settlements. A promise to transfer property to a husband or wife or to a third person or a promise regulating the property interests of husband and wife is within the Statute of Frauds if the consideration includes marriage or a promise to marry, whether or not mutual promises to marry are part of the agreement. Such a promise may be made by one of the parties to the contemplated marriage or by a third person.

Illustrations

1. In consideration of A's promise to marry B, B orally promises to marry A and to settle Blackacre upon A. B's promise is within the Statute of Frauds.

2. B offers to marry A. To induce A to accept the offer, B orally promises to settle property upon A. A accepts the offer. Both promises to marry and B's promise to make a settlement are within the Statute of Frauds.

3. In consideration of A's promise to marry B, B orally promises to marry A and to forego the rights which the law allows B with reference to A's property. B's promise is within the Statute of Frauds.

4. In consideration of A's marrying B, C orally promises A a settlement. C's promise is within the Statute of Frauds.

c. Promise in contemplation of marriage. A promise is not within the Statute merely because it is conditional on marriage, or because marriage is contemplated by the promisor or the promisee or both. The marriage or promise to marry must be bargained for and given in exchange for the promise. See § 71.

Illustrations

5. A and B mutually promise that each will settle $5,000 on A's daughter when she marries B's son. The promises are not within the Statute of Frauds, since the marriage is a condition rather than consideration.

6. A and B are engaged to marry. In consideration of A's promise that when married they will live in a house owned by A, B promises to settle $10,000 upon her. The promises are not within the marriage provision of the Statute of Frauds.

d. Part performance; subsequent memorandum. An oral contract between prospective spouses made upon consideration of marriage does not become enforceable merely because the marriage has taken place in reliance on it, nor by virtue of subsequent action incident to the marriage relation, since a contrary rule would deprive the marriage provision of the Statute of any significant effect. But the agreement may be enforced if there has been such additional part performance or action in reliance that justice requires enforcement. See § 139. A promise of a marriage settlement made by a third person involves less danger of interference in the marriage relation and may be enforced as in other cases of reliance. See, e.g., § 129. Particularly in the latter type of case the marriage provision of the Statute performs a cautionary as well as an evidentiary function, and a subsequent writing is not sufficient compliance with the Statute unless made as a memorandum of the agreement. See § 133. A new agreement not in consideration of the marriage may fail for want of consideration or as a fraud on creditors even though an antenuptial agreement would have been binding and enforceable but for the Statute.

TOPIC 4. THE LAND CONTRACT PROVISION

§ 125. Contract to Transfer, Buy, or Pay for an Interest in Land.

(1) A promise to transfer to any person any interest in land is within the Statute of Frauds.

(2) A promise to buy any interest in land is within the Statute of Frauds, irrespective of the person to whom the transfer is to be made.

(3) When a transfer of an interest in land has been made, a promise to pay the price, if originally within the Statute of Frauds, ceases to be within it unless the promised price is itself in whole or in part an interest in land.

(4) Statutes in most states except from the land contract and one-year provisions of the Statute of Frauds short-term leases and contracts to lease, usually for a term not longer than one year.

Comment

a. Conveyance of land. The English Statute of Frauds in §§ 1 and 3 required a writing for the creation, transfer or surrender of an interest in land. The words "contract or sale" in § 4, therefore, have been read as "contract for sale" and not applied to present conveyances. American statutes modeled on § 4 commonly use such phrases as "any agreement for the sale of real estate or any interest in or concerning it," and are similarly read to exclude present conveyances. The formal requisites of a conveyance of land are beyond the scope of this Restatement. See § 1; Restatement of Property §§ 467, 522. What is an interest in land is the subject of § 127.

b. Short-term leases. A lease is both a conveyance and a contract. As conveyances, leases "not exceeding the term of three years from the making thereof" were excepted by § 2 from § 1 of the English statute, providing that interests in land created without a writing had the effect of estates at will. Leases thus exempted as conveyances were also held not within either the land contract provision or the one-year provision of § 4. In most states statutes reduce to one year the term of a valid oral lease and eliminate the words "from the making thereof." The usual result is to validate an oral lease or contract to lease for a one-year term even though made before the term begins. In some states the statute modeled on § 4 of the English statute applies expressly to "an agreement for the leasing for a longer period than one year" of real property and thus applies neither to a lease nor to a contract to make a lease for a year or less, even though made before the term begins. An agreement related to a lease, however, if it is not itself a lease or contract to lease, is not within the exception.

Illustration

1. A leases land to B under a written lease terminable at the end of any year by written notice given by either party. During the third year of the lease, in consideration of a loan by B, A orally promises not to terminate the lease before the end of the fourth year. The oral agreement is not a lease or contract to lease but is a contract not to be performed within a year, and is within the one-year provision of a Statute of Frauds enacted in the original English form.

c. Contract to sell. The land contract provision applies to any executory promise to transfer an interest in land, whether the consideration is money, chattels, services, other land, or something else, and whether the land is to be transferred to the promisee or to someone else. "Transfer" for this purpose includes the creation or extinguishing of an interest with the effect of giving another an interest he did not previously have, and "promise to transfer" includes an option contract. But the provision does not apply to a promise to refrain from making a transfer, or to a promise to divide profits if land is sold. In some cases, despite a failure to satisfy the Statute, a resulting or constructive trust is imposed on one who has acquired land or other property under the contract. See Restatement, Second, Trusts §§ 404–60; Restatement of Restitution §§ 180–83.

Illustrations

2. A promises B to transfer Blackacre to B or to C for a price to be paid by B. A's promise is within the Statute of Frauds, whether or not B is committed to buy.

3. A owes B $1,000. In consideration of B's promise to extend the time of payment three months, A promises orally that he will sell his land and apply the proceeds as far as necessary to pay the debt. A's promise to sell the land is within the Statute of Frauds.

4. A and B orally promise C a share in a partnership of which A and B are partners. C orally promises to contribute his services to the firm business. A and B own land as part of the partnership assets. The promises are within the Statute.

5. For consideration, A promises B to devise Blackacre to B. A's promise is within the Statute.

6. A promises B, his daughter, that he will die intestate so that B will inherit a share in a parcel of land. A's promise is not within the land contract provision of the Statute of Frauds. The contemplated transfer to B is a transfer by operation of law, not a transfer by virtue of the contract.

7. A orally promises B to share with him whatever proceeds A obtains from the sale of Blackacre. A's promise is not within the land contract provision of the Statute of Frauds.

d. Contract to buy. The land contract provision applies to a contract to buy as well as to a contract to sell. It covers a promise to pay for a conveyance of an interest in land, so long as the conveyance has not been made, whether the price is to be paid in money, in goods, services or other land, or otherwise, and whether the conveyance is to be made to the promisor or to a third person. But the Statute does not prevent enforcement of a negotiable instrument given in part payment under an oral land contract.

Illustrations

8. A promises to pay $5,000 to B for a conveyance of Blackacre either to A or to a third person. A's promise is within the Statute of Frauds.

9. A promises to support B during B's life in consideration of B's promise to convey Blackacre to A. A's promise is within the Statute of Frauds.

10. A and B make an oral contract for the sale of Blackacre by B for $10,000, and A gives B a check for $1,000 as a down payment. B is ready and willing to perform, but A stops payment of the check. The Statute of Frauds does not prevent enforcement of A's obligation on the check. See § 78.

e. Effect of conveyance. Payment of the price for land does not of itself take a land contract out of the Statute of Frauds. See § 129. But once the transfer has been made, the promise to pay the price becomes enforceable, unless the price is land. Compare § 147.

Illustrations

11. A promises B to transfer Blackacre to B, in consideration of B's promise to pay A $5,000. A tenders a deed of Blackacre to B and B accepts the deed. B's promise is no longer within the land contract provision of the Statute of Frauds.

12. A owes B $10,000. A promises to convey Blackacre to B in full settlement of the debt, and B promises to accept the conveyance in full settlement. A tenders to B a deed to Blackacre and B accepts the deed. The Statute of Frauds does not prevent enforcement of B's promise.

13. A owes B $1,000. In consideration of B's promise to extend the time of payment three months, A promises orally that he will sell a parcel of land and apply the proceeds as far as necessary to pay the debt. A sells the parcel. A's promise is no longer within the land contract provision of the Statute of Frauds.

§ 126. Contract to Procure Transfer or to Act as Agent.

(1) A contract to procure the transfer of an interest in land by a person other than the promisor is within the Statute of Frauds.

(2) A contract to act as agent for another in endeavoring to procure the transfer of any interest in land by someone other than the promisor is not within the Statute of Frauds as a contract for the sale of an interest in land.

Comment

a. Contract to procure transfer. A promise that a third person will convey land to the promisee is within the Statute, even though the promisee is to pay the price. The Statute also applies if the third person is to convey the land to the promisor for the benefit of the promisee or his nominee, or is to convey directly to the promisee's nominee. But if the conveyance is made, the contract may cease to be within the Statute under the rule stated in § 125, or a resulting or constructive trust may arise.

Illustrations

1. A promises B that C, A's wife, will transfer her land to B's son D on payment by D of $5,000. In consideration of A's promise, B promises to pay A a commission of $100. A's promise is within the Statute of Frauds.

2. A orally promises B that A will buy Blackacre from C. The promise is within the Statute of Frauds, but ceases to be within it if A accepts a conveyance from C. See § 125.

3. A orally promises B to buy a parcel of land from C and to hold it in trust for B, subject to the payment of the price by B. B orally promises A a commission for so doing. A's promise to buy the parcel is within the Statute of Frauds. If A purchases the parcel, however, he holds it upon a constructive trust for B. See Restatement of Restitution § 194.

b. Agency contracts. A contract to employ a real estate broker and to pay him a commission is not within the Statute of Frauds as a contract for the sale of an interest in land unless the commission is to take the form of an interest in land. In such a case the broker's promise to act as agent is not within the Statute, unless he promises to make or procure a transfer. A promise to use best efforts to procure a transfer is not such a promise. In many states, however, statutes explicitly require a writing for a contract to pay a commission to a real estate broker or business opportunity broker. See Statutory Note preceding § 110.

Illustrations

4. A orally promises B to pay him $500 if he succeeds in inducing C to agree to transfer Blackacre to A for $5,000. A's promise is not within the Statute of Frauds as a contract for the sale of an interest in land. In many states, however, a separate statute makes such a promise unenforceable in the absence of a writing.

5. A orally promises B to pay B a commission of $100 if B induces C to transfer Blackacre to B's son D, and B orally promises A to use his best efforts to that end. Neither promise is within the Statute of Frauds as a contract for the sale of an interest in land.

6. A orally promises B that A will convey Blackacre to any purchaser procured by B, at a price stated "net" of B's 5 per cent commission. B procures an offer by C to buy on A's terms and to pay B's commission, but A refuses to convey. A's promise to B is within the Statute of Frauds.

§ 127. Interest in Land.

An interest in land within the meaning of the Statute is any right, privilege, power or immunity, or combination thereof, which is an interest in land under the law of property and is not "goods" within the Uniform Commercial Code.

Comment

a. Property interests. In applying the land contract provision of the Statute of Frauds, the test of what is an interest in land is in general that furnished by the law of property. See Restatement of Property §§ 1–9. Leaseholds are included unless within an exception for short-term leases. Both present and future interests, legal and equitable, are interests in land for this purpose, including the interests of mortgagor and mortgagee or of vendor and purchaser under a specifically enforceable contract.

Illustrations

1. A, a mortgagor of Blackacre, promises B, the mortgagee, to release A's right to redeem the mortgaged property, in consideration of B's promise to accept the release in full satisfaction of the mortgage debt. The promises of A and B are within the Statute of Frauds.

2. A, holding a note made by B and secured by mortgage on B's land, promises to assign the note to C. A's promise to C is not within the land contract provision of the Statute. Though the assignment will give C an interest in land, the interest is transferred by operation of law rather than by agreement. See § 340.

3. By written agreement A promises to sell and B promises to buy Blackacre. B promises to assign to C B's right to a conveyance. B's promise to C is within the Statute of Frauds.

b. Servitudes. Interests in land subject to the Statute of Frauds include easements and profits and interests created by restrictive covenants and agreements affecting the use of land. Creation and transfer of an easement or profit are subject to the formal requisites of a conveyance as well as those of a land contract. See Restatement of Property §§ 467, 494. A license to use land, however, is not subject to the

Statute of Frauds (see Restatement of Property § 515), and an oral attempt to create an easement may take effect as a revocable license. See Restatement of Property § 514. A promise that certain land will be used in a particular way is subject to the land contract provision of the Statute of Frauds, except that a grantee who accepts a deed may be bound by a promise therein even though he does not sign. If the Statute is satisfied by the promisor, successors to his title may be bound without further formality. See Restatement of Property §§ 522, 532.

Illustrations

4. A orally promises B to allow B during B's life to maintain a drain, or to carry away gravel, or to erect and maintain a dam on a parcel of land. In consideration thereof B orally promises to pay A $1,000. Both promises are within the Statute of Frauds.

5. A, a boarding-house keeper, orally promises B to give B board and lodging in A's house for the ensuing year, in consideration of B's promise to pay A $20 a week. Neither promise is within the Statute of Frauds.

6. A orally promises B to allow B to paste advertisements on A's wall during the ensuing month, in consideration of B's promise to pay A $100. Neither promise is within the Statute of Frauds.

7. A transfers Blackacre to B by deed and orally promises that he will insert restrictions in the deeds to subsequent grantees of adjoining land belonging to A, prohibiting the erection of buildings within a certain distance from the street. A's promise is within the Statute of Frauds.

c. Sale of goods to be severed from realty. Uniform Commercial Code § 2–107(1) provides that a contract for the sale of "minerals or the like (including oil and gas) or a structure or its materials to be removed from realty" is a contract for the sale of goods if they are to be severed by the seller. But before severance a purported present sale is effective only as a contract to sell unless it complies with the formal requisites of a conveyance of land. If the buyer is to sever, the Code Comment says that the land contract provision of the Statute of Frauds applies. As to goods not described in Subsection (1), § 2–107(2) provides that a contract for the sale apart from the land of "growing crops or other things attached to realty and capable of severance without material harm thereto" is a contract for the sale of goods whether the buyer or the seller is to sever. In such a case the parties can by identification effect a present sale before severance.

d. Security interests in fixtures. Uniform Commercial Code § 9–203 provides a Statute of Frauds for a "security agreement" creating a "security interest" in personal property or fixtures. For this purpose § 9–105 defines "goods" differently from § 2–105 on sale of goods. See also §§ 1–201, 9–102, 9–313.

§ 128. Boundary and Partition Agreements.

(1) A contract between owners of adjoining tracts of land fixing a dividing boundary is within the Statute of Frauds but if the location of the boundary was honestly disputed the contract becomes enforceable notwithstanding the Statute when the agreed boundary has been marked or has been recognized in the subsequent use of the tracts.

(2) A contract by joint tenants or tenants in common to partition land into separate tracts for each tenant is within the Statute of Frauds but becomes enforceable notwithstanding the Statute as to each tract when possession of it is taken in severalty in accordance with the agreement.

Comment

a. Rationale. Boundary and partition agreements have the effect of an agreement to convey land and are within the land contract provision of the Statute of Frauds. The rules making them enforceable on the basis of action taken under the agreement are similar to the "part performance" doctrine stated in § 129. In cases not within the rules of this Section, relief may be granted under the more general doctrine of § 129.

§ 129. Action in Reliance; Specific Performance.

A contract for the transfer of an interest in land may be specifically enforced notwithstanding failure to comply with the Statute of Frauds if it is established that the party seeking enforcement, in reasonable reliance on the contract and on the continuing assent of the party against whom enforcement is sought, has so changed his position that injustice can be avoided only by specific enforcement.

Comment

a. Historical note and modern justifications. This Section restates what is widely known as the "part performance doctrine." Part performance is not an accurate designation of such acts as taking possession and making improvements when the contract does not provide for such acts, but such acts regularly bring the doctrine into play. The doctrine is contrary to the words of the Statute of Frauds, but it was established by English courts of equity soon after the enactment of the Statute. Payment of purchase-money, without more, was once thought sufficient to justify specific enforcement, but a contrary view now prevails, since in such cases restitution is an adequate remedy. English decisions treated a transfer of possession of the land as sufficient, if unequivocally referable to the oral agreement, apparently on the ground that the promise to transfer had been executed by a common-law conveyance. Such decisions are not generally followed in the United States. Enforcement has instead been justified on the ground that repudiation after "part performance" amounts to a "virtual fraud." A more accurate statement is that courts with equitable powers are vested by tradition with what in substance is a dispensing power based on the promisee's reliance, a discretion to be exercised with caution in the light of all the circumstances. Compare § 90.

b. Rationale. Two distinct elements enter into the application of the rule of this Section: first, the extent to which the evidentiary function of the statutory formalities is fulfilled by the conduct of the parties; second, the reliance of the promisee, providing a compelling substantive basis for relief in addition to the expectations created by the promise. The evidentiary element can be satisfied by painstaking examination of the evidence and realistic appraisal of the probabilities on the part of the trier of fact; this is commonly summarized in a standard that calls upon the trier of the facts to be satisfied by "clear and convincing evidence." The substantive element requires consideration of the adequacy of the remedy of restitution.

Illustrations

1. A and B agree by an unsigned writing that A will sell Blackacre to B for $5,000. B pays the price to A as agreed, and A accepts the payment but refuses to transfer the land as agreed. B is not entitled to specific performance, but can recover the amount of the payment.

2. A orally leases A's farm to B for five years, agreeing that B will repair the premises at prevailing wages to be credited on the rent. B takes possession of the farm and does $1,000 worth of repair work, using material furnished by A. A then seeks to evict B. B is entitled to $1,000 less the fair rental of the farm for the period of his occupancy, but is not entitled to specific performance or damages.

3. A and B make an oral agreement for the sale of Blackacre by A to B. With A's consent B takes possession of the land, pays part of the price, builds a dwelling house on the land and occupies it. Two years later, as a result of a dispute over the amount still to be paid, A repudiates the agreement. B may obtain a decree of specific performance.

4. A orally promises to make a gift of Blackacre to his son B and puts B in possession. With A's consent B builds a dwelling house on the land and lives in it for twenty years until A dies, paying all taxes on the land. B may obtain a decree of specific performance against A's heir or personal representative.

c. Monetary relief. Unlike the rule of § 125(3), under which a contract ceases to be subject to the Statute of Frauds when the land is conveyed, the present rule is limited to equitable relief, and does not make available an ordinary action for damages for breach of contract. The remedy of restitution is not ordinarily affected by the Statute of Frauds. See § 375. Where a contract is specifically enforceable under the rule of this Section, damages or other relief may be awarded if specific performance is prevented by the intervention of an innocent purchase for value, by condemnation of the land, or by other circumstances. Or monetary relief may be granted on the basis of fraud, estoppel, or other doctrines. See § 139. Even in jurisdictions where the rule of this Section is repudiated, an equitable lien may be imposed on the land as security for restitution of the value of benefits conferred.

d. Transfer of possession and reasonable reliance. Where specific enforcement is rested on a transfer of possession plus either part payment of the price or the making of improvements, it is commonly said that the action taken by the purchaser must be unequivocally referable to the oral agreement. But this requirement is not insisted on if the making of the promise is admitted or is clearly proved. The promisee must act in reasonable reliance on the promise, before the promisor has repudiated it, and the action must be such that the remedy of restitution is inadequate. If these requirements are met, neither taking of possession nor payment of money nor the making of improvements is essential. Thus, the rendering of peculiar services not readily compensable in money may justify specific performance, particularly if the promisee has also taken other action in reliance on the promise.

Illustrations

5. A owns an unsightly vacant lot adjoining B's home in a residential suburb. A's agent and B orally agree that A will sell the lot to B for $1,500. B, a lawyer aware of the doctrine of part performance, expends $1,000 in grading and planting on the lot, but makes no payments and does not communicate with A for two years. A observes the grading and planting, but later denies concluding a contract or knowing that B claimed under a contract. B is not entitled to specific performance, since his actions are not unequivocally referable to a contract for sale and recovery of the value of the improvements is an adequate remedy.

6. A leases a residence to B for $9 per month. After four months A and B agree to a written contract for sale of the premises for $1,000 in monthly installments of $12.89, but the contract is not signed. B pays $12.89 each month for thirteen months and pays for taxes and insurance. Then the land increases in value because an air base is located nearby, and A repudiates the contract. B is entitled to specific performance.

7. A orally agrees to lease shop space in a new hotel to B for five years and to give B an option to renew the lease for another five years. At A's request B moves in before formal execution of a lease, deposits $5,000 with A, and expends $50,000 on fixtures and improvements. Later A and B agree on pencil corrections to a written lease and return it to A's attorney for redrafting, but no redrafted lease is submitted or executed. B occupies the premises and pays rent for five years, and notifies A of B's election to renew, but A denies the existence of an option to renew. B is entitled to specific performance.

8. A leaves 1,000 acres of land to his cousin B by will. A's heirs contest the will, and B retains his uncle C, an attorney, agreeing orally that C is to receive as his fee, contingent upon success, a specific 180 acres of the land. C successfully defends the will, but B refuses to convey the land as agreed. In C's suit for specific performance, B admits the making of the contract, but defends under the Statute of Frauds. Specific performance may be granted.

9. A promises to give C, an adjoining landowner, first refusal in the event that A sells a tract of land. Later B and C agree orally that C will consent to a sale by A to B and that B will then convey to C a fifteen-foot strip adjoining C's land, C paying a proportionate part of the price. C notifies A that C consents, and A conveys the tract to B, but B repudiates his promise to convey the strip to C. C is entitled to a decree of specific performance against B.

10. A, aged 55, orally promises B, his adopted daughter, that if B will quit school, live with A and his sick wife and refrain from marrying until B is 25, help A run his farm, and take care of the wife until the wife dies, A will leave B all his property by will. B performs as requested until the wife dies 12 years later, except for an eight-month trip with A's consent. After the wife's death, B at age 28 marries a man of whom A disapproves; A thereafter refuses to have anything to do with B, revokes a will carrying out his promise, and makes a new will leaving his property to others. Four years after the marriage A dies. B is entitled to specific performance.

e. Action by landowner. Specific performance may be granted to a seller or lessor of land under the rule of this Section. But it must be justified by his own part performance or other action in reliance on the contract rather than by the avoidance of injustice to the buyer or lessee.

Illustrations

11. A and B orally agree that A will sell a house and lot to B for $10,000. A signs a memorandum of the contract but B does not; B pays $1,000 on account of the price. A prepares a conveyance and delivers it in escrow to await payment, delivers possession of the land to B, and sells him the furniture

in the house. B lives in the house for six months and plants a substantial garden, but refuses to pay the balance of the price because of defects in A's title, and finally repudiates the contract shortly after the defects are cured. Whether or not B would have been entitled to specific performance, A is not.

12. A orally leases a storeroom to B for six years at a rental of $400 per month. In accordance with the agreement A builds a balcony at a cost of $1500 which does not add to the value of the premises. B takes possession and pays rent for three years, and then repudiates the lease at a time when tenants have become scarce. A is entitled to specific performance.

f. Other clauses of the Statute. Ordinarily the various clauses of the Statute of Frauds apply separately. See Comment b to § 110. Thus a contract for the sale of land may also be a contract in consideration of marriage, a contract not to be performed within a year, and a contract for the sale of goods. When the contract is specifically enforceable under the rule of this Section, however, the other clauses of the Statute do not prevent enforcement.

TOPIC 5. THE ONE-YEAR PROVISION

§ 130. Contract Not to Be Performed Within a Year.

(1) Where any promise in a contract cannot be fully performed within a year from the time the contract is made, all promises in the contract are within the Statute of Frauds until one party to the contract completes his performance.

(2) When one party to a contract has completed his performance, the one-year provision of the Statute does not prevent enforcement of the promises of other parties.

Comment

a. Possibility of performance within one year. The English Statute of Frauds applied to an action "upon any agreement that is not to be performed within the space of one year from the making thereof." The design was said to be not to trust to the memory of witnesses for a longer time than one year, but the statutory language was not appropriate to carry out that purpose. The result has been a tendency to construction narrowing the application of the statute. Under the prevailing interpretation, the enforceability of a contract under the one-year provision does not turn on the actual course of subsequent events, nor on the expectations of the parties as to the probabilities. Contracts of uncertain duration are simply excluded; the provision covers only those contracts whose performance cannot possibly be completed within a year.

Illustrations

1. A, an insurance company, orally promises to insure B's house against fire for five years, B promising to pay the premium therefor within the week. The contract is not within the Statute of Frauds, since if the house burns and the insurer pays within a year the contract will be fully performed.

2. A orally promises to work for B, and B promises to employ A during A's life at a stated salary. The promises are not within the one-year provision of the Statute, since A's life may terminate within a year.

3. A and B, a railway, agree that A will provide grading and ties and B will construct a switch and maintain it as long as A needs it for shipping purposes. A plans to use it for shipping lumber from adjoining land which contains enough lumber to run a mill for 30 years, and uses the switch for 15 years. The contract is not within the one-year provision of the Statute.

4. A orally promises B to sell him five crops of potatoes to be grown on a specified farm in Minnesota, and B promises to pay a stated price on delivery. The contract is within the Statute of Frauds. It is impossible in Minnesota for five crops of potatoes to mature in one year.

b. Discharge within a year. Any contract may be discharged by a subsequent agreement of the parties, and performance of many contracts may be excused by supervening events or by the exercise of a power to cancel granted by the contract. The possibility that such a discharge or excuse may occur within a year is not a possibility that the contract will be "performed" within a year. This is so even though the excuse is articulated in the agreement. This distinction between performance and excuse for nonperformance is sometimes tenuous; it depends on the terms and the circumstances, particularly on whether the essential purposes of the parties will be attained. Discharge by death of the promisor may be the equivalent of performance in the case of a promise to forbear, such as a contract not to compete.

Illustrations

5. A orally promises to work for B, and B promises to employ A for five years at a stated salary. The promises are within the Statute of Frauds. Though the duties of both parties will be discharged if A dies within a year, the duties cannot be "performed" within a year. This conclusion is not affected by a term in the oral agreement that the employment shall terminate on A's death.

6. The facts being otherwise as stated in Illustration 5, the agreement provides that either party may terminate the contract by giving 30 days notice at any time. The agreement is one of uncertain duration and is not within the one-year provision of the Statute.

7. The facts being otherwise as stated in Illustration 5, the agreement provides that A may quit at any time. The agreement is within the Statute.

8. A, the maternal grandmother of a new-born illegitimate child, agrees with B, the father, that A will care for the child and B will make support payments until the child becomes 21 years old. The agreement is not within the one-year provision of the Statute. If the child dies within a year, the primary object of furnishing necessaries to the child will be fully "performed".

9. A sells his grocery business to B, who pays part of the price and promises to pay the balance in a month, A agreeing orally not to engage in the grocery business in the same town for five years. The contract is not within the one-year provision of the Statute, since A's death within one year will give B the equivalent of full performance.

c. The one-year period. The period of a year begins when agreement is complete, ordinarily when the offer is accepted. Compare §§ 63, 64. But a subsequent restatement of the terms starts the period again if the manifestation of mutual assent is such that it would be sufficient in the absence of prior agreement. The one-year period ends at midnight of the anniversary of the day on which the contract is made, on the theory that fractions of a day are disregarded in the way most favorable to the enforceability of the contract. If complete performance is possible before that time, the contract is not within the one-year provision, regardless of what hour of the day the contract is entered into.

Illustrations

10. Without consideration A promises B that, so long as B buys through A B's requirements for gasoline and A accepts B's orders, A will pay B an amount equal to the discount other distributors would allow B. For several years A accepts orders from B. A's promise is not within the one-year provision, since a separate contract is made each time A accepts an order.

11. On December 1, 1966, A and B contract orally for A's employment by B at a stated salary for a year beginning the following day. The contract is not within the one-year provision, since the promised performance will be fully rendered before midnight of December 1, 1967.

12. On December 1, 1966, A and B enter into an oral contract for the employment of A at a stated salary for the calendar year 1967. On the first working day in 1967, A presents himself for work, says "I understand these are the terms on which I am to be employed," and restates the terms. B replies, "That is right." Though the original contract was within the Statute of Frauds, the subsequent restatement makes a new contract performable within a year.

d. Full performance on one side. If either party promises a performance that cannot be completed within a year, the Statute applies to all promises in the contract, including those which can or even must be performed within a year. But unlike other provisions of the Statute, the one-year provision does not apply to a contract which is performed on one side at the time it is made, such as a loan of money, nor to any contract which has been fully performed on one side, whether the performance is completed within a year or not. This rule, by permitting an action for the agreed price, avoids the problem of valuation which would otherwise arise in an action for the value of benefits conferred; but the rule goes further and makes available the usual contract remedies.

Illustrations

13. A sells and delivers goods to B in return for B's promise to pay $1,000 in six months, $1,000 in a year and $1,000 in eighteen months. B's promises are not within the one-year provision of the Statute.

Illustrations 14:

14. A promises to pay B $5,000 in two years in return for B's promise to render a stated performance for five years. A pays the $5,000 as agreed. B then refuses further performance. The contract is withdrawn from the operation of the Statute.

e. Part performance. Part performance not amounting to full performance on one side does not in general take a contract out of the one-year provision. Restitution is available in such cases, and doctrines of estoppel and fraud may be applicable. See §§ 139, 375. Where the contract provides the price or rate to be paid for the part performance, the performing party will normally recover according to the contract; in other cases, the contract terms are evidence of reasonable value.

Illustrations

15. A and B contract orally for A's employment by B at a stated salary for the ensuing two years. A works under the contract for 15 months when B discharges him without cause. The contract is not withdrawn from the operation of the Statute, and A may not recover damages for wrongful discharge. But A may recover any unpaid salary.

16. A and B agree on the sale of the output of A's creamery to B for five years at stated prices. After four years B refuses further deliveries. The contract is not withdrawn from the operation of the Statute, but A may recover the contract price of goods delivered and accepted.

f. Other clauses of the Statute. Ordinarily the one-year provision of the Statute applies independently of the other provisions. See Comment b to § 110. But statutes in most states have the effect of excepting leases of land for one year even though they begin at a future date. See § 125. And the one-year provision does not prevent specific enforcement of a land contract under the rule stated in § 129.

TOPIC 6. SATISFACTION OF THE STATUTE BY A MEMORANDUM

§ 131. General Requisites of a Memorandum.

Unless additional requirements are prescribed by the particular statute, a contract within the Statute of Frauds is enforceable if it is evidenced by any writing, signed by or on behalf of the party to be charged, which

(a) reasonably identifies the subject matter of the contract,

(b) is sufficient to indicate that a contract with respect thereto has been made between the parties or offered by the signer to the other party, and

(c) states with reasonable certainty the essential terms of the unperformed promises in the contract.

Comment

a. The statutory language. This Section restates the law developed by judicial interpretation of the requirement of § 4 of the English Statute of Frauds that "the agreement . . . or some memorandum or note thereof" be in writing and signed. Despite slight variations in wording in § 17 of the English Statute and in American statutes, they have generally been read to establish the same requisites. Where the statute requires that "the contract" be in writing, however, a mere memorandum is not sufficient; and statutory provisions sometimes explicitly require a statement of the consideration or explicitly negate such a requirement, either with respect to contracts of suretyship or in all cases.

b. The Uniform Commercial Code. Paragraphs (a) and (b) follow the phrasing of Uniform Commercial Code §§ 1–206 and 2–201. Compare §§ 8–319, 9–203. Section 1–206 requires in addition an indication that the contract has been made "at a defined or stated price." Section 2–201 omits this requirement and also any reference to identification of subject matter, and adds "A writing is not insufficient because it omits or incorrectly states a term agreed upon but the contract is not enforceable under this paragraph beyond the quantity of goods shown in such writing." Section 8–319 refers to "a stated quantity of described securities at a defined or stated price." Section 9–203 requires "a security agreement which contains a description of the collateral" and in certain cases "a description of the land concerned." The description is sufficient "if it reasonably identifies what is described." See § 9–110.

   c. Rationale. The primary purpose of the Statute is evidentiary, to require reliable evidence of the existence and terms of the contract and to prevent enforcement through fraud or perjury of contracts never in fact made. The contents of the writing must be such as to make successful fraud unlikely, but the possibility need not be excluded that some other subject matter or person than those intended will also fall within the words of the writing. Where only an evidentiary purpose is served, the requirement of a memorandum is read in the light of the dispute which arises and the admissions of the party to be charged; there is no need for evidence on points not in dispute.

   The suretyship and marriage provisions of the Statute perform a cautionary as well as an evidentiary function. See §§ 112, 124. The land contract provision performs a channeling function. See Statutory Note preceding § 110. Even where these provisions are involved, however, there is no evidence of a statutory purpose to facilitate repudiation of firm oral agreements fairly made, to protect a promisor from temptation to perjure himself by false denial of the promise, or to reward a candid contract-breaker by denying enforcement.

   d. Types of documents. The statutory memorandum may be a written contract, but under the traditional statutory language any writing, formal or informal, may be sufficient, including a will, a notation on a check, a receipt, a pleading, or an informal letter. Neither delivery nor communication is essential. See § 133. Writing for this purpose includes any intentional reduction to tangible form. See Uniform Commercial Code § 1–201.

Illustrations

   1. A makes an oral contract with B to devise Blackacre to B, and executes a will containing the devise and a recital of the contract. The will is revoked by a later will. The revoked will is a sufficient memorandum to charge A's estate.

   2. A publishes in a newspaper an offer to buy certain goods, stating the terms of his proposal, and his name is printed under the advertisement. B accepts the offer. The advertisement is a sufficient memorandum to charge A. See § 136.

   3. A writes and signs in pencil a receipt for $1,000 which recites that the money is received from B as part payment of the price of $5,000 for a parcel of land. The receipt is a sufficient memorandum to charge A on the agreement recited.

   e. Subject matter. A memorandum, like a contract, must be read in its context and need not be comprehensible to persons not familiar with the particular type of transaction. Without reference to executory oral promises, the memorandum in context must indicate with reasonable certainty the nature of the transaction and must provide a basis for identifying the land, goods or other subject matter.

Illustrations

   4. A Company executes a written contract with B by which B purchases certain accounts owned by A Company. As part of the same transaction, C, the president of A Company, signs a contract of guaranty printed at the foot of the same paper: "In order to induce B to enter into an agreement dated _____ with _____ (hereinafter referred to as the client), the undersigned agrees to be liable for due performance of all the client's agreements with B." The blanks are not filled in. The quoted words are sufficient to identify the obligation guaranteed.

   5. A and B make an oral contract for the sale of goods and sign the following memorandum:

"Sept. 19th B, 12 mos.

300 bales S. F. drills	7¼
100 cases blue do	8¾

Credit to commence when ship sails; not after December 1—delivered free of charge for truckage.

                                               (Signed)   A

                                                                                                                                   B"

If persons acquainted with the usages of the business would understand its meaning, the memorandum is sufficient.

    6. A and B enter into an oral contract by which A promises to sell and B to buy such of A's iron in his millyard as he may decide to sell. A memorandum describes the subject matter of the contract as "all A's iron which he may decide to sell." The description is sufficient.

    7. A and B enter into a contract by which A promises to sell and B to buy a certain lot of hops belonging to A. A telegram from B refers to the subject matter as "number 13." This refers to a sample submitted by A to B by mail with a numbered tag attached and referring by trade usage to a specific lot. The description is sufficient.

    8. A and B enter into an oral contract for the sale and purchase of Blackacre. An otherwise sufficient memorandum, signed by A and B, describes the subject matter as "the land on the corner of X and Y Streets," omitting any statement as to the city or state. A owns only one of the four lots at the intersection. The description is sufficient.

    9. A and B enter into a written contract for the employment of B as A's sales manager for a term of two years. At the end of the two years, A and B orally agree to extend the employment for three more years at an increased salary. A year later A signs the following memorandum: "It is understood that the arrangements made for employment of B in our business on January 1, 1977, for a period of three years from that date at a salary of $30,000 per year, continues in force until January 1, 1980." The memorandum sufficiently identifies the nature of B's employment.

    f. Contract between the parties. A memorandum must be sufficient to indicate that a contract has been made between the parties with respect to an identified subject matter or that the signer has offered such a contract to the other party. The parties must be reasonably identified; the identification may consist of a name or initials, even though there may be others with the same name or initials, or of any other reasonably accurate mode of description. Identification of the agent of a party in the memorandum sufficiently refers to the party, whether or not the agent is himself a party. See Restatement, Second, Agency § 153. Where there is no dispute as to the parties, a party may be sufficiently identified by possession of a memorandum signed by the other party. A signed written offer to the public may be sufficient even though the offeree is not identified.

Illustrations

    10. A and B are negotiating for the sale of A's restaurant to B. B gives A a check for $500 bearing the notation "Tentative deposit on tentative purchase of 1415 City Line Ave., Phila. Restaurant, Fixtures, Equipment, Good Will." Later A and B orally agree on terms of sale. The quoted memorandum is not sufficient to indicate that a contract for sale has been made.

    11. C and D make an oral contract for the sale of Blackacre and sign the following memorandum: "C agrees to sell and D agrees to buy Blackacre for $10,000." C is agent for A, D is agent for B, and each is acting on behalf of his principal. The memorandum is sufficient to charge A and B.

    12. An otherwise sufficient memorandum of an oral contract for the sale of Blackacre states that "the owner of Blackacre" promises to sell it. The memorandum is signed by B, and B is the agent of A, the owner of Blackacre, acting on A's behalf. The memorandum is sufficient to charge A.

13. A, president and principal stockholder of A Company, gives B his personal check for $10,000 and a written offer to buy Blackacre from B on stated terms. The offer, signed by A, states that "the offer to purchase is from a company owned by A." B accepts the offer by a signed writing. Neither the offer nor the acceptance identifies the purchaser except by the quoted language. The identification is sufficient.

14. A and B make an oral agreement for the sale of a parcel of land by A to B. B pays A $50 and A signs and delivers to B a receipt which identifies the parcel and accurately states the terms of payment but does not name or describe B or his agent. In B's suit for specific performance, A defends on the ground of B's inequitable conduct in the negotiations. B is sufficiently identified by his possession of the memorandum.

g. *Terms; accuracy.* The degree of particularity with which the terms of the contract must be set out cannot be reduced to a formula. The writing must be the agreement or a memorandum "thereof"; a memorandum of a different agreement will not suffice. The "essential" terms of unperformed promises must be stated; "details or particulars" need not. What is essential depends on the agreement and its context and also on the subsequent conduct of the parties, including the dispute which arises and the remedy sought. Omission or erroneous statement of an agreed term makes no difference if the same term is supplied by implication or by rule of law. Erroneous statement of a term can sometimes be corrected by reformation. See § 155. Otherwise omission or misstatement of an essential term means that the memorandum is insufficient. Uniform Commercial Code § 2–201, however, states a different rule for sale of goods.

Illustrations

15. A and B enter into an oral contract for the sale of Blackacre by A to B. A memorandum is made and signed which states sufficiently the parties, subject matter and terms of the oral bargain except that, though the parties in fact orally agreed that the price should be payable on delivery of a deed, the memorandum contains no statement as to when the price is payable. The memorandum is sufficient.

16. A and B enter into an oral contract for the sale of Blackacre by A to B, and both sign a memorandum providing for a "purchase money mortgage in the amount of $18,000 payable for 15 years at 5%." B claims a right to pay $142.35 per month; A claims a payment of $100 a month plus monthly interest at 5%. No usage is shown. The memorandum is not sufficient to support an action by B for specific performance on his terms.

h. *Statement of consideration.* In Wain v. Warlters, 5 East 10 (K.B. 1804), a promise in writing to pay the debt of another was held unenforceable because the writing failed to state the consideration, which had been fully executed. Where that view is followed, the words "for value received" or an implication of consideration may validate the memorandum. But the decision has not been generally followed in the United States, and the English law was changed by statute in 1856. Uniform Commercial Code § 3–408 eliminates the requirement of consideration for a negotiable instrument or obligation thereon given in payment of or as security for an antecedent obligation, and § 3–416 exempts from the Statute of Frauds any guaranty written on a negotiable instrument. Aside from explicit statutory provisions, the prevailing view is that error or omission in the recital of past events does not affect the sufficiency of a memorandum.

Where, on the other hand, the consideration for a promise consists of a return promise not yet performed, performance of the return promise is commonly a condition of the promisor's duty, and an adequate memorandum will ordinarily reveal the consideration. A memorandum of a contract for the sale of land for an agreed price is not sufficient unless it discloses the price. Compare Uniform Commercial Code §§ 1–206 and 3–319, referring to "a defined or stated price" for intangible personal property or for investment securities. But § 2–201 dispenses with statement of the price of goods sold.

Illustrations

17. A lends $1,000 to B, and as part of the transaction C orally agrees to guarantee repayment. To evidence the guaranty, C signs a written promise to pay A $1,000. The written promise is a sufficient memorandum without any statement of consideration.

18. A agrees not to sue B Company on a debt for goods sold and delivered, in consideration of C's guaranty of payment for past and future deliveries to B up to $3,000. C signs the following

guaranty: "I, C, do hereby guarantee to A the payment of any sums due or that may become due up to the sum of $3,000 on such goods as B may have bought or shall buy from A. [Signed] C." A makes no further deliveries. The memorandum is not sufficient to charge C, since it omits any mention of A's return promise.

19. A and B orally agree on the sale of a farm by A to B for $155 an acre. A dates and signs the following memorandum: "Received from B $100 as payment on 84 acres farm, [at $155 an acre] balance to be paid when deed and abstract are presented." The memorandum is sufficient to charge A if the bracketed words are included but not if they are omitted.

§ 132. Several Writings.

The memorandum may consist of several writings if one of the writings is signed and the writings in the circumstances clearly indicate that they relate to the same transaction.

Comment

a. Rationale. The requirements of the Statute of Frauds, designed primarily to serve an evidentiary purpose, are less rigorous than those of the Statute of Wills, which is designed to serve cautionary and channeling purposes as well. See Comment c to § 72; Statutory Note preceding § 110. A will may refer to facts which have independent significance, and in some States a will may incorporate by reference an unattested existing document. See Restatement Second, Trusts § 54. A memorandum of a contract need only give assurance that the contract enforced was in fact made and provide evidence of its terms. It may consist of several separate documents, even though not all of them are signed and even though no one of them is itself a sufficient memorandum. At least one must be signed by the party to be charged, and the documents and circumstances must be such that the documents can be read together as "some memorandum or note" of the agreement. Explicit incorporation by reference is unnecessary, but if the connection depends on evidence outside the writings, the evidence of connection must be clear and convincing.

b. Several signed writings. Where two or more documents are signed by the party to be charged, they may be read together even though neither contains any reference to the other. The question whether they constitute a sufficient memorandum is substantially the same as if they had been incorporated in a single document.

Illustration

1. A signs and sends to B a letter stating that he is interested in leasing a parcel of land from B. After six months of negotiations A and B orally agree on an eight-year lease of the parcel with an option to purchase, and both sign a memorandum which is sufficient except that it does not identify the land. The two documents together constitute a sufficient memorandum to charge A.

c. Reference to unsigned writing: physical connection. Where the signature of the party to be charged is made or adopted with reference to an unsigned writing, the signed and unsigned writings together may constitute a memorandum. It is sufficient that the signed writing refers to the unsigned writing explicitly or by implication, or that the party to be charged physically attaches one document to the other or encloses them in the same envelope. Even if there is no internal reference or physical connection, the documents may be read together if in the circumstances they clearly relate to the same transaction and the party to be charged has acquiesced in the contents of the unsigned writing.

Illustrations

2. A and B make an oral contract within the Statute. A writes and signs a letter to B which is a sufficient memorandum except that it does not identify B. The deficiency may be supplied by the name and address on the envelope in which the letter arrives.

3. A and B make an oral contract within the Statute. A memorandum of the contract is made on two sheets of paper which are not connected physically, and A signs one of the sheets. The two sheets may be read together as a memorandum to charge A if an incomplete sentence on one is completed on the other, if the contract partially disclosed by one is clearly the same contract partially

disclosed by the other, or if the fact that one is a continuation of the other is otherwise shown by clear and convincing evidence.

4. A and B enter into an oral contract within the Statute. A memorandum of the contract is made on two sheets of paper. The contents of the sheets do not show that they belong together, but A signs one and then fastens the sheets together with a clip. Even though the clip is later removed, the fastening is a sufficient adoption of A's signature with reference to both sheets to charge A, but only if the evidence of the fastening is clear and convincing.

5. A agrees orally to employ B for two years. An unsigned memorandum of the contract, stating its terms, is prepared at A's direction. Later B begins work and payroll cards are made and initialed by A which state some of the terms but not the duration of the employment. If it is clear that the unsigned memorandum and the payroll cards refer to the same agreement, they may be read together as a sufficient memorandum to charge A.

d. Reference to future writings. Ordinarily a signature does not authenticate a document not in existence at the time the signature is made. But when several documents are executed by different parties in a single transaction, the signature of one may have reference to a subsequent signature of another. In some such cases the earlier signature may be adopted with reference to a document prepared later, whether signed by anyone or not. In other cases the reference is to an event of independent significance, or to the exercise of a power granted by the signer. Thus a signed offer authenticates the acceptance invited by it.

Illustrations

6. A and B enter into a contract within the Statute and sign a memorandum, otherwise sufficient, stating that the price to be paid shall be the same as the price agreed upon by C and D in a similar contract expected to be made on the following day. The memorandum is sufficient if it accurately states the entire agreement between A and B. The contract made between C and D is an event of independent significance, and may be referred to for the price whether or not there is a memorandum signed by C or D.

7. A and B enter into an oral contract for the purchase and sale of a tract of land and sign a memorandum, otherwise sufficient, stating that the contract is "contingent upon A's ability to arrange $7,000 purchase money mortgage." A subsequently applies in writing to a financial institution for such a mortgage loan on specific terms as to duration, interest rate and payment. The mortgage loan application may be read with the memorandum to satisfy the Statute against either party.

§ 133. Memorandum Not Made as Such.

Except in the case of a writing evidencing a contract upon consideration of marriage, the Statute may be satisfied by a signed writing not made as a memorandum of a contract.

Comment

a. Rationale. The rule of this Section reflects the general assumption that the primary purpose of the Statute is evidentiary, that it was not intended to facilitate repudiation of oral contracts. The marriage provision, however, performs a cautionary function as well, and a subsequent writing does not satisfy the Statute unless made as a memorandum of the agreement. See § 124 Comment d. More than a merely evidentiary writing is also required to satisfy a statutory provision that "the contract" be in writing.

b. Communication; delivery. There is no requirement that a memorandum be communicated or delivered to the other party to the contract, or even that it be known to him or to anyone but the signer. A memorandum may consist of an entry in a diary or in the minutes of a meeting, of a communication to or from an agent of the party, of a public record, or of an informal letter to a third person. Where a written offer serves as a memorandum to charge the offeror, however, communication of the offer is essential; written instructions to an agent to make an offer do not suffice. And where the statute requires only the vendor's signature the memorandum is not effective to charge the vendee until he manifests assent to it.

Illustrations

1. A and B enter into an oral contract for the sale of Blackacre. A writes and signs a letter to his friend C containing an accurate statement of the contract. The letter is a sufficient memorandum to charge A even though it is never mailed.

2. A writes to B the following letter:

"Dear B: I will employ you as superintendent of my mill for a term of three years from date, at a salary of $28,000 a year. Let me know if you wish to accept this offer. [Signed] A."

B accepts the offer orally. The letter is a sufficient memorandum to charge A.

3. A writes and signs a letter to his agent C authorizing C to make the offer stated in Illustration 2. C orally makes the offer, and B orally accepts it. A's letter is not a sufficient memorandum to charge him.

c. Repudiating memorandum. A signed writing which is otherwise a sufficient memorandum of a contract is not rendered insufficient by the fact that it also repudiates or cancels the contract, or asserts that it is not binding because not in writing. But a writing denying the making of the contract is not a memorandum of it.

Illustration

4. A and B enter into an oral contract by which A promises to sell and B promises to buy Blackacre for $5,000. A writes and signs a letter to B in which he states accurately the terms of the bargain, but adds "our agreement was oral. It, therefore, is not binding upon me, and I shall not carry it out." The letter is a sufficient memorandum to charge A.

d. Pleadings and testimony. A written pleading, stipulation or deposition may serve as a memorandum if otherwise sufficient as to contents and signature. An oral statement before the court is treated in some states as the equivalent of a signed writing. See Uniform Commercial Code §§ 2–201(3) (b), 8–319(d). Where the writing or oral statement is made under legal compulsion, it is nonetheless effective unless there is a contrary procedural policy in the state. But a motion to dismiss a complaint or a failure to deny an allegation, though given the procedural effect of an admission, is not the equivalent of a signed writing for the purposes of the Statute of Frauds.

§ 134. Signature.

The signature to a memorandum may be any symbol made or adopted with an intention, actual or apparent, to authenticate the writing as that of the signer.

Comment

a. Types of symbol. The traditional form of signature is of course the name of the signer, handwritten in ink. But initials, thumbprint or an arbitrary code sign may also be used; and the signature may be written in pencil, typed, printed, made with a rubber stamp, or impressed into the paper. Signed copies may be made with carbon paper or by photographic process.

b. Place of signature; "subscribed." Under a statute in the traditional English form, the signature need not appear on any particular part of the writing. Although it is usual to sign at the end of a document, a printed letterhead or billhead may be adopted as a signature. See Uniform Commercial Code § 1–201(39) Comment. Even where the statute uses the word "subscribe," there is an ambiguity: the word "subscribe" is sometimes read as a synonym for "sign," sometimes as requiring signing at the end or foot. Wherever the signature appears, it must be made or adopted with the requisite intention, but in the absence of contrary evidence the intention may be inferred from the conventional form of the writing.

Illustrations

1. A and B make an oral contract within the Statute. A sends to B a written acceptance, stating the terms, on a form bearing A's name as a printed heading. At the foot of the form is the word

"Accepted" followed by a blank space for signature, which is not filled in. In the absence of other evidence of intention, the form is not signed by A.

2. A and B make an oral contract within the Statute. A writes a memorandum stating the terms which begins, "I, A, make the following contract with B." A then delivers the memorandum to B. This is A's signature if the trier of fact infers A's intent to authenticate the writing.

3. A and B make an oral contract within the Statute. A clerk makes a written statement of the contract, and A writes at the top thereof—"O.K." followed by A's initials. This is a signature by A.

c. Time of signing; blanks and alterations. Commonly a document is signed after it is completed, but blanks may be left to be filled in later. If the signer fills a blank or adds a postscript or if another does so with his authority, the prior signature is effectively adopted with reference to the added portion. Alterations are often separately initialed, but re-adoption of the prior signature is equally effective for the purposes of the Statute of Frauds. Compare Uniform Commercial Code §§ 3–115, 3–407.

Illustration

4. A has a number of forms of letters printed ending with the words, "Yours very truly, A." With A's authority a clerk fills in one of the forms with the terms of an offer to B and sends it to B. B accepts orally. A's printed name is his signature.

§ 135. Who Must Sign.

Where a memorandum of a contract within the Statute is signed by fewer than all parties to the contract and the Statute is not otherwise satisfied, the contract is enforceable against the signers but not against the others.

Comment

a. The "party to be charged." Section 4 of the English Statute of Frauds required signature of the agreement, or some memorandum or note thereof, "by the party to be charged therewith, or some other person thereunto by him lawfully authorized." Section 17 referred to signature "by the parties to be charged by such contract or their agents thereunto lawfully authorized." Both forms of words are generally read to refer to the party to be charged in the legal proceeding, not the party or parties to be bound by the contract. In a few states, however, either by statute or by decision, the memorandum of a land contract is required to be signed only by the lessor or vendor. See Comment b to § 133.

b. Agency. A memorandum may be signed by an agent of a party with the same effect as if the party had signed personally. Unless the Statute so provides, written authorization is unnecessary, but the power to sign cannot be orally conferred on the other party to the transaction. The same third person may be the agent of both parties to sign a memorandum, and an auctioneer has irrevocable power to sign for both buyer and seller for a reasonable time on the day of sale. See Restatement, Second, Agency §§ 24, 30.

§ 136. Time of Memorandum.

A memorandum sufficient to satisfy the Statute may be made or signed at any time before or after the formation of the contract.

Comment

a. Pre-contract memorandum. A written offer signed by the offeror may constitute a sufficient memorandum to bind him. See Illustration 2 to § 131; Illustrations 2 and 3 to § 133. In other cases a memorandum or signature made before the formation of the contract may be adopted thereafter. See §§ 132, 134.

b. Subsequent memorandum. There is no requirement that the memorandum be made contemporaneously with the contract. It may be made even after breach or repudiation. The language "No action shall be brought" has sometimes been read to require a memorandum made before the action is begun, but such a procedural defect is curable under modern statutes or rules of court. See Comment d to § 133.

§ 137. Loss or Destruction of a Memorandum.

The loss or destruction of a memorandum does not deprive it of effect under the Statute.

Comment

a. Not a rule of evidence. Although the Statute of Frauds was designed to serve an evidentiary purpose, it is not a rule of evidence. In cases of loss or destruction, the contents of a memorandum may be shown by an unsigned copy or by oral evidence. See Uniform Rules of Evidence Rule 70; cf. Fed. R. Ev. 1001–04; compare Uniform Commercial Code § 3–804 (negotiable instrument).

TOPIC 7. CONSEQUENCES OF NON-COMPLIANCE

§ 138. Unenforceability.

Where a contract within the Statute of Frauds is not enforceable against the party to be charged by an action against him, it is not enforceable by a set-off or counterclaim in an action brought by him, or as a defense to a claim by him.

Comment

a. Contracts within the Statute. Section 110 lists the classes of contracts which are subject to the Statute of Frauds, and Topics 1–5, §§ 111–30 elaborate the descriptions of some of those classes and the circumstances in which certain contracts originally within the Statute may cease to be within it.

b. Unenforceability. Despite variations in wording, the American statutes based on the English Statute of Frauds are read to make contracts unenforceable by action or defense unless the Statute is satisfied by a signed memorandum. See § 8, defining "unenforceable contract." Satisfaction by a memorandum is the subject of Topic 6, §§ 131–37. Under the rule stated in § 135, the Statute may be satisfied as against one party and not as against another; in that event the Statute does not prevent enforcement by action, set-off, counterclaim or defense against the former party.

c. Exceptions. In many situations a contract within the Statute becomes enforceable even though the Statute is not satisfied by a memorandum. Of particular importance are cases where denial of enforcement would be unjust because of part or full performance or other reliance by the aggrieved party. Some such cases are dealt with by rules withdrawing the case from the class of contracts within the Statute (see, e.g., §§ 125, 130), others by a rule making particular remedies available (see, e.g., §§ 129, 375). Exceptions relating to particular classes of contracts are stated in appropriate sections in the Topics relating to those classes.

§ 139. Enforcement by Virtue of Action in Reliance.

(1) A promise which the promisor should reasonably expect to induce action or forbearance on the part of the promisee or a third person and which does induce the action or forbearance is enforceable notwithstanding the Statute of Frauds if injustice can be avoided only by enforcement of the promise. The remedy granted for breach is to be limited as justice requires.

(2) In determining whether injustice can be avoided only by enforcement of the promise, the following circumstances are significant:

   (a) the availability and adequacy of other remedies, particularly cancellation and restitution;

   (b) the definite and substantial character of the action or forbearance in relation to the remedy sought;

   (c) the extent to which the action or forbearance corroborates evidence of the making and terms of the promise, or the making and terms are otherwise established by clear and convincing evidence;

   (d) the reasonableness of the action or forbearance;

   (e) the extent to which the action or forbearance was foreseeable by the promisor.

Comment

a. Relation to other rules. This Section is complementary to § 90, which dispenses with the requirement of consideration if the same conditions are met, but it also applies to promises supported by consideration. Like § 90, this Section overlaps in some cases with rules based on estoppel or fraud; it states a basic principle which sometimes renders inquiry unnecessary as to the precise scope of other policies.

Sections 128 and 129 state particular applications of the same principle to land contracts; §§ 125(3) and 130(2) also rest on it in part. See also Uniform Commercial Code §§ 2–201(3), 8–319(b). Where a promise is made without intention to perform, remedies under this Section may be alternative to remedies for fraud. See Comment b to § 313; Restatement, Second, Torts § 530.

b. Avoidance of injustice. Like § 90 this Section states a flexible principle, but the requirement of consideration is more easily displaced than the requirement of a writing. . . . Subsection (2) lists some of the relevant factors in applying the latter requirement. Each factor relates either to the extent to which reliance furnishes a compelling substantive basis for relief in addition to the expectations created by the promise or to the extent to which the circumstances satisfy the evidentiary purpose of the Statute and fulfill any cautionary, deterrent and channeling functions it may serve.

Illustrations

1. A is lessee of a building for five years at $75 per month and has sublet it for three years at $100 per month. A seeks to induce B to purchase the building, and to that end orally promises to assign to B the lease and sublease and to execute a written assignment as soon as B obtains a deed. B purchases the building in reliance on the promise. B is entitled to the rentals from the sublease.

2. A is a pilot with an established airline having rights to continued employment, and could take up to six months leave without prejudice to those rights. He takes such leave to become general manager of B, a small airline which hopes to expand if a certificate to operate over an important route is granted. When his six months leave is about to expire, A demands definite employment because of that fact, and B orally agrees to employ A for two years and on the granting of the certificate to give A an increase in salary and a written contract. In reliance on this agreement A lets his right to return to his prior employer expire. The certificate is soon granted, but A is discharged in breach of the agreement. The Statute of Frauds does not prevent recovery of damages by A.

c. Particular factors. The force of the factors listed varies in different types of cases, and additional factors may affect particular types of contracts. Thus reliance of the kinds usual in suretyship transactions is not sufficient to justify enforcement of an oral guaranty, where the evidentiary and cautionary functions performed by the statutory formalities are not fulfilled. See Comment a to § 112. In the case of a contract between prospective spouses made upon consideration of marriage, the policy of the Statute is reinforced by a policy against legal interference in the marriage relation, and reliance incident to the marriage relation does not make the contract enforceable. See Comment d to § 124. Where restitution is an unavailable remedy because to grant it would nullify the statutory purpose, a remedy based on reliance will ordinarily also be denied. See Comment a to § 375.

Illustration

3. A orally promises to pay B a commission for services in negotiating the sale of a business opportunity, and B finds a purchaser to whom A sells the business opportunity. A statute extends the Statute of Frauds to such promises, and is interpreted to preclude recovery of the reasonable value of such services. The promise is not made enforceable by B's reliance on it.

d. Partial enforcement; particular remedies. The same factors which bear on whether any relief should be granted also bear on the character and extent of the remedy. In particular, the remedy of restitution is not ordinarily affected by the Statute of Frauds (see § 375); where restitution is an adequate remedy, other remedies are not made available by the rule stated in this Section. Again, when specific enforcement is available under the rule stated in § 129, an ordinary action for damages is commonly less satisfactory, and justice then does not require enforcement in such an action. See Comment c to § 129. In some cases it may be appropriate to measure relief by the extent of the promisee's reliance rather than by the terms of the promise. See § 90 Comment e and Illustrations.

Illustration

4. A renders services to B under an oral contract within the Statute by which B promises to pay for the services. On discharge without cause in breach of the contract, A is entitled to the reasonable value of the services, but in the absence of additional circumstances is not entitled to damages for wrongful discharge.

§ 140. Defense of Failure to Perform.

The Statute of Frauds does not invalidate defenses based on the plaintiff's failure to perform a condition of his claim or defenses based on his present or prospective breach of the contract he seeks to enforce.

Comment

a. Affirmative relief; independent claims. Since the Statute of Frauds requires signature "by the party to be charged," the question whether a contract is enforceable against the plaintiff in an action is distinct from the question whether it is enforceable against the defendant. See § 135. If a contract is unenforceable against the plaintiff, the defendant cannot use it as a basis for affirmative relief by way of counterclaim. Nor can he assert it defensively against an independent claim of the plaintiff.

Illustration

1. A owes B $1,000. In consideration of B's oral agreement to discharge the debt, A promises to transfer Blackacre to B. A tenders B a deed of Blackacre. B refuses the tender and sues for $1,000. Whether or not A has signed a memorandum sufficient to charge him, B can recover.

b. Conditions; present or prospective breach. A contractual right may be limited by the agreed terms or by virtue of considerations of fairness or public policy. Thus a failure of the promisee to perform a return promise commonly discharges the promisor's duty in whole or in part or gives him an offsetting claim. Where a plaintiff seeks to enforce a contract, the defendant may assert defensively any defense or claim arising from the terms of that contract, whether or not the Statute makes the contract unenforceable against the plaintiff, and whether or not the defendant has or asserts a defense under the Statute.

Illustration

2. A promises to sell Blackacre to B, and B promises to pay $5,000 for it. B signs a memorandum sufficient to charge him, but A does not and the contract is not enforceable against A. A sues B for damages for breach of the contract. B may defend on the ground that A repudiated the contract before tendering a deed, or may recoup damages resulting from a defect in A's title.

§ 141. Action for Value of Performance Under Unenforceable Contract.

(1) In an action for the value of performance under a contract, except as stated in Subsection (2), the Statute of Frauds does not invalidate any defense which would be available if the contract were enforceable against both parties.

(2) Where a party to a contract which is unenforceable against him refuses either to perform the contract or to sign a sufficient memorandum, the other party is justified in suspending any performance for which he has not already received the agreed return, and such a suspension is not a defense in an action for the value of performance rendered before the suspension.

Comment

a. Restitution as a contract remedy. Subsection (1) applies to the remedy of restitution the same rule stated in § 140 for actions for damages or specific performance. Restitution is a standard remedy for breach of contract, and is dealt with in §§ 370–77. In some situations a plaintiff who has broken a contract is nevertheless entitled to restitution of the value of his part performance, less the harm caused by his breach. See § 374. An action for restitution in either type of case is not regarded as an action "upon" the contract within the meaning or purpose of the Statute of Frauds, and the remedy is not in general affected by the Statute. See § 375. Whether or not the contract is enforceable against the plaintiff, his action is subject to the same limitations and defenses as if the contract were fully enforceable against both parties.

Illustration

1. A contracts to transfer land to B for $10,000, and B pays $1,000. B does not sign a memorandum, and sues to recover the $1000 payment on the ground that the contract is unenforceable under the Statute of Frauds. A is willing and able to perform. B cannot recover. See § 375.

   b. *Refusal to sign a memorandum.* The Statute of Frauds does not affect the defense of actual or prospective failure of consideration. See § 140. Where a contract is unenforceable against one party, whether or not it is enforceable against the other, the latter has reasonable grounds for insecurity and may demand performance or adequate assurance of performance, including the signing of a sufficient memorandum. Compare Uniform Commercial Code § 2–609; § 251. If his demand for such assurance is refused without excuse, he may suspend his own performance and maintain an action for the reasonable value of any part performance he has rendered. In such an action, his suspension of performance is neither a complete nor a partial defense. Compare §§ 251, 253, 255; Restatement, Second, Agency § 468(3); Restatement of Restitution § 108(d).

Illustration

2. A and B enter into an oral contract for the performance of services by A extending over a period of two years, B promising to pay $5,000 on completion of the services. After six months work A demands that B sign a written memorandum of the contract. B refuses, and A quits work and sues for the value of the work done. A can recover without deduction for damages caused by A's quitting.

§ 142. Tort Liability for Acts Under Unenforceable Contract.

Where because of the existence of a contract conduct would not be tortious, unenforceability of the contract under the Statute of Frauds does not make the conduct tortious if it occurs without notice of repudiation of the contract.

Comment

   a. *Scope.* An unenforceable contract may include authority or consent to do acts which would otherwise constitute a tort. The authority or consent is effective notwithstanding the Statute of Frauds to bar tort remedies for acts done pursuant to the contract, but the authority or consent may be revoked without liability. Acts subsequent to revocation are not protected.

Illustration

1. A enters into an oral contract with B by which A promises to transfer Blackacre to B and B promises to pay $5,000, B to have an immediate license to go upon land. B does so. A sues for trespass; B tenders $5,000 and demands a transfer. A need not accept the money or make a transfer, but B has a good defense to A's action for trespass.

§ 143. Unenforceable Contract as Evidence.

The Statute of Frauds does not make an unenforceable contract inadmissible in evidence for any purpose other than its enforcement in violation of the Statute.

Comment

   a. *Procedure.* The Statute of Frauds makes non-complying contracts unenforceable by action or defense, subject to certain exceptions. See § 138. The procedure for asserting the bar of the Statute is beyond the scope of this Restatement. Rule 8(c) of the Federal Rules of Civil Procedure requires it to be pleaded as an affirmative defense. If the defense is properly pleaded, or if it is not required to be pleaded, evidence offered for the purpose of enforcing an unenforceable contract may be excluded as immaterial. But the Statute, despite occasional statements to the contrary, does not lay down a rule of evidence, and an unenforceable contract may be proved for any legitimate purpose.

Illustrations

1. A renders services to B under an oral contract within the Statute by which B promises to pay for the services. On B's refusal to pay, A sues for the value of the services. The oral contract is admissible as evidence that the services were not rendered officiously or as a gift, and as evidence of the value of the services.

2. A sues B on a debt and garnishes C, who had borrowed money from B. In defense C offers to prove an oral contract with B whereby B agreed to discharge C in return for C's oral promise to transfer Blackacre to D at a future day. Since the oral contract, though unenforceable, would establish a good defense to the garnishment under § 144, it is admissible in evidence against A.

3. A owns goods in B's possession and sells the goods to C on credit. The Statute is not satisfied. At C's request B ships the goods to C before any repudiation by A. The goods are lost in transit, C repudiates the sale, and A sues B for conversion. The contract is admissible in evidence to prove that C rather than A was the owner of the goods. See § 142.

§ 144. Effect of Unenforceable Contract as to Third Parties.

Only a party to a contract or a transferee or successor of a party to the contract can assert that the contract is unenforceable under the Statute of Frauds.

Comment

a. Successor to contract duty. Where a contract is unenforceable under the Statute, the Statute provides a defense to a party who is sued for specific performance of the contract or for damages for its breach. A person who assumes the contractual duty and agrees to perform it may assert the defense only if the terms of the contract of assumption permit. See § 309. The personal representative, trustee in bankruptcy or like successor to the duty has the benefit of the defense. See, e.g., Bankruptcy Reform Act of 1978, 11 U.S.C. § 541(e) (1978).

b. Assignee or successor to claim. Where an unenforceable contract is asserted as a defense to an independent claim by a party to the contract, the Statute enables the party to reply that the defense is invalid. See § 140. The same reply is available to an assignee of the claim or to a successor such as a personal representative or trustee in bankruptcy.

c. Transferee of property. Where a party who has made an unenforceable contract to sell property transfers the property to a third person, the third person has the benefit of the Statute as a defense to any claim based on the contract. See § 146. A successor such as a personal representative or trustee in bankruptcy of the seller also has the benefit of the defense. Bankruptcy Reform Act of 1978, 11 U.S.C. § 544(a)(3) (1978).

d. Other third parties. Only parties to a contract and their transferees and successors can take advantage of the Statute of Frauds. As against others the unenforceable contract creates the same rights, powers, privileges and immunities as if it were enforceable. See Uniform Commercial Code § 2–201 Comment. For this purpose, where one party has sold or contracted to sell property to the other and has not repudiated the sale or contract, the seller's attaching or levying creditor is a successor only to the interest the seller has apart from the Statute. See § 143 Illustration 2.

Illustrations

1. A and B make a contract which is unenforceable by virtue of the Statute. C prevents B from performing, and C's conduct would be tortious if the contract were enforceable. The Statute does not impair C's tort liability to A or B.

2. A contracts to sell a ship to B. The Statute is not satisfied. B insures the ship with C, an insurance company. The ship is lost. The Statute provides no defense to C.

3. A contracts to sell specific goods to B, title to pass at once. A retains possession and the contract is unenforceable, but the sale is not fraudulent under any rule of law. C, A's creditor, attaches the goods as A's before any repudiation of the contract. The attachment is invalid as against B.

4. A promises orally to sell Blackacre to B and B pays A the price. Later A incurs debts which render him insolvent. A then signs a sufficient memorandum, or conveys the land to B. A's creditor cannot set aside the contract or the transfer as in fraud of creditors.

§ 145. Effect of Full Performance.

Where the promises in a contract have been fully performed by all parties, the Statute of Frauds does not affect the legal relations of the parties.

Comment

a. Rationale. The Statute of Frauds renders certain contracts unenforceable by action or defense; it does not forbid the making or performance of such contracts, or authorize their rescission after full performance on both sides. After such full performance, neither party can maintain an action for restitution merely because the contract was unenforceable under the Statute. See § 141. The Statute has no further function to perform, and the legal relations of the parties are the same as if the contract had been enforceable. Compare § 147.

Illustrations

1. A owes B a debt of $20,000. A's land, worth $10,000, is about to be sold on foreclosure under a mortgage held by C. B contracts to bid in the land and to deduct from A's debt to B $10,000 less the amount B pays. B bids in the land for $6,000. A's debt is reduced by $4,000.

2. At D's request S orally guarantees to C that D will pay a debt D owes to C. On D's failure to pay at maturity, S pays the debt. C's claim against D is discharged, and S has the same rights against D as if S's promise to C had been enforceable.

§ 146. Rights of Competing Transferees of Property.

(1) Where a contract to transfer property or a transfer was unenforceable against the transferor under the Statute of Frauds but subsequently becomes enforceable, the contract or transfer has whatever priority it would have had aside from the Statute of Frauds over an intervening contract by the transferor to transfer the same property to a third person.

(2) If the third person obtains title to the property by an enforceable transaction before the prior contract becomes enforceable, the prior contract is unenforceable against him and does not affect his title.

Comment

a. Competing contracts. Where an owner of property makes two agreements to sell the same property to two different buyers, both agreements may be enforceable against him, or the second agreement may be unenforceable as a bargain interfering with a contract with a third person. See § 194. Where each agreement standing alone would be specifically enforceable, the first in time ordinarily has priority, but the second may achieve priority by consent of the first transferee, by estoppel, by a recording act, or by the doctrine of bona fide purchase. See, e.g., § 342.

b. Priority of unenforceable contract. Where the first contract is unenforceable by virtue of the Statute of Frauds, it does not render the second agreement illegal or prevent the second agreement from being an enforceable contract, unless enforcement of the second would be a tortious interference with the first. See §§ 179, 180, 194. The second transferee, as a successor of the transferor, has the benefit of the transferor's statutory defense. See § 144. But the unenforceable contract is not void or voidable; if the Statute is satisfied by a memorandum or the contract becomes enforceable by virtue of action taken in reliance on it, it has the same priority as if it had been enforceable from the beginning. Compare Restatement, Second, Trusts §§ 41, 42.

Illustration

1. A orally contracts to sell Blackacre to B. Later A contracts in a signed writing to sell Blackacre to C. Thereafter A signs a memorandum of his contract with B. B can enforce the contract specifically against A and C, whether or not C entered into his contract with knowledge of B's, and

whether or not B knew of C's contract when the memorandum was signed. C may recover damages from A.

c. Rights of a transferee. Where the second transferee obtains title to the property, he becomes a successor of the transferor, and has the benefit of the transferor's statutory defense. See § 144. He need not be a bona fide purchaser; whether or not he gives value and whether or not he knows of the prior unenforceable contract, he is given the benefit of the defense so as to preserve the value of the defense to the transferor. Compare Restatement, Second, Trusts §§ 41, 42. For this purpose an attaching or levying creditor is not treated as a transferee unless the property has been sold on execution before the prior contract becomes enforceable. An interest arising by virtue of the transferor's marriage is not protected by the rule.

Illustrations

2. A orally contracts to sell Blackacre to B. He transfers Blackacre to C by deed as a gift, C having knowledge of the contract with B. A subsequently signs a memorandum of the contract with B. B may recover damages from A, but cannot enforce the contract specifically against C.

3. The facts being otherwise as stated in Illustration 2, A signs the memorandum before the conveyance to C. B can enforce the contract specifically against A and C.

4. A orally contracts to sell Blackacre to B. Later a creditor of A attaches Blackacre. Thereafter A signs a memorandum of the contract. B can enforce the contract specifically against A and the creditor.

5. A, a bachelor, orally contracts to sell Blackacre to B. A marries. Thereafter A signs a memorandum of the contract. A's wife has no dower interest in Blackacre.

§ 147. Contract Containing Multiple Promises.

(1) Where performance of the promises in a contract which subject it to the Statute of Frauds is exclusively beneficial to one party, that party by agreeing to forego the performance may render the remainder of the contract enforceable, but this rule does not apply to a contract to transfer property on the promisor's death.

(2) Where the promises in a contract which subject it to the Statute have become enforceable or where the duty to perform them has been discharged by performance or otherwise, the Statute does not prevent enforcement of the remaining promises.

(3) Except as stated in this Section, where some of the unperformed promises in a contract are unenforceable against a party under the Statute of Frauds, all the promises in the contract are unenforceable against him.

Comment

a. Waiver of unenforceable part by party seeking enforcement. Where the part of the contract which renders it subject to the Statute is exclusively beneficial to the party seeking enforcement, he may agree to forego that part and enforce the rest. This rule has particular application to cases where the party seeking enforcement has paid the entire consideration. But the rule is not applied to a promise to make a will covering both real and personal property for a single consideration, even though the entire consideration has been given, presumably because of the policy of the Statute of Wills and because of the availability of the remedy of restitution.

Illustrations

1. In consideration of A's oral promise to marry B and to settle $5,000 upon her, B promises to marry A. If A refuses to marry B after B expresses assent to forego the settlement, the Statute of Frauds does not preclude an action by B against A for breach of promise to marry.

2. For a single premium A orally insures a shipment of B's goods against fire and also orally agrees to answer for certain defaults of the carrier. The goods are damaged by fire. The Statute of Frauds does not prevent enforcement of the fire insurance.

3. A promises to make a will leaving real and personal property to B in return for services to be rendered by B. B renders the services, but A dies leaving the property to someone else. If the Statute

of Frauds makes the contract unenforceable as to the real property, it is equally unenforceable as to the personal property.

b. Performance or discharge of the part within the Statute. Where a contract includes promises within the Statute and also promises not within it, the objection to enforcement disappears when the part within the Statute becomes enforceable or is performed or where performance is excused. The part remaining unperformed, if not of itself within the Statute, can be enforced as if it were a separate contract. On the effect of part performance, compare §§ 125(3), 129, 130, 139; Uniform Commercial Code §§ 2–201(3), 8–319(b).

Illustrations

4. A and B orally agree that A will work for B for six months and that B will transfer to A an automobile valued at $2,400 and pay A $600 a month salary. Later the Statute is satisfied with respect to the sale of the automobile by receipt and acceptance. The balance of the contract becomes enforceable.

5. A employs B as plant manager under an oral agreement that B will be paid $600 a month and given an option to buy the plant, including real and personal property, on stated terms, but that A may substitute for the option an additional payment of $900 per month from the time B starts work. The amounts involved are not disproportionate. B works for several months and gives notice of his exercise of the option, but A refuses to sell. The Statute of Frauds does not prevent B's recovery of the additional payment.

c. Unenforceability of multiple promises. Where an undischarged part of a contract is unenforceable by virtue of the Statute of Frauds, the whole contract is unenforceable, unless the party to be charged has signed a memorandum. As to the situation where a memorandum is signed by fewer than all parties to the contract, see § 135. Whether an agreement creates a single contract or more than one for the present purpose depends primarily on the terms of the agreement, the interdependence of its parts, and the possibility of apportioning the consideration on one side among several promises on the other without doing violence to the expectations of the parties.

Illustrations

6. A and B orally agree that A will work for B for six months and that B will transfer to A an automobile worth $2,400 and pay A $600 a month salary. The Statute is not satisfied with respect to the sale of the automobile. In the absence of a waiver by A, the entire contract is unenforceable.

7. A written agreement between A and B provides that A's manufacturing facilities will be shipped to B and set up and operated by B, that within one year A will buy from B for $70,000 certain goods to be manufactured by B, and that for two years A and B will engage in a joint selling enterprise with respect to other goods on terms to be mutually agreed upon. A and B later agree orally on the terms for the joint enterprise. After B begins manufacture, A repudiates the agreement. The Statute of Frauds does not prevent B's recovery of damages for refusal to complete the $70,000 purchases.

§ 148. Rescission by Oral Agreement.

Notwithstanding the Statute of Frauds, all unperformed duties under an enforceable contract may be discharged by an oral agreement of rescission. The Statute may, however, apply to a contract to rescind a transfer of property.

Comment

a. Rescission of an executory contract. This Section may be regarded as a particular application of the rules stated in §§ 145 and 149. In determining whether the Statute applies to a contract modifying a prior contract, the second contract is treated as creating a single new contract containing the terms as modified. So treated, it is not within the Statute if there is no remaining unperformed promise.

Illustration

1. A and B enter into a written contract of employment for a term exceeding a year. Later they orally agree to rescind the contract. The oral agreement is effective and the written contract is rescinded.

b. *Sale of goods.* A contract for the sale of goods may be unenforceable under Uniform Commercial Code § 2–201 or because the contract is also a contract to answer for the debt of another or a land contract or a contract not to be performed within a year. Each provision of the Statute of Frauds must be considered separately, and this Section is applicable no matter which provision is under consideration. Uniform Commercial Code § 2–209(2), however, gives effect to a signed agreement which excludes modification "or rescission" except by a signed writing. That provision, applicable to "transactions in goods" (§ 2–102), by its terms negates the rule stated in this Section.

Where title to goods passes to the buyer under a contract for sale, or where the buyer acquires a special property in the goods (Uniform Commercial Code § 2–401), the rule stated in the first sentence of this Section applies if the contract is unenforceable. If the contract is enforceable by virtue of a sufficient memorandum, a contract to rescind the transfer of property may be within the Statute. Compare Uniform Commercial Code § 2–326(4) on contracts for "sale or return." If the seller retains possession, the contract to rescind may be enforceable on the ground that the goods "have been received and accepted" by the seller. See Uniform Commercial Code § 2–201(3) (c). But if the original contract for sale is enforceable because the buyer has "received and accepted" the goods, a contract to rescind is treated as a contract for resale by the buyer to the seller in applying the Statute of Frauds.

Illustration

2. A contracts to sell and B to buy a refrigerator for the price of $500, and the refrigerator is delivered and paid for. One week later A and B orally agree that if B is not satisfied after a week's further trial the transaction will be rescinded. There is no redelivery or repayment. The contract of rescission is unenforceable.

c. *Land contracts; right to specific performance.* Where land has been transferred by an effective deed, an agreement to rescind the transaction is a contract for the transfer of an interest in land within the Statute of Frauds. The same rule has sometimes been applied to executory land contracts which were enforceable by virtue of a memorandum or of action in reliance, on the ground that a specifically enforceable contract creates an equitable property interest in the purchaser. But the reasoning is circular: if the rule of the first sentence of this Section is applied, an oral contract to rescind is a defense to an action for specific enforcement of the executory contract, and there is no equitable property interest. The prevailing rule is that an executory land contract may be rescinded orally like other contracts within the Statute, even though enforceable. Compare Restatement of Property § 557, Comment e. In any event the contract to rescind becomes enforceable when there has been a material change of position in reliance on it. See § 150. The same reasoning applies to specifically enforceable contracts to transfer property other than land.

Illustration

3. A and B contract in writing that A will sell and B will buy Blackacre for $140,000. Later A and B orally rescind the written contract. The written contract is not enforceable.

§ 149. Oral Modification.

(1) For the purpose of determining whether the Statute of Frauds applies to a contract modifying but not rescinding a prior contract, the second contract is treated as containing the originally agreed terms as modified. The Statute may, however, apply independently of the original terms to a contract to modify a transfer of property.

(2) Where the second contract is unenforceable by virtue of the Statute of Frauds and there has been no material change of position in reliance on it, the prior contract is not modified.

Comment

a. Modification. Where one contract modifies another, the terms of the new contract are found partly in the original contract and partly in the modifying contract. In applying the Statute of Frauds, the new contract is viewed as a whole. See Uniform Commercial Code § 2–209(3) (sale of goods). But where a transfer of property has been made, the modifying contract must be viewed separately in applying the Statute insofar as there is a new transfer of property. See § 148; compare Restatement of Property § 557, Comment e; Restatement, Second, Property (Landlord and Tenant) § 2.4 (modification of a lease).

Illustrations

1. A and B make a written contract that A will employ B for two years at $500 a month. At the time B begins work, they agree orally to substitute a contract for six months at $600 a month. The second contract is not within the Statute, is enforceable, and at once discharges the prior contract.

2. A and B make a written contract that A will repair and sell to B two specific appliances for $3,000. Later they agree orally to eliminate one appliance and to reduce the price. Whether the second contract is within the Statute depends on whether the reduced price is $500 or more. See Uniform Commercial Code § 2–201.

3. A and B make mutual promises to marry within one month. Later they orally agree that the marriage will be postponed for two years. The oral agreement is not enforceable.

b. Effect of unenforceable modification. Subsection (2) is an application of the rule stated in § 147: where part of a contract is unenforceable by virtue of the Statute, the whole contract is ordinarily unenforceable. An agreement to rescind a prior contract and to substitute a new contract is normally indivisible; if the substitution is unenforceable, the rescission is also unenforceable. There is no difference for this purpose between modification of a term and substitution of an entire new contract. But it is possible for the parties to include in a single agreement two separate contracts, one to rescind a prior contract and the other to make a new contract; in such a case they may intend the rescission to be effective even though the new contract is unenforceable. See § 148.

Illustrations

4. In Illustration 3 the original promises to marry are not within the Statute. They remain enforceable unless there is a material change of position. See § 150.

5. A promises to sell and B to buy a specific automobile for $3,000, delivery to be made in 30 days and payment in 60 days. Both parties sign a sufficient memorandum. The next day they orally agree on delivery in 45 days and payment in 90 days. Before any change of position B repudiates the oral agreement. The oral agreement is not enforceable; the original contract remains enforceable.

6. A and B make an enforceable oral contract that A will work for B for 30 days at $20 a day. The next day A and B orally contract to substitute employment for two years at $6,000 a year. The first contract remains enforceable; the second is not.

7. A contracts with B that A will manufacture and sell to B described goods in installments at stated prices. Later A and B agree in a writing signed by B but not by A that the undelivered balance of the goods will be cancelled and that A will deliver a different type of goods at different prices. Even though the later agreement is not enforceable against A and even though no action is taken under it, the original contract is rescinded.

c. Change of position. The effect of a change of position in reliance on an oral modification is stated in § 150.

§ 150. Reliance on Oral Modification.

Where the parties to an enforceable contract subsequently agree that all or part of a duty need not be performed or of a condition need not occur, the Statute of Frauds does not prevent enforcement of the subsequent agreement if reinstatement of the original terms would be unjust in view of a material change of position in reliance on the subsequent agreement.

Comment

a. Relation to other rules. This Section states a particular application of the broader principle stated in § 139. Just as § 139 is complementary to § 90, so this Section is complementary to §§ 84 and 89, which like § 90 dispense with the requirement of consideration in similar circumstances. But this Section like § 139 also applies to promises supported by consideration. Enforcement of a promise or agreement under the present rule is often said to rest on "waiver" or "estoppel," or on excuse by prevention or hindrance. See §§ 84, 153; Uniform Commercial Code § 2–209(5).

b. Waiver. Where a contract is modified by subsequent agreement and the contract as modified is within a provision of the Statute of Frauds, the modified contract is unenforceable unless the Statute is satisfied. In such a case, if the original contract was enforceable it is not rescinded or modified but remains enforceable. See § 149. But the unenforceable modification may operate as a waiver. See Uniform Commercial Code § 2–209(4). To the extent that the waiver is acted on before it is revoked, it excuses the other party from performance of his own duty and of conditions of the duty of the waiving party. Cf. §§ 246, 247, 278–80.

Illustration

1. A and B contract in writing that A will sell specific goods to B for $1,000, delivery to be made in 30 days and payment in 60 days. Ten days later B orally requests that delivery be delayed until 45 days, and A so delays in reliance on the request. The delay is not a breach of A's duty and does not excuse B from performing.

c. Reinstatement after waiver. Where an unenforceable modification of an enforceable contract operates as a waiver affecting an executory portion of the contract, the waiving party may retract the waiver by reasonable notification received by the other party. The original terms are then reinstated unless reinstatement would be unjust in view of a material change of position in reliance on the waiver. See Uniform Commercial Code § 2–209(5).

Illustration

2. The facts being otherwise as stated in Illustration 1, B retracts his request for delay early enough to enable A without difficulty to deliver in accordance with the original terms. A is no longer justified in relying on B's request for delay, either to excuse performance of A's duty or to deny B an excuse for non-performance.

d. Requirement of reliance. The change of position which prevents retraction of the waiver and reinstatement of the original terms may consist of action or forbearance, and may result from reliance either by the other party to the modifying agreement or by a beneficiary. But it must be a change of position in reliance on the modifying agreement, and it must be such that reinstatement of the original terms would be unjust. See § 84 on the effect of an extension of time by the party retracting a waiver. If the duty or condition would not have been performed in any event, or if there is a waiver of performance after a failure of performance, the failure is not in reliance on the modifying agreement.

Illustrations

3. The facts being otherwise as stated in Illustration 1, A is unable to deliver for reasons independent of B's request for delay. The request does not excuse A's delay.

4. A and B contract in writing that A will sell and B will buy a parcel of land on stated terms. B's promise to buy is conditional on delivery by A within three days of a certificate showing his title. A does not furnish the certificate, and after three days B orally tells A that he need not furnish the certificate. Though B's implied promise to buy without the certificate is binding without consideration (see § 84), in the absence of reliance the promise is unenforceable by virtue of the Statute of Frauds.

e. Interpretation, modification and waiver. A waiver under this Section may be found in a course of performance. Where there are repeated occasions for performance by one party and the other has knowledge of the nature of the performance and opportunity to object, a course of performance accepted or not objected to may be relevant to show the meaning of the contract, or a modification of it, or a waiver. Where a claim or defense based on interpretation fails, and a claim or defense based on modification is unenforceable by virtue of the Statute of Frauds, a claim or defense based on waiver may nevertheless succeed. But the waiver, unlike the other bases, is subject to the possibility of reinstatement of rights waived. In case of doubt, the policy of the Statute combines with the need for flexibility in an on-going relationship to establish a preference for the claim or defense based on waiver. See Uniform Commercial Code § 2–208 and Comment.

CHAPTER 6

MISTAKE

§ 151. Mistake Defined.

A mistake is a belief that is not in accord with the facts.

Comment

a. Belief as to facts. In this Restatement the word "mistake" is used to refer to an erroneous belief. A party's erroneous belief is therefore said to be a "mistake" of that party. The belief need not be an articulated one, and a party may have a belief as to a fact when he merely makes an assumption with respect to it, without being aware of alternatives. The word "mistake" is not used here, as it is sometimes used in common speech, to refer to an improvident act, including the making of a contract, that is the result of such an erroneous belief. This usage is avoided here for the sake of clarity and consistency. Furthermore, the erroneous belief must relate to the facts as they exist at the time of the making of the contract. A party's prediction or judgment as to events to occur in the future, even if erroneous, is not a "mistake" as that word is defined here. An erroneous belief as to the contents or effect of a writing that expresses the agreement is, however, a mistake. Mistake alone, in the sense in which the word is used here, has no legal consequences. The legal consequences of mistake in connection with the creation of contractual liability are determined by the rules stated in the rest of this Chapter.

Illustrations

1. A contracts with B to raise and float B's boat which has run aground on a reef. At the time of making the contract, A believes that the sea will remain calm until the work is completed. Several days later, during a sudden storm, the boat slips into deep water and fills with mud, making it more difficult for A to raise it. Although A may have shown poor judgment in making the contract, there was no mistake of either A or B, and the rules stated in this Chapter do not apply. Whether A is discharged by supervening impracticability is governed by the rules stated in Chapter 11. See Illustration 5 to § 261. If, however, the boat had already slipped into deep water at the time the contract was made, although they both believed that it was still on the reef, there would have been a mistake of both A and B. Its legal consequences, if any, would be governed by the rule stated in § 152.

2. A contracts to sell and B to buy stock amounting to a controlling interest in C Corporation. At the time of making the contract, both A and B believe that C Corporation will have earnings of $1,000,000 during the following fiscal year. Because of a subsequent economic recession, C Corporation earns less than $500,000 during that year. Although B may have shown poor judgment in making the contract, there was no mistake of either A or B, and the rules stated in this Chapter do not apply. See Uniform Commercial Code § 8–306(2).

b. Facts include law. The rules stated in this Chapter do not draw the distinction that is sometimes made between "fact" and "law." They treat the law in existence at the time of the making of the contract as part of the total state of facts at that time. A party's erroneous belief with respect to the law, as found in statute, regulation, judicial decision, or elsewhere, or with respect to the legal consequences of his acts, may, therefore, come within these rules.

Illustration

3. A contracts to sell a tract of land to B. Both parties understand that B plans to erect an office building on the land and believe that he can lawfully do so. Unknown to them, two days earlier a municipal ordinance was enacted requiring a permit for lawful erection of such a building. There is a mistake of both A and B. Its legal consequences, if any, are governed by the rule stated in § 152. See Illustration 7 to § 152.

§ 152. When Mistake of Both Parties Makes a Contract Voidable.

(1) Where a mistake of both parties at the time a contract was made as to a basic assumption on which the contract was made has a material effect on the agreed exchange of performances, the contract is voidable by the adversely affected party unless he bears the risk of the mistake under the rule stated in § 154.

(2) In determining whether the mistake has a material effect on the agreed exchange of performances, account is taken of any relief by way of reformation, restitution, or otherwise.

Comment

a. Rationale. Before making a contract, a party ordinarily evaluates the proposed exchange of performances on the basis of a variety of assumptions with respect to existing facts. Many of these assumptions are shared by the other party, in the sense that the other party is aware that they are made. The mere fact that both parties are mistaken with respect to such an assumption does not, of itself, afford a reason for avoidance of the contract by the adversely affected party. Relief is only appropriate in situations where a mistake of both parties has such a material effect on the agreed exchange of performances as to upset the very basis for the contract.

This Section applies to such situations. Under it, the contract is voidable by the adversely affected party if three conditions are met. First, the mistake must relate to a "basic assumption on which the contract was made." Second, the party seeking avoidance must show that the mistake has a material effect on the agreed exchange of performances. Third, the mistake must not be one as to which the party seeking relief bears the risk. The parol evidence rule does not preclude the use of prior or contemporaneous agreements or negotiations to establish that the parties were mistaken. See § 214(d). However, since mistakes are the exception rather than the rule, the trier of the facts should examine the evidence with particular care when a party attempts to avoid liability by proving mistake. See Comment c to § 155. The rule stated in this Section is subject to that in § 157 on fault of the party seeking relief. It is also subject to the rules on exercise of the power of avoidance stated in §§ 378–85.

b. Basic assumption. A mistake of both parties does not make the contract voidable unless it is one as to a basic assumption on which both parties made the contract. The term "basic assumption" has the same meaning here as it does in Chapter 11 in connection with impracticability (§§ 261, 266(1)) and frustration (§§ 265, 266(2)). See Uniform Commercial Code § 2–615(a). For example, market conditions and the financial situation of the parties are ordinarily not such assumptions, and, generally, just as shifts in market conditions or financial ability do not effect discharge under the rules governing impracticability, mistakes as to market conditions or financial ability do not justify avoidance under the rules governing mistake. See Comment b to § 261. The parties may have had such a "basic assumption," even though they were not conscious of alternatives. See Introductory Note to Chapter 11. Where, for example, a party purchases an annuity on the life of another person, it can be said that it was a basic assumption that the other person was alive at the time, even though the parties never consciously addressed themselves to the possibility that he was dead. See Illustration 6.

Illustrations

1. A contracts to sell and B to buy a tract of land, the value of which has depended mainly on the timber on it. Both A and B believe that the timber is still there, but in fact it has been destroyed by fire. The contract is voidable by B.

2. A contracts to sell and B to buy a tract of land, on the basis of the report of a surveyor whom A has employed to determine the acreage. The price is, however, a lump sum not calculated from the acreage. Because of an error in computation by the surveyor, the tract contains ten per cent more acreage than he reports. The contract is voidable by A. Compare Illustrations 8 and 11 to this Section and Illustration 2 to § 158.

3. A contracts to sell and B to buy a tract of land. B agrees to pay A $100,000 in cash and to assume a mortgage that C holds on the tract. Both A and B believe that the amount of the mortgage is $50,000, but in fact it is only $10,000. The contract is voidable by A, unless the court supplies a term under which B is entitled to enforce the contract if he agrees to pay an appropriate additional sum, and B does so. See Illustration 2 to § 158.

4. A contracts to sell and B to buy a debt owed by C to A, and secured by a mortgage. Both A and B believe that there is a building on the mortgaged land so that the value of the mortgaged property exceeds that of the debt, but in fact there is none so that its value is less than half that of the debt. The contract is voidable by B. See § 333.

5. A contracts to assign to B for $100 a $10,000 debt owed to A by C, who is insolvent. Both A and B believe that the debt is unsecured and is therefore, virtually worthless, but in fact it is secured by stock worth approximately $5,000. The contract is voidable by A.

6. A pays B, an insurance company, $100,000 for an annuity contract under which B agrees to make quarterly payments to C, who is 50 years old, in a fixed amount for the rest of C's life. A and B believe that C is in good health and has a normal life expectancy, but in fact C is dead. The contract is voidable by A.

c. Material effect on agreed exchange. A party cannot avoid a contract merely because both parties were mistaken as to a basic assumption on which it was made. He must, in addition, show that the mistake has a material effect on the agreed exchange of performances. It is not enough for him to prove that he would not have made the contract had it not been for the mistake. He must show that the resulting imbalance in the agreed exchange is so severe that he can not fairly be required to carry it out. Ordinarily he will be able to do this by showing that the exchange is not only less desirable to him but is also more advantageous to the other party. Sometimes this is so because the adversely affected party will give, and the other party will receive, something more than they supposed. Sometimes it is so because the other party will give, and the adversely affected party will receive, something less than they supposed. In such cases the materiality of the effect on the agreed exchange will be determined by the overall impact on both parties. In exceptional cases the adversely affected party may be able to show that the effect on the agreed exchange has been material simply on the ground that the exchange has become less desirable for him, even though there has been no effect on the other party. Cases of hardship that result in no advantage to the other party are, however, ordinarily appropriately left to the rules on impracticability and frustration. See Illustration 9 and § 266. The standard of materiality here, as elsewhere in this Restatement (e.g., § 237), is a flexible one to be applied in the light of all the circumstances.

Illustrations

7. The facts being as stated in Illustration 3 to § 151, in determining whether the effect on the agreed exchange is material, and the contract therefore voidable by B, the court will consider not only the decrease in its desirability to B but also any advantage to A through his receiving a higher price than the land would have brought on the market had the facts been known. See Illustration 3 to § 151.

8. A contracts to sell and B to buy a tract of land, which they believe contains 100 acres, at a price of $1,000 an acre. In fact the tract contains 110 acres. The contract is not voidable by either A or B, unless additional facts show that the effect on the agreed exchange of performances is material.

9. A contracts to sell and B to buy a dredge which B tells A he intends to use for a special and unusual purpose, but B does not rely on A's skill and judgment. A and B believe that the dredge is fit for B's purpose, but in fact it is not, although it is merchantable. The contract is not voidable by B because the effect on the agreed exchange of performances is not material. If B's purpose is substantially frustrated, he may have relief under § 266(2). See also Uniform Commercial Code §§ 2–314, 2–315.

d. Significance of other relief. Under the rule stated in Subsection (2), before determining the effect on the agreed exchange, the court will first take account of any relief that may be available to him or granted to the other party under the rules stated in §§ 155 (see Illustration 10) and 158 (see Illustration 11). A party may choose to seek relief by means of reformation even though it makes his own performance more onerous when, absent reformation, the contract would be voidable by the other party. See Introductory Note and Comment e to § 155.

Illustrations

10. A and B agree that A will sell and B will buy a tract of land for $100,000, payable by $50,000 in cash and the assumption of an existing mortgage of $50,000. In reducing the agreement to writing,

B's lawyer erroneously omits the provision for assumption of the mortgage, and neither A nor B notices the omission. Under the rule stated in § 155, at the request of either party, the court will decree that the writing be reformed to add the provision for assumption of the mortgage. The contract is, therefore, not voidable by A because, when account is taken of the availability to him of reformation, the effect on the agreed exchange of performances is not material. See Illustration 1 to § 155.

11. A contracts to sell and B to buy a tract of land, described in the contract as containing 100 acres, at a price of $100,000, calculated from the acreage at $1,000 an acre. In fact the tract contains only 90 acres. If B is entitled to a reduction in price of $10,000, under the rule stated in § 158(2), the contract is not voidable by B because when account is taken of the availability to him of a reduction in price, the effect on the agreed exchange of performances is not material. See Illustration 1 to § 158. As to the possibility of an argument based on frustration, see § 266(2).

e. Allocation of risk. A party may be considered to have undertaken to perform in spite of a mistake that has a material effect on the agreed exchange of performances. He then bears the risk of the mistake. Because of the significance of the allocation of risk in the law of mistake, the scope of this exception is spelled out in detail in § 154. (It is assumed in the illustrations to the present Section that the adversely affected party does not bear the risk of the mistake under the rule stated in § 154. See, e.g., Illustration 14.)

f. Releases. Releases of claims have afforded particularly fertile ground for the invocation of the rule stated in this Section. It is, of course, a traditional policy of the law to favor compromises as a means of settling claims without resort to litigation. See Comment a to § 74. Nevertheless, a claimant who has executed such a release may later wish to attack it. The situation may arise with respect to any claim, but a particularly common example involves claims for personal injury, where the claimant may have executed the release without full knowledge of the extent or, perhaps, even of the nature of his injuries. Such a claimant has a variety of possible grounds for attacking the release on discovering that his injuries are more serious than he had initially supposed. He may seek to have the release interpreted against the draftsman so as to be inapplicable to the newly discovered injuries (§ 206). He may seek to have the release reformed on the ground that it does not correctly express the prior agreement of the parties (§ 155). He may seek to avoid the release on the ground that it was unfairly obtained through misrepresentation, duress or undue influence (Chapter 7). He may seek to have the release, or at least that part purporting to cover the newly discovered injuries, held unenforceable as unconscionable (§ 208). Or he may seek to avoid the release on the ground that both he and the other party were mistaken as to the nature or extent of his injuries. Assuming that the release is properly interpreted to cover unknown injuries and that it was not unfairly obtained or unconscionable, his case will turn on the application of the rule stated in this Section to his claim of mistake. In dealing with such attacks on releases, a court should be particularly sensitive to obscure or misleading language and especially alert to the possibility of unfairness or unconscionability. However, the same rules relating to mistake apply to such releases as apply to other contracts, and if the results sometimes seem at variance with those rules, the variance can usually be attributed to the presence of one of the alternative grounds listed above.

A claimant's attempt at avoidance based on mistake of both parties, therefore, will frequently turn on a determination, in the light of all the circumstances, of the basic assumptions of the parties at the time of the release. These circumstances may include the fair amount that would be required to compensate the claimant for his known injuries, the probability that the other party would be held liable on that claim, the amount received by the claimant in settlement of his claim, and the relationship between the known injuries and the newly discovered injuries. If, for example, the amount received by the claimant is reasonable in comparison with the fair amount required to compensate him for his known injuries and the probability of the other party being held liable on that claim, this suggests that the parties assumed that his injuries were only those known. Furthermore, even if the parties do not assume that his injuries are only those known, they may assume that any unknown injuries are of the same general nature as the known ones, while differing in extent. Although the parties may fix the assumptions on which the contract is based by an express provision, fairly bargained for, the common recital that the release covers all injuries, known or unknown and of whatever nature or extent, may be disregarded as unconscionable if, in view of the circumstances of the parties, their legal representation, and the setting of the negotiations, it flies in the face of what would otherwise be regarded as a basic assumption of the parties. What has been said here with respect to releases of claims for personal injury is generally true for releases executed in other contexts.

Illustrations

12. A has a claim against B for B's admitted negligence, which appears to have caused damage to A's automobile in an amount fairly valued at $600. In consideration of B's payment of $600, A executes a release of "all claims for injury to person or property" that he may have against B. Both A and B believe that A has suffered damage to property only, but A later discovers that he has also suffered personal injuries in the extent of $20,000. The release is voidable by A.

13. A has a claim against B for B's admitted negligence, which appears to have caused personal injuries to A's back in an amount fairly valued at $10,000, although the parties are aware that A may require further treatment. In consideration of B's payment of $15,000, A executes a release of "all claims for injury to person or property" that he may have against B. A later incurs additional expenses of $20,000 in connection with his back, which was injured more seriously than he had believed. The release is not voidable by A.

g. Relation to breach of warranty. The rule stated in this Section has a close relationship to the rules governing warranties [in a] sale by a seller of goods or of other kinds of property. A buyer usually finds it more advantageous to rely on the law of warranty than on the law of mistake. Because of the broad scope of a seller's warranties, a buyer is more often entitled to relief based on a claim of breach of warranty than on a claim based on mistake. Furthermore, because relief for breach of warranty is generally based on the value that the property would have had if it had been as warranted (see Uniform Commercial Code § 2–714(2)), it is ordinarily more extensive than that afforded if he merely seeks to avoid the contract on the ground of mistake. Nevertheless, . . . warranties are not necessarily exclusive and, even absent a warranty, a buyer may be able to avoid on the ground of mistake if he brings himself within the rule stated in this Section. The effect, on a buyer's claim of mistake, of language purporting to disclaim the seller's responsibility for the goods is governed by the rules on interpretation stated in Chapter 9.

Illustration

14. A, a violinist, contracts to sell and B, another violinist, to buy a violin. Both A and B believe that the violin is a Stradivarius, but in fact it is a clever imitation. A makes no express warranty and, because he is not a merchant with respect to violins, makes no implied warranty of merchantibility under Uniform Commercial Code § 2–314. The contract is voidable by B.

h. Mistakes as to different assumptions. The rule stated in this Section applies only where both parties are mistaken as to the same basic assumption. Their mistakes need not be, and often they will not be, identical. If, however, the parties are mistaken as to different assumptions, the rule stated in § 153, rather than that stated in this Section, applies.

§ 153. When Mistake of One Party Makes a Contract Voidable.

Where a mistake of one party at the time a contract was made as to a basic assumption on which he made the contract has a material effect on the agreed exchange of performances that is adverse to him, the contract is voidable by him if he does not bear the risk of the mistake under the rule stated in § 154, and

   (a) the effect of the mistake is such that enforcement of the contract would be unconscionable, or

   (b) the other party had reason to know of the mistake or his fault caused the mistake.

Comment

a. Rationale. Courts have traditionally been reluctant to allow a party to avoid a contract on the ground of mistake, even as to a basic assumption, if the mistake was not shared by the other party. Nevertheless, relief has been granted where the other party actually knew (see §§ 160, 161) or had reason to know of the mistake at the time the contract was made or where his fault caused the mistake. There has, in addition, been a growing willingness to allow avoidance where the consequences of the mistake are so grave that enforcement of the contract would be unconscionable. This Section states a rule that permits avoidance on this latter basis, as well as on the more traditional grounds. The rules stated in this Section also apply to option contracts, under which a party's offer is irrevocable either under a statute, such as one applying to bids for public works, or on other grounds. The parol evidence rule does not preclude the use of prior or contemporaneous agreements or negotiations to establish that a party was mistaken. See § 214(d). Nevertheless, because mistakes are the exception rather than the rule, the trier of the facts should examine the evidence with particular care when a party attempts to avoid liability by proving mistake. See Comment c to § 155. The rule stated in this Section is subject to that stated in § 157 on fault of the party seeking relief. It is also subject to the rules on exercise of the power of avoidance stated in §§ 380–85.

b. Similarity to rule where both are mistaken. In order for a party to have the power to avoid a contract for a mistake that he alone made, he must at least meet the same requirements that he would have had to meet had both parties been mistaken (§ 152). The mistake must be one as to a basic assumption on which the contract was made; it must have a material effect on the agreed exchange of performances; and the mistaken party must not bear the risk of the mistake. The most common sorts of such mistakes occur in bids on construction contracts and result from clerical errors in the computation of the price or in the omission of component items. . . . The rule stated in this Section is not, however, limited to such cases. It also applies, for example, to a misreading of specifications . . . or such misunderstanding as does not prevent a manifestation of mutual assent. . . . Where only one party is mistaken, however, he must meet either the additional requirement stated in Subparagraph (a) or one of the additional requirements stated in Subparagraph (b).

c. Additional requirement of unconscionability. Under Subparagraph (a), the mistaken party must in addition show that enforcement of the contract would be unconscionable. The reason for this additional requirement is that, if only one party was mistaken, avoidance of the contract will more clearly disappoint the expectations of the other party than if he too was mistaken. . . . Although § 208, Unconscionable Contract or Term, is not itself applicable to such cases since the unconscionability does not appear at the time the contract is made, the standards of unconscionability in such cases are similar to those under § 208 (see Comment c to § 208). The mistaken party bears the substantial burden of establishing unconscionability and must ordinarily show not only the position he would have been in had the facts been as he believed them to be but also the position in which he finds himself as a result of his mistake. For example, in the typical case of a mistake as to the price in a bid, the builder must show the profit or loss that will result if he is required to perform, as well as the profit that he would have made had there been no mistake.

Illustrations

1. In response to B's invitation for bids on the construction of a building according to stated specifications, A submits an offer to do the work for $150,000. A believes that this is the total of a column of figures, but he has made an error by inadvertently omitting a $50,000 item, and in fact the total is $200,000. B, having no reason to know of A's mistake, accepts A's bid. If A performs for $150,000, he will sustain a loss of $20,000 instead of making an expected profit of $30,000. If the court determines that enforcement of the contract would be unconscionable, it is voidable by A.

2. The facts being otherwise as stated in Illustration 1, the item that A inadvertently omits is a $35,000 item which would have made the total $185,000, so that if he does the work for $150,000 he will sustain a loss of $5,000 rather than make a profit of $30,000. The court may reach a result contrary to that in Illustration 1, on the ground that enforcement of the contract would not be unconscionable, and hold that it is not voidable by A.

3. The facts being otherwise as stated in Illustration 1, B has not accepted A's bid before notification of the mistake, but by statute A's bid is an irrevocable option contract because B is a state agency. In addition, A has posted a $10,000 bidder's bond with S as surety. If the court determines that enforcement of the option contract would be unconscionable, it is voidable by A and, on avoidance by A, S is not liable on the bond.

4. The facts being otherwise as stated in Illustration 1, the $50,000 error in A's bid is the result of A's mistake in interpreting B's specifications. If the court determines that enforcement of the contract would be unconscionable, it is voidable by A.

5. A writes B offering to sell for $100,000 a tract of land that A owns known as "201 Lincoln Street." B, who mistakenly believes that this description includes an additional tract of land worth $30,000, accepts A's offer. If the court determines that enforcement of the contract would be unconscionable, it is voidable by B.

6. A offers to sell B goods shipped from Bombay ex steamer "Peerless." B accepts. There are two steamers of the name "Peerless" sailing from Bombay at materially different times. B means Peerless No. 2, and A has reason to know this. A means Peerless No. 1, but B has no reason to know this. Under the rule stated in § 20 there is a contract for the sale of goods from Peerless No. 2, but, under the rule stated in this Section, if the court determines that its enforcement would be unconscionable, it is voidable by A. See Illustration 4 to § 20.

d. Effect of reliance on unconscionability. Reliance by the other party may make enforcement of a contract proper although enforcement would otherwise be unconscionable. If the mistake is discovered and the other party notified before he has relied on the contract, avoidance by the mistaken party deprives the other party only of his expectation, the "benefit of the bargain," (see § 344). If, however, the other party has relied on the contract in some substantial way, avoidance may leave that reliance uncompensated. In such a case, enforcement of the contract would not be unconscionable, even if it otherwise would be. If, however, the court can adequately protect the other party by compensating him for his reliance under the rules stated in § 158, avoidance is not then precluded on this ground.

Illustrations

7. In response to an invitation from B, a general contractor, for bids from subcontractors, A submits an offer to B to do paving work for $10,000, to be used by B as a partial basis for B's bid on a large building. As A knows, B is required to name his subcontractors in his general bid. Because of the short time in which A has to prepare his bid, A inadvertently totals his bid as $10,000 rather than $15,000. B uses A's bid in arriving at his offer of $100,000, making A's offer irrevocable as an option contract (§ 87). B's offer is accepted, but A discovers his mistake before B accepts his bid. The option contract is not voidable by A because of B's reliance by using A's offer in making up his own offer. See Illustration 6 to § 87.

8. The facts being otherwise as stated in Illustration 1, on A's refusal to perform for $150,000, B is no longer able to accept the next lowest bid and has to re-advertise for bids at a cost of $1,000 before getting a bid that he accepts. If the court determines that enforcement of the contract would be unconscionable, the contract is voidable by A in spite of B's reliance, because B can be adequately protected by holding A liable for the $1,000 cost of re-advertising (see § 158(1) and Comment b to that Section).

e. Had reason to know of or caused the mistake. If the other party had reason to know of the mistake, the mistaken party can avoid the contract regardless of whether its enforcement would be unconscionable. (The terminology "reason to know" is used instead of "should know" on the ground explained in Comment b to § 19. The situation in which the other party actually knows of the mistake is covered in § 161. See Comment d to § 161.) Similar results follow where the other party's fault caused the mistake. (If the mistake was the fault of both parties, it was not caused by the other party within the meaning of this Section and the court may exercise its discretion under the rule stated in § 158(2). See Comment c to § 158.) In attempting to unscramble a partially or completely executed transaction, the court may allow the mistaken party recovery under the rules stated in § 158(1).

Illustrations

9. The facts being otherwise as stated in Illustration 1, A does not prove what his profit or loss will be if he performs, but B had estimated the expected cost as $180,000 before advertising for bids and the ten other bids were all in the range between $180,000 and $200,000. If it is determined, because of the discrepancy between A's bid on the one hand and B's estimate and the ten other bids on the other, that B had reason to know of A's mistake, the contract is voidable by A.

10. The facts being otherwise as stated in Illustration 7, if it is determined that B had reason to know of A's mistake, the contract is voidable by A.

f. Allocation of risk. Here, as under § 152, a party may undertake to perform in spite of a mistake that would otherwise allow him to avoid the contract. It is, of course, unusual for a party to bear the risk of a mistake that the other party had reason to know of or that was caused by his fault within Subparagraph (b). Because of the significance of allocation of risk in the law of mistake, the scope of this exception is spelled out in detail in § 154. (It is assumed in the illustrations to the present Section that the adversely affected party does not bear the risk under the rule stated in § 154.)

g. Mistake as to identity. Mistakes as to the identity of a party have sometimes been treated as distinct from other mistakes, but the modern trend is to apply the rules applicable to other mistakes. Cf. Uniform Commercial Code § 2–403(1)(a). Such a mistake is therefore subject generally to the rules stated in this Chapter and, since it is by its nature a mistake of only one of the parties, particularly to the rule stated in this Section. The identity of the other party, as distinguished, for example, from his financial standing (see Comment b to § 152), is usually a basic assumption on which a contract is made. If the other party knows that he is not the intended offeree, he cannot accept an offer. That case is governed by § 52. If, however, he accepts without knowing that he is not the intended offeree, a contract may result. See Comment b to § 52. Whether that contract is voidable by the offeror on the ground of mistake is governed by the rule stated in this Section. The contract is voidable by the mistaken party, under the rule stated in Subparagraph (b), if the other party has caused a mistake as to his identity or if he had reason to know of the mistake, as long as it has a material effect on the agreed exchange of performances. Otherwise it is not voidable unless enforcement of the contract would be unconscionable, under the rule stated in Subparagraph (a). In some transactions the identity of the other party is of sufficient importance that he will be able to show unconscionability, but often he will not.

The situation in which a party deals with an agent acting secretly for an undisclosed principal is governed by the Restatement, Second, of Agency and not by the Restatement of this Subject. The basic principles there applied are not, however, inconsistent with the rule stated in this Section. The party who deals with such an agent gets that which he expects, the liability of the agent on the contract. See Restatement, Second, Agency § 322. Indeed, he gets more, for on disclosure of the agent's principal he can also hold the principal. See Restatement, Second, Agency § 186. Although it is also true that he may himself be liable to the principal, as well as to the agent, on the contract, this additional burden has not been regarded by the law of agency as sufficiently important to make enforcement of the contract against him unconscionable, since it does not change the terms of the contract.

Illustrations

11. In answer to an inquiry from "J. B. Smith Company," A offers to sell goods for cash on delivery. A mistakenly believes that the offeree is John B. Smith, who has an established business of good repute, but in fact it is a business run by his son, whose business is new and near insolvency. The son accepts, not knowing of A's mistake. If the court concludes that, because payment is to be cash on delivery, enforcement of the contract would not be unconscionable, the contract is not voidable by A.

12. The facts being otherwise as stated in Illustration 11, A's offer is to sell goods on 90 days credit. If the court determines that, because payment is to be on 90 days credit, enforcement of the contract would be unconscionable, the contract is voidable by A. See §§ 251, 252; Uniform Commercial Code §§ 2–609, 2–702(1).

13. The facts being otherwise as stated in Illustration 11, A's offer contains references to "your long established business" from which the son had reason to know of A's mistake. The contract is voidable by A.

§ 154. When a Party Bears the Risk of a Mistake.

A party bears the risk of a mistake when

(a) the risk is allocated to him by agreement of the parties, or

(b) he is aware, at the time the contract is made, that he has only limited knowledge with respect to the facts to which the mistake relates but treats his limited knowledge as sufficient, or

(c) the risk is allocated to him by the court on the ground that it is reasonable in the circumstances to do so.

Comment

a. Rationale. Absent provision to the contrary, a contracting party takes the risk of most supervening changes in circumstances, even though they upset basic assumptions and unexpectedly affect the agreed exchange of performances, unless there is such extreme hardship as will justify relief on the ground of impracticability of performance or frustration of purpose. A party also bears the risk of many mistakes as to existing circumstances even though they upset basic assumptions and unexpectedly affect the agreed exchange of performances. For example, it is commonly understood that the seller of farm land generally cannot avoid the contract of sale upon later discovery by both parties that the land contains valuable mineral deposits, even though the price was negotiated on the basic assumption that the land was suitable only for farming and the effect on the agreed exchange of performances is material. In such a case a court will ordinarily allocate the risk of the mistake to the seller, so that he is under a duty to perform regardless of the mistake. The rule stated in this Section determines whether a party bears the risk of a mistake for the purposes of both §§ 152 and 153. Stating these rules in terms of the allocation of risk avoids such artificial and specious distinctions as are sometimes drawn between "intrinsic" and "extrinsic" mistakes or between mistakes that go to the "identity" or "existence" of the subject matter and those that go merely to its "attributes," "quality" or "value." Even though a mistaken party does not bear the risk of a mistake, he may be barred from avoidance if the mistake was the result of his failure to act in good faith and in accordance with reasonable standards of fair dealing. See § 157.

b. Allocation by agreement. The most obvious case of allocation of the risk of a mistake is one in which the parties themselves provide for it by their agreement. Just as a party may agree to perform in spite of impracticability or frustration that would otherwise justify his non-performance, he may also agree, by appropriate language or other manifestations, to perform in spite of mistake that would otherwise justify his avoidance. An insurer, for example, may expressly undertake the risk of loss of property covered as of a date already past. Whether the agreement places the risk on the mistaken party is a question to be answered under the rules generally applicable to the scope of contractual obligations, including those on interpretation, usage and unconscionability. See Chapter 9.

Illustration

1. A contracts to sell and B to buy a tract of land. A and B both believe that A has good title, but neither has made a title search. The contract provides that A will convey only such title as he has, and A makes no representation with respect to title. In fact, A's title is defective. The contract is not voidable by B, because the risk of the mistake is allocated to B by agreement of the parties.

c. Conscious ignorance. Even though the mistaken party did not agree to bear the risk, he may have been aware when he made the contract that his knowledge with respect to the facts to which the mistake relates was limited. If he was not only so aware that his knowledge was limited but undertook to perform in the face of that awareness, he bears the risk of the mistake. It is sometimes said in such a situation that, in a sense, there was not mistake but "conscious ignorance."

Illustration

2. The facts being otherwise as stated in Illustration 2 to § 152, A proposes to B during the negotiations the inclusion of a provision under which the adversely affected party can cancel the contract in the event of a material error in the surveyor's report, but B refuses to agree to such a provision. The contract is not voidable by A, because A bears the risk of the mistake.

d. Risk allocated by the court. In some instances it is reasonably clear that a party should bear the risk of a mistake for reasons other than those stated in Subparagraphs (a) and (b). In such instances, under the rule stated in Subparagraph (c), the court will allocate the risk to that party on the ground that it is reasonable to do so. A court will generally do this, for example, where the seller of farm land seeks to avoid the contract of sale on the ground that valuable mineral rights have newly been found. See Comment a. In dealing with such issues, the court will consider the purposes of the parties and will have recourse to its own general knowledge of human behavior in bargain transactions, as it will in the analogous situation in which it is asked to supply a term under the rule stated in § 204. The rule stated in Subsection (c) is subject to contrary agreement and to usage (§ 221).

Illustrations

3. The facts being otherwise as stated in Illustration 6 to § 152, C is not dead but is afflicted with an incurable fatal disease and cannot live more than a year. The contract is not voidable by A, because the court will allocate to A the risk of the mistake.

4. A, an owner of land, and B, a builder, make a contract under which B is to take from A's land, at a stated rate per cubic yard, all the gravel and earth necessary for the construction of a bridge, an amount estimated to be 114,000 cubic yards. A and B believe that all of the gravel and earth is above water level and can be removed by ordinary means, but in fact about one quarter of it is below water level, so that removal will require special equipment at an additional cost of about twenty percent. The contract is not voidable by B, because the court will allocate to B the risk of the mistake. Compare Illustration 5 to § 266.

5. A contracts with B to build a house on B's land. A and B believe that subsoil conditions are normal, but in fact some of the land must be drained at an expense that will leave A no profit under the contract. The contract is not voidable by A, because the court will allocate to A the risk of the mistake. Compare Illustration 8 to § 266.

6. The facts being otherwise as stated in Illustration 1 to § 153, the $50,000 error in A's bid is the result of A's mistaken estimate as to the amount of labor required to do the work. A cannot avoid the contract, because the court will allocate to A the risk of the mistake.

§ 155. When Mistake of Both Parties as to Written Expression Justifies Reformation.

Where a writing that evidences or embodies an agreement in whole or in part fails to express the agreement because of a mistake of both parties as to the contents or effect of the writing, the court may at the request of a party reform the writing to express the agreement, except to the extent that rights of third parties such as good faith purchasers for value will be unfairly affected.

Comment

a. Scope. The province of reformation is to make a writing express the agreement that the parties intended it should. Under the rule stated in this Section, reformation is available when the parties, having reached an agreement and having then attempted to reduce it to writing, fail to express it correctly in the writing. Their mistake is one as to expression—one that relates to the contents or effect of the writing that is intended to express their agreement—and the appropriate remedy is reformation of that writing properly to reflect their agreement. For the rule stated in this Section to be invoked, therefore, there must have been some agreement between the parties prior to the writing. The prior agreement need not, however, be complete and certain enough to be a contract. Compare § 1 with § 3; see § 33. If the parties reach agreement as to only part of a prospective bargain, and if they are later mistaken in their attempt to put in writing this agreement together with such other terms as will make a contract, reformation is still an appropriate remedy. The agreement must, of course, be certain enough to permit a court to frame relief in terms of reformation. The writing that is reformed may purport to embody their entire agreement (i.e., a completely integrated agreement under § 210(1)), or only part of their agreement (i.e., a partially integrated agreement under § 210(2)), since the parol evidence rule does not preclude such a showing of mistake. See § 214(d). It may be a writing evidencing a contract within the Statute of Frauds, since the Statute does not bar reformation. See § 156. (If neither the parol evidence rule nor the Statute of Frauds applies, the writing itself will not ordinarily have sufficient legal significance for its reformation to be necessary.) The error in expressing the agreement may consist in the omission or erroneous reduction to writing of a term agreed upon or the inclusion of a term not agreed upon. If the parties are mistaken with respect to the legal effect of the language that they have used, the writing may be reformed to reflect the intended effect. Reformation is available even though the effect of the error is to make it appear from the writing that there is no enforceable agreement. See Illustration 2 and Comment a and Illustration 3 to § 156. Reformation is not precluded by the mere fact that the party who seeks it failed to exercise reasonable care in reading the writing, but the right to reformation is subject to the rule on fault stated in § 157. With the merger of law and equity under modern codes of procedure, it is generally unnecessary to seek reformation as a condition to enforcing the true contract, and a party may be granted both reformation and enforcement in a single suit.

Illustrations

1. A and B agree that A will sell and B will buy a tract of land for $100,000 and that B will assume an existing mortgage of $50,000. In reducing the agreement to writing, B's lawyer erroneously omits the provision for assumption, and neither A nor B notices the omission. At the request of either A or B, the court will reform the writing to add the provision for assumption.

2. A and B agree that A will sell and B will buy all the coal that B shall require in his business during a five year period. In reducing the agreement to writing, B mistakenly provides that he will buy all the coal that he shall desire to buy during that period, and A fails to notice the error. At the request of either A or B, the court will reform the writing to provide that B will buy all the coal that he shall require rather than all that he shall desire to buy.

3. A agrees with B to guarantee the collectibility of a debt owed by C to B. In reducing the agreement to writing, the parties mistakenly choose words that, unknown to both of them, have the effect of making A an ordinary guarantor rather than a guarantor of collectibility only. At the request of either A or B, the court will reform the writing to limit A's obligation to that of a guarantor of collectibility.

b. Relation to other rules. The rule stated in this Section applies only where both parties are mistaken with respect to the reduction to writing. (In the case of a promise under seal to make a gift, since the intention of only one party is involved, his mistake alone will entitle him to reformation, at least if there has been no reliance by the donee that cannot be compensated for. See Comment d.) A mistake as to expression is a mistake as to a basic assumption, but the contract is not voidable unless reformation is unavailable to protect the interests of the parties. See § 152. One party may, therefore, seek reformation in order to prevent avoidance by the other. See Comment e to this Section and Illustration 10 to § 152. If, however, the parties make a written agreement that they would not otherwise have made because of a mistake other than one as to expression, the court will not reform a writing to reflect the agreement that it thinks they would have made. The remedy in that case is avoidance. See Illustrations 4 and 5. The discretionary relief authorized under the rule stated in § 158 may involve some reshaping of the contract duties by the court but is different from reformation.

Several other related cases must also be distinguished. If one party sends to the other an offer which, because of a mistake, does not reflect the offeror's intention, the rule stated in this Section does not apply both because only one party is mistaken and because there was no prior agreement. The mistaken party's remedy, if any, in that case is not reformation but avoidance under the rule stated in § 153. See Illustration 6 to § 153. Similarly, when the parties to a bargain, sufficiently certain to be a contract, are silent with respect to a term that is essential to a determination of their rights and duties, the court will not decree reformation but will supply a term under the rule stated in § 204. See Illustration 6. Furthermore, even where there is a prior agreement that is not properly expressed in the writing, if only one party is mistaken and the other actually knows this, the mistaken party's right to reformation is governed by the rule on fraudulent misrepresentation stated in § 166. In some instances where it might appear that both parties are mistaken with respect to the reduction to writing of a prior agreement, interpretation of the writing will show that the mistake is only apparent and not real. Where, for example, the parties use language in the writing in an unusual way, interpretation of the writing in accord with the meaning attached by the parties will protect their expectations, and reformation is unnecessary. See Illustration 7. In a borderline case a court may avoid the necessity of reforming the writing by viewing the issue as one of interpretation. Finally, in the case of a standardized agreement, the special rule stated in § 211(3) may operate to exclude a term that is not only unknown to a party but beyond the range of reasonable expectations. See Comment f to § 211.

Illustrations

4. A and B make a written contract for the sale by A to B for $15,000 of a claim by A against C. Both parties mistakenly believe that the claim is an unliquidated one for about $20,000, but in fact it does not exceed $10,000. A court will not, at the request of B, reform the writing, because the mistake of the parties was not one as to its contents or effect. B's right to avoidance is governed by the rule stated in § 152. See Illustration 4 to § 152.

5. A contracts to sell and B to buy a tract of land, described in the contract as containing 100 acres, at a price of $100,000. Both parties believe that the area is 100 acres but in fact it is only 90 acres. The court will not, at the request of B, reform the writing, because the mistake of the parties was not one as to its contents or effect. B's right to avoidance is governed by the rules stated in §§ 152 and 158. See Illustration 11 to § 152 and Illustration 1 to § 158.

6. A and B agree that A shall have the exclusive right to market goods manufactured by B and that A shall pay B half of any profits he derives from their sale. The agreement is then reduced to writing. Each party understands that A is to use best efforts to promote sale of the goods and that B will use best efforts to supply them, but nothing is said on this subject. Under the rule stated in § 204 a court will supply a term imposing on both A and B an obligation to use best efforts, and it will not reform the writing. See Illustration 9 to § 77 and Uniform Commercial Code § 2–306(2).

7. A agrees to sell and B to buy the American patent rights on an invention as to which A holds American, British and French patent rights. In reducing their agreement to writing, the parties use the term "all patent rights," meaning all American rights. A court will interpret the writing in the light of the circumstances to cover only the American and not the British or French patent rights, and it will not reform the writing. See Illustration 2 to § 212.

c. Proof required. Because experience teaches that mistakes are the exception and not the rule, the trier of the facts should examine the evidence with particular care when it relates to a party's assertion of mistake as the basis for his claim or defense. Care is all the more necessary when the asserted mistake relates to a writing, because the law of contracts, as is indicated by the parol evidence rule and the Statute of Frauds, attaches great weight to the written expression of an agreement. This is commonly summarized in a standard that requires the trier of the facts to be satisfied by "clear and convincing evidence" before reformation is granted. Each case must, however, turn on its particular facts, and the evidentiary weight to be attached to a writing will depend, in part, on its inherent credibility in the light of those facts. Once the court is convinced that the writing fails to express the agreement of the parties, the writing loses its usual evidentiary effect with respect to other matters, such as the ascertainment of the parties' actual agreement. Because this Restatement is concerned with rules of substantive law and not with rules of procedure, including proof, this question of the proof required for reformation is not dealt with in this Section.

d. Equitable discretion. This Section states the circumstances in which a court "may" grant reformation. Since the remedy of reformation is equitable in nature, a court has the discretion to withhold it, even if it would otherwise be appropriate, on grounds that have traditionally justified courts of equity in withholding relief. No attempt is made here to define the limits of this traditional equitable discretion. One such limit, however, has been that equity will not ordinarily aid a volunteer, and it is for this reason that the promisee of a promise under seal to make a gift is generally barred from obtaining reformation. See Comment b.

e. Who is entitled to reformation. Reformation may be granted at the request of any party to the contract, including an intended beneficiary, or of a party's successor in interest. In contrast to the rules for avoidance stated in §§ 152 and 153, the party seeking relief need not show that the mistake has resulted in an inequality that adversely affects him. A party may, for example, seek and be granted reformation even though it makes his own performance more onerous when, absent reformation, the agreement would be unenforceable for lack of consideration (see Illustration 2) or where the agreement would be voidable by the other party (see Illustration 10 to § 152). A court will, however, deny reformation where the effect of the mistake is trivial.

f. Protection of innocent third parties. The claim of a mistaken party to reformation, being equitable in its origin, is subject to the rights of good faith purchasers for value and other third parties who have similarly relied on the finality of a consensual transaction in which they have acquired an interest in property. Cf. Restatement of Restitution § 13. Such other third parties include those who have given value and come within the definition of "purchaser" in Uniform Commercial Code § 1–201(33), (32), notably mortgagees, pledgees and other holders of a security interest. Judgment creditors and trustees in bankruptcy are not included.

Illustrations

8. A gives B a note for $50,000, loaned to him by B, and also gives B a written contract by which A promises to execute a mortgage on land that he owns as security for the note. Because of a mistake of both parties as to the contents of the writing, it fails to express their agreement that the mortgage is to be subject to another mortgage for $30,000 for which A is then bargaining. B negotiates the note and assigns the contract to C, a good faith purchaser for value. The court will not, at the request of A, reform the writing because to do so would adversely affect C, a good faith purchaser.

9. The facts being otherwise as stated in Illustration 8, B does not transfer the note and contract to C, a good faith purchaser, but D, a judgment creditor of B, attaches the claim. The court will, at the request of A, reform the writing so that the mortgage is to be subject to the $30,000 mortgage, because D is not a good faith purchaser or other third party taking an interest in property in a voluntary transaction. The result would be the same if B instead went into bankruptcy and D were B's trustee.

§ 156. Mistake as to Contract Within the Statute of Frauds.

If reformation of a writing is otherwise appropriate, it is not precluded by the fact that the contract is within the Statute of Frauds.

Comment

a. Rationale and scope. The premise underlying the rule stated in this Section is that a writing evidencing an agreement may be reformed under the rule stated in § 155 before it is subjected to the requirements of the Statute of Frauds. If the parties have prepared an integrated agreement which, because of a mistake of both of them, incorrectly states an essential term that would have to be contained in a writing in order to satisfy the Statute, the court will reform the writing before determining whether it satisfies the Statute. The Statute of Frauds does not bar reformation in such a case. See Illustration 1. The court will similarly reform a writing that is a mere memorandum and not an integrated agreement before determining whether it satisfies the Statute. See Illustration 2. Reformation is also available where the parties have by mistake omitted an essential term, as distinguished from stating it incorrectly. No meaningful distinction can be drawn in this respect between errors of omission and those of commission. See Illustration 3. If reformation is to be an appropriate remedy in the case of omission, however, the failure of the writing to contain the omitted term must, under the rule stated in § 155, be the result of mistake of both parties as to its contents; they must have believed that the writing contained the term. Reformation will not be granted where the parties simply failed to include a required term in the writing and one party, having discovered the failure, later seeks to reform it so that it will satisfy the Statute. The Statute is neither a basis for denying nor one for granting reformation. See Illustration 4. The rule stated in this Section applies to reformation under the rules stated in § 166 as well as under the rules stated in this Chapter.

Illustrations

1. A agrees to sell and B to buy a tract of land for $100,000. In preparing a writing that the parties intend to be a completely integrated agreement, A's secretary erroneously types "$10,000" instead of "$100,000," and both A and B sign without noticing the error. Although the agreement is within the Statute of Frauds (§ 125), at the request of either A or B, the court will reform the writing to read "$100,000."

2. The facts being otherwise as stated in Illustration 1, the parties do not intend the writing to be an integrated agreement but a mere memorandum evidencing the agreement. Although the agreement is within the Statute of Frauds (§ 125), at the request of either A or B, the court will reform the writing to read "$100,000" before determining whether the statute is satisfied.

3. The facts being otherwise as stated in Illustration 1, instead of typing "$10,000" by mistake, the secretary erroneously omits an entire line of the agreement so that no price is stated, and both A and B sign without noticing the error. Although the agreement is within the Statute of Frauds (§ 125), at the request of either A or B, the court will reform the writing to include the omitted line containing the agreed price of $100,000 before determining whether the Statute is satisfied.

4. A agrees to sell and B to buy a tract of land for $100,000. They prepare and sign a document that does not, as they both realize, contain the price, although neither party is aware of the legal consequences of this omission. Because, apart from the Statute of Frauds, reformation would not otherwise be appropriate, a court will not, at the request of either A or B, reform the writing to include the price.

§ 157. Effect of Fault of Party Seeking Relief.

A mistaken party's fault in failing to know or discover the facts before making the contract does not bar him from avoidance or reformation under the rules stated in this Chapter, unless his fault amounts to a failure to act in good faith and in accordance with reasonable standards of fair dealing.

Comment

a. Rationale. The mere fact that a mistaken party could have avoided the mistake by the exercise of reasonable care does not preclude either avoidance (§§ 152, 153) or reformation (§ 155). Indeed, since a party can often avoid a mistake by the exercise of such care, the availability of relief would be severely circumscribed if he were to be barred by his negligence. Nevertheless, in extreme cases the mistaken party's fault is a proper ground for denying him relief for a mistake that he otherwise could have avoided. Although the critical degree of fault is sometimes described as "gross" negligence, that term is not well defined and is avoided in this Section as it is in the Restatement, Second, of Torts. Instead, the rule is stated in terms of good faith and fair dealing. The general duty of good faith and fair dealing, imposed under the rule stated in § 205, extends only to the performance and enforcement of a contract and does not apply to the negotiation stage prior to the formation of the contract. See Comment c to § 205. Therefore, a failure to act in good faith and in accordance with reasonable standards of fair dealing during pre-contractual negotiations does not amount to a breach. Nevertheless, under the rule stated in this Section, the failure bars a mistaken party from relief based on a mistake that otherwise would not have been made. During the negotiation stage each party is held to a degree of responsibility appropriate to the justifiable expectations of the other. The terms "good faith" and "fair dealing" are used, in this context, in much the same sense as in § 205 and Uniform Commercial Code [§ 1–304].

Illustrations

1. The facts being otherwise as stated in Illustration 1 to § 153, A's mistake is caused by his failure to exercise reasonable care in totalling and verifying his figures. A's negligence does not amount to a failure to act in good faith and in accordance with reasonable standards of fair dealing, and he is not precluded from avoiding the contract.

2. The facts being otherwise as stated in Illustration 1 to § 153 B, on finding that A's bid is the lowest, asks A to check his figures to make certain that there has been no mistake. A states that he has done so although he has not and although such a check would have revealed his mistake. B then accepts A's bid. A's conduct amounts to a failure to act in good faith and in accordance with reasonable standards of fair dealing, and he cannot avoid the contract.

b. Failure to read writing. Generally, one who assents to a writing is presumed to know its contents and cannot escape being bound by its terms merely by contending that he did not read them; his assent is deemed to cover unknown as well as known terms. See Comment b to § 23; Comment b to § 211. But see the special rule of § 211(3) for the case of standardized agreements. The exceptional rule stated in the present Section with regard to reformation has no application to the common case in which the term in question was not the subject of prior negotiations. It only affects cases that come within the scope of § 155, under which there must have been an agreement that preceded the writing. In such a case, a party's negligence in failing to read the writing does not preclude reformation if the writing does not correctly express the prior agreement. See Illustration 3. Where there was no prior agreement, however, this Section does not apply because reformation is not available under § 155. See Illustration 4.

Illustrations

3. The facts being otherwise as stated in Illustration 1 to § 155, neither A nor B reads the writing before signing it, although the omission would be obvious to either if he read it. Neither A's nor

B's conduct amounts to a failure to act in good faith and in accordance with reasonable standards of fair dealing, and neither A nor B is precluded from obtaining a decree reforming the writing.

4. A mails B a written offer to sell B a tract of land for $100,000, with a provision that B will assume an existing mortgage of $50,000. B fails to read all of the terms of A's offer and sends his acceptance without knowing of the provision for assumption of the mortgage. B is bound by the provision for assumption. Since B cannot obtain a decree of reformation under the rule stated in § 155, this Section does not apply.

§ 158. Relief Including Restitution.

(1) In any case governed by the rules stated in this Chapter, either party may have a claim for relief including restitution under the rules stated in §§ 240 and 376.

(2) In any case governed by the rules stated in this Chapter, if those rules together with the rules stated in Chapter 16 will not avoid injustice, the court may grant relief on such terms as justice requires including protection of the parties' reliance interests.

Comment

a. Scope. A court may use several techniques to adjust the rights of the parties after discovery of a mistake. Subsection (1) speaks to claims for relief such as that provided by the rule on part performances as agreed equivalents stated in § 240 and those on restitution and other relief stated in Chapter 16. Subsection (2) speaks to supplying a term to avoid injustice. See the analogous rule stated in § 272.

b. Relief including restitution. Avoidance of a contract ideally involves a reversal of any steps that the parties may have taken by way of performance, so that each party returns such benefit as he may have received. This is not, however, possible in all cases. Occasionally a party who has performed may be entitled to recover on the contract for the part that he has performed under the rule on part performances as agreed equivalents (§ 240). Even where this is not so, it may be appropriate to permit avoidance coupled with a money claim for restitution to the extent that one party's performance has benefited the other. Such claims are governed by the rules stated in §§ 370–77. A party may also have a claim that goes beyond mere restitution and includes elements of reliance by the claimant. See, e.g., Illustration 8 to § 153.

c. Supplying a term to avoid injustice. Under the rule stated in § 204, when the parties have not agreed with respect to a term that is essential to a determination of their rights and duties, the court will supply a term that is reasonable in the circumstances. Ordinarily the rules stated in this Chapter, coupled with those stated in Chapter 16, will be adequate to allow the court to arrive at a just result. See Subsection (1). If, however, these rules will not suffice to avoid injustice, the court may supply a term just as it may in cases of impracticability of performance and frustration of purpose. See § 272(2) and Comment c to that section. Here, as there, a particularly significant application occurs when the just solution is to "sever" the agreement and require that some unexecuted part of it be performed on both sides, rather than to relieve both parties of all their duties. The situation differs from that envisioned in § 240, under which the court merely allows recovery at the contract rate for performance that has already been rendered. The question under this Section is whether the court can salvage a part of the agreement that is still executory on both sides. See Illustration 1.

Sometimes the party who is not adversely affected by a mistake can, by assenting to a modification of the contract, eliminate the effect of the mistake on the agreed exchange. He should generally be allowed to do so and thereby to preclude avoidance by the party who would otherwise be adversely affected. A court may, under Subsection (2), grant the party who has not been adversely affected what is, in effect, an option to enforce the contract on new terms. See Illustration 2.

The Court may also exercise its discretion under Subsection (2) where both parties have been responsible for the mistake. It may do so, for example, where a mistake of one party resulted both from his failure to act in good faith and in accordance with reasonable standards of fair dealing (§ 157) and from the fault of the other party (§ 153(b)). See Comment f to § 153. Furthermore, for the sake of simplicity, the rules stated in this Chapter have been formulated in terms of the typical contract based on an exchange of consideration by two parties, and it does not, therefore, deal exhaustively with problems of mistake involving several parties (§ 9) including intended beneficiaries (§ 302), promises enforceable because of reliance (§ 90), promises enforceable because under seal (§ 95), and other less typical situations. In such cases, the court will apply rules analogous to those stated in this Chapter. See Comments b, d, and e to § 155. The situations dealt with in Subsection (2) are to be distinguished from those envisioned by § 155, where a writing is reformed to carry out the intentions of the parties.

Illustrations

1. A contracts to sell and B to buy a tract of land, described in the contract as containing 100 acres, at a price of $100,000, calculated from the acreage at $1,000 an acre. In fact the tract contains only 90 acres. Under the rule stated in § 152, the contract would be voidable by B. If, however, the court decides that this rule will not avoid injustice, it is within the discretion of the court to grant relief on such terms as justice requires. The contract is not then voidable by B. See Illustration 11 to § 152.

2. The facts being otherwise as stated in Illustration 1, the tract in fact contains 110 acres. Under the rule stated in § 152, the contract would be voidable by A. If, however, the court decides that this rule will not avoid injustice, it is within the discretion of the court to grant relief on such terms as justice requires. Compare Illustration 2 to § 152.

3. A sends B two different offers of a contract, one with an option for renewal by A and one without such an option. B signs the one with an option, believing that it is the other one. Under the rule stated in § 153, if the court found that enforcement of the contract would be unconscionable, the contract would be voidable by B. If, however, the court decides that this rule will not avoid injustice, it may supply a term, if reasonable, under which B is entitled to avoid the contract only if he accepts the other offer.

CHAPTER 7

MISREPRESENTATION, DURESS AND UNDUE INFLUENCE

TOPIC 1. MISREPRESENTATION

§ 159. Misrepresentation Defined.

A misrepresentation is an assertion that is not in accord with the facts.

Comment

a. Nature of the assertion. A misrepresentation, being a false assertion of fact, commonly takes the form of spoken or written words. Whether a statement is false depends on the meaning of the words in all the circumstances, including what may fairly be inferred from them. An assertion may also be inferred from conduct other than words. Concealment or even non-disclosure may have the effect of a misrepresentation under the rules stated in §§ 160 and 161. Whether a misrepresentation is fraudulent is determined by the rule stated in § 162(1). However, an assertion need not be fraudulent to be a misrepresentation. Thus a statement intended to be truthful may be a misrepresentation because of ignorance or carelessness, as when the word "not" is inadvertently omitted or when inaccurate language is used. But a misrepresentation that is not fraudulent has no consequences under this Chapter unless it is material. Whether an assertion is material is determined by the rule stated in § 162(2). The consequences of a misrepresentation are dealt with in §§ 163, 164 and 166.

Illustrations

1. A, seeking to induce B to make a contract to buy a used car, turns the odometer back from 60,000 to 18,000 miles. B makes the contract. A's conduct in setting the odometer is a misrepresentation. Whether the contract is voidable by B is determined by the rule stated in § 164.

2. A, seeking to induce B to make a contract to lease a particular generator, writes B a letter with the intention of describing its output correctly as "1200 kilowatts." Because of an error of A's typist, unnoticed by A, the letter states that the output of the generator is "2100 kilowatts." B makes the contract. A's statement is a misrepresentation. Whether the contract is voidable by B is determined by the rule stated in § 164.

b. Half-truths. A statement may be true with respect to the facts stated, but may fail to include qualifying matter necessary to prevent the implication of an assertion that is false with respect to other facts. For example, a true statement that an event has recently occurred may carry the false implication that the situation has not changed since its occurrence. Such a half-truth may be as misleading as an assertion that is wholly false.

Illustrations

3. A, seeking to induce B to make a contract to buy land, tells B that his title to the land has been upheld in a court decision. A knows that the decision has been appealed but does not tell this to B. B makes the contract. A's statement omits matter necessary to prevent the implied assertion that A's title is clearly established, and this assertion is a misrepresentation. Whether the contract is voidable by B is determined by the rule stated in § 164.

4. A, seeking to induce B to make a contract to buy an apartment house, tells B that the apartments are all rented to tenants at $200 a month. A knows that the rent of $200 has not been approved by the local rent control authorities and that without this approval it is illegal but does not tell this to B. B makes the contract. A's statement omits matter needed to prevent the implied assertion that the rent is legal, and this assertion is a misrepresentation (see § 170). Whether the contract is voidable by B is determined by the rules stated in § 164.

c. Meaning of "fact." An assertion must relate to something that is a fact at the time the assertion is made in order to be a misrepresentation. Such facts include past events as well as present circumstances but do not include future events. An assertion limited to future events (see § 2), may be a basis of liability for breach of contract, but not of relief for misrepresentation. However, a promise or a prediction of future events may by implication involve an assertion that facts exist from which the promised or predicted consequences will follow, which may be a misrepresentation as to those facts. Thus, from a statement that a particular machine will attain a specified level of performance when it is used, it may be inferred that its present design and condition make it capable of such a level. Such an inference may be drawn even if the statement is not legally binding as a promise.

Illustrations

5. A, seeking to induce B to make a contract to buy land, promises B to build an expensive house on an adjoining tract. A knows that he neither owns nor has such an interest in the tract that he can perform the promise, although he hopes to perform it. B makes the contract. A's promise implies an assertion that he owns the tract or has such an interest in the adjoining tract that he can perform his promise, and this assertion is a misrepresentation. Whether the contract is voidable by B is determined by the rule stated in § 164.

6. A, seeking to induce B to buy a furnace, tells B that it will give a stated amount of heat while consuming only a stated amount of fuel. A knows that the furnace is not capable of such efficiency. B makes the contract. A's statement implies an assertion that the furnace has an existing capability of such efficiency, and this assertion is a misrepresentation. Whether the contract is voidable by B is determined by the rule stated in § 164.

d. State of mind as a fact. A person's state of mind is a fact, and an assertion as to one's opinion or intention, including an intention to perform a promise, is a misrepresentation if the state of mind is other than as asserted. The extent to which the recipient is justified in relying on an assertion of opinion or intention is dealt with in §§ 168, 169 and 171.

§ 160. When Action Is Equivalent to an Assertion (Concealment).

Action intended or known to be likely to prevent another from learning a fact is equivalent to an assertion that the fact does not exist.

Comment

a. Scope. Concealment is an affirmative act intended or known to be likely to keep another from learning of a fact of which he would otherwise have learned. Such affirmative action is always equivalent to a misrepresentation and has any effect that a misrepresentation would have under the rules stated in §§ 163, 164 and 166. The rule stated in the following section applies to non-disclosure, where one person simply fails to inform another of a fact relating to the transaction. Non-disclosure is equivalent to a misrepresentation only in the circumstances enumerated in that section.

b. Common situations. The rule stated in this Section is commonly applied in two situations, although it is not limited to them. In the first, a party actively hides something from the other, as when the seller of a building paints over a defect. See Illustration 1. In such a case his conduct has the same effect as an assertion that the defect does not exist, and it is therefore a misrepresentation. Similarly, if the offeror reads a written offer to the offeree and omits a portion of it, his conduct has the same effect as an assertion that the omitted portion is not contained in the writing and is therefore a misrepresentation. In the second situation, a party prevents the other from making an investigation that would have disclosed a defect. An analogous situation arises where a party frustrates an investigation made by the other, for example by sending him in search of information where it cannot be found. Even a false denial of knowledge by a party who has possession of the facts may amount to a misrepresentation as to the facts that he knows, just as if he had actually misstated them, if its effect on the other is to lead him to believe that the facts do not exist or cannot be discovered. Action may be considered as likely to prevent another from learning of a fact even though it does not make it impossible to learn of it.

Illustrations

1. A, seeking to induce B to make a contract to buy his house, paints the basement floor in order to prevent B from discovering that the foundation is cracked. B is prevented from discovering the defect and makes the contract. The concealment is equivalent to an assertion that the foundation is not cracked, and this assertion is a misrepresentation. Whether the contract is voidable by B is determined by the rule stated in § 164.

2. A, seeking to induce B to make a contract to buy his house, convinces C, who, as A knows, is about to tell B that the foundation is cracked, to say nothing to B about the foundation. B is prevented from discovering the defect and makes the contract. A's conduct is equivalent to an assertion that the foundation is not cracked, and this assertion is a misrepresentation. Whether the contract is voidable by B is determined by the rule stated in § 164.

§ 161. When Non-Disclosure Is Equivalent to an Assertion.

A person's non-disclosure of a fact known to him is equivalent to an assertion that the fact does not exist in the following cases only:

(a) where he knows that disclosure of the fact is necessary to prevent some previous assertion from being a misrepresentation or from being fraudulent or material.

(b) where he knows that disclosure of the fact would correct a mistake of the other party as to a basic assumption on which that party is making the contract and if non-disclosure of the fact amounts to a failure to act in good faith and in accordance with reasonable standards of fair dealing.

(c) where he knows that disclosure of the fact would correct a mistake of the other party as to the contents or effect of a writing, evidencing or embodying an agreement in whole or in part.

(d) where the other person is entitled to know the fact because of a relation of trust and confidence between them.

Comment

a. Concealment distinguished. Like concealment, non-disclosure of a fact may be equivalent to a misrepresentation. Concealment necessarily involves an element of non-disclosure, but it is the act of preventing another from learning of a fact that is significant and this act is always equivalent to a misrepresentation (§ 160). Non-disclosure without concealment is equivalent to a misrepresentation only in special situations. A party making a contract is not expected to tell all that he knows to the other party, even if he knows that the other party lacks knowledge on some aspects of the transaction. His nondisclosure, as such, has no legal effect except in the situations enumerated in this Section. He may not, of course, tell half-truths and his assertion of only some of the facts without the inclusion of such additional matters as he knows or believes to be necessary to prevent it from being misleading is itself a misrepresentation.... In contrast to the rule applicable to liability in tort for misrepresentation, it is not enough, where disclosure is expected, merely to make reasonable efforts to disclose the relevant facts. Actual disclosure is required. Compare Restatement, Second, Torts § 551, Comment d.

b. Fraudulent or material. In order to make the contract voidable under the rule stated in § 164(1), the non-disclosure must be either fraudulent or material. The notion of disclosure necessarily implies that the fact in question is known to the person expected to disclose it. But the failure to disclose the fact may be unintentional, as when one forgets to disclose a known fact, and it is then equivalent to an innocent misrepresentation. Furthermore, one is expected to disclose only such facts as he knows or has reason to know will influence the other in determining his course of action. See § 162(2). Therefore, he need not disclose facts that the ordinary person would regard as unimportant unless he knows of some peculiarity of the other person that is likely to lead him to attach importance to them. There is, however, no such requirement of materiality if it can be shown that the non-disclosure was actually fraudulent. If a fact is intentionally withheld for the purpose of inducing action, this is equivalent to a fraudulent misrepresentation.

c. Failure to correct. One who has made an assertion that is neither a fraudulent nor a material misrepresentation may subsequently acquire knowledge that bears significantly on his earlier assertion. He is expected to speak up and correct the earlier assertion in three cases. First, if his assertion was not a misrepresentation because it was true, he may later learn that it is no longer true. . . . Second, his assertion may have been a misrepresentation but may not have been fraudulent. If this was because he believed that it was true, he may later learn that it was not true. . . . Third, if his assertion was a misrepresentation but was not material because he had no reason to know of the other's special characteristics that made reliance likely, he may later learn of such characteristics. If a person fails to correct his earlier assertion in these situations, the result is the same as it would have been had he had his newly acquired knowledge at the time he made the assertion. The rule stated in Clause (a), like that stated in Clause (d), extends to non-disclosure by persons who are not parties to the transaction.

Illustrations

1. A makes to B, a credit rating company, a true statement of his financial condition, intending that its substance be published to B's subscribers. B summarizes the information and transmits the summary to C, a subscriber. Shortly thereafter, A's financial condition becomes seriously impaired, but he does not disclose this to B. C makes a contract to lend money to A. A's non-disclosure is equivalent to an assertion that his financial condition is not seriously impaired, and this assertion is a misrepresentation. Whether the contract is voidable by B is determined by the rule stated in § 164.

2. A, seeking to induce B to make a contract to buy a thoroughbred mare, tells B that the mare is in foal to a well-known stallion. Unknown to A, the mare has miscarried. A learns of the miscarriage but does not disclose it to B. B makes the contract. A's non-disclosure is equivalent to an assertion that the mare has not miscarried, and this assertion is a misrepresentation. Whether the contract is voidable by B is determined by the rule stated in § 164.

A, in casual conversation with B, tells B that a tract of land owned by A contains thirty acres. A knows that i3. t contains only twenty-nine acres but misstates its area because he does not regard the figure as important. A's statement is not fraudulent because it is not made with the intention of inducing B to buy the land (§ 162(1)). B later offers to buy the tract from A. A does not disclose its true area to B, for fear that B will not buy it, and accepts B's offer. A's non-disclosure is equivalent to a new assertion that the tract contains thirty acres, and this assertion is a fraudulent misrepresentation (§ 162(1)). Whether the contract is voidable by B is determined by the rule stated in § 164.

d. Known mistake as to a basic assumption. In many situations, if one party knows that the other is mistaken as to a basic assumption, he is expected to disclose the fact that would correct the mistake. A seller of real or personal property is, for example, ordinarily expected to disclose a known latent defect of quality or title that is of such a character as would probably prevent the buyer from buying at the contract price. An owner is ordinarily expected to disclose a known error in a bid that he has received from a contractor. See Comment e to § 153. The mistake must be as to a basic assumption, as is also required by the rules on mistake stated in § 152 (see Illustrations 4, 5 and 6) and § 153 (see Illustrations 8 and 9). The rule stated in Clause (b), is, however, broader than these rules for mistake because it does not require a showing of a material effect on the agreed exchange and is not affected by the fact that the party seeking relief bears the risk of the mistake (§ 154). Nevertheless, a party need not correct all mistakes of the other and is expected only to act in good faith and in accordance with reasonable standards of fair dealing, as reflected in prevailing business ethics. A party may, therefore, reasonably expect the other to take normal steps to inform himself and to draw his own conclusions. If the other is indolent, inexperienced or ignorant, or if his judgment is bad or he lacks access to adequate information, his adversary is not generally expected to compensate for these deficiencies. A buyer of property, for example, is not ordinarily expected to disclose circumstances that make the property more valuable than the seller supposes. . . . In contrast to the rules stated in Clauses (a) and (d), that stated in Clause (b) is limited to non-disclosure by a party to the transaction. Actual knowledge is required for the application of the rule stated in Clause (b). The case of a party who does not know but has reason to know of a mistake is governed by the rule stated in § 153(b). As to knowledge in the case of an organization, see the analogous rule in Uniform Commercial Code § 1–201(27).

Illustrations

4. A, seeking to induce B to make a contract to buy land, knows that B does not know that the land has been filled with debris and covered but does not disclose this to B. B makes the contract. A's

non-disclosure is equivalent to an assertion that the land has not been filled with debris and covered, and this assertion is a misrepresentation. Whether the contract is voidable by B is determined by the rule stated in § 164.

5. A, seeking to induce B to make a contract to buy A's house, knows that B does not know that the house is riddled with termites but does not disclose this to B. B makes the contract. A's non-disclosure is equivalent to an assertion that the house is not riddled with termites, and this assertion is a misrepresentation. Whether the contract is voidable by B is determined by the rule stated in § 164.

6. A, seeking to induce B to make a contract to buy a food-processing business, knows that B does not know that the health department has given repeated warnings that a necessary license will not be renewed unless expensive improvements are made but does not disclose this to B. B makes the contract. A's non-disclosure is equivalent to an assertion that no warnings have been given by the health department, and this assertion is a misrepresentation. Whether the contract is voidable by B is determined by the rule stated in § 164.

7. A, seeking to induce B to make a contract to sell land, knows that B does not know that the land has appreciably increased in value because of a proposed shopping center but does not disclose this to B. B makes the contract. Since B's mistake is not one as to a basic assumption ... A's non-disclosure is not equivalent to an assertion that the value of the land has not appreciably increased. ... The contract is not voidable by B.

8. In response to B's invitation for bids on the construction of a building according to stated specifications, A submits an offer to do the work for $150,000. A believes that this is the total of a column of figures, but he has made an error by inadvertently omitting a $5,000 item, and in fact the total is $155,000. B knows this but accepts A's bid without disclosing it. B's non-disclosure is equivalent to an assertion that no error has been made in the total, and this assertion is a misrepresentation. Whether the contract is voidable by A is determined by the rule stated in § 164. See Illustrations 1 and 2 to § 153. See also Comment a to § 167.

9. In answer to an inquiry from "J. B. Smith Company," A offers to sell goods for cash on delivery. A mistakenly believes that the offeree is John B. Smith, who has an established business of good repute, but in fact it is a business run by his son, with whom A has refused to deal because of previous disputes. The son learns of A's mistake but accepts A's offer without disclosing his identity. The son's non-disclosure is equivalent to an assertion that the business is run by the father, and this assertion is a misrepresentation. Whether the contract is voidable by A is determined by the rule stated in § 164. See Illustration 11 to § 153. See also Comment a to § 167.

10. A, seeking to induce B to make a contract to sell A land, learns from government surveys that the land contains valuable mineral deposits and knows that B does not know this, but does not disclose this to B. B makes the contract. A's non-disclosure does not amount to a failure to act in good faith and in accordance with reasonable standards of fair dealing and is therefore not equivalent to an assertion that the land does not contain valuable mineral deposits. The contract is not voidable by B.

11. The facts being otherwise as stated in Illustration 10, A learns of the valuable mineral deposits from trespassing on B's land and not from government surveys. A's non-disclosure is equivalent to an assertion that the land does not contain valuable mineral deposits, and this assertion is a misrepresentation. Whether the contract is voidable by B is determined by the rule stated in § 164.

e. Known mistake as to a writing. One party cannot hold the other to a writing if he knew that the other was mistaken as to its contents or as to its legal effect. He is expected to correct such mistakes of the other party and his failure to do so is equivalent to a misrepresentation, which may be grounds either for avoidance under § 164 or for reformation under § 166. (Compare the rule on reformation for mistake of both parties as to their written expression stated in § 155. See Comment a to § 155.) The failure of a party to use care in reading the writing so as to discover the mistake may not preclude such relief (§ 172). In the case of standardized agreements, these rules supplement that of § 211(3), which applies, regardless of actual knowledge, if there is reason to believe that the other party would not manifest assent if he knew that the writing contained a particular term. Like the rule stated in Clause (b), that stated in Clause (c) requires actual knowledge and is limited to non-disclosure by a party to the transaction. See Comment d.

Illustration

12. A, seeking to induce B to make a contract to sell a tract of land to A for $100,000, makes a written offer to B. A knows that B mistakenly thinks that the offer contains a provision under which A assumes an existing mortgage, and he knows that it does not contain such a provision but does not disclose this to B. B signs the writing, which is an integrated agreement. A's non-disclosure is equivalent to an assertion that the writing contains such a provision, and this assertion is a misrepresentation. Whether the contract is voidable by B is determined by the rule stated in § 164. Whether, at the request of B, the court will decree that the writing be reformed to add the provision for assumption is determined by the rule stated in § 166. See Illustration 4 to § 166.

f. Relation of trust and confidence. The rule stated in Clause (d) supplements that stated in § 173 with respect to contracts between parties in a fiduciary relation. Where the latter rule applies, as in the case of a trustee, an agent, a guardian, or an executor or administrator, its more stringent requirements govern. Even where a party is not, strictly speaking, a fiduciary, he may stand in such a relation of trust and confidence to the other as to give the other the right to expect disclosure. Such a relationship normally exists between members of the same family and may arise, in other situations as, for example, between physician and patient. In addition, some types of contracts, such as those of suretyship or guaranty, marine insurance and joint adventure, are recognized as creating in themselves confidential relations and hence as requiring the utmost good faith and full and fair disclosure. As to contracts of suretyship, see Restatement of Security § 124.

The rule stated in Clause (d) is not limited to cases in which the non-disclosure is by a party to the transaction. In contrast, the rule stated in § 173 applies only to non-disclosure by a fiduciary who is a party. Therefore the rule stated in Clause (d) covers the residual case of a fiduciary who is not a party. As to the duty of a trustee to disclose to his beneficiary matters important for him to know in dealing with others, see Restatement, Second, Trusts § 173, Comment d. As to the duty of an agent to disclose to his principal matters important for him to know in dealing with others, see Restatement, Second, Agency § 381.

Illustration

13. A, who is experienced in business, has raised B, a young man, in his household, and B has habitually followed his advice, although A is neither his parent nor his guardian. A, seeking to induce B to make a contract to sell land to A, knows that the land has appreciably increased in value because of a planned shopping center but does not disclose this to B. B makes the contract. A's non-disclosure is equivalent to an assertion that the value of the land has not appreciably increased, and this assertion is a misrepresentation. Whether the contract is voidable by B is determined by the rule stated in § 164. See Illustration 7.

§ 162. When a Misrepresentation Is Fraudulent or Material.

(1) A misrepresentation is fraudulent if the maker intends his assertion to induce a party to manifest his assent and the maker

    (a) knows or believes that the assertion is not in accord with the facts, or

    (b) does not have the confidence that he states or implies in the truth of the assertion, or

    (c) knows that he does not have the basis that he states or implies for the assertion.

(2) A misrepresentation is material if it would be likely to induce a reasonable person to manifest his assent, or if the maker knows that it would be likely to induce the recipient to do so.

Comment

a. Meaning of "fraudulent." The word "fraudulent" is used in various senses in the law. In order that a misrepresentation be fraudulent within the meaning of this Section, it must not only be consciously false but must also be intended to mislead another. Compare Restatement, Second, Torts § 526. Consequences are intended if a person either acts with the desire to cause them or acts believing that they are substantially certain to result. See Restatement, Second, Torts § 8A. Thus one who believes that another is substantially certain to be misled as a result of a misrepresentation intends to mislead even though he may not desire to do so. See Comment c to Restatement, Second, Torts § 531. If the maker knows that his statement is misleading because it is subject to two interpretations, it is fraudulent if he makes it with the intention that it be understood in the false sense. See Restatement, Second, Torts § 527. If the recipient continues to rely on a misrepresentation made in an earlier transaction, the misrepresentation is fraudulent if the maker knows that the recipient is still relying. See Restatement, Second, Torts § 535. Furthermore, the maker need not have a particular person in mind as the recipient at the time the misrepresentation is made. He may merely have reason to expect that it will reach any of a class of persons, of which the recipient is a member, as in the case of the merchant who furnishes information to a credit agency. See Illustration 1. In order that a fraudulent representation have legal effect within this Chapter, it need not be material. Compare §§ 163, 164, 166 with Restatement, Second, Torts § 538. It is, however, essential that it actually induce assent. See §§ 163, 164, 166.

Illustration

1. A makes to B, a credit rating company, a statement of his financial condition that he knows is untrue, intending that its substance be published to B's subscribers. B summarizes the information and transmits the summary to C, a subscriber. C is thereby induced to make a contract to lend money to A. A's statement is a fraudulent misrepresentation and the contract is voidable by C under the rule stated in § 164.

b. *"Scienter."* The word "scienter" is often used by courts to refer to the requirement that the maker know of the untrue character of his assertion. Subsection (1) states three ways in which this requirement can be met. First, it is clearly met if the maker knows the fact to be otherwise than as stated. However, knowledge of falsity is not essential, and it is sufficient under the rule stated in Clause (a) if he believes the assertion to be false. It will not suffice merely to show that the misrepresentation is one that a person of ordinary care and intelligence would have recognized as false, although this is evidence from which his belief in its falsity may be inferred. Second, the requirement is met under the rule stated in Clause (b), if the maker, lacking confidence in the truth of his assertion that he states or implies, nevertheless chooses to make it as one of his own knowledge rather than one merely of his opinion. This is so when he is conscious that he has only a belief in its truth and recognizes that there is some chance that it may not be true. This conclusion is often expressed by saying that the misrepresentation has been made without belief in its truth or that it has been made recklessly, without regard to whether it is true or false. Third, the requirement is met under the rule stated in Clause (c), if the maker has said or implied that the assertion is made on some particular basis, such as his personal knowledge or his personal investigation, when it is not so made. This is so even though the maker is honestly convinced of its truth from hearsay or other source that he believes is reliable.

Illustration

2. A, seeking to induce B to make a contract to buy his house, tells B that the plumbing is of pipe of a specified quality. A does not know the quality of the pipe, and it is not of the specified quality. B is induced by A's statement to make the contract. The statement is a fraudulent misrepresentation, both because A does not have the confidence that he implies in its truth, and because he knows that he does not have the basis for it that he implies. The contract is voidable by B under the rule stated in § 164.

c. *Meaning of "material."* Although a fraudulent misrepresentation need not be material in order to entitle the recipient to relief under the rule stated in § 164, a non-fraudulent misrepresentation will not entitle him to relief unless it is material. The materiality of a misrepresentation is determined from the viewpoint of the maker, while the justification of reliance is determined from the viewpoint of the recipient. (Contrast also the concept of a "material" failure to perform. See § 241.) The requirement of materiality may be met in either of two ways. First, a misrepresentation is material if it would be likely to induce a reasonable person to manifest his assent. Second, it is material if the maker knows that for some special reason it is likely to induce the particular recipient to manifest his assent. There may be personal considerations that the recipient regards as important even though they would not be expected to affect others in his situation, and if the maker is aware of this the misrepresentation may be material even though it would not be expected to induce a reasonable person to make the proposed contract. One who preys upon another's known idiosyncrasies cannot complain if the contract is held voidable when he succeeds in what he is endeavoring to accomplish. Cf. Restatement, Second, Torts § 538. Although a nonfraudulent misrepresentation that is not material does not make the contract voidable under the rules stated in this Chapter, the recipient may have a claim to relief under other rules, such as those relating to breach of warranty. See Introductory Note to this Topic.

Illustrations

3. A, while negotiating with B for the sale of A's race horse, tells him that the horse has run a mile in a specified time. A is honestly mistaken, and, unknown to him, the horse has never come close to that time. B is induced by A's assertion to make a contract to buy the horse. A's statement, although not fraudulent, is a material misrepresentation, and the contract is voidable by B under the rule stated in § 164.

4. A, while negotiating with B for the sale of A's race horse, tells him that the horse was bred in a specified stable. A is honestly mistaken, and, unknown to him, it was bred in another stable of better reputation. The specified stable was, unknown to A, founded by B's grandfather, and B is therefore induced by A's assertion to make a contract to buy the horse. A's misrepresentation is neither fraudulent nor material, and the contract is not voidable by B.

5. The facts being otherwise as in Illustration 4, A knows that the named stable was founded by B's grandfather and that B would like to own a horse bred there. A's misrepresentation, although not fraudulent, is material, and the contract is voidable by B under the rule stated in § 164.

§ 163. When a Misrepresentation Prevents Formation of a Contract.

If a misrepresentation as to the character or essential terms of a proposed contract induces conduct that appears to be a manifestation of assent by one who neither knows nor has reasonable opportunity to know of the character or essential terms of the proposed contract, his conduct is not effective as a manifestation of assent.

Comment

a. Rationale. Under the general principle stated in § 19(2), a party's conduct is not effective as a manifestation of his assent unless he knows or has reason to know that the other party may infer from it that he assents. This Section involves an application of that principle where a misrepresentation goes to what is sometimes called the "factum" or the "execution" rather than merely the "inducement." If, because of a misrepresentation as to the character or essential terms of a proposed contract, a party does not know or have reasonable opportunity to know of its character or essential terms, then he neither knows nor has reason to know that the other party may infer from his conduct that he assents to that contract. In such a case there is no effective manifestation of assent and no contract at all. Compare § 174. This result only follows, however, if the misrepresentation relates to the very nature of the proposed contract itself and not merely to one of its nonessential terms. The party may believe that he is not assenting to any contract or that he is assenting to a contract entirely different from the proposed contract. The mere fact that a party is deceived as to the identity of the other party, as when a buyer of goods obtains credit by impersonating a person of means, does not bring the case within the present Section, unless it affects the very nature of the contract. See Uniform Commercial Code § 2–403(1)(a). It is immaterial under the rule stated in this Section whether the misrepresentation is made by a party to the transaction or by a third person. See Comment e to § 164.

Illustration

1. A, seeking to induce B to make a contract to sell him goods on credit, tells B that he is C, a well-known millionaire. B is induced by the statement to make the proposed contract with A. B's apparent manifestation of assent is effective. However, the contract is voidable by B under the rule stated in § 164(1). Contrast Illustrations 2 and 4.

b. Effect of fault. If the recipient had a reasonable opportunity to know the character or essential terms of the proposed contract, the rule stated in this Section does not apply, and his conduct is effective as a manifestation of assent. Compare § 172. The case then comes within § 164 on avoidance or § 166 on reformation. In deciding whether the recipient has had such an opportunity, less care will ordinarily be expected of him if he did not intend to assume a legal obligation at all than if he intended to assume a legal obligation, although one of a different nature.

Illustrations

2. A and B reach an understanding that they will execute a written contract containing terms on which they have agreed. It is properly prepared and is read by B, but A substitutes a writing containing essential terms that are different from those agreed upon and thereby induces B to sign it in the belief that it is the one he has read. B's apparent manifestation of assent is not effective.

3. A and B reach an understanding that they will execute a written contract containing terms on which they have agreed. A prepares a writing containing essential terms that are different from those agreed upon and induces B to sign it by telling him that it contains the terms agreed upon and that it is not necessary for him to read it. B's apparent manifestation of assent is effective if B had a reasonable opportunity to read the writing. However, the contract is voidable by B under the rule stated in § 164. See Illustration 3 to § 164. In the alternative, at the request of B, the court will decree that the writing be reformed to conform to their understanding under the rule stated in § 166. See Illustration 1 to § 166.

4. The facts being otherwise as stated in Illustration 3, B is blind and gets C to read the writing to him, but C, in collusion with A, reads it wrongly. B's apparent manifestation of assent is not effective.

c. "Void" rather than voidable. It is sometimes loosely said that, where the rule stated in this Section applies, there is a "void contract" as distinguished from a voidable one. See Comment a to § 7. This distinction has important consequences. For example, the recipient of a misrepresentation may be held to have ratified the contract if it is voidable but not if it is "void." Furthermore, a good faith purchaser may acquire good title to property if he takes it from one who obtained voidable title by misrepresentation but not if he takes it from one who obtained "void title" by misrepresentation.

§ 164. When a Misrepresentation Makes a Contract Voidable.

(1) If a party's manifestation of assent is induced by either a fraudulent or a material misrepresentation by the other party upon which the recipient is justified in relying, the contract is voidable by the recipient.

(2) If a party's manifestation of assent is induced by either a fraudulent or a material misrepresentation by one who is not a party to the transaction upon which the recipient is justified in relying, the contract is voidable by the recipient, unless the other party to the transaction in good faith and without reason to know of the misrepresentation either gives value or relies materially on the transaction.

Comment

a. Requirements. A misrepresentation may make a contract voidable under the rule stated in this Section, even though it does not prevent the formation of a contract under the rule stated in the previous section. Three requirements must be met in addition to the requirement that there must have been a misrepresentation. First, the misrepresentation must have been either fraudulent or material. See Comment b. Second, the misrepresentation must have induced the recipient to make the contract. See Comment c. Third, the recipient must have been justified in relying on the misrepresentation. See Comment d. Even if the contract is voidable, exercise of the power of avoidance is subject to the limitations stated in Chapter 16 on remedies.

b. Fraudulent and non-fraudulent misrepresentation. A representation need not be fraudulent in order to make a contract voidable under the rule stated in this Section. However, a non-fraudulent misrepresentation does not make the contract voidable unless it is material, while materiality is not essential in the case of a fraudulent misrepresentation. One who makes a non-fraudulent misrepresentation of a seemingly unimportant fact has no reason to suppose that his assertion will induce assent. But a fraudulent misrepresentation is directed to attaining that very end, and the maker cannot insist on his bargain if it is attained, however unexpectedly, as long as the additional requirements of inducement and justifiable reliance are met. See Illustration 1. Compare Restatement, Second, Torts § 538, which limits liability for fraudulent misrepresentation to cases in which the matter misrepresented is material.

Illustrations

1. A, seeking to induce B to make a contract to buy a tract of land at a price of $1,000 an acre, tells B that the tract contains 100 acres. A knows that it contains only 90 acres. B is induced by the statement to make the contract. Because the statement is a fraudulent misrepresentation (§ 162(1)), the contract is voidable by B, regardless of whether the misrepresentation is material.

2. The facts being otherwise as stated in Illustration 1, A is mistaken and does not know that the tract contains only 90 acres. Because the statement is not a fraudulent misrepresentation, the contract is voidable by B only if the misrepresentation is material (§ 162(2)).

3. A and B agree that A will buy a tract of land from B for $100,000 and will assume an existing mortgage of $50,000. In reducing the agreement to writing, A intentionally omits the provision for assumption but tells B that the writing correctly expresses their agreement. B does not notice the omission and is induced by A's statement to sign the writing. The misrepresentation is both fraudulent and material, and the contract is voidable by B. Compare Illustration 1 to § 166 and see Illustration 10 to § 161.

c. Inducement. No legal effect flows from either a non-fraudulent or a fraudulent misrepresentation unless it induces action by the recipient, that is, unless he manifests his assent to the contract in reliance on it. Whether a misrepresentation is an inducement is a question of fact governed by the rule stated in § 167. In general, the recipient of a misrepresentation need not show that he has actually been harmed by relying on it in order to avoid the contract. But see § 165.

d. Justification. A misrepresentation, even if relied upon, has no legal effect unless the recipient's reliance on it is justified. The most significant and troublesome applications of this principle occur in connection with assertions of opinion (§§ 168, 169), assertions as to matters of law (§ 170), assertions of intention (§ 171), and fault (§ 172). In other situations the requirement of justification is usually met unless, for example, the fact to which the misrepresentation relates is of only peripheral importance to the transaction or is one as to which the maker's assertion would not be expected to be taken seriously.

e. Misrepresentation by a third party. The rule stated in Subsection (2) makes a contract voidable for a misrepresentation by a third party, subject to the general principle of law that if an innocent person has in good faith and without notice given value or changed his position in reliance on the contract, it is not voidable on that ground. This is the same principle that protects an innocent person who purchases goods or commercial paper in good faith, without notice and for value from one who has obtained them from the original owner by a misrepresentation. See Uniform Commercial Code §§ 2–403(1), 3–305. In the cases that fall within Subsection (2), however, the innocent person deals directly with the recipient of the misrepresentation, which is made by one not a party to their contract. The contract is not voidable by the recipient if the innocent person gives value or relies materially on the transaction before learning or acquiring reason to know of the misrepresentation. The term "value" has the same meaning here as it does under Uniform Commercial Code § 1–201(44), and therefore the consideration given by the innocent party is value for this purpose. The rule does not protect a person who is responsible under the law of agency for the maker's misrepresentation. See Restatement, Second, Agency § 259. Assignees and intended beneficiaries, who derive their rights from a contract that is voidable for misrepresentation, take subject to the right of avoidance under §§ 309, 336. The rule stated in Subsection (2) does not preclude avoidance for mistake under the rules stated in Chapter 6.

Illustrations

4. A, who is not C's agent, induces B by a fraudulent misrepresentation to make a contract with C to sell land to C. C promises to pay the agreed price, not knowing or having reason to know of the fraudulent misrepresentation. Since C's promise to pay is value, the contract is not voidable by B. The contract would be voidable by B if C learned or acquired reason to know of the fraudulent misrepresentation before promising to pay the price.

5. A, who is not C's agent, induces B by a fraudulent misrepresentation to sign a pledge by which B promises C, a charitable corporation, to contribute a sum of money. C does not know or have reason to know of the fraudulent representation. B's promise, although binding under § 90(2), is

voidable by B. B's promise would not be voidable if C materially changed its position in reliance on B's promise before learning or acquiring reason to know of the fraudulent misrepresentation.

§ 165. Cure by Change of Circumstances.

If a contract is voidable because of a misrepresentation and, before notice of an intention to avoid the contract, the facts come into accord with the assertion, the contract is no longer voidable unless the recipient has been harmed by relying on the misrepresentation.

Comment

a. Rationale. In general, the recipient of a misrepresentation need not show that he has actually been harmed by relying on it in order to avoid the contract. If, however, the effect of misrepresentation has been cured because the facts have been brought or have otherwise come into accord with the assertion before he has notified the maker of his intention to avoid the contract, there is ordinarily little likelihood of harm. The rule stated in this Section precludes avoidance in such a case, unless the recipient shows that he has actually been harmed. It applies to fraudulent as well as to non-fraudulent misrepresentations.

Illustrations

1. A, seeking to induce B to make a contract to buy land, tells B that the land is unencumbered. A knows that the land is subject to a lien. B is induced by A's statement to make the proposed contract. A then removes the lien. If B has not been harmed by the misrepresentation, the contract is no longer voidable by B.

2. A, seeking to induce B to make a contract to buy land from C, tells B that he has authority from C to sell land. A knows that he has no such authority. B is induced by C's statement to make the proposed contract. C later ratifies A's sale of the land. If B has not been harmed by the misrepresentation, the contract is no longer voidable by B.

§ 166. When a Misrepresentation as to a Writing Justifies Reformation.

If a party's manifestation of assent is induced by the other party's fraudulent misrepresentation as to the contents or effect of a writing evidencing or embodying in whole or in part an agreement, the court at the request of the recipient may reform the writing to express the terms of the agreement as asserted,

  (a) if the recipient was justified in relying on the misrepresentation, and

  (b) except to the extent that rights of third parties such as good faith purchasers for value will be unfairly affected.

Comment

a. Scope. Reformation is more broadly available for fraudulent misrepresentation than for mistake. Compare § 155. Reformation for mistake is limited to the situation in which the parties, having already reached an agreement, later fail to express it correctly in a writing. That limitation, stated in § 155, applies to all cases where both parties are mistaken, including those where one of the mistaken parties has made a non-fraudulent misrepresentation as to the contents or effect of a writing. Where, however, only one party is mistaken and the other has fraudulently misrepresented the writing's contents or effect, reformation may be granted even though there was no prior agreement. Compare Comment a to § 155. The writing must be one that evidences or embodies, at least in part, the agreement of the parties. Otherwise it will not ordinarily have sufficient legal significance for its reformation to be necessary, and the dispute can be resolved simply in accordance with the general rules applicable to offer and acceptance. The rule stated in this Section also applies to the case where only one party is mistaken and the other, although aware of the mistake, says nothing to correct it. In that case his non-disclosure is equivalent to an assertion that the writing is as the other understands it to be (§ 161(c)). (Where only one party is mistaken and the other is not aware of the mistake, the rule stated in § 153, on mistake of only one party, applies.) The misrepresentation must, of course, be certain enough to permit a court to know how the writing should be reformed. Reformation is not precluded by the mere fact that the party who seeks it failed to exercise reasonable care in reading the writing, but his reliance on the misrepresentation must be justified and the right to reformation is therefore subject to the rule on fault stated in § 172. This Section, like § 155, only states the circumstances in which a court "may" grant reformation, and, since the remedy is equitable, a court has the discretion to withhold it, even if it would otherwise be appropriate, on grounds traditionally considered by courts of equity in exercising their discretion. See Comment d to § 155.

Illustrations

1. A and B agree that A will buy a tract of land from B for $100,000 and will assume an existing mortgage of $50,000. In reducing the agreement to writing, A intentionally omits the provision for assumption and tells B that the writing correctly expresses their agreement. B does not notice the omission and is induced by A's fraudulent misrepresentation to sign the writing, which is an integrated agreement. At the request of B, the court will reform the writing to add the provision for assumption. Compare Illustration 3 to § 164. See Illustration 1 to § 155.

2. A, seeking to induce B to make a contract to sell a tract of land to A for $100,000, makes a written offer to B and tells B that it includes a provision under which A assumes an existing mortgage. A knows that the writing does not contain such a provision. B does not notice the omission and is induced by A's fraudulent misrepresentation to sign the writing, which is an integrated agreement. At the request of B, the court will reform the writing to add the provision for assumption.

3. A, seeking to induce B to make a contract to sell a tract of land to A for $100,000, makes a written offer to B and tells B that the legal effect of a particular provision is that A assumes an existing mortgage. A, who is a lawyer, knows that this is not the legal effect of the provision. B does not realize that the legal effect of the provision is not as asserted and is induced by A's fraudulent misrepresentation to sign the writing, which is an integrated agreement. See § 170. At the request of B, the court will reform the writing to add the provision for assumption.

4. A, seeking to induce B to make a contract to sell a tract of land to A for $100,000, makes a written offer to B. A knows that B mistakenly thinks that the offer contains a provision under which A assumes an existing mortgage and that it does not contain such a provision, but does not disclose this to B for fear that B will not accept. B is induced by A's non-disclosure to sign the writing, which is an integrated agreement. A's non-disclosure is equivalent to an assertion that the writing contains such a provision (§ 161(e)) and amounts to a fraudulent misrepresentation. At the request of B, the court will reform the writing to add the provision for assumption. See Illustration 13 to § 161.

b. *Relation to other rules.* The rule stated in this Section applies only to misrepresentations as to the contents or effect of a writing. If the misrepresentation relates to some other fact, the contract may be voidable under § 164, but reformation is not appropriate. See also § 163. The availability of reformation based on a fraudulent misrepresentation does not, however, preclude the alternative of avoidance, and the recipient has a choice of remedies. See Illustration 12 to § 161 and compare Illustration 3 to § 164 with Illustration 1 to the present Section. This is in contrast to the rule for mutual mistake. See Introductory Note to Chapter 6 and Comment d to § 152. In some instances, however, the problem may be merely one of interpretation of the writing, so that neither reformation nor avoidance is appropriate. See § 20.

Illustration

5. A, seeking to induce B to make a contract to buy a tract of land at a price of $100,000, makes a written offer to B and tells B that the tract contains 100 acres. A knows that it contains only 90 acres. B is induced by A's fraudulent misrepresentation to sign the writing. The court will not, at the request of B, reform the writing because the mistake of the parties was not one as to the contents or effect of the writing. B's right to avoidance is governed by the rule stated in § 164(1). See Illustration 1 to § 164 and Illustration 5 to § 155.

c. *Parol evidence rule and Statute of Frauds.* The parol evidence rule does not preclude proof of a fraudulent misrepresentation to justify reformation. See § 214(d). Furthermore, if reformation of a writing is otherwise appropriate, it is not precluded by the fact that the contract is within the Statute of Frauds. See § 156.

d. Protection of innocent third parties. The right to reformation under the rule stated in this Section is subject to the rights of good faith purchasers for value and other third parties who have similarly relied on the finality of a consensual transaction in which they have acquired an interest in property. Such other third parties include those who have given value and come within the definition of "purchaser" in Uniform Commercial Code § 1–201(33), (32), notably mortgagees, pledgees and other holders of a security interest. Judgment creditors and trustees in bankruptcy are not included. This is the same exception as that under § 155 where third parties have intervened. See Comment f to § 155 and Illustrations 8 and 9 to that Section.

§ 167. When a Misrepresentation Is an Inducing Cause.

A misrepresentation induces a party's manifestation of assent if it substantially contributes to his decision to manifest his assent.

Comment

a. Scope. The rule stated in this Section determines whether a misrepresentation in fact induced a party's actual or apparent manifestation of assent, as required under §§ 163, 164 and 166. A misrepresentation is not a cause of a party's making a contract unless he relied on the misrepresentation in manifesting his assent. His reliance will usually consist of his acceptance, an affirmative act, but may also consist of his refraining from revoking an outstanding offer. See Illustrations 8 and 9 to § 161. It is not necessary that this reliance have been the sole or even the predominant factor in influencing his conduct. It is not even necessary that he would not have acted as he did had he not relied on the assertion. It is enough that the manifestation substantially contributed to his decision to make the contract. It is, therefore, immaterial that he may also have been influenced by other considerations. As to the effect of the recipient's fault, see § 172. The misrepresentation need not be made directly to the recipient but may be made to a third person for the purpose of having him transmit it, or its substance, to the recipient in order to induce action. See Illustration 1 to § 162.

Illustrations

1. A, seeking to induce B to make a contract to buy land, makes a fraudulent misrepresentation. Although he believes A's assertion, B wishes to confirm it and therefore inspects the land and inquires of third persons. B then makes the contract. The misrepresentation substantially contributes to his decision to make the contract, although he is also induced to do so by his investigation and inquiries. B's manifestation of assent is induced by the misrepresentation, and the contract is voidable by B.

2. A, seeking to induce B to make a contract to buy land, makes two statements to B about the land, one a true assertion and one a fraudulent misrepresentation. B makes the contract. The fraudulent misrepresentation substantially contributes to his decision to make the contract, although he is also induced to do so by the true assertion. B's manifestation of assent is induced by the misrepresentation, and the contract is voidable by B.

b. Criteria. Circumstantial evidence is often important in determining whether a misrepresentation has been an inducing cause. The materiality of the misrepresentation is a particularly significant factor in this determination. It is assumed, in the absence of facts showing the contrary, that the recipient attached importance to the truth of a misrepresentation if it was material, but not if it was immaterial. The extent of a party's investigation also bears on the question of causation. If he relies solely on his investigation and not on the misrepresentation, he is not entitled to relief. One who makes an investigation will often be taken to rely on it alone as to all facts disclosed to him in the course of it. On the other hand, if the fact is not one that the investigation disclosed or would have been likely to disclose, the recipient may still be relying on the misrepresentation as well as on the investigation. Particularly when the investigation produces results that tend to confirm the misrepresentation but are still somewhat inconclusive, it may be found that the recipient relied on both and that he attached importance to the truth of the misrepresentation in making the contract. A party who, having made a misrepresentation, intentionally frustrates the other's investigation of its truth, will be precluded from claiming that the other relied on the investigation to the exclusion of the misrepresentation. See Restatement, Second, Torts § 547(2).

Illustrations

3. A, seeking to induce B to make a contract to buy his race horse, tells him that the horse has run a mile in a specified time. A is honestly mistaken, and, unknown to him, the horse has never come close to that time. B makes the contract. Because A's misrepresentation is material, it will be assumed, in the absence of facts showing the contrary, that B attached importance to its truth in deciding to make the contract. The contract is therefore voidable by B. See Illustration 3 to § 162.

4. A, seeking to induce B to make a contract to buy his race horse, tells him that the horse was bred in a particular stable. A knows that it was bred in another stable. B makes the contract. If A's misrepresentation is not material, it will not be assumed that B attached importance to its truth in deciding to make the contract. Unless other evidence shows that B relied on the misrepresentation, the contract is not voidable by B. See Illustration 4 to § 162.

§ 168. Reliance on Assertions of Opinion.

(1) An assertion is one of opinion if it expresses only a belief, without certainty, as to the existence of a fact or expresses only a judgment as to quality, value, authenticity, or similar matters.

(2) If it is reasonable to do so, the recipient of an assertion of a person's opinion as to facts not disclosed and not otherwise known to the recipient may properly interpret it as an assertion

   (a) that the facts known to that person are not incompatible with his opinion, or

   (b) that he knows facts sufficient to justify him in forming it.

Comment

a. Knowledge and opinion. A statement of opinion is also a statement of fact because it states that a person has a particular state of mind concerning the matter to which his opinion relates. But it also implies that he does not have such definite information, that he is not certain enough of what he says, to make an assertion of his own knowledge as to that matter. It implies at most that he knows of no facts incompatible with the belief or that he knows of facts that justify him in holding it. The difference is that between "This is true," and "I think this is true, but I am not sure." The important distinction is between assertions of knowledge and those of opinion, rather than assertions of fact and those of opinion. The person whose opinion is asserted is usually the maker of the assertion himself, but the opinion may also be that of a third person. See Comment b to § 169.

b. Criteria. The fact that points of view may be expected to differ on the subject of a statement suggests that the statement is one of opinion. Statements of judgment as to quality, value, authenticity, or similar matters are common examples. For instance, the statement that an automobile is a "good" car relates to a matter on which views may be expected to differ. The maker of such a statement will normally be understood as expressing only his own judgment and not as making assertions concerning such matters as horsepower or riding qualities. But see Comment d and Illustration 3. The form of the statement is important but not controlling. A statement that is in form an assertion of the maker's knowledge may be made in circumstances that suggest that it expresses only a belief, that he is not free from doubt. This may be so, for example, when the recipient knows that the maker has no information concerning the fact asserted and therefore can be stating only his belief. The problem is one of interpretation of the language used.

c. Statements of quantity, quality, value and price. A seller's statement of the quantity of land or goods is virtually never a statement of opinion, even though he does not suggest that it is based on a survey, weighing or other measurement. The words "more or less" do not change such a statement into one of opinion, and the recipient is justified in believing that the quantity is substantially as stated although the measurement expressed may not be exact. In contrast, a seller's general statement of quality is usually one of opinion. There are, however, instances in which the gradations of quality are so marked that goods are usually sold as of a specified grade and an assertion of grade is not one of opinion. A statement of value is, like one of quality, ordinarily a statement of opinion. However, a statement of the price at which something has been offered for sale or sold is not one of opinion.

Illustrations

1. A, seeking to induce B to make a contract to buy goods, tells B that he paid $10,000 for them. A knows that he paid only $8,000 for the goods. The statement is not one of opinion.

2. The facts being otherwise as stated in Illustration 1, A tells B only that the goods are worth $10,000. The statement is one of opinion.

d. Implication of a statement of opinion. In some circumstances the recipient may reasonably understand a statement of opinion to be more than an assertion as to the maker's state of mind. Under the rule stated in Subsection (2), if the statement of opinion relates to facts not known to the recipient, he may be justified in inferring that there are facts that justify the opinion, or at least that there are no facts that are incompatible with it. In such a case, the statement of opinion becomes, in effect, an assertion as to those facts and may be relied on as such. The rule is, however, applied in the light of the realities of the market place. The propensity of sellers and buyers to exaggerate the advantages to the other party of the bargains they promise is well recognized, and to some extent their assertions of opinion must be discounted. Nevertheless, while some allowance must be made for seller's puffing and buyer's depreciation, the other party is entitled to assume that a statement of opinion is not so far removed from the truth as to be incompatible with the facts known to the maker. Where circumstances justify it, a statement of opinion may also be reasonably understood as carrying with it an assertion that the maker knows facts sufficient to justify him in forming it. However, the rule stated in Subsection (2) applies only when the facts to which the opinion relates are not disclosed and not otherwise known to the recipient. An assertion of opinion that does not fall within Subsection (2) is one of opinion only. As to the circumstances in which reliance on such an assertion is justified, see § 169.

Illustrations

3. A, seeking to induce B to make a contract to buy real property, tells B that the sewage system is "good." A knows that the sewage system is unworkable. B interprets A's statement of opinion as an assertion that the facts known to A are not incompatible with his opinion and is induced by this assertion to make the contract. B's interpretation is reasonable, the assertion is a fraudulent misrepresentation, and the contract is voidable by B.

4. The facts being otherwise as stated in Illustration 3, A knows that the sewage system is not very good but is workable. There is no misrepresentation because the facts known to A are not incompatible with his opinion, and the contract is not voidable by B.

5. A, seeking to induce B to make a contract to become A's partner in A's business, tells B that the business is "a money-maker." A knows that the business has been unprofitable since its inception. B interprets A's statement of opinion as an assertion that the facts known to A are not incompatible with his opinion and is induced by this assertion to make the contract. B's interpretation is reasonable, the assertion is a fraudulent misrepresentation, and the contract is voidable by B.

6. A, who is knowledgeable in financial matters, seeking to induce B, who is also knowledgeable in such matters, to make a contract to buy A's shares of stock in C Corporation, tells B that within five years the shares will pay dividends that will amount to the purchase price of the stock. Neither A nor B has information about the finances of C, which is, in fact, hopelessly insolvent. B interprets A's statement of opinion as an assertion that A knows facts sufficient to justify him in forming that opinion and is induced by this assertion to make the contract. B's interpretation is reasonable, the assertion is a fraudulent misrepresentation, and the contract is voidable by B.

7. A, seeking to induce B to make a contract to buy land, tells B, "There is water under this land and if you dig a well anywhere on the land, you will strike it." A does not know whether there is water under the land, and there is none. B knows that no water survey has been made and that A has no information concerning the presence or absence of subterranean water, but interprets A's statement of opinion as an assertion that A knows facts sufficient to justify him in forming that opinion and is induced by this assertion to make the contract. B's interpretation is not reasonable, and the contract is not voidable by B. See also § 169.

§ 169. When Reliance on an Assertion of Opinion Is Not Justified.

To the extent that an assertion is one of opinion only, the recipient is not justified in relying on it unless the recipient

    (a) stands in such a relation of trust and confidence to the person whose opinion is asserted that the recipient is reasonable in relying on it, or

    (b) reasonably believes that, as compared with himself, the person whose opinion is asserted has special skill, judgment or objectivity with respect to the subject matter, or

    (c) is for some other special reason particularly susceptible to a misrepresentation of the type involved.

Comment

a. Scope: The rule stated in this Section applies only to the extent that an assertion amounts to nothing more than an assertion of opinion, whether that of the maker or a third person. As is stated in § 168(2), an assertion of opinion as to facts not known to the recipient may, in proper circumstances, reasonably be interpreted to include an assertion as to those facts themselves. If that assertion is false, it may be the basis of avoidance regardless of the rule stated in this Section. The rule stated here determines whether reliance is justified whenever the assertion of opinion does not carry with it an assertion as to facts under the rule stated in § 168(2).

b. Rationale. If the subject matter of the transaction is one on which the two parties have roughly equal skill and judgment, each must generally form his own opinions and neither is justified in relying on the other's. The law assumes that the ordinary person is reasonably competent to form his own opinions as to the advisability of entering into those transactions that form part of the ordinary routine of life. The mere fact that one of the parties is less astute than the other does not justify him in relying on the other's opinion. This is true even though one party knows that the other is somewhat more conversant with the value and quality of the subject matter, since expressions of opinion by the other party are generally to be discounted. It may be assumed, for example, that a seller will express a favorable opinion concerning what he has to sell. When he praises it in general terms, commonly known as "puffing" or "sales talk," without specific content or reference to facts, buyers are expected to understand that they are not entitled to rely. See Uniform Commercial Code § 2–313(2). A similar assumption applies to deprecating statements by buyers. See Comment d to § 168.

c. Confidential relationship. In some situations a relationship of trust and confidence between the parties justifies the reliance of one on the other's opinion. Where there is a true fiduciary relation, the more stringent requirements of § 173 apply. But even where a party is not, strictly speaking, a fiduciary, he may stand in a relation of trust and confidence to the recipient. Such a relation often arises, for example, between members of the same family. See Comment f to § 161. It may also arise where one party has taken steps to induce the other to believe that he can safely rely on the first party's judgment, as where he has gained the other's confidence by stressing their common membership in a religious denomination, fraternal order or social group, or the fact that they were born in the same locality. In addition, some types of contracts, such as marine insurance and joint adventure, are recognized as creating in themselves a confidential relation and hence as requiring the utmost good faith and full and fair disclosure. As to contracts of suretyship, see Restatement of Security § 124(1). As to undue influence, see § 177.

Illustration

1. A, professing friendship, offers to advise B, an elderly widow inexperienced in business, concerning her investments. He does so for five years, giving her good advice and acquiring her trust and confidence. At the end of this time he advises her to buy his worthless shares of stock, telling her that in his opinion it is a "good investment." B is induced by A's statement to make the contract. B's reliance on A's statement is justified, and the contract is voidable by B.

d. Special skill, judgment or objectivity. Ordinarily the recipient is not justified in relying on the other party's assertion of opinion because the recipient has as good a basis for forming his own opinion and the other party's opinion must be discounted because of his self-interest. Clause (b) applies to situations where this is not the case because the recipient reasonably believes that the other party has special skill or judgment, relative to that of the recipient, with respect to the subject matter. In modern commercial life, situations often occur in which special training or experience are necessary to the formation of a sound judgment. Often, in such a case, the recipient will be able to base a claim to relief on one of the assertions as to facts that arise under the rule stated in § 168(2). This will not be so, however, if the facts are known to both parties. In that event, the recipient's reliance may be justified under the rule stated in Clause (b). Compare Uniform Commercial Code § 2–315.

Clause (b) also applies to instances in which the recipient reasonably believes that the person whose opinion is asserted has special objectivity with respect to the subject matter that would give his opinion particular weight. This includes situations in which one who is not a party to the transaction and has no other adversary interest misrepresents his opinion. See § 164(2). It also includes situations in which the maker has an adversary interest but conceals this from the recipient. In such cases, the recipient's reasonable although erroneous belief that the maker is disinterested may be sufficient to justify his reliance. Finally, it applies to situations where a party to the transaction misrepresents that an apparently disinterested person holds a particular opinion. Thus an assertion that a third person has paid or offered a particular price for something, in addition to being a misrepresentation as to the conduct of that person, implies that that person holds an appropriate opinion of its value, and a prospective purchaser may be justified in taking this into account in determining whether to buy. Whether a person's apparent disinterest gives him the special objectivity required to justify reliance on this implied assertion of opinion depends on the circumstances of the particular case, including any special skill or judgment that may accompany his disinterest.

Illustrations

2. A, the proprietor of a dance studio, seeking to induce B, a 60-year-old widow with no background in dancing, to make a contract for dance lessons, tells B that she has "dance potential" and would develop into a "beautiful dancer." A knows that B has little aptitude as a dancer. B is induced by A's statement of opinion to make the proposed contract. B's reliance on A's statement of opinion is justified, and the contract is voidable by B.

3. A, seeking to induce B to make a contract to buy land, tells B that C, a local businessman, shortly before his death offered him $50,000 for the land. A knows that C offered only $40,000 for the land. B infers from A's statement that in C's opinion the land was worth $50,000 and, believing that C had special objectivity, is induced by the statement to make the contract. B's reliance is justified, and the contract is voidable by B.

e. Particularly susceptible recipient. If the recipient is for some special reason, other than those covered by Clause (b), particularly vulnerable to misrepresentation of the kind practiced on him, his reliance on it is justified under Clause (c). Examples of such reasons include lack of intelligence, illiteracy, and unusual credulity or gullibility. One whose misrepresentation of opinion induces reliance because of such a characteristic will not be heard to say that the reliance he sought to induce was not justified because his statement was one of opinion and therefore should have been mistrusted.

Illustration

4. A, seeking to induce B, who is particularly inexperienced and gullible, to make a contract to buy property, tells B that its value is $35,000. A knows that it is practically worthless. B is induced by A's statement to make the contract. If B's reliance is justified because his inexperience and gullibility make him particularly susceptible to such a misrepresentation, the contract is voidable by B.

§ 170. Reliance on Assertions as to Matters of Law.

If an assertion is one as to a matter of law, the same rules that apply in the case of other assertions determine whether the recipient is justified in relying on it.

Comment

a. Law as fact. A statement as to a matter of law is subject to the same rules as are other assertions. Such a statement may or may not be one of opinion. Thus, an assertion that a particular statute has been enacted or repealed or that a particular decision has been rendered by a court is generally not a statement of opinion. The rules that determine the consequences of a misrepresentation of such a matter of law are the same as those that determine the consequences of a similar misrepresentation of any other fact.

Illustration

1. A, seeking to sell goods to B, tells B that the government authorities have not fixed a maximum price for such goods. A knows that the authorities have fixed a maximum price for the goods. The assertion is a fraudulent misrepresentation, and the contract is voidable by B.

b. Law as opinion. Many statements of law involve assertions as to what a court would determine to be the legal consequences of a dispute if it were litigated, and such a statement is one of opinion. Such a statement may, as may any other statement of opinion, carry with it the assertion that the facts known to the maker are not incompatible with his opinion, or that he does know facts that justify him in forming it. See § 168(2). However, a statement that is limited to the maker's opinion as to the legal consequences of a state of facts and does not amount to an assertion as to the facts themselves is an assertion of opinion only. This is particularly true if all of the facts are known to both parties or are assumed by both of them to exist. Such a statement may be relied on, but to no greater extent than any other statement of opinion only (§ 169). Thus, as between the two parties to a contract, the recipient is ordinarily expected to draw his own conclusions or to seek his own independent legal advice. On the other hand, if the maker of the representation purports to have special expertise in the law which the recipient does not have, reliance on the opinion may be justified (§ 167(b)). If a lawyer states his opinion of law to a layman, the layman is entitled to assume his professional honesty and may justifiably rely on his opinion even though the two have an adverse relation in negotiating a contract. Even if the maker is not a lawyer, he may purport to have special knowledge that will enable him to form a reliable opinion, as where a real estate broker or an insurance agent gives his opinion on a routine problem within his competence to a layman.

Illustration

2. A, seeking to induce B to make a contract to buy land from him tells B, "I have good title to this land." Unknown to A, the person from whom he purchased the land had no title to it. B interprets A's statement as an assertion that he knows of conveyances sufficient to vest good title in him and is induced to make the contract. Although A's statement is in the form of a legal conclusion, B's interpretation is reasonable, the assertion is a material misrepresentation, and the contract is voidable by B. See § 168(2).

c. Foreign law. The rule stated in this Section applies to statements of foreign as well as domestic law. Some courts have refused to recognize that statements of the law of a state or country where the recipient neither resides nor habitually does business are mere statements of opinion, even though they purport to cover only the legal consequences of facts known to both parties. This refusal may often be explained on the ground that, although the statement is of opinion only, the recipient's reliance is more likely to be justified because he is less able to draw his own conclusions as to foreign law. Nevertheless, he is not justified in relying on a statement of opinion as to foreign law absent one of the circumstances enumerated in § 169. If the maker resides or habitually does business in the foreign jurisdiction, he may be expected to have special expertise as to its law. See § 169(b).

§ 171. When Reliance on an Assertion of Intention Is Not Justified.

(1) To the extent that an assertion is one of intention only, the recipient is not justified in relying on it if in the circumstances a misrepresentation of intention is consistent with reasonable standards of dealing.

(2) If it is reasonable to do so, the promisee may properly interpret a promise as an assertion that the promisor intends to perform the promise.

Comment

a. Assertions of intention. A statement as to the intention of either the maker or a third person is an assertion of a fact, his state of mind, just as a statement of his opinion is such an assertion. It is therefore a misrepresentation if that state of mind is not as asserted. However, the truth of a statement as to a person's intention depends on his intention at the time that the statement is made and is not affected if he subsequently, for any reason, changes his mind. In order for reliance on an assertion of intention to be justified, the recipient's expectation that the maker's intention will be carried out must be reasonable. If he knows facts that will make it impossible for the maker to carry out his intention, then his reliance cannot be justified. See Illustration 1. As with statements of opinion (§ 169), not all statements of intention are to be taken seriously. In some situations, courts have accorded the maker considerable latitude in misrepresenting his intention, for the reason that such statements are generally regarded as unreliable. A court will take account of all the circumstances, including any usage and the relationship of the parties. A prospective buyer of land may, for example, misrepresent his intended use of the land in order to conceal from the seller some special advantage that the buyer will derive from its purchase, which if known to the seller, would cause him to demand a higher price. The contract is not voidable on this ground if the court concludes that, in all the circumstances, the buyer's misrepresentation is not contrary to reasonable standards of dealing. See Illustration 2. The result will ordinarily be different, however, if the prospective buyer misrepresents his intended use so as to conceal from the seller some harm to the seller's other interests that will be caused if the buyer carries out his actual intention. See Illustration 3.

Illustrations

1. A, the owner of a real estate development, seeking to induce B to make a contract to buy a lot in it, tells B that he intends to construct a golf course in the development. A has no such intention. B is induced by A's statement to make the contract. The contract is voidable by B. If, however, B knows that the terrain is not suitable for a golf course, that there is not enough land for it, and that it could only be constructed by purchase of a large quantity of additional land quite beyond A's means, B's reliance is not justified, and the contract is not voidable by B.

2. A, seeking to induce B to make a contract to sell a tract of land, tells B that he intends to hold the tract as an investment. A intends instead to combine the tract with others as part of a large development but declines to tell B this in order to prevent B from asking a higher price. B is induced by A's statement to make the contract. If the court concludes that, in all the circumstances, A's statement was not contrary to reasonable standards of dealing, the contract is not voidable by B.

3. A, seeking to induce B to make a contract to sell a tract of land, tells B that he intends to use the tract for the construction of a residence. A intends instead to use it for the construction of an industrial building but declines to tell B this because B owns an adjacent tract that will be adversely affected if A carries out his real intention. B is induced by A's non-disclosure to make the contract. The contract is voidable by B.

b. A promise as a statement of intention. It is ordinarily reasonable for the promisee to infer from the making of a promise that the promisor intends to perform it. If, therefore, the promise is made with the intention of not performing it, this implied assertion is false and is a misrepresentation. The promise itself need not be made in words but may be inferred from conduct or even supplied by law. Nor does it need to be a legally enforceable promise. The promisor's intention not to perform his promise cannot be established merely by proof of its non-performance. Nevertheless, the probable inability of a party, at the time the contract is made, to perform it, for instance the insolvency of one who buys land, is evidence bearing on the question of intent not to perform. If the promisor knows or should know that he cannot at least substantially perform his promise, this is strong although not conclusive evidence of an intent not to carry it out. (The effect of a buyer's misrepresentation of solvency or of intent to pay in the case of a contract for the sale of goods is the subject of the special rule of Uniform Commercial Code § 2–702(2).) If a party is entitled to avoid the contract on this ground, he may do so immediately and need not await the time for performance. The application of the rule stated in Subsection (2) does not turn on whether the promisor is the offeror or the offeree. When the parties exchange promises as consideration for each other, each promise is properly regarded as the inducement for the other. Therefore, if the offeree has no intention of performing his promise when he accepts, the contract is voidable by the offeror on the ground that his promise was made in reliance on that of the offeree. See Comment a to § 167. As with other assertions, the recipient's reliance must be justified. It is not justified if the promisor has disclosed his intention not to perform or if performance is known not to be within his control.

Illustration

4. A, seeking to induce B to make a contract to have work done on his house, and to make a part payment of $1,000, promises to do the work for a stated price. A does not intend to perform the contract. B is induced by A's promise to make the contract and the part payment. B may interpret A's promise as an assertion of his intention to perform. This assertion is a fraudulent misrepresentation, and the contract is voidable by B.

§ 172. When Fault Makes Reliance Unjustified.

A recipient's fault in not knowing or discovering the facts before making the contract does not make his reliance unjustified unless it amounts to a failure to act in good faith and in accordance with reasonable standards of fair dealing.

Comment

a. Rationale. The recipient's reliance on the misrepresentation must be justified in order to entitle him to avoidance (§ 164) or reformation (§ 166). He is not entitled to relief if his reliance was unreasonable in the light of his particular circumstances. See Comment b to § 164. But the mere fact that he could, by the exercise of reasonable care, have avoided the mistake caused by the misrepresentation does not bar him from relief. The rule is similar to that applicable to mistake in general (§ 157), and its justification is particularly strong since here the recipient's mistake is the result of a misrepresentation. However, the recipient's fault will prevent the application of the rule stated in § 163, under which a misrepresentation as to the very nature of a proposed contract makes his apparent manifestation of assent ineffective. That rule applies only if he has neither knowledge nor reasonable opportunity to obtain knowledge of the character or essential terms of the proposed contract. But even in such a case, lack of reasonable care will not preclude the recipient from avoiding or from obtaining reformation. See Illustration 1. The recipient's fault makes his reliance unjustified only in extreme cases where he has failed to act in good faith and in accordance with reasonable standards of fair dealing.

Illustration

1. A and B reach an understanding that they will execute a written contract containing terms on which they have agreed. A prepares a writing containing essential terms different from those agreed upon and induces B to sign it by telling him that it contains the agreed terms and that it is not necessary for him to read it. Although B's apparent manifestation of assent is effective if he had a reasonable opportunity to read the writing (see Illustration 3 to § 163), his reliance is justified since his fault does not amount to a failure to act in good faith and in accordance with reasonable standards of fair dealing. The contract is voidable by B. In the alternative he may have the writing reformed.

b. Good faith and fair dealing. In determining whether the recipient of a misrepresentation has conformed to the standard of good faith and fair dealing, account is taken of his peculiar qualities and characteristics, including his credulity and gullibility, and the circumstances of the particular case, including the fraudulent or innocent nature of the misrepresentation. However, in contrast to the rules that govern a damage action in deceit, the rule stated in this Section applies to innocent as well as to fraudulent misrepresentations. Compare Restatement, Second, Torts § 545A with § 552A. If the recipient knows that the assertion is false or should have discovered its falsity by making a cursory examination, his reliance is clearly not justified and he is not entitled to relief. See Restatement, Second, Torts § 541. He is expected to use his senses and not rely blindly on the maker's assertion. On the other hand, he is not barred by the mere failure to investigate the truth of a misrepresentation, even where it might be reasonable to do so. See Restatement, Second, Torts § 540. The fact that the recipient took advantage of an opportunity to investigate may be relevant under the rules relating to assertions of opinion (see Comment b to § 168) or as indicating that he did not rely on the misrepresentation (see Comment b to § 167). For the purposes of the rule stated in this Section, however, the recipient is generally entitled to rely on the maker's assertions as to his knowledge without undertaking an investigation as to their truthfulness.

Illustrations

2. A, seeking to induce B to make a contract to buy land, tells B that the land is free from encumbrances. Unknown to either A or B, C holds a recorded and unsatisfied mortgage on the land. B

could easily learn this by walking across the street to the register of deeds in the courthouse but does not do so. B is induced by A's statement to make the contract. B's reliance is justified since his fault does not amount to a failure to act in good faith and in accordance with reasonable standards of fair dealing, and the contract is voidable by B.

3. A, seeking to induce B to make a contract to buy furniture for B's house, hands B a printed order form and tells B that the total price for the furniture is $550 and that this is stated in the form. A knows that in the form additional furniture is described and that the total price stated is $1,050. B is induced by A's statement to sign the form without reading it, and A accepts B's offer. B's reliance is justified since his fault does not amount to a failure to act in good faith and in accordance with reasonable standards of fair dealing. The contract is voidable by B. In the alternative he may have the writing reformed.

§ 173. When Abuse of a Fiduciary Relation Makes a Contract Voidable.

If a fiduciary makes a contract with his beneficiary relating to matters within the scope of the fiduciary relation, the contract is voidable by the beneficiary, unless

(a) it is on fair terms, and

(b) all parties beneficially interested manifest assent with full understanding of their legal rights and of all relevant facts that the fiduciary knows or should know.

Comment

a. Equal footing. The rule stated in this Section applies to any fiduciary, including a trustee, an agent, a guardian, or an executor or administrator. See Restatement, Second, Trusts § 170(2). It is more severe than the rule relating to non-disclosure in the case of one who stands in a relation of trust and confidence but who is not a fiduciary. See § 161(b); cf. § 169(a). When a fiduciary makes a contract with the person beneficially interested, it is not enough that he make a complete disclosure of the facts known to him. The person beneficially interested must be put on an equal footing, with full understanding of his legal rights and of all relevant facts that the fiduciary knows or should know. If that person is not of competent age and understanding, this may be difficult if not impossible to achieve. If it is impossible, the fiduciary is precluded from making a contract with him within the scope of the fiduciary relation.

b. Fairness. In addition to assuring itself that the parties were placed on an equal footing, a court will inquire into the fairness of the resulting agreement. What is required is not merely the absence of unconscionability, as is the case for contracts in general. The contract is voidable unless it is shown to be on fair terms in the light of the circumstances at the time of its making.

Illustration

1. A, the executor of a will under which a tract of land has been devised to B, makes a contract with B to buy the tract from him. Before making the contract, A tells B all relevant facts about the transaction. The contract is voidable by B unless the court concludes that it is on fair terms.

c. Relation to other rules. The rule stated in this Section applies only where the fiduciary is a party to the contract. As to the effect of misrepresentation or non-disclosure by a fiduciary who is not a party to the contract, see §§ 161(a), 169(a), which apply to any relation of trust and confidence, including a fiduciary relation. The rule stated in this Section, like those stated in §§ 164, 175 and 177, only makes the contract voidable, and the power of avoidance is subject to the rights of good faith purchasers and to the rules stated in Chapter 16 on remedies.

TOPIC 2. DURESS AND UNDUE INFLUENCE

§ 174. When Duress by Physical Compulsion Prevents Formation of a Contract.

If conduct that appears to be a manifestation of assent by a party who does not intend to engage in that conduct is physically compelled by duress, the conduct is not effective as a manifestation of assent.

Comment

a. Rationale. Under the general principle stated in § 21(2), a party's conduct is not effective as a manifestation of his assent if he does not intend to engage in it. This Section involves an application of that principle to those relatively rare situations in which actual physical force has been used to compel a party to appear to assent to a contract. Compare § 163. The essence of this type of duress is that a party is compelled by physical force to do an act that he has no intention of doing. He is, it is sometimes said, "a mere mechanical instrument." The result is that there is no contract at all, or a "void contract" as distinguished from a voidable one. See Comment a to § 7. Cases, such as those involving hypnosis, in which conduct is compelled without physical force, are left to be governed by the general rule stated in § 19(2).

Illustration

1. A presents to B, who is physically weaker than A, a written contract prepared for B's signature and demands that B sign it. B refuses. A grasps B's hand and compels B by physical force to write his name. B's signature is not effective as a manifestation of his assent, and there is no contract.

b. "Void" rather than voidable. The distinction between "void contract" and a voidable contract has important consequences. For example, a victim of duress may be held to have ratified the contract if it is voidable, but not if it is "void." Furthermore, a good faith purchaser may acquire good title to property if he takes it from one who obtained voidable title by duress but not if he takes it from one who obtained "void title" by duress. It is immaterial under the rule stated in this Section whether the duress is exercised by a party to the transaction or by a third person. See Comment d to § 175.

§ 175. When Duress by Threat Makes a Contract Voidable.

(1) If a party's manifestation of assent is induced by an improper threat by the other party that leaves the victim no reasonable alternative, the contract is voidable by the victim.

(2) If a party's manifestation of assent is induced by one who is not a party to the transaction, the contract is voidable by the victim unless the other party to the transaction in good faith and without reason to know of the duress either gives value or relies materially on the transaction.

Comment

a. Improper threat. The essence of the type of duress dealt with in this Section is inducement by an improper threat. The threat may be expressed in words or it may be inferred from words or other conduct. Past events often import a threat. Thus, if one person strikes or imprisons another, the conduct may amount to duress because of the threat of further blows or continued imprisonment that is implied. Courts originally restricted duress to threats involving loss of life, mayhem or imprisonment, but these restrictions have been greatly relaxed and, in order to constitute duress, the threat need only be improper within the rule stated in § 176.

b. No reasonable alternative. A threat, even if improper, does not amount to duress if the victim has a reasonable alternative to succumbing and fails to take advantage of it. It is sometimes said that the threat must arouse such fear as precludes a party from exercising free will and judgment or that it must be such as would induce assent on the part of a brave man or a man of ordinary firmness. The rule stated in this Section omits any such requirement because of its vagueness and impracticability. It is enough if the threat actually induces assent (see Comment c) on the part of one who has no reasonable alternative. The alternative may take the form of a legal remedy. For example, the threat of commencing an ordinary civil action to enforce a claim to money may be improper. See § 176(1)(c). However, it does not usually amount to duress because the victim can assert his rights in the threatened action, and this is ordinarily a reasonable alternative to succumbing to the threat, making the proposed contract, and then asserting his rights in a later civil action. See Illustration 1; cf. Restatement of Restitution § 71. This alternative may not, however, be reasonable if the threat involves, for instance, the seizure of property, the use of oppressive tactics, or the possibility of emotional consequences. See Illustration 2. The standard is a practical one under which account must be taken of the exigencies in which the victim finds himself, and the mere availability of a legal remedy is not controlling if it will not afford effective relief to one in the victim's circumstances. See Illustrations 3 and 4. The alternative to succumbing to the threat need not, however, involve a legal remedy at all. In the case of a threatened denial of needed goods or services, the availability on the market of similar goods or services may afford a reasonable means of avoiding the threat. Compare Illustrations 5 and 6. Since alternative sources of funds are ordinarily available, a refusal to pay money is not duress, absent a showing of peculiar necessity. See Illustration 7. Where the threat is one of minor vexation only, toleration of the inconvenience involved may be a reasonable alternative. Whether the victim has a reasonable alternative is a mixed question of law and fact, to be answered in clear cases by the court.

Illustrations

1. A makes an improper threat to commence civil proceedings against B unless B agrees to discharge a claim that B has against A. In order to avoid defending the threatened suit, B is induced to make the contract. Defense of the threatened suit is a reasonable alternative, the threat does not amount to duress, and the contract is not voidable by B.

2. A makes an improper threat to commence a civil action and to file a lis pendens against a tract of land owned by B, unless B agrees to discharge a claim that B has against A. Because B is about to make a contract with C for the sale of the land and C refuses to make the contract if the levy is made, B agrees to discharge the claim. B has no reasonable alternative, A's threat is duress, and the contract is voidable by B.

3. A, with whom B has left a machine for repairs, makes an improper threat to refuse to deliver the machine to B, although B has paid for the repairs, unless B agrees to make a contract to have additional repair work done. B can replevy the machine, but because he is in urgent need of it and delay would cause him heavy financial loss, he is induced by A's threat to make the contract. B has no reasonable alternative, A's threat amounts to duress, and the contract is voidable by B.

4. A, who has promised B to vacate leased premises in return for $10,000 in order to permit B to demolish the building and construct another, refuses to do so unless B agrees to purchase his worthless furniture for $5,000. B can resort to regular eviction proceedings, but because this will materially delay his construction schedule and cause him heavy financial loss, he is induced by A's threat to make the contract. B has no reasonable alternative, A's threat amounts to duress, and the contract is voidable by B.

5. A, who has contracted to sell goods to B, makes an improper threat to refuse to deliver the goods to B unless B modifies the contract to increase the price. B attempts to buy substitute goods elsewhere but is unable to do so. Being in urgent need of the goods, he makes the modification. See Uniform Commercial Code § 2–209(1). B has no reasonable alternative, A's threat amounts to duress, and the modification is voidable by B.

6. The facts being otherwise as stated in Illustration 5, B could buy substitute goods elsewhere but does not attempt to do so. The purchase of substitute goods and a claim for any damages is a reasonable alternative, the threat does not amount to duress, and the contract is not voidable by B.

7. A, who has contracted to pay for goods delivered by B, makes an improper threat to refuse to pay B unless B modifies the contract to reduce the price. B attempts to borrow money elsewhere but is unable to do so. Being in urgent need of cash to avoid foreclosure of a mortgage, he makes the modification. See Uniform Commercial Code § 2–209(1). B has no reasonable alternative, A's threat amounts to duress, and the modification is voidable by B.

c. Subjective test of inducement. In order to constitute duress, the improper threat must induce the making of the contract. The rule for causation in cases of misrepresentation stated in § 167 is also applied to analogous cases of duress. No special rule for causation in cases of duress is stated here because of the infrequency with which the problem arises. A party's manifestation of assent is induced by duress if the duress substantially contributes to his decision to manifest his assent. Compare § 167. The test is subjective and the question is, did the threat actually induce assent on the part of the person claiming to be the victim of duress. Threats that would suffice to induce assent by one person may not suffice to induce assent by another. All attendant circumstances must be considered, including such matters as the age, background and relationship of the parties. Persons of a weak or cowardly nature are the very ones that need protection; the courageous can usually protect themselves. Timid and inexperienced persons are particularly subject to threats, and it does not lie in the mouths of the unscrupulous to excuse their imposition on such persons on the ground of their victims' infirmities. However, here as under § 167 circumstantial evidence may be useful in determining whether a threat did in fact induce assent. For example, although it is not essential that a reasonable person would have believed that the maker of the threat had the ability to execute it, this may be relevant in determining whether the threat actually induced assent. Similarly, such factors as the availability of disinterested advice and the length of time that elapses between the making of the threat and the assent may also be relevant in determining whether the threat actually induced the assent.

Illustrations

8. A, seeking to induce B to make a contract to sell land to A, threatens to poison B unless B makes the contract. The threat would not be taken seriously by a reasonable person, but B is easily frightened and attaches importance to the threat in deciding to make the contract. The contract is voidable by B.

9. A seeks to induce B, A's wife, who has a history of severe emotional disturbances, to sign a separation agreement on unfavorable terms. B has no lawyer, while A does. A tells B that if she does not sign the agreement he will charge her with desertion, she will never see her children again and she will get back none of her personal property, which is in A's possession. B signs the separation agreement. The agreement is voidable by B.

d. *Voidable.* Duress by threat results in a contract voidable by the victim. It differs in this important respect from duress by physical compulsion, which results in there being no contract at all. See Comment b to § 174. The power of avoidance for duress is subject to limitations that are similar to those applicable to avoidance on other grounds, such as mistake and misrepresentation. These limitations are stated in §§ 378–84. The person making the threat may, of course, pursue any civil claim that he has against the victim independently of the contract induced by the threat. Furthermore, to the extent that such a claim is valid, the maker of the threat may be entitled to retain what he has actually received through performance of such a contract. These matters are not dealt with in this Section.

e. *Duress by a third person.* If a party's assent has been induced by the duress of a third person, rather than that of the other party to the contract, the contract is nevertheless voidable by the victim. There is, however, an important exception if the other party has, in good faith and without reason to know of the duress, given value or changed his position materially in reliance on the transaction. "Value" includes a performance or a return promise that is consideration under the definition stated in § 71, so that the other party is protected if he has made the contract in good faith before learning of the duress. See Uniform Commercial Code § 1–201(44). The rule stated in this Section does not, however, protect a party to whom the duress is attributable under the law of agency. The rule is similar to that for misrepresentation (§ 163) and is analogous to the rule that protects against the original owner the good faith purchaser of property from another who obtained it by duress.

Illustrations

10. A, who is not C's agent, induces B by duress to contract with C to sell land to C. C, in good faith, promises B to pay the agreed price. The contract is not voidable by B.

11. The facts being otherwise as stated in Illustration 10, C learns of the duress before he promises to pay the agreed price. The contract is voidable by B.

§ 176. When a Threat Is Improper.

(1) A threat is improper if

    (a) what is threatened is a crime or a tort, or the threat itself would be a crime or a tort if it resulted in obtaining property,

    (b) what is threatened is a criminal prosecution,

    (c) what is threatened is the use of civil process and the threat is made in bad faith, or

    (d) the threat is a breach of the duty of good faith and fair dealing under a contract with the recipient.

(2) A threat is improper if the resulting exchange is not on fair terms, and

(a) the threatened act would harm the recipient and would not significantly benefit the party making the threat,

(b) the effectiveness of the threat inducing the manifestation of assent is significantly increased by prior unfair dealing by the party making the threat, or

(c) what is threatened is otherwise a use of power for illegitimate ends.

Comment

a. Rationale. An ordinary offer to make a contract commonly involves an implied threat by one party, the offeror, not to make the contract unless his terms are accepted by the other party, the offeree. Such threats are an accepted part of the bargaining process. A threat does not amount to duress unless it is so improper as to amount to an abuse of that process. Courts first recognized as improper threats of physical violence and later included wrongful seizure or detention of goods. Modern decisions have recognized as improper a much broader range of threats, notably those to cause economic harm.

Comment

a. Rationale. An ordinary offer to make a contract commonly involves an implied threat by one party, the offeror, not to make the contract unless his terms are accepted by the other party, the offeree. Such threats are an accepted part of the bargaining process. A threat does not amount to duress unless it is so improper as to amount to an abuse of that process. Courts first recognized as improper threats of physical violence and later included wrongful seizure or detention of goods. Modern decisions have recognized as improper a much broader range of threats, notably those to cause economic harm. The rules stated in this Section recognize as improper both the older categories and their modern extensions under developing notions of "economic duress" or "business compulsion." The fairness of the resulting exchange is often a critical factor in cases involving threats. The categories within Subsection (1) involve threats that are either so shocking that the court will not inquire into the fairness of the resulting exchange (see Clauses (a) and (b)) or that in themselves necessarily involve some element of unfairness (see Clauses (c) and (d)). Those within Subsection (2) involve threats in which the impropriety consists of the threat in combination with resulting unfairness. Such a threat is not improper if it can be shown that the exchange is one on fair terms. Of course a threat may be improper for more than one reason. Any threat that comes within Subsection (1) as well as Subsection (2) is improper without an inquiry, under the rule stated in Subsection (2), into the fairness of the resulting exchange.

b. Crime or tort. A threat is improper if the threatened act is a crime or a tort, as in the traditional examples of threats of physical violence and of wrongful seizure or retention of goods. See Comment a. Where physical violence is threatened, it need not be to the recipient of the threat, nor even to a person related to him, if the threat in fact induces the recipient to manifest his assent. See Illustration 2. The threatened act need not involve harm to person or goods but may, for example, involve a tortious interference with another's contractual rights. Where the crime or tort is a minor one, however, the claim of duress may fail, even though the threat is improper, on the ground that the victim had a reasonable alternative (see Comment b to § 175) or that the threat was not an inducing cause (see Comment c to § 175). The threatened act need not be a crime or tort if the threat itself would have been one had it resulted in the obtaining of property. Therefore, in jurisdictions where a broad modern extortion statute has been enacted, many of the threats that come within Subsection (2) are elements of the crime of extortion and therefore also fall within Clause (1)(a). See Model Penal Code § 223.4. The fairness of the exchange is immaterial in such cases.

Illustrations

1. A is a good faith purchaser for value of a valuable painting stolen from B. When B demands the return of the painting, A threatens to poison B unless he releases all rights to the painting for $1,000. B, having no reasonable alternative, is induced by A's threat to sign the release, and A pays him $1,000. The threatened act is both a crime and a tort, and the release is voidable by B.

2. A threatens B that he will kill C, an employee of B, unless B makes a contract to sell A a tract of land that B owns. B, having no reasonable alternative, is induced by A's threat to make the contract. The threatened act is both a crime and a tort, and the contract is voidable by B.

343

3. A, a pawnbroker, has possession of a valuable heirloom pledged by B. B offers to redeem the pledge, but A threatens not to surrender it unless B signs a promissory note in compromise of another claim, the validity of which is in dispute. B, having no reasonable alternative, is induced by A's threat to sign the note. The threatened act is a tort, and the note is voidable by B.

c. *Threat of prosecution.* Under the rule stated in Clause (1)(b), a threat of criminal prosecution is improper as a means of inducing the recipient to make a contract. An explanation in good faith of the criminal consequences of another's conduct may not involve a threat. But if a threat is made, the fact that the one who makes it honestly believes that the recipient is guilty is not material. The threat involves a misuse, for personal gain, of power given for other legitimate ends. See Comment f. The threat may be to instigate prosecution against the recipient or some third person, who is commonly although not necessarily a relative of the recipient. The guilt or innocence of the person whose prosecution is threatened is immaterial in determining whether the threat is improper, although it may be easier to show that the threat actually induced assent in the case of guilt. A bargain to suppress prosecution may be unenforceable on grounds of public policy. See the Introductory Note to Chapter 8 on agreements against public policy.

Illustrations

4. A, who believes that B, his employee, has embezzled money from him, threatens B that a criminal complaint will be filed and he will be prosecuted immediately unless he executes a promissory note for $5,000 in satisfaction of A's claim. B, having no reasonable alternative, is induced by A's threat to sign the note. The note is voidable by B. A may, however, have a claim against B for restitution of any money embezzled. See Comment d to § 175.

5. A is the payee of a valid $5,000 promissory note executed by B for the repayment of money embezzled by B. A makes a threat to C, a friend of B, that a criminal complaint will be filed and B will be prosecuted immediately unless C becomes a surety on the note in consideration of an extension of time for its payment. C is induced by A's threat to become a surety. The suretyship contract is voidable by C.

d. *Threat of civil process.* The policy in favor of free access to the judicial system militates against the characterization as improper of threats to commence civil process, even if the claim on which the process is based eventually proves to be without foundation. Nevertheless, if the threat is shown to have been made in bad faith, it is improper. Bad faith may be shown by proving that the person making the threat did not believe there was a reasonable basis for the threatened process, that he knew the threat would involve a misuse of the process or that he realized the demand he made was exorbitant. See Comment f. However, a threat to commence civil process, even if improper, may not amount to duress since defense of the threatened action is often a reasonable alternative. See Comment b to § 175.

Illustrations

6. A threatens to commence a civil action and file a lis pendens against a tract of land owned by B, unless B makes a contract to discharge a disputed claim that B has against A. A knows that the threatened action is without foundation. B, having no reasonable alternative, is induced by A's threat to make the contract. Since A does not believe that there is a reasonable basis for the threatened process, his threat is made in bad faith. A's threat is improper, and the contract is voidable by B. If, however, A believes that there is a reasonable basis for the threatened process and if the proposed contract is not exorbitant, the threat is not improper, and the contract is not voidable by B.

7. A, who has a valid claim for damages against B, threatens to attach a shipment of perishable goods unless B makes a contract to sell a machine to A. As A knows, other non-perishable goods are available for attachment. B, having no reasonable alternative, is induced by A's threat to make the contract. Since A knows that the threatened attachment would involve a misuse of that process to force a settlement rather than to preserve assets, his threat is made in bad faith. A's threat is improper and the contract is voidable by B.

e. *Breach of contract.* A threat by a party to a contract not to perform his contractual duty is not, of itself, improper. Indeed, a modification induced by such a threat may be binding, even in the absence of consideration, if it is fair and equitable in view of unanticipated circumstances. See § 89. The mere fact that the modification induced by the threat fails to meet this test does not mean that the threat is necessarily improper. However, the threat is improper if it amounts to a breach of the duty of good faith and fair dealing imposed by the contract. See § 205. As under the Uniform Commercial Code, the "extortion of a 'modification' without legitimate commercial reason is ineffective as a violation of the duty of good faith. . . . The test of 'good faith' between merchants or as against merchants includes 'observance of reasonable commercial standards of fair dealing in the trade' (Section 2–103), and may in some situations require an objectively demonstrable reason for seeking a modification. But such matters as a market shift which makes performance come to involve a loss may provide such a reason even though there is no such unforeseen difficulty as would make out a legal excuse from performance under Sections 2–615 and 2–616." Comment 2 to Uniform Commercial Code § 2–209. However, a threat of non-performance made for some purpose unrelated to the contract, such as to induce the recipient to make an entirely separate contract, is ordinarily improper. See Illustration 9. Furthermore, a threat may be a breach of the duty of good faith and fair dealing under the contract even though the threatened act is not itself a breach of the contract. See Illustrations 10 and 11. This is particularly likely to be the case if the threat is effective because of power not derived from the contract itself. See Comment f.

Illustrations

8. A contracts to excavate a cellar for B at a stated price. A unexpectedly encounters solid rock and threatens not to finish the excavation unless B modifies the contract to state a new price that is reasonable but is nine times the original price. B, having no reasonable alternative, is induced by A's threat to make the modification by a signed writing that is enforceable by statute without consideration. A's threat is not a breach of his duty of good faith and fair dealing, and the modification is not voidable by B. See Illustration 1 to § 89.

9. A contracts to excavate a cellar for B at a stated price. A begins the excavation and then threatens not to finish it unless B makes a separate contract to excavate the cellar of another building. B, having no reasonable alternative, is induced by A's threat to make the contract. A's threat is a breach of his duty of good faith and fair dealing, and the proposed contract is voidable by B. See Illustration 5 to § 175.

10. A contracts to sell part of a tract of land to B. B, solely to induce A to discharge him from his contract duty on favorable terms, threatens to resell the land to a purchaser whose industrial use will have an undesirable effect on A's remaining land, unless A releases B in return for a stated sum. A, having no reasonable alternative, signs the release. B's threat is a breach of his duty of good faith and fair dealing, and the modification is voidable by A.

11. A makes a threat to discharge B, his employee, unless B releases a claim that he has against A. The employment agreement is terminable at the will of either party, so that the discharge would not be a breach by A. B, having no reasonable alternative, releases the claim. A's threat is a breach of his duty of good faith and fair dealing, and the release is voidable by B. *f. Other improper threats.* The proper limits of bargaining are difficult to define with precision. Hard bargaining between experienced adversaries of relatively equal power ought not to be discouraged. Parties are generally held to the resulting agreement, even though one has taken advantage of the other's adversity, as long as the contract has been dictated by general economic forces. See Illustration 14. Where, however, a party has been induced to make a contract by some power exercised by the other for illegitimate ends, the transaction is suspect. For example, absent statute, a threat of refusal to deal with another party is ordinarily not duress, but if other factors are present an agreement that results from such a threat may be called into question. Subsection (2) deals with threats that are improper if the resulting exchange is not on fair terms. Clause (a) is concerned with cases in which a party threatens to do an act that would not significantly benefit him but would harm the other party. If, on the recipient's refusal to contract, the maker of the threat were to do the threatened act, it would therefore be done maliciously and unconscionably, out of pure vindictiveness. A typical example is a threat to make public embarrassing information concerning the recipient unless he makes a proposed contract. See Illustration 12 and Model Penal Code § 223.4(g). Clause (b) is concerned with cases in which the party making the threat has by unfair dealing achieved an advantage over the recipient that makes his threat unusually effective. Typical examples involve manipulative conduct during the bargaining stage that leaves one person at the mercy of the other. . . . Clause (c) is concerned with other cases in which the threatened act involves the use of power for illegitimate ends. Many of the situations encompassed

by clauses (1)(b), (1)(c), (2)(a) and (2)(b) involve extreme applications of this general rule, but it is more broadly applicable to analogous cases.... If, in any of these cases, the threat comes within Subsection (1), as where the threatened act or the threat itself is criminal or tortious (Clause (1)(a)), it is improper without an inquiry into the fairness of the resulting exchange under Subsection 2. See Comment *a*.

Illustrations

12. A makes a threat to B, his former employee, that he will try to prevent B's employment elsewhere unless B agrees to release a claim that he has against A. B, having no reasonable alternative, is thereby induced to make the contract. If the court concludes that the attempt to prevent B's employment elsewhere would harm B and would not significantly benefit A, A's threat is improper and the contract is voidable by B.

13. A, who has sold goods to B on several previous occasions, intentionally misleads B into thinking that he will supply the goods at the usual price and thereby causes B to delay in attempting to buy them elsewhere until it is too late to do so. A then threatens not to sell the goods to B unless he agrees to pay a price greatly in excess of that charged previously. B, being in urgent need of the goods, makes the contract. If the court concludes that the effectiveness of A's threat in inducing B to make the contract was significantly increased by A's prior unfair dealing, A's threat is improper and the contract is voidable by B.

14. The facts being otherwise as stated in Illustration 13, A merely discovers that B is in great need of the goods and that they are in short supply but does not mislead B into thinking that he will supply them. A's threat is not improper, and the contract is not voidable by B.

15. A operates a fur storage concession for customers of B's store. A becomes bankrupt and fails to pay C $1,000 for charges for storing furs of B's customers. C makes a threat to B not to deliver the furs to B's customers unless B makes a contract to pay C the $1,000 plus $2,000 that A owes C for storage of other furs. B, afraid of offending its customers and having no reasonable alternative, makes the contract. If the court concludes that C's threat to B is a use for illegitimate ends of its power as against B to retain the furs for the $1,000 owed for the storage of furs for B's customers, C's threat is improper and the contract is voidable by B.

16. A, a municipal water company, seeking to induce B, a developer, to make a contract for the extension of water mains to his development at a price greatly in excess of that charged to those similarly situated, threatens to refuse to supply to B unless B makes the contract. B, having no reasonable alternative, makes the contract. Because the threat amounts to a use for illegitimate ends of A's power not to supply water, the contract is voidable by B.

§ 177. When Undue Influence Makes a Contract Voidable.

(1) Undue influence is unfair persuasion of a party who is under the domination of the person exercising the persuasion or who by virtue of the relation between them is justified in assuming that that person will not act in a manner inconsistent with his welfare.

(2) If a party's manifestation of assent is induced by undue influence by the other party, the contract is voidable by the victim.

(3) If a party's manifestation of assent is induced by one who is not a party to the transaction, the contract is voidable by the victim unless the other party to the transaction in good faith and without reason to know of the undue influence either gives value or relies materially on the transaction.

Comment

a. Required domination or relation. The rule stated in this Section protects a person only if he is under the domination of another or is justified, by virtue of his relation with another in assuming that the other will not act inconsistently with his welfare. Relations that often fall within the rule include those of parent and child, husband and wife, clergyman and parishioner, and physician and patient. In each case it is a question of fact whether the relation is such as to give undue weight to the other's attempts at persuasion. The required relation may be found in situations other than those enumerated. However, the mere fact that a party is weak, infirm or aged does not of itself suffice, although it may be a factor in determining whether the required relation existed.

   b. Unfair persuasion. Where the required domination or relation is present, the contract is voidable if it was induced by any unfair persuasion on the part of the stronger party. The law of undue influence therefore affords protection in situations where the rules on duress and misrepresentation give no relief. The degree of persuasion that is unfair depends on a variety of circumstances. The ultimate question is whether the result was produced by means that seriously impaired the free and competent exercise of judgment. Such factors as the unfairness of the resulting bargain, the unavailability of independent advice, and the susceptibility of the person persuaded are circumstances to be taken into account in determining whether there was unfair persuasion, but they are not in themselves controlling. Compare § 173.

Illustrations

   1. A, who is not experienced in business, has for years been accustomed to rely in business matters on the advice of his friend, B, who is experienced in business. B constantly urges A to make a contract to sell to C, B's confederate, a tract of land at a price that is well below its fair value. A is thereby induced to make the contract. Even though B's conduct does not amount to misrepresentation, it amounts to undue influence because A is justified in assuming that B will not act in a manner inconsistent with his welfare, and the contract is voidable.

   2. A, an elderly and illiterate man, lives with and depends for his support on B, his nephew. B tells A that he will no longer support him unless A makes a contract to sell B a tract of land. A is thereby induced to make the proposed contract. Even though B's conduct does not amount to duress, it amounts to undue influence because A is under the domination of B, and the contract is voidable by A.

   c. Undue influence by a third person. If a party's assent has been induced by the undue influence of a third person rather than that of the other party to the contract, the contract is nevertheless voidable by the victim, unless the other party has in good faith either given value or changed his position materially in reliance on the transaction. The rule is similar to that for misrepresentation (see Comment c to § 164) and duress (see Comment b to § 175). Compare Illustration 1.

CHAPTER 8

UNENFORCEABILITY ON GROUNDS OF PUBLIC POLICY

TOPIC 1. UNENFORCEABILITY IN GENERAL

§ 178. When a Term Is Unenforceable on Grounds of Public Policy.

(1) A promise or other term of an agreement is unenforceable on grounds of public policy if legislation provides that it is unenforceable or the interest in its enforcement is clearly outweighed in the circumstances by a public policy against the enforcement of such terms.

(2) In weighing the interest in the enforcement of a term, account is taken of

(a) the parties' justified expectations,

(b) any forfeiture that would result if enforcement were denied, and

(c) any special public interest in the enforcement of the particular term.

(3) In weighing a public policy against enforcement of a term, account is taken of

(a) the strength of that policy as manifested by legislation or judicial decisions,

(b) the likelihood that a refusal to enforce the term will further that policy,

(c) the seriousness of any misconduct involved and the extent to which it was deliberate, and

(d) the directness of the connection between that misconduct and the term.

Comment

a. Legislation providing for unenforceability. Occasionally, on grounds of public policy, legislation provides that specified kinds of promises or other terms are unenforceable. Whether such legislation is valid and applicable to the particular term in dispute is beyond the scope of this Restatement. Assuming that it is, the court is bound to carry out the legislative mandate with respect to the enforceability of the term. But with respect to such other matters as the enforceability of the rest of the agreement (§§ 183, 184) and the possibility of restitution (Topic 5), a court will be guided by the same rules that apply to other terms unenforceable on grounds of public policy (see Illustration 1), absent contrary provision in the legislation itself (see Illustration 3). The term "legislation" is used here in the broadest sense to include any fixed text enacted by a body with authority to promulgate rules, including not only statutes, but constitutions and local ordinances, as well as administrative regulations issued pursuant to them. It also encompasses foreign laws to the extent that they are applicable under conflict of laws rules. See Restatement, Second, Conflict of Laws §§ 202, 203.

Illustrations

1. A promises to pay B $1,000 if the Buckets win their basketball game with the Hoops, and B promises to pay A $2,000 if the Hoops win. A state statute makes wagering a crime and provides that a promise such as A's or B's is "void." A's and B's promises are unenforceable on grounds of public policy. Any claims of A or B to restitution for money paid under the agreement are governed by the rules stated in Topic 5. See § 199(b) and Illustrations 4 and 5 to that section.

2. A and B make an agreement by which A agrees to sell and B to buy, at a fixed price per bushel, one thousand bushels of wheat from A at any time that A shall choose during the following month. The state statute that makes wagering a crime does not apply to such an agreement and it does not offend any judicially declared public policy. Enforcement of A's and B's promises is not precluded on grounds of public policy.

3. A borrows $10,000 from the B Bank, promising to repay it with interest at the rate of twelve per cent. A state statute that fixes the maximum legal rate of interest on such loans at ten per cent provides that a promise to pay a greater sum is "void" as usurious as to all the promised interest but not as to the principal. A's promise to pay the interest is unenforceable on grounds of public policy. The rule stated in § 184(2) does not make A's promise to pay interest enforceable up to ten per cent because the legislation provides otherwise. Compare Illustration 5 to § 184.

b. Balancing of interests. Only infrequently does legislation, on grounds of public policy, provide that a term is unenforceable. When a court reaches that conclusion, it usually does so on the basis of a public policy derived either from its own perception of the need to protect some aspect of the public welfare or from legislation that is relevant to that policy although it says nothing explicitly about unenforceability. See § 179. In some cases the contravention of public policy is so grave, as when an agreement involves a serious crime or tort, that unenforceability is plain. In other cases the contravention is so trivial as that it plainly does not preclude enforcement. In doubtful cases, however, a decision as to enforceability is reached only after a careful balancing, in the light of all the circumstances, of the interest in the enforcement of the particular promise against the policy against the enforcement of such terms. The most common factors in the balancing process are set out in Subsections (2) and (3). Enforcement will be denied only if the factors that argue against enforcement clearly outweigh the law's traditional interest in protecting the expectations of the parties, its abhorrence of any unjust enrichment, and any public interest in the enforcement of the particular term.

c. Strength of policy. The strength of the public policy involved is a critical factor in the balancing process. Even when the policy is one manifested by legislation, it may be too insubstantial to outweigh the interest in the enforcement of the term in question. See Illustrations 4 and 5. A court should be particularly alert to this possibility in the case of minor administrative regulations or local ordinances that may not be indicative of the general welfare. A disparity between a relatively modest criminal sanction provided by the legislature and a much larger forfeiture that will result if enforcement of the promise is refused may suggest that the policy is not substantial enough to justify the refusal. See Illustration 4.

Illustrations

4. A and B make an agreement for the sale of goods for $10,000, in which A promises to deliver the goods in his own truck at a designated time and place. A municipal parking ordinance makes unloading of a truck at that time and place an offense punishable by a fine of up to $50. A delivers the goods to B as provided. Because the public policy manifested by the ordinance is not sufficiently substantial to outweigh the interest in the enforcement of B's promise, enforcement of his promise is not precluded on grounds of public policy.

5. A promises to employ B and B promises to work for A, all work to be done on weekdays. The agreement is made on Sunday in violation of a statute that makes the doing of business on Sunday a misdemeanor. If the court decides that the public policy manifested by the statute is not sufficiently substantial to outweigh the interests in enforcement of A's and B's promises, it will hold that enforcement of their promises is not precluded on grounds of public policy.

d. Connection with term. The extent to which a refusal to enforce a promise or other term on grounds of public policy will further that policy depends not only on the strength of the policy but also on the relation of the term to that policy and to any misconduct involved. In most cases there is a promise that involves conduct offensive to the policy. The promise may be one to engage in such conduct. See Illustration 6. Or it may be one that tends to induce the other party to engage in such conduct. This tendency may result from the fact that the promise is made in return for the promisee's engaging in the conduct (see Illustration 7) or in return for the promisee's return promise to engage in the conduct (see Illustration 8). Or it may result from the fact that the duty to perform the promise is conditional on the promisee's engaging in the conduct (see Illustration 9). In such cases, it is the tendency itself that makes the promise unenforceable, even though the promise does not actually induce the conduct. There are other situations in which the conduct is not itself against public policy, but it is against public policy to promise to engage in such conduct or to attempt to induce it. It is sometimes objectionable to make a commitment to engage in conduct that is not in itself objectionable. This is the case, for example, for a promise to vote in a particular way. See Illustration 10. It is sometimes objectionable to attempt to induce conduct that is not in itself objectionable. This is the case, for example, for a promise made in consideration of the promisee's voting in a particular way. See

Illustration 11. This list does not exhaust all of the possible relations between the conduct and the promise that may justify a decision that the promise is unenforceable. But as the relation between the conduct and the promise becomes tenuous, it becomes difficult to justify unenforceability unless serious misconduct is involved. A party will not be barred from enforcing a promise because of misconduct that is so remote or collateral that refusal to enforce the promise will not deter such conduct and enforcement will not amount to an inappropriate use of the judicial process. See Illustrations 15 and 16. However, a new promise to perform an earlier promise that was unenforceable on grounds of public policy is also unenforceable on those grounds unless the circumstances that made the first promise unenforceable no longer exist. The rules stated in §§ 183 and 184 involve special applications of these general principles concerning the relation between the conduct and the promise.

Illustrations

6. A, the owner of a newspaper, promises B that he will publish a statement about C known by A and B to be false and defamatory if B pays him $10,000. B pays A $10,000. A's promise is one to commit a tort (§ 192) and is unenforceable on grounds of public policy.

7. B promises to pay A, the owner of a newspaper, $10,000 if he will publish a statement about C known by A and B to be false and defamatory. A publishes the libel. B's promise is one tending to induce A to commit a tort (§ 192) and is unenforceable on grounds of public policy.

8. A, the owner of a newspaper, promises B that he will publish a statement about C known by A and B to be false and defamatory if B will promise to pay him $10,000. B makes the promise. A's promise is one tending to induce A to commit a tort (§ 192). Both promises are unenforceable on grounds of public policy.

9. B promises to convey a tract of land worth $11,000 to A, the owner of a newspaper, if A pays B $1,000, B's duty to be conditional on A's publishing a statement about C known by A and B to be false and defamatory. A pays B $1,000 and publishes the libel. B's promise is one tending to induce A to commit a tort (§ 192) and is unenforceable on grounds of public policy. Compare § 185.

10. A pays B, a competitor, $10,000 for B's promise not to compete with A for a year. Although B's refraining from competition with A would not in itself be improper, B's promise not to compete with A unreasonably restrains B from competition (§ 186) and is unenforceable on grounds of public policy.

11. A promises to pay B, a competitor, $10,000 if he will refrain from competing with A for a year. Although B's refraining from competing with A would not in itself be improper, A's promise unreasonably tends to induce B to refrain from competition (§ 186) and is unenforceable on grounds of public policy.

12. A induces B to make an agreement to buy goods on credit from A by bribing B's purchasing agent. A delivers the goods to B. A's bribe tends to induce the agent to violate his fiduciary duty. B's promise to pay the price is unenforceable on grounds of public policy. See § 193.

13. A, who wants to induce B to buy goods from him, promises to pay C $1,000 if he will bribe B's purchasing agent to arrange the sale. C does so. C's bribe tends to induce the agent to violate his fiduciary duty. A's promise is unenforceable on grounds of public policy. See § 193.

14. A, who wants to induce B to buy goods from him, promises to pay C $1,000 if he arranges the sale. C arranges the sale by bribing B's purchasing agent. C's bribe tends to induce the agent to violate his fiduciary duty. A's promise is unenforceable on grounds of public policy. See § 193.

15. A and B make an agreement for exclusive dealing that is unenforceable because unreasonably in restraint of trade (§ 186). A sells and delivers goods pursuant to the unenforceable agreement to C, who promises to pay the price. Because the relation between C's promise to pay the price and the unreasonable restraint is too remote, enforcement of C's promise is not precluded on grounds of public policy.

16. A and B make a wagering agreement in violation of a statute that makes such agreements "void." When A loses, C pays B at A's request, and A promises C to pay him that amount. Because the relation between A's promise to pay C and the improper wager is too remote, enforcement of A's promise is not precluded on grounds of public policy.

e. Other factors. A court will be reluctant to frustrate a party's legitimate expectations unless there is a corresponding benefit to be gained in deterring misconduct or avoiding an inappropriate use of the judicial process. See Illustration 17. The promisee's ignorance or inadvertence, even if it does not bring him within the rule stated in § 180, is one factor in determining the weight to be attached to his expectations. See Illustration 4 to § 181. To the extent, however, that he engaged in misconduct that was serious or deliberate, his claim to protection of his expectations fails. The interest in favor of enforcement becomes much stronger after the promisee has relied substantially on those expectations as by preparation or performance. The court will then take into account any enrichment of the promisor and any forfeiture by the promisee if he should lose his right to the agreed exchange after he has relied substantially on those expectations. See Comment b to § 227. The possibility of restitution may be significant in this connection. See Topic 5. In addition to the interest of the promisee, the court will also weigh any interest that the public or third parties may have in the enforcement of the term in question. Such an interest may be particularly evident where the policy involved is designed to protect third parties. See Illustrations 18 and 19.

Illustrations

17. A agrees to reimburse B for any legal expenses incurred if B will go on C's land in order to test a right of way that is disputed by A and C. B goes on C's land. Enforcement of A's promise is not precluded on grounds of public policy, even if it is later determined that B has committed a trespass. Compare § 192.

18. A, a trustee under a will, makes an agreement with B in violation of A's fiduciary duty. If enforcement of A's and B's promises is desirable for the protection of the beneficiaries, it is not precluded on grounds of public policy. Compare § 193.

19. A, B, and C, directors of a bank, make notes payable to the bank in order to deceive the bank examiner. They agree that the notes shall be returned and cancelled after they have served their purpose. Enforcement of the promises of A, B and C embodied in the notes is not precluded on grounds of public policy.

f. Effect on rest of agreement. The rules stated in this Section determine only whether a particular promise or other term is unenforceable. The question of the effect of such a determination on the rest of the agreement is sometimes a complex one. If there is only one promise in the transaction and it is unenforceable, then the question will not arise. (As to the divisibility of such a promise, however, see §§ 184, 185). This is the case for offers that have been accepted by a performance rather than by a promise (§ 53), for promises enforceable because of reliance by the promisee (§ 90), and for promises under seal (§ 95). Furthermore, even when there is another promise, it too is often unenforceable under the rules stated in this Section. This is the case, for example, where one party's promise is unenforceable because the promised conduct offends public policy and the other party's return promise is unenforceable because it tends to induce that conduct. See Illustration 8. There are, however, situations in which only one party's promise is unenforceable while the other party's return promise is enforceable, as is the case where the promisee of the return promise belongs to the class sought to be protected by the policy in question. See Illustrations 3, 4 and 5 to § 179 and Illustration 5 to § 181. (That an unenforceable promise may be consideration for a return promise, see § 78.) Finally, there are circumstances in which the unenforceability of one part of an agreement does not entail the unenforceability of the rest of the agreement, and these are dealt with in §§ 183 and 184. As to the effect of public policy on conditions, see § 185.

§ 179. Bases of Public Policies Against Enforcement.

A public policy against the enforcement of promises or other terms may be derived by the court from

    (a) legislation relevant to such a policy, or

    (b) the need to protect some aspect of the public welfare, as is the case for the judicial policies against, for example,

        (i) restraint of trade (§§ 186–188),

        (ii) impairment of family relations (§§ 189–191), and

        (iii) interference with other protected interests (§§ 192–196, 356).

Comment

a. Development of the judicial role. Historically, the public policies against enforcement of terms were developed by judges themselves on the basis of their own perception of the need to protect some aspect of the public welfare. Some of these policies are now rooted in precedents accumulated over centuries. Important examples are the policies against restraint of trade, impairment of domestic relations, and interference with duties owed to individuals. These are singled out for mention in Paragraph (b) because they are dealt with in detail in Topics 2–4 of this Chapter. Society has, however, many other interests that are worthy of protection, and as society changes so do these interests. Courts remain alert to other and sometimes novel situations in which enforcement of a term may contravene those interests. See Illustration 1. At the same time, courts should not implement obsolete policies that have lost their vigor over the course of years. The rule of this Section is therefore an open-ended one that does not purport to exhaust the categories of recognized public policies.

Illustration

1. A and B make a written agreement that contains a term providing that "no prior negotiations shall be used to interpret this agreement." Prior negotiations would otherwise be admissible to establish the meaning of the writing (§ 214(c)). If the court decides that the term would unreasonably deprive it of relevant evidence that would enable it to resolve an ambiguity in the agreement and thereby hamper it in the fair administration of justice, it will hold that the term is unenforceable on grounds of public policy.

b. Modern role of legislation. The declaration of public policy has now become largely the province of legislators rather than judges. This is in part because legislators are supported by facilities for factual investigations and can be more responsive to the general public. When proscribing conduct, however, legislators seldom address themselves explicitly to the problems of contract law that may arise in connection with such conduct. See § 178(a). Usually they do not even have these problems in mind and say nothing as to the enforceability of terms. In such situations it is pointless to search for the "intention of the legislature," and the court's task is to determine on its own whether it should, by refusing to enforce the promise, add a sanction to those already provided by the legislature. This is a question of "law," in the conventional sense, rather than one of "fact." The legislation is significant, not as controlling the disposition of the case, but as enlightening the court concerning some specific policy to which it is relevant. A court will examine the particular statute in the light of the whole legislative scheme in the jurisdiction to see, for example, if similar statutes in the same area contain explicit provisions making comparable promises unenforceable. It will look to the purpose and history of the statute. The fact that the statute explicitly prohibits the making of a promise or the engaging in the promised conduct may be persuasive in showing a policy against enforcement of a promise but it is not necessarily conclusive. On the other hand, the fact that the statute provides a civil sanction, whether in addition to a criminal penalty or not, may suggest that no other civil sanction such as unenforceability is intended, but this is not necessarily conclusive either. See Illustration 2. Furthermore, even though a field is the subject of legislation, a court may decide that the legislature has not entirely occupied the field and may refuse to enforce a term on grounds of a judicially developed public policy even though there is no contravention of the legislation. The term "legislation" is used here in the same broad sense as in the preceding section. See Comment a to § 178. Although no attempt is made in this Restatement to state rules to deal with any of the myriad of specific pieces of legislation that may be involved in such controversies, § 181 deals with the important cases involving licensing requirements.

Illustration

2. A induces B to make an agreement to buy goods on credit from A by bribing B's purchasing agent. A delivers the goods to B. A state statute makes such bribery a crime and gives B a civil action to recover the amount of the bribe against A. Although the statute already provides for a civil sanction, a court may decide that B's promise to pay the price is unenforceable on grounds of public policy. Cf. Illustration 12 to § 178.

c. When refusal to enforce may frustrate policy. In some instances, refusal to enforce a term may frustrate rather than further public policy. This is likely to be the case where legislation was enacted to protect a class of persons to which the promisee belongs in transactions of the kind involved. In such instances, there is no policy against the enforcement of the promise by one who belongs to that class.

Illustrations

3. A, a corporation, makes an agreement to do work for B, a city. C, an official of B, is also a principal shareholder of A, and a statute prohibits the making of such agreements and subjects those who make them to penalties. A's performance of the agreement is defective. Since the statute was enacted to protect a class of persons to which B belongs against a class to which A belongs, enforcement of A's promise is not precluded on grounds of public policy and B can recover damages from A for breach of contract.

4. A, an insurance company, issues a policy of fire insurance to B on his house. The policy differs from that required by a state statute prescribing a standard fire policy. B's house is destroyed by fire. Since the statute was enacted to protect a class of persons to which B belongs against a class to which A belongs, enforcement of A's promise is not precluded on grounds of public policy and B can recover the insurance proceeds from A.

5. A employs B to work in his factory and promises to pay him double for the overtime if B works ten hours a day instead of the usual eight. A state statute, designed to protect the health of workers in such factories, provides a maximum period of employment of eight hours a day and makes violation a crime for both employer and employee. B works ten hours a day but A refuses to pay him extra for the overtime. A court may decide that the statute was enacted to protect a class of persons to which B belongs against a class to which A belongs and that therefore enforcement of A's promise is not precluded on grounds of public policy.

6. A, a bank, invests in a real estate mortgage. A statute prohibits it from making such investments and subjects it to penalties for doing so. Since otherwise the creditors and shareholders of the bank, for whose protection the statute was enacted, would be injured, enforcement of the mortgage debt is not precluded on grounds of public policy and the bank may recover on the debt and foreclose the mortgage.

d. Change of circumstances. Whether a promise is unenforceable on grounds of public policy is determined as of the time that the promise is made and is not ordinarily affected by a subsequent change of circumstances, whether of fact or law. If, however, both parties were excusably ignorant of facts or of legislation of a minor character that made it unenforceable, a change as to these may make the promise enforceable. Compare § 180.

§ 180. Effect of Excusable Ignorance.

If a promisee is excusably ignorant of facts or of legislation of a minor character, of which the promisor is not excusably ignorant and in the absence of which the promise would be enforceable, the promisee has a claim for damages for its breach but cannot recover damages for anything that he has done after he learns of the facts or legislation.

Comment

a. Excusable ignorance. At the time a promise is made, the promisee may be excusably ignorant of facts that contravene the public policy in question. Furthermore, although for the purposes of this Chapter, parties are generally charged with knowledge of policies affecting enforceability, this Section states a limited exception for a party who is excusably ignorant of legislation of a minor character from which the policy is derived. Such ignorance is more likely to be excusable where the legislation is of a local, specialized or technical nature and where the other party may be assumed to have knowledge as to such matters. In determining whether ignorance of fact or law is excusable, any misrepresentations made by the other party are relevant. However, good faith is expected on the part of the party who claims ignorance and he cannot blind his eyes because he does not wish to see. Furthermore, the matter of which he is ignorant must not be one as to which he is expected to have knowledge because of his expertise or his relation to the transaction.

b. Promisor must not be excusably ignorant. The promisee's excusable ignorance is not by itself enough to give him the right to enforce the promise under this Section. The promisor must not be excusably ignorant as to the matter in question. (That an unenforceable promise can be consideration for a return promise, see § 78.) If the promisor has specialized knowledge of the field involved, he is likely to be charged with knowledge as to legislation of even a minor character. It is not necessary that the promisor make any misrepresentation, although a misrepresentation by him may be significant as bearing on whether the promisee's ignorance is excusable. See Comment a. Furthermore, on learning the truth, the promisee is expected promptly to withdraw from the transaction and render no further performance.

Illustrations

1. A and B make an agreement under which B promises to deliver to A goods. B already has a contract to deliver the goods to C, but A neither knows nor has reason to know this. On learning of B's contract with C, A refuses to take the goods or pay the price. Enforcement of B's promise to deliver the goods to A is not precluded on grounds of public policy and A has a claim against B for damages. But see § 194.

2. A and B make an agreement under which A promises to pay B $10,000 in return for B's promise to cut down trees on a specified tract of land. A knows that the land belongs to C rather than to A, but B neither knows nor has reason to know this. C prohibits entry on the land. Enforcement of A's promise to pay B $10,000 is not precluded on grounds of public policy and B has a claim against A for damages. As to the rights of A and B if A neither knows nor has reason to know that C is the owner, see § 198(b).

3. A, an insurance company, makes an agreement with B under which it promises to employ B for a year. A has not obtained a license required for it lawfully to do business, but B neither knows nor has reason to know this. On discovering it after he has begun to work, B promptly refuses further services. Enforcement of A's promise to employ B is not precluded on grounds of public policy and B has a claim against A for damages.

4. A and B make an agreement under which A, a builder, promises to build a house for B for $100,000. The plan and specifications involve violations of local building ordinances of which B neither knows nor has reason to know. On discovering the violations, B promptly refuses to allow A to proceed with the work. Enforcement of A's promise to build the house is not precluded on grounds of public policy and B has a claim against A for damages.

5. A, the owner of a newspaper, promises B that he will publish a statement about C that A knows is false and defamatory if B pays him $10,000. B, who is ignorant of the law of torts and does not know the statement is actionable as libel, pays A $10,000. A's promise to publish the statement is unenforceable on grounds of public policy.

c. Other effects of ignorance. If both the promisor and the promisee are excusably ignorant, the promisee may have a claim in restitution under the rule stated in § 198 even though he has no claim for damages under this Section. Furthermore, a court may take account of a party's ignorance, even if it is not excusable, in applying the rule stated in § 178. See Comment e to § 178.

§ 181. Effect of Failure to Comply With Licensing or Similar Requirement.

If a party is prohibited from doing an act because of his failure to comply with a licensing, registration or similar requirement, a promise in consideration of his doing that act or of his promise to do it is unenforceable on grounds of public policy if

(a) the requirement has a regulatory purpose, and

(b) the interest in the enforcement of the promise is clearly outweighed by the public policy behind the requirement.

Comment

a. Scope. One of the most frequent applications of the general rule stated in § 178 occurs where a party seeks to enforce an agreement although he has failed to obtain a license, to register or to comply with a similar requirement. This Section states a specific version of that general rule as it applies to such cases.

Whether there has been a violation of legislation that imposes the requirement is a matter of interpretation of the legislation itself and is beyond the scope of this Restatement.

   b. Regulatory purpose. In deciding whether a party can enforce an agreement in spite of his failure to comply with such a requirement, courts distinguish between requirements that have a regulatory purpose and those that do not. The policy behind a requirement that has a regulatory purpose may be regarded as sufficiently substantial to preclude enforcement, while the policy behind one that is merely designed to raise revenue will not be. In determining whether a measure has a regulatory purpose, a court will consider the entire legislative scheme, including any relevant declaration of purpose. Common indications of regulation include provisions for examination or apprenticeship to ensure minimum standards on entrance and provisions for the posting of a bond or procedures for license revocation to ensure that standards are maintained.

Illustration

   1. A, an unlicensed broker, agrees to arrange a transaction for B, for which B promises to pay A $1,000. A city ordinance requires persons arranging such transactions to be licensed as a result of paying a fee, with no inquiry into competence or responsibility. A arranges the transaction. Since the licensing requirement is designed merely to raise revenue and does not have a regulatory purpose, enforcement of B's promise is not precluded on grounds of public policy.

   c. Balancing where purpose is regulatory. If the court decides that the requirement has a regulatory purpose, it must then weigh the interests favoring enforcement of the promise against the public policy behind the requirement. The factors listed in § 178 are taken into account in this process. If the party who has failed to comply with the requirement has done nothing by way of preparation or performance, the interest in enforcement of the promise is easily outweighed. But if, as is usually the case, he has completely performed and is seeking the promised compensation for that performance, forfeiture to himself and enrichment to the other party may result from a refusal to enforce the other party's promise. In determining the extent to which forfeiture and enrichment will result, a court will consider the possibilities that part of the agreement may be enforceable (see § 183 and Illustration 1 to that section) and that restitution may be available (see § 197 and Illustration 4 to that section). In evaluating the gravity of the public policy involved, the court will look to the interest that the regulation is designed to protect and will give greater weight, for example, to a measure intended to protect the public health or safety than one intended to have only an economic effect. Compare Illustrations 2 and 3. It will consider the magnitude of the penalty provided by the legislature as some indication of the weight that it attached to that interest. It will also take account of the extent to which the misconduct was deliberate or inadvertent. See Illustration 4.

Illustrations

   2. A, an unlicensed plumber, agrees to repair plumbing in B's home, for which B promises to pay A $1,000. A state statute, enacted to prevent the public from being victimized by incompetent plumbers and to protect the public health, requires persons doing plumbing to be licensed on the basis of an examination, the posting of a bond, and the payment of a fee, and makes violation a crime. A does the agreed work. A court may decide that the public policy against enforcement of B's promise outweighs the interest in its enforcement, and that B's promise is unenforceable on grounds of public policy. Compare Illustration 1 to § 183.

   3. A, an unlicensed milk dealer, promises to deliver to B, a licensed milk dealer, milk for which B promises to pay $20,000. A state statute designed for the purpose of economic regulation of the milk industry provides that "no dealer shall buy or sell milk without a license," and makes violation a misdemeanor punishable by a fine of up to $500 and imprisonment for up to 6 months. A delivers the milk to B, but B refuses to pay the price. In view of all the circumstances, including the discrepancy between the forfeiture by A if B's promise were not enforced and the penalty provided by the statute, a court may decide that the public policy against enforcement of B's promise does not outweigh the interest in its enforcement and that enforcement of B's promise is not precluded on grounds of public policy.

   4. The facts being otherwise as stated in Illustration 2, A had once been licensed but his license had expired the week before because, unknown to him, his clerk had inadvertently forgotten to send

in the renewal fee, although the bond had been extended. The court may decide that in all the circumstances including A's ignorance of the fact that he was unlicensed, enforcement of B's promise is not precluded on grounds of public policy.

d. Enforcement by the other party. The rule stated in this Section deals only with the right of the non-complying party to enforce the other party's promise. The enforceability of the non-complying party's promise is governed by the general rule stated in § 178. Regulatory legislation may be designed to protect a class of persons to which the other party belongs against a class to which the non-complying party belongs. See Comment c to § 179. In that case the policy behind the legislation will usually best be served by holding the non-complying party liable in damages for any defective performance. See Illustration 5.

Illustration

5. The facts being otherwise as stated in Illustration 2, A's work is defective. Since the ordinance was enacted to protect a class of persons to which B belongs against a class to which A belongs, enforcement of A's promise is not precluded on grounds of public policy and B can recover damages from A for breach of contract.

§ 182. Effect of Performance if Intended Use Is Improper.

If the promisee has substantially performed, enforcement of a promise is not precluded on grounds of public policy because of some improper use that the promisor intends to make of what he obtains unless the promisee

(a) acted for the purpose of furthering the improper use, or

(b) knew of the use and the use involves grave social harm.

Comment

a. Scope. A significant application of the general rule stated in § 178 occurs where one party intends to use goods, money, or something else that he acquires in the transaction in a manner contrary to public policy. Whether that party's promise to render his own performance is unenforceable on grounds of public policy depends on the balancing process required under that rule. Even if his promise would be unenforceable if the agreement were wholly executory, however, his receipt of performance may justify enforcement. This Section states a rule that determines when this is so by resolving the problem of balancing in such a case. Situations that do not come within it because the promisee has not substantially performed are governed by the general rule stated in § 178.

b. Action for purpose of furthering use. If the improper use involves grave social harm, as where it threatens human life, the promisee's mere knowledge of the use is sufficient to bar him from recovering for his performance. If the improper use does not involve grave social harm, the promisee is not barred from recovery unless he not only knew of the use but acted for the purpose of furthering it. Whether the promisee acted for such a purpose is a question of fact. It may be evidenced by his doing of specific acts to facilitate the improper use. It may also be evidenced by a course of dealing with persons engaged in improper conduct. In close cases, a court will consider whether denial of recovery will deter the improper conduct or, on the contrary, encourage persons engaging in such conduct to enter into transactions knowing that their promises are unenforceable.

Illustrations

1. A sells and delivers to B a shotgun on credit. The sale of firearms is legal, but B plans to use the gun in hunting without a license required by law and A knows this. Enforcement of B's promise to pay the price is not precluded on grounds of public policy. If B planned to use the gun to commit a robbery and A knew this, B's promise to pay the price would be unenforceable on those grounds.

2. A, who has lost $1,000 by playing faro, promises B, who regularly makes loans to gamblers, that he will repay B with interest in thirty days if B will make him three loans: $1,000 to cover his losses, $4,000 to recoup them by continuing to play faro, and $2,000 to support his family while he does so. B lends A a total of $7,000, and A loses it all playing faro. A state statute makes playing faro for money a crime. Enforcement of A's promise to repay the $1,000 to cover his losses and the $2,000 to

support his family is not precluded on grounds of public policy. Since A lent him the $4,000 for the purpose of furthering B's gambling, B's promise to repay the $4,000 is unenforceable on those grounds.

3. A sells and delivers to B a quantity of plants. The sale of such plants is legal, but B plans to transport them to a country where quarantine regulations forbid their importation. A not only knows this, but so packs and marks them as to conceal their character in order to aid B's plan. B's promise to pay the price is unenforceable on grounds of public policy.

§ 183. When Agreement Is Enforceable as to Agreed Equivalents.

If the parties' performances can be apportioned into corresponding pairs of part performances so that the parts of each pair are properly regarded as agreed equivalents and one pair is not offensive to public policy, that portion of the agreement is enforceable by a party who did not engage in serious misconduct.

Comment

a. Concept of "divisibility" or "severability." This Section deals with the situation in which a party is allowed to enforce one part of an agreement even though another part of the same agreement is unenforceable on grounds of public policy, for the reason that the first part does not materially advance the improper purpose. It illustrates a general technique by which a court can mitigate the harshness of a rule that bars a party from enforcing an agreement by apportioning the performances into corresponding pairs of part performances and then enforcing the agreement as to only one part. Another common illustration of this technique occurs when a party is allowed to insist on his right to a return performance under one part of an agreement even though he has committed a material breach under another part of the same agreement. See § 240. In situations where this mitigating technique is applied, the agreement is sometimes said to be "divisible" or "severable." This terminology is avoided here as wrongly suggesting that an agreement itself can be characterized as "divisible" or "severable" for all purposes and in any circumstances. A court may conclude that an agreement that is "divisible" or "severable" for one purpose or in some circumstances is not "divisible" or "severable" for another purpose or in other circumstances. The concept is a flexible one, to be applied on a case by case basis.

b. Requirements. The rule stated in this Section applies when four requirements are met. The first is that it must be possible to apportion the parties' performances into corresponding pairs of part performances. This process of apportionment is essentially one of calculation and the rule cannot be applied unless calculation is feasible. But it is enough in a contract for the sale of goods, for example, if the price of separate items is separately stated in the agreement itself or in a price list on which the agreement was based, or can be reliably ascertained from stated prices for components or from a total price for similar items. See Comment d to § 240. The second requirement is that the corresponding pairs of part performances must be properly regarded as agreed equivalents. This means that the parts of the pair must be of roughly equivalent value to the injured party in terms of his expectation with respect to the total agreed exchange. Fairness requires that a party, having received only a fraction of the performance that he expected under an agreement, not be asked to pay an identical fraction of the price that he originally promised on the expectation of full performance, unless it appears that the performance that he actually received is worth to him roughly the same fraction of what full performance would have been worth to him. Because the rule is based on considerations of fairness, it is necessarily somewhat imprecise and flexible. Its application may be especially attractive where it will avoid forfeiture by a party who has already relied on the agreement, as by preparation or performance. In this connection, the availability of restitution as an alternative means of avoiding forfeiture is relevant. See Topic 5. Decisions holding that part performances are not properly regarded as agreed equivalents for some other purpose, for example in the case of material breach (§ 240) are not determinative under this Section. See Comment a; Comment e to § 240. The third requirement is that one of the pairs of performances must not be offensive to public policy. If the entire agreement is part of an integrated scheme to contravene public policy, none of it will be enforced. The fourth requirement is that the party seeking enforcement must not have engaged in serious misconduct. This will depend on the gravity of the public policy involved and the extent of the party's involvement in its contravention. A court will not use the mitigating technique of this Section in favor of a party whose misconduct is so serious that a refusal to enforce the entire agreement is a proper sanction to discourage such conduct. In such a case enforcement of any part of the agreement would amount to a misuse of official authority.

Illustrations

1. A, an unlicensed plumber, agrees to install plumbing in B's home for which B agrees to pay $1,000 for labor and $500 for materials. A city ordinance, designed to prevent the public from being victimized by incompetent plumbers and to protect the public health, requires persons doing plumbing to be licensed on the basis of an examination, the posting of a bond, and the payment of a fee, and makes violation a misdemeanor. A does the agreed work. Even if the court decides that B's promise to pay $1,000 for labor is unenforceable on grounds of public policy, it may decide that B's promise to pay $500 for materials is not. If the price for materials is not separately stated, the court may reach the same decision if it can reliably ascertain it from A's price lists or from market prices.

2. A promises to deliver fish to B in ten equal monthly installments in return for B's promise to pay for each installment within 90 days. After three installments have been delivered, B decides to resell the fish as sardines in violation of a statute that makes such mislabelling a misdemeanor, and A agrees to pack them so as to aid B in doing so. Even though B's promise to pay for the last seven installments is unenforceable on grounds of public policy (§ 182) his promise to pay for the first three is not.

c. When apportionment not possible. Even if the parties' performances cannot be apportioned into corresponding pairs of part performances under the rule stated in this Section, the unenforceability of a single promise or other term on grounds of public policy does not necessarily mean that the entire agreement is unenforceable. If the unenforceable term is relatively unimportant in relation to the entire agreement, the rest of the agreement may be salvaged under the rule stated in the following section.

§ 184. When Rest of Agreement Is Enforceable.

(1) If less than all of an agreement is unenforceable under the rule stated in § 178, a court may nevertheless enforce the rest of the agreement in favor of a party who did not engage in serious misconduct if the performance as to which the agreement is unenforceable is not an essential part of the agreed exchange.

(2) A court may treat only part of a term as unenforceable under the rule stated in Subsection (1) if the party who seeks to enforce the term obtained it in good faith and in accordance with reasonable standards of fair dealing.

Comment

a. Refusal to enforce a promise. Under the rule stated in the preceding Section, an agreement may be unenforceable as to corresponding equivalents on each side but enforceable as to the rest. If it is not possible to apportion the parties' performances in this way so that corresponding concessions are made on both sides, a refusal to enforce only part of the agreement will necessarily result in some inequality. If the performance as to which the agreement is unenforceable is an essential part of the agreed exchange, the inequality will be so great as to make the entire agreement unenforceable. Under Subsection (1), however, if that performance is not an essential part of the agreed exchange, a court may enforce all but the part that contravenes public policy. For example, a promise not to compete that is unreasonably in restraint of trade will often not invalidate the entire agreement of which it is a part. Whether the performance is an essential part of the agreed exchange depends on its relative importance in the light of the entire agreement between the parties. A party who has engaged in such serious misconduct that the entire agreement is unenforceable cannot take advantage of the rule stated in Subsection (1). See Comment d to § 178.

Illustration

1. A employs B as head bookkeeper of his retail clothing store under an employment agreement in which B promises not to work in the retail clothing business in the same town for three years after the termination of his employment. B works for A for five years but does not deal directly with customers and acquires no confidential information in his work. Although B's promise is unreasonably in restraint of trade and is unenforceable on grounds of public policy, enforcement of the rest of the employment agreement is not precluded on those grounds. See Illustration 8 to § 188.

b. Refusal to enforce part of a term. Sometimes a term is unenforceable on grounds of public policy because it is too broad, even though a narrower term would be enforceable. In such a situation, under Subsection (2), the court may refuse to enforce only part of the term, while enforcing the other part of the term as well as the rest of the agreement. The court's power in such a case is not a power of reformation, however, and it will not, in the course of determining what part of the term to enforce, add to the scope of the term in any way. A court will not exercise this discretion in favor of a party unless it appears that he made the agreement in good faith and in accordance with reasonable standards of fair dealing. Compare §§ 157, 205. For example, a court will not aid a party who has taken advantage of his dominant bargaining power to extract from the other party a promise that is clearly so broad as to offend public policy by redrafting the agreement so as to make a part of the promise enforceable. The fact that the term is contained in a standard form supplied by the dominant party argues against aiding him in this request. Whether a particular dispute involves a single term, so that it comes under Subsection (2), or separate terms, so that it comes under Subsection (1), will be determined from the substance of the agreement as well as from its language.

Illustrations

2. A, who is engaged in business as a baker and confectioner, sells the business to B, and as part of the bargain promises not to engage in the business of "baker, confectioner, or other business" within the same town for three years. The provision is fairly bargained for. A's promise is so broad as to be unreasonably in restraint of trade because A's business is only that of baker and confectioner. Although part of A's promise is unenforceable on grounds of public policy (§ 188), it is enforceable with respect to the business of baker or confectioner.

3. A sells his grocery business to B and as part of the agreement promises not to engage in that business "within the city where the business is situated or within a radius of fifty miles." The provision is fairly bargained for. A's promise involves an unreasonable restraint of trade because the business extends within the city and over a radius of only twenty-five miles. Although part of A's promise is unenforceable on grounds of public policy (§ 188), it is enforceable with respect to the city and twenty-five miles.

4. A and B make an agreement for A to repair B's building under which B promises not to hold A liable for a "willful or negligent breach of duty." The provision is fairly bargained for. Although part of B's promise is unenforceable on grounds of public policy (§ 195), it is enforceable with respect to negligence.

5. A lends B $10,000, taking a promissory note for that sum plus interest. In calculating the rate of interest, the parties make an error so that the amount of interest exceeds the highest permissible legal rate. Although part of B's promise to pay the stipulated interest is unenforceable on grounds of public policy, it is enforceable up to the highest permissible rate. If A knew when he made the loan that the amount exceeded the highest permissible legal rate, B's promise to pay interest would be unenforceable in its entirety.

§ 185. Excuse of a Condition on Grounds of Public Policy.

To the extent that a term requiring the occurrence of a condition is unenforceable under the rule stated in § 178, a court may excuse the non-occurrence of the condition unless its occurrence was an essential part of the agreed exchange.

Comment

a. Relationship to other rules. This Section is concerned with the situation in which a promisor seeks to induce the promisee to do an act by conditioning his own promise on the promisee's doing that act. If it is contrary to public policy to do the act or to encourage the doing of it, the court will first go through the same process of balancing competing interests as it does under the rule stated in § 178. If it concludes that the public interest is paramount, it may react in one of two ways. First, it may hold that the promise itself is unenforceable on grounds of public policy under the rule stated in § 178. See Comment d to § 178 and Illustration 9 to that Section. Whether the rest of the agreement is also unenforceable is then determined by the rules stated in §§ 183 and 184. Second, it may disregard the term requiring the occurrence of the condition by excusing the non-occurrence of the condition under the rule stated in this Section. See Illustration 1. The promise itself is not then unenforceable on grounds of public policy and the rest of the agreement is not affected.

b. *Essential part of the agreed exchange.* Whether a court will take the first or the second course will depend on whether occurrence of the condition was an essential part of the agreed exchange. If it was an essential part, the court will hold that the promise itself, and perhaps the entire agreement, is unenforceable on grounds of public policy under the rule stated in § 178. If it was not an essential part, the court will simply disregard the term by excusing the non-occurrence of the condition on grounds of public policy under the rule stated in this Section. In determining whether occurrence of a condition is an essential part of the agreed exchange, a court will look at the entire agreement in the light of all the circumstances and will be guided by basically the same factors that govern that determination under the rules stated in §§ 84 and 229. The fundamental question is, how central was the condition to the agreement reached by the parties? It is not enough that the actual non-occurrence happened to involve a departure that was not an essential part of the agreed exchange, if the occurrence of the condition was an essential part of that exchange. A court need not entirely excuse the non-occurrence of the condition, but may merely excuse it to the extent required by public policy. In doing so it will be guided by principles analogous to those applicable under § 184. See Illustration 2.

Illustrations

1. A employs B as advertising manager of his retail clothing store. As part of the employment agreement, A promises to pay B a pension on B's retirement on condition that B not work in the retail clothing business in the same town. B works for A for fifteen years, but does not deal with customers and acquires no confidential trade information in his work. The restraint is unreasonable under the rule stated in § 188, but the condition is not an essential part of the agreed exchange and its non-occurrence will be excused. A's promise to pay the pension is enforceable even though B works as an advertising manager in the retail clothing business in the same town. Compare Illustration 8 to § 188.

2. A employs B as a research chemist in his nationwide pharmaceutical business. As part of the employment agreement, A promises to pay B a pension on B's retirement on condition that B not work in any branch of the chemical industry at any place in the country for three years after retirement. B works for fifteen years and acquires valuable confidential information that would be useful to A's competitors and would harm A's business. B can find employment as a research chemist outside of the pharmaceutical industry. The restraint is unreasonably broad under the rule stated in § 188, but the condition is not an essential part of the agreed exchange and its non-occurrence will be excused. If the court concludes that the confidential information acquired by B is such as unreasonably to harm A's business, that B can find employment as a research chemist outside the pharmaceutical industry, and that B obtained the term in good faith and in accordance with fair dealing (see § 184), the court will hold that A's promise to pay the pension is conditional on B's not working in the pharmaceutical industry at any place in the country within three years of his retirement. Compare Illustration 7 to § 188.

TOPIC 2. RESTRAINT OF TRADE

§ 186. Promise in Restraint of Trade.

(1) A promise is unenforceable on grounds of public policy if it is unreasonably in restraint of trade.

(2) A promise is in restraint of trade if its performance would limit competition in any business or restrict the promisor in the exercise of a gainful occupation.

Comment

a. *Rule of reason.* Every promise that relates to business dealings or to a professional or other gainful occupation operates as a restraint in the sense that it restricts the promisor's future activity. Such a promise is not, however, unenforceable unless the restraint that it imposes is unreasonably detrimental to the smooth operation of a freely competitive private economy. A rule of reason of this kind necessarily has somewhat vague outlines. Whether a restraint is reasonable is determined in the light of the circumstances of the transaction, including not only the particular facts but general social and economic conditions as well. The promise is viewed in terms of the effects that it could have had and not merely what actually occurred. Account is taken of such factors as the protection that it affords for the promisee's legitimate interests, the hardship that it imposes on the promisor, and the likely injury to the public. See § 188 and Comments b and c to that Section. A restraint that is reasonable in some circumstances may be unreasonable in others.

b. Typical restraints. The rule stated in this Section has little impact on some of the most significant promises in restraint of trade. Among the leading examples are promises that are intended to or that tend to create a monopoly, in the sense of control or domination of a market, and those that significantly lessen competition by, for example, tying the purchase of one product to another controlling prices or limiting production. The effect of such restraints is largely governed by federal and state legislation. See Introductory Note to this Topic. (No implication is intended in the Illustrations in this Topic with respect to the application of such legislation.) Another example consists of promises that restrict the alienation of a property interest. These promises usually involve land and such restraints are dealt with as part of the larger problem of restraints on alienation of land in general. See Restatement of Property, Division IV, Part II. Among the residue of promises that are left to be governed by the general common law restriction on promises in restraint of trade, the most commonly litigated are those to refrain from competition. They are given special treatment in the two sections that follow.

Illustrations

1. A, B and C, competing manufacturers, promise each other not to sell goods in which they deal at prices below fixed minimums. Their promises are unreasonably in restraint of trade and are unenforceable on grounds of public policy.

2. A, B and C, who are competing merchants in a city where there are many competitors, promise to become partners in order to reduce the expense of doing business. The economic situation of A, B and C is such as to make the partnership reasonable. Their implied promises not to compete individually in the same market are not unreasonably in restraint of trade and enforcement is not precluded on grounds of public policy.

3. A transfers a tract of land in fee simple to B. As part of the transaction, B promises never to transfer the land. B's promise is unreasonably in restraint of trade and is unenforceable on grounds of public policy. See Restatement of Property § 406.

§ 187. Non-Ancillary Restraints on Competition.

A promise to refrain from competition that imposes a restraint that is not ancillary to an otherwise valid transaction or relationship is unreasonably in restraint of trade.

Comment

a. Importance of rules. The common law on restraint of trade has played a particularly important role with respect to promises to refrain from competition. Parties who have challenged such promises have ordinarily been content to assert their unenforceability under the common law and have not sought relief under federal or state legislation. There is, therefore, an especially well-developed and significant body of judicial decisions applying the general rule of reason stated in the preceding section to such promises. Because of the importance of these decisions, the rules that they embody are given special attention in this Section and the one that follows. (No implication is intended with respect to the application of federal or state legislation to such promises.)

b. Non-ancillary restraints. In order for a promise to refrain from competition to be reasonable, the promisee must have an interest worthy of protection that can be balanced against the hardship on the promisor and the likely injury to the public. See § 188 and Comments b and c to that Section. The restraint must, therefore, be subsidiary to an otherwise valid transaction or relationship that gives rise to such an interest. A restraint that is not so related to an otherwise valid transaction or relationship is necessarily unreasonable. The promisee's interest may arise out of his acquisition from the promisor of a business. See § 188(2)(a). It may arise out of a relation between himself as employer or principal and the promisor as employee or agent. See § 188(2)(b). Or it may arise out of a relation between himself and the promisor as partners. See § 188(2)(c). This enumeration does not purport to be exhaustive, but a promise not to complete that is not ancillary to some such transaction or relationship as these is unreasonable because it protects no legitimate interest of the promisee. This is so even though the promise would be enforceable if it were an ancillary promise. In order for a restraint to be ancillary to a transaction or relationship the promise that imposes it must be made as part of that transaction or relationship. A promise made subsequent to the transaction or relationship is not ancillary to it. In the case of an ongoing transaction or relationship, however, it is enough if the promise is made before its termination, as long as it is supported by consideration and meets the other requirements of enforceability.

Illustrations

1. A is about to go into a business that would compete with B's business in the same city. B pays A $50,000 in return for A's promise not to compete. A's promise is unreasonably in restraint of trade and is unenforceable on grounds of public policy.

2. A and B, competing manufacturers, promise each other that A will not sell goods in one designated territory and that B will not sell goods in another designated territory. Their promises are unreasonably in restraint of trade and are unenforceable on grounds of public policy.

c. Promises to stifle competition in bidding. An important application of the rule stated in this Section occurs in connection with promises not to bid at auctions or at other competitive sales, since such restraints are generally not, by their nature, ancillary to an otherwise valid transaction or relationship. See Illustration 3. The same principle applies to promises to bid so as to affect adversely the final result, even though the number of bidders is not diminished. See Illustration 4. However, two or more persons may agree to bid for something for their collective benefit, either because they intend to hold it collectively or to divide it later into such parts as each wishes to hold, neither desiring outright ownership of the whole. Such restraints are ancillary to a relationship of joint venture, in the nature of partnership, between the parties and such promises are not unenforceable if they do not otherwise offend the test of reasonableness. See Illustration 15 to § 188.

Illustrations

3. A and B attend an art auction. Both intend to bid on a valuable painting, but A, desiring to buy it himself at as low a price as possible, pays B $1,000 in return for B's promise to refrain from bidding on the painting. B's promise is unreasonably in restraint of trade and is unenforceable on grounds of public policy. The result would be the same if the promise were made in connection with a private rather than a public sale of the painting.

4. A, B and C, building contractors, make an agreement under which they will bid individually but each promises to pay to a fund 2 per cent of the gross amount of the contract price on any successful bid by one of them, the total amount of the fund to be divided equally among the three at the end of each year. Their promises are unreasonably in restraint of trade and are unenforceable on grounds of public policy.

§ 188. Ancillary Restraints on Competition.

(1) A promise to refrain from competition that imposes a restraint that is ancillary to an otherwise valid transaction or relationship is unreasonably in restraint of trade if

(a) the restraint is greater than is needed to protect the promisee's legitimate interest, or

(b) the promisee's need is outweighed by the hardship to the promisor and the likely injury to the public.

(2) Promises imposing restraints that are ancillary to a valid transaction or relationship include the following:

(a) a promise by the seller of a business not to compete with the buyer in such a way as to injure the value of the business sold;

(b) a promise by an employee or other agent not to compete with his employer or other principal;

(c) a promise by a partner not to compete with the partnership.

Comment

a. Rule of reason. The rules stated in this Section apply to promises not to compete that, because they impose ancillary restraints, are not necessarily invalid. Subsection (1) restates in more detail the general rule of reason of § 186 as it applies to such promises. Under this formulation the restraint may be unreasonable in either of two situations. The first occurs when the restraint is greater than necessary to protect the legitimate interests of the promisee. The second occurs when, even though the restraint is not greater than necessary to protect those interests, the promisee's need for protection is outweighed by the hardship to the promisor and the likely injury to the public. In the second situation the court may be faced with a particularly difficult task of balancing competing interests. No mathematical formula can be offered for this process.

b. Need of the "promisee. If a restraint is not ancillary to some transaction or relationship that gives rise to an interest worthy of protection, the promise is necessarily unreasonable under the rule stated in the preceding Section. In some instances, however, a promise to refrain from competition is a natural and reasonable means of protecting a legitimate interest of the promisee arising out of the transaction to which the restraint is ancillary. In those instances the same reasons argue for its enforceability as in the case of any other promise. For example, competitors who are combining their efforts in a partnership may promise as part of the transaction not to compete with the partnership. Assuming that the combination is not monopolistic, such promises, reasonable in scope, will be upheld in view of the interest of each party as promisee. See Subsection (2)(c) and Comment h. (It is assumed in the Illustrations to this Section that the arrangements are not objectionable on grounds other than those that come within its scope.) The extent to which the restraint is needed to protect the promisee's interests will vary with the nature of the transaction. Where a sale of good will is involved, for example, the buyer's interest in what he has acquired cannot be effectively realized unless the seller engages not to act so as unreasonably to diminish the value of what he has sold. The same is true of any other property interest of which exclusive use is part of the value. See Subsection (2)(a) and Comment f. In the case of a post-employment restraint, however, the promisee's interest is less clear. Such a restraint, in contrast to one accompanying a sale of good will, is not necessary in order for the employer to get the full value of what he has acquired. Instead, it must usually be justified on the ground that the employer has a legitimate interest in restraining the employee from appropriating valuable trade information and customer relationships to which he has had access in the course of his employment. Arguably the employer does not get the full value of the employment contract if he cannot confidently give the employee access to confidential information needed for most efficient performance of his job. But it is often difficult to distinguish between such information and normal skills of the trade, and preventing use of one may well prevent or inhibit use of the other. See Subsection (2)(b) and Comment g. Because of this difference in the interest of the promisee, courts have generally been more willing to uphold promises to refrain from competition made in connection with sales of good will than those made in connection with contracts of employment.

c. Harm to the promisor and injury to the public. Even if the restraint is no greater than is needed to protect the promisee's interest, the promisee's need may be outweighed by the harm to the promisor and the likely injury to the public. In the case of a sale of a business, the harm caused to the seller may be excessive if the restraint necessitates his complete withdrawal from business; the likely injury to the public may be too great if it has the effect of removing a former competitor from competition. See Comment f. In the case of a post-employment restraint, the harm caused to the employee may be excessive if the restraint inhibits his personal freedom by preventing him from earning his livelihood if he quits; the likely injury to the public may be too great if it is seriously harmed by the impairment of his economic mobility or by the unavailability of the skills developed in his employment. See Comment g. Not every restraint causes injury to the public, however, and even a post-employment restraint may increase efficiency by encouraging the employer to entrust confidential information to the employee.

d. Extent of the restraint. The extent of the restraint is a critical factor in determining its reasonableness. The extent may be limited in three ways: by type of activity, by geographical area, and by time. If the promise proscribes types of activity more extensive than necessary to protect those engaged in by the promisee, it goes beyond what is necessary to protect his legitimate interests and is unreasonable. If it covers a geographical area more extensive than necessary to protect his interests, it is also unreasonable. And if the restraint is to last longer than is required in light of those interests, taking account of such factors as the permanent or transitory nature of technology and information, it is unreasonable. Since, in any of these cases, the restraint is too broad to be justified by the promisee's need, a court may hold it to be unreasonable without the necessity of weighing the countervailing interests of the promisor and the public. What limits as to activity, geographical area, and time are appropriate in a particular case depends on all the circumstances. As to the possibility of divisibility, see § 183.

e. Examples of ancillary restraints. The rule stated in Subsection (1) has its most significant applications with respect to the three types of promises set out in Subsection (2). In each of these situations the promisee may have need for protection sufficient to sustain a promise to refrain from competition as long as it is reasonable in extent. They involve promises by the seller of a business, by an employee or agent, and by a partner. The list is not an exclusive one and there may be other situations in which a valid transaction or relationship gives the promisee a legitimate interest sufficient to sustain a promise not to compete.

f. Promise by seller of a business. A promise to refrain from competition made in connection with a sale of a business may be reasonable in the light of the buyer's need to protect the value of the good will that he has acquired. In effect, the seller promises not to act so as to diminish the value of what he has sold. An analogous situation arises when the value of a corporation's business depends largely on the good will of one or more of the officers or shareholders. In that situation, officers or shareholders, either on the sale of their shares or on the sale of the corporation's business, may make an enforceable promise not to compete with the corporation or with the purchaser of its business, just as the corporation itself could on sale of its business make an enforceable promise to refrain from competition.

Illustrations

1. A sells his grocery business to B and as part of the agreement promises not to engage in a business of the same kind within a hundred miles for three years. The business of both A and B extends to a radius of a hundred miles, so that competition anywhere within that radius would harm B's business. The restraint is not more extensive than is necessary for B's protection. A's promise is not unreasonably in restraint of trade and enforcement is not precluded on grounds of public policy.

2. The facts being otherwise as stated in Illustration 1, neither A's nor B's business extends to a radius of a hundred miles. The area fixed is more extensive than is necessary for B's protection. A's promise is unreasonably in restraint of trade and is unenforceable on grounds of public policy. As to the possibility of refusal to enforce limited to part of the promise, see § 184(2).

3. A sells his grocery business to B and as part of the agreement promises not to engage in business of any kind within the city for three years. The activity proscribed is more extensive than is necessary for B's protection. A's promise is unreasonably in restraint of trade and is unenforceable on grounds of public policy. As to the possibility of refusal to enforce only part of the promise, see § 184(2).

4. A sells his grocery business to B and as part of the agreement promises not to engage in a business of the same kind within the city for twenty-five years, although B has ample opportunity to make A's former good will his own in a much shorter period of time. The time fixed is longer than is necessary for A's protection. A's promise is unreasonably in restraint of trade and is unenforceable on grounds of public policy. As to the possibility of refusal to enforce only part of the promise, see § 184(2).

5. A, a corporation, sells its business to B. As part of the agreement, C and D, officers and large shareholders of A, promise not to compete with B within the territory in which A did business for three years. Their promises are not unreasonably in restraint of trade and enforcement is not precluded on grounds of public policy.

g. Promise by employee or agent. The employer's interest in exacting from his employee a promise not to compete after termination of the employment is usually explained on the ground that the employee has acquired either confidential trade information relating to some process or method or the means to attract customers away from the employer. Whether the risk that the employee may do injury to the employer is sufficient to justify a promise to refrain from competition after the termination of the employment will depend on the facts of the particular case. Post-employment restraints are scrutinized with particular care because they are often the product of unequal bargaining power and because the employee is likely to give scant attention to the hardship he may later suffer through loss of his livelihood. This is especially so where the restraint is imposed by the employer's standardized printed form. Cf. § 208. A line must be drawn between the general skills and knowledge of the trade and information that is peculiar to the employer's business. If the employer seeks to justify the restraint on the ground of the employee's knowledge of a process or method, the confidentiality of that process or method and its technological life may be critical. The public interest in workable employer-employee relationships with an efficient use of employees must be balanced against the interest in individual economic freedom. The court will take account of any diminution in competition likely to result from slowing down the dissemination of ideas and of any impairment of the function of the market in shifting manpower to areas of greatest productivity. If the employer seeks to justify the restraint on the ground of the employee's ability to attract customers, the nature, extent and locale of the employee's contacts with customers are relevant. A restraint is easier to justify if it is limited to one field of activity among many that are available to the employee. The same is true if the restraint is limited to the taking of his former employer's customers as contrasted with competition in general. A restraint may be ancillary to a relationship although, as in the case of an employment at will, no contract of employment is involved. Analogous rules apply to restraints imposed on agents by their principals. As to the duty of an agent not to compete with his principal during the agency relationship, see Restatement, Second, Agency §§ 393, 394.

Illustrations

6. A employs B as a fitter of contact lenses under a one-year employment contract. As part of the employment agreement, B promises not to work as a fitter of contact lenses in the same town for three years after the termination of his employment. B works for A for five years, during which time he has close relationships with A's customers, who come to rely upon him. B's contacts with A's customers are such as to attract them away from A. B's promise is not unreasonably in restraint of trade and enforcement is not precluded on grounds of public policy.

7. A employs B as advertising manager of his retail clothing store. As part of the employment agreement, B promises not to work in the retail clothing business in the same town for three years after the termination of his employment. B works for A for five years but does not deal with customers and acquires no confidential trade information in his work. B's promise is unreasonably in restraint of trade and is unenforceable on grounds of public policy. Compare Illustration 1 to § 185.

8. A employs B as an instructor in his dance studio. As part of the employment agreement, B promises not to work as a dance instructor in the same town for three years after the termination of his employment. B works for five years and deals directly with customers but does not work with any customer for a substantial period of time and acquires no confidential information in his work. B's promise is unreasonably in restraint of trade and is unenforceable on grounds of public policy.

9. A employs B as a research chemist in his nationwide pharmaceutical business. As part of the employment agreement, B promises not to work in the pharmaceutical industry at any place in the country for three years after the termination of his employment. B works for five years and acquires valuable confidential information that would be useful to A's competitors and would unreasonably harm A's business. B can find employment as a research chemist outside of the pharmaceutical industry. B's promise is not unreasonably in restraint of trade and enforcement is not precluded on grounds of public policy.

10. A employs B to work with rapidly changing technology, some parts of which entail valuable confidential information. As part of the agreement B promises not to work for any competitor of A for ten years after the termination of the employment. The confidential information made available to A will probably remain valuable for only a much shorter period. The time fixed is longer than is necessary for A's protection. B's promise is unreasonably in restraint of trade and is unenforceable on grounds of public policy. As to the possibility of refusal to enforce only part of the promise, see § 184(2).

h. *Promise by partner.* A rule similar to that applicable to an employee or agent applies to a partner who makes a promise not to compete that is ancillary to the partnership agreement or to an agreement by which he disposes of his partnership interest. The same is true of joint adventurers, who are treated as partners in this respect.

Illustrations

11. A, B and C form a partnership to practice veterinary medicine in a town for ten years. In the partnership agreement, each promises that if, on the termination of the partnership, the practice is continued by the other two members, he will not practice veterinary medicine in the same town during its continuance up to a maximum of three years. The restraint is not more extensive than is necessary for the protection of each partner's interest in the partnership. Their promises are not unreasonably in restraint of trade and enforcement is not precluded on grounds of public policy.

12. A, an experienced dentist and oral surgeon, takes into partnership B, a younger dentist and oral surgeon. In the partnership agreement, B promises that, if he withdraws from the partnership, he will not practice dentistry or oral surgery in the city for three years. Their practice is limited to oral surgery, and does not include dentistry. The activity proscribed is more extensive than is necessary for A's protection. B's promise is unreasonably in restraint of trade and is unenforceable on grounds of public policy. As to the possibility of refusal to enforce only part of the promise, see § 184(2).

13. A works for five years as a partner in a nationwide firm of accountants. In the partnership agreement, A promises not to engage in accounting in any city where the firm has an office for three years after his withdrawal from the partnership. The firm has offices in the twenty largest cities in the United States. A's promise imposes great hardship on him because this area includes almost all that in which he could engage in a comparable accounting practice. The promise is unreasonably in restraint of trade and is unenforceable on grounds of public policy. As to the possibility of refusal to enforce only part of the promise, see § 184(2).

14. A, a doctor who has a general practice in a remote area, takes into partnership B, a younger doctor. In the partnership agreement, B promises that, if he withdraws from the partnership, he will not engage in the practice of medicine within the area for three years. If B's unavailability in the area will be likely to cause injury to the public because of the shortage of doctors there, the court may determine that B's promise is unreasonably in restraint of trade and is unenforceable on grounds of public policy.

15. A and B attend an art auction and each plans to bid on a valuable painting. They decide to acquire it as a joint venture and each promises the other to bid for its purchase jointly and, if successful, to deal with it jointly. Their promises are not unreasonably in restraint of trade and are not unenforceable on grounds of public policy. Compare Illustrations 3 and 4 to § 187.

TOPIC 3. IMPAIRMENT OF FAMILY RELATIONS

§ 189. Promise in Restraint of Marriage.

A promise is unenforceable on grounds of public policy if it is unreasonably in restraint of marriage.

Comment

a. Rule of reason. Marriage is regarded by the common law as of concern to the state as well as to the individual, and the freedom of individuals to marry should not be impaired except for good reason. A promise in restraint of marriage is not necessarily unenforceable, but is subject to a rule of reason, analogous to that applicable to promises in restraint of trade. See § 186. Here, as there, the duration of the restraint and its extent, in terms of the narrowing of the likely area of choice, are important. In order for the restraint to be reasonable, it must serve some purpose other than that of merely discouraging marriage. The most common acceptable purpose is that of providing support until marriage. Courts are, therefore, relatively tolerant of restraints on marriages that condition a promise of support on the promisee's not marrying and thereby acquiring another provider. Particularly is this so when the restraint is imposed by one spouse on remarriage by the other spouse, since both the close family relationship and the limitation of the restraint to a subsequent marriage argue in favor of enforceability.

Illustrations

1. A pays B, his twenty-one-year-old child, $100,000 in return for B's promise not to marry for ten years. B's promise is unreasonably in restraint of marriage and is unenforceable on grounds of public policy.

2. A, a man of seventy years, promises B, his fifty-year-old unmarried niece, that if she will remain in his home as house-keeper and will not marry, he will leave her $50,000 in his will. B does so until A's death. A's promise is not unreasonably in restraint of marriage and its enforcement is not precluded on grounds of public policy.

3. A and B, who are about to marry, make an antenuptial agreement in which A promises B that in case of A's death B shall receive a specified income from A's estate as long as B remains unmarried. A's promise is not unreasonably in restraint of marriage and its enforcement is not precluded on grounds of public policy.

§ 190. Promise Detrimental to Marital Relationship.

(1) A promise by a person contemplating marriage or by a married person, other than as part of an enforceable separation agreement, is unenforceable on grounds of public policy if it would change some essential incident of the marital relationship in a way detrimental to the public interest in the marriage relationship. A separation agreement is unenforceable on grounds of public policy unless it is made after separation or in contemplation of an immediate separation and is fair in the circumstances.

(2) A promise that tends unreasonably to encourage divorce or separation is unenforceable on grounds of public policy.

Comment

a. Change in essential incident of marital relationship. Although marriage is sometimes loosely referred to as a "contract," the marital relationship has not been regarded by the common law as contractual in the usual sense. Many terms of the relationship are seen as largely fixed by the state and beyond the power of the parties to modify. Two reasons support this view. One is that there is a public interest in the relationship, and particularly in such matters as support and child custody, that makes it inappropriate to subject it to modification by the parties. Another is that the courts lack workable standards and are not an appropriate forum for the types of contract disputes that would arise if such promises were enforceable. The rule stated in Subsection (1) reflects this view by making a promise unenforceable if it changes an essential incident of marriage in a way detrimental to the public interest in the relationship. This rule, however, does not prevent persons contemplating marriage or married persons from making contracts between themselves for the disposition of property, since this is not ordinarily regarded as an essential incident of the marital relationship. Nor does it prevent their making contracts for services that are not an essential incident of the marital relationship within the rule stated here. But it does, for example, preclude them from changing in a way detrimental to the public interest in the relationship the duty imposed by law on one spouse to support the other. Whether a change in the duty of support is detrimental in this way will depend on the circumstances of each case. The presence of an unenforceable promise in an otherwise enforceable antenuptial or separation agreement does not, of course, necessarily entail the unenforceability of the entire agreement. See §§ 183, 184. The principles underlying this Section also apply to an agreement under which a third person as trustee is to hold sums in trust for the other spouse on separation. The rules stated in this Section apply only to the relations between the parties and do not govern the enforceability of promises relating to the duty of support owed to children. Even though enforcement of a promise is not precluded under the rule stated in Subsection (1), it may be precluded under the rule stated in Subsection (2).

Illustration

1. A and B, who are about to marry, make an antenuptial agreement in which A promises to leave their home at any time on notice by B and to make no further claims against B, and B promises thereupon to pay A $100,000. The promises of A and B alter an essential incident of the marital relationship in a way detrimental to the public interest in that relationship and are unenforceable on grounds of public policy.

b. Separation agreements. The policy that limits the parties in modifying the marital relationship does not apply if that relationship has ended. The rule stated in Subsection (1) thus does not apply to a promise that is part of an enforceable separation agreement. A separation agreement, to be enforceable, must be made after the parties have separated or when they contemplate immediate separation, so that the marriage has, in effect, already disintegrated. It must also be fair in the circumstances, a matter as to which the court may exercise its continuing discretionary powers. Separation agreements commonly deal with such matters as support and are generally enforceable because the parties could usually accomplish the same result through a judicial separation. They are still subject to the rule stated in Subsection (2) if they tend unreasonably to encourage divorce.

Illustration

2. A and B, who are married but have decided to separate, make a separation agreement that is fair in the circumstances, in which A promises to pay B a stated sum each month in return for B's promise to relinquish all other claims to support. Although the promises of A and B change an essential incident of the marital relationship, their enforcement is not for that reason precluded on grounds of public policy because they are part of a separation agreement. But see Subsection (2) and Comment c.

c. Tending to encourage divorce or separation. When persons contemplating marriage or married persons seek to determine by agreement their rights in the event of a divorce or separation, the rule stated in Subsection (2) comes into play, along with that stated in Subsection (1). See Illustration 2. Because of the public interest in the marriage relationship (see Comment a), a promise that undermines that relationship by tending unreasonably to encourage divorce or separation is unenforceable. Although the parties are free, if they choose, to terminate their relationship under the law providing for divorce or separation, a commitment that tends unreasonably in this direction will not be enforced. Whether a promise tends unreasonably to encourage divorce or separation in a particular case is a question of fact that depends on all the circumstances, including the state of disintegration of the marriage at the time the promise is made. A promise that merely disposes of property rights in the event of divorce or separation does not of itself tend unreasonably to encourage either.

Illustrations

3. A, who is married to B, promises to pay B $50,000 in return for B's promise to obtain a divorce. The promises of A and B tend unreasonably to encourage divorce and are unenforceable on grounds of public policy. The result does not depend on whether or not there are grounds for divorce or on whether or not B has performed.

4. A, who was married to B but has obtained a divorce that can possibly be set aside for fraud, promises to pay B $50,000 in return for B's promise not to attempt to have the divorce set aside. The promises of both A and B tend unreasonably to encourage divorce and are unenforceable on grounds of public policy. The result does not depend on whether or not B has performed.

5. A and B, who are about to be married, make an antenuptial agreement in which A promises that in case of divorce, he will settle $1,000,000 on B. A court may decide that, in view of the large sum promised, A's promise tends unreasonably to encourage divorce and is unenforceable on grounds of public policy.

6. A, who has begun divorce proceedings against B, promises B that if divorce is granted, alimony shall be fixed at a stated sum, in return for B's agreement to relinquish all other claims to alimony. A court may decide that in view of the disintegration of the marriage relationship, the promises of A and B do not tend unreasonably to encourage divorce and their enforcement is not precluded on grounds of public policy.

§ 191. Promise Affecting Custody.

A promise affecting the right of custody of a minor child is unenforceable on grounds of public policy unless the disposition as to custody is consistent with the best interest of the child.

Comment

a. Rationale. The custody of minor children is, like marriage, an important subject of public concern. A promise by one entitled to the custody of a minor child to transfer the custody to another or not to reclaim custody already transferred to another is unenforceable unless it is consistent with the child's best interest. Such promises are typically found in separation agreements between parents, and the fact that the person to whom custody is transferred is a parent is an important, although not controlling, factor in showing that the transfer is in the interest of the child. Even where enforcement of a promise disposing of custody is not precluded on grounds of public policy, the disposition is still subject to the plenary supervision of the court. Similar rules apply to visitation rights.

Illustrations

1. A and B, the parents of a child of ten, make an otherwise valid separation agreement in which A promises to give up custody of the child to B. Whether or not A's promise is enforceable depends on whether custody by B is consistent with the best interest of the child.

2. A and B, the parents of a child of ten, promise to give up custody of the child to C, a stranger, in return for C's promise to support the child. The promises of A, B and C affect A's and B's custody rights in a minor child and unless the court finds that these promises are consistent with the best interest of the child, they are unenforceable on grounds of public policy.

TOPIC 4. INTERFERENCE WITH OTHER PROTECTED INTERESTS

§ 192. Promise Involving Commission of a Tort.

A promise to commit a tort or to induce the commission of a tort is unenforceable on grounds of public policy.

Comment

a. Scope. A promise to commit a tort is plainly unenforceable on grounds of public policy. See Illustration 6 and 8 to § 178. So is a promise made in return for the commission of a tort or a promise to commit a tort. See Illustrations 7, 8 and 9 to § 178. The same is true if the act is a tortious interference with a third person's interest in property. The rule does not, however, apply to an agreement made in good faith merely to test another's claim to property. See Illustration 17 to § 178. It is also subject to the rule on excusable ignorance stated in § 180. See Illustration 2 to § 180. This Section does not purport to be exhaustive and there are other types of conduct, involving neither the commission of a tort nor the interference with property, that so jeopardize an individual's life or freedom as to render promises involving them unenforceable on grounds of public policy. See Restatement, Second, Torts §§ 892–92D.

Illustrations

1. A and B make an agreement under which A promises to bring an action against a corporation, and have its assets seized, although there is no reasonable ground to believe that there is a cause of action, for the sole purpose of lowering the price of its stock so that B can buy it at an advantageous price. A's promise is to commit a tort and is unenforceable on grounds of public policy.

2. A makes an agreement with B under which A promises that he will excavate a city street without permission from the city. A's promise is to interfere tortiously with an interest in property of the city and is unenforceable on grounds of public policy.

b. Promise to indemnify. A promise to indemnify another against the consequences of his committing a tort is unobjectionable if the tortious act is only an undesired possibility and the promise does not tend to induce its commission. See Illustrations 3 and 4. In some circumstances, however, the promise may tend to induce the commission of the act. Where this is so, it is unenforceable for the same reason as is a promise to commit a tort or a promise in return for the commission of a tort. See Illustration 5.

Illustrations

3. A, an insurance company, in consideration of a premium paid by B, promises to indemnify B against liability for injury to the persons or property of others whether caused by B's negligence or not. Enforcement of A's promise is not precluded on grounds of public policy.

4. A, a publisher, and B, an author, make an agreement for the publication of a book that B is about to write. Although it is neither expected nor desired that the book will contain false and defamatory matter, A is concerned about that possibility and requires a bond on which C, a surety company, promises to indemnify A for any liability that A may incur for such matter in the book. Enforcement of C's promise is not precluded on grounds of public policy.

5. A, the owner of a newspaper, promises B that he will publish a statement about C known to be false and defamatory if B pays him $10,000 and furnishes a bond with B as principal and D as surety to indemnify A against liability for publishing the statement. B's and D's promises on the bond tend to induce the commission of a tort and are unenforceable on grounds of public policy. That A's promise is one to commit a tort and is unenforceable on grounds of public policy, see Illustration 6 to § 178.

§ 193. Promise Inducing Violation of Fiduciary Duty.

A promise by a fiduciary to violate his fiduciary duty or a promise that tends to induce such a violation is unenforceable on grounds of public policy.

Comment

a. Scope. A fiduciary is expected to refrain from acting for his private advantage or otherwise contrary to the interests of his beneficiary or principal in matters affecting the fiduciary relation, and he is liable in tort for breach of his duty. Restatement, Second, Torts § 874, cf. Restatement, Second, Agency § 312. A promise by a fiduciary to violate his duty as a fiduciary is unenforceable on grounds of public policy, as is a promise that tends to induce such a violation. In an exceptional case, however, a court may conclude that the interests of third parties require enforcement. See Illustration 18 to § 178. Directors and other officials of a corporation act in a fiduciary capacity and are subject to the rule stated in this Section. The rule applies by analogy to shareholders with reference to their voting powers, although it does not preclude agreements where the only advantage bargained for is one that will accrue to all shareholders through the ownership of shares. See Illustration 3. The details of the duties of various types of fiduciaries and the extent to which the beneficiary or principal can authorize a fiduciary to bargain for private advantages not directly accruing to him by virtue of his fiduciary relation are beyond the scope of this Restatement. See Restatement, Second, Agency §§ 387, 393, Restatement, Second, Trusts §§ 169, 170. If there has been effective consent by the beneficiary or principal so that no violation of a fiduciary duty is involved, the rule stated in this Section does not apply. In determining whether consent is effective, such matters as capacity to contract and undue influence are taken into account.

Illustrations

1. A, in consulting with B, his lawyer, informs B of some facts. Later C promises B $1,000 if B will disclose those facts. B discloses them to C. C's promise is one that tends to induce a violation of B's fiduciary duty to A and is unenforceable on grounds of public policy.

2. A sells all of his shares of stock in a corporation to B, who pays the price and promises to exercise his voting power in accordance with A's instructions. B's promise is one to violate a fiduciary duty and is unenforceable on grounds of public policy.

3. A, B and C, shareholders in a corporation who are dissatisfied with the policy of the directors, promise each other to vote for other directors. Their promises are not ones to violate a fiduciary duty and their enforcement is not precluded on grounds of public policy.

§ 194. Promise Interfering With Contract With Another.

A promise that tortiously interferes with performance of a contract with a third person or a tortiously induced promise to commit a breach of contract is unenforceable on grounds of public policy.

Comment

a. Scope. Interfering with performance of a contract may be a tort. See Restatement, Second, Torts § 766. A promise that tortiously interferes with performance of a contract with a third person is therefore unenforceable on grounds of public policy. The same is true of a promise to commit a breach of contract that has been tortiously induced. The rule stated in this Section applies even though the contract interfered with is unenforceable because of the Statute of Frauds.

Illustrations

1. A and B make an agreement under which A promises to employ B to work full time and B promises to begin to work immediately. As A knows, B is under an existing contract of full time employment with C. A's promise tends tortiously to interfere with B's contract with C, and B's is a tortiously induced promise to commit a breach of that contract. Both promises are unenforceable on grounds of public policy. Compare Illustration 1 to § 180.

2. A induces B, a member of a stock exchange, to make an agreement under which B promises to charge A reduced commissions that A knows are in violation of the rules of the exchange by which B agreed to be bound when he became a member. B's promise is a tortiously induced promise to commit a breach of his contract with the exchange and is unenforceable on grounds of public policy. Compare Illustration 1 to § 180.

§ 195. Term Exempting From Liability for Harm Caused Intentionally, Recklessly or Negligently.

(1) A term exempting a party from tort liability for harm caused intentionally or recklessly is unenforceable on grounds of public policy.

(2) A term exempting a party from tort liability for harm caused negligently is unenforceable on grounds of public policy if

(a) the term exempts an employer from liability to an employee for injury in the course of his employment;

(b) the term exempts one charged with a duty of public service from liability to one to whom that duty is owed for compensation for breach of that duty, or

(c) the other party is similarly a member of a class protected against the class to which the first party belongs.

(3) A term exempting a seller of a product from his special tort liability for physical harm to a user or consumer is unenforceable on grounds of public policy unless the term is fairly bargained for and is consistent with the policy underlying that liability.

Comment

a. Rationale. The law of torts imposes standards of conduct for the protection of others against unreasonable risk of harm. One cannot exempt himself from such liability for harm that is caused either intentionally or recklessly. See Restatement, Second, Torts § 500. (As to the possibility that one party's consent may give the other a defense under the law of torts, see Restatement, Second, Torts §§ 892–92D.) However, a party to a contract can ordinarily exempt himself from liability for harm caused by his failure to observe the standard of reasonable care imposed by the law of negligence. See Restatement, Second, Torts § 282. This rule is subject to an exception if the other party is a member of a protected class. Two examples of this exception are widely recognized. First, an employer is not permitted to exempt himself from liability to his employee for negligently caused injury (paragraph (a)). Second, one who is charged with a duty of public service, such as a common carrier or a public utility, and who undertakes to perform it for compensation, is not permitted to exempt himself from liability to the one to be served for negligent breach of that duty (paragraph (b)). The rigor of this rule may, however, be mitigated by a fairly bargained for agreement to limit liability to a reasonable agreed value in return for a lower rate. In most jurisdictions legislation has altered the rule in specific situations, usually by restricting the power to limit liability. The two examples given under Subsection (2) are not intended as an exhaustive list of situations in which such terms are unenforceable. If, for example, a statute imposes a standard of conduct, a court may decide on the basis of an analysis of the statute, that a term exempting a party from liability for failure to conform to that standard is unenforceable. See § 179(a).

Illustrations

1. A, a common carrier, issues a pass to B, one of its employees. A term of the pass exempts A from liability to B for any injury caused by A's negligence. The term is unenforceable on grounds of public policy. Enforcement of a similar term in a pass given gratuitously to one who is not an employee would not be precluded on those grounds.

2. A term in an agreement between A, a railroad, and B, an adjacent land owner, exempts A from liability to B for fires negligently caused by sparks from its engines. Because the term does not exempt A from liability for breach of its duty of public service, its enforcement is not precluded on grounds of public policy. The term would be unenforceable on those grounds if it exempted A from liability for harm caused either willfully, intentionally or recklessly.

b. *Relation to other rules.* Language inserted by a party in an agreement for the purpose of exempting him from liability for negligent conduct is scrutinized with particular care and a court may require specific and conspicuous reference to negligence under the general principle that language is interpreted against the draftsman. See § 206. Furthermore, a party's attempt to exempt himself from liability for negligent conduct may fail as unconscionable. See § 208. The rule stated in this Section does not apply to an agreement by a third person to indemnify a party against liability in tort. The effect of a term purporting to exempt a party from the consequences of a misrepresentation is governed by the rule stated in § 196.

c. *Strict product liability.* One who sells a product in a defective condition unreasonably dangerous to the user or consumer or to his property is subjected to liability for resulting physical harm under the rule stated in Restatement, Second, Torts § 402A. In general, a term exempting the seller from this liability is unenforceable on grounds of public policy. See Comment m to Restatement, Second, Torts § 402A. Subsection (3) states an exception for the rare situation in which the term is consistent with the policy underlying the liability. This might be the case, for example, for a term in a fairly negotiated contract between two merchants for the sale of an experimental product. Such a term would not, however, affect the rights of one who was not a party to the contract.

§ 196. Term Exempting From Consequences of Misrepresentation.

A term unreasonably exempting a party from the legal consequences of a misrepresentation is unenforceable on grounds of public policy.

Comment

a. *Rationale.* A misrepresentation that induces the formation of a contract may have the effect of giving the recipient of the misrepresentation the power to avoid the contract (§ 164; cf. § 163). It may also give him a claim for damages in tort (Restatement, Second, Torts chs. 22, 23). Sometimes a party to a contract includes language to negate or limit these consequences. Under the general rules governing the interpretation of agreements, such language is interpreted wherever reasonable as consistent with the representations themselves. See § 202(5); see also Uniform Commercial Code § 2–316(1). To the extent that there is a conflict, however, a party's attempt unreasonably to exempt himself, in whole or in part, from the consequences of his misrepresentation is inoperative. See Uniform Commercial Code § 2–316(1). The rule stated in this Section applies to non-fraudulent as well as fraudulent misrepresentations. It does not, however, apply to language that prevents the making of any misrepresentation in the first place, such as that disclosing the truth (see § 161). Nor does it apply to language that prevents reliance by the recipient on a misrepresentation (see § 167) or that makes his reliance unjustified (see § 172), but such language is not effective unless it actually has the asserted effect and is not a mere recital that it does. Furthermore, the parties can limit the time within which a misrepresentation can be asserted, as long as the time is a reasonable one. The rule stated in this Section does not apply to an agreement by a third person to indemnify a party against liability for misrepresentation.

Illustration

1. A and B sign a written agreement containing a term precluding B from asserting any misrepresentations made by A. The term is unenforceable on grounds of public policy with respect to both fraudulent and non-fraudulent misrepresentations. As to the effect of the parol evidence rule on prior or contemporaneous non-fraudulent misrepresentations, see Comment b and § 214(d).

b. Relation to other rules. The rule stated in this Section does not alter the effect of an integrated agreement on prior agreements under the parol evidence rule (§ 213), which is subject to an exception for fraudulent, but not for non-fraudulent, misrepresentations (§ 214). It does not preclude the possibility that the parties may effectively limit the remedies that are available for misrepresentation (see Uniform Commercial Code § 2–719), as long as this is not unconscionable (§ 208). In many situations it will be subject to specific statutory provisions, such as those governing warranties under the Uniform Commercial Code. See Uniform Commercial Code § 2–316.

TOPIC 5. RESTITUTION

§ 197. Restitution Generally Unavailable.

Except as stated in §§ 198 and 199, a party has no claim in restitution for performance that he has rendered under or in return for a promise that is unenforceable on grounds of public policy unless denial of restitution would cause disproportionate forfeiture.

Comment

a. Rationale. In general, if a court will not, on grounds of public policy, aid a promisee by enforcing the promise, it will not aid him by granting him restitution for performance that he has rendered in return for the unenforceable promise. Neither will it aid the promisor by allowing a claim in restitution for performance that he has rendered under the unenforceable promise. It will simply leave both parties as it finds them, even though this may result in one of them retaining a benefit that he has received as a result of the transaction.

Illustrations

1. A, the owner of a newspaper, promises B that he will publish a statement about C known to A and B to be false and defamatory, if B pays him $10,000. B pays A $10,000. Since A's promise is unenforceable on grounds of public policy (§ 192), B has no claim in restitution against A. See Illustration 6 to § 178.

2. A induces B to make an agreement to buy goods on credit from A by bribing B's purchasing agent. A's bribe tends to induce the agent to violate his fiduciary duty. A delivers the goods to B. Since B's promise to pay the price is unenforceable on grounds of public policy, A has no claim in restitution against B. See § 193 and Illustration 14 to § 178.

b. Exceptions. Exceptions to the rule denying restitution are made in favor of a party who is excusably ignorant or is not equally in the wrong (§ 198) and in favor of a party who has withdrawn or where the situation is contrary to public policy (§ 199). These exceptions are dealt with in the two sections that follow. In addition, the rule is subject to the exception stated in this Section that allows restitution in favor of a party who would otherwise suffer a forfeiture that is disproportionate in relation to the contravention of public policy involved. Account will be taken of such factors as the extent of the party's deliberate involvement in any misconduct, the gravity of that misconduct, and the strength of the public policy. See § 178(3). The exception is especially appropriate in the case of technical rules or regulations that are drawn so that their strict application would result in such forfeiture if restitution were not allowed. Here, as elsewhere in this Restatement, the term "forfeiture" is used to refer to the denial of compensation that results when the obligee loses his right to the agreed exchange after he has relied substantially, as by preparation or performance, on the expectation of that exchange. See Comment b to § 227 and Comment b to § 229. Whether the forfeiture is "disproportionate" for the purposes of this Section will depend on the extent of that denial of compensation as compared with the gravity of the public interest involved and the extent of the contravention. If the claimant has threatened grave social harm, no forfeiture will be disproportionate. Restitution under this Section is subject to the rules of §§ 370–77.

Illustrations

3. A makes an agreement with B to sell to B for $10,000 a painting that A, as B knows, has already contracted to sell to C. B pays A $5,000 in advance of delivery. Although B's promise to pay the price is unenforceable on grounds of public policy (§ 194), denial of restitution would cause B disproportionate forfeiture. B has a claim in restitution against A for $5,000.

4. A, a foreign corporation, makes an agreement with B to sell B goods for $1,000. A delivers the goods but does not comply with a state statute that prohibits a foreign corporation from doing business in the state without appointing an agent for service of process and provides that contracts made in violation of the statute are unenforceable. Although B's promise to pay the price is unenforceable on grounds of public policy, denial of restitution would cause A disproportionate forfeiture. A has a claim in restitution against B for the goods or their value to B.

5. A, a city, makes an agreement with B under which B is to install traffic signals for $50,000. In making the agreement, A fails to comply with a state statute that prescribes procedures for making municipal contracts, so that A's promise is unenforceable on grounds of public policy. Although B knows this, he installs the signals. In determining whether B has a claim in restitution against A for the value of the signals to A, the court will consider the extent of the forfeiture that would result from the denial of such a claim in relation to the gravity of the public policy involved and the extent of the contravention.

§ 198. Restitution in Favor of Party Who Is Excusably Ignorant or Is Not Equally in the Wrong.

A party has a claim in restitution for performance that he has rendered under or in return for a promise that is unenforceable on grounds of public policy if

  (a) he was excusably ignorant of the facts or of legislation of a minor character, in the absence of which the promise would be enforceable, or

  (b) he was not equally in the wrong with the promisor.

Comment

a. Ignorance of facts or legislation. A party's excusable ignorance of facts or of legislation of a minor character may enable him to enforce a promise that would otherwise be unenforceable on grounds of public policy. See § 180. In the alternative, he may have a claim in restitution under the rule stated in paragraph (a). In some cases, however, he will not be able to enforce the promise because the other party is also excusably ignorant of the facts or legislation. See Comment b to § 180. In such cases, he is nevertheless entitled to restitution under the rule stated in paragraph (b). Whether ignorance is excusable is governed by the same considerations that apply under the rule stated in § 180. Restitution under this Subsection is subject to the rules of §§ 370–77.

Illustration

1. A, an insurance company, issues a policy of fire insurance to B on a building. A state statute makes A's promise unenforceable as a wager because B has no insurable interest in the building. B pays A the premium but neither A nor B knows nor has reason to know that B has no legally insurable interest in the building. Although A's promise is unenforceable on grounds of public policy, B was excusably ignorant of the facts that make it unenforceable, and B has a claim in restitution against A for the amount of the premium paid.

b. Not equally in the wrong. The general rule that neither party is entitled to restitution is subject to an exception in favor of a party who is not equally in the wrong, or as it is sometimes said is not in pari delicto, with the party from whom he seeks restitution. For the most part, the exception is applied in two types of cases. In the first, the claimant is regarded as being less in the wrong because the public policy is intended to protect persons of the class to which he belongs and, as a member of that protected class, he is regarded as less culpable. See Illustration 2. Even if the claimant cannot enforce the promise, he is nevertheless entitled to restitution. A claimant who can enforce the promise can, in the alternative, have restitution on the ground that he is not equally in the wrong. See Comment b to § 197. In the second type of case, the claimant is regarded as being less in the wrong because he has been the victim of misrepresentation or oppression practiced on him by the other party. See Illustration 3. It is not necessary that the misrepresentation or oppression be sufficient to give a right to avoidance under the rules on misrepresentation, duress and undue influence stated in Chapter 7. The fact that the other party engages in improper transactions as a business or that he occupies a special position of trust or confidence may be critical. The exception stated in paragraph (b) is not usually available to a claimant whose misconduct is serious when viewed in the light of the threatened social harm. However, if the other party's conduct is especially reprehensible, the court may decide that it is more important to deprive him of his ill-gotten gains. This may be so, for example, where he has enticed the claimant into the transaction, where he has devised a scheme to defraud the claimant, or where he engages in the misconduct professionally. Restitution under this paragraph is subject to the rules stated in §§ 370–77.

Illustrations

2. A deposits $1,000 with B on terms that both A and B know are prohibited by a state statute. Although B's promise is unenforceable on grounds of public policy, if the court decides that A belongs to the class of persons that the policy is intended to protect and is therefore not equally in the wrong with B, it will allow A a claim in restitution against B for $1,000.

3. A, a lawyer, promises B, an uneducated person, that he will attempt to use his personal influence with city councilmen to secure the passage of an ordinance desired by B, in return for B's promise to pay $5,000 immediately and $10,000 if the ordinance is passed. B believes A's assurances that the agreement is not improper and pays A $5,000. Although A's promise is unenforceable on grounds of public policy, B is not equally in the wrong with A because of A's misrepresentation and B's ignorance. B has a claim in restitution against A for $5,000. The result does not depend on whether or not A has done anything to secure passage of the ordinance.

§ 199. Restitution Where Party Withdraws or Situation Is Contrary to Public Interest.

A party has a claim in restitution for performance that he has rendered under or in return for a promise that is unenforceable on grounds of public policy if he did not engage in serious misconduct and

(a) he withdraws from the transaction before the improper purpose has been achieved, or

(b) allowance of the claim would put an end to a continuing situation that is contrary to the public interest.

Comment

a. Restitution on withdrawal. The rule stated in paragraph (a) gives a right of restitution to a party, who, after having become involved in an improper transaction, withdraws from the transaction before the improper purpose has been achieved. There are two reasons for giving a party such a "time for repentance," or locus poenitentiae, as it is sometimes called. First, the rule may encourage a party to abandon an improper transaction before the improper purpose is carried out. Second, the granting of relief may not be regarded as a misuse of official authority if the wrongdoer who asks for relief has withdrawn in time. To come within the rule, a party must actually withdraw by refusing any further participation in or benefits from the transaction. It is not enough that the achievement of the purpose has been prevented by circumstances beyond his control. The time when an improper purpose has been so substantially achieved that withdrawal should no longer give a right to restitution depends on the gravity of the social harm threatened under the facts of the particular case. The exception is not available in favor of a party whose misconduct is serious when viewed in the light of the threatened social harm. Restitution under this Section is subject to the rules stated in §§ 370–77.

Illustrations

1. A, an insurance company, issues a policy of fire insurance to B on a building. A state statute makes A's promise unenforceable as a wager because B has no legally insurable interest in the building. B pays A the premium but, before the coverage becomes effective, B notifies A that he cancels the policy. Although A's promise is unenforceable on grounds of public policy, B withdrew from the transaction before the improper purpose had been achieved. B has a claim in restitution against A for the amount of the premium paid.

2. A lends money to B for the purpose of enabling B to bet on a horse race in return for B's promise to repay it in six months. A state statute makes betting on a horse race a crime. Before B has made the bet, A tells B that he wants the money back so that it will not be used for this purpose. Although B's promise to repay the money is unenforceable on grounds of public policy (§ 178), A withdrew from the transaction before the improper purpose had been achieved. A is entitled to restitution from B of the amount lent. The result does not depend on whether or not B makes the bet.

3. A, who is engaged in organizing a prize contest, promises B that if B pays A $500, A will see that B wins a $5,000 automobile in the contest. Although organizing the contest is not itself a crime, a state statute makes participation in the fraudulent operation of such a contest a crime. B pays A $500, but when A demands another $100 from B, before the contest, B refuses, tells A that he does not want the automobile, and demands the return of the $500. Although A's promise that B will get an automobile is unenforceable on grounds of public policy, B withdrew from the transaction before the improper purpose had been achieved. B has a claim in restitution against A for $500.

b. Situation against public interest. The exception stated in paragraph (b) is applicable when the denial of restitution would leave property in the hands of one whose control of it would be contrary to the public interest, for example, because its status would be rendered so uncertain as seriously to restrain its alienation. The exception may be invoked to recover money deposited with a stakeholder under an unenforceable wagering agreement. Even after the event that is the subject of the wager has occurred, either party can claim restitution from the stakeholder. The stakeholder is not, however, liable to the loser for anything that he pays over to the winner before notice by the loser of his claim.

Illustrations

4. A and B make a wagering agreement under which each deposits $1,000 with C, who as a stakeholder promises to pay the total sum of $2,000 to the winner. Under a state statute it is a crime to make such a wager. A wins the wager, but before C has paid A, B notifies C that he claims restitution. B has a claim in restitution against C for $1,000, the amount that he paid C. The result is the same even if C pays A after notice from B.

5. The facts being otherwise as stated in Illustration 4, C refuses to pay A, although not requested by B to do so. Although C's promise to pay the total sum of $2,000 to A is unenforceable on grounds of public policy, A has a claim in restitution against C for $1,000, the amount that he paid C.

CHAPTER 9

THE SCOPE OF CONTRACTUAL OBLIGATIONS

TOPIC 1. THE MEANING OF AGREEMENTS

§ 200. Interpretation of Promise or Agreement.

Interpretation of a promise or agreement or a term thereof is the ascertainment of its meaning.

Comment

a. Formation of contract. Questions of interpretation arise in determining whether there is a contract as well as in determining rights and duties under a contract. Chapter 3 states rules applicable in determining whether the parties have manifested the mutual assent necessary to a contract enforceable as a bargain. The rules stated in the present Topic overlap with those rules, but also apply where the making of a contract is not disputed.

b. Manifestation of intention. As is made clear in Chapter 3, particularly §§ 17–20, the intention of a party that is relevant to formation of a contract is the intention manifested by him rather than any different undisclosed intention. The definitions of "promise," "agreement," and "term" in §§ 2, 3 and 5 also refer to "manifestation of intention." It follows that the meaning of the words or other conduct of a party is not necessarily the meaning he expects or understands. He is not bound by a meaning unless he has reason to know of it, but the expectation and understanding of the other party must also be taken into account. See § 201.

c. Interpretation and legal operation. Interpretation is not a determination of the legal effect of words or other conduct. Properly interpreted, an agreement may not be enforceable as a contract, or a term such as a promise to pay a penalty may be denied legal effect, or it may have a legal effect different from that agreed upon, as in a case of employment at less than a statutory minimum wage.

§ 201. Whose Meaning Prevails.

(1) Where the parties have attached the same meaning to a promise or agreement or a term thereof, it is interpreted in accordance with that meaning.

(2) Where the parties have attached different meanings to a promise or agreement or a term thereof, it is interpreted in accordance with the meaning attached by one of them if at the time the agreement was made

    (a) that party did not know of any different meaning attached by the other, and the other knew the meaning attached by the first party; or

    (b) that party had no reason to know of any different meaning attached by the other, and the other had reason to know the meaning attached by the first party.

(3) Except as stated in this Section, neither party is bound by the meaning attached by the other, even though the result may be a failure of mutual assent.

Comment

a. The meaning of words. Words are used as conventional symbols of mental states, with standardized meanings based on habitual or customary practice. Unless a different intention is shown, language is interpreted in accordance with its generally prevailing meaning. See § 202(3). Usages of varying degrees of generality are recorded in dictionaries, but there are substantial differences between English and American usages and between usages in different parts of the United States. Differences of usage also exist in various localities and in different social, economic, religious and ethnic groups. All these usages change over time, and persons engaged in transactions with each other often develop temporary usages peculiar to themselves. Moreover, most words are commonly used in more than one sense.

b. The problem of context. Uncertainties in the meaning of words are ordinarily greatly reduced by the context in which they are used. The same is true of other conventional symbols, and the meaning of conduct not used as a conventional symbol is even more dependent on its setting. But the context of words and other conduct is seldom exactly the same for two different people, since connotations depend on the entire past experience and the attitudes and expectations of the person whose understanding is in question. In general, the context relevant to interpretation of a bargain is the context common to both parties. More precisely, the question of meaning in cases of misunderstanding depends on an inquiry into what each party knew or had reason to know, as stated in Subsections (2) and (3). See § 20 and Illustrations. Ordinarily a party has reason to know of meanings in general usage.

c. Mutual understanding. Subsection (1) makes it clear that the primary search is for a common meaning of the parties, not a meaning imposed on them by the law. . . . The objective of interpretation in the general law of contracts is to carry out the understanding of the parties rather than to impose obligations on them contrary to their understanding: "the courts do not make a contract for the parties." Ordinarily, therefore, the mutual understanding of the parties prevails even where the contractual term has been defined differently by statute or administrative regulation. But parties who used a standardized term in an unusual sense obviously run the risk that their agreement will be misinterpreted in litigation.

Illustrations

1. A and B agree that A will sell goods to B "f.o.b." the place of destination. Prior correspondence shows that the price has been adjusted on the assumption that B's insurance policies will cover the goods during shipment. Notwithstanding the normal meaning of the "f.o.b." term declared in Uniform Commercial Code § 2–319, it may be found that the parties have "otherwise agreed" under that section and that B bears the risk in transit.

2. A signs a negotiable promissory note payable to B's order, and C signs his name on the back without more. Under Uniform Commercial Code § 3–402, C's signature is an indorsement, and evidence of a contrary understanding is not admissible except for the purpose of reformation of the instrument. This conclusion does not rest on interpretation of the writing.

3. A agrees to sell beer to B at a specified price per barrel. At the time of the agreement both parties and others in their trade use as standard barrels wooden barrels which originally hold 31 gallons and hold less as they continue in use. A statute defines a barrel as 31½ gallons. The statute does not prevent interpretation of the agreement as referring to the barrels in use.

d. Misunderstanding. Subsection (2) follows the terminology of § 20, referring to the understanding of each party as the meaning "attached" by him to a term of a promise or agreement. Where the rules stated in Subsections (1) and (2) do not apply, neither party is bound by the understanding of the other. The result may be an entire failure of agreement or a failure to agree as to a term. There may be a binding contract despite failure to agree as to a term, if the term is not essential or if it can be supplied. See § 204. In some cases a party can waive the misunderstanding and enforce the contract in accordance with the understanding of the other party.

Illustrations

4. A agrees to sell and B to buy a quantity of eviscerated "chicken." A tenders "stewing chicken" or "fowl"; B rejects on the ground that the contract calls for "broilers" or "fryers." Each party makes a claim for damages against the other. It is found that each acted in good faith and that neither had reason to know of the difference in meaning. Both claims fail.

5. A orders goods from B, using A's standard form. B acknowledges the order, using his own standard form. Each form provides that no terms are agreed to except those on the form and that the other party agrees to the form. One form contains an arbitration clause; the other does not. The goods are delivered and paid for. Later a dispute arises as to their quality. There is no agreement to arbitrate the dispute.

§ 202. Rules in Aid of Interpretation.

(1) Words and other conduct are interpreted in the light of all the circumstances, and if the principal purpose of the parties is ascertainable it is given great weight.

(2) A writing is interpreted as a whole, and all writings that are part of the same transaction are interpreted together.

(3) Unless a different intention is manifested,

(a) where language has a generally prevailing meaning, it is interpreted in accordance with that meaning;

(b) technical terms and words of art are given their technical meaning when used in a transaction within their technical field.

(4) Where an agreement involves repeated occasions for performance by either party with knowledge of the nature of the performance and opportunity for objection to it by the other, any course of performance accepted or acquiesced in without objection is given great weight in the interpretation of the agreement.

(5) Wherever reasonable, the manifestations of intention of the parties to a promise or agreement are interpreted as consistent with each other and with any relevant course of performance, course of dealing, or usage of trade.

Comment

a. Scope of special rules. The rules in this Section are applicable to all manifestations of intention and all transactions. The rules are general in character, and serve merely as guides in the process of interpretation. They do not depend upon any determination that there is an ambiguity, but are used in determining what meanings are reasonably possible as well as in choosing among possible meanings.

b. Circumstances. The meaning of words and other symbols commonly depends on their context; the meaning of other conduct is even more dependent on the circumstances. In interpreting the words and conduct of the parties to a contract, a court seeks to put itself in the position they occupied at the time the contract was made. When the parties have adopted a writing as a final expression of their agreement, interpretation is directed to the meaning of that writing in the light of the circumstances. See §§ 209, 212. The circumstances for this purpose include the entire situation, as it appeared to the parties, and in appropriate cases may include facts known to one party of which the other had reason to know. See § 201.

Illustrations

1. A contracts with B to do concrete work on a bridge, to be paid for according to "the number of square yards of concrete surface included in the bridge deck." An estimate included in the proposal for bids and an estimate submitted by A to B after award are shown to have been based on the top surface only, not including the side and bottom surfaces. On a finding that this was the mutual understanding, the contract is to be so interpreted.

2. In a written agreement between A and B it is stated that B owns half of the stock of C Company, that "A has rendered valuable services to C Company for which B desires to compensate A in the sum of $25,000 payable in the manner hereinafter set forth," and that B will pay A "one-half of all money received from C Company, such as dividends, or profits until A has been paid the said amount of $25,000." It is shown that the written agreement was executed after the services were rendered, that there was no prior explicit understanding that A would be compensated, and that before signing the written agreement A and B orally agreed that the $25,000 was to be a "bonus out of B's profit," "double or nothing," "a gamble." The written agreement is to be interpreted in accordance with the oral agreement.

c. Principal purpose. The purposes of the parties to a contract are not always identical; particularly in business transactions, the parties often have divergent or even conflicting interests. But up to a point they commonly join in a common purpose of attaining a specific factual or legal result which each regards as necessary to the attainment of his ultimate purposes. Moreover, one party may know or have reason to know the purpose of the other and thus that his meaning is one consistent with that purpose. Determination that the parties have a principal purpose in common requires interpretation, but if such a purpose is disclosed further interpretation is guided by it. Even language which is otherwise explicit may be read with a modification needed to make it consistent with such a purpose.

Illustrations

3. A promises B as follows: "In consideration of your supplying my nephew C with china and earthenware during the coming year, I guarantee the payment of any bills you may draw on him on account thereof to the amount of $200." C is engaged in the business of selling such goods. B sells C $2,000 of china during the year and draws bills for their price in varying amounts. C pays $1,000 and then defaults. A's promise is to be interpreted as a continuing undertaking, not limited to the first $200 of purchases.

4. A agrees with his divorced wife B and C, trustee, to pay to C $1,200 each year for the benefit of D, the 10-year-old son of A and B, until D enters college, and to pay $2,200 each year for the period of D's higher education but not more than four years. At age 19 D completes high school and is inducted into the army. Upon a finding that the main purpose of the agreement is to provide for D's maintenance and education, the agreement is to be interpreted as not requiring payments during D's military service.

d. Interpretation of the whole. Meaning is inevitably dependent on context. A word changes meaning when it becomes part of a sentence, the sentence when it becomes part of a paragraph. A longer writing similarly affects the paragraph, other related writings affect the particular writing, and the circumstances affect the whole. Where the whole can be read to give significance to each part, that reading is preferred; if such a reading would be unreasonable, a choice must be made. See § 203. To fit the immediate verbal context or the more remote total context particular words or punctuation may be disregarded or supplied; clerical or grammatical errors may be corrected; singular may be treated as plural or plural as singular.

Illustrations

5. A written agreement between A and B for the exchange of real estate provides that A and B will each pay a $200 commission to C, a broker, "upon the signing of this agreement by both parties hereto." The last sentence of the agreement states, "The commission being due and payable upon the transfer of the properties." It is shown that A refused to sign the agreement until the last sentence was added. The agreement is to be interpreted to make the commission due only when both the signing and the transfer take place.

6. A agrees to appoint B exclusive distributor in a specified area for a new product to be manufactured by A, and B agrees to use his best efforts to promote sale of the product. The written agreement includes an initial retail price list and a provision that A will sell to B at the lowest price and highest discount it gives to any distributor. Whether the parties intend to be bound before any other distributor is appointed or any price fixed is a question of the meaning of the entire agreement in its context. If they do, the agreement has the effect of an agreement to sell at a reasonable price at the time for delivery. See Uniform Commercial Code § 2–305.

7. A contracts in writing to build a house for B according to specifications, and C, a surety company, guarantees A's performance. After completion and acceptance the house and its contents are damaged by hot water because of defective work by the plumbing and heating subcontractor. In determining the responsibility of A and C, the contract, specifications and surety bond are to be read together.

e. General usage. In the United States the English language is used far more often in a sense which would be generally understood throughout the country than in a sense peculiar to some locality or group. In the absence of some contrary indication, therefore, English words are read as having the meaning given them by general usage, if there is one. This rule is a rule of interpretation in the absence of contrary evidence, not a rule excluding contrary evidence. It may also yield to internal indications such as inconsistency, absurdity, or departure from normal grammar, punctuation, or word order.

Illustrations

8. A issues to B a fire insurance policy covering lumber stored in "sheds." In the absence of contrary indication, lumber in the basement of a two-story warehouse is not covered.

9. A leases restaurant premises to B. The lease provides that A will pay for electricity and that B will "pay for gas or fuel used in the preparation of food." In the absence of contrary indication, "fuel" should be read not to include electricity.

f. Technical terms. Parties to an agreement often use the vocabulary of a particular place, vocation or trade, in which new words are coined and common words are assigned new meanings. But technical terms are often misused, and it may be shown that a technical word or phrase was used in a non-technical sense. Moreover, the same word may have a variety of technical and other meanings. "Mules" may mean animals, shoes or machines; a "ram" may mean an animal or a hydraulic ram; "zebra" may refer to a mammal, a butterfly, a lizard, a fish, a type of plant, tree or wood, or merely to the letter "Z".

Illustrations

10. The facts being otherwise as stated in Illustration 9, there is a local usage in the restaurant trade that "fuel" includes electricity used in cooking. In the absence of contrary indication, "fuel" may be read in accordance with the usage. But a provision in the lease that if B installs a new electric range he will also install a special meter and pay for electricity used by the range would show that the parties did not adopt the local usage.

11. A contract for the sale of horsemeat scraps calls for "minimum 50% protein." As both parties know, by a usage of the business in which they are engaged, 49.5 per cent is treated as the equivalent of 50 per cent. The contract is to be interpreted in accordance with the usage.

g. Course of performance. The parties to an agreement know best what they meant, and their action under it is often the strongest evidence of their meaning. But such "practical construction" is not conclusive of meaning. Conduct must be weighed in the light of the terms of the agreement and their possible meanings. Where it is unreasonable to interpret the contract in accordance with the course of performance, the conduct of the parties may be evidence of an agreed modification or of a waiver by one party. See Uniform Commercial Code § 2–208. Or there may be simply a mistake which should be corrected. The rule of Subsection (4) does not apply to action on a single occasion or to action of one party only; in such cases the conduct of a party may be evidence against him that he had knowledge or reason to know of the other party's meaning, but self-serving conduct is not entitled to weight.

Illustrations

12. A discloses to B a secret formula for an antiseptic liquid and B agrees to pay monthly royalties based on amounts sold. Fifty years later the formula has been published in medical journals. After continuing to pay for 25 years more, B contends that the duty to pay royalties ended when the formula ceased to be secret. B's conduct strongly negates the contention.

13. Several railroads agree in writing to share working expenses and taxes of X, another railroad, on a "wheelage basis." For several years they pay shares in proportion to their stock ownership in the other railroad. Then all but one agree that they have been mistaken and that future payments will be made on a basis of use of X's physical properties. Stock ownership is so plainly unrelated to any possible meaning of "wheelage" that the course of performance does not support an interpretation of "wheelage basis" as requiring payments in proportion to stock ownership.

h. Preference for consistency. Subsection (5) states a rule fairly implied in Subsections (1) and (2); words and conduct are interpreted in the light of the circumstances, and writings are interpreted as a whole. A meaning consistent with all the circumstances is preferred to a meaning which requires that part of the context be disregarded. But the parties may have agreed to displace normal meanings, may have modified a prior understanding, or may have agreed to confusing or self-contradictory terms. They may even have entirely failed to agree, though each thought there was an agreement. See §§ 20, 201.

§ 203. Standards of Preference in Interpretation.

In the interpretation of a promise or agreement or a term thereof, the following standards of preference are generally applicable:

> (a) an interpretation which gives a reasonable, lawful, and effective meaning to all the terms is preferred to an interpretation which leaves a part unreasonable, unlawful, or of no effect;
>
> (b) express terms are given greater weight than course of performance, course of dealing, and usage of trade, course of performance is given greater weight than course of dealing or usage of trade, and course of dealing is given greater weight than usage of trade;
>
> (c) specific terms and exact terms are given greater weight than general language;
>
> (d) separately negotiated or added terms are given greater weight than standardized terms or other terms not separately negotiated.

Comment

a. Scope. The rules of this Section are applicable to all manifestations of intention and all transactions. They apply only in choosing among reasonable interpretations. They do not override evidence of the meaning of the parties, but aid in determining meaning or prescribe legal effect when meaning is in doubt.

b. Superfluous terms. Since an agreement is interpreted as a whole, it is assumed in the first instance that no part of it is superfluous. The parties may of course agree to supersede prior manifestations of intention; indeed, this is the normal effect of an integrated agreement. See § 213. But, particularly in cases of integrated agreements, terms are rarely agreed to without reason. Where an integrated agreement has been negotiated with care and in detail and has been expertly drafted for the particular transaction, an interpretation is very strongly negated if it would render some provisions superfluous. On the other hand, a standard form may include provisions appropriate only to some of the transactions in which the form is to be used; or the form may be used for an inappropriate transaction. Even agreements tailored to particular transactions sometimes include overlapping or redundant or meaningless provisions.

The preference for an interpretation which gives meaning to every part of an agreement does not mean that every part is assumed to have legal consequences. Parties commonly direct their attention to performance rather than breach, and it is enough that each provision has meaning to them as a guide to performance. Stipulations against particular legal consequences are not uncommon. Thus it is not unusual to define the intended performance with precision and then to provide for tolerances within which variation is permitted. See Uniform Commercial Code § 2–508(2).

c. Unreasonable and unlawful terms. In the absence of contrary indication, it is assumed that each term of an agreement has a reasonable rather than an unreasonable meaning, and that the agreement is intended to be lawful rather than unconscionable, fraudulent or otherwise illegal. But parties are free to make agreements which seem unreasonable to others, and circumstances may show that even an agreement innocent on its face has an illegal purpose. The search is for the manifested intention of the parties. If a term or a contract is unconscionable or otherwise against public policy, it should be dealt with directly rather than by spurious interpretation. See § 208 and Uniform Commercial Code § 2–302 and Comment.

Illustration

1. A licenses B to manufacture pipes under A's patents, and B agrees to pay "a royalty of 50 cents per 1,000 feet for an output of 5,000,000 or less feet per year, and for an output of over 5,000,000 feet per year at the rate of 30 cents per thousand feet." The 50 cent rate is payable on the first 5,000,000 feet, the 30 cent rate only on the excess. The more literal reading is unreasonable, since it would involve a smaller payment for 6,000,000 feet than for 4,000,000 feet.

d. Priority of express terms. Just as parties to agreements often depart from general usage as to the meaning of words or other conduct, so they may depart from a usage of trade. Similarly, they may change a pattern established by their own prior course of dealing. Their meaning in such cases is ordinarily to be ascertained as a fact; no penalty is attached by the law of contracts to their failure to conform to the usages of others or to their own prior usage. Course of performance may establish meaning, or it may show mistake or oversight or modification or waiver. See § 202. The priorities stated in Subsection (b) are those stated in Uniform Commercial Code §§ 1–205 and 2–208, rephrased to fit the different context of the Restatement.

   e. General and specific terms. People commonly use general language without a clear consciousness of its full scope and without awareness that an exception should be made. Attention and understanding are likely to be in better focus when language is specific or exact, and in case of conflict the specific or exact term is more likely to express the meaning of the parties with respect to the situation than the general language. If the specific or exact can be read as an exception or qualification of the general, both are given some effect, in accordance with the rule stated in Subsection (a). Compare Uniform Commercial Code § 2–317. But the rule yields to manifestation of a contrary intention.

   f. Superseded standard terms. The rule stated in Subsection (d) has frequent application in cases of standardized documents. Printed forms are often misused, and there may be a question whether the parties manifested assent to a printed term on a writing. A printed provision that is clearly part of an integrated contract is normally to be interpreted as consistent with other terms, but in cases of inconsistency a handwritten or typewritten term inserted in connection with the particular transaction ordinarily prevails. Similarly, a typewritten term may be superseded by drawing a line through it, modified by interlineation, or controlled by an inconsistent handwritten insertion in another part of the agreement. It is sometimes said generally that handwritten terms control typewritten and printed terms, and typewritten control printed. See Uniform Commercial Code § 3–118(b); compare § 2–316(1) (disclaimer of express warranty), § 3–110(3) (instrument payable both to order and to bearer). But the rule yields to manifestation of a contrary intention.

Illustrations

   2. A, an agent of C, authorized to make contracts for C, writes a letter to B beginning "We offer," and stating a proposal in detailed and clear language, signed "C by A, Agent." At the bottom of the office stationery which A uses for the offer there is printed "All contracts and orders taken are subject to the approval of the executive office." A portion of the letter is typed over a portion of this printing. A jury's finding that the printed words were not part of the letter and that it is therefore an offer will not be set aside.

   3. A charter party contains the printed provision "vessel to have turn in loading." There is written below this, "vessel to be loaded promptly." The printed and written provisions are given the consistent meaning that the vessel shall take its turn in loading, though this involves considerable delay, but when its turn arrives, the vessel shall be loaded promptly.

   4. A's agent B draws checks on the C bank, imprinting the amounts with perforations made by a checkwriting machine. The amounts are also handwritten in figures. In case of conflict, since the perforated amounts are more difficult to alter, they control the handwritten figures. See Uniform Commercial Code § 3–118(b), (c).

§ 204. Supplying an Omitted Essential Term.

When the parties to a bargain sufficiently defined to be a contract have not agreed with respect to a term which is essential to a determination of their rights and duties, a term which is reasonable in the circumstances is supplied by the court.

Comment

   a. Scope; relation to other rules. This Section states a principle governing the legal effect of a binding agreement. The supplying of an omitted term is not technically interpretation, but the two are closely related; courts often speak of an "implied" term. In many common situations the principle has been elaborated in more detailed rules, applicable unless otherwise agreed. See the rules on the effect of failure of performance stated in §§ 231–49 and the rules on impossibility and frustration stated in Chapter 11, and compare §§ 158 and 272, regarding the supplying of terms in cases of mistake and impracticability or frustration. A similar principle is often applicable in determining whether the terms of an agreement are sufficiently certain to constitute a contract. See §§ 33, 34. In both situations the supplying of an omitted term may resemble or overlap interpretation (see § 200) or the effect given to usage (see §§ 219–23).

b. How omission occurs. The parties to an agreement may entirely fail to foresee the situation which later arises and gives rise to a dispute; they then have no expectations with respect to that situation, and a search for their meaning with respect to it is fruitless. Or they may have expectations but fail to manifest them, either because the expectation rests on an assumption which is unconscious or only partly conscious, or because the situation seems to be unimportant or unlikely, or because discussion of it might be unpleasant or might produce delay or impasse.

c. Interpretation and omission. Interpretation may be necessary to determine that the parties have not agreed with respect to a particular term, but the supplying of an omitted term is not within the definition of interpretation in § 200. Where there is tacit agreement or a common tacit assumption or where a term can be supplied by logical deduction from agreed terms and the circumstances, interpretation may be enough. But interpretation may result in the conclusion that there was in fact no agreement on a particular point, and that conclusion should be accepted even though the omitted term could be supplied by giving agreed language a meaning different from the meaning or meanings given it by the parties.

d. Supplying a term. The process of supplying an omitted term has sometimes been disguised as a literal or a purposive reading of contract language directed to a situation other than the situation that arises. Sometimes it is said that the search is for the term the parties would have agreed to if the question had been brought to their attention. Both the meaning of the words used and the probability that a particular term would have been used if the question had been raised may be factors in determining what term is reasonable in the circumstances. But where there is in fact no agreement, the court should supply a term which comports with community standards of fairness and policy rather than analyze a hypothetical model of the bargaining process. Thus where a contract calls for a single performance such as the rendering of a service or the delivery of goods, the parties are most unlikely to agree explicitly that performance will be rendered within a "reasonable time;" but if no time is specified, a term calling for performance within a reasonable time is supplied. See Uniform Commercial Code §§ 1–204, 2–309(1). Similarly, where there is a contract for the sale of goods but nothing is said as to price the price is a reasonable price at the time for delivery. See Uniform Commercial Code § 2–305.

e. Effect of the parol evidence rule. The fact that an essential term is omitted may indicate that the agreement is not integrated or that there is partial rather than complete integration. In such cases the omitted term may be supplied by prior negotiations or a prior agreement. See § 216. But omission of a term does not show conclusively that integration was not complete and a completely integrated agreement, if binding, discharges prior agreements within its scope. See § 213. Where there is complete integration and interpretation of the writing discloses a failure to agree on an essential term, evidence of prior negotiations or agreements is not admissible to supply the omitted term, but such evidence may be admissible, if relevant, on the question of what is reasonable in the circumstances.

Illustration

1. A and his wife convey their ranch to A's sister and her husband, reserving an option to repurchase. The parties agree orally that the property will be kept in the family, but the deed says nothing as to assignment of the option. If the deed is found to be a partial integration, the oral agreement is effective to show that the option is not assignable. If the deed is found to be a complete integration, the oral agreement is discharged and the option is assignable.

TOPIC 2. CONSIDERATIONS OF FAIRNESS AND THE PUBLIC INTEREST

§ 205. Duty of Good Faith and Fair Dealing.

Every contract imposes upon each party a duty of good faith and fair dealing in its performance and its enforcement.

Comment

a. Meanings of "good faith." Good faith is defined in Uniform Commercial Code § 1–201(19) as "honesty in fact in the conduct or transaction concerned." "In the case of a merchant" Uniform Commercial Code § 2–103(1)(b) provides that good faith means "honesty in fact and the observance of reasonable commercial standards of fair dealing in the trade." The phrase "good faith" is used in a variety of contexts, and its meaning varies somewhat with the context. Good faith performance or enforcement of a contract emphasizes faithfulness to an agreed common purpose and consistency with the justified expectations of the other party; it excludes a variety of types of conduct characterized as involving "bad faith" because they violate community standards of decency, fairness or reasonableness. The appropriate remedy for a breach of the duty of good faith also varies with the circumstances.

b. Good faith purchase. In many situations a good faith purchaser of property for value can acquire better rights in the property than his transferor had. See, e.g., § 342. In this context "good faith" focuses on the honesty of the purchaser, as distinguished from his care or negligence. Particularly in the law of negotiable instruments inquiry may be limited to "good faith" under what has been called "the rule of the pure heart and the empty head." When diligence or inquiry is a condition of the purchaser's right, it is said that good faith is not enough. This focus on honesty is appropriate to cases of good faith purchase; it is less so in cases of good faith performance.

c. Good faith in negotiation. This Section, like **Uniform Commercial Code § 1–203**, does not deal with good faith in the formation of a contract. Bad faith in negotiation, although not within the scope of this Section, may be subject to sanctions. Particular forms of bad faith in bargaining are the subjects of rules as to capacity to contract, mutual assent and consideration and of rules as to invalidating causes such as fraud and duress. See, for example, §§ 90 and 208. Moreover, remedies for bad faith in the absence of agreement are found in the law of torts or restitution. For examples of a statutory duty to bargain in good faith, see, e.g., National Labor Relations Act § 8(d) and the federal Truth in Lending Act. In cases of negotiation for modification of an existing contractual relationship, the rule stated in this Section may overlap with more specific rules requiring negotiation in good faith. See §§ 73, 89; Uniform Commercial Code § 2–209 and Comment.

d. Good faith performance. Subterfuges and evasions violate the obligation of good faith in performance even though the actor believes his conduct to be justified. But the obligation goes further: bad faith may be overt or may consist of inaction, and fair dealing may require more than honesty. A complete catalogue of types of bad faith is impossible, but the following types are among those which have been recognized in judicial decisions: evasion of the spirit of the bargain, lack of diligence and slacking off, willful rendering of imperfect performance, abuse of a power to specify terms, and interference with or failure to cooperate in the other party's performance.

Illustrations

1. A, an oil dealer, borrows $100,000 from B, a supplier, and agrees to buy all his requirements of certain oil products from B on stated terms until the debt is repaid. Before the debt is repaid, A makes a new arrangement with C, a competitor of B. Under the new arrangement A's business is conducted by a corporation formed and owned by A and C and managed by A, and the corporation buys all its oil products from C. The new arrangement may be found to be a subterfuge or evasion and a breach of contract by A.

2. A, owner of a shopping center, leases part of it to B, giving B the exclusive right to conduct a supermarket, the rent to be a percentage of B's gross receipts. During the term of the lease A acquires adjoining land, expands the shopping center, and leases part of the adjoining land to C for a competing supermarket. Unless such action was contemplated or is otherwise justified, there is a breach of contract by A.

3. A Insurance Company insures B against legal liability for certain bodily injuries to third persons, with a limit of liability of $10,000 for an accident to any one person. The policy provides that A will defend any suit covered by it but may settle. C sues B on a claim covered by the policy and offers to settle for $9,500. A refuses to settle on the ground that the amount is excessive, and judgment is rendered against B for $20,000 after a trial defended by A. A then refuses to appeal, and offers to pay $10,000 only if B satisfies the judgment, impairing B's opportunity to negotiate for settlement. B

prosecutes an appeal, reasonably expending $7,500, and obtains dismissal of the claim. A has failed to deal fairly and in good faith with B and is liable for B's appeal expense.

4. A and B contract that A will perform certain demolition work for B and pay B a specified sum for materials salvaged, the contract not to "become effective until" certain insurance policies "are in full force and effect." A makes a good faith effort to obtain the insurance, but financial difficulty arising from injury to an employee of A on another job prevents A from obtaining them. A's duty to perform is discharged.

5. B submits and A accepts a bid to supply approximately 4000 tons of trap rock for an airport at a unit price. The parties execute a standard form of "Invitation, Bid, and Acceptance (Short Form Contract)" supplied by A, including typed terms "to be delivered to project as required," "delivery to start immediately," "cancellation by A may be effected at any time." Good faith requires that A order and accept the rock within a reasonable time unless A has given B notice of intent to cancel.

6. A contracts to perform services for B for such compensation "as you, in your sole judgment, may decide is reasonable." After A has performed the services, B refuses to make any determination of the value of the services. A is entitled to their value as determined by a court.

7. A suffers a loss of property covered by an insurance policy issued by B, and submits to B notice and proof of loss. The notice and proof fail to comply with requirements of the policy as to form and detail. B does not point out the defects, but remains silent and evasive, telling A broadly to perfect his claim. The defects do not bar recovery on the policy.

e. Good faith in enforcement. The obligation of good faith and fair dealing extends to the assertion, settlement and litigation of contract claims and defenses. See, e.g., §§ 73, 89. The obligation is violated by dishonest conduct such as conjuring up a pretended dispute, asserting an interpretation contrary to one's own understanding, or falsification of facts. It also extends to dealing which is candid but unfair, such as taking advantage of the necessitous circumstances of the other party to extort a modification of a contract for the sale of goods without legitimate commercial reason. See Uniform Commercial Code § 2–209, Comment 2. Other types of violation have been recognized in judicial decisions: harassing demands for assurances of performance, rejection of performance for unstated reasons, willful failure to mitigate damages, and abuse of a power to determine compliance or to terminate the contract. For a statutory duty of good faith in termination, see the federal Automobile Dealer's Day in Court Act, 15 U.S.C. §§ 1221–25 (1976).

Illustrations

8. A contracts to sell and ship goods to B on credit. The contract provides that, if B's credit or financial responsibility becomes impaired or unsatisfactory to A, A may demand cash or security before making shipment and may cancel if the demand is not met. A may properly demand cash or security only if he honestly believes, with reason, that the prospect of payment is impaired.

9. A contracts to sell and ship goods to B. On arrival B rejects the goods on the erroneous ground that delivery was late. B is thereafter precluded from asserting other unstated grounds then known to him which A could have cured if stated seasonably.

§ 206. Interpretation Against the Draftsman.

In choosing among the reasonable meanings of a promise or agreement or a term thereof, that meaning is generally preferred which operates against the party who supplies the words or from whom a writing otherwise proceeds.

Comment

a. Rationale. Where one party chooses the terms of a contract, he is likely to provide more carefully for the protection of his own interests than for those of the other party. He is also more likely than the other party to have reason to know of uncertainties of meaning. Indeed, he may leave meaning deliberately obscure, intending to decide at a later date what meaning to assert. In cases of doubt, therefore, so long as other factors are not decisive, there is substantial reason for preferring the meaning of the other party. The rule is often invoked in cases of standardized contracts and in cases where the drafting party has the stronger bargaining position, but it is not limited to such cases. It is in strictness a rule of legal effect, sometimes called construction, as well as interpretation: its operation depends on the positions of the parties as they appear in litigation, and sometimes the result is hard to distinguish from a denial of effect to an unconscionable clause.

b. Compulsory contract or term. The rule that language is interpreted against the party who chose it has no direct application to cases where the language is prescribed by law, as is sometimes true with respect to insurance policies, bills of lading and other standardized documents. In some cases, however, the statute or regulation adopts language which was previously used without compulsion and was interpreted against the drafting party, and there is normally no intention to change the established meaning. Moreover, insurers are more likely than insureds to participate in drafting prescribed forms and to review them carefully before putting them into use.

§ 207. Interpretation Favoring the Public.

In choosing among the reasonable meanings of a promise or agreement or a term thereof, a meaning that serves the public interest is generally preferred.

Comment

a. Scope. The rule preferring an interpretation which favors an interest of the public applies only to agreements which affect a public interest. It is a rule of legal effect as well as interpretation, and rests more on considerations of public policy than on the probable intention of the parties. It has often been relied on to justify narrow construction of a grant of a public franchise or an agreement for a tax exemption. In general, it does not prefer the interest of a governmental agency as a party to a contract; government contracts are likely to be construed against the government as the drafting party.

Illustration

1. A is employed by B as an inventor. In an agreement settling their disputes on termination of the employment, A promises to assign to B all A's rights in a pending patent application and all improvements on the invention covered. Thereafter A makes an invention and applies for a patent, and B claims it as an improvement. The public interest in encouraging invention supports an interpretation of the agreement excluding future improvements unless future improvements were specifically included.

§ 208. Unconscionable Contract or Term.

If a contract or term thereof is unconscionable at the time the contract is made a court may refuse to enforce the contract, or may enforce the remainder of the contract without the unconscionable term, or may so limit the application of any unconscionable term as to avoid any unconscionable result.

Comment

a. Scope. Like the obligation of good faith and fair dealing (§ 205), the policy against unconscionable contracts or terms applies to a wide variety of types of conduct. The determination that a contract or term is or is not unconscionable is made in the light of its setting, purpose and effect. Relevant factors include weaknesses in the contracting process like those involved in more specific rules as to contractual capacity, fraud, and other invalidating causes; the policy also overlaps with rules which render particular bargains or terms unenforceable on grounds of public policy. Policing against unconscionable contracts or terms has sometimes been accomplished "by adverse construction of language, by manipulation of the rules of offer and acceptance or by determinations that the clause is contrary to public policy or to the dominant purpose of the contract." Uniform Commercial Code § 2–302 Comment 1. Particularly in the case of standardized agreements, the rule of this Section permits the court to pass directly on the unconscionability of the contract or clause rather than to avoid unconscionable results by interpretation. Compare § 211.

b. Historic standards. Traditionally, a bargain was said to be unconscionable in an action at law if it was "such as no man in his senses and not under delusion would make on the one hand, and as no honest and fair man would accept on the other;" damages were then limited to those to which the aggrieved party was "equitably" entitled. Hume v. United States, 132 U.S. 406 (1889), quoting Earl of Chesterfield v. Janssen, 2 Ves. Sen. 125, 155, 28 Eng. Rep. 82, 100 (Ch. 1750). Even though a contract was fully enforceable in an action for damages, equitable remedies such as specific performance were refused where "the sum total of its provisions drives too hard a bargain for a court of conscience to assist." Campbell Soup Co. v. Wentz, 172 F.2d 80, 84 (3d Cir. 1948). Modern procedural reforms have blurred the distinction between remedies at law and in equity. For contracts for the sale of goods, Uniform Commercial Code § 2–302 states the rule of this Section without distinction between law and equity. Comment 1 to that section adds, "The principle is one of the prevention of oppression and unfair surprise (Cf. Campbell Soup Co. v. Wentz, . . .) and not of disturbance of allocation of risks because of superior bargaining power."

c. Overall imbalance. Inadequacy of consideration does not of itself invalidate a bargain, but gross disparity in the values exchanged may be an important factor in a determination that a contract is unconscionable and may be sufficient ground, without more, for denying specific performance. . . . Such a disparity may also corroborate indications of defects in the bargaining process. . . . Theoretically it is possible for a contract to be oppressive taken as a whole, even though there is no weakness in the bargaining process and no single term which is in itself unconscionable. Ordinarily, however, an unconscionable contract involves other factors as well as overall imbalance.

Illustrations

1. A, an individual, contracts in June to sell at a fixed price per ton to B, a large soup manufacturer, the carrots to be grown on A's farm. The contract, written on B's standard printed form, is obviously drawn to protect B's interests and not A's; it contains numerous provisions to protect B against various contingencies and none giving analogous protection to A. Each of the clauses can be read restrictively so that it is not unconscionable, but several can be read literally to give unrestricted discretion to B. In January, when the market price has risen above the contract price, A repudiates the contract, and B seeks specific performance. In the absence of justification by evidence of commercial setting, purpose, or effect, the court may determine that the contract as a whole was unconscionable when made, and may then deny specific performance.

2. A, a homeowner, executes a standard printed form used by B, a merchant, agreeing to pay $1,700 for specified home improvements. A also executes a credit application asking for payment in 60 monthly installments but specifying no rate. Four days later A is informed that the credit application has been approved and is given a payment schedule calling for finance and insurance charges amounting to $800 in addition to the $1,700. Before B does any of the work, A repudiates the agreement, and B sues A for $800 damages, claiming that a commission of $800 was paid to B's salesman in reliance on the agreement. The court may determine that the agreement was unconscionable when made, and may then dismiss the claim.

d. Weakness in the bargaining process. A bargain is not unconscionable merely because the parties to it are unequal in bargaining position, nor even because the inequality results in an allocation of risks to the weaker party. But gross inequality of bargaining power, together with terms unreasonably favorable to the stronger party, may confirm indications that the transaction involved elements of deception or compulsion, or may show that the weaker party had no meaningful choice, no real alternative, or did not in fact assent or appear to assent to the unfair terms. Factors which may contribute to a finding of unconscionability in the bargaining process include the following: belief by the stronger party that there is no reasonable probability that the weaker party will fully perform the contract; knowledge of the stronger party that the weaker party will be unable to receive substantial benefits from the contract; knowledge of the stronger party that the weaker party is unable reasonably to protect his interests by reason of physical or mental infirmities, ignorance, illiteracy or inability to understand the language of the agreement, or similar factors. See Uniform Consumer Credit Code § 6.111.

Illustration

3. A, literate only in Spanish, is visited in his home by a salesman of refrigerator-freezers for B. They negotiate in Spanish; A tells the salesman he cannot afford to buy the appliance because his job will end in one week, and the salesman tells A that A will be paid numerous $25 commissions on sales to his friends. A signs a complex installment contract printed in English. The contract provides for a cash price of $900 plus a finance charge of $250. A defaults after paying $32, and B sues for the

balance plus late charges and a 20% attorney's fee authorized by the contract. The appliance cost B $350. The court may determine that the contract was unconscionable when made, and may then limit B's recovery to a reasonable sum.

e. Unconscionable terms. Particular terms may be unconscionable whether or not the contract as a whole is unconscionable. Some types of terms are not enforced, regardless of context; examples are provisions for unreasonably large liquidated damages, or limitations on a debtor's right to redeem collateral. See Uniform Commercial Code §§ 2–718, 9–501(3). Other terms may be unconscionable in some contexts but not in others. Overall imbalance and weaknesses in the bargaining process are then important.

Illustrations

4. A, a packer, sells and ships 300 cases of canned catsup to B, a wholesale grocer. The contract provides, "All claims other than swells must be made within ten days from receipt of goods." Six months later a government inspector, upon microscopic examination of samples, finds excessive mold in the cans and obtains a court order for destruction of the 270 remaining cases in B's warehouse. In the absence of justifying evidence, the court may determine that the quoted clause is unconscionable as applied to latent defects and does not bar a claim for damages for breach of warranty by B against A.

5. A, a retail furniture store, sells furniture on installment credit to B, retaining a security interest. As A knows, B is a woman of limited education, separated from her husband, maintaining herself and seven children by means of $218 per month public assistance. After 13 purchases over a period of five years for a total of $1,200, B owes A $164. B then buys a stereo set for $514. Each contract contains a paragraph of some 800 words in extremely fine print, in the middle of which are the words "all payments . . . shall be credited pro rata on all outstanding . . . accounts." The effect of this language is to keep a balance due on each item until all are paid for. On B's default, A sues for possession of all the items sold. It may be determined that either the quoted clause or the contract as a whole was unconscionable when made.

6. A, a corporation with its principal office in State X, contracts with B, a resident of State X, to make improvements on B's home in State X. The contract is made on A's standard printed form, which contains a clause by which the parties submit to the jurisdiction of a court in State Y, 200 miles away. No reason for the clause appears except to make litigation inconvenient and expensive for B. The clause is unconscionable.

f. Law and fact. A determination that a contract or term is unconscionable is made by the court in the light of all the material facts. Under Uniform Commercial Code § 2–302, the determination is made "as a matter of law," but the parties are to be afforded an opportunity to present evidence as to commercial setting, purpose and effect to aid the court in its determination. Incidental findings of fact are made by the court rather than by a jury, but are accorded the usual weight given to such findings of fact in appellate review. An appellate court will also consider whether proper standards were applied.

Illustration

7. A, a finance company, lends money to B, a manufacturing company, on the security of an assignment by B of its accounts receivable. The agreement provides for loans of 75% of the value of assigned accounts acceptable to A, and forbids B to dispose of or hypothecate any assets without A's written consent. The agreed interest rate of 18% would be usurious but for a statute precluding a corporation from raising the defense of usury. Substantial advances are made, and the balance owed is $14,000 when B becomes bankrupt, three months after the first advance. A determination that the agreement is unconscionable on its face, without regard to context, is error. The agreement is unconscionable only if it is not a reasonable commercial device in the light of all the circumstances when it was made.

g. Remedies. Perhaps the simplest application of the policy against unconscionable agreements is the denial of specific performance where the contract as a whole was unconscionable when made. If such a contract is entirely executory, denial of money damages may also be appropriate. But the policy is not penal: unless the parties can be restored to their pre-contract positions, the offending party will ordinarily be awarded at least the reasonable value of performance rendered by him. Where a term rather than the entire contract is unconscionable, the appropriate remedy is ordinarily to deny effect to the unconscionable term. In such cases as that of an exculpatory term, the effect may be to enlarge the liability of the offending party.

TOPIC 3. EFFECT OF ADOPTION OF A WRITING

§ 209. Integrated Agreements.

(1) An integrated agreement is a writing or writings constituting a final expression of one or more terms of an agreement.

(2) Whether there is an integrated agreement is to be determined by the court as a question preliminary to determination of a question of interpretation or to application of the parol evidence rule.

(3) Where the parties reduce an agreement to a writing which in view of its completeness and specificity reasonably appears to be a complete agreement, it is taken to be an integrated agreement unless it is established by other evidence that the writing did not constitute a final expression.

Comment

a. Significance of integration. Where the parties to an agreement have reduced a term of the agreement to specific words or other symbols, interpretation of that term relates to the meaning of the words and symbols used. See § 212. An integrated agreement supersedes contrary prior statements, and a completely integrated agreement supersedes even consistent additional terms. See §§ 213–16. But both integrated and unintegrated agreements are to be read in the light of the circumstances and may be explained or supplemented by operative usages of trade, by the course of dealing between the parties, and by the course of performance of the agreement.

b. Form of integrated agreement. No particular form is required for an integrated agreement. Written contracts, signed by both parties, may include an explicit declaration that there are no other agreements between the parties, but such a declaration may not be conclusive. The intention of the parties may also be manifested without explicit statement and without signature. A letter, telegram or other informal document written by one party may be orally assented to by the other as a final expression of some or all of the terms of their agreement. Indeed, the parties to an oral agreement may choose their words with such explicit precision and completeness that the same legal consequences follow as where there is a completely integrated agreement.

Illustrations

1. A and B enter into an oral contract, and prepare and sign a writing to incorporate its terms. Though the writing contains substantially all the orally agreed terms, they are not fully satisfied with it, and they agree to have it redrafted. There is no integrated agreement.

2. A orally agrees to employ B on certain terms. B immediately writes and A receives a letter beginning, "Confirming our oral arrangement this morning," and fully stating the contract as he understands it. A makes no reply but with knowledge of B's understanding accepts services from B under the contract. The letter is a completely integrated agreement. Even though the letter is not in all respects accurate, it operates as an offer of substituted terms, and A's acquiescence manifests assent to those terms.

c. Proof of integration. Whether a writing has been adopted as an integrated agreement is a question of fact to be determined in accordance with all relevant evidence. The issue is distinct from the issues whether an agreement was made and whether the document is genuine, and also from the issue whether it was intended as a complete and exclusive statement of the agreement. See § 210; compare Uniform Commercial Code § 2–202. Ordinarily the issue whether there is an integrated agreement is determined by the trial judge in the first instance as a question preliminary to an interpretative ruling or to the application of the parol evidence rule. See §§ 212, 213. After the preliminary determination, such questions as whether the agreement was in fact made may remain to be decided by the trier of fact. Subsection (3) states the rule that a written agreement complete on its face is taken to be an integrated agreement in the absence of contrary evidence.

Illustration

3. A sells and delivers a hotel to B. Later A takes possession of the hotel furniture, and B sues to recover it. B claims the furniture under an oral agreement; A proves an apparently complete written agreement for the sale of the real property, and objects to consideration of the oral agreement. In the absence of contrary evidence, the writing is taken to be an integration; whether it is a complete integration is decided on the basis of all relevant evidence. If the oral agreement contradicts the writing, or if the writing is a complete integration, evidence of the oral agreement is excluded; otherwise the trier of fact is to decide whether the oral agreement was made.

§ 210. Completely and Partially Integrated Agreements.

(1) A completely integrated agreement is an integrated agreement adopted by the parties as a complete and exclusive statement of the terms of the agreement.

(2) A partially integrated agreement is an integrated agreement other than a completely integrated agreement.

(3) Whether an agreement is completely or partially integrated is to be determined by the court as a question preliminary to determination of a question of interpretation or to application of the parol evidence rule.

Comment

a. Complete integration. The definition in Subsection (1) is to be read with the definition of integrated agreement in § 209, to reject the assumption sometimes made that because a writing has been worked out which is final on some matters, it is to be taken as including all the matters agreed upon. Even though there is an integrated agreement, consistent additional terms not reduced to writing may be shown, unless the court finds that the writing was assented to by both parties as a complete and exclusive statement of all the terms. Upon such a finding, however, evidence of the alleged making of consistent additional terms must be kept from the trier of fact. See § 216; Uniform Commercial Code § 2–202 Comment 3.

b. Proof of complete integration. That a writing was or was not adopted as a completely integrated agreement may be proved by any relevant evidence. A document in the form of a written contract, signed by both parties and apparently complete on its face, may be decisive of the issue in the absence of credible contrary evidence. But a writing cannot of itself prove its own completeness, and wide latitude must be allowed for inquiry into circumstances bearing on the intention of the parties.

Illustration

1. A, a college, owns premises which have no toilet or plumbing facilities or heating equipment. In negotiating a lease to B for use of the premises as a radio station, A orally agrees to permit the use of facilities in an adjacent building and to provide heat. The parties subsequently execute a written lease agreement which makes no mention of facilities or heat. The question whether the written lease was adopted as a completely integrated agreement is to be decided on the basis of all relevant evidence of the prior and contemporaneous conduct and language of the parties.

c. Partial integration. It is often clear from the face of a writing that it is incomplete and cannot be more than a partially integrated agreement. Incompleteness may also be shown by other writings, which may or may not become part of a completely or partially integrated agreement. Or it may be shown by any relevant evidence, oral or written, that an apparently complete writing never became fully effective, or that it was modified after initial adoption.

Illustration

2. A writes to B a letter offer containing four provisions. B replies by letter that three of the provisions are satisfactory, but makes a counter proposal as to the fourth. After further discussion of the fourth provision, the parties come to oral agreement on a revision of it, but make no further statements as to the other three terms. A's letter is a partially integrated agreement with respect to the first three provisions.

§ 211. Standardized Agreements.

(1) Except as stated in Subsection (3), where a party to an agreement signs or otherwise manifests assent to a writing and has reason to believe that like writings are regularly used to embody terms of agreements of the same type, he adopts the writing as an integrated agreement with respect to the terms included in the writing.

(2) Such a writing is interpreted wherever reasonable as treating alike all those similarly situated, without regard to their knowledge or understanding of the standard terms of the writing.

(3) Where the other party has reason to believe that the party manifesting such assent would not do so if he knew that the writing contained a particular term, the term is not part of the agreement.

Comment

a. Utility of standardization. Standardization of agreements serves many of the same functions as standardization of goods and services; both are essential to a system of mass production and distribution. Scarce and costly time and skill can be devoted to a class of transactions rather than to details of individual transactions. Legal rules which would apply in the absence of agreement can be shaped to fit the particular type of transaction, and extra copies of the form can be used for purposes such as record-keeping, coordination and supervision. Forms can be tailored to office routines, the training of personnel, and the requirements of mechanical equipment. Sales personnel and customers are freed from attention to numberless variations and can focus on meaningful choice among a limited number of significant features: transaction-type, style, quantity, price, or the like. Operations are simplified and costs reduced, to the advantage of all concerned.

b. Assent to unknown terms. A party who makes regular use of a standardized form of agreement does not ordinarily expect his customers to understand or even to read the standard terms. One of the purposes of standardization is to eliminate bargaining over details of individual transactions, and that purpose would not be served if a substantial number of customers retained counsel and reviewed the standard terms. Employees regularly using a form often have only a limited understanding of its terms and limited authority to vary them. Customers do not in fact ordinarily understand or even read the standard terms. They trust to the good faith of the party using the form and to the tacit representation that like terms are being accepted regularly by others similarly situated. But they understand that they are assenting to the terms not read or not understood, subject to such limitations as the law may impose.

c. Review of unfair terms. Standardized agreements are commonly prepared by one party. The customer assents to a few terms, typically inserted in blanks on the printed form, and gives blanket assent to the type of transaction embodied in the standard form. He is commonly not represented in the drafting, and the draftsman may be tempted to overdraw in the interest of his employer. The obvious danger of overreaching has resulted in government regulation of insurance policies, bills of lading, retail installment sales, small loans, and other particular types of contracts. Regulation sometimes includes administrative review of standard terms, or even prescription of terms. Apart from such regulation, standard terms imposed by one party are enforced. But standard terms may be superseded by separately negotiated or added terms (§ 203), they are construed against the draftsman (§ 206), and they are subject to the overriding obligation of good faith (§ 205) and to the power of the court to refuse to enforce an unconscionable contract or term (§ 208). Moreover, various contracts and terms are against public policy and unenforceable. See Chapter 8.

d. Non-contractual documents. The same document may serve both contractual and other purposes, and a party may assent to it for other purposes without understanding that it embodies contract terms. He may nevertheless be bound if he has reason to know that it is used to embody contract terms. Insurance policies, steamship tickets, bills of lading, and warehouse receipts are commonly so obviously contractual in form as to give the customer reason to know their character. But baggage checks or automobile parking lot tickets may appear to be mere identification tokens, and a party without knowledge or reason to know that the token purports to be a contract is then not bound by terms printed on the token. Documents such as invoices, instructions for use, and the like, delivered after a contract is made, may raise similar problems.

Illustrations

3. A agrees orally with B, a stockbroker, that in transactions between them "abracadabra" shall mean X Company. A sends a signed written order to B to buy 100 shares "abracadabra," and B buys 100 shares of X Company. The parties are bound in accordance with the oral agreement.

4. A and B are engaged in buying and selling shares of stock from each other, and agree orally to conceal the nature of their dealings by using the word "sell" to mean "buy" and using the word "buy" to mean "sell." A sends a written offer to B to "sell" certain shares, and B accepts. The parties are bound in accordance with the oral agreement.

c. Statements of intention. The rule of Subsection (1) permits reference to the negotiations of the parties, including statements of intention and even positive promises, so long as they are used to show the meaning of the writing. A contrary rule in the interpretation of wills is sometimes stated broadly enough to apply to the interpretation of contracts, but that rule is subject to exceptions and rests in part on the more rigorous formal requirements to which wills are subject. Statements of a contracting party subsequent to the adoption of an integration are admissible against him to show his understanding of the meaning asserted by the other party.

Illustrations

5. In an integrated agreement A promises B to insert B's "business card" in A's "advertising chart" for a price to be paid when the chart is "published." The quoted terms are to be read in the light of the circumstances known to the parties, including their oral statements as to their meaning.

6. In an integrated agreement A contracts to sell "my horse," and B contracts to buy it. A owns two horses. It may be shown by oral evidence, including statements of the parties, that both A and B meant the same horse.

d. "Question of law." Analytically, what meaning is attached to a word or other symbol by one or more people is a question of fact. But general usage as to the meaning of words in the English language is commonly a proper subject for judicial notice without the aid of evidence extrinsic to the writing. Historically, moreover, partly perhaps because of the fact that jurors were often illiterate, questions of interpretation of written documents have been treated as questions of law in the sense that they are decided by the trial judge rather than by the jury. Likewise, since an appellate court is commonly in as good a position to decide such questions as the trial judge, they have been treated as questions of law for purposes of appellate review. Such treatment has the effect of limiting the power of the trier of fact to exercise a dispensing power in the guise of a finding of fact, and thus contributes to the stability and predictability of contractual relations. In cases of standardized contracts such as insurance policies, it also provides a method of assuring that like cases will be decided alike.

e. Evaluation of extrinsic evidence. Even though an agreement is not integrated, or even though the meaning of an integrated agreement depends on extrinsic evidence, a question of interpretation is not left to the trier of fact where the evidence is so clear that no reasonable person would determine the issue in any way but one. But if the issue depends on evidence outside the writing, and the possible inferences are conflicting, the choice is for the trier of fact.

§ 213. Effect of Integrated Agreement on Prior Agreements (Parol Evidence Rule).

(1) A binding integrated agreement discharges prior agreements to the extent that it is inconsistent with them.

(2) A binding completely integrated agreement discharges prior agreements to the extent that they are within its scope.

(3) An integrated agreement that is not binding or that is voidable and avoided does not discharge a prior agreement. But an integrated agreement, even though not binding, may be effective to render inoperative a term which would have been part of the agreement if it had not been integrated.

Comment

a. Parol evidence rule. This Section states what is commonly known as the parol evidence rule. It is not a rule of evidence but a rule of substantive law. Nor is it a rule of interpretation; it defines the subject matter of interpretation. It renders inoperative prior written agreements as well as prior oral agreements. Where writings relating to the same subject matter are assented to as parts of one transaction, both form part of the integrated agreement. Where an agreement is partly oral and partly written, the writing is at most a partially integrated agreement. See § 209.

b. Inconsistent terms. Whether a binding agreement is completely integrated or partially integrated, it supersedes inconsistent terms of prior agreements. To apply this rule, the court must make preliminary determinations that there is an integrated agreement and that it is inconsistent with the term in question. See § 209. Those determinations are made in accordance with all relevant evidence, and require interpretation both of the integrated agreement and of the prior agreement. The existence of the prior agreement may be a circumstance which sheds light on the meaning of the integrated agreement, but the integrated agreement must be given a meaning to which its language is reasonably susceptible when read in the light of all the circumstances. See §§ 212, 214.

Illustrations

1. D Corporation regularly borrows money from C Bank. S, the principal stockholder in D, offers to guarantee payment if C will increase the amounts lent. There is a bank custom to make such loans only on adequate collateral supplied by the borrower, and C promises S to follow the custom. S then executes a written agreement with C guaranteeing payment of future loans to D "with or without security." If the written agreement is a binding integrated agreement, C's prior promise is discharged.

2. A orally agrees to sell a city lot to B. The city is installing a sidewalk in front of the lot, and A orally agrees to pay the cost to be assessed by the city in an amount not exceeding $45. B then retains a lawyer to draw up a written agreement, and A and B execute it, A without reading it. The agreement provides that A will pay all costs of the installation of the sidewalk, but does not mention any dollar limit. If the written agreement is a binding integrated agreement, any agreement for a $45 limit is discharged.

c. Scope of a completely integrated agreement. Where the parties have adopted a writing as a complete and exclusive statement of the terms of the agreement, even consistent additional terms are superseded. See § 216. But there may still be a separate agreement between the same parties which is not affected. To apply the rule of Subsection (2) the court in addition to determining that there is an integrated agreement and that it is completely integrated, must determine that the asserted prior agreement is within the scope of the integrated agreement. Those determinations are made in accordance with all relevant evidence, and require interpretation both of the integrated agreement and of the prior agreement.

Illustrations

3. In May A and B exchange properties and agree orally that A will make certain repairs on the property to be conveyed by A to B, the repairs to be finished by October 1. A and B then draw up and sign a memorandum of the repair agreement, specifying all the terms except that the memorandum is silent as to time of performance. If the memorandum is a binding completely integrated agreement, the agreement to finish by October 1 is discharged, and the repairs are to be finished within a reasonable time. The oral agreement as to October 1 may be relevant evidence as to what is a reasonable time.

4. A and B make an oral agreement for the sale of land and a hotel thereon, together with the hotel furniture. They employ a lawyer to prepare a written contract. He does so, and they sign it. It contains no mention of personal property. The agreement as to furniture is discharged if there is a binding completely integrated agreement covering the entire transaction, but not if only the part of the agreement relating to real property is integrated.

d. Effect of non-binding integration. An integrated agreement does not supersede prior agreements if it is not binding, for example, by reason of lack of consideration, or if it is voidable and avoided. The circumstances may, however, show an agreement to discharge a prior agreement without regard to whether the integrated agreement is binding, and such an agreement may be effective. Moreover, an integrated agreement may be effective to render inoperative an oral term which would have been part of the agreement if it had not been integrated. The integrated agreement may then be without consideration, even though the inoperative oral term would have furnished consideration.

Illustrations

5. A and B enter into a contract that B will build a house on A's land for a price. Later they enter into an oral contract by which B promises to add a porch and A promises to pay an extra $2,000. Still later they enter into an integrated agreement in which B promises to build according to the original plans and A promises to pay the extra $2,000. The integrated agreement is not binding for lack of consideration, and the oral intermediate agreement is not discharged.

6. A and B enter into a contract that B will build a house on A's land for a price. Later B offers to add a porch if A will sign a new contract. They then enter into an integrated agreement in which B promises to build according to the original plans and A promises to pay an extra $2,000. If the integrated agreement is inconsistent with the porch offer, or if it is a completely integrated agreement and the matter of the porch is within its scope, the integrated agreement is effective to discharge the porch offer but is not binding for lack of consideration.

§ 214. Evidence of Prior or Contemporaneous Agreements and Negotiations.

Agreements and negotiations prior to or contemporaneous with the adoption of a writing are admissible in evidence to establish

(a) that the writing is or is not an integrated agreement;

(b) that the integrated agreement, if any, is completely or partially integrated;

(c) the meaning of the writing, whether or not integrated;

(d) illegality, fraud, duress, mistake, lack of consideration, or other invalidating cause;

(e) ground for granting or denying rescission, reformation, specific performance, or other remedy.

Comment

a. Integrated agreement and completely integrated agreement. Whether a writing has been adopted as an integrated agreement and, if so, whether the agreement is completely or partially integrated are questions determined by the court preliminary to determination of a question of interpretation or to application of the parol evidence rule. See §§ 209–13. Writings do not prove themselves; ordinarily, if there is dispute, there must be testimony that there was a signature or other manifestation of assent. The preliminary determination is made in accordance with all relevant evidence, including the circumstances in which the writing was made or adopted. It may require preliminary interpretation of the writing; the court must then consider the evidence which is relevant to the question of interpretation.

b. Interpretation. Words, written or oral, cannot apply themselves to the subject matter. The expressions and general tenor of speech used in negotiations are admissible to show the conditions existing when the writing was made, the application of the words, and the meaning or meanings of the parties. Even though words seem on their face to have only a single possible meaning, other meanings often appear when the circumstances are disclosed. In cases of misunderstanding, there must be inquiry into the meaning attached to the words by each party and into what each knew or had reason to know. See § 201.

Illustrations

1. A and B in an integrated contract agree that A shall serve as captain of B's ship, and shall have a certain rate of pay instead of "privilege and primage." Previous negotiations showing that the meaning to the parties of the quoted words when used was the privilege of transporting goods in the captain's cabin establish that as the meaning in the contract.

2. In an integrated contract with A, B promises to buy "your wool." Previous negotiations of the parties related to both wool from A's sheep and wool that A had contracted to buy from other

persons. The negotiations are admissible to establish both classes as the meaning of the words "your wool" in the contract.

3. A, in an integrated contract with B, promises B to sell certain goods to be manufactured by A, and B promises to pay the "total cost." Previous negotiations may establish the meaning of "total cost."

4. A and B make an integrated contract by which A promises to sell and B to buy goods "ex Peerless." Evidence is admissible to show that there are two ships of that name, which one each party meant, and, in case of misunderstanding, whether either had knowledge or reason to know of the other's meaning.

c. Invalidating cause. What appears to be a complete and binding integrated agreement may be a forgery, a joke, a sham, or an agreement without consideration, or it may be voidable for fraud, duress, mistake, or the like, or it may be illegal. Such invalidating causes need not and commonly do not appear on the face of the writing. They are not affected even by a "merger" clause. See Comment e to § 216.

Illustrations

5. A and B make an integrated agreement by which A promises to complete an unfinished building according to certain plans and specifications, and B promises to pay A $2,000 for so doing. It may be shown that, by a contract made previously with B, A had promised to erect and complete the building for $10,000; that he had not fully completed it though paid the whole price. This evidence is admissible to show that there is no consideration for B's new promise, since A is promising no more than he is bound by his original contract to perform.

6. A and B make an integrated agreement by which A promises to sell and B promises to buy a large quantity of rifles. It may be shown that A and B had previously agreed that the rifles when bought by B should be used in fomenting a rebellion in violation of law.

d. Remedies. A contract which is fully enforceable in an action for damages may be subject to equitable remedies such as rescission or reformation by reason of fraud, mistake or the like. Specific performance may be denied by reason of oppression or unfairness, or other remedies may be withheld or limited where the contract or a term is unconscionable. See § 208. Evidence of the circumstances in which the contract was made may be relevant to such remedial issues, even though it also shows an agreement or proposal superseded by a later integrated contract.

Illustration

7. A and B make an integrated agreement by which A promises to sell and B promises to buy a tract of land described in the agreement. Owing to a mutual mistake the description is not an accurate one of the tract in regard to which both A and B were bargaining. Prior oral agreements may be shown to establish the right to reformation of the integration so that it shall accurately describe the tract intended.

§ 215. Contradiction of Integrated Terms.

Except as stated in the preceding Section, where there is a binding agreement, either completely or partially integrated, evidence of prior or contemporaneous agreements or negotiations is not admissible in evidence to contradict a term of the writing.

Comment

a. Relation to other rules. Like § 216, this Section states an evidentiary consequence of § 213. A binding integrated agreement discharges inconsistent prior agreements, and evidence of a prior agreement is therefore irrelevant to the rights of the parties when offered to contradict a term of the writing. The same evidence may be properly considered on the preliminary issues whether there is an integrated agreement and whether it is completely or partially integrated. See §§ 209, 210. If there is a finding that there is an integrated agreement or a completely integrated agreement, the evidence may nevertheless be relevant to a question of interpretation, to a question of invalidating cause, or to a question of remedy. See § 214. But the earlier agreement, no matter how clear, cannot override a later agreement which supersedes or amends it.

b. Interpretation and contradiction. An earlier agreement may help the interpretation of a later one, but it may not contradict a binding later integrated agreement. Whether there is contradiction depends, as is stated in § 213, on whether the two are consistent or inconsistent. This is a question which often cannot be determined from the face of the writing; the writing must first be applied to its subject matter and placed in context. The question is then decided by the court as part of a question of interpretation. Where reasonable people could differ as to the credibility of the evidence offered and the evidence if believed could lead a reasonable person to interpret the writing as claimed by the proponent of the evidence, the question of credibility and the choice among reasonable inferences should be treated as questions of fact. But the asserted meaning must be one to which the language of the writing, read in context, is reasonably susceptible. If no other meaning is reasonable, the court should rule as a matter of law that the meaning is established. See § 212(2).

§ 216. Consistent Additional Terms.

(1) Evidence of a consistent additional term is admissible to supplement an integrated agreement unless the court finds that the agreement was completely integrated.

(2) An agreement is not completely integrated if the writing omits a consistent additional agreed term which is

   (a) agreed to for separate consideration, or

   (b) such a term as in the circumstances might naturally be omitted from the writing.

Comment

a. Relation to other rules. Like § 215, this Section states an evidentiary consequence of § 213. It also limits the concept of a completely integrated agreement set forth in § 210. Compare Uniform Commercial Code § 2–202(b). Where the limitation is not applicable, the court must decide whether the agreement is completely integrated on the basis of all relevant evidence, including the evidence of consistent additional terms.

b. Consistency. Terms of prior agreements are superseded to the extent that they are inconsistent with an integrated agreement, and evidence of them is not admissible to contradict a term of the integration. See §§ 213, 215. The determination whether an alleged additional term is consistent or inconsistent with the integrated agreement requires interpretation of the writing in the light of all the circumstances, including the evidence of the additional term. For this purpose, the meaning of the writing includes not only the terms explicitly stated but also those fairly implied as part of the bargain of the parties in fact. It does not include a term supplied by a rule of law designed to fill gaps where the parties have not agreed otherwise, unless it can be inferred that the parties contracted with reference to the rule of law. There is no clear line between implications of fact and rules of law filling gaps; although fairly clear examples of each can be given, other cases will involve almost imperceptible shadings. See § 204.

Illustrations

1. A check states no date of payment, but it is orally agreed that the check will be paid only after six months. The oral agreement contradicts the check. Under Uniform Commercial Code § 3–108 the check is payable on demand, and most competent adults in the United States have reason to know the rule.

2. A owes B two debts, and sends a check for an amount less than the amount of either. In the absence of any contrary manifestation of intention by either party, the rule of law would be that the check is applied to the debt which first matured. An agreement that the other debt is to be paid is not inconsistent with the check.

c. Separate consideration. Where there is a binding completely integrated agreement, even consistent additional terms are superseded if they are within the scope of the agreement. See § 213. A separate contract, not covered by the integrated agreement, is not superseded. The rule of Subsection (2)(a) goes further; it limits the scope of the integrated agreement by excluding a consistent additional term made for separate consideration even though the additional term and its consideration are part of the same contract. This rule may be regarded as a particular application of the rule of Subsection (2)(b).

Illustration

3. A and B in an integrated writing promise to sell and buy a specific automobile. As part of the transaction they orally agree that B may keep the automobile in A's garage for one year, paying $15 a month. The oral agreement is not within the scope of the integration and is not superseded.

d. Terms omitted naturally. If it is claimed that a consistent additional term was omitted from an integrated agreement and the omission seems natural in the circumstances, it is not necessary to consider further the questions whether the agreement is completely integrated and whether the omitted term is within its scope, although factual questions may remain. This situation is especially likely to arise when the writing is in a standardized form which does not lend itself to the insertion of additional terms. Thus agreements collateral to a negotiable instrument if written on the instrument might destroy its negotiability or otherwise make it less acceptable to third parties; the instrument may not have space for the additional term. Leases and conveyances are also often in a standard form which leads naturally to the omission of terms which are not standard. These examples are not exclusive. Moreover, there is no rule or policy penalizing a party merely because his mode of agreement does not seem natural to others. Even though the omission does not seem natural, evidence of the consistent additional terms is admissible unless the court finds that the writing was intended as a complete and exclusive statement of the terms of the agreement. See § 210.

Illustrations

4. A owes B $1,000. They agree orally that A will sell B Blackacre for $3,000 and that the $1,000 will be credited against the price, and then sign a written agreement, complete on its face, which does not mention the $1,000 debt or the credit. The written agreement is not completely integrated, and the oral agreement for a credit is admissible in evidence to supplement the written agreement.

5. A and B sign a written agreement, complete on its face, that A will sell B Blackacre for $3,000, conveyance and payment to be made within 60 days. It is claimed that B was about to render services for A and that the written agreement was signed on the oral understanding that B would be permitted to pay the price by rendering the services at $50 an hour. The oral understanding is admissible in evidence unless it is found that the written agreement was completely integrated.

6. A and B sign a standard form of written agreement for the sale of goods, complete on its face except that a blank for time and place of delivery is not filled in. It is claimed that the writing was signed on the oral understanding that delivery would be made within 30 days at the buyer's place of business. Under Uniform Commercial Code §§ 2–308 and 2–309, the goods would be deliverable, unless otherwise agreed, within a reasonable time at the seller's place of business. The written agreement is not completely integrated, and the oral understanding is admissible in evidence to supplement its terms.

7. A and B sign a written agreement complete on its face, for the sale of goods to be shipped by A from Chicago to New York. It is claimed that the written agreement was signed on the oral understanding that the shipment would be made by a specified route. Under Uniform Commercial Code §§ 2–311 and 2–504, unless otherwise agreed, A could properly ship by any reasonable route. The written agreement is not completely integrated, and the oral understanding is admissible in evidence to supplement its terms.

8. A and B orally agree that A shall work for B in specified employment for $3,000. B delivers to A an absolute written promise to pay $3,000 in six months. The terms of the oral agreement are admissible in evidence to supplement the written promise and to qualify B's duty to pay $3,000.

9. A and B sign a written agreement, complete on its face, for the sale of a specific machine by A to B. The writing describes the machine and warrants that it is new, but contains no other terms relevant to warranty. Warranties of title, conformity to the description, merchantability, or fitness for a particular purpose, arising under Uniform Commercial Code §§ 2–312 through 2–315, are not

excluded. Whether an additional oral warranty of quality is superseded depends on whether the agreement is completely integrated.

e. Written term excluding oral terms ("merger" clause). Written agreements often contain clauses stating that there are no representations, promises or agreements between the parties except those found in the writing. Such a clause may negate the apparent authority of an agent to vary orally the written terms, and if agreed to is likely to conclude the issue whether the agreement is completely integrated. Consistent additional terms may then be excluded even though their omission would have been natural in the absence of such a clause. But such a clause does not control the question whether the writing was assented to as an integrated agreement, the scope of the writing if completely integrated, or the interpretation of the written terms.

§ 217. Integrated Agreement Subject to Oral Requirement of a Condition.

Where the parties to a written agreement agree orally that performance of the agreement is subject to the occurrence of a stated condition, the agreement is not integrated with respect to the oral condition.

Comment

a. Relation to other rules. This Section states a rule for unsealed writings which is similar in operation to the rules governing delivery of a sealed promise in escrow or its conditional delivery to the promisee. See § 103. If an unrestricted power of revocation is reserved by either party, there is no contract until he acts further. But if performance of the written agreement is subject to an oral requirement of a condition not within the control of either party, there may be a binding contract creating immediate conditional rights. In such a case the precise legal consequences may turn on inquiry into what the parties in fact agreed to. The writing, if so intended, may be a partially integrated agreement and may automatically become a completely integrated agreement on the occurrence of the oral requirement of a condition. See §§ 209, 210.

Illustrations

1. A and B agree that A will sell a patent to B for $10,000 if C, an engineer advising B, approves. A and B sign a written agreement covering all of the agreement except C's approval, and agree orally that it will take effect only if C approves. There is an immediate contract, but B's duty is conditional on C's approval.

2. A and B sign a written agreement for an exchange of real property and leave it with C, an attorney, on the oral understanding that it is not to take effect until each has consulted his wife and notified C that he still wishes to close the exchange. There is no contract until each has notified C.

b. Requirement of a condition inconsistent with a written term. The rule of this Section may be regarded as a particular application of the rule of § 216(2)(b), giving effect to consistent additional terms omitted naturally from a writing. So regarded, it has sometimes been limited to requirements of conditions consistent with the written terms. But an oral requirement of a condition is never completely consistent with a signed written agreement which is complete on its face; in such cases evidence of the oral requirement bears directly on the issues whether the writing was adopted as an integrated agreement and if so whether the agreement was completely integrated or partially integrated. Inconsistency is merely one factor in the preliminary determination of those issues. If the parties orally agreed that performance of the written agreement was subject to a condition, either the writing is not an integrated agreement or the agreement is only partially integrated until the condition occurs. Even a "merger" clause in the writing, explicitly negating oral terms, does not control the question whether there is an integrated agreement or the scope of the writing. See Comment e to § 216.

Illustrations

3. A and B sign a written agreement for the sale of goods, and orally agree that the writing shall not take effect unless railroad cars are available within ten days. The oral agreement is effective.

4. Evidence of the facts stated in Illustration 3 is offered, and the writing contains a provision that "delivery shall be made within 30 days." Evidence of the oral agreement is excluded only if the

court makes a preliminary determination that performance of the written agreement could not in the circumstances reasonably be found to have been subject to the oral agreement.

5. A and B make and sign an elaborate written agreement for the merger of their corporate holdings into a single new company. The writing provides that all obligations under it will terminate unless agreed subscriptions to the stock of the new company are accepted within twenty days. It is also orally agreed that the project is not to be operative unless the parties raise $600,000 additional capital. If the additional capital is not raised, there is no contract.

§ 218. Untrue Recitals; Evidence of Consideration.

(1) A recital of a fact in an integrated agreement may be shown to be untrue.

(2) Evidence is admissible to prove whether or not there is consideration for a promise, even though the parties have reduced their agreement to a writing which appears to be a completely integrated agreement.

Comment

a. Fact and transaction. The parol evidence rule (§ 213) relates to the effect of an integrated agreement on prior agreements. An integrated agreement may have the effect of discharging a prior promise, conveyance or discharge; it does not establish fictitious events.

b. Effect of recital. A recital of fact in an integrated agreement is evidence of the fact, and its weight depends on the circumstances. Contrary facts may be proved. The result may be that the integrated agreement is not binding, or that it has a different effect from the effect if the recital had been true. In the absence of estoppel, the true facts have the same operation as if stated in the writing.

c. Estoppel. In some circumstances a recital may embody a representation of fact by one party to the other, and the party making such a representation may be barred by estoppel from showing the truth contrary to the representation after another has relied on the representation. See Comment a to § 90.

d. Omission of consideration. Where a written agreement requires consideration and none is stated in the writing, a finding that the writing is a completely integrated agreement would mean that it is not binding for want of consideration. Since only a binding integrated agreement brings the parol evidence rule into operation, evidence is admissible to show that there was consideration and what it was.

Illustration

1. A gives B a written promise to pay $100. The writing states no consideration. B promises orally to build a fence in consideration of the promise of $100. Both promises are operative.

e. Incorrect recital of consideration. Where a writing shows a promise in consideration of a return promise and it is determined that the writing is a binding integrated agreement, inconsistent prior agreements are discharged. See § 213. But an integrated agreement which is not binding does not ordinarily discharge prior agreements, and the parol evidence rule does not apply to recitals of facts. Where consideration is required, the requirement is not satisfied by a false recital of consideration, although in some circumstances a recital of consideration may make a promise binding without consideration. See §§ 71, 87, 88. An incorrect statement of a consideration does not prevent proof either that there was no consideration or that there was a consideration different from that stated. In some such cases the recital may imply a promise not explicitly stated.

Illustrations

2. A, an insurance company, issues a fire insurance policy to B. The policy provides that A is not bound until the premium is paid, and falsely recites payment. On accepting the policy, B impliedly promises to pay the premium and A is bound by the policy.

3. A, desiring to make a gift of Blackacre to his daughter B, delivers to B a written promise to transfer Blackacre to her in consideration of $1,000 paid by B, receipt of which is acknowledged. No money is in fact paid by B, and the circumstances do not justify implication of a promise to pay. A's promise is not binding for want of consideration.

TOPIC 4. SCOPE AS AFFECTED BY USAGE

§ 219. Usage.

Usage is habitual or customary practice.

Comment

a. Scope of usage. Although rules of law are often founded on usage, usage is not in itself a legal rule but merely habit or practice in fact. A particular usage may be more or less widespread. It may prevail throughout an area, and the area may be small or large—a city, a state or a larger region. A usage may prevail among all people in the area, or only in a special trade or other group. Usages change over time, and persons in close association often develop temporary usages peculiar to themselves.

b. Usage of words. A word usage exists when few or many people use a word or phrase to convey a standard meaning or several standard meanings and develop a common understanding of the meaning or meanings. Dictionaries record word usages which have achieved some generality, with varying degrees of completeness and accuracy. See § 201.

§ 220. Usage Relevant to Interpretation.

(1) An agreement is interpreted in accordance with a relevant usage if each party knew or had reason to know of the usage and neither party knew or had reason to know that the meaning attached by the other was inconsistent with the usage.

(2) When the meaning attached by one party accorded with a relevant usage and the other knew or had reason to know of the usage, the other is treated as having known or had reason to know the meaning attached by the first party.

Comment

a. Relation to other rules. Usage may "give particular meaning to" an agreement, or may "supplement or qualify" it. See Uniform Commercial Code § 1–205. This Section deals with usage as an element in interpretation and states rules consistent with the general rules on agreement and interpretation stated in §§ 20 and 201. Usage supplementing or qualifying an agreement is the subject of the following section, and §§ 222 and 223 apply the general rules of this Section and § 221 to the particular cases of usage of trade and course of dealing. Where there are conflicting usages of words and no different intention is shown, § 202 provides guides for the process of interpretation; where there is conflict between usage of trade and express terms, course of performance or course of dealing, § 203 states standards of preference.

b. Interpretation of language. An agreement may have a legal effect not intended by either party, but interpretation is limited to meanings intended by at least one party. Neither party is bound by a meaning unless he knows or has reason to know of it. See §§ 200, 201. Usage is subject to the same rule: a party is not bound by a usage unless he knows or has reason to know of it. Hence a party who asserts a meaning based on usage must show either that the other party knew of the usage or that the other party had reason to know of it. Analytically, the meaning of language is a question of fact, but in the absence of extrinsic evidence the meaning of language in an integrated writing is to be determined as a question of law. See § 212. Where a usage of words is sufficiently well known, a court will take judicial cognizance of it without proof; otherwise the burden of establishing a usage is on the party asserting it. See § 202. Ordinarily there is no requirement that a usage relevant to the interpretation of language be pleaded, but a party against whom evidence of usage is offered may be entitled to a continuance or to notice sufficient to prevent unfair surprise. See Uniform Commercial Code § 1–205(6).

Illustrations

1. A contracts to sell and B to buy ten bushels of oats. By very general usage 32 pounds constitutes a bushel of oats. In the absence of contrary evidence, ten bushels in the contract means 320 pounds.

2. A contracts with B to "sponsor" a bowling team and to pay B "the usual sponsoring fees." In an action against A for repudiating the contract in a dispute over the fees, B cannot recover without proving a usage as to "usual sponsoring fees."

3. A employs B as exclusive broker to sell business premises subject to a one-year lease back to A. B submits an agreement for sale to C subject to a one-year lease, with a provision for termination of the lease on six months notice. A rejects the agreement. In an action for the agreed commission B claims that by local usage all business leases contain such a provision. B has the burden of establishing the usage and A's knowledge or reason to know of it.

c. Agreed but unstated terms. An agreement or term thereof need not be stated in words if the parties manifest assent to it by other conduct, and such assent is often manifested by conduct in accordance with usage. Where there is an integrated agreement, an agreed but unstated term may be annexed by usage on the same principle which controls consistent additional terms generally. See § 216. But it is so common to contract with reference to usage, leaving the usage unstated, that no inquiry is necessary as to whether it is natural in the particular circumstances to omit the term from the writing. See Uniform Commercial Code § 2–202(a). Where it is claimed that the usage contradicts the express terms, the issue is resolved as a question of interpretation. See § 203(b). Whether a usage is reasonable may bear on the issue whether the parties contracted with reference to it, but if they did they are not in general forbidden to make agreements which seem unreasonable to others.

Illustrations

4. A and B contract for a year's employment of B by A. As both parties know, there is a usage that such a contract may be terminated by a month's notice. Unless a contrary intention is manifested, the usage is part of the contract.

5. A sends goods to B by C, a private carrier, receiving a bill of lading from C. B rejects the shipment. The usage of such carriers, known to A and C, is to notify the shipper of such a rejection. Unless a contrary intention is manifested, the requirement of notification is added to the terms of the bill of lading.

6. A contracts to sell and B to buy 100 barrels of flour at $8 a barrel. By a usage of the trade known to A and B payment under such contracts is due ten days after delivery unless otherwise agreed. The usage is part of the contract.

7. A contracts to sell and B to buy 100 barrels of mackerel. By a usage of trade known to A and B, sellers of mackerel, unless they agree otherwise, warrant that the fish are not below a certain size. The usage is part of the contract. See Uniform Commercial Code §§ 2–314(3), 2–316(3)(c).

d. Ambiguity and contradiction. Language and conduct are in general given meaning by usage rather than by the law, and ambiguity and contradiction likewise depend upon usage. Hence usage relevant to interpretation is treated as part of the context of an agreement in determining whether there is ambiguity or contradiction as well as in resolving ambiguity or contradiction. There is no requirement that an ambiguity be shown before usage can be shown, and no prohibition against showing that language or conduct have a different meaning in the light of usage from the meaning they might have apart from the usage. The normal effect of a usage on a written contract is to vary its meaning from the meaning it would otherwise have.

Illustrations

8. A leases a rabbit warren to B. The written lease contains a covenant that at the end of the term A will buy and B will sell the rabbits at "60£ per thousand." The parties contract with reference to a local usage that 1,000 rabbits means 100 dozen. The usage is part of the contract.

9. In an integrated contract, A promises to sell and B to buy a certain quantity of "white arsenic" for a stated price. The parties contract with reference to a usage of trade that "white arsenic" includes arsenic colored with lamp black. The usage is part of the contract.

10. A, a bank in New York City, issues to B a letter of credit promising a payment on presentation of documents including a "full set of bills of lading." By a general banking usage in New

York City, banks accept less than a full set in such cases if there is a guaranty by a responsible New York bank in lieu of the missing part. Unless otherwise agreed, the usage is part of the contract. Uniform Commercial Code § 5–109.

§ 221. Usage Supplementing an Agreement.

An agreement is supplemented or qualified by a reasonable usage with respect to agreements of the same type if each party knows or has reason to know of the usage and neither party knows or has reason to know that the other party has an intention inconsistent with the usage.

Comment

a. Agreed terms and omitted terms. Where the parties have in fact agreed to incorporate a usage into their agreement, the case is within § 220. This Section extends the same principle to cases where the parties did not advert to the problem with which the usage deals, or where one or each separately foresaw the problem but failed to manifest any intention with respect to it. In such cases, in the absence of usage, the court would supply a reasonable term. See § 204. But if there is a reasonable usage which supplies an omitted term and the parties know or have reason to know of the usage, it is a surer guide than the court's own judgment of what is reasonable. Thus a usage may make it unnecessary to inquire into or prove what the actual intentions of the parties were with respect to an unstated term. Compare Uniform Commercial Code §§ 1–205(3), 2–202(a).

Illustrations

1. A, a canner, and B, a wholesale grocer, contract for the sale by A to B of canned fruit products, using a standard form of contract approved by canning and wholesale grocer trade associations. By uniform usage among canners, where the standard form is used title to unshipped goods passes on billing dates specified on the form. In the absence of contrary indication, the usage is part of the contract.

2. A, an ordained rabbi, is employed by B, an orthodox Jewish congregation, to officiate as cantor at specified religious services. At the time the contract is made, it is the practice of such congregations to seat men and women separately at services, and a contrary practice would violate A's religious beliefs. At a time when it is too late for A to obtain substitute employment, B adopts a contrary practice. A refuses to officiate. The practice is part of the contract, and A is entitled to the agreed compensation.

b. Reason to know and reasonableness. The more general and well-established a usage is, the stronger is the inference that a party knew or had reason to know of it. Similarly, the fact that a usage is reasonable may tend to show that the parties contracted with reference to it or that a particular party knew or had reason to know of it. Where the parties in fact agree to a usage, there is no general requirement that their usage seem reasonable to others; but where there is no agreement only a reasonable usage supplies an omitted term. What is reasonable for this purpose depends on the circumstances; it may be reasonable to hold a nonmerchant to mercantile standards if he is represented by a mercantile agent. See Uniform Commercial Code § 2–104, defining "merchant." Ordinarily an agent is authorized to comply with relevant usages of business if the principal has notice that usages of such a nature may exist. See Restatement, Second, of Agency § 36.

Illustrations

3. A, in Washington, sends an order to B, a broker in Baltimore, to be executed on the New York Stock Exchange. Unless both A and B give the order a different and identical interpretation or B has reason to know that A has a different intention, the order is interpreted in accordance with the reasonable usages of the New York Stock Exchange.

4. A, a publisher, contracts with B to publish a two-volume work. The contract provides for binding "10,000 copies at .538," which by usage of the publishing business refers to the number of volumes rather than the number of sets. The usage is part of the contract even though the work is B's first and he does not know of the usage.

c. Effect of usage on law. It is often said that usage cannot change a rule of law, but a distinction must be drawn. If the rule of law is one which overrides contrary agreement, it also overrides usage; but if the law merely supplies a term in the absence of contrary agreement, usage can have the same effect as contrary agreement. See Uniform Commercial Code § 1–201(3).

Illustrations

5. A and B, both members of a Mercantile Exchange, enter into an oral contract within the Statute of Frauds. By usage of the Exchange oral agreements between members of the Exchange are enforceable. The usage does not make the contract enforceable if it is otherwise unenforceable.

6. A makes B a promise without consideration. By usage such promises are binding without consideration. The usage does not make the promise legally binding.

7. A makes an offer to B by telephone, and B accepts by telephone. By usage known to both parties such an agreement is not binding unless promptly confirmed in writing by the acceptor. Unless a contrary intention is indicated, the usage is part of the agreement, and there is no contract unless B gives prompt written confirmation.

d. Intention inconsistent with usage. The parties to an agreement are not bound to follow the usages of others or their own prior usages. If either party has reason to know that the other has an intention inconsistent with a particular usage, the usage is not applicable. Such an intention need not be manifested in any particular way; whether the parties contracted with reference to a usage is determined on the basis of all the circumstances, and a usage may be excluded by the same type of proof which would include it.

Illustrations

8. A, a resident of Philadelphia, makes a contract with B, a resident of New York, by which A promises to build a brick wall in Philadelphia. There is a local usage in Philadelphia as to measuring brick which differs from that elsewhere. B is not aware of the Philadelphia usage, as A has reason to know. The usage is not part of the contract.

9. A, a bank, issues a letter of credit promising to honor drafts accompanied by bills of lading covering "Coromandel groundnuts." Dealers in groundnuts understand "Coromandel groundnuts" to mean "machine-shelled groundnut kernels." A is not bound to honor drafts accompanied by bills of lading covering "machine-shelled groundnut kernels." See Uniform Commercial Code § 5–109(1)(c).

§ 222. Usage of Trade.

(1) A usage of trade is a usage having such regularity of observance in a place, vocation, or trade as to justify an expectation that it will be observed with respect to a particular agreement. It may include a system of rules regularly observed even though particular rules are changed from time to time.

(2) The existence and scope of a usage of trade are to be determined as questions of fact. If a usage is embodied in a written trade code or similar writing the interpretation of the writing is to be determined by the court as a question of law.

(3) Unless otherwise agreed, a usage of trade in the vocation or trade in which the parties are engaged or a usage of trade of which they know or have reason to know gives meaning to or supplements or qualifies their agreement.

Comment

a. Relation to other rules. This Section follows Uniform Commercial Code § 1–205 and states a particular application of the rules stated in §§ 220 and 221. As to conflicting usages of words, see § 202; as to conflict between usage of trade and express terms, course of performance or course of dealing, see § 203.

b. Regularity of observance. A usage of trade need not be "ancient or immemorial," "universal," or the like. Unless agreed to in fact, it must be reasonable, but commercial acceptance by regular observance makes out a prima facie case that a usage of trade is reasonable. There is no requirement that an agreement be ambiguous before evidence of a usage of trade can be shown, nor is it required that the usage of trade be consistent with the meaning the agreement would have apart from the usage. When the usage consists of a system of rules, the parties need not be aware of a particular rule if they know or have reason to know the system and the particular rule is within the scheme of the system. A change within the system may have effect promptly, even though there has been no time for regular observance of the change.

Illustrations

1. A contracts to sell B 10,000 shingles. By usage of the lumber trade, in which both are engaged, two packs of a certain size constitute 1,000, though not containing that exact number. Unless otherwise agreed, 1,000 in the contract means two packs.

2. A contracts to sell B 1,000 feet of San Domingo mahogany. By usage of dealers in mahogany, known to A and B, good figured mahogany of a certain density is known as San Domingo mahogany, though it does not come from San Domingo. Unless otherwise agreed, the usage is part of the contract.

3. A promises to act as B's agent in a certain business, and B promises to pay a certain commission for each "order." By a local usage in that business, "order" means only an order on which the purchaser has paid a certain price. Unless otherwise agreed, the usage is part of the contract.

4. A and B enter into a contract for the sawing of logs during the "winter season." Usage in the logging business may show that "winter season" means the period between the closing of a sawmill in the autumn and the arrival of logs in the spring.

5. A and B enter into a contract of charter party in which A promises to discharge the vessel "in 14 days." Usage in the shipping business may show this means 14 working days.

6. A and B enter into a contract for the purchase and sale of "No. 1 heavy book paper guaranteed free from ground wood." Usage in the paper trade may show that this means paper not containing over 3% ground wood.

   c. *Local usages of trade.* Where usages vary from place to place, there may be a problem in deciding which usage is applicable. Even though local residents regularly contract with reference to a local usage of trade, others are not bound by the usage unless they know or have reason to know of it. If that condition is satisfied and no contrary intention is shown, a usage of trade in a particular place is ordinarily used to interpret the agreement as to that part of the performance which is to occur there. See Uniform Commercial Code § 1–205(5).

Illustrations

7. A contracts to employ B for 20 days. In the kind of work to which the employment relates, in the place where both reside and the work is to be performed, a day's work is eight hours. Unless otherwise agreed, B's employment is for 20 eight-hour days.

8. A leases to B a portion of a building for "confectionery store purposes." By local usage at the time and place where the lease is made and the building is located, "confectionery store purposes" include the giving of light lunches. Unless otherwise agreed, the usage is part of the contract.

9. A promises B to keep certain premises "fully insured." At the time and place where the contract is made and to be performed and where the parties reside, insurance companies will not insure such premises for more than three-fourths of their value, and such premises insured for three-fourths of their value are called "fully insured." Unless otherwise agreed, the local usage is part of the contract.

10. A of Chicago negotiates and concludes in South Carolina an integrated contract to sell and deliver to B in South Carolina "ground sheep manure." These words mean a finer grinding in South Carolina than they do in Chicago, and A has reason to know of the South Carolina usage. Unless otherwise agreed, the contract is taken to refer to the South Carolina usage.

§ 223. Course of Dealing.

(1) A course of dealing is a sequence of previous conduct between the parties to an agreement which is fairly to be regarded as establishing a common basis of understanding for interpreting their expressions and other conduct.

(2) Unless otherwise agreed, a course of dealing between the parties gives meaning to or supplements or qualifies their agreement.

Comment

a. Relation to other rules. This Section follows Uniform Commercial Code § 1–205 and states a particular application of the rules stated in §§ 220 and 221. As to conflict between course of dealing and express terms, course of performance or usage of trade, see § 203.

b. Common basis of understanding. Course of dealing may become part of an agreement either by explicit provision or by tacit recognition, or it may guide the court in supplying an omitted term. Like usage of trade, it may determine the meaning of language or it may annex an agreed but unstated term. There is no requirement that an agreement be ambiguous before evidence of a course of dealing can be shown, nor is it required that the course of dealing be consistent with the meaning the agreement would have apart from the course of dealing.

Illustrations

1. A, a sugar company, enters into a written agreement with B, a grower of sugar beets, by which B agrees to raise and deliver and A to purchase specified quantities of beets during the coming season. No price is fixed. The agreement is on a standard form used for B and many other growers in prior years. A's practice is to pay all growers uniformly on a formula based on A's "net return" according to A's established accounting system. Unless otherwise agreed, the established pattern of pricing is part of the agreement.

2. A, a manufacturer, sends a price quotation on goods to B, a dealer, together with printed "conditions of sale." B then sends orders to A; and A fills them. B takes advantage of discount terms of the quotation not referred to in B's orders. Unless otherwise agreed, the "conditions of sale" are part of each contract.

TOPIC 5. CONDITIONS AND SIMILAR EVENTS

§ 224. Condition Defined.

A condition is an event, not certain to occur, which must occur, unless its non-occurrence is excused, before performance under a contract becomes due.

Comment

a. "Condition" limited to event. "Condition" is used in this Restatement to denote an event which qualifies a duty under a contract. See the Introductory Note to this Topic. It is recognized that "condition" is used with a wide variety of other meanings in legal discourse. Sometimes it is used to denote an event that limits or qualifies a transfer of property. In the law of trusts, for example, it is used to denote an event such as the death of the settlor that qualifies his disposition of property in trust. See Restatement, Second, Trusts § 360. See also the rules on "conditional" delivery (§ 103) and "conditional" assignment (§§ 103, 331). Sometimes it is used to refer to a term (§ 5) in an agreement that makes an event a condition, or more broadly to refer to any term in an agreement (e.g., "standard conditions of sale"). For the sake of precision, "condition" is not used here in these other senses.

Illustration

1. A contracts to sell and B to buy goods pursuant to a writing which provides, under the heading "Conditions of Sale," that "the obligations of the parties are conditional on B obtaining from X Bank by June 30 a letter of credit" on stated terms. The quoted language is a term of the agreement

(§ 5), not a condition. The event referred to by the term, obtaining the letter of credit by June 30, is a condition.

b. Uncertainty of event. Whether the reason for making an event a condition is to shift to the obligee the risk of its non-occurrence, or whether it is to induce the obligee to cause the event to occur (see Introductory Note to this Topic), there is inherent in the concept of condition some degree of uncertainty as to the occurrence of the event. Therefore, the mere passage of time, as to which there is no uncertainty, is not a condition and a duty is unconditional if nothing but the passage of time is necessary to give rise to a duty of performance. Moreover, an event is not a condition, even though its occurrence is uncertain, if it is referred to merely to measure the passage of time after which an obligor is to perform. See Comment b to § 227. Performance under a contract becomes due when all necessary events, including any conditions and the passage of any required time, have occurred so that a failure of performance will be a breach. See §§ 231–43.

The event need not, in order to be a condition, be one that is to occur after the making of the contract, although that is commonly the case. It may relate to the present or even to the past, as is the case where a marine policy insures against a loss that may already have occurred. Furthermore, a duty may be conditioned upon the failure of something to happen rather than upon its happening, and in that case its failure to happen is the event that is the condition.

Illustrations

2. A tells B, "If you will paint my house, I will pay you $1,000 on condition that 30 days have passed after you have finished." B paints A's house. Although A is not under a duty to pay B $1,000 until 30 days have passed, the passage of that time is not a condition of A's duty to pay B $1,000.

3. A contracts to sell and B to buy goods to be shipped "C.I.F.," payment to be "on arrival of goods." Risk of loss of the goods passes from A to B when A, having otherwise complied with the C.I.F. term of the contract, puts the goods in the possession of the carrier (Uniform Commercial Code § 2–320(2)). If the goods are lost in transit, B is under a duty to pay the price when the goods should have arrived (Uniform Commercial Code §§ 2–709(1)(a), 2–321(3)). The arrival of the goods is not a condition of B's duty to pay for the goods.

c. Necessity of a contract. In order for an event to be a condition, it must qualify a duty under an existing contract. Events which are part of the process of formation of a contract, such as offer and acceptance, are therefore excluded under the definition in this section. It is not customary to call such events conditions. But cf. § 36(2) ("condition of acceptance"). For the most part, they are required by law and may not be dispensed with by the parties, while conditions are the result of, or at least subject to, agreement. Where, however, an offer has become an option contract, e.g., by the payment of a dollar (§ 87), the acceptance is a condition under the definition in this section.

Illustration

4. A tells B, "I promise to pay you $1,000 if you paint my house." B begins to paint A's house. Since B's beginning of the invited performance gives rise to an option contract, B's completion of performance is a condition of A's duty under that contract to pay B $1,000. See § 45.

d. Relationship of conditions. A duty may be subject to any number of conditions, which may be related to each other in various ways. They may be cumulative so that performance will not become due unless all of them occur. They may be alternative so that performance may become due if any one of them occurs. Or some may be cumulative and some alternative. Furthermore, a condition may qualify the duties of both parties. Cf. § 217.

Illustrations

5. A, as the result of financial reverses, sells B a valuable painting for $1,000,000, but reserves a right to repurchase it by tendering the same price on or before August 18 if he again finds himself in such a financial condition that he can keep it for his personal enjoyment. A's tender of $1,000,000 by August 18 and his being in such financial condition that he can keep the painting for his personal

enjoyment are cumulative conditions and redelivery of the painting does not become due unless both of them occur.

6. A purchases land from Mrs. B, who is unable to get Mr. B to join her in signing the deed because they are engaged in divorce proceedings. A takes possession under a deed signed by Mrs. B, pays Mrs. B $10,000 and promises to pay an additional $5,000 "if, within one year, (1) Mr. and Mrs. B execute a quitclaim deed to A, or (2) Mrs. B furnishes A with a certificate of the death of Mr. B with Mrs. B surviving him, or (3) Mrs. B as a single person executes a quitclaim deed to A after having been awarded the land following the entry of a final decree of divorce from Mr. B." The three enumerated events are alternative conditions and A's payment of $5,000 to Mrs. B becomes due if any of them occurs.

7. A and B contract to merge their corporate holdings into a single new company. It is agreed that the project is not to be operative unless the parties raise $600,000 additional capital. The raising of the additional capital is a condition of the duties of both A and B. If it is not raised, neither A's nor B's performance becomes due.

e. Occurrence of event as discharge. Parties sometimes provide that the occurrence of an event, such as the failure of one of them to commence an action within a prescribed time, will extinguish a duty after performance has become due, along with any claim for breach. Such an event has often been called a "condition subsequent," while an event of the kind defined in this section has been called a "condition precedent." This terminology is not followed here. Since a "condition subsequent," so-called, is subject to the rules on discharge in § 230, and not to the following rules on conditions, it is not called a "condition" in this Restatement. Occasionally, although the language of an agreement says that if an event does not occur a duty is "extinguished," "discharged," or "terminated," it can be seen from the circumstances that the event must ordinarily occur before performance of the duty can be expected. When a court concludes that, for this reason, performance is not to become due unless the event occurs, the event is, in spite of the language, a condition of the duty. See § 227(3). See also Comment a to § 230.

Illustrations

8. A insures B's property against theft. The policy provides that B's failure to notify A within 30 days after loss shall "terminate" A's duty to pay and that suit must be brought within one year after loss. Since it can be seen from the circumstances that notice must ordinarily be given before payment by A can be expected, B's notification of A within 30 days after loss is a condition of A's duty. B's bringing suit against A within a year after loss is not a condition of A's duty. B's failure to bring suit within that time will discharge A's duty after payment has become due, along with any claim for breach.

9. A and B make a contract under which A promises to pay B $10,000 in annual installments of $1,000 each, beginning the following January 1, with a provision that "no installments whether or not overdue and unpaid shall be payable in case of A's death within the 10 years." A's being alive is a condition of his duty to pay any installment. A's death within ten years will discharge his duty to pay any installment after payment has become due, along with any claim for breach.

f. Sealed contracts. The rules governing conditions stated in the Restatement of this Subject are applicable to sealed as well as unsealed contracts. The same rules have traditionally been applied to both types of contract with technical exceptions that are no longer of significance.

§ 225. Effects of the Non-Occurrence of a Condition.

(1) Performance of a duty subject to a condition cannot become due unless the condition occurs or its non-occurrence is excused.

(2) Unless it has been excused, the non-occurrence of a condition discharges the duty when the condition can no longer occur.

(3) Non-occurrence of a condition is not a breach by a party unless he is under a duty that the condition occur.

Comment

a. Two effects. The unexcused non-occurrence of a condition has two possible effects on the duty subject to that condition. The first effect always follows and the second often does. The first, stated in Subsection (1), is that of preventing performance of the duty from becoming due. This follows from the definition of "condition" in § 224. Performance of the duty may still become due, however, if the condition occurs later within the time for its occurrence. The non-occurrence of the condition within that time has the additional effect, stated in Subsection (2), of discharging the duty. The time within which the condition can occur in order for the performance of the duty to become due may be fixed by a term of the agreement or, in the absence of such a term, by one supplied by the court (§ 204). Where discharge would produce harsh results, this second effect may be avoided by rules of interpretation (§§ 226, 228) or of excuse of conditions (Comment b and § 229).

Illustrations

1. A contracts to sell and B to buy A's business. The contract provides that B is to pay in installments over a five-year period following the conveyance, and that A is to convey on condition that B pledge specified collateral to secure his payment. Conveyance by A does not become due until B pledges the collateral. If the agreement does not provide for the time within which the collateral is to be pledged, A's duty is discharged if it is not pledged within a reasonable time.

2. B gives A $10,000 to use in perfecting an invention, and A promises to repay it only out of royalties received during his lifetime from the sale of the patent rights. In spite of diligent efforts, A is unable to perfect his invention and obtain a patent, and no royalties are received. A dies after six years. B has no claim against A's estate. Receipt of royalties is a condition of A's duty to repay the money and A's duty is discharged by the non-occurrence of that condition during his lifetime.

b. Excuse. The non-occurrence of a condition of a duty is said to be "excused" when the condition need no longer occur in order for performance of the duty to become due. The non-occurrence of a condition may be excused on a variety of grounds. It may be excused by a subsequent promise, even without consideration, to perform the duty in spite of the non-occurrence of the condition. See the treatment of "waiver" in § 84, and the treatment of discharge in §§ 273–85. It may be excused by acceptance of performance in spite of the non-occurrence of the condition, or by rejection following its non-occurrence accompanied by an inadequate statement of reasons. See §§ 246–48. It may be excused by a repudiation of the conditional duty or by a manifestation of an inability to perform it. See § 255; §§ 250–51. It may be excused by prevention or hindrance of its occurrence through a breach of the duty of good faith and fair dealing (§ 205). See § 239. And it may be excused by impracticability. See § 271. These and other grounds for excuse are dealt with in other chapters of this Restatement. This Chapter deals only with one general ground, excuse to avoid forfeiture. See § 229.

c. Effect of excuse. When the non-occurrence of a condition of a duty is excused, the damages for breach of the duty will depend on whether or not the occurrence of the condition was also part of the performances to be exchanged under the exchange of promises. If it was not part of the agreed exchange, the obligor is liable for the same damages for which he would have been liable had the duty originally been unconditional. If it was part of the agreed exchange, however, the saving to the obligee resulting from the non-occurrence of the condition must be subtracted in determining the obligor's liability for damages. Rules for determining damages are set out in § 347; see generally §§ 346–56. If the obligee is under a duty that the condition occur, the ground for the excuse of the non-occurrence of the condition may not be a ground for discharge of that duty. He may therefore be liable for breach of the duty in spite of the excuse of the non-occurrence of the condition. Not only may a party excuse entirely the non-occurrence of a condition of his duty, but he may merely excuse its non-occurrence during the period of time in which it would otherwise have to occur. If he does this, the non-occurrence of the condition during that period will not discharge the duty under Subsection (2), although its non-occurrence will ultimately have that effect. See Illustration 8 to § 84.

Illustrations

3. A contracts with B to build a house for $50,000, payable on condition that A present a certificate from C, B's architect, showing that the work has been properly completed. A properly

completes the work, but C refuses to give the certificate because of collusion with B, and the non-occurrence of the condition is therefore excused. See § 239. Since the presentation of the architect's certificate is not part of the performances to be exchanged under the exchange of promises, A has a claim against B for $50,000.

4. Under an option contract, A promises to sell B a painting "on condition that B pay $100,000" by a stated date. Before that date, the non-occurrence of the condition is excused by A's repudiation of the contract. See § 255. Since the payment of the $100,000 is B's part of the performances to be exchanged under the exchange of promises, B saved that amount when the non-occurrence of the condition was excused, and it should be subtracted in determining damages. B has a claim against A for the value of the painting to B less $100,000.

5. A leases property to B for a stated monthly rental. The lease provides that A is under a duty to remove described property from the premises, and that its removal is a condition of B's duty to pay the rent. After A has removed most of the property from the premises, B says that he will pay the rent even though not all of it has been removed. The non-occurrence of the condition is excused and B is under a duty to pay the rent even though A does not remove the rest of the property. See § 84. But A's duty to remove the rest of the property is not discharged and his failure to remove the rest is a breach.

d. Imposition of duty distinguished. When one party chooses to use the institution of contract to induce the other party to cause an event to occur, he may do so by making the event a condition of his own duty (Introductory Note to this Topic). Or he may do so by having the other party undertake a duty that the event occur. Or he may do both. But, as Subsection (3) makes clear, a term making an event a condition of an obligor's duty does not of itself impose a duty on the obligee and the non-occurrence of the event is not of itself a breach by the obligee. Unless the obligee is under such a duty, the non-occurrence of the event gives rise to no claim against him. The same term may, however, be interpreted not only to make an event a condition of the obligor's duty, but also to impose a duty on the obligee that it occur. And even where no term of the agreement imposes a duty that a condition occur, the court may supply such a term. See § 204.

Illustrations

6. A, a shipowner, promises to carry B's cargo on his ship to Portsmouth. B promises to pay A the stipulated freight on condition that A's ship sail directly there on its next sailing. A's ship carries B's cargo to Portsmouth, but puts into port on the way. Since carrying B's cargo directly to Portsmouth is a condition of B's duty, no duty to pay arises, and, since the condition can no longer occur, B's duty is discharged. Since A is under no duty to carry B's cargo directly to Portsmouth, however, his failure to do so is not a breach.

7. The facts being otherwise as stated in Illustration 6, A promises to carry B's cargo on his ship directly to Portsmouth on its next sailing. Since carrying B's cargo directly to Portsmouth is a condition of B's duty, no duty to pay arises and, since the condition can no longer occur, B's duty is discharged. Since A is under a duty to carry B's cargo directly to Portsmouth, his failure to do so is also a breach.

8. A contracts to sell and B to buy a house for $50,000, with the provision, "This contract is conditional on approval by X Bank of B's pending mortgage application." Approval by X Bank is a condition of B's duty. B is under no duty that the X Bank approve his application, but a court will supply a term imposing on him a duty to make reasonable efforts to obtain approval. See §§ 204, 205.

e. Ignorance immaterial. The rules stated in this Section apply without regard to whether a party knows or does not know of the non-occurrence of a condition of his duty.

Illustration

9. The facts being otherwise as stated in Illustration 6, B refuses to pay the freight without knowing that A's ship has put into port on the way. B's refusal is not a breach since his duty is discharged.

§ 226. How an Event May Be Made a Condition.

An event may be made a condition either by the agreement of the parties or by a term supplied by the court.

Comment

a. By agreement of the parties. No particular form of language is necessary to make an event a condition, although such words as "on condition that," "provided that" and "if" are often used for this purpose. An intention to make a duty conditional may be manifested by the general nature of an agreement, as well as by specific language. Whether the parties have, by their agreement, made an event a condition is determined by the process of interpretation. That process is subject to the general rules that are contained in previous topics of this Chapter. For example, as in other instances of interpretation, the purpose of the parties is given great weight (§ 202(1)), and, in choosing between reasonable meanings, that meaning is generally preferred which operates against the draftsman (§ 206). There are also some special standards of preference that are of particular applicability to conditions, and these are set out in § 227.

Illustrations

1. A partnership agreement among physicians provides that A may withdraw from the partnership on three months' written notice to the partnership's executive committee, "but in the event that the committee requests him to revoke his notice of withdrawal prior to its effective date, and he refuses to comply, he shall not upon his withdrawal engage in the practice of medicine within a twenty-five mile radius." A gives notice of his withdrawal. A request by the committee that A revoke his notice is a condition of A's duty not to practice medicine within a twenty-five mile radius.

2. A, a tenant of B, promises to pay $1,000 for "such repairs as an architect appointed by B shall approve." The appointment by B of an architect and the architect's approval of repairs are conditions of A's duty to pay for repairs.

3. A sells an automobile to B, for which B promises to pay $5,000 "on demand." A sues B for the $5,000 without first making a demand. A can recover. The quoted language is to be interpreted in the light of the purpose of the parties (§ 202(1)), and the purpose of such language, in connection with a promise that is one to pay money and is otherwise unconditional, is to fix the time after which interest at the legal rate is payable. A's suit should therefore not be dismissed merely because he did not demand payment, and a demand by A is not a condition of B's duty. The same interpretation follows by analogy from the rule of Uniform Commercial Code § 3–122(1)(b), under which a claim on a demand instrument arises on its date or date of issue.

4. A contracts to sell and B to buy a house for $50,000. The contract contains the provision, "This contract is conditional on approval by X Bank of B's pending mortgage application." Approval by X Bank is a condition of B's duty but not of A's duty. The quoted language is to be interpreted in the light of the purpose of the parties (§ 202(1)), and their purpose in including such a provision is to protect B and not A in the event that the application is not approved. If X Bank does not approve B's application, performance by B will not become due even if A makes a conditional offer to deliver a deed, but performance by A will become due if, in spite of X Bank's failure to approve B's application, B makes a conditional offer to pay the $50,000. Cf. Illustration 8 to § 225.

b. Nature of event. Just as the process of interpretation determines whether the parties have by their agreement made an event a condition, it also determines the nature of that event. Here too the process is subject to the general rules of interpretation stated earlier in the present Chapter, and here too there are some special standards of preference. These standards are set out in §§ 227(1) and 228.

Illustrations

5. A, an insurance company, insures B, a storekeeper, against safe burglary, "provided entry be made by actual force and violence, of which there are visible marks upon the exterior of all of the doors of the safe if entry is made through such doors." A burglar robs B's safe by picking the lock of the outer door, leaving no visible marks, and punching out the lock of the inner door. If the requirement of visible marks on both doors is merely evidentiary, the condition occurs when there is as here, adequate

evidence of force and violence to prevent fraudulent claims, even though there are no visible marks on the outer door. Since A was the draftsman of the policy, the meaning favorable to B is preferred (§ 206).

6. A contracts to sell and B to buy a house for $50,000. The contract recites that financing is to take the form of "$30,000 mortgage from X Bank" on stated terms and provides that B's duty is "conditional upon B's ability to arrange above described financing." B is unable to get the mortgage from X Bank but A offers to take a $30,000 purchase money mortgage on the stated terms and makes a conditional offer to deliver a deed. B refuses to perform. Although circumstances may show a contrary intention, the quoted language will ordinarily be interpreted so that the condition occurs only if B is able to get the mortgage from X Bank, and not if B is able to get a similar mortgage from A. Under this interpretation, B's refusal is not a breach.

c. By a term supplied by court. When the parties have omitted a term that is essential to a determination of their rights and duties, the court may supply a term which is reasonable in the circumstances (§ 204). Where that term makes an event a condition, it is often described as a "constructive" (or "implied in law") condition. This serves to distinguish it from events which are made conditions by the agreement of the parties, either by their words or by other conduct, and which are described as "express" and as "implied in fact" (inferred from fact) conditions. See Comments a and b to § 4. It is useful to distinguish "constructive" conditions, even though the distinction is necessarily somewhat arbitrary. For one thing, it is helpful in analysis and description to have terminology that reflects the two distinctive processes, sometimes called "interpretation" and "construction," that give rise to conditions. See Uniform Commercial Code §§ 2–313 to 2–315, in which an analogous distinction is made between express and implied warranties. For another, to the extent that the parties have, by a term of their agreement, clearly made an event a condition, they can be confident that a court will ordinarily feel constrained strictly to apply that term, while the same court may regard itself as having considerable latitude in tailoring a similar term that it has itself supplied.

One example of such a term supplied by the court is the requirement of § 45(2) that the offeree, under an option contract, complete or tender the invited performance as a condition of the offeror's duty. A more common example occurs where an obligor's duty cannot be performed without some act by the obligee, and the court supplies a term making that act a condition of the obligor's duty. In most such situations, the obligee's own obligation of good faith and fair dealing (§ 205) imposes on him a duty to do the act, so that a material failure to perform that duty would, in any case, have the same effect as the non-occurrence of a condition under the rules relating to performances to be exchanged under an exchange of promises (§ 239). The examples given in the following illustrations involve situations where no duty to do the act is imposed.

Illustrations

7. A promises to make necessary interior repairs on a building that he has leased to B, but reserves no privilege of entering the building. B's giving reasonable notice to A of any necessary interior repairs of which A would otherwise be unaware is a condition of A's duty to make those repairs, although B is under no duty to give notice.

8. A, a general contractor, contracts with B, a town, to construct a sewer system, agreeing in addition to defend any action against the town arising out of the work and to pay any damages recovered in such an action. B's giving reasonable notice to A of the commencement of any action of which A would otherwise be unaware is a condition of A's duties to defend and pay damages, although B is under no duty to give notice.

§ 227. Standards of Preference With Regard to Conditions.

(1) In resolving doubts as to whether an event is made a condition of an obligor's duty, and as to the nature of such an event, an interpretation is preferred that will reduce the obligee's risk of forfeiture, unless the event is within the obligee's control or the circumstances indicate that he has assumed the risk.

(2) Unless the contract is of a type under which only one party generally undertakes duties, when it is doubtful whether

    (a) a duty is imposed on an obligee that an event occur, or

(b) the event is made a condition of the obligor's duty, or

(c) the event is made a condition of the obligor's duty and a duty is imposed on the obligee that the event occur, the first interpretation is preferred if the event is within the obligee's control. . . .

Comment

a. Scope. The present Section states three standards of preference used in the process of interpretation with regard to conditions. They supplement the standards of preference in § 203, as well as the other rules set out in Topics 1 through 4 of this Chapter.

b. Condition or not. The non-occurrence of a condition of an obligor's duty may cause the obligee to lose his right to the agreed exchange after he has relied substantially on the expectation of that exchange, as by preparation or performance. The word "forfeiture" is used in this Restatement to refer to the denial of compensation that results in such a case. The policy favoring freedom of contract requires that, within broad limits (see § 229), the agreement of the parties should be honored even though forfeiture results. When, however, it is doubtful whether or not the agreement makes an event a condition of an obligor's duty, an interpretation is preferred that will reduce the risk of forfeiture. For example, under a provision that a duty is to be performed "when" an event occurs, it may be doubtful whether it is to be performed only if that event occurs, in which case the event is a condition, or at such time as it would ordinarily occur, in which case the event is referred to merely to measure the passage of time. In the latter case, if the event does not occur some alternative means will be found to measure the passage of time, and the non-occurrence of the event will not prevent the obligor's duty from becoming one of performance. If the event is a condition, however, the obligee takes the risk that its non-occurrence will discharge the obligor's duty. See § 225(2). When the nature of the condition is such that the uncertainty as to the event will be resolved before either party has relied on its anticipated occurrence, both parties can be entirely relieved of their duties, and the obligee risks only the loss of his expectations. When, however, the nature of the condition is such that the uncertainty is not likely to be resolved until after the obligee has relied by preparing to perform or by performing at least in part, he risks forfeiture. If the event is within his control, he will often assume this risk. If it is not within his control, it is sufficiently unusual for him to assume the risk that, in case of doubt, an interpretation is preferred under which the event is not a condition. The rule is, of course, subject to a showing of a contrary intention, and even without clear language, circumstances may show that he assumed the risk of its non-occurrence.

Although the rule is consistent with a policy of avoiding forfeiture and unjust enrichment, it is not directed at the avoidance of actual forfeiture and unjust enrichment. Since the intentions of the parties must be taken as of the time the contract was made, the test is whether a particular interpretation would have avoided the risk of forfeiture viewed as of that time, not whether it will avoid actual forfeiture in the resolution of a dispute that has arisen later. Excuse of the non-occurrence of a condition because of actual forfeiture is dealt with in § 229, and rules for the avoidance of unjust enrichment as such are dealt with in the Restatement of Restitution and in Chapter 16 of this Restatement, particularly §§ 370–77.

Illustrations

1. A, a general contractor, contracts with B, a subcontractor, for the plumbing work on a construction project. B is to receive $100,000, "no part of which shall be due until five days after Owner shall have paid Contractor therefor." B does the plumbing work, but the owner becomes insolvent and fails to pay A. A is under a duty to pay B after a reasonable time.

2. A, a mining company, hires B, an engineer, to help reopen one of its mines for "$10,000 to be payable as soon as the mine is in successful operation." $10,000 is a reasonable compensation for B's service. B performs the required services, but the attempt to reopen the mine is unsuccessful and A abandons it. A is under a duty to pay B $10,000 after the passage of a reasonable time.

3. A, a mining company, contracts with B, the owner of an untested experimental patented process, to help reopen one of its mines for $5,000 paid in advance and an additional "$15,000 to be payable as soon as the mine is in successful operation." $10,000 is a reasonable compensation for B's services. B performs the required services, but because the process proves to be unsuccessful, A abandons the attempt to reopen the mine. A is under no duty to pay B any additional amount. In all the circumstances the risk of failure of the process was, to that extent, assumed by B.

4. A contracts to sell and B to buy land for $100,000. At the same time, A contracts to pay C, a real estate broker, as his commission, $5,000 "on the closing of title." B refuses to consummate the sale. Absent a showing of a contrary intention, a court may conclude that C assumed this risk, and that A's duty is conditional on the sale being consummated. A is then under no duty to pay C.

c. *Nature of event.* In determining the nature of the event that is made a condition by the agreement, as in determining whether the agreement makes an event a condition in the first place (see Comment b), it will not ordinarily be supposed that a party has assumed the risk of forfeiture. Where the language is doubtful, an interpretation is generally preferred that will avoid this risk. This standard of preference finds an important application in the case of promises to pay for work done if some independent third party, such as an architect, surveyor or engineer, is satisfied with it, where the risk of forfeiture in the case of a judgment that is dishonest or based on a gross mistake as to the facts is substantial. The standard does not, however, help a party if the condition is within his control or if the circumstances otherwise indicate that he assumed that risk.

Illustrations

5. A contracts with B to repair B's building for $20,000, payment to be made "on the satisfaction of C, B's architect, and the issuance of his certificate." A makes the repairs, but C refuses to issue his certificate, and explains why he is not satisfied. Other experts in the field consider A's performance to be satisfactory and disagree with C's explanation. A has no claim against B. The quoted language is sufficiently clear that Subsection (1) does not apply. If C is honestly not satisfied, B is under no duty to pay A, and it makes no difference if his dissatisfaction was not reasonable.

6. The facts being otherwise as stated in Illustration 5, C refuses to issue his certificate although he admits that he is satisfied. A has a claim against B for $20,000. The quoted language will be interpreted so that the requirement of the certificate is merely evidentiary and the condition occurs when there is, as here, adequate evidence that C is honestly satisfied.

7. The facts being otherwise as stated in Illustration 5, C does not make a proper inspection of the work and gives no reasons for his dissatisfaction. A has a claim against B for $20,000. In using the quoted language, A and B assumed that C would exercise an honest judgment and by failing to make a proper inspection, C did not exercise such a judgment. Since the parties have omitted an essential term to cover this situation, the court will supply a term (see § 204) requiring A to pay B if C ought reasonably to have been satisfied.

8. The facts being otherwise as stated in Illustration 5, C makes a gross mistake with reference to the facts on which his refusal to give a certificate is based. A has a claim against B for $20,000. In using the quoted language, A and B assumed that C would exercise his judgment without a gross mistake as to the facts. Since the parties have omitted an essential term to cover this situation, the court will supply a term (see § 204) requiring A to pay B if C ought reasonably to have been satisfied.

d. *Condition or duty.* When an obligor wants the obligee to do an act, the obligor may make his own duty conditional on the obligee doing it and may also have the obligee promise to do it. Or he may merely make his own duty conditional on the obligee doing it. Or he may merely have the obligee promise to do it. (See Introductory Note to this Topic and Comment d to § 225). It may not be clear, however, which he has done. The rule in Subsection (2) states a preference for an interpretation that merely imposes a duty on the obligee to do the act and does not make the doing of the act a condition of the obligor's duty. The preferred interpretation avoids the harsh results that might otherwise result from the non-occurrence of a condition and still gives adequate protection to the obligor under the rules of Chapter 10 relating to performances to be exchanged under an exchange of promises. Under those rules, particularly §§ 237–41, the obligee's failure to perform his duty has, if it is material, the effect of the non-occurrence of a condition of the obligor's duty. Unless the agreement makes it clear that the event is required as a condition, it is fairer to apply these more flexible rules. The obligor will, in any case, have a remedy for breach. In many instances the rule in Subsection (1) will also apply and will reinforce the preference stated in Subsection (2).

This standard of preference applies only where the event is within the obligee's control. Where it is within the obligor's control (e.g., his honest satisfaction with the obligee's performance), within a third party's control (e.g., an architect's satisfaction with performance), or within no one's control (e.g., the accidental destruction of the subject matter), the preferential rule does not apply since it is not usual for the obligee to undertake a duty that such an event will occur. Although the obligee can, by appropriate language, undertake a duty that an event that is not within his control will occur, such an undertaking must be derived from the agreement of the parties under the general rules of interpretation stated earlier in the present Chapter without resort to this standard of preference.

Furthermore, this standard of preference does not apply when the contract is of a type under which only the obligor generally undertakes duties. It therefore does not apply to the typical insurance contract under which only the insurer generally undertakes duties, and a term requiring an act to be done by the insured is not subject to this standard of preference. In view of the general understanding that only the insurer undertakes duties, the term will be interpreted as making that event a condition of the insurer's duty rather than as imposing a duty on the insured.

Illustrations

9. On August 1, A contracts to sell and B to buy goods, "selection to be made by buyer before September 1." B merely has a duty to make his selection by September 1, and his making it by that date is not a condition of A's duty. A failure by B to make a selection by September 1 is a breach, and if material it operates as the non-occurrence of a condition of A's duty. See §§ 237, 241.

10. A, B, and C make a contract under which A agrees to buy the inventory of B's grocery business, C agrees to finance A's down payment, and B agrees to subordinate A's obligation to him to pay the balance to A's obligation to C to repay the amount of the down payment. The contract provides that "C shall maintain the books of account for A, and shall inventory A's stock of merchandise every two months, rendering statements to B." C merely has a duty to do these acts and doing them is not a condition of B's duty. A failure by C to do them is a breach, and if material it operates as the non-occurrence of a condition of B's duty. See §§ 237, 241.

11. A insures B's house against fire for $50,000 under a policy providing, "other insurance is prohibited." Because the insured has undertaken no other duties under the contract, Subsection (2) does not apply. Because a policy of fire insurance is a type of contract under which only the insurer generally undertakes duties, the absence of other insurance is merely a condition of A's duty, and B is not under a duty not to procure other insurance.

e. Condition or discharge. Circumstances may show that the parties intended to make an event a condition of an obligor's duty even though their language appears to make the non-occurrence of the event a ground for discharge of his duty after performance has become due. See Comment e to § 224. An example is the traditional form of bond, which states that the obligor is under a duty to perform, but that the duty will be discharged if something happens. The language, in spite of its form, is interpreted so that the failure of that thing to happen is a condition of the obligor's duty. Unless that condition occurs, no performance is due. Although this form of expression persists in legal documents, only rarely do the parties intend that one of them shall be under a duty to perform which is to cease on the occurrence of something that is still uncertain. The clearest language is therefore necessary to justify such an interpretation, and if the language is doubtful a contrary interpretation is preferred.

Illustrations

12. In return for a fee paid by X, A signs and delivers to B a bond which reads: "I acknowledge myself to be indebted to B in the sum of $50,000. The condition of this obligation is such that if X shall faithfully perform his duties as executor of the will of Y, this obligation shall be void, but otherwise of full effect." X's failure faithfully to perform his duties is a condition of A's duty under the bond.

13. A promises to pay B $10,000 for a quantity of oil, and promises to pay B an additional $5,000 "but if a greater quantity of oil arrives in vessels during the first quarter of the year than arrived during the same quarter last year, then this obligation to be void." A's payment of the additional $5,000 is not due until the end of the first quarter, and the failure of a greater quantity of oil to arrive by that time is a condition of A's duty to pay the additional $5,000.

§ 228. Satisfaction of the Obligor as a Condition.

When it is a condition of an obligor's duty that he be satisfied with respect to the obligee's performance or with respect to something else, and it is practicable to determine whether a reasonable person in the position of the obligor would be satisfied, an interpretation is preferred under which the condition occurs if such a reasonable person in the position of the obligor would be satisfied.

Comment

a. Conditions of satisfaction. This Section sets out a special standard of preference for a type of condition that has long been of particular interest and importance—the satisfaction of the obligor himself, rather than a third party. Usually it is the obligee's performance as to which the obligor is to be satisfied, but it may also be something else, such as the propitiousness of circumstances for his enterprise. The agreement will often use language such as "satisfaction" or "complete satisfaction," without making it clear that the test is merely one of honest satisfaction rather than of reasonable satisfaction. Under any interpretation, the exercise of judgment must be in accordance with the duty of good faith and fair dealing (§ 205), and for this reason, the agreement is not illusory (§ 77). If the agreement leaves no doubt that it is only honest satisfaction that is meant and no more, it will be so interpreted, and the condition does not occur if the obligor is honestly, even though unreasonably, dissatisfied. Even so, the dissatisfaction must be with the circumstance and not with the bargain and the mere statement of the obligor that he is not satisfied is not conclusive on the question of his honest satisfaction.

Illustrations

1. A grants to B an exclusive license in a designated territory to bottle and sell a soft drink on specified terms for a five-year period. The contract describes in detail B's duty diligently to represent A in the territory and provides that A may terminate the license at any time if in A's "sole, exclusive and final judgment made in good faith" B does not perform that duty. After a year, A terminates, honestly telling B that in A's judgment B has not performed his duty under the contract. B has no claim against A since the agreement clearly provides a test of honest satisfaction.

2. A contracts to sell and B to buy 500 barrels of cherries in syrup "quality to be satisfactory in buyer's honest judgment," delivery to be in installments. After deliveries of and payments for a total of 100 barrels, B states that he is not satisfied and refuses to take more. Since the agreement clearly provides a test of honest satisfaction, B's termination is effective if his judgment is in fact made honestly in accordance with his duty of good faith and fair dealing (§ 205). However, A may show that B's rejection was for other reasons by proving, for example, that B expressed satisfaction at the time of the first deliveries, that B's demand had dropped sharply, and that A's cherries are selected and put up with great care and are of the highest quality.

b. Preference for objective standard. When, however, the agreement does not make it clear that it requires merely honest satisfaction, it will not usually be supposed that the obligee has assumed the risk of the obligor's unreasonable, even if honest, dissatisfaction. In such a case, to the extent that it is practicable to apply an objective test of reasonable satisfaction, such a test will be applied. The situation differs from that where the satisfaction of a third party such as an architect, surveyor or engineer is concerned. See Comment c to § 227. These professionals, even though employed by the obligor, are assumed to be capable of independent judgment, free from the selfish interests of the obligor. But if the obligor would subject the obligee's right to compensation to his own idiosyncrasies, he must use clear language. When, as is often the case, the preferred interpretation will reduce the obligee's risk of forfeiture, so that § 227(1) also applies, there is an additional argument in its favor. This argument is particularly strong where the obligor will be left with a benefit which he cannot return. If, however, the circumstance with respect to which a party is to be satisfied is such that the application of an objective test is impracticable, the rule of this Section is not applicable. A court will then, for practical reasons, apply a subjective test of honest satisfaction, even if the agreement admits of doubt on the point and even if the result will be to increase the obligee's risk of forfeiture.

Illustrations

3. A contracts with B to install a heating system in B's factory, for a price of $20,000 to be paid "on condition of satisfactory completion." A installs the heating system, but B states that he is not satisfied with it and refuses to pay the $20,000. B gives no reason except that he does not approve of the heating system, and according to experts in the field the system as installed is entirely satisfactory. A has a claim against B for $20,000 since it is practicable to apply an objective test to the installation of the heating system. This interpretation is also preferred because it reduces A's risk of forfeiture.

4. A contracts with B to paint a portrait of B's daughter, for which B promises to pay $5,000 "if entirely satisfied." A paints the portrait, but B honestly states that he is not satisfied with it and refuses to pay the $5,000. B gives no reason except that the portrait does not please him, and according to experts in the field the portrait is an admirable work of art. A has no claim against B since it is not practicable to apply an objective test to the painting.

5. A contracts to have B furnish a four-piece band to play in A's inn for six months, with a provision, "If band proves unsatisfactory to A contract is subject to two weeks' notice." A occasionally objects when B is absent and a guitar is substituted for B's string bass. After two months, A gives notice of termination, stating that he is dissatisfied for this reason. B has no claim against A since it is not practicable to apply an objective test to the band's performance.

§ 229. Excuse of a Condition to Avoid Forfeiture.

To the extent that the non-occurrence of a condition would cause disproportionate forfeiture, a court may excuse the non-occurrence of that condition unless its occurrence was a material part of the agreed exchange.

Comment

a. Relation to other rules. Although both this Section and § 208, on unconscionable contract or term, limit freedom of contract, they are designed to reach different types of situations. While § 208 speaks of unconscionability "at the time the contract is made," this Section is concerned with forfeiture that would actually result if the condition were not excused. It is intended to deal with a term that does not appear to be unconscionable at the time the contract is made but that would, because of ensuing events, cause forfeiture.

b. Disproportionate forfeiture. The rule stated in the present Section is, of necessity, a flexible one, and its application is within the sound discretion of the court. Here, as in § 227(1), "forfeiture" is used to refer to the denial of compensation that results when the obligee loses his right to the agreed exchange after he has relied substantially, as by preparation or performance on the expectation of that exchange. See Comment *b* to § 227. The extent of the forfeiture in any particular case will depend on the extent of that denial of compensation. In determining whether the forfeiture is "disproportionate," a court must weigh the extent of the forfeiture by the obligee against the importance to the obligor of the risk from which he sought to be protected and the degree to which that protection will be lost if the non-occurrence of the condition is excused to the extent required to prevent forfeiture. The character of the agreement may, as in the case of insurance agreements, affect the rigor with which the requirement is applied.

Illustrations

1. A contracts to build a house for B, using pipe of Reading manufacture. In return, B agrees to pay $75,000 in progress payments, each payment to be made "on condition that no pipe other than that of Reading manufacture has been used." Without A's knowledge, a subcontractor mistakenly uses pipe of Cohoes manufacture which is identical in quality and is distinguishable only by the name of the manufacturer which is stamped on it. The mistake is not discovered until the house is completed, when replacement of the pipe will require destruction of substantial parts of the house. B refuses to pay the unpaid balance of $10,000. A court may conclude that the use of Reading rather than Cohoes pipe is so relatively unimportant to B that the forfeiture that would result from denying A the entire balance would be disproportionate, and may allow recovery by A subject to any claim for damages for A's breach of his duty to use Reading pipe.

2. A, an ocean carrier, carries B's goods under a contract providing that it is a condition of A's liability for damage to cargo that "written notice of claim for loss or damage must be given within 10 days after removal of goods." B's cargo is damaged during carriage and A knows of this. On removal of the goods, B notes in writing on the delivery record that the cargo is damaged, and five days later informs A over the telephone of a claim for that damage and invites A to participate in an inspection within the ten day period. A inspects the goods within the period, but B does not give written notice of its claim until 25 days after removal of the goods. Since the purpose of requiring the condition of written notice is to alert the carrier and enable it to make a prompt investigation, and since this purpose had been served by the written notice of damage and the oral notice of claim, the court may excuse the non-occurrence of the condition to the extent required to allow recovery by B.

c. Limitation on scope. The rule of this Section applies only where occurrence of the condition was not a material part of the agreed exchange. These are situations where, under § 84, the non-occurrence of the condition could have been excused by a promise to perform the duty in spite of its non-occurrence. It is not enough that the actual non-occurrence happened to involve a departure that was not a material part of the agreed exchange, if the occurrence of the condition was a material part of that exchange. A court may, of course, ignore trifling departures.

A court need not excuse entirely the non-occurrence of the condition, but may merely excuse its non-occurrence during the period of time in which it would otherwise have to occur (see Comment c to § 225), if it concludes that the time of its occurrence is not a material part of the agreed exchange. This conclusion is sometimes summed up by the phrase that "time is not of the essence."

Illustrations

3. A contracts to make repairs on B's house, in return for which B agrees to pay $10,000 "on condition that the repairs are completed by October 1." The repairs are not completed until October 2. A court may decide that there are two cumulative conditions, repair of the house and completion of the repairs by October 1, and that the non-occurrence of the second condition is excused to the extent of one day.

4. On July 1, A makes an option contract with B, under which B has the right to buy land for $200,000, on condition that he exercise it no later than June 30 five years later. B makes an initial payment of $10,000 and agrees to make additional $10,000 payments on or before June 30 of each of the four succeeding years, unless he has already exercised the option, his right being "conditional on his paying the $10,000 on or before the prescribed date." These payments are not to be applied to the purchase price. After paying for two years and building on adjacent land, substantially increasing the value of the land subject to the option, B mails a $10,000 check for the third year on June 30. A receives it on July 1 and returns it to B, stating that the option contract is cancelled. A court may decide that there are two cumulative conditions, payment of $10,000 and payment on or before June 30, and that the non-occurrence of the second condition is excused to the extent of one day.

5. The facts being otherwise as in Illustration 4, B makes the payments on June 30 of each of the four succeeding years, but does not exercise the option by tendering the $200,000 until July 1, following the June 30 expiration date. Even if a court decides that there are two cumulative conditions, payment of $200,000 and payment on or before June 30, it may not decide that the non-occurrence of the second condition is excused to the extent of one day because that would give B a more extensive option than that on which the parties agreed.

CHAPTER 10

PERFORMANCE AND NON-PERFORMANCE

TOPIC 1. PERFORMANCES TO BE EXCHANGED
UNDER AN EXCHANGE OF PROMISES

§ 230. Event That Terminates a Duty.

(1) Except as stated in Subsection (2), if under the terms of the contract the occurrence of an event is to terminate an obligor's duty of immediate performance or one to pay damages for breach, that duty is discharged if the event occurs.

(2) The obligor's duty is not discharged if occurrence of the event

    (a) is the result of a breach by the obligor of his duty of good faith and fair dealing, or

    (b) could not have been prevented because of impracticability and continuance of the duty does not subject the obligor to a materially increased burden. . . .

Comment

a. Scope. Parties sometimes provide that an obligor's matured duty will be extinguished on the occurrence of a specified event, which is sometimes referred to as a "condition subsequent." See Comment e to § 224. They may, for example, provide that an obligor's duty to reimburse the obligee for some loss or to compensate him for a breach will be extinguished if the obligee does not take some action, such as bringing suit, within a stated period of time. Under such a provision, the duty is generally discharged if the event occurs. The same result follows if its occurrence becomes inevitable. Subsection (2) states exceptions to this general rule for cases in which the occurrence of the event is due to the obligor's breach of his duty of good faith and fair dealing (§ 205) or could not have been prevented by the obligee because of impracticability (§ 261). See Subsection (2). The rule stated in this Section applies only to matured duties and to duties to make compensation. If performance under the contract is not to become due until occurrence of an event, that event is a condition of the duty and is governed by the rules stated in §§ 224–29. The difference is one of substance and not merely of the form in which the provision is stated.

Illustrations

1. A, an insurance company, insures the property of B under a policy providing that no recovery can be had if suit is not brought on the policy within two years after a loss. A loss occurs and B lets two years pass before bringing suit. A's duty to pay B for the loss is discharged and B cannot maintain the action on the policy.

2. The facts being otherwise as stated in Illustration 1, B lives in a foreign country and is prevented by the outbreak of war from bringing suit against A for two years. A's duty to pay B for the loss is not discharged and B can maintain an action on the policy when the war is ended.

b. Promise to perform in spite of occurrence. Under the rule stated in Subsection (3), a promise by the obligor to perform the duty regardless of the occurrence of the event is binding if the obligee has materially changed his position in reliance on it. The promise need not be in words and may be inferred from other conduct. The rule, like that stated in § 84, is sometimes thought of in terms of "waiver" or "estoppel." See Comments a and b to § 84. It supplements the general rules on modification of contracts by agreement of the parties.

Illustration

3. The facts being otherwise as stated in Illustration 1, after the loss occurs, A tells B that it is not necessary to bring suit within two years, and B relies on the statement in refraining from suing for two years. A's duty to pay B for the loss is not discharged and B can maintain an action on the policy even after two years have passed.

§ 231. Criterion for Determining When Performances Are to Be Exchanged Under an Exchange of Promises.

Performances are to be exchanged under an exchange of promises if each promise is at least part of the consideration for the other and the performance of each promise is to be exchanged at least in part for the performance of the other.

Comment

a. Expectation of an exchange of performances. Agreements involving an exchange of promises play a vital role in an economically advanced society. Ordinarily when parties make such an agreement, they not only regard the promises themselves as the subject of an exchange (§ 71(2)), but they also intend that the performances of those promises shall subsequently be exchanged for each other. Even without a showing of such an actual intention, a court will often, out of a sense of fairness, assume that it was their expectation that there would be a subsequent exchange of the performance of each party for that of the other. Cf. 204. This Chapter consists, in substantial part, of rules designed to secure that expectation of a subsequent exchange of performances.

b. Performances need not be simultaneous. It is often expected that performances will be exchanged under an exchange of promises even though those performances are not to take place at the same time. Under a contract for the sale of goods, for example, the parties expect an exchange of the delivery of the goods by the seller and the payment of the price by the buyer, regardless of whether the price is payable before, at the same time as, or after delivery of the goods. As long as this is their expectation, the delivery of the goods and the payment of the price are to be exchanged under the exchange of promises, and it is immaterial when the price is payable.

Illustrations

1. A, a shipowner, promises to carry B's cargo on his ship. B promises to pay A the stipulated freight. They exchange these promises in the expectation that there will be a subsequent exchange of those performances. A fails to carry B's cargo, and B thereupon refuses to pay the freight. A's carrying the cargo and B's paying the freight are to be exchanged under the exchange of promises. Therefore, under the rule stated in § 237, A has no claim against B.

2. In return for A's promise to deliver a machine, B promises to pay A $10,000 within 30 days. They exchange these promises in the expectation that there will be a subsequent exchange of those performances. A fails to deliver the machine, and B thereupon refuses to pay any part of the $10,000. A's delivery of the machine and B's payment of the $10,000 are to be exchanged under the exchange of promises. Therefore, under the rule stated in § 237, A has no claim against B.

c. Consideration need not be exclusively promises. The parties may expect that their performances will be exchanged under their exchange of promises even though that exchange does not consist exclusively of promises. The consideration given by one or both parties may consist in part of some performance.

Illustration

3. In return for A's promise to deliver a machine priced at $10,000, B pays A $5,000 as a down payment and promises to pay A the $5,000 balance within 30 days after delivery of the machine. They exchange these promises in the expectation that delivery of the machine will be exchanged, at least in part, for the $5,000 balance and that the $5,000 balance will be exchanged for the machine. A fails to deliver the machine, and B thereupon refuses to pay the $5,000 balance. A's delivery of the machine and B's payment of the $5,000 balance within 30 days are to be exchanged under the exchange of promises. Therefore, under the rule stated in § 237, A has no claim against B. B is entitled to restitution of the $5,000 he paid (see §§ 370–77) in addition to his claim against A for damages for breach (§ 243).

d. Separate contracts. The rules that protect parties whose performances are to be exchanged under an exchange of promises apply only when the promises are exchanged as part of a single contract. When each party gives more than one promise, or gives some performance in addition to a promise, it may not be clear whether there is a single exchange of promises resulting in a single contract or separate exchanges resulting in separate contracts. If every promise by one party is at least part of the consideration for every promise by the other party, there is a single exchange in which all of the promises on each side are exchanged for all of those on the other side. This is so, for example, where a buyer and a seller make a single bargain for the sale of several related kinds of goods. But if one or more promises by each party are no part of the consideration for one or more promises by the other party, there are instead separate exchanges. In that case all of the promises on each side cannot be regarded as exchanged for all of those on the other side. This is so, for example, where a buyer and a seller make several bargains at the same time for the sale of several unrelated kinds of goods. In deciding whether there is a single contract rather than separate contracts, the court must look to the actual bargain of the parties, in accordance with § 71(2), to decide whether each promise on one side was sought and given as at least part of the exchange for each promise on the other side. The form of the agreement is not controlling, and the actual bargain of the parties is not to be determined merely by reference to such criteria as whether separate performances are made the subject of a single promise or of separate promises, whether separate promises are contained in a single writing or in separate writings, or whether the understanding of the parties is entirely written or oral or is partly written and partly oral.

Illustrations

4. A promises to sell and B to buy a food freezer priced at $1,200 to be paid for in monthly installments over an eighteen-month period. A also promises to sell B frozen food at greatly reduced prices, and B promises to buy an initial quantity, deliverable at the same time as the freezer, for $200, with additional quantities to be available in the future at B's option. Although two separate writings are executed, one entitled "Freezer Contract" and, the other, entitled "Food Contract," the promises are made as part of the same bargain, and payment for the freezer, for example, is to be exchanged at least in part for the delivery of the food. A tenders the freezer but fails to supply the food although B tenders the $200. B thereupon refuses to take the freezer or to pay anything. The performances promised in the two writings, A's delivery of the freezer and the food and B's payment for the freezer and the food, are to be exchanged under a single exchange of promises. Therefore, under the rule stated in § 238, A has no claim against B.

5. A, the owner of a small publishing business, makes a written contract with B, a large publishing company, to sell A's business to B in exchange for 10,000 shares of B's stock, having a market price equal to the fair value of A's business. At the same time, A and B execute a separate writing under which A is to work for B for 5 years, subject to renewal at B's option, at a salary of $30,000 a year plus a bonus based on sales. B unjustifiably discharges A after one month, and A thereupon refuses to complete the transfer of his business to B. Whether or not A's refusal to complete the exchange is a breach depends on whether, under the bargain of the parties, there are two contracts or only one contract. If the court determines that the promise of A to work for B is no part of the consideration for B's promise to buy A's business, and that the promise of B to employ A is no part of the consideration for A's promise to sell his business, there are two separate exchanges of promises. The performance promised in the one writing and the performance promised in the other cannot then be performances to be exchanged under a single exchange of promises. B then has a claim against A for damages for breach of the contract to sell A's business to B, and A has a claim against B for damages for breach of the contract to employ A (§ 243). If, however, the court determines that each of the promises is at least part of the consideration for the other, there is only one exchange of promises. Under the rule stated in § 232 all of the performances of each party taken collectively are treated as performances to be exchanged under that exchange of promises. Under the rule stated in § 238, B then has no claim against A for damages for A's refusal to complete the transfer of his business to B, but A has a claim against B for damages because of his unjustifiable discharge of A (§ 243).

e. *Leases and other conveyances.* The applicability of the rules stated in this Chapter to covenants in leases and other conveyances of land is not dealt with in this Restatement.

§ 232. When It Is Presumed That Performances Are to Be Exchanged Under an Exchange of Promises.

Where the consideration given by each party to a contract consists in whole or in part of promises, all the performances to be rendered by each party taken collectively are treated as performances to be exchanged under an exchange of promises, unless a contrary intention is clearly manifested.

Comment

a. Reason for presumption. The rules applicable to performances to be exchanged under an exchange of promises are designed to give the parties maximum protection, consistent with freedom of contract, against disappointment of their expectation of a subsequent exchange of those performances. When the parties have exchanged promises, there is ordinarily every reason to suppose that they contracted on the basis of such an expectation since the exchange of promises would otherwise have little purpose. Even absent a showing of their actual intentions, fairness dictates that such an expectation be assumed. This Section therefore states a presumption in favor of the conclusion that, in such a case, the performances are to be exchanged under the exchange of promises. For one of the parties to show that the expectation was otherwise, the contrary intention must be clearly manifested. The presumption applies regardless of whether the promises are written or oral or both, and even where a negotiable instrument is involved. See Uniform Commercial Code § 3–408. It also applies even though the consideration given by a party consists partly of some performance and only partly of a promise (see Comment c to § 231), although it is possible that in such a case the promise may be so minor and incidental that its non-performance would not be a material failure of performance. See Comment b to § 241.

Illustrations

1. A, a wholesaler, promises to sell and B, a retailer, promises to buy goods together with related advertising material, payment to be made within 30 days of delivery. A also promises not to sell similar advertising material to any other retailer in B's city. A sells similar advertising material to another retailer in B's city, and B thereupon refuses to take or pay for the goods. A's selling B goods together with advertising material and not selling others similar advertising material, taken collectively, and B's payment are to be exchanged under the exchange of promises. Therefore, under the rule stated in § 237, if A's failure of performance is material, A has no claim against B.

2. A promises to sell to B a lot in a subdivision for $8,000. B promises to pay in four annual installments of $2,000 each, beginning one year after execution of the contract. A promises to begin to make improvements and pave the streets within 60 days and to complete work within a reasonable time and promises to deliver a deed at the time of the final payment. A fails to pave the streets, and B thereupon refuses to pay any installments. A's making improvements, paving streets, and delivering a deed, taken collectively, and B's paying installments are to be exchanged under the exchange of promises. Therefore, under the rule stated in § 237, if A's failure of performance is material, A has no claim against B.

3. A employs B under a five-year employment contract, which contains a valid covenant under which B promises not to engage in the same business in a designated area for two years after the termination of the employment. It expressly provides that "this covenant is independent of any other provision in this agreement." After B has begun work, A unjustifiably discharges him, and B thereupon engages in business in violation of the covenant. A's employing B and B's working for A are to be exchanged under the exchange of promises. The quoted words indicate an intention that A's employing B is not to be exchanged for B's refraining from engaging in the same business. If the court concludes that this intention is clearly manifested, A has a claim against B for damages for breach of his promise not to compete.

4. A contracts to sell and B to buy a machine, to be delivered immediately, for $10,000. As part of the same bargain, B gives A his negotiable promissory note for $10,000 to A's order, payable in 90 days, but the note makes no reference to the transaction out of which it arises. A fails to deliver the machine. A's delivering the machine and B's paying the note are to be exchanged under the exchange of promises. Therefore, under the rule stated in § 237, A has no claim on the note or the contract against B. See Uniform Commercial Code §§ 3–306, 3–408, and 3–307(3).

b. Promises taken collectively. When the rule stated in this Section applies, all of the performances to be rendered by each party taken collectively are to be exchanged under the exchange of promises. A court need not determine whether separate performances on either side are the subject of a single promise or of separate promises. Nor need a court concern itself with the relationship among separate promises viewed as of the time of their making. Instead the court is to focus on the relative importance of the failure of performance in the light of the situation of the parties at the time of that failure. See §§ 237, 238, 241.

c. Performances need not be treated as equivalent. When an exchange consists exclusively of promises, the values of the performances to be subsequently exchanged are usually regarded by the parties as equivalent. This is not always so since a party may make what is often called an "aleatory" promise, under which his duty to perform is conditional on the occurrence of a fortuitous event. Or it may be understood that the value of one party's performance will be affected by chance, as where he promises to deliver his output or to pay during another's lifetime. Even when one or both of the parties makes such a promise, however, they contemplate a subsequent exchange of performances, subject of course to the occurrence of the required conditions. Such cases are therefore subject to the rules stated in this Chapter (see § 239), along with some special rules relating to the election of remedies which are stated in §§ 378–80.

Illustration

5. A, an insurance company, issues to B a group health insurance policy covering B's employees for one year beginning January 1 in return for B's promise to pay the premium on February 1. During the month of January A unjustifiably rejects proper claims filed by B's employees under the policy. B refuses to pay the premium on February 1. A's paying proper claims of B's employees and B's paying the premium are to be exchanged under the exchange of promises. Therefore, under the rule stated in § 237, if A's breach is material, A has no claim against B.

§ 233. Performance at One Time or in Installments.

(1) Where performances are to be exchanged under an exchange of promises, and the whole of one party's performance can be rendered at one time, it is due at one time, unless the language or the circumstances indicate the contrary.

(2) Where only a part of one party's performance is due at one time under Subsection (1), if the other party's performance can be so apportioned that there is a comparable part that can also be rendered at that time, it is due at that time, unless the language or the circumstances indicate the contrary.

Comment

a. Performance at one time. Subsection (1) states the established rule that a party who can give his whole performance at one time is expected to do so. He is not entitled to perform a part at a time, nor is the other party entitled to demand that he do so. Uniform Commercial Code § 2–307 so provides for contracts for the sale of goods. The rule expresses the usual understanding of parties in such cases. A party who asserts a different understanding may establish a contrary intention by an express agreement such as one for delivery in installments, or by usage of trade (§ 221; Uniform Commercial Code § 1–205) or by course of dealing (§ 223; Uniform Commercial Code § 1–205). Or he may establish it by showing special circumstances, as where under a contract for brick to be used to build a building it is understood that the buyer's storage space is so limited that it would be impossible for him to receive the entire amount at once. See Comment 3 to Uniform Commercial Code § 2–307. The rule does not apply where performance requires a period of time. The requirement that performance be possible at one time may, however, be met even though the performance, as in the case of delivery of a large quantity of bulky goods, cannot be instantaneous.

Illustrations

1. A contracts to sell and B to buy ten identical carloads of coal for $100,000. Delivery by A of all ten carloads is due in a single lot.

2. The facts being otherwise as stated in Illustration 1, it is known by both A and B that only one carload of coal will be available at a time. A may deliver one carload at a time.

b. Right to other party's performance. If the language or circumstances indicate that, contrary to the general rule stated in Subsection (1), only a part of one party's performance is due at one time, a question then arises as to when the other party's performance is due. Under the rule stated in Subsection (2), if the other party's performance can be so apportioned that there is a comparable part that can also be given at that time, part performance by both parties is due at that time. See § 234(1). In the typical case the other party's performance will consist of the price and the question is whether the price can be apportioned. See

Comment d to § 240. This is the way in which the rule is stated for the sale of goods in Uniform Commercial Code § 2–307.

Illustration

3. The facts being as stated in Illustration 2, payment of $10,000 by B is due at the same time that A delivers each carload of coal.

§ 234. Order of Performances.

(1) Where all or part of the performances to be exchanged under an exchange of promises can be rendered simultaneously, they are to that extent due simultaneously, unless the language or the circumstances indicate the contrary.

(2) Except to the extent stated in Subsection (1), where the performance of only one party under such an exchange requires a period of time, his performance is due at an earlier time than that of the other party, unless the language or the circumstances indicate the contrary.

Comment

a. Advantages of simultaneous performance. A requirement that the parties perform simultaneously where their performances are to be exchanged under an exchange of promises is fair for two reasons. First, it offers both parties maximum security against disappointment of their expectations of a subsequent exchange of performances by allowing each party to defer his own performance until he has been assured that the other will perform. This advantage is implemented by the rule stated in § 238, which deals with offers to perform. Second, it avoids placing on either party the burden of financing the other before the latter has performed. Subsection (1) therefore imposes a requirement of simultaneous performance whenever this is feasible under the contract, in the absence of language or circumstances indicating a contrary intention. A notable example of such a requirement is that laid down for contracts for the sale of goods by Uniform Commercial Code §§ 2–507 and 2–511. The requirement is subject to the agreement of the parties, as by an express provision extending credit to the buyer, or one requiring him to pay against documents or to furnish a letter of credit. Even absent an express provision, a contrary intention may be shown by circumstances including usage of trade and course of dealing (§§ 221, 223; Uniform Commercial Code § 1–205).

b. When simultaneous performance possible under agreement. In the absence of language or circumstances showing a contrary intention, the requirement of simultaneous performance stated in Subsection (1) applies whenever such performance is possible, consistent with the terms of the contract. A major instance where simultaneous performance is not possible occurs when one party's performance is continuous over some substantial period of time, a situation that is dealt with in Subsection (2). However, as is the case for the requirement of the preceding section that the whole performance be possible at one time, the requirement of simultaneous performance is not to be applied so literally as to exclude instances in which the objectives of the requirement can be fulfilled although performance cannot be instantaneous. See Comment a to § 233. A less important instance where simultaneous performance is not possible occurs when distance and lack of adequate communications make it impossible to assure the parties that performance is taking place at the same time, so that although the performance of each party can be instantaneous, the two performances cannot be simultaneous within the meaning of Subsection (1). Cases in which simultaneous performance is possible under the terms of the contract can be grouped into five categories: (1) where the same time is fixed for the performance of each party; (2) where a time is fixed for the performance of one of the parties and no time is fixed for the other; (3) where no time is fixed for the performance of either party; (4) where the same period is fixed within which each party is to perform; (5) where different periods are fixed within which each party is to perform. The requirement of simultaneous performance applies to the first four categories. The requirement does not apply to the fifth category, even if simultaneous performance is possible, because in fixing different periods for performance the parties must have contemplated the possibility of performance at different times under their agreement. Therefore in cases in the fifth category the circumstances show an intention contrary to the rule stated in Subsection (1).

Illustrations

1. A promises to sell land to B, delivery of the deed to be on July 1. B promises to pay A $50,000, payment to be made on July 1. Delivery of the deed and payment of the price are due simultaneously.

2. A promises to sell land to B, the deed to be delivered on July 1. B promises to pay A $50,000, no provision being made for the time of payment. Delivery of the deed and payment of the price are due simultaneously.

3. A promises to sell land to B and B promises to pay A $50,000, no provision being made for the time either of delivery of the deed or of payment. Delivery of the deed and payment of the price are due simultaneously.

4. A promises to sell land to B, delivery of the deed to be on or before July 1. B promises to pay A $50,000, payment to be on or before July 1. Delivery of the deed and payment of the price are due simultaneously.

5. A promises to sell land to B, delivery of the deed to be on or before July 1. B promises to pay A $50,000, payment to be on or before August 1. Delivery of the deed and payment of the prices are not due simultaneously.

c. When simultaneous performance possible in part. The requirement of simultaneous performance stated in Subsection (1) also applies where only part rather than all of the performance of one party can be performed simultaneously with either part or all of the performance of the other party. It therefore applies to the situations discussed in Comment b to § 233 and exemplified by Illustration 3 to that section. But it is broader than this and also applies, for example, to instances where some part performance of one party can be rendered simultaneously with the entire performance of the other party. See Comment f and Illustration 12.

Illustrations

6. A promises to sell land to B, delivery of the deed to be four years from the following July 1. B promises to pay A $50,000 in installments of $10,000 on each July 1 for five years. Delivery of the deed and payment of the last installment are due simultaneously.

7. A promises to sell land to B, delivery of the deed to be one year from July 1. B promises to pay A $50,000 in installments of $10,000 on each July 1 for five years. Delivery of the deed and payment of the second installment are due simultaneously.

d. When simultaneous performance later becomes possible. Although different times or periods were originally fixed for the performance of each party, performance by the party who is to perform first may sometimes be delayed until the time for performance by the other party has arrived. If the latter party is entitled to and does assert that his remaining duties of performance are discharged because of the delay, under the rule stated in § 237, no question of the order of performance remains. Unless the delay is justified, he will also have a claim for damages for total breach based on all of his remaining rights to performance. (§§ 236(1), 243(1)). If, however, he is not entitled to assert that his remaining duties of performance are discharged, or if he does not assert this even though he is entitled to do so, a question of the order of performances remains. Unless the delay is justified he will, of course, have a claim for damages for partial breach because of the delay. Whether or not the delay is justified, he can at least insist on simultaneous performance. (As to judicial supervision of the requirement of simultaneous performance where the injured party has brought an action before the time when his own performance is due and that time then arrives before he has obtained and enforced a judgment, see Comment c and Illustration 5 to § 238.) There may be circumstances, however, in which it is appropriate for him to require the other party to perform first, as where the parties to a sale of goods contemplate that the buyer will need the time specified between delivery and payment to resell the goods in order to pay the price. In such a case the right of the party in delay to receive payment may be subject to postponement.

Illustration

8. The facts being otherwise as stated in Illustration 6, B duly pays the first three installments, but unjustifiably does not pay the fourth until the fifth is due. If B's failure to pay the fourth

installment discharges A's remaining duties of performance under the rule stated in § 237, A has a claim for damages for total breach (§ 243(1)), and no further performance is due from either party. Otherwise B's failure to pay the fourth installment gives rise to only a claim for damages for partial breach because of the delay, and, unless circumstances make it appropriate for A to require B to pay the fourth installment first, delivery of the deed and payment of the fourth and fifth installments are then due simultaneously.

e. Where performance requires a period of time. Where the performance of one party requires a period of time and the performance of the other party does not, their performance can not be simultaneous. Since one of the parties must perform first, he must forego the security that a requirement of simultaneous performance affords against disappointment of his expectation of an exchange of performances, and he must bear the burden of financing the other party before the latter has performed. See Comment a. Of course the parties can by express provision mitigate the harshness of a rule that requires that one completely perform before the other perform at all. They often do this, for example, in construction contracts by stating a formula under which payment is to be made at stated intervals as work progresses. But it is not feasible for courts to devise such formulas for the wide variety of such cases that come before them in which the parties have made no provision. Centuries ago, the principle became settled that where work is to be done by one party and payment is to be made by the other, the performance of the work must precede payment, in the absence of a showing of a contrary intention. It is sometimes supposed, that this principle grew out of employment contracts, and reflects a conviction that employers as a class are more likely to be responsible than are workmen paid in advance. Whether or not the explanation is correct, most parties today contract with reference to the principle, and unless they have evidenced a contrary intention it is at least as fair as the opposite rule would be.

f. Applicability of rule. The rule stated in Subsection (2) usually finds its application to contracts involving services, such as construction and employment contracts. The common practice of making express provision for progress payments has diminished its importance with regard to the former, and the widespread enactment of state wage statutes giving the employee a right to the frequent periodic payment of wages has lessened its significance with regard to the latter. Nevertheless, it is a helpful rule for residual cases not otherwise provided for. It applies not only to contracts under which the performance of one party is more or less continuous, but also to contracts where performance consists of a series of acts with an interval of time between them. See Comment c. Under a contract of the latter type, simultaneity may be possible in part and, to the extent that it is possible, the rule stated in Subsection (2) is subject to that stated in Subsection (1). See Illustrations 6 and 12.

Illustrations

9. A contracts to do the concrete work on a building being constructed by B for $10 a cubic yard. In the absence of language or circumstances indicating the contrary, payment by B is not due until A has finished the concrete work.

10. The facts being otherwise as stated in Illustration 9, B promises to furnish a bond to secure his payment. No provision is made as to the time for furnishing the bond. No performance by A is due until B has furnished the bond. Although the doing of the concrete work by A requires a period of time and the furnishing of the bond by B does not, the circumstance that the bond is required to secure payment by B indicates that B must furnish the bond first.

11. A contracts to make alterations in B's home for $5,000. $500 is to be paid on the signing of the contract, $1,500 on the starting of work, $2,000 on the completion of rough carpentry and rough plumbing, and $1,000 on the completion of the job. Payment by B is due as the work progresses according to the terms of the contract.

12. A promises to sell land to B, in return for which B promises to pay A $10,000 a year for five years on July 1 of each year. No provision is made as to the time for delivery of a deed. Delivery of a deed is not due until July 1 of the fifth year, at which time delivery of the deed and payment of the last installment are due simultaneously. See Illustration 6.

TOPIC 2. EFFECT OF PERFORMANCE AND NON-PERFORMANCE

§ 235. Effect of Performance as Discharge and of Non-Performance as Breach.

(1) Full performance of a duty under a contract discharges the duty.

(2) When performance of a duty under a contract is due any non-performance is a breach.

Comment

a. Discharge by performance. Under the rule stated in Subsection (1), a duty is discharged when it is fully performed. Nothing less than full performance, however, has this effect and any defect in performance, even an insubstantial one, prevents discharge on this ground. The defect need not be wilful or even negligent. Although a court may ignore trifling departures, performance that is merely substantial does not result in discharge under Subsection (1). See Comment d to § 237. A duty may, of course, be discharged on some other ground. See Chapter 12. For example, a duty that has not been fully performed may be discharged on the ground of impracticability of performance. See Chapter 11.

Illustration

1. A contracts to build a house for B for $50,000 according to specifications furnished by B. A builds the house according to the specifications. A's duty to build the house is discharged.

b. Effect of non-performance. Non-performance is not a breach unless performance is due. Performance may not be due because a required period of time has not passed, or because a condition has not occurred (§ 225), or because the duty has already been discharged (Chapter 12) as, for example, by impracticability of performance (Chapter 11). In such a case non-performance is justified. When performance is due, however, anything short of full performance is a breach, even if the party who does not fully perform was not at fault and even if the defect in his performance was not substantial. Non-performance of a duty when performance is due is a breach whether the duty is imposed by a promise stated in the agreement or by a term supplied by the court (§ 204), as in the case of the duty of good faith and fair dealing (§ 205). Non-performance includes defective performance as well as an absence of performance.

Illustrations

2. The facts being otherwise as stated in Illustration 1, A builds the house according to the specifications except for an inadvertent variation in kitchen fixtures which can easily be remedied for $100. A's non-performance is a breach.

3. A contracts with B to manufacture and deliver 100,000 plastic containers for a price of $100,000. The colors of the containers are to be selected by B from among those specified in the contract. B delays in making his selection for an unreasonable time, holding up their manufacture and causing A loss. B's delay is a breach. His duty of good faith and fair dealing (§ 205) includes a duty to make his selection within a reasonable time.

4. A contracts with B to repair B's building for $20,000, payment to be made "on the satisfaction of C, B's architect, and the issuance of his certificate." A makes the repairs but does not ask C for his certificate. B does not pay A. B's non-performance is not a breach. It is justified on the ground that performance is not due because of the non-occurrence of a condition. See Illustration 5 to § 227.

c. Statute of Frauds. Non-performance can be a breach of a contract even though, at the time of the non-performance, the contract is unenforceable because of the Statute of Frauds (§§ 8, 138). Non-performance when performance is due still gives rise to a claim for damages for which a court will grant relief if the Statute is subsequently satisfied as, for example, by the later signing of a memorandum or by an admission in court. See Comments c and d to § 133 and Comment b to § 136. If the Statute is subsequently satisfied, the claim is one for damages for a breach that occurred previously, at the time of the actual non-performance, and not for one that occurred at the time of the later satisfaction of the Statute.

Illustration

5. A and B make an oral contract, unenforceable under the Statute of Frauds (§ 125), by which A promises to sell and B to buy land for $50,000. Although B tenders the money, A fails to tender a deed and later writes a letter to B which satisfies the Statute of Frauds. A's non-performance is a breach and gives rise to a claim for damages, even though the claim is unenforceable until A writes the letter. See Illustration 4 to § 133.

§ 236. Claims for Damages for Total and for Partial Breach.

(1) A claim for damages for total breach is one for damages based on all of the injured party's remaining rights to performance.

(2) A claim for damages for partial breach is one for damages based on only part of the injured party's remaining rights to performance.

Comment

a. Breach. A breach may be one by non-performance (§ 235(2)), or by repudiation (§ 253), or by both (§ 243). Every breach gives rise to a claim for damages, and may give rise to other remedies. Even if the injured party sustains no pecuniary loss or is unable to show such loss with sufficient certainty, he has at least a claim for nominal damages. See § 346(2). If a court chooses to ignore a trifling departure (Comment a to § 235), there is no breach and no claim arises.

b. Total and partial breach distinguished. Although every breach gives rise to a claim for damages, not every claim for damages is one for damages based on all of the injured party's remaining rights to performance under the contract. Such a claim is said to be one for damages for total breach. (The injured party's remaining duties under the contract are not necessarily discharged, however. Even if performances are to be exchanged under an exchange of promises, a duty of the injured party to give a performance that is not part of that exchange of performances is not discharged (§ 237). And a duty of the injured party to give a performance that is the agreed equivalent of performance that has been given by the other party is not discharged (§ 240).) If the injured party elects to or is required to await the balance of the other party's performance under the contract, his claim is said instead to be one for damages for partial breach. For example, an injured party who claims damages in addition to specific performance claims damages for partial breach. Rules for determining whether a particular breach gives rise to a claim for damages for partial breach, for total breach, or for either partial or total breach at the election of the injured party are stated in §§ 243 and 253.

Illustrations

1. A contracts with B to build a building on B's land, work to commence on May 1 and to be completed by October 1. On May 10, A has not yet commenced work. If the court concludes that A's breach, although material (§ 241), has not continued for such a length of time that B is discharged (§ 242), B has a claim against A for damages caused by the delay, but this is not a claim for damages based on all of B's remaining rights to performance. B's claim is one for damages for partial breach. See § 243.

2. The facts being otherwise as stated in Illustration 1, B cancels the contract. If the court concludes that A's breach is not only material but has continued for such a length of time that B is discharged (§ 242), B has a claim against A for damages based on all of his remaining rights to performance. B's claim is one for damages for total breach. See § 243.

§ 237. Effect on Other Party's Duties of a Failure to Render Performance.

Except as stated in § 240, it is a condition of each party's remaining duties to render performances to be exchanged under an exchange of promises that there be no uncured material failure by the other party to render any such performance due at an earlier time.

Comment

a. Effect of non-occurrence of condition. Under the rule stated in this Section, a material failure of performance, including defective performance as well as an absence of performance, operates as the non-occurrence of a condition. Under § 225, the non-occurrence of a condition has two possible effects on the duty subject to that condition. See Comment a to § 225. The first is that of preventing performance of the duty from becoming due, at least temporarily (§ 225(1)). The second is that of discharging the duty when the condition can no longer occur (§ 225(2)). A material failure of performance has, under this Section, these effects on the other party's remaining duties of performance with respect to the exchange. It prevents performance of those duties from becoming due, at least temporarily, and it discharges those duties if it has not been cured during the time in which performance can occur. The occurrence of conditions of the type dealt with in this Section is required out of a sense of fairness rather than as a result of the agreement of the parties. Such conditions are therefore sometimes referred to as "constructive conditions of exchange." Cf. § 204. What is sometimes referred to as "failure of consideration" by courts and statutes (e.g., Uniform Commercial Code § 3–408) is referred to in this Restatement as "failure of performance" to avoid confusion with the absence of consideration. Circumstances significant in determining whether a failure is material are set out in § 241. Circumstances significant in determining the period of time after which remaining duties are discharged, if a material failure has not been cured, are set out in § 242. The rules stated in this Section and the one following apply without regard to whether or not the failure of performance is a breach. They apply, for example, even though the failure is justified on the ground of impracticability of performance (Chapter 11). Illustrations of the operation of these rules in situations in which the failure is justified are given in other chapters under the sections that deal with the particular justification, such as impracticability. See, e.g., §§ 267, 268. The illustrations in this Chapter concern, for the most part, their operation in situations where the failure is a breach. But see, e.g., Illustration 3. The rules of this Section and the one following apply even when the promise of the party in default is unenforceable under the Statute of Frauds, while the promise of the other party is enforceable. See § 140. They are, of course, subject to variation by agreement of the parties.

Illustrations

1. A contracts to build a house for B for $50,000, progress payments to be made monthly in an amount equal to 85% of the price of the work performed during the preceding month, the balance to be paid on the architect's certificate of satisfactory completion of the house. Without justification B fails to make a $5,000 progress payment. A thereupon stops work on the house and a week goes by. A's failure to continue the work is not a breach and B has no claim against A. B's failure to make the progress payment is an uncured material failure of performance which operates as the non-occurrence of a condition of A's remaining duties of performance under the exchange. If B offers to make the delayed payment and in all the circumstances it is not too late to cure the material breach, A's duties to continue the work are not discharged. A has a claim against B for damages for partial breach because of the delay.

2. The facts being otherwise as stated in Illustration 1, B fails to make the progress payment or to give any explanation or assurances for one month. If, in all the circumstances, it is now too late for B to cure his material failure of performance by making the delayed payment, A's duties to continue the work are discharged. Because B's failure to make the progress payment was a breach, A also has a claim against B for total breach of contract (§ 243).

3. A, a theater manager, contracts with B, an actress, for performance by her for a period of six months in a play that A is about to present. B dies during the first week of the performance. A's remaining duties with respect to the exchange of performances are discharged by B's uncured material failure of performance. Because B's failure is justified on the ground of impossibility (§ 262), A has no claim against B's estate.

b. First material failure of performance. In many disputes over failure of performance, both parties fail to finish performance, and the question is whether one of them is justified in so doing by the other party's failure. (Compare Comment d.) This Section states the fundamental rule under which that question is to be answered. (The liability of the other party for damages for total breach is governed by the rule stated in § 243.) The rule is based on the principle that where performances are to be exchanged under an exchange of promises, each party is entitled to the assurance that he will not be called upon to perform his remaining duties of performance with respect to the expected exchange if there has already been an uncured material failure of performance by the other party. The central problem is in determining which party is chargeable with the first uncured material failure of performance. In determining the relative times when performance is due, the terms of the agreement and the supplementary rules on time for performance should be considered (§§ 233, 234). In determining whether there has been a failure of performance, the terms of the agreement and the supplementary rules such as those on omitted essential terms (§ 204) and the duty of good faith and fair dealing (§ 205) should be considered. In determining whether a failure of performance is material, the circumstances listed in § 241 should be considered. Even if the failure is material, it may still be possible to cure it by subsequent performance without a material failure. In the event of cure the injured party may still have a claim for any remaining non-performance as well as for any delay. In determining when it is too late to cure a failure of performance, the circumstances listed in § 242 should be considered. In making all of these determinations the situation of the parties is to be viewed as of the time for performance and in terms of the actual failure. If, for example, under the terms of the agreement the order of performance depends on an event subsequent to the time of the making of the contract, that event is to be taken into account.

Illustrations

4. A contracts to sell and B to buy at a stated price four parcels of land which A does not own but which the parties expect A to acquire by purchase at a foreclosure sale. A bids on the four parcels at the foreclosure sale, but each time B bids against him and acquires all four for less than the contract price. A does not convey the four parcels to B. B has no claim against A. B's bidding at the sale was a material breach of his duty of good faith and fair dealing (§ 205), which operated as the non-occurrence of a condition of A's duties and discharged them.

5. A, a contractor, and B, a subcontractor, make a contract under which B promises to install sewer pipe in a trench which A is to dig and maintain during installation. A unjustifiably so fails to maintain the trench that it fills with water, severely hindering installation. B thereupon stops work and refuses to continue unless the breach is cured. A does not cure his breach. If A's breach is material (§ 241), it operates as the non-occurrence of a condition of B's duty to build the sewer, discharging it, and A has no claim against B. If A's breach is not material, B's duties are not discharged, and B's stopping work and refusing to continue is a breach.

6. A contracts to sell and B to buy on 30 days credit 3,000 tons of iron rails at a stated price. B purchases iron rails heavily from various sources for use in his business, and in consequence A has difficulty in securing 3,000 tons and the market price is substantially increased. A fails to deliver the rails. B has a claim against A for breach of contract. B's purchase of iron rails from other sources for use in his business is not a failure of performance because B is under no duty to refrain from purchasing for that purpose. A's failure to deliver the rails is therefore a breach.

7. The facts being otherwise as stated in Illustration 6, B maliciously buys iron rails heavily from various sources in order to prevent A from performing his contract with B. B has no claim against A. B's malicious purchase of iron rails from other sources is a material breach of his duty of good faith and fair dealing (§ 204), which operates as the non-occurrence of a condition of A's duty to deliver the rails, discharging it.

c. Ignorance immaterial. The non-occurrence of a condition of a party's duty has the effects stated in § 225 even though that party does not know of its non-occurrence. See Comment e to § 225. It follows that one party's material failure of performance has the effect of the non-occurrence of a condition of the other party's remaining duties, under the rule stated in this Section, even though that other party does not know of the failure. If the other party is discharged as the result of an unjustified material failure of which he is ignorant, he has a claim for damages for total breach (§ 245). But any loss that he has suffered as a result of his own actions taken in ignorance of the breach cannot be recovered since his actions were not caused by the other's breach. See Illustrations 8 and 9.

A party's ignorance may, however, cause him to lose rights under rules other than the one stated in this section. He may, for example, be precluded from relying on a condition where, through ignorance, he fails to make timely objection. So, under Uniform Commercial Code § 2–608, a buyer of goods who accepts them in ignorance of their defects loses his right to insist upon strict performance as a condition of his duty to pay the price. Other rules may preclude a party from relying on a failure of performance as the non-occurrence of a condition where, because of unreasonable ignorance, he has accepted the other party's performance or has given no reasons or the wrong reasons for its rejection. See, e.g., §§ 246 and 248; Uniform Commercial Code §§ 2–605, 2–607.

Illustrations

8. A and B make an employment contract. After the service has begun, A, the employee, commits a material breach of his duty to give efficient service that would justify B in discharging him. B is not aware of this but discharges A for an inadequate reason. A has no claim against B for discharging him. B has a claim against A for damages for total breach (§ 243) based on B's loss due to A's failure to give efficient service up to the time of discharge, but not for damages based on the loss of A's services after that time, because that loss was caused by B's discharge of A and not by A's failure to give efficient service.

9. A contracts to sell and B to buy goods on 30 days credit. A delivers defective goods, which B rejects in ignorance of their defects. A has no claim against B. B has a claim against A for total breach (§ 243), but can recover nominal damages only since the unavailability of the goods to B was caused by B's rejection and not by their defects.

10. The facts being otherwise as stated in Illustration 9, when B rejects the goods he states an insufficient reason, which induces a failure by A to cure the defects in the goods. B is precluded from relying on the defects to justify his rejection, not because of his ignorance itself, but because his giving of an insufficient reason for rejection excused the non-occurrence of the condition of his duty to take and pay for the goods (§ 248; Uniform Commercial Code § 2–605).

d. Substantial performance. In an important category of disputes over failure of performance, one party asserts the right to payment on the ground that he has completed his performance, while the other party refuses to pay on the ground that there is an uncured material failure of performance. (Compare Comment b.) A typical example is that of the building contractor who claims from the owner payment of the unpaid balance under a construction contract. In such cases it is common to state the issue, not in terms of whether there has been an uncured material failure by the contractor, but in terms of whether there has been substantial performance by him. This manner of stating the issue does not change its substance, however, and the rule stated in this Section also applies to such cases. If there has been substantial although not full performance, the building contractor has a claim for the unpaid balance and the owner has a claim only for damages. If there has not been substantial performance, the building contractor has no claim for the unpaid balance, although he may have a claim in restitution (§ 374). The considerations in determining whether performance is substantial are those listed in § 241 for determining whether a failure is material. See Comment b to § 241. If, however, the parties have made an event a condition of their agreement, there is no mitigating standard of materiality or substantiality applicable to the non-occurrence of that event. If, therefore, the agreement makes full performance a condition, substantial performance is not sufficient and if relief is to be had under the contract, it must be through excuse of the non-occurrence of the condition to avoid forfeiture. See § 229 and Illustration 1 to that section.

Illustration

11. A contracts to build a house for B, for which B promises to pay $50,000 in monthly progress payments equal to 85% of the value of the work with the balance to be paid on completion. When A completes construction, B refuses to pay the $7,500 balance claiming that there are defects that amount to an uncured material breach. If the breach is material, A's performance is not substantial and he has no claim under the contract against B, although he may have a claim in restitution (§ 374). If the breach is not material, A's performance is said to be substantial, he has a claim under the contract against B for $7,500, and B has a claim against A for damages because of the defects.

e. Duties affected. Under the rule stated in this Section, only duties with respect to the performances to be exchanged under the particular exchange of promises are affected by a failure of one of those performances. A duty under a separate contract is not affected (see Comment d to § 231 and Illustration 5 to that section), nor is a duty under the same contract affected if it was not one to render a performance to be exchanged under an exchange of promises (see Illustrations 3 and 4 to § 232). Furthermore, only duties to render performance are affected. A claim for damages that has already arisen as a result of a claim for partial breach is not discharged under the rule stated in this Section.

Illustration

12. A contracts to build a building for B. B delays making the site available to A, giving A a claim against B for damages for partial breach. A then commits a material breach and B properly cancels the contract. B has a claim against A for damages for total breach, but A still has a claim against B for damages for partial breach.

§ 238. Effect on Other Party's Duties of a Failure to Offer Performance.

Where all or part of the performances to be exchanged under an exchange of promises are due simultaneously, it is a condition of each party's duties to render such performance that the other party either render or, with manifested present ability to do so, offer performance of his part of the simultaneous exchange.

Comment

a. Effect of offer to perform. Where the performances are to be exchanged simultaneously under an exchange of promises, each party is entitled to refuse to proceed with that simultaneous exchange until he is reasonably assured that the other party will perform at the same time. If a party actually performs, his performance both discharges his own duty (§ 235(1)) and amounts to the occurrence of a condition of the other party's duty (§ 237). But it is not necessary that he actually perform in order to produce this latter effect. It is enough that he make an appropriate offer to perform, since it is a condition of each party's duties of performance with respect to the exchange that there be no uncured material failure by the other party at least to offer performance. Circumstances significant in determining whether a failure is material are set out in § 241. Such an offer of performance by a party amounts to the occurrence of a condition of the other party's duty to render performance, although it does not amount to performance by the former. Until a party has at least made such an offer, however, the other party is under no duty to perform, and if both parties fail to make such an offer, neither party's failure is a breach. (If one of the parties is already in breach, as where he has repudiated or has failed to go to the place appointed for the simultaneous exchange, the other party's duty to render performance may already have been discharged under §§ 253(2) or 237, giving him a claim for damages for total breach under §§ 253(1) or 243(1).) When it is too late for either to make such an offer, both parties are discharged by the non-occurrence of a condition. A failure to offer performance can be cured, if an appropriate offer is made in time (§ 242). Cf. Comment b to § 237. The fact that a party is ignorant of a defect in the other party's offer is immaterial. See Comment c to § 237.

Illustrations

1. A contracts to sell and B to buy a machine for $10,000, delivery of the machine and payment of the price to be made at a stated place on July 1. On July 1 both parties are present at that place, but A neither delivers nor offers to deliver the machine and B neither pays nor offers to pay the price. A has no claim against B, and B has no claim against A. See Uniform Commercial Code §§ 2–507(1) and 2–511(1). If, however, B had committed a material breach by failing to go to the stated place, A would have had a claim against B for damages for total breach. See §§ 237, 243.

2. The facts being otherwise as stated in Illustration 1, on July 2, B, with manifested present ability to do so, offers to pay the price if A simultaneously delivers the machine, but A refuses to deliver the machine. If the delay of one day does not exceed the time after which A is discharged (§ 242), A's refusal is a breach. If it exceeds that time, B has no claim against A.

b. What amounts to an offer to perform. An offer of performance meets the requirement stated in this Section even though it is conditional on simultaneous performance by the other party. The offer must be accompanied with manifested present ability to make it good, but the offeror need not go so far as actually to hold out that which he is to deliver. (On the meaning of the term "manifested," see Comment b to § 2.) Thus the Uniform Commercial Code § 2–503(1) requires only "that the seller put and hold conforming goods at the buyer's disposition and give the buyer any notice reasonably necessary to enable him to take delivery." In this respect the requirement of this Section is less exacting than that of tender under, for example, § 45 or § 62. Any conduct, including tender, that goes beyond an offer of performance will, of course, also satisfy the requirement. The requirement of an offer of performance is to be applied in the light of what is reasonably to be expected by the parties in view of the practical difficulties of absolute simultaneity (see Comment b to § 234) and is subject to the agreement of the parties, as supplemented or qualified by usage (§§ 221, 222) and course of dealing (§ 223).

Illustration

3. A contracts to sell and B to buy land for $50,000. The land is to be conveyed free of liens and encumbrances, but B knows that it is subject to a $30,000 mortgage held by C which A expects to satisfy out of the $50,000 purchase price. A, in the presence of B and C, makes a conditional offer of a deed of the property subject to the mortgage, and both A and C present documents that are legally sufficient to satisfy the mortgage debt to be delivered immediately on payment of the price by B. B thereupon refuses to pay the price. In view of the circumstances at the time the contract was made, A's offer is sufficient, and A has a claim against B for damages for total breach of contract.

c. Judicial supervision. In an action for specific performance or for the price, a court may ensure that the party seeking relief makes an offer of performance that meets the requirements of this Section by granting relief conditional on such an offer. Uniform Commercial Code § 2–709(2), for example, provides that "where the seller sues for the price, he must hold for the buyer any goods which have been identified to the contract and are still in his control. . . ." See Illustration 4. See also Comment a to § 358 with respect to specific performance. If performances, although not originally due simultaneously, have become due simultaneously after the commencement of the action because the earlier performance has been delayed, the granting of such relief is equally appropriate. Even though the performances do not become due simultaneously until after judgment, the court may exercise its power on either the defendant's request or on its own motion. See Illustration 5.

Illustrations

4. The facts being otherwise as stated in Illustration 1, on July 1, A puts the machine at B's disposition and requests that he pay for it. B refuses to pay and A, after attempting unsuccessfully to resell the machine, brings an action for the price under Uniform Commercial Code § 2–709. A court will award judgment for the full price only if A holds the machine for the buyer during the action. See Uniform Commercial Code § 2–709(2).

5. A promises to sell real estate to B, delivery of the deed to be four years from July 1. B promises to pay $50,000 in installments of $10,000 on each July 1 for five years. B duly pays the first three installments but does not pay the fourth, and A brings an action to recover it. A has judgment but the judgment is not collected until after the July 1 when the payment of the fifth installment and the delivery are due. The court will restrain collection of the judgment until A makes an offer to transfer the real estate conditional on being paid the amount of the judgment and also the fifth installment of the price. See Illustration 8 to § 234 and Illustration 2 to § 358.

§ 239. Effect on Other Party's Duties of a Failure Justified by Non-Occurrence of a Condition.

(1) A party's failure to render or to offer performance may, except as stated in Subsection (2), affect the other party's duties under the rules stated in §§ 237 and 238 even though failure is justified by the non-occurrence of a condition.

(2) The rule stated in Subsection (1) does not apply if the other party assumed the risk that he would have to perform in spite of such a failure.

Comment

a. General rule. The rules stated in §§ 237 and 238 apply to any uncured material failure, whether or not it is a breach. They therefore apply even when a party's failure is justified on the ground that performance has not become due because of the non-occurrence of a condition of his duty (§ 224). Subsection (1) makes it clear that this is so, as a general rule. The general rule is based on the premise that the other party did not assume the risk that he would have to perform even if the expected exchange was not forthcoming because of the non-occurrence of the condition. His expectation is that even if the condition does not occur, he will not be called upon to perform unless that exchange is forthcoming. He is therefore entitled to refuse to perform if there is a failure of the return performance, even if that failure is not a breach because of the non-occurrence of the condition. In that case, he has, of course, no claim for damages, although he may have one in restitution. See §§ 370–77.

Illustration

1. A contracts to sell and B to buy a house for $50,000. The contract contains the provision, "This contract is conditional on approval by X Bank of B's pending mortgage application." Approval by X Bank is a condition of B's duty, and therefore if X Bank does not approve B's application, performance by B will not become due, even if A makes an offer of a deed. But it is not a condition of A's duty and therefore performance by A will become due if, although X Bank does not approve B's application, B makes an offer to pay $50,000. See Illustration 4 to § 226. Under the rule stated in this Section, performance by A will not become due if B does not pay or offer to pay $50,000 because A did not assume the risk that he would nonetheless have to perform.

b. Assumption of risk. Subsection (2) states an exception to the general rule to cover the case in which a party assumes the risk that he will have to perform even if the agreed exchange is not forthcoming because of the non-occurrence of a condition. Since a condition is by definition not certain to occur (§ 224), every obligee of a conditional duty assumes a risk. It is the premise of the general rule that he assumes only the risk that if the condition does not occur, the expected exchange will not be carried out on either side. See Illustration 1. But sometimes he assumes the greater risk that, if the condition does not occur, he will have to carry out his side of the exchange even though it is not carried out on the other side. If he has assumed this greater risk, then conduct on the other side which would otherwise operate as a failure to perform under § 237 or to offer to perform under § 238 does not so operate. The nature of the risk taken by a party who enters into such an exchange of promises is sometimes indicated by describing the promise that he receives as "aleatory." See Comment c to § 232.

Illustrations

2. A, a general contractor, contracts with B, a subcontractor, for the plumbing work on a construction project. B is to receive $100,000, payable monthly as the work progresses "on condition that Owner shall have paid Contractor therefor." B works for three months and makes monthly requests for payment of a total of $60,000 from A. When A does not pay B because the owner has not paid A for the plumbing work, B stops work and a month later notifies A that he cancels the contract. If the court determines, in the light of the quoted language and other circumstances, that B assumed the risk that he would have to perform even if A did not pay him on the ground that the owner did not pay A, A's justifiable non-payment on that ground does not operate as a failure to perform under § 237 and therefore B's cancellation is a breach. Compare Illustration 1 to § 227 and Illustration 2 to § 237.

3. The facts being otherwise as stated in Illustration 2, A unjustifiably refuses to pay B, although the owner has paid A for the plumbing work. Although B assumed the risk that he would have to perform even if A did not pay on the ground that the owner did not pay A, A's non-payment is not justified on that ground and therefore operates as a failure to perform under § 237. If a court concludes that the failure is material and that B's cancellation came when it was too late for A to cure it, B's cancellation is not a breach. Compare Illustration 1 to § 227 and Illustration 2 to § 237.

§ 240. Part Performances as Agreed Equivalents.

If the performances to be exchanged under an exchange of promises can be apportioned into corresponding pairs of part performances so that the parts of each pair are properly regarded as agreed equivalents, a party's performance of his part of such a pair has the same effect on the other's duties to render performance of the agreed equivalent as it would have if only that pair of performances had been promised.

Comment

a. Mitigating effect of the rule. Under the rule stated in § 237, a party's failure to perform may cause him to lose his right to the agreed exchange after he has relied substantially on the expectation of that exchange, as by either preparation or performance. The risk of forfeiture is similar to that which arises on the non-occurrence of a condition stated in the agreement. See Comment a to § 227. But because the failure must be material in order to have this effect under § 237, courts can temper the application of those sections in appropriate cases to avoid forfeiture in a way that is not possible where the agreement itself states the condition. Compare §§ 241 and 242 with § 229. In addition, forfeiture may sometimes be reduced or avoided by allowing a party whose failure has been material to have restitution in accordance with the policy favoring avoidance of unjust enrichment. See §§ 370–77. This Section embodies another mitigating doctrine which reduces the risk of forfeiture in that important class of cases in which it is proper to regard corresponding parts of the performances of each party as agreed equivalents. Its effect is to give a party who has performed one of these parts the right to its agreed equivalent just as if the parties had made a separate contract with regard to that pair of corresponding parts. A failure as to some other part does not affect this right. See Comment d to § 231. Of course, if the failure amounts to a breach, the injured party has a claim for damages. Substantial performance of such a part has the same effect with regard to such a pair of agreed equivalents as substantial performance of the whole has under § 237 with respect to the entire contract. See Comment d to § 237.

  b. *Separate contracts distinguished.* When it is proper to regard parts of pairs of corresponding performances under a contract as agreed equivalents, the contract is sometimes loosely said to be "divisible" or "severable." But under the rule stated in this Section, the pairs of corresponding parts are not treated as if they were separate contracts. If there are two separate contracts, one party's performance under the first and the other party's performance under the second are not to be exchanged under a single exchange of promises, and even a total failure of performance by one party as to the first has no necessary effect on the other party's duty to perform the second. Comment d to § 231. (On the situation if the failure gives reasonable grounds to believe that the other party will commit a breach of the second, see §§ 251 and 252.) This is not so, however, if there is a single contract under which the parties are to exchange performances, even though it is proper to regard pairs of corresponding parts of those performances as agreed equivalents. If there is an uncured material failure by either party, he can claim compensation for any parts that he has already performed, but he cannot enforce the contract with respect to any other pair of corresponding parts, including the part or parts that he has failed to perform. See Illustration 3. With respect to those parts the rule of § 237 still applies, for the parties are bound by a single contract and not by a series of separate contracts for each pair of corresponding parts. Although the pairs of performances may be regarded as agreed equivalents, the parties exchanged promises for an exchange of their whole performances.

Illustrations

  1. A contracts to sell and B to buy a quantity of dressed hogs and a quantity of live hogs at stated prices for each quantity. A is to deliver the dressed hogs first and the live hogs 15 days later, and B is to pay for each delivery within 30 days after it is made. A delivers the dressed hogs, but unjustifiably refuses to deliver the live ones. If a court finds that delivery of the dressed hogs and payment of the price stated for them are agreed equivalents, A can recover the stated price for the dressed hogs under the contract. B then has a claim against A for damages for his failure to deliver the live hogs.

  2. The facts being otherwise as stated in Illustration 1, A has no right to payment for either the dressed or the live hogs until 30 days after delivery of the live ones, but A unjustifiably refuses to deliver the live hogs until B pays for the dressed ones. If a court finds that delivery of the dressed hogs and the price stated for them are agreed equivalents, A can recover the stated price for the dressed hogs under the contract. See § 227(1). B then has a claim against A for damages for his failure to deliver the live hogs.

  3. The facts being otherwise as stated in Illustration 1, before A delivers the dressed hogs, he repudiates the contract by stating that he will not deliver the live ones. B then refuses to accept the dressed hogs. Even if a court finds that delivery of the dressed hogs and payment of the price stated for them are agreed equivalents, A has no claim against B. B has a claim against A for damages for total breach of contract (§ 253).

  c. *Order of performance distinguished.* The terms "divisible" and "severable" are sometimes used, not only in determining whether the rule stated in this Section is applicable, but also in determining whether a party's performance is due at one time or in installments (§ 233). Many of the contracts covered by the rule stated in this Section happen also to be contracts in which performance of each party is to be given in installments, corresponding to the times of the other party's performance. Indeed, the fact that the order of performance involves such pairs of corresponding parts may suggest that it is proper to regard those pairs as agreed equivalents. But it does not necessarily follow that it is proper, and in many contracts under which performance is to be in pairs of corresponding parts, it is not proper to regard the parts of those pairs as agreed equivalents. See Illustrations 7 and 9. Conversely, in many contracts under which performance of one or both parties is to be at one time, it is proper to regard those performances as composed of pairs of agreed equivalents. See Illustrations 2, 8 and 10. Two distinct determinations are involved and it is undesirable to obscure this by employing the same terminology for both.

d. Apportionment. The rule stated in this Section cannot be applied unless the parties' performances can be apportioned into corresponding pairs of part performances. The process of apportionment is essentially one of calculation and the rule can only be applied where calculation is feasible. It is enough, however, if the price of separate items is separately stated in the agreement itself or in a price list on which the agreement was based, or can be reliably ascertained from stated prices for components or from a total price for similar items.

Illustrations

4. A contracts with B to work for one year as a real estate salesman and to devote his full time to this work. A is to receive half of the real estate commission on all sales that he effects. A devotes full time to this work for ten months, but unjustifiably devotes only part time for the last two months. A court may apportion the unpaid commissions earned by A into those earned during the first ten months and those earned under the last two months according to the formula stated in the contract and, if it finds that working full time for ten months and the commissions on the sales over those months are agreed equivalents, A can recover the unpaid commissions for those months under the contract. B then has a claim against A for damages for his failure to devote full time during the last two months.

5. A contracts with B to furnish the rights to 23 motion pictures to be selected by B from a much larger list over a period of five years. The contract states a total price of $23,000, but does not break it down into $1,000 for each picture. A furnishes B with the rights to only 14 pictures, which B shows, and then A unjustifiably refuses to furnish the rights to 9 others. A court may apportion the price as $1,000 for each picture and, if it finds that the furnishing of rights to 14 pictures and the payment of $14,000 are agreed equivalents, A can recover that amount under the contract. B has a claim for damages against A for his failure to furnish the rights to the 9 other pictures.

e. Agreed equivalents. The corresponding pairs of performances so apportioned only come within the rule stated in this Section if it is proper to regard the parts of each pair as agreed equivalents. The parties may, by express provision, determine either that it is or is not proper so to regard them. But they do not often do this, and, because separate pairs of corresponding parts are not the subjects of separate bargains (see Comment b), the parties usually cannot even be said to have had any actual intention on the point. Whether it is proper to regard the parts of each pair as agreed equivalents will usually depend on considerations of fairness, similar to those that guide a court in deciding whether to supply a term under § 204. Decisions holding that a contract is or is not "divisible" or "severable" for some other purpose, for example in connection with the rules in Chapter 8, Unenforceability on Grounds of Public Policy, are not determinative under this Section. See also Comments b and c. The standard under this Section, like that of materiality under § 237, is necessarily a somewhat imprecise and flexible one. It requires that the parts of a pair be of roughly equivalent value to the injured party in terms of his expectation with respect to the total agreed exchange. This is because fairness requires that a party, having received only a fraction of the performance that he expected under a contract, not be asked to pay an identical fraction of the price that he originally promised on the expectation of full performance, unless it appears that the performance that he actually received is worth to him roughly that same fraction of what full performance would have been worth to him. Therefore the mere fact that the subject of the contract is sold by weight or measure and the total price determined by a unit price (e.g., per pound or cubic yard or acre) does not result in agreed equivalents. The injured party will not be required to pay for a part of the performance that he has received if he cannot make full use of that part without the remainder of the performance, as, for example, where a buyer has received a machine but not an attachment necessary for its operation. In deciding whether the injured party can make full use of only part, a court must, of course, take account of the possibility that the remainder of the performance can be easily obtained from some other source, as, for example, where the attachment is available on the market.

Illustrations

6. A contracts with B to do specified work on B's subdivision. A is to do the excavation and grading of lots and streets for a lump sum price of $75,000, payable on completion of that part of the work. A is then to make street improvements, including the installation of curbs and gutters, for stated unit prices, payable on completion of that part of the work. A is to provide separate performance bonds for each part. A does the excavation and grading of lots and streets but then unjustifiably refuses to make street improvements. B refuses to pay A for excavation and grading, although he can easily have the street improvements made by another contractor. The excavation and grading of lots and streets and the payment of $75,000 are agreed equivalents. A has a claim against B for $75,000 under the contract for the excavation and grading. B has a claim for damages against A for his unjustified failure to make street improvements.

7. A contracts to build a house for B for $50,000, progress payments to be made monthly in an amount equal to 85% of the price of the work performed during the preceding month, the balance to be paid on the architect's certificate of satisfactory completion of the house. A unjustifiably stops work at the end of a month before the work is substantially completed and sues for the progress payment for that month. The performance during that month and the corresponding progress payment are not agreed equivalents. A can recover nothing under the contract for that performance. B has a claim against A for damages for breach. Whether A has a claim against B in restitution is determined under the rules stated in §§ 370–77.

8. A contracts with B to drive 10,000 logs from various points down a river to B's boom at one cent per log mile. Because of a flood, A drives only 5,763 logs an average distance of 100 miles each to B's boom, and leaves the other 4,237 logs on the banks part of the way to B's boom. B expects to resell the logs and can resell the 5,763 at the same unit price as the entire 10,000. The driving of the logs to B's boom and the corresponding price at the contract rate are agreed equivalents, but the driving of logs part way and the corresponding price at the contract rate are not. A can recover $5,763 under the contract for the 5,763 logs that he has driven to B's boom, but can recover nothing for the remaining 4,237 logs that he has driven only part of the way. If A's failure to drive the remaining logs to B's boom is unjustified, it is a breach, and B has a claim against A for damages. Whether A's failure is justified on the ground of impracticability of performance is determined under the rules stated in §§ 261 and 263.

9. The United States contracts with A under an "Industrial Preparedness Contract" for the production in volume of an electronic device. The work is to be done in three steps. Step I requires A to draw up plans and make a pilot run. Step II requires A to acquire equipment for production. Step III, to be taken only in case of national emergency and after receipt of an order from the United States, requires volume production and delivery in accordance with a stated schedule. A is required to maintain a state of readiness for this step over a six-year period. Specified payments are to be made on the completion of Steps I and II and against deliveries during Step III. A completes Steps I and II and, after having been paid $150,000, repudiates the contract when $50,000 is still unpaid on Step II. A sues for that unpaid balance of $50,000. The completion of Steps I and II and the payment of the amounts specified in the contract for those steps are not agreed equivalents. A has no claim against the United States for that performance. The United States has a claim against A for damages for breach.

10. A contracts with B to construct and maintain ten signs advertising B's motel for $1,600 a year, $100 each for eight smaller signs and $400 each for two larger signs. The signs are of a special design not easily obtainable elsewhere. A constructs and maintains only seven of the smaller and one of the larger signs, unjustifiably failing to construct the other two. A's failure to construct the remaining two signs will not appreciably diminish the effect of the other eight. The construction and maintenance of the eight signs and the corresponding price at the contract rate are agreed equivalents. A can recover $1,100 a year under the contract for the signs that he constructs and maintains. B has a claim against A for damages for breach.

11. The facts being otherwise as stated in Illustration 10, the signs are part of a series beginning "10 more miles to B's place," so that the failure to construct the remaining two will appreciably diminish the effect of the other eight. The construction and maintenance of each sign and the corresponding price at the contract rate are not agreed equivalents. A can recover nothing under the contract for the signs that he constructs and maintains. B has a claim against A for damages for breach. Whether A has a claim against B in restitution is determined under the rules stated in §§ 370–77.

§ 241. Circumstances Significant in Determining Whether a Failure Is Material.

In determining whether a failure to render or to offer performance is material, the following circumstances are significant:

(a) the extent to which the injured party will be deprived of the benefit which he reasonably expected;

(b) the extent to which the injured party can be adequately compensated for the part of that benefit of which he will be deprived;

(c) the extent to which the party failing to perform or to offer to perform will suffer forfeiture;

(d) the likelihood that the party failing to perform or to offer to perform will cure his failure, taking account of all the circumstances including any reasonable assurances;

(e) the extent to which the behavior of the party failing to perform or to offer to perform comports with standards of good faith and fair dealing.

Comment

a. Nature of significant circumstances. The application of the rules stated in §§ 237 and 238 turns on a standard of materiality that is necessarily imprecise and flexible. (Contrast the situation where the parties have, by their agreement, made an event a condition. See § 226 and Comments a and c thereto and § 229.) The standard of materiality applies to contracts of all types and without regard to whether the whole performance of either party is to be rendered at one time or part performances are to be rendered at different times. See Uniform Commercial Code § 2–612. It also applies to pairs of agreed equivalents under § 240. See Illustration 2. It is to be applied in the light of the facts of each case in such a way as to further the purpose of securing for each party his expectation of an exchange of performances. This Section therefore states circumstances, not rules, which are to be considered in determining whether a particular failure is material. A determination that a failure is not material means only that it does not have the effect of the non-occurrence of a condition under §§ 237 and 238. Even if not material, the failure may be a breach and give rise to a claim for damages for partial breach (§§ 236, 243).

Illustrations

1. A, a subcontractor, contracts to do excavation and earth moving on a housing subdivision project for B, the owner and general contractor, and to do all work "in a workmanlike manner." B is to make monthly progress payments for the work performed during the preceding month less a retainer of ten percent. A negligently damages a building with his bulldozer causing serious damage and denies any liability for B's loss. When B refuses to make further progress payments until A repairs the damage or admits liability, A notifies B that he cancels the contract. If the court determines that A's breach is material, A has no claim against B. B has a claim against A for damages for breach of contract.

2. The facts being otherwise as stated in Illustration 6 to § 240, A completes the part concerned with the excavation and grading of lots and streets but fails in a minor respect to comply with the specifications. If a court determines that the failure is not material, A has a claim against B for $75,000 under the contract for the excavation and grading. B has a claim for damages against A for his failure fully to perform as to excavation and grading and also for his unjustified refusal to make street improvements.

b. Loss of benefit to injured party. Since the purpose of the rules stated in §§ 237 and 238 is to secure the parties' expectation of an exchange of performances, an important circumstance in determining whether a failure is material is the extent to which the injured party will be deprived of the benefit which he reasonably expected from the exchange (Subsection (a)). If the consideration given by either party consists partly of some performance and only partly of a promise (see Comment a to § 232), regard must be had to the entire exchange, including that performance, in applying this criterion. Although the relationship between the monetary loss to the injured party as a result of the failure and the contract price may be significant, no simple rule based on the ratio of the one to the other can be laid down, and here, as elsewhere under this Section, all relevant circumstances must be considered. In construction contracts, for example, defects affecting structural soundness are ordinarily regarded as particularly significant. In the sale of goods a particularly exacting standard has evolved. There it has long been established that, in the absence of a showing of a contrary intention, a buyer is entitled to expect strict performance of the contract, and Uniform Commercial Code § 2–601 carries forward this expectation by allowing the buyer to reject "if the goods or the tender of delivery fail in any respect to conform to the contract." The Code, however, compensates to some extent for the severity of this standard by extending the seller's right to cure beyond the point when the time for performance has expired in some instances (§ 2–508(2)), by allowing revocation of acceptance only if a nonconformity "substantially impairs" the value of the goods to the buyer (§ 2–608(1)), and by allowing the injured party to treat a nonconformity or default as to one installment under an installment contract as a breach of the whole only if it "substantially impairs" the value of the whole (§ 2–612(3)).

c. Adequacy of compensation for loss. The second circumstance, the extent to which the injured party can be adequately compensated for his loss of benefit (Subsection (b)), is a corollary of the first. Difficulty that he may have in proving with sufficient certainty the amount of that loss will affect the adequacy of compensation. If the failure is a breach, the injured party always has a claim for damages, and the question becomes one of the adequacy of that claim to compensate him for the lost benefit. Where the failure is not a breach, the question becomes one of the adequacy of any claim, such as one in restitution, to which the injured party may be entitled. This is a particularly important circumstance when the party in breach seeks specific performance. Such relief may be granted if damages can adequately compensate the injured party for the defect in performance. See Comment c to § 242.

d. Forfeiture by party who fails. Because a material failure acts as the non-occurrence of a condition, the same risk of forfeiture obtains as in the case of conditions generally if the party who fails to perform or tender has relied substantially on the expectation of the exchange, as through preparation or performance. Therefore a third circumstance is the extent to which the party failing to perform or to make an offer to perform will suffer forfeiture if the failure is treated as material. For this reason a failure is less likely to be regarded as material if it occurs late, after substantial preparation or performance, and more likely to be regarded as material if it occurs early, before such reliance. For the same reason the failure is more likely to be regarded as material if such preparation or performance as has taken place can be returned to and salvaged by the party failing to perform or tender, and less likely to be regarded as material if it cannot. These factors argue against a finding of material failure and in favor of one of substantial performance where a builder has completed performance under a construction contract and, because the building is on the owner's land, can salvage nothing if he is denied recovery of the balance of the price. Even in such a case, however, the potential forfeiture may be mitigated if the builder has a claim in restitution (§§ 370–77, especially § 374) or if he has already received progress payments under a provision of the contract. The same factors argue for a finding of material failure where a seller tenders goods and can salvage them by resale to others if they are rejected and he is denied recovery of the price. This helps to explain the severity of the rule as applied to the sale of goods. See Comment b. Even in such a case, however, the potential forfeiture may be aggravated if the seller has manufactured the goods specially for the buyer or has spent substantial sums in shipment.

Illustrations

3. A contracts to sell and B to buy 300 crates of Australian onions, shipment to be from Australia in March. A has 300 crates ready for shipment in March, but government requisitions prevent him from loading more than 240 crates on the only ship available in March. B refuses to accept or pay for the onions when they are tendered. Under the circumstances stated in Subsections (a) and (c), A's failure is material and A has no claim against B. If A's failure is unjustified, B has a claim against A for damages for partial breach because of the delay even if A cures his failure, and has a claim against A for damages for total breach if A does not cure his failure (§ 243).

4. The facts being otherwise as stated in Illustration 2 to § 232, B can have the part of the street in front of his own lot paved for $500, but this will not give him the expected access to his lot

because the rest of the street is not paved. Under the circumstances stated in Subsections (a), (b), and (c), the failure of performance is material and A has no claim against B. If A's failure is unjustified, B has a claim against A for damages for partial breach because of the delay even if A cures his failure, and has a claim against A for damages for total breach if A does not cure his failure (§ 243).

e. Uncertainty. A material failure by one party gives the other party the right to withhold further performance as a means of securing his expectation of an exchange of performances. To the extent that that expectation is already reasonably secure, in spite of the failure, there is less reason to conclude that the failure is material. The likelihood that the failure will be cured is therefore a significant circumstance in determining whether it is material (Subsection (d)). The fact that the injured party already has some security for the other party's performance argues against a determination that the failure is material. So do reasonable assurances of performance given by the other party after his failure. So does a shift in the market that makes performance of the contract more favorable to the other party. On the other hand, defaults by the other party under other contracts or as to other installments under the same contract argue for a determination of materiality. So does such financial weakness of the other party as suggests an inability to cure. This circumstance differs from the notion of reasonable grounds for insecurity (§ 251), in that the former can become relevant only after there has been an actual failure to perform or to tender. On discharge by repudiation, see § 253(2).

Illustration

5. A contracts to sell and B to buy land for $25,000. B is to make a $5,000 down payment and pay the balance in four annual installments of $5,000 each. A is to proceed immediately to have abstracts of title prepared showing a marketable title and to deliver them prior to the time for payment of the first annual installment. Without explanation, A fails to have abstracts prepared for delivery prior to the time for payment of the first annual installment. B refuses to pay that installment. Under the circumstances stated in Subsections (a)-(d), the failure of performance is material and A has no claim against B. B has a claim against A for damages for partial breach based on the delay if A cures his failure and a claim for damages for total breach if he does not (§ 243).

f. Absence of good faith or fair dealing. A party's adherence to standards of good faith and fair dealing (§ 205) will not prevent his failure to perform a duty from amounting to a breach (§ 236(2)). Nor will his adherence to such standards necessarily prevent his failure from having the effect of the non-occurrence of a condition (§ 237; cf. § 238). The extent to which the behavior of the party failing to perform or to offer to perform comports with standards of good faith and fair dealing is, however, a significant circumstance in determining whether the failure is material (Subsection (e)). In giving weight to this factor courts have often used such less precise terms as "wilful." Adherence to the standards stated in Subsection (e) is not conclusive, since other circumstances may cause a failure to be material in spite of such adherence. Nor is non-adherence conclusive, and other circumstances may cause a failure not to be material in spite of such non-adherence.

Illustrations

6. A contracts to build a house for B, using pipe of Reading manufacture. In return, B agrees to pay $75,000, with provision for progress payments. Without B's knowledge, a subcontractor mistakenly uses pipe of Cohoes manufacture which is identical in quality and is distinguishable only by the name of the manufacturer which is stamped on it. The substitution is not discovered until the house is completed, when replacement of the pipe will require destruction of substantial parts of the house. B refuses to pay the unpaid balance of $10,000. Under the circumstances stated in Subsections (a), (c), and (e), the failure of performance is not material and A has a claim against B for the unpaid balance of $10,000, subject to a claim by B against A for damages for A's breach of his duty to use Reading pipe. See Illustration 1 to § 229.

7. A contracts to build a supermarket for B. In return B agrees to pay $250,000, with provision for progress payments. A completes performance except that, angered by a dispute over an unrelated transaction, he refuses to build a cover over a compressor. B can have the cover built by another builder for $300. B refuses to pay the unpaid balance of $40,000. In spite of the circumstances stated in Subsection (e), under the circumstances stated in Subsections (a), (b), and (c), the failure of

performance is not material and A has a claim against B for the unpaid balance of $40,000, subject to a claim by B against A for damages for A's breach of his duty to build a cover over the compressor.

§ 242. Circumstances Significant in Determining When Remaining Duties Are Discharged.

In determining the time after which a party's uncured material failure to render or to offer performance discharges the other party's remaining duties to render performance under the rules stated in §§ 237 and 238, the following circumstances are significant:

(a) those stated in § 241;

(b) the extent to which it reasonably appears to the injured party that delay may prevent or hinder him in making reasonable substitute arrangements;

(c) the extent to which the agreement provides for performance without delay, but a material failure to perform or to offer to perform on a stated day does not of itself discharge the other party's remaining duties unless the circumstances, including the language of the agreement, indicate that performance or an offer to perform by that day is important.

Comment

a. Cure. Under §§ 237 and 238, a party's uncured material failure to perform or to offer to perform not only has the effect of suspending the other party's duties (§ 225(1)) but, when it is too late for the performance or the offer to perform to occur, the failure also has the effect of discharging those duties (§ 225(2)). Ordinarily there is some period of time between suspension and discharge, and during this period a party may cure his failure. Even then, since any breach gives rise to a claim, a party who has cured a material breach has still committed a breach, by his delay, for which he is liable in damages. Furthermore, in some instances timely performance is so essential that any delay immediately results in discharge and there is no period of time during which the injured party's duties are merely suspended and the other party can cure his failure.

b. Significant circumstances. This Section states circumstances which are to be considered in determining whether there is still time to cure a particular failure, or whether the period of time for discharge has expired. They are similar to the circumstances stated in the preceding section. The importance of delay to the injured party will depend on the extent to which it will deprive him of the benefit which he reasonably expected (§ 241(a)) and on the extent to which he can be adequately compensated (§ 241(b)). The extent of the forfeiture by the party failing to perform or to offer to perform (§ 241(c)) is also significant in determining the importance of delay. The likelihood that the injured party's withholding of performance will induce the other party to cure his failure is particularly important (§ 241(d)), because the very reason for suspending rather than immediately discharging the injured party's duties is that this will induce cure. The reasonableness of the injured party's conduct in communicating his grievances and in seeking satisfaction is a factor to be considered in this connection. Where performance is to extend over a period of time, as where delivery of goods is to be in installments, so that a continuing relationship between the parties is contemplated, the injured party may be expected to give more opportunity for cure than in the case of an isolated exchange. On discharge by repudiation, see § 253(2). Finally, the nature of the behavior of the party failing to perform or to offer to perform may be considered here as under the preceding section (§ 241(e)).

Illustration

1. The facts being otherwise as stated in Illustration 1 to § 237, B tenders the progress payment after a two-day delay along with damages for the delay. A refuses to accept the payment and resume work and notifies B that he cancels the contract. B's tender cured his breach before A's remaining duties to render performance were discharged, and B has a claim against A for total breach of contract, subject to a claim by A against B for damages for partial breach because of the delay.

c. Substitute arrangements. It is often said that in commercial transactions, notably those for the sale of goods, prompt performance by a party is essential if he is to be allowed to require the other to perform or, as it is sometimes put, "time is of the essence." The importance of prompt delivery by a seller of goods generally derives from the circumstance that goods, as contrasted for example with land, are particularly likely to be subject to rapid fluctuations in market price. Therefore, even a relatively short delay in a rising market may adversely affect the buyer by causing a sharp increase in the cost of "cover." See Uniform Commercial Code §§ 2–712, 2–713. A less rigid standard applies to contracts for the sale of goods to be delivered in installments or to be specially manufactured for the buyer. On the other hand, considerable delay does not preclude enforcement of a contract for the sale of land if damages are adequate to compensate for the delay and there are no special circumstances indicating that prompt performance was essential and no express provision requiring such performance. But these are all merely particular applications of a more general principle. Subsection (b) states that principle. Under any contract, the extent to which it reasonably appears to the injured party that delay may prevent or hinder him from making reasonable substitute arrangements is a consideration in determining the effect of delay. Cf. § 241(a), (b). As in the case of § 241 (see Comment c), a party in breach who seeks specific performance may be granted relief with compensation for the delay, in circumstances where he would have no claim for damages.

Illustrations

2. A, a theater manager, contracts with B, an actress, for her performance for six months in a play that A is about to present. B becomes ill during the second month of the performance, and A immediately engages another actress to fill B's place during the remainder of the six months. B recovers at the end of ten days and offers to perform the remainder of the contract, but A refuses. Whether B's failure to render performance due to illness immediately discharges A's remaining duties of performance, instead of merely suspending them, depends on the circumstances stated in Subsection (b) and in § 241(b) and (d), and in particular on the possibility as it reasonably appears to A when B becomes ill of the illness being only temporary and of A's obtaining an adequate temporary substitute.

3. A contracts to sell and B to buy 1,000 shares of stock traded on a national securities exchange, delivery and payment to be on February 1. B offers to pay the price on February 1, but A unjustifiably and without explanation fails to offer to deliver the stock until February 2. B then refuses to accept the stock or pay the price. Under the circumstances stated in Subsection (b) and in § 241(a) and (c), the period of time has passed after which B's remaining duties to render performance are discharged because of A's material breach and A therefore has no claim against B. B has a claim against A for breach.

4. A contracts to sell and B to buy land, the transfer to be on February 1. B tenders the price on February 1, but A does not tender a deed until February 2. B then refuses to accept the deed or pay the price. Under the circumstances stated in Subsections (b) and (c) and in § 241(a), in the absence of special circumstances, the period of time has not passed after which B's remaining duties to render performance are discharged. Although A's breach is material, it has been cured. A has a claim against B for damages for total breach of contract, subject to a claim by B against A for damages for partial breach because of the delay.

5. A agrees to sell and B to buy land, the transfer to be on February 1. A tenders a sufficient deed on February 1, but B explains that although he wants to carry out the contract he would like to have a few weeks more to raise the amount of the price. A replies that unless B tenders the price immediately he will not deliver the deed. On February 15, B sues for specific performance, offering in his pleading to pay the agreed price with interest to compensate A for the delay. In the circumstances stated in Subsection (b) and in § 241(a), (b), and (d), the period of time has not passed after which A's remaining duties to render performance are discharged. Although B's breach is material, the court may decree specific performance subject to B's tender of the price and payment by B of damages for partial breach to compensate A for the delay.

6. A contracts to sell and B to buy 5,000 tons of iron at a stated price, delivery to be in five monthly installments of 1,000 tons each on the first of each month and payment for each installment to be made on the tenth of that month. A makes the first three deliveries on the first of the month but, although the market price for iron is falling, he delays twelve days in making the fourth delivery, explaining to B that temporary labor troubles have caused the delay. B notifies A that he refuses to take or pay for the fourth delivery and that he cancels the contract. Whether the period of time has passed after which B's remaining duties to render performance are discharged, so that B's notification

is not a repudiation, depends on the circumstances stated in Subsection (b) and in § 241(a), (b), (d), and (e). See Uniform Commercial Code § 2–612.

7. A contracts to sell and B to buy 5,000 tons of iron at a stated price, delivery to be in five monthly installments of 1,000 tons each on the first of each month and payment for each installment to be made on the tenth of that month. A makes the first four deliveries on the first of the month, and B makes the first three payments by the tenth but does not make the fourth payment. The market price for iron is falling and B gives no assurances or explanation for the delay. On the twentieth of the month A notifies B that he will make no further deliveries and that he cancels the contract. Whether the period of time has passed after which A's remaining duties to render performance are discharged, so that A's notification is not a repudiation, depends on the circumstances stated in Subsection (b) and in § 241(a), (b), (d), and (e). See Uniform Commercial Code § 2–612.

d. Effect of agreement. The agreement of the parties often contains a provision for the time of performance or tender. It may simply provide for performance on a stated date. In that event, a material breach on that date entitles the injured party to withhold his performance and gives him a claim for damages for delay, but it does not of itself discharge the other party's remaining duties. Only if the circumstances, viewed as of the time of the breach, indicate that performance or tender on that day is of genuine importance are the injured party's remaining duties discharged immediately, with no period of time during which they are merely suspended. It is, of course, open to the parties to make performance or tender by a stated date a condition by their agreement, in which event, absent excuse (see Comment b to § 225 and Comment c to § 229), delay beyond that date results in discharge (§ 225(2)). Such stock phrases as "time is of the essence" do not necessarily have this effect, although under Subsection (c) they are to be considered along with other circumstances in determining the effect of delay.

Illustrations

8. A contracts to charter a vessel belonging to B and to pay stipulated freight "on condition that the vessel arrive in New York ready for loading by March 1." B promises that the vessel will arrive by that date and carry A's cargo. B unjustifiably fails to have the vessel in New York to be loaded until March 2. A refuses to load the vessel. Whether or not the period of time has passed after which B's uncured material failure would discharge A's remaining duties to render performance, A's duties are discharged under § 225(2) by the non-occurrence of an event that is made a condition by the agreement of the parties. B has no claim against A. A has a claim against B for damages for total breach.

9. The facts being otherwise as stated in Illustration 4, the parties use a printed form contract that provides that "time is of the essence." Absent other circumstances indicating that performance by February 1 is of genuine importance, A has a claim against B for damages for total breach of contract.

10. The facts being otherwise as stated in Illustration 4, the contract provides that A's rights are "conditional on his tendering a deed on or before February 1." A has no claim against B. But cf. Illustration 4 to § 229.

e. Excuse and reinstatement. Just as a party may under § 84 promise to perform in spite of the complete non-occurrence of a condition, he may under that section promise to perform in spite of a delay in its occurrence. If he places no limit on the delay, his power to impose a time limit by later notification of the other party is subject to the rules on reinstatement stated in § 84(2).

§ 243. Effect of a Breach by Non-Performance as Giving Rise to a Claim for Damages for Total Breach.

(1) With respect to performances to be exchanged under an exchange of promises, a breach by non-performance gives rise to a claim for damages for total breach only if it discharges the injured party's remaining duties to render such performance, other than a duty to render an agreed equivalent under § 240.

(2) Except as stated in Subsection (3), a breach by non-performance accompanied or followed by a repudiation gives rise to a claim for damages for total breach.

(3) Where at the time of the breach the only remaining duties of performance are those of the party in breach and are for the payment of money in installments not related to one another, his breach by non-performance as to less

§ 243

than the whole, whether or not accompanied or followed by a repudiation, does not give rise to a claim for damages for total breach.

(4) In any case other than those stated in the preceding subsections, a breach by non-performance gives rise to a claim for total breach only if it so substantially impairs the value of the contract to the injured party at the time of the breach that it is just in the circumstances to allow him to recover damages based on all his remaining rights to performance.

Comment

a. Promises exchanged in an expectation of an exchange of performances. Under § 236, a claim for damages for total breach is one for damages based on all of the injured party's remaining rights to performance while a claim for damages for partial breach is one that is based on only part of those rights. No precise general rule can be stated for determining in all cases when a breach gives rise to a claim for damages for total breach and when it gives rise to a claim merely for damages for partial breach. Subsection (1), however, states a rule for the most significant type of case—the case in which performances are to be exchanged under an exchange of promises, and the breach occurs before the injured party has fully performed his duties with respect to the expected exchange. The breach, if it is material (§ 241), will operate as the non-occurrence of a condition of those remaining duties (§ 237). This will at least justify the injured party in suspending his performance (§ 225(1)), and will, if the breach is not cured in time (§ 242), discharge his remaining duties of performance (§ 225(2)). Under the rule stated in Subsection (1), the injured party has a claim for damages for total breach if, but only if, those remaining duties are discharged. See Comment b to § 236 and Illustration 2 to § 237. (The injured party also has a claim for damages for total breach as the result of a material breach in, for example, Illustrations 4, 5, and 6 to § 237 and Illustrations 2 and 6 to § 240). There is, of course, an exception where the injured party has already, at the time of the breach, come under a duty to render performance of an agreed equivalent under the rule stated in § 240. Such a duty is not discharged, even if there is a material breach, and its survival does not prevent the injured party from claiming damages for total breach under Subsection (1). In contrast to the situation where there is a repudiation (see Comment b), the injured party has a choice in the situation contemplated in Subsection (1). If, in spite of the breach, he wishes to await performance by the party in breach and to have merely a claim for damages for partial breach rather than for total breach, he can excuse the non-occurrence of the condition of his remaining duties (§ 237) by promising to perform them in spite of its non-occurrence (§ 84). His remaining duties are then not discharged, and the rule stated in Subsection (1) does not apply. The injured party need not do this expressly (see Comment e to § 84), but may do so by his actions in the course of performance. See §§ 246, 247.

Illustrations

1. A promises to sell to B a lot in a subdivision for $8,000. B promises to pay in four installments of $2,000 each, beginning one year after execution of the contract. A promises to begin to make improvements and pave the streets within 60 days and to complete work within a reasonable time and promises to deliver a deed at the time of the final payment. A commits a material breach by unjustifiably failing to pave the streets, and B thereupon refuses to pay any installments. After a reasonable time for A to cure his material breach has passed (§ 242), B's duty to pay the price is discharged, and he has a claim against A for damages for total breach.

2. The facts being otherwise as stated in Illustration 1, B pays the first installment although he knows of A's material breach. B's payment operates as a promise to pay the remaining installments in spite of the non-occurrence of a condition of his duty to do so. See § 237; Illustration 5 to § 84. B's duty to pay the price is not discharged, and he has a claim against A merely for damages for partial breach because of the delay.

b. Effect of repudiation. Under the rule stated in Subsection (2), if a repudiation (§ 250) accompanies or follows a breach by non-performance, the injured party generally has a claim for damages for total breach. A repudiation does not, however, have this effect in those circumstances in which, under the rule stated in Subsection (3), nothing less than a breach as to the whole gives rise to such a claim (see Comment c and Illustrations 4 and 5). A repudiation together with a breach by non-performance, therefore, has this effect in all cases in which a repudiation alone would give rise to a claim for total breach (§ 253) and in some additional cases (see Illustrations 3 and 8). An injured party who has a claim for damages for total breach as a result of a repudiation, and who asserts a claim merely for damages for partial breach, runs the risk that if he prevails he will be barred under the doctrine of merger from further recovery, even in the event of a subsequent breach, because he has "split a cause of action." See Restatement, Second, Judgments §§ 24–26. His position differs from that of the injured party under the rule stated in Subsection (1), who can, by promising to perform in spite of a breach (§ 84), prevent the breach from discharging his remaining duties of performance, avoid its giving rise to a claim for damages for total breach at all, and thereby treat it as giving rise to a claim merely for damages for partial breach (see Comment a). Where a repudiation accompanies or follows a breach that would, if the injured party so chose, give rise to a claim for damages for total breach under Subsection (1), both Subsections (1) and (2) apply. In that case, the injured party cannot avoid the consequence described above of having a claim for damages for total breach under the rule stated in Subsection (2). Even under the rule stated in Subsection (2), however, the injured party can assert a claim for damages for a partial breach without prejudice to a claim for damages arising out of a subsequent breach if he and the repudiator agree that the latter's performance under the contract is to be continued. Furthermore, he is not barred from claiming specific relief under the contract merely because he has a claim for damages for total breach (see Comment a to § 359). If the repudiator nullifies his repudiation (§ 256(1)), the injured party still has a claim for damages for the breach by nonperformance but it may then be a claim merely for damages for partial breach (see Comment a to § 256).

Illustration

3. A contracts to sell and B to buy for $8,000 a subdivision lot on which B plans to build a house for himself. Delivery of the deed and payment of the price are to be made within 30 days, and A promises to make improvements and pave the streets within one year. A delivers the deed and B pays the price within 30 days. A paves the streets and makes most but not all of the improvements within one year, but then repudiates by unjustifiably telling B that he refuses to make the rest of the improvements. B has a claim against A for damages for total breach, even though absent a repudiation B's claim might be merely one for damages for partial breach. See Illustration 8. If A and B then agree that A will make the rest of the improvements, B has a claim against A merely for damages for partial breach because of the delay.

c. Duties on one side. The rule stated in Subsection (3) applies only where all the remaining duties at the time of the breach are those of the party in breach. It therefore applies where the parties have exchanged promise for performance (§ 72), and where the parties have exchanged promise for promise (§ 74) and the injured party has fully performed. It is well established that if those duties of the party in breach at the time of the breach are simply to pay money in installments, not related to one another in some way, as by the requirement of the occurrence of a condition with respect to more than one of them, then a breach as to any number less than the whole of such installments gives rise to a claim merely for damages for partial breach. Whether there is a relationship between installments or other acts depends on the extent to which, in the circumstances, a breach as to less than the whole of such installments or acts can substantially affect the injured party's expectation under the contract.

d. Avoiding harsh results of limitations. Dissatisfaction with the rule stated in Subsection (3) often manifests itself by the inclusion in the agreement of an acceleration clause under which the remaining installments become due, either automatically or at the option of the injured party, on a breach as to one installment, so that such non-performance gives rise to a claim for damages for total breach. Even when the injured party has no claim for damages for total breach, he may be entitled to equitable relief, a declaratory judgment, an installment judgment, or restitution (see Comment b to § 359), to the extent that these remedies are permitted. The degree to which the limitation might yield on a showing of manifest injustice, as where the refusal to pay is not in good faith or where fraud on creditors is involved, is unclear. Problems of assuring performance of such obligations to pay in installments on the debtor's death, dissolution, or bankruptcy arise even where no breach by non-performance has occurred, and are not dealt with in this Restatement. See Comment c to § 250.

Illustrations

4. A borrows $10,000 from B and promises to repay with interest in ten monthly installments. A unjustifiably fails to pay the first four installments. B has a claim against A merely for damages for

partial breach for non-payment of the four unpaid installments. The result is the same even if A repudiates by telling B that he will not make the payments.

5. A, an insurer, issues a policy of disability insurance to B under which monthly payments are to be made to B and the payment of additional premiums waived if B is totally and permanently disabled. B suffers total and permanent disability. A makes monthly payments for a year and then unjustifiably fails to make further payments. After A has been in default for a year, B sues A. B has a claim against A merely for damages for partial breach for non-payment during the second year. The result is the same even if A repudiates by telling B that he will not make the payments.

e. General criterion. The rules stated in Subsections (1), (2) and (3) cover most of the significant cases. Subsection (4) states a general rule for residual cases. Under that rule the criterion is whether the breach so substantially impairs the value of the contract to the injured party at the time of the breach that it is just to allow him to recover damages based on all his remaining rights to performance. This determination is to be made in the light of all the circumstances, taking account of the difficulty of calculating damages for total breach and of any uncertainties that could be avoided if the injured party were given a claim merely for damages for partial breach. The criterion is essentially that of Uniform Commercial Code § 2–610 and, here as there, "The most useful test of substantial value is to determine whether material inconvenience or injustice will result if the aggrieved party is forced to wait . . ." (Comment 3). Although the considerations listed in §§ 241 and 242 are intended for use in determining whether the injured party is discharged, not in determining whether he has a claim for damages for total breach, some of them are relevant to this latter determination. Among these are the extent to which the injured party will be deprived of the benefit that he reasonably expected (§ 241(a)), the likelihood that the party in breach will cure his breach (§ 241(d)), the extent to which the behavior of the party in breach comports with standards of good faith and fair dealing (§ 241(e)), and the extent to which further delay will prevent or hinder the injured party in making reasonable substitute arrangements (§ 242(b)).

Illustrations

6. For a fee of $25,000, paid in advance, A contracts with B, an impresario, to sing in five concerts offered to the public as a series. A unjustifiably fails to sing in the first two concerts. A's breach so substantially impairs the value of the contract to B that B has a claim against A for damages for total breach.

7. The facts being otherwise as stated in Illustration 3, A does not repudiate but, in spite of repeated requests from B, does not make improvements or pave streets for two years. A's breach so substantially impairs the value of the contract to B that B has a claim against A for damages for total breach.

8. The facts being otherwise as stated in Illustration 3, A does not repudiate and gives B reasonable assurances that the remaining improvements will be completed with a delay of no more than one month. B has a claim against A merely for damages for partial breach because of the delay.

§ 244. Effect of Subsequent Events on Duty to Pay Damages.

A party's duty to pay damages for total breach by non-performance is discharged if it appears after the breach that there would have been a total failure by the injured party to perform his return promise.

Comment

a. Rationale. If the parties are to exchange performances under an exchange of promises, each party's duties to render performance are generally regarded as conditional on the other party's performance, or at least on his readiness to perform (§§ 237, 238, 251, 253). This principle applies even though one party is already in breach by non-performance. His duty to pay damages is discharged if it subsequently appears that there would have been a total failure of performance by the injured party. A failure is total in this context if it would have been sufficient to have discharged any remaining duties of the party in breach to render his performance. See § 242. The result follows even if it appears that the failure would have been justified and not a breach. Cf. § 254 (1).

Illustration

1. A contracts to sell and B to buy a particular machine. B is to pay the price on June 15 and A is to deliver the machine on July 1, at which time risk of loss is to pass to B. B does not pay on June 15, and on June 20 the machine is accidentally destroyed. B's duty to pay damages to A for his non-payment is discharged.

§ 245. Effect of a Breach by Non-Performance as Excusing the Non-Occurrence of a Condition.

Where a party's breach by non-performance contributes materially to the non-occurrence of a condition of one of his duties, the non-occurrence is excused.

Comment

a. Excuse of non-occurrence of condition. Where a duty of one party is subject to the occurrence of a condition, the additional duty of good faith and fair dealing imposed on him under § 205 may require some cooperation on his part, either by refraining from conduct that will prevent or hinder the occurrence of that condition or by taking affirmative steps to cause its occurrence. Under § 235(2), non-performance of that duty when performance is due is a breach. See Illustration 3 to § 235. Under this Section it has the further effect of excusing the non-occurrence of the condition itself, so that performance of the duty that was originally subject to its occurrence can become due in spite of its non-occurrence. See Comments b and c to § 225. The rule stated in this Section only applies, however, where the lack of cooperation constitutes a breach, either of a duty imposed by the terms of the agreement itself or of a duty imposed by a term supplied by the court. There is no breach if the risk of such a lack of cooperation was assumed by the other party or if the lack of cooperation is justifiable.

Illustrations

1. A contracts with B to repair B's building for $20,000, payment to be made "on the satisfaction of C, B's architect, and the issuance of his certificate." A fully performs his duty to make the repairs, but B induces C to refuse to issue his certificate. A has a claim against B for $20,000. B's breach of his duty of good faith and fair dealing contributed materially to the non-occurrence of the condition, the issuance of the certificate, excusing it. Cf. Illustrations 5, 6, 7, and 8 to § 227.

2. A contracts to sell and B to buy land for $100,000. At the same time A contracts to pay C, a real estate broker, as his commission, $5,000 "on the closing of title." A unjustifiably refuses to consummate the sale. C has a claim against A for $5,000, less any expenses that C saved because the sale was not consummated. A's breach of his duty of good faith and fair dealing contributed materially to the non-occurrence of the condition, the closing of title, excusing it. See Illustration 4 to § 227.

3. A contracts to sell and B to buy a house for $50,000, with the provision, "This contract is conditional on approval by X Bank of B's pending mortgage application." B fails to make reasonable efforts to obtain approval and, when the X Bank disapproves the application, refuses to perform when A tenders a deed. A has a claim against B for total breach of contract. B's breach of his duty of good faith and fair dealing contributed materially to the non-occurrence of the condition, approval of the application, excusing it. Cf. Illustration 8 to § 225.

4. A contracts to sell and B to buy A's rights as one of three lessees under a mining lease in Indian lands. The contract states that it is "subject only to approval by the Secretary of the Interior," which is required by statute. B files a request for approval but A fails to support B's request by giving necessary cooperation. Approval is denied and A cannot convey his rights. B has a claim against A for total breach of contract. A's breach of his duty of good faith and fair dealing contributed materially to the non-occurrence of the condition, approval by the Secretary of the Interior, excusing it.

b. Contribute materially. Although it is implicit in the rule that the condition has not occurred, it is not necessary to show that it would have occurred but for the lack of cooperation. It is only required that the breach have contributed materially to the non-occurrence. Nevertheless, if it can be shown that the condition would not have occurred regardless of the lack of cooperation, the failure of performance did not contribute materially to its non-occurrence and the rule does not apply. The burden of showing this is properly thrown on the party in breach.

Illustrations

5. A and B, about to become man and wife, make an antenuptial contract under which A is to pay B $100,000 if B survives A. Four years after their marriage, A shoots both B and himself. B dies instantly and A dies the following day. B's estate has a claim against A's estate for $100,000. A's breach of his duty of good faith and fair dealing contributed materially to the non-occurrence of the condition, B's surviving A, excusing it. The fact that B's estate cannot show that B would otherwise have survived A does not prevent it from recovering the $100,000. Compare the rule on certainty in § 352.

6. A, the owner of a manufacturing plant, contracts to transfer the plant to B. B is to pay A $500,000 plus a bonus of $100,000 if the profits from the plant exceed a stated amount during the first year of its operation. Six months after the transfer B sells the plant to C, who dismantles it. B refuses to pay the bonus. Whether A has a claim against B depends on whether B's failure to operate the plant for a year is a breach of his duty of good faith and fair dealing which contributed materially to the non-occurrence of the condition, the profits exceeding the stated amount during the first year, excusing it. The fact that A cannot show that the profits would otherwise have exceeded the stated amount does not prevent him from recovering. If, however, B shows that they would not have exceeded that amount, A cannot recover. Compare the rule on certainty in § 352.

7. The facts being otherwise as stated in Illustration 4, A shows that even if he had given his cooperation, the Secretary of the Interior would have withheld approval on other grounds. B has no claim against A for breach of contract. A's breach of his duty of good faith and fair dealing did not contribute materially to the non-occurrence of the condition, and its non-occurrence is not excused.

c. Exceptions. Under §§ 237 and 238, it may be required as a condition of one party's duty that the other party perform or offer to perform his duty. A breach by the first party of his duty of good faith and fair dealing will, if material and not cured in time, discharge that duty of the other party (§ 237), eliminating the requirement that the other party perform or offer to perform it. The discharge of the duty has the additional effect of excusing the non-occurrence of the condition. But non-occurrence of the condition is excused only if the duty is discharged. The rule stated in this Section is, therefore, not applicable to such situations. See Illustrations 4, 5, and 7 to § 237.

§ 246. Effect of Acceptance as Excusing the Non-Occurrence of a Condition.

(1) Except as stated in Subsection (2), an obligor's acceptance or his retention for an unreasonable time of the obligee's performance, with knowledge of or reason to know of the non-occurrence of a condition of the obligor's duty, operates as a promise to perform in spite of that non-occurrence, under the rules stated in § 84.

(2) If at the time of its acceptance or retention the obligee's performance involves such attachment to the obligor's property that removal would cause material loss, the obligor's acceptance or retention of that performance operates as a promise to perform in spite of the non-occurrence of the condition, under the rules stated in § 84, only if the obligor with knowledge of or reason to know of the defects manifests assent to the performance.

Comment

a. Acceptance or retention as a promise. Section 84 states the circumstances in which a promise to perform a duty in spite of the non-occurrence of a condition is binding. Non-verbal conduct, such as continued performance with knowledge of the non-occurrence, may amount to a promise under that section. See Comment e and Illustration 4 to § 84. Because acceptance and retention of the other party's performance in spite of the non-occurrence of a condition are both particularly important kinds of such conduct, this Section sets out in detail the circumstances in which acceptance or retention amounts to a promise under the rules stated in § 84. In this context, acceptance of performance means merely voluntary receipt of it, with no implication that it is received in full satisfaction. The acceptance or retention must, of course, be with knowledge of or reason to know of the non-occurrence of the condition.

b. Effect of promise. The rule stated in this Section applies to all conditions other than those excepted by § 84. A particularly important situation in which it finds application occurs where performances are being exchanged under an exchange of promises, and the party who has accepted or retained the other's performance asserts that because of defects in that performance there has been a non-occurrence of a condition of his remaining duties to perform (§ 237). If the rule stated in this Section applies, however, the non-occurrence of the condition is excused, and even if the defects amount to a material failure they do not have the asserted effect. Under the Uniform Commercial Code §§ 2–607, 2–608, and 2–709, for example, the buyer must pay the price for goods accepted and retained in spite of a defective tender if the acceptance was with knowledge of or reason to know of the defect. But it does not follow from one party's mere voluntary receipt of performance that the other party's defective performance has discharged his own duty under § 235(1). Therefore, subject to the rules on discharge in Chapter 12, he is liable for damages for partial breach because of his defective performance. Under Uniform Commercial Code §§ 2–607(2) and 2–714, for example, the buyer's acceptance and retention of the goods does not preclude him from recovering damages for any non-conformity of tender. Not only may a party excuse entirely the non-occurrence of a condition of his duty, but he may excuse a delay in its occurrence. See Comment c to § 225. He may then claim damages for partial breach because of the delay. See Illustration 1.

Illustrations

1. A, a subcontractor, contracts to do excavation and earth moving on a housing subdivision project for B, the owner and general contractor, and to do all work "in a workmanlike manner." B is to make monthly progress payments for the work performed during the preceding month less a retainer of ten percent. A negligently damages a building with his bulldozer causing serious damage and denies any liability for B's loss. B refuses to make further progress payments until A repairs the damage or admits liability, but allows A to continue work on the project. Without any advance notice, B then notifies A that he cancels the contract. A has a claim against B for total breach of contract. Even if a court would otherwise have determined that A's uncured material failure had continued long enough to discharge B's remaining duties of performance, B's acceptance of performance by A operated as a promise to perform, excusing the delay in cure. Cf. Illustration 1 to § 241.

2. A contracts to sell and B to buy a machine for $10,000, delivery to be on March 1 and payment to be within 30 days thereafter. A does not deliver the machine until March 10, in such circumstances that the delay is a material breach. B accepts the machine but refuses to pay the price. A has a claim against B for the price of $10,000 under Uniform Commercial Code § 2–709, subject to a claim by B against A for damages for partial breach because of the delay under Uniform Commercial Code §§ 2–607(2) and 2–714.

c. Acceptance or retention of part. The rule stated in this Section also applies where there has been only a part performance and this has been accepted or retained. Therefore the acceptance of an installment has the same effect as to defects in that installment and in prior installments as the acceptance of the whole performance would have. See Uniform Commercial Code § 2–612(3). Furthermore, the recipient of a whole performance has no right as a general rule to accept part and reject part, and therefore his acceptance of part has the same effect as to defects in the whole as the acceptance of the whole would have. (But cf. Uniform Commercial Code § 2–601(c), which permits a buyer of goods to accept "some commercial units" and reject the rest.) But sometimes a party will accept a conforming part of the other party's performance without knowing or having reason to know that there will subsequently be a failure as to the balance of the performance. Such an acceptance of part will not amount to a promise under the rule stated in this Section. But if the injured party retains that part for an unreasonable time after he knows or has reason to know of the failure with respect to the balance, that retention will amount to a promise, unless it comes within the exception stated in this Section. A comparable rule governs revocation of acceptance under Uniform Commercial Code § 2–608.

Illustrations

3. A contracts to sell and B to buy 10,000 tons of steel, to be delivered in installments of 1,000 tons a month for ten months, payment to be made 90 days after each delivery. A commits a material breach by delay in delivery of the first two installments under such circumstances that B's remaining duties of performance are discharged (§ 237). B nevertheless accepts delivery of the third installment without complaining of the previous breach. B's acceptance amounts to a promise to accept future installments in spite of the material breach. A has a claim against B for the price of each of the three

installments, after the 90 day period has passed, under Uniform Commercial Code § 2–709, subject to a claim by B against A for damages for partial breach because of the delay under Uniform Commercial Code §§ 2–607(2) and 2–714. See Uniform Commercial Code § 2–612(3).

  4. A contracts to sell and B to buy a machine and governor that are sold as a single unit for $10,000, payment to be within 30 days of delivery. A delivers the machine with a defective governor, which constitutes a material breach. B accepts the machine but tenders back the defective governor. B's acceptance of the machine amounts to a promise to pay $10,000 in spite of the defect in the governor. A has a claim against B for the price of $10,000, subject to a claim by B against A for damages for partial breach because of the defect in the governor. See Uniform Commercial Code §§ 2–601 and 2–607.

  5. The facts being otherwise as stated in Illustration 4, A is entitled under the contract to deliver the machine first and the governor later. B accepts the machine, but when he receives the governor he promptly revokes his acceptance and tenders back both the machine and the governor. B's acceptance of the machine does not amount to a promise. A has no claim against B. B has a claim against A for damages for total breach of contract. See Uniform Commercial Code § 2–608.

  d. Performance attached to obligor's property. If the performance is so attached to the obligor's property, real or personal, that removal would cause him material expense or injury, it would be unfair to put him to the choice of either removing the performance or excusing the non-occurrence of the condition. The Section therefore makes an exception for that case. (See § 373 as to the possibility of a right to restitution in that case.) If, however, the obligor goes beyond mere acceptance and retention of the performance and manifests assent to it in spite of the non-occurrence of the condition, Subsection (2) provides that his conduct amounts to a promise under the rule stated in § 84. In order to have this effect his assent need only be to treat the performance as the occurrence of the condition; it need not be to receive it in full satisfaction of the other's duty. See Comment b.

Illustrations

  6. A contracts to build a house for B on B's land for $50,000, payable in part in monthly progress payments with the balance due on completion. A builds the house but unjustifiably departs from the specifications in a number of respects. B moves into and uses the house, knowing of some of the departures and not knowing or having reason to know of others. B refuses to pay the balance of $10,000. B can rely on all of the departures, including those of which he knew, to show that A's breach is material and that A has no claim against B for the $10,000 balance under the contract.

  7. The facts being otherwise as stated in Illustration 6, B tells A that he "will take" the house in spite of those departures of which he knows. B can rely on the departures of which he did not know or have reason to know, but not on the departures of which he knew, to show that A's breach is material and that A has no claim against B to the $10,000 balance under the contract. If B fails to show that A's breach is material, A's claim against B for the $10,000 balance is subject to B's claim against A for damages for partial breach because of all of the departures, including those of which he knew.

§ 247. Effect of Acceptance of Part Performance as Excusing the Subsequent Non-Occurrence of a Condition.

An obligor's acceptance of part of the obligee's performance, with knowledge or reason to know of the non-occurrence of a condition of the obligor's duty, operates as a promise to perform in spite of a subsequent non-occurrence of the condition under the rules stated in § 84 to the extent that it justifies the obligee in believing that subsequent performances will be accepted in spite of that non-occurrence.

Comment

  a. Acceptance or retention of part. An obligor's acceptance or retention of part performance in spite of the non-occurrence of a condition of his duty may have two effects. First, it may operate as a promise to perform that duty in spite of that non-occurrence under the rule stated in the preceding section. Second, it may operate as a promise to perform in spite of a subsequent non-occurrence of the condition under the rule stated in this Section. It only has this second effect, however, to the extent that it justifies the obligee in believing that subsequent performance will be accepted in spite of that non-occurrence. Where, for example, there have been successive acceptances of defective installments, the obligee may be justified in believing that subsequent installments will be accepted in spite of similar defects. Not only may a party excuse entirely the non-occurrence of a condition of his duty, but he may excuse its non-occurrence during the period of time in which it would otherwise have to occur. See Comment c to § 225 and Illustration 1.

Illustrations

1. A contracts to sell and B to buy land for $10,000, the price to be payable in a down payment and 36 monthly installments and the deed to be delivered on payment of the last installment. The agreement provides that payment of installments on the dates due is a condition of A's duty to deliver a deed. B does not pay any of the first twelve installments on the dates due, but A accepts them without comment. B tenders the thirteenth installment after the date due, but not later than was generally the case for the previous payments. The non-occurrence of the condition during the period of time in which it would otherwise have to occur, failure to pay the thirteenth installment on the date due, is excused and A's duty is not discharged. A has, however, a claim against B for damages for partial breach because of the delay.

2. A contracts to build a house for B for $50,000, payable in part in monthly progress payments with the balance due on completion, all payments to be made on condition that A present a certificate from B's architect showing that the work has been properly completed. B makes the last six out of seven progress payments without presentation of an architect's certificate and without asking for one, and A materially changes his position in reliance on this. Although A fully performs, B refuses to pay the $10,000 balance because of A's failure to present an architect's certificate. The non-occurrence of the condition, presentation of the architect's certificate, is excused and A has a claim against B for $10,000.

b. Reinstatement. Since, under this Section, acceptance or retention amounts to a promise under the rules stated in § 84, the obligor can again make his duty subject to the condition by notifying the obligee of his intention to do so. His right to reinstate the requirement of the condition is, however, subject to the restrictions stated in § 84(2), and he cannot reinstate it if, for example, to do so will be unjust because of a material change of position by the obligee.

Illustrations

3. The facts being otherwise as stated in Illustration 1, A notifies B at the time that the twelfth installment is due that he intends to require prompt payment of the thirteenth and subsequent installments. The non-occurrence of the condition during the period of time in which it would otherwise have to occur, failure to pay the thirteenth installment on the date due, is not excused by A's previous acceptance without comment of delayed installments.

4. The facts being otherwise as stated in Illustration 2, B notifies A shortly before completion of construction and after A has materially relied that he intends to require presentation of the architect's certificate before paying the balance. The non-occurrence of the condition, presentation of the architect's certificate, is nevertheless excused and A has a claim against B for $10,000.

§ 248. Effect of Insufficient Reason for Rejection as Excusing the Non-Occurrence of a Condition.

Where a party rejecting a defective performance or offer of performance gives an insufficient reason for rejection, the non-occurrence of a condition of his duty is excused only if he knew or had reason to know of that non-occurrence and then only to the extent that the giving of an insufficient reason substantially contributes to a failure by the other party to cure.

Comment

a. Failure to give a reason for rejection. Ordinarily a party whose performance or offer of performance has been rejected must determine at his peril the reason for that rejection. Whether or not he is under a duty to give that performance, he is not entitled to a statement of reasons from the other party and the other party is not prejudiced if he refuses to give such a statement. The following section states a limited exception to this for the case in which the payment of legal tender is required. (And cf. Uniform Commercial Code § 2–605, under which a buyer who fails to particularize his reasons for rejection is precluded, in some circumstances, from relying on an unstated defect.)

b. Giving insufficient reason for rejection. Just as the injured party is not, as a general rule, precluded from relying on a reason for rejection because he stated no reasons (Comment a), he is not precluded by the mere fact that he stated an insufficient reason, even though he knew or had reason to know of a sufficient one. The giving of an insufficient reason may, however, so mislead the other party as to induce his failure to cure the defective performance or offer of performance within the time allowed by the agreement. If it does so, the non-occurrence of the condition is excused, although the injured party still has a claim for damages. This is a specific application of the general rule that requires good faith and fair dealing in the enforcement of contracts. See § 205 and Illustration 10 to that section. As to the requirement that the giving of the insufficient reason contribute materially to the failure to cure, see Comment b to § 245. Where there is a question of fact as to whether performance was defective or not, the failure to state a reason or the stating of an insufficient reason may be considered in resolving that question, but this Section does not deal with such problems of proof.

Illustrations

1. The facts being otherwise as stated in Illustration 6 to § 246, on moving into the house B gives A a list of seventeen defects to be cured, but omits three others of which he knew or had reason to know. Absent a showing that A could have cured the three defects in time if B had specified them then, B can rely on all of the defects to show that A's breach is material and that A has no claim to $10,000 under the contract.

2. A, a subcontractor, makes a contract with B, a contractor, to install a roof on a school that B is building. After A has begun work, B notifies him that the contract is cancelled because of A's failure to provide enough skilled workmen as required by the contract. A sues B. B attempts to show that, although A may have provided enough skilled workmen, A so failed to follow specifications as to constitute a material breach. B is not precluded from showing this, even if he knew it at the time of the cancellation, unless A could have cured the defects in time if B had specified them then.

§ 249. When Payment Other Than by Legal Tender Is Sufficient.

Where the payment or offer of payment of money is made a condition of an obligor's duty, payment or offer of payment in any manner current in the ordinary course of business satisfies the requirement unless the obligee demands payment in legal tender and gives any extension of time reasonably necessary to procure it.

Comment

a. Rationale. Ordinarily a party whose performance or offer of performance has been rejected is not entitled to a reason for its rejection (Comment a to § 248). However, money claims are so generally paid by means other than legal tender that, absent a specific demand, the debtor is not likely to suppose that an insistence on legal tender is the reason behind a refusal to accept payment or offer to pay by check or in some other manner current in the ordinary course of business. Moreover, if the debtor is informed that this is the reason for rejection, he can ordinarily obtain legal tender and cure his defective performance or offer of performance, at least if he is given a reasonable extension of time. This Section, therefore, states an exceptional rule applicable to such cases. What manner of payment is current in the ordinary course of business depends on the nature of the transaction involved. Whether payment or an offer of payment must be in money is beyond the scope of this Section, and is to be determined by the rules of Chapter 9 on interpretation, including those on usage (§§ 221, 222) and course of dealing (§ 223). Cf. Comment b to § 238. If the contract explicitly requires payment in legal tender, this requirement will be given effect as a demand for legal tender given in advance of the time for performance, and renders any further demand or extension of time unnecessary.

Illustrations

1. A contracts to sell and B to buy land for $10,000, payment of the price and delivery of the deed to be "not later than July 30." On the morning of July 30, B offers to give A his certified check for $10,000. A, giving no reason, rejects B's check and refuses to offer to deliver a deed. B's offer to give his certified check satisfies the requirement of § 238 that B offer to pay A $10,000.

2. The facts being otherwise as stated in Illustration 1, A demands legal tender when he rejects B's certified check, but his demand comes after banking hours and he refuses to give B the necessary time to procure it. B's offer to give his certified check satisfies the requirement of § 238 that B offer to pay A $10,000.

TOPIC 3. EFFECT OF PROSPECTIVE NON-PERFORMANCE

§ 250. When a Statement or an Act Is a Repudiation.

A repudiation is

   (a) a statement by the obligor to the obligee indicating that the obligor will commit a breach that would of itself give the obligee a claim for damages for total breach under § 243, or

   (b) a voluntary affirmative act which renders the obligor unable or apparently unable to perform without such a breach.

Comment

a. Consequences of repudiation. A statement by a party to the other that he will not or cannot perform without a breach, or a voluntary affirmative act that renders him unable or apparently unable to perform without a breach may impair the value of the contract to the other party. It may have several consequences under this Restatement. If it accompanies a breach by non-performance that would otherwise give rise to only a claim for damages for partial breach, it may give rise to a claim for damages for total breach instead (§ 243). Even if it occurs before any breach by non-performance, it may give rise to a claim for damages for total breach (§ 253(1)), discharge the other party's duties (§ 253(2)), or excuse the non-occurrence of a condition (§ 255).

b. Nature of statement. In order to constitute a repudiation, a party's language must be sufficiently positive to be reasonably interpreted to mean that the party will not or cannot perform. Mere expression of doubt as to his willingness or ability to perform is not enough to constitute a repudiation, although such an expression may give an obligee reasonable grounds to believe that the obligor will commit a serious breach and may ultimately result in a repudiation under the rule stated in § 251. However, language that under a fair reading "amounts to a statement of intention not to perform except on conditions which go beyond the contract" constitutes a repudiation. Comment 2 to Uniform Commercial Code § 2–610. Language that is accompanied by a breach by non-performance may amount to a repudiation even though, standing alone, it would not be sufficiently positive. See § 243(2). The statement must be made to an obligee under the contract, including a third party beneficiary or an assignee.

Illustrations

1. On April 1, A contracts to sell and B to buy land, delivery of the deed and payment of the price to be on July 30. On May 1, A tells B that he will not perform. A's statement is a repudiation.

2. A contracts to build a house for B for $50,000, progress payments to be made monthly in an amount equal to 85% of the price of the work performed during the preceding month, the balance to be paid on the architect's certificate of satisfactory completion of the house. Without justification B fails to make a $5,000 progress payment and tells A that because of financial difficulties he will be unable to pay him anything for at least another month. If, after a month, it would be too late for B to cure his material failure of performance by making the delayed payment, B's statement is a repudiation. See Illustration 2 to § 237.

3. The facts being otherwise as stated in Illustration 1, A does not tell B that he will not perform but says, "I am not sure that I can perform, and I do not intend to do so unless I am legally bound to." A's statement is not a repudiation.

4. The facts being otherwise as in Illustration 1, A tells C, a third person having no right under the contract, and not B, that he will not perform. C informs B of this conversation, although not requested by A to do so. A's statement is not a repudiation. But see Comments b and c to § 251.

c. Nature of act. In order to constitute a repudiation, a party's act must be both voluntary and affirmative, and must make it actually or apparently impossible for him to perform. An act that falls short of these requirements may, however, give reasonable grounds to believe that the obligor will commit a serious breach for the purposes of the rule stated in § 251. The effect of bankruptcy is governed in large part by federal law. In liquidation cases, for example, Bankruptcy Reform Act § 365(a), (d) and (e) gives the trustee the power to assume or reject an executory contract within a statutory period, and the obligee must give him the time to exercise this power. A contract not assumed during this period is deemed to be rejected. Under Bankruptcy Reform Act § 365(g)(1), notwithstanding state law, the trustee's rejection of a contract "constitutes a breach of such contract . . . immediately before the date of the filing of the petition . . . ." The rules stated in this Restatement apply to the extent that they are consistent with federal bankruptcy law.

Illustrations

5. The facts being otherwise as stated in Illustration 1, A says nothing to B on May 1, but on that date he contracts to sell the land to C. A's making of the contract with C is a repudiation.

6. The facts being otherwise as stated in Illustration 1, A says nothing to B on May 1, but on that date he mortgages the land to C as security for a $40,000 loan which is not payable until one year later. A's mortgaging the land is a repudiation. Compare Illustration 4 to § 251.

7. A contracts to employ B, and B to work for A, the employment to last a year beginning in ten days. Three days after making the contract B embarks on a ship for a voyage around the world. B's embarking for the voyage is a repudiation.

d. Gravity of threatened breach. In order for a statement or an act to be a repudiation, the threatened breach must be of sufficient gravity that, if the breach actually occurred, it would of itself give the obligee a claim for damages for total breach under § 243(1). Generally, a party acts at his peril if, insisting on what he mistakenly believes to be his rights, he refuses to perform his duty. His statement is a repudiation if the threatened breach would, without more, have given the injured party a claim for damages for total breach. Modern procedural devices, such as the declaratory judgment, may be used to mitigate the harsh results that might otherwise result from this rule. Furthermore, if the threatened breach would not itself have given the injured party a claim for damages for total breach, the statement or voluntary act that threatens it is not a repudiation. But where a party wrongfully states that he will not perform at all unless the other party consents to a modification of his contract rights, the statement is a repudiation even though the concession that he seeks is a minor one, because the breach that he threatens in order to exact it is a complete refusal of performance.

Illustrations

8. On April 1, A contracts to sell and B to buy land for $50,000, delivery of the deed and payment of the price to be on August 1. On May 1, the parties make an enforceable modification under which delivery of the deed and payment of the price are to be on July 30 instead of August 1. On June 1, A tells B that he will not deliver a deed until August 1. A's statement is not a repudiation unless the one-day delay would, in the absence of a repudiation, have given B a claim for damages for total breach. See Illustration 4 to § 242.

9. The facts being otherwise as stated in Illustration 8, A tells B that he will not deliver a deed at all unless B agrees to accept it on August 1. A's statement is a repudiation. The result is the same even though A acts in the erroneous belief that the modification has no legal effect.

§ 251. When a Failure to Give Assurance May Be Treated as a Repudiation.

(1) Where reasonable grounds arise to believe that the obligor will commit a breach by non-performance that would of itself give the obligee a claim for damages for total breach under § 243, the obligee may demand adequate assurance of due performance and may, if reasonable, suspend any performance for which he has not already received the agreed exchange until he receives such assurance.

(2) The obligee may treat as a repudiation the obligor's failure to provide within a reasonable time such assurance of due performance as is adequate in the circumstances of the particular case.

Comment

a. Rationale. Ordinarily an obligee has no right to demand reassurance by the obligor that the latter will perform when his performance is due. However, a contract "imposes an obligation on each party that the other's expectation of receiving due performance will not be impaired." Uniform Commercial Code § 2–609(1). When, therefore, an obligee reasonably believes that the obligor will commit a breach by non-performance that would of itself give him a claim for damages for total breach (§ 243), he may, under the rule stated in this Section, be entitled to demand assurance of performance. The rule is a generalization, applicable without regard to the subject matter of the contract, from that of Uniform Commercial Code § 2–609. The latter applies only to contracts for the sale of goods and gives a party a right to adequate assurance of performance where "reasonable grounds for insecurity arise with respect to the performance" of the other party. Both rules rest on the principle that the parties to a contract look to actual performance "and that a continuing sense of reliance and security that the promised performance will be forthcoming when due, is an important feature of the bargain." Comment 1 to Uniform Commercial Code § 2–609. This principle is closely related to the duty of good faith and fair dealing in the performance of the contract (§ 205). See also Comment b to § 141. The rule stated in this Section may be modified by agreement of the parties, and where they have done so their rights depend on the application of the rules on interpretation stated in Chapter 9, The Scope of Contractual Obligations.

b. Relation to other rules. An obligee who believes, for whatever reason, that the obligor will not or cannot perform without a breach, is always free to act on that belief. If he is not himself under a duty to perform before the obligor, he may simply await the obligor's performance and, if his belief is confirmed, he will have a claim for damages for breach by non-performance. If he can prove that his belief would have been confirmed, he is at least shielded from liability even if he has failed to give a performance that is due before that of the obligor or has, by making alternative arrangements, done an act that amounts to a repudiation. For example, under § 254, the obligee's duty to pay damages for total breach by repudiation is discharged if the obligor himself would not or could not have performed when his performance was due. If, however, the obligee's belief is incorrect, his own failure to perform or his making of alternate arrangements may subject him to a claim for damages for total breach. This Section affords him an opportunity, in appropriate cases, to demand assurance of due performance and thereby avoid the uncertainties that would otherwise inhere in acting on his belief. If it is then reasonable for the obligee to suspend his own performance while he awaits assurance by the obligor, he may do so under Subsection (1). Under the special rule stated in § 252, the obligee may always suspend his own performance where his belief that the obligor will commit a breach is based on the obligor's insolvency. If the obligee does not, within a reasonable time, obtain adequate assurance of due performance, he may under Subsection (2) treat the obligor's failure to provide such an assurance as a repudiation. His right to do so is, however, subject to the rule stated in § 256 under which the manifestation of doubt or the apparent inability, on which the obligee bases his belief that the obligor will commit a breach, may be nullified. In contrast to the situation where the obligor has actually repudiated under § 250, the obligee may choose not to treat the failure to provide assurances as a repudiation and may continue to perform without affecting his right to recover damages for subsequent loss that he could have avoided by so treating it. See Comment a to § 257 and § 350. If he chooses to treat the obligor's failure as a repudiation, it may have any of the three effects that any other repudiation may have: it may give him a claim for damages for total breach (§ 253(1)), it may discharge his own remaining duties of performance (§ 253(2)), and it may excuse the non-occurrence of a condition of the other party's duty (§ 255). The effect on the obligee's remaining duties of performance of prospective non-performance by the obligor that would not be a breach because it would be justified on the ground of impracticability of performance is dealt with in § 268.

Illustrations

1. A contracts to let B use his concert hall on the evening of May 7 for a performance by B's string quartet, in return for B's promise to perform and to pay A a percentage of the receipts. The contract provides that B is not discharged even if he is unable to transport his quartet to A's hall. On May 6, because of an unexpected airline strike, A reasonably believes that B's quartet will be unable to come the 3,000 miles necessary to perform in his hall as scheduled. Without demanding adequate assurance of due performance under the rule stated in this Section, A then contracts with C to let C hold a meeting in the hall on the evening of May 7. A's contract with C is a repudiation of his contract with B (§ 250), which gives rise to a claim by B against A for damages for total breach (§ 253). If, however, B is in fact unable to bring his quartet to A's hall on May 7, B's claim against A is discharged (§ 254).

2. The facts being otherwise as stated in Illustration 1, B succeeds in chartering a plane and flies the 3,000 miles with his quartet in his private plane. He arrives in time to perform, but is unable to do so because C is using the hall. B has a claim against A for damages for total breach (§ 243).

c. Reasonable grounds for belief. Whether "reasonable grounds" have arisen for an obligee's belief that there will be a breach must be determined in the light of all the circumstances of the particular case. The grounds for his belief must have arisen after the time when the contract was made and cannot be based on facts known to him at that time. Nor, since the grounds must be reasonable, can they be based on events that occurred after that time but as to which he took the risk when he made the contract. But minor breaches may give reasonable grounds for a belief that there will be more serious breaches, and the mere failure of the obligee to press a claim for damages for those minor breaches will not preclude him from basing a demand for assurances on them. Compare § 241(d), Comment e to that section, and Comment b to § 242. Even circumstances that do not relate to the particular contract, such as defaults under other contracts, may give reasonable grounds for such a belief. See Comment a to § 252. Conduct by a party that indicates his doubt as to his willingness or ability to perform but that is not sufficiently positive to amount to a repudiation (see Comment b to § 250), may give reasonable grounds for such a belief. And events that indicate a party's apparent inability, but do not amount to a repudiation because they are not voluntary acts, may also give reasonable grounds for such a belief. One important application of the rule stated in this Section occurs when a party who has contracted to buy specific property, land or goods, discovers that the seller has neither present ownership of the property nor a right to become or at least a reasonable expectation of becoming the owner in time to perform. Another important application of the rule occurs when an obligor who is allowed a period of time within which to perform makes an offer of defective performance. It may still be possible for him, if the offer is refused, to make an offer of conforming performance within the period allowed. Nevertheless, the offer of defective performance may give the obligee reasonable grounds to believe that the obligor will commit a breach under this Section. A third important application of the rule occurs when a party becomes insolvent. The effect of insolvency will vary according to the nature of the obligor's duty. If, for example, it is merely to perform personal services, the fact of insolvency alone may not give reasonable grounds to believe that the obligor will commit a breach, but if it is to pay for goods on credit it will. See Uniform Commercial Code § 2–702(1). A special rule on insolvency is stated in § 252. In any case, in order for this Section to apply, the breach that the obligee believes the obligor will commit must be a breach by non-performance that would so substantially impair the value of the contract to the obligee that it would of itself, unaccompanied by a repudiation, give him a claim for damages for total breach under § 243.

Illustrations

3. On May 1, A contracts to sell and B to buy a parcel of land for $50,000, delivery of the deed and payment of the price to be on July 30. Unknown to both A and B, C has a dower interest in the land. On May 15, B discovers this and demands that A give him adequate assurance of due performance. A fails to do so, and B commences an action against A on July 1. B had reasonable grounds to believe that A would commit a breach by non-performance that would of itself have given B a claim for damages for total breach. If the court concludes that a reasonable time for A to give assurances had passed on July 1, B properly treated A's failure to give assurances as a repudiation. B then has a claim for damages against A for total breach.

4. The facts being otherwise as stated in Illustration 3, C's interest in the land is that of mortgagee under a mortgage that A can discharge at any time by payment of the mortgage debt. B had no reasonable grounds to believe that A would commit a breach, B could not treat A's failure to give assurances as a repudiation, and B has no claim for damages against A. Compare Illustration 6 to § 250.

5. A contracts to sell and B to buy A's house, delivery of the deed and payment of the price to be made during September. On September 1, A offers to deliver a deed to B which is defective in that a fence projects beyond the front line of the house and the swimming pool lacks a certificate of occupancy. Both defects can be cured by A within the month, but A fails to reply to a demand by B that A assure B that A will cure them within that time. On September 20, B notifies A that he cancels the contract. On September 30, A, having cured the defects, offers to deliver a conforming deed to B. A court may conclude that, as a result of A's apparent inability to perform, B had reasonable grounds to believe that A would commit a breach by non-performance that would of itself have given B a claim for damages for total breach, that A failed upon demand by B to give adequate assurance of due performance within a reasonable time, and therefore that B properly treated A's failure as a repudiation. B then has a claim against A for damages for total breach.

d. Nature of demand. A party who demands assurances must do so in accordance with his duty of good faith and fair dealing in the enforcement of the contract (§ 205). Whether a particular demand for assurance conforms to that duty will depend on the circumstances. The demand need not be in writing. Although a written demand is usually preferable to an oral one, if time is of particular importance the additional time required for a written demand might necessitate an oral one. Compare Uniform Commercial Code § 2–609(1), which controls in the case of a sale of goods and which requires a demand "in writing." Harrassment by means of frequent unjustified demands may amount to a violation of the duty of good faith and fair dealing.

Illustration

6. The facts being otherwise as stated in Illustration 1, before contracting with C, A telephones B on May 6 and asks B to assure him that he will be there on May 7. B says only "We will do our best to get there." B succeeds in chartering a plane and flies the 3,000 miles with his quartet. He arrives in time to perform, but is unable to do so because C is using the hall. In the absence of countervailing circumstances, a court should conclude that, as a result of B's apparent inability to perform, A had reasonable grounds to believe that B would commit a breach by non-performance that would of itself have given A a claim for damages for total breach, that because of the shortness of time a demand by telephone conformed to the duty of good faith and fair dealing (§ 205), that B failed upon such a demand to give adequate assurance of due performance, and therefore that A properly treated B's failure as a repudiation. A then has a claim against B for damages for total breach.

e. Nature and time of assurance. Whether an assurance of due performance is "adequate" depends on what it is reasonable to require in a particular case taking account of the circumstances of that case. The relationship between the parties, any prior dealings that they have had, the reputation of the party whose performance has been called into question, the nature of the grounds for insecurity, and the time within which the assurance must be furnished are all relevant factors. (If the obligor's insolvency constitutes the grounds for the obligee's insecurity, the special rule stated in § 252 empowers him to suspend performance until he receives assurance in the form of actual performance, an offer of performance, or reasonable security.) What is a "reasonable time" within which to give assurance under Subsection (2) will also depend on the particular circumstances. Like the demand, the assurance is subject to the general requirement of good faith and fair dealing in the enforcement of the contract (§ 205; see Comment d).

7. The facts being otherwise as stated in Illustration 1, before contracting with C, A telephones B on May 6 and asks B to assure him that he will be there on May 7. B explains over the telephone that he has been able to charter a plane and expects to come as planned. B then flies the 3,000 miles with his quartet. He arrives in time to perform, but is unable to do so because C is using the hall. The assurance given by B was adequate in view of what it was reasonable to require, and therefore A could not treat B's failure to do more as a repudiation. B then has a claim against A for damages for total breach.

8. The facts being otherwise as stated in Illustration 1, before contracting with C, A telephones B on May 6 and asks B to assure him that he will be there on May 7. B replies that he hopes to be able to charter a plane and that he will telephone A to let him know. A tells B that he must know by noon on May 7 in order to make alternative arrangements with C. B succeeds in chartering a plane and flies the 3,000 miles with his quartet. After he has arrived on the afternoon of May 7, he telephones A to assure him that he will perform. A court may conclude that, as a result of B's apparent inability to perform, A had reasonable grounds to believe that B would commit a breach by non-performance that would of itself have given A a claim for damages for total breach, that the assurances given by B were not within a reasonable time, and therefore that B properly treated B's delay in giving them as a repudiation. A then has a claim against B for damages for total breach.

§ 252. Effect of Insolvency.

(1) Where the obligor's insolvency gives the obligee reasonable grounds to believe that the obligor will commit a breach under the rule stated in § 251, the obligee may suspend any performance for which he has not already received the agreed exchange until he receives assurance in the form of performance itself, an offer of performance, or adequate security.

(2) A person is insolvent who either has ceased to pay his debts in the ordinary course of business or cannot pay his debts as they become due or is insolvent within the meaning of the federal bankruptcy law.

Comment

a. Insolvency. An obligor's insolvency is not a repudiation (Comment c to § 250) and may not even give the obligee reasonable grounds to believe that the obligor will commit a breach (Comment c to § 251). It does, however, have this latter effect when the obligee is to pay for goods on credit, and Uniform Commercial Code § 2–702(1) states a specific statutory rule for that situation. This Section states a rule that applies more broadly to similar situations in which insolvency gives reasonable grounds to believe that the obligor will commit a breach. It supplements the rule stated in § 251 by giving the obligee the unqualified power to suspend his own performance until he receives from the obligor performance, an offer of performance (see Comment b to § 238), or reasonable security, which may, in an appropriate case, be by a guarantee of performance. He need not show, as he must under § 251(1), that it is "reasonable" to suspend, and he need not perform unless he receives the assurance required by this Section. Mere evidence of an ability to perform in spite of insolvency or a favorable report from a credit rating agency will not suffice. However, the rule stated in this Section only empowers the obligee to suspend his own performance. If he would treat the failure to give assurance as a repudiation, he must proceed under § 251. Furthermore, in order for the obligee to have the benefit of this Section, the obligor must actually be insolvent. The obligee who merely has doubts as to the obligor's solvency should also proceed under § 251. See Comment b to § 251. A party is insolvent for the purpose of this Section only if one of the three tests of insolvency stated in Subsection (2) is satisfied. This statement follows the definition of insolvency under Uniform Commercial Code § 1–201(23). Mere doubts about the solvency of the other party or uncertainty as to his ability to perform may amount, under the rule stated in § 251, to reasonable grounds to believe that he will commit a serious breach, but they do not amount to insolvency. The rule stated in this Section may be modified by agreement of the parties.

Illustrations

1. On April 1, A, a subcontractor, contracts with B, a contractor, to furnish labor and materials for the floors of an apartment building that B is building. A is to begin work on May 1 and be paid 85% of the price in monthly payments as the work progresses and the balance on his completion of the work. On April 10, A discovers that B is insolvent and demands that B pay for the work in advance or give reasonable security. When B refuses to do so, A refuses to begin work on May 1. B has no claim against A.

2. On February 1, A contracts to work for B as a salesman for a year beginning March 1, for a monthly salary and $5,000 to be paid in advance on February 15. On February 10, A becomes insolvent. B refuses to pay the $5,000 on February 15 unless A gives reasonable security. Because A's insolvency

did not give reasonable grounds to believe that A would commit a breach, A has a claim against B for damages.

§ 253. Effect of a Repudiation as a Breach and on Other Party's Duties.

(1) Where an obligor repudiates a duty before he has committed a breach by non-performance and before he has received all of the agreed exchange for it, his repudiation alone gives rise to a claim for damages for total breach.

(2) Where performances are to be exchanged under an exchange of promises, one party's repudiation of a duty to render performance discharges the other party's remaining duties to render performance.

Comment

a. Breach. An obligee under a contract is ordinarily entitled to the protection of his expectation that the obligor will perform. For this reason, a repudiation by the obligor under § 250 or § 251 generally gives rise to a claim for damages for total breach even though it is not accompanied or preceded by a breach by non-performance. Such a repudiation is sometimes elliptically called an "anticipatory breach," meaning a breach by anticipatory repudiation, because it occurs before there is any breach by non-performance. If there is a breach by non-performance, in addition to the repudiation under § 250 or § 251 the breach is not one by repudiation alone and the rules stated in § 243 rather than those stated in Subsection (1) apply. If, under § 251, it was a breach by non-performance that gave the obligee grounds to believe that the obligor would commit a more serious breach, the obligor's failure to give assurances cannot give rise to a breach by repudiation alone. The measure of damages in the case of a claim under this Section is governed by the rules stated in Topic 2 of Chapter 16.

Illustrations

1. On April 1, A and B make a contract under which B is to work for A for three months beginning on June 1. On May 1, A repudiates by telling B he will not employ him. On May 15, B commences an action against A. B's duty to work for A is discharged and he has a claim against A for damages for total breach.

2. On July 1, A contracts to sell and B to buy a quantity of barrel staves, delivery and payment to be on December 1. On August 1, A repudiates by writing B that he will be unable to deliver staves at the contract price. On September 1, B commences an action against A. B's duty to pay for the staves is discharged and he has a claim against A for damages for total breach. See Uniform Commercial Code § 2–610.

b. Discharge. Under Subsection (1) a breach by repudiation alone can only give rise to a claim for total breach, although a breach by non-performance, even if coupled with a repudiation, can generally give rise to either a claim for partial breach or to one for total breach (§§ 236, 237). Of course, in appropriate circumstances, the injured party can, after a breach by repudiation alone, pursue alternative relief by seeking, for example, a decree of specific performance or an injunction. See Topic 3 of Chapter 16. Nevertheless, the rule stated in Subsection (1) is one of those rules that are peculiar to breach by repudiation alone and differ from those applicable to a breach by non-performance. (Another such rule is that a breach by repudiation alone can be totally nullified by the party in breach (§ 257), while a breach by non-performance, whether coupled with a repudiation or not, cannot be.) Subsection (2) states a corollary of this rule that a breach by repudiation always gives rise to a claim for damages for total breach: where performances are to be exchanged under an exchange of promises, one party's repudiation discharges any remaining duties of performance of the other party with respect to the expected exchange.

c. Scope. If an obligor repudiates under § 250 or § 251 before he has received all of the agreed exchange for his promise, the repudiation alone gives rise to a claim for damages for total breach under Subsection (1). The most important example of such a case occurs when performances are to be exchanged under an exchange of promises and one party repudiates a duty with respect to the expected exchange before the other party has fully performed that exchange. See Illustrations 1 and 2. (A repudiation of a duty whose performance is not part of the expected exchange, and for which there is therefore no agreed exchange, does not come within the rule stated in Subsection (1). See, e.g., Illustration 3 to § 232.) Another example occurs when one party repudiates a duty under an option contract before the other party has exercised the option by giving the agreed exchange. See Illustration 3. However, it is one of the established limits on the doctrine of "anticipatory breach" that an obligor's repudiation alone, whether under § 250 or § 251, gives rise to no claim for damages at all if he has already received all of the agreed exchange for it. The rule stated in Subsection (1) does not, therefore, allow a claim for damages for total breach in such a case.

Illustrations

3. On February 1, A and B make an option contract under which, in consideration for B's payment of $100, A promises to convey to B a parcel of land on May 1 for $50,000, if B tenders that sum by that date. On March 1, A repudiates by selling the parcel to C. On April 1, B commences an action against A. Since A has not received the $50,000, the agreed exchange for his duty to sell the parcel to B, B has a claim against A for damages for total breach.

4. On February 1, A and B make a contract under which, as consideration for B's immediate payment of $50,000, A promises to convey to B a parcel of land on May 1. On March 1, A repudiates by selling the parcel to C. On April 1, B commences an action against A. Since A has received the $50,000, the agreed exchange for his duty to sell the parcel to B, B has no claim against A for damages for breach of contract until performance is due on May 1.

5. On February 1, A and B make a contract under which, as consideration for A's conveying a parcel of land to B, B promises to make annual payments of $10,000 for five years. B makes the payments for the first two years and on March 1 of the third year repudiates by telling A that he will not make any further payments. A commences an action against B. Since B has received the land, the agreed exchange for his duty to pay the remaining installments, A has no claim against B for damages for breach of contract until performance is due on the following February 1.

6. On January 15, A and B make a contract under which A promises to convey to B a parcel of land on February 1, and B promises to pay A $10,000 at that time and the balance of $40,000 in four annual installments. A conveys the parcel to B and B pays A $10,000. On March 1, B repudiates by telling A that he will not make any further payments. A commences an action against B. Since B has received the land, the agreed exchange for his duty to make the remaining payments, A has no claim against B for damages for breach of contract, until performance is due on the following February 1.

d. Avoiding harsh results of limitation. The limitation described in Comment c sometimes avoids difficult problems of forecasting damages and is supported by the clear weight of authority. It has, however, been subjected to considerable criticism, and instances of its actual application are infrequent. Compare, for example, Illustration 3 with Illustration 4. A court can often avoid harsh results by making available other types of relief, such as a declaratory judgment or restitution. See §§ 345, 373 and Comment a to § 373. Insurance contracts are subject to special considerations which may make it appropriate to grant equitable relief in, for example, a suit for reinstatement. The degree to which the limitation might yield on a showing of manifest injustice, as where the refusal to pay is not in good faith, is unclear. Compare Comment d to § 243. Furthermore, if the repudiation is coupled with a breach by non-performance that would otherwise give rise to a claim for damages for only partial breach, it may give rise instead to a claim for damages for total breach, but whether it does so is governed by § 243 and not by this Section.

§ 254. Effect of Subsequent Events on Duty to Pay Damages.

(1) A party's duty to pay damages for total breach by repudiation is discharged if it appears after the breach that there would have been a total failure by the injured party to perform his return promise.

(2) A party's duty to pay damages for total breach by repudiation is discharged if it appears after the breach that the duty that he repudiated would have been discharged by impracticability or frustration before any breach by non-performance.

Comment

a. Non-performance by injured party after repudiation. If the parties are to exchange performances under an exchange of promises, each party's duties to render performance are generally regarded as conditional on the other party's performance, or at least on his readiness to perform (§§ 237, 238, 251, 253). This principle applies even though one party is already in breach by repudiation. His duty to pay damages is discharged if it subsequently appears that there would have been a total failure of performance by the injured party. A failure is total in this context if it would have been sufficient to have discharged any remaining duties of the party in breach to render his performance. See § 242. The result follows even if it appears that the failure would have been justified and not a breach. Cf. § 244.

Illustration

1. On April 1, A and B make a personal service contract under which A promises to employ B for six months beginning July 1 and B promises to work for A during that period. On May 1, A repudiates the contract. On June 1, B falls ill and is unable to perform during the entire period. A's duty to pay B damages for total breach by repudiation is discharged.

b. Impracticability or frustration after repudiation. Under the rule stated in § 253(1), a party's breach by anticipatory repudiation immediately gives rise to a claim for damages for total breach. If it subsequently appears that the duty that he repudiated would have been discharged by supervening impracticability (§ 261) or frustration (§ 265) before any breach by non-performance, his duty to pay damages is discharged. Impracticability or frustration that would have occurred after breach by non-performance may affect the measure of damages but does not discharge the duty to pay damages; cf. §§ 344, 347, 352.

Illustration

2. On April 1, A and B make a personal service contract under which A promises to employ B for 6 months beginning July 1 and B promises to work for A during that period. On May 1, B repudiates the contract. On June 1, B falls ill and is unable to perform during the entire period. B's duty to pay damages to A for his anticipatory repudiation is discharged.

§ 255. Effect of a Repudiation as Excusing the Non-Occurrence of a Condition.

Where a party's repudiation contributes materially to the non-occurrence of a condition of one of his duties, the non-occurrence is excused.

Comment

a. Rationale. This Section accords the same effect to a repudiation that § 245 accords to a breach by non-performance. No one should be required to do a useless act, and if, because of a party's repudiation, it appears that the occurrence of a condition of a duty would not be followed by performance of the duty, the non-occurrence of the condition is generally excused. In judging whether occurrence of the condition would be followed by performance of the duty the obligee may take the obligor at his word. Nevertheless, the repudiation must contribute materially to the non-occurrence of the condition, and if the condition would not have occurred in any event, its non-occurrence is not excused. In such a case both parties are discharged.

Illustrations

1. A, an insurance company, issues a policy insuring B against theft, and providing that no payment will be made unless written notice is given within 60 days after loss. A loss occurs, and B immediately notifies A by telephone. A repudiates by informing B without adequate reason that it will not pay the loss. Because of this, B does not give written notice to A. B has a claim against A for the amount of the loss.

2. On February 1, A contracts to sell and B to buy a house for $50,000, B's duty being "conditional on approval by X Bank of B's pending mortgage application." On March 1, B repudiates by telling A that he will not buy the house. On March 10, the X Bank, which is unaware of B's repudiation, disapproves B's application on financial grounds. A has no claim against B. The non-occurrence of the condition, approval by X Bank, is not excused because B's repudiation did not contribute materially to its non-occurrence.

b. Exceptions. Under §§ 237 and 238, it may be required as a condition of one party's duty that the other party perform or offer to perform his duty. A repudiation by the first party will, in those circumstances, discharge that duty of the other party (§ 253(2)), eliminating the requirement that the other party perform or offer to perform it. The discharge has the additional effect of excusing the non-occurrence of the condition. But non-occurrence of the condition is excused only if the duty is discharged. See Comment c to § 245 and Illustrations 1 and 2 to § 253.

Illustration

3. A, a contractor, makes a contract with B, a subcontractor, under which B is to be paid $300,000 for furnishing heating and air conditioning units for a housing project to be built by A, "on condition that Contractor is furnished with a performance bond within two weeks." No provision is made for progress payments. A week after the making of the contract, A repudiates by telling B that he will not perform the contract. Because of the repudiation, B does not furnish a performance bond. B has a claim against A for damages for total breach. The non-occurrence of one condition, B's furnishing of a performance bond, is excused under this Section because A's repudiation contributed materially to its non-occurrence. The non-occurrence of another condition, B's furnishing heating and air conditioning units, is excused because B's duty to furnish the units was discharged when A repudiated (§ 253(2)), and its performance was therefore no longer a condition under § 237.

§ 256. Nullification of Repudiation or Basis for Repudiation.

(1) The effect of a statement as constituting a repudiation under § 250 or the basis for a repudiation under § 251 is nullified by a retraction of the statement if notification of the retraction comes to the attention of the injured party before he materially changes his position in reliance on the repudiation or indicates to the other party that he considers the repudiation to be final.

(2) The effect of events other than a statement as constituting a repudiation under § 250 or the basis for a repudiation under § 251 is nullified if, to the knowledge of the injured party, those events have ceased to exist before he materially changes his position in reliance on the repudiation or indicates to the other party that he considers the repudiation to be final.

Comment

a. Effect of nullification. A repudiation may have three consequences: it may give rise to a claim for damages for total breach (§ 253(1)), discharge duties (§ 253(2)), and excuse the non-occurrence of a condition (§ 255). A party's manifestation of doubt or apparent inability may entitle the other party to demand adequate assurance of due performance and to treat a failure to give such assurance as a repudiation under the rule stated in § 251. If, however, the effect of the statement or other events constituting the repudiation under § 250 or the basis for the repudiation under § 251 is nullified as provided in this Section, none of these consequences follows. Such a nullification does not, of course, alter the consequences of any breach by non-performance that may have taken place. If, for example, a repudiation accompanies a breach by non-performance, nullification of the repudiation leaves the injured party a claim for damages for the breach, although the claim may no longer be one for damages for total breach (see Comment b to § 243). If the repudiation is wholly anticipatory, nullification leaves the injured party with no claim at all. Compare the effect of events subsequent to a total breach by repudiation (§ 254).

Illustrations

1. On February 1, A contracts to supply B with natural gas for one year beginning on May 1, payment to be made each month. On June 1, A repudiates and fails to supply gas under the contract. On June 2, before B has taken any action in response to the repudiation, A resumes the supply of gas and notifies B that he retracts his repudiation. B has no claim against A based on the repudiation. B has a claim against A for damages for A's breach by non-performance for one day. Whether B's claim is one for damages for partial breach or for total breach is determined by the rule stated in § 243(1).

2. On February 1, A contracts to supply B with natural gas for one year beginning on May 1, payment to be made each month. On March 1, A repudiates. On April 1, before B has taken any action in response to the repudiation, A notifies B that he retracts his repudiation. B's duties under the contract are not discharged, and B has no claim against A.

b. Manner of retraction. It is not necessary for the repudiator to use words in order to retract his statement. Conduct, such as an offer of performance, may be adequate to convey the idea of retraction to the injured party.

c. Time for nullification. Once the injured party has materially changed his position in reliance on the repudiation, nullification would clearly be unjust. In the interest of certainty, however, it is undesirable to make the injured party's rights turn exclusively on such a vague criterion, and he may therefore prevent subsequent nullification by indicating to the other party that he considers the repudiation final. It is, for example, enough under Uniform Commercial Code § 2–612 that "the aggrieved party has since the repudiation cancelled or materially changed his position or otherwise indicated that he considers the repudiation final." Cancellation of the contract or the commencement of an action claiming damages for total breach would be sufficient. (See Comment 1 to Uniform Commercial Code § 2–611.)

Illustrations

3. The facts being otherwise as stated in Illustration 2, on March 15, B makes a contract with C for the supply of gas to replace that which he was to receive from A. B's duties under the contract are discharged and B has a claim against A for damages for total breach (§ 253).

4. The facts being otherwise as stated in Illustration 2, on March 15, B notifies A that he cancels the contract. B's duties under the contract are discharged and B has a claim against A for damages for total breach (§ 253).

5. On April 1, A contracts to sell and B to buy a parcel of land, delivery of the deed and payment of the price to be on July 30. On May 1, A sells the parcel to C and B learns of this. On June 1, before B has taken any action in response to the sale to C, A reacquires the land and B learns of this. B's duties under the contract are not discharged and B has no claim against A. Compare Illustrations 5 and 6 to § 250.

§ 257. Effect of Urging Performance in Spite of Repudiation.

The injured party does not change the effect of a repudiation by urging the repudiator to perform in spite of his repudiation or to retract his repudiation.

Comment

a. Effects of rule. Although the effects of a repudiation may be nullified as stated in § 256, a repudiation operates until nullified not only as a breach (§ 253(1)), but as a ground for discharge (§ 253(2)) and for excuse of the non-occurrence of a condition (§ 255). Under the rule stated in this Section, these effects continue although the injured party has urged that the repudiator perform or that he retract his repudiation. This rule is in accord with that of Uniform Commercial Code § 2–610(b), which allows the injured party to "resort to any remedy for breach . . . even though he has notified the repudiating party that he would await the latter's performance and has urged retraction." Any possibility that the injured party might unfairly mislead the repudiator is avoided by the duty of good faith and fair dealing (§ 205). An injured party who continues to perform in spite of a repudiation may, however, be precluded under § 350 from claiming damages for loss that he could have avoided.

Illustration

1. A contracts to sell and B to buy a parcel of land for $50,000, delivery of the deed and payment of the price to be on July 1. On June 1, A repudiates the contract. B writes A urging him to perform, but A does not reply. B thereupon buys another parcel of land in its place and makes no conditional offer of the $50,000 on July 1. A, however, having changed his mind makes a conditional offer of a deed on July 1. B has a claim against A for damages for total breach. A has no claim against B.

TOPIC 4. APPLICATION OF PERFORMANCES

§ 258. Obligor's Direction of Application.

(1) Except as stated in Subsection (2), as between two or more contractual duties owed by an obligor to the same obligee, a performance is applied according to a direction made by the obligor to the obligee at or before the time of performance.

(2) If the obligor is under a duty to a third person to devote a performance to the discharge of a particular duty that the obligor owes to the obligee and the obligee knows or has reason to know this, the obligor's performance is applied to that duty.

Comment

a. Obligor's power. As a general rule, an obligor has the power to direct the obligee's application of a payment or other performance. The direction is effective immediately on the obligee's acceptance of the performance, the performance is considered to be applied as directed, and the obligor's duty is discharged accordingly. A contrary statement or other inconsistent action by an obligee who has accepted the performance does not affect this result. The obligor cannot, however, effectively direct an application in breach of a contract with the obligee as to how performances should be applied if the contract is specifically enforceable, as may be the case if application as directed will deprive the obligee of security. See § 363. The obligor can effectively direct that a performance be applied to a duty that is not matured, to one that is unsecured, and even to one that is unenforceable on grounds of public policy. As to state statutes governing consumer credit transactions, see the Introductory Note to this Topic.

Illustrations

1. A makes two contracts to sell identical cargoes of sugar to B, delivery under the first to be not later than July 1 and under the second not later than August 1. In June A delivers a conforming cargo of sugar, directing that it be applied to the second contract. A's duty under that contract is discharged.

2. A owes B two debts of $1,000 each, one secured and the other unsecured. A sends B $1,000 with a letter stating that the payment is to discharge the secured debt. B keeps the money but replies, "I shall apply your payment to the unsecured debt." The secured debt is discharged.

3. A owes B $1,000 for goods sold. He has also promised to pay B $1,000 that he lost to B at gambling, but his promise is unenforceable on grounds of public policy. A pays B $1,000, stating that it is in payment of his gambling losses. A's duty to pay B $1,000 for goods sold is not discharged.

b. Direction. The obligor must manifest his direction to the obligee, but he need not manifest it in words. A direction may be inferred from other circumstances, including the performance itself. It is often clear from the nature of the performance that it is to be applied to a particular duty, as is the case if goods delivered by a seller conform to only one of several contracts with the buyer. In resolving doubts as to whether a direction has been made, the fact that one application is obviously more advantageous to the obligor than another is a factor to be given weight. In extreme situations a particular application may be so disadvantageous to the obligor that it is not permitted to the obligee even absent a contrary direction by the obligor. See § 259(2). An obligor's direction may be made before as well as at the time of performance, but it is the time of performance that is controlling, and a direction made earlier can be changed or revoked.

Illustrations

4. The facts being otherwise as stated in Illustration 2, A does not send B a letter but merely makes an entry in his account book crediting the payment to the secured debt. Because A has not manifested his intention to B, his purported direction is ineffective. Under the rules stated in § 260, the unsecured debt is discharged.

5. The facts being otherwise as stated in Illustration 1, A delivers no sugar until July 1, when he delivers a conforming cargo of sugar without saying anything about its application. In the absence of a contrary indication, the coincidence of the dates and the fact that application of the performance

to the first contract will avoid breach sufficiently manifest A's intention that it be so applied. A's duty under that contract is discharged.

   6. A owes B two matured debts, one of $1,221, which will soon be barred by a statute of limitations, and the other of $1,193, which will not soon be barred. A pays B $1,193 with no further direction of its application. In the absence of a contrary indication, the coincidence of the amount of the payment and that of one of the debts sufficiently manifest A's intention that the payment be applied to the $1,193 debt. The $1,193 debt is discharged.

   c. Interests of third persons. Sometimes an obligor owes a duty to a third person to devote a performance to the discharge of a particular duty that the obligor owes to the obligee. If the obligee knows or has reason to know that this is so, an inconsistent direction by the obligor is ineffective and the performance is applied to that duty to the obligee. The obligor's duty to the third person may be a fiduciary one, as where the obligor is a trustee who has received money in trust to pay a debt. Or it may be a contractual duty, as where a debtor has a duty to devote to the debt the very money received from the third party. But the duty to the third party must relate to the disposition of the third party's performance and not be merely one to pay the debt. Compare Illustrations 7 and 8; cf. § 260(2)(a).

Illustrations

   7. A contracts with B to build a building, to be completed free of liens. C obtains a mechanic's lien on the building to secure payment for labor and materials that he has furnished under a subcontract with A. A owes C on other accounts as well as under this subcontract. A, on receiving progress payments from B, uses the money to pay C, and directs C, who knows its source, to apply it to the other accounts. If A is under no duty to B to use the progress payments in a particular way, A's direction is effective regardless of C's knowledge. A's duty to pay the other accounts is discharged to the extent of the payments to C. Compare Illustration 1 to § 260.

   8. The facts being otherwise as stated in Illustration 7, the progress payments, as C knows, are paid pursuant to an agreement between A and B that they are to be used to discharge A's duty to pay C for labor and materials on the building. A's direction is not effective and his duty to pay the other accounts is not discharged. A's duty to pay C for the labor and materials is discharged to the extent of the payments to C.

§ 259. Creditor's Application.

   (1) Except as stated in Subsections (2) and (3), if the debtor has not directed application of a payment as between two or more matured debts, the payment is applied according to a manifestation of intention made within a reasonable time by the creditor to the debtor.

   (2) A creditor cannot apply such a payment to a debt if

   (a) the debtor could not have directed its application to that debt, or

   (b) a forfeiture would result from a failure to apply it to another debt and the creditor knows or has reason to know this, or

   (c) the debt is disputed or is unenforceable on grounds of public policy.

   (3) If a creditor is owed one such debt in his own right and another in a fiduciary capacity, he cannot, unless empowered to do so by the beneficiary, effectively apply to the debt in his own right a greater proportion of a payment than that borne by the unsecured portion of that debt to the unsecured portions of both claims.

Comment

   a. Creditor's power of application. If the debtor has not directed the application of his payment by the time payment is made, the creditor has a power to apply it himself. Subject to some limitations (see Comments c and d), he can apply it to any matured debt or distribute it among several matured debts and can do so to his own advantage, without regard to the effect on the debtor. He can, for example, apply it to an unsecured debt, to one that is barred by a statute of limitations, or to one that is unenforceable because of the Statute of Frauds. He cannot, however, apply it to a debt that is not matured at the time of payment.

The creditor's power may be limited by a direction given by the debtor at or before the time of payment that it not be applied to a particular debt or debts. As to the extension of these principles to performances other than payments and as to state statutes governing consumer credit transactions, see the Introductory Note to this Topic.

Illustrations

1. A owes B two matured debts, one of which is barred by a statute of limitations. A makes a payment to B without directing its application. B can apply it to the barred debt and the debt is discharged to that extent. If the payment is insufficient to pay that debt in full, however, the bar of the statute is not removed as to the remainder. See § 82 and Comment e to that section.

2. A owes B two matured debts, one of which is voidable because A was an infant when it was incurred. A makes a payment to B without directing its application. B can apply it to the voidable debt and the debt is discharged to that extent.

3. A owes B two matured debts, on one of which there is a surety. A makes a payment to B without directing its application. B can apply it to the debt for which there is no surety and the debt is discharged to that extent.

4. A owes B a matured debt and makes a payment without directing its application. The next day another debt from A to B matures. B cannot apply the payment to the latter debt. The payment is applied to the former debt and it is discharged to that extent.

5. A owes B three matured debts. On making a payment to B, A says, "You may apply this payment to either the first or the second of my debts." If B applies the payment to either the first or the second debt, A's duty is discharged to that extent. An attempt by B to apply the payment to the third debt would be ineffective, and its application as between the first and second debts would be determined by the rules stated in § 260.

b. Manifestation of intent. Although application by the creditor requires no consent by the debtor, it is not effective unless within a reasonable time the creditor notifies the debtor or otherwise manifests to him his intention to make the application. Mere entry by the creditor on his books is not enough. What length of time is reasonable depends on the circumstances. Action taken by the creditor after a controversy has arisen between the parties regarding application of the payment is not within a reasonable time.

Illustration

6. A owes B two matured debts of $1,000 each. A pays B $1,000 without directing its application. B promptly credits the payment in his books to one of the debts. Because B has not manifested his intention to A, his purported application is ineffective. The application of the payment is determined by the rules stated in § 260. However, if promptly after payment B sends A a letter demanding payment of one of the debts, this is a manifestation to A of B's intention to apply the payment to the other debt.

c. Limitations on creditor's power of application. The creditor's power of application is more limited than the debtor's power in a number of ways. The creditor cannot apply a payment to a debt to which the debtor himself could not direct its application because of a duty to a third party (§ 258(2)). See Illustration 8 to § 258. Furthermore, he must in some situations take the debtor's interests into account. He cannot apply the payment to a debt if he knows or has reason to know that the failure to apply it to another debt will result in a forfeiture. Nor can he apply the payment to a debt that is disputed or is unenforceable on grounds of public policy. The creditor is also subject to the duty of good faith and fair dealing imposed by the rule stated in § 205. Insofar as the creditor's power is in these ways limited, his purported application is ineffective, and application is determined under the rules stated in § 260.

Illustrations

7. A owes B two matured debts, one of which is for rent under a lease providing that A's rights as lessee are forfeit for non-payment of rent. A makes a payment to B sufficient to pay the debt for rent without directing its application. B notifies A that he has applied it to the other debt. B's purported

application is ineffective and the other debt is not discharged. Under the rules stated in § 260, the payment is applied to the debt for the rent and it is discharged.

8. A owes B two matured debts of $1,000 each, one of which A has consistently disputed. A pays B $1,000 without directing its application. B notifies A that he has applied it to the disputed claim. B's purported application is ineffective, and the disputed debt is not discharged. Under the rules stated in § 260, the payment is applied to the other debt and it is discharged.

9. A owes B two matured debts, on one of which no interest is due because the note representing it is usurious. A makes a payment to B without directing its application. B notifies A that he has applied it to the payment of interest on the debt represented by the usurious note. B's purported application is ineffective. The application of the payment is determined by the rules stated in § 260.

d. Creditor having claims in two capacities. If a creditor is owed one debt in his own right and another debt as fiduciary, and the latter debt is at least partly unsecured, he must apply to that debt no less a proportion of the payment than that borne by its unsecured amount to the total unsecured amount of both debts. Since this limitation is to protect the beneficiary, it may be removed with his consent.

10. A owes B two matured unsecured debts, one for $1,000 in B's own right and one for $2,000 on a contract made by A with B, who was acting for C, an undisclosed principal. A makes a $900 payment to B without directing its application. B must apply no less than $600 to the debt arising out of the agency contract. To the extent that he does not, his application is not effective. The debt arising out of the agency contract is then discharged to the extent of $600 under the rules stated in § 260.

e. Mutual assent to change application. Once an effective application of a payment has been made by either party, it cannot be changed without the assent of the other. Assent may validate the change even if the original application was not permissible, unless it was one that even the debtor lacked the power to direct (§ 258(2)). Silence for more than a reasonable time after receipt of notice from the obligee of a changed application or of one not otherwise permissible is a manifestation of assent in the absence of circumstances indicating the contrary. Compare § 69.

Illustration

11. The facts being otherwise as stated in Illustration 8, A does not reply for six months after he receives B's statement. B's application is validated. The disputed debt is discharged and the other debt is not discharged.

§ 260. Application of Payments Where Neither Party Exercises His Power.

(1) If neither the debtor nor the creditor has exercised his power with respect to the application of a payment as between two or more matured debts, the payment is applied to debts to which the creditor could have applied it with just regard to the interests of third persons, the debtor and the creditor.

(2) In applying payments under the rule stated in Subsection (1), a payment is applied to the earliest matured debt and ratably among debts of the same maturity, except that preference is given

    (a) to a debt that the debtor is under a duty to a third person to pay immediately, and

    (b) if he is not under such a duty,

        (i) to overdue interest rather than principal, and

        (ii) to an unsecured or precarious debt rather than one that is secured or certain of payment.

Comment

a. General rule. If neither the debtor nor the creditor exercises his power with respect to the application of a payment it is applied with just regard to the interests of third persons, the debtor and the creditor. This general principle supplements the specific rules stated in Subsection (2) and gives guidance in their application. However, a payment will not be applied to a duty to which the creditor himself could not have applied it because of the limitations stated in § 259. As to the extension of these principles to performances other than payments and as to state statutes governing consumer credit transactions other than payments, see the Introductory Note to this Topic.

b. Interests of third persons. The interests of third persons are served by precluding application to debts to which the creditor could not have applied the payment (Subsection (1)), thereby incorporating the rule as to debts owed to him in a fiduciary capacity stated in § 259(3). Furthermore, Paragraph (2)(a) states a rule for the protection of third persons that is much broader than the limitation of § 258(2) that is imposed on the creditor under the rule stated in § 259(2)(a). If the obligor owes a duty to a third person to pay a particular debt, preference is given to that debt. The duty to the third person may be based on a fiduciary relationship or on contract. Such a duty is owed by a principal debtor to a surety, as a result of the surety's right of exoneration, even though the surety became bound by a contract with the obligee without a request of the principal debtor. This preference applies to all cases of payments made by a principal debtor, even though his duty to exonerate the surety is merely a general one and does not require him to use for that purpose the particular money with which payment is made. Compare Comment c to § 258.

Illustration

1. A contracts with B to build a building. To secure A's payment for labor and materials, A gives B a surety bond that is enforceable against the surety by laborers and materialmen. A uses the progress payments that he receives from B to pay C, whom he owes for other materials as well as for materials for the building. Neither A nor C exercises his power of application as to these payments. The payments are applied to the debts for materials for the building because A owes a duty to the surety on the bond, who has a right of exoneration against A, to pay that debt. The result does not depend on whether C knew or had reason to know the source of the money used as payment. Compare Illustrations 7 and 8 to § 258.

c. Other interests. The interests of the debtor are served by precluding application to debts to which the creditor could not have applied the payment (Subsection (1)), thereby incorporating the rules as to forfeiture and disputed and unenforceable debts stated in § 259(2)(b) and (c). In the absence of any paramount interest of third persons or of the debtor, the interests of the creditor are served by the preferences stated in Paragraph (2)(b). There is a preference for paying overdue interest, on which interest may not be payable, rather than principal. There is also a preference for paying unsecured or precarious debts rather than those that are secured or certain of payment (Paragraph (2)(b)). If these preferences are not applicable, then the payment is applied to the debt that matured first and ratably among debts that matured at the same time.

Illustrations

2. A owes B several matured interest-bearing debts, on all of which interest is overdue. A makes a payment as to which neither A nor B exercises his power of application. The payment is applied to interest on all of the debts before it is applied to the overdue principal of any one.

3. A owes B two matured debts, one of which is secured by collateral belonging to the debtor. A makes a payment as to which neither A nor B exercises his power of application. The payment is applied to the unsecured debt even though it matured later.

CHAPTER 11

IMPRACTICABILITY OF PERFORMANCE AND FRUSTRATION OF PURPOSE

§ 261. Discharge by Supervening Impracticability.

Where, after a contract is made, a party's performance is made impracticable without his fault by the occurrence of an event the non-occurrence of which was a basic assumption on which the contract was made, his duty to render that performance is discharged, unless the language or the circumstances indicate the contrary.

Comment

a. Scope. Even though a party, in assuming a duty, has not qualified the language of his undertaking, a court may relieve him of that duty if performance has unexpectedly become impracticable as a result of a supervening event (see Introductory Note to this Chapter). This Section states the general principle under which a party's duty may be so discharged. The following three sections deal with the three categories of cases where this general principle has traditionally been applied: supervening death or incapacity of a person necessary for performance (§ 262), supervening destruction of a specific thing necessary for performance (§ 263), and supervening prohibition or prevention by law (§ 264). But, like Uniform Commercial Code § 2–615(a), this Section states a principle broadly applicable to all types of impracticability and it "deliberately refrains from any effort at an exhaustive expression of contingencies" (Comment 2 to Uniform Commercial Code § 2–615). The principle, like others in this Chapter, yields to a contrary agreement by which a party may assume a greater as well as a lesser obligation. By such an agreement, for example, a party may undertake to achieve a result irrespective of supervening events that may render its achievement impossible, and if he does so his non-performance is a breach even if it is caused by such an event. See Comment c. The rule stated in this Section applies only to discharge a duty to render a performance and does not affect a claim for breach that has already arisen. The effect of events subsequent to a breach on the amount of damages recoverable is governed by the rules on remedies stated in Chapter 16. See Comment e to § 347. Their effect on a claim for breach by anticipatory repudiation is governed by the rules on discharge stated in Chapter 12. Cases of existing, as opposed to supervening, impracticability are governed by § 266 rather than this Section.

b. Basic assumption. In order for a supervening event to discharge a duty under this Section, the non-occurrence of that event must have been a "basic assumption" on which both parties made the contract (see Introductory Note to this Chapter). This is the criterion used by Uniform Commercial Code § 2–615(a). Its application is simple enough in the cases of the death of a person or destruction of a specific thing necessary for performance. The continued existence of the person or thing (the non-occurrence of the death of destruction) is ordinarily a basic assumption on which the contract was made, so that death or destruction effects a discharge. Its application is also simple enough in the cases of market shifts or the financial inability of one of the parties. The continuation of existing market conditions and of the financial situation of the parties are ordinarily not such assumptions, so that mere market shifts or financial inability do not usually effect discharge under the rule stated in this Section. In borderline cases this criterion is sufficiently flexible to take account of factors that bear on a just allocation of risk. The fact that the event was foreseeable, or even foreseen, does not necessarily compel a conclusion that its non-occurrence was not a basic assumption. See Comment c to this Section and Comment a to § 265.

Illustrations

1. On June 1, A agrees to sell and B to buy goods to be delivered in October at a designated port. The port is subsequently closed by quarantine regulations during the entire month of October, no commercially reasonable substitute performance is available (see Uniform Commercial Code § 2–614(1)), and A fails to deliver the goods. A's duty to deliver the goods is discharged, and A is not liable to B for breach of contract.

2. A contracts to produce a movie for B. As B knows, A's only source of funds is a $100,000 deposit in C bank. C bank fails, and A does not produce the movie. A's duty to produce the movie is not discharged, and A is liable to B for breach of contract.

3. A and B make a contract under which B is to work for A for two years at a salary of $50,000 a year. At the end of one year, A discontinues his business because governmental regulations have made it unprofitable and fires B. A's duty to employ B is not discharged, and A is liable to B for breach of contract.

4. A contracts to sell and B to buy a specific machine owned by A to be delivered on July 30. On July 29, as a result of a creditor's suit against A, a receiver is appointed and takes charge of all of A's assets, and A does not deliver the goods on July 30. A's duty to deliver the goods is not discharged, and A is liable to B for breach of contract.

c. Contrary indication. A party may, by appropriate language, agree to perform in spite of impracticability that would otherwise justify his non-performance under the rule stated in this Section. He can then be held liable for damages although he cannot perform. Even absent an express agreement, a court may decide, after considering all the circumstances, that a party impliedly assumed such a greater obligation. In this respect the rule stated in this Section parallels that of Uniform Commercial Code § 2–615, which applies "Except so far as a seller may have assumed a greater obligation . . ." Circumstances relevant in deciding whether a party has assumed a greater obligation include his ability to have inserted a provision in the contract expressly shifting the risk of impracticability to the other party. This will depend on the extent to which the agreement was standardized (cf. § 211), the degree to which the other party supplied the terms (cf. § 206), and, in the case of a particular trade or other group, the frequency with which language so allocating the risk is used in that trade or group (cf. § 219). The fact that a supplier has not taken advantage of his opportunity expressly to shift the risk of a shortage in his supply by means of contract language may be regarded as more significant where he is middleman, with a variety of sources of supply and an opportunity to spread the risk among many customers on many transactions by slight adjustment of his prices, than where he is a producer with a limited source of supply, few outlets, and no comparable opportunity. A commercial practice under which a party might be expected to insure or otherwise secure himself against a risk also militates against shifting it to the other party. If the supervening event was not reasonably foreseeable when the contract was made, the party claiming discharge can hardly be expected to have provided against its occurrence. However, if it was reasonably foreseeable, or even foreseen, the opposite conclusion does not necessarily follow. Factors such as the practical difficulty of reaching agreement on the myriad of conceivable terms of a complex agreement may excuse a failure to deal with improbable contingencies. See Comment b to this Section and Comment a to § 265.

Illustration

5. A, who has had many years of experience in the field of salvage, contracts to raise and float B's boat, which has run aground. The contract, prepared by A, contains no clause limiting A's duty in the case of unfavorable weather, unforeseen circumstances, or otherwise. The boat then slips into deep water and fills with mud, making it impracticable for A to raise it. If the court concludes, on the basis of such circumstances as A's experience and the absence of any limitation in the contract that A prepared, that A assumed an absolute duty, it will decide that A's duty to raise and float the boat is not discharged and that A is liable to B for breach of contract.

d. Impracticability. Events that come within the rule stated in this Section are generally due either to "acts of God" or to acts of third parties. If the event that prevents the obligor's performance is caused by the obligee, it will ordinarily amount to a breach by the latter and the situation will be governed by the rules stated in Chapter 10, without regard to this Section. See Illustrations 4–7 to § 237. If the event is due to the fault of the obligor himself, this Section does not apply. As used here "fault" may include not only "willful" wrongs, but such other types of conduct as that amounting to breach of contract or to negligence. See Comment 1 to Uniform Commercial Code § 2–613. Although the rule stated in this Section is sometimes phrased in terms of "impossibility," it has long been recognized that it may operate to discharge a party's duty even though the event has not made performance absolutely impossible. This Section, therefore, uses "impracticable," the term employed by Uniform Commercial Code § 2–615(a), to describe the required extent of the impediment to performance. Performance may be impracticable because extreme and unreasonable difficulty, expense, injury, or loss to one of the parties will be involved. A severe shortage of raw materials or of supplies due to war, embargo, local crop failure, unforeseen shutdown of major sources of supply, or the like, which either causes a marked increase in cost or prevents performance altogether may bring the case within the rule stated in this Section. Performance may also be impracticable because it will involve a risk of injury to person or to property, of one of the parties or of others, that is disproportionate to the ends to be attained by performance. However, "impracticability" means more than "impracticality." A mere change in the degree of difficulty or expense due to such causes as increased wages, prices of raw materials, or costs of construction, unless well beyond the normal range, does not amount to impracticability since it is this sort of risk that a fixed-price contract is intended to cover. Furthermore, a party is expected to use reasonable efforts to surmount obstacles to performance (see § 205), and a performance is impracticable only if it is so in spite of such efforts.

Illustrations

6. A contracts to repair B's grain elevator. While A is engaged in making repairs, a fire destroys the elevator without A's fault, and A does not finish the repairs. A's duty to repair the elevator is discharged, and A is not liable to B for breach of contract. See Illustration 3 to § 263.

7. A contracts with B to carry B's goods on his ship to a designated foreign port. A civil war then unexpectedly breaks out in that country and the rebels announce that they will try to sink all vessels bound for that port. A refuses to perform. Although A did not contract to sail on the vessel, the risk of injury to others is sufficient to make A's performance impracticable. A's duty to carry the goods to the designated port is discharged, and A is not liable to B for breach of contract. Compare Illustration 5 to § 262.

8. The facts being otherwise as stated in Illustration 7, the rebels announce merely that they will confiscate all vessels found in the designated port. The goods can be bought and sold on markets throughout the world. A refuses to perform. Although there is no risk of injury to persons, the court may conclude that the risk of injury to property is disproportionate to the ends to be attained. A's duty to carry the goods to the designated port is then discharged, and A is not liable to B for breach of contract. If, however, B is a health organization and the goods are scarce medical supplies vital to the health of the population of the designated port, the court may conclude that the risk is not disproportionate to the ends to be attained and may reach a contrary decision.

9. Several months after the nationalization of the Suez Canal, during the international crisis resulting from its seizure, A contracts to carry a cargo of B's wheat on A's ship from Galveston, Texas to Bandar Shapur, Iran for a flat rate. The contract does not specify the route, but the voyage would normally be through the Straits of Gibraltar and the Suez Canal, a distance of 10,000 miles. A month later, and several days after the ship has left Galveston, the Suez Canal is closed by an outbreak of hostilities, so that the only route to Bandar Shapur is the longer 13,000 mile voyage around the Cape of Good Hope. A refuses to complete the voyage unless B pays additional compensation. A's duty to carry B's cargo is not discharged, and A is liable to B for breach of contract.

10. The facts being otherwise as in Illustration 9, the Suez Canal is closed while A's ship is in the Canal, preventing the completion of the voyage. A's duty to carry B's cargo is discharged, and A is not liable to B for breach of contract.

11. A contracts to construct and lease to B a gasoline service station. A valid zoning ordinance is subsequently enacted forbidding the construction of such a station but permitting variances in appropriate cases. A, in breach of his duty of good faith and fair dealing (§ 205), makes no effort to obtain a variance, although variances have been granted in similar cases, and fails to construct the station. A's performance has not been made impracticable. A's duty to construct is not discharged, and A is liable to B for breach of contract.

e. "Subjective" and "objective" impracticability. It is sometimes said that the rule stated in this Section applies only when the performance itself is made impracticable, without regard to the particular party who is to perform. The difference has been described as that between "the thing cannot be done" and "I cannot do it," and the former has been characterized as "objective" and the latter as "subjective." This Section recognizes that if the performance remains practicable and it is merely beyond the party's capacity to render it, he is ordinarily not discharged, but it does not use the terms "objective" and "subjective" to express this. Instead, the rationale is that a party generally assumes the risk of his own inability to perform his duty. Even if a party contracts to render a performance that depends on some act by a third party, he is not ordinarily discharged because of a failure by that party because this is also a risk that is commonly understood to be on the obligor. See Comment c. But see Comment a to § 262.

Illustrations

12. A, a milkman, and B, a dairy farmer, make a contract under which B is to sell and A to buy all of A's requirements of milk, but not less than 200 quarts a day, for one year. B may deliver milk from any source but expects to deliver milk from his own herd. B's herd is destroyed because of hoof and mouth disease and he fails to deliver any milk. B's duty to deliver milk is not discharged, and B is liable to A for breach of contract. See Illustration 1 to § 263; compare Illustration 7 to § 263.

13. A contracts to sell and B to buy on credit 1,500,000 gallons of molasses "of the usual run from the C sugar refinery." C delivers molasses to others but fails to deliver any to A, and A fails to deliver any to B. A's duty to deliver molasses is not discharged, and A is liable to B for breach of contract. If A has a contract with C, C may be liable to A for breach of contract.

14. A, a general contractor, is bidding on a construction contract with B which gives B the right to disapprove the choice of subcontractors. A makes a contract with C, a subcontractor, under which, if B awards A the contract, A will obtain B's approval of C and C will do the excavation for A. A is awarded the contract by B, but B disapproves A's choice of C, and A has the excavation work done by another subcontractor. A's duty to have C do the excavation is not discharged, and A is liable to C for breach of contract.

f. Alternative performances. A contract may permit a party to choose to perform in one of several different ways, any of which will discharge his duty. Where the duty is to render such an alternative performance, the fact that one or more of the alternatives has become impracticable will not discharge the party's duty to perform if at least one of them remains practicable. The form of the promise is not controlling, however, and not every promise that is expressed in alternative form gives rise to a duty to render an alternative performance. For example, a surety's undertaking that either the principal will perform or the surety will compensate the creditor does not ordinarily impose such a duty. See Restatement of Security § 117. Nor does a promise either to render a performance or pay liquidated damages impose such a duty. Furthermore, a duty that is originally one to render alternative performances ceases to be such a duty if all but one means of performance have been foreclosed, as by the lapse of time or the occurrence of a condition including election by the obligor, or on the grounds of public policy (Chapter 8) or unconscionability (§ 208).

Illustrations

15. On June 1, A contracts to sell and B to buy whichever of three specified machines A chooses to deliver on October 1. Two of the machines are destroyed by fire on July 1, and A fails to deliver the third on October 1. A's duty to deliver a machine is not discharged, and A is liable to B for breach of contract. If all three machines had been destroyed, A's duty to deliver a machine would have been discharged, and A would not have been liable to B for breach of contract. See Uniform Commercial Code § 2–613.

16. A contracts to repair B's building. The contract contains a valid provision requiring A to pay liquidated damages if he fails to make any of the repairs. S is surety for A's performance. Before A is able to begin, B's building is destroyed by fire. Neither A's nor S's duty is one to render an alternative performance. A's duty to repair the building is discharged, and A is not liable to B for liquidated damages or otherwise for breach of contract. S's duty as surety for A is also discharged, and S is not liable to B for breach of contract.

§ 262. Death or Incapacity of Person Necessary for Performance.

If the existence of a particular person is necessary for the performance of a duty, his death or such incapacity as makes performance impracticable is an event the non-occurrence of which was a basic assumption on which the contract was made.

IMPRACTICABILITY OF PERFORMANCE AND FRUSTRATION OF PURPOSE

Comment

a. Rationale. This Section states a common specific instance for the application of the rule stated in § 261. If, as both parties understand, the existence of a particular person is necessary for the performance of a duty, it is a "basic assumption on which the contract was made" that he will neither die nor be deprived of the necessary capacity before the time for performance. Therefore, the death of that person or his loss of capacity discharges the obligor's duty to render the performance, subject to the qualifications stated in § 261. Usually, the person in question will be the obligor, but he may also be the obligee or a third person. Where the obligor is personally to perform the duty, his death or incapacity results in "objective," not merely in "subjective," impracticability (Comment e to § 261), since it is no longer practicable for anyone to perform the duty. The result is, of course, different if the language or the circumstances indicate the contrary (Comment c to § 261), but it is sufficiently rare for a party to undertake a duty to render personal service in spite of his death or incapacity that an intention to do so must be clearly manifested. Although the obligor's fault will prevent his disability from discharging that duty, it is often so difficult to foresee the effect of conduct on health that fault in bringing about disability must be clear in order to prevent the disability from resulting in discharge. The rule applies not only to the disability of a natural person but also, by analogy, to the dissolution of a legal person such as a corporation. However, it is seldom applicable to such cases in practice because the dissolution ordinarily must not be due to its financial inability (see Comment b to § 261) and, since it must not be due to its own fault, it must not be within its control. If the disability exists at the time the contract is made, the rule stated in § 266(1) rather than that stated in § 261 controls, and this Section applies for the purpose of that rule as well.

Illustrations

1. A contracts to employ B as his confidential secretary for a year. B dies before the end of the year. B's duty to work for A is discharged, and B's estate is not liable to A for breach of contract.

2. The facts being otherwise as stated in Illustration 1, A rather than B dies before the end of the year, and B takes other employment. B's duty to work for A is discharged, and B is not liable to A's estate for breach of contract.

3. A, a corporation, contracts to employ B as its secretary for five years. Within that time the state legislature enacts a law requiring the dissolution of corporations engaged in A's business. On dissolution, A's duty to employ B is discharged, and A is not liable to B for breach of contract. See also § 264. B may have a claim against A under the rule stated in § 272(1).

4. The facts being otherwise as in Illustration 3, A's dissolution is voluntary or the result of insolvency. A's duty to employ B is not discharged, and A is liable to B for breach of contract. See Comment b and Illustration 3 to § 261. Cf. Illustration 5 to § 319.

5. A contracts with B to produce a play starring C, a famous actor, in B's theater on December 16. Early in December, while the play is being performed elsewhere, C experiences a worsening throat condition and, although it does not prevent his performing, he is advised by his doctor to cancel his further performances and have a minor operation. On December 12, A notifies B that the December 16 performance of the play is cancelled for this reason. A's duty to produce the play is discharged, and A is not liable to B for breach of contract. Compare Illustration 7 to § 261.

b. Where particular person is necessary. The parties may effectively provide that a particular person is or is not necessary for performance. The agreement may, for example, require the obligor's personal service. Where, as is often the case, the agreement is silent on the subject, all the circumstances will be considered to determine whether the duty, as understood by the parties, sufficiently involves elements of personal service or discretion to require performance by a particular person. In this connection, resort may be had to the rules laid down in Chapter 9, The Scope of Contractual Obligations, including those on usage and course of dealing (§§ 219–23). The question whether a duty requires performance by a particular person is essentially the same question that arises where a party seeks to delegate performance of his duty to another and is to be determined by the same criteria. See § 318 and Comment b to that Section. If an obligor can discharge his duty by the performance of another, his own disability will not discharge him.

Illustrations

6. A contracts with B to cut a tract of standing timber. A dies, and his estate refuses to complete performance. In the absence of special circumstances showing that A's personal service or supervision is necessary to performance of his duty, A's duty to cut the timber is not discharged, and A's estate is liable to B for breach of contract.

7. A and B make a contract under which A is to devote full time to prospecting for coal on B's land, and, if he is successful, B personally is to finance and manage a corporation for the exploitation of the coal. B is to pay A a salary and convey to him a one-quarter interest in any resulting corporation. A locates coal and is paid his salary, but B dies before he is able to finance and manage a corporation to exploit it, and no such corporation is formed. Whether performance of B's duty to finance and manage a corporation became impracticable on B's death depends on whether that duty, as understood by the parties, could only be performed by B himself. If the court concludes that it could, B's duty to convey an interest in any resulting corporation is discharged, and B's estate is not liable to A for breach of contract. A may have a claim against B under the rule stated in § 272(1).

8. A and B, a firm of architects, contract with C to design a building for C. It is understood by the parties that both A and B shall render services under the contract. A dies and B fails to complete performance. Both A's and B's duties to design the building are discharged, and neither A's estate nor B is liable to C for breach of contract.

9. A and B, a firm of contractors doing an extensive business in many localities, contract with C to fill a tract of low land. A dies and B fails to complete performance. Neither A's nor B's duty to fill the land is discharged, and both A's estate and B are liable to C for breach of contract.

§ 263. Destruction, Deterioration or Failure to Come Into Existence of Thing Necessary for Performance.

If the existence of a specific thing is necessary for the performance of a duty, its failure to come into existence, destruction, or such deterioration as makes performance impracticable is an event the non-occurrence of which was a basic assumption on which the contract was made.

Comment

a. Rationale. This Section, like the preceding one, states a common specific instance for the application of the rule stated in § 261. If, as both parties understand, the existence of a specific thing is necessary for the performance of a duty it is "a basic assumption on which the contract was made" that that thing will come into existence if it does not already exist and will remain in existence until the time for performance. Therefore, if its failure to come into existence or its destruction or deterioration makes performance impracticable, the obligor's duty to render that performance is discharged, subject to the qualifications stated in § 261. Each party bears some of the risk that the transaction will not be carried out for such a reason. The rule does not apply, however, where an obligor merely happens to have at his disposal only one means of performance, which is destroyed, since the parties do not then make the contract on the basis of such an assumption. See Comment b to § 261. Nor does it apply if the language or the circumstances indicate the contrary. See Comment c to § 261. If the parties contract on an erroneous assumption that a specific thing necessary for performance is then in existence, the rule stated in § 266(1) rather than that stated in § 261 controls, and this Section applies for the purpose of that rule as well.

Illustrations

1. A contracts to sell and B to buy cloth. A expects to manufacture the cloth in his factory, but before he begins manufacture the factory is destroyed by fire without his fault. Although cloth meeting the contract description is available on the market, A refuses to buy and deliver it to B. A's duty to deliver the cloth is not discharged, and A is liable to B for breach of contract. See Illustration 12 to § 261; compare Illustration 7 to this Section.

2. The facts being otherwise as stated in Illustration 1, A contracts to sell cloth to be manufactured in the factory that is later destroyed. A's duty to deliver the cloth is discharged, and A is not liable to B for breach of contract. Cf. Illustration 13 to § 261.

3. A contracts with B to shingle the roof of B's house. When A has done part of the work, much of the house including the roof is destroyed by fire without his fault, so that he is unable to complete the work. A's duty to shingle the roof is discharged, and A is not liable to B for breach of contract. Compare Illustration 6 to § 261.

4. A contracts with B to build a house for B. When A has done part of the work, much of the structure is destroyed by fire without his fault. A refuses to finish building the house. A's duty to build the house is not discharged, and A is liable to B for breach of contract.

5. A contracts to sell a specified machine to B for $10,000. Before A tenders the machine to B, a fire destroys it without A's fault. A's duty to deliver the machine is discharged (Uniform Commercial Code § 2–613), and A is not liable for breach of contract. Compare Illustration 4 to § 267.

b. When specific thing is necessary. The rule stated in this Section applies not only when the terms of the contract make the specific thing necessary, but also when, although the contract is silent, the parties understand that it is necessary. In proving such an understanding, prior negotiations may be used to show the meaning of a writing, even though it takes the form of a completely integrated agreement. See § 214(c).

Illustrations

6. A contracts with B to drive logs to B's mill during the following spring. Although the contract does not specify a particular stream, the parties know that there is only one stream down which the logs can be driven. An extraordinary drought dries that stream up during the time for performance. A's duty to drive the logs is discharged, and A is not liable to B for breach of contract.

7. A, a farmer, contracts with B in the spring to sell a large quantity of beans to B during the following season. Although the contract does not state where the beans are to be grown, A owns but one tract of land, on which he has in the past raised beans, and both parties understand that the beans will be raised on this tract. A properly plants and cultivates beans on the tract in sufficient quantity to perform the contract, but an extraordinary flood destroys the crop. A delivers no beans to B. A's duty to deliver beans is discharged, and A is not liable to B for breach of contract. Compare Illustration 1 to this Section; Illustration 12 to § 261.

8. The facts being otherwise as stated in Illustration 7, A and B have no common understanding as to where the beans will be grown. A's duty to deliver beans is not discharged, and A is liable to B for breach of contract. Cf. Comment f to § 261.

§ 264. Prevention by Governmental Regulation or Order.

If the performance of a duty is made impracticable by having to comply with a domestic or foreign governmental regulation or order, that regulation or order is an event the non-occurrence of which was a basic assumption on which the contract was made.

Comment

a. Rationale. This Section, like the two that precede it, states a specific instance for the application of the rule stated in § 261. It is "a basic assumption on which the contract was made" that the law will not directly intervene to make performance impracticable when it is due. Therefore, if supervening governmental action prohibits a performance or imposes requirements that make it impracticable, the duty to render that performance is discharged, subject to the qualifications stated in § 261. The fact that it is still possible for a party to perform if he is willing to break the law and risk the consequences does not bar him from claiming discharge. The rule stated in this Section does not apply if the language or the circumstances indicate the contrary. With the trend toward greater governmental regulation, however, parties are increasingly aware of such risks, and a party may undertake a duty that is not discharged by such supervening governmental actions, as where governmental approval is required for his performance and he assumes the risk that approval will be denied (Illustration 3). Such an agreement is usually interpreted as one to pay damages if performance is prevented rather than one to render a performance in violation of law. See §§ 180, 198. If the prohibition or prevention already exists at the time of the making of the contract, the rule stated in § 266(1) rather than that stated in § 261 controls, and this Section applies for the purpose of that rule as well. See Comment a to § 266. See also Chapter 8 on agreements unenforceable on grounds of public policy. The effect of a governmental regulation or order on a claim for breach is governed by the rules on discharge stated in Chapter 12.

Illustrations

1. A sells land to B, who, as part of the contract, promises that the land shall not be built upon. The land is taken by eminent domain under statutory authority and a building is built on it. B's duty not to build on the land is discharged, and B is not liable to A for breach of contract.

2. A, a railroad, promises to give B annual passes for life, in consideration for a conveyance of land by B to A. After thirteen years, a statute is enacted forbidding railroads to grant such passes, and A refuses to give further passes to B. A's duty to give passes is discharged, and A is not liable to B for breach of contract. B may have a claim against A under the rule stated in § 272(1).

3. A, a manufacturer of sewage treatment equipment, contracts to design and install a central sewage treatment plant, for which B, a developer of a residential subdivision, contracts to pay. The parties understand that A must obtain the approval of the state Department of Health before installation. A is unable to install the plant because the Department of Health disapproves the plans. If the court concludes, on the basis of A's experience and the absence of any limitation in the contract, that A assumed the risk that approval would be denied, it will decide that A's duty to install the plant is not discharged and that A is liable to B for breach of contract. Cf. Illustration 3 to § 266.

4. A contracts with B to sell him a specific machine on a stated day, time being of the essence. C, by false allegations of ownership of the machine, induces a court to enjoin A from delivering the machine. In spite of diligent efforts, A is unable to have the injunction dissolved in time to fulfill his contract with B. A's duty to deliver the machine is discharged, and A is not liable to B for breach of contract. The result would be different if due to A's fault C had just grounds for obtaining the injunction, or if A, in breach of his duty of good faith and fair dealing (§ 205), failed to use diligent efforts which could have secured its dissolution. See Comment d to § 261 and Illustration 11 to that section.

5. A and B make a contract under which A is to employ B for a year. B is unable to complete his performance because he is arrested and imprisoned for a burglary that he has committed. Because his inability was due to his own fault, B's duty to work for a year is not discharged, and B is liable to A for breach of contract. See Comment d to § 261.

b. Nature of regulation or order. Under the rule stated in this Section, the regulation or order may be domestic or foreign. It may emanate from any level of government and may be, for example, a municipal ordinance or an order of an administrative agency. Any governmental action is included and technical distinctions between "law," "regulation," "order" and the like are disregarded. It is not necessary that the regulation or order be valid, but a party who seeks to justify his non-performance under this Section must have observed the duty of good faith and fair dealing imposed by § 205 in attempting, where appropriate, to avoid its application. The requirement is like that of Uniform Commercial Code § 2–615, under which compliance in good faith is sufficient regardless of the validity of the regulation or order. See Comment 10 to Uniform Commercial Code § 2–615. The regulation or order must directly affect a party's performance in such a way that it is impracticable for him both to comply with the regulation or order and to perform. Governmental action that has the indirect effect of making performance more burdensome by, for example, contributing to a scarcity of supply, is governed by the general rule stated in § 261 and not by the specific rule stated in this Section.

Illustration

6. A, a citizen of a foreign country, contracts with B to sell him the output of A's mill for one year. War breaks out, and A's government orders him to sell the output of his mill to it instead. A complies with the order in good faith and fails to deliver to B. A's duty to deliver his output to B is discharged, and A is not liable for breach of contract. The result does not depend on the legal validity of the order.

§ 265. Discharge by Supervening Frustration.

Where, after a contract is made, a party's principal purpose is substantially frustrated without his fault by the occurrence of an event the non-occurrence of which was a basic assumption on which the contract was made, his remaining duties to render performance are discharged, unless the language or the circumstances indicate the contrary.

Comment

a. Rationale. This Section deals with the problem that arises when a change in circumstances makes one party's performance virtually worthless to the other, frustrating his purpose in making the contract. It is distinct from the problem of impracticability dealt with in the four preceding sections because there is no impediment to performance by either party. Although there has been no true failure of performance in the sense required for the application of the rule stated in § 237, the impact on the party adversely affected will be similar. The rule stated in this Section sets out the requirements for the discharge of that party's duty. First, the purpose that is frustrated must have been a principal purpose of that party in making the contract. It is not enough that he had in mind some specific object without which he would not have made the contract. The object must be so completely the basis of the contract that, as both parties understand, without it the transaction would make little sense. Second, the frustration must be substantial. It is not enough that the transaction has become less profitable for the affected party or even that he will sustain a loss. The frustration must be so severe that it is not fairly to be regarded as within the risks that he assumed under the contract. Third, the non-occurrence of the frustrating event must have been a basic assumption on which the contract was made. This involves essentially the same sorts of determinations that are involved under the general rule on impracticability. See Comments b and c to § 261. The foreseeability of the event is here, as it is there, a factor in that determination, but the mere fact that the event was foreseeable does not compel the conclusion that its non-occurrence was not such a basic assumption.

Illustrations

1. A and B make a contract under which B is to pay A $1,000 and is to have the use of A's window on January 10 to view a parade that has been scheduled for that day. Because of the illness of an important official, the parade is cancelled. B refuses to use the window or pay the $1,000. B's duty to pay $1,000 is discharged, and B is not liable to A for breach of contract.

2. A contracts with B to print an advertisement in a souvenir program of an international yacht race, which has been scheduled by a yacht club, for a price of $10,000. The yacht club cancels the race because of the outbreak of war. A has already printed the programs, but B refuses to pay the $10,000. B's duty to pay $10,000 is discharged, and B is not liable to A for breach of contract. A may have a claim under the rule stated in § 272(1).

3. A, who owns a hotel, and B, who owns a country club, make a contract under which A is to pay $1,000 a month and B is to make the club's membership privileges available to the guests in A's hotel free of charge to them. A's building is destroyed by fire without his fault, and A is unable to remain in the hotel business. A refuses to make further monthly payments. A's duty to make monthly payments is discharged, and A is not liable to B for breach of contract.

4. A leases neon sign installations to B for three years to advertise and illuminate B's place of business. After one year, a government regulation prohibits the lighting of such signs. B refuses to make further payments of rent. B's duty to pay rent is discharged, and B is not liable to A for breach of contract. See Illustration 7.

5. A contracts to sell and B to buy a machine, to be delivered to B in the United States. B, as A knows, intends to export the machine to a particular country for resale. Before delivery to B, a government regulation prohibits export of the machine to that country. B refuses to take or pay for the machine. If B can reasonably make other disposition of the machine, even though at some loss, his principal purpose of putting the machine to commercial use is not substantially frustrated. B's duty to take and pay for the machine is not discharged, and B is liable to A for breach of contract.

6. A leases a gasoline station to B. A change in traffic regulations so reduces B's business that he is unable to operate the station except at a substantial loss. B refuses to make further payments of rent. If B can still operate the station, even though at such a loss, his principal purpose of operating a

gasoline station is not substantially frustrated. B's duty to pay rent is not discharged, and B is liable to A for breach of contract. The result would be the same if substantial loss were caused instead by a government regulation rationing gasoline or a termination of the franchise under which B obtained gasoline.

b. Limitations on scope. The rule stated in this Section is subject to limitations similar to those stated in § 261 with respect to impracticability. It applies only when the frustration is without the fault of the party who seeks to take advantage of the rule, and it does not apply if the language or circumstances indicate the contrary. Frustration by circumstances existing at the time of the making of the contract rather than by supervening circumstances is governed by the similar rule stated in § 266(2).

Illustration

7. The facts being otherwise as in Illustration 4, the government regulation provides for a procedure under which B can apply for an exemption, but B, in breach of his duty of good faith and fair dealing (§ 205), fails to make such an application. Unless it is found that such an application would have been unsuccessful, B's duty to pay rent is not discharged, and B is liable to A for breach of contract. Cf. Illustration 11 to § 261; Illustration 3 to § 264.

§ 266. Existing Impracticability or Frustration.

(1) Where, at the time a contract is made, a party's performance under it is impracticable without his fault because of a fact of which he has no reason to know and the non-existence of which is a basic assumption on which the contract is made, no duty to render that performance arises, unless the language or circumstances indicate the contrary.

(2) Where, at the time a contract is made, a party's principal purpose is substantially frustrated without his fault by a fact of which he has no reason to know and the non-existence of which is a basic assumption on which the contract is made, no duty of that party to render performance arises, unless the language or circumstances indicate the contrary.

Comment

a. Relation to other rules. A party's performance may be as easily affected by impracticability existing at the time the contract was made, because of some fact of which he was ignorant, as by supervening impracticability. Indeed, it is sometimes difficult to characterize a situation as involving either existing or changed circumstances, as, for example, where a judicial decision is handed down after the time that the contract was made giving an unanticipated interpretation to a statute enacted before that time. Cf. Illustration 3. The rules stated in this Section for cases of existing impracticability and frustration therefore parallel those for supervening impracticability and frustration (§§ 261, 265). The rules stated in §§ 262–64 for determining when the non-occurrence of an event is a basic assumption on which a contract is made for the purpose of § 261 apply by analogy in determining when the non-existence of a fact is such a basic assumption for the purpose of this Section. There are two respects in which the rules stated in this Section differ from those applicable to supervening impracticability and frustration. First, under the rules stated in this Section, the affected party must have had no reason to know at the time the contract was made of the facts on which he later relies. Second, the effect of these rules is to prevent a duty from arising in the first place rather than to discharge a duty that has already arisen. Where a party has partly performed before discovery of the impracticability or frustration, he may claim relief including restitution under the rules stated in §§ 240 and 370–77. See Illustration 5 and § 272(1). In many of the cases that come under this Section, relief based on the rules relating to mistake stated in Chapter 6 will also be appropriate. See Introductory Note to Chapter 6. In that event, the party entitled to relief may, of course, choose the ground on which he will rely. In other cases that come under the rules stated in this Section, the rules on agreements unenforceable on grounds of public policy stated in Chapter 8 will also apply. To the extent that the latter bar relief for reasons based on public policy, they are controlling.

Illustrations

1. A contracts to sell a specified machine to B for $10,000. At the time the contract is made, the machine has been destroyed by fire without A's fault but A has no reason to know this. Under the

rule stated in Subsection (1) no duty arose under which A is to deliver the machine, and A is not liable to B for breach of contract. Cf. Illustration 7 to this Section and Illustration 5 to § 263.

2. A and B make a contract under which A is to sell B a house. B, an experienced real estate dealer, insists on the inclusion of a provision under which A is to procure a permit for its conversion into a two family dwelling. Two days earlier, a local zoning ordinance was enacted prohibiting such a conversion, but A has no reason to know this. A is unable to procure the permit. Under the rule stated in Subsection (1), no duty arose under which A is to procure the permit, and A is not liable to B for breach of contract. See § 264.

3. A, in public bidding, is awarded a contract to build a hospital for the State. A makes a subcontract with B for the installation of glass. Before B begins performance, a court declares the contract between A and the State to be invalid because of departures, of which A had no reason to know, from administrative procedure required for public bidding. A notifies B that he will be unable to perform his contract with B. Under the rule stated in Subsection (1), no duty arose under which A is to perform his contract with B, and A is not liable to B for breach of contract. See § 264. Cf. Illustration 3 to § 264. B may have a claim against A under the rule stated in § 272(1).

4. A, an engineering firm, contracts with B to lay water mains under a river. After diligent effort, A is unable to do the work, although other, more experienced firms could do it. Performance is not impracticable. A is under a duty to lay the mains, and A is liable to B for breach of contract. See Comment e to § 261.

5. A, an owner of land, and B, a builder, make a contract under which B is to take from A's land, at a stated rate per cubic yard, all the gravel and earth necessary for the construction of a bridge, an amount estimated to be 114,000 cubic yards. Much of the gravel and earth is below water level and cannot be removed by ordinary means, so that removal would require the use of special equipment at ten times the usual cost per cubic yard, but B has no reason to know this. After removing 50,000 yards, B discovers that this is the case for the remaining gravel and earth, and refuses to take or pay for it. Under the rule stated in Subsection (1), no duty arose under which B is to take or pay for the gravel, and B is not liable to A for breach of contract. A may have a claim against B under the rule stated in § 272(1).

6. A contracts to sell land to B for B's use as a health resort and milk farm. Two days earlier, a local zoning ordinance was enacted forbidding its use for this purpose, but B has no reason to know this. On discovery of the ordinance, B refuses to take or pay for the land. Under the rule stated in Subsection (2), no duty arose under which B is to take or pay for the land, and B is not liable to A for breach of contract.

b. Contrary indication. As under the rules stated in §§ 261 and 265, the language or circumstances may indicate that a party has assumed a greater obligation than that imposed on him under this Section. It is somewhat more usual for a party to undertake such an obligation with respect to existing facts than it is with respect to supervening events. A common and important instance occurs when a seller warrants specific goods against defects (Illustration 7). Whether a party has assumed such an obligation is a particularly troublesome question where the parties make a contract calling for technological development under a mistaken assumption that such development either is feasible under the existing state of the art or will become feasible as a result of a technological breakthrough (Illustrations 9 and 10). In such a case the court will determine whether the obligor took the risk that development might not be practicable by looking at such factors as the history of the negotiations, the relative expertise and bargaining power of the parties, their respective roles with regard to plans and specifications, the nature of the performances and the state of technology in the industry. If the obligee has undertaken an obligation as to the accuracy and sufficiency of the plans and specifications, then the consequences of their inaccuracy or insufficiency are governed by the rules stated in Chapter 10, Performance and Non-Performance.

Illustrations

7. A contracts to sell a specified machine to B for $10,000, warranting its merchantability. At the time the contract is made, the machine is not merchantable because of an uncurable defect not due to the fault of A, but A has no reason to know this. Because of A's warranty, he is under a duty to

deliver a merchantable machine in spite of the impracticability of doing so, and A is liable to B for breach of contract.

8. A contracts with B to build a house on B's land according to plans furnished by A. Because of subsoil conditions, of which A has no reason to know, this cannot be done unless the land is drained at great expense. After the house is partly completed, it collapses because of these conditions, and A refuses to continue the work. The court may determine from all the circumstances, including the fact that A furnished the plans, that A is under a duty to build the house in spite of the impracticability of doing so, and that A is liable to B for breach of contract. Compare Illustration 4 to § 263.

9. A contracts with B to develop, manufacture, and deliver a light weight electronic device according to A's own specifications by means of what both A and B understand will be a revolutionary technological breakthrough. No breakthrough occurs, and A is unable to deliver the device because it is not possible for any manufacturer, under the state of the art, to keep the weight within the contract specifications. The court may determine from all the circumstances, including the facts that A furnished the specifications and that the parties understand that A will achieve a breakthrough, that A is under a duty to deliver the device in spite of the impracticability of doing so, and that A is liable to B for breach of contract.

10. A contracts with B to manufacture and deliver a light weight electronic device according to specifications furnished by B's engineers. It is not possible for any manufacturer to keep the weight within the contract specifications, but A has no reason to know this. A does not deliver the device. The court may determine from all the circumstances, including the fact that B furnished the specifications, that A is under no duty to deliver the device because of the impracticability of doing so and that A is not liable to B for breach of contract.

§ 267. Effect on Other Party's Duties of a Failure Justified by Impracticability or Frustration.

(1) A party's failure to render or to offer performance may, except as stated in Subsection (2), affect the other party's duties under the rules stated in §§ 237 and 238 even though the failure is justified under the rules stated in this Chapter.

(2) The rule stated in Subsection (1) does not apply if the other party assumed the risk that he would have to perform despite such a failure.

Comment

a. General rule. The rules stated in §§ 237 and 238 apply to any uncured material failure, whether or not it is a breach. They therefore apply even when a party's non-performance is justified because performance has not become due, his duty having been discharged or not having arisen on the ground of impracticability or frustration (§§ 261, 265, 266). Subsection (1) makes it clear that this is so, as a general rule. Its function in this Chapter is similar to that of § 239(1) in Chapter 10, Performance and Non-Performance. See Comment a to § 239.

Illustrations

1. A contracts with B to paint a continuous mural around a room in B's house for $10,000. A dies after he has finished three of the four walls, and B refuses to pay A's estate anything. Although A's duty as to the fourth wall has been discharged, with the result that his performance never became due, his failure to render it nevertheless may affect B's duty under the rule stated in § 237. Since his failure was material and cannot be cured, A's estate has no claim under the contract for the three painted walls. The estate may have a claim under the rule stated in § 272(1).

2. A, a school teacher, contracts with B to teach in B's school for a year. A is to work from September through May, with June, July and August as vacation, during which A's duties are insignificant. B is to pay A monthly from September through August. A dies at the beginning of June, and B refuses to pay A's salary for June, July or August. A's estate has a claim against B under the contract for the salary for those three months. Although A's duty as to the last three months has been discharged with the result that his performance as to those months never became due, his failure to

render performance nevertheless may affect B's duty under the rule stated in § 237. But since his failure was not material, A's estate has a claim against B for the salary for those three months.

b. Assumption of risk. The rule stated in Subsection (2) is similar to that of § 239(2). Sometimes a party will undertake a greater obligation than that imposed by Subsection (1) and will assume the risk that he will have to carry out his side of the exchange even though it is not carried out on the other side. If he has assumed this greater risk, then conduct on the other side which would otherwise affect his duty under the rules stated in § 237 or § 238 does not affect his duty. See Comment b to § 239.

Illustrations

3. A contracts with B to furnish bus service to students attending B's school during the school year, from September through May, for a stated sum payable monthly. In March the school is closed until further notice because of an epidemic. Although the school remains closed during April and May, A is required under the contract to remain ready to resume performance. B refuses to pay A for April and May. Since in the circumstances, including the requirement that A remain ready to resume performance, B assumed the risk that he would have to perform in spite of such non-performance by A, the rule stated in Subsection (1) does not apply and A's failure to render performance does not affect B's duty under the rule stated in § 237. A has a claim against B under the contract for the monthly sums for April and May.

4. A, who is not a merchant, contracts to sell a specified machine to B for $10,000 on 30 days credit. Before A tenders the machine to B, a fire destroys it without A's fault. Under Uniform Commercial Code § 2–509(3), risk of loss does not pass to the buyer until tender if the seller is not a merchant. Since the risk of loss did not pass to B until tender, the rule stated in Subsection (1) applies and A's failure of performance may affect B's duty under the rule stated in § 237. Since his failure was material and cannot be cured, A has no claim against B under the contract. Compare Illustration 5 to § 263.

5. The facts being otherwise as stated in Illustration 4, the machine is destroyed after A tenders it to B, but before B receives it. Since the risk of loss passed to B on tender, the rule stated in Subsection (1) does not apply, and A's failure to render performance does not affect B's duty under the rule stated in § 237. A has a claim against B under the contract, even though B does not receive the machine.

6. A contracts to sell a house to B for $50,000 in a state having the Uniform Vendor and Purchaser Risk Act. Under the Act, risk of loss does not pass to the buyer until there has been a transfer of either legal title or possession. Before A has transferred either the legal title to or the possession of the house to B, a fire destroys it without A's fault. Since the risk of loss did not pass to B until transfer of title or possession, the rule stated in Subsection (1) applies, and A's failure to offer performance may affect B's duty under the rule stated in § 238. Since his failure was material and cannot be cured, A has no claim under the contract against B.

7. The facts being otherwise as stated in Illustration 6, the house is destroyed after B has taken possession but before title has been transferred. Since the risk of loss passed to B on transfer of possession, the rule stated in Subsection (1) does not apply, and A's failure to offer performance does not affect B's duty under the rule stated in § 238. A has a claim against B for $50,000, even though B does not receive title to the house.

§ 268. Effect on Other Party's Duties of a Prospective Failure Justified by Impracticability or Frustration.

(1) A party's prospective failure of performance may, except as stated in Subsection (2), discharge the other party's duties or allow him to suspend performance under the rules stated in §§ 251(1) and 253(2) even though the failure would be justified under the rules stated in this Chapter.

(2) The rule stated in Subsection (1) does not apply if the other party assumed the risk that he would have to perform in spite of such a failure.

Comment

a. Relation to other rules. This Restatement adopts the principle "that a continuing sense of reliance and security that the promised performance will be forthcoming when due, is an important feature of the bargain." Comment 1 to Uniform Commercial Code § 2–609; see Comment a to § 251. If there is reason to expect that a party will not perform as promised, the other party has the protection afforded by the rules stated in §§ 250 and 253 if the first party has repudiated, and by the rule stated in § 251 if reasonable grounds for insecurity have arisen with respect to the first party's future performance. However, those sections apply only if such prospective non-performance would amount to a breach. This Section applies when the prospective non-performance would not be a breach because of the rules on impracticability of performance or frustration of purpose stated in this Chapter. Subsection (2) makes it clear that if the other party has assumed the risk that he will have to perform although he receives no return performance, his duties are not discharged.

b. Statement or voluntary act. If a party properly states that he will not perform because of impracticability of his performance or frustration of his purpose, the other party cannot treat that statement as a repudiation under the rule stated in § 250(a) because the threatened non-performance would not be a breach. It therefore gives him no claim for breach of contract. Nevertheless, under the rule stated in this Section it discharges his remaining duties to render the agreed exchange. The same rule applies to a voluntary affirmative act that would otherwise be a repudiation under the rule stated in § 250(b). The rules on nullification of a repudiation (§ 256) and urging performance (§ 257) also apply to situations that come under this Section.

Illustration

1. A, an impresario, contracts with B, a singer, for an engagement for three months beginning on January 1. On the preceding November 30, B contracts pneumonia, and states to A that he will be unable to sing before February 1. A employs another singer to fill B's place. On January 1, B, having recovered, offers to perform but A refuses. Since B's statement would have been a repudiation under the rule stated in § 250 but for the operation of the rules on impracticability of performance stated in §§ 261 and 262, A's duty to employ B is discharged, and A is not liable to B for breach of contract. Cf. Illustration 2 to § 242.

c. Failure to give assurances. If reasonable grounds arise to believe that a party will not perform because of impracticability of his performance or frustration of his purpose, the other party cannot demand assurances and treat a failure to give them as a repudiation under the rule stated in § 251, because the prospective non-performance would not be a breach. It therefore gives him no claim for breach of contract. Nevertheless, under the rule stated in this Section, he may in a proper case suspend his own performance and treat a failure to give assurance as discharging any remaining duties that he has to render the agreed exchange.

Illustrations

2. A, an impresario, contracts with B, a singer, for an engagement for three months beginning on January 1. On the preceding November 30, B contracts pneumonia, and A is advised by competent medical authority that B will not be able to sing before February 1. A reasonably demands assurances of due performance by B. B ignores the demand, and A employs another singer to fill B's place. On January 1, B, having recovered, offers to perform, but A refuses. Since B's failure to furnish assurance of due performance would have been a repudiation under the rule stated in § 251 but for the operation of the rules on impracticability of performance stated in §§ 261 and 262, A's duty to employ B is discharged, and A is not liable to B for breach of contract.

3. A contracts to sell land to B, title to be conveyed one year from the date of the contract. B then learns from reliable sources that the state plans to condemn the land for a highway before that time and reasonably demands assurance of due performance by A. A ignores the demand, and B acquires other land as a substitute for that which A contracted to convey. The state then abandons its plans to build the highway and A tenders the deed one year from the date of the contract. B refuses to perform. Since A's failure to furnish assurance of due performance would have been a repudiation under the rule stated in § 251 but for the operation of the rules on impracticability of performance

stated in §§ 261 and 264, B's duty to take and pay for the land is discharged, and B is not liable to A for breach of contract.

§ 269. Temporary Impracticability or Frustration.

Impracticability of performance or frustration of purpose that is only temporary suspends the obligor's duty to perform while the impracticability or frustration exists but does not discharge his duty or prevent it from arising unless his performance after the cessation of the impracticability or frustration would be materially more burdensome than had there been no impracticability or frustration.

Comment

a. Rationale. Impracticability of performance or frustration of purpose may be only temporary. While it lasts, the affected party's duty is at least suspended. When the circumstances giving rise to the impracticability or frustration cease to exist, he must then perform. He is usually expected to perform in full and is entitled to an appropriate extension of time for performance. When the delay has made full performance impracticable, the rules stated in § 270 for partial impracticability and in § 272(2) on supplying a term apply. In some cases, however, delay will make his performance materially more burdensome for him than had there been no impracticability or frustration, and when it appears that this will be so, his duty is discharged and not merely suspended. In applying the standard of materiality, a court will consider whether the delay has seriously upset the allocation of risks under the agreement of the parties. The rule stated in this Section is, of course, subject to contrary agreement. It applies only to the duty of the party adversely affected by the impracticability or frustration; the effect on the duty of the other party, as to a performance to be exchanged under an exchange of promises, is governed by the rules stated in §§ 267, 268, 237 and 238. Compare Illustration 2 to § 242.

Illustrations

1. A contracts with B to build an electric power plant, completion to be within two years, for $10,000,000. Before the commencement of performance, a shortage of materials due to a sudden outbreak of war makes it temporarily impracticable for A to perform. A's duty is suspended until it is no longer impracticable for him to obtain materials, and he is then under a duty to perform with an appropriate extension of time, unless B's duty to pay is discharged by the delay under the rules stated in §§ 237 and 267. However, if circumstances including increased prices then make it materially more burdensome for A to perform, A's duty to build the plant is discharged regardless of whether B's duty would otherwise be discharged by the delay.

2. On July 5, A charters his vessel to B for a voyage from New York to Liverpool, contracting that the vessel shall be ready for loading July 10. On July 8, the government requisitions the vessel for the stated period of a week, returning the vessel to A in New York on July 15. A's duty to have the vessel ready is suspended until July 15 and he is then under a duty to perform with an appropriate extension of time, unless B's duty to pay is then discharged by the delay under the rules stated in §§ 237 and 267. However, if circumstances including his other contracts then make it materially more burdensome for A to perform, A's duty is discharged regardless of whether B's duty would otherwise be discharged by the delay.

§ 270. Partial Impracticability.

Where only part of an obligor's performance is impracticable, his duty to render the remaining part is unaffected if

 (a) it is still practicable for him to render performance that is substantial, taking account of any reasonable substitute performance that he is under a duty to render; or

 (b) the obligee, within a reasonable time, agrees to render any remaining performance in full and to allow the obligor to retain any performance that has already been rendered.

Comment

a. Relation to other rules. An obligor's performance may be impracticable only in part. (If impracticability as to part makes his performance of the rest so much more burdensome that it is also impracticable, then the entire performance is impracticable and the rules stated in §§ 261 and 266 apply.) If he has done all that is practicable, he may have a claim for relief including restitution under the rules stated in §§ 240 and 370–77. See § 272(1) and Comment a. If, however, further performance is practicable, it may be possible to salvage at least some of the unexecuted part of the agreement. This Section states rules for two situations in which it is relatively easy to do this because the obligee has already performed in full, or is willing to do so, or can be required to do so. In more complex situations where the obligee's duty to perform must be adjusted to avoid injustice, a court may nevertheless salvage some of the agreement by supplying a term under the rule stated in § 272(2). Analogous problems involving frustration of purpose are also dealt with in § 272(2).

b. Substantial performance practicable. If the part of the obligor's performance that is impracticable is so minor that it is still practicable for him to render substantial performance, his duty to do so is unaffected. Whether his performance would be substantial depends on the impact on the reasonable expectations of the obligee, who either has performed in full or remains liable to perform in full (§ 237). Two means of reducing this impact are significant. First, if the obligor can render a reasonable substitute performance in place of the impracticable part, he must do so under his duty of good faith in performance (§ 205), and that substitute performance will be considered in determining whether his performance would be substantial. Second, if the obligee has a claim in restitution against the obligor under the rules stated in § 272(1), on the ground that the obligor will otherwise receive a performance from the obligee for which he has not rendered the agreed exchange in full, the adequacy of this claim as compensation for the obligee must also be considered in determining whether the obligor's performance would be substantial. In the common case where performances are to be exchanged under an exchange of promises, performance would be substantial if the failure of performance would not be material. See Comment d to § 237. Both parties then remain bound to complete the exchange, subject to discharge of the duty to perform the impracticable part and a compensating claim for restitution.

Illustrations

1. A contracts to build a supermarket for B for $250,000. Included in the plans are numerous lighted signs, including one next to an adjacent highway. Before A begins performance, a local ordinance prohibits the installation of this sign. Since A's failure to install it would not be material, his performance would be substantial, and A's duty to build the rest of the supermarket is unaffected. B is still under a duty to pay $250,000, subject to a claim under the rule stated in § 272(1) based on A's failure to build the sign for which he has been paid.

2. A contracts with B to deliver all of B's requirements of milk during the following year at B's loading platform at 200 Lincoln Street. Before A begins performance, the loading platform is accidentally destroyed by fire, but B has an equally suitable platform across the street at 201 Lincoln Street. Neither A's nor B's duties are affected, except that A is to deliver and B is to accept milk at 201 Lincoln Street.

3. A contracts to sell and B to buy a quantity of wheat "f.o.b. Kosmos Steamer at Seattle." Before delivery, an outbreak of war makes Kosmos line ships unavailable at Seattle, but delivery on that line's loading dock remains possible and is a commercially reasonable substitute. Neither A's nor B's duties are affected, except that A is to deliver and B is to accept wheat at the Kosmos line's loading dock. B may have a claim under the rules stated in § 272(1) based on A's failure to load the wheat for which he has been paid.

c. Agreement. Even if it is not practicable to render substantial performance, the obligee may salvage the agreement under the rule stated in Subsection (b). If he assures the obligor that the latter will receive in full the performance that he originally expected from the obligee, the obligor must render the rest of his performance. The obligee can make a legally binding commitment of this kind by agreeing (cf. § 3) to render to the obligor any remaining performance and to allow the obligor to retain any performance that has already been rendered. See §§ 18, 19, 89. When performances are to be exchanged under an exchange of promises, and the obligor's non-performance will be a material failure, such agreement will prevent the discharge of the obligee's duties (§§ 237, 238) and the consequent discharge of the obligor's duties, and the agreement will be salvaged. It will also bar any claim for restitution with respect to the obligor's non-performance. See Comment b. Under an exchange of any type, such agreement will bar a claim by the obligee for restitution with respect to any performance that he has already rendered.

Illustration

4. A contracts with B to service seven different areas at B's airport for a lump sum. Before performance is to begin, a government regulation forbids the servicing of one of the areas, discharging A's duty as to that area under the rules stated in §§ 261 and 264. Under § 267(1), A's non-performance would operate as a failure of performance for the purpose of the rule stated in § 237, and B's remaining duties would be discharged. If, however, B within a reasonable time agrees to pay A the lump sum in full, B's remaining duties are not discharged and A's duty to service the other six areas is unaffected.

§ 271. Impracticability as Excuse for Non-Occurrence of a Condition.

Impracticability excuses the non-occurrence of a condition if the occurrence of the condition is not a material part of the agreed exchange and forfeiture would otherwise result. . . .

Comment

a. Relation to other rules. This is one of several sections in this Restatement that serve to avoid the forfeiture that might otherwise result from the non-occurrence of a condition. Under the rule stated in § 227(1), when it is doubtful whether or not an agreement makes an event a condition of an obligor's duty, an interpretation that it does not do so is generally preferred if this will reduce the obligee's risk of forfeiture (see Comment b to § 227). Under the rule stated in § 229, even if the parties do make an event a condition in spite of the risk of forfeiture, the non-occurrence of the condition may still be excused if actual forfeiture would otherwise result, but only if the forfeiture would be extreme. Under the rule stated in this Section, if the non-occurrence of the condition is the result of impracticability, it is excused if forfeiture, even if not extreme, would otherwise result. The impracticability must, of course, be such as would suffice to discharge a duty or prevent it from arising. See §§ 261, 262, 263, 264, 266(1). Here, as in §§ 227 and 229, "forfeiture" is used to refer to the denial of compensation that results when the obligee loses his right to the agreed exchange, after he has relied substantially on the expectation of that exchange, as by preparation or performance. See Comment b to § 227 and Comment b to § 229.

Illustrations

1. A contracts with B to repair B's building for $20,000, payment to be made "on the satisfaction of C, B's architect, and the issuance of his certificate." A properly makes the repairs, but C dies before he is able to give a certificate. Since presentation of the architect's certificate is not a material part of the agreed exchange and forfeiture would otherwise result, the occurrence of the condition is excused, and A has a claim against B for $20,000. Cf. Illustration 3 to § 225.

2. A, an insurance company, issues to B a policy of accidental injury insurance which provides that notice within 14 days of an accident is a condition of A's duty. B is injured as a result of an accident covered by the policy but is so mentally deranged that he is unable to give notice for 20 days. B gives notice as soon as he is able. Since the giving of notice within 14 days is not a material part of the agreed exchange, and forfeiture would otherwise result, the non-occurrence of the condition is excused and B has a claim against A under the policy.

b. Limitation on scope. The rule of this Section, like that of § 229, applies only where occurrence of the condition was not a material part of the agreed exchange. See § 84 and Comment c to § 229. If the occurrence of the condition is impracticable only in part, its non-occurrence is, of course, excused only to that extent.

Illustration

3. A, an insurance company, issues to B a policy of whole life insurance making it a condition of A's duty that premiums be paid annually. B is imprisoned in a foreign country for five years, and is

unable to pay the premiums during that time. On his release, he tenders the overdue premiums, but A refuses to accept them. Since the annual payment of premiums is a material part of the agreed exchange, its non-occurrence is not excused because of impracticability even though forfeiture will result. B has no claim against A.

§ 272. Relief Including Restitution.

(1) In any case governed by the rules stated in this Chapter, either party may have a claim for relief including restitution under the rules stated in §§ 240 and 377.

(2) In any case governed by the rules stated in this Chapter, if those rules together with the rules stated in Chapter 16 will not avoid injustice, the court may grant relief on such terms as justice requires including protection of the parties' reliance interests.

Comment

a. Mitigating doctrines. Because the rules stated in this Chapter might otherwise appear to have the harsh effect of denying either party any recovery following the discharge of one party's duty based on impracticability or frustration, this Section makes it clear that several mitigating doctrines may be used to allow at least some recovery in a proper case. Subsection (1) speaks to claims for relief such as that provided by the rule on part performances as agreed equivalents stated in § 240 and those on restitution and other relief stated in § 377. Subsection (2) speaks to supplying a term to avoid injustice.

b. Relief including restitution. A party whose duty has never arisen or has been discharged because of impracticability of performance or frustration of purpose may already have rendered some of his own performance or received some of the other party's performance or both. In some cases the party who has performed is entitled to recovery for what he has done under the rule on part performances as agreed equivalents (§ 240). See Illustration 8 to § 240. Even where this is not so, it will generally be appropriate to allow him a claim for restitution to the extent that his performance has benefited the other. Such claims, whether for restitution in kind or for the equivalent in money, are governed by the rules stated in Chapter 16. In a proper case recovery may go beyond mere restitution and include elements of reliance by the claimant even though they have not benefited the other party. See § 377. Special mention has been made of the possibility of such claims in those illustrations in the present Chapter in which the facts make it likely that one party's performance has benefited the other (Illustrations 3 and 7 to § 262, Illustration 2 to § 264, Illustration 2 to § 265, Illustration 1 to § 267). In appropriate circumstances such claims might be allowed in other illustrations as well. The rule stated in Subsection (1) is, of course, subject to the agreement of the parties and does not apply if a contrary intention is manifested.

c. Supplying a term to avoid injustice. Under the rule stated in § 204, when the parties have not agreed with respect to a term that is essential to a determination of their rights and duties, the court will supply a term that is reasonable in the circumstances. Since it is the rationale of this Chapter that, in a case of impracticability or frustration, the contract does not cover the case that has arisen, the court's function can be viewed generally as that set out in § 204 of supplying a term to deal with that omitted case. See Introductory Note to this Chapter. Ordinarily the rules stated in this Chapter, coupled with those stated in Chapter 16, will be adequate to allow the court to arrive at a just result (Subsection (1)). In some instances, however, these rules will not suffice to avoid injustice. A particularly significant example occurs where the just solution is to "sever" the agreement and require that some unexecuted part of it be performed on both sides, rather than to relieve both parties of all of their duties. This situation differs from that envisioned in § 240, under which the court merely allows recovery at the contract rate for performance that has already been rendered. The question under this Section is whether the court can salvage a part of the agreement that is still executory on both sides. See Illustrations 1, 2, 3 and 4. The rule stated in Subsection (2) makes it clear that it can do so by supplying a term which is reasonable in the circumstances when the rules stated in this Chapter together with those stated in Chapter 16 will not avoid injustice. The rule operates in other situations as well and may, for example, be invoked to require an obligor to prorate among several obligees that part of his performance that remains practicable. See Illustration 5.

IMPRACTICABILITY OF PERFORMANCE AND FRUSTRATION OF PURPOSE

Illustrations

1. A contracts with B to work for him for one year for $60,000. Illness prevents A from working for the first eleven months, and he refuses to work for the twelfth month although B manifests his assent to paying him $5,000. Under the rule stated in § 270, only a manifestation of assent to payment of $60,000, B's remaining performance in full, would prevent the discharge of A's duty to work for the twelfth month. If, however, the court decides that this rule will not avoid injustice, it may supply a term, if reasonable, under which A is to work for the twelfth month in return for B's payment of $5,000. A would then be liable to B for breach of contract.

2. A contracts with B to service seven different areas at B's airport at prices that are stated separately for each area. Before performance is to begin, a government regulation forbids the servicing of one of the areas. A does not service that area, but offers to service the other six areas in return for the stated prices. B refuses to allow A to do so. Under § 267(1), A's non-performance would operate as a failure of performance for the purpose of the rule stated in § 237, and B's remaining duties would be discharged. If, however, the court decides that this rule will not avoid injustice, it may supply a term, if reasonable, under which B is to accept A's servicing of the other areas and pay the stated prices. B would then be liable to A for breach of contract.

3. A contracts to sell and B to buy A's accounting business for a specified sum. A agrees to remain active in the business for two years during which B agrees to pay A an additional specified sum. After transferring the business to B and receiving a down payment, A dies. B offers to transfer the business to A's estate, refuses to pay the balance due, and demands the return of his down payment. Under the rule stated in § 267(1), not remaining active in the business would operate as a failure of performance for the purpose of the rule stated in § 237, and B's remaining duties would be discharged. If, however, the court decides that this rule will not avoid injustice, it may supply a term, if reasonable, under which B is to keep and pay for the business, but both parties' duties with respect to the two-year period are discharged. B would then be liable to A's estate for breach of contract.

4. A, an inventor, makes a contract with B, a manufacturer of washing machines, giving B the exclusive right to use a transmission on which A holds a patent that has 14 years to run. In return, B agrees to pay A royalties, the minimum annual payment to be $10,000. As the result of an outbreak of war, the government prohibits the manufacture of washing machines for a two-year period, frustrating B's purpose during that time. When B refuses to pay royalties for the two-year period, A notifies B that B no longer has the exclusive right to the transmission. Under the rule stated in § 269, B's duty is suspended until the manufacture of washing machines is no longer prohibited, and if circumstances, including other contractual commitments, do not make it materially more burdensome for B to perform after the suspension of payments, B's duty to pay is not thereby discharged. Nevertheless, under § 267(1), a failure by B to pay royalties for a period of two years would operate as a failure of performance for the purpose of the rule stated in § 237, and A's remaining duties would be discharged. If, however, the court decides that this rule will not avoid injustice, it may supply a term, if reasonable, under which A is to give B the exclusive right to use his patented transmission for the remainder of the life of the patent, after the two-year period, in return for B's payment of the agreed royalties during that time. A would then be liable to B for breach of contract.

5. By two separate contracts, A agrees to sell and B and C to buy identical quantities of peaches grown in A's orchard. Although A has no contract with D, he regularly sells D the same quantity. An unusual drought prevents A from growing more than one third the total amount required by B, C and D. A delivers all of the peaches to D, although both B and C manifest assent to paying A for what he can deliver. Because the rules stated in this Chapter will not avoid injustice, the court will, under Uniform Commercial Code § 2–615(b), supply a term under which A must allocate the peaches fairly and reasonably between B and C but may at his option include his regular customer D. A is liable to B and C for breach of contract for failure so to allocate the peaches.

6. A, the owner of an opera company that is heavily in debt, transfers half of its stock to B, who promises to manage the company. B is to have the right to sell the stock only if through his management the debt is paid off. After seven years, during which B is able to pay off only 15 per cent of the debt, the opera house is accidentally destroyed by fire. The insurance proceeds are used to pay off the debt, leaving a balance in the treasury, and the opera house is not rebuilt, preventing the

occurrence of the condition of B's right to sell his stock. A seeks an accounting for the stock transferred to B. Under the rule stated in § 271, the non-occurrence of the condition is not excused because its occurrence is a material part of the agreed exchange. If, however, the court decides that this rule will not avoid injustice, it may supply a term, under which B is entitled to a reasonable compensation for his services, giving due regard to the terms of the contract.

CHAPTER 12

DISCHARGE BY ASSENT OR ALTERATION

TOPIC 1. THE REQUIREMENT OF CONSIDERATION

§ 273. Requirement of Consideration or a Substitute.

Except as stated in §§ 274–77, an obligee's manifestation of assent to a discharge is not effective unless

(a) it is made for consideration,

(b) it is made in circumstances in which a promise would be enforceable without consideration, or

(c) it has induced such action or forbearance as would make a promise enforceable.

Comment

a. Rationale. This Section states the traditional requirement of consideration or one of its substitutes in order that the obligee's assent to even a present discharge be effective. The requirement is analogous to that of consideration or some substitute in order that even a present transfer of a right by assignment be irrevocable (§ 332). Subject to some exceptions, a gratuitous discharge is not effective, just as a gratuitous promise is not enforceable and a gratuitous assignment is not irrevocable. The use of words suggesting present transfer, such as those of gift or of assignment, does not affect the result. See Illustration 1.

Illustration

1. A, whom B owes $1,000 for goods delivered, gives B a signed writing that states, "I hereby irrevocably give, transfer, assign and release my right to the $1,000 that you owe me." B's debt is not discharged. Compare § 284 with § 332(1)(a).

b. Consideration and its substitutes. For centuries the seal was used to make a discharge of a duty effective, and in a few states the legislation that has generally deprived the seal of its effect makes an exception for executed transactions such as releases. See Reporter's Note to Introductory Note, Topic 3, Chapter 4. In a few other states legislation makes a signed writing a substitute for a seal in this respect. Today, however, the requirement stated in this Section is usually satisfied by consideration. The rules on consideration that apply generally to the enforceability of promises apply here. These include those set out in Topic 2 of Chapter 4 for situations where a promise is enforceable without consideration. A transaction need not follow one of the traditional forms set out in Topics 4 and 5 in order to be effective. Furthermore, a discharge that is originally ineffective may become effective if it has induced such action or forbearance as would make a promise enforceable (§ 90). See Illustration 2. The rule stated in this Section does not preclude the discharge of a duty by means of a gift of tangible property. See Illustration 3.

Illustrations

2. A pays B $1,000 in return for B's promise to paint a landscape for A. Before B is to begin, A says, "I don't want the painting, but you can keep the $1,000." B relies on A's statement by making conflicting commitments to do other work. B's duty to A is discharged. Compare § 275.

3. A contracts to sell to B a particular machine that B has in his possession as bailee in return for B's promise to pay $1,000. Before B pays the $1,000, A says, "You can keep the machine as a gift." Since A has made an effective gift of the machine to B, B's duty to pay for it is discharged. Compare § 276.

§ 274. Cancellation, Destruction or Surrender of a Writing.

An obligee's cancellation, destruction or surrender to the obligor of a writing of a type customarily accepted as a symbol or as evidence of his right discharges without consideration the obligor's duty if it is done with the manifested intention to discharge it.

Comment

a. Rationale. A duty under a formal contract (§ 6) has traditionally been regarded as so bound up in the writing embodying it that it will not survive the document's cancellation, destruction or surrender if that act is done by the obligee with a manifested intention to discharge the duty. With the decline of the seal and the increased use of other writings, these methods of discharge have been extended to writings that are symbolic or evidentiary of the duties that they embody. Cancellation, destruction or surrender of such a writing is regarded as an appropriate formality to show the offeree's serious intent to discharge the duty that it represents. Whether a particular type of writing is symbolic or evidentiary under this Section is the same question as is raised under § 332(1)(b) relating to the revocability of a gratuitous assignment. See Comments c and d to § 332; cf. Uniform Commercial Code § 9–105(1)(i). In the case of such a writing, the rule stated in this Section is available in addition to the other methods of discharge. Cancellation requires such mutilation by defacing or obliterating the writing, by tearing off signatures or by such other methods as manifest an intention that the writing be no longer legally effective. It may be partial as well as total. Surrender to the obligee includes surrender to someone in his behalf. A court decreeing that a third person has no enforceable rights under a document in his possession may order him to surrender it to prevent its possible wrongful use. The rule stated in this Section then applies. In the case of negotiable instruments and documents and letters of credit, the rule stated in this Section is subject to the provisions of the Uniform Commercial Code, Articles 3 5 7. See particularly Uniform Commercial Code §§ 3–605, 3–602. As to the effect of alteration, see §§ 286, 287.

Illustrations

1. A makes B a promise to pay $1,000 that is enforceable because it is in a sealed writing delivered to B (§ 95). B redelivers the writing to A and says "You don't owe me anything." A's duty to pay B is discharged.

2. A makes a written contract with B under which B pays A $15,000 and promises to pay A $10,000 more for land conveyed by A. Later A gratuitously delivers to B the written contract, signed by B, with the expressed intent of discharging B's duty to pay the balance of the price. B's duty to pay A the $10,000 is discharged.

§ 275. Assent to Discharge Duty of Return Performance.

If a party, before he has fully performed his duty under a contract, manifests to the other party his assent to discharge the other party's duty to render part or all of the agreed exchange, the duty is to that extent discharged without consideration.

Comment

a. Rationale. A gift of tangible property may be made by delivery of possession. If, therefore, one party is under a duty to transfer such property to another who is under a duty to pay for it, the former can manifest his assent when he transfers it to do so as a gift, thereby discharging the other party's duty to pay for it. The rule stated in this Section extends this principle to performances other than the transfer of tangible property such as, for example, the furnishing of services. The assent may be to discharge the other party's duty wholly or in part. The assent must be manifested before the completion of performance, by analogy to the rule as to a donor of tangible property, who must manifest his assent at the time of the transfer. It may be manifested before performance, as long as it continues to the time of performance, but assent manifested after performance is completed does not come within the rule. Under the discredited concept of "merger by deed" it has sometimes been held that the contract duties of a seller of land are discharged by the buyer's mere acceptance of a non-conforming deed of conveyance. That concept is rejected in this Restatement, but the seller's duties may be discharged under the rule stated in this Section if the buyer manifests his assent to take the deed as full performance. See Illustration 3; Uniform Land Transactions Act § 1–309.

Illustrations

1. A and B make a contract under which A promises to sell land to B and B promises to pay A $100,000. A delivers to B a deed to the land, saying as he does so, "This is a gift." B's duty to pay A $100,000 is discharged.

2. A and B make a contract under which A promises to build a fence and B promises to pay A $1,000. As A begins to build the fence, he says to B, "The price we agreed on was too high, and you need pay only $900 for the fence." A then builds the fence. B's duty to pay A to the extent of $100 is discharged and B owes A only $900. See also § 89.

3. A and B make a contract under which A promises to convey title to land by a warranty deed. A tenders a deed to B under which A warrants only against incumbrances made or suffered by himself. B, when paying the price, tells A, "That is all right, I will accept it as full performance instead of a warranty deed." A's duty to convey good title to the land is discharged. If B remains silent, without more, however, A's duty is not discharged.

§ 276. Assent to Discharge Duty to Transfer Property.

A duty of an obligor in possession of identified personal property to transfer an interest in that property is discharged without consideration if the obligee manifests to the obligor his assent to the discharge of that duty.

Comment

a. Rationale. A gift of tangible property may be made by delivery of possession. If, therefore, an obligor is under a duty to transfer an interest in identified personal property that is in his possession and the obligee wishes to surrender his right to receive it, the property could first be delivered to the obligee pursuant to the duty and then redelivered to the obligor as a gift. The rule stated in this Section allows the obligee to relinquish his right simply by manifesting his assent rather than by going through the formalities of delivery and redelivery. It applies to all personal property capable of possession and is not limited to chattels.

Illustration

1. A contracts to sell to B a particular machine that A has in his possession. B pays the price but before B takes delivery, he says to A, "I give you that machine." A's duty to deliver the machine is discharged.

§ 277. Renunciation.

(1) A written renunciation signed and delivered by the obligee discharges without consideration a duty arising out of a breach of contract.

(2) A renunciation by the obligee on his acceptance from the obligor of some performance under a contract discharges without consideration a duty to pay damages for a breach that gives rise only to a claim for damages for partial breach of contract.

Comment

a. Scope. Under the rules stated in this Section, a party injured by a breach of contract can renounce his claim for damages for that breach and thereby discharge without consideration the other party's duty. He can do so in whole or in part. The concept of renunciation presupposes that the injured party is aware of his claim at the time he renounces it. Furthermore, because these rules apply only to duties arising under a contract, the obligor is held to a duty of good faith and fair dealing with respect to the obligee (§ 205). Discharge by renunciation of a negotiable instrument is beyond the scope of this Restatement. See Uniform Commercial Code § 3–605.

b. *Written renunciation.* Under the rule stated in Subsection (1), the obligee can renounce a claim arising out of a breach of contract, including a claim for damages for either partial or total breach (§ 236), and may do so even though the obligor renders no further performance under the contract. Although no consideration is required, the obligee must deliver a signed writing to the obligor.

Illustrations

1. A and B make a contract under which A promises to employ B and B promises to work for A for six months beginning on June 1. After B has begun work, A wrongfully discharges B. B writes A, "I am glad to leave you and I give up any right to sue you." A's duty to pay B damages for total breach is discharged. A's duty to pay B wages earned during the time B has worked is not discharged.

2. A contracts to sell and B to buy wheat to be delivered on June 1. A fails to deliver the wheat on that day. After sufficient delay to discharge B's remaining duties of performance, B writes A, "Since you are so late in delivery, I cancel our deal and waive all my rights against you." A's duty to pay B damages for total breach is discharged.

3. A and B make a contract under which A promises to build a house on B's land and B promises to pay A $50,000. A fails to follow the plans in some particulars, giving B a claim against A for damages for partial breach. After B takes possession of the house, he gives a signed writing to A stating, "I do not care about these specified defects in your performance; you have done pretty well on the whole, and I am satisfied with the house." A's duty to pay B damages for partial breach is discharged. As to B's right to restitution, see § 253.

c. *Oral renunciation.* Under the rule stated in Subsection (2), the obligee can renounce his right to damages for a breach that is sufficient to give rise to a claim for damages for partial breach but not serious enough to give rise to a claim for damages for total breach (§ 236). However, he can do so only on his acceptance from the obligor of some performance under the contract. A renunciation may occur before performance as long as it continues to the time of performance. No consideration is required and the renunciation may be oral. Mere silent acceptance, however, is not a renunciation. A claim for the unpaid balance of a debt is not one for damages for partial breach under the rule stated in this Section, but a claim for damages caused by delay in payment of a debt is such a claim. See Illustration 3 to § 278. See § 246 for the effect of acceptance of performance on the obligee's right to claim damages for total breach.

Illustrations

4. The facts being otherwise as stated in Illustration 3, B's renunciation is oral rather than written and occurs before B has taken possession of the house rather than after. A's duty to pay B damages for partial breach is discharged. The result does not depend on whether or not B has paid the price in full before his renunciation. As to B's right to restitution, see § 253.

5. A and B make a contract under which A promises to employ B and B promises to work for A for six months. After B has begun work, he commits a breach of the contract giving A a claim for damages for partial breach. A says, "Never mind, I excuse that failure in view of your generally excellent performance," and B continues to work for A. A's claim for damages for partial breach is discharged. The result would be different if A's renunciation occurred after B had finished working for A.

d. *Other situations distinguished.* If the injured party's renunciation is supported by consideration or by reliance, it can be sustained without resort to the rule stated in this Section. If, for example, each of the parties believes that he has a claim against the other for damages for total breach, the renunciation by one of his disputed claim for damages will furnish the consideration for the renunciation by the other of his disputed claim. If a party having a claim for damages for partial breach renounces his claim and the other party relies on the renunciation so that it would be unjust not to enforce the renunciation, the reliance will make the renunciation enforceable.

Illustration

6. The facts being otherwise as stated in Illustration 3, B's statement to A is oral rather than written. A's duty to pay damages for partial breach is not discharged. If, however, A relied on the

statement by moving from the site men and material that might have been used to remedy the defects, a court might hold that A's reliance was such that his duty to pay B damages for partial breach was discharged.

§ 278. Substituted Performance.

(1) If an obligee accepts in satisfaction of the obligor's duty a performance offered by the obligor that differs from what is due, the duty is discharged.

(2) If an obligee accepts in satisfaction of the obligor's duty a performance offered by a third person, the duty is discharged, but an obligor who has not previously assented to the performance for his benefit may in a reasonable time after learning of it render the discharge inoperative from the beginning by disclaimer.

Comment

a. Substituted performance by the obligor. If the obligor offers a performance that differs from what is due in full or partial satisfaction of his duty, the obligee need not accept it. If he chooses to accept it, however, the obligor is discharged in accordance with the terms of the offer. The obligee generally cannot avoid the consequences of such an exercise of dominion by a declaration that he does not assent to the condition attached by the debtor. Uniform Commercial Code § 1–207, providing for acceptance of performance under reservation of rights, need not be read as changing this well-established rule. See Comment d to § 281.

Illustration

1. A owes B $1,000. A offers B a machine in full satisfaction of his debt, and B accepts it. A's debt is discharged. The result is the same if, before accepting the machine, B writes A that he does not accept it in full satisfaction of the debt.

b. Substituted performance by third person. The obligee need not accept a performance that is offered in full or partial satisfaction of the obligor's duty by a third person who does not do so on behalf of the obligor. If he chooses to accept it, however, the obligor is discharged in accordance with the terms of the third person's offer. The performance may be the same as or different from that originally due from the obligor. The transaction is regarded as one for the benefit of the obligor, who, like any intended beneficiary, has the power to disclaim the benefit of the third person's performance and deprive it of its effect as a discharge. See § 306.

Illustration

2. A owes B $1,000. C offers B a machine in full satisfaction of A's debt, and B accepts it. A's debt is discharged.

c. Consideration for discharge. Under the rule stated in § 273, although the discharge is an immediate change in the legal relations between the obligor and the obligee and involves no promise by the obligee, it is not effective unless it is supported by consideration or some substitute for consideration. Under the rules on performance of a legal duty and settlement of claims stated in §§ 73 and 74, part performance by an obligor of a duty that is liquidated and undisputed is not consideration for a discharge of that duty in full, even if the obligee so accepts it. This result has been much criticized and slight variations of circumstance are often held to take a case out of the rule. See Comment c to § 73. Thus part performance of such a duty by a third party is regarded as different in this respect and may be consideration for a discharge in full. This does not, however, extend to the situation where the third party acts as the obligor's agent or to the one where he purports to do so and the obligor later ratifies his act. Nor does it extend to the case where a debtor simply offers payment by means of a third person's check.

Illustrations

3. A owes B a liquidated and undisputed matured debt of $1,000. A offers B $500 in full satisfaction of the debt, and B accepts the $500. A's debt is discharged only to the extent of $500.

4. The facts being otherwise as stated in Illustration 3, the $500 is offered by C, a third person, instead of A. A's debt is discharged in full.

§ 279. Substituted Contract.

(1) A substituted contract is a contract that is itself accepted by the obligee in satisfaction of the obligor's existing duty.

(2) The substituted contract discharges the original duty and breach of the substituted contract by the obligor does not give the obligee a right to enforce the original duty.

Comment

a. Nature and effect of a substituted contract. A substituted contract is one that is itself accepted by the obligee in satisfaction of the original duty and thereby discharges it. A common type of substituted contract is one that contains a term that is inconsistent with a term of an earlier contract between the parties. If the parties intend the new contract to replace all of the provisions of the earlier contract, the contract is a substituted contract. If a substituted contract brings in a new party it is called a "novation" (§ 280).

Illustrations

1. A is under a duty to deliver a tractor to B on July 1. On June 1, A offers to deliver a bulldozer to B on July 1 if B will accept his promise in satisfaction of A's duty to deliver the tractor, and B accepts. The contract is a substituted contract. A's duty to deliver the tractor is discharged. If A does not deliver the bulldozer, B can enforce the duty to deliver it but not the original duty to deliver the tractor.

2. A and B make a contract under which A promises to build on a designated spot a building, for which B promises to pay $100,000. Later, before this contract is performed, A and B make a new contract under which A is to build on the same spot a different building, for which B is to pay $200,000. The new contract is a substituted contract and the duties of A and B under the original contract are discharged.

b. Validity of substituted contract. Under the rule stated in § 273, although the discharge that results from a substituted contract is an immediate change in the legal relations between the obligor and the obligee and involves no promise by the obligee, it is not effective unless it is supported by consideration or some substitute for consideration. See Comment c to § 278. Furthermore, to the extent that the substituted contract is vulnerable on such grounds as mistake, misrepresentation, duress or unconscionability, recourse may be had on the original duty. Thus, if the substituted contract is voidable, it discharges the original duty until avoidance, but on avoidance of the substituted contract the original duty is again enforceable. If the substituted contract is unenforceable because of the Statute of Frauds, it does not bar enforcement of the original duty. Cf. § 149.

Illustrations

3. A owes B a liquidated and undisputed matured debt of $1,000. A offers to pay B $500 in 30 days if B will accept his promise in full satisfaction of the debt, and B accepts. A's debt is not discharged. See Illustration 3 to § 278.

4. The facts being otherwise as stated in Illustration 1, A by fraudulent misrepresentations induces B to make the contract for delivery of the bulldozer. B may avoid the substituted contract and enforce the original contract, or he may enforce the substituted contract.

c. Accord distinguished. Because the original duty is discharged regardless of whether the substituted contract is performed, a substituted contract differs from an accord, under which the original duty is discharged only if the accord is performed. See § 281. Whether a contract is a substituted contract or an accord is a question of interpretation, subject to the general rules stated in Chapter 9. In resolving doubts in this regard, a court is less likely to conclude that an obligee was willing to accept a mere promise in satisfaction of an original duty that was clear than in satisfaction of one that was doubtful. It will therefore be less likely to find a substituted contract and more likely to find an accord if the original duty was one to pay money, if it was undisputed, if it was liquidated and if it was matured. Compare Illustration 1 with Illustration 1 to § 281.

§ 280. Novation.

A novation is a substituted contract that includes as a party one who was neither the obligor nor the obligee of the original duty.

Comment

a. Definition of novation. The word "novation" is used in this Restatement to refer to a type of substituted contract that has the effect of adding a party, either as obligor or obligee, who was not a party to the original duty. See Comment a to § 279. A novation may involve more than three parties. The performance to be rendered under the new duty may be the same as or different from that to be rendered under the original duty. It is also possible to have an accord that adds a new party, but that is less often the case and such an accord is not termed a novation. See Illustration 1.

b. Effect of novation. A novation discharges the original duty, just as any other substituted contract does, so that breach of the new duty gives no right of action on the old duty. Most novations simply substitute a new obligor for an old obligor or, less commonly, a new obligee for an old obligee. Sometimes these are termed simple novations, to distinguish them from more complex transactions that are termed compound novations.

c. Consideration. A novation is subject to the same requirements as any other contract, including that of consideration. However, since consideration need not be given to the promisor and need not be given by the promisee (§ 71 (4)), consideration to support the discharge of the original duty can usually be found in the promise to undertake a new duty. It is not necessary for this purpose that all of the parties to the novation manifest their assent simultaneously nor that they all be in the same place, but their manifestations of assent must have reference to one another (§ 23). Although all parties usually assent to a novation, a novation is possible without the assent of the obligor of the original duty or of the obligee of the new duty if that party is an intended beneficiary and does not disclaim (§ 306). See Illustrations 2 and 5. Assent of the obligee of the original duty and of the obligor of the new duty is always necessary.

d. Substitution of obligor. A simple novation involving a substitution of obligors results when an obligee promises the obligor that he will discharge the obligor's duty in consideration for a third person's promise to pay the obligee. See Illustration 1. As to the analogous situation of an obligee who takes in payment from the obligor a negotiable instrument on which a third person is liable, see Uniform Commercial Code § 3–802. A substitution of obligors may also result when an obligee promises a third person that he will discharge the obligor's duty in consideration for the third person's promise to render either the performance that was due from the obligor or some other performance. Even a promise to render part performance is consideration in that situation. See Comment c to § 278. If the obligor is an intended beneficiary (§ 302), there is a novation. The assent of the obligor is not required. However, his rights are governed by the rules stated in Chapter 14, Contract Beneficiaries, and if he has not assented he can by disclaimer render the transaction inoperative from the beginning (§ 306). See Illustration 2. Such a novation also results when a third person promises an obligor to assume, immediately and in substitution for the obligor's duty, a duty to the obligee to render the performance that was due from the obligor or some other performance, and the obligee agrees with the obligor or with the third person to that substitution. The third person then comes under a new duty to the obligee, who is an intended beneficiary of his promise to assume (§ 302), and this is consideration for the obligee's agreement to discharge the original obligor. The obligee, having already assented to the discharge of the duty in this way, has no power to disclaim it. See Illustration 3. However, a mere promise by a third party to assume the obligor's duty, not offered in substitution for that duty, does not result in a novation, and the new duty that the third party may owe to the obligee as an intended beneficiary is in addition to and not in substitution for the obligor's original duty. For a novation to take place, the obligee must assent to the discharge of the obligor's duty in consideration for the promise of the third party to undertake that duty. As to the effect of an obligee's acceptance of performance from an assignee after a repudiation by the obligor, see § 329(2).

Illustrations

1. A owes B $1,000. B promises A that he will discharge the debt immediately if C will promise B to pay B $1,000. C so promises. There is a novation under which B's and C's promises are consideration for each other and A is discharged.

2. A owes B $1,000. B promises C that he will discharge the debt immediately if C will promise him to pay him $1,000. Intending to benefit A, C so promises. There is a novation under which B's and C's promises are consideration for each other, and A's duty to pay B is discharged. A is an intended beneficiary of B's promise (§ 302) and can by disclaimer render the transaction, including the discharge, inoperative from the beginning (§ 306). The result is the same if B's promise is made in return for C's promise to pay $500. See Illustration 4 to § 278.

3. A owes B a duty to service B's machine for a year. A sells part of his business to C, who promises A that he will assume A's duty to B if B promises to accept it immediately and in substitution for A's duty. B so promises A. There is a novation under which B's and C's promises are consideration for each other, and A's duty to service B's machine is discharged. B is an intended beneficiary of C's promise (§ 302), but cannot disclaim because he has assented. The result is the same if B's promise is made to C.

e. Substitution of obligee. A simple novation involving a substitution of obligees results when an obligee promises his obligor to discharge the obligor's duty in consideration for the obligor's promise to a third person to render either the performance that was due from the obligor or some other performance. See Illustration 4. A substitution of obligees may also result when the obligor's promise is one made directly to the obligee but is one to render the performance to a third person as beneficiary. If the third person is an intended beneficiary (§ 302), there is a novation. Illustration 5. The assent of the third person is not required. However, his rights are subject to the rules stated in Chapter 14, Contract Beneficiaries, and if he has not assented he can by disclaimer render the transaction, including the discharge, inoperative from the beginning. Obligees may also be substituted by assignment of a right, which differs from novation in that assignment requires neither the knowledge nor the assent of the obligor and cannot change the performance to be rendered by him. For other differences, see Chapter 15, Assignment and Delegation.

Illustrations

4. A owes B $1,000. B promises A that he will discharge the debt immediately if A will promise C to perform stated services to C. A so promises C. There is a novation under which A's and B's promises are consideration for each other and A's duty to pay B is discharged. If B's promise were to discharge A when A performed the services, there would be an accord rather than a novation.

5. A owes B $1,000. Intending to benefit C, B promises A that he will discharge the debt immediately if A will promise him to perform stated services to C. A so promises B. There is a novation under which A's and B's promises are consideration for each other and A's duty to pay B is discharged. C is an intended beneficiary of A's promise (§ 302) and can by disclaimer render the transaction, including the discharge, inoperative from the beginning.

f. Compound novations. The novations already described involve a simple substitution of one obligor or obligee for another. More complex transactions, sometimes called compound novations, are possible. If, for example, there are two duties and the obligee of the first is the obligor of the second, the three parties may agree that one party shall drop out altogether. See Illustration 6. Furthermore, if each of two parties has a right against the other, they may agree with a third party that the third party shall immediately acquire a right against and be subject to a duty to one of them in substitution for the original right of and duty due the other. The new right and duty may be for performances that are the same as or different from the original ones. See Illustration 7.

Illustrations

6. A owes B $1,000 and B owes C $1,000. A promises B and C that he will assume B's debt to C if B promises to discharge A's debt to B and if C promises to discharge B's debt to C and accept A as his debtor. B and C so promise. There is a novation under which A's promise and B's and C's promises are consideration for each other, and A's debt to B and B's debt to C are discharged.

7. A and B make a contract under which A promises to deliver a tractor to B and B promises to pay A $1,000. A promises to deliver a bulldozer to C and to discharge B's duty if B promises to discharge A's duty and C promises to pay A $2,000. B and C so promise. There is a novation and A's duty to deliver a tractor to B and B's duty to pay $1,000 are discharged.

§ 281. Accord and Satisfaction.

(1) An accord is a contract under which an obligee promises to accept a stated performance in satisfaction of the obligor's existing duty. Performance of the accord discharges the original duty.

(2) Until performance of the accord, the original duty is suspended unless there is such a breach of the accord by the obligor as discharges the new duty of the obligee to accept the performance in satisfaction. If there is such a breach, the obligee may enforce either the original duty or any duty under the accord.

(3) Breach of the accord by the obligee does not discharge the original duty, but the obligor may maintain a suit for specific performance of the accord, in addition to any claim for damages for partial breach.

Comment

a. Nature of an accord. An accord is a contract under which an obligee promises to accept a substituted performance in future satisfaction of the obligor's duty. Because an accord is a contract, it differs from a mere revocable offer by the obligee to accept a substituted performance in satisfaction of the duty (§ 278). The typical accord involves an exchange of promises (Illustration 1), although an accord may also take the form of an option contract (Illustration 2). It is the essence of an accord that the original duty is not satisfied until the accord is performed, a result that is sometimes suggested by use of the term "executory accord." See Comment e.

b. Suspensory effect. The accord entitles the obligor to a chance to render the substituted performance in satisfaction of the original duty. Under the rule stated in Subsection (2), the obligee's right to enforce that duty is suspended subject to the terms of the accord until the obligor has had that chance. If the obligor is under a duty to perform the accord, his performance discharges both his original duty and his duty under the accord (§ 235). If, however, there is such a breach of the accord by the obligor as discharges the obligee's duty under the accord to accept the stated performance in satisfaction, he is no longer bound by the accord. He may then choose between enforcement of the original duty and any duty under the accord. Whether a breach by the obligor discharges the obligee's duty under the accord is governed by the rules stated in Chapter 10, Performance and Non-Performance.

Illustrations

1. A owes B $10,000. They make a contract under which A promises to deliver to B a specific machine within 30 days and B promises to accept it in satisfaction of the debt. The contract is an accord. A's debt is suspended and is discharged if A delivers the machine within 30 days.

2. A owes B $10,000. In consideration of $10 paid by A, not as part of the debt, B promises to accept in satisfaction of the debt a specific machine from A within 30 days. The contract is an accord. A's debt is suspended for 30 days and is discharged if A delivers the machine within 30 days, although A is under no duty to deliver the machine.

3. A, B and C, who are creditors of D, enter into a voluntary composition with D under which D promises to pay and A, B and C promise to accept 50% of their debts in full satisfaction. The composition is an accord. D's debts are suspended and are discharged if D pays the 50%.

4. The facts being otherwise as stated in Illustration 1, A fails to deliver the machine within 30 days and tells B that he will not deliver it. B can enforce either the original $10,000 debt or the duty to deliver the machine.

c. Effect of obligee's breach. If a breach of the accord by the obligee prevents the obligor from performing the accord, the original duty is not discharged, but the obligor has a claim for damages for total breach of the accord. However, the obligor's damages cannot be measured simply by his original duty, but must take account of what he has saved by not performing. To avoid imposing on the innocent obligor the burden of proving these damages, specific performance of the accord will be granted unless for some reason that remedy is inappropriate. In addition, the obligor may have a claim for damages for partial breach.

Illustration

5. The facts being otherwise as stated in Illustration 1, A tenders the machine within 30 days, but B refuses to receive it. If B then sues on the original $10,000 debt, A can obtain a decree of specific performance providing for the concurrent delivery of the machine and the discharge of the debt.

d. Validity of accord. The enforceability of an accord is governed by the rules applicable to the enforceability of contracts in general. The obligee's promise to accept the substituted performance in satisfaction of the original duty may be supported by consideration because that performance differs significantly from that required by the original duty (§ 73) or because the original duty is in fact doubtful or is believed by the obligor to be so (§ 74). It may also be supported by the obligor's reliance even in the absence of consideration (§ 90). A recurring situation involves the creditor who indorses and cashes a check sent by the debtor and marked "payment in full." The debtor then argues that the creditor, by exercising dominion over the check, has made an accord under which he has promised to accept payment of the check in satisfaction of the debt. Assuming that the transaction is not subject to objections such as those based on the absence of consideration (§§ 73, 74), on lack of good faith and fair dealing (§ 205) and on unconscionability (§ 208), such a notation by the debtor, if prominent enough to meet the requirements of § 19(2), may form the basis of an enforceable accord pursuant to the general rule stated in § 69(2). The creditor cannot generally avoid the consequences of his exercise of dominion by a declaration that he does not assent to the condition attached by the debtor. Uniform Commercial Code § 1–207, providing for acceptance of performance under reservation of rights, need not be read as changing this well-established rule. See Comment a to § 278.

Illustration

6. A contracts with B to have repairs made on A's house, no price being fixed. B sends A a bill for $1,000. A honestly disputes this amount and sends a letter explaining that he thinks the amount excessive and is enclosing a check for $800 as payment in full. B, after reading the letter, indorses the check and deposits it in his bank for collection. B is bound by an accord under which he promises to accept payment of the check as satisfaction of A's debt for repairs. The result is the same if, before indorsing the check, B adds the words "Accepted under protest as part payment." The result would be different, however, if B's claim were liquidated, undisputed and matured. See § 74.

e. Substituted contract distinguished. Because the obligor's original duty is not satisfied until the accord is performed, an accord differs from a substituted contract, under which a promise of substituted performance is accepted in satisfaction of the original duty. See § 279. Whether a contract is an accord or a substituted contract is a question of interpretation, subject to the general rules stated in Chapter 9. In resolving doubts in this regard, a court is less likely to conclude that an obligee was willing to accept a mere promise in satisfaction of an original duty that was clear than in satisfaction of one that was doubtful. It is therefore less likely to find a substituted contract and more likely to find an accord if the original duty was one to pay money, if it was undisputed, if it was liquidated and if it was matured. Compare Illustration 1 with Illustration 1 to § 279.

TOPIC 2. SUBSTITUTED PERFORMANCE, SUBSTITUTED CONTRACT, ACCORD AND ACCOUNT STATED

§ 282. Account Stated.

(1) An account stated is a manifestation of assent by debtor and creditor to a stated sum as an accurate computation of an amount due the creditor. A party's retention without objection for an unreasonably long time of a statement of account rendered by the other party is a manifestation of assent.

(2) The account stated does not itself discharge any duty but is an admission by each party of the facts asserted and a promise by the debtor to pay according to its terms.

Comment

a. Computation not compromise or liquidation. If a debtor and a creditor make an agreement in the nature of a compromise or liquidation of a disputed or unliquidated debt, the agreement may be either a substituted contract or an accord resulting in discharge under the rules stated in §§ 279 and 280. If, however, they make an agreement in the nature of a computation rather than of compromise of the debt, the agreement is called an "account stated." An account stated must be founded on previous transactions that have given rise to the relation of debtor and creditor and is usually based on a number of items. If each party is indebted to the other an account stated may be founded on the difference between their indebtedness.

b. Manifestation of assent. Usually it is the creditor who submits the statement, but it may be the debtor who does so. In either case, the recipient's assent may be inferred from his conduct. Under the rule stated in Subsection (1), his retention of the statement for an unreasonably long time is a manifestation of his assent. How long a time is unreasonable is a question of fact to be answered in the light of all the circumstances. The parties, subject to rules such as that on unconscionability (§ 208), may fix by agreement a time after which the recipient will be considered to have assented to a statement of account. However, the party sending the statement cannot impose such a time limit on the recipient merely by a clause on the statement. For federal legislation on credit billing, see 15 U.S.C. § 1666 (1975).

c. Effect of account stated. An account stated does not itself result in discharge, but operates as an admission of its contents for evidentiary purposes. It also operates as a promise to pay. It may therefore become binding as the result of reliance under the rule stated in § 90. It may also be effective as a promise to pay an antecedent indebtedness under the rule stated in § 82, although statutes in many states require that it be in writing and signed if it is to have this effect. See Comment a to § 82. If it is in writing it may also satisfy the Statute of Frauds. In the absence of a requirement of a writing, however, an account stated may be oral. The effect of an account stated as a promise is subject to the rules on mistake (Chapter 6).

Illustrations

1. A regularly sells goods to B. From time to time B returns some of the goods for credit and makes payments for the rest. At the end of each month, A sends B itemized statements of B's outstanding balance. One of the statements incorrectly gives an outstanding balance of $5,500 because of A's oversight in failing to debit B with a $1,000 delivery and to credit B with a $500 payment both made during the preceding month. Before either mistake is discovered, B writes A that the statement is "correct." There is an account stated, but it does not prevent A from proving the $1,000 delivery or B from proving the $500 payment. B owes A $6,000.

2. A regularly sells goods to B. From time to time B returns some of the goods for credit and makes payments for the rest. At the end of each month, A sends B itemized statements of B's outstanding balance. One of the statements incorrectly gives an outstanding balance of $5,500 because of A's failure to credit B with a $1,000 payment that was stolen by one of A's employees. B writes A that the statement is "correct" without verifying it, and the resulting delay in discovering the mistake prevents A from obtaining restitution from the employee. B is precluded from showing the mistake. B owes A $5,500.

3. The facts being otherwise as stated in Illustration 2, B does not write A that the statement is "correct." B's retention of the statement for an unreasonable time is a manifestation of assent to it. B owes A $5,500.

TOPIC 3. AGREEMENT OF RESCISSION, RELEASE AND CONTRACT NOT TO SUE

§ 283. Agreement of Rescission.

(1) An agreement of rescission is an agreement under which each party agrees to discharge all of the other party's remaining duties of performance under an existing contract.

(2) An agreement of rescission discharges all remaining duties of performance of both parties. It is a question of interpretation whether the parties also agree to make restitution with respect to performance that has been rendered.

Comment

a. Nature of agreement of rescission. Sometimes the parties to a contract that is at least partly executory on each side make an agreement under which each party agrees to discharge all of the other party's duties of performance. Such an agreement is called an "agreement of rescission" in this Restatement. Consideration is provided by each party's discharge of the duties of the other. This is so even though one or both parties have partly performed their duties or one or both have a claim for damages for partial breach. The surrender of a doubtful claim may be enough under the rule stated in § 74. The agreement need not be expressed in words. Other conduct may show an intent by both parties to abandon their contract. If one party, even wrongfully, expresses a wish or an intention to cease performance and the other party fails to object, circumstances may justify the inference that there has been an agreement of rescission. Sometimes mere inaction on both sides, such as the failure to take any steps looking toward performance or enforcement, may indicate an intent to abandon the contract. Mere failure to object to a repudiation, however, is not a manifestation of assent to an agreement of rescission. See § 257. The term "agreement of rescission" is used in this Restatement to avoid confusion with the word "rescission," which courts sometimes use to refer to the exercise by one party of a power of avoidance (§ 7). An agreement of "partial rescission" that would discharge less than all the parties' remaining duties of performance is treated as a modification. See Comment b. An agreement of rescission differs from a "termination," which "occurs when either party pursuant to a power created by agreement or law puts an end to the contract otherwise than for its breach" and from a "cancellation," which "occurs when either party puts an end to the contract for breach by the other." Uniform Commercial Code § 2–106.

Illustrations

1. A and B make a contract under which A promises to paint B's house and B promises to pay A $1,000. A finds, after beginning the work, that he will lose more money by finishing than by giving up at once and makes B an offer to rescind the contract. B accepts. There is an agreement of rescission and the duties of both A and B are discharged.

2. A and B make a contract under which A promises to paint B's house and B promises to pay A $1,000. After A has finished the work, B's financial condition has become impaired, and A tells B, "You need never pay me the $1,000 that you owe me." There is no agreement of rescission and B's duty to pay A $1,000 is not discharged. The result is the same if the original contract results from B's offer to pay A $1,000 if A paints B's house and A's acceptance by doing the work.

b. The Statute of Frauds and oral agreement of rescission. Under the rule stated in § 148, the Statute of Frauds does not affect the enforceability of an oral agreement of rescission unless rescission of a transfer of property is involved. An attempt to make an agreement of "partial rescission" that would discharge less than all of their remaining duties under the existing contract is considered a modification, subject to the rule stated in § 149, and not an agreement of rescission. Even a provision of the earlier contract to the effect that it can be rescinded only in writing does not impair the effectiveness of an oral agreement of rescission. In the absence of statute, such a self-imposed limitation does not limit the power of the parties subsequently to contract. A different rule is laid down in Uniform Commercial Code § 2–209(2) for contracts for the sale of goods.

c. Whether promise of restitution is included. If the original contract has been partly performed on one or both sides at the time of the agreement of rescission, a question arises as to whether a party is entitled to restitution for such performance as he has rendered. There is no rule of law establishing a presumption to answer this question. It is a question of interpretation of the agreement of rescission that is to be determined on the facts of each case.

Illustration

3. A and B make a contract under which A promises to sell B land for $100,000, payable in five installments of $20,000 each. B pays the first installment and takes possession under the contract. A and B then make an agreement of rescission. Whether A has a duty to return the $20,000 payment, either in full or less the fair rental value of the land for the time that B was in possession, is a question of interpretation of the agreement of rescission.

§ 284. Release.

(1) A release is a writing providing that a duty owed to the maker of the release is discharged immediately or on the occurrence of a condition.

(2) The release takes effect on delivery as stated in §§ 101–03 and, subject to the occurrence of any condition, discharges the duty.

Comment

a. Nature of release. Although no particular form is required for an agreement to discharge a duty, the term "release" has traditionally been reserved for a formal written statement by an obligee that the obligor's duty is discharged. That usage is preserved in this Section. No special words are required and the writing may state, for example, that it releases the obligor, that it releases the obligor's duties or that it releases the obligee's rights. It must, however, take effect immediately or on the occurrence of a condition. A promise to discharge in the future an existing duty merely creates a new duty that can itself be discharged by the parties. Such a promise is not a release. The duty that is released need not be matured. A purported release of a duty that does not yet exist, however, is not a release but a promise to discharge a duty in the future. See Illustration 3. A purported release of a duty that is revived on the occurrence of a condition is not a release but a contract not to sue.

b. Effectiveness of release. A release was traditionally made under seal and this may still be done in jurisdictions where the seal has not been deprived of its effect in this respect. A release may also be supported by consideration or the obligor's reliance. Furthermore, statutes in some states give an unsealed release the same effect that a sealed release had at common law. As a formal instrument, a release is subject to the same requirements of delivery as is a contract under seal. Delivery may be to the obligor conditionally or unconditionally or in escrow. See §§ 101–03. A release is usually authenticated by the obligee's signature.

Illustrations

1. A owes B $1,000. B delivers to A, in a state where the seal retains its effect, a sealed writing stating that B releases A from the debt. The writing is a release. A's duty to pay B is discharged whether it was due when the release was given or not. The result is the same if the release is not under seal but is supported by consideration.

2. The facts being otherwise as stated in Illustration 1, the writing states that B releases A from the debt if B dies before it is due. The writing is a conditional release. The debt is discharged if B dies before it is due.

3. A, who is engaged in business transactions with B, receives from B a writing supported by consideration stating that B releases A from all debts that A owes or may in the future owe to B. One month later B sells goods to A, for which A promises to pay $10,000. With respect to debts not yet in existence, the writing is not a release but a contract to discharge A. The subsequent inconsistent contract operates as a modification of this earlier contract and A is under a duty to pay B $10,000.

c. Interpretation. The rules of interpretation that apply to contracts generally apply also to writings that purport to be releases. The principal purpose of the obligee is given great weight if it can be ascertained (§ 202(1)). If a literal interpretation of a writing that purports to be a release would frustrate that purpose, the writing may be interpreted as a contract not to sue. This is particularly likely in the case of a purported release of one joint debtor that states that all rights against another joint debtor are reserved. If the effect of a literal interpretation of the writing as a release would be to release the other joint debtor (§ 294) and frustrate the obligee's purpose as indicated by his attempted reservation of rights, the writing will be interpreted as a contract not to sue. See also Restatement of Security § 122.

Illustration

4. A and B are bound jointly to pay C $1,000. C delivers to A a writing supported by consideration stating that C releases A from the debt but that C reserves his rights against B. If a release of A would discharge B under the rules stated in § 294, the writing will be interpreted as a contract not to sue and not as a release.

§ 285. Contract Not to Sue.

(1) A contract not to sue is a contract under which the obligee of a duty promises never to sue the obligor or a third person to enforce the duty or not to do so for a limited time.

(2) Except as stated in Subsection (3), a contract never to sue discharges the duty and a contract not to sue for a limited time bars an action to enforce the duty during that time.

(3) A contract not to sue one co-obligor bars levy of execution on the property of the promisee during the agreed time but does not bar an action or the recovery of judgment against any co-obligor.

Comment

a. Nature of contract not to sue. Sometimes an obligee does not manifest an intention to discharge the obligor but merely makes a contract by which he promises not to sue him. See § 295. Such a contract is often called "a covenant not to sue," a term that is not used in this Restatement in order to avoid any suggestion that it must be under seal. Although a contract never to sue an obligor does not in terms discharge the obligor's duty immediately, it is given this effect in order to avoid circuity of action. A contract not to sue for a limited time bars an action to enforce the duty during that time. As to a contract not to sue one co-obligor, see Comment b.

Illustration

1. A owes B $1,000 payable immediately. B assigns his right to C, receiving in return C's promise not to sue A for one year. C cannot maintain an action against A before the end of the year.

b. Co-obligors. If an obligee makes a contract not to sue one co-obligor and then joins that co-obligor in an action merely for the purpose of obtaining judgment against the other co-obligors, this is not regarded as a breach of the contract not to sue the one co-obligor if none of his assets are seized in satisfaction of the judgment. See Comment b to § 295. Therefore, the effect of the contract is merely to bar levy of execution on his property during the agreed time.

TOPIC 4. ALTERATION

§ 286. Alteration of Writing.

(1) If one to whom a duty is owed under a contract alters a writing that is an integrated agreement or that satisfies the Statute of Frauds with respect to that contract, the duty is discharged if the alteration is fraudulent and material.

(2) An alteration is material if it would, if effective, vary any party's legal relations with the maker of the alteration or adversely affect that party's legal relations with a third person. The unauthorized insertion in a blank space in a writing is an alteration.

Comment

a. Effect of alteration. The rule on alteration stated in this Section applies to writings that are completely or partially integrated agreements under the parol evidence rule (§§ 209, 210) and to memoranda that are necessary to satisfy the Statute of Frauds (§ 131). If a party to whom a duty is owed under a contract represented by such a writing fraudulently and materially alters the writing, that duty is discharged. An alteration that is not both fraudulent and material does not have this effect and the duty remains enforceable according to its original terms. Once a duty has been discharged by alteration, an attempt by the maker of the alteration to revive the duty by restoring the writing is ineffective unless the party whose duty is discharged forgives the alteration (§ 287(2)). An alteration by one who is not a party to the contract does not result in a discharge, however, even if it is fraudulent and material. An alteration by a party never discharges his own duty and therefore never terminates any right of the other party, unless the other manifests his assent under the rule stated in § 287(1). This Restatement does not apply to the alteration of commercial paper or documents of title, which are the subjects of Uniform Commercial Code §§ 3–407, 7–208, 7–306.

b. What is a material alteration. An alteration may be by addition, deletion or substitution. An unauthorized insertion in a space that has been left blank in a writing is an alteration, but to come within the rule stated in Subsection (1) the writing must, in spite of the blank space, be an integrated agreement or satisfy the Statute of Frauds. An alteration is not material, however, unless it purports to change the legal relationships under the contract. If two or more persons are under duties to perform separate acts, an alteration that affects the duty of only one of them does not discharge the duty of another. An alteration may be material even though it purports to be to the disadvantage of the person making it, although such an alteration will rarely be fraudulent as required by the rule stated in Subsection (1). A mere change in the spelling of a party's name or the addition of the date of the writing is not material if it does not purport to have legal effect.

Illustrations

1. A and B make an integrated agreement for the sale of goods to be delivered by A for which B is to pay the price of $1,100 on July 1. A fraudulently erases "July 1" and substitutes "June 1." The alteration is both fraudulent and material, and B's duty is discharged.

2. The facts being otherwise as stated in Illustration 1, instead of altering the date A fraudulently alters the amount by erasing $1,100 and substituting "$1,000" to enable him to sue in a local court whose jurisdiction is limited to claims not exceeding $1,000. The alteration is both fraudulent and material, and B's duty is discharged.

3. The facts being otherwise as stated in Illustration 1, the agreement, although partially integrated, contains a blank for the amount of interest if the price is not paid when due, and A, instead of altering the date, fraudulently and without authority from B inserts "8%" although they had agreed on 6%. The insertion without authority is an alteration that is both fraudulent and material, and B's duty is discharged.

4. A and B sign a memorandum that satisfies the Statute of Frauds with respect to their oral contract for the sale of land from A to B for $10,000, the date of closing to be July 1. B fraudulently erases "July 1" and substitutes "June 1." The alteration is both fraudulent and material, and A's duty is discharged.

5. The facts being otherwise as stated in Illustration 4, B makes the alteration innocently, in the erroneous belief that they agreed on June 1 and that the words "July 1" are the result of a mistake. Because the alteration, although material, is not fraudulent, A's duty is not discharged, and A is bound by the contract made before the alteration.

6. The facts being otherwise as stated in Illustration 4, the alteration is made by C, with whom B has left the writing for safekeeping, with the fraudulent intent of aiding B. Because the alteration, although fraudulent and material, is not made by one to whom a duty is owed under the contract, A's duty is not discharged, and A is bound by the contract without the alteration.

§ 287. Assent to or Forgiveness of Alteration.

(1) If a party, knowing of an alteration that discharges his duty, manifests assent to the altered terms, his manifestation is equivalent to an acceptance of an offer to substitute those terms.

(2) If a party, knowing of an alteration that discharges his duty, asserts a right under the original contract or otherwise manifests a willingness to remain subject to the original contract or to forgive the alteration, the original contract is revived.

Comment

a. Assent to alteration. An alteration may be regarded as manifesting a desire on the part of its maker to have a contract in the altered form, and assent by the other party will be treated as if it were acceptance of an offer to substitute the altered terms. The same requirements must be met as in the case of any substituted contract, including those imposed by the doctrine of consideration and by the Statute of Frauds. If two or more persons are under duties to perform the same act and only one of them assents to an alteration, the fact that the others are discharged does not affect the liability of the one who assents, and his assent has the same effect as to him as it would have had if no duties of the others had been discharged.

Illustrations

1. A and B make an integrated agreement under which B promises to employ A for one year from the date of the contract at a stated monthly salary. B fraudulently erases "one year" and substitutes "two years." A, on learning of the alteration, writes B, "I shall be glad to work for you for two years at the stated salary." Although the alteration was both fraudulent and material, A's manifestation of assent is equivalent to an acceptance of an offer by B to employ A for two years, and both A and B are bound by a contract on those terms.

2. The facts being otherwise as stated in Illustration 1, A manifests his assent over the telephone instead of in writing. A's assent is not enforceable against him because of the Statute of Frauds (§ 130).

b. Forgiveness of alteration. The innocent party loses none of his rights as the result of an alteration made without his consent and can always assert them under the original contract. If he does assert them, however, he is regarded as having forgiven the alteration and the original contract is revived. Any other manifestation of a willingness to remain subject to the duties under the original contract or to forgive the alteration has the same effect. Forgiveness need not be supported by consideration. If two or more persons are under duties to perform the same act, the effect of forgiveness by one of them is the same as the effect of assent as discussed in Comment a.

Illustrations

3. A and B make an integrated contract for the sale of goods to be delivered by A for which B promises to pay a price of $1,000. A fraudulently erases "$1,000" and substitutes "$1,100." B, on learning of the alteration, writes A that he must deliver the goods as promised. Although the alteration is both fraudulent and material, A can enforce the contract against B.

4. The facts being otherwise as stated in Illustration 3, B instead of writing A that he must deliver the goods, writes A that he forgives the alteration. Although the alteration is both fraudulent and material, A can enforce the contract against B.

CHAPTER 13

JOINT AND SEVERAL PROMISORS AND PROMISEES

TOPIC 1. JOINT AND SEVERAL PROMISORS

§ 288. Promises of the Same Performance.

(1) Where two or more parties to a contract make a promise or promises to the same promisee, the manifested intention of the parties determines whether they promise that the same performance or separate performances shall be given.

(2) Unless a contrary intention is manifested, a promise by two or more promisors is a promise that the same performance shall be given.

Comment

a. "Same performance." Where there are more promisors than one in a contract, some or all of them may promise the same performance. See § 10. Thus A and B may both promise that $100 lent by C will be repaid, or that certain goods will be delivered to C, or that certain services will be rendered to C. On the other hand, each promisor may promise a separate performance, which may be similar to that promised by another. Thus where C lends $100 to A and B, A may promise to repay $50 and B may promise to repay $50. As used in §§ 288–96, "same performance" refers to the first of these two types of situations but not to the second.

b. The performances promised. The question whether two promisors promise the same or separate performances is distinct from the question whether two promisors of the same performance are bound by "joint" or by "several" duties or by both, but the two questions are sometimes confused. The question what performances are promised is entirely a question of interpretation of the promises, while the distinction between "joint" and "several" duties is primarily remedial and procedural and is substantially abolished by statute in many jurisdictions.

c. Presumption that the same performance is promised. It has often been said that when two or more persons undertake a contractual obligation they are presumed to undertake it jointly and that "words of severance" are necessary to overcome the presumption. Such statements combine the rule of Subsection (2) with that of § 289(2). Even though the rule of § 289(2) is abolished by statute, the rule of Subsection (2) operates in the rare case of absence of any evidence of intention; it yields to manifestations of contrary intention, whether or not there are "words of severance." The fact that the interests of the promisors are different, that one receives all or most of the consideration, or that one is merely a surety does not necessarily rebut the presumption. But promises to subscribe for a common purpose sums of money set opposite the names of the promisors are ordinarily promises of separate performances.

Illustrations

1. A, B and C sign a paper reading "Each of us guarantees to D that he shall be duly repaid $100, which he has this day lent E." A, B and C promise the same performance, the payment of the whole sum of $100 to D. Performance by one of them discharges the duties of the others to D, though the guarantors who have not paid may be liable for contribution to the one who pays.

2. A and B sign a written contract which provides "A and B will take charge of C's plant and provide it with proper management." In the absence of any contrary indication, the quoted words will be taken to mean that A and B promise the same performance and that each is to be fully responsible for the proper management of the plant.

3. A and B, "the railroad companies," and C, "the coal company," enter into a written agreement under which "the railway companies hereby purchase" a specified quantity of coal, and "the railroad companies agree to remit" in a specified way. In the absence of any contrary indication, the quoted words will be taken to mean that A and B promise the same performance, and that each is to be fully

responsible for the price of the coal. The words "one-half bill to each" would be a sufficient contrary indication.

4. A, B and C sign a subscription contract reading "A, B and C hereby undertake to pay the following sums." Opposite the name of each signer is a separate sum. Each promises only a separate performance, the payment of the sum opposite his name.

d. "Several" promises. The word "several" is used in two different senses with reference to promises and duties. First, if one party promises one performance, and another promises a different performance, each may be bound independently of the other and the promisee may be entitled to both performances. The promises and the duties of the promisors may then be described as "several," but this Chapter does not hereafter deal with promises which are "several" in this sense. Second, in traditional usage promises of the same performance by different promisors are said to create "several" duties if "words of severance" are used, even though performance by any one of the promisors is to discharge the duties of all. The legal consequences of such promises of the same performance are the subject of §§ 289–96. Promises of the same performance may be treated as "joint," "several," or "joint and several."

Illustration

5. A and B sign a written promise "A and B severally promise C $100." A and B are each bound to the extent of $100, but the quoted words are ambiguous as to whether payment of $100 by one is to discharge the duty of the other.

§ 289. Joint, Several, and Joint and Several Promisors of the Same Performance.

(1) Where two or more parties to a contract promise the same performance to the same promisee, each is bound for the whole performance thereof, whether his duty is joint, several, or joint and several.

(2) Where two or more parties to a contract promise the same performance to the same promisee, they incur only a joint duty unless an intention is manifested to create several duties or joint and several duties.

(3) By statute in most states some or all promises which would otherwise create only joint duties create joint and several duties.

Comment

a. Liability of each for the whole performance. In the civil-law system of Louisiana, derived from the Roman and French law, promises of the same performance create "joint" liability on the part of each promisor unless an intention is manifested to create a "solidary" obligation. "Joint" liability means liability only for an aliquot share of the total obligation; a "solidary" obligation is substantially the same as a "joint and several" obligation at common law. Common-law terminology and results are quite different: promises of the same performance may create joint duties, several duties, or joint and several duties; and each promisor is liable for the whole performance promised. A contrary agreement may be effective either to show that separate performances are promised or to limit the liability which would otherwise be created.

Illustrations

1. A and B owe $100 to C jointly, and C obtains a judgment against A and B for $100. Execution may be levied wholly on the property of either A or B, or partially on the property of each.

2. A and B severally promise to pay C the same $100. C may obtain separate judgments against each for $100, and may levy execution under either judgment until $100 is collected.

3. A and B and several others make a written offer to guarantee the repayment of loans to be made to C by D, "provided that our total liability shall not at any time exceed $4,000 and our individual liability shall not exceed $200." D lends C $100 in reliance on the guaranty. Each signer of the guaranty is responsible for the entire $100, whether the liability is joint, several, or joint and several.

b. The presumption of joint obligation. The question whether promisors of the same performance undertake "several" duties in addition to or instead of a "joint" duty has traditionally been treated as a question of the application of deductions from legal concepts rather than as a question of manifested intention. Where a "joint" duty differs from "joint and several" duties, the joint duty is invariably less advantageous to the promisee, while the advantage to the promisor does not normally serve any legitimate interest. Joint duties, as distinguished from joint and several duties, are likely to reflect ignorance or inadvertence on the part of the promisee. But in the absence of statute both common-law courts and courts of equity long held promises of the same performance to be joint only unless the promises took a linguistic form appropriate to several duties. The modern tendency is to treat the question as one of interpretation and therefore to give weight to manifestations of contrary intention in whatever form. Subsection (2) reflects this tendency.

c. Severance. The fact that one promisor is under a duty to another to perform the promise or that one promisor has received all or the greater portion of the consideration does not prevent their duty from being joint rather than several or joint and several. But the fact that the promises are made in separate documents or are separately stated in the same document sufficiently shows an intention to undertake several duties. The standard modern form to create duties which are both joint and several is "We jointly and severally promise," but any equivalent words will do as well. In particular, a promise in the first person singular, signed by several persons, creates joint and several duties.

Illustrations

4. A, B and C sign a contract stating that "A as principal, and B and C as sureties, promise" a certain performance. A, B and C are jointly bound. In the absence of statute, the statement of the suretyship relation does not manifest an intention to create several duties or joint and several duties.

5. A and B sign a contract in these terms: "We, and each of us, promise D that C shall be paid the sum of $100" on a certain date. This creates joint and several duties on the part of the signers.

6. A, B and C sign a contract in writing in these words: "I promise to pay D $100" on a certain date. This creates joint and several duties on the part of A, B and C to see that D is paid $100.

7. A, B and C sign a paper reading: "Each of us guarantees to D that he shall be duly repaid $100, which he has this day lent E." A, B and C promise the same performance, but their duties are several.

d. Statutes. As is indicated in the Statutory Note preceding § 288, statutes in a sizable number of jurisdictions provide that joint promises have the effect of creating joint and several duties, and statutes in others create a presumption of joint and several duties either in all cases or where all promisors receive a benefit from the consideration. Although Uniform Partnership Act § 15 provides a presumption of joint liability on partnership contracts, that section has been modified in several states to provide instead a presumption of joint and several liability. Uniform Commercial Code § 3–118(e) provides that, unless the instrument otherwise specifies, two or more persons who sign a negotiable instrument as maker, acceptor or drawer or indorser and as a part of the same transaction are jointly and severally liable. In addition, the consequences of joint liability have been modified by statute in most of the States where it retains significance.

Illustration

8. A makes a negotiable promissory note payable to B and C. B and C indorse and sell the note to D. Under Uniform Commercial Code § 3–118(e), B and C are jointly and severally liable to D. If B and C are partners, notice of dishonor to one is notice to each under Uniform Commercial Code § 3–508(5). But Uniform Partnership Act § 15 provides that partners are liable jointly.

§ 290. Compulsory Joinder of Joint Promisors.

(1) By statute in most states where the distinction between joint duties and joint and several duties retains significance, an action can be maintained against one or more promisors who incur only a joint duty, even though other promisors subject to the same duty are not served with process.

(2) In the absence of statute, an action can be maintained against promisors who incur only a joint duty without joinder of those beyond the jurisdiction of the court, the representatives of deceased promisors, or those against whom the duty is not enforceable at the time of suit.

Comment

a. Historical note. Compulsory joinder of joint promisors is a remnant of a procedural system which was largely displaced by nineteenth-century reforms. In the English common-law courts the objection was waived unless non-joinder appeared from the plaintiff's declaration or was asserted by plea in abatement naming those not joined. Absent waiver, except in cases of infancy or death, the requirement was strictly enforced that all those originally jointly bound be joined as defendants. Where some were beyond the jurisdiction of the court and did not appear, the plaintiff's proper course was to proceed to outlaw them; judgment could then be had against those who did appear. Even in cases of joint and several duties, the plaintiff had to elect to sue all or one; he could not sue two or more unless he sued all.

b. Statutes. The requirement of joinder has been modified by statute in at least four different ways in various states. Perhaps the most common change is a provision that when less than all joint promisors are served with process, the action may in the discretion of the court proceed against those served, the judgment binding the joint property of all and the separate property of those served. A second common provision simply permits the action to proceed against those served as if they were the sole defendants. Third, in some states suit may be brought against any or all of a number of joint promisors; such provisions differ from the first two types in eliminating any requirement that all be named as defendants. Finally, whatever the rule as to joint obligors generally, partners may in many states be sued in the firm name.

c. Judicial mitigation. Unless changed by statute a requirement of joinder of promisors who incur only a joint duty remains in force in those states where the distinction between joint duties and joint and several duties retains significance. But the strict common-law requirement was mitigated by judicial decision in the United States in a number of situations which required statutory relief in England. Thus joinder of parties not within the jurisdiction of the court has not been required in the United States. Exceptions have been made for dormant partners, bankrupt co-promisors, and promisors against whom the claim is barred by the statute of limitations. Compare § 291. Modern procedure commonly permits joinder of several as well as joint claims, and misjoinder or nonjoinder can be cured by amendment.

Illustrations

1. A and B are jointly indebted to C. C sues A, who makes no objection to the nonjoinder of B. C is entitled to judgment against A for the full amount of the debt.

2. The facts being otherwise as stated in Illustration 1, A makes proper objection to the nonjoinder of B, and C joins B by amendment. C is entitled to judgment against A and B.

3. A, B and C jointly contract to pay money to D. C was an infant when he made the promise, or has since been discharged in bankruptcy, or has a defense under the statute of limitations. D may sue A and B without joining C as a defendant.

§ 291. Judgment in an Action Against Co-Promisors.

In an action against promisors of the same performance, whether their duties are joint, several, or joint and several, judgment can properly be entered for or against one even though no judgment or a different judgment is entered with respect to another, except that judgment for one and against another is improper where there has been a determination on the merits and the liability of one cannot exist without the liability of the other.

Comment

a. Historical note. Before the procedural reforms of the nineteenth century, promisors could only be joined as defendants if they were jointly bound, and joinder of all those jointly bound was ordinarily required. See § 290. The judgment and execution were joint, although levy could be made on the separate property of one defendant. Hence a successful defense by one defendant operated for the benefit of all. If one joint promisor defaulted, the practice was to enter an interlocutory judgment against him and to proceed against those who appeared; if they prevailed, the interlocutory judgment was discharged. Final judgment either for or against one defendant was a discharge of all defendants in that action, although a new action might be brought when a defendant was successful on a ground peculiar to him. Compare § 292. The same rules were applied in a joint action against joint and several promisors.

Illustration

1. A sues B and C on their joint promise. B asserts performance as a defense; C denies making the promise. Findings are made for B and against C on these issues. Judgment will be rendered for both B and C.

   b. Individual defenses. When one defendant pleaded a defense peculiar to himself, the plaintiff was permitted to discontinue against him and continue the action against the others. In the nineteenth century it was established that final judgment for the defendant on such a plea did not discharge his co-defendants, and discontinuance became unnecessary. This exception was established for cases of lack of jurisdiction, contractual incapacity, discharge in bankruptcy, and statute of limitations, but under modern procedure there is no reason why it should not apply to any case where a joint promisor succeeds in a defense peculiar to himself.

Illustration

2. A sues B and C on their joint promise. B pleads a contract not to sue as a defense. Judgment may be given for B and against C.

   c. Effect of procedural reforms and statutes. Modern procedural reforms and statutes relating to joint obligations have eliminated the foundations on which the all-or-none rule rested. In most States joinder of promisors of the same performance is permitted but not required, and judgment against one does not bar action against his co-obligor, whether there is a joint duty or several duties or both. Legislation has often not dealt specifically with the rule, and the proper procedure on the default of one of several defendants is beyond the scope of this Restatement. This Section embodies the rational remainder of the all-or-none rule; it permits the court to insist that verdict and judgment be free of caprice, bias, or obvious misunderstanding. Its application may be influenced by the extent to which inconsistent verdicts are tolerated in the jurisdiction in other situations. Compare Restatement, Second, Torts § 883.

Illustration

3. A sues B and C on their joint promise. They deny that any promise was made. An instruction to the jury that verdict must be for or against both is called for; and a verdict for one and against the other should be set aside on motion of an aggrieved party.

§ 292. Effect of Judgment for or Against Co-Promisors.

(1) A judgment against one or more promisors does not discharge other promisors of the same performance unless joinder of the other promisors is required by the rule stated in § 290. By statute in most states judgment against one promisor does not discharge co-promisors even where such joinder is required.

(2) The effect of judgment for one or more promisors of the same performance is determined by the rules of res judicata relating to suretyship or vicarious liability.

Comment

a. Merger of joint duties by judgment. During the nineteenth century the rule was established, contrary to earlier authority, that judgment against one joint promisor merged the entire claim and barred a subsequent action against a co-promisor. The co-promisor remained liable for contribution if the defendant in the action satisfied the judgment. Yet the discharge was rigorously enforced both at law and in equity: no exception was made when the plaintiff had judgment against the only promisors known to him, they proved insolvent, and suit was brought against a subsequently discovered partner. The same logic applied to the joint duty of joint and several promisors: either a joint judgment or a several judgment against one barred a subsequent joint action, but not a several action against a promisor not joined in the first action.

b. Mitigation of the merger doctrine. Procedural reforms have permitted joinder of defendants whose duty is not joint. Thus in cases of joint and several promisors claims based on the several promises of those not joined in a prior action can be joined, and the merger of the joint duty is academic. As to joint promises, the doctrine did not apply when the omitted promisor was dead (see § 296), and exceptions were made for promisors out of the jurisdiction, for foreign judgments, for cases of estoppel, for judgments on promises given as conditional payment or collateral security. Today statutes in most states have given some or all joint promises the effect of joint and several promises, or have directly provided that judgment against one or more joint promisors does not bar an action against the others, or have permitted judgments binding the joint property of those not served, who may later be summoned to show cause why they should not be bound. . . .

   c. *Judgment based on personal defense.* Also in the nineteenth century, it was established that a judgment for one joint promisor did not discharge the joint duty of all if it was based on a defense peculiar to him. Originally applied to cases of lack of jurisdiction, contractual incapacity, discharge in bankruptcy, and statute of limitations, this rule now applies to any defense not applicable to the co-promisors. Compare § 291.

   d. *Suretyship and vicarious liability.* "Res judicata" is used in Subsection (2) in a broad sense as including merger, bar, collateral estoppel and direct estoppel. See Introductory Note to Restatement, Second, Judgments, Chapter 3. The rules governing the effects of a judgment on parties and others are stated in Restatement, Second, Judgments, Chapters 3 and 4, and in Restatement, Second, Conflict of Laws §§ 96–97, and are not repeated here. Particularly applicable to promisors of the same performance are rules relating to the effect of a judgment for or against a principal obligor upon a subsequent action against a surety. The judgment may impair or destroy the surety's right to indemnity or contribution, and the surety is discharged to the extent of the impairment or destruction. See Restatement, Second, Judgments § 51; cf. Restatement of Security § 139, Restatement, Second, Agency § 184. Regardless of indemnity or contribution, a judgment for one obligor may also bar a subsequent action against another whose liability is based entirely on breach by the first. See Restatement, Second, Judgments § 51.

§ 293. Effect of Performance or Satisfaction on Co-Promisors.

Full or partial performance or other satisfaction of the contractual duty of a promisor discharges the duty to the obligee of each other promisor of the same performance to the extent of the amount or value applied to the discharge of the duty of the promisor who renders it.

Comment

   a. *Rationale.* This Section makes explicit what is meant by "promises of the same performance": performance by any one of the promisors discharges the duty of the others. See § 288. Satisfaction by the acceptance of a substituted performance (§ 278) has the same effect, since the promisee or beneficiary has a right only to the single performance or to an agreed equivalent. For this purpose it does not matter whether the promisors are bound jointly, severally, or jointly and severally. One of the promisors is not permitted by a subsequent agreement with a promisee or beneficiary to confer on him a right against the other promisors to receive more than was originally promised. A release (§ 284) or contract not to sue (§ 285) is not of itself satisfaction within the meaning of this Section, but is dealt with in §§ 294 and 295.

Illustrations

   1. A borrows $100 from D for the common benefit of A, B and C in equal shares, and A, B and C promise that D will be repaid. A pays $25 to D pursuant to an express agreement that it shall apply only to A's duty and shall not limit D's rights against B or C. D's rights against B and C, as well as his right against A, are reduced by $25.

   2. The facts being otherwise as stated in Illustration 1, A delivers to D a set of books worth $25, and D accepts the books in full satisfaction of A's duty. A, B and C are discharged.

   3. The facts being otherwise as stated in Illustration 1, A delivers to D a set of books worth $200, and D accepts the books in satisfaction of $25 of A's duty. D's rights against B and C, as well as his right against A, are reduced by $25.

   4. A, B and C are bound jointly, or jointly and severally, to D for the payment of an unliquidated claim. A and B agree with D to liquidate the claim at $100, reserving C's rights. D subsequently sues C on the claim, recovers a judgment for $75 without prejudice to his claim against A and B, and collects $75 from C. The liability of A and B is reduced to $25.

b. "Obligee." The word "obligee" is used in this Section and in succeeding sections of this Chapter to include both a promisee and a beneficiary who under the rules of §§ 302–15 has the right to enforce a promise.

§ 294. Effect of Discharge on Co-Promisors.

(1) Except as stated in § 295, where the obligee of promises of the same performance discharges one promisor by release, rescission or accord and satisfaction,

(a) co-promisors who are bound only by a joint duty are discharged unless the discharged promisor is a surety for the co-promisor;

(b) co-promisors who are bound by joint and several duties or by several duties are not discharged except to the extent required by the law of suretyship.

(2) By statute in many states a discharge of one promisor does not discharge other promisors of the same performance except to the extent required by the law of suretyship.

(3) Any consideration received by the obligee for discharge of one promisor discharges the duty of each other promisor of the same performance to the extent of the amount or value received. An agreement to the contrary is not effective unless it is made with a surety and expressly preserves the duty of his principal.

Comment

a. The common-law rule. The English rule that release of one joint obligor releases all was applied to joint and several obligations as well as joint obligations, and to tort as well as contract obligations. See Restatement, Second, Torts § 885. Historically the rule rested on the unitary character of the obligee's right and possibly on the principle that a deed is construed against the grantor. It has been suggested that a contrary rule might permit the obligee to obtain more than just compensation, and that the legitimate expectations of the released obligor might be frustrated by claims of co-obligors for contribution. None of these considerations justifies the rule, however, and it has often been denounced as anomalous and unjust. It has long been possible to avoid it by use of the form of a contract not to sue. See § 295(1). Modern decisions have converted it from a rule defeating intention to a rule of presumptive intention: where an intention contrary to the rule of Subsection (1)(a) is manifested, the purported release or other discharge has the effect of a contract not to sue. See § 295(2).

b. Discharge of a surety. Where the released promisor is surety for a co-promisor, the co-promisor is adequately protected against double recovery by the rule of Subsection (3), since the surety loses his right to reimbursement to the extent that he agrees that consideration given by him is not credited to the principal. There is no danger of indirect attack on the surety, since the principal has no right to contribution from the surety. Thus the only basis for discharge of the co-promisor is the unitary character of the obligation. The obsolescence of that concept has therefore led to the exception stated in Subsection (1)(a).

c. Joint and several promises. Where the English view is followed, joint and several promisors have the benefit of the rule stated in Subsection (1)(a) for joint promisors. Statutes converting joint obligations into joint and several obligations do not, in this view, affect the rule on releases. See Introductory Note to this Chapter. But the English view is out of harmony with the rule stated in § 292(1) as to the effect of a judgment against one joint and several obligor, and is not supported either by logic or by convenience. Subsection (1)(b) therefore rejects the English view and follows the contrary authorities and the analogy of the rule governing judgments.

d. Suretyship defenses. Where a promisee knows that a promisor is surety for a co-promisor, release of the principal discharges the surety unless the surety consents or the promisee reserves his rights against the surety. Restatement of Security § 122. In modern times similar rules have been applied to agreements between the promisee and the principal modifying their contract, including agreements to extend the time of payment. See Restatement of Security §§ 128, 129; Uniform Commercial Code §§ 3–415, 3–606. These rules of suretyship developed independently of the rules for joint obligations; they are beyond the scope of this Restatement.

e. Statutes. The Model Joint Obligations Act provides explicitly in § 4 that a release of one co-obligor does not discharge others if there is an express reservation of the obligee's rights. In the absence of a reservation of rights, § 5 provides that an obligee's claim is satisfied to the extent that he knows that a released obligor paid less than he was bound to pay by his contract or relation with the co-obligor, or in the absence of such knowledge to the lesser extent of the fractional share of the released obligor. Compare Restatement of Security §§ 114, 122. Other statutes vary in clarity and in their terms, but substantially similar rules seem to have been adopted by statute or decision in about half the states. See Introductory Note to this Chapter.

f. Consideration for discharge. If the circumstances are such that a co-promisor is not discharged under the rules stated in Subsections (1) and (2), he is nevertheless entitled to the benefit of consideration received by the obligee as stated in Subsection (3). This pro tanto discharge relates only to the co-promisor's duty to the obligee; it does not affect any right the promisor giving the consideration may have as a surety, whether by way of indemnity or contribution or subrogation. The co-promisor is not deprived of the right to the pro tanto discharge by an agreement to which he is not a party except in the suretyship cases mentioned below.

g. Settlement with a surety. Under Subsection (1) discharge of a surety does not discharge a co-promisor who is the principal obligor. In the absence of a contrary agreement, the principal must be credited with any consideration received from the surety. But the surety is entitled to reimbursement from the principal, and upon full satisfaction of the obligation he is subrogated to the obligee's rights against the principal to secure his right to reimbursement. See Restatement of Security §§ 104, 141. If the surety buys his peace by paying the obligee under an agreement that the payment is not to be credited on the obligation, he has no right to reimbursement from the principal and violates no duty to him. The agreement is therefore effective. See Model Joint Obligations Act § 3. The payment either has the effect of an assignment to the obligee of the surety's right to reimbursement or enlists the obligee's cooperation in securing reimbursement.

Illustrations

1. A as principal and B as surety owe C $100 for money lent to A. B pays C $25 for a contract not to sue B, under an agreement that the payment is not to be deducted from the amount of the debt. C may enforce the full claim for $100 against A. Unless otherwise agreed, B is entitled to any amount over $75 which C receives from A.

2. A and B owe C $100 for money lent for their common benefit in equal shares. B pays C $75 for a contract not to sue B, under an agreement that only $50 is to be deducted from the amount of the debt. C may enforce the claim for $50 against A. Unless otherwise agreed, B is entitled to any amount over $25 which C receives from A.

§ 295. Effect of Contract Not to Sue; Reservation of Rights.

(1) Where the obligee of promises of the same performance contracts not to sue one promisor, the other promisors are not discharged except to the extent required by the law of suretyship.

(2) Words which purport to release or discharge a promisor and also to reserve rights against other promisors of the same performance have the effect of a contract not to sue rather than a release or discharge.

(3) Any consideration received by the obligee for a contract not to sue one promisor discharges the duty of each other promisor of the same performance to the extent of the amount or value received. An agreement to the contrary is not effective unless it is made with a surety and expressly preserves the duty of his principal.

Comment

a. The distinction between discharge and contract not to sue. Discharge by release, rescission or accord and satisfaction has long been regarded as an executed transaction rather than an executory promise. It has also long been held that release of one joint promisor discharges his co-promisors, and the rule has been extended to other types of discharges. See § 294. In its origin the rule was regarded as a logical consequence of the nature of the right created by a joint promise; it did not depend on the intention of the parties to the release, and regularly operated to defeat their manifest intention. But the rule could be avoided by use of the form of a contract not to sue, also known as a covenant not to sue. Such a contract was treated as an executory promise; although a single promisor could plead the contract as a defense to prevent circuity of action, it did not discharge the right and hence did not discharge co-promisors.

b. Joinder of one not to be sued in action against co-promisor. If a promisee contracts not to sue one promisor and then sues one or more co-promisors, joinder of the obligee under the contracts is not required by the rule of § 290. Where a contrary view was taken and the co-promisor was held entitled to have the one not to be sued joined as a defendant, the formal joinder so required was not regarded as a breach of the contract not to sue. The promisee could without violating the contract join the one not to be sued and take a joint judgment against all the co-promisors, provided he took no steps to enforce the judgment against the assets of the one not to be sued.

c. Reservation of rights. Until the nineteenth century, words in a release of one joint promisor which purported to reserve rights against co-promisors were regarded as repugnant to the nature of the release and void. But in modern times, in order to give effect to the manifested intention, courts have interpreted releases containing such words as contracts not to sue. This rule has been extended to other types of discharge, and has greatly reduced the significance of the rule that release of one releases all.

So far as the rules governing joint promisors are concerned, no reservation of rights is necessary in an instrument taking the form of a contract not to sue. But for the purposes of the law of suretyship, which developed independently, a contract not to sue is treated like a release: an unqualified contract not to sue the principal debtor is treated as impairing the surety's right to assert the creditor's right by way of subrogation and hence as discharging the surety. See Comment d to § 294. This result can be avoided by a reservation of rights, which is regarded as preserving not only the surety's right to reimbursement from the principal but also his right to subrogation. Thus the reservation subjects the one not to be sued to the risk that the protection the contract affords may be illusory. See Restatement of Security § 122; Uniform Commercial Code § 3–606.

d. Consideration received. Subsection (3) applies to consideration received by the obligee for a contract not to sue the same rule stated in § 294(3) for consideration for discharge. See Comments f and g to § 294.

§ 296. Survivorship of Joint Duties.

On the death of one of two or more promisors of the same performance in a contract, the estate of the deceased promisor is bound by the contract, whether the duty was joint, several, or joint and several.

Comment

a. Historical note. By the common law of England, joint duties bound only the surviving obligors or the estate of the last survivor. The same rule was applied to the joint part of a joint and several duty, and the representative of a deceased promisor could not be joined in an action against survivors. Where a joint debt could be collected from a solvent survivor, no injustice was done; the survivor could then enforce contribution by the estate. But if the survivor was insolvent, the rule as to joint duties left the obligee without a legal remedy. Equitable relief was given in some such cases, but such relief has sometimes been denied where the deceased promisor was a surety.

b. The modern rule. The survivorship rule has been abolished in most states by statute or decision. Statutes making joint duties joint and several have this effect, and specific statutes on the point have been widely enacted. See Introductory Note to this Chapter. General statutes on the survival of actions have sometimes been given the same effect, and a number of judicial decisions have simply negated the rule. The question whether the representatives of deceased promisors may be joined in an action against survivors may be resolved by specific statute or left to general procedural statutes or rules.

TOPIC 2. JOINT AND SEVERAL PROMISEES

§ 297. Obligees of the Same Promised Performance.

(1) Where a party to a contract makes a promise to two or more promisees or for the benefit of two or more beneficiaries, the manifested intention of the parties determines whether he promises the same performance to all, a separate performance to each, or some combination.

(2) Except to the extent that a different intention is manifested or that the interests of the obligees in the performance or in the remedies for breach are distinct, the rights of obligees of the same performance are joint.

Comment

a. "Several" rights. The word "several" is used in two different senses with reference to rights created by a promise. First, the promisor may promise a distinct performance to each obligee, creating entirely separate rights. Second, even though the same performance is promised to a number of obligees, they may in the event of breach have separate claims for relief. In the first sense, the same right cannot be both "several" and "joint;" which it is is entirely a question of interpretation. In the second sense, rights may be either "joint" or "several" or some combination, but the parties cannot control entirely the remedies and procedures available.

b. Distinct interests. The interests referred to in Subsection (2) are the material or pecuniary interests of the obligees rather than their sentimental interests or desires. Partners, for example, are jointly concerned with the welfare of the partnership and are co-owners of the partnership property; they have a joint interest in the performance of a promise made to or by them with reference to partnership matters and in the consideration given or received for such a promise. A principal and surety, on the other hand, are affected differently by the performance of a promise made by them, and the principal often has the beneficial interest in the performance of a return promise to the exclusion of the surety.

Illustrations

1. A, B, and C are partners or engaged in a joint venture. D promises to pay them $100 for goods sold by the partnership or joint venture. D's duty is to make a single payment, and the right of A, B and C is joint.

2. A, B, C and D own four separate tracts of adjoining land. D contracts with A, B and C to build a flood-control dam to protect all four tracts. D fails to build, and flood damages the tracts of A, B and C in varying amounts. Their claims for damages are separately enforceable unless the contract provides otherwise.

3. A contracts with B and C to pay an annuity to D, B's mother. A's duty is to render a single annual performance. The right of B and C is joint. D has a several right.

§ 298. Compulsory Joinder of Joint Obligees.

(1) In an action based on a joint right created by a promise, the promisor by making appropriate objection can prevent recovery of judgment against him unless there are joined either as plaintiffs or as defendants all the surviving joint obligees.

(2) Except in actions on negotiable instruments and except as stated in § 300, any joint obligee unless limited by agreement may sue in the name of all the joint obligees for the enforcement of the promise by a money judgment.

Comment

a. Common-law procedure. Before the procedural reforms of the nineteenth century, promisees of the same performance could not join as plaintiffs in an action at law unless their right was joint. If the right was joint, failure to join all surviving joint promisees was ground for dismissing the action. But any joint promisee had an irrevocable power to sue in the names of all. Unless the power was used fraudulently (see § 300), a dissenting co-plaintiff in such a case could apply for a stay until security for costs was given by the party using his name, or he could in good faith release or settle the claim (see § 299), but he could not otherwise prevent use of his name.

b. Modern procedure. Modern statutes and rules of court follow the more flexible procedure which formerly prevailed in courts of equity. Joinder is permitted much more freely, and non-joinder and misjoinder can be cured by adding or dropping parties; partial or conditional relief can be given. But joint promisees are still required to join as plaintiffs or to be joined as defendants or involuntary plaintiffs. By statute in some states, partners may sue in the firm name. Whether or not there is proper joinder of plaintiffs, a judgment for or against one joint promisee bars subsequent actions against the same defendant by the others unless there is fraud or collusion. See Restatement, Second, Judgments § 53.

    c. Control over litigation. In an action for recovery of a promised sum of money or for damages, the judgment can take proper account of any divergent interests of joint plaintiffs, and any disputes among the plaintiffs can be decided separately. Where specific relief is sought, however, or where relief is conditional on some performance by plaintiffs, lack of unanimity among the plaintiffs may be fatal to the action. In some situations an impasse can be broken pursuant to a prior agreement among the plaintiffs. See Uniform Partnership Act § 18(h), providing for majority decision unless other provision is made. Otherwise, the plaintiff may be remitted to monetary relief. Where a negotiable instrument is payable to the order of two or more persons, not in the alternative, Uniform Commercial Code § 3–116 provides that it may be enforced only by all of them.

Illustration

    1. A and B, joint owners of property, convey it to C in exchange for a cash payment and C's promise to develop the property and pay to A and B a percentage of the profits. A can join B as a party and recover damages for a breach by C even though B objects, but cannot maintain an action to rescind the contract if B in good faith refuses to join.

§ 299. Discharge by or Tender to One Joint Obligee.

    Except where the promise is made in a negotiable instrument and except as stated in § 300, any joint obligee, unless limited by agreement, has power to discharge the promisor by receipt of the promised performance or by release or otherwise, and tender to one joint obligee is equivalent to a tender to all.

Comment

    a. Interpretation of the promise. The rule of this Section rests on a conventional interpretation of words of promise. If, for example, A promises to pay a sum of money to B and C, partners, it is ordinarily understood that payment may be made either to B or to C, and that each has authority to receive the payment on behalf of the other. If this is the understanding, the power of one to receive the payment cannot be revoked by the other, since both have an interest. Compare Restatement, Second, Agency, § 139. If an intention is manifested that the payment is to be made to B and not to C, they are not joint obligees, and this Section does not apply.

    b. Negotiable instruments. Where a negotiable instrument is made payable to the order of A and B, the usual purpose is to require the indorsement of both for negotiation of the instrument or the execution of a receipt on the instrument, signed by both, in the event of direct presentment to the payor. See Uniform Commercial Code § 3–505. In furtherance of that purpose, Uniform Commercial Code § 3–116 creates an exception to the rule of this Section, providing that the instrument can be discharged only by all the co-obligees.

    c. Interpretation of agreement for discharge. Where one joint obligee settles with the promisor for something less than full performance, he may purport to settle the claim of all the obligees or only his own share. Which agreement is made depends on the manifested intention of the parties to the settlement. If only a partial settlement is made, it does not bar joinder of the joint obligee in a later action by the others. See § 298. A settlement of one obligee's share which purported to discharge the claim of all would ordinarily be invalid. See § 300.

Illustrations

    1. A owes $1000 to B and C jointly. At B's request A in good faith renders services and delivers goods worth a total of $1200 to B and third persons in satisfaction of the debt, having no reason to know that C is not getting the benefit of the goods and services. A's obligation to both B and C is discharged.

    2. A promises to convey property to B and C jointly in exchange for $10,000, and B and C each pay A $5,000. On A's failure to convey the property, he repays $5,000 to B in return for a release of B's

interest in the contract and a covenant not to sue thereon. C's right to return of the $5,000 paid by him is not discharged.

§ 300. Effect of Violation of Duty to a Co-Obligee.

(1) If an obligee attempts or threatens to discharge the promisor in violation of his duty to a co-obligee of the same performance, the co-obligee may obtain an injunction forbidding the discharge.

(2) A discharge of the promisor by an obligee in violation of his duty to a co-obligee of the same performance is voidable to the extent necessary to protect the co-obligee's interest in the performance, except to the extent that the promisor has given value or otherwise changed his position in good faith and without knowledge or reason to know of the violation.

Comment

a. Duties among co-obligees. The interests of co-obligees among themselves depend upon the agreement or other relation among them. Commonly each has a beneficial interest, but one or more may be a nominal party or a mere agent. An obligee who has power to affect the rights of co-obligees has at least a duty to act in good faith; often he is subject to more rigorous fiduciary duties. For example, he may be an agent for a co-obligee, or they may be partners or co-trustees.

b. Liability of the promisor. A promisor who participates in a breach of a duty owed by one co-obligee to another cannot retain any advantage thereby obtained at the expense of the injured co-obligee unless he is in the position of a bona fide purchaser. See Restatement of Restitution §§ 202, 208; compare Restatement, Second, Agency §§ 27, 159–78, 300. Where the promise is to pay money, an improper discharge is effective to the extent of the interest of the obligee giving it. But in a case of improper discharge of a duty to convey land, the injured co-obligee may nevertheless be granted specific performance on such terms as may be equitable in the circumstances.

Illustration

1. A owes a single payment of $1,000 to B, C and D. As A knows, B, C and D have agreed to share the money equally. In exchange for a discharge by A of $1,000 owed him by B individually, B purports to release A from the obligation to B, C and D. The release is operative only to the extent of B's one-third interest.

§ 301. Survivorship of Joint Rights.

On the death of a joint obligee, unless a contrary intention was manifested, the surviving obligees are solely entitled as against the promisor to receive performance, to discharge the promisor, or to sue for the enforcement of the promise by a money judgment. On the death of the last surviving obligee, only his estate is so entitled.

Comment

a. Duty to account. Whether the estate of a deceased joint obligee succeeds to his beneficial interest in the promise depends upon agreement or the law governing the relationship among the obligees. The survivors have the right to receive performance or to settle, but may be required to account to those beneficially interested. See, e.g., Uniform Partnership Act §§ 37, 38. The powers of the survivors must be exercised in good faith and in accordance with their duty to those beneficially interested.

b. Joinder. The rule of this Section was a rule of the English common-law courts, and was not applied in courts of equity. It is justified today by the convenience of its principal consequence: it is unnecessary to join the personal representative of a deceased co-obligee in an action for a money judgment. See § 299. Where equitable relief is sought, joinder of such a representative is permitted and when necessary to complete adjudication it is required.

CHAPTER 14

CONTRACT BENEFICIARIES

§ 302. Intended and Incidental Beneficiaries.

(1) Unless otherwise agreed between promisor and promisee, a beneficiary of a promise is an intended beneficiary if recognition of a right to performance in the beneficiary is appropriate to effectuate the intention of the parties and either

    (a) the performance of the promise will satisfy an obligation of the promisee to pay money to the beneficiary; or

    (b) the circumstances indicate that the promisee intends to give the beneficiary the benefit of the promised performance.

(2) An incidental beneficiary is a beneficiary who is not an intended beneficiary.

Comment

a. Promisee and beneficiary. This Section distinguishes an "intended" beneficiary, who acquires a right by virtue of a promise, from an "incidental" beneficiary, who does not. See §§ 304, 315. Section 2 defines "promisee" as the person to whom a promise is addressed, and "beneficiary" as a person other than the promisee who will be benefitted by performance of the promise. Both terms are neutral with respect to rights and duties: either or both or neither may have a legal right to performance. Either promisee or beneficiary may but need not be connected with the transaction in other ways: neither promisee nor beneficiary is necessarily the person to whom performance is to be rendered, the person who will receive economic benefit, or the person who furnished the consideration.

b. Promise to pay the promisee's debt. The type of beneficiary covered by Subsection (1)(a) is often referred to as a "creditor beneficiary." In such cases the promisee is surety for the promisor, the promise is an asset of the promisee, and a direct action by beneficiary against promisor is normally appropriate to carry out the intention of promisor and promisee, even though no intention is manifested to give the beneficiary the benefit of the promised performance. Promise of a performance other than the payment of money may be governed by the same principle if the promisee's obligation is regarded as easily convertible into money, as in cases of obligations to deliver commodities or securities which are actively traded in organized markets. Less liquid obligations are left to Subsection (1)(b).

A suretyship relation may exist even though the duty of the promisee is voidable or is unenforceable by reason of the statute of limitations, the Statute of Frauds, or a discharge in bankruptcy, and Subsection (1)(a) covers such cases. The term "creditor beneficiary" has also sometimes been used with reference to promises to satisfy a supposed or asserted duty of the promisee, but there is no suretyship if the promisee has never been under any duty to the beneficiary. Hence such cases are not covered by Subsection (1)(a). The beneficiary of a promise to discharge a lien on the promisee's property, or of a promise to satisfy a duty of a third person, is similarly excluded from Subsection (1)(a). Such beneficiaries may, however, be "intended beneficiaries" under Subsection (1)(b).

Illustrations

1. A owes C a debt of $100. The debt is barred by the statute of limitations or by a discharge in bankruptcy, or is unenforceable because of the Statute of Frauds. B promises A to pay the barred or unenforceable debt. C is an intended beneficiary under Subsection (1)(a).

2. B promises A to furnish support for A's minor child C, whom A is bound by law to support. C is an intended beneficiary under Subsection (1)(a).

3. B promises A to pay whatever debts A may incur in a certain undertaking. A incurs in the undertaking debts to C, D and E. If the promise is interpreted as a promise that B will pay C, D and

E, they are intended beneficiaries under Subsection (1)(a); if the money is to be paid to A in order that he may be provided with money to pay C, D and E, they are at most incidental beneficiaries.

c. Gift promise. Where the promised performance is not paid for by the recipient, discharges no right that he has against anyone, and is apparently designed to benefit him, the promise is often referred to as a "gift promise." The beneficiary of such a promise is often referred to as a "donee beneficiary"; he is an intended beneficiary under Subsection (1)(b). The contract need not provide that performance is to be rendered directly to the beneficiary: a gift may be made to the beneficiary, for example, by payment of his debt. Nor is any contact or communication with the beneficiary essential.

Illustrations

4. A, an insurance company, promises B in a policy of insurance to pay $10,000 on B's death to C, B's wife. C is an intended beneficiary under Subsection (1)(b).

5. C is a troublesome person who is annoying A. A dislikes him but, believing the best way to obtain freedom from annoyance is to make a present, secures from B a promise to give C a box of cigars. C is an intended beneficiary under Subsection (1)(b).

6. A's son C is indebted to D. With the purpose of assisting C, A secures from B a promise to pay the debt to D. Both C and D are intended beneficiaries under Subsection (1)(b).

7. A owes C $100 for money lent. B promises A to pay C $200, both as a discharge of the debt and as an indication of A's gratitude to C for making the loan. C is an intended beneficiary under Subsection (1)(a) as to the amount of the debt and under Subsection (1)(b) as to the excess.

8. A conveys land to B in consideration of B's promise to pay $15,000 as follows: $5,000 to C, A's wife, on whom A wishes to make a settlement, $5,000 to D to whom A is indebted in that amount, and $5,000 to E, a life insurance company, to purchase an annuity payable to A during his life. C is an intended beneficiary under Subsection (1)(b); D is an intended beneficiary under Subsection (1)(a); E is an incidental beneficiary.

9. A owes C $100. Not knowing of any such debt, B promises A to pay $100 to C. C is an intended beneficiary under Subsection (1)(a) if A manifests an intention that the payment is to satisfy the debt, an intended beneficiary under Subsection (1)(b) if A manifests an intention to make a gift of $100, leaving outstanding the original debt.

d. Other intended beneficiaries. Either a promise to pay the promisee's debt to a beneficiary or a gift promise involves a manifestation of intention by the promisee and promisor sufficient, in a contractual setting, to make reliance by the beneficiary both reasonable and probable. Other cases may be quite similar in this respect. Examples are a promise to perform a supposed or asserted duty of the promisee, a promise to discharge a lien on the promisee's property, or a promise to satisfy the duty of a third person. In such cases, if the beneficiary would be reasonable in relying on the promise as manifesting an intention to confer a right on him, he is an intended beneficiary. Where there is doubt whether such reliance would be reasonable, considerations of procedural convenience and other factors not strictly dependent on the manifested intention of the parties may affect the question whether under Subsection (1) recognition of a right in the beneficiary is appropriate. In some cases an overriding policy, which may be embodied in a statute, requires recognition of such a right without regard to the intention of the parties.

Illustrations

10. A, the operator of a chicken processing and fertilizer plant, contracts with B, a municipality, to use B's sewage system. With the purpose of preventing harm to landowners downstream from its system, B obtains from A a promise to remove specified types of waste from its deposits into the system. C, a downstream landowner, is an intended beneficiary under Subsection (1)(b).

11. A, a corporation, contracts with B, an insurance company, that B shall pay to any future buyer of a car from A the loss he may suffer by the burning or theft of the car within one year after sale. Later A sells a car to C, telling C about the insurance. C is an intended beneficiary.

12. B contracts to build a house for A. Pursuant to the contract, B and his surety S execute a payment bond to A by which they promise A that all of B's debts for labor and materials on the house

will be paid. B later employs C as a carpenter and buys lumber from D. C and D are intended beneficiaries of S's promise to A, whether or not they have power to create liens on the house.

13. C asserts that A owes him $100. A does not owe this money, or think that he owes it, but rather than engage in litigation and in order to obtain peace of mind A secures a promise from B to pay C $100. C is an intended beneficiary.

14. A, a labor union, enters into a collective bargaining agreement with B, an employer, in which B promises not to discriminate against any employee because of his membership in A. All B's employees who are members of A are intended beneficiaries of the promise.

15. A buys food from B, a grocer, for household use, relying on B's express warranty. C, A's minor child, is injured in person by breach of the warranty. Under Uniform Commercial Code § 2–318, without regard to the intention of A or B, the warranty extends to C.

e. Incidental beneficiaries. Performance of a contract will often benefit a third person. But unless the third person is an intended beneficiary as here defined, no duty to him is created. See § 315.

Illustrations

16. B contracts with A to erect an expensive building on A's land. C's adjoining land would be enhanced in value by the performance of the contract. C is [only] an incidental beneficiary [and cannot bring suit under the contract].

17. B contracts with A to buy a new car manufactured by C. C is [only] an incidental beneficiary [and cannot bring suit under the contract], even though the promise can only be performed if money is paid to C.

18. A, a labor union, promises B, a trade association, not to strike against any member of B during a certain period. One of the members of B charters a ship from C on terms under which such a strike would cause financial loss to C. C is [only] an incidental beneficiary of A's promise [and cannot bring suit under the contract].

19. A contracts to erect a building for C. B then contracts with A to supply lumber needed for the building. C is [only] an incidental beneficiary of B's promise, and B is [only] an incidental beneficiary of C's promise to pay A for the building [and neither can bring suit under the other's contract].

f. Trust and agency. Where money or property is transferred from one person to another with an intention to benefit a third person, the manifested intention of the parties determines whether the transferee is an agent for the transferor or the third person or a trustee for the third person or whether the third person is the beneficiary of a promise made by the transferee. See Restatement, Second, Agency §§ 14B, 14L; Restatement, Second, Trusts §§ 8, 14. Similarly, an agreement between two parties may constitute one the agent of the other to confer a benefit on a third person, or the promise of one may be made to the other as trustee for a third person, or a third person may be the beneficiary of a promise of either or both; the manifested intention of the parties determines which of these possible relations is created for the particular purpose involved. There is a fiduciary relation between agent and principal or between trustee and beneficiary, but not between promisor or promisee and beneficiary of a contract. Agency requires the consent of the principal and the agent; a trust or a contract for the benefit of a third person does not require the consent of the beneficiary. Either the promisee or the beneficiary of a promise may be made a trustee of rights arising by virtue of the promise; although the beneficiary of such a trust is a beneficiary of the promise under this Section, his rights must be enforced in accordance with the law of Trusts. See Restatement, Second, Trusts §§ 26, 177, 199.

Illustration

20. A, an insurance company, promises B in a policy of insurance to pay $10,000 on B's death to C as trustee for B's wife D. C is an intended beneficiary and may enforce his rights as trustee; D's rights as beneficiary of the trust and the contract are enforceable only in the manner in which rights of other trust beneficiaries are enforced.

§ 303. Conditional Promises; Promises Under Seal.

The statements in this Chapter are applicable to both conditional and unconditional promises and to sealed and unsealed promises.

Comment

a. Conditional promises. A conditional promise may be made for the benefit of the beneficiary of a promise to pay a debt, or the beneficiary of a gift promise, or one who is otherwise an intended beneficiary. It is enough that the debt will be satisfied or the gift made or the right conferred if the condition occurs so that the promised performance becomes due.

Illustrations

1. A owes C $100. B promises A to pay the debt if Dancer wins the Derby. C is an intended beneficiary of the conditional promise.

2. C asserts and A denies that A owes C $100. B promises to pay the debt if it is legally recoverable. C is an intended beneficiary of B's conditional promise.

3. A obtains from B, an insurance company, a policy on A's life, payable to A's wife, C. The policy is conditional on the payment of annual premiums. C is an intended beneficiary, but her right is conditional.

4. A's son C has formed the X Automobile Company. For the stated purpose of benefiting C, A obtains B's promise to buy twenty automobiles from the company. The company is an intended beneficiary, though B's duty to pay the price is conditional on delivery of the automobiles. Compare Illustration 17 to § 302.

b. Promises under seal. Historically a right under a sealed instrument could be asserted only by a party named in the document or so described as to be capable of identification when it was delivered. Compare § 108. A person so named or described may have rights as a promisee even though the instrument is delivered to a third person. See § 103. But in modern times, even in States where the seal is still recognized, no distinction is made between sealed and unsealed contracts respecting the rights of beneficiaries.

§ 304. Creation of Duty to Beneficiary.

A promise in a contract creates a duty in the promisor to any intended beneficiary to perform the promise, and the intended beneficiary may enforce the duty.

Comment

a. Intended and incidental beneficiaries. "Beneficiary" is defined in § 2, "intended beneficiary" and "incidental beneficiary" in § 302. The terms are defined in relation to a "promise," a term which is neutral with respect to legal consequences; this Section states that a duty to an intended beneficiary is created if the promise is otherwise binding. The related proposition that an incidental beneficiary acquires no right is stated in § 315.

b. Creation and termination of duty. This Section reflects the basic principle that the parties to a contract have the power, if they so intend, to create a right in a third person. The requirements for formation of a contract must of course be met, and the right of the beneficiary, like that of the promisee, may be conditional, voidable, or unenforceable. See § 309. Whether the right of the beneficiary can be varied without his consent by action taken by the promisee or by agreement between promisee and promisor is a separate question which depends on the terms of the contract. See § 311.

c. Promise to pay the promisee's debt. Where the performance of the promise will satisfy an obligation of the promisee to pay money to the beneficiary, the promisee is surety for the promisor. The contract is an asset of the promisee, and on grounds of simplicity and convenience of remedy the beneficiary is allowed a direct action against the promisor without joining the promisee, instead of a procedure like garnishment or a suit to realize on an asset of the debtor not available to seizure by ordinary legal process.

The direct remedy also protects the beneficiary in reliance on the promise; his reliance is likely to take the form of inaction and to be difficult or impossible to prove. Promises to render performances other than the payment of money may be similar but require a manifestation of intention to give the benefit of the performance to the beneficiary.

Illustrations

1. A owes C $100. For consideration B promises A to pay the debt. B breaks his contract. C may sue B and obtain judgment for the amount of the debt.

2. A transfers Blackacre to B subject to a mortgage in favor of C, which B assumes and agrees to pay. After default C may sue B and get judgment for the amount of the mortgage debt, or, after foreclosure by sale, for the amount of any deficiency in the sum realized by the sale.

3. A owes C $100. For consideration B promises A to pay $100 to C in satisfaction of the debt. Later the statute of limitations bars an action by C against A. That fact is not of itself a defense in an action by C against B.

4. A promises C to have a fence built between their lands, and C pays A the price. B contracts with A to assume A's obligation to C, and A promises to pay B on completion of the work. On B's failure to build the fence, C may recover damages from B. But a contract by B to build the fence for A would ordinarily not be a contract to assume A's obligation to C.

d. Gift promise. Where the promisee manifests an intention to make a gift of the promised performance to a beneficiary, recognition of a duty to the beneficiary means that the beneficiary has available for his own benefit the usual remedies for breach of contract. An action by the beneficiary is commonly a convenient way to enforce the right of the promisee as well as to redress any injury to the beneficiary. This is so even though the promisee has reserved a power to vary the beneficiary's right, so long as that power has not been exercised.

Illustration

5. A gives money to B, his son, who promises in consideration thereof to pay A's daughter C, $5000 on A's death. A dies and B fails to pay C. C may sue on the promise and obtain judgment for $5000.

e. Other intended beneficiaries. The considerations which lead to the recognition of the right of a beneficiary of a promise to pay the promisee's debt or of a gift promise operate in varying degrees in other cases. Where the promisee clearly manifests an intention to confer on the beneficiary a legal right to enforce the contract, recognition of the beneficiary's right rests on the same grounds as recognition of the promisee's right. In cases of doubt, the question whether such an intention is to be attributed to the promisee may be influenced by the likelihood that recognition of the right will further the legitimate expectations of the promisee, make available a simple and convenient procedure for enforcement, or protect the beneficiary in his reasonable reliance on the promise.

Illustrations

6. A owes C $1000. For consideration B promises A to pay C $1000 for an assignment of C's right. On tender of such an assignment C can recover from B on his promise.

7. A's son C is indebted to D. With the purpose of assisting C, A secures from B for consideration a promise to pay the debt to D. D may enforce B's promise for D's own benefit.

8. A owns property subject to a mortgage in favor of C. C asserts and A denies that A is personally liable for the mortgage debt. To resolve the dispute, A transfers the property to B on B's promise to pay the mortgage debt. C may enforce B's promise for C's own benefit whether or not A is personally liable.

9. A, a common carrier, is required as a condition of its license to maintain liability insurance covering claims for bodily injury arising out of A's operations, and files a policy written by B. C claims to have been injured under circumstances covered by the policy. C may maintain a direct action against B.

10. A transfers property to B. A promises to use money received from B to discharge all A's obligations "including C's fees" up to $20,000; B promises to discharge all obligations in excess of $20,000 which A "is found to be responsible to pay including C's fees." C cannot maintain an action against B on the promise before A's liability has been established.

§ 305. Overlapping Duties to Beneficiary and Promisee.

(1) A promise in a contract creates a duty in the promisor to the promisee to perform the promise even though he also has a similar duty to an intended beneficiary.

(2) Whole or partial satisfaction of the promisor's duty to the beneficiary satisfies to that extent the promisor's duty to the promisee.

Comment

a. The promisee's right. The promisee of a promise for the benefit of a beneficiary has the same right to performance as any other promisee, whether the promise is binding because part of a bargain, because of his reliance, or because of its formal characteristics. If the promisee has no economic interest in the performance, as in many cases involving gift promises, the ordinary remedy of damages for breach of contract is an inadequate remedy, since only nominal damages can be recovered. In such cases specific performance is commonly appropriate. See § 307. In the ordinary case of a promise to pay the promisee's debt, on the other hand, the promisee may suffer substantial damages as a result of breach by the promisor. So long as there is no conflict with rights of the beneficiary or the promisor, he is entitled to recover such damages. See § 310.

Illustrations

1. In consideration of A's promise to transfer to his brother C A's interest in his mother's estate, A's father B promises A to pay a like amount to C. A makes the promised transfer, but B dies without performing his promise. A may maintain a suit for specific performance against B's personal representative.

2. A owes C an unliquidated sum. In consideration of $100 paid to B by A, B promises A to pay C whatever is due. B breaks his promise, and A pays C a reasonable sum in discharge of C's claim. A can at his election recover from B either $100 or the amount paid C.

3. A promises C to have a fence built between their lands, and C pays A the price of the fence. A informs B of the contract between A and C and of the danger that C's cattle will harm A's property if the fence is not properly built, and B contracts with A to carry out A's contract with C to build the fence. Because of B's breach of contract C's cattle damage A's property. A may recover the damage from B.

b. Conflicting claims and double liability. In the ordinary case of a promise to pay a debt owed by the promisee to a beneficiary, a single payment by the promisor will discharge both his duty to the promisee and his duty to the beneficiary. But a breach by the promisor can damage both promisee and beneficiary in the full amount of the debt. The promisor and his other creditors are entitled to protection against such doubling of liability so long as the injuries to both promisee and beneficiary can be redressed by a single payment. Moreover, when the promisor is insolvent, the promisee as surety is not permitted to compete with the beneficiary for the assets of the principal debtor. Hence the general creditors of the promisee, so far as they are asserting his rights, cannot reach his claim against the promisor until the beneficiary's claim is satisfied.

Illustrations

4. A owes C $100. For consideration B promises A to pay the debt to C. On B's breach A may obtain a judgment for $100 against B. But the court may protect B against double payment by permitting joinder of C, by an order that money collected by A is to be applied to reduce A's debt to C, by giving B credit on the judgment for payments to C which reduce A's obligation, or by enjoining enforcement of the judgment to the extent of such payment.

5. A owes C $100. For consideration B promises A to pay the debt to C. A subsequently becomes bankrupt. C may recover from B to the exclusion of A's trustee in bankruptcy.

c. Variation of beneficiary's right. Subsection (2) states that satisfaction of the duty to the beneficiary satisfies the duty to the promisee. The converse is not always true: satisfaction of the duty to the promisee may not satisfy the duty to the beneficiary. Whether and to what extent the promisor's duty to the beneficiary is subject to variation or discharge by the promisee or by agreement between promisor and promisee is governed by the rules stated in § 311. One consequence of a right not subject to such variation or discharge is that the promisor's duty to the beneficiary cannot be satisfied without the beneficiary's consent except by rendering the promised performance.

Illustration

6. A deposits money in B, a bank, to the joint credit of A and his wife C, payable to either A or C or the survivor. A and C make withdrawals. On A's death B owes the balance to C, and is not entitled to credit for a payment to A's personal representative.

§ 306. Disclaimer by a Beneficiary.

A beneficiary who has not previously assented to the promise for his benefit may in a reasonable time after learning of its existence and terms render any duty to himself inoperative from the beginning by disclaimer.

Comment

a. Acceptance unnecessary. No assent by a beneficiary to the contract and no knowledge on his part is necessary to give him a right of action on it. Compare §§ 53, 104; Restatement, Second, Trusts § 36. Of course, the promise may be conditional on knowledge or assent, or the performance promised may be such that it can only be rendered with the cooperation of the beneficiary.

b. Disclaimer. Like an offeree, a beneficiary is entitled to reject a promised benefit, whether or not there is a related burden. Compare § 38. No particular formality is required for disclaimer, and its effect on the promisor's duty to the beneficiary is the same as if no promise had been made. But once the beneficiary has manifested assent, disclaimer is operative only if the requirements are met for discharge of a contractual duty. Compare § 37.

c. Rights of promisee. This Section does not deal with the effect on the rights of the promisee of a disclaimer by the beneficiary. That effect depends on the circumstances. In some situations there may be a discharge by non-occurrence of a condition (see § 225(2)), by impossibility or frustration (see §§ 261, 265), or by virtue of the law of suretyship (see § 314; Restatement of Security § 116; Uniform Commercial Code § 3–604). In such situations, if the promisor would otherwise be unjustly enriched, the promisee may have a right to restitution of benefits conferred on the promisor; see Comment a to § 370.

d. Rights of third persons. The effect of disclaimer on other claims which have intervened, such as a claim for taxes owed by the beneficiary, is beyond the scope of this Restatement. A disclaimer may be ineffective against third persons if it is a breach of duty to them. Examples are disclaimer in fraud of creditors and disclaimer by a trustee. Compare Restatement, Second, Trusts §§ 35, 102.

§ 307. Remedy of Specific Performance.

Where specific performance is otherwise an appropriate remedy, either the promisee or the beneficiary may maintain a suit for specific enforcement of a duty owed to an intended beneficiary.

Comment

a. Suit by beneficiary. Whether specific performance is an appropriate remedy is determined by the rules stated in §§ 357–69. Where a contract creates a duty to a beneficiary under the rule stated in § 304, the beneficiary is a proper party plaintiff either in an action for damages or in a suit for specific performance. He is the real party in interest within the meaning of any statute requiring suit to be brought by such a party. There is no general requirement that the promisee be made a party, but the promisee is ordinarily a proper party and the circumstances may be such that a final decree should await joinder of the promisee. As to grant of an injunction instead of specific performance, see § 357(2).

b. Suit by promisee. Even though a contract creates a duty to a beneficiary, the promisee has a right to performance. See § 305. The promisee cannot recover damages suffered by the beneficiary, but the promisee is a proper party to sue for specific performance if that remedy is otherwise appropriate under the rules stated in §§ 357–69. Where a statute requires suit to be prosecuted in the name of the real party in interest, the promisee is commonly permitted to sue either as the "trustee of an express trust" or by an express provision for "a party with whom or in whose name a contract has been made for the benefit of another." See Federal Rules of Civil Procedure Rule 17. There is no general requirement that the beneficiary be joined in such a suit; whether he should or must be made a party depends on the circumstances.

c. Promise to pay the promisee's debt. Where the promised performance will satisfy an obligation of the promisee to pay money to the beneficiary, the promisee may suffer substantial damages as a result of breach. He is entitled to recover such damages so long as there is no conflict with rights of the beneficiary or the promisor. But the promisee as surety for the promisor is not permitted to compete with the beneficiary for the assets of the promisor, and the promisor is ordinarily entitled to protection against enforced double liability. See §§ 305, 310. These difficulties can be avoided by specific performance of the surety's right to exoneration. See Restatement of Security § 112.

Illustration

1. A, a stockholder of X, a corporation, guarantees payment of a debt owed by X to C. A sells his stock to B, who agrees to assume and pay A's obligation on the guaranty. B fails to pay, and C sues A on the guaranty. A may obtain a decree directing B to pay the debt to C.

d. Gift promise. Where the promisee intends to make a gift of the promised performance to the beneficiary, the beneficiary ordinarily has an economic interest in the performance but the promisee does not. Thus the promisee may suffer no damages as the result of breach by the promisor. In such cases the promisee's remedy in damages is not an adequate remedy within the rules stated in §§ 359 and 360, and specific performance may be appropriate. See Illustration 1 to § 305. The court may of course so fashion its decree as to protect the interests of the promisee and beneficiary without unnecessary injury to the promisor or innocent third persons. See § 358.

Illustration

2. As part of a separation agreement B promises his wife A not to change the provision in B's will for C, their son. A dies and B changes his will to C's detriment, adding also a provision that C will forfeit any bequest if he questions the change before any tribunal. A's personal representative may sue for specific performance of B's promise.

§ 308. Identification of Beneficiaries.

It is not essential to the creation of a right in an intended beneficiary that he be identified when a contract containing the promise is made.

Comment

a. The fact that a beneficiary cannot be identified when the contract is made may have a bearing on the question whether the promisee intended to make a gift to him or otherwise to confer on him a right to the promised performance, and thus may determine whether he is an intended beneficiary or an incidental beneficiary. See § 302. It may also bear on the question whether the right created is revocable or not. See § 311. But there is no requirement of identification prior to the time for enforcement of the right. Notwithstanding the rule stated in § 108 as to promisees, the rule of this Section applies to beneficiaries of sealed as well as unsealed promises. See § 303.

Illustrations

1. A takes out a policy issued by B, an insurance company, the principal sum being payable to A at the age of 60, or if he dies before that age to his wife C, if she survives him; otherwise to such

children as he may have surviving at the time of his death. C dies when A is 50. A dies at the age of 55. D, A's only child then surviving, is entitled to the policy and its proceeds to the exclusion of the estates of A and C.

2. B promises A to pay anyone to whom A may become indebted for the purchase of an automobile. A buys an automobile from C. B is under a duty to C.

§ 309. Defenses Against the Beneficiary.

(1) A promise creates no duty to a beneficiary unless a contract is formed between the promisor and the promisee; and if a contract is voidable or unenforceable at the time of its formation the right of any beneficiary is subject to the infirmity.

(2) If a contract ceases to be binding in whole or in part because of impracticability, public policy, non-occurrence of a condition, or present or prospective failure of performance, the right of any beneficiary is to that extent discharged or modified.

(3) Except as stated in Subsections (1) and (2) and in § 311 or as provided by the contract, the right of any beneficiary against the promisor is not subject to the promisor's claims or defenses against the promisee or to the promisee's claims or defenses against the beneficiary.

(4) A beneficiary's right against the promisor is subject to any claim or defense arising from his own conduct or agreement.

Comment

a. Necessity of contract. Subsection (1) makes explicit a negative fairly implied in § 304: the right of an intended beneficiary is created by contract, and in the absence of contract there is no such right. Moreover, where there is a contract, the beneficiary's right is subject to any limitations imposed by the law. Thus absence of mutual assent or consideration, lack of capacity, fraud, mistake and the like may be asserted by the promisor against the beneficiary.

Illustrations

1. B promises A to pay C $100. B's promise, owing to lack of consideration or illegality, gives A no right. Whether at the time of B's promise C had a right against A to be paid $100 or not, C acquires no right against B.

2. B orally contracts with A to convey Blackacre to C. The promise is unenforceable because not in writing. Whether or not at the time of B's promise C had a right against A to have Blackacre conveyed to him, C cannot maintain an action on B's promise.

3. The facts being otherwise as stated in Illustration 2, B subsequently delivers to A a written memorandum of the contract. C can now maintain an action on B's promise.

b. Conditions; failure of performance. Where there is a contract, the right of a beneficiary is subject to any limitations imposed by the terms of the contract. Such a limitation may be imposed by the agreed terms, or it may be imposed in the absence of contrary agreement by virtue of considerations of fairness and public policy. Thus a failure of the promisee to perform a return promise ordinarily discharges the promisor's duty to a beneficiary to the same extent that it discharges his duty to the promisee. But not every condition of the promisee's right is necessarily a condition of the right of the beneficiary. The agreement may effectively provide that the right of the beneficiary is not to be affected by the act or neglect of the promisee. Aside from such an agreed term, where the beneficiary's right is not subject to variation by agreement between promisor and promisee under the rules stated in § 311 there may be an implicit limitation on the extent to which such variation can be effected by the act or neglect of the promisee.

Illustrations

4. B, a life insurance company, issues a policy to A insuring A's life, the insurance money being payable to C. The policy reserves to A a power to change the beneficiary. C's right is subject to termination by A's changing the beneficiary before the maturity of the policy.

5. B promises A to pay C $100 in consideration of A's promise to B to perform stated services for him. A substantially breaks his promise to perform these services. Whether or not at the time of B's promise C had a right against A to be paid $100 he has no right against B.

6. A insures goods against fire with B, an insurance company. Later A mortgages the goods to C to secure a loan, and the insurance policy is amended to provide that loss is payable to A and C "as their interest may appear, subject to all the terms and conditions of the policy." A deliberately sets fire to the goods. Neither A nor C may recover from B for the resulting damage.

7. The facts being otherwise as stated in Illustration 6, the policy provides that C's interest shall not be invalidated by any act or neglect of the mortgagor. C may recover the amount of the loss from B.

8. B and his surety S contract with A, a city, to grade streets and to pay all laborers and materialmen on the job. The contract provides that any laborer working under the contract shall be entitled to sue and recover from S. A extends B's time for performance without S's consent. In a suit by C, a laborer, against S, the extension of time is not a defense.

c. Other claims and defenses. The position of a beneficiary is comparable to that of an assignee after knowledge of the assignment by the obligor. See § 336. His right, like that of an assignee, is subject to limitations inherent in the contract, and to supervening defenses arising by virtue of its terms. Partial defenses by way of recoupment for breach by the promisee may be asserted against the beneficiary, unless precluded by the terms of the agreement or considerations of fairness or public policy. Compare Uniform Commercial Code § 2–717. But the beneficiary's right is direct, not merely derivative, and claims and defenses of the promisor against the promisee arising out of separate transactions do not affect the right of the beneficiary except in accordance with the terms of the contract. Similarly, the beneficiary's right against the promisor is not subject to claims and defenses of the promisee against the beneficiary unless the contract so provides. The conduct of the beneficiary, however, like that of any obligee, may give rise to claims and defenses which may be asserted against him by the obligor, and his right may be affected by the terms of an agreement made by him.

Illustrations

9. In exchange for a conveyance of one parcel of land by B to A, A conveys another parcel of land to B subject to a mortgage in favor of C, which B assumes and agrees to pay, and A also agrees to pay money to B at a later date. In an action by C on B's promise, B can offset any part of the sum payable by A which is due and unpaid.

10. A collective bargaining agreement between A, a labor union, and many coal operators including B provides that each operator will pay 40 cents to C, trustee of a welfare fund for coal miners, for each ton of coal mined. In violation of the agreement A calls a strike of B's employees. B is not entitled to deduct the resulting damage from the payments due to C.

11. A, a bank, goes out of business, transferring assets to B, another bank, in consideration of B's promise to pay A's deposit liabilities. The applicable statute of limitations does not bar deposit liabilities of a going bank until six years after demand. In an action by C, a depositor of A, it is no defense to B that C's claim against A is barred by the statute of limitations.

§ 310. Remedies of the Beneficiary of a Promise to Pay the Promisee's Debt; Reimbursement of Promisee.

(1) Where an intended beneficiary has an enforceable claim against the promisee, he can obtain a judgment or judgments against either the promisee or the promisor or both based on their respective duties to him. Satisfaction in whole or in part of either of these duties, or of a judgment thereon, satisfies to that extent the other duty or judgment, subject to the promisee's right of subrogation.

(2) To the extent that the claim of an intended beneficiary is satisfied from assets of the promisee, the promisee has a right of reimbursement from the promisor, which may be enforced directly and also, if the beneficiary's claim is fully satisfied, by subrogation to the claim of the beneficiary against the promisor, and to any judgment thereon and to any security therefor.

Comment

a. Promisee as surety. The claim of a beneficiary against the promisee is not discharged by the promisor's agreement to assume the promisee's obligation. Unless the beneficiary consents to a novation, the promisee remains liable as surety for the promisor. In accordance with the usual rule of suretyship, the creditor may enforce his claim against both surety and principal obligor and need not first have recourse against the principal. See Restatement of Security § 130. The question whether joinder of surety and principal in a single action is permitted or required, and the form of the judgment in case of joinder are beyond the scope of this Restatement.

Illustrations

1. A owes C $100. For consideration B promises A to pay the debt. B breaks his contract. C can sue A and can also sue B and get judgment against each of them for $100, and can enforce either judgment until he has collected $100. Entire or partial satisfaction of a judgment against either A or B precludes to that extent enforcement of a judgment against the other, subject to A's right of subrogation.

2. A transfers Blackacre to B subject to a mortgage in favor of C, which B assumes and contracts to pay. C can sue A and he can also sue B and get judgment against each for the amount of the mortgage or, if the mortgaged property has been sold on foreclosure, for the amount of any deficiency in the sum realized by the sale.

3. B contracts with A to pay A's debt to C. D contracts with B to pay the debt. E contracts with D to pay it. C can bring actions against A, B, D and E and obtain judgment against each of them.

b. Suretyship defenses. Once a creditor knows that his debtor has become a surety, he is required to take account of the suretyship in his subsequent dealings. See § 314; Restatement of Security § 114; compare Uniform Commercial Code §§ 3–415, 3–604, 3–606. Thus a release of the promisor, or a binding extension of his time to perform, may discharge the surety-promisee. See Restatement of Security §§ 122, 129. Where the surety is threatened with unusual hardship and prior enforcement of the creditor's right against the promisor will not prejudice the creditor, the creditor may be required to utilize available assets of the promisor before having recourse to the surety. See Restatement of Security § 131.

c. Reimbursement of the promisee. Like any surety, the promisee who pays a debt to a beneficiary is entitled to reimbursement from the principal obligor, the promisor. The promisee is not permitted to compete with the beneficiary for the assets of the promisor, but once the beneficiary's claim is satisfied the promisee is entitled as subrogee to assert the beneficiary's claim against the promisor. See Restatement of Restitution § 162; Restatement of Security § 141. In addition, the promisee has a right to exoneration. See § 307.

Illustration

4. A owes C $1000. For consideration B promises A to pay the debt. B gives C a bond as security, but fails to pay the debt. C sues A and B and obtains a judgment against each of them, and obtains full payment by a levy of execution on A's property. A is subrogated to C's judgment against B and to the security of the bond.

§ 311. Variation of a Duty to a Beneficiary.

(1) Discharge or modification of a duty to an intended beneficiary by conduct of the promisee or by a subsequent agreement between promisor and promisee is ineffective if a term of the promise creating the duty so provides.

(2) In the absence of such a term, the promisor and promisee retain power to discharge or modify the duty by subsequent agreement.

(3) Such a power terminates when the beneficiary, before he receives notification of the discharge or modification, materially changes his position in justifiable reliance on the promise or brings suit on it or manifests assent to it at the request of the promisor or promisee.

(4) If the promisee receives consideration for an attempted discharge or modification of the promisor's duty which is ineffective against the beneficiary, the beneficiary can assert a right to the consideration so received. The promisor's duty is discharged to the extent of the amount received by the beneficiary.

Comment

a. The power to create an irrevocable duty. The parties to a contract cannot by agreement preclude themselves from varying their duties to each other by subsequent agreement. Nor can they force a right on an unwilling beneficiary, or prevent the beneficiary from joining with them in an agreement varying the duty to him. Compare Restatement, Second, Trusts § 338. But they can by agreement create a duty to a beneficiary which cannot be varied without the beneficiary's consent. Compare § 104; Restatement, Second, Trusts §§ 330, 331.

b. Express and implied terms. Agreements precluding variation of a duty to a beneficiary before the beneficiary knows of the promise are unusual and would often be unwise. See Comment f. But the power of the parties to make such an agreement is not restricted by special formal requirements. The agreement need not be explicit: omission of a standard clause reserving a power of modification may manifest an intention to preclude modification; reservation of a limited power may negate a broader power; usage of trade or course of dealing may supply a term precluding modification. See § 5, defining "term."

c. Life insurance. Partly on the basis of statutes, the rule was established in a number of states in the latter part of the nineteenth century that the ordinary life insurance policy in the form then in use belonged to the beneficiary the moment it was issued, and that the insured had no power to transfer the right to any other person unless the power was reserved. That rule was not applied to fraternal benefit insurance, partly again because of statutes and partly because of charter and by-law provisions. Standard policy forms were revised to avoid the rule by reserving to the insured the power to change the beneficiary. Modern policies also provide for powers to surrender for cash, to borrow against the policy, and to assign the policy. Deletion of such a standard provision may manifest an intention that the power is not to exist.

Illustrations

1. A insures his life for $10,000 with the B Insurance Company, designating C as beneficiary but reserving power to change the beneficiary. The policy provides for surrender of the policy by the insured for a stated cash value. Subsequently A by appropriate indorsement on the policy irrevocably designates C as beneficiary. A's power to surrender for cash is terminated.

2. A insures his life for $10,000 with the B Insurance Company, designating C as beneficiary but reserving power to change the beneficiary. The policy provides for assignment by the insured, and A assigns it to D as security for a loan. On A's death C's right is limited to the excess over the amount due to D.

d. Infant beneficiaries. Where the beneficiary has full contractual capacity, a duty to him can be made irrevocable by his assent under Subsection (3). Or he may be made a promisee. See § 71(4) as to consideration in such cases. Failure to procure such assent or to make him a promisee may be an indication that the right is to be revocable. But where the beneficiary lacks capacity, as in the case of an infant, such an inference is less clearly justified. It is therefore sometimes said that in such a case the infant's assent is "presumed." The true test rests not on fictitious assent but on the manifested intention of the original parties; other circumstances, such as the fact that the consideration for the promise is executory, may rebut the inference that the beneficiary's right is irrevocable.

Illustrations

3. A is employed by the B corporation, and designates his infant son C as beneficiary of a death benefit under a plan set up by B. No provision is made for a power to change the beneficiary. A later notifies B that the designation of C is revoked and that the benefit is to be paid to D, to whom A is newly married. C's right is not affected.

4. A and his wife and his infant son C move onto the farm of A's uncle B under an agreement between A and B that they will care for B and the farm until B dies and that B will pay A good wages and will convey a specified portion of the farm to C when C becomes 21 years old. B is unable to pay

wages and conveys a different portion of the farm to A in satisfaction of his obligations under the original agreement. C's right is discharged.

   e. Effect of loss under insurance policy. The terms of the promise may make the beneficiary's right irrevocable in whole or in part or only upon a condition. Thus a reserved power to change the beneficiary of a life insurance policy terminates on the death of the insured. In general the power of promisor and promisee to vary the duty to a beneficiary under other types of insurance policies is understood to be subject to a similar limitation: when an insured loss occurs, the power to vary the terms of the policy with respect to that loss is terminated.

Illustration

   5. A contracts with B for liability insurance covering any person operating A's automobile with A's permission. C incurs liability covered by the policy. Thereafter A and B agree to rescind the policy. The attempted rescission does not affect the rights of C or the person to whom he is liable.

   f. The power to vary. Under the rule stated in Subsection (1), a promisor and a promisee can by agreement create a duty to a beneficiary which cannot be varied without his consent. But in the absence of such an agreement the parties retain control over the contractual relation they have created. Loss of control over a policy of life insurance, for example, may prevent perfectly proper readjustments in the light of misconduct of the beneficiary or the birth of children, or a family financial crisis; the practice of reserving a power to change the beneficiary has therefore become almost universal. Other types of contracts normally remain subject to variation by the parties without express provision at least until there is some possibility of reliance by the beneficiary.

Illustrations

   6. A contracts with B to pay B $200 in return for B's delivery of goods to C as a gift from A. Before any goods are identified to the contract or any payment is made and before C learns of the contract, A and B rescind it. After learning of the rescission, C has no right against B.

   7. B contracts with A to pay C $200 which A owes C. Before C learns of this contract, in consideration of a horse worth $200, A releases B from his contract. After learning of the release, C has no right against B.

   8. A conveys land to B and B assumes and agrees to pay to C a debt owed by A which is secured by a mortgage on the land. Before C learns of the contract, B resells the land to D, who assumes and agrees to pay the debt. As part of the transaction between B and D and in consideration thereof, A releases B from his promise to pay C. After learning of the release, C has no right against B.

   g. Reliance. In the absence of some contrary indication, an intended beneficiary is justified in relying on the promise. It is immaterial whether he learns of the promise from the promisor, the promisee or a third party, and whether the promise is one to satisfy the promisee's duty or is a gift promise or is neither. If there is a material change of position in justifiable reliance on the promise, the change of position precludes discharge or modification of the contract without the beneficiary's consent. In the case of a promise to pay a debt of the promisee or another person, it is not necessary that the beneficiary enter into a novation with the promisor, though a novation would a fortiori be effective. See § 280. As to what constitutes receipt of a notification sufficient to preclude reliance, see § 68; compare Uniform Commercial Code § 1–201(26) and (27).

   h. Assent. Even though there is no novation and no change of position by the beneficiary, the power of promisor and promisee to vary the promisor's duty to an intended beneficiary is terminated when the beneficiary manifests assent to the promise in a manner invited by the promisor or promisee. This rule rests in part on an analogy to the law of offer and acceptance and in part on the probability that the beneficiary will rely in ways difficult or impossible to prove. In the case of a promise to discharge a duty of the promisee or a third person, the latter basis is supported by the analogy of the rule that a creditor gives "value" for rights acquired as security for a pre-existing claim. See Uniform Commercial Code § 1–201(44). As to terms of the promise inviting or requiring the beneficiary to manifest assent in a particular way, the law of offer and acceptance provides appropriate analogies. See §§ 60, 63–67. Indeed, the promise may in some cases be an offer to the beneficiary by the promisor or promisee or both. The bringing of suit against the promisor is a sufficient manifestation of assent to preclude discharge or modification.

Illustrations

9. The facts being otherwise as stated in Illustration 6, 7 or 8, C brings suit against B before receiving notification of the rescission or release. Judgment should be given for C.

10. B contracts with A to pay C $200 which A owes C, and A notifies C of the contract by mail. C mails a letter to A assenting to the contract before receiving notification of a rescission by A and B. The rescission is ineffective against C. Compare §§ 42, 63.

11. A and B, two affiliated corporations, contract that upon surrender of outstanding bonds issued by A new bonds will be issued, bond for bond, paying less interest but guaranteed by B. Forty years later, shortly before the old bonds mature, only a small number of the old bonds have been surrendered, and A and B release each other from the contract with respect to any new bonds not yet issued. The releases are effective against any holder of old bonds who receives notification of the releases before he surrenders his bonds.

i. Fraud on creditors. The rules of Subsections (1) and (2) refer to a subsequent agreement which is otherwise valid, and are subject to the law relating to any invalidating cause. In particular, a promise for the benefit of a creditor of the promisee is an asset of the promisee. A release of the promisor may be a fraud on the beneficiary or on other creditors of the promisee if the promisee is insolvent and the release is made without fair consideration, or if the release is made with actual intent to hinder, delay or defraud creditors. See Uniform Fraudulent Conveyance Act §§ 4, 7. In that event, even though the beneficiary has not assented or relied, the release is not effective except to the extent that the promisor has innocently given consideration for it. See Uniform Fraudulent Conveyance Act § 9(2). Similar considerations may be applicable in a case of a promise to satisfy the duty of another person than the promisee.

Illustration

12. B contracts with A to pay C $200 which A owes C. Before C learns of this contract, A, in consideration of B's proposing him for admission to a social club, releases B from his contract. A has no assets other than this contract worth $200. The release does not impair C's right against B.

j. The beneficiary's right to proceeds. Where a promise creates rights in a beneficiary, the promisee may retain power to discharge or modify the promisor's duty. Whether the exercise of such a power is rightful or wrongful may depend on facts other than the promise. If it is wrongful, the promisee is under a duty of restitution to the beneficiary for any amount received by him therefor. See Restatement of Restitution §§ 131, 165. Subsection (4) applies a similar principle to cases where the beneficiary's right against the promisor is not discharged or modified. In the latter type of case, the promisor may also have a right of restitution. Compare Restatement of Restitution §§ 124, 126. Which right prevails in the event of conflict and the extent to which assertion of the right against the promisee bars a claim against the promisor depends on what is equitable in the circumstances.

§ 312. Mistake as to Duty to Beneficiary.

The effect of an erroneous belief of the promisor or promisee as to the existence or extent of a duty owed to an intended beneficiary is determined by the rules making contracts voidable for mistake.

Comment

a. Supposed creditor as beneficiary. When performance of the promise will satisfy an obligation of the promisee to pay money to a beneficiary, the beneficiary is normally treated as an intended beneficiary. In cases of a duty other than to pay money, in cases of a duty of someone other than the promisee, or in cases of a supposed or asserted duty of the promisee, whether the beneficiary is an intended beneficiary depends on the intention manifested by the promisee. See §§ 302, 304 and Comments. If the beneficiary would be reasonable in relying on the promise as manifesting an intention to confer a right on him, he is an intended beneficiary. Compare § 20.

b. Existence of mistake. Nonexistence of the supposed duty does not establish a mistake where the terms of the promise provide for the case. Thus if the promisor promises to perform whatever duty is owed and none is owed, the beneficiary has no right against the promisor. Likewise, a promise to render a performance whether or not there is a pre-existing duty is effective according to its terms. Prima facie an unqualified promise to render the performance has the same effect, but mistake as to the existence of the duty may make the contract voidable. See §§ 309, 151–58.

Illustrations

1. A, a stockholder in X, a corporation, guarantees the payment of a debt owed by X to C and agrees to pay interest and an attorney's fee. Subsequently A sells his stock to B, who agrees to assume and pay the debt owed by X. B is liable for interest and an attorney's fee only to the extent of X's liability.

2. The facts being otherwise as stated in Illustration 1, B agrees to assume and pay the debt owed by X and to pay interest and an attorney's fee. B's liability for interest and an attorney's fee is not affected by the nonliability of X or A or both.

3. A, the owner of Blackacre, mortgages it to C for $5000. A transfers Blackacre subject to the mortgage to X, who does not assume or agree to pay the mortgage debt. X transfers Blackacre to B, who with knowledge of all the facts assumes and agrees to pay the mortgage debt. B is liable to C for the amount of the debt.

4. The facts being otherwise as stated in Illustration 3, B shows by clear and convincing evidence that his promise was inserted in the deed by mistake of the scrivener, contrary to the contract between X and B and without their knowledge. In the absence of a change of circumstances making reformation inequitable, the deed will be reformed to strike out the promise. See § 155.

§ 313. Government Contracts.

(1) The rules stated in this Chapter apply to contracts with a government or governmental agency except to the extent that application would contravene the policy of the law authorizing the contract or prescribing remedies for its breach.

(2) In particular, a promisor who contracts with a government or governmental agency to do an act for or render a service to the public is not subject to contractual liability to a member of the public for consequential damages resulting from performance or failure to perform unless

 (a) the terms of the promise provide for such liability; or

 (b) the promisee is subject to liability to the member of the public for the damages and a direct action against the promisor is consistent with the terms of the contract and with the policy of the law authorizing the contract and prescribing remedies for its breach.

Comment

a. Rationale. Beneficiaries of government contracts have often been denied rights because of the doctrinal difficulties referred to in the Introductory Note to this Chapter. Subsection (1) reflects the disappearance of those difficulties, but leaves room for the weighing of considerations peculiar to particular situations. Subsection (2) applies to a particular class of contracts the classification of beneficiaries in § 302. Government contracts often benefit the public, but individual members of the public are treated as incidental beneficiaries unless a different intention is manifested. In case of doubt, a promise to do an act for or render a service to the public does not have the effect of a promise to pay consequential damages to individual members of the public unless the conditions of Subsection (2)(b) are met. Among factors which may make inappropriate a direct action against the promisor are arrangements for governmental control over the litigation and settlement of claims, the likelihood of impairment of service or of excessive financial burden, and the availability of alternatives such as insurance.

Illustrations

1. B contracts with the United States to carry mail over a certain route. C, a member of the public, is injured by B's failure to perform his contract. B is under no contractual duty to C.

2. B, a water company, contracts with A, a municipality, to maintain a certain pressure of water at the hydrants on the streets of the municipality. A owes no duty to the public to maintain that pressure. The house of C, an inhabitant of the municipality, is destroyed by fire, owing to B's failure to maintain the agreed pressure. B is under no contractual duty to C.

b. Tort liability. Whether or not members of the public are intended beneficiaries of a government contract, the contractor may be subject to tort liability to them. The question whether the contractor has an affirmative duty to act may arise in connection with tort liability, and the answer may or may not turn upon the same considerations which determine whether the member of the public is an intended beneficiary. See Restatement, Second, Torts §§ 314–25; compare Restatement, Second, Agency §§ 354, 378.

c. Promise to pay damages. Government contractors sometimes make explicit promises to pay damages to third persons, and such promises are enforced. If there is no explicit promise, and no government liability, the question whether a particular claimant is an intended beneficiary is one of interpretation, depending on all the circumstances of the contract. When there is government liability, and the question of interpretation is in doubt, there is liability if a direct action is appropriate in view of the factors referred to in Comment a.

Illustrations

3. A, a municipality, enters into a contract with B, by which B promises to build a subway and to pay damages directly to any person who may be injured by the work of construction. Because of the work done in the construction of the subway, C's house is injured by the settling of the land on which it stands. D suffers personal injuries from the blasting of rock during the construction. B is under a contractual duty to C and D.

4. A, a county, enters into a contract with B, a surety company, by which B promises indemnity to a stated amount for any damages caused by clerical errors of clerks in the Registry of Deeds. C is injured by an error of such a clerk. C can recover damages from B.

5. A, a municipality, owes a duty to the public to keep its streets in repair. B, a street railway company, contracts to keep a portion of these streets in repair but fails to do so. C, a member of the public, is injured thereby. He may bring actions against A and B and can recover judgment against each of them.

6. A, a municipality, awards a construction contract to B. The contract provides that if through B's act or neglect another contractor on the same project suffers loss and makes a claim against A, B will defend at B's own expense any suit based on the claim and will pay any resulting judgment against A. C, another contractor on the same project, makes a claim against A based on breach by B of B's contract with A. The described provision does not enable C to bring a direct action as an intended beneficiary of B's promise.

§ 314. Suretyship Defenses.

An intended beneficiary who has an enforceable claim against the promisee is affected by the incidents of the suretyship of the promisee from the time he has knowledge of it.

Comment

a. Effect of knowledge. This Section states a principle of suretyship. See Restatement of Security § 114; compare Uniform Commercial Code § 3–415. Under the definitions in § 302 a contract to satisfy a duty of the promisee to an intended beneficiary makes the promisee a surety for the promisor. Even though he has not consented to the suretyship relation, the beneficiary must recognize it and take it into account when he learns of it.

b. Impairment of recourse or collateral. Where the beneficiary knows that the promisee is surety for the promisor, release of the promisor discharges the surety unless the surety consents or the beneficiary reserves his rights against the surety. Compare §§ 293–94; see Restatement of Security § 122. Similar rules apply to agreements between beneficiary and promisor modifying their contract, including agreements to extend the time of payment, and to surrender or other impairment of collateral security. See Restatement of Security §§ 128, 129, 132; Uniform Commercial Code § 3–606. These rules of suretyship are beyond the scope of this Restatement.

Illustration

1. A owes C a debt of $10,000, secured by a mortgage on A's land. A sells Blackacre to B, who assumes and agrees to pay the mortgage debt. C, knowing of this assumption, releases a portion of the mortgaged premises from the lien of the mortgage. The remaining portion of Blackacre is then worth $12,000, but at the date of maturity of the mortgage is worth $8,000. The released land is then worth $2,000. B makes default in paying the debt. C can recover from A only $8,000. Since C's own act has diminished by $2,000 the value of the security applicable to the debt, his right against A is subject to diminution by that amount. If the released land is then worth $1,000, C can recover $9,000 from A.

§ 315. Effect of a Promise of Incidental Benefit.

An incidental beneficiary acquires by virtue of the promise no right against the promisor or the promisee.

Comment

a. An incidental beneficiary is a person who will be benefited by performance of a promise but who is neither a promisee nor an intended beneficiary. See §§ 2, 302. Illustrations 3, 8, 16–19 to § 302 also illustrate the rule stated in this Section.

CHAPTER 15

ASSIGNMENT AND DELEGATION

§ 316. Scope of This Chapter.

(1) In this Chapter, references to assignment of a right or delegation of a duty or condition, to the obligee or obligor of an assigned right or delegated duty, or to an assignor or assignee, are limited to rights, duties, and conditions arising under a contract or for breach of a contract.

(2) The statements in this Chapter are qualified in some respects by statutory and other rules governing negotiable instruments and documents, relating to interests in land, and affecting other classes of contracts.

Comment

a. Contractual right; chose in action. Statements in this Chapter are limited to contractual rights and duties. Such rights include debts, rights to non-monetary performance and rights to damages and other contractual remedies, whether or not a right to payment has been earned. On the other hand, "chose in action" is a much broader term. In its primary sense it includes debts of all kinds, tort claims, and rights to recover ownership or possession of real or personal property; it has been extended to instruments and documents embodying intangible property rights, to such intangible property as patents and copyrights, and even to equitable rights in tangible property. The rules stated here may have some application to non-contractual choses in action, but the transfer of non-contractual rights is beyond the scope of the Restatement of this Subject.

b. Negotiable instruments and documents; conveyances of land. The rules governing negotiable instruments and documents and the benefits and burdens attached to successive owners of real property by virtue of a contract in a prior conveyance or lease are to some extent different from the law governing contracts in general. The law governing negotiable instruments and documents derives from the law merchant and is now largely statutory. See Comment to § 6. The law relating to covenants in conveyances and leases of land grew up as part of the law of real property and is left to the Restatement, Second, of Property.

c. Assignment and delegation. In this Chapter rights are said to be "assigned"; duties are said to be "delegated." The phrase "assignment of the contract," which may refer to either or both, is avoided because "contract" is defined in § 1 in terms of the act or acts of promising. See § 328. "Assignment" is the transfer of a right by the owner (the obligee or assignor) to another person (the assignee). See § 317. A person subject to a duty (the obligor) does not ordinarily have such a power to substitute another in his place without the consent of the obligee; this is what is meant when it is said that duties cannot be assigned. "Delegation" of performance may be effective to empower a substitute to perform on behalf of the obligor, but the obligor remains subject to the duty until it has been discharged by performance or otherwise. Compare the usage of terms in Uniform Commercial Code § 2–210. Delegation of performance of a condition is similar in effect to delegation of performance of duty.

d. Involuntary transfer. In accordance with common usage, assignment and delegation in this Chapter include only transfers made or powers created by virtue of a manifestation of intention of the assignor or obligor. The manifestation may be made to the assignee or the person delegated or to another person on his behalf, but transfers made and powers created by operation of law are excluded. Such transfers and powers, including transfers to and powers of an executor, administrator, trustee in bankruptcy or receiver by virtue of his office, are in general beyond the scope of this Restatement. As to the equitable remedies of constructive trust, equitable lien, and subrogation, which sometimes operate much like an assignment, see Restatement of Restitution §§ 160–62; Restatement of Security § 141.

TOPIC 1. WHAT CAN BE ASSIGNED OR DELEGATED

§ 317. Assignment of a Right.

(1) An assignment of a right is a manifestation of the assignor's intention to transfer it by virtue of which the assignor's right to performance by the obligor is extinguished in whole or in part and the assignee acquires a right to such performance.

(2) A contractual right can be assigned unless

    (a) the substitution of a right of the assignee for the right of the assignor would materially change the duty of the obligor, or materially increase the burden or risk imposed on him by his contract, or materially impair his chance of obtaining return performance, or materially reduce its value to him, or

    (b) the assignment is forbidden by statute or is otherwise inoperative on grounds of public policy, or

    (c) assignment is validly precluded by contract.

Comment

a. "Assignment." The word "assignment" is sometimes used to refer to the act of the owner of a right (the obligee or assignor) purporting to transfer it, sometimes to the resulting change in legal relations, sometimes to a document evidencing the act or change. In this Chapter "assign" and "assignment" refer to an act which has the effect stated in Subsection (1). To avoid ambiguity, such an assignment is said to be "effective"; a similar act which does not have the stated effect is referred to as an "attempted" or "purported" assignment. In either case the actor is referred to as the "assignor" and the transferee or intended or purported transferee is referred to as the "assignee."

Illustrations

1. A has a right to $100 against B. A assigns his right to C. A's right is thereby extinguished, and C acquires a right against B to receive $100.

2. A purports to assign to C a right to receive $100 from B. A has no such right. The assignment is ineffective, and C can recover damages from A under the rules stated in § 333.

b. Assignment to obligor. A purported assignment by a creditor to his debtor of the indebtedness owed by the debtor is not covered by this Chapter. Such an "assignment" may or may not be effective to extinguish the assignor's right and thus to discharge the debtor; it cannot create in the debtor a right to performance by himself. Compare § 9.

c. Historical note. As is indicated in the Introductory Note to this Chapter, the historic common-law rule that a chose in action could not be assigned has largely disappeared. It remains applicable to some non-contractual rights, particularly claims for damages for personal injury, and to certain claims against the Government. This Section is limited by § 316 to contractual rights, and the historic rule now has very limited application to such rights. Except as stated in this Section, they may be effectively assigned. Notwithstanding the historical background, recourse need no longer be had to the law merchant, to doctrines peculiar to courts of equity, or to the concept of a power of attorney irrevocable because coupled with an interest. The restrictions in paragraphs (2)(a) and (c) rest on the basic principle that rights based on agreement are limited by the agreement.

d. Material variation. What is a material variation, an increase in burden or risk, or an impairment of the obligor's expectation of counter-performance under paragraph (2)(a) depends on the nature of the contract and on the circumstances. Both assignment of rights and delegation of performance are normal and permissible incidents of many types of contracts. See, for example, as to contracts for the sale of goods, Uniform Commercial Code § 2–210 Comment. When the obligor's duty is to pay money, a change in the person to whom the payment is to be made is not ordinarily material. Compare § 322; Uniform Commercial Code § 9–318. But if the duty is to depend on the personal discretion of one person, substitution of the personal discretion of another is likely to be a material change. The clause on material impairment of the chance of obtaining return performance operates primarily in cases where the assignment is accompanied by an improper delegation under § 318 or § 319: if the obligor is to perform in exchange for the promise of one person to render a return performance at a future time, substitution of the return promise of another impairs the obligor's expectation of counter-performance. But in cases of doubt, adequate assurance of due performance may prevent such an impairment. Compare § 251; Uniform Commercial Code § 2–609.

Illustrations

3. B contracts to support A for the remainder of A's life. A cannot by assignment confer on C a right to have B support C.

4. B contracts to support A for the remainder of A's life. B commits a material breach of the contract, and A assigns his right of action to C. The assignment is effective.

5. B contracts to sell to A for three years 250 tons of ice a week, and A contracts to pay on delivery a stated price per ton. A assigns his right under the contract to C. The assignment is effective. C's right to delivery is conditional on payment, but payment by C satisfies the condition.

6. B sells his business to A and makes a valid contract not to compete. A sells the business to C and assigns to C the right to have B refrain from competition. The assignment is effective with respect to competition with the business derived from B. The good will of the business, with contractual protection against its impairment, is treated as an assignable asset.

e. Public policy and statutory limitations. The rules for promises and other terms of an agreement stated in Chapter 8 apply by analogy in determining whether an assignment is inoperative on grounds of public policy under paragraph (2)(b) of this Section. Additional statutory restrictions are common. Uniform Commercial Code § 5–116 prevents assignment of the right to draw under a letter of credit unless the credit is expressly designated as transferable or assignable, and renders ineffective an assignment of the beneficiary's right to proceeds until the letter of credit or advice of credit is delivered to the assignee. As is stated in the Statutory Note preceding § 316, wage-assignment statutes often contain a variety of limitations, and there are statutes forbidding or limiting the assignment of rights under government contracts.

Illustrations

7. For value A, a public official, assigns to C salary or fees already earned and also his unearned salary for the ensuing month. The assignment of the earned salary or fees is effective, in the absence of a contrary statute, but the assignment of unearned salary is against public policy.

8. A contracts with B, a physician, for medical services, and later claims that B's negligence in performing the services caused personal injury to A in violation of B's contractual duty to use due care. A assigns the claim to C. The assignment is ineffective.

9. A, a retired officer of the United States Army, borrows money from C and as security for the loan assigns to C whatever is due or shall become due to A as retired pay. The assignment is ineffective except as permitted by statute under regulations prescribed by the Secretary of the Army.

f. Contractual prohibition. The effect of a term in a contract forbidding the assignment of rights arising under the contract is the subject of § 322. Such a term may resolve doubts as to whether an assignment violates paragraph (2)(a) of this Section. Where it seems to forbid an assignment clearly outside the scope of paragraph (2)(a), it may be read restrictively to permit the assignment, or to give the obligor a claim against the assignor rather than a defense against the assignee, or the term may be invalid by statute or decision. See Uniform Commercial Code §§ 2–210, 9–318. Even if the term gives the obligor a defense against the assignee, the assignment is usually partially effective as an assignment conditional on the assent of the obligor.

§ 318. Delegation of Performance of Duty.

(1) An obligor can properly delegate the performance of his duty to another unless the delegation is contrary to public policy or the terms of his promise.

(2) Unless otherwise agreed, a promise requires performance by a particular person only to the extent that the obligee has a substantial interest in having that person perform or control the acts promised.

(3) Unless the obligee agrees otherwise, neither delegation of performance nor a contract to assume the duty made with the obligor by the person delegated discharges any duty or liability of the delegating obligor.

Comment

a. Duty and condition. A contractual performance may discharge the duty of a performing obligor, or it may satisfy a condition of the right of a performing obligee to a return performance. Where the same person is both obligor and obligee, the same performance may both discharge his duty and satisfy a condition of his right. The propriety of delegation is in general governed by the same standard whether the issue is performance of a duty or performance of a condition. In the interest of simplicity of statement, however, the rules are stated in two separate sections. This Section deals with delegation of performance of a duty; delegation of performance of a condition is the subject of § 319.

Illustrations

1. A owes B $100, and asks C to pay B. Payment or tender to B by C has the effect of payment or tender by A.

2. A contracts to deliver to B coal of specified kind and quality. A delegates the performance of this duty to C, who tenders to B coal of the specified kind and quality. The tender has the effect of a tender by A.

3. A contracts to build a building for B in accordance with specifications, and delegates the plumbing work to C. Performance by C has the effect of performance by A.

b. The duty of the person delegated. The rules stated in this Section apply without regard to whether the person delegated has a legal duty to render the performance in question or whether he acquires a legal right to render it or to receive a return performance. The person delegated may be an agent, gratuitous or otherwise, of the delegating obligor. For such cases this Section is a particular application of Restatement, Second, Agency § 17. Or the person delegated may be an assignee of a related right, entitled to enforce it for his own benefit. See Restatement, Second Agency §§ 14G, 14H. In either case he may or may not promise the obligor to render the performance. If he does so promise, the obligee may in some cases be an intended beneficiary of the promise, with the consequences stated in Chapter 14.

Illustration

4. In Illustrations 1, 2 and 3, the stated consequences are not affected by the fact that C is an agent of A or an assignee of A's right to return performance or that C has or has not assumed A's duty.

c. Non-delegable duties. Delegation of performance is a normal and permissible incident of many types of contract. See Uniform Commercial Code § 2–210, Comment. The principal exceptions relate to contracts for personal services and to contracts for the exercise of personal skill or discretion. Compare § 317. Even where delegation is normal, a particular contract may call for personal performance. Or the contract may permit delegation where personal performance is normally required. In the absence of contrary agreement, Subsection (2) precludes delegation only where a substantial reason is shown why delegated performance is not as satisfactory as personal performance.

Illustrations

5. A, a teacher employed in a public or private school, attempts to delegate the performance of his duties to B, a competent person. An offer by B to perform A's duties need not be accepted, and actual performance by B without the assent of the employer will create no right in either A or B to the salary stated in A's contract.

6. A contracts with B, a corporation, to sing three songs over the radio as part of an advertisement of B's product. A's performance is not delegable unless B assents.

7. A contracts with B that A will personally cut the grass on B's meadow. A cannot effectively delegate performance of the duty to C, however competent C may be.

8. A, a corporation, contracts with B to build a building. A delegates the entire performance to X and Y, the sole stockholders of A. Performance by X and Y in accordance with specifications discharges A's duty, since the supervision is not materially changed.

d. Delegation and novation. An obligor is discharged by the substitution of a new obligor only if the contract so provides or if the obligee makes a binding manifestation of assent, forming a novation. See §§ 280, 328 and 329. Otherwise, the obligee retains his original right against the obligor, even though the obligor manifests an intention to substitute another obligor in his place and the other purports to assume the duty. The obligee may, however, have rights against the other as an intended beneficiary of the promise to assume the duty. See Chapter 14.

Illustrations

9. A borrows $50,000 from B and contracts to repay it. The contract provides that, if a corporation C is organized and assumes the debt under described conditions, A will be under no further obligation. C is organized and in good faith assumes the debt as provided. A is discharged.

10. A contracts with B to cut the grass on B's meadow. A delegates performance to C, who contracts with A to assume A's duty and perform the work. C begins performance with B's assent, but later breaks the contract. C is liable to B, but A is not discharged.

§ 319. Delegation of Performance of Condition.

(1) Where a performance by a person is made a condition of a duty, performance by a person delegated by his satisfies that requirement unless the delegation is contrary to public policy or the terms of the agreement.

(2) Unless otherwise agreed, an agreement requires performance of a condition by a particular person only to the extent that the obligor has a substantial interest in having that person perform or control the acts required.

Comment

a. Types of conditions; related duties. A promissory duty may be subject to a condition either by virtue of a term of the promise or agreement or by virtue of a term of the contract supplied by a rule of law. See § 5; Comment c to § 226. This Section applies only to a particular type of condition, a performance by the obligee or some other person. When a promise is subject to such a condition, there may or may not be a return promise by the obligee or another that the performance will be rendered. If there is such a return promise, a breach of it often does not have the effect of the non-occurrence of a condition unless the failure of performance is material. See § 245. This Section deals with delegation as it affects performance of a condition; delegation affecting performance of a duty is the subject of § 318.

Illustration

1. A contracts with B, a city, to clean the streets of B weekly for five years in return for monthly payments. A delegates performance to C, and C substantially performs until B cancels the contract. C's performance satisfies the condition of B's duty to pay, whether C is A's agent or an assignee from A.

b. Non-delegable performance. The propriety of delegation of performance that is made a condition is in general governed by the same standard as the propriety of delegation of performance of a duty. Indeed, the same delegation may involve both. See, e.g., Illustration 5 to § 318. Delegation is generally permissible unless otherwise agreed, but performance of personal services and the exercise of personal skill and discretion are not ordinarily delegable. Where the condition consists of the making of a promise, delegation substituting a different promisor is ordinarily not effective.

Illustrations

2. Under an option contract A has a right to a conveyance of Blackacre on terms including execution of a promissory note secured by a mortgage on Blackacre. A assigns the contract to C, and C tenders a note executed by C but not by A. B is not bound to convey.

3. A, a corporation, contracts with B to convey Blackacre to B upon completion of installment payments B contracts to make. The deed is to include a covenant against incumbrances which gives rights only to the immediate grantee. A assigns the contract and conveys the land to C. B's duty is conditional on adequate assurance that he will receive a deed directly from A.

4. The facts being otherwise as stated in Illustration 3, B defaults and A becomes insolvent because land values are greatly reduced. The assignment and conveyance to C are made as a result of insolvency proceedings in which A is dissolved. In the absence of a showing that an incumbrance exists, C may obtain a decree of specific performance against B conditional on deposit by C of a deed containing a covenant against incumbrances by C only.

5. A, a corporation of State X, has a contract to act as B's exclusive sales agent for two years in a region including State X. A liquidates and assigns the contract and delegates the duties under it to C, a corporation of State Y, a state outside the region. B can properly treat the contract as terminated.

§ 320. Assignment of Conditional Rights.

The fact that a right is created by an option contract or is conditional on the performance of a return promise or is otherwise conditional does not prevent its assignment before the condition occurs.

Comment

a. Offers and option contracts. An offer can be accepted only by a person whom it invites to furnish the consideration, or by his agent. See §§ 29, 52. The power to accept can be exercised by a transferee only if the transferee is such a person. But an option contract, limiting the power to revoke an offer, is treated as creating a right which is assignable like other contractual rights. See § 25. Of course the assignment may be ineffective if it materially varies the obligor's duty, or if it is contrary to the terms of the option contract. See § 317.

Illustrations

1. In return for $100 paid by A, B promises to convey Blackacre for $10,000 on receipt of that amount within thirty days. A assigns the option to C. On C's tender of $10,000 within thirty days, B is under a duty to convey Blackacre to C.

2. In return for $100 paid by A, B promises to convey Blackacre to A, if A gives notice of acceptance within thirty days, for $10,000 of which $2,000 is to be paid on conveyance and the balance in four annual installments represented by notes. A assigns the option to C. The assignment is effective, but C's right is conditional on tender of notes signed by A.

b. Conditional right and conditional assignment. Not every conditional right is capable of effective assignment. The fact that the right is conditional does not prevent effective assignment, but assignment is subject to the same restrictions as in cases of unconditional rights. See § 317. Either the assignment or the right assigned, or both, may be subject to a condition. See § 331. Thus there may be a conditional assignment of a conditional right.

Illustrations

3. A holds an insurance policy in which the insurer promises to pay him $1000 at the end of twenty years if A makes specified payments of premiums. A can assign his conditional right.

4. A has a contract with B under which certain payments are to be made to A by B under a fixed schedule and other payments are to be made if B's earnings exceed stated amounts. As security for a loan to A by C, A assigns to C A's rights to payments by B, A to retain any payments falling due before default by A under the loan agreement. The assignment is effective according to its terms.

c. Return performance. The parties to an exchange of promises ordinarily contemplate an exchange of performances, and the right of each is often conditional on his own performance. See §§ 231–39. Or the right may be conditional on a performance by another, or on some other event. Such a condition does not prevent assignment by a promisee or beneficiary of his conditional right. Whether or not the return performance is delegable, and whether or not the assignor is under a duty to render it, the assignee's right is subject to the same conditions as was the assignor's.

Illustrations

5. A, a builder, and B, an owner of land, enter into a building contract. A assigns to C payments due or to become due him under the contract. The assignment is effective.

6. In Illustration 5, B sells the land to D and assigns to D his right to performance by A. The assignment is effective.

7. A, a teacher employed in a public or private school, assigns to C the salary to be earned the following month. In the absence of statute, the assignment is effective.

d. Delegation and assumption. The question whether a return performance is delegable arises only if the assignor attempts to delegate it. Often an assignor delegates performance to the assignee, and the assignee assumes the assignor's duty to perform, promising the assignor that the delegated performance will be rendered. See §§ 318–19. If the performance is delegable, such an assignment does not of itself materially vary a condition of the right assigned. The assignor remains subject to the same duty as before, and the obligor of the assigned right acquires a new right as an intended beneficiary of the assignee's promise. In effect the assignor becomes a surety for the assignee.

Illustrations

8. A contracts with B, a city, to clean the streets of B weekly for five years in return for monthly payments. A assigns his rights under the contract to C, and C promises A to perform A's duties under it. The assignment is effective. A is still bound to B, but as surety for C.

9. A, a builder, and B, an owner of land, enter into a building contract. A enters into a contract with C that C will take A's place in the building contract and that A will be freed from his obligation under it. B does not manifest assent or accept any performance from C. A is still bound to B.

10. A and B contract that B will sell and deliver goods to A in monthly installments for six months and A will pay for them on delivery. A assigns his rights under the contract to C, who assumes the duty of payment. C refuses to accept any goods from B. Both A and C are subject to liability to B, A as surety for C.

11. After the assignment in Illustration 10, C and B, without consulting A, agree to and do postpone deliveries for three months. A's duty is discharged.

e. Prospective failure of performance. An assignment is not effective if its effect is to impair materially the obligor's chance of obtaining return performance. See § 317. Thus an assignment accompanied by the assignor's repudiation of his duty to render a return performance may justify the obligor in suspending his own performance, in so changing his position that his duty is discharged, or even in bringing an immediate action for breach. See §§ 329 and 235–38. An attempt to delegate to an assignee a non-delegable performance may have a similar effect. Under Uniform Commercial Code § 2–210, the obligor may treat any assignment of rights under a contract for the sale of goods as creating reasonable grounds for insecurity if the assignor delegates performance. Under § 2–609 of the Code, the obligor may then demand adequate assurance of due performance, and failure of the assignor or assignee to furnish such assurance within a reasonable time has the effect of a repudiation. See also § 251.

Illustrations

12. A and C, partners, contract with B to act as the exclusive distributor of B's product in a specified territory. The contract is to last for one year, and they are to have an option to renew it from year to year. After six months A sells his interest in the contract to C and withdraws from the business. C gives notice of intention to renew, and B refuses to renew. B is not subject to liability to C for the refusal.

13. A, a corporation, leases railway cars to B by a contract providing that A will keep the cars in repair. A becomes insolvent, and as a result of insolvency proceedings A's rights under the lease contract and A's repair facilities and staff are transferred to C, a solvent corporation, which assumes

the duty of repair and assures B of its readiness and willingness to carry out the terms of the lease. A remains in existence under court supervision. B remains obligated by the lease.

§ 321. Assignment of Future Rights.

(1) Except as otherwise provided by statute, an assignment of a right to payment expected to arise out of an existing employment or other continuing business relationship is effective in the same way as an assignment of an existing right.

(2) Except as otherwise provided by statute and as stated in Subsection (1), a purported assignment of a right expected to arise under a contract not in existence operates only as a promise to assign the right when it arises and as a power to enforce it.

Comment

a. Rights under existing contracts. This Section does not apply to rights in existence at the time of assignment. Such rights are assignable under the rules stated in §§ 317 and 320 even though they are conditional or have not matured. For this purpose rights arising under a contract are treated as existing from the moment of its formation, even though the chance is slight that there will ever be a duty of immediate performance.

Illustration

1. A contracts to build a house for B for a stated price. The contract provides that if A performs any work on the house beyond what the specifications require, he shall have compensation therefor, to be determined by the architect. Before any such work has been agreed upon, A, for value, assigns his right to compensation for extra work to C. Subsequently A becomes bankrupt, and still later extra work under the contract is agreed upon and performed. Immediately on completion of the work A assigns the right to compensation to D. The assignment to C is effective and is not defeated by A's bankruptcy or the assignment to D.

b. Rationale. The conceptual difficulty posed by transfer of a right which does not exist can be met by giving effect to the attempted transfer when the right later arises. Uniform Commercial Code § 9–204, for example, provides that with certain exceptions a security agreement may provide that all obligations covered by the security agreement are to be secured by after-acquired collateral; in an appropriate case, the security interest is said by § 9–203 to "attach" when it becomes enforceable against the debtor with respect to the collateral.

The effect given in such cases is limited, not because of any logical necessity, but by virtue of a public policy which seeks to protect the assignor and third parties against transfers which may be improvident or fraudulent. Similar limitations are placed on attempted transfers of future rights in property other than contractual rights. See Restatement of Property § 316; Restatement of Security § 10; Restatement, Second, Trusts § 86; Uniform Commercial Code §§ 2–401, 2–501, 9–203(4), 9–204(2).

c. Continuing relationships. Subsection (1) gives effect to an assignment of a right to compensation for services expected to be rendered in the course of an existing employment, even though there is no contract to continue the employment, and states a similar rule for rights expected to arise out of other continuing business relationships. Even where there is no continuing relationship, a purported assignment of a right expected to arise out of a subsequent transaction may sometimes become a part of the subsequent transaction and take effect as such a part.

Illustrations

2. B employs A from week to week in his factory at a salary of $50 a week. A, in the first week of January, assigns to C any salary which he may earn during the last week in that month in his employment by B. The assignment is effective, and if A works for B during that week B will come under a duty to C to pay him $50.

3. B employs A at a stated rate of pay from day to day. A assigns to C whatever A may become entitled to from work done for B during the ensuing month. During the ensuing month A not only earns

his regular pay but acquires a right to extra compensation in the course of his employment. The assignment is effective both as to the right to regular pay and the right to extra compensation.

4. In January A assigns to C as security for a loan the salary he expects to earn in March under his existing employment by B, though A has no contract with B to work during that month. A becomes bankrupt in February, and later receives a discharge in bankruptcy. He continues his employment during March. Even though the assignment is otherwise effective, A's debt to C is discharged, and A's March salary belongs to A free of C's claim.

5. A receives from B an order for brick to be used by B in performing an existing contract with D to build a school, with an assurance that A "has been awarded the job of furnishing bricks for the school." Before prices or specifications for the brick have been determined, A assigns to C as security for a loan the money to become due from B for material for the school. The brick is later delivered as expected. The assignment is effective.

6. A is negotiating to sell to B property part of which is subject to a mortgage from A to C. In consideration of C's release of the mortgage, A assigns to C a payment to be made by B. Later the same day A and B sign a contract to sell the property which provides for the payment expected. Notwithstanding the lack of a continuing business relationship, the assignment to C is effective when the contract to sell is made.

d. Other future rights. In the absence of statute, a purported assignment of a future right not within the rule stated in Subsection (1) has only the effect stated in Subsection (2). That effect is that the assignee has enforceable rights against the assignor only to the extent that contractual remedies are available, as in the case of a promise to make a future assignment. See § 330. As against third parties, the purported assignment operates as a grant to the assignee of the assignor's power to enforce the right. But unless specific enforcement against the assignor is appropriate, the grant of power is revocable and can be defeated by the assignor's creditors until it is exercised.

Illustrations

7. A is employed as a teacher for the school year by X, a municipality. A, in the expectation of employment by B, another municipality, for the following school year, assigns to C the salary for the first month of service which A may render for B. A is subsequently employed by B as expected, and A's salary for the first month becomes due. C makes demand upon B for payment of the salary. B refuses and pays A. In the absence of statute, B has violated no right of C.

8. The facts being otherwise as stated in Illustration 7, D, a creditor of A, garnishes A's salary after it becomes due. C intervenes, claiming the funds as assignee. In the absence of statute, D's claim is prior to C's.

e. Statutory provisions. The limitations imposed by this Section on the assignment of future rights are not the only possible mode of safeguarding the interests of the assignor and third parties. Particularly when a method is provided for giving public notice of the transaction, statutes commonly relax the limitations stated here. For transactions subject to Article 9 of the Uniform Commercial Code, the Code provides a notice-filing system, and § 9–204 gives effect to a security agreement (not involving consumer goods) providing that a security interest shall attach to after-acquired collateral. Such collateral may include contractual rights. Somewhat similar variations from the rules of this Section have been made in other statutes relating to the assignment of accounts receivable. Again, wage-assignment statutes sometimes limit amount and duration, but within the limits set may permit assignment of wages to be earned under future engagements. See Introductory Note to Chapter 15.

§ 322. Contractual Prohibition of Assignment.

(1) Unless the circumstances indicate the contrary, a contract term prohibiting assignment of "the contract" bars only the delegation to an assignee of the performance by the assignor of a duty or condition.

(2) A contract term prohibiting assignment of rights under the contract, unless a different intention is manifested,

(a) does not forbid assignment of a right to damages for breach of the whole contract or a right arising out of the assignor's due performance of his entire obligation;

(b) gives the obligor a right to damages for breach of the terms forbidding assignment but does not render the assignment ineffective;

(c) is for the benefit of the obligor, and does not prevent the assignee from acquiring rights against the assignor or the obligor from discharging his duty as if there were no such prohibition.

Comment

a. Rationale. In the absence of statute or other contrary public policy, the parties to a contract have power to limit the rights created by their agreement. The policy against restraints on the alienation of property has limited application to contractual rights. . . .

b. Ineffective terms. In some circumstances where contractual prohibitions of assignment are regularly limited by construction, explicit contractual provision would not change the result. Where a right to the payment of money is fully earned by performance, for example, a provision that an attempt to assign forfeits the right may be invalid as a contractual penalty. See § 356. If there is no forfeiture, and the obligee joins in demanding payment to the assignee, a contractual prohibition which serves no legitimate interest of the obligor is disregarded. Uniform Commercial Code §§ 2–210 and 9–318 render contractual prohibitions ineffective in additional circumstances, and in some situations a prohibition is invalid as a restraint on alienation aside from statute. See Uniform Commercial Code § 9–311.

Illustrations

1. A holds a policy of industrial insurance issued to him by the B Insurance Company. After lapse for failure to pay premiums, B refuses to pay the "cash surrender value" provided for in the policy. A and others similarly situated assign their claims to C for collection. The assignment is effective without regard to any contractual prohibition of assignment.

2. A and B contract for the sale of land by B to A. A fully performs the contract, becomes entitled to specific performance on B's refusal to convey the land, and then assigns his rights to C. C is entitled to specific performance against B without regard to any contractual prohibition of assignment.

c. Construction. The rules stated in this Section do not exhaust the factors to be taken into account in construing and applying a prohibition against assignment. "Not transferable" has a clear meaning in a theatre ticket; in a certificate of deposit the same words may refer to negotiability rather than assignability. Where there is a promise not to assign but no provision that an assignment is ineffective, the question whether breach of the promise discharges the obligor's duty depends on all the circumstances. See §§ 237, 241.

d. Consent of the obligor. Ordinarily a contractual prohibition of assignment is for the benefit of the obligor. In such cases third parties cannot assert the invalidity of a prohibited assignment if the obligor makes no objection. Where, however, the prohibition is not solely for the benefit of the obligor, waiver by the obligor may not validate the assignment. The validity of restraints on alienation in such cases is governed by considerations similar to those governing the validity of spendthrift trusts. See Restatement, Second, Trusts §§ 153–57.

Illustrations

3. B contracts to transfer land to A on payment of $5000. The contract provides that A shall not assign his right. A assigns his right to C. B, on receiving $5000 from C, conveys the land to him. B's duty under his contract with A is discharged.

4. A Manufacturing Company contracts with B Insurance Company for group insurance on the lives of A's employees. The policy and certificates issued under it to individual employees limit the class of permitted beneficiaries, permit the employee to change the beneficiary, forbid irrevocable designation of a beneficiary, and provide that the certificate is not assignable. A certificate is issued to C, a widower, who designates his son D as beneficiary and delivers the certificate to D as a gift. Later C remarries and designates his second wife E as beneficiary. On C's death B interpleads D and E, paying the insurance money into court. E is entitled to the fund.

§ 323. Obligor's Assent to Assignment or Delegation.

(1) A term of a contract manifesting an obligor's assent to the future assignment of a right or an obligee's assent to the future delegation of the performance of a duty or condition is effective despite any subsequent objection.

(2) A manifestation of such assent after the formation of a contract is similarly effective if made for consideration or in circumstances in which a promise would be binding without consideration, or if a material change of position takes place in reliance on the manifestation.

Comment

a. Effect of assent. The assent of the obligor is not ordinarily necessary to make an assignment effective. But his assent may operate to preclude objection based on a change in his duty, burden or risk or in his chance of obtaining return performance. See § 317. It may permit a separate action by a partial assignee. See § 326. It may be an offer of a new contract by novation, or the acceptance of an offer of novation, and may thus terminate the assignor's power to revoke a gratuitous assignment (see § 332), or may discharge or modify a duty of the assignor or a condition of the right assigned (see §§ 318–19). Which of these effects is produced depends on the circumstances and the scope of the assent manifested.

b. Promises to or by "assigns." Contracts often refer to the "assigns" of one or both parties. A purported promise by a promisor "and his assigns" does not mean that the promisor can terminate his duty by making an assignment, nor does it of itself show an assumption of duties by any assignee. It tends to indicate that the promised performance is not personal, just as a promise to a promisee "and his assigns" tends to indicate that the promisor is willing to render performance to an assignee. Whether there is a manifestation of assent to assignment or delegation, however, depends on the interpretation of the contract as a whole. Notwithstanding references to "assigns," other terms and the circumstances may show that the assent is limited or even that there is no assent.

Illustration

1. A and C, partners, contract with B to act as exclusive distributor of B's product in a specified territory. The terms of the contract show that B reposes personal trust and confidence in both A and C. A term, "This agreement shall bind and benefit the respective successors and assigns of the parties hereto," may be read as inapplicable to an assignment by A or C which delegates performance unless B makes a further manifestation of assent.

c. Assent subsequent to contract. Assent to assignment or delegation may be manifested after the formation of a contract, and may have effects similar to those of a term in the contract. Indeed, such assent may be a practical construction of the contract, relevant to determine its meaning. See Uniform Commercial Code § 2–208. In addition, subsequent assent may waive a prohibition contained in the contract. Unless consideration is given or unless the circumstances are such as to make a new promise binding without consideration, however, such a manifestation of assent can be withdrawn before it has been acted on. See §§ 84, 89, 90. Assent to assignment and delegation, even though irrevocable, does not of itself establish a novation discharging duties of the assignor.

Illustrations

2. A and B enter into a contract binding A personally to do some delicate cabinet work. A assigns his rights and delegates performance of his duties to C. On being informed of this, B agrees with C in consideration of C's promise to do the work that B will accept C's work, if properly done, instead of the performance promised by A. Later without cause B refuses to allow C to proceed with the work, though C is ready to do so, and makes demand on A that A perform. A refuses. C can recover damages from B and B cannot recover from A.

3. A contracts to employ B in A's business for one year at a specified salary. A contemplates selling the business, and the contract provides that the contract may be transferred with the business, but B is not informed of the identity of the purchaser. A month later A sells the business to C and assigns his rights and delegates his duties under the contract to C, who agrees to assume A's duties. After the sale B works for C and is paid by C for two weeks. C then discharges B because B refuses to accept a reduction in salary. There is a breach of contract by A as well as C.

§ 324. Mode of Assignment in General.

It is essential to an assignment of a right that the obligee manifest an intention to transfer the right to another person without further action or manifestation of intention by the obligee. The manifestation may be made to the other or to a third person on his behalf and, except as provided by statute or by contract, may be made either orally or by a writing.

Comment

a. Requisites of assignment. Assignment requires an assignable right. See § 317. Aside from statute, the assignor of such a right may make an assignment by manifestation of intention without any particular formality. A manifestation of intention or a promise to make a transfer in the future is not an assignment, however. See § 330. Where the manifestation is made to a third person on behalf of the assignee, the assignment may not take effect unless there is an acceptance by the assignee; or it may take effect subject to disclaimer by the assignee. See § 327. Lack of formality may mean that the assignment is revocable (see § 332), or that it is subject to defenses or claims of the obligor which accrue subsequently (see §§ 336, 338), or that it can be defeated by creditors of the assignor or by subsequent assignees of the same right (see §§ 341, 342).

b. Statutory formalities: the Statute of Frauds. The Statute of Frauds is the subject of Chapter 5 of this Restatement. Section 4 of the Uniform Sales Act included a Statute of Frauds for "a contract to sell or a sale of any . . . choses in action of the value of five hundred dollars or upwards." The Uniform Commercial Code substitutes a general provision that "a contract for the sale of personal property is not enforceable by way of action or defense beyond five thousand dollars in amount or value of remedy" in the absence of a writing, with exceptions for the sale of goods or investment securities and for "security agreements," which are covered by more specific sections. Uniform Commercial Code § 1–206. Such provisions prevent enforcement against an assignor unless there is a memorandum in writing or some substitute formality, but under the rule stated in § 144 of this Restatement they cannot ordinarily be asserted by third persons, including the obligor of an assigned right. Notwithstanding non-compliance with the Statute, therefore, the assignment is effective against the obligor. Moreover, the obligor discharges his duty by performing in accordance with the assignment, and the assignee can keep the benefit of the performance.

c. Security agreements; wage assignments. Uniform Commercial Code § 9–203 provides that with stated exceptions "a security interest is not enforceable against the debtor or third parties" unless the collateral is in the possession of the secured party or the debtor has signed a security agreement. This provision applies not only where the "debtor" assigns contractual rights as security for an obligation, but also where the "debtor" is a "seller of accounts or chattel paper." §§ 1–201(37), 9–102(1)(b), 9–105(1)(d); see the Statutory Note at the beginning of this Chapter and the Reporter's Note to § 317. Transactions subject to this provision are not enforceable against anyone unless the statutory formalities are met. Statutes regulating assignments of wages may go further and deny all effect to a non-complying assignment.

§ 325. Order as Assignment.

(1) A written order drawn upon an obligor and signed and delivered to another person by the obligee is an assignment if it is conditional on the existence of a duty of the drawee to the drawer to comply with the order and the drawer manifests an intention that a person other than the drawer is to retain the performance.

(2) An order which directs the drawee to render a performance without reference to any duty of the drawee is not of itself an assignment, even though the drawee is under a duty to the drawer to comply with the order and even though the order indicates a particular account to be debited or any other fund or source from which reimbursement is expected.

Comment

a. Order on particular fund. The principal application of Subsection (1) is to rights to the payment of money, but it also applies to other rights. The creditor typically delivers to the assignee a written instrument addressed to the debtor, directing the debtor to pay all or part of the debt to the assignee. The instrument may be delivered instead to some other person on the assignee's behalf. See § 327. It may or may not indicate the ultimate disposition of the proceeds. Facts aside from the instrument may show that the recipient is to act as the creditor's agent rather than as assignee. An order communicated only to the debtor is not an assignment unless there is some additional manifestation of intention to assign.

Illustrations

1. A delivers to C the following writing addressed to B, "Pay C for his own use $100 out of the amount you owe me." The writing is an assignment.

2. A gives C, acting as A's agent, an order to collect from B whatever B owes A. The order is not an assignment.

3. A writes to B, "Please pay to C the balance due me." This is insufficient to establish an assignment or to give B notice of an assignment. But the letter would be an effective assignment if delivered to C to pay or secure a debt owed by A to C.

b. Drafts and delivery orders. A check or other draft is an unconditional order for the payment of money meeting formal requisites of certainty in amount and time of payment. If payable to order or bearer, it is negotiable; whether or not negotiable, it is not of itself an assignment of a right against the drawee, and the drawee is not liable on the instrument until he accepts it. Additional facts may show that an assignment is intended, and the instrument may then be the means by which the assignment is effected. See Uniform Commercial Code §§ 3–104, 3–409, 3–805. Similar principles apply to unaccepted orders for the delivery of goods, whether or not conditional, if in negotiable form. See Uniform Commercial Code §§ 7–502, 7–503, 7–504. They also apply to any order which is treated as chargeable against the general credit of the drawer and independent of any particular fund or obligation. As to what terms render an order conditional for this purpose, see Uniform Commercial Code § 3–105.

Illustrations

4. A draws and delivers to C for value either a negotiable or a non-negotiable check upon his bank, B, payable to C, for the full amount of A's balance, or for part of it. B dishonors the check in violation of its duty to A. C has no right against B.

5. In Illustration 4, B accepts the check by signing a certification on its face and redelivering it to C. There is a novation substituting C for A as B's creditor to the amount of the check.

6. In Illustration 4, A and C agree that the check will operate as an assignment. The agreement is effective as between A and C. Its effect on B is subject to the rules relating to adverse claims to bank deposits.

§ 326. Partial Assignment.

(1) Except as stated in Subsection (2), an assignment of a part of a right, whether the part is specified as a fraction, as an amount, or otherwise, is operative as to that part to the same extent and in the same manner as if the part had been a separate right.

(2) If the obligor has not contracted to perform separately the assigned part of a right, no legal proceeding can be maintained by the assignor or assignee against the obligor over his objection, unless all the persons entitled to the promised performance are joined in the proceeding, or unless joinder is not feasible and it is equitable to proceed without joinder.

Comment

a. Other types of divided interests. The partial assignment covered by this Section is to be distinguished from other transactions creating divided interests in a contractual right: (1) A conditional assignment leaves the assignor with an interest if the condition is not met. (2) A total assignment may empower the assignee to enforce the entire right wholly or partially for the benefit of the assignor or others. Examples are assignment to secure an obligation and assignment to a trustee. (3) The obligee may promise to enforce the right wholly or partially for the benefit of others, or to pay to others all or part of any proceeds collected. Such a promise may amount to a declaration of trust or may create an equitable interest in the promisee by virtue of a right to specific performance of the promise.

b. Partial assignment. The distinguishing feature of a partial assignment is a manifestation of intention to make an immediate transfer of part but not all of the assignor's right, and to confer on the assignee a direct right against the obligor to the performance of that part. Historically, the right of a partial assignee could be enforced only by a suit in a court of equity, and it was therefore sometimes described as an "equitable" right. But the right of a total assignee also had historically an "equitable" character. Under the rule stated in Subsection (1), a partial assignment and a total assignment are equally effective, subject to the protection of the obligor under the rule stated in Subsection (2).

Illustrations

1. B owes A $100. A assigns $25 to C. With knowledge of the assignment, B pays the entire debt to A. B's duty to C is not discharged. See § 338.

2. B owes A $100. A assigns $25 to C, and later assigns the entire debt to D, who pays value without notice of the assignment to C. C has the same priority as to the $25 assigned to him as if the entire debt had been assigned to him. See § 342.

c. Joinder. The obligee of a right cannot bring successive actions to enforce parts of it. The right is merged in a judgment enforcing it in part, and subsequent actions are barred. See Restatement, Second, Judgments § 24. But where the obligor has notice of an assignment, a judgment for or against the assignor does not bar a subsequent action by the assignee. See Restatement, Second, Judgments §§ 37, 55; compare § 338, infra. To protect the obligor against multiple actions in a case of partial assignment, therefore, the rule stated in Subsection (2) entitles him to require joinder of all the obligees. This protection is limited by its reason: it is not available if the obligor has assented to the partial assignment. Moreover, it yields to equitable considerations if joinder is not feasible; in such cases the question whether an action may proceed depends on the probability of material prejudice to the obligor, the extent to which relief can be so shaped as to avoid such prejudice, the adequacy of the relief which can be afforded to the parties before the court, and the availability of adequate alternative remedies. See Rule 19 of the Federal Rules of Civil Procedure.

Illustrations

3. B owes A $100. A assigns $25 to C. Neither A nor C can maintain an action against B over B's objection unless the other is joined in the proceeding.

4. The facts being otherwise as stated in Illustration 3, B pays the $75 balance to A. C can maintain an action against B for $25 without joining A.

§ 327. Acceptance or Disclaimer by the Assignee.

(1) A manifestation of assent by an assignee to the assignment is essential to make it effective unless

(a) a third person gives consideration for the assignment, or

(b) the assignment is irrevocable by virtue of the delivery of a writing to a third person.

(2) An assignee who has not manifested assent to an assignment may, within a reasonable time after learning of its existence and terms, render it inoperative from the beginning by disclaimer.

Comment

a. Necessity of acceptance. Sale of a contractual right, like sale of goods, requires a bargain in which there is a manifestation of mutual assent to the exchange. Ordinarily the person who furnishes the consideration is the transferee of the right sold, but where consideration is given by one person for an assignment to another, it is not necessary that the assignee know of the bargain or assent to it. Compare §§ 17, 71(2). Where there is no bargain, an irrevocable gift can be made without the assent of the donee by the delivery of a written assignment or a symbolic or evidentiary writing to a third person. Compare §§ 104, 306; Restatement, Second, Trusts §§ 35, 36. The circumstances in which such a delivery makes the assignment irrevocable are stated in § 332.

Illustrations

1. A has a contractual right against D. For consideration received from B, A assigns the right to B's son C. C has no knowledge of the assignment. The assignment is effective immediately, subject to C's power of disclaimer.

2. A delivers his savings bank book to B, saying "I deliver this book to you as a gift to C." C has no knowledge of the gift. An attempted revocation by A before C learns of the gift is ineffective.

   b. *Disclaimer.* As in other cases of rights created without the assent of the obligee, an assignee is entitled to reject the right, whether or not there is a related burden. Compare §§ 38, 104, 306. No particular formality is required for disclaimer, and its usual effect is the same as if no assignment had been made. But it cannot make tortious acts lawful when done, and in some cases it may give rise to a right of restitution. See Comment a to § 306. The effect of intervening claims of third persons is beyond the scope of this Restatement.

3. A, the payee of a negotiable or non-negotiable note or certificate of deposit, delivers it to B without indorsement as a gift to C, who has no knowledge of the delivery. Upon learning of the gift C refuses it. A is the owner of the note or certificate.

§ 328. Interpretation of Words of Assignment; Effect of Acceptance of Assignment.

(1) Unless the language or the circumstances indicate the contrary, as in an assignment for security, an assignment of "the contract" or of "all my rights under the contract" or an assignment in similar general terms is an assignment of the assignor's rights and a delegation of his unperformed duties under the contract.

(2) Unless the language or the circumstances indicate the contrary, the acceptance by an assignee of such an assignment operates as a promise to the assignor to perform the assignor's unperformed duties, and the obligor of the assigned rights is an intended beneficiary of the promise.

Caveat: The Institute expresses no opinion as to whether the rule stated in Subsection (2) applies to an assignment by a purchaser of his rights under a contract for the sale of land.

Comment

   a. *"Assignment" of duty.* A duty cannot be "assigned" in the sense in which "assignment" is used in this Chapter. The parties to an assignment, however, may not distinguish between assignment of rights and delegation of duties. A purported "assignment" of duties may simply manifest an intention that the assignee shall be substituted for the assignor. Such an intention is not completely effective unless the obligor of the assigned right joins in a novation, but the rules of this Section give as full effect as can be given without the obligor's assent. As to contracts for the sale of goods, see Uniform Commercial Code § 2–210.

Illustration

1. A, an oil company, has a contract to sell and deliver oil to B. A delivers to C, another oil company, a writing assigning to C "the contract" or "all A's rights and duties under the contract." C is under a duty to B to deliver the oil called for by the contract, and A is surety for C.

   b. *Contrary agreement; assignment for security.* This Section states rules of presumptive interpretation which yield to a manifestation of a different intention. In particular delegation and assumption of the assignor's duties is not ordinarily implied where the contract calls for personal performance by the assignor. Again, an assignment as security does not ordinarily delegate performance to the secured party, and the secured party does not assume the assignor's duties. See Uniform Commercial Code §§ 2–210, 9–317. Under §§ 9–102 and 9–104 of the Code a sale of "accounts or chattel paper" is treated as a secured transaction unless it is part of the sale of a business or unless the assignee is to perform the contract. The quoted terms are limited by definitions in §§ 9–105 and 9–106 to "monetary obligations" or "rights to payment." See Reporter's Note to § 317.

Illustrations

2. In Illustration 1, A assigns "the contract" or "all A's rights under the contract" to C, a financial institution. Delivery of the oil is not delegated to C, and C is under no duty to deliver oil.

3. A sells and delivers an automobile to B, the price to be paid in installments, and assigns to C for value "all A's rights under the contract." After B has made all the payments, the automobile is discovered to have been stolen and is retaken by the owner. C is not liable to B for breach of warranty of title; A is.

c. Land contracts. By virtue of the right of either party to obtain specific performance of a contract for the sale of land, such contracts are treated for many purposes as creating a property interest in the purchaser and thus as partially executed. The vendor's interest resembles the interest of a mortgagee under a mortgage given as security for the purchase price. An assignment of the vendor's rights under the contract is similar to an assignment of a right to payment for goods or services: ordinarily no assumption of the vendor's duties by the assignee is implied merely from the acceptance of the assignment.

When the purchaser under a land contract assigns his rights, the assignment has commonly been treated like a sale of land "subject to" a mortgage. In this view acceptance of the assignment does not amount to an assumption of the assignor's duties unless the contract of assignment so provides either expressly or by implication. . . . Decisions refusing to infer an assumption of duties by the assignee have been influenced by doctrinal difficulties in the recognition of rights of assignees and beneficiaries. Those difficulties have now been overcome, and it is doubtful whether adherence to such decisions carries out the probable intention of the parties in the usual case. But since the shift in doctrine has not yet produced any definite change in the body of decisions, the Institute expresses no opinion on the application of Subsection (2) to an assignment by a purchaser under a land contract.

Illustration

4. A contracts to purchase land from B. The contract provides that it is to bind the assigns of the parties. A assigns "the contract" to C, and B assigns "the contract" to D. These facts themselves do not show a promise by D; the Institute expresses no opinion as to whether they show a promise by C.

§ 329. Repudiation by Assignor and Novation With Assignee.

(1) The legal effect of a repudiation by an assignor of his duty to the obligor of the assigned right is not limited by the fact that the assignee is a competent person and has promised to perform the duty.

(2) If the obligor, with knowledge of such a repudiation, accepts any performance from the assignee without reserving his rights against the assignor, a novation arises by which the duty of the assignor is discharged and a similar duty of the assignee is substituted.

Comment

a. Repudiation and its effects. In some cases a repudiation by one party to a contract discharges the duty of the other party; in some cases it requires the other to treat as total a breach which might otherwise be partial, or it may itself be a total breach. See § 253; Uniform Commercial Code § 2–610. For these purposes repudiation includes a positive statement by an assignor that he will not or cannot substantially perform his duties, or any voluntary affirmative action which renders substantial performance apparently impossible. In some circumstances a statement that he doubts whether he will substantially perform, or that he takes no responsibility for performance, or even a failure to give adequate assurance of performance may have a similar effect. See §§ 250–51.

b. Scope of obligor's assent. The assignment of a contractual right and delegation to the assignee of the assignor's duty is often a matter of course. The obligor of the assigned right may then have a right to withhold performance until he receives adequate assurance of performance by the assignee. Section 251. Failure to demand such assurance and acceptance of performance by the assignee manifest the obligor's assent to the assignment and delegation (see § 323), but not to the discharge of the assignor's duty. However, when the obligor knows that the delegating assignor has repudiated his duty he has reason to know that the performance of the assignee is offered by way of novation, and his silent acceptance of the performance operates as acceptance of the offer of novation. Compare § 69.

Illustrations

1. A is under a contract with B to build a house for $10,000. A assigns his rights under the contract to C, who agrees to assume A's duty to build the house. B is informed of the assignment and assumption, and makes no objection as C partly performs. A remains bound to B as surety for C's performance.

2. In Illustration 1, A withdraws from the construction business and informs B that he takes no further responsibility for C's performance. B makes no objection and C proceeds with the work. A is discharged.

   c. *Reservation of rights.* The obligor of an assigned right cannot be forced to assent to a repudiation by the assignor or to an offer of a substituted contract with the assignee. To avoid the implication that his silence gives assent, he must manifest either to the assignor or to the assignee his intention to retain unimpaired his rights against the assignor, but no particular form is required. See Uniform Commercial Code §§ 1–207, 3–606; § 281. If the terms of the assignment so provide, the delegation or assumption of duty may be defeated in such a case, and the repudiation may be retracted before it has been acted on. See Uniform Commercial Code § 2–611. Where the assignee continues performance, the reservation of rights by the obligor means that the assignor, if compelled to pay for the assignee's default, will have a right over against the assignee.

Illustration

3. In Illustration 2, on being informed of A's repudiation, B notifies A or C that further performance is "without prejudice." A is not discharged.

§ 330. Contracts to Assign in the Future, or to Transfer Proceeds to Be Received.

(1) A contract to make a future assignment of a right, or to transfer proceeds to be received in the future by the promisor, is not an assignment.

(2) Except as provided by statute, the effect of such a contract on the rights and duties of the obligor and third persons is determined by the rules relating to specific performance of contracts.

Comment

   a. *Contract to assign.* As to a right in existence, it is a question of interpretation whether the obligee manifests an intention to make a present transfer or only an intention to bind himself to make a future transfer. A present assignment may be coupled with a promise to provide future evidence of the transfer, but there is no assignment if the transfer is not to take place until the obligee acts further. Whether or not there is a present assignment, the assignee may be empowered to enforce the right. Such a power is ordinarily fairly implied when there is a purported present assignment of a future right, and once the right arises in such a case the situation is substantially similar to that created by a revocable assignment. See § 321.

Illustration

1. A holds a promissory note made by B and secured by a mortgage on Blackacre. A enters into a written agreement with C which recites that A has sold the note and mortgage to C for a price payable in installments and that A is to hold the note and mortgage as security for the price and to indorse the note and execute an assignment of the mortgage when the price is paid. There is a present assignment to C, subject to the security interest retained by A.

   b. *Contract to transfer proceeds.* A promise by an obligee that he will collect money due him and pay over all or part of it to the promisee is not an assignment. The same rule applies to a promise to transfer proceeds other than money. Thus if a purchaser under a contract for the sale of land contracts to resell the land, there is a subcontract rather than an assignment of the original contract. But if the prospective transferee is authorized to receive performance on behalf of the obligee-transferor and to retain it, there may be an assignment of the contractual right. The test is whether an intention is manifested to transfer present ownership of the right.

Illustrations

2. A sells property to B and authorizes B to pay the price to X, a bank, on A's behalf. Later A borrows money from C and agrees to repay C out of the money received from B. A then instructs X to hold for the account of A and C all sums received from B, stating "C does not claim this money as owner, but you are to hold it until you have been advised in writing by both parties." There is no assignment to C.

3. A, the holder of a note payable by B, delivers it to C, A's attorney, for collection, agreeing that C is co-owner of the claim to the extent of half of what he collects. C is a partial assignee of the right against B.

c. *Contracts specifically enforceable.* In some circumstances a contract to assign or a contract to transfer proceeds may create a right in the promisee very similar to that of an assignee. Even though there is no present assignment, the promisee may have a right to specific performance of the promise. If it can be enforced against third parties, such a right resembles that of an assignee, and it is sometimes referred to as an "equitable assignment" or "equitable lien." In general the remedy of specific performance is available if the promisee's remedy in damages would be inadequate. See §§ 359, 360. In particular, specific performance is decreed if the promise is one to transfer an interest in specific land or to transfer a specified right as security for an obligation.

Illustrations

4. A, a real estate broker, is employed by B to find a purchaser for B's land. In consideration of C's help in finding a purchaser, A promises to pay C one-half of the commission earned. The land is sold and the commission earned. C has no right against B.

5. B, the owner of a parcel of land, contracts to sell the parcel to A. A contracts to assign the contract to C or to convey the parcel to C. Even though C is not an assignee, C can sue A and B to compel A to assert for C's benefit A's right to specific performance by B.

6. As part of a property settlement in divorce proceedings A contracts with his wife C to make an irrevocable change in the beneficiary of a policy of insurance on A's life to D, their minor child. A fails to do so and later gratuitously makes his second wife E the beneficiary of the policy. On A's death B, the insurance company, pays the amount of the policy into court and interpleads C, D and E. D is entitled to the money.

d. *After-acquired rights.* In general a contract to give security is specifically enforceable as between the parties even as to rights arising after the contract is made. By statute or decision, however, an exception has been made for contracts to assign wages under future employments. See § 321. And in some states, on the analogy of rules applied to mortgages of after-acquired tangible property, an "equitable assignment" of rights not in existence is subordinate to the claims of creditors of the assignor whose rights attach after the rights have arisen and before the assignor has made a present assignment. In the absence of statutory provision for public notice, the rights of the promisee are inferior to those of a subsequent good faith purchaser for value without notice of the prior contract.

Illustrations

7. A "assigns" to C as security for a loan "all the book debts due and owing or which may during the continuance of this security become due and owing" to A. B subsequently becomes indebted to A on a contract made after the "assignment," and thereafter a creditor of A garnishes the debt. In the absence of a statute, C is entitled to the debt to the exclusion of the creditor.

8. The facts being otherwise as stated in Illustration 7, A assigns the debt to D after it arises. D takes the assignment in good faith as a purchaser for value, without notice of the "assignment" to C. In the absence of statute, D is entitled to the debt to the exclusion of C.

e. The Uniform Commercial Code. The provisions of Article 9 of the Uniform Commercial Code apply to "accounts" and "general intangibles," but not to insurance, bank accounts or wages. See Introductory Note to this Chapter. Under § 9–204(1) a security agreement "may provide that any or all obligations covered by the security agreement are to be secured by after-acquired collateral." When a security interest "attaches" is governed by § 9–203, "unless explicit agreement postpones the time of attaching." § 9–203(2). The security interest is subordinate to the rights of creditors of the debtor and purchasers from him if it is unperfected. See § 9–301. But if the filing provisions of the Code have been complied with beforehand, the security interest is perfected when it attaches. See § 9–303.

TOPIC 3. EFFECT BETWEEN ASSIGNOR AND ASSIGNEE

§ 331. Partially Effective Assignments.

An assignment may be conditional, revocable, or voidable by the assignor, or unenforceable by virtue of a Statute of Frauds.

Comment

a. Assignor's power to destroy assignee's right. In this Restatement "assignment" is used to refer to an act which extinguishes in whole or in part the assignor's right and creates a similar right in the assignee. See §§ 317, 324. On proof of an unconditional assignment, the assignee can recover on an assigned right; the assignor cannot. The assignor may be entitled to revoke the assignment because it is gratuitous or by virtue of a reserved power, or the assignment may be voidable for fraud or other invalidating cause. Even if destruction of the assignee's right is a violation of the assignor's duty, he retains by virtue of his former ownership certain powers which may have that effect. See §§ 338, 342.

b. Conditional assignment; conditional and future rights. A conditional assignment does not wholly extinguish the assignor's right until the condition occurs. A conditional right may be effectively assigned either conditionally or unconditionally; a conditional assignment of a conditional right means that the rights of the assignee and assignor are both subject to one condition and that the right of the assignee is subject to an additional condition. See § 323. Strictly there cannot be an effective assignment of a right not yet in existence, but after the right arises the assignment may for some purposes be treated as if it had been effective when made. See §§ 321, 330.

Illustration

1. A has a right to $400 against B and assigns the right to C in payment for an automobile on condition that the car run 1,000 miles without needing repairs. The assignment is conditional and is effective according to its terms. If the car does not run 1,000 miles without needing repairs, the right to the $400 belongs to A, not to C.

§ 332. Revocability of Gratuitous Assignments.

(1) Unless a contrary intention is manifested, a gratuitous assignment is irrevocable if

    (a) the assignment is in a writing either signed or under seal that is delivered by the assignor; or

    (b) the assignment is accompanied by delivery of a writing of a type customarily accepted as a symbol or as evidence of the right assigned.

(2) Except as stated in this Section, a gratuitous assignment is revocable and the right of the assignee is terminated by the assignor's death or incapacity, by a subsequent assignment by the assignor, or by notification from the assignor received by the assignee or by the obligor.

(3) A gratuitous assignment ceases to be revocable to the extent that before the assignee's right is terminated he obtains

    (a) payment or satisfaction of the obligation, or

    (b) judgment against the obligor, or

(c) a new contract of the obligor by novation.

(4) A gratuitous assignment is irrevocable to the extent necessary to avoid injustice where the assignor should reasonably expect the assignment to induce action or forbearance by the assignee or a subassignee and the assignment does induce such action or forbearance.

(5) An assignment is gratuitous unless it is given or taken

(a) in exchange for a performance or return promise that would be consideration for a promise; or

(b) as security for or in total or partial satisfaction of a pre-existing debt or other obligation.

Comment

a. Historical note. Before the assignment of a contractual right was recognized as effective by common-law courts, an assignment was treated as a power of attorney. Exercise of the power to create a new legal right in the assignee was recognized as effective by the common-law courts in the seventeenth century. But in the event of revocation by the assignor before the power was exercised, the assignee's right was enforceable only by a court of equity. See the Introductory Note to this Chapter. A power of attorney requires no consideration, but the maxim that equity will not aid a volunteer precluded relief to a gratuitous assignee in the event of revocation before the power was exercised. In modern times an assignment is recognized as an effective conveyance without regard to the distinction between law and equity. But a gratuitous conveyance remains revocable unless the formal requisites of a valid gift are met. The owner of a contractual right, like the owner of a chattel, can effectively and irrevocably declare himself trustee of it without consideration or formality, but an attempted informal gift which is ineffective does not create a trust. See Restatement, Second, Trusts §§ 28, 31. In certain cases, however, where the donor has died believing he has made an effective gratuitous conveyance to a natural object of his bounty, a constructive trust for the intended donee may arise. See Restatement of Restitution § 164.

b. Formal requisites of gift; written assignment. Historically, a gift of a chattel could be made either by delivery of the chattel or by delivery of a deed of gift under seal. This rule has been extended by analogy to gifts of intangible personal property, including contractual rights. As the seal has come to seem archaic, the delivery of a signed written assignment has by statute or decision been given the same effect. The assignment may be delivered either conditionally or unconditionally, and either to the donee or to a third person on his behalf. Compare §§ 101–103. The writing must of course fully manifest an intention to make a present transfer rather than to promise or authorize a future transfer. Compare §§ 325, 330. As to investment securities, Uniform Commercial Code § 8–309 requires delivery of a certificated security, and an attempted transfer without delivery amounts only to a promise to transfer.

Illustrations

1. B owes A four million dollars. A signs, seals and delivers to C a deed of gift of the debt to the extent of one million dollars. There is an effective and irrevocable assignment.

2. B owes A $70,000 represented by a promissory note payable to the order of A in installments. A signs and delivers to C, his sister, a written instrument not under seal reciting that in consideration of love and affection for C A gives and assigns to C fifty per cent of the note, reserving all installments due or paid during A's life. The note is retained in A's possession. The gift is effective and irrevocable.

3. A has a savings account in the B bank which is represented by a passbook. While in the hospital and about to undergo a serious operation, A signs the following note and gives it to a nurse for her husband C: "Dear Papa, the bank book is in my letter box in the kitchen. It is yours. Look out for yourself. My will is in the lawyer's office. Your loving wife." A dies before C takes possession of the passbook. There is no effective gift.

c. Delivery of a symbolic writing. In the regular course of business certain writings are treated as adequately evidencing that a person in possession of the writing is entitled to receive performance and to dispose of the right and its proceeds. See Uniform Commercial Code § 1–201(15), defining "document of title," § 3–104, defining certain types of negotiable instrument, § 8–102, defining "security," § 9–105(1)(b), defining "chattel paper." In some circumstances the right to performance is conditional on exhibition or surrender of such a writing. See Uniform Commercial Code § 3–505 (negotiable instrument), § 5–116 (letter of credit), § 7–403(3) (negotiable document of title), § 8–401 (certificated security). A gift of a right embodied in such a writing may be made by delivery in accordance with rules governing gifts of chattels by delivery.

Illustration

4. A gratuitously delivers to B a savings bank book, a non-negotiable promissory note, a life insurance policy and a registered bond with the expressed intent of making B the owner of the rights of which these documents are evidence. The delivery operates as an effective and irrevocable assignment of both the rights and the documents.

d. Delivery of an evidentiary writing. Even though a right is not conditional on exhibition or surrender of a document, it may be so integrated in a writing that contradictory terms of prior agreements and contemporaneous oral agreements are superseded. See §§ 213, 216; Uniform Commercial Code § 2–202. The "best evidence" or original document rule, permitting secondary evidence to prove the contents of a writing only when an explanation is given for nonproduction of the original, has been largely eviscerated by modern evidence practice. See, e.g., Fed. R. Evidence 1001–04. Even though the traditional rule does not apply, an evidentiary writing may be of such importance in the enforcement of the right that its delivery is an appropriate formality to validate a gift of the right. Accordingly, the rule validating a gift by delivery of an essential instrument has been extended to some evidentiary writings. The test is whether the writing is of a type customarily accepted as evidence of the right.

Illustrations

5. A makes a written contract with B to convey land to B for $25,000. Later A gratuitously delivers to C the written contract, signed by B, with the expressed intent of making C the owner of the right to the purchase money. The gift is effective and irrevocable.

6. A deposits a draft with B bank for collection and is given a receipt signed by B which describes the draft and recites that it is "received from A for collection." A writes on the receipt, "Pay this to C," signs his name, and delivers the receipt to C with the expressed intent of making a gift to C of the proceeds of the draft. The gift is effective and irrevocable.

7. A has a checking account in B bank and delivers the bank pass book to C with the expressed intent of making a gift to C of the balance in the account. The gift is revocable in view of the customary practice of making withdrawals without notation in the pass book, even though A has in fact made no such withdrawals.

8. A deposits various sums of money with B, and keeps a list of the amounts on a sheet of paper. A delivers the list, bearing a total and a date but no signature or other writing, to C with the expressed intent of making a gift to C of the amount due. The gift is revocable.

e. What constitutes delivery. Where a gift of a contractual right by delivery of a symbolic or evidentiary writing is in issue, the concept of delivery is the same as that employed with respect to gifts of tangible personal property. Delivery may be made either conditionally or unconditionally, and either to the donee or to a third person on his behalf. Compare §§ 101–03. A writing in the possession of a third person may be delivered by means of a symbolic or evidentiary writing or by means of a token or symbol such as a key to a safe deposit box. Or the third person may agree to hold on behalf of the donee. A gift of a writing already in the possession of the donee for another purpose may be made by mere oral manifestation of intention. Redelivery to the donor for safekeeping does not defeat the delivery. Where a different rule is applied to gifts of chattels, it is applied equally to gifts of contractual rights by delivery: thus if it is held that a gift causa mortis by mere spoken words is ineffective in the case of a chattel in the donee's possession, the same rule is applied to a gift of a contractual writing.

f. Effect of acts subsequent to assignment. A gratuitous assignment, even though revocable, may authorize the assignee to take action which will complete the gift. If, pursuant to the authority given, the assignee obtains performance or other satisfaction from the obligor or a judgment against the obligor or a new contract by novation, the assignor's power of revocation terminates and the assignee may keep for his own benefit what he has acquired. Whatever he obtains after revocation can be recovered from him by the assignor. Revocation is also precluded to the extent that it would be unjust in view of a material change of position in reliance on the assignment. Compare § 90.

Illustration

9. A draws a check on his account in B bank payable to the order of C and delivers it to C with the expressed intent of making a gift to C of part of the account. C negotiates the check to D for value, or obtains payment from B. Meanwhile A dies. C can retain what he received before the death, but A's personal representative can recover what C received thereafter.

g. Effect of bankruptcy. Under § 541 of the Bankruptcy Reform Act of 1978, 11 U.S.C. § 541 (1978), the commencement of a case under the Act creates an estate, which includes with certain inapplicable exceptions all legal or equitable interests of the debtor in property as of the commencement of the case. Hence if a gratuitous assignment is revocable by an assignor at the time when he becomes bankrupt, his trustee in bankruptcy may exercise the power of revocation. Even if the assignment is otherwise irrevocable, the trustee in bankruptcy has the right of any creditor to set it aside if the assignor is insolvent or is rendered insolvent or if it is made with actual intent to hinder, delay, or defraud creditors. See Uniform Fraudulent Conveyance Act §§ 4, 7; Bankruptcy Reform Act of 1978, 11 U.S.C. § 548 (1978).

h. Gratuitous assignment. Whether an assignment is gratuitous for the purposes of the rules stated in this Section is not necessarily the same question as whether the assignment is for value so as to constitute the assignee a bona fide purchaser for value within such rules as that stated in § 342. See Comment c to § 338. For example, where an assignment is made in exchange for a return promise which would be consideration under the rule stated in § 75, the assignment is not gratuitous, whether or not the promise is value under the rules stated in Restatement, Second, Trusts § 302. A new loan or other obligation is consideration for this purpose if bargained for and given in exchange for the assignment. Moreover, an assignment as security for or in total or partial satisfaction of a pre-existing obligation is not gratuitous, whether or not there is consideration under § 73 or value under Restatement, Second, Trusts § 304 and Restatement of Restitution § 173. Such an assignment is not gratuitous even if the pre-existing obligation is unenforceable, to the extent that in the circumstances a promise to pay the obligation would be binding under §§ 82–85.

§ 333. Warranties of an Assignor.

(1) Unless a contrary intention is manifested, one who assigns or purports to assign a right by assignment under seal or for value warrants to the assignee

(a) that he will do nothing to defeat or impair the value of the assignment and has no knowledge of any fact which would do so;

(b) that the right, as assigned, actually exists and is subject to no limitations or defenses good against the assignor other than those stated or apparent at the time of the assignment;

(c) that any writing evidencing the right which is delivered to the assignee or exhibited to him to induce him to accept the assignment is genuine and what it purports to be.

(2) An assignment does not of itself operate as a warranty that the obligor is solvent or that he will perform his obligation.

(3) An assignor is bound by affirmations and promises to the assignee with reference to the right assigned in the same way and to the same extent that one who transfers goods is bound in like circumstances.

(4) An assignment of a right to a subassignee does not operate as an assignment of the assignee's rights under his assignor's warranties unless an intention is manifested to assign the rights under the warranties.

Comment

a. Implied warranties. The warranties of an assignor of a contractual right arise by operation by law and are similar to those of one who transfers a negotiable instrument without indorsement or who transfers a document of title or investment security. See Uniform Commercial Code §§ 3–417, 7–507, 8–306. Unlike an indorser of commercial paper or a collecting bank or its customer, an assignor is not liable for defaults of the obligor and does not warrant his solvency. Compare Uniform Commercial Code §§ 3–414, 4–207 with § 7–505 (document of title), § 8–308(9) (certificated investment security). An assignor does warrant his lack of knowledge of facts and his future abstention from conduct which would impair the value of the assigned right.

Illustrations

1. A has a right against B and assigns it for value to C. Thereafter A gives B a release. C can recover damages from A for any harm this causes C. The amount of harm may be greater if B is released for value before he receives notification of the assignment than if B remains liable to C.

2. A has a right against B, performance of which B has repudiated without excuse. A assigns his right to C for value without disclosing B's repudiation. C can recover from A damages for any harm the repudiation causes C.

3. A reasonably and in good faith believes he has a right against B, and assigns it to C for value as an actual right. In fact the right does not exist. C can recover damages from A.

b. *Express warranties and disclaimers.* The rules stated in this Section can be varied by express or implied agreement. Express warranties are created in the same ways as express warranties in the transfer of goods, and implied warranties may be excluded or modified in the same ways. See Uniform Commercial Code §§ 2–312, 2–313, 2–316, 2–317. The words "without recourse" may be ambiguous in this context: ordinarily they are used to disclaim the liability of an indorser but do not eliminate implied warranties. See Uniform Commercial Code §§ 3–414, 3–417(3).

Illustration

4. A believes that there is only a slight possibility that he may have a right against B. A assigns to C for value "Any claim or right" which he may have against B without disclosing how seriously he doubts the validity of the claim. A is under no duty to C if the claim is invalid.

c. *Warranty to a sub-assignee.* A sub-assignee may be an intended beneficiary of an assignor's warranty to an intermediate assignee, or the intermediate assignee may assign to the sub-assignee a claim for breach of warranty. But unless such an intention is manifested, the warranties of an assignor run only to his assignee, and are not transferred by a sub-assignment. Compare Uniform Commercial Code §§ 2–318, 2–607(5), 3–803.

I When a warranty of an assignor is broken, the assignee is entitled to the usual remedies for breach of contract. He can recover damages not only for harm caused but also for the amount by which he would have been benefited if the assigned right had been as warranted. But if the assigned right would have been worthless aside from the breach of warranty, there are no damages. The assignor is also subject to liability, at the assignee's election, for the value of anything received by him from the assignee on account of the assignment, or for any amount wrongfully collected from the obligor. In an appropriate case such equitable remedies as injunction and constructive trust are also available.

TOPIC 4. EFFECT ON THE OBLIGOR'S DUTY

§ 334. Variation of Obligor's Duty by Assignment.

(1) If the obligor's duty is conditional on the personal cooperation of the original obligee or another person, an assignee's right is subject to the same condition.

(2) If the obligor's duty is conditional on cooperation which the obligee could properly delegate to an agent, the condition may occur if there is similar cooperation by an assignee.

Comment

a. *Scope.* This Section relates to the consequences of assignment of a right, stating corollaries of the statement in § 317 that a right cannot be assigned if the effect would be to change materially the duty of the obligor. Delegation of the performance of a duty or requirement of a condition is the subject of §§ 318 and 319. Those Sections apply the same principles applied by this Section to determine when the obligor's duty is conditional on the obligee's personal cooperation and when the obligee could properly delegate cooperation to an agent. See also Restatement, Second, Agency § 17.

b. Terms of assignment. Whether there is a material change in the obligor's duty depends not only on the terms of the contract creating the duty and on the circumstances, but also on the terms of the assignment. Commonly an assignment manifests an intention that the obligor render performance to the assignee rather than to the assignor. Such a change is immaterial in the usual case of a duty to pay money, but material where personal cooperation is made a condition of the duty. Even in the latter case, however, it is at least theoretically possible to assign the right without departing from the requirement.

Illustrations

1. B contracts to sell A specified goods for a stated price. A effectively assigns his right to C. On tender of the agreed price, C has a right to take delivery of the goods at the agreed time and place.

2. B contracts to sell and deliver 100 gallons of fuel oil to A at A's house. C lives next door to A and has equal facility for receiving delivery of oil. A assigns his right under the contract to C and directs B to deliver the oil at C's house. B is under a duty to do so. The change in the required performance is too slight to give B a valid objection.

3. B contracts with A to furnish A's family with all the oil it shall need for the ensuing year at a fixed price. A assigns his rights under the contract to C. C can acquire no right against B that C's family shall be supplied with oil, but may acquire a right that A's family shall be supplied, if such is the intention of the parties.

4. B contracts with A to serve A as a valet. A, for value, assigns his rights under the contract to C. C acquires no right to have B act as valet to C. If the assignment manifests an intent to give C a right to have B act as valet to A, C acquires such a right.

c. Conditions of cooperation. This Section refers to conditions of cooperation, and does not apply to performances which do not involve the cooperation of anyone, such as going to Rome, forbearing from suit, or refraining from competition. Performances involving the cooperation of third persons, such as paying money to, selling to, buying from, or working for a third person, may bring into play the same principles as conditions of cooperation by the obligee. Contracts to pay money to the obligee or to sell to or buy from him seldom require his personal cooperation, but may do so. Typically, Subsection (1) applies to contracts to serve under the personal direction of the obligee or to give personal direction to his work.

Illustrations

5. B, a silver mining company, contracts with A, a smelting company, to deliver B's ore to A for smelting. A contracts to smelt the ore and to deliver the metal thereby obtained to B, receiving an agreed price for the work. A's right to receive the ore is assigned for value by him to C. A remains financially responsible but ceases to operate a smelter. The assignment is ineffective. The contract to deliver valuable ore to the assignor involves a degree of personal confidence which precludes the substitution of an assignee to receive the ore. C, therefore, has no right to have the ore delivered to himself, and as A has ceased to carry on the smelting business, C has no right to require B to deliver the ore to A.

6. B contracts to sell to A, an ice cream manufacturer, the amount of ice A may need in his business for the ensuing three years, to the extent of not more than 250 tons a week, at a stated price a ton. A makes a corresponding promise to B to buy such an amount of ice. A sells his ice cream plant to C and assigns to C all A's rights under the contract with B. Whether the assignment is effective depends on the terms of the contract between A and B and on the likelihood that C's requirements will be different from A's. If the contract is read as a contract to furnish such ice as the plant requires, B is bound to furnish C ice up to the agreed maximum even though C requires more or less ice than B would have required.

7. B contracts to build a wall on A's land at a place to be selected by A personally. A sells the land and assigns his rights under the contract to C and joins C in selecting the place. B is bound to build the wall.

§ 335. Assignment by a Joint Obligee.

A joint obligee may effectively assign his right, but the assignee can enforce it only in the same manner and to the same extent as the assignor could have enforced it.

Comment

a. The extent to which the rights of obligees of the same performance are joint depends on the intention manifested and on the extent to which their interests in the performance or in the remedies for breach are distinct. See § 297(2). In an action based on a joint right, the obligor can require joinder of all surviving joint obligees, but any joint obligee may sue in the name of all. See § 298. This power to enforce the joint right, the related power to discharge the obligor, and any right to receive and retain the proceeds as against the co-obligees are assignable, subject to limitations imposed by the relationship of the obligees. See §§ 299–301.

§ 336. Defenses Against an Assignee.

(1) By an assignment the assignee acquires a right against the obligor only to the extent that the obligor is under a duty to the assignor; and if the right of the assignor would be voidable by the obligor or unenforceable against him if no assignment had been made, the right of the assignee is subject to the infirmity.

(2) The right of an assignee is subject to any defense or claim of the obligor which accrues before the obligor receives notification of the assignment, but not to defenses or claims which accrue thereafter except as stated in this Section or as provided by statute.

(3) Where the right of an assignor is subject to discharge or modification in whole or in party by impracticability, public policy, non-occurrence of a condition, or present or prospective failure of performance by an obligee, the right of the assignee is to that extent subject to discharge or modification even after the obligor receives notification of the assignment.

(4) An assignee's right against the obligor is subject to any defense or claim arising from his conduct or to which he was subject as a party or a prior assignee because he had notice.

Comment

a. Negotiable instruments and documents. The rules stated in this Section do not apply to the negotiation or transfer of a negotiable instrument or document. See § 316. The Uniform Commercial Code provides for the rights of a holder in due course of a negotiable instrument, a holder to whom a negotiable document has been duly negotiated and a purchaser for value who has taken an investment security without notice of a particular defense. Such a holder or purchaser takes free of many defenses of the obligor. See §§ 3–305, 7–502, 8–202. Compare Comment f. Where those provisions do not apply, transfer of a negotiable instrument or document vests in the transferee the rights which the transferor had or had authority to convey. See §§ 3–201, 3–306, 7–504, 8–301.

b. Accrued defenses. Unlike the negotiation of a negotiable instrument, the assignment of a non-negotiable contractual right ordinarily transfers what the assignor has but only what he has. The assignee's right depends on the validity and enforceability of the contract creating the right, and is subject to limitations imposed by the terms of that contract and to defenses which would have been available against the obligee had there been no assignment. Until the obligor receives notification of an assignment, he is entitled to treat the obligee as owner of the right, and the assignee's right is subject to defenses and claims arising from dealings between assignor and obligor in relation to the contract before notification. See § 338.

Illustrations

1. A holds B's unsealed written promise, unenforceable because given without consideration. A assigns this to C, who pays value on the faith of the writing, with reasonable belief that A had given B consideration and that the promise is legally binding. C has no right against B.

2. A has a right against B voidable because created when B was an infant. A assigns his right to C, who is ignorant of the facts making the right voidable. C's right against B is voidable.

3. A lends money to B and assigns his right to C. C's right is barred by the Statute of Limitations when A's right would have been.

4. A, who is not C's agent, fraudulently induces B to buy lumber from C. C does not know of the fraud and acts in good faith. C later assigns his rights under the contract to D, who knows of the fraud but was not a party to it. B cannot avoid the contract against D.

c. Accrued claims. Statutes or rules of court commonly permit an obligor when sued to assert by way of set-off or counterclaim in the same action such claims as he has against the plaintiff, whether related to the plaintiff's claim or not. See, e.g., Rule 13 of the Federal Rules of Civil Procedure. In appropriate circumstances the obligor may use defensively against an assignee an offsetting claim against the assignor, although the assignee is not subject to affirmative liability on such a claim unless he contracts to assume such liability. See § 328; Uniform Commercial Code §§ 2–210, 9–317. Courts of equity exercised jurisdiction in set-off at an early date, but set-off in actions at law stems from an English statute enacted in 1729 and applicable to "mutual debts"; counterclaim statutes first appeared in the nineteenth century. Set-off against an assignee has sometimes been limited to cases where both offsetting claims were fully matured at the time of assignment. The modern rule, however, unless a statute provides otherwise, turns on the time the obligor receives notification of assignment and applies even though the assigned right has not then matured. See Uniform Commercial Code § 9–318.

Illustration

5. A lends money to B, who regularly sells goods to A on credit and expects to repay the loan by making such sales. A assigns his right to C. Thereafter B sells goods to A as expected, and the price becomes due before B receives notification of the assignment. Unless a statute provides otherwise, B can set off his claim for the price in an action by C as assignee.

d. Defenses and claims accruing after notification. After receiving notification of an assignment, an obligor must treat the assignee as owner of the right and cannot assert against him a defense or claim arising out of a subsequent transaction except as stated in § 338. Moreover, the obligor cannot under the usual statute or rule of court set off an unrelated claim which matures after notification is received. Section 553 of the Bankruptcy Reform Act of 1978, 11 U.S.C. § 553 (1978), provides for the set-off of unmatured claims. The extent to which a similar rule is applicable to assignment for the benefit of creditors or to other insolvency proceedings is often affected by statute and is beyond the scope of this Restatement. Notification, however, does not enlarge the obligor's duty, and the possibility remains that the assigned right will become subject to a defense or to a claim by way of recoupment. The assignee's right is subject to such a defense or claim if it arises from the terms of the contract between the assignor and the obligor. See Uniform Commercial Code § 9–318.

Illustrations

6. A contracts to market goods for B in return for payment to be made by B. A then assigns his right to payment to C, and B receives notification of the assignment. Subsequently A becomes insolvent and wholly fails to perform the contract. B has a defense against C.

7. A contracts to build a structure for B, and becomes entitled to progress payments. A assigns the money due to C, and B receives notification of the assignment. Thereafter, in breach of his contract, A abandons the work. In an action by C against B, B is entitled to recoup damages caused by A's breach.

e. Claims against a prior assignee. The rules stated in this Section apply to a sub-assignee. Just as an assignee is subject to defenses and claims accruing before the obligor receives notification, so a sub-assignee is subject to defenses and claims accruing between assignee and obligor before the obligor receives notification of a sub-assignment. Defenses and claims arising from the terms of the contract creating the right are available to the obligor regardless of when they accrue.

Illustration

8. B owes A $100. A assigns the right to C, and C assigns it to D. C owes B $50. Unless a statute provides otherwise, B can set off against D the debt owed by C only if it becomes due before B receives notification of the assignment by C.

f. Agreement not to assert defenses. The obligor may undertake a greater obligation to an assignee than to the assignor by direct contract with the assignee, and may confer on the assignor an agency power to bind him to such an agreement. Section 9–206 of the Uniform Commercial Code gives effect to an agreement by a buyer or lessee that he will not assert against an assignee any claim or defense which he may have against the seller or lessor, making it enforceable by a good faith assignee for value without notice of a claim or defense, except as to defenses of a type which may be asserted against a holder in due course of a negotiable instrument. The Assignment of Claims Act of 1940, 31 U.S.C. § 203 (1979), contains a more limited authorization for a no-setoff agreement by the United States. The Code provision is subject to any statute or decision which establishes a different rule for buyers or lessees of consumer goods, and a number of retail installment sales acts limit the power of a buyer to make such an agreement. In addition, the Federal Trade Commission has issued a Trade Regulation Rule barring such agreements with respect to consumers. See 16 C.F.R. §§ 433.1–.3 (1975). In the absence of statute, administrative rule or court decision, such an agreement can take effect to give the assignee greater rights than the assignor as to matters governed by the terms of the contract; but if the agreement not to assert defenses or claims is itself voidable or unenforceable, the assignee takes subject to the defect.

Illustrations

9. B, doing business under the name A, executes a purported contract with A reciting the delivery of goods by A to B and B's promise to pay A for them. B then executes on behalf of A an assignment to C of A's rights under the contract and delivers it to C for consideration. Whether or not C knows the facts, B's purported promise is binding in favor of C.

10. A sells and delivers goods to B, and B agrees that in the event of an assignment to C, B will pay the price to C without asserting any defense or claim based on breach of warranty by A. A assigns his rights under the contract to C, who takes in good faith and without notice of any defense or claim. In the absence of statute or administrative rule, B is barred from asserting against C a defense or claim based on breach of warranty by A.

11. A contracts to sell goods to B, and B agrees that in the event of an assignment to C B will pay the price to C without asserting any defense or claim that B has against A. A assigns his rights under the contract to C and absconds without delivering any goods to B. In the absence of statute, administrative rule or of facts giving rise to an estoppel, B has a defense against C.

g. Estoppel. Even though an obligor's agreement not to assert a defense or claim is not binding or is voidable or unenforceable, he may be estopped to assert the claim or defense against an assignee. Where he makes a representation of fact with the intention of inducing an assignee or prospective assignee to act in reliance on the representation, and an assignee does so act, the doctrine of estoppel bars the obligor from contradicting the representation in litigation against the assignee if contradiction would be inequitable. Compare § 90. Application of the doctrine depends on all the circumstances. The representation may be express or it may be implied from conduct, in unusual cases even from failure to act. In some circumstances estoppel may rest on the obligor's reason to know that the assignee may rely, even though there is no intention to induce reliance.

Illustrations

12. A contracts to do construction work for B, a subcontractor, and becomes entitled to progress payments. A assigns the progress payments to C, who advances money to A in reliance on B's assertion to C that the work has been done and that the payments will be made when received from the general contractor. In an action by C for the payments, B is estopped to offset B's claim against A for A's defaults subsequent to the assignment.

13. A contracts to sell furniture to B for a price payable in installments. A assigns his rights under the contract to C, who buys the rights and pays for them in reliance on B's written statement addressed to C that the furniture has been received and accepted by B. In an action by C for the balance due on the price, B is estopped to assert that no furniture had been received. But there is no such estoppel if at the time of the assignment C has reason to know that A has made a practice of obtaining false statements of receipt and acceptance.

14. In May A contracts to deliver described goods to B on credit in October. In June A assigns his rights and delegates his duties under the contract to C. With knowledge of the assignment B accepts the goods from C in October, making no claim of an offset. B is estopped to assert against C claims for prior defective deliveries by A.

h. Conduct of the assignee. The conduct of the assignee or his agents may, like that of any obligee, give rise to defenses and claims which may be asserted against him by the obligor. An obligee who is subject to such a defense or claim cannot improve his position by assigning the right to an assignee who is not subject to the defense or claim and then taking a reassignment. Compare Uniform Commercial Code § 3–201.

Illustration

15. A is fraudulently induced by B, the agent of C, to sell goods to C. C assigns his rights to D, who pays value in good faith and without notice. D assigns to E, who knows of the fraud. A cannot avoid the contract as against E, who succeeded to D's rights. But if E assigns to C, A's power of avoidance will revive.

§ 337. Elimination of Defenses by Subsequent Events.

Where the right of an assignor is limited or voidable or unenforceable or subject to discharge or modification, subsequent events which would eliminate the limitation or defense have the same effect on the right of the assignee.

Comment

a. Rationale. The rule of this Section is the converse of the rules stated in § 336. An assignment ordinarily transfers only what the assignor has, but limitations and defenses are not enlarged by the transfer. If a condition of the obligor's duty is met or excused, for example, the condition ceases to limit the assignee's right just as it would have ceased to limit the right of the assignor in the absence of assignment.

Illustrations

1. A has a right against B, voidable for A's fraud. A assigns the right to C. Thereafter B learns of the fraud but does not within a reasonable time notify either A or C of his intention to avoid the transaction. Whether or not B knows of the assignment, C's right ceases to be voidable.

2. A has a right against B, unenforceable because of noncompliance with the Statute of Frauds. A assigns the right to C. Thereafter B makes a memorandum sufficient to satisfy the Statute. Whether or not B knows of the assignment, C's right is enforceable.

b. New promises. The rule of this Section does not apply to new transactions between the obligor and the assignor after the obligor has received notification of the assignment. See § 338. Moreover, the effect of a new promise by the obligor of a kind referred to in §§ 82–85 is governed by those Sections. A new promise of such a kind, made to the assignor, is binding only if the assignor is then an obligee of the antecedent duty or is acting as agent for the assignee. See § 92.

Illustration

3. A is the payee of B's negotiable note for $200. A indorses and delivers the note to C. After maturity, without knowledge of C's rights, B pays A $50 on account of the note. The part payment is not effective to extend the period of the statute of limitations in favor of C. If the part payment were made before assignment, the period would be so extended.

§ 338. Discharge of an Obligor After Assignment.

(1) Except as stated in this Section, notwithstanding an assignment, the assignor retains his power to discharge or modify the duty of the obligor to the extent that the obligor performs or otherwise gives value until but not after the obligor receives notification that the right has been assigned and that performance is to be rendered to the assignee.

(2) So far as an assigned right is conditional on the performance of a return promise, and notwithstanding notification of the assignment, any modification of or substitution for the contract made by the assignor and obligor in good faith and in accordance with reasonable commercial standards is effective against the assignee. The assignee acquires corresponding rights under the modified or substituted contract.

(3) Notwithstanding a defect in the right of an assignee, he has the same power his assignor had to discharge or modify the duty of the obligor to the extent that the obligor gives value or otherwise changes his position in good faith and without knowledge or reason to know of the defect.

(4) Where there is a writing of a type customarily accepted as a symbol or as evidence of the right assigned, a discharge or modification is not effective

(a) against the owner or an assignor having a power of avoidance, unless given by him or by a person in possession of the writing with his consent and any necessary indorsement or assignment;

(b) against a subsequent assignee who takes possession of the writing and gives value in good faith and without knowledge or reason to know of the discharge or modification.

Comment

a. Discharge by true obligee. Rules governing the discharge of a contractual right by one who is actually the owner of the right are stated in Chapter 12. Such a discharge is effective against the obligee who gives it, whether he is the original promisee, a beneficiary, or an assignee, and against any person who has no greater rights. Under § 336 a subsequent assignee is ordinarily such a person; but the law governing negotiable instruments and documents in some circumstances gives to a bona fide holder a greater right than his transferor had. See Uniform Commercial Code §§ 3–305, 7–502, 8–202. Estoppel and related doctrines have a similar effect. See Subsection (4)(b); § 336 Comments f, g; Uniform Commercial Code § 9–206.

Illustration

1. B owes A $100. A assigns the right to C. C gives B a gratuitous release under seal and subsequently assigns the right to D for value. D acquires no right against B.

b. Discharge by apparent obligee. This Section covers discharge by one who reasonably seems to the obligor to own the right, though in fact he does not. The obligor is ordinarily protected in such a case of a discharge wrongfully given, but only if he renders performance or otherwise gives value or changes his position in good faith and without knowledge or reason to know that the appearance is false.

Illustrations

2. B owes A $100. A assigns the right to C. C assigns it to D, and D assigns it to E. Before receiving notification of the assignment to E, B pays D. B is discharged.

3. B owes A $100. A assigns the right for value to C and subsequently by way of oral gift to D. Before receiving notification of the assignment to C, B pays D. B is discharged.

c. Value; antecedent debt. The rules as to what constitutes value in this Chapter are the same as the rules stated in §§ 298–309 of the Restatement, Second, of Trusts, except as stated in § 173 of the Restatement of Restitution and except as modified by statute. See also Restatement of Security § 10 Comment e. The exception, which conforms to the provisions of Uniform Commercial Code §§ 1–201(44) and 3–303 and earlier uniform acts, is that a transfer of property other than land in satisfaction of or as security for a preexisting debt or other obligation is a transfer for value. Compare § 332.

d. Promise as value. Restatement, Second, Trusts § 302 and Restatement of Restitution § 173 state that a transfer of property in consideration of a promise to make payment in the future is not a transfer for value unless the transferee would be liable upon his promise even if he were compelled to surrender the property, or unless he has so changed his position that it would be inequitable to compel him to surrender the property. Uniform Commercial Code § 3–303 embodies a similar rule for some transactions in negotiable instruments. But for other transactions Uniform Commercial Code § 1–201(44) provides that value is given for rights acquired "in return for a binding commitment to extend credit or for the extension of immediately available credit whether or not drawn upon and whether or not a chargeback is provided for in the event of difficulties in collection"; or "generally, in return for any consideration sufficient to support a simple contract." Compare §§ 4–208 and 4–209 on bank collections. Under those provisions an executory promise is value for the purposes of bona fide purchase of goods, negotiable documents, or investment securities from a person with voidable title. Uniform Commercial Code §§ 2–403(1), 7–501(4), 7–502, 8–301, 8–302. The extent to which by analogy this statutory rule may be applicable to purchases of contractual rights not subject to the statutory provisions is beyond the scope of this Restatement.

e. Receipt of notification. Subsection (1), like § 336, follows Uniform Commercial Code § 9–318 in stating that the assignor's power to discharge terminates when the obligor "receives notification." This phrase is used with the meaning prescribed by Uniform Commercial Code § 1–201(26): a person receives a notification when it comes to his attention or is duly delivered at a place held out by him as the place for receipt of such communications. No particular formality is required, but under § 9–318 the notification must reasonably identify the rights assigned, and if the assignee fails upon request to furnish reasonable proof an account debtor may pay the assignor. For the greater protection given to banks of deposit, see § 339 Comment c. Receipt of notification does not include all facts which would give "reason to know." See Restatement, Second, Agency §§ 9, 268.

Illustration

4. A assigns to C a debt owed by B. Pursuant to Uniform Commercial Code §§ 9–401 and 9–402, C files a financing statement describing the collateral as "debt owed by B." Without knowledge of the filing and without any other reason to know of the assignment, B pays A. B is discharged.

f. Modification of executory contract. Subsection (2) follows Uniform Commercial Code § 9–318 in stating that so far as a contract is executory the assignor and obligor retain power to make good faith modifications without the assignee's consent even after notification. The assignee is protected by automatic corresponding rights in the modified or substituted contract. As in the case of a discharge by the assignor before notification, exercise of the power may be a breach of the contract of assignment. See § 333. Contrary agreement between obligor and assignee is effective.

Illustrations

5. A contracts to do construction work for B, and assigns to C the payments to become due. C notifies B of the assignment. A becomes financially unable to perform, and B makes advance payments to A which are necessary to enable A to perform. B is liable to C only for the balance due after deducting the amount of the advances.

6. A Company contracts to supply electricity to B for twenty years. Later A assigns to C for value certain fixed monthly payments to be made by B under the contract. After ten years B ceases to require electricity and A and B agree in good faith to terminate all performance under the contract. B is not liable to C for payments which would have accrued thereafter.

g. Revocable or voidable assignment. Where an assignment is revocable because gratuitous or is voidable because of infancy, insanity, fraud, duress, mistake, or public policy, the assignee nevertheless has power to discharge or modify the duty of an obligor who pays value in good faith and without notice. In the case of a revocable gratuitous assignment, the obligor may assume until he has reason to know otherwise that the assignor desires him to complete the gift by performance or novation. See § 332. But if the obligor has reason to know that a revocable assignment has been revoked or that the assignment is voidable by the assignor, he cannot safely perform. If the facts or law are in dispute in such a case, or if the assignor has not yet exercised a power to avoid, the obligor is entitled to protection by interpleader or like remedy. See § 339. Where an assignor's right is voidable by or held in trust for a third person, an assignee may or may not take subject to the defect. See § 343. If he is subject to it, the same principles apply as in a case of voidable assignment.

Illustrations

7. B owes A $100. A makes a revocable gratuitous assignment to C, and subsequently makes a similar assignment to D. B with knowledge of the facts pays C. B is not discharged. The assignment to D gives B reason to know that A intends to revoke the assignment to C.

8. B owes A $100. A is induced by C's fraud to assign the right to C. B in good faith and without notice of the fraud enters into a novation with C in satisfaction of the debt. B's duty under the original contract is discharged. But if C holds a substituted right under the novation in constructive trust for A, performance by B with reason to know the facts does not discharge his duty to A.

9. A, as trustee for X, has a right against B. A, in violation of his trust, assigns his right to C gratuitously. B pays C with reason to know of A's breach of trust. B's duty to X is not discharged.

h. Symbolic writings. Certain writings are treated in the ordinary course of business as symbols of contractual rights. See Comment c to § 332. Discharge of duties under some such writings is affected by statute. See Uniform Commercial Code §§ 3–601 (commercial paper), 7–403 (document of title), 8–207 (registered investment security). These and other writings are "chattel paper", "documents" or "instruments" under Uniform Commercial Code § 9–105; still others, such as insurance policies are excluded from Article 9 by § 9–104. In either case they are not subject to § 9–318 on assignment of "accounts." See § 9–106.

Aside from statute, an obligor who renders performance without requiring production of such a symbolic writing takes the risk that the person receiving performance does not have possession of the writing either because he has assigned it or because his right is defective. Non-production has the same effect as receipt of notification of assignment or reason to know of a defect in an assignee's right. In addition, the obligor who performs without surrender or cancellation of or appropriate notation on the writing takes the risk of further obligation to an assignee who takes possession of the writing as a bona fide purchaser. The latter rule may be regarded as an application of a broader doctrine of estoppel. See Restatement, Second, Agency §§ 8B, 176.

Illustrations

10. A gives or sells to C a savings bank book on the B bank and delivers the book to C. C gives or sells the book to D, but D allows C to retain or resume possession of it. The B bank pays C in good faith and before receipt of notification of the assignment from C to D. B's debt is discharged.

11. The facts being otherwise as stated in Illustration 10, the B bank pays A in good faith and before notification of any assignment. B's debt is not discharged.

12. The facts being otherwise as stated in Illustration 10, B pays C without surrender or cancellation of or notation in the book. Subsequently C sells and delivers the book to E, a bona fide purchaser for value. B owes the debt to E.

13. B owes A $100. A executes and delivers a written assignment of the debt to C, but a separate written agreement provides that the assignment shall only take effect if C renders a specified service. C does not render the service, but presents the assignment to B, who pays C in good faith. A is estopped to deny the effectiveness of the assignment to support discharge of B, though A may recover the payment from C.

§ 339. Protection of Obligor in Cases of Adverse Claims.

Where a claim adverse to that of an assignee subjects the obligor to a substantial risk beyond that imposed on him by his contract, the obligor will be granted such relief as is equitable in the circumstances.

Comment

a. Rationale. Like the rules stated in §§ 317 and 334, the rule of this Section rests on the basic principle that rights based on agreement are limited by the agreement. An obligor who has contracted to render a performance should not be required to render it twice because of uncertainties of law and fact relating to the person entitled to receive it, or because a person having a power of avoidance has not yet elected whether to exercise it. In most situations the obligor is protected against double liability by the rules permitting him to disregard an assignment until he receives notification of it and to honor it thereafter. See §§ 336, 338. But additional safeguards may be needed when the obligor has received such notification and also has reason to know of an adverse claim.

b. Proof of assignment. Even in the absence of an adverse claim, the obligor may request that the assignee furnish reasonable proof that the assignment has been made. Uniform Commercial Code § 9–318(3) permits an account debtor to pay the assignor in such a case unless the proof is seasonably furnished. Compare § 5–116 (letters of credit). Where the obligation is embodied in a commercial instrument or document, the obligor may without dishonor require its production. See Uniform Commercial Code §§ 3–505 (commercial paper), 5–116 (letters of credit), 7–403(3) (negotiable document of title). If it is lost, security may be required indemnifying the obligor against loss by reason of further claims. See Uniform Commercial Code §§ 3–804 (commercial paper), 7–601 (documents of title), 8–405 (investment securities).

Illustration

1. A assigns to C a debt owed A by B, and C notifies B of the assignment. B requests C to furnish reasonable proof of the assignment, but C fails to do so. After a reasonable time B pays A. B's duty to C is discharged.

c. Bank deposits; commercial instruments. In the absence of statute, a bank of deposit pays at its peril on its depositor's order after it has received a proper notification of an adverse claim. To be safe, the bank must promptly notify its depositor and must hold the deposit for a reasonable time to permit the adverse claimant to bring an action. If no process is served within a reasonable time it may pay its depositor or honor his order. By statute in many states the bank is permitted to continue to honor the depositor's instructions even with knowledge of an adverse claim, unless the adverse claimant supplies indemnity or obtains an injunction. Similar provisions are made by the Uniform Commercial Code for payments to holders of certain commercial instruments. See §§ 3–603 (commercial paper), 5–114(2) (letters of credit), 8–403 (investment securities). Such statutes may expressly or by implication limit the right of the obligor to defend on the basis of the claim of a third person. See Uniform Commercial Code § 3–306(d).

Illustrations

2. A deposits money in the B bank and later assigns the deposit to C. C notifies B of the assignment, but does not serve B with process or supply B with indemnity or deliver to B an instrument of assignment signed by A. After nine days B pays A. In the absence of statute B is discharged from liability to C only if nine days is found to be a reasonable time.

3. A deposits money in the B bank and orally assigns the deposit to C. C applies for an injunction against payment by B to A. A denies making the assignment. The injunction should be granted only if C gives security to protect both A and B.

d. Interpleader and like remedies. The classical remedy for an innocent and neutral stakeholder confronted by conflicting claims was a bill in equity to compel the claimants to interplead. That remedy was subject to a number of technical restrictions, and was ineffective if one or more claimants were not within the jurisdiction of the court. A distinct remedy, the bill in the nature of interpleader, was sometimes available when the obligor had an interest in the dispute between claimants but could establish an independent basis of equity jurisdiction. The extent to which such restrictions and distinctions survive modern procedural reforms is beyond the scope of this Restatement. Under Rule 22 of the Federal Rules of Civil Procedure and 28 U.S.C. §§ 1335, 1397, 2361, for example, interpleader is an appropriate remedy for an obligor confronted by a claim adverse to that of an assignee.

Where no statute like those relating to adverse claims to bank deposits is applicable, the obligor is excused from performance until he has had a reasonable time to ascertain the validity of adverse claims or to compel the claimants to interplead. See Uniform Commercial Code § 7–603 (documents of title). Even though an adverse-claims statute applies, interpleader is appropriate if it is otherwise available, either by way of defense or by original action. The effect of interpleader can also be obtained if an adverse claimant takes over the defense of an action against the obligor in such a way that he is bound by the judgment. See Restatement, Second, Judgments § 39. In many situations an adverse claimant who receives a notification by the obligor thus to take over the defense and who fails to do so is barred by a judgment against the obligor from making further claim against the obligor. See, e.g., Restatement, Second, Judgments § 57. If the situation is such that the adverse claimant cannot be so barred by a judgment against the obligor, the obligor is entitled to equitable protection.

Illustrations

4. A deposits money with B and later makes an irrevocable gratuitous assignment of the deposit to C, who gives notice to B. X notifies B that A held the money as X's agent. If sued by either C or X, B can protect himself by notifying the other to take over the defense. If the other unreasonably refuses to do so, and judgment is rendered against B, the other is barred by the judgment from making further claim against B.

5. The facts being otherwise as stated in Illustration 4, the circumstances are such that the other claimant is not subject to the jurisdiction of the court and cannot be barred by a judgment against B from making further claim against B. Such a judgment will be denied or its enforcement restrained unless the plaintiff gives security to protect B against the outstanding claim.

6. A is drilling a well for B under contract. C notifies B that A has assigned to C his rights under the contract. X, claiming that A is indebted to X, serves B with garnishment process in an action against A. B files an answer alleging the assignment, and promptly notifies A and C of the proceedings. C then sues B in an adjoining state. C's action will be stayed until X's action is determined.

e. Types of adverse claim; voidable assignment. The rule stated in this Section applies to all the cases suggested by §§ 338–43: to disputes between assignee and assignor, between assignee and attaching creditor of the assignor, between successive assignees, and between assignee and a claimant against an assignor. In particular, when the obligor has reason to know that an assignment is voidable by the assignor, he renders performance to the assignee at his peril. See § 338(3). In such a case he may by interpleader or like remedy ascertain whether the assignor desires to exercise his power of avoidance. If the assignor elects to exercise his power the obligor is under no duty to the assignee.

TOPIC 5. PRIORITIES BETWEEN ASSIGNEE AND ADVERSE CLAIMANTS

§ 340. Effect of Assignment on Priority and Security.

(1) An assignee is entitled to priority of payment from the obligor's insolvent estate to the extent that the assignor would have been so entitled in the absence of assignment.

(2) Where an assignor holds collateral as security for the assigned right and does not effectively transfer the collateral to the assignee, the assignor is a constructive trustee of the collateral for the assignee in accordance with the rules stated for pledges in §§ 29–34 of the Restatement of Security.

Comment

a. Priority. The principle that an assignment transfers to the assignee the same right held by the assignor, with its advantages and disadvantages, applies to priority of payment in insolvency proceedings.

Illustration

1. By the Bankruptcy Reform Act of 1978, the wages of employees in certain cases are given priority of payment over most other provable claims. A, an employee of B of the class entitled to priority, effectively assigns his wages to C either before or after B's bankruptcy. C is entitled to priority of payment from B's estate.

b. Security follows the debt. Where a secured claim is assigned, the collateral is ordinarily assigned as well. The obligor then has the same right to redeem from the assignee that he previously had to redeem from the assignor. If the assignor retains the collateral, he has no right to hold it as security for any other claim without the consent of the owner of the collateral. An attempt so to hold it or to dispose of it for the assignor's own benefit is a breach of the assignor's duty to the obligor, and the obligor can offset his damages against the assignee just as he could have against the assignor. See § 336; compare Restatement of Security §§ 20, 24. Such an impairment of the assignee's right is a breach of the assignor's warranty to the assignee. See § 333. To avoid these difficulties and the unjust enrichment of either assignor or obligor, a constructive trust for the assignee is imposed on the collateral.

Illustrations

2. A is entitled to receive $1000 from B, and as security for the right has a certificate for 25 shares of the X railroad, indorsed by B in blank. A effectively assigns his right to C, who is ignorant of the existence of the security. C is entitled to the shares as security.

3. A holds a bond issued by B, secured by collateral held by X as trustee for the benefit of the bondholders. X wrongfully fails to preserve the collateral. Later A sells the bond to C, who does not know of the wrong. When the wrong is discovered, B is insolvent. C is entitled to A's claim against X.

c. Agreements affecting security. A constructive trust arises by operation of law and does not depend on agreement. Even though a transfer of collateral is articulated in the agreement between assignor and assignee, a constructive trust arises to the extent that the transfer by agreement is inoperative. But the constructive trust can be avoided by agreement. If the assignment is a breach of a condition of the assignor's interest in the collateral, that interest is terminated and the beneficial owner of the collateral is the obligor rather than the assignee. An agreement between assignor and assignee or between obligor and assignee that the collateral is not to be transferred has a similar effect. On the other hand, with the obligor's consent the collateral can be held as security for another claim of the assignor. See Restatement of Security § 29.

Illustration

4. The facts being otherwise as stated in Illustration 2, A and C agree that the pledge of shares is not to be transferred to C. B is entitled to return of the shares.

d. Rights of creditors and purchasers. Where an assignor wrongfully exercises dominion over collateral for the assigned right, he and those who succeed only to his rights remain subject to the rights of both the assignee and the obligor. Both his creditors and purchasers of the collateral with notice remain subject both to any constructive trust for an assignee and to the obligor's rights to redeem and to offset his claim for damages. Even a bona fide purchaser of the collateral gets no greater rights than the assignor unless the collateral is negotiable or there is an agreement or estoppel binding the assignee or obligor or both. But where negotiable collateral is duly negotiated by the assignor, the purchaser takes free of the rights of assignee and obligor, and estoppel or agreement may have similar consequences. In such cases the assigned right is subject to the obligor's offsetting claim unless the offset is barred by the law of negotiable instruments or documents or by estoppel or agreement.

Illustrations

5. The facts being otherwise as stated in Illustration 2, A sells and delivers the share certificate to D, a bona fide purchaser. D acquires it free of any adverse claim. Uniform Commercial Code §§ 8–302, 9–309. C's right against B is subject to the offset of B's claim for damages against A for conversion.

6. A has a right to receive $1,000 from B for money lent, secured by a pledge of B's savings bank book on the X bank, with an unconditional written assignment of the bank account to A signed by B. A sells and assigns 25 per cent of the right to C for value, but retains possession of the savings bank book and the assignment by B. Later A sells the savings bank account to D, who takes possession of the book as a bona fide purchaser for value. D's right is prior to C's under § 342, and B is estopped to redeem from D. C's right against B is subject to the offset of B's claim for damages against A.

§ 341. Creditors of an Assignor.

(1) Except as provided by statute, the right of an assignee is superior to a judicial lien subsequently obtained against the property of the assignor, unless the assignment is ineffective or revocable or is voidable by the assignor or by the person obtaining the lien or is in fraud of creditors.

(2) Notwithstanding the superiority of the right of an assignee, an obligor who does not receive notification of the assignment until after he has lost his opportunity to assert the assignment as a defense in the proceeding in which the judicial lien was obtained is discharged from his duty to the assignee to the extent of his satisfaction of the lien.

Comment

a. Priority of assignee. An effective assignment extinguishes the assignor's right without any notification of the obligor. Any proceeds of the assigned right received by the assignor thereafter are held in constructive trust for the assignee. See Restatement of Restitution § 165. A creditor of the assignor who claims the assigned right by garnishment, levy of execution or like process is not a bona fide purchaser, even though he has no notice of the assignment. Unless protected by statute or by estoppel or like doctrine, he is subject to the assignee's right. Compare § 342; see Restatement of Restitution § 173. "Judicial lien," as used in this Section, has the same meaning as it does in the Bankruptcy Reform Act of 1978.

b. Defective assignment. An assignor's trustee in bankruptcy can in general reach all of the assignor's legal or equitable interest in any of his property, including powers that he might have exercised for his own benefit and property transferred by him in fraud of creditors. See Bankruptcy Reform Act of 1978, 11 U.S.C. §§ 541(a), (b), 548 (1978). In addition, a person against whom a transfer is voidable can reach the property transferred. In such cases, therefore, the assignee's right is not superior to that of the lien obtained by garnishment or like process. A revocable gratuitous assignment, for example, does not limit the power of the assignor's creditors to levy on the assigned claim. See § 332.

c. Protection of obligor. An obligor garnished by a creditor of the assignor cannot safely pay even in response to a judgment if he has received notification of the assignment, but he is entitled to protection against double liability by interpleader or like remedy. See § 339. If the garnished obligor has not received notification, the assignee's right against him is discharged to the same extent as the assignor's right would have been in the absence of assignment. See §§ 336, 338.

Such a discharge of the obligor does not necessarily terminate the assignee's rights against the assignor and the garnishing creditor. The assignee is entitled to restitution from the assignor to the extent that the assignor has been unjustly enriched by the discharge of his debt. See Restatement of Restitution § 118. The garnishing creditor takes free of the assignee's right to the extent that he becomes a bona fide purchaser or that the assignee is barred by estoppel, laches, res judicata, or other defense. See Restatement of Restitution §§ 131, 173, 179.

Illustration

1. A has a right against B and assigns it to C for value. X, a creditor of A, serves garnishment process on B in an action against A, and obtains judgment against B before B receives notification of the assignment. A month later, before any payment or satisfaction or issue of execution and within the time specified in local procedural rules, B and C move to reopen the judgment. The motion should be granted, and C is entitled to judgment against B to the exclusion of X.

d. Filing statutes. Creditors are commonly among the beneficiaries of statutes requiring public filing of notices of certain types of transactions. The Uniform Commercial Code makes a general requirement of filing to "perfect" a nonpossessory "security interest" in personal property, including "any sale of accounts or chattel paper." See §§ 9–102, 9–302. An unperfected security interest is subordinate to the rights of "a person who becomes a lien creditor before the security interest is perfected." See § 9–301. Transfers of wage claims, rights under insurance policies or deposit accounts, and various other transactions are excluded from coverage. See § 9–104. With respect to certain international open accounts receivable, § 9–103(3)(c) provides alternatives of the application of the filing law of the American jurisdiction in which the debtor has its executive offices or perfection "by notification to the account debtor." Wage assignment statutes also often provide for public filing or for notification of the obligor or both. See Statutory Note preceding § 316.

§ 342. Successive Assignees From the Same Assignor.

Except as otherwise provided by statute, the right of an assignee is superior to that of a subsequent assignee of the same right from the same assignor, unless

    (a) the first assignment is ineffective or revocable or is voidable by the assignor or by the subsequent assignee; or

    (b) the subsequent assignee in good faith and without knowledge or reason to know of the prior assignment gives value and obtains

(i) payment or satisfaction of the obligation,

(ii) judgment against the obligor,

(iii) a new contract with the obligor by novation, or

(iv) possession of a writing of a type customarily accepted as a symbol or as evidence of the right assigned.

Comment

a. Scope. No attempt is made in this Section to state the effect of statutory changes, which often make priority depend on filing in a public office. In the absence of statute, the rules stated in this Section are applicable to both total and partial assignments and to assignments as security for an obligation as well as to outright sales of contractual rights. If the first assignment is partial, or if the assignor retains a beneficial interest, the subsequent assignee is entitled to any balance after the first assignee has been satisfied.

b. Dearle v. Hall. In England and in a number of states, aside from statute, a different rule has been followed, giving priority to the assignee who first gives notice to the obligor, regardless of the order in which the assignments were made. That rule stems from the leading case of Dearle v. Hall, 3 Russ. 1, 48 (1828), involving successive assignments of the interest of a beneficiary of a trust. The English rule has consequences similar to that of a system of public filing, except that the obligor acts as the filing office; it is somewhat more convenient where a single obligor is involved such as a trustee or the owner or prime contractor on a construction project than in cases of multiple obligors, as where a business concern assigns its accounts receivable. The English rule was not adopted in Restatement, Second, Trusts § 163.

c. Filing statutes. In modern times the rules of this Section have been greatly affected by statute. From 1938 to 1950 Section 60 of the Bankruptcy Act made the validity of an assignment in the assignor's bankruptcy turn on perfection of the assignment as against a hypothetical subsequent assignee. As a result numerous state statutes were enacted, directed particularly at assignments of accounts receivable. In 1950 amendments to the Bankruptcy Act reduced the significance of the problem of successive assignments. The current formulation is found in Bankruptcy Reform Act of 1978, 11 U.S.C. § 547(e)(1)(B) (1978):

a transfer of a fixture or property other than real property is perfected when a creditor on a simple contract cannot acquire a judicial lien that is superior to the interest of the transferee.

The subject is now largely governed by the Uniform Commercial Code, except in cases of wage claims, some rights under insurance policies, deposit accounts, and certain other excluded types of transactions. See § 9–104.

Under the Code, filing or the taking of possession is generally required to "perfect" a "security interest," which includes the interest of a buyer of accounts or chattel paper. Sections 1–201(37), 9–302. An unperfected security interest is subordinate to the rights of a person who is not a secured party to the extent that he gives value for accounts or general intangibles without knowledge of the security interest and before it is perfected. Section 9–301. As between secured parties, priority is determined by the order of filing or perfection, or if neither security interest is filed or perfected, by the order of attachment. Sections 9–312(5) and (6).

d. Defective assignment. If the prior assignment is revocable or voidable by the assignor a subsequent assignment is an effective manifestation of an intent to revoke or avoid. The subsequent assignment therefore has priority. A subsequent assignment may be similarly used to effectuate a power of avoidance of the subsequent assignee.

Illustrations

1. A has a right to the payment of $100 by B, and orally assigns it to C by way of gift. Subsequently A assigns the right to D, who gives value but knows of the assignment to C. Unless B has paid C without notice of D's assignment, B must pay D.

2. B owes A $100. A is an infant in a state where an infant may avoid his contract without restoring any consideration received. A assigns his right to C for value. Subsequently, on becoming of

age, A assigns his right to D, who gives value but knows of the assignment to C. Unless B has paid C without notice of D's assignment, B must pay D.

e. Payment, judgment or novation. Where the subsequent assignee as a bona fide purchaser for value obtains performance by the obligor, judgment against him, or a new contract with him by novation, he is entitled to retain what he has received and to enforce the judgment or novation against the obligor, free of any obligation to account to the prior assignee. Historically, this rule was justified on the ground that the right of an assignee was equitable and was not enforceable against a bona fide purchaser of the legal right. In modern times the doctrine of bona fide purchase has been extended in the interest of the security of transactions. But where the interest of the first assignee has been perfected pursuant to statute, whether by filing or otherwise, subsequent bona fide purchasers are not protected unless the statute so provides or there is an estoppel. See Uniform Commercial Code §§ 1–103, 9–306, 9–309, 9–312.

Illustration

3. B owes $100 to A. A assigns the right to C for value. Later A assigns it for value to D, who takes it in good faith. D notifies B of the assignment to him before C notifies B of his assignment. C's right is superior to D's. But if D, still without knowledge or reason to know of the assignment to C, receives $50 from B, D can retain what he receives.

f. Symbolic writings. Certain writings are treated in the ordinary course of business as symbols of contractual rights. See Comment c to § 332; Comment h to § 338. To the extent that such writings are negotiable by common law or by statute, they are beyond the scope of this Section. The rights of bona fide purchasers of some such writings, both negotiable and non-negotiable, are governed by the Uniform Commercial Code. See, e.g., § 9–308 (chattel paper). Aside from statute, a person who takes possession of such a writing as a bona fide purchaser is protected in his reasonable expectations arising from the apparent ownership of his assignor. This rule may be regarded as an application of a broader doctrine of estoppel. See Restatement, Second, Agency §§ 8B, 176.

Illustrations

4. A, the holder of a savings bank book which records a deposit of $100 in the B savings bank, assigns the deposit to C for value without delivering the book. A then delivers the book to D, who pays value therefore in ignorance of the assignment to C. D is entitled to the deposit.

5. A holds a life insurance policy issued by the B insurance company. By written assignment A assigns the policy to C as security for a debt, but does not deliver the policy. Later A assigns the policy to D as security for a loan of $3,000, and delivers the policy to D. Still later D lends an additional $1,000 to A on A's note, relying in good faith on a notation added to the note without A's authority that the note is secured by the policy. C is entitled to redeem the policy from D on payment of $3,000.

g. Relation to discharge of obligor. Priority between successive assignees is independent of the protection of the obligor under § 338. An assignee who acts in good faith may take priority under this Section by receiving payment from an obligor who acts in bad faith and hence is not discharged. Conversely, an assignee who receives a payment with knowledge of a prior assignment must account to the prior assignor even though the obligor acts in good faith and is discharged to the extent of the payment.

h. Value. As to what constitutes value, see Comments c and d to § 338.

§ 343. Latent Equities.

If an assignor's right against the obligor is held in trust or constructive trust for or subject to a right of avoidance or equitable lien of another than the obligor, an assignee does not so hold it if he gives value and becomes an assignee in good faith and without notice of the right of the other.

Comment

a. Scope. The rule stated in this Section is an application to contractual rights of the rules stated in Restatement, Second, Trusts §§ 284–85 and Restatement of Restitution § 172 as applying to property generally. See also Restatement, Second, Agency § 307A. The rule does not apply to defenses or claims of the obligor, but protects the bona fide purchaser against all other equitable claims adverse to the right of the assignor. The bona fide purchaser may be a purchaser for value of the entire right or only of a fractional or otherwise limited interest, such as a security interest. But the rule does not apply to cases of successive assignments by the same assignor, and does not protect a promisee or beneficiary of a contract to assign or a declaration of trust until he becomes an assignee. See Restatement, Second, Trusts § 286; Restatement of Restitution § 175.

Illustrations

1. A, as trustee for X, has a right against B. In violation of his trust A assigns the right gratuitously to C. C assigns to D, a purchaser for value in good faith and without notice of the breach of trust. D holds the right free of the trust.

2. A has a right against B and is induced to assign it to C by C's fraud. C assigns it to D, a purchaser for value in good faith and without notice of the fraud. Even after discovering the fraud D can enforce the right against B and retain the proceeds free of A's claim.

b. Equities of the obligor. The rule of this Section is not applied where the protection of the bona fide purchaser would impair the rights of the obligor. Thus where the assignor of a debt holds collateral in constructive trust for the assignee under the rule stated in § 340, a subsequent bona fide purchaser of the collateral from the assignor takes subject to the debtor's right to redeem the collateral by paying the debt to the assignee; the rule of this Section is not applicable unless the collateral is negotiable or the debtor is bound by agreement or estoppel. See Restatement of Security §§ 29, 31. Again, where a surety for the assignor is subrogated to the rights of the obligor, the assignee does not have priority by virtue of the rule stated in this Section. Priorities in such cases arising in connection with public construction contracts are affected by statute and are beyond the scope of this Restatement. Compare Restatement of Restitution § 162; Restatement of Security §§ 141, 165–68.

c. Negotiable instruments and documents. The rule of this Section is negated with respect to negotiable instruments and documents of title which are transferred but not duly negotiated by Uniform Commercial Code §§ 3–306, 7–504, 8–301. Compare § 9–308 (chattel paper).

d. Value. As to what constitutes value, see Comments c and d to § 338.

CHAPTER 16

REMEDIES

TOPIC 1. IN GENERAL

§ 344. Purposes of Remedies.

Judicial remedies under the rules stated in this Restatement serve to protect one or more of the following interests of a promisee:

    (a) his "expectation interest," which is his interest in having the benefit of his bargain by being put in as good a position as he would have been in had the contract been performed,

    (b) his "reliance interest," which is his interest in being reimbursed for loss caused by reliance on the contract by being put in as good a position as he would have been in had the contract not been made, or

    (c) his "restitution interest," which is his interest in having restored to him any benefit that he has conferred on the other party.

Comment

a. Three interests. The law of contract remedies implements the policy in favor of allowing individuals to order their own affairs by making legally enforceable promises. Ordinarily, when a court concludes that there has been a breach of contract, it enforces the broken promise by protecting the expectation that the injured party had when he made the contract. It does this by attempting to put him in as good a position as he would have been in had the contract been performed, that is, had there been no breach. The interest protected in this way is called the "expectation interest." It is sometimes said to give the injured party the "benefit of the bargain." This is not, however, the only interest that may be protected.

The promisee may have changed his position in reliance on the contract by, for example, incurring expenses in preparing to perform, in performing, or in foregoing opportunities to make other contracts. In that case, the court may recognize a claim based on his reliance rather than on his expectation. It does this by attempting to put him back in the position in which he would have been had the contract not been made. The interest protected in this way is called "reliance interest." Although it may be equal to the expectation interest, it is ordinarily smaller because it does not include the injured party's lost profit.

In some situations a court will recognize yet a third interest and grant relief to prevent unjust enrichment. This may be done if a party has not only changed his own position in reliance on the contract but has also conferred a benefit on the other party by, for example, making a part payment or furnishing services under the contract. The court may then require the other party to disgorge the benefit that he has received by returning it to the party who conferred it. The interest of the claimant protected in this way is called the "restitution interest." Although it may be equal to the expectation or reliance interest, it is ordinarily smaller because it includes neither the injured party's lost profit nor that part of his expenditures in reliance that resulted in no benefit to the other party. . . .

Illustrations

    1. A contracts to build a building for B on B's land for $100,000. B repudiates the contract before either party has done anything in reliance on it. It would have cost A $90,000 to build the building. A has an expectation interest of $10,000, the difference between the $100,000 price and his savings of $90,000 in not having to do the work. Since A has done nothing in reliance, A's reliance interest is zero. Since A has conferred no benefit on B, A's restitution interest is zero.

    2. The facts being otherwise as stated in Illustration 1, B does not repudiate until A has spent $60,000 of the $90,000. A has been paid nothing and can salvage nothing from the $60,000 that he has spent. A now has an expectation interest of $70,000, the difference between the $100,000 price and his saving of $30,000 in not having to do the work. A also has a reliance interest of $60,000, the amount

that he has spent. If the benefit to B of the partly finished building is $40,000, A has a restitution interest of $40,000.

b. Expectation interest. In principle, at least, a party's expectation interest represents the actual worth of the contract to him rather than to some reasonable third person. Damages based on the expectation interest therefore take account of any special circumstances that are peculiar to the situation of the injured party, including his personal values and even his idiosyncrasies, as well as his own needs and opportunities. See Illustration 3. In practice, however, the injured party is often held to a more objective valuation of his expectation interest because he may be barred from recovering for loss resulting from such special circumstances on the ground that it was not foreseeable or cannot be shown with sufficient certainty. See §§ 351 and 352. Furthermore, since he cannot recover for loss that he could have avoided by arranging a substitute transaction on the market (§ 350), his recovery is often limited by the objective standard of market price. See Illustration 4. The expectation interest is not based on the injured party's hopes when he made the contract but on the actual value that the contract would have had to him had it been performed. . . . It is therefore based on the circumstances at the time for performance and not those at the time of the making of the contract. See Illustration 5.

Illustrations

3. A, who is about to produce a play, makes a contract with B, an actor, under which B is to play the lead in the play at a stated salary for the season. A breaks the contract and has the part played by another actor. B's expectation interest includes the extent to which B's reputation would have been enhanced if he had been allowed to play the lead in A's play, as well as B's loss in salary, both subject to the limitations stated in Topic 2.

4. A contracts to construct a monument in B's yard for $10,000 but abandons the work after the foundation has been laid. It will cost B $6,000 to have another contractor complete the work. The monument planned is so ugly that it would decrease the market price of the house. Nevertheless, B's expectation interest is the value of the monument to him, which, under the rule stated in § 348(2)(b), would be measured by the cost of completion, $6,000.

5. A makes a contract with B under which A is to pay B for drilling an oil well on B's land, adjacent to that of A, for development and exploration purposes. Both A and B believe that the well will be productive and will substantially enhance the value of A's land in an amount that they estimate to be $1,000,000. Before A has paid anything, B breaks the contract by refusing to drill the well. Other exploration then proves that there is no oil in the region. A's expectation interest is zero.

c. Reliance interest. If it is reliance that is the basis for the enforcement of a promise, a court may enforce the promise but limit the promisee to recovery of his reliance interest. See §§ 87, 89, 90, 139. There are also situations in which a court may grant recovery based on the reliance interest even though it is consideration that is the basis for the enforcement of the promise. These situations are dealt with in §§ 349 and 353.

d. Restitution interest. Since restitution is the subject of a separate Restatement, this Chapter is concerned with problems of restitution only to the extent that they arise in connection with contracts. Such problems arise when a party, instead of seeking to enforce an agreement, claims relief on the ground that the other party has been unjustly enriched as a result of some benefit conferred under the agreement. In some cases a party's choice of the restitution interest is dictated by the fact that the agreement is not enforceable, perhaps because of his own breach (§ 374), as a result of impracticability of performance or frustration of purpose (§ 377(1)), under the Statute of Frauds (§ 375), or in consequence of the other party's avoidance for some reason as misrepresentation, duress, mistake or incapacity (§ 376). Occasionally a party chooses the restitution interest even though the contract is enforceable because it will give a larger recovery than will enforcement based on either the expectation or reliance interest. These rare instances are dealt with in § 373. Sometimes the restitution interest can be protected by requiring restoration of the specific thing, such as goods or land, that has resulted in the benefit. See § 372. Where restitution in kind is not appropriate, however, a sum of money will generally be allowed based on the restitution interest. See § 371.

§ 345. Judicial Remedies Available.

The judicial remedies available for the protection of the interests stated in § 344 include a judgment or order

    (a)   awarding a sum of money due under the contract or as damages,

    (b)   requiring specific performance of a contract or enjoining its non-performance,

    (c)   requiring restoration of a specific thing to prevent unjust enrichment,

    (d)   awarding a sum of money to prevent unjust enrichment,

    (e)   declaring the rights of the parties, and

    (f)   enforcing an arbitration award.

Comment

a. Nature of remedies. This Section enumerates the principal judicial remedies available for the protection of the interests defined in the preceding section. It is not intended to be exhaustive, since other remedies such as replevin of a chattel or reformation or cancellation of a writing supplement those listed here. As to reformation, see §§ 155, 166. Nor are the remedies listed mutually exclusive, since a court may in the same action, for example, both require specific performance of a promise and award a sum of money as damages for delay in its performance. The details of the procedure by which such remedies are obtained and enforced vary from one jurisdiction to another and are beyond the scope of this Restatement. In some circumstances a party to a contract is empowered to protect himself or to obtain satisfaction by methods not involving recourse to a court, such as retaking goods or foreclosing on security. The exercise of such a power, whether under a term of the contract or otherwise, is not a judicial remedy and is not dealt with in this Section. But see Topic 5 as to election and avoidance.

b. Enforcement. In most contract cases, what is sought is enforcement of a contract. Enforcement usually takes the form of an award of a sum of money due under the contract or as damages. Damages may be based on either the expectation or reliance interest of the injured party. See § 344. They are subject to the rules stated in Topic 2. A court may also enforce a promise by ordering that it be specifically performed or, in the alternative, by enjoining its nonperformance. In doing so, it protects the promisee's expectation interest. The rules governing the granting of such relief are stated in Topic 3.

c. Restitution. Sometimes a party, instead of seeking to enforce a contract under the rules stated in Topics 2 and 3, seeks protection of his restitution interest. If this can be accomplished by requiring the other party to restore a specific thing that is in his hands, a court may order restoration or make restoration a condition of granting relief to the other party. If restoration of the specific thing is not appropriate, the restitution interest may be protected by requiring the other party to pay a sum of money equivalent to the benefit that he has derived from that thing. The rules relating to the prevention of unjust enrichment by restitution, in either kind or money, are stated in Topic 4.

d. Declaratory judgments. Declaratory judgments play an important and growing role in the resolution of disputes arising out of contracts. Courts may render declaratory judgments under statutes adopted in nearly all states, and, in some instances, without the aid of statute. Such a judgment declares the legal relations between the parties but does not award damages or order other relief and may be rendered even though no breach of contract has occurred. In most states, including those that have adopted the Uniform Declaratory Judgment Act, courts may also render declaratory judgments in conjunction with other relief. In all states, and in the federal courts under the Federal Declaratory Judgment Act, the decision whether to render a declaratory judgment is discretionary. Because questions relating to declaratory judgments depend largely on statute and are not confined to contract cases, they are not considered in detail in this Restatement.

e. Enforcement of arbitration awards. Arbitration also plays an important and growing role in the resolution of contract disputes. Although arbitration is not in itself a judicial remedy, enforcement by a court of an award of an arbitral tribunal is. Statutes relating to the enforcement of such awards, based on either an agreement to arbitrate a future dispute or a submission of an existing dispute, have been enacted in many states. These statutes provide for the transformation of an award into a judgment by means of a summary procedure, without the necessity of bringing an action on the award as was required at common

TOPIC 2. ENFORCEMENT BY AWARD OF DAMAGES

§ 346. Availability of Damages.

(1) The injured party has a right to damages for any breach by a party against whom the contract is enforceable unless the claim for damages has been suspended or discharged.

(2) If the breach caused no loss or if the amount of the loss is not proved under the rules stated in this Chapter, a small sum fixed without regard to the amount of loss will be awarded as nominal damages.

Comment

a. Right to damages. Every breach of contract gives the injured party a right to damages against the party in breach, unless the contract is not enforceable against that party, as where he is not bound because of the Statute of Frauds. The resulting claim may be one for damages for total breach or one for damages for only partial breach. See § 236. Although a judgment awarding a sum of money as damages is the most common judicial remedy for breach of contract, other remedies, including equitable relief in the form of specific performance or an injunction, may be also available, depending on the circumstances. See Topic 3. In the exceptional situation of a contract for transfer of an interest in land that is unenforceable under the Statute of Frauds, action in reliance makes the contract enforceable by specific performance even though it gives rise to no claim for damages for breach. See Comment c to § 129. A duty to pay damages may be suspended or discharged by agreement or otherwise, and if it is discharged the claim for damages is extinguished. See Introductory Note to Chapter 12. When this happens, the right to enforcement by other means such as specific performance or an injunction is also extinguished. If the duty of performance, as distinguished from the duty to pay damages, has been suspended or discharged, as by impracticability of performance or frustration of purpose, there is then no breach and this Section is not applicable.

The parties can by agreement vary the rules stated in this Section, as long as the agreement is not invalid for unconscionability (§ 208) or on other grounds. The agreement may provide for a remedy such as repair or replacement in substitution for damages. See Uniform Commercial Code § 2–719.

b. Nominal damages. Although a breach of contract by a party against whom it is enforceable always gives rise to a claim for damages, there are instances in which the breach causes no loss. See Illustration 1. There are also instances in which loss is caused but recovery for that loss is precluded because it cannot be proved with reasonable certainty or because of one of the other limitations stated in this Chapter. See §§ 350–53. In all these instances the injured party will nevertheless get judgment for nominal damages, a small sum usually fixed by judicial practice in the jurisdiction in which the action is brought. Such a judgment may, in the discretion of the court, carry with it an award of court costs. Costs are generally awarded if a significant right was involved or the claimant made a good faith effort to prove damages, but not if the maintenance of the action was frivolous or in bad faith. Unless a significant right is involved, a court will not reverse and remand a case for a new trial if only nominal damages could result.

Illustration

1. A contracts to sell to B 1,000 shares of stock in X Corporation for $10 a share to be delivered on June 1, but breaks the contract by refusing on that date to deliver the stock. B sues A for damages, but at trial it is proved that B could have purchased 1,000 shares of stock in X Corporation on the market on June 1 for $10 a share and therefore has suffered no loss. In an action by B against A, B will be awarded nominal damages.

c. Beneficiaries of gift promises. If a promisee makes a contract, intending to give a third party the benefit of the promised performance, the third party may be an intended beneficiary who is entitled to enforce the contract. See § 302(1)(b). Such a gift promise creates overlapping duties, one to the beneficiary and the other to the promisee. If the performance is not forthcoming, both the beneficiary and the promisee have claims for damages for breach. If the promisee seeks damages, however, he will usually be limited to nominal damages: although the loss to the beneficiary may be substantial, the promisee cannot recover for that loss and he will ordinarily have suffered no loss himself. In such a case the remedy of specific performance will often be an appropriate one for the promisee. See § 307.

Illustration

2. As part of a separation agreement B promises his wife A not to change the provision in B's will for C, their son. A dies and B changes his will to C's detriment, adding also a provision that C will forfeit any bequest if he questions the change before any tribunal. In an action by A's personal representative against B, the representative can get a judgment for nominal damages. As to the representative's right to specific performance, see Illustration 2 to § 307.

§ 347. Measure of Damages in General.

Subject to the limitations stated in §§ 350–53, the injured party has a right to damages based on his expectation interest as measured by

    (a) the loss in the value to him of the other party's performance caused by its failure or deficiency, plus

    (b) any other loss, including incidental or consequential loss, caused by the breach, less

    (c) any cost or other loss that he has avoided by not having to perform.

Comment

a. Expectation interest. Contract damages are ordinarily based on the injured party's expectation interest and are intended to give him the benefit of his bargain by awarding him a sum of money that will, to the extent possible, put him in as good a position as he would have been in had the contract been performed. See § 344(1)(a). In some situations the sum awarded will do this adequately as, for example, where the injured party has simply had to pay an additional amount to arrange a substitute transaction and can be adequately compensated by damages based on that amount. In other situations the sum awarded cannot adequately compensate the injured party for his disappointed expectation as, for example, where a delay in performance has caused him to miss an invaluable opportunity. The measure of damages stated in this Section is subject to the agreement of the parties, as where they provide for liquidated damages (§ 356) or exclude liability for consequential damages.

b. Loss in value. The first element that must be estimated in attempting to fix a sum that will fairly represent the expectation interest is the loss in the value to the injured party of the other party's performance that is caused by the failure of, or deficiency in, that performance. If no performance is rendered, the loss in value caused by the breach is equal to the value that the performance would have had to the injured party. See Illustrations 1 and 2. If defective or partial performance is rendered, the loss in value caused by the breach is equal to the difference between the value that the performance would have had if there had been no breach and the value of such performance as was actually rendered. In principle, this requires a determination of the values of those performances to the injured party himself and not their values to some hypothetical reasonable person or on some market. See Restatement, Second, Torts § 911. They therefore depend on his own particular circumstances or those of his enterprise, unless consideration of these circumstances is precluded by the limitation of foreseeability (§ 351). Where the injured party's expected advantage consists largely or exclusively of the realization of profit, it may be possible to express this loss in value in terms of money with some assurance. In other situations, however, this is not possible and compensation for lost value may be precluded by the limitation of certainty. See § 352. In order to facilitate the estimation of loss with sufficient certainty to award damages, the injured party is sometimes given a choice between alternative bases of calculating his loss in value. The most important of these are stated in § 348. See also §§ 349 and 373.

Illustrations

1. A contracts to publish a novel that B has written. A repudiates the contract and B is unable to get his novel published elsewhere. Subject to the limitations stated in §§ 350–53, B's damages

include the loss of royalties that he would have received had the novel been published together with the value to him of the resulting enhancement of his reputation. But see Illustration 1 to § 352.

2. A, a manufacturer, contracts to sell B, a dealer in used machinery, a used machine that B plans to resell. A repudiates and B is unable to obtain a similar machine elsewhere. Subject to the limitations stated in §§ 350–53, B's damages include the net profit that he would have made on resale of the machine.

c. Other loss. Subject to the limitations stated in §§ 350–53, the injured party is entitled to recover for all loss actually suffered. Items of loss other than loss in value of the other party's performance are often characterized as incidental or consequential. Incidental losses include costs incurred in a reasonable effort, whether successful or not, to avoid loss, as where a party pays brokerage fees in arranging or attempting to arrange a substitute transaction. See Illustration 3. Consequential losses include such items as injury to person or property resulting from defective performance. See Illustration 4. The terms used to describe the type of loss are not, however, controlling, and the general principle is that all losses, however described, are recoverable.

Illustrations

3. A contracts to employ B for $10,000 to supervise the production of A's crop, but breaks his contract by firing B at the beginning of the season. B reasonably spends $200 in fees attempting to find other suitable employment through appropriate agencies. B can recover the $200 incidental loss in addition to any other loss suffered, whether or not he succeeds in finding other employment.

4. A leases a machine to B for a year, warranting its suitability for B's purpose. The machine is not suitable for B's purpose and causes $10,000 in damage to B's property and $15,000 in personal injuries. B can recover the $25,000 consequential loss in addition to any other loss suffered. See Uniform Commercial Code § 2–715(2)(b).

d. Cost or other loss avoided. Sometimes the breach itself results in a saving of some cost that the injured party would have incurred if he had had to perform. See Illustration 5. Furthermore, the injured party is expected to take reasonable steps to avoid further loss. See § 350. Where he does this by discontinuing his own performance, he avoids incurring additional costs of performance. See Illustrations 6 and 8. This cost avoided is subtracted from the loss in value caused by the breach in calculating his damages. If the injured party avoids further loss by making substitute arrangements for the use of his resources that are no longer needed to perform the contract, the net profit from such arrangements is also subtracted. See Illustration 9. The value to him of any salvageable materials that he has acquired for performance is also subtracted. See Illustration 7. Loss avoided is subtracted only if the saving results from the injured party not having to perform rather than from some unrelated event. See Illustration 10. If no cost or other loss has been avoided, however, the injured party's damages include the full amount of the loss in value with no subtraction, subject to the limitations stated in §§ 350–53. See Illustration 11. The intended "donee" beneficiary of a gift promise usually suffers loss to the full extent of the value of the promised performance, since he is ordinarily not required to do anything, and so avoids no cost on breach. See § 302(1)(b).

Illustrations

5. A contracts to build a hotel for B for $500,000 and to have it ready for occupancy by May 1. B's occupancy of the hotel is delayed for a month because of a breach by A. The cost avoided by B as a result of not having to operate the hotel during May is subtracted from the May rent lost in determining B's damages.

6. A contracts to build a house for B for $100,000. When it is partly built, B repudiates the contract and A stops work. A would have to spend $60,000 more to finish the house. The $60,000 cost avoided by A as a result of not having to finish the house is subtracted from the $100,000 price lost in determining A's damages. A has a right to $40,000 in damages from B, less any progress payments that he has already received. See Illustration 2 to § 344.

7. The facts being otherwise as stated in Illustration 6, A has bought materials that are left over and that he can use for other purposes, saving him $5,000. The $5,000 cost avoided is subtracted in determining A's damages, resulting in damages of only $35,000 rather than $40,000.

8. A contracts to convey land to B in return for B's working for a year. B repudiates the contract before A has conveyed the land. The value to A of the land is subtracted from the value to A of B's services in determining A's damages.

9. A contracts to employ B for $10,000 to supervise the production of A's crop, but breaks his contract by firing B at the beginning of the season. B instead takes another job as a supervisor at $9,500. The $9,500 is subtracted from the $10,000 loss of earnings in determining B's damages. See Illustration 8 to § 350.

10. A contracts to build a machine for B and deliver it to be installed in his factory by June 30. A breaks the contract and does not deliver the machine. B's factory is destroyed by fire on December 31 and the machine, if it had been installed there, would also have been destroyed. The fact that the factory was burned is not considered in determining B's damages.

11. A contracts to send his daughter to B's school for $5,000 tuition. After the academic year has begun, A withdraws her and refuses to pay anything. A's breach does not reduce B's instructional or other costs and B is unable to find another student to take the place of A's daughter. B has a right to damages equal to the full $5,000.

e. Actual loss caused by breach. The injured party is limited to damages based on his actual loss caused by the breach. If he makes an especially favorable substitute transaction, so that he sustains a smaller loss than might have been expected, his damages are reduced by the loss avoided as a result of that transaction. See Illustration 12. If he arranges a substitute transaction that he would not have been expected to do under the rules on avoidability (§ 350), his damages are similarly limited by the loss so avoided. See Illustration 13. Recovery can be had only for loss that would not have occurred but for the breach. See § 346. If, after the breach, an event occurs that would have discharged the party in breach on grounds of impracticability of performance or frustration of purpose, damages are limited to the loss sustained prior to that event. See Illustration 15. Compare § 254(2). The principle that a party's liability is not reduced by payments or other benefits received by the injured party from collateral sources is less compelling in the case of a breach of contract than in the case of a tort. See Restatement, Second, Torts § 920A. The effect of the receipt of unemployment benefits by a discharged employee will turn on the court's perception of legislative policy rather than on the rule stated in this Section. See Illustration 14.

Illustrations

12. A contracts to build a house for B for $100,000, but repudiates the contract after doing part of the work and having been paid $40,000. Other builders would charge B $80,000 to finish the house, but B finds a builder in need of work who does it for $70,000. B's damages are limited to the $70,000 that he actually had to pay to finish the work less the $60,000 cost avoided or $10,000, together with damages for any loss caused by the delay. See Illustration 2 to § 348.

13. A contracts to employ B for $10,000 to supervise the production of A's crop. A breaks the contract by firing B at the beginning of the season, and B, unable to find another job, instead takes a job as a farm laborer for the entire season at $6,000. The $6,000 that he made as a farm laborer is subtracted from the $10,000 loss of earnings in determining B's damages. See Illustration 8 to § 350.

14. A contracts to employ B for $10,000 to supervise the production of A's crop, but breaks his contract by firing B at the beginning of the season. B is unable to find another similar job but receives $3,000 in state unemployment benefits. Whether the $3,000 will be subtracted from the $10,000 loss of earnings depends on the state legislation under which it was paid and the policy behind it.

15. On April 1, A and B make a personal service contract under which A is to employ B for six months beginning July 1 and B is to work for A during that period. On May 1, B repudiates the contract. On August 1, B falls ill and is unable to perform the contract for the remainder of the period. A can only recover damages based on his loss during the month of July since his loss during subsequent months was not caused by B's breach. Compare Illustration 2 to § 254.

f. Lost volume. Whether a subsequent transaction is a substitute for the broken contract sometimes raises difficult questions of fact. If the injured party could and would have entered into the subsequent contract, even if the contract had not been broken, and could have had the benefit of both, he can be said to have "lost volume" and the subsequent transaction is not a substitute for the broken contract. The injured party's damages are then based on the net profit that he has lost as a result of the broken contract. Since entrepreneurs try to operate at optimum capacity, however, it is possible that an additional transaction would not have been profitable and that the injured party would not have chosen to expand his business by undertaking it had there been no breach. It is sometimes assumed that he would have done so, but the question is one of fact to be resolved according to the circumstances of each case.... See also Uniform Commercial Code § 2–708(2).

Illustration

16. A contracts to pave B's parking lot for $10,000. B repudiates the contract and A subsequently makes a contract to pave a similar parking lot for $10,000. A's business could have been expanded to do both jobs. Unless it is proved that he would not have undertaken both, A's damages are based on the net profit he would have made on the contract with B, without regard to the subsequent transaction.

§ 348. Alternatives to Loss in Value of Performance.

(1) If a breach delays the use of property and the loss in value to the injured party is not proved with reasonable certainty, he may recover damages based on the rental value of the property or on interest on the value of the property.

(2) If a breach results in defective or unfinished construction and the loss in value to the injured party is not proved with sufficient certainty, he may recover damages based on.

    (a) the diminution in the market price of the property caused by the breach, or

    (b) the reasonable cost of completing performance or of remedying the defects if that cost is not clearly disproportionate to the probable loss in value to him.

(3) If a breach is of a promise conditioned on a fortuitous event and it is uncertain whether the event would have occurred had there been no breach, the injured party may recover damages based on the value of the conditional right at the time of breach.

Comment

a. Reason for alternative bases. Although in principle the injured party is entitled to recover based on the loss in value to him caused by the breach, in practice he may be precluded from recovery on this basis because he cannot show the loss in value to him with sufficient certainty. See § 352. In such a case, if there is a reasonable alternative to loss in value, he may claim damages based on that alternative....

b. Breach that delays the use of property. If the breach is one that prevents for a period of time the use of property from which profits would have been made, the loss in value to the injured party is based on the profits that he would have made during that period. If those profits cannot be proved with reasonable certainty (§ 352), two other bases for recovery are possible. One is the fair rental value of the property during the period of delay. Damages based on fair rental value include an element of profit since the fair rental value of property depends on what it would command on the market and this turns on the profit that would be derived from its use. For this reason, uncertainty as to profits may result in uncertainty in fair rental value. Another possible basis for recovery, as a last resort, is the interest on the value of the property that has been made unproductive by the breach, if that value can be shown with reasonable certainty. Although these two other bases will ordinarily give a smaller recovery than loss in value, it is always open to the party in breach to show that this is not so and to hold the injured party to a smaller recovery based on loss in value to him.

Illustration

1. A contracts with B to construct an outdoor drive-in theatre, to be completed by June 1. A does not complete the work until September 1. If B cannot prove his lost profits with reasonable certainty, he can recover damages based on the rental value of the theatre property or based on the interest on the value of the theatre property itself if he can prove either of these values with reasonable certainty. See Illustration 2 to § 352.

c. Incomplete or defective performance. If the contract is one for construction, including repair or similar performance affecting the condition of property, and the work is not finished, the injured party will usually find it easier to prove what it would cost to have the work completed by another contractor than to prove the difference between the values to him of the finished and the unfinished performance. Since the cost to complete is usually less than the loss in value to him, he is limited by the rule on avoidability to damages based on cost to complete. See § 350(1). If he has actually had the work completed, damages will be based on his expenditures if he comes within the rule stated in § 350(2).

Sometimes, especially if the performance is defective as distinguished from incomplete, it may not be possible to prove the loss in value to the injured party with reasonable certainty. In that case he can usually recover damages based on the cost to remedy the defects. Even if this gives him a recovery somewhat in excess of the loss in value to him, it is better that he receive a small windfall than that he be undercompensated by being limited to the resulting diminution in the market price of his property.

Sometimes, however, such a large part of the cost to remedy the defects consists of the cost to undo what has been improperly done that the cost to remedy the defects will be clearly disproportionate to the probable loss in value to the injured party. Damages based on the cost to remedy the defects would then give the injured party a recovery greatly in excess of the loss in value to him and result in a substantial windfall. Such an award will not be made. It is sometimes said that the award would involve "economic waste," but this is a misleading expression since an injured party will not, even if awarded an excessive amount of damages, usually pay to have the defects remedied if to do so will cost him more than the resulting increase in value to him. If an award based on the cost to remedy the defects would clearly be excessive and the injured party does not prove the actual loss in value to him, damages will be based instead on the difference between the market price that the property would have had without the defects and the market price of the property with the defects. This diminution in market price is the least possible loss in value to the injured party, since he could always sell the property on the market even if it had no special value to him.

Illustrations

2. A contracts to build a house for B for $100,000 but repudiates the contract after doing part of the work and having been paid $40,000. Other builders will charge B $80,000 to finish the house. B's damages include the $80,000 cost to complete the work less the $60,000 cost avoided or $20,000, together with damages for any loss caused by delay. See Illustration 12 to § 347.

3. A contracts to build a house for B for $100,000. When it is completed, the foundations crack, leaving part of the building in a dangerous condition. To make it safe would require tearing down some of the walls and strengthening the foundation at a cost of $30,000 and would increase the market value of the house by $20,000. B's damages include the $30,000 cost to remedy the defects.

4. A contracts to build a house for B for $100,000 according to specifications that include the use of Reading pipe. After completion, B discovers that A has used Cohoes pipe, an equally good brand. To replace the Cohoes pipe with Reading pipe would require tearing down part of the walls at a cost of over $20,000 and would not affect the market price of the house. In an action by B against A, A gives no proof of any special value that Reading pipe would have to him. B's damages do not include the $20,000 cost to remedy the defects because that cost is clearly disproportionate to the loss in value to B. B can recover only nominal damages.

d. Fortuitous event as condition. In the case of a promise conditioned on a fortuitous event (see Comment a to § 379), a breach that occurs before the happening of the fortuitous event may make it impossible to determine whether the event would have occurred had there been no breach. It would be unfair to the party in breach to award damages on the assumption that the event would have occurred, but equally unfair to the injured party to deny recovery of damages on the ground of uncertainty. The injured party has, in any case, the remedy of restitution (see § 373). Under the rule stated in Subsection (3) he also has the alternative remedy of damages based on the value of his conditional contract right at the time of breach, or what may be described as the value of his "chance of winning." The value of that right must itself be proved with reasonable certainty, as it may be if there is a market for such rights or if there is a suitable basis for determining the probability of the occurrence of the event.

The rule stated in this Subsection is limited to aleatory promises and does not apply if the promise is conditioned on some event, such as return performance by the injured party, that is not fortuitous. If, for example, an owner repudiates a contract to pay for repairs to be done by a contractor and then maintains that the contractor could not or would not have done the work had he not repudiated, the contractor must prove that he could and would have performed. If he fails to do this, he has no remedy in damages. He is not entitled to claim damages under the rule stated in Subsection (3).

Illustration

5. A offers a $100,000 prize to the owner whose horse wins a race at A's track. B accepts by entering his horse and paying the registration fee. When the race is run, A wrongfully prevents B's horse from taking part. Although B cannot prove that his horse would have won the race, he can prove that it was considered to have one chance in four of winning because one fourth of the money bet on the race was bet on his horse. B has a right to damages of $25,000 based on the value of the conditional right to the prize.

§ 349. Damages Based on Reliance Interest.

As an alternative to the measure of damages stated in § 347, the injured party has a right to damages based on his reliance interest, including expenditures made in preparation for performance or in performance, less any loss that the party in breach can prove with reasonable certainty the injured party would have suffered had the contract been performed.

Comment

a. Reliance interest where profit uncertain. . . . Under the rule stated in this Section, the injured party may, if he chooses, ignore the element of profit and recover as damages his expenditures in reliance. He may choose to do this if he cannot prove his profit with reasonable certainty. He may also choose to do this in the case of a losing contract, one under which he would have had a loss rather than a profit. In that case, however, it is open to the party in breach to prove the amount of the loss, to the extent that he can do so with reasonable certainty under the standard stated in § 352, and have it subtracted from the injured party's damages. The resulting damages will then be the same as those under the rule stated in § 347. . . .

Illustrations

1. A gives B a "dealer franchise" to sell A's products in a stated area for one year. In preparation for performance, B spends money on advertising, hiring sales personnel, and acquiring premises that cannot be used for other purposes. A then repudiates before performance begins. If neither party proves with reasonable certainty what profit or loss B would have made if the contract had been performed, B can recover as damages his expenditures in preparation for performance. See Illustration 8 to § 90.

2. A contracts with B to stage a series of performances in B's theater, each to have 50 per cent of the gross receipts. After A has spent $20,000 in getting ready for the performances, B rents the theater to others and repudiates the contract, and A stages the performance at another theater. A's expenditures in preparation for performance of the contract with B are worth $8,000 to him in connection with staging the performances at the other theater. If neither party proves with reasonable certainty what profit or loss A would have made if the contract had been performed, A can recover as damages the $12,000 balance of his expenditures in preparation for performance.

3. A contracts to build for B a factory of experimental design for $1,000,000. After A has spent $250,000 and been paid $150,000 in progress payments, B repudiates the contract and A stops work. A's expenditures include materials worth $10,000 that he can use on other jobs. If neither party proves with reasonable certainty what profit or loss A would have made if the contract had been performed, A can recover as damages the $90,000 balance of his expenditures in preparation for performance.

4. A contracts to sell his retail store to B. After B has spent $100,000 for inventory, A repudiates the contract and B sells the inventory for $60,000. If neither party proves with reasonable certainty what profit or loss B would have made if the contract had been performed, B can recover as damages the $40,000 loss that he sustained on the sale of the inventory.

b. Reliance interest in other cases. There are other instances in which damages may be based on the reliance interest. Under the rules stated in §§ 87, 89, 90 and 139, if a promise is enforceable because it has induced action or forbearance, the remedy granted for breach may be limited as justice requires. Under these rules, relief may be limited to damages measured by the extent of the promisee's reliance rather than by the terms of the promise. See Comment e to § 87, Comment d to § 89, Comment d to § 90 and Comment d to § 139. Furthermore, even when the contract is enforceable because of consideration, a court may, under the rule stated in § 353, conclude that the circumstances require that damages be limited to losses incurred in reliance. See Comment a to § 353.

§ 350. Avoidability as a Limitation on Damages.

(1) Except as stated in Subsection (2), damages are not recoverable for loss that the injured party could have avoided without undue risk, burden or humiliation.

(2) The injured party is not precluded from recovery by the rule stated in Subsection (1) to the extent that he has made reasonable but unsuccessful efforts to avoid loss.

Comment

a. Rationale. The rules stated in this Section reflect the policy of encouraging the injured party to attempt to avoid loss. The rule stated in Subsection (1) encourages him to make such efforts as he can to avoid loss by barring him from recovery for loss that he could have avoided if he had done so. See Comment b. The exception stated in Subsection (2) protects him if he has made actual efforts by allowing him to recover, regardless of the rule stated in Subsection (1), if his efforts prove to be unsuccessful. See Comment h. See also Comment c to § 347.

b. Effect of failure to make efforts to mitigate damages. As a general rule, a party cannot recover damages for loss that he could have avoided by reasonable efforts. Once a party has reason to know that performance by the other party will not be forthcoming, he is ordinarily expected to stop his own performance to avoid further expenditure. See Illustrations 1, 2, 3 and 4. Furthermore, he is expected to take such affirmative steps as are appropriate in the circumstances to avoid loss by making substitute arrangements or otherwise. It is sometimes said that it is the "duty" of the aggrieved party to mitigate damages, but this is misleading because he incurs no liability for his failure to act. The amount of loss that he could reasonably have avoided by stopping performance, making substitute arrangements or otherwise is simply subtracted from the amount that would otherwise have been recoverable as damages.

Illustrations

1. A contracts to build a bridge for B for $100,000. B repudiates the contract shortly after A has begun work on the bridge, telling A that he no longer has need for it. A nevertheless spends an additional $10,000 in continuing to perform. A's damages for breach of contract do not include the $10,000.

2. A contracts to lease a machine to B and to deliver it at B's factory. B repudiates the contract, but A nevertheless ships the machine to B, who refuses to receive it. A's damages for breach of contract do not include the cost of shipment of the machine.

3. A sells oil to B in barrels. B discovers that some of the barrels are leaky, in breach of warranty, but does not transfer the oil to good barrels that he has available. B's damages for breach of contract do not include the loss of the oil that could have been saved by transferring the oil to the available barrels.

4. A contracts to sell flour to B. The flour is defective, in breach of warranty, as B discovers after delivery. B nevertheless uses it to bake bread to supply his customers. B's damages for breach of contract do not include his loss of business caused by delivering inferior bread made from the flour.

c. Substitute transactions. When a party's breach consists of a failure to deliver goods or furnish services, for example, it is often possible for the injured party to secure similar goods or services on the market. If a seller of goods repudiates, the buyer can often buy similar goods elsewhere. See Illustration 5. If an employee quits his job, the employer can often find a suitable substitute. See Illustration 6. Similarly, when a party's breach consists of a failure to receive goods or services, for example, it is often possible for the aggrieved party to dispose of the goods or services on the market. If a buyer of goods repudiates, the seller can often sell the goods elsewhere. See Illustration 7. If an employer fires his employee, the employee can often find a suitable job elsewhere. See Illustration 8. In such cases as these, the injured party is expected to make appropriate efforts to avoid loss by arranging a substitute transaction. If he does not do so, the amount of loss that he could have avoided by doing so is subtracted in calculating his damages. In the case of the sale of goods, this principle has inspired the standard formulas under which a buyer's or seller's damages are based on the difference between the contract price and the market price on that market where the injured party could have arranged a substitute transaction for the purchase or sale of similar goods. See Uniform Commercial Code §§ 2–708, 2–713. Similar rules are applied to other contracts, such as contracts for the sale of securities, where there is a well-established market for the type of performance involved, but the principle extends to other situations in which a substitute transaction can be arranged, even if there is no well-established market for the type of performance. However, in those other situations, the burden is generally put on the party in breach to show that a substitute transaction was available, as is done in the case in which an employee has been fired by his employer.

Illustrations

5. A contracts to sell to B a used machine to be delivered at B's factory by June 1 for $10,000. A breaks the contract by repudiating it on May 1. By appropriate efforts B could buy a similar machine from another seller for $11,000 in time to be delivered at his factory by June 1, but he does not do so and loses a profit of $25,000 that he would have made from use of the machine. B's damages do not include the loss of the $25,000 profit, but he can recover $1,000 from A. See Uniform Commercial Code §§ 2–713(1), 2–715(2)(a).

6. A contracts to supervise the production of B's crop for $10,000, but breaks his contract and leaves at the beginning of the season. By appropriate efforts, B could obtain an equally good supervisor for $11,000, but he does not do so and the crop is lost. B's damages for A's breach of contract do not include the loss of his crop, but he can recover $1,000 from A.

7. A contracts to buy from B a used machine from B's factory for $10,000. A breaks the contract by refusing to receive or pay for the machine. By appropriate efforts, B could sell the machine to another buyer for $9,000, but he does not do so. B's damages for A's breach of contract do not include the loss of the $10,000 price, but he can recover $1,000 from A. See Uniform Commercial Code § 2–708(1).

8. A contracts to employ B for $10,000 to supervise the production of A's crop, but breaks his contract by firing B at the beginning of the season. By appropriate efforts, B could obtain an equally good job as a supervisor at $100 less than A had contracted to pay him, but he does not do so and remains unemployed. B's damages for A's breach of contract do not include his $10,000 loss of earnings, but he can recover $100 from A. See Illustration 9 to § 347.

d. *"Lost volume."* The mere fact that an injured party can make arrangements for the disposition of the goods or services that he was to supply under the contract does not necessarily mean that by doing so he will avoid loss. If he would have entered into both transactions but for the breach, he has "lost volume" as a result of the breach. See Comment f to § 347. In that case the second transaction is not a "substitute" for the first one. See Illustrations 9 and 10.

Illustrations

9. A contracts to buy grain from B for $100,000, which would give B a net profit of $10,000. A breaks the contract by refusing to receive or pay for the grain. If B would have made the sale to A in addition to other sales, B's efforts to make other sales do not affect his damages. B's damages for A's breach of contract include his $10,000 loss of profit.

10. A contracts to pay B $20,000 for paving A's parking lot, which would give B a net profit of $3,000. A breaks the contract by repudiating it before B begins work. If B would have made the contract with A in addition to other contracts, B's efforts to obtain other contracts do not affect his damages. B's damages for A's breach of contract include his $3,000 loss of profit.

e. What is a "substitute." Whether an available alternative transaction is a suitable substitute depends on all the circumstances, including the similarity of the performance and the times and places that they would be rendered. See Illustration 11. If discrepancies between the transactions can be adequately compensated for in damages, the alternative transaction is regarded as a substitute and such damages are awarded. See Illustrations 12 and 13. If the party in breach offers to perform the contract for a different price, this may amount to a suitable alternative. See Illustration 14. But this is not the case if the offer is conditioned on surrender by the injured party of his claim for breach. See Illustration 15.

Illustrations

11. The facts being otherwise as stated in Illustration 8, by appropriate efforts B could only obtain a job as a farm laborer at $6,000, but he does not do so and remains unemployed. B's damages for breach of contract include his $10,000 loss of earnings.

12. The facts being otherwise as stated in Illustration 5, the other seller will not deliver the similar machine to B's factory, and insists that B take possession of it two weeks earlier than he can install it in his factory, but B can arrange to have it stored for two weeks and shipped to his factory for $1,500. B's damages do not include the loss of the $25,000 profit, but he can recover the $1,500 as well as the $1,000 from A.

13. A contracts to bale hay on B's farm so that B can use it later to feed his livestock. A does the work so defectively that the hay is worthless. B can buy similar hay in bales in Central City, 100 miles from his farm, for $10,000. The cost to ship the bales between Central City and his farm is $1,000. B's damages include the $10,000 market price and the $1,000 cost of shipment. If B had intended to ship his bales of hay to Central City for sale there, rather than to feed it to his livestock, the $1,000 cost of shipment would be subtracted from the $10,000 market price as cost avoided under § 347(c).

14. A contracts to sell to B a used machine from A's factory for $10,000. A breaks the contract by refusing to deliver the machine at that price, but offers to sell it to B for $11,000 without prejudice to B's right to damages. B refuses to buy it at that price and, since he cannot find a similar machine elsewhere, loses a profit of $25,000 that he would have made from use of the machine. B's damages do not include the loss of the $25,000 profit, but he can recover $1,000 from A.

15. The facts being otherwise as stated in Illustration 14, A's offer to sell the machine at $11,000 is conditioned on B's surrendering any claim that he may have against A for breach of contract. B's damages may include the loss of the $25,000 profit.

f. Time for arranging substitute transaction. The injured party is expected to arrange a substitute transaction within a reasonable time after he learns of the breach. He is expected to do this even if the breach takes the form of an anticipatory repudiation, since under the rule stated in Subsection (2) he is then protected against the possibility of a change in the market before the time for performance. See Comment g. The injured party may, however, make appropriate efforts to urge the repudiating party to perform in spite of his repudiation or to retract his repudiation, and these efforts will be taken into account in determining what is a reasonable time. Although the injured party is expected to arrange a substitute transaction without unreasonable delay following the anticipatory repudiation, the time for performance under the substitute transaction will ordinarily be the same time as it would have been under the original contract.

Illustrations

16. On May 1, A contracts to sell to B a stated quantity of grain for $100,000, delivery and payment to be made on July 1. On July 1, A breaks the contract by refusing to deliver the grain, but B does not buy substitute grain on the market on that date although he could do so for $110,000. On July 10, B buys substitute grain on the market for $120,000. B's damages for A's breach of contract do not include the $20,000 above the contract price that he paid on July 10, but he can recover $10,000 from A.

17. The facts being otherwise as stated in Illustration 16, A breaks the contract by repudiating it on June 1 and on the same day B tells A that he considers the repudiation final. B does not buy substitute grain on the market on that date although he could do so for $105,000 for delivery and

payment on July 1. B's damages for A's breach of contract do not include the $20,000 above the contract price that he paid on July 10, but he can recover $5,000 from A.

g. Efforts expected. In some situations, it is reasonable for the injured party to rely on performance by the other party even after breach. This may be true, for example, if the breach is accompanied by assurances that performance will be forthcoming. In such a situation the injured party is not expected to arrange a substitute transaction although he may be expected to take some steps to avoid loss due to a delay in performance. Nor is it reasonable to expect him to take steps to avoid loss if those steps may cause other serious loss. He need not, for example, make other risky contracts, incur unreasonable expense or inconvenience or disrupt his business. In rare instances the appropriate course may be to complete performance instead of stopping. Finally the aggrieved party is not expected to put himself in a position that will involve humiliation, including embarrassment or loss of honor and respect.

Illustrations

18. A contracts to build a building for B for $100,000. B repudiates the contract shortly before A has finished work. Because A has duties to subcontractors and will have difficulty in calculating his damages, A spends an additional $10,000 and completes the building. If stopping work would not have been reasonable in the circumstances, A can recover the full $100,000, including the $10,000 that he spent after B's repudiation. Compare Illustration 1.

19. A contracts to supervise the production of B's crop for $10,000, but commits a material breach of the contract by failing to begin on time. By appropriate efforts, B could obtain an equally good supervisor for $1,000 more than he had contracted to pay A, but he does not do so because A assures him that the delay is only temporary. By the time that B discovers that A will be unavailable for the entire season, it is too late to hire another supervisor and the crop is lost. If B's delay in hiring another supervisor was reasonable in the circumstances, B's damages for A's breach of contract may include the loss of his crop.

20. A, a motion picture company, contracts to have B star in a musical comedy for $100,000. A breaks the contract and engages C, a rival of B, to star in the musical comedy, but offers B an equally good role under an identical contract as a star in another musical comedy for $100,000. Because B would be humiliated to work for A after A hired a rival in B's place, B refuses to accept the offer. If rejection of the offer was reasonable in the circumstances, B can recover the full $100,000. Compare Illustration 8.

h. Actual efforts to mitigate damages. Sometimes the injured party makes efforts to avoid loss but fails to do so. The rule stated in Subsection (2) protects the injured party in that situation if the efforts were reasonable. If, for example, a seller who is to manufacture goods for a buyer decides, on repudiation by the buyer, "in the exercise of reasonable commercial judgment for the purpose of avoiding loss" to complete manufacture of the goods, he is protected under Uniform Commercial Code § 2–704(2) even if it later appears that he could have better avoided loss by stopping manufacture. Similarly, if a buyer of goods who decides, on repudiation by the seller, to " 'cover' by making in good faith and without unreasonable delay any reasonable purchase of or contract to purchase goods in substitution for those due from the seller," he is protected under Uniform Commercial Code § 2–712. See also Uniform Commercial Code § 2–706 for the seller's comparable right of resale. The rule stated in Subsection (2) reflects the policy underlying these Code provisions, one encouraging the injured party to make reasonable efforts to avoid loss by protecting him even when his efforts fail. To this extent, his failure to avoid loss does not have the effect stated in Subsection (1). Under the rule stated in § 347, costs incurred in a reasonable but unsuccessful effort to avoid loss are recoverable as incidental losses. See Comment c to § 347.

Illustrations

21. A contracts to sell to B a used machine to be delivered at A's factory by June 1 for $10,000. A breaks the contract by repudiating it on May 1. B makes a reasonable purchase of a similar machine for $12,000 in time to be delivered at his factory by June 1. It later appears that, unknown to B, a similar machine could have been found for only $11,000. Nevertheless, B can recover $2,000 from A. Compare Illustration 5. See Uniform Commercial Code § 2–712.

22. A contracts to supervise the production of B's crop for $10,000, but breaks his contract and leaves at the beginning of the season. B makes a reasonable substitute contract with another supervisor for $12,000 in time to save his crop. It later appears that, unknown to B, a suitable supervisor could have been found for only $11,000. Nevertheless, B can recover $2,000 from A. Compare Illustration 6.

23. A pays a premium to B, an insurance company, for a policy of fire insurance on his house for a period of five years. B later repudiates the policy and A reasonably gets a similar policy from another insurer for the balance of the period. A has a right to damages against B based on the cost of the new policy.

§ 351. Unforeseeability and Related Limitations on Damages.

(1) Damages are not recoverable for loss that the party in breach did not have reason to foresee as a probable result of the breach when the contract was made.

(2) Loss may be foreseeable as a probable result of a breach because it follows from the breach

(a) in the ordinary course of events, or

(b) as a result of special circumstances, beyond the ordinary course of events, that the party in breach had reason to know.

(3) A court may limit damages for foreseeable loss by excluding recovery for loss of profits, by allowing recovery only for loss incurred in reliance, or otherwise if it concludes that in the circumstances justice so requires in order to avoid disproportionate compensation.

Comment

a. Requirement of foreseeability. A contracting party is generally expected to take account of those risks that are foreseeable at the time he makes the contract. He is not, however, liable in the event of breach for loss that he did not at the time of contracting have reason to foresee as a probable result of such a breach. The mere circumstance that some loss was foreseeable, or even that some loss of the same general kind was foreseeable, will not suffice if the loss that actually occurred was not foreseeable. It is enough, however, that the loss was foreseeable as a probable, as distinguished from a necessary, result of his breach. Furthermore, the party in breach need not have made a "tacit agreement" to be liable for the loss. Nor must he have had the loss in mind when making the contract, for the test is an objective one based on what he had reason to foresee. There is no requirement of foreseeability with respect to the injured party. In spite of these qualifications, the requirement of foreseeability is a more severe limitation of liability than is the requirement of substantial or "proximate" cause in the case of an action in tort or for breach of warranty. Compare Restatement, Second, Torts § 431, Uniform Commercial Code § 2–715(2)(b). Although the recovery that is precluded by the limitation of foreseeability is usually based on the expectation interest and takes the form of lost profits. . ., the limitation may also preclude recovery based on the reliance interest.

Illustrations

1. A, a carrier, contracts with B, a miller, to carry B's broken crankshaft to its manufacturer for repair. B tells A when they make the contract that the crankshaft is part of B's milling machine and that it must be sent at once, but not that the mill is stopped because B has no replacement. Because A delays in carrying the crankshaft, B loses profit during an additional period while the mill is stopped because of the delay. A is not liable for B's loss of profit. That loss was not foreseeable by A as a probable result of the breach at the time the contract was made because A did not know that the broken crankshaft was necessary for the operation of the mill.

2. A contracts to sell land to B and to give B possession on a stated date. Because A delays a short time in giving B possession, B incurs unusual expenses in providing for cattle that he had already purchased to stock the land as a ranch. A had no reason to know when they made the contract that B had planned to purchase cattle for this purpose. A is not liable for B's expenses in providing for the cattle because that loss was not foreseeable by A as a probable result of the breach at the time the contract was made.

b. "General" and "special" damages. Loss that results from a breach in the ordinary course of events is foreseeable as the probable result of the breach. See Uniform Commercial Code § 2–714(1). Such loss is sometimes said to be the "natural" result of the breach, in the sense that its occurrence accords with the common experience of ordinary persons. For example, a seller of a commodity to a wholesaler usually has reason to foresee that his failure to deliver the commodity as agreed will probably cause the wholesaler to lose a reasonable profit on it. See Illustrations 3 and 4. Similarly, a seller of a machine to a manufacturer usually has reason to foresee that his delay in delivering the machine as agreed will probably cause the manufacturer to lose a reasonable profit from its use, although courts have been somewhat more cautious in allowing the manufacturer recovery for loss of such profits than in allowing a middleman recovery for loss of profits on an intended resale. See Illustration 5. The damages recoverable for such loss that results in the ordinary course of events are sometimes called "general" damages.

If loss results other than in the ordinary course of events, there can be no recovery for it unless it was foreseeable by the party in breach because of special circumstances that he had reason to know when he made the contract. See Uniform Commercial Code § 2–715(2)(a). For example, a seller who fails to deliver a commodity to a wholesaler is not liable for the wholesaler's loss of profit to the extent that it is extraordinary nor for his loss due to unusual terms in his resale contracts unless the seller had reason to know of these special circumstances. See Illustration 6. Similarly, a seller who delays in delivering a machine to a manufacturer is not liable for the manufacturer's loss of profit to the extent that it results from an intended use that was abnormal unless the seller had reason to know of this special circumstance. See Illustration 7. In the case of a written agreement, foreseeability is sometimes established by the use of recitals in the agreement itself. The parol evidence rule (§ 213) does not, however, preclude the use of negotiations prior to the making of the contract to show for this purpose circumstances that were then known to a party. The damages recoverable for loss that results other than in the ordinary course of events are sometimes called "special" or "consequential" damages. These terms are often misleading, however, and it is not necessary to distinguish between "general" and "special" or "consequential" damages for the purpose of the rule stated in this Section.

Illustrations

3. A and B make a written contract under which A is to recondition by a stated date a used machine owned by B so that it will be suitable for sale by B to C. A knows when they make the contract that B has contracted to sell the machine to C but knows nothing of the terms of B's contract with C. Because A delays in returning the machine to B, B is unable to sell it to C and loses the profit that he would have made on that sale. B's loss of reasonable profit was foreseeable by A as a probable result of the breach at the time the contract was made.

4. A, a manufacturer of machines, contracts to make B his exclusive selling agent in a specified area for the period of a year. Because A fails to deliver any machines, B loses the profit on contracts that he would have made for their resale. B's loss of reasonable profit was foreseeable by A as a probable result of the breach at the time the contract was made.

5. A and B make a contract under which A is to recondition by a stated date a used machine owned by B so that it will be suitable for use in B's canning factory. A knows that the machine must be reconditioned by that date if B's factory is to operate at full capacity during the canning season, but nothing is said of this in the written contract. Because A delays in returning the machine to B, B loses its use for the entire canning season and loses the profit that he would have made had his factory operated at full capacity. B's loss of reasonable profit was foreseeable by A as a probable result of the breach at the time the contract was made.

6. The facts being otherwise as stated in Illustration 3, the profit that B would have made under his contract with A was extraordinarily large because C promised to pay an exceptionally high price as a result of a special need for the machine of which A was unaware. A is not liable for B's loss of profit to the extent that it exceeds what would ordinarily result from such a contract. To that extent the loss was not foreseeable by A as a probable result of the breach at the time the contract was made.

7. The facts being otherwise as stated in Illustration 5, the profit that B would have made from the use of the machine was unusually large because of an abnormal use to which he planned to put it of which A was unaware. A is not liable for B's loss of profit to the extent that it exceeds what would

ordinarily result from the use of such a machine. To that extent the loss was not foreseeable by A at the time the contract was made as a probable result of the breach.

c. Litigation or settlement caused by breach. Sometimes a breach of contract results in claims by third persons against the injured party. The party in breach is liable for the amount of any judgment against the injured party together with his reasonable expenditures in the litigation, if the party in breach had reason to foresee such expenditures as the probable result of his breach at the time he made the contract. See Illustrations 8, 10, 11 and 12. This is so even if the judgment in the litigation is based on a liquidated damage clause in the injured party's contract with the third party. See Illustration 8. A failure to notify the party in breach in advance of the litigation may prevent the result of the litigation from being conclusive as to him. But to the extent that the injured party's loss resulting from litigation is reasonable, the fact that the party in breach was not notified does not prevent the inclusion of that loss in the damages assessed against him. In furtherance of the policy favoring private settlement of disputes, the injured party is also allowed to recover the reasonable amount of any settlement made to avoid litigation, together with the costs of settlement. See Illustration 9.

Illustrations

The facts being otherwise as stated in Illustration 3, B not only loses the profit that he would have made on sale of the machine to C, but is held liable for damages in an action brought by C for breach of contract. The damages paid to C and B's reasonable expenses in defending the action were also foreseeable by A as a probable result of the breach at the time he made the contract with B. The result is the same even though they were based on a liquidated damage clause in the contract between B and C if A knew of the clause or if the use of such a clause in the contract between B and C was foreseeable by A at the time he made the contract with B.

9. The facts being otherwise as stated in Illustration 3, B not only loses the profit that he would have made on sale of the machine to C, but settles with C by paying C a reasonable sum of money to avoid litigation. The amount of the settlement paid to C and B's reasonable expenses in settling were also foreseeable by A at the time he made the contract with B as a probable result of the breach.

10. A contracts to supply B with machinery for unloading cargo. A, in breach of contract, furnishes defective machinery, and C, an employee of B, is injured. C sues B and gets a judgment, which B pays. The amount of the judgment and B's reasonable expenditures in defending the action were foreseeable by A at the time the contract was made as a probable result of the breach.

11. A contracts to procure a right of way for B, for a railroad. Because A, in breach of contract, fails to do this, B has to acquire the right of way by condemnation proceedings. B's reasonable expenditures in those proceedings were foreseeable by A at the time the contract was made as a probable result of the breach.

12. A leases land to B with a covenant for quiet enjoyment. C brings an action of ejectment against B and gets judgment. B's reasonable expenditures in defending the action were foreseeable by A as the probable result of the breach at the time the contract was made.

d. Unavailability of substitute. If several circumstances have contributed to cause a loss, the party in breach is not liable for it unless he had reason to foresee all of them. Sometimes a loss would not have occurred if the injured party had been able to make substitute arrangements after breach, as, for example, by "cover" through purchase of substitute goods in the case of a buyer of goods (see Uniform Commercial Code § 2–712). If the inability of the injured party to make such arrangements was foreseeable by the party in breach at the time he made the contract, the resulting loss was foreseeable. See Illustration 13. On the impact of this principle on contracts to lend money, see Comment e.

Illustrations

13. A contracts with B, a farmer, to lease B a machine to be used harvesting B's crop, delivery to be made on July 30. A knows when he makes the contract that B's crop will be ready on that date and that B cannot obtain another machine elsewhere. Because A delays delivery until August 10, B's crop is damaged and he loses profit. B's loss of profit was foreseeable by A at the time the contract was made as a probable result of the breach.

e. Breach of contract to lend money. The limitation of foreseeability is often applied in actions for damages for breach of contracts to lend money. Because credit is so widely available, a lender often has no reason to foresee at the time the contract is made that the borrower will be unable to make substitute arrangements in the event of breach. See Comment d. In most cases, then, the lender's liability will be limited to the relatively small additional amount that it would ordinarily cost to get a similar loan from another lender. However, in the less common situation in which the lender has reason to foresee that the borrower will be unable to borrow elsewhere or will be delayed in borrowing elsewhere, the lender may be liable for much heavier damages based on the borrower's inability to take advantage of a specific opportunity (see Illustration 14), his having to postpone or abandon a profitable project (see Illustration 15), or his forfeiture of security for failure to make prompt payment (see Illustration 16).

Illustrations

14. A contracts to lend B $100,000 for one year at eight percent interest for the stated purpose of buying a specific lot of goods for resale. B can resell the goods at a $20,000 profit. A delays in making the loan, and although B can borrow money on the market at ten percent interest, he is unable to do so in time and loses the opportunity to buy the goods. Unless A had reason to foresee at the time that he made the contract that such a delay in making the loan would probably cause B to lose the opportunity, B can only recover damages based on two percent of the amount of the loan.

15. A contracts to lend $1,000,000 to B for the stated purpose of enabling B to build a building and takes property of B as security. After construction is begun, A refuses to make the loan or release the security. Because B lacks further security, he is unable to complete the building, which becomes a total loss. B's loss incurred in partial construction of the building was foreseeable by A at the time of the contract as a probable result of the breach.

16. A, who holds B's land as security for a loan, contracts to lend B a sum of money sufficient to pay off other liens on the land at the current rate of interest. A repudiates and informs B in time to obtain money elsewhere on the market, but B is unable to do so. The liens are foreclosed and the land sold at a loss. Unless A knew when he made the contract that B would probably be unable to borrow the money elsewhere, B's loss on the foreclosure sale was not foreseeable as a probable result of A's breach.

f. Other limitations on damages. It is not always in the interest of justice to require the party in breach to pay damages for all of the foreseeable loss that he has caused. There are unusual instances in which it appears from the circumstances either that the parties assumed that one of them would not bear the risk of a particular loss or that, although there was no such assumption, it would be unjust to put the risk on that party. One such circumstance is an extreme disproportion between the loss and the price charged by the party whose liability for that loss is in question. The fact that the price is relatively small suggests that it was not intended to cover the risk of such liability. Another such circumstance is an informality of dealing, including the absence of a detailed written contract, which indicates that there was no careful attempt to allocate all of the risks. The fact that the parties did not attempt to delineate with precision all of the risks justifies a court in attempting to allocate them fairly. The limitations dealt with in this Section are more likely to be imposed in connection with contracts that do not arise in a commercial setting. Typical examples of limitations imposed on damages under this discretionary power involve the denial of recovery for loss of profits and the restriction of damages to loss incurred in reliance on the contract. Sometimes these limits are covertly imposed, by means of an especially demanding requirement of foreseeability or of certainty. The rule stated in this Section recognizes that what is done in such cases is the imposition of a limitation in the interests of justice.

Illustrations

17. A, a private trucker, contracts with B to deliver to B's factory a machine that has just been repaired and without which B's factory, as A knows, cannot reopen. Delivery is delayed because A's truck breaks down. In an action by B against A for breach of contract the court may, after taking into consideration such factors as the absence of an elaborate written contract and the extreme disproportion between B's loss of profits during the delay and the price of the trucker's services, exclude recovery for loss of profits.

18. A, a retail hardware dealer, contracts to sell B an inexpensive lighting attachment, which, as A knows, B needs in order to use his tractor at night on his farm. A is delayed in obtaining the attachment and, since no substitute is available, B is unable to use the tractor at night during the delay. In an action by B against A for breach of contract, the court may, after taking into consideration such factors as the absence of an elaborate written contract and the extreme disproportion between B's loss of profits during the delay and the price of the attachment, exclude recovery for loss of profits.

§ 352. Uncertainty as a Limitation on Damages.

Damages are not recoverable for loss beyond an amount that the evidence permits to be established with reasonable certainty.

Comment

a. Requirement of certainty. A party cannot recover damages for breach of a contract for loss beyond the amount that the evidence permits to be established with reasonable certainty. See Illustration 1. Courts have traditionally required greater certainty in the proof of damages for breach of a contract than in the proof of damages for a tort. The requirement does not mean, however, that the injured party is barred from recovery unless he establishes the total amount of his loss. It merely excludes those elements of loss that cannot be proved with reasonable certainty. The main impact of the requirement of certainty comes in connection with recovery for lost profits. Although the requirement of certainty is distinct from that of foreseeability (§ 351), its impact is similar in this respect. Although the requirement applies to damages based on the reliance as well as the expectation interest, there is usually little difficulty in proving the amount that the injured party has actually spent in reliance on the contract, even if it is impossible to prove the amount of profit that he would have made. In such a case, he can recover his loss based on his reliance interest instead of on his expectation interest. See § 349 and Illustrations 1, 2 and 3.

Doubts are generally resolved against the party in breach. A party who has, by his breach, forced the injured party to seek compensation in damages should not be allowed to profit from his breach where it is established that a significant loss has occurred. A court may take into account all the circumstances of the breach, including willfulness, in deciding whether to require a lesser degree of certainty, giving greater discretion to the trier of the facts. Damages need not be calculable with mathematical accuracy and are often at best approximate. See Comment 1 to Uniform Commercial Code § 1–106. This is especially true for items such as loss of good will as to which great precision cannot be expected. See Illustration 4. Furthermore, increasing receptiveness on the part of courts to proof by sophisticated economic and financial data and by expert opinion has made it easier to meet the requirement of certainty.

Illustrations

1. A contracts to publish a novel that B has written. A repudiates the contract and B is unable to get his novel published elsewhere. If the evidence does not permit B's loss of royalties and of reputation to be estimated with reasonable certainty, he cannot recover damages for that loss, although he can recover nominal damages. See Illustration 1 to § 347.

2. A contracts to sell B a tract of land on which B plans to build an outdoor drive-in theatre. A breaks the contract by selling the land to C, and B is unable to build the theatre. If, because of the speculative nature of the new enterprise the evidence does not permit B's loss of profits to be estimated with reasonable certainty, his recovery will be limited to expenses incurred in reliance or, if none can be proved with reasonable certainty, to nominal damages.

3. A and B make a contract under which A is to construct a building of radical new design for B for $5,000,000. After A has spent $3,000,000 in reliance, B repudiates the contract and orders A off the site. If the evidence does not permit A's lost profits to be estimated with reasonable certainty, he can recover the $3,000,000 that he has spent in reliance. He must, however, then prove that amount with reasonable certainty.

4. A, a manufacturer, makes a contract with B, a wholesaler, to sell B a quantity of plastic. B resells the plastic to dealers. The plastic is discovered to be defective and B has many complaints from dealers, some of which refuse to place further orders with him. B can recover the loss of good will if his

loss can be estimated with reasonable certainty by such evidence as his business records before and after the transaction and the testimony of his salespersons and that of dealers.

b. Proof of profits. The difficulty of proving lost profits varies greatly with the nature of the transaction. If, for example, it is the seller who claims lost profit on the ground that the buyer's breach has caused him to lose a sale, proof of lost profit will ordinarily not be difficult. If, however, it is the buyer who claims lost profit on the ground that the seller's breach has caused him loss in other transactions, the task of proof is harder. Furthermore, if the transaction is more complex and extends into the future, as where the seller agrees to furnish all of the buyer's requirements over a period of years, proof of the loss of profits caused by the seller's breach is more difficult. If the breach prevents the injured party from carrying on a well-established business, the resulting loss of profits can often be proved with sufficient certainty. Evidence of past performance will form the basis for a reasonable prediction as to the future. See Illustration 5. However, if the business is a new one or if it is a speculative one that is subject to great fluctuations in volume, costs or prices, proof will be more difficult. Nevertheless, damages may be established with reasonable certainty with the aid of expert testimony, economic and financial data, market surveys and analyses, business records of similar enterprises, and the like. See Illustration 6. Under a contract of exclusive agency for the sale of goods on commission, the agent can often prove with sufficient certainty the profits that he would have made had he not been discharged. Proof of the sales made by the agent in the agreed territory before the breach, or of the sales made there by the principal after the breach, may permit a reasonably accurate estimate of the agent's loss of commissions. However, if the agency is not an exclusive one, so that the agent's ability to withstand competition is in question, such a showing will be more difficult, although the agent's past record may give a sufficient basis for judging this. See Illustration 7.

Illustrations

5. A contracts with B to remodel B's existing outdoor drive-in theatre, work to be completed on June 1. A does not complete the work until September 1. B can use records of the theatre's prior and subsequent operation, along with other evidence, to prove his lost profits with reasonable certainty.

6. A contracts with B to construct a new outdoor drive-in theatre, to be completed on June 1. A does not complete the theatre until September 1. Even though the business is a new rather than an established one, B may be able to prove his lost profits with reasonable certainty. B can use records of the theatre's subsequent operation and of the operation of similar theatres in the same locality, along with other evidence including market surveys and expert testimony, in attempting to do this.

7. A contracts with B to make B his exclusive agent for the sale of machine tools in a specified territory and to supply him with machine tools at stated prices. After B has begun to act as A's agent, A repudiates the agreement and replaces him with C. B can use evidence as to sales and profits made by him before the repudiation and made by C after the repudiation in attempting to prove his lost profits with reasonable certainty. It would be more difficult, although not necessarily impossible, for B to succeed in this attempt if his agency were not exclusive.

c. Alternative remedies. The necessity of proving damages can be avoided if another remedy, such as a decree of specific performance or an injunction, is granted instead of damages. Although the availability of such a remedy does not preclude an award of damages as an alternative, it may justify a court in requiring greater certainty of proof if damages are to be awarded. See Illustration 8.

Illustration

8. A, a steel manufacturer, and B, a dealer in scrap steel, contract for the sale by A to B of all of A's output of scrap steel for five years at a price fixed in terms of the market price. B's profit will depend largely on the amount of A's output and the cost of transporting the scrap to B's purchasers. A repudiates the contract at the end of one year. Whether B can recover damages based on lost profits over the remaining four years will depend on whether he can prove A's output and the transportation costs with reasonable certainty. If he can do so for part of the remaining four years, he can recover damages based on lost profits for that period. The availability of the remedy of specific performance is a factor that will influence a court in requiring greater certainty.

§ 353. Loss Due to Emotional Disturbance.

Recovery for emotional disturbance will be excluded unless the breach also caused bodily harm or the contract or the breach is of such a kind that serious emotional disturbance was a particularly likely result.

Comment

a. Emotional disturbance. Damages for emotional disturbance are not ordinarily allowed. Even if they are foreseeable, they are often particularly difficult to establish and to measure. There are, however, two exceptional situations where such damages are recoverable. In the first, the disturbance accompanies a bodily injury. In such cases the action may nearly always be regarded as one in tort, although most jurisdictions do not require the plaintiff to specify the nature of the wrong on which his action is based and award damages without classifying the wrong. See Restatement, Second, Torts §§ 436, 905. In the second exceptional situation, the contract or the breach is of such a kind that serious emotional disturbance was a particularly likely result. Common examples are contracts of carriers and innkeepers with passengers and guests, contracts for the carriage or proper disposition of dead bodies, and contracts for the delivery of messages concerning death. Breach of such a contract is particularly likely to cause serious emotional disturbance. Breach of other types of contracts, resulting for example in sudden impoverishment or bankruptcy, may by chance cause even more severe emotional disturbance, but, if the contract is not one where this was a particularly likely risk, there is no recovery for such disturbance.

Illustrations

1. A contracts to construct a house for B. A knows when the contract is made that B is in delicate health and that proper completion of the work is of great importance to him. Because of delays and departures from specifications, B suffers nervousness and emotional distress. In an action by B against A for breach of contract, the element of emotional disturbance will not be included as loss for which damages may be awarded.

2. A, a hotel keeper, wrongfully ejects B, a guest, in breach of contract. In doing so, A uses foul language and accuses B of immorality, but commits no assault. In an action by B against A for breach of contract, the element of B's emotional disturbance will be included as loss for which damages may be awarded.

3. A makes a contract with B to conduct the funeral for B's husband and to provide a suitable casket and vault for his burial. Shortly thereafter, B discovers that, because A knowingly failed to provide a vault with a suitable lock, water has entered it and reinterment is necessary. B suffers shock, anguish and illness as a result. In an action by B against A for breach of contract, the element of emotional disturbance will be included as loss for which damages may be awarded.

4. The facts being as stated in Illustration 19 to § 351, the element of emotional disturbance resulting from the additional operation will be included as loss for which damages may be awarded.

§ 354. Interest as Damages.

(1) If the breach consists of a failure to pay a definite sum in money or to render a performance with fixed or ascertainable monetary value, interest is recoverable from the time for performance on the amount due less all deductions to which the party in breach is entitled.

(2) In any other case, such interest may be allowed as justice requires on the amount that would have been just compensation had it been paid when performance was due.

Comment

a. Scope. This Section deals with an injured party's right to interest as damages in compensation for the deprivation of a promised performance. Had the performance been rendered when it was due, the injured party would have been able to make use of it. Interest is a standardized form of compensation to the injured party for the loss of that use, in the absence of agreement to the contrary. It is payable without compounding at the rate, commonly called the "legal rate," fixed by statute for this purpose.

This Section does not deal with the injured party's right to interest to compensate him for expenditures occasioned by the breach. If, following an anticipatory repudiation, he loses the use of money through making reasonable substitute arrangements, he is entitled to interest as incidental damages under the rule stated in § 347. Nor does this Section deal with the injured party's right to interest under the terms of the contract. If the parties have agreed on the payment of interest, it is payable not as damages but pursuant to a contract duty that is enforceable as is any other such duty, subject to legal restrictions on the rate of interest. Nor does this Section deal with interest on a judgment once rendered.

b. Performance must be due. Interest is not payable as damages for non-performance until performance is due. If there is a period of time before performance is due, such as a definite or indefinite period of credit, interest does not begin to run until the period is over. If the performance is to be rendered on demand, interest does not begin to run until a demand is made, even though an action might be maintained without a demand. See Illustration 3 to § 226. If the action itself is considered to be the required demand, interest begins to run from the time the action is brought. If the performance is subject to the occurrence of an event as a condition, interest does not begin to run until that condition occurs or is excused.

c. Where amount due is sufficiently definite. Under the rule stated in Subsection (1), a party is not chargeable with interest on a sum unless its amount is fixed by the contract or he could have determined its amount with reasonable certainty so that he could have made a proper tender. Unless otherwise agreed, interest is always recoverable for the non-payment of money once payment has become due and there has been a breach. This rule applies to debts due for money lent, goods sold or services performed, including installments due on a construction contract. The fact that the breach has spared some expense that is uncertain in amount does not prevent the recovery of interest. The sum due is sufficiently definite if it is ascertainable from the terms of the contract, as where the contract fixes a price per unit of performance, even though the number of units performed must be proved and is subject to dispute. The same is true, even if the contract does not of itself create a money debt, if it fixes a money equivalent of the performance. It is also true, even if the contract does not fix a money equivalent of the performance, if such an equivalent can be determined from established market prices. The fact that the extent of the performance rendered and the existence of the market price must be proved by evidence extrinsic to the contract does not prevent the application of these rules.

Illustrations

1. A lends B $10,000 to be repaid in 30 days without interest. B fails to pay the debt. A sues B and recovers $10,000. A is also entitled to simple interest on the $10,000 at the legal rate from the date of maturity.

2. A contracts to sell B goods for $10,000 on 30 days credit, nothing being said as to interest. A delivers the goods but B fails to pay for them at the end of 30 days. A sues B and recovers $10,000. A is also entitled to simple interest on the $10,000 at the legal rate from the expiration of the credit period.

3. A contracts to sell B all the berries to be grown on A's farm during one year for $5 a quart. A delivers 2,000 quarts. No part of the price is paid. B wrongly claims that only 1,000 quarts were delivered and that they were all paid for when received. A sues B and recovers $10,000. A is also entitled to simple interest on the $10,000 at the legal rate from the date when payment was due.

4. A contracts to sell machinery to B for $10,000, the price to be paid by B in wheat at the market price on July 1. A delivers the machinery but B fails to deliver the wheat. A sues B and recovers $10,000. A is also entitled to simple interest on the $10,000 at the legal rate from July 1. The result would be the same if the price were not expressed in dollars but in terms of 1,000 bushels of wheat to be delivered on July 1 and the market price on that day was $10 a bushel.

5. On February 1 A makes a contract to sell a ship to B for $10,000,000, payment and delivery to be October 1. On September 1, B repudiates the contract and A promptly makes a reasonable contract to resell the ship for $8,000,000, payment and delivery to take place on October 1. A sues B and recovers $2,000,000. A is entitled to simple interest on the $2,000,000 at the legal rate from October 1.

6. A contracts to cut and deliver to B 1 million feet of lumber from trees on B's land. Delivery is to be by June 1 and the price is $100 per thousand feet payable on delivery. After A has spent $30,000 in cutting the timber, but before he has delivered any of it, B repudiates the contract. As a result of his expenditure, A has $1,000 worth of materials left over that he can use on other contracts. It would have cost A an additional $60,000 to cut and deliver all of the timber. A sues B and recovers $39,000. See § 347. A is entitled to simple interest on the $39,000 at the legal rate from June 1.

7. A contracts to work for B at a weekly salary of $2,000. B wrongfully discharges A ten weeks before the contract ends and refuses to pay A anything for the four weeks preceding the discharge. By reasonable efforts, A can find similar work paying $1,500 a week for the last ten weeks. A sues B and recovers $2,000 for each of the first four weeks and $500 for each of the last ten, or $13,000. A is entitled to simple interest on each instalment at the legal rate from the date that it was payable.

d. Discretionary in other cases. Damages for breach of contract include not only the value of the promised performance but also compensation for consequential loss. The amount to be awarded for such loss is often very difficult to estimate in advance of trial and cannot be determined by the party in breach with sufficient certainty to enable him to make a proper tender. In such cases, the award of interest is left to judicial discretion, under the rule stated in Subsection (2), in the light of all the circumstances, including any deficiencies in the performance of the injured party and any unreasonableness in the demands made by him.

Illustrations

8. A sells seed to B, warranting that it is Bristol cabbage seed. It is an inferior type of cabbage seed instead, and B suffers a loss of profit. B sues A and recovers $10,000, the difference between the value to B of a crop of Bristol cabbage and the crop actually grown. That amount was not, however, sufficiently definite to give B a right to interest on it. The allowance of interest is in the discretion of the court.

9. A contracts to build a bungalow for B for $30,000. After completion but before B has paid the final $6,000, B occupies the bungalow but refuses to pay the balance because the workmanship and materials are unsatisfactory. A sues B and recovers only $4,000 on the ground that B's claim entitles him to compensation in the amount of $2,000. The sum of $4,000 was not sufficiently definite to give A a right to interest on it. The allowance of interest is within the discretion of the court. The fact that A was himself in breach will be considered.

§ 355. Punitive Damages.

Punitive damages are not recoverable for a breach of contract unless the conduct constituting the breach is also a tort for which punitive damages are recoverable.

Comment

a. Compensation not punishment. The purposes of awarding contract damages is to compensate the injured party. See Introductory Note to this Chapter. For this reason, courts in contract cases do not award damages to punish the party in breach or to serve as an example to others unless the conduct constituting the breach is also a tort for which punitive damages are recoverable. Courts are sometimes urged to award punitive damages when, after a particularly aggravated breach, the injured party has difficulty in proving all of the loss that he has suffered. In such cases the willfulness of the breach may be taken into account in applying the requirement that damages be proved with reasonable certainty (Comment a to § 352); but the purpose of awarding damages is still compensation and not punishment, and punitive damages are not appropriate. In exceptional instances, departures have been made from this general policy. A number of states have enacted statutes that vary the rule stated in this Section, notably in situations involving consumer transactions or arising under insurance policies.

Illustrations

1. A is employed as a school teacher by B. In breach of contract and without notice B discharges A by excluding him from the school building and by stating in the presence of the pupils that he is

discharged. Regardless of B's motive in discharging A, A cannot recover punitive damages from B. A can recover compensatory damages under the rule stated in § 347, including any damages for emotional disturbance that are allowable under the rule stated in § 353.

 2. A and B, who are neighbors, make a contract under which A promises to supply water to B from A's well for ten years in return for B's promise to make monthly payments and share the cost of repairs. After several years, the relationship between A and B deteriorates and A, in breach of contract and to spite B, shuts off the water periodically. B cannot recover punitive damages from A. B can recover compensation damages under the rule stated in § 347 if he can prove them with reasonable certainty (§ 352), and the court may take into account the willfulness of A's breach in applying that requirement. See Comment a to § 352.

 b. Exception for tort. In some instances the breach of contract is also a tort, as may be the case for a breach of duty by a public utility. Under modern rules of procedure, the complaint may not show whether the plaintiff intends his case to be regarded as one in contract or one in tort. The rule stated in this Section does not preclude an award of punitive damages in such a case if such an award would be proper under the law of torts. See Restatement, Second, Torts § 908. The term "tort" in the rule stated in this Section is elastic, and the effect of the general expansion of tort liability to protect additional interests is to make punitive damages somewhat more widely available for breach of contract as well. Some courts have gone rather far in this direction.

Illustrations

 3. A, a telephone company, contracts with B to render uninterrupted service. A, tortiously as well as in breach of contract, fails to maintain service at night and B is unable to telephone a doctor for his sick child. B's right to recover punitive damages is governed by Restatement, Second, Torts § 908.

 4. A borrows money from B, pledging jewelry as security for the loan. B, tortiously as well as in breach of contract, sells the jewelry to a good faith purchaser for value. A's right to recover punitive damages is governed by Restatement, Second, Torts § 908.

§ 356. Liquidated Damages and Penalties.

 (1) Damages for breach by either party may be liquidated in the agreement but only at an amount that is reasonable in the light of the anticipated or actual loss caused by the breach and the difficulties of proof of loss. A term fixing unreasonably large liquidated damages is unenforceable on grounds of public policy as a penalty.

 (2) A term in a bond providing for an amount of money as a penalty for non-occurrence of the condition of the bond is unenforceable on grounds of public policy to the extent that the amount exceeds the loss caused by such non-occurrence.

Comment

 a. Liquidated damages or penalty. The parties to a contract may effectively provide in advance the damages that are to be payable in the event of breach as long as the provision does not disregard the principle of compensation. The enforcement of such provisions for liquidated damages saves the time of courts, juries, parties and witnesses and reduces the expense of litigation. This is especially important if the amount in controversy is small. However, the parties to a contract are not free to provide a penalty for its breach. The central objective behind the system of contract remedies is compensatory, not punitive. Punishment of a promisor for having broken his promise has no justification on either economic or other grounds and a term providing such a penalty is unenforceable on grounds of public policy. See Chapter 8. The rest of the agreement remains enforceable, however, under the rule stated in § 184(1), and the remedies for breach are determined by the rules stated in this Chapter. See Illustration 1. A term that fixes an unreasonably small amount as damages may be unenforceable as unconscionable. See § 208. As to the liquidation of damages and modification or limitation of remedies in contracts of sale, see Uniform Commercial Code §§ 2–718, 2–719.

 b. Test of penalty. Under the test stated in Subsection (1), two factors combine in determining whether an amount of money fixed as damages is so unreasonably large as to be a penalty. The first factor is the anticipated or actual loss caused by the breach. The amount fixed is reasonable to the extent that it approximates the actual loss that has resulted from the particular breach, even though it may not approximate the loss that might have been anticipated under other possible breaches. See Illustration 2. Furthermore, the amount fixed is reasonable to the extent that it approximates the loss anticipated at the time of the making of the contract, even though it may not approximate the actual loss. See Illustration 3. The second factor is the difficulty of proof of loss. The greater the difficulty either of proving that loss has occurred or of establishing its amount with the requisite certainty (see § 351), the easier it is to show that the amount fixed is reasonable. To the extent that there is uncertainty as to the harm, the estimate of the court or jury may not accord with the principle of compensation any more than does the advance estimate of the parties. A determination whether the amount fixed is a penalty turns on a combination of these two factors. If the difficulty of proof of loss is great, considerable latitude is allowed in the approximation of anticipated or actual harm. If, on the other hand, the difficulty of proof of loss is slight, less latitude is allowed in that approximation. If, to take an extreme case, it is clear that no loss at all has occurred, a provision fixing a substantial sum as damages is unenforceable. See Illustration 4.

Illustrations

1. A and B sign a written contract under which A is to act in a play produced by B for a ten week season for $4,000. A term provides that "if either party shall fail to perform as agreed in any respect he will pay $10,000 as liquidated damages and not as a penalty." A leaves the play before the last week to take another job. The play is sold out for that week and A is replaced by a suitable understudy. The amount fixed is unreasonable in the light of both the anticipated and the actual loss and, in spite of the use of the words "liquidated damages," the term provides for a penalty and is unenforceable on grounds of public policy. The rest of the agreement is enforceable (§ 184(1)), and B's remedies for A's breach are governed by the rules stated in this Chapter.

2. A, B and C form a partnership to practice veterinary medicine in a town for ten years. In the partnership agreement, each promises that if, on the termination of the partnership, the practice is continued by the other two members, he will not practice veterinary medicine in the same town during its continuance up to a maximum of three years. A term provides that for breach of this duty "he shall forfeit $50,000 to be collected by the others as damages." A leaves the partnership, and the practice is continued by B and C. A immediately begins to practice veterinary medicine in the same town. The loss actually caused to B and C is difficult of proof and $50,000 is not an unreasonable estimate of it. Even though $50,000 may be unreasonable in relation to the loss that might have resulted in other circumstances, it is not unreasonable in relation to the actual loss. Therefore, the term does not provide for a penalty and its enforcement is not precluded on grounds of public policy. See Illustration 14 to § 188.

3. A contracts to build a grandstand for B's race track for $1,000,000 by a specified date and to pay $1,000 a day for every day's delay in completing it. A delays completion for ten days. If $1,000 is not unreasonable in the light of the anticipated loss and the actual loss to B is difficult to prove, A's promise is not a term providing for a penalty and its enforcement is not precluded on grounds of public policy.

4. The facts being otherwise as stated in Illustration 3, B is delayed for a month in obtaining permission to operate his race track so that it is certain that A's delay of ten days caused him no loss at all. Since the actual loss to B is not difficult to prove, A's promise is a term providing for a penalty and is unenforceable on grounds of public policy.

c. Disguised penalties. Under the rule stated in this Section, the validity of a term providing for damages depends on the effect of that term as interpreted according to the rules stated in Chapter 9. Neither the parties' actual intention as to its validity nor their characterization of the term as one for liquidated damages or a penalty is significant in determining whether the term is valid. Sometimes parties attempt to disguise a provision for a penalty by using language that purports to make payment of the amount an alternative performance under the contract, that purports to offer a discount for prompt performance, or that purports to place a valuation on property to be delivered. Although the parties may in good faith contract for alternative performances and fix discounts or valuations, a court will look to the substance of the agreement to determine whether this is the case or whether the parties have attempted to disguise a provision for a penalty that is unenforceable under this Section. In determining whether a contract is one for alternative performances, the relative value of the alternatives may be decisive.

Illustration

5. A contracts to build a house for B for $50,000 by a specified date or in the alternative to pay B $1,000 a week during any period of delay. A delays completion for ten days. If $1,000 a week is unreasonable in the light of both the anticipated and actual loss, A's promise to pay $1,000 a week is, in spite of its form, a term providing for a penalty and is unenforceable on grounds of public policy.

d. Related types of provisions. This Section does not purport to cover the wide variety of provisions used by parties to control the remedies available to them for breach of contract. A term that fixes as damages an amount that is unreasonably small does not come within the rule stated in this Section, but a court may refuse to enforce it as unconscionable under the rule stated in § 208. A mere recital of the harm that may occur as a result of a breach of contract does not come within the rule stated in this Section, but may increase damages by making that harm foreseeable under the rule stated § 351. As to the effect of a contract provision on the right to equitable relief, see Comment a to § 359. As to the effect of a term requiring the occurrence of a condition where forfeiture would result, see § 229. Although attorneys' fees are not generally awarded to the winning party, if the parties provide for the award of such fees the court will award a sum that it considers to be reasonable. If, however, the parties specify the amount of such fees, the provision is subject to the test stated in this Section.

e. Penalties in bonds. Bonds often fix a flat sum as a penalty for non-occurrence of the condition of the bond. A term providing for a penalty is not unenforceable in its entirety but only to the extent that it exceeds the loss caused by the non-occurrence of the condition.

Illustration

6. A executes a bond obligating himself to pay B $10,000, on condition that the bond shall be void, however, if C, who is B's cashier, shall properly account for all money entrusted to him. C defaults to the extent of $500. A's promise is unenforceable on grounds of public policy to the extent that it exceeds the actual loss, $500.

TOPIC 3. ENFORCEMENT BY SPECIFIC PERFORMANCE AND INJUNCTION

§ 357. Availability of Specific Performance and Injunction.

(1) Subject to the rules stated in §§ 359–69, specific performance of a contract duty will be granted in the discretion of the court against a party who has committed or is threatening to commit a breach of the duty.

(2) Subject to the rules stated in §§ 359–69, an injunction against breach of a contract duty will be granted in the discretion of the court against a party who has committed or is threatening to commit a breach of the duty if

(a) the duty is one of forbearance, or

(b) the duty is one to act and specific performance would be denied only for reasons that are inapplicable to an injunction.

Comment

a. Specific performance. An order of specific performance is intended to produce as nearly as is practicable the same effect that the performance due under a contract would have produced. It usually, therefore, orders a party to render the performance that he promised. (On the form of the order, see § 358.) Such relief is seldom granted unless there has been a breach of contract, either by nonperformance or by repudiation. In unusual circumstances, however, it may be granted where there is merely a threatened breach. See Subsection (1).

b. Injunction. A court may by injunction direct a party to refrain from doing a specified act. This is appropriate in two types of cases.

In the first, the performance due under the contract consists simply of forbearance, and the injunction in effect orders specific performance. See Paragraph (2)(a). Duties of forbearance are often imposed not as a matter of agreement but as a matter of law, as is usually the case for the duty not to interfere with the other party's performance of the contract. Duties of forbearance are ordinarily accompanied by other duties that require affirmative action by both parties. The presence of such other duties does not, of itself, preclude issuance of an injunction ordering forbearance only, but an injunction will not be issued if the performance of those other duties cannot be secured. See § 363.

In the second type of case, the performance due under the contract consists of the doing of an act rather than of forbearance, and the injunction is used as an indirect means of enforcing the duty to act. See Paragraph (2)(b). Instead of ordering that the act be done, the court orders forbearance from inconsistent action. This is appropriate in situations where an injunction will afford a measure of relief and the duty to act would have been specifically enforced were it not for some objection that can be avoided by ordering forbearance from inconsistent action. For example, the difficulties involved in supervising compliance with the order may be less in the case of an injunction that in the case of specific performance. See § 366. An injunction will not be issued, however, if the reason for refusing specific performance is not merely that the practical difficulties of such relief are too great but that compelling performance of the duty is itself undesirable. For example, an injunction is not ordinarily appropriate as an indirect means of enforcing a duty to render personal service. See Comment c to § 367.

Illustrations

1. A contracts with B to give B the "first refusal" of A's house on stated terms. A later offers to sell the house to others without first offering it to B and B sues A to enjoin him from doing this. An injunction may properly be granted.

2. A, B and C form a partnership to practice veterinary medicine in a town for ten years. In the partnership agreement each makes an enforceable promise that if, on the termination of the partnership, the practice is continued by the other two members, he will not practice veterinary medicine in the same town during its continuance up to a maximum of three years. See Illustration 11 to § 188. A leaves the partnership and the practice is continued by B and C. A immediately threatens to begin the practice of veterinary medicine in the same town, and B and C sue to enjoin A from doing so. An injunction may properly be granted.

3. A, the owner of a large factory, contracts to take all of his requirements of electricity from B, who promises to build a new electric plant at a place where it would not otherwise be profitable. A repudiates the contract and B sues A to enjoin him from using electricity that is not supplied by B. An injunction may properly be granted.

4. A makes a contract with B under which A promises to sell exclusively B's dress patterns in A's stores for a period of five years. The contract provides details as to manner of exhibition and division of profits. On anticipatory repudiation of the contract by A, B sues A for specific performance of his duty to sell B's patterns and to enjoin him from selling competing dress patterns. Even if the court refuses specific performance on the ground that enforcement and supervision would be too difficult (§ 366), it may properly grant an injunction.

5. A, a fruit growers' cooperative, contracts to sell to B, a fruit processor, 1,000 tons of loganberries a year for five years. In reliance on the contract, B substantially expands his plant and engages in an extensive advertising campaign. A then repudiates the contract. The loss to B is difficult to estimate but will probably exceed $500,000. A's entire assets do not exceed $100,000. B sues A for specific performance and to enjoin A from selling loganberries to anyone other than B. Even if the court refuses specific performance on the ground that enforcement and supervision would be too difficult (§ 366), it may properly grant an injunction.

c. Discretionary nature of relief. The granting of equitable relief has traditionally been regarded as within judicial discretion. The exercise of that discretion is subject to the rules stated in §§ 359–69. It is also subject to general principles of equity that are not peculiar to contract disputes, such as those that bar relief to one who has been guilty of laches or who has come into court with unclean hands. Furthermore, it is subject to principles of common sense so that, for example, a court will not order a performance that is impossible. In granting relief, as well as in denying it, a court may take into consideration the public interest.

§ 358. Form of Order and Other Relief.

(1) An order of specific performance or an injunction will be so drawn as best to effectuate the purposes for which the contract was made and on such terms as justice requires. It need not be absolute in form and the performance that it requires need not be identical with that due under the contract.

(2) If specific performance or an injunction is denied as to part of the performance that is due, it may nevertheless be granted as to the remainder.

(3) In addition to specific performance or an injunction, damages and other relief may be awarded in the same proceeding and an indemnity against future harm may be required.

Comment

a. Flexibility of order. The objective of the court in granting equitable relief is to do complete justice to the extent that this is feasible. Under the rule stated in Subsection (1), the court has the power to mold its order to this end. The form and terms of the order are to a considerable extent within the discretion of the court. Its order may be directed at the injured party as well as at the party in breach. It may be conditional on some performance to be rendered by the injured party or a third person, such as the payment of money to compensate for defects or the giving of security. It may even be conditional on the injured party's assent to the modification of the contract that he seeks to enforce.

The exact performance that is promised in a contract may be, in whole or in part, very difficult of enforcement, or it may have become unreasonably burdensome or unlawful. Nevertheless, by exercising its discretion in fashioning the order, the court may be able substantially to assure the expectations of the parties, without undue difficulty of enforcement, unreasonable hardship to the party in breach, or violation of the law. It may command a performance by the party in breach that is not identical with the one that he promised to render. It may indirectly induce the party in breach to do an act by enjoining him from doing inconsistent acts. See § 357(2)(b). If a court cannot, because of the promisor's death or disability, compel performance of a contract to give a child rights as an heir, whether by adoption or otherwise, it may nevertheless be able to give the child those rights. Statutes in most states empower the court to transfer the title to land by virtue of its own decree or the deed of an officer of the court without the execution of a deed by the previous owner. In appropriate cases, a court may issue a preliminary injunction to prevent an undesirable change in the situation.

Illustrations

1. A, a water company, contracts with B, a city, to construct a water supply system and to supply sufficient water for public and private use, including any increase in demand. In return B gives A the exclusive right to supply water at rates fixed according to a schedule. A constructs the system substantially as agreed with the exception of a few defects, which can be corrected. B repudiates and A sues B for specific performance. Specific performance may properly be granted, conditional on correction of the defects. See § 369. If changing circumstances require it, the order may also be conditional on A's consent to modification of the terms of the contract, if this should become necessary to avoid unreasonable hardship to B.

2. A contracts to sell land to B, who promises to pay the price in eight installments on stated dates. Conveyance is to be made on payment of the third installment, and the balance is to be secured by a mortgage and paid with interest in five annual installments. After B has paid the third installment, A delays and finally refuses to convey, and B sues for specific performance. Specific performance may properly be granted. The order will be conditional on execution of the mortgage for the balance and may provide for equitable adjustment of rents and profits, interest on the unpaid part of the price, and extension of the times fixed for the last five payments to allow for time lost by A's delay.

b. Order as to part. Sometimes the requirements are met for specific performance of part of the performance due from the party in breach, but the remaining part of the performance has become impracticable or is otherwise of such a character as to preclude such relief. A court may properly issue an order as to the first part, together with any compensation that is appropriate for non-performance of the second part. This will not be done, however, if compelling performance of only part would impose unreasonable hardship on the party in breach.

c. Damages and other relief. In addition to any equitable relief granted, a court may also award damages or other relief. Since an order seldom results in performance within the time the contract requires, damages for the delay will usually be appropriate. A seller of land who cannot perform as agreed because of a deficiency in area or a defect in title may be ordered to transfer all that he can, with compensation for the resulting claim for partial breach. The compensation may take the form of damages, restitution of money already paid or an abatement of the price not yet paid. A claimant who sues for specific performance or an injunction and who is denied that relief, may be awarded damages or restitution in the same proceeding. In appropriate cases, an indemnity may be required against future harm, and in some cases such an indemnity may be the only remedy that is necessary.

Illustrations

3. A contracts to sell B a tract of land warranted to contain 200 acres for $100,000. The tract contains only 160 acres, substantially uniform in value. A refuses to perform and B sues for specific performance. Specific performance will be granted with an abatement of $20,000, conditional on B paying $80,000. See Illustration 1 to § 369. If the price had already been paid in full, the decree would order the restitution of $20,000.

4. A contracts to transfer land to B and to make specified repairs and complete an unfinished building on the land. A repudiates and B sues for specific performance. Specific performance of A's duty to transfer the land may be granted with an abatement in the price or other compensation sufficient to enable him to make the repairs and complete the building himself.

§ 359. Effect of Adequacy of Damages.

(1) Specific performance or an injunction will not be ordered if damages would be adequate to protect the expectation interest of the injured party.

(2) The adequacy of the damage remedy for failure to render one part of the performance due does not preclude specific performance or injunction as to the contract as a whole.

(3) Specific performance or an injunction will not be refused merely because there is a remedy for breach other than damages, but such a remedy may be considered in exercising discretion under the rule stated in § 357.

Comment

a. Bases for requirement. The underlying objective in choosing the form of relief to be granted is to select a remedy that will adequately protect the legally recognized interest of the injured party. If, as is usually the case, that interest is the expectation interest, the remedy may take the form either of damages or of specific performance or an injunction. As to the situation in which the interest to be protected is the restitution interest, see § 373.

During the development of the jurisdiction of courts of equity, it came to be recognized that equitable relief would not be granted if the award of damages at law was adequate to protect the interests of the injured party. There is, however, a tendency to liberalize the granting of equitable relief by enlarging the classes of cases in which damages are not regarded as an adequate remedy. This tendency has been encouraged by the adoption of the Uniform Commercial Code, which "seeks to further a more liberal attitude than some courts have shown in connection with the specific performance of contracts of sale." Comment 1 to Uniform Commercial Code § 2–716. In accordance with this tendency, if the adequacy of the damage remedy is uncertain, the combined effect of such other factors as uncertainty of terms (§ 362), insecurity as to the agreed exchange (§ 363) and difficulty of enforcement (§ 366) should be considered. Adequacy is to some extent relative, and the modern approach is to compare remedies to determine which is more effective in serving the ends of justice. Such a comparison will often lead to the granting of equitable relief. Doubts should be resolved in favor of the granting of specific performance or injunction.

Because the availability of equitable relief was historically viewed as a matter of jurisdiction, the parties cannot vary by agreement the requirement of inadequacy of damages, although a court may take appropriate notice of facts recited in their contract. See also Comment b to § 361.

b. Damages adequate as to part. The fact that damages would be an adequate remedy for failure to render one part of the promised performance does not preclude specific performance of the contract as a whole. In such a case, complete relief should be granted in a single action and that relief may properly be a decree ordering performance of the entire contract if the other requisites for such relief are met.

Illustration

1. A contracts to sell his business, including land, buildings and stock in trade, to B. A repudiates the contract and B sues for specific performance. Specific performance of the entire contract may be granted, even though the stock in trade is of a kind that could be purchased elsewhere. However, in that case it is also within the court's discretion to require A to convey the land and buildings and to pay damages for failure to deliver the stock in trade.

c. Other legal remedies. Common-law remedies other than damages may be available to the injured party, but they will seldom afford as complete relief as will specific performance. Restitution of the value in money of the performance rendered by the injured party is one of those remedies, but it does not purport to be the equivalent of a promised performance, and its availability is not a sufficient reason for denying specific enforcement. Replevin is another of those remedies, but its effectiveness is reduced by rules allowing the giving of a bond in place of surrendering of the goods sought to be replevied. The availability of such a remedy will not preclude the granting of equitable relief, although it may be considered by a court in the exercise of its discretion in that regard. The availability of other forms of equitable relief, such as a decree for specific restitution, for reformation, and for rescission or cancellation, may also be considered in choosing the remedy best suited to the circumstances of the case.

§ 360. Factors Affecting Adequacy of Damages.

In determining whether the remedy in damages would be adequate, the following circumstances are significant:

(a) the difficulty of proving damages with reasonable certainty,

(b) the difficulty of procuring a suitable substitute performance by means of money awarded as damages, and

(c) the likelihood that an award of damages could not be collected.

Comment

a. Principal factors. Under the rule stated in § 359, specific performance or an injunction will not be ordered if damages would be adequate to protect the injured party's expectation interest. This Section lists the principal factors that enter into a decision as to the adequacy of damages. The enumeration does not purport to be exclusive of other factors. A court may also consider, for example, the probability that full compensation cannot be had without multiple litigation, although this is an unusual circumstance in contract cases.

b. Difficulty in proving damages. The damage remedy may be inadequate to protect the injured party's expectation interest because the loss caused by the breach is too difficult to estimate with reasonable certainty (§ 352). If the injured party has suffered loss but cannot sustain the burden of proving it, only nominal damages will be awarded. If he can prove some but not all of his loss, he will not be compensated in full. In either case damages are an inadequate remedy. Some types of interests are by their very nature incapable of being valued in money. Typical examples include heirlooms, family treasures and works of art that induce a strong sentimental attachment. Examples may also be found in contracts of a more commercial character. The breach of a contract to transfer shares of stock may cause a loss in control over the corporation. The breach of a contract to furnish an indemnity may cause the sacrifice of property and financial ruin. The breach of a covenant not to compete may cause the loss of customers of an unascertainable number or importance. The breach of a requirements contract may cut off a vital supply of raw materials. In such situations, equitable relief is often appropriate.

Illustrations

1. A contracts to sell to B a painting by Rembrandt for $1,000,000. A repudiates the contract and B sues for specific performance. Specific performance will be granted.

2. A contracts to sell to B the racing sloop "Columbia," this sloop being one of a class of similar boats manufactured by a particular builder. Although other boats of this class are easily obtainable, their racing characteristics differ considerably and B has selected the "Columbia" because she is regarded as a witch in light airs and, therefore, superior to most of the others. A repudiates the contract and B sues for specific performance. Specific performance may properly be granted.

3. A contracts to sell to B his interest as holder of a franchise to operate a hamburger stand. Because A has not yet opened his stand for business, it would be difficult to prove his expected profits with reasonable certainty. A repudiates the contract and B sues for specific performance. Specific performance may properly be granted.

4. A, a manufacturer of steel, contracts to sell B all of its output of steel scrap for a period of five years. After one year, A repudiates the contract and B sues A for specific performance. The uncertainty in A's output over the remaining four years would make it very difficult for B to prove damages. Specific performance may properly be granted.

5. A contracts to supply B with water for irrigation. In reliance on his contract, B sows his land with rice. A repudiates the contract although he has water that he can supply and B sues for specific performance. The loss that B will suffer as a result of A's failure to supply water is difficult of estimation. Specific performance may properly be granted.

c. Difficulty of obtaining substitute. If the injured party can readily procure by the use of money a suitable substitute for the promised performance, the damage remedy is ordinarily adequate. Entering into a substitute transaction is generally a more efficient way to prevent injury than is a suit for specific performance or an injunction and there is a sound economic basis for limiting the injured party to damages in such a case. Furthermore, the substitute transaction affords a basis for proving damages with reasonable certainty, eliminating the factor stated in Paragraph (a)....

Illustrations

6. A contracts to sell B 10,000 bales of cotton. A repudiates the contract on the day for delivery. B can buy cotton on the market at a somewhat higher price. B will not be granted specific performance.

7. A contracts to sell to B 1,000 shares of stock in the X Corporation for $10,000. A repudiates the contract and B sues for specific performance. Other shares of X Corporation are not readily obtainable and B will suffer an uncertain loss as a result of diminished voting power. Specific performance may properly be granted. If other shares were readily obtainable, even though at a considerably higher price, specific performance would be refused.

8. A contracts to obtain a patent for his invention and to assign a half interest in it to B, who promises to pay A's expenses and $100,000. A repudiates the contract and threatens to assign the patent when it is issued to others. B sues A for specific performance. Specific performance may properly be granted. The decree may enjoin A from assigning the patent to others and order him to proceed with the application and, on its issuance to execute an assignment to B, all conditional on appropriate payment by B.

d. Difficulty of collecting damages. Even if damages are adequate in other respects, they will be inadequate if they cannot be collected by judgment and execution. The party in breach may be judgment proof or may conceal his assets. Statutes may exempt some or all of his property from execution. If he is insolvent, specific performance may result in a preferential transfer to the party seeking relief and will then be denied on grounds of public policy. See Comment b to § 365 and Illustration 4 to that Section. If, however, the contract is unperformed on both sides and provides for a fair exchange, performance will not result in a preferential transfer and may benefit other creditors and help prevent insolvency.

Illustrations

9. A contracts to sell his stock of goods together with good will to B for $100,000, a fair price, payable on delivery. Before the time for performance, A becomes insolvent and repudiates the contract. B sues A for specific performance. A's insolvency is a factor tending to show that damages are inadequate. But see Illustration 4 to § 365.

10. A owns an interest in a shop, the title to which is held by B in trust for A and others. B is insolvent. A assigns his interest to C and B contracts with C to effectuate the transfer of that interest to C and to terminate his own power. B then refuses to do so and C sues B for specific performance. B's insolvency is a factor tending to show that damages are inadequate.

e. Contracts for the sale of land. Contracts for the sale of land have traditionally been accorded a special place in the law of specific performance. A specific tract of land has long been regarded as unique and impossible of duplication by the use of any amount of money. Furthermore, the value of land is to some extent speculative. Damages have therefore been regarded as inadequate to enforce a duty to transfer an interest in land, even if it is less than a fee simple. Under this traditional view, the fact that the buyer has made a contract for the resale of the land to a third person does not deprive him of the right to specific performance. If he cannot convey the land to his purchaser, he will be held for damages for breach of the resale contract, and it is argued that these damages cannot be accurately determined without litigation. Granting him specific performance enables him to perform his own duty and to avoid litigation and damages.

Similarly, the seller who has not yet conveyed is generally granted specific performance on breach by the buyer. Here it is argued that, because the value of land is to some extent speculative, it may be difficult for him to prove with reasonable certainty the difference between the contract price and the market price of the land. Even if he can make this proof, the land may not be immediately convertible into money and he may be deprived of funds with which he could have made other investments. Furthermore, before the seller gets a judgment, the existence of the contract, even if broken by the buyer, operates as a clog on saleability, so that it may be difficult to find a purchaser at a fair price. The fact that specific performance is available to the buyer has sometimes been regarded as of some weight under the now discarded doctrine of "mutuality of remedy" (see Comment c to § 363), but this is today of importance only because it enables a court to assure the vendee that he will receive the agreed performance if he is required to pay the price. The fact that legislation may have prohibited imprisonment as a means of enforcing a decree for the payment of money does not affect the seller's right to such a decree. After the seller has transferred the interest in the land to the buyer, however, and all that remains is for the buyer to pay the price, a money judgment for the amount of the price is an adequate remedy for the seller.

Illustrations

11. On February 1, A contracts to sell his farm to B for $500,000, of which $100,000 is paid when the contract is signed and $400,000 is to be paid on A's delivery of a deed on August 1. On March 1, A repudiates the contract. B sues A for specific performance. Specific performance will be granted immediately, A's performance not to take place until August 1 and to be conditional on the simultaneous payment by B of the $400,000 balance when the deed is tendered at that time. A may also be enjoined from making a conveyance to anyone else.

12. The facts being otherwise as stated in Illustration 11, B rather than A repudiates the contract on March 1 and A sues B for specific performance. Specific performance will be granted immediately, B's performance not to take place until August 1 and to be conditional on the simultaneous tender by A of the deed when the $400,000 balance is tendered at that time.

13. A contracts to sell land to B, a dealer in land, who contracts to sell it to C. C plans to build a home on the land and would be granted specific performance against B if B refused to convey the land to him. A repudiates the contract and refuses to convey the land to B and B sues A for specific performance. Specific performance will be granted.

§ 361. Effect of Provision for Liquidated Damages.

Specific performance or an injunction may be granted to enforce a duty even though there is a provision for liquidated damages for breach of that duty.

Comment

a. Rationale. A contract provision for payment of a sum of money as damages may not afford an adequate remedy even though it is valid as one for liquidated damages and not a penalty (§ 356). Merely by providing for liquidated damages, the parties are not taken to have fixed a price to be paid for the privilege not to perform. The same uncertainty as to the loss caused that argues for the enforceability of the provision may also argue for the inadequacy of the remedy that it provides. Such a provision does not, therefore, preclude the granting of specific performance or an injunction if that relief would otherwise be granted. If the provision is unenforceable as one for a penalty, the same result follows, but because of the ineffectiveness of the clause rather than the operation of the rule here stated. If equitable relief is granted, damages for such breach as has already occurred may also be awarded in accordance with the rule stated in § 358. These damages will ordinarily be limited to the actual loss suffered unless the provision for liquidated damages affords a suitable basis for calculating such damages.

Illustration

1. A, B and C form a partnership to practice veterinary medicine in a town for ten years. In the partnership agreement each makes an enforceable promise that if, on the termination of the partnership, the practice is continued by the other two members, he will not practice veterinary medicine in the same town during its continuance up to a maximum of three years. See Illustration 11 to § 188 and Illustration 2 to § 357. Each also makes an enforceable promise that for breach of this duty he will pay $50,000 as liquidated damages. See Illustration 2 to § 356. A leaves the partnership, and the practice is continued by B and C. A immediately begins to practice veterinary medicine in the same town. B and C sue A for an injunction and damages. In spite of the liquidated damage clause, A will be enjoined from practicing veterinary medicine in violation of his promise not to compete. B and C may not then recover damages under the liquidated damage clause but may recover damages for any actual loss caused by A's breach, but not more than $50,000.

b. Provision for alternative performance distinguished. Although parties who merely provide for liquidated damages are not taken to have fixed a price for the privilege not to perform, there is no reason why parties may not fix such a price if they so choose. If a contract contains a provision for the payment of such a price as a true alternative performance, specific performance or an injunction may properly be granted on condition that the alternative performance is not forthcoming. But if the obligor chooses to pay the price, equitable relief will not be granted.

Illustration

2. A sells his grocery business to B for $200,000, of which $100,000 is payable immediately and $100,000 at the end of a year. Under the agreement A makes an enforceable promise not to engage in a business of the same kind within a hundred miles for three years unless he reduces the balance from $100,000 to $50,000. See Illustration 1 to § 188. Before the end of the year, A writes B that the balance is reduced to $50,000 and immediately opens a competing business. A will not be enjoined from operating the competing business.

§ 362. Effect of Uncertainty of Terms.

Specific performance or an injunction will not be granted unless the terms of the contract are sufficiently certain to provide a basis for an appropriate order.

Comment

a. Reason for requirement. One of the fundamental requirements for the enforceability of a contract is that its terms be certain enough to provide the basis for giving an appropriate remedy. See § 33. If this minimum standard of certainty is not met, there is no contract at all. It may be, however, that the terms are certain enough to provide the basis for the calculation of damages but not certain enough to permit the court to frame an order of specific performance or an injunction and to determine whether the resulting performance is in accord with what has been ordered. In that case there is a contract but it is not enforceable by specific performance or an injunction.

b. Degree of certainty required. If specific performance or an injunction is to be granted, it is important that the terms of the contract are sufficiently certain to enable the order to be drafted with precision because of the availability of the contempt power for disobedience. Before concluding that the required certainty is lacking, however, a court will avail itself of all of the usual aids in determining the scope of the agreement. See Chapter 9, The Scope of Contractual Obligations. Apparent difficulties of enforcement due to uncertainty may disappear in the light of courageous common sense. Expressions that at first appear incomplete may not appear so after resort to usage (§ 221) or the addition of a term supplied by law (§ 204). A contract is not too uncertain merely because a promisor is given a choice of performing in several ways, whether expressed as alternative performances or otherwise. He may be ordered to make the choice and to perform accordingly, and, if he fails to make the choice, the court may choose for him and order specific performance. Even though subsidiary terms have been left to determination by future agreement, if performance has begun by mutual consent, equitable relief may be appropriate with the court supplying the missing terms so as to assure the promisor all advantages that he reasonably expected.

Illustrations

1. A and B make a contract under which A promises to convey part of a tract of land to B and B promises to pay $100,000 and to build "a first class theatre" on it. Building the theatre will enhance the value of A's remaining land. A conveys the land to B, who pays the price but refuses to build the theatre. A sues B for specific performance. Specific performance will be refused because of the uncertainty of the terms of the contract, although A can receive damages from B based on the failure to enhance the value of his land if he can prove them with reasonable certainty (§ 352). See also § 366 on the effect of difficulty in supervision.

2. A leases land to B for three years, with an option to buy for $100,000 on terms of payment to be agreed upon. B occupies the land, making substantial repairs and improvements, and then accepts the option, tendering $100,000 in cash. A repudiates and B sues A for specific performance. Specific performance will not be refused on the ground of uncertainty. Although the terms of payment are uncertain and the parties may have contemplated a period of credit, refusal of specific performance would result in a forfeiture because B has made improvements and the payment tendered is on terms sufficiently favorable to A. See Illustration 2 to § 33.

3. A contracts to lease an apartment, with heat and light, to B as soon as the apartment building is completed. After the building is completed, A refuses to install sufficient equipment for heat and light. B sues A for specific performance. Specific performance will not be refused on the ground of uncertainty.

§ 363. Effect of Insecurity as to the Agreed Exchange.

Specific performance or an injunction may be refused if a substantial part of the agreed exchange for the performance to be compelled is unperformed and its performance is not secured to the satisfaction of the court.

Comment

a. Importance of security. The rule stated in this Section is intended to make sure that a party is not compelled to render his own performance without receiving substantially the agreed exchange from the other party. This problem does not arise in an action for damages for total breach because the party in breach is only required to pay money, and the amount is always reduced by the amount the injured party saves by not having to proceed with his own performance. If the party in breach is to be required to perform specifically, however, the injured party is expected to do the same, and some security to assure that performance is desirable. Even if performance by the party in breach would have been due under the contract before that of the injured party, such security is desirable since, after controversy has developed, the risk of non-performance is increased. In some situations, the injured party may already have so far partly performed and so committed his funds and labor that his own self-interest furnishes adequate security. In other situations, however, it will be reasonable, in the exercise of judicial discretion, to require the injured party to furnish further security.

b. Means of securing performance. The desired security can often be afforded by the terms of the order itself. If performance by the injured party is already due or will be due simultaneously with the performance of the party in breach, the order may be made conditional on the injured party's rendition of his performance. This can be done even if a series of simultaneous exchanges is involved. If performance by the injured party is not due under the contract until after performance by the party in breach or is not due until an undetermined time, the injured party may nevertheless consent to have the order conditioned on his simultaneous performance, and even absent his consent it may be just to require him to perform simultaneously if he is to be granted equitable relief rather than damages. In such situations a discount may be allowed to compensate the injured party for the advancement in the time for his performance. If security cannot be afforded by fashioning the order in one of these ways, it may be made conditional on the injured party's execution of a mortgage as security for future performance or on his giving other collateral.

If it is impossible to assure performance by the injured party, an order may be refused, especially if there is reason to fear that the injured party will not perform. For example, a contract to render personal service exclusively for one employer will not be indirectly enforced by an injunction against serving another employer unless the court is convinced that the employer is ready and willing to perform his part of the contract.

The question of security does not arise until the time for issuance of an order. At the pleading stage, a mere allegation by the plaintiff that he is ready and willing to perform is usually sufficient in a suit for specific performance or an injunction. Actual performance or tender is not generally required.

Illustrations

1. A contracts to sell land to B, part of the purchase price to be paid in installments after the time fixed for the conveyance of the land. A refuses to convey the land and B sues for specific performance. Specific performance may properly be granted, conditional on B executing a mortgage or giving other satisfactory security that the payments will be made. This is so even though the contract provides for no security.

2. A contracts to transfer land to B immediately in return for B's promise to render personal services to A for ten years. A dispute between them causes unfriendly relations, A refuses to convey the land, and B sues for specific performance. Specific performance will be refused because of the increased risk that B's services will not be rendered and because sufficient security that they will be rendered is lacking.

3. A contracts to transfer land to B on performance by B of his promise to render personal services to A for ten years. After B has performed for six years, A repudiates the contract and B, who is able and willing to finish performance, sues for specific performance. A may properly be enjoined from conveying the land to anyone else and ordered to convey it to B upon full performance by B. But see § 367(2).

4. A contracts to transfer land to B for $100,000. B promises to pay $20,000 in cash on conveyance, to pay the balance in four annual installments secured by a mortgage and, immediately on conveyance, to improve the land by building a suitable brick residence. The contract provides that if B does not build the residence, title to the land will revert to A. A refuses to convey and B sues for specific performance. Specific performance may properly be granted. Even though B's promise to build the residence may not be specifically enforceable, the provision for reversion of title affords A sufficient security. The order may be made defeasible if B does not build the residence.

5. A, a fruit growers cooperative association, organized to improve economic conditions in the industry, contracts with its members to market their fruit, each member promising to deal exclusively with the association. B, one of the members, threatens to deal with others, imperilling the association's success. There is no indication that A will fail to market B's fruit as agreed. A sues to enjoin B from dealing with others. The injunction may properly be granted without requiring additional security.

c. "Mutuality of remedy." It has sometimes been said that there is a requirement of "mutuality of remedy." However, the law does not require that the parties have similar remedies in case of breach, and the fact that specific performance or an injunction is not available to one party is not a sufficient reason for refusing it to the other party. The rationale of the supposed requirement of "mutuality of remedy" is to make sure that the party in breach will not be compelled to perform without being assured that he will receive any remaining part of the agreed exchange from the injured party. It is therefore enough if adequate security can be furnished.

Illustrations

6. A contracts to sell a tract of land to B for $100,000. The contract when made is unenforceable against B because the only memorandum of the contract is signed by A but not B. A repudiates the contract and B sues for specific performance. Specific performance may properly be granted because the commencement of the action by B makes the contract enforceable against him.

7. A contracts to sell a tract of land to B for $100,000. A is unable to convey the agreed title because C owns a part interest in the tract. A repudiates the contract and B sues for specific performance. Specific performance as to A's interest may properly be granted even though A could not have obtained such a decree against B because of his own breach. See § 369.

d. Assignments. A special application of the rule stated in this Section occurs where a party to a contract assigns his rights to an assignee. The assignee can get specific performance or an injunction on the same terms that the assignor could. The fact that the other party to the contract cannot get such relief against the assignee is not in itself a sufficient reason for refusing it when it is sought by the assignee. The assignment does not relieve the assignor from his contractual duty and may not make it less likely that the agreed exchange will be rendered. However, specific performance or an injunction may be refused if there is no satisfactory security that it will be rendered. The order may, as in any other case, be fashioned to provide this security. Furthermore, if the assignee assumes the assignor's duty, the other party acquires additional security for the performance due him. Even if the assignor repudiates his duty or becomes unable to perform it, the assignee may be able to get an order by making a tender and keeping it good.

§ 364. Effect of Unfairness.

(1) Specific performance or an injunction will be refused if such relief would be unfair because

　(a) the contract was induced by mistake or by unfair practices,

　(b) the relief would cause unreasonable hardship or loss to the party in breach or to third persons, or

　(c) the exchange is grossly inadequate or the terms of the contract are otherwise unfair.

(2) Specific performance or an injunction will be granted in spite of a term of the agreement if denial of such relief would be unfair because it would cause unreasonable hardship or loss to the party seeking relief or to third persons.

Comment

a. Types of unfairness. Courts have traditionally refused equitable relief on grounds of unfairness ... in situations where they would not necessarily refuse to award damages. Some of these situations involve ... elements of substantive unfairness in the exchange itself or in its terms that fall short of what is required for unenforceability on grounds of unconscionability. . . .

Illustrations

1. A is an aged, illiterate farmer, inexperienced in business. B is an experienced speculator in real estate who knows that a developer wants to acquire a tract of land owned by A and will probably pay a price considerably above the previous market price. B takes advantage of A's ignorance of this fact and of his general inexperience and persuades A not to seek advice. He induces A to contract to sell the land at the previous market price, which is considerably less than the developer later agrees to pay B. A refuses to perform, and B sues A for specific performance. Specific performance may properly be refused on the ground of unfairness.

2. A and B make a contract under which A is to sell B a tract of land for $100,000. B does not tell A that he intends to combine the tract with others as part of a large development in order to prevent A from asking a higher price. $100,000 is a fair price for the tract at existing market prices. A refuses to perform and B sues A for specific performance. Specific performance will not be refused on the ground of unfairness. Cf. Illustration 2 to § 171.

3. A writes B offering to sell for $100,000 a tract of land that A owns known as "201 Lincoln Street." B, who mistakenly believes that this description contains an additional tract of land worth $30,000, accepts A's offer. On discovery of his mistake, B refuses to perform and A sues for specific performance. Even if the court determines that enforcement of the contract would not be unconscionable under the rule stated in § 153, specific performance may properly be refused on the ground of unfairness. Cf. Illustration 5 to § 153.

4. A, a milkman, and B, a dairy farmer make a contract under which B is to sell and A to buy all of A's requirements of milk, but not less than 200 quarts a day, for one year. B may deliver milk from any source but expects to deliver milk from his own herd. B's herd is destroyed because of hoof and mouth disease and he fails to deliver any milk. A sues B for specific performance. Even though B's duty to deliver milk is not discharged and B is liable to A for breach of contract, specific performance may properly be refused on the ground of unfairness. Cf. Illustration 12 to § 261.

b. Unfairness in the exchange. Unfairness in the exchange does not of itself make an agreement unenforceable. . . . If it is extreme, however, it may be a sufficient ground, without more, for denying specific performance or an injunction. . . .

Illustrations

5. A, an individual, contracts in June to sell at a fixed price per ton to B, a large soup manufacturer, carrots to be grown on A's farm. The contract, written on B's standard printed form, is obviously drawn to protect B's interests and not A's; it contains numerous provisions to protect B against various contingencies and none giving analogous protection to A. Each of the clauses can be read restrictively so that it is not unconscionable, but several can be read literally to give unrestricted discretion to B. In January, when the market price has risen above the contract price, A repudiates the contract, and B seeks specific performance. In the absence of justification by evidence of commercial setting, purpose or effect, the court may determine that the contract as a whole was unconscionable when made and may properly deny specific performance on the ground of unfairness regardless of whether it would award B damages for breach.

6. A, a childless widow in her seventies suffering from Parkinson's disease, contracts with B, her niece, to leave B her farm in her will in return for B's promise to care for A for the rest of her life. B immediately resigns her job and begins to care for A, but deterioration of A's condition requires her to go to the hospital within a week and she dies without changing her will. B sues A's estate for specific performance. If the court concludes that the contract was fair when made, in view of the burden of caring for A in her condition and the risk that she might live for a considerable time, it will order specific performance.

c. Unfair term. Sometimes a party relies upon an unfair term as a defense in a suit for specific performance or injunction. Even if the term is not unconscionable (§ 208), the court may disregard it and grant the relief sought. See Illustration 7.

Illustration

7. A contracts to sell land to B for $100,000, payable in five annual $20,000 installments with conveyance to be at the time of the last payment. The contract contains a term providing that "time is of the essence with respect to each installment, and B shall lose all his rights under the contract if he fails to pay any installment when due." See Comment d to § 242. B pays the first installment and takes possession, making improvements and paying the next two installments on time. When he tenders the fourth payment one month late, A refuses it and brings an action of ejectment. B sues for specific performance. The court may refuse to enforce the quoted term on the ground of unfairness. Specific performance may then properly be granted conditional on payment into court of the fourth installment with interest from maturity and on payment of the last installment on conveyance.

§ 365. Effect of Public Policy.

Specific performance or an injunction will not be granted if the act or forbearance that would be compelled or the use of compulsion is contrary to public policy.

Comment

a. Act or forbearance against public policy. If the performance of a contract is contrary to public policy, the contract will often be unenforceable under the rules stated in Chapter 8, Unenforceability on Grounds of Public Policy. Its performance may, for example, involve a breach of a duty to a third person arising under tort law, out of a fiduciary relation or under a contract. See §§ 192, 193 and 194. There are, however, situations in which the contract is enforceable but it would be an improper use of judicial power to grant specific performance or an injunction because the act or forbearance that would be compelled would adversely affect some aspect of the public interest or would otherwise be contrary to public policy. In such situations, equitable relief will be refused even though a judgment for damages will be granted. See Illustration 1.

Illustration

1. A is induced to make a contract to sell land to B, to be paid for out of funds of C that B holds as trustee, by B's false representation that such use of C's money is within B's authority as trustee. A sues B for specific performance. Specific performance will be refused on grounds of public policy, since the act that would be ordered would involve a breach of trust, even though B will be held liable in damage for breach of contract.

b. Compulsion against public policy. Even though the act or forbearance that would be compelled is not contrary to public policy, the use of compulsion to require that act or forbearance may be contrary to public policy. One example of this general principle is the rule under which a court will refuse to grant specific performance if the character of performance is such that enforcement will impose a disproportionate burden on the court (§ 366). Another is the rule under which a court will refuse to grant specific performance of a promise to render personal services or supervision (§ 367). The general principle is not, however, limited to these situations and another important application occurs where equitable relief is denied on the ground that to grant it would give a preference with respect to the assets of an insolvent party.

Illustrations

2. A contracts to give B, a railroad company, a right of way in return for B's promise to locate a station and stop its express trains at a designated place. It later turns out that that place is an inconvenient one for the public and that the disadvantage to B as well as the public of B's promise is performed will be disproportionate to any advantage to A. B refuses to locate the station as promised, and A sues B for specific performance. Specific performance will be refused on grounds of public policy, even though B will be held liable in damages for breach of contract.

3. A borrows money from B and contracts to transfer to him as security 100 shares of stock in X Corporation but does not create a security interest in specific shares. A dies insolvent without having kept his promise. B sues A's administrator for specific performance. Specific performance will be refused on grounds of public policy because it would compel the administrator to commit a breach of his duty as trustee of the asset in his charge, even though A's estate will be held liable in damages for breach of contract.

4. A contracts to manufacture and deliver to B, for a price paid in advance, 100 articles as to which A has a monopoly under a patent. A manufactures 1,000 such articles but refuses to deliver any of them to B. B sues A for specific performance. A becomes insolvent and his other creditors file a petition in bankruptcy. A's trustee intervenes in the suit to protect A's assets. Specific performance will be refused because it would result in a preference, even though A will be held liable for breach of contract. But see Uniform Commercial Code § 2–502.

§ 366. Effect of Difficulty in Enforcement or Supervision.

A promise will not be specifically enforced if the character and magnitude of the performance would impose on the court burdens in enforcement or supervision that are disproportionate to the advantages to be gained from enforcement and to the harm to be suffered from its denial.

Comment

a. Burden on court as a factor. Granting specific performance may impose on the court heavy burdens of enforcement or supervision. Difficult questions may be raised as to the quality of the performance rendered under the decree. Supervision may be required for an extended period of time. Specific relief will not be granted if these burdens are disproportionate to the advantages to be gained from enforcement and the harm to be suffered from its denial. A court will not, however, shrink from assuming these burdens if the claimant's need is great or if a substantial public interest is involved. In such cases, for example, structures may be ordered to be built and facilities may be required to be maintained. Experience has shown that potential difficulties in enforcement or supervision are not always realized and the significance of this factor is peculiarly one for judicial discretion. Because of the limited scope appropriate to judicial review of arbitration awards, a court will be less hesitant in confirming such an award that grants specific performance than it would in granting specific performance itself.

Illustrations

1. A contracts to modernize and expand B's steel fabricating plant at a cost of $50,000,000. A falls behind the schedule fixed in the agreement, and B seeks specific performance to compel A to requisition 300 more workmen for the night shift and take other steps to speed up the work. A court may properly refuse specific performance on the ground that the difficulty of supervision by the court would be disproportionate to the benefits to be gained from enforcement.

2. The facts being otherwise as stated in Illustration 1, the dispute between A and B is referred, under a clause in the contract or a subsequent submission, to arbitration pursuant to rules stating that the arbitrator may grant any appropriate remedy including specific performance. The arbitrators award B specific performance. A court may properly confirm the award even though it would not have granted specific performance itself.

3. A, a real estate developer, sells a lot to B, contracting with him to build a sewer system to serve it. B pays the price and builds a house on the lot. A builds a sewer system that is inadequate and endangers the health and comfort of B's family. Specific performance will not be refused on the grounds that supervision by the court would be disproportionately difficult.

4. A, a manufacturer of steel, contracts to sell B all of its output of steel scrap for a period of five years. After one year, A repudiates the contract and B sues A for specific performance. Specific performance will not be refused on the ground that supervision by the court over the balance of the five-year period would be disproportionately difficult.

§ 367. Contracts for Personal Service or Supervision.

(1) A promise to render personal service will not be specifically enforced.

(2) A promise to render personal service exclusively for one employer will not be enforced by an injunction against serving another if its probable result will be to compel a performance involving personal relations the enforced continuance of which is undesirable or will be to leave the employee without other reasonable means of making a living.

Comment

a. Rationale of refusal of specific performance. A court will refuse to grant specific performance of a contract for service or supervision that is personal in nature. The refusal is based in part upon the undesirability of compelling the continuance of personal association after disputes have arisen and confidence and loyalty are gone and, in some instances, of imposing what might seem like involuntary servitude. To this extent the rule stated in Subsection (1) is an application of the more general rule under which specific performance will not be granted if the use of compulsion is contrary to public policy (§ 365).

The refusal is also based upon the difficulty of enforcement inherent in passing judgment on the quality of performance. To this extent the rule stated in Subsection (1) is an application of the more general rule on the effect of difficulty of enforcement (§ 366).

b. What is personal service. A performance is not a personal service under the rule stated in Subsection (1) unless it is personal in the sense of being non-delegable (§ 318). However, not every non-delegable performance is properly described as a service. An act such as the writing of an autograph or the signing of a diploma may be personal in the sense of being non-delegable even though it is not a personal service, and if that is so specific performance is not precluded. In determining what is a personal service, the policies reflected in the more general rules on the effect of public policy (§ 365) and of the difficulty of enforcement (§ 366) are relevant. The importance of trust and confidence in the relation between the parties, the difficulty of judging the quality of the performance rendered and the length of time required for performance are significant factors. Among the parties that have been held to render what are personal services within the rule stated in Subsection (1) are actors, singers and athletes, and the rule applies generally to contracts of employment that create the intimate relation traditionally known as master and servant. See Restatement, Second, Agency § 2.

The rule that bars specific enforcement of the employee's promise to render personal service has sometimes been extended to bar specific enforcement of the employer's promise where personal supervision is considered to be involved. The policies against compelling an employer to retain an employee have not, however, prevented courts from ordering reinstatement of employees discharged in contravention of statutes prohibiting discrimination or in violation of collective bargaining agreements.

Illustrations

1. A, a noted opera singer, contracts with B to sing exclusively at B's opera house during the coming season. A repudiates the contract before the time for performance in order to sing at C's competing opera house, and B sues A for specific performance. Even though A's singing at C's opera house will cause B great loss that he cannot prove with reasonable certainty, and even though A can find suitable jobs singing at opera houses not in competition with B's, specific performance will be refused.

2. The facts being otherwise as stated in Illustration 1, B discharges A and A sues for specific performance. Even though singing at B's opera house would have greatly enhanced A's reputation and earning power in an amount that A cannot prove with reasonable certainty, specific performance will be refused.

c. Availability of injunction. A contract for personal service is usually exclusive in the sense that it imposes not only a duty to render the service to the other party but also a duty to forbear from rendering it to anyone else. Because specific performance of the duty to render the service is precluded by the rule stated in Subsection (1), the availability of injunctive relief to enforce the duty of forbearance takes on special importance. Subsection (2) indicates the application of the general rule on injunctive relief stated in § 357(2) to this important situation. Under that general rule, an injunction will not be ordered if the remedy in damages would be adequate (§ 359). Damages are likely to be adequate to protect the employer's interest unless the employee's services are unique or extraordinary, either because of special skill that he possesses or because of special knowledge that he has acquired of the employer's business.

Even if damages are not adequate, however, an injunction will not be granted if its probable result will be to leave the employee without other reasonable means of making a living. It is not the purpose in granting the injunction to enforce the duty to render the service and, to justify granting it, it should appear that the employee is not being forced to perform the contract as the only reasonable means of making a living. Furthermore, if the probable result of an injunction will be the employee's performance of the contract, it should appear that the employer is prepared to continue the employment in good faith so that performance will not involve personal relations the enforced continuance of which is undesirable. These issues are for the exercise of judicial discretion based on such factors as the character and duration of the service, the probability of the renewal of good relations, the extent to which other remedies are adequate, and the probable hardship that will result from an injunction.

Illustrations

3. A contracts to serve exclusively as sales manager in B's clothing store for a year. A repudiates the contract shortly after beginning performance and goes to work for C, a competitor of B. B sues A for an injunction ordering A not to work for C. Unless A's services are unique or extraordinary, the injunction will be refused. If, however, A has special knowledge of B's customers that will cause a substantial number of them to leave B and patronize C, the injunction may properly be granted.

4. The facts being otherwise as stated in Illustration 1, B sues A for an injunction ordering A not to sing in C's opera house. The injunction may properly be granted. If, however, C is not a competitor of B, the injunction will not be granted because its principal effect would be indirectly to compel A to continue in B's service.

§ 368. Effect of Power of Termination.

(1) Specific performance or an injunction will not be granted against a party who can substantially nullify the effect of the order by exercising a power of termination or avoidance.

(2) Specific performance or an injunction will not be denied merely because the party seeking relief has a power to terminate or avoid his duty unless the power could be used, in spite of the order, to deprive the other party of reasonable security for the agreed exchange for his performance.

Comment

a. Power in party against whom relief is sought. Specific performance or an injunction will not be granted against a party who, by exercising a power of termination or avoidance, can substantially nullify the effect of the order. The power of termination or avoidance may be derived from a term of the agreement or from a rule of law. If a term of the agreement allows the party to terminate at will so as to make his promise illusory, no contract is created and no question of enforcement arises. See Comment e to § 2. Even if the term requires that notice of termination be given some period of time before it takes effect, so that the promise is not illusory and the contract is enforceable, the period may be so short that specific performance or an injunction would be pointless. If, however, the period is a substantial one, for example thirty days, and the performance that would have to be rendered during that period would be substantial even if notice were given immediately, equitable relief may properly be granted. As to the situation in which the power can be exercised only at the cost of rendering some significant alternative performance, see Comment b to § 361.

Illustrations

1. A, a noted opera singer, contracts with B to sing exclusively at B's opera house for two seasons, reserving the power to terminate the contract at any time after the end of the first season by giving 24 hours' written notice, A repudiates the contract when the second season is half over in order to sing at C's competing opera house, and B sues to enjoin A from doing so. The injunction will not be granted. If, however, A repudiates when the first season is half over, the injunction may be granted.

2. A sells his business to B and makes a valid promise not to carry on a competing business, reserving the power to terminate his duty not to compete by paying B $50,000. A repudiates his duty not to compete and threatens to operate a competing business, and B sues A to enjoin him from doing so. The injunction may be granted, conditional on A not having paid the $50,000.

b. Power in party seeking relief. The existence of a power of termination or avoidance in the party who seeks specific performance or an injunction does not preclude such relief unless the power will seriously threaten the other party's security that the agreed exchange will be rendered. This is a specific application of the general rule stated in § 363. If the power is reserved by a term of the agreement, the court can protect the other party by providing that either the decree itself or the other party's performance shall extinguish the power. If the party seeking relief has already rendered part performance or otherwise materially changed his position in reliance on the contract, this may give him a stronger economic interest in carrying out the agreement and thus increase the other party's security. If the other party's security cannot be reasonably assured, however, equitable relief will be refused.

Illustrations

3. A, a minor, makes a contract to transfer a farm to B for $100,000. B repudiates the contract and A sues B for specific performance. Specific performance, even on condition of payment of the $100,000, will be refused if A has not reached the age of majority, unless the jurisdiction is one in which the court's decree is conclusive on A so as to terminate his power of avoidance. After A reaches the age of majority and has ratified the contract, specific performance will be granted.

4. A makes a contract with B under which B obtains rights to all the oil and gas that he can produce from A's land for 10 years and promises to sink specific wells and pay A a fixed royalty on all oil and gas produced. The contract provides that B may at any time surrender his rights and terminate his duties on payment of $1. After B has sunk one well, A repudiates the contract and threatens to make a similar contract with C. B sues to enjoin A from interfering with his right to oil and gas as long as he continues to render substantial performance. The injunction may be granted. The result would be different if A repudiated before any performance by B and there was no way reasonably to secure B's performance.

5. A, a noted opera singer, contracts with B to sing exclusively at B's opera house during the coming season, B reserving the right to terminate the contract on 10 days' written notice. A repudiates the contract when the season is half over, after having been paid for that part of the season, in order to sing at C's competing opera house, and B sues to enjoin A from singing at C's opera house. The injunction may be granted, conditional on B's continued readiness and willingness to perform his part of the contract.

§ 369. Effect of Breach by Party Seeking Relief.

Specific performance or an injunction may be granted in spite of a breach by the party seeking relief, unless the breach is serious enough to discharge the other party's remaining duties of performance.

Comment

a. Seriousness of breach. If a party has himself committed such a serious breach of contract, whether by non-performance or repudiation, as to discharge the other party's remaining duties under the contract, the party in breach is not entitled to relief, equitable or otherwise, if the other party refuses further performance. Whether a breach is serious enough to have this effect is determined by the rules stated in Chapter 10, Performance and Non-Performance. However, the fact that a party has committed a minor breach, one not serious enough to discharge the other party's remaining duties, does not preclude specific performance or an injunction. The party seeking relief may be required to cure the breach as a condition of the decree (see Illustration 1 to § 358) or may be held accountable for damages caused by his breach, either through a payment of money to the other party or by an abatement in the price that the other party is compelled to pay.

Illustrations

1. A contracts to sell B his farm, said to contain 150 acres and to have a house on it in good repair. The farm contains 149 acres and the house is in slight disrepair. A tenders a deed but B refuses to accept it or pay although the defects are not such as would discharge his remaining duties of performance (see § 241), and A sues B for specific performance. Specific performance may properly be granted with an abatement of the price in an amount equal to damages for the defects. See Illustration 3 to § 358.

2. A contracts to sell to B his farm, conveyance and payment to be made on May 1. A tenders a deed on May 1 but B is not then able to pay. B tenders payment on May 10 but A refuses to convey although the delay is not such as would discharge his remaining duties of performance (see § 242), and B sues A for specific performance. Specific performance may properly be granted, conditional on B paying A any damages caused by the delay.

3. The facts being otherwise as stated in Illustration 2, B does not tender payment until September 1, a delay sufficient to discharge A's remaining duties of performance (see § 242). Specific performance will be refused on the ground of B's breach.

TOPIC 4. RESTITUTION

§ 370. Requirement That Benefit Be Conferred.

A party is entitled to restitution under the rules stated in this Restatement only to the extent that he has conferred a benefit on the other party by way of part performance or reliance. . . .

Illustrations

1. A, who holds a mortgage on B's house, makes a contract with B under which A promises not to foreclose the mortgage for a year. In reliance on this promise, B invests money that he would have used to pay the mortgage in improving other land that he owns. A repudiates the contract and forecloses. B cannot get restitution based on the improvements since making them conferred no benefit on A. But see Illustration 4 to § 373 and Illustration 11 to § 90.

2. A contracts to sell B a machine for $100,000. After A has spent $40,000 on the manufacture of the machine but before its completion, B repudiates the contract. A cannot get restitution of the $40,000 because no benefit was conferred on B.

3. A promises to deposit $100,000 to B's credit in the X Bank in return for B's promise to render services. A deposits the $100,000, the X Bank fails, and B refuses to perform. A can get restitution of the $100,000 because a benefit was to that extent conferred on B even though it was lost by B when the X Bank failed. See § 373.

4. A contracts to work full time for B as a bookkeeper. In breach of this contract, A uses portions of the time that he should spend working for B in keeping books for C, who pays him an additional salary. B sues A for breach of contract. B cannot recover from A the amount of the salary paid by C because it was not a benefit conferred by B.

5. A, a social worker, promises B to render personal services to C in return for B's promise to educate A's children. B repudiates the contract after A has rendered part of the services. A can get restitution from B for the services, even though they were not rendered to B, because they conferred a benefit on B. See Illustration 3 to § 371.

§ 371. Measure of Restitution Interest.

If a sum of money is awarded to protect a party's restitution interest, it may as justice requires be measured by either

(a) the reasonable value to the other party of what he received in terms of what it would have cost him to obtain it from a person in the claimant's position, or

(b) the extent to which the other party's property has been increased in value or his other interests advanced.

Comment

a. Measurement of benefit. Under the rules stated in §§ 344 and 370, a party who is liable in restitution for a sum of money must pay an amount equal to the benefit that has been conferred upon him. If the benefit consists simply of a sum of money received by the party from whom restitution is sought, there is no difficulty in determining this amount. If the benefit consists of something else, however, such as services or property, its measurement in terms of money may pose serious problems. . . .

A particularly significant circumstance is whether the benefit has been conferred by way of performance or by way of reliance in some other way. . . . Recovery is ordinarily more generous for a benefit that has been conferred by performance. To the extent that the benefit may reasonably be measured in different ways, the choice is within the discretion of the court. Thus a court may take into account the value of opportunities for benefit even if they have not been fully realized in the particular case.

An especially important choice is that between the reasonable value to a party of what he received in terms of what it would have cost him to obtain it from a person in the claimant's position and the addition to the wealth of that party as measured by the extent to which his property has been increased in value or his other interests advanced. In practice, the first measure is usually based on the market price of such a substitute. Under the rule stated in this Section, the court has considerable discretion in making the choice between these two measures of benefit. Under either choice, the court may properly consider the purposes of the recipient of the benefit when he made the contract, even if those purposes were later frustrated or abandoned.

b. Choice of measure. The reasonable value to the party against whom restitution is sought (Paragraph (a)) is ordinarily less than the cost to the party seeking restitution, since his expenditures are excluded to the extent that they conferred no benefit. See Comment *a* to § 344. Nor can the party against whom restitution is sought reduce the amount for which he may himself be liable by subtracting such expenditures from the amount of the benefit that he has received. . . . The reasonable value to the party from whom restitution is sought (Paragraph (a)), is, however, usually greater than the addition to his wealth (Paragraph (b)). If this is so, a party seeking restitution for part performance is commonly allowed the more generous measure of reasonable value, unless that measure is unduly difficult to apply, except when he is in breach (§ 374). . . . In the case of services rendered in an emergency or to save life, however, restitution based on addition to wealth will greatly exceed that based on expense saved and recovery is invariably limited to the smaller amount. See Illustration 2. In the case of services rendered to a third party as the intended beneficiary of a gift promise, restitution from the promisee based on his enrichment is generally not susceptible of measurement and recovery based on reasonable value is appropriate. . . .

Illustrations

1. A, a carpenter, contracts to repair B's roof for $3,000. A does part of the work at a cost of $2,000, increasing the market price of B's house by $1,200. The market price to have a similar carpenter do the work done by A is $1,800. A's restitution interest is equal to the benefit conferred on B. That benefit may be measured either by the addition to B's wealth from A's services in terms of the $1,200 increase in the market price of B's house or the reasonable value to B of A's services in terms of the $1,800 that it would have cost B to engage a similar carpenter to do the same work. If the work was not completed because of a breach by A . . . $1,200 is appropriate. If the work was not completed because of a breach by B . . . $1,800 is appropriate. . . .

2. A, a surgeon, contracts to perform a series of emergency operations on B for $3,000. A does the first operation, saving B's life, which can be valued in view of B's life expectancy at $1,000,000. The market price to have an equally competent surgeon do the first operation is $1,800. A's restitution interest is equal to the benefit conferred on B. That benefit is measured by the reasonable value to B of A's services in terms of the $1,800 that it would have cost B to engage a similar surgeon to do the operation regardless of the rule on which restitution is based.

3. A, a social worker, promises B to render personal services to C in return for B's promise to educate A's children. A renders only part of the services and B then refuses to educate A's children. The market price to have a similar social worker do the services rendered by A is $1,800. If A recovers in restitution under the rule stated in § 373, an appropriate measure of the benefit conferred on B is the reasonable value to B of A's services in terms of the $1,800 that it would have cost B to engage a similar social worker to do the same work.

§ 372. Specific Restitution.

(1) Specific restitution will be granted to a party who is entitled to restitution, except that:

(a) specific restitution based on a breach by the other party under the rule stated in § 373 may be refused in the discretion of the court if it would unduly interfere with the certainty of title to land or otherwise cause injustice, and

(b) specific restitution in favor of the party in breach under the rule stated in § 374 will not be granted.

(2) A decree of specific restitution may be made conditional on return of or compensation for anything that the party claiming restitution has received.

(3) If specific restitution, with or without a sum of money, will be substantially as effective as restitution in money in putting the party claiming restitution in the position he was in before rendering any performance, the other party can discharge his duty by tendering such restitution before suit is brought and keeping his tender good.

Comment

a. Specific restitution on avoidance or in similar circumstances. A party who has a right to restitution under the rule stated in § 376 because he has avoided the contract, generally has a choice of either claiming a sum of money in restitution or seeking specific restitution if the benefit is something that can be returned to him. The same is true of a party who has a right to restitution under the rule stated in § 377 on one of the grounds there stated, even though this rule does not, strictly speaking, result in avoidance of the contract. The right to specific restitution may, however, be subject to rights of third parties. Their rights are not dealt with in this Restatement. For special rules governing the right of a seller under a contract for the sale of goods, see Uniform Commercial Code §§ 2–507, 2–702.

Illustration

1. A is induced by B's misrepresentation to sell a tract of land to B for $100,000. On discovery of the misrepresentation, A tenders back the $100,000 and sues B for specific restitution of the land. Specific restitution will be granted.

b. Specific restitution on other grounds. A party whose right to restitution is based on the other party's breach also has a right to specific restitution, subject to the limitation stated in Paragraph (a). In the case of a contract for the sale of goods, the Uniform Commercial Code limits much more severely the seller's right to specific restitution, although the seller can protect himself by taking a security interest in the goods. See Uniform Commercial Code § 2–703. The most important problems of specific restitution that remain usually arise in connection with contracts to transfer land. If the buyer of land fails or refuses to pay the price after the transfer of the land to him, the seller is limited to his claim for the price, which may be secured by a vendor's lien as a matter of law or by a security interest that he has reserved. The question of his right to specific restitution does not arise in that situation (§ 373(2)). Specific restitution may, however, be appropriate where there is a right to restitution because the return promise is to do something other than pay money. See Illustrations 2 and 3. In that case, however, a court may refuse specific restitution if it would unduly interfere with the certainty of title to the land. In resolving that question, a court will take into account all the circumstances, including the inadequacy of other relief. A court may also refuse specific restitution if it would otherwise cause injustice as where, for example, it would result in a preference over other creditors in bankruptcy. Specific restitution under the rule stated in this Section is available to the injured party even though enforcement of the contract is barred by the Statute of Frauds. See § 375. Under the exception stated in Paragraph (b), however, it is never available to a party who is himself in breach. See § 374.

Illustrations

2. A contracts to transfer a tract of land to B in return for B's promise to transfer a tract of land to A at the same time. After A has transferred his tract to B and received a deed from B, A learns that B does not have title to the other tract. A sues B for specific restitution. Specific restitution will be granted, together with compensation to A for the value to B of the use of the land, because the right to specific restitution will not unduly interfere with the certainty of title to land. If B's promise is to transfer his tract to A ten years after A's transfer of his tract, specific restitution will be denied because a right to specific restitution would unduly interfere with the certainty of title to land during the ten years.

3. A contracts to transfer a tract of land to B in return for B's promise to support A for life. B repudiates the contract after he has supported A for a time and A has transferred the land to him, and A sues B for specific restitution. Specific restitution will be granted, conditional on compensation by A for any support that he has received less the value to B of the use of the land, because the right to specific restitution will not unduly interfere with the certainty of title to land given the inadequacy of A's right to damages because of the difficulty of proving damages with sufficient certainty (§ 352).

4. A contracts to transfer a tract of land to B in return for B's promise to transfer a tract of land to A at a later date. After A has transferred his tract of land to B, B sells both tracts to C, a good faith purchaser for value, taking a mortgage to secure the balance of the price on the tract transferred by A. A sues B and C for specific restitution. Specific restitution will be denied but A can get a decree subrogating him to B's right to the balance of the price and to his rights under the purchase money mortgage that secures it.

5. A contracts to transfer to B half of his 20,000 shares of stock in the X Corporation in return for B's promise to pay $100,000, to organize a holding company to control X Corporation and to protect A's remaining interest as a shareholder. After A has transferred the stock and B has paid the $100,000, B refuses to organize the holding company. A sues B for specific restitution. Specific restitution may properly be granted conditional on repayment by A of the $100,000.

c. *Tender of specific restitution.* In some circumstances, a party who is liable for restitution can discharge his duty by tendering specific restitution and keeping his tender good. The tender has this result only if specific restitution will be substantially as effective as restitution in money in putting the party claiming restitution in the position he was in before rendering any performance. If tender of a sum of money in addition to specific restitution will do this, such a tender discharges the other party's duty. See Illustration 6. The tender must, however, be made before suit has been brought.

Illustration

6. A makes an oral contract with B under which A transfers 1,000 shares of stock to B in return for B's promise to convey a tract of land to A. B repudiates the contract before he has conveyed the land and tenders back the stock and the dividends received from it and keeps his tender good. A rejects the tender and sues B for restitution of the value to B of the stock. A cannot recover the value of the stock.

§ 373. Restitution When Other Party Is in Breach.

(1) Subject to the rule stated in Subsection (2), on a breach by non-performance that gives rise to a claim for damages for total breach or on a repudiation, the injured party is entitled to restitution for any benefit that he has conferred on the other party by way of part performance or reliance.

(2) The injured party has no right to restitution if he has performed all of his duties under the contract and no performance by the other party remains due other than payment of a definite sum of money for that performance.

Comment

a. *Restitution as alternative remedy for breach.* An injured party usually seeks, through protection of either his expectation or his reliance interest, to enforce the other party's broken promise. See § 344(1). However, he may, as an alternative, seek, through protection of his restitution interest, to prevent the unjust enrichment of the other party. See § 344(2). This alternative is available to the injured party as a remedy for breach under the rule stated in this Section. It is available regardless of whether the breach is by non-performance or by repudiation. If, however, the breach is by non-performance, restitution is available only if the breach gives rise to a claim for damages for total breach and not merely to a claim for damages for partial breach. Compare Illustration 1 with Illustration 2. A party who has lost the right to claim damages for total breach by, for example, acceptance or retention of performance with knowledge of defects (§ 246), has also lost the right to restitution. Restitution is available on repudiation by the other party, even in those exceptional situations in which no claim for damages for total breach arises as a result of repudiation alone. See Comment d to § 253. See Illustration 3. The rule stated in this Section applies to all enforceable promises, including those that are enforceable because of reliance. See Illustration 4. An injured party's right to restitution may be barred by election under the rules stated in §§ 378 and 379.

Illustrations

1. A contracts to sell a tract of land to B for $100,000. After B has made a part payment of $20,000, A wrongfully refuses to transfer title. B can recover the $20,000 in restitution. The result is

the same even if the market price of the land is only $70,000, so that performance would have been disadvantageous to B.

2. A contracts to build a house for B for $100,000, progress payments to be made monthly. After having been paid $40,000 for two months, A commits a breach that is not material by inadvertently using the wrong brand of sewer pipe. B has a claim for damages for partial breach but cannot recover the $40,000 that he has paid A.

3. On February 1, A and B make a contract under which, as consideration for B's immediate payment of $50,000, A promises to convey to B a parcel of land on May 1. On March 1, A repudiates by selling the parcel to C. On April 1, B commences an action against C. Although under the rule stated in § 253(1), B has no claim against A for damages for breach of contract until performance is due on May 1, B can recover $50,000 from A in restitution. See Illustration 4 to § 253.

4. A, who holds a mortgage on B's land, promises B that he will not foreclose the mortgage for another year, even if B makes no payments. In reliance on A's promise, B makes valuable improvements. A forecloses in breach of his promise and buys the land at a judicial sale for the amount of the mortgage debt. B can recover in restitution for the value of the improvements. Compare Illustration 1 to § 370; see also Illustration 12 to § 90.

b. When contract price is a limit. The rule stated in Subsection (1) is subject to an important exception. If, after one party has fully performed his part of the contract, the other party then refuses to pay a definite sum of money that has been fixed as the price for that performance, the injured party is barred from recovery of a greater sum as restitution under the rule stated in Subsection (2). Since he is entitled to recover the price in full together with interest, he has a remedy that protects his expectation interest by giving him the very thing that he was promised. Even if he asserts that the benefit he conferred on the other party exceeds the price fixed by the contract, justice does not require that he have the right to recover this larger sum in restitution. To give him that right would impose on the court the burden of measuring the benefit in terms of money in spite of the fact that this has already been done by the parties themselves when they made their contract. See Illustration 5. If, however, the performance to be rendered by the party in breach is something other than the payment of a definite sum in money, this burden is less of an imposition on the court since, even if damages were sought by the injured party, the court would have to measure the value to him of the performance due from the party in breach. The clearest case occurs where the injured party has paid the full price in money for the performance that the party in breach has subsequently failed to render. To allow restitution of the sum paid in that case imposes no burden of measurement on the court and relieves it of the burden that it would have if damages were awarded of measuring the value to the injured party of the performance due from the party in breach. See Illustration 6. For this reason, the rule stated in Subsection (2) is limited to the situation where the only remaining performance due from the party in breach is the payment of a definite sum of money. See Illustrations 6 and 7. If the performance promised by the party in breach consists in part of money and in part of something else, full performance by the injured party does not bar him from restitution unless the party in breach has rendered all of his performance except a money payment.

Illustrations

5. A contracts to work for B for one month for $10,000. After A has fully performed, B repudiates the contract and refuses to pay the $10,000. A can get damages against B for $10,000, together with interest, but cannot recover more than that sum even if he can show that the benefit to B from the services was greater than $10,000.

6. A contracts to sell a tract of land to B for $100,000. After B has paid the full $100,000, A repudiates and refuses to transfer title. B has a right to $100,000 in restitution.

7. A contracts to build a building for B in return for B's promise to transfer a tract of land to A and to pay $10,000. After A has built the building, B refuses to transfer title or to pay the $10,000. A has a right to the reasonable value of his work and materials.

c. Effect of "divisibility." Sometimes a contract is "divisible" in the sense that parts of the performances to be exchanged on each side are properly regarded as a pair of agreed equivalents. See § 240. The rule stated in Subsection (2) applies by analogy to such contracts. If one party has fully performed his side of such a pair and all that remains on the other side is for the other party to pay a definite sum of money, recovery for the performance rendered is limited to that sum. Restitution is not available as an alternative even if there has been a breach as to other parts of the contract. See Illustration 8. If both parties have fully performed, so that nothing with respect to the pair of agreed equivalents remains to be done on either side, no recovery can be had as to that pair.

Illustrations

8. A contracts to work as a consultant for B for a fee of $50,000, payable at the end of the year, together with a payment of $200 a month for A's use of his own car and reimbursement of A's expenses. B wrongfully discharges A at the end of six months. A cannot recover in restitution for the use of his car or for his expenses, but can recover for these items as provided in the contract. As to his recovery for his services, see Illustration 12.

9. A contracts to build a house for B for $50,000, progress payments to be made monthly in an amount equal to 85% of the price of the work performed during the preceding month, the balance to be paid on the architect's certificate of satisfactory completion of the house. B makes the first three payments and then repudiates the contract and has another builder finish the house. A can recover in restitution for the reasonable value of his work, labor and materials, less the amount of the three payments. The performance during each month and the corresponding progress payments are not agreed equivalents under the rule stated in § 240. See Illustration 7 to § 240.

d. Losing contracts. An injured party who has performed in part will usually prefer to seek damages based on his expectation interest (§ 347) instead of a sum of money based on his restitution interest because such damages include his net profit and will give him a larger recovery. Even if he cannot prove what his net profit would have been, he will ordinarily seek damages based on his reliance interest (§ 348), since this will compensate him for all of his expenditures, regardless of whether they resulted in a benefit to the party in breach. See Comment a to § 344. In the case of a contract on which he would have sustained a loss instead of having made a profit, however, his restitution interest may give him a larger recovery than would damages on either basis. The right of the injured party under a losing contract to a greater amount in restitution than he could have recovered in damages has engendered much controversy. The rules stated in this Section give him that right. He is entitled to such recovery even if the contract price is stated in terms of a rate per unit of work and the recovery exceeds that rate. There are, however, two important limitations. The first limitation is one that is applicable to any claim for restitution: the party in breach is liable only to the extent that he has benefited from the injured party's performance. If he has, for example, taken advantage of the injured party's part performance by having the rest of the work completed after his breach, the extent of his benefit is easy to measure in terms of the reasonable value of the injured party's performance. See Illustration 10. If, however, he has abandoned the project and not completed the work, that measurement will be more difficult. See Illustration 11. In that situation, the court may exercise its sound discretion in choosing between the two measures stated in § 371. In doing so it will take account of all the circumstances including the observance by the parties of standards of good faith and fair dealing during any negotiations leading up to the rupture of contractual relations (§ 208). See Introductory Note to Chapter 10. Since a contract that is a losing one for the injured party is often an advantageous one for the party in breach, the possibility should not be overlooked that the breach was provoked by the injured party in order to avoid having to perform. The second limitation is that stated in Subsection (2). If the injured party has completed performance and nothing remains for the party in breach to do but to pay him the price, his recovery is limited to the price. See Comment b.

Illustrations

10. A, a plumbing subcontractor, contracts with B, a general contractor, to install the plumbing in a factory being built by B for C. B promises to pay A $100,000. After A has spent $40,000, B repudiates the contract and has the plumbing finished by another subcontractor at a cost of $80,000. The market price to have a similar plumbing subcontractor do the work done by A is $40,000. A can recover the $40,000 from B in restitution.

11. A contracts to build a house for B for $100,000. After A has spent $40,000, B discovers that he does not have good title to the land on which the house is to be built. B repudiates the contract and abandons the project. A's work results in no actual benefit to B. A cannot recover in restitution from

B, but under the rule stated in § 349 he can recover as damages the $40,000 that he has spent unless B proves with reasonable certainty that A would have sustained a net loss if the contract had been performed. See Illustration 4 to § 349.

12. A contracts to work as a consultant for B for a fee of $50,000, payable at the end of the year. B wrongfully discharges A at the end of eleven months. A can recover in restitution based on the reasonable value of his services. The terms of the contract are evidence of this value but are not conclusive.

e. Avoidability as a limit on restitution. The rule that precludes restitution for a benefit that has been conferred officiously (Restatement of Restitution § 2), applies to preclude recovery for performances that a party has rendered following a repudiation by the other party. Compare the rule stated in § 350.

Illustration

13. A contracts to build a bridge for B for $100,000. B repudiates the contract shortly after A has begun work on the bridge, telling A that he no longer has need for it. A nevertheless spends an additional $10,000 in continuing to perform. A's restitution interest under the rule stated in § 370 does not include the benefit conferred on B by the $10,000. See Illustration 1 to § 350.

§ 374. Restitution in Favor of Party in Breach.

(1) Subject to the rule stated in Subsection (2), if a party justifiably refuses to perform on the ground that his remaining duties of performance have been discharged by the other party's breach, the party in breach is entitled to restitution for any benefit that he has conferred by way of part performance or reliance in excess of the loss that he has caused by his own breach.

(2) To the extent that, under the manifested assent of the parties, a party's performance is to be retained in the case of breach, that party is not entitled to restitution if the value of the performance as liquidated damages is reasonable in the light of the anticipated or actual loss caused by the breach and the difficulties of proof of loss.

Comment

a. Restitution in spite of breach. The rule stated in this Section applies where a party, after having rendered part performance, commits a breach by either non-performance or repudiation that justifies the other party in refusing further performance. It is often unjust to allow the injured party to retain the entire benefit of the part performance rendered by the party in breach without paying anything in return. The party in breach is, in any case, liable for the loss caused by his breach. If the benefit received by the injured party does not exceed that loss, he owes nothing to the party in breach. If the benefit received exceeds that loss, the rule stated in this Section generally gives the party in breach the right to recover the excess in restitution. If the injured party has a right to specific performance and remains willing and able to perform, he may keep what he has received and sue for specific performance of the balance.

The rule stated in this Section is of particular importance in connection with breach by the buyer under a land sale contract (see Illustration 1) and breach by the builder under a construction contract (see Illustrations 2, 3 and 4). It is less important in the case of the defaulting employee, who has the protection afforded by statutes that require salary payments at relatively short intervals. The case of defaulting buyer of goods is governed by Uniform Commercial Code § 2–718(2), which generally allows restitution of all but an amount fixed by that section. Furthermore, to the extent that the contract is "divisible" so that pairs of part performances on each side are agreed equivalents (§ 240), the party in breach can recover under the terms of the contract and does not need restitution to obtain relief.

b. Measurement of benefit. If the party in breach seeks restitution of money that he has paid, no problem arises in measuring the benefit to the other party. See Illustration 1. If, however, he seeks to recover a sum of money that represents the benefit of services rendered to the other party, measurement of the benefit is more difficult. Since the party seeking restitution is responsible for posing the problem of measurement of benefit, doubts will be resolved against him and his recovery will not exceed the less generous of the two measures stated in § 370, that of the other party's increase in wealth. See Illustration 3. If no value can be put on this, he cannot recover. See Illustration 5. Although the contract price is evidence of the benefit, it is not conclusive. However, in no case will the party in breach be allowed to recover more than a ratable portion of the total contract price where such a portion can be determined.

A party who intentionally furnishes services or builds a building that is materially different from what he promised is properly regarded as having acted officiously and not in part performance of his promise and will be denied recovery on that ground even if his performance was of some benefit to the other party. This is not the case, however, if the other party has accepted or agreed to accept the substitute performance. See §§ 278, 279.

Illustrations

1. A contracts to sell land to B for $100,000, which B promises to pay in $10,000 installments before transfer of title. After B has paid $30,000 he fails to pay the remaining installments and A sells the land to another buyer for $95,000. B can recover $30,000 from A in restitution less $5,000 damages for B's breach of contract, or $25,000. If A does not sell the land to another buyer and obtains a decree of specific performance against B, B has no right to restitution.

2. A contracts to make repairs to B's building in return for B's promise to pay $10,000 on completion of the work. After spending $8,000 on the job, A fails to complete it because of insolvency. B has the work completed by another builder for $4,000, increasing the value of the building to him by a total of $9,000, but he loses $500 in rent because of the delay. A can recover $5,000 from B in restitution less $500 in damages for the loss caused by the breach, or $4,500.

3. A contracts to make repairs to B's building in return for B's promise to pay $10,000 on completion of the work. A makes repairs costing him $8,000 but inadvertently fails to follow the specifications in such material respects that there is no substantial performance. See Comment d to § 237. The defects cannot be corrected without the destruction of large parts of the building, but the work confers a benefit on B by increasing the value of the building to him by $4,000. A can recover $4,000 from B in restitution.

4. The facts being otherwise as stated in Illustration 3, the defects do not require destruction of large parts of the building and can be corrected for $4,000, which will confer a benefit on B by increasing the value of the building to him by a total of $9,000. A can recover $5,000 from B in restitution.

5. A contracts to tutor B's son for six months in preparation for an examination, in return for which B promises to pay A $2,000 at the end of that time. After A has worked for three months, he leaves to take another job and B is unable to find a suitable replacement. In the absence of any reliable basis for measuring the benefit to B from A's part performance, restitution will be denied.

c. Exception for money paid. Instead of promising to pay a fixed sum as liquidated damages in case of breach, a promisor may actually pay a sum of money that the parties understand is to be retained by the promisee if the promise is not performed. If the sum is a reasonable one that would be sustained as liquidated damages under the rule stated in § 356, the promisee is entitled to retain it. If it is not, the promisor is entitled to restitution under the rule stated in Subsection (1). The test of reasonableness is the same as that applicable to a provision for liquidated damages. See Comment b to § 356. The understanding of the parties may be shown by the terms of their agreement, by description of the sum as "earnest money" or by usage. The sum may or may not be part of the price to be paid by the promisor. The same principle applies if what is to be retained by the promisee is property other than money.

Illustrations

6. The facts being otherwise as stated in Illustration 1, the contract provides that on default by B, A has the right to retain the first $10,000 installment paid by B. If $10,000 is a reasonable amount, B can recover only $20,000 from A in restitution.

7. The facts being otherwise as stated in Illustration 1, the contract provides that on default by B, A has the right to retain any installments paid by B. The provision is not valid, and B can still recover $30,000 from A in restitution less $5,000 damages for B's breach of contract, or $25,000.

§ 375. Restitution When Contract Is Within Statute of Frauds.

A party who would otherwise have a claim in restitution under a contract is not barred from restitution for the reason that the contract is unenforceable by him because of the Statute of Frauds unless the Statute provides otherwise or its purpose would be frustrated by allowing restitution.

Comment

a. Restitution generally available. Parties to a contract that is unenforceable under the Statute of Frauds frequently act in reliance on it before discovering that it is unenforceable. A party may, for example, render services under the contract or may make improvements on land that is the subject of the contract. The rule stated in this Section allows restitution in such cases. See Illustrations 1 and 2. If the party claiming restitution is in breach, the right to restitution is subject to the rule stated in § 374. If the other party is in breach it is subject to the rule stated in § 373. Since allowing restitution does not amount to enforcement of the contract, it ordinarily does not contravene the policy behind the Statute. Restitution will not be allowed, however, if the Statute so provides or if restitution would frustrate the purpose of the Statute. See Illustration 3. However, the mere fact that the particular wording of the Statute makes the contract "void" is not controlling in this respect.

For the purposes of this Section, the measure of the benefit conferred is generally the same as that applicable to similar situations under enforceable contracts. See Comment b to § 373 and Comment b to § 374. The agreement, although unenforceable, may be evidence of this benefit. As to the possibility of recovery based on the reliance interest, see § 139.

Illustrations

1. A makes an oral contract to furnish services to B that are not to be performed within a year (§ 130). After A has worked for two months B discharges him without paying him anything. A can recover from B as restitution the reasonable value of the services rendered during the two months.

2. A makes an oral contract to sell a tract of land to B for $100,000 (§ 125). B pays $50,000, takes possession and makes improvements. A then refuses to convey the land to B, and B sues A for restitution of $50,000 plus $20,000, the reasonable value of the improvements, less $5,000, the value to B of the use of the land. B can recover $65,000 from A.

3. A, a home owner, makes an oral contract with B, a real estate broker, to pay B the usual 5% commission if B succeeds in selling A's house. The state Statute of Frauds contains a provision providing that a real estate broker shall have no right to such a commission unless there is a written memorandum of the contract. B sells A's house for $100,000 and sues A in restitution for $5,000, the reasonable value of B's services. B cannot recover in restitution because the purpose of the Statute would be frustrated if B were allowed to recover as restitution the same amount that had been promised under the contract.

b. Limits on restitution. The rule stated in this Section gives a right to restitution only to one who would have such a right if the contract were enforceable. It is therefore subject to the rules stated in §§ 370–72. A party's right to restitution may, for example, be terminated by the other party's tender of specific restitution. See § 373(4). Furthermore, the rule stated in this Section governs the right to restitution only if the Statute makes the contract unenforceable. If the party seeking restitution under a land sale contract has a right to enforce the contract by a suit for specific performance on the ground of reliance (§ 129), his right to restitution is governed by the rules stated in §§ 373 and 374. Similarly, if a party seeking restitution under a contract not to be performed within a year has a right to enforce it because he has completely performed, his right to restitution is governed by the rule stated in § 373. Finally, under the rule stated in § 138(1), the right to restitution is subject to the same defenses that would be available if the Statute were satisfied. A party has no right to restitution, therefore, if the other party is not in breach and is prepared to perform, except to the extent that such a right would exist if the Statute were satisfied. A party has, however, a right to restitution under the rule stated in § 141 if the other party will neither perform nor sign a sufficient memorandum. See Illustration 4.

The rule stated in this Section is not intended as an exclusive statement of the right to restitution under provisions of the Statute of Frauds other than those contained in Chapter 5 of this Restatement. For example, in the case of a contract that is unenforceable because of a statutory requirement that contracts not performable within a lifetime be evidenced by a writing, full performance by one party may not make such a contract enforceable by him. He may therefore be unable to enforce the contract and yet not be entitled to restitution under the rule stated in § 373 because of the limitation in Subsection (2) of that section. His right to restitution is not dealt with in this Restatement.

Illustration

4. A makes an oral contract to buy a tract of land from B for $100,000 (§ 125). Payment is to be made in $10,000 installments, conveyance to be made on the payment of the third installment. A pays $10,000 and then refuses to pay any more and sues B to recover in restitution the $10,000 that he has paid. If B signs a sufficient memorandum, A's refusal to pay is a defense to his action under the rule stated in § 141(1) and A cannot get restitution. See Illustration 6 to § 374. If B refuses to sign a sufficient memorandum, A's refusal to pay is not a defense under the rule stated in § 141(2) and A can get restitution. See Illustration 1 to § 373.

§ 376. Restitution When Contract Is Voidable.

A party who has avoided a contract on the ground of lack of capacity, mistake, misrepresentation, duress, undue influence or abuse of a fiduciary relation is entitled to restitution for any benefit that he has conferred on the other party by way of part performance or reliance.

Comment

a. Recovery of benefit on avoidance. A party who exercises his power of avoidance is entitled to recover in restitution for any benefit that he has conferred on the other party through part performance of or reliance on the contract. The benefit from his part performance includes that resulting from the use by the other party of whatever he has received up to the time that it is returned on avoidance. Furthermore, under the rule stated in § 384, a party seeking restitution must generally return any benefit that he has himself received. If he has received and must return land, for example, he may have made improvements on the land in reliance on the contract and he is entitled, on avoidance and return of the land, to recover the reasonable value of those improvements (§ 371(b)). The rule stated in this Section applies to avoidance on any ground, including lack of capacity (§§ 14–16), mistake (§§ 152, 153), misrepresentation (§ 164), duress (§ 175), undue influence (§ 177) or abuse of a fiduciary relation (§ 173). Uncertainties in measuring the benefit, however, are more likely to be resolved in favor of the party seeking restitution if the other party engaged in misconduct, as in cases of fraudulent misrepresentation, duress or undue influence. In cases of mental incompetency the rule stated in this Section is supplemented by that stated in § 15(2) and in cases of mistake it is supplemented by that stated in § 158.

Illustrations

1. A contracts to sell an automobile to B, an infant, for $2,000. After A has delivered the automobile and B has paid the $2,000, B disaffirms the contract on the ground of infancy (§ 14), tenders the automobile back to A, and sues A for $2,000. B can recover the $2,000 from A in restitution.

2. A contracts to sell and B to buy for $100,000 a tract of land, the value of which has depended mainly on the timber on it. Both A and B believe that the timber is still there, but in fact it has been destroyed by fire. After A has conveyed the land to B and B has paid the $100,000, B discovers the mistake. B disaffirms the contract for mistake (§ 152), tenders a deed to the land to A, and sues A for $100,000. B can recover $100,000 from A in restitution. See Illustration 1 to § 152.

3. A submits a $150,000 offer in response to B's invitation for bids on the construction of a building. A believes that this is the total of a column of figures, but he has made an error by inadvertently omitting $50,000, and in fact the total is $200,000. Because B had estimated the expected cost as $180,000 and the 10 other bids were all in the range between $180,000 and $200,000, B had reason to know of A's mistake. A discovers the mistake after he has done part of the work, disaffirms the contract on the ground of mistake (§ 153), and sues B in restitution for the benefit conferred on B as measured by the reasonable value of A's performance. A can recover the reasonable value of his

performance in restitution and if the cost of the work done can be determined under the next lowest bid, that cost is evidence of its reasonable value. See Illustration 9 to § 153.

    4.   A fraudulently induces B to make a contract to buy a tract of land for $100,000. After A has conveyed the land and B has paid the price, B makes improvements on the land with a reasonable value of $20,000. B then discovers the fraud, disaffirms the contract for misrepresentation (§ 164), tenders a deed to the land to A, and sues A for $100,000 plus $20,000, the reasonable value of the improvements, less $5,000, the value to B of the use of the land. B can recover $115,000 in restitution from A. See Illustration 1 to § 164.

    5.   A fraudulently induces B to make a contract to sell a tract of land for $100,000. After B has conveyed the land and A has paid the price, A farms the land at a net profit of $10,000. B then discovers the fraud, disaffirms the contract for misrepresentation, tenders back the $100,000, and sues A for specific restitution plus the $10,000 profit that A made by farming the land. B can recover the land and $10,000 in restitution from A.

§ 377. Restitution in Cases of Impracticability, Frustration, Non-Occurrence of Condition or Disclaimer by Beneficiary.

A party whose duty of performance does not arise or is discharged as a result of impracticability of performance, frustration of purpose, non-occurrence of a condition or disclaimer by a beneficiary is entitled to restitution for any benefit that he has conferred on the other party by way of part performance or reliance.

Comment

    a. Scope. A party whose duty of performance is discharged on grounds of supervening impracticability of performance (§ 261) or frustration of purpose (§ 265) may already have performed in part or otherwise relied on the contract before the occurrence of the supervening event. A party whose duty never arises on those grounds (§ 266) may have taken similar action before discovery of the relevant circumstances. Under the rule stated in this Section such a party is entitled to restitution. Furthermore, in cases of impracticability or frustration the other party is also ordinarily relieved of any obligation of rendering the return performance that he has promised on the ground of failure of performance (§ 267). Under the rule stated in this Section that party is also entitled to restitution. The same is true where the parties are relieved of their obligations on the ground of the non-occurrence of a condition (§ 225) or because of a disclaimer by a beneficiary (§ 306). If both parties have rendered some performance, each is entitled to restitution against the other. The rule stated in this Section is subject to contrary agreement to the extent that the agreement does not violate the rules relating to unfairness (§ 364), unconscionability (§ 208) and forfeiture (§ 229).

Illustrations

    1.   A contracts to employ B as a confidential secretary for a month for $2,000, to be paid at the end of that time. B falls ill after working for two weeks and the duties of performance of both A and B are discharged as a result of impracticability of performance (§ 262). B is entitled to restitution from A for the services that he has performed. See Illustration 1 to § 262. The result is the same if B's duty is discharged as a result of A's illness rather than B's. See Illustration 2 to § 262.

    2.   A contracts to employ B as a confidential secretary for a month for $2,000, to be paid in advance. B falls ill after A has paid the $2,000 but before B has begun work and the duties of performance of both A and B are discharged as a result of impracticability of performance (§ 262). A is entitled to restitution of $2,000 from B. If B had fallen ill after working for two weeks, B would also be entitled to restitution from A for the services that he has performed.

    3.   A contracts to sell and B to buy a house for $50,000, conditional on approval by X Bank of B's pending mortgage application. B pays A $5,000 when the contract is signed. In spite of reasonable efforts by B, the X Bank does not approve his application and his duty of performance is discharged (§ 225). B is entitled to restitution of $5,000 from A. See Illustration 8 to § 225.

    b. Measure of benefit. Cases of impracticability and frustration may pose particularly difficult problems of adjustment after the occurrence of a disrupting event that was ordinarily unforeseeable when the contract was made. The rule stated in § 272(2) gives a court discretion in an extreme case to do justice by supplying a term that is reasonable in the circumstance. In most cases, however, restitution is all that is required, given the choice open to the court in measuring benefit (§ 371). Usually the measure of reasonable value is appropriate. A benefit may be found if it was conferred before the occurrence of the event even though the event later resulted in its destruction, and in that case recovery may be limited to the measure of increase in wealth prior to the event, if this is less than reasonable value. Compare Illustrations 4 and 6. A party cannot, however, recover his reliance interest under the rule stated in this Section, and his expenditures in reliance are not subtracted from what he has received in calculating the benefit for which he is liable. See Illustration 5; see also Comment b to § 371. Furthermore, to the extent that the contract price can be roughly apportioned to the work done, recovery will not be allowed in excess of the appropriate amount of the price.

Illustrations

4. A contracts with B to shingle the roof of B's house for $5,000, payable as the work progresses. After A has spent $2,000 doing part of the work and has been paid $1,800, much of the house including the roof is destroyed by fire without his fault, and the duties of performance of both A and B are discharged as a result of impracticability of performance (§ 263). The work done before the fire increased the market price and the insurable value of the house by $1,500. A is entitled to restitution of $1,500 from B and B is entitled to restitution of $1,800 from A. See Illustration 3 to § 263.

5. The facts being otherwise as stated in Illustration 4, the fire also destroyed shingles that had cost A $500 and that were piled near the house for the rest of the work. A is not entitled to restitution of this loss from B. Nor can A subtract the $500 from the $1,800 he has been paid in determining the benefit that he has received. The court may, however, take this loss into consideration in deciding whether to allow A restitution of $1,500 or $2,000. See also § 272.

6. A contracts to paint some bizarre frescoes in B's house for $10,000. The frescoes will not increase the market value of the house. A dies after the frescoes have been partly completed. Other artists can adequately complete the work and will do so for $6,000. A's executors are entitled to restitution of $4,000 from B. If they can prove that A's price was unusually low because of A's lack of employment and an economic depression and that the work was roughly half finished, the court may properly allow restitution of $5,000.

7. A contracts to tutor B's son for six months in preparation for an examination, in return for which B promises to pay A $2,000 at the end of that time. After A has worked for three months, B's son becomes ill and the duties of performance of both A and B are discharged as a result of impracticability of performance. Other tutors would have charged $800 to do the work that A has done. A is entitled to restitution of $800 from B. Even if other tutors would have charged $1,200, A is entitled to restitution of only $1,000 from B unless he can show that the first half of the work was more burdensome.

TOPIC 5. PRECLUSION BY ELECTION AND AFFIRMANCE

§ 378. Election Among Remedies.

If a party has more than one remedy under the rules stated in this Chapter, his manifestation of a choice of one of them by bringing suit or otherwise is not a bar to another remedy unless the remedies are inconsistent and the other party materially changes his position in reliance on the manifestation.

Comment

a. Election among remedies. The rules stated in this Chapter give a party three basic types of remedies: damages (Topic 2), specific performance or an injunction (Topic 3), and restitution (Topic 4). The rule stated in this Section precludes a party who has manifested his choice of one of those remedies from shifting to another remedy if such a shift would be unjust because of the other party's reliance on the earlier manifestation. The mere manifestation of an intention to pursue one remedy rather than another does not, however, preclude a party from making such a shift. Nor must the shift be made within any particular time. Only if the other party has materially changed his position in reliance on the original choice is a shift to another remedy precluded by the election of the first. A change of position is "material" within the meaning of this Section if it is such that in all the circumstances a shift in remedies would be unjust. This rejection of any doctrine of election in the absence of reliance is consistent with a similar policy in the Uniform Commercial Code. See Uniform Commercial Code § 2–703 and Comment 1; § 2–711 and § 2–721. Even if the bringing of an action for one remedy is a manifestation of choice of that remedy, it does not preclude the plaintiff from shifting to another remedy as long as the defendant has not materially changed his position. Alternative counts seeking inconsistent remedies are generally permitted in the same complaint and a change in remedy may often be made by amendment of the complaint, even at an advanced stage of the action.

Illustrations

1. A contracts to sell a tract of land to B. A repudiates and B brings an action for damages. While this action is pending, A makes valuable improvements on the land reasonably believing that B does not intend to pursue his remedy of specific performance. B then amends his complaint to ask specific performance. If A's change of position is material, B's claim for specific performance is precluded.

2. A contracts to transfer his farm to B in return for B's promise to support A for life. After A has transferred the farm, B repudiates the contract and A sues for specific restitution. Before any change in B's position, A learns that a part of the farm has been sold by B and amends his complaint to ask for damages for the breach. A's claim for damages is not precluded.

3. A contracts to transfer his farm to B in return for B's promise to support A for life. After A has transferred the farm, B repudiates the contract and A sues for damages. Before any change in B's position, A discovers that it will be difficult to prove his damages with reasonable certainty and that a judicial sale of B's property including the farm would be unlikely to realize enough to satisfy a judgment and amends his complaint to ask specific restitution. Specific restitution is not precluded.

b. Additional circumstances. In two situations a party is not precluded from seeking a different remedy, even after reliance on his first choice by the other party, because his shift is justified by additional circumstances. The first situation is that in which the party made his original choice while ignorant of facts that give him a remedy based on, for example, misrepresentation or mistake and later discovers those facts. In that situation he is not bound by his original choice because he made it when mistaken. The second situation is that in which after a party makes his original choice, a later breach by the other party occurs. In that situation he can pursue any remedy based on the later breach without regard to his original choice.

c. Remedy not available. The rule stated in this Section applies only where a party pursues a remedy that he actually has. A party is not precluded from pursuing other remedies by the fact that he has made a mistaken attempt to obtain a remedy that is not available to him, even if his original choice has been relied on by the other party.

Illustrations

4. A makes an oral contract to transfer his farm to B in return for B's promise to support A for life. After A has transferred the farm, B repudiates the contract and A sues for damages. B pleads the Statute of Frauds and A's action is about to be dismissed. A then amends his complaint to ask specific restitution. Regardless of whether B has changed his position, specific restitution is not precluded.

5. A makes a written contract to sell a tract of land to B. A repudiates the contract and B, claiming that both parties were mistaken as to the contents of the writing, sues A for reformation of the writing and for specific performance of the contract as reformed. The court refuses to reform the writing on the ground that mistake was not proved and B amends his complaint to ask damages for breach of the contract as written. B's claim for damages is not precluded.

d. Other remedy not inconsistent. The rule stated in this Section applies only where a party seeks to shift to a remedy that is inconsistent with the one he has chosen. A party who seeks specific performance or an injunction may, for example, be entitled to damages to compensate him for delay in performance. See Comment c to § 358. Similarly, a party who seeks restitution may, for example, be entitled to damages to compensate him for costs of transportation of goods that he has incurred. A later request for such damages in a suit for specific performance or an injunction or in one for restitution is not precluded because it is not inconsistent with that suit. However, the remedy of specific performance or an injunction and that of damages for total breach of contract are inconsistent. The remedy of specific performance or an injunction and that of restitution are also inconsistent. And the remedy of restitution and that of damages for total breach are inconsistent.

Illustration

6. A contracts to sell a tract of land to B. A fails to convey the tract and B sues A for specific performance. B later amends his complaint to add a claim for damages resulting from the delay caused by A's failure. Regardless of whether A has changed his position, such a further claim is not precluded.

e. Other situations distinguished. The rule stated in this Section applies only as among the remedies provided for in this Chapter. It does not, for example preclude a party from pursuing a claim in tort for misrepresentation or a claim for breach of warranty in the sale of goods. See Uniform Commercial Code § 2–721. It does not determine whether a party is barred by election from treating his remaining duties of performance as discharged (§ 379). Nor does it apply in the many instances in which a party makes a choice that affects his substantive rights, such as the choice of an offeree between acceptance (§ 50) and rejection (§ 38), the choice of an intended beneficiary between disclaiming the contract and not doing so (§ 306), or the choice of an infant between affirmance and disaffirmance (§§ 14, 380). Furthermore, this rule does not apply to situations in which a party is precluded by his delay from enforcing a substantive right, as is the case where one having the power of avoidance loses it by delay (§ 381). Finally this Section is inapplicable to matters of procedure, such as the requirement that a party choose between inconsistent remedies at some stage of a judicial proceeding, and to matters governed by the law of judgments, such as merger and bar. See Restatement, Second, Judgments §§ 17, 18, 19.

§ 379. Election to Treat Duties of Performance Under Aleatory Contract as Discharged.

If a right or duty of the injured party is conditional on an event that is fortuitous or is supposed by the parties to be fortuitous, he cannot treat his remaining duties to render performance as discharged on the ground of the other party's breach by non-performance if he does not manifest to the other party his intention to do so before any adverse change in the situation of the injured party resulting from the occurrence of that event or a material change in the probability of its occurrence.

Comment

a. Election under an aleatory contract. An aleatory contract is one in which at least one party is under a duty that is conditional on the occurrence of an event that, so far as the parties to the contract are aware, is dependent on chance. Its occurrence may be within the control of third persons or beyond the control of any person. The event may have already occurred, as long as that fact is unknown to the parties. It may be the failure of something to happen as well as its happening. Common examples are contracts of insurance and suretyship, as well as gambling contracts. If the injured party's duty is conditional on such an event, it would be unfair if, after the breach, he were allowed to take advantage of a material change in the likelihood of its occurrence when deciding whether to treat his remaining duties as discharged. If it was more likely that it would occur it would be to his advantage to treat those duties as discharged. For this reason, he is precluded from treating them as discharged if there has been an adverse change in his situation because the event has occurred or because there has been a material increase in the probability of its occurrence. The same principle applies to the case where a right rather than a duty of the injured party is conditional on the occurrence of such an event.

Illustrations

1. A, an insurance company, issues to B a policy of fire insurance on B's house for a year in the amount of $100,000. In consideration, B gives A his promissory note for the premium, payable in three months. B fails to pay the note at maturity. Four months later, before A has given notice of cancellation, B's house burns. A cannot treat B's failure to pay as discharging it from its duty to pay for the loss under the policy. A is liable for the loss less the amount of the note.

2. A makes a contract with B under which A guarantees that C will pay a $100,000 debt owed B by C and due on July 1. In consideration, B promises to pay A $1,000 on May 1. B fails to pay on that date. Before A manifests to B his intention to treat B's failure as discharging him from his duty to honor his guarantee of C's debt, C becomes insolvent. A cannot treat B's failure as discharging him from that duty and is liable on his $100,000 guarantee less the $1,000.

3. A and B make a contract under which A guarantees a $50,000 debt owed to B by C and due on July 1 in consideration of a guarantee by B of a $100,000 debt owed to A by D and due on August 1. C fails to pay on July 1 and A fails to honor his guarantee. Before B manifests his intention to treat A's failure as discharging B from his duty to honor his guarantee of D's debt, D becomes insolvent. B cannot treat A's failure as discharging him from that duty and is liable on his $100,000 guarantee less the $50,000 that A owes on his guarantee.

§ 380. Loss of Power of Avoidance by Affirmance.

(1) The power of a party to avoid a contract for incapacity, duress, undue influence or abuse of a fiduciary relation is lost if, after the circumstances that made the contract voidable have ceased to exist, he manifests to the other party his intention to affirm it or acts with respect to anything that he has received in a manner inconsistent with disaffirmance.

(2) The power of a party to avoid a contract for mistake or misrepresentation is lost if after he knows or has reason to know of the mistake or of the misrepresentation if it is non-fraudulent or knows of the misrepresentation if it is fraudulent, he manifests to the other party his intention to affirm it or acts with respect to anything that he has received in a manner inconsistent with disaffirmance.

(3) If the other party rejects an offer by the party seeking avoidance to return what he has received, the party seeking avoidance if entitled to restitution can, after the lapse of a reasonable time, enforce a lien on what he has received by selling it and crediting the proceeds toward his claim in restitution.

Comment

a. Ratification by affirmance. A party who has the power of avoidance may lose it by action that manifests a willingness to go on with the contract. Such action is known as "affirmance" and has the effect of ratifying the contract. See Restatement of Restitution § 68. The rule stated in this Section is a special application of that stated in § 85, under which a promise to perform a voidable duty is binding. On ratification, the affirming party is bound as from the outset and the other party continues to be bound.

b. Manner and time of affirmance. A party may manifest his intention to affirm by words or other conduct, including the exercise of dominion over what he has received in a manner inconsistent with avoidance of the contract. Compare Uniform Commercial Code § 2–606. If he offers to return the performance that he has received and if such an offer is rejected, he must hold that performance for the other party. Because the party seeking restitution has a lien on any performance that he has himself received, however, he is entitled to enforce that lien under the rule stated in Subsection (3) after he has waited a reasonable time. A party's power of avoidance for incapacity, duress, undue influence or abuse of a fiduciary relation is not lost by conduct while the circumstances that made the contract voidable continue to exist. Nor is his power of avoidance for misrepresentation or mistake lost until he knows of the misrepresentation if it is fraudulent, or knows or ought to know of a non-fraudulent misrepresentation or mistake.

Illustrations

1. A is induced by B's misrepresentation to make a contract to repair B's house, payment to be made when the services have been rendered. When A discovers the facts, he accuses B of fraud and threatens to avoid the transaction unless B pays in advance or furnishes security. Before A receives any response from B, A notifies B that he avoids the contract. A's conduct did not amount to affirmance and the contract is avoided. The result would be different, however, if A demanded that B perform the contract or accepted security from B.

2. A is induced by B's misrepresentation to make a contract to employ B for a year. When A discovers the facts, he continues to employ B for two weeks and then discharges him in violation of the

contract, notifying B that he avoids the contract. A's conduct amounted to affirmance and he is liable to B for breach of contract. The result would not be affected if A did not learn until the end of the two weeks that the law gave him the power to avoid the contract. The result would be different, however, if B had persuaded A to continue the employment for another two weeks as a trial period and A discharged B at the end of that time because A was still dissatisfied.

3. A is induced by B's fraudulent and material misrepresentation to buy land from B. When A discovers the fraud he brings an action in deceit against B. A later discontinues the action and notifies B that he avoids the contract. Since A's bringing of the action was a manifestation of his intention to affirm the contract only if damages are paid, it did not without more amount to affirmance. A's subsequent attempt to avoid the contract was effective.

4. A contracts to sell and B to buy a tract of land, the value of which has depended mainly on the timber on it. Both A and B believe that the timber is still there, but in fact it has been destroyed by fire so that the contract is voidable by B on the ground of mistake. See Illustration 1 to § 152. On discovery of the mistake, B tenders a deed back to A, who refuses to accept it. B continues to occupy and to use the land. B's conduct amounts to affirmance and he is precluded from avoiding the contract.

§ 381. Loss of Power of Avoidance by Delay.

(1) The power of a party to avoid a contract for incapacity, duress, undue influence or abuse of a fiduciary relation is lost if, after the circumstances that made it voidable have ceased to exist, he does not within a reasonable time manifest to the other party his intention to avoid it.

(2) The power of a party to avoid a contract for misrepresentation or mistake is lost if after he knows of a fraudulent misrepresentation or knows or has reason to know of a non-fraudulent misrepresentation or mistake he does not within a reasonable time manifest to the other party his intention to avoid it. The power of a party to avoid a contract for non-fraudulent misrepresentation or mistake is also lost if the contract has been so far performed or the circumstances have otherwise so changed that avoidance would be inequitable and if damages will be adequate compensation.

(3) In determining what is a reasonable time, the following circumstances are significant:

(a) the extent to which the delay enabled or might have enabled the party with the power of avoidance to speculate at the other party's risk;

(b) the extent to which the delay resulted or might have resulted in justifiable reliance by the other party or by third persons;

(c) the extent to which the ground for avoidance was the result of any fault by either party; and

(d) the extent to which the other party's conduct contributed to the delay.

(4) If a right or duty of the party who has the power of avoidance for non-fraudulent misrepresentation or mistake is conditional on an event that is fortuitous or is supposed by the parties to be fortuitous, a manifestation of intention under Subsection (1) or (2) is not effective unless it is made before any adverse change in his situation resulting from the occurrence of that event or a material change in the probability of its occurrence.

Comment

a. Effect of delay. A party who has the power to avoid a contract may lose that power by delay alone, even without such conduct as amounts to affirmance (§ 380). Under the rule stated in this Section the power is lost if it is not exercised within a reasonable time. The rule is similar in its purpose to that stated in § 380 on the loss of the power to treat one's remaining duties as discharged on breach. Here, as under § 379, what time is reasonable depends on all the circumstances, including the extent to which the delay was or was likely to be prejudicial to the other party or to third persons. Such prejudice may result if the delay enables the party with the power of avoidance to speculate at the other party's risk, affirming if the course of the market makes the contract advantageous to him and disaffirming if it makes it disadvantageous. Such prejudice may also result from reliance or the likelihood of reliance by the other party or by third persons. The reliance must be justifiable and the fact that the one who relied knew of the ground for avoidance is a consideration in this connection. If the ground for avoidance was to any extent the fault of either party, this is also a factor. For example, the fault of the party with the power of avoidance in not discovering a mistake or a misrepresentation will shorten the period for avoidance. Compare §§ 157, 172. The misconduct of the other party in cases of fraudulent misrepresentation or duress will lengthen it. A consumer is not generally expected to avoid as promptly as is a merchant in similar circumstances. Furthermore, if the other party contributes to the delay, as by promising to remedy defects or by urging a further period of testing before avoidance, this will lengthen the period. Ordinarily, if the party with the power of avoidance retains during the delay something that he has received from the other party, avoidance will be precluded by the rule stated in § 380. The importance of the present Section is, therefore, chiefly in cases in which the party with that power has received nothing.

b. When reasonable time begins. A party who has the power of avoidance for incapacity, duress, undue influence or abuse of a fiduciary relation is not expected to act until the circumstances that have made the contract voidable have ceased to exist, and the reasonable time does not begin to run until then. In the case of a party who has the power of avoidance for misrepresentation or mistake, it does not begin to run until he knows of the misrepresentation if it is fraudulent, or knows or has reason to know of a non-fraudulent misrepresentation or mistake. However, in determining whether a party acted within a reasonable time once he was expected to do so, the fact that a considerable period of time had elapsed after the original transaction is significant. Nevertheless, if the power of avoidance is then exercised within a reasonable time, avoidance is not ordinarily precluded even though the other party has relied. Compare Illustration 2 with Illustration 3. But see Comment c. The rights of third parties who may have relied are not dealt with in this Restatement. See Introductory Note to this Chapter. Where a party seeks to avoid a contract on the ground of a mistake that he alone has made, he must show that enforcement of the contract would be unconscionable, unless the other party had reason to know of the mistake or his fault caused it. See § 153. The lapse of time before the mistaken party discovers his mistake may invite reliance by the other party that will make it more difficult to show unconscionability even though it would not preclude avoidance under the present Section. A party need not specify in detail the bases of his disaffirmance unless this is necessary in order for the other party to know the ground of avoidance or to take appropriate action in response. Compare Illustration 5 with Illustration 6. As to the requirement that he return what he has received, see § 384.

Illustrations

1. A is induced by B's misrepresentation to contract in January to sell B 1,000 shares of stock in the X Corporation for $100,000, delivery and payment to be on May 1. A discovers the fraud in February but does not manifest his intention to avoid the transaction until April. In view of the extent to which A's delay of two months enabled him to speculate at B's expense, A has lost his power of avoidance, and his manifestation is not effective to avoid the transaction. Compare Illustration 2 to § 379. The result does not depend on whether the market price of the stock has risen or fallen.

2. A, a noted opera singer, is induced by B's nonfraudulent misrepresentation to contract in April to sing the leading role in a new production designed for A at B's opera house in October. A soon discovers the misrepresentation but does not manifest an intention to avoid the transaction until June. By that time B has made substantial commitments for the production in reliance on A's singing the leading role. In view of the likelihood and the extent of such reliance, A has lost the power of avoidance, and A's manifestation is not effective to avoid the contract.

3. The facts being otherwise as stated in Illustration 2, A does not discover the misrepresentation until June, immediately before A's manifestation of intention to avoid the contract. In spite of B's reliance, A has not lost the power of avoidance and A's manifestation is effective.

4. A contracts to buy from B a farm that B misrepresents as containing 100 acres of cleared land, 100 acres of brush, and a well with an adequate supply of water. A week later A discovers that only 80 acres have been cleared, but he does not discover that the well is dry, although a careful inspection would have revealed this. When he moves onto the farm six months later, he discovers that the well is dry and promptly notifies B that he avoids the contract. A has not lost his power to avoidance on the ground of the misrepresentation as to the well, even though he may have lost his power of avoidance on the ground of the misrepresentation as to the cleared land.

5. A contracts to sell and B to buy a tract of land, the value of which has depended mainly on the timber on it, delivery of the deed and payment of the price to be made in a week. Both A and B believe that the timber is still there, but in fact it has been destroyed by fire, so that the contract is voidable by B. See Illustration 1 to § 152. B discovers the mistake and when the next day, A tenders a deed to the tract, B refuses to perform without giving any reason. B's refusal of performance is a sufficient manifestation of his intention to avoid the contract even though no reason was given.

6. The facts being otherwise as stated in Illustration 5, A makes no offer to deliver a deed to the tract on the day fixed for performance. B's refusal of performance is not a sufficient manifestation of his power of avoidance because it was justified by A's failure to offer to deliver a deed.

c. When avoidance would be inequitable. In some situations where a party has a power of avoidance for non-fraudulent misrepresentation or mistake, the circumstances may have so changed after the contract was made that it would be inequitable to allow avoidance if damages would adequately compensate him. This may be so where performance in whole or in part makes avoidance excessively burdensome for the other party. It may also be so where, because of a drastic shift in market prices, avoidance will throw onto the other party a heavy loss unrelated to the misrepresentation or mistake. In such situations the party having the power of avoidance loses it and is limited to a claim for damages under the rule stated in Subsection (2). A similar rule as to avoidance for mental incompetency is stated in § 15(2).

Illustration

7. A, seeking to induce B to make a contract to buy his house for $50,000, tells B that the roof is in "good condition." A is mistaken and unknown to him the roof has a hidden defect that can be fully remedied for $1,000. B is induced by the statement to make the proposed contract, and, two years after taking possession, he discovers the defect. Even if the court considers the statement a material misrepresentation, it may conclude that the contract is no longer voidable and limit B's relief to the recovery of $1,000 in damages from A.

d. Aleatory contracts. Under an aleatory contract, at least one party is under a duty that is conditional on the occurrence of an event that, so far as the parties are aware, is dependent on chance. See Comment a to § 379. If the duty of the party having a power of avoidance for non-fraudulent misrepresentation or mistake is conditional on such an event, it would be unfair if he could take advantage of a material change in the likelihood of its occurrence when deciding whether to exercise that power. If it were more likely that it would occur it would be to his advantage to exercise it. If it were less likely that it would occur, it would be to his advantage not to exercise it. For this reason, he is precluded from exercising it if there has been an adverse change in his situation because the event has occurred or because there has been a material increase in the probability of its occurrence. The same principle applies to the case when a right of the party with the power of avoidance is conditional on the occurrence of such an event.

Illustration

8. A and B make a contract under which A guarantees a debt owed to B by C in consideration of a guarantee by B of a debt owed to A by D. B is induced to make the contract by A's non-fraudulent material misrepresentation. Before the truth is discovered, C, who was in bad financial circumstances when the contract was made, has received a large legacy. B cannot avoid the contract because the bargain has become less advantageous to B. If D rather than C receives the legacy, there is no adverse change in B's situation and he can still avoid the contract.

§ 382. Loss of Power to Affirm by Prior Avoidance.

(1) If a party has effectively exercised his power of avoidance, a subsequent manifestation of intent to affirm is inoperative unless the other party manifests his assent to affirmance by refusal to accept a return of his performance or otherwise.

(2) A party has not exercised his power of avoidance under the rule stated in Subsection (1) until

(a) he has regained all or a substantial part of what he would be entitled to by way of restitution on avoidance,

(b) he has obtained a final judgment of or based on avoidance, or

(c) the other party has materially relied on or manifested his assent to a statement of disaffirmance.

Comment

a. Conclusive effect of avoidance. Effective exercise of the power of avoidance is conclusive and precludes subsequent affirmance. An exercise of the power is not effective if it is itself avoided on such grounds as mistake, misrepresentation, duress or mental incompetency. Exercise of the power by an infant is not, however, voidable on the ground of his infancy. Even after a party's effective exercise of the power of avoidance, the other party may wish to have the transaction sustained and, if both parties manifest this intention their new agreement is effective.

b. What amounts to exercise of power. A mere statement of disaffirmance, even if coupled with ineffective attempts to regain what one has given, is not such an exercise of the power of avoidance as will preclude affirmance. There is no exercise of the power by a party until he has regained all or part of what he gave, has obtained a judgment that will put him back into his original position, has caused the other party to change his position in reliance on the disaffirmance, or has contracted with the other party on the basis of the disaffirmance.

Illustrations

1. A, an infant, contracts to sell B an automobile on credit. After delivering it to B, A writes B that he disaffirms and demands its return. B does not return the automobile and A sues B for the price. A can recover the price because A's letter was not an exercise of his power of avoidance.

2. The facts being otherwise as stated in Illustration 1, A brings an action to replevy the automobile but discontinues it before he gets a final judgment and sues B for the price. A can recover the price because A's action in replevin was not an exercise of his power of avoidance.

3. The facts being otherwise as stated in Illustration 1, A sees the automobile parked on the street and drives it back to his garage and sues B for the price. A cannot recover the price because his regaining possession of the automobile was an exercise of his power of avoidance.

§ 383. Avoidance in Part.

A contract cannot be avoided in part except that where one or more corresponding pairs of part performances have been fully performed by one or both parties the rest of the contract can be avoided.

Comment

a. No avoidance in part. A party who has the power of avoidance must ordinarily avoid the entire contract, including any part that has already been performed. He cannot disaffirm part of the contract that is particularly disadvantageous to himself while affirming a more advantageous part, and an attempt to do so is ineffective as a disaffirmance. The rule stated in this Section does not preclude avoidance of only one of two or more entirely separate contracts. Nor does it prevent reformation of a part of a contract for either mistake or misrepresentation. See §§ 155 and 166.

1. A makes a contract to work for B for a year and is induced by B's fraud to assent to a covenant under which he agrees to refrain from entering into a similar business in the same town for three years after the termination of the employment. A discovers the fraud after he has worked for a month. A cannot avoid the covenant not to compete without avoiding the rest of the contract.

b. Exception for "divisible" contracts. There is an exception to the general rule stated in this Section if the contract is "divisible" in the sense that the performances to be exchanged can be apportioned into corresponding pairs of part performances under the rule stated in § 240. In that situation, if one or more pairs of part performances have been fully performed by one or both parties, the party who has the power of avoidance can avoid the rest of the contract only or can avoid the whole contract.

Illustration

2. A is induced by B's fraud to contract to sell B 1,200 tons of coal to be delivered in monthly installments of 100 tons, payment for each installment to be made on delivery. A discovers the fraud after the second delivery. If A avoids the contract, he must avoid the entire unperformed part, but he does not have to avoid the part that has been performed unless he chooses to do so.

§ 384. Requirement That Party Seeking Restitution Return Benefit.

(1) Except as stated in Subsection (2), a party will not be granted restitution unless

    (a) he returns or offers to return, conditional on restitution, any interest in property that he has received in exchange in substantially as good condition as when it was received by him, or

    (b) the court can assure such return in connection with the relief granted.

(2) The requirement stated in Subsection (1) does not apply to property

    (a) that was worthless when received or that has been destroyed or lost by the other party or as a result of its own defects,

    (b) that either could not from the time of receipt have been returned or has been used or disposed of without knowledge of the grounds for restitution if justice requires that compensation be accepted in its place and the payment of such compensation can be assured, or

    (c) as to which the contract apportions the price if that part of the price is not included in the claim for restitution.

Comment

a. Duty to return benefit. A party who seeks restitution of a benefit that he has conferred on the other party is expected to return what he has received from the other party. The objective is to return the parties, as nearly as is practicable, to the situation in which they found themselves before they made the contract. If a party has received land, goods or other property, he is expected to return it. The fact that he has benefited from possession of them does not preclude restitution since he can compensate the other party in money for this benefit. The property itself, however, must generally be returned. If it has been used, destroyed or substantially altered in character while in his possession, restitution is generally not available. Mere depreciation in market value, however, is not such a change as will preclude restitution. Cf. Uniform Commercial Code § 2-608.

b. Necessity of offer to return. If a party seeking restitution offers to return what he has received, he may make his offer conditional on restitution being made to him. To this end, the law gives him a lien on what he has received. See § 380(3). In equity, his failure to make such an offer before commencing a suit for rescission did not preclude relief. The decree could be made conditional on an offer. At law, however, an offer was traditionally regarded as a condition of the right to commence an action based on rescission. The merger of law and equity and modern procedural reforms have made this distinction undesirable, and the rule stated in this Section reflects the increasing criticism of the rule at law. If the court has the power to assure the required return in connection with the relief that it grants, it is not necessary that there have been a prior return or offer to return. If all that is to be returned is money, a credit against a larger sum allowed in restitution will suffice. In other cases a conditional judgment will be proper. A court may, in awarding costs, take account of any failure by the party seeking restitution to afford the other party an adequate opportunity to make restitution without the commencement of legal process. This is particularly appropriate in cases, such as mutual mistake, impracticability of performance or frustration of purpose, in which the other party is in no way at fault. Even though an offer to return property is not necessary under the rule stated in this Section, the retention of property together with the exercise of dominion over it may preclude avoidance under the rule stated in § 380.

Illustrations

1. A contracts to sell to B a factory and a patent and B makes a part payment of $100,000. A assigns the patent but fails to transfer the factory to B. B sues A asking restitution of $100,000 without

offering to reassign the patent. B is entitled to a judgment for that amount conditional on his tender of a reassignment of the patent.

2. A is induced by B's fraudulent misrepresentations to contract to sell to B for $10,000 an antique worth $100,000. A delivers the antique and B pays the $10,000. On discovery of the fraud, A demands the return of the antique without offering to repay the $10,000. On B's refusal, A sues B in conversion for the value of the antique. A is entitled to a judgment for $90,000, the value of the antique less $10,000.

3. The facts being otherwise as stated in Illustration 2, A sues B in replevin and posts a bond. If the procedure in replevin does not permit an adequate opportunity for the determination of A's claim of fraud before return of the antique to him, replevin will be denied on the ground that he has not offered to return the $10,000.

c. Where no offer of return required. In some instances there is no requirement of an offer to return. This is so if the property was worthless when received or if its destruction or loss was caused by the other party or by its own defects. See Illustration 4. It may also be so if it was never possible to return the property or if it has become impossible because the recipient used or disposed of it before he had knowledge of the grounds for restitution. See Illustrations 5 and 6. In those cases no offer need to be made if justice requires that compensation be accepted in place of the property and if the payment of such compensation can be assured. In determining what justice requires, consideration will be given to all the circumstances, including any misconduct such as fraud or duress by the other party. A party who receives only property that he already owned receives no interest and is not subject to the rule stated in Subsection (1) at all. Furthermore, if the contract apportions the price among various pieces of property, restitution of the price as to part of the property may be had on a return of only that part if the price as to the unreturned property is not included in the claim for restitution. See Illustration 7.

Illustrations

4. A contracts to work on B's ranch in return for a number of cattle warranted by B to be sound. After A has done the work and B has delivered the cattle, they are discovered to have hoof and mouth disease and are destroyed by government order. A is entitled to restitution of the reasonable value of his services.

5. A puts his son in B's private school, paying a year's tuition in advance. During the first month of school, the son is wrongfully expelled by B. A is entitled to restitution of the amount of tuition paid less the benefit to A of B's services during the first month.

6. A contracts to buy from B his seat on the stock exchange, his good will and the furniture in his office and pays $10,000 as part of the price. B delivers the furniture and A sells it to others. Later B refuses to perform the rest of the contract. A is entitled to restitution of $10,000 less compensation to B for the furniture.

7. A contracts to lease a plow and a tractor to B, to be used together. The price is stated to be $200 for the plow and $500 for the tractor, and B pays the full $700 in advance. A delivers the plow but fails to deliver the tractor. B can offer to return the plow and get restitution of $700. Because the prices are apportioned, B can also keep the plow and get restitution of $500.

§ 385. Effect of Power of Avoidance on Duty of Performance or on Duty Arising Out of Breach.

(1) Unless an offer to restore performance received is a condition of avoidance, a party has no duty of performance while his power of avoidance exists.

(2) If an offer to restore performance received is a condition of avoidance, a duty to pay damages is terminated by such an offer made before the power of avoidance is lost.

Comment

a. No duty of performance. If a party has the power to avoid the contract simply by disaffirmance, without offering to restore performance received, his refusal or failure to perform is not a breach under the rule stated in Subsection (1). This is so even if he is ignorant of his power of avoidance and believes that his refusal or failure is a breach. As a general rule, the legal consequences of a party's refusal or failure to perform are not affected by the fact that he is ignorant of some justification or excuse for his refusal or failure. See Comment e to § 225 and Comment c to § 237.

Illustrations

1. A is induced by B's fraud to make a contract to buy goods from B. While A is still ignorant of the fraud and before he has received the goods from B, A writes a letter telling him that he refuses to perform. B sues A for damages for total breach by repudiation. A is not liable to B because, since A has no duty of performance, his letter was not a repudiation.

2. A is induced by B's fraud to make a contract to buy goods from B. A delays for an unreasonable time after discovery of the fraud and then, before he has received the goods, writes B a letter telling him that he refuses to perform on the ground of fraud. B sues A for damages for total breach by repudiation. A is liable to B because, A's power of avoidance having been lost by delay, he had a duty of performance and his letter was a repudiation.

b. Duty arising out of breach terminated. If an offer to restore performance received is a condition of avoidance (§ 384), a party with a power of avoidance is under a duty of performance until such an offer is made. His refusal or failure to perform is therefore a breach. A subsequent offer to restore performance, however, terminates the duty to pay damages that arises from that breach if the offer is made before the power of avoidance is lost.

3. A is induced by B's fraud to make a contract to buy goods from B. While A is still ignorant of the fraud but after he has received the goods from B, A commits a material breach by failure to pay B. A then discovers the fraud and tenders the goods back to B. B sues A for damages for total breach of contract. Even if an offer to return the goods was a condition of avoidance by A, A is not liable to B because A's breach was nullified by the tender of what he had received.

PART III

RESTATEMENT (THIRD) OF EMPLOYMENT LAW (EXCERPTS) (2015)

RESTATEMENT (THIRD) EMPLOYMENT LAW (EXCERPTS)*

(2015)

[Many federal and state statutes regulate aspects of relationships between employees and their employers. The minimum wage statutes, for example, establish floors for the price terms in employment contracts. Nonetheless, the common law continues to govern the unregulated terms of the relationship. There have been dramatic changes in this body of law over the last few decades, especially with respect to an employer's right to terminate an employee. These changes, however, are not uniform from state to state. Even within a state, the highest court may not yet have fully developed the implications of the changes. Employment law, consequently, is not as clear as it could be in important respects, which can result in avoidable uncertainty in the law.

[In 2000, the American Law Institute ("ALI") began work on a Restatement of the Law (Third), Employment Law. Its aim is to clarify the common law of employment by, among other things, restating the law to reflect, and detail the implications of, the recent changes. The following excerpts, concerning termination qualify the traditional common law default rule, which provides that in the absence of a fixed contractual duration, either party may terminate an employment relationship at will, with or without a reason. The Restatement lays out several significant exceptions to this rule. Most notable among these exceptions are the effect of statutes and public policy, and the ways in which an employer's employment-policy statements can become binding on the employer, and can be changed, without complying with the traditional common law rules of contract formation, modification, and consideration.]

---

§ 2.01. Default Rule of an At-Will Employment Relationship.

Either party may terminate an employment relationship with or without cause unless the right to do so is limited by a statute, other law or public policy, or an agreement between the parties, a binding employer promise, or a binding employer policy statement (§ 2.02).

§ 2.02. Agreements and Binding Employer Promises or Statements Providing for Terms Other Than At-Will Employment.

The employment relationship is not terminable at will by an employer if:

(a) an agreement between the employer and the employee provides for (1) a definite term of employment, or (2) an indefinite term of employment and requires cause (defined in § 2.04) to terminate the employment (§ 2.03); or

(b) a promise by the employer to limit termination of employment reasonably induces detrimental reliance by the employee (§ 2.02, Comment c); or

(c) a binding policy statement made by the employer limits termination of employment (§ 2.05); or

(d) the implied duty of good faith and fair dealing applicable to all employment relationships; (§ 2.07) limits termination of employment; or

(e) other established principles recognized in the general law of contracts limit termination of employment (§ 2.02, comment d).

---

* © by The American Law Institute. All Rights Reserved.

§ 2.03. Agreements for a Definite or Indefinite Term.

(a) An employer must have cause (§ 2.04) for terminating

(1) an unexpired agreement for a definite term of employment, or

(2) an agreement for an indefinite term of employment requiring cause for termination.

(b) In the absence of an express agreement providing otherwise, the employee is under no reciprocal obligation to have cause to terminate the employment relationship.

§ 2.04. Cause for Termination of Employment Agreements.

Unless otherwise provided for in the agreement:

(a) An employer has cause for early termination of an agreement for a definite term of employment if the employee has materially breached the agreement, including by persistent neglect of duties; by engaging in misconduct or other malfeasance, including gross negligence; or by being unable to perform the duties of the position due to a long-term disability.

(b) In addition to the grounds stated in subsection (a), an employer has a ground for terminating an agreement for an indefinite term of employment requiring cause for termination when a significant change in the employer's economic circumstances means that the employer no longer has a business need for the employee's services.

§ 2.05. Binding Employer Policy Statements.

Policy statements by an employer in documents such as employee manuals, personnel handbooks, and employment policy directives that are provided or made accessible to employees, whether by physical or electronic means, and that, reasonably read in context, establish limits on the employer's power to terminate the employment relationship, are binding on the employer until modified or revoked (as provided in § 2.06).

§ 2.06. Modification or Revocation of Binding Employer Policy Statements.

(a) An employer may prospectively modify or revoke its binding policy statements if it provides reasonable advance notice of, or reasonably makes accessible, the modified statement or revocation to the affected employees.

(b) Modifications and revocations apply to all employees hired, and all employees who continue working, after the notice is given and the modification or revocation becomes effective.

(c) Modifications and revocations cannot adversely affect vested or accrued employee rights that may have been created by the statement, an agreement based on the statement (covered by § 2.03), or reasonable detrimental reliance on a promise in the statement (covered by § 2.02, Comment c).

§ 2.07. Implied Duty of Good Faith and Fair Dealing.

(a) Each party to an employment relationship, including at-will employment owes a nonwaivable duty of good faith and fair dealing to each other party, which includes a party's obligation not to hinder the other party's performance under, or to deprive the other of the benefit of, their contractual relationship (§ 3.05(a)).

(b) The implied duty of good faith and fair dealing applies to at-will employment relationships in manner consistent with the essential nature of such an at-will relationship.

(c) In any employment relationship, including at-will employment, the employer's implied duty of good faith and fair dealing includes the duty not to terminate or seek to terminate the employment relationship for the purpose of

(1) preventing the vesting or accrual of an employee right or benefit; or

(2) retaliating against the employee for performing the employee's obligations under the employment contract or law.

PART IV

RESTATEMENT (THIRD) OF RESTITUTION AND UNJUST ENRICHMENT

RESTATEMENT (THIRD) OF RESTITUTION AND UNJUST ENRICHMENT

(2011)

(Excerpts)

TOPIC 1
RESTITUTION TO A PERFORMING PARTY WITH NO CLAIM ON THE CONTRACT

Sec.
31. Unenforceability.
32. Illegality.
33. Incapacity of Recipient.
34. Mistake or Supervening Change of Circumstances.
35. Performance of Disputed Obligation.
36. Restitution to a Party in Default.

---

§ 31. Unenforceability.

(1) A person who renders performance under an agreement that cannot be enforced against the recipient by reason of

    (a) indefiniteness, or

    (b) the failure to satisfy an extrinsic requirement of enforceability such as the Statute of Frauds, has a claim in restitution against the recipient as necessary to prevent unjust enrichment. There is no unjust enrichment if the claimant receives the counterperformance specified by the parties' unenforceable agreement.

(2) There is no claim under this section if enforcement of the agreement is barred by the applicable statute of limitations, nor in any other case in which the allowance of restitution would defeat the policy of the law that makes the agreement unenforceable. Restitution is appropriate except to the extent that forfeiture is an intended or acceptable consequence of unenforceability.

§ 32. Illegality.

A person who renders performance under an agreement that is illegal or otherwise unenforceable for reasons of public policy may obtain restitution from the recipient in accordance with the following rules:

    (1) Restitution will be allowed, whether or not necessary to prevent unjust enrichment, if restitution is required by the policy of the underlying prohibition.

    (2) Restitution will also be allowed, as necessary to prevent unjust enrichment, if the allowance of restitution will not defeat or frustrate the policy of the underlying prohibition. There is no unjust enrichment if the claimant receives the counterperformance specified by the parties' unenforceable agreement.

    (3) Restitution will be denied, notwithstanding the enrichment of the defendant at the claimant's expense, if a claim under subsection (2) is foreclosed by the claimant's inequitable conduct. . . .

§ 33. Incapacity of Recipient.

(1) A person who renders performance under an agreement that is unenforceable by reason of the other party's legal incapacity has a claim in restitution against the recipient as necessary to prevent unjust enrichment. There is no unjust enrichment if the claimant receives the counterperformance specified by the parties' unenforceable agreement.

(2) Restitution under this section is available only to a person who has dealt with the recipient in good faith on reasonable terms.

(3) Notwithstanding the unjust enrichment of the recipient, restitution may be limited or denied if it would be inconsistent with the protection that the doctrine of incapacity is intended to afford in the circumstances of the case.

§ 34. Mistake or Supervening Change of Circumstances.

(1) A person who renders performance under a contract that is subject to avoidance by reason of mistake or supervening change of circumstances has a claim in restitution to recover the performance or its value, as necessary to prevent unjust enrichment. . . .

(2) For purposes of subsection (1):

(a) the value of a nonreturnable contractual performance is measured by reference to the recipient's contractual expectations; and

(b) the recipient's liability in restitution may be reduced to allow for loss incurred in reliance on the contract.

§ 35. Performance of Disputed Obligation.

(1) If one party to a contract demands from the other a performance that is not in fact due by the terms of their agreement, under circumstances making it reasonable to accede to the demand rather than to insist on an immediate test of the disputed obligation, the party on whom the demand is made may render such performance under protest or with reservation of rights, preserving a claim in restitution to recover the value of the benefit conferred in excess of the recipient's contractual entitlement.

(2) The claim described in subsection (1) is available only to a party acting in good faith and in the reasonable protection of its own interests. It is not available where there has been an accord and satisfaction, or where a performance with reservation of rights is inadequate to discharge the claimant's obligation to the recipient.

§ 36. Restitution to a Party in Default.

(1) A performing party whose material breach prevents a recovery on the contract has a claim in restitution against the recipient of performance, as necessary to prevent unjust enrichment.

(2) Enrichment from receipt of an incomplete or defective contractual performance is measured by comparison to the recipient's position had the contract been fully performed. The claimant has the burden of establishing the fact and amount of any net benefit conferred.

(3) A claim under this section may be displaced by a valid agreement of the parties establishing their rights and remedies in the event of default.

(4) If the claimant's default involves fraud or other inequitable conduct, restitution may on that account be denied. . . .

TOPIC 2
ALTERNATIVE REMEDIES FOR BREACH OF AN ENFORCEABLE CONTRACT

Sec.
37. Rescission for Material Breach.
38. Performance-Based Damages.
39. Profit From Opportunistic Breach.

§ 37. Rescission for Material Breach.

(1) Except as provided in subsection (2), a plaintiff who is entitled to a remedy for the defendant's material breach or repudiation may choose rescission as an alternative to enforcement if the further requirements of § 54 can be met.

(2) Rescission as a remedy for breach of contract is not available against a defendant whose defaulted obligation is exclusively an obligation to pay money.

§ 38. Performance-Based Damages.

(1) As an alternative to damages based on the expectation interest . . ., a plaintiff who is entitled to a remedy for material breach or repudiation may recover damages measured by the cost or value of the plaintiff's performance.

(2) Performance-based damages are measured by

(a) uncompensated expenditures made in reasonable reliance on the contract, including expenditures made in preparation for performance or in performance, less any loss the defendant can prove with reasonable certainty the plaintiff would have suffered had the contract been performed . . .; or

(b) the market value of the plaintiff's uncompensated contractual performance, not exceeding the price of such performance as determined by reference to the parties' agreement.

(3) A plaintiff whose damages are measured by the rules of subsection (2) may also recover for any other loss, including incidental or consequential loss, caused by the breach.

§ 39. Profit From Opportunistic Breach.

(1) If a deliberate breach of contract results in profit to the defaulting promisor and the available damage remedy affords inadequate protection to the promisee's contractual entitlement, the promisee has a claim to restitution of the profit realized by the promisor as a result of the breach. Restitution by the rule of this section is an alternative to a remedy in damages.

(2) A case in which damages afford inadequate protection to the promisee's contractual entitlement is ordinarily one in which damages will not permit the promisee to acquire a full equivalent to the promised performance in a substitute transaction.

(3) Breach of contract is profitable when it results in gains to the defendant (net of potential liability in damages) greater than the defendant would have realized from performance of the contract. Profits from breach include saved expenditure and consequential gains that the defendant would not have realized but for the breach, as measured by the rules that apply in other cases of disgorgement. . . .

PART V
ELECTRONIC CONTRACTING

UNIFORM ELECTRONIC TRANSACTIONS ACT

(Excerpts)

[The National Conference of Commissioners on Uniform State Laws ("NCCUSL," now the Uniform Law Commission) proposed the Uniform Electronic Transactions Act ("UETA") in 1999. As of May 15, 2018, forty-seven states, the District of Columbia, and the Virgin Islands have enacted it. (Other states, notably New York and Illinois, have similar statutes.) Prior to enactment, state statutes of frauds provided that, generally speaking, an action could not be brought on certain types of contracts unless the contract was in writing and signed by the party to be charged. UETA removes the resulting barriers to electronic commerce, including contracting by email, over the Internet, between computers without human intervention, and by using a wide variety of other electronic means. UETA applies when parties have agreed to conduct their transaction in electronic form, UETA § 5(b), although whether the parties have so agreed is to be determined from the context and other surrounding circumstances, including the conduct of the parties. UETA establishes that electronic records and signatures generally are equivalent to paper writings and manual signatures, thereby displacing statutes of frauds in a great many cases. UETA must be construed and applied to further its purposes—"(1) to facilitate electronic transactions consistent with other applicable law; (2) to be consistent with reasonable practices concerning electronic transactions and with the continued expansion of those practices; and (3) to effectuate its general purpose to make uniform the law with respect to the subject of [the Act] among States enacting it." *Id.* at § 6.

[Where enacted, UETA is state law. In 2000, just a year after NCCUSL proposed UETA, Congress enacted a federal statute, the Electronic Signatures in Global Commerce Act ("E-Sign"), below. E-Sign's purposes are essentially the same as UETA's. This development raised a question whether E-Sign "preempts"—supersedes—UETA, because federal statutes are "the supreme law of the land," U.S. Const., Art. VI(2), and E-Sign applies very broadly to "any transaction in or affecting interstate or foreign commerce." 15 U.S.C. § 7001(a). However, E-Sign provides that under most circumstances it does not preempt UETA (and some other state statutes with similar effect). 15 U.S.C. § 7002(a).

[UETA addresses some issues that E-Sign does not mention, and it treats a few issues differently. Consequently, UETA and E-Sign are both important parts of the law governing contracts.]

Table of Contents

Sec.
1. Short Title.
2. Definitions.
3. Scope.
4. Prospective Application.
5. Use of Electronic Records and Electronic Signatures; Variation by Agreement.
6. Construction and Application.
7. Legal Recognition of Electronic Records, Electronic Signatures, and Electronic Contracts.
8. Provision of Information in Writing; Presentation of Records.
9. Attribution and Effect of Electronic Record and Electronic Signature.
10. Effect of Change or Error.
11. Notarization and Acknowledgment.
12. Retention of Electronic Records; Originals.
13. Admissibility in Evidence.
14. Automated Transaction.
15. Time and Place of Sending and Receipt.

§ 1. Short Title.

This [Act] may be cited as the Uniform Electronic Transactions Act.

§ 2. Definitions.

In this [Act]:

(1) "Agreement" means the bargain of the parties in fact, as found in their language or inferred from other circumstances and from rules, regulations, and procedures given the effect of agreements under laws otherwise applicable to a particular transaction.

(2) "Automated transaction" means a transaction conducted or performed, in whole or in part, by electronic means or electronic records, in which the acts or records of one or both parties are not reviewed by an individual in the ordinary course in forming a contract, performing under an existing contract, or fulfilling an obligation required by the transaction.

(3) "Computer program" means a set of statements or instructions to be used directly or indirectly in an information processing system in order to bring about a certain result.

(4) "Contract" means the total legal obligation resulting from the parties' agreement as affected by this [Act] and other applicable law.

(5) "Electronic" means relating to technology having electrical, digital, magnetic, wireless, optical, electromagnetic, or similar capabilities.

(6) "Electronic agent" means a computer program or an electronic or other automated means used independently to initiate an action or respond to electronic records or performances in whole or in part, without review or action by an individual.

(7) "Electronic record" means a record created, generated, sent, communicated, received, or stored by electronic means.

(8) "Electronic signature" means an electronic sound, symbol, or process attached to or logically associated with a record and executed or adopted by a person with the intent to sign the record.

(9) "Governmental agency" means an executive, legislative, or judicial agency, department, board, commission, authority, institution, or instrumentality of the federal government or of a State or of a county, municipality, or other political subdivision of a State.

(10) "Information" means data, text, images, sounds, codes, computer programs, software, databases, or the like.

(11) "Information processing system" means an electronic system for creating, generating, sending, receiving, storing, displaying, or processing information.

(12) "Person" means an individual, corporation, business trust, estate, trust, partnership, limited liability company, association, joint venture, governmental agency, public corporation, or any other legal or commercial entity.

(13) "Record" means information that is inscribed on a tangible medium or that is stored in an electronic or other medium and is retrievable in perceivable form.

(14) "Security procedure" means a procedure employed for the purpose of verifying that an electronic signature, record, or performance is that of a specific person or for detecting changes or errors in the information in an electronic record. The term includes a procedure that requires the use of algorithms or other codes, identifying words or numbers, encryption, or callback or other acknowledgment procedures.

(15) "State" means a State of the United States, the District of Columbia, Puerto Rico, the United States Virgin Islands, or any territory or insular possession subject to the jurisdiction of the United States. The term includes an Indian tribe or band, or Alaskan native village, which is recognized by federal law or formally acknowledged by a State.

(16) "Transaction" means an action or set of actions occurring between two or more persons relating to the conduct of business, commercial, or governmental affairs.

Comment

1. **"Agreement."**

Whether the parties have reached an agreement is determined by their express language and all surrounding circumstances. The Restatement 2d Contracts § 3 provides that, "An agreement is a manifestation of mutual assent on the part of two or more persons." See also Restatement 2d Contracts, Section 2, Comment b. The Uniform Commercial Code specifically includes in the circumstances from which an agreement may be inferred "course of performance, course of dealing and usage of trade . . ." as defined in the UCC. Although the definition of agreement in this Act does not make specific reference to usage of trade and other party conduct, this definition is not intended to affect the construction of the parties' agreement under the substantive law applicable to a particular transaction. Where that law takes account of usage and conduct in informing the terms of the parties' agreement, the usage or conduct would be relevant as "other circumstances" included in the definition under this Act.

Where the law applicable to a given transaction provides that system rules and the like constitute part of the agreement of the parties, such rules will have the same effect in determining the parties agreement under this Act. For example, UCC Article 4 (Section 4–103(b)) provides that Federal Reserve regulations and operating circulars and clearinghouse rules have the effect of agreements. Such agreements by law properly would be included in the definition of agreement in this Act.

The parties' agreement is relevant in determining whether the provisions of this Act have been varied by agreement. In addition, the parties' agreement may establish the parameters of the parties' use of electronic records and signatures, security procedures and similar aspects of the transaction. See Model Trading Partner Agreement, 45 Business Lawyer Supp. Issue (June 1990). See Section 5(b) and Comments thereto.

2. **"Automated Transaction."**

An automated transaction is a transaction performed or conducted by electronic means in which machines are used without human intervention to form contracts and perform obligations under existing contracts. Such broad coverage is necessary because of the diversity of transactions to which this Act may apply.

As with electronic agents, this definition addresses the circumstance where electronic records may result in action or performance by a party although no human review of the electronic records is anticipated. Section 14 provides specific rules to assure that where one or both parties do not review the electronic records, the resulting agreement will be effective.

The critical element in this definition is the lack of a human actor on one or both sides of a transaction. For example, if one orders books from Bookseller.com through Bookseller's website, the transaction would be an automated transaction because Bookseller took and confirmed the order via its machine. Similarly, if Automaker and supplier do business through Electronic Data Interchange, Automaker's computer, upon receiving information within certain pre-programmed parameters, will send an electronic order to supplier's computer. If Supplier's computer confirms the order and processes the shipment because the order falls within pre-programmed parameters in Supplier's computer, this would be a fully automated transaction. If, instead, the Supplier relies on a human employee to review, accept, and process the Buyer's order, then only the Automaker's side of the transaction would be automated. In either case, the entire transaction falls within this definition.

3. **"Computer program."**

This definition refers to the functional and operating aspects of an electronic, digital system. It relates to operating instructions used in an electronic system such as an electronic agent. (See definition of "Electronic Agent.")

4. **"Electronic."**

The basic nature of most current technologies and the need for a recognized, single term warrants the use of "electronic" as the defined term. The definition is intended to assure that the Act will be applied broadly as new technologies develop. The term must be construed broadly in light of developing technologies in order to fulfill the purpose of this Act to validate commercial transactions regardless of the medium used by the parties. Current legal requirements for "writings" can be satisfied by almost any tangible media, whether paper, other fibers, or even stone. The purpose and applicability of this Act covers intangible media which are technologically capable of storing, transmitting and reproducing information in human perceivable form, but which lack the tangible aspect of paper, papyrus or stone.

While not all technologies listed are technically "electronic" in nature (e.g., optical fiber technology), the term "electronic" is the most descriptive term available to describe the majority of current technologies. For example, the development of biological and chemical processes for communication and storage of data, while not specifically mentioned in the definition, are included within the technical definition because such processes operate on electromagnetic impulses. However, whether a particular technology may be characterized as technically "electronic," i.e., operates on electromagnetic impulses, should not be determinative of whether records and signatures created, used and stored by means of a particular technology are covered by this Act. This Act is intended to apply to all records and signatures created, used and stored by any medium which permits the information to be retrieved in perceivable form.

5. **"Electronic agent."**

This definition establishes that an electronic agent is a machine. As the term "electronic agent" has come to be recognized, it is limited to a tool function. The effect on the party using the agent is addressed in the operative provisions of the Act (e.g., Section 14). An electronic agent, such as a computer program or other automated means employed by a person, is a tool of that person. As a general rule, the employer of a tool is responsible for the results obtained by the use of that tool since the tool has no independent volition of its own. However, an electronic agent, by definition, is capable within the parameters of its programming, of initiating, responding or interacting with other parties or their electronic agents once it has been activated by a party, without further attention of that party.

While this Act proceeds on the paradigm that an electronic agent is capable of performing only within the technical strictures of its preset programming, it is conceivable that, within the useful life of this Act, electronic agents may be created with the ability to act autonomously, and not just automatically. That is, through developments in artificial intelligence, a computer may be able to "learn through experience, modify the instructions in their own programs, and even devise new instructions." Allen and Widdison, "Can Computers Make Contracts?" *9 Harv. J.L. & Tech 25* (Winter, 1996). If such developments occur, courts may construe the definition of electronic agent accordingly, in order to recognize such new capabilities.

The examples involving Bookseller.com and Automaker in the Comment to the definition of Automated Transaction are equally applicable here. Bookseller acts through an electronic agent in processing an order for books. Automaker and the supplier each act through electronic agents in facilitating and effectuating the just-in-time inventory process through EDI.

6. **"Electronic record."**

An electronic record is a subset of the broader defined term "record." It is any record created, used or stored in a medium other than paper (see definition of electronic). The defined term is also used in this Act as a limiting definition in those provisions in which it is used.

Information processing systems, computer equipment and programs, electronic data interchange, electronic mail, voice mail, facsimile, telex, telecopying, scanning, and similar technologies all qualify as electronic under this Act. Accordingly information stored on a computer hard drive or floppy disc, facsimiles, voice mail messages, messages on a telephone answering machine, audio and video tape recordings, among other records, all would be electronic records under this Act.

7. **"Electronic signature."**

The idea of a signature is broad and not specifically defined. Whether any particular record is "signed" is a question of fact. Proof of that fact must be made under other applicable law. This Act simply assures that the signature may be accomplished through electronic means. No specific technology need be used in order to create a valid signature. One's voice on an answering machine may suffice if the requisite intention is present. Similarly, including one's name as part of an electronic mail communication also may suffice, as may the firm name on a facsimile. It also may be shown that the requisite intent was not present and accordingly the symbol, sound or process did not amount to a signature. One may use a digital signature with the requisite intention, or one may use the private key solely as an access device with no intention to sign, or otherwise accomplish a legally binding act. In any case the critical element is the intention to execute or adopt the sound or symbol or process for the purpose of signing the related record.

The definition requires that the signer execute or adopt the sound, symbol, or process with the intent to sign the record. The act of applying a sound, symbol or process to an electronic record could have differing meanings and effects. The consequence of the act and the effect of the act as a signature are determined under other applicable law. However, the essential attribute of a signature involves applying a sound, symbol or process with an intent to do a legally significant act. It is that intention that is understood in the law as a part of the word "sign", without the need for a definition.

This Act establishes, to the greatest extent possible, the equivalency of electronic signatures and manual signatures. Therefore the term "signature" has been used to connote and convey that equivalency. The purpose is to overcome unwarranted biases against electronic methods of signing and authenticating records. The term "authentication," used in other laws, often has a narrower meaning and purpose than an electronic signature as used in this Act. However, an authentication under any of those other laws constitutes an electronic signature under this Act.

The precise effect of an electronic signature will be determined based on the surrounding circumstances under Section 9(b).

This definition includes as an electronic signature the standard webpage click through process. For example, when a person orders goods or services through a vendor's website, the person will be required to provide information as part of a process which will result in receipt of the goods or services. When the customer ultimately gets to the last step and clicks "I agree," the person has adopted the process and has done so with the intent to associate the person with the record of that process. The actual effect of the electronic signature will be determined from all the surrounding circumstances[. However,] the person adopted a process which the circumstances indicate s/he intended to have the effect of getting the goods/services and being bound to pay for them. The adoption of the process carried the intent to do a legally significant act, the hallmark of a signature.

Another important aspect of this definition lies in the necessity that the electronic signature be linked or logically associated with the record. In the paper world, it is assumed that the symbol adopted by a party is attached to or located somewhere in the same paper that is intended to be authenticated, e.g., an allonge firmly attached to a promissory note, or the classic signature at the end of a long contract. These tangible manifestations do not exist in the electronic environment, and accordingly, this definition expressly provides that the symbol must in some way be linked to, or connected with, the electronic record being signed. This linkage is consistent with the regulations promulgated by the Food and Drug Administration. 21 CFR Part 11 (March 20, 1997).

A digital signature using public key encryption technology would qualify as an electronic signature, as would the mere inclusion of one's name as a part of an e-mail message—so long as in each case the signer executed or adopted the symbol with the intent to sign. . . .

9. **"Information processing system."**

This definition is consistent with the UNCITRAL Model Law on Electronic Commerce. The term includes computers and other information systems. It is principally used in Section 15 in connection with the sending and receiving of information. In that context, the key aspect is that the information enter a system from which a person can access it.

10. **"Record."**

This is a standard definition designed to embrace all means of communicating or storing information except human memory. It includes any method for storing or communicating information, including "writings." A record need not be indestructible or permanent, but the term does not include oral or other communications which are not stored or preserved by some means. Information that has not been retained other than through human memory does not qualify as a record. As in the case of the terms "writing" or "written," the term "record" does not establish the purposes, permitted uses or legal effect which a record may have under any particular provision of substantive law. ABA Report on Use of the Term "Record," October 1, 1996.

11. **"Security procedure."**

A security procedure may be applied to verify an electronic signature, verify the identity of the sender, or assure the informational integrity of an electronic record. The definition does not identify any particular technology. This permits the use of procedures which the parties select or which are established by law. It permits the greatest flexibility among the parties and allows for future technological development.

The definition in this Act is broad and is used to illustrate one way of establishing attribution or content integrity of an electronic record or signature. The use of a security procedure is not accorded operative legal effect, through the use of presumptions or otherwise, by this Act. In this Act, the use of security procedures is simply one method for proving the source or content of an electronic record or signature.

A security procedure may be technologically very sophisticated, such as an asymmetric cryptographic system. At the other extreme the security procedure may be as simple as a telephone call to confirm the identity of the sender through another channel of communication. It may include the use of a mother's maiden name or a personal identification number (PIN). Each of these examples is a method for confirming the identity of a person or accuracy of a message.

12. **"Transaction."**

The definition has been limited to actions between people taken in the context of business, commercial or governmental activities. The term includes all interactions between people for business, commercial, including specifically consumer, or governmental purposes. However, the term does not include unilateral or non-transactional actions. As such it provides a structural limitation on the scope of the Act as stated in the next section.

It is essential that the term commerce and business be understood and construed broadly to include commercial and business transactions involving individuals who may qualify as "consumers" under other applicable law. If Alice and Bob agree to the sale of Alice's car to Bob for $2000 using an internet auction site, that transaction is fully covered by this Act. Even if Alice and Bob each qualify as typical "consumers" under other applicable law, their interaction is a transaction in commerce. Accordingly their actions would be related to commercial affairs, and fully qualify as a transaction governed by this Act.

Other transaction types include:

1. A single purchase by an individual from a retail merchant, which may be accomplished by an order from a printed catalog sent by facsimile, or by exchange of electronic mail.

2. Recurring orders on a weekly or monthly basis between large companies which have entered into a master trading partner agreement to govern the methods and manner of their transaction parameters.

3. A purchase by an individual from an online internet retail vendor. Such an arrangement may develop into an ongoing series of individual purchases, with security procedures and the like, as a part of doing ongoing business.

4. The closing of a business purchase transaction via facsimile transmission of documents or even electronic mail. In such a transaction, all parties may participate through electronic conferencing technologies. At the appointed time all electronic records are executed electronically and transmitted to the other party. In such a case, the electronic records and electronic signatures are validated under this Act, obviating the need for "in person" closings.

A transaction must include interaction between two or more persons. Consequently, to the extent that the execution of a will, trust, or a health care power of attorney or similar health care designation does not involve another person and is a unilateral act, it would not be covered by this Act because not occurring as a part of a transaction as defined in this Act. However, this Act *does* apply to all electronic records and signatures *related* to a transaction, and so does cover, for example, internal auditing and accounting records related to a transaction.

§ 3. Scope.

(a) Except as otherwise provided in subsection (b), this [Act] applies to electronic records and electronic signatures relating to a transaction.

(b) This [Act] does not apply to a transaction to the extent it is governed by:

(1) a law governing the creation and execution of wills, codicils, or testamentary trusts;

(2) [The Uniform Commercial Code other than Sections 1–107 and 1–206, Article 2, and Article 2A];

(3) [the Uniform Computer Information Transactions Act]; and

(4) [other laws, if any, identified by State].

(c) This [Act] applies to an electronic record or electronic signature otherwise excluded from the application of this [Act] under subsection (b) to the extent it is governed by a law other than those specified in subsection (b).

(d) A transaction subject to this [Act] is also subject to other applicable substantive law.

§ 4. Prospective Application.

This [Act] applies to any electronic record or electronic signature created, generated, sent, communicated, received, or stored on or after the effective date of this [Act].

§ 5. Use of Electronic Records and Electronic Signatures; Variation by Agreement.

(a) This [Act] does not require a record or signature to be created, generated, sent, communicated, received, stored, or otherwise processed or used by electronic means or in electronic form.

(b) This [Act] applies only to transactions between parties each of which has agreed to conduct transactions by electronic means. Whether the parties agree to conduct a transaction by electronic means is determined from the context and surrounding circumstances, including the parties' conduct.

(c) A party that agrees to conduct a transaction by electronic means may refuse to conduct other transactions by electronic means. The right granted by this subsection may not be waived by agreement.

(d) Except as otherwise provided in this [Act], the effect of any of its provisions may be varied by agreement. The presence in certain provisions of this [Act] of the words "unless otherwise agreed", or words of similar import, does not imply that the effect of other provisions may not be varied by agreement.

(e) Whether an electronic record or electronic signature has legal consequences is determined by this [Act] and other applicable law.

Comment

This section limits the applicability of this Act to transactions which parties have agreed to conduct electronically. Broad interpretation of the term agreement is necessary to assure that this Act has the widest possible application consistent with its purpose of removing barriers to electronic commerce.

1. This section makes clear that this Act is intended to facilitate the use of electronic means, but does not require the use of electronic records and signatures. This fundamental principle is set forth in subsection (a) and elaborated by subsections (b) and (c), which require an intention to conduct transactions electronically and preserve the right of a party to refuse to use electronics in any subsequent transaction.

2. The paradigm of this Act is two willing parties doing transactions electronically. It is therefore appropriate that the Act is voluntary and preserves the greatest possible party autonomy to refuse electronic transactions. The requirement that party agreement be found from all the surrounding circumstances is a limitation on the scope of this Act.

3. If this Act is to serve to facilitate electronic transactions, it must be applicable under circumstances not rising to a full fledged contract to use electronics. While absolute certainty can be accomplished by obtaining an explicit contract before relying on electronic transactions, such an explicit contract should not be necessary before one may feel safe in conducting transactions electronically. Indeed, such a requirement would itself be an unreasonable barrier to electronic commerce, at odds with the fundamental purpose of this Act. Accordingly, the requisite agreement, express or implied, must be determined from all available circumstances and evidence.

4. Subsection (b) provides that the Act applies to transactions in which the parties have agreed to conduct the transaction electronically. In this context it is essential that the parties' actions and words be broadly construed in determining whether the requisite agreement exists. Accordingly, the Act expressly provides that the party's agreement is to be found from all circumstances, including the parties' conduct. The critical element is the intent of a party to conduct a transaction electronically. Once that intent is established, this Act applies. See Restatement 2d Contracts, Sections 2, 3, and 19.

Examples of circumstances from which it may be found that parties have reached an agreement to conduct transactions electronically include the following:

A. Automaker and supplier enter into a Trading Partner Agreement setting forth the terms, conditions and methods for the conduct of business between them electronically.

B. Joe gives out his business card with his business e-mail address. It may be reasonable, under the circumstances, for a recipient of the card to infer that Joe has agreed to communicate electronically for business purposes. However, in the absence of additional facts, it would not necessarily be reasonable to infer Joe's agreement to communicate electronically for purposes outside the scope of the business indicated by use of the business card.

C. Sally may have several e-mail addresses—home, main office, office of a non-profit organization on whose board Sally sits. In each case, it may be reasonable to infer that Sally is willing to communicate electronically with respect to business related to the business/purpose associated with the respective e-mail addresses. However, depending on the circumstances, it may not be reasonable to communicate with Sally for purposes other than those related to the purpose for which she maintained a particular e-mail account.

D. Among the circumstances to be considered in finding an agreement would be the time when the assent occurred relative to the timing of the use of electronic communications. If one orders books from an on-line vendor, such as Bookseller.com, the intention to conduct that transaction and to receive any correspondence related to the transaction electronically can be inferred from the conduct. Accordingly, as to information related to that transaction it is reasonable for Bookseller to deal with the individual electronically.

The examples noted above are intended to focus the inquiry on the party's agreement to conduct a transaction electronically. Similarly, if two people are at a meeting and one tells the other to send an e-mail to confirm a transaction—the requisite agreement under subsection (b) would exist. In each case, the use of a business card, statement at a meeting, or other evidence of willingness to conduct a transaction electronically must be viewed in light of all the surrounding circumstances with a view toward broad validation of electronic transactions.

5. Just as circumstances may indicate the existence of agreement, express or implied from surrounding circumstances, circumstances may also demonstrate the absence of true agreement. For example:

A. If Automaker, Inc. were to issue a recall of automobiles via its Internet website, it would not be able to rely on this Act to validate that notice in the case of a person who never logged on to the website, or indeed, had no ability to do so, notwithstanding a clause in a paper purchase contract by which the buyer agreed to receive such notices in such a manner.

B. Buyer executes a standard form contract in which an agreement to receive all notices electronically in set forth on page 3 in the midst of other fine print. Buyer has never communicated with Seller electronically, and has not provided any other information in the contract to suggest a willingness to deal electronically. Not only is it unlikely that any but the most formalistic of agreements may be found, but nothing in this Act prevents courts from policing such form contracts under common law doctrines relating to contract formation, unconscionability and the like.

6. Subsection (c) has been added to make clear the ability of a party to refuse to conduct a transaction electronically, even if the person has conducted transactions electronically in the past. The effectiveness of a party's refusal to conduct a transaction electronically will be determined under other applicable law in light of all surrounding circumstances. Such circumstances must include an assessment of the transaction involved.

A party's right to decline to act electronically under a specific contract, on the ground that each action under that contract amounts to a separate "transaction," must be considered in light of the purpose of the contract and the action to be taken electronically. For example, under a contract for the purchase of goods, the giving and receipt of notices electronically, as provided in the contract, should not be viewed as discreet transactions. Rather such notices amount to separate actions which are part of the "transaction" of purchase evidenced by the contract. Allowing one party to require a change of medium in the middle of the transaction evidenced by that contract is not the purpose of this subsection. Rather this subsection is intended to preserve the party's right to conduct the next purchase in a non-electronic medium.

7. Subsection (e) is an essential provision in the overall scheme of this Act. While this Act validates and effectuates electronic records and electronic signatures, the legal effect of such records and signatures is left to existing substantive law outside this Act except in very narrow circumstances. . . . Even when this Act operates to validate records and signatures in an electronic medium, it expressly preserves the substantive rules of other law applicable to such records. See, e.g., Section 11.

For example, beyond validation of records, signatures and contracts based on the medium used, Section 7(a) and (b) should not be interpreted as establishing the legal effectiveness of any given record, signature or contract. Where a rule of law requires that the record contain minimum substantive content, the legal effect of such a record will depend on whether the record meets the substantive requirements of other applicable law.

Section 8 expressly preserves a number of legal requirements in currently existing law relating to the presentation of information in writing. Although this Act now would allow such information to be presented in an electronic record, Section 8 provides that the other substantive requirements of law must be satisfied in the electronic medium as well.

§ 6. Construction and Application.

This [Act] must be construed and applied:

(1) to facilitate electronic transactions consistent with other applicable law;

(2) to be consistent with reasonable practices concerning electronic transactions and with the continued expansion of those practices; and

(3) to effectuate its general purpose to make uniform the law with respect to the subject of this [Act] among States enacting it.

§ 7. Legal Recognition of Electronic Records, Electronic Signatures, and Electronic Contracts.

(a) A record or signature may not be denied legal effect or enforceability solely because it is in electronic form.

(b) A contract may not be denied legal effect or enforceability solely because an electronic record was used in its formation.

(c) If a law requires a record to be in writing, an electronic record satisfies the law.

(d) If a law requires a signature, an electronic signature satisfies the law.

Comment

1. This section sets forth the fundamental premise of this Act: namely, that the medium in which a record, signature, or contract is created, presented or retained does not affect it's legal significance. Subsections (a) and (b) are designed to eliminate the single element of medium as a reason to deny effect or enforceability to a record, signature, or contract. The fact that the information is set forth in an electronic, as opposed to paper, record is irrelevant.

2. Under Restatement 2d Contracts Section 8, a contract may have legal effect and yet be unenforceable. Indeed, one circumstance where a record or contract may have effect but be unenforceable is in the context of the Statute of Frauds. Though a contract may be unenforceable, the records may have collateral effects, as in the case of a buyer that insures goods purchased under a contract unenforceable under the Statute of Frauds. The insurance company may not deny a claim on the ground that the buyer is not the owner, though the buyer may have no direct remedy against seller for failure to deliver. See Restatement 2d Contracts, Section 8, Illustration 4.

While this section would validate an electronic record for purposes of a statute of frauds, if an agreement to conduct the transaction electronically cannot reasonably be found (see Section 5(b)) then a necessary predicate to the applicability of this Act would be absent and this Act would not validate the electronic record. Whether the electronic record might be valid under other law is not addressed by this Act.

3. Subsections (c) and (d) provide the positive assertion that electronic records and signatures satisfy legal requirements for writings and signatures. The provisions are limited to requirements in laws that a record be in writing or be signed. This section does not address requirements imposed by other law in addition to requirements for writings and signatures. See, e.g., Section 8.

Subsections (c) and (d) are particularized applications of subsection (a). The purpose is to validate and effectuate electronic records and signatures as the equivalent of writings, subject to all of the rules applicable to the efficacy of a writing, except as such other rules are modified by the more specific provisions of this Act.

Illustration 1: A sends the following e-mail to B: "I hereby offer to buy widgets from you, delivery next Tuesday. /s/ A." B responds with the following e-mail: "I accept your offer to buy widgets for delivery next Tuesday. /s/ B." The e-mails may not be denied effect solely because they are electronic. In addition, the e-mails do qualify as records under the Statute of Frauds. However, because there is no quantity stated in either record, the parties' agreement would be unenforceable under existing UCC Section 2–201(1).

Illustration 2: A sends the following e-mail to B: "I hereby offer to buy 100 widgets for $1000, delivery next Tuesday. /s/ A." B responds with the following e-mail: "I accept your offer to purchase 100 widgets for $1000, delivery next Tuesday. /s/ B." In this case the analysis is the same as in Illustration 1 except that here the records otherwise satisfy the requirements of UCC Section 2–201(1). The transaction may not be denied legal effect solely because there is not a pen and ink "writing" or "signature".

4. Section 8 addresses additional requirements imposed by other law which may affect the legal effect or enforceability of an electronic record in a particular case. For example, in Section 8(a) the legal requirement addressed is *the provision of information* in writing. The section then sets forth the standards to be applied in determining whether the provision of information by an electronic record is the equivalent of the provision of information in writing. The requirements in Section 8 are in addition to the bare validation that occurs under this section.

5. Under the substantive law applicable to a particular transaction within this Act, the legal effect of an electronic record may be separate from the issue of whether the record contains a signature. For example, where notice must be given as part of a contractual obligation, the effectiveness of the notice will turn on whether the party provided the notice regardless of whether the notice was signed (see Section 15). An electronic record attributed to a party under Section 9 and complying with the requirements of Section 15 would suffice in that case, notwithstanding that it may not contain an electronic signature.

§ 8. Provision of Information in Writing; Presentation of Records.

(a) If parties have agreed to conduct a transaction by electronic means and a law requires a person to provide, send, or deliver information in writing to another person, the requirement is satisfied if the information is provided, sent, or delivered, as the case may be, in an electronic record capable of retention by the recipient at the time of receipt. An electronic record is not capable of retention by the recipient if the sender or its information processing system inhibits the ability of the recipient to print or store the electronic record.

(b) If a law other than this [Act] requires a record (i) to be posted or displayed in a certain manner, (ii) to be sent, communicated, or transmitted by a specified method, or (iii) to contain information that is formatted in a certain manner, the following rules apply:

(1) The record must be posted or displayed in the manner specified in the other law.

(2) Except as otherwise provided in subsection (d)(2), the record must be sent, communicated, or transmitted by the method specified in the other law.

(3) The record must contain the information formatted in the manner specified in the other law.

(c) If a sender inhibits the ability of a recipient to store or print an electronic record, the electronic record is not enforceable against the recipient.

(d) The requirements of this section may not be varied by agreement, but:

(1) to the extent a law other than this [Act] requires information to be provided, sent, or delivered in writing but permits that requirement to be varied by agreement, the requirement under subsection (a) that the information be in the form of an electronic record capable of retention may also be varied by agreement; and

(2) a requirement under a law other than this [Act] to send, communicate, or transmit a record by [first-class mail, postage prepaid] [regular United States mail], may be varied by agreement to the extent permitted by the other law.

§ 9. Attribution and Effect of Electronic Record and Electronic Signature.

(a) An electronic record or electronic signature is attributable to a person if it was the act of the person. The act of the person may be shown in any manner, including a showing of the efficacy of any security procedure applied to determine the person to which the electronic record or electronic signature was attributable.

(b) The effect of an electronic record or electronic signature attributed to a person under subsection (a) is determined from the context and surrounding circumstances at the time of its creation, execution, or adoption, including the parties' agreement, if any, and otherwise as provided by law.

Comment

1. Under subsection (a), so long as the electronic record or electronic signature resulted from a person's action it will be attributed to that person—the legal effect of that attribution is addressed in subsection (b). This section does not alter existing rules of law regarding attribution. The section assures that such rules will be applied in the electronic environment. A person's actions include actions taken by

human agents of the person, as well as actions taken by an electronic agent, i.e., the tool, of the person. Although the rule may appear to state the obvious, it assures that the record or signature is not ascribed to a machine, as opposed to the person operating or programming the machine.

In each of the following cases, both the electronic record and electronic signature would be attributable to a person under subsection (a):

A. The person types his/her name as part of an e-mail purchase order;

B. The person's employee, pursuant to authority, types the person's name as part of an e-mail purchase order;

C. The person's computer, programmed to order goods upon receipt of inventory information within particular parameters, issues a purchase order which includes the person's name, or other identifying information, as part of the order.

In each of the above cases, law other than this Act would ascribe both the signature and the action to the person if done in a paper medium. Subsection (a) expressly provides that the same result will occur when an electronic medium is used.

2. Nothing in this section affects the use of a signature as a device for attributing a record to a person. Indeed, a signature is often the primary method for attributing a record to a person. In the foregoing examples, once the electronic signature is attributed to the person, the electronic record would also be attributed to the person, unless the person established fraud, forgery, or other invalidating cause. However, a signature is not the only method for attribution.

3. The use of facsimile transmissions provides a number of examples of attribution using information other than a signature. A facsimile may be attributed to a person because of the information printed across the top of the page that indicates the machine from which it was sent. Similarly, the transmission may contain a letterhead which identifies the sender. Some cases have held that the letterhead actually constituted a signature because it was a symbol adopted by the sender with intent to authenticate the facsimile. However, the signature determination resulted from the necessary finding of intention in that case. Other cases have found facsimile letterheads NOT to be signatures because the requisite intention was not present. The critical point is that with or without a signature, information within the electronic record may well suffice to provide the facts resulting in attribution of an electronic record to a particular party.

In the context of attribution of records, normally the content of the record will provide the necessary information for a finding of attribution. It is also possible that an established course of dealing between parties may result in a finding of attribution. Just as with a paper record, evidence of forgery or counterfeiting may be introduced to rebut the evidence of attribution.

4. Certain information may be present in an electronic environment that does not appear to attribute but which clearly links a person to a particular record. Numerical codes, personal identification numbers, public and private key combinations all serve to establish the party to whom an electronic record should be attributed. Of course security procedures will be another piece of evidence available to establish attribution.

The inclusion of a specific reference to security procedures as a means of proving attribution is salutary because of the unique importance of security procedures in the electronic environment. In certain processes, a technical and technological security procedure may be the best way to convince a trier of fact that a particular electronic record or signature was that of a particular person. In certain circumstances, the use of a security procedure to establish that the record and related signature came from the person's business might be necessary to overcome a claim that a hacker intervened. The reference to security procedures is not intended to suggest that other forms of proof of attribution should be accorded less persuasive effect. It is also important to recall that the particular strength of a given procedure does not affect the procedure's status as a security procedure, but only affects the weight to be accorded the evidence of the security procedure as tending to establish attribution.

5. This section does apply in determining the effect of a "click-through" transaction. A "click-through" transaction involves a process which, if executed with an intent to "sign," will be an electronic signature. See definition of Electronic Signature. In the context of an anonymous "click-through," issues of

proof will be paramount. This section will be relevant to establish that the resulting electronic record is attributable to a particular person upon the requisite proof, including security procedures which may track the source of the click-through.

6. Once it is established that a record or signature is attributable to a particular party, the effect of a record or signature must be determined in light of the context and surrounding circumstances, including the parties' agreement, if any. Also informing the effect of any attribution will be other legal requirements considered in light of the context. Subsection (b) addresses the effect of the record or signature once attributed to a person.

§ 10. Effect of Change or Error.

If a change or error in an electronic record occurs in a transmission between parties to a transaction, the following rules apply:

(1) If the parties have agreed to use a security procedure to detect changes or errors and one party has conformed to the procedure, but the other party has not, and the nonconforming party would have detected the change or error had that party also conformed, the conforming party may avoid the effect of the changed or erroneous electronic record.

(2) In an automated transaction involving an individual, the individual may avoid the effect of an electronic record that resulted from an error made by the individual in dealing with the electronic agent of another person if the electronic agent did not provide an opportunity for the prevention or correction of the error and, at the time the individual learns of the error, the individual:

(A) promptly notifies the other person of the error and that the individual did not intend to be bound by the electronic record received by the other person;

(B) takes reasonable steps, including steps that conform to the other person's reasonable instructions, to return to the other person or, if instructed by the other person, to destroy the consideration received, if any, as a result of the erroneous electronic record; and

(C) has not used or received any benefit or value from the consideration, if any, received from the other person.

(3) If neither paragraph (1) nor paragraph (2) applies, the change or error has the effect provided by other law, including the law of mistake, and the parties' contract, if any.

(4) Paragraphs (2) and (3) may not be varied by agreement.

§ 11. Notarization and Acknowledgment.

If a law requires a signature or record to be notarized, acknowledged, verified, or made under oath, the requirement is satisfied if the electronic signature of the person authorized to perform those acts, together with all other information required to be included by other applicable law, is attached to or logically associated with the signature or record.

§ 12. Retention of Electronic Records; Originals.

(a) If a law requires that a record be retained, the requirement is satisfied by retaining an electronic record of the information in the record which:

(1) accurately reflects the information set forth in the record after it was first generated in its final form as an electronic record or otherwise; and

(2) remains accessible for later reference.

(b) A requirement to retain a record in accordance with subsection (a) does not apply to any information the sole purpose of which is to enable the record to be sent, communicated, or received.

(c) A person may satisfy subsection (a) by using the services of another person if the requirements of that subsection are satisfied.

(d) If a law requires a record to be presented or retained in its original form, or provides consequences if the record is not presented or retained in its original form, that law is satisfied by an electronic record retained in accordance with subsection (a).

(e) If a law requires retention of a check, that requirement is satisfied by retention of an electronic record of the information on the front and back of the check in accordance with subsection (a).

(f) A record retained as an electronic record in accordance with subsection (a) satisfies a law requiring a person to retain a record for evidentiary, audit, or like purposes, unless a law enacted after the effective date of this [Act] specifically prohibits the use of an electronic record for the specified purpose.

(g) This section does not preclude a governmental agency of this State from specifying additional requirements for the retention of a record subject to the agency's jurisdiction.

§ 13. Admissibility in Evidence.

In a proceeding, evidence of a record or signature may not be excluded solely because it is in electronic form.

§ 14. Automated Transaction.

In an automated transaction, the following rules apply:

(1) A contract may be formed by the interaction of electronic agents of the parties, even if no individual was aware of or reviewed the electronic agents' actions or the resulting terms and agreements.

(2) A contract may be formed by the interaction of an electronic agent and an individual, acting on the individual's own behalf or for another person, including by an interaction in which the individual performs actions that the individual is free to refuse to perform and which the individual knows or has reason to know will cause the electronic agent to complete the transaction or performance.

(3) The terms of the contract are determined by the substantive law applicable to it.

Comment

1. This section confirms that contracts can be formed by machines functioning as electronic agents for parties to a transaction. It negates any claim that lack of human intent, at the time of contract formation, prevents contract formation. When machines are involved, the requisite intention flows from the programing and use of the machine. As in other cases, these are salutary provisions consistent with the fundamental purpose of the Act to remove barriers to electronic transactions while leaving the substantive law, e.g., law of mistake, law of contract formation, unaffected to the greatest extent possible.

2. The process in paragraph (2) validates an anonymous click-through transaction. It is possible that an anonymous click-through process may simply result in no recognizable legal relationship, e.g., A goes to a person's website and acquires access without in any way identifying herself, or otherwise indicating agreement or assent to any limitation or obligation, and the owner's site grants A access. In such a case no legal relationship has been created.

On the other hand it may be possible that A's actions indicate agreement to a particular term. For example, A goes to a website and is confronted by an initial screen which advises her that the information at this site is proprietary, that A may use the information for her own personal purposes, but that, by clicking below, A agrees that any other use without the site owner's permission is prohibited. If A clicks "agree" and downloads the information and then uses the information for other, prohibited purposes, should not A be bound by the click? It seems the answer properly should be, and would be, yes.

If the owner can show that the only way A could have obtained the information was from his website, and that the process to access the subject information required that A must have clicked the "I agree" button after having the ability to see the conditions on use, A has performed actions which A was free to refuse, which A knew would cause the site to grant her access, i.e., "complete the transaction." The terms of the resulting contract will be determined under general contract principles, but will include the limitation on A's use of the information, as a condition precedent to granting her access to the information.

3. In the transaction set forth in Comment 2, the record of the transaction also will include an electronic signature. By clicking "I agree" A adopted a process with the intent to "sign," i.e., bind herself to a legal obligation, the resulting record of the transaction. If a "signed writing" were required under otherwise applicable law, this transaction would be enforceable. If a "signed writing" were not required, it may be sufficient to establish that the electronic record is attributable to A under Section 9. Attribution may be shown in any manner reasonable including showing that, of necessity, A could only have gotten the information through the process at the website.

§ 15. Time and Place of Sending and Receipt.

(a) Unless otherwise agreed between the sender and the recipient, an electronic record is sent when it:

(1) is addressed properly or otherwise directed properly to an information processing system that the recipient has designated or uses for the purpose of receiving electronic records or information of the type sent and from which the recipient is able to retrieve the electronic record;

(2) is in a form capable of being processed by that system; and

(3) enters an information processing system outside the control of the sender or of a person that sent the electronic record on behalf of the sender or enters a region of the information processing system designated or used by the recipient which is under the control of the recipient.

(b) Unless otherwise agreed between a sender and the recipient, an electronic record is received when:

(1) it enters an information processing system that the recipient has designated or uses for the purpose of receiving electronic records or information of the type sent and from which the recipient is able to retrieve the electronic record; and

(2) it is in a form capable of being processed by that system.

(c) Subsection (b) applies even if the place the information processing system is located is different from the place the electronic record is deemed to be received under subsection (d).

(d) Unless otherwise expressly provided in the electronic record or agreed between the sender and the recipient, an electronic record is deemed to be sent from the sender's place of business and to be received at the recipient's place of business. For purposes of this subsection, the following rules apply:

(1) If the sender or recipient has more than one place of business, the place of business of that person is the place having the closest relationship to the underlying transaction.

(2) If the sender or the recipient does not have a place of business, the place of business is the sender's or recipient's residence, as the case may be.

(e) An electronic record is received under subsection (b) even if no individual is aware of its receipt.

(f) Receipt of an electronic acknowledgment from an information processing system described in subsection (b) establishes that a record was received but, by itself, does not establish that the content sent corresponds to the content received.

(g) If a person is aware that an electronic record purportedly sent under subsection (a), or purportedly received under subsection (b), was not actually sent or received, the legal effect of the sending or receipt is determined by other applicable law. Except to the extent permitted by the other law, the requirements of this subsection may not be varied by agreement.

Comment

1. This section provides default rules regarding when and from where an electronic record is sent and when and where an electronic record is received. This section does not address the efficacy of the record that is sent or received. That is, whether a record is unintelligible or unusable by a recipient is a separate issue from whether that record was sent or received. The effectiveness of an illegible record, [and] whether it binds any party, are questions left to other law.

2. Subsection (a) furnishes rules for determining when an electronic record is sent. The effect of the sending and its import are determined by other law once it is determined that a sending has occurred.

In order to have a proper sending, the subsection requires that information be properly addressed or otherwise directed to the recipient. In order to send within the meaning of this section, there must be specific information which will direct the record to the intended recipient. Although mass electronic sending is not precluded, a general broadcast message, sent to systems rather than individuals, would not suffice as a sending.

The record will be considered sent once it leaves the control of the sender, or comes under the control of the recipient. Records sent through e-mail or the internet will pass through many different server systems. Accordingly, the critical element when more than one system is involved is the loss of control by the sender.

However, the structure of many message delivery systems is such that electronic records may actually never leave the control of the sender. For example, within a university or corporate setting, e-mail sent within the system to another faculty member is technically not out of the sender's control since it never leaves the organization's server. Accordingly, to qualify as a sending, the e-mail must arrive at a point where the recipient has control. This section does not address the effect of an electronic record that is thereafter "pulled back," e.g., removed from a mailbox. The analog in the paper world would be removing a letter from a person's mailbox. As in the case of providing information electronically under Section 8, the recipient's ability to receive a message should be judged from the perspective of whether the sender has done any action which would preclude retrieval. This is especially the case in regard to sending, since the sender must direct the record to a system designated or used by the recipient.

3. Subsection (b) provides simply that when a record enters the system which the recipient has designated or uses and to which it has access, in a form capable of being processed by that system, it is received. Keying receipt to a system accessible by the recipient removes the potential for a recipient leaving messages with a server or other service in order to avoid receipt. However, the section does not resolve the issue of how the sender proves the time of receipt.

To assure that the recipient retains control of the place of receipt, subsection (b) requires that the system be specified or used by the recipient, and that the system be used or designated for the type of record being sent. Many people have multiple e-mail addresses for different purposes. Subsection (b) assures that recipients can designate the e-mail address or system to be used in a particular transaction. For example, the recipient retains the ability to designate a home e-mail for personal matters, work e-mail for official business, or a separate organizational e-mail solely for the business purposes of that organization. If A sends B a notice at his home which relates to business, it may not be deemed received if B designated his business address as the sole address for business purposes. Whether actual knowledge upon seeing it at home would qualify as receipt is determined under the otherwise applicable substantive law.

4. Subsections (c) and (d) provide default rules for determining where a record will be considered to have been sent or received. The focus is on the place of business of the recipient and not the physical location of the information processing system, which may bear absolutely no relation to the transaction between the parties. It is not uncommon for users of electronic commerce to communicate from one State to another without knowing the location of information systems through which communication is operated. In addition, the location of certain communication systems may change without either of the parties being aware of the

change. Accordingly, where the place of sending or receipt is an issue under other applicable law, e.g., conflict of laws issues, tax issues, the relevant location should be the location of the sender or recipient and not the location of the information processing system.

Subsection (d) assures individual flexibility in designating the place from which a record will be considered sent or at which a record will be considered received. Under subsection (d) a person may designate the place of sending or receipt unilaterally in an electronic record. This ability, as with the ability to designate by agreement, may be limited by otherwise applicable law to places having a reasonable relationship to the transaction.

5. Subsection (e) makes clear that receipt is not dependent on a person having notice that the record is in the person's system. Receipt occurs when the record reaches the designated system whether or not the recipient ever retrieves the record. The paper analog is the recipient who never reads a mail notice.

6. Subsection (f) provides legal certainty regarding the effect of an electronic acknowledgment. It only addresses the fact of receipt, not the quality of the content, nor whether the electronic record was read or "opened."

7. Subsection (g) limits the parties' ability to vary the method for sending and receipt provided in subsections (a) and (b), when there is a legal requirement for the sending or receipt. As in other circumstances where legal requirements derive from other substantive law, to the extent that the other law permits variation by agreement, this Act does not impose any additional requirements, and provisions of this Act may be varied to the extent provided in the other law.

ELECTRONIC SIGNATURES IN GLOBAL AND NATIONAL COMMERCE ACT

(2000)

[Congress enacted the Electronic Signatures in Global and National Commerce Act ("E-Sign") in 2000. Its purpose is much like that of the Uniform Electronic Transactions Act ("UETA")—to facilitate contracting using electronic records, including electronic contracts, and electronic signatures. E-Sign prevents challenges to the legal effect, validity, or enforceability of contracts that are based only on their electronic form. As indicated in the annotation to UETA in this pamphlet, above, E-Sign applies very broadly to "any transaction in or affecting interstate or foreign commerce." 15 U.S.C. § 7001(a). Consequently, Congress considered whether, as a federal statute, E-Sign should pre-empt UETA and similar state statutes. E-Sign provides that it does not pre-empt UETA if UETA is enacted in its original version (1999), or a state enacts a similar statute. 15 U.S.C. § 7002(a). By superseding state statutes of frauds for many transactions, E-Sign was another important step in modernizing and making uniform the law governing many contracts, including international contracts, to which U.S. law applies. (*See also* the United Nations Convention on the Use of Electronic Communications in International Contracts, below.)

[E-Sign and UETA each addresses some issues that the other does not, and they treat a few issues differently. For example, E-Sign contains special provisions to protect consumers. *See* 15 U.S.C. § 7001(c). Consequently, E-Sign and UETA are both important parts of the law governing contracts.]

Table of Contents

Sec.
7001. General Rule of Validity.
7002. Exemption to Preemption.
7003. Specific Exceptions.
7006. Definitions.

§ 7001. General Rule of Validity.

(a) **In General.** Notwithstanding any statute, regulation, or other rule of law (other than this title and title II), with respect to any transaction in or affecting interstate or foreign commerce—

(1) a signature, contract, or other record relating to such transaction may not be denied legal effect, validity, or enforceability solely because it is in electronic form; and

(2) a contract relating to such transaction may not be denied legal effect, validity, or enforceability solely because an electronic signature or electronic record was used in its formation.

(b) **Preservation of Rights and Obligations.** This title does not—

(1) limit, alter, or otherwise affect any requirement imposed by a statute, regulation, or rule of law relating to the rights and obligations of persons under such statute, regulation, or rule of law other than a requirement that contracts or other records be written, signed, or in nonelectronic form; or

(2) require any person to agree to use or accept electronic records or electronic signatures, other than a governmental agency with respect to a record other than a contract to which it is a party.

(c) **Consumer Disclosures.**

(1) **Consent to Electronic Records.** Notwithstanding subsection (a), if a statute, regulation, or other rule of law requires that information relating to a transaction or transactions in or affecting interstate or foreign commerce be provided or made available to a consumer in writing, the use of an electronic record to provide or make available (whichever is required) such information satisfies the requirement that such information be in writing if—

(A) the consumer has affirmatively consented to such use and has not withdrawn such consent;

(B) the consumer, prior to consenting, is provided with a clear and conspicuous statement—

(i) informing the consumer of (I) any right or option of the consumer to have the record provided or made available on paper or in nonelectronic form, and (II) the right of the consumer to withdraw the consent to have the record provided or made available in an electronic form and of any conditions, consequences (which may include termination of the parties' relationship), or fees in the event of such withdrawal;

(ii) informing the consumer of whether the consent applies (I) only to the particular transaction which gave rise to the obligation to provide the record, or (II) to identified categories of records that may be provided or made available during the course of the parties' relationship;

(iii) describing the procedures the consumer must use to withdraw consent as provided in clause (i) and to update information needed to contact the consumer electronically; and

(iv) informing the consumer (I) how, after the consent, the consumer may, upon request, obtain a paper copy of an electronic record, and (II) whether any fee will be charged for such copy;

(C) the consumer—

(i) prior to consenting, is provided with a statement of the hardware and software requirements for access to and retention of the electronic records; and

(ii) consents electronically, or confirms his or her consent electronically, in a manner that reasonably demonstrates that the consumer can access information in the electronic form that will be used to provide the information that is the subject of the consent; and

(D) after the consent of a consumer in accordance with subparagraph (A), if a change in the hardware or software requirements needed to access or retain electronic records creates a material risk that the consumer will not be able to access or retain a subsequent electronic record that was the subject of the consent, the person providing the electronic record—

(i) provides the consumer with a statement of (I) the revised hardware and software requirements for access to and retention of the electronic records, and (II) the right to withdraw consent without the imposition of any fees for such withdrawal and without the imposition of any condition or consequence that was not disclosed under subparagraph (B)(i); and

(ii) again complies with subparagraph (C).

(2) **Other Rights.**

(A) **Preservation of Consumer Protections.** Nothing in this title affects the content or timing of any disclosure or other record required to be provided or made available to any consumer under any statute, regulation, or other rule of law.

(B) **Verification or Acknowledgment.** If a law that was enacted prior to this Act expressly requires a record to be provided or made available by a specified method that requires verification or acknowledgment of receipt, the record may be provided or made available electronically only if the method used provides verification or acknowledgment of receipt (whichever is required).

(3) **Effect of Failure to Obtain Electronic Consent or Confirmation of Consent.** The legal effectiveness, validity, or enforceability of any contract executed by a consumer shall not be denied solely because of the failure to obtain electronic consent or confirmation of consent by that consumer in accordance with paragraph (1)(C)(ii).

(4) **Prospective Effect.** Withdrawal of consent by a consumer shall not affect the legal effectiveness, validity, or enforceability of electronic records provided or made available to that consumer in accordance with paragraph (1) prior to implementation of the consumer's withdrawal of consent. A consumer's withdrawal of consent shall be effective within a reasonable period of time after receipt of the withdrawal by the provider of the record. Failure to comply with paragraph (1)(D) may, at the election of the consumer, be treated as a withdrawal of consent for purposes of this paragraph.

(5) **Prior Consent.** This subsection does not apply to any records that are provided or made available to a consumer who has consented prior to the effective date of this title to receive such records in electronic form as permitted by any statute, regulation, or other rule of law.

(6) **Oral Communications.** An oral communication or a recording of an oral communication shall not qualify as an electronic record for purposes of this subsection except as otherwise provided under applicable law. . . .

(e) **Accuracy and Ability to Retain Contracts and Other Records.** Notwithstanding subsection (a), if a statute, regulation, or other rule of law requires that a contract or other record relating to a transaction in or affecting interstate or foreign commerce be in writing, the legal effect, validity, or enforceability of an electronic record of such contract or other record may be denied if such electronic record is not in a form that is capable of being retained and accurately reproduced for later reference by all parties or persons who are entitled to retain the contract or other record. . . .

(h) **Electronic Agents.** A contract or other record relating to a transaction in or affecting interstate or foreign commerce may not be denied legal effect, validity, or enforceability solely because its formation, creation, or delivery involved the action of one or more electronic agents so long as the action of any such electronic agent is legally attributable to the person to be bound.

§ 7002. Exemption to Preemption.

(a) **In General.** A State statute, regulation, or other rule of law may modify, limit, or supersede the provisions of section 101 with respect to State law only if such statute, regulation, or rule of law—

(1) constitutes an enactment or adoption of the Uniform Electronic Transactions Act as approved and recommended for enactment in all the States by the National Conference of Commissioners on Uniform State Laws in 1999, except that any exception to the scope of such Act enacted by a State under section 3(b)(4) of such Act shall be preempted to the extent such exception is inconsistent with this title or title II, or would not be permitted under paragraph (2)(A)(ii) of this subsection; or

(2)(A) specifies the alternative procedures or requirements for the use or acceptance (or both) of electronic records or electronic signatures to establish the legal effect, validity, or enforceability of contracts or other records, if—

(i) such alternative procedures or requirements are consistent with this title and title II; and

(ii) such alternative procedures or requirements do not require, or accord greater legal status or effect to, the implementation or application of a specific technology or technical specification for performing the functions of creating, storing, generating, receiving, communicating, or authenticating electronic records or electronic signatures; and

(B) if enacted or adopted after the date of the enactment of this Act, makes specific reference to this Act. . . .

(c) **Prevention of Circumvention.** Subsection (a) does not permit a State to circumvent this title or title II through the imposition of nonelectronic delivery methods under section 8(b)(2) of the Uniform Electronic Transactions Act.

§ 7003. Specific Exceptions.

(a) **Excepted Requirements.** The provisions of section 101 shall not apply to a contract or other record to the extent it is governed by—

(1) a statute, regulation, or other rule of law governing the creation and execution of wills, codicils, or testamentary trusts;

(2) a State statute, regulation, or other rule of law governing adoption, divorce, or other matters of family law; or

(3) the Uniform Commercial Code, as in effect in any State, other than sections 1–107 and 1–206 and Articles 2 and 2A. . . .

§ 7006. Definitions.

For purposes of this title:

(1) **Consumer.** The term "consumer" means an individual who obtains, through a transaction, products or services which are used primarily for personal, family, or household purposes, and also means the legal representative of such an individual.

(2) **Electronic.** The term "electronic" means relating to technology having electrical, digital, magnetic, wireless, optical, electromagnetic, or similar capabilities.

(3) **Electronic Agent.** The term "electronic agent" means a computer program or an electronic or other automated means used independently to initiate an action or respond to electronic records or performances in whole or in part without review or action by an individual at the time of the action or response.

(4) **Electronic Record.** The term "electronic record" means a contract or other record created, generated, sent, communicated, received, or stored by electronic means.

(5) **Electronic Signature.** The term "electronic signature" means an electronic sound, symbol, or process, attached to or logically associated with a contract or other record and executed or adopted by a person with the intent to sign the record.

(6) **Federal Regulatory Agency.** The term "Federal regulatory agency" means an agency, as that term is defined in section 552(f) of title 5, United States Code.

(7) **Information.** The term "information" means data, text, images, sounds, codes, computer programs, software, databases, or the like.

(8) **Person.** The term "person" means an individual, corporation, business trust, estate, trust, partnership, limited liability company, association, joint venture, governmental agency, public corporation, or any other legal or commercial entity.

(9) **Record.** The term "record" means information that is inscribed on a tangible medium or that is stored in an electronic or other medium and is retrievable in perceivable form.

(10) **Requirement.** The term "requirement" includes a prohibition.

(11) **Self-Regulatory Organization.**—The term "self-regulatory organization" means an organization or entity that is not a Federal regulatory agency or a State, but that is under the supervision of a Federal regulatory agency and is authorized under Federal law to adopt and administer rules applicable to its members that are enforced by such organization or entity, by a Federal regulatory agency, or by another self-regulatory organization.

(12) **State.** The term "State" includes the District of Columbia and the territories and possessions of the United States.

(13) **Transaction.** The term "transaction" means an action or set of actions relating to the conduct of business, consumer, or commercial affairs between two or more persons, including any of the following types of conduct—

(A) the sale, lease, exchange, licensing, or other disposition of (i) personal property, including goods and intangibles, (ii) services, and (iii) any combination thereof; and

(B) the sale, lease, exchange, or other disposition of any interest in real property, or any combination thereof. . . .

AMERICAN LAW INSTITUTE PRINCIPLES OF THE LAW OF SOFTWARE CONTRACTS

As Adopted and Promulgated
by
THE AMERICAN LAW INSTITUTE AT WASHINGTON D.C.
May 19, 2009

[Unlike the American Law Institute's ("ALI's") restatements of the law, its more recently developed "Principles" series does not purport to state the rules and standards of existing law. Instead, the Principles aim to make the law better by advising courts, legislatures, and governmental agencies about what the law should be. Accordingly, like the Restatements, the Principles are not binding until some law-making institution adopts one or more of them. However, the ALI is a highly respected organization. Its works go through an extremely thorough process of development, in which eminent professors of law, judges, and practicing lawyers participate. Its restatements of the law have been influential. Consequently, the ALI hopes that its Principles series will also guide the development of the law, especially where the law needs modernization.

[The Principles of the Law of Software Contracts ("PLSC") addresses the law that should apply to contracting in one specific, rapidly changing technological environment. These Principles apply broadly to agreements for the transfer of software for a consideration, including sales, leases, licenses, and sharing arrangements. PLSC § 1.06. Some provisions concern issues that some courts have addressed, such as contracting over the Internet when a transferee signifies agreement by clicking on a button placed ahead of a standard form contract's terms. *Id.* at § 2.02(c)(3). Other provisions concern issues not yet adjudicated or otherwise decided.

[The future influence of the PLSC must be considered cloudy. Other major efforts to introduce new law governing software and similar new-technology contracts have been so controversial that the efforts failed. Two examples are the National Conference of Commissioners on Uniform State Law's Uniform Computer Information Act (2002) (enacted by only two states) and the amendments to Article 2 of the Uniform Commercial Code (2003) (not enacted by any state). The latter failed mainly because the text left it unclear whether the amended Article 2 would apply to software and similar contracts when the software was not in a tangible form, such as a computer disc.]

TABLE OF CONTENTS

CHAPTER 1. DEFINITIONS, SCOPE, AND GENERAL TERMS

TOPIC 1. DEFINITIONS

§ 1.01.   Definitions.
    (a)   Access Agreement.
    (b)   Agreement.
    (c)   Computer.
    (d)   Consumer Agreement.
    (e)   Contract.
    (f)   Digital Content.
    (g)   Digital-Content Player.
    (h)   Electronic.
    (i)   Record.
    (j)   Software.

(k) Standard Form and Standard Term.
(*l*) Standard-Form Transfer of Generally Available Software.
(m) Transfer.
(n) Transferor and Transferee.

TOPIC 2. SCOPE

§ 1.06. Scope; Generally.
§ 1.07. Scope; Embedded Software.
§ 1.08. Scope; Mixed Transfers Including Non-Embedded Software.
§ 1.09. Enforcement of Terms under Federal Intellectual Property Law.
§ 1.10. Public Policy.
§ 1.11. Unconscionability.
§ 1.12. Relation to Outside Law.

TOPIC 3. GENERAL TERMS

§ 1.13. Choice of Law in Standard-Form Transfers of Generally Available Software.
§ 1.14. Forum-Selection Clauses.

CHAPTER 2. FORMATION AND ENFORCEMENT

TOPIC 1. FORMATION, GENERALLY

§ 2.01. Formation, Generally.

TOPIC 2. STANDARD-FORM TRANSFERS OF GENERALLY AVAILABLE SOFTWARE: ENFORCEMENT OF THE STANDARD FORM

§ 2.02. Standard-Form Transfers of Generally Available Software: Enforcement of the Standard Form.

TOPIC 3. CONTRACT MODIFICATION

§ 2.03 Contract Modification.

CHAPTER 3. PERFORMANCE

TOPIC 1. INDEMNIFICATION AND WARRANTIES

§ 3.01. Implied Indemnification Against Infringement.
§ 3.02. Express Quality Warranties.
§ 3.03. Implied Warranty of Merchantability.
§ 3.04. Implied Warranty of Fitness for a Particular Purpose.
§ 3.05. Other Implied Quality Warranties.
§ 3.06. Disclaimer of Express and Implied Quality Warranties.
§ 3.07. Third-Party Beneficiaries of Warranty.

TOPIC 2. PAROL-EVIDENCE RULE AND INTERPRETATION

§ 3.08. Integration, Ambiguity, and Parol Evidence.
§ 3.09. General Principles of Interpretation.
§ 3.10. Whose Meaning Prevails.

TOPIC 3. BREACH

§ 3.11. Breach and Material Breach.
§ 3.12. Cure of Breach.

CHAPTER 4. REMEDIES

TOPIC 1. AGREEMENTS WITH RESPECT TO REMEDY

§ 4.01. Contractual Modification or Limitation of Remedy.
§ 4.02. Liquidation and Limitation of Damages.
§ 4.03. Use of Automated Disablement to Impair Use.

TOPIC 2. REMEDIES IN THE ABSENCE OF AGREEMENT

§ 4.04. Cancellation.
§ 4.05. Expectation Damages.
§ 4.06. Specific Performance.

CHAPTER 1

DEFINITIONS, SCOPE, AND GENERAL TERMS

TOPIC 1. DEFINITIONS

§ 1.01. Definitions.

As used in these Principles

(a) Access Agreement

An "access agreement" is an agreement that authorizes the user of software to access the provider's software via a data-transmission system, such as the Internet, or via a private network or another intermediary now known or hereafter developed.

(b) Agreement

An "agreement" is the bargain of the parties in fact as found in their language or other circumstances, including course of performance, course of dealing, or usage of trade.

(c) Computer

A "computer" is an electronic device that processes information and follows instructions to accomplish a result.

(d) Consumer Agreement

A "consumer agreement" is an agreement for the transfer of software or access to software primarily for personal, family, or household purposes.

(e) Contract

A "contract" is the total legal obligation that results from the parties' agreement, these Principles, and any other applicable law.

(f) Digital Content

"Digital content" consists of "digital art" or a "digital database."

   (1) "Digital art" is literary and artistic information stored electronically, such as music, photographs, motion pictures, books, newspapers, and other images and sounds.

   (2) A "digital database" is a compilation of facts arranged in a systematic manner and stored electronically. A digital database does not include digital art.

(g) Digital-Content Player

A "digital-content player" consists of software that renders digital content visible, audible, or otherwise perceivable.

(h) Electronic

"Electronic" means technology having electrical, digital, magnetic, wireless, optical, electromagnetic, or similar capabilities.

(i) Record

A "record" is information that is inscribed on a tangible medium or that is stored in an electronic or other medium and is retrievable in perceivable form.

(j) Software

(1) "Software" consists of statements or instructions that are executed by a computer to produce a certain result.

(2) Software does not include digital content, but does include a digital-content player.

(k) Standard Form and Standard Term

(1) A "standard form" is a record regularly used to embody terms of agreements of the same type.

(2) A "standard term" is a term appearing in a standard form and relating to a particular matter.

(*l*) Standard-Form Transfer of Generally Available Software

A "standard-form transfer of generally available software" is a transfer using a standard form of

(1) a small number of copies of software to an end user; or

(2) the right to access software to a small number of end users if the software is generally available to the public under substantially the same standard terms.

(m) Transfer

A "transfer" is a conveyance of rights in software or an authorization to access software, including by way of sale, license, lease, or access agreement.

(n) Transferor and Transferee

(1) Except where otherwise provided, a "transferor" is a party who, pursuant to an agreement with the transferee, has transferred or has agreed to transfer software.

(2) Except where otherwise provided, a "transferee" is party who, pursuant to an agreement with the transferor, has received or has agreed to receive rights in or access to software.

TOPIC 2. SCOPE

§ 1.06. Scope; Generally.

(a) These Principles apply to agreements for the transfer of software for a consideration. Software agreements include agreements to sell, lease, license, access, or otherwise transfer or share software.

(b) These Principles do not apply to

(1) the transfer of any disk, CD-ROM, or other tangible medium that stores the software, or

(2) the transfer of a security interest in software.

§ 1.07. Scope; Embedded Software.

(a) Subject to § 1.06, these Principles apply to agreements for the transfer of software embedded in goods if a reasonable transferor would believe the transferee's predominant purpose for engaging in the transfer is to obtain the software.

(b) These Principles apply to agreements for the transfer of embedded software only if these Principles applied to the transfer of the embedded software being upgraded or replaced.

§ 1.08. Scope; Mixed Transfers Including Non-Embedded Software.

(a) For purposes of this section,

(1) "goods" include any embedded software, and

(2) A "mixed transfer" constitutes a single transaction that consists of the transfer of non-embedded software and any combination of goods, digital content, and services.

(b) Subject to § 1.06, in the case of an agreement for a mixed transfer, these Principles apply to the transfer of the non-embedded software unless the transfer also includes digital content or services and a reasonable transferor would believe the transferee's predominant purpose for engaging in the transfer is to obtain the digital content or services.

§ 1.09. Enforcement of Terms under Federal Intellectual Property Law.

A term of an agreement is unenforceable if it (a) conflicts with a mandatory rule of federal intellectual property law; or (b) conflicts impermissibly with the purposes and policies of federal intellectual property law; or (c) would constitute federal intellectual property misuse in an infringement proceeding.

§ 1.10. Public Policy.

A term of an agreement is unenforceable if the interest in enforcement of the term is clearly outweighed in the circumstances by a public policy against its enforcement.

§ 1.11. Unconscionability.

(a) If the court as a matter of law finds the agreement of any term of the agreement to have been unconscionable at the time it was made, the court may refuse to enforce the agreement, or it may enforce the remainder of the agreement without the unconscionable term, or it may so limit the application of any unconscionable term to avoid any unconscionable result.

(b) When it is claimed or appears to the court that the agreement or any term thereof may be unconscionable, the parties shall be afforded a reasonable opportunity to present evidence as to its commercial setting, purpose, and effect to aid the court in making the determination.

§ 1.12. Relation to Outside Law.

These Principles should be considered in the context of other applicable law.

TOPIC 3. GENERAL TERMS

§ 1.13. Choice of Law in Standard-Form Transfers of Generally Available Software.

(a) The parties to a standard-form transfer of generally available software may by agreement select the law of a domestic or foreign jurisdiction to govern their rights and duties with respect to an issue in contract if their transaction bears a reasonable relationship to the selected jurisdiction. However, if application of the selected law to an issue would lead to a result that is repugnant to public policy as expressed in the law of the jurisdiction that would otherwise govern under subsection (b), then the law of the jurisdiction chosen by subsection (b) governs with respect to that issue.

(b) In the absence of an enforceable agreement on choice of law, the rights and duties of the parties to a standard-form transfer of generally available software with respect to an issue in contract are determined

(1) in the case of a consumer agreement, by the law of the jurisdiction where the consumer is located; and

(2) in all other cases, by the law of the jurisdiction where the transferor is located.

(c) For purposes of subsection (b):

(1) an individual is located at the individual's principal residence.

(2) an organization that has only one place of business is located at its place of business.

(3) an organization that has more than one place of business is located at its chief executive office.

(4) an organization that does not have a physical place of business is located at its place of incorporation or primary registration.

§ 1.14. Forum-Selection Clauses.

The parties may by agreement choose an exclusive forum unless the choice is unfair or unreasonable. A forum choice may be unfair or unreasonable if:

(a) the forum is unreasonably inconvenient for a party;

(b) the agreement as to the forum was obtained by misrepresentation, duress, the abuse of economic power, or other unconscionable means;

(c) the forum does not have power under its domestic law to entertain the action or to award remedies otherwise available; or

(d) enforcement of the forum-selection clause would be repugnant to public policy as expressed in the law of the forum in which suit is brought.

CHAPTER 2

FORMATION AND ENFORCEMENT

TOPIC 1. FORMATION GENERALLY

§ 2.01. Formation, Generally.

(a) Subject to § 2.02, a contract may be formed in any manner sufficient to show an agreement, including by offer and acceptance and by conduct.

(b) A contract may be formed under subsection (a) even though

(1) one or more terms are left open, if there is a reasonably certain basis for granting an appropriate remedy in the event of a breach; or

(2) the parties' records are different. In such a case, the terms of the contract are

(A) terms, whether in a record or not, to which both parties agree;

(B) terms that appear in the records of both parties; and

(C) terms supplied by these Principles or other law.

TOPIC 2. STANDARD-FORM TRANSFERS OF GENERALLY AVAILABLE SOFTWARE; ENFORCEMENT OF THE STANDARD FORM

§ 2.02. Standard-Form Transfers of Generally Available Software: Enforcement of the Standard Form.

(a) This Section applies to standard-form transfers of generally available software as defined in § 1.01(1).

(b) A transferee adopts a standard form as a contract when a reasonable transferor would believe the transferee intends to be bound to the form.

(c) A transferee will be deemed to have adopted a standard form as a contract if

(1) the standard form is reasonably accessible electronically prior to initiation of the transfer at issue;

(2) upon initiating the transfer, the transferee has reasonable notice of and access to the standard form before payment or, if there is no payment, before completion of the transfer;

(3) in the case of an electronic transfer of software, the transferee signifies agreement at the end of or adjacent to the electronic standard form, or in the case of a standard form printed on or attached to packaged software or separately wrapped from the software, the transferee does not exercise the opportunity to return the software unopened for a full refund within a reasonable time after the transfer; and

(4) the transferee can store and reproduce the standard form if presented electronically.

(d) Subject to § 1.10 (public policy), § 1.11 (unconscionability), and other invalidating defenses supplied by these Principles or outside law, a standard term is enforceable if reasonably comprehensible.

(e) If a transferee asserts that it did not adopt a standard form as a contract under subsection (b) or asserts a failure of the transferor to comply with subsection (c) or (d), the transferor has the burden of production and persuasion on the issue of compliance with the subsections.

TOPIC 3. CONTRACT MODIFICATION

§ 2.03. Contract Modification.

(a) Subject to subsection (c), an agreement modifying a contract is enforceable without consideration and may be formed in any manner sufficient to show an agreement, including by offer and acceptance and by conduct.

(b) In the case of an electronic transfer of software, a transferee will be deemed to have agreed to a modification of the transferee receives reasonable electronic notice of the modification and the transferee signifies agreement to the modification electronically at the end of or adjacent to the electronic notice.

(c) An agreement modifying a contract is not enforceable if

(1) A party agrees to the modification as a result of fraud, duress, or another invalidating cause, or

(2) The contract being modified is in a record that includes a no-oral-modification or other clause excluding modification except by an authenticated record, and the modifications oral or unauthenticated by the party contesting the modification, unless the other party has reasonably relied on a waiver of the no-oral-modification or other clause.

(d) Subject to subsection (a) through (c), the parties may agree in their contract to procedures for unmodifying it. However, in the case of a standard-form transfer of generally available software, mere notice of a material modification sent by one party is insufficient to prove agreement by the other party, even if the original contract authorizes this manner of modifying the contract.]

CHAPTER 3

PERFORMANCE

TOPIC 1. INDEMNIFICATION AND WARRANTIES

§ 3.01. Implied Indemnification Against Infringement.

(a) Except as provided in (d) or as excluded or modified under (e), a transferor that deals in software of the kind transferred or holds itself out by occupation as having knowledge or skill peculiar to the software, and that receives money or a right to payment of a monetary obligation in exchange for the software, must indemnify and hold the transferee harmless against any claim of a third party based on infringement of an intellectual property or like right which right exists at the time of transfer and is based on the laws of the United States or a State thereof. The transferor must pay those costs and damages incurred by the transferee that are specifically attributable to such claim or those costs and damages agreed to in a monetary settlement of such claim.

(b) If a court enjoins the transferee's use of the software or holds the software infringing or otherwise in violation of a like right under subsection (a), the transferor may be liable for damages under § 4.05 and must at its own expense and on reasonable notice from the transferee of its desire for a remedy provide the transferee with one of the following remedies as the transferor chooses:

   (1) procure for the transferee at no cost to the transferee the continued right to use the software under the terms of the applicable agreement;

   (2) replace or modify the software with non-infringing software of substantially equivalent functionality; or

   (3) cancel the applicable agreement and refund to the transferee the fees actually paid by the transferee for the infringing components of the software. If the infringement renders the software substantially unusable, the transferor must refund the entire fee. In either case, the transferor must also reimburse the transferee for incidental expenses incurred in replacing the software, but the transferor may deduct from the amounts due to the transferee under this section a reasonable allowance for the period of time the transferee used the software.

(c) The indemnification law of the state whose law applies to the agreement under § 1.13 or under otherwise applicable law applies to the duty of indemnification of subsection (a).

(d) Unless otherwise agreed, a transferor has no obligations under subsections (a) and (b) if

   (1) the transferee uses or modifies the software in a manner not in accordance with the terms of the agreement where such use or modification gives rise to the claim; or

   (2) the infringement arises from the transferor's compliance with (i) transferee-provided functional specifications; and (ii) a transferee-provided method or process for implementation of those specifications, unless the transferor knows of potential infringement or a claim of infringement at the time of transfer and does not notify the transferee that compliance with the specifications and method or process may result in an infringement.

(e) Indemnification under subsection (a) and the duties of subsection (b) may be excluded or modified

   (1) if the exclusion or modification is in a record, is conspicuous, and uses language that gives the transferee reasonable notice of the modification or notice that the transferor has no obligation to indemnify the transferee; or

   (2) by course of performance, course of dealing, or usage of trade.

§ 3.02. Express Quality Warranties.

(a) In this Section "transferee" includes both an "immediate transferee" that enters an agreement with the transferor and a "remote transferee" that receives the software or access to the software in the normal chain of distribution.

(b) Except as provided in subsection (d), the transferor creates an express warranty to the transferee as follows:

(1) An affirmation of fact or promise made by the transferor to the transferee, including by advertising or by a record packaged with or accompanying the software, that relates to the software and on which a reasonable transferee could rely creates an express warranty that the software will conform to the affirmation of fact or promise.

(2) Any description of the software made by the transferor to the transferee on which a reasonable transferee could rely creates an express warranty that the software will conform to the description.

(3) Any demonstration of software shown by the transferor to the transferee on which a reasonable transferee could rely creates an express warranty that the software will conform to the demonstration.

(c) A transferor can create an express warranty without using formal words, such as "warrant" or "guarantee," or without intending to create an express warranty. However, a mere opinion or commendation of the software does not create an express warranty.

(d) A distributor or dealer that merely transfers software covered by a warranty in a record made by another party, which warranty identifies the maker of the record as the warrantor, is not liable for breach of the warranty. The distributor or dealer is liable for any express warranties of its own or if it adopts the maker's warranty.

§ 3.03. Implied Warranty of Merchantability.

(a) Unless excluded or modified, a transferor that deals in software of the kind transferred or that holds itself out by occupation as having knowledge or skill peculiar to the software warrants to the transferee that the software is merchantable.

(b) Merchantable software at minimum must

(1) pass without objection in the trade under the contract description; and

(2) be fit for the ordinary purposes for which such software is used; and

(3) be adequately packaged and labeled.

§ 3.04. Implied Warranty of Fitness for a Particular Purpose.

(a) Unless excluded or modified, if a transferor at the time of contracting has reason to know any particular purpose for which the transferee requires the software and the transferee relies on the transferor's skill or judgment to select, develop, or furnish the software, the transferor warrants that the software is fit for the transferee's purpose.

(b) Unless excluded or modified, if an agreement requires a transferor to provide or select a system of hardware and software and the transferor at the time of contracting has reason to know that the transferee is relying on the skill or judgment of the transferor to select the components of the system, the transferor warrants that the software provided or selected will function together with the hardware as a system.

§ 3.05. Other Implied Quality Warranties.

(a) Unless modified or excluded, implied warranties may arise from course of dealing or usage of trade.

(b) A transferor that receives money or a right to payment of a monetary obligation in exchange for the software warrants to any party in the normal chain of distribution that the software contains no material hidden defects of which the transferor was aware at the time of the transfer. This warranty may not be excluded. In addition, this warranty does not displace an action for misrepresentation or its remedies.

§ 3.06. Disclaimer of Express and Implied Quality Warranties.

A statement intending to exclude or modify an express quality warranty is unenforceable if a reasonable transferee would not expect the exclusion or modification.

(a) Unless the circumstances suggest otherwise, all implied quality warranties other than the warranty of no material hidden defects (§ 3.05(b)) are excluded by language in a record communicated to the transferee such as "as is," "with all faults," or other language that a reasonable transferee would believe excludes all implied quality warranties.

(b) The implied warranty of merchantability is excluded if the exclusion is in a record communicated to the transferee, is conspicuous, and mentions "merchantability."

(c) The implied warranty of fitness for a particular purpose is excluded if the exclusion is in a record communicated to the transferee, is conspicuous, and mentions "fitness for a particular purpose."

(d) If before entering an agreement a transferee has tested the software as fully as desired or unreasonably has refused to test it, there are no implied quality warranties with regard to defects that a test should have or would have revealed.

(e) An implied quality warranty other than the warranty of no material hidden defects (§ 3.05(b)) may be excluded or modified by course performance, course dealing, or usage of trade.

(f) Remedies for breach of quality warranties may be limited in accordance with § 4.01 of these Principles.

§ 3.07. Third-Party Beneficiaries of Warranty.

(a) A transferor's warranty extends to any person for whose benefit the transferor intends to supply the software if the person uses the software in a manner contemplated or that should have been contemplated by the transferor.

(b) A transferor's warranty to a consumer extends to the consumer's immediate family, household members, or guests if the transferor reasonably should expect such persons to use the software.

(c) Except as provided in (b), a contractual term that excludes or limits the third parties to which a warranty extends is enforceable.

(d) An exclusion or modification of a warranty that is effective against the transferee is also effective against third parties to which the warranty extends under this Section.

TOPIC 2. PAROL-EVIDENCE RULE AND INTERPRETATION

§ 3.08. Integration, Ambiguity, and Parol Evidence.

(a) A full integration constitutes a record or records intended by the parties as a complete and exclusive statement of the terms of an agreement. A partial integration constitutes a record or records intended by the parties as the complete and exclusive statement of one or more terms of an agreement.

(b) The court should determine whether a record is fully integrated, partially integrated, or not integrated prior to applying subsections (e) and (f). In making this determination, the court should consider all credible and relevant extrinsic evidence, including evidence of agreements and negotiations prior to or contemporaneous with the adoption of the record.

(c) If the transfer is a standard-form transfer of generally available software, a term in a record indicating that the record is fully integrated or partially integrated should be probative but not conclusive on the issue.

(d) The court should determine whether a term in a record is ambiguous prior to applying subsections (e) and (f). In making this determination, the court should consider all credible and relevant extrinsic evidence, including evidence of agreements and negotiations prior to or contemporaneous with the adoption of the record. If a term or terms is ambiguous, extrinsic evidence is admissible to prove the meaning of the term or terms.

(e) Unambiguous terms set forth in a fully integrated record may not be contradicted by evidence of any prior agreement or of a contemporaneous oral agreement, but may be explained by evidence of a course of performance, course of dealing, or usage of trade.

(f) Unambiguous terms set forth in a partially integrated record may not be contradicted by evidence of prior or contemporaneous oral conflicting terms, but may be explained by evidence of course of performance, course of dealing, usage of trade, or consistent additional terms.

(g) Notwithstanding subsections (e) and (f),

(1) evidence is admissible to prove

(A) illegality, fraud, duress, mistake, or other invalidating causes; and

(B) independent agreements; and

(2) evidence of course of performance, course of dealing, and usage of trade is admissible to supplement a record.

§ 3.09. General Principles of Interpretation.

(a) Words or conduct should be interpreted in accordance with the meaning intended by both parties. Subject to § 3.10, if the parties disagree over that meaning, words or conduct should be interpreted reasonably in light of all of the circumstances.

(b) In determining a reasonable interpretation of the words or conduct, significant factors include:

(1) each party's purpose or purposes in making the contract;

(2) any course of performance, course of dealing, or usage of trade; and

(3) the language of the entire agreement.

§ 3.10. Whose Meaning Prevails.

(a) If the parties disagree over the meaning of words or conduct, the meaning intended by one of them should be enforced if at the time the parties made the agreement that party did not know or have reason to know any different meaning intended by the other party, and the other party knew or had reason to know the meaning intended by the first party.

(b) The parties have not made an enforceable agreement if

(1) the parties disagree over the meaning of a fundamental term or terms;

(2) the term or terms is ambiguous; and

(3) neither party knew or should have known of the other's meaning.

(c) In all other cases of disagreement as to the meaning of a term or terms, § 3.09 applies.

TOPIC 3. BREACH

§ 3.11. Breach and Material Breach.

(a) A breach occurs if a party without legal excuse fails to perform an obligation as required by the agreement.

(b) An uncured breach, whether or not material, entitles the aggrieved party to remedies.

(c) In determining whether a breach is material, significant factors include:

(1) the terms of the agreement;

(2) usage of trade, course of dealing, and course of performance;

(3) the extent to which the aggrieved party will be deprived of the benefit reasonably expected;

(4) the extent to which the aggrieved party can be adequately compensated for the part of the benefit deprived;

(5) the degree of harm or likely harm to the aggrieved party; and

(6) the extent to which the behavior of the party failing to perform or to offer to perform departs from standards of good faith and fair dealing.

(d) Notwithstanding subsection (c) or any provision to the contrary in the agreement, a material breach occurs if:

(1) the transferor breaches the warranty of § 3.05(b);

(2) a limited remedy fails of its essential purpose under § 4.01; or

(3) the transferor breaches the agreement by failing to comply with § 4.03.

(e) The cumulative effect of nonmaterial breaches may be material.

§ 3.12. Cure of Breach.

(a) Unless otherwise agreed, a party in breach of contract may, on seasonable notice to the aggrieved party and at its own expense, cure the breach by making a conforming performance if:

(1) the time for performance has not yet expired and the conforming performance occurs within the time for performance; or

(2) the breaching party had reasonable grounds to believe the nonconforming performance would be acceptable with or without money allowance and provides a conforming performance within a further reasonable time after performance was due; or

(3) the breaching party seasonably notifies the aggrieved party of its intent to cure and promptly provides a conforming performance before the aggrieved party cancels under § 4.04.

(b) If a breaching party fails to cure a material breach, the aggrieved party's obligation to perform any remaining duties is suspended except with respect to restrictions on the use of the software. The aggrieved party also may cancel under § 4.04.

(c) A party may not cancel or refuse to perform because of a breach that has been seasonably cured under subsection (a).

(d) The cumulative effect of repeated attempts to cure may be a material breach.

CHAPTER 4

REMEDIES

TOPIC 1. AGREEMENTS WITH RESPECT TO REMEDY

§ 4.01. Contractual Modification or Limitation of Remedy.

(a) Subject to the provisions of subsections (b) and (c) of this Section, § 4.02 (liquidation and limitation of damages), § 4.03(e) (unauthorized automated disablement), and except for damages for breach of the warranty of § 3.05(b) (no material hidden defects),

(1) the agreement may provide for remedies in addition to or in substitution for those provided in these Principles and may limit or alter the measure of damages recoverable under these Principles, as by limiting the transferee's remedy to return of the software and repayment of the price or to repair and replacement of nonconforming software; and

(2) resort to a remedy as provided is optional unless the remedy is expressly agreed to be exclusive, in which case it is the sole remedy.

(b) If circumstances cause an exclusive or limited remedy to fail of its essential purpose, the aggrieved party may recover a remedy as provided in these Principles or applicable outside law.

(c) Subject to the provisions of § 4.03(e) (unauthorized automated disablement), and except for damages for breach of the warranty of § 3.05(b) (no material hidden defects), consequential damages may be limited or excluded unless the limitation or exclusion is unconscionable at the time of contracting or operates in an unconscionable way. This rule applies even if circumstances cause an exclusive or limited remedy to fail of its essential purpose under subsection (b). Limitation of consequential damages for personal injury in the case of consumer software is prima facie unconscionable but limitation of consequential damages where the loss is commercial is not.

§ 4.02. Liquidation and Limitation of Damages.

(a) Damages for breach by either party may be liquidated in the agreement but only at an amount that is reasonable in light of the anticipated or actual harm caused by the breach, the difficulties of proof of loss, and the inconvenience or nonfeasibility of otherwise obtaining an adequate remedy. Section 4.01 determines the enforceability of a term that limits but does not liquidate damages.

(b) If a term liquidating damages is unenforceable under this Section, the aggrieved party may recover a remedy as provided in these Principles, except as limited by other terms of the agreement.

§ 4.03. Use of Automated Disablement to Impair Use.

(a) "Automated disablement" means the use of electronic means to disable or materially impair the functionality of software.

(b) A transferor may not use automated disablement if the process results in the loss of rights granted in the agreement or the loss of use of other software or digital content.

(c) Notwithstanding anything to the contrary in the agreement, a transferor may not use automated disablement as a remedy for breach if the agreement is a standard-form transfer of generally available software or if the transaction is a consumer agreement.

(d) Subject to subsection (c), if the transferor has a right to cancel under § 4.04, it may do so using automated disablement only if such authorization is provided for in the agreement and under the following circumstances:

(1) the term authorizing automated disablement is conspicuous; and

(2) the transferor provides timely notice of the breach and its intent to use automated disablement and provides the transferee with a reasonable opportunity to cure the breach and the transferee has not so cured; and

(3) the transferor has obtained a court order permitting it to use automated disablement.

(e) A transferee may recover direct, incidental, and consequential damages caused by use of automated disablement in violation of this Section notwithstanding any agreement to the contrary.

(f) Obligations of the transferor and rights of the transferee under this Section may not be waived.

TOPIC 2. REMEDIES IN THE ABSENCE OF AGREEMENT

§ 4.04. Cancellation.

(a) An aggrieved party may cancel a contract on a material breach of the whole contract if the breach has not been cured under § 3.12 or waived.

(b) Cancellation is not effective unless the canceling party gives reasonable notice of cancellation to the party in breach.

(c) Except as otherwise provided in the agreement, upon effective cancellation by the transferor:

(1) of an access contract, any rights of access are discontinued; and

(2) all rights of the transferee in the software provided under the agreement terminate and the transferee must destroy any physical copies of the software or seasonably return them to the transferor, delete all electronic copies on its systems, and refuse delivery of any physical copies.

(d) Except as otherwise provided in the agreement, upon cancellation by either party, all executory obligations of both parties are discharged except those based on a previous breach or performance or those that the parties agreed would survive termination or cancellation.

(e) A cancellation is ineffective if it fails to meet the standard of subsection (a) or the requirements of subsection (b).

§ 4.05. Expectation Damages.

Unless otherwise agreed, damages under these Principles should put the aggrieved party in as good a position as if the other party had fully performed. Damages for lost expectancy include direct, incidental, and consequential damages, less expenses saved in consequence of the breach.

§ 4.06. Specific Performance.

(a) Specific performance may be decreed when the software to be transferred is unique, or in other proper circumstances. Specific performance is not available if it would require the performance of personal services or if an award of damages would be adequate to protect the expectation interest of the transferee.

(b) The decree for specific performance may include such terms and conditions as to payment of the price, damages, confidentiality, and rights in the software as the court may deem just.

(c) An aggrieved transferor who does not cancel may be entitled to a decree requiring adherence to the terms of the agreement as against a breaching transferee, but not if the decree would require the performance of personal services or if an award of damages would be adequate to protect the expectation interest of the transferor.

PART VI
INTERNATIONAL CONTRACT LAW

UNITED NATIONS CONVENTION ON CONTRACTS FOR THE INTERNATIONAL SALE OF GOODS

(1980)

[In 1969, the United Nations Commission on International Trade Law (UNCITRAL) appointed a working group to prepare a draft of an international convention (treaty) on the sale of goods. The United States was an active participant in the working group. The ultimate result was the Convention for the International Sale of Goods (the CISG), which was adopted in 1980, and came into force in 1988 when it had been ratified by the requisite ten countries.]

The CISG aims to do for international sales of goods essentially what Article 2 of the Uniform Commercial Code did for sales within the U.S. Prior to adoption of the CISG, the parties could agree on which nation's law would apply to their contract by including a choice-of-law provision in the contract. Many contracts, however, did not contain such provisions, and the courts of some nations were (and continue to be) more likely than others to give choice-of-law provisions full effect. In either case, the law that determined the applicable law was (and, for other kinds of international contracts, is) vague and undependable. Moreover, different nations' laws can differ dramatically, especially when different legal traditions shaped them. The result of these complications was considerable uncertainty in the law, which discouraged contracting by making it more costly.

[The CISG's principal purpose is to establish a uniform law and to reduce legal uncertainties for international sales of goods. Because it is an international treaty, it is binding only on Contracting States—those that have ratified, accepted, approved, or acceded to the treaty. CISG, Art. 99(1). As of May 15, 2018, there were more than 80 Contracting States, including the United States and most other major trading nations.

[Following the Senate's advice and consent, the U.S. ratified the CISG in 1986 (subject to certain reservations). It then became part of the "supreme law of the land," pre-empting inconsistent state contract law. U.S. Const., Art. VI(2). Until 2008, it was settled that this treaty is "self-executing;" therefore, federal and state courts applied it as domestic law even though Congress had not acted to make it domestic law. In that year, the U.S. Supreme Court narrowed the self-executing treaty doctrine in a way that unsettles this issue. Medellin v. Texas, 128 S.Ct. 1346, 1368–69 (2008).

[Although in form the CISG is an international treaty, in substance it is a code, much like Article 2 of the UCC. Article 2 governs contracts for the sale of goods between a seller and a buyer in the United States. The CISG governs contracts for the sale of goods (with certain exclusions, such as consumer contracts) between parties who have their places of business in two different countries, both of which have ratified the CISG. Accordingly, if, for example, a United States seller with its place of business in New York enters into a contract for the sale of goods to a buyer with its place of business in France (one of the countries that has ratified the CISG), then unless the parties otherwise provide, the contract is governed by the provisions of the CISG. However, under CISG Article 6 the parties to a contract that would otherwise fall within the CISG may exclude the application of the CISG to the contract or, with certain exceptions, derogate from or vary the effect of any CISG provisions.[1]

[Like the UCC, the CISG does not govern the issue whether a contract is substantively valid; that is, it does not govern matters such as fraud, capacity, duress, mistake, legality, or the like. However, the CISG does govern whether a contract satisfies requisite formal requirements, such as whether a contract is required to be in writing, and also governs matters such as whether a contract was formed and whether a contract is sufficiently definite to be enforceable.]

---

[1] The CISG is potentially applicable to international sale-of-goods contracts even though one of the parties resides in a country that has not ratified the Convention. However, when the United States ratified the CISG it filed a "reservation" under which it does not adhere to that portion of the CISG that makes the CISG applicable in such cases. Accordingly, the CISG is not applicable to a contract for the sale of goods between a firm with its place of business in the United States and a firm with its place of business in a country that has not ratified the CISG.

CONVENTION ON CONTRACTS FOR THE INTERNATIONAL SALE OF GOODS

THE STATES PARTIES TO THIS CONVENTION

BEARING IN MIND the broad objectives in the resolutions adopted by the sixth special session of the General Assembly of the United Nations on the establishment of a New International Economic Order,

CONSIDERING that the development of international trade on the basis of equality and mutual benefit is an important element in promoting friendly relations among States,

BEING OF THE OPINION that the adoption of uniform rules which govern contracts for the international sale of goods and take into account the different social, economic and legal systems would contribute to the removal of legal barriers in international trade and promote the development of international trade,

HAVE AGREED as follows:

PART I. SPHERE OF APPLICATION AND GENERAL PROVISIONS

CHAPTER I. SPHERE OF APPLICATION

Article 1

(1) This Convention applies to contracts of sale of goods between parties whose places of business are in different States:

(a) when the States are Contracting States; or

(b) when the rules of private international law lead to the application of the law of a Contracting State.

(2) The fact that the parties have their places of business in different States is to be disregarded whenever this fact does not appear either from the contract or from any dealings between, or from information disclosed by, the parties at any time before or at the conclusion of the contract.

(3) Neither the nationality of the parties nor the civil or commercial character of the parties or of the contract is to be taken into consideration in determining the application of this Convention.

[The United States has declared a reservation under Article 95, and therefore is not bound by Article 1(1)(b).]

Article 2

This Convention does not apply to sales:

(a) of goods bought for personal, family or household use, unless the seller, at any time before or at the conclusion of the contract, neither knew nor ought to have known that the goods were bought for any such use;

(b) by auction;

(c) on execution or otherwise by authority of law;

(d) of stocks, shares, investment securities, negotiable instruments or money;

(e) of ships, vessels, hovercraft or aircraft;

(f) of electricity.

Article 3

(1) Contracts for the supply of goods to be manufactured or produced are to be considered sales unless the party who orders the goods undertakes to supply a substantial part of the materials necessary for such manufacture or production.

(2) This Convention does not apply to contracts in which the preponderant part of the obligations of the party who furnishes the goods consists in the supply of labour or other services.

Article 4

This Convention governs only the formation of the contract of sale and the rights and obligations of the seller and the buyer arising from such a contract. In particular, except as otherwise expressly provided in this Convention, it is not concerned with:

(a) the validity of the contract or of any of its provisions or of any usage;

(b) the effect which the contract may have on the property in the goods sold.

Article 5

This Convention does not apply to the liability of the seller for death or personal injury caused by the goods to any person.

Article 6

The parties may exclude the application of this Convention or, subject to Article 12, derogate from or vary the effect of any of its provisions.

CHAPTER II. GENERAL PROVISIONS

Article 7

(1) In the interpretation of this Convention, regard is to be had to its international character and to the need to promote uniformity in its application and the observance of good faith in international trade.

(2) Questions concerning matters governed by this Convention which are not expressly settled in it are to be settled in conformity with the general principles on which it is based or, in the absence of such principles, in conformity with the law applicable by virtue of the rules of private international law.

Article 8

(1) For the purposes of this Convention statements made by and other conduct of a party are to be interpreted according to his intent where the other party knew or could not have been unaware what that intent was.

(2) If the preceding paragraph is not applicable, statements made by and other conduct of a party are to be interpreted according to the understanding that a reasonable person of the same kind as the other party would have had in the same circumstances.

(3) In determining the intent of a party or the understanding a reasonable person would have had, due consideration is to be given to all relevant circumstances of the case including the negotiations, any practices which the parties have established between themselves, usages and any subsequent conduct of the parties.

CONVENTION ON CONTRACTS FOR THE INTERNATIONAL SALE OF GOODS

Article 9

(1) The parties are bound by any usage to which they have agreed and by any practices which they have established between themselves.

(2) The parties are considered, unless otherwise agreed, to have impliedly made applicable to their contract or its formation a usage of which the parties knew or ought to have known and which in international trade is widely known to, and regularly observed by, parties to contracts of the type involved in the particular trade concerned.

Article 10

For the purposes of this Convention:

(a) if a party has more than one place of business, the place of business is that which has the closest relationship to the contract and its performance, having regard to the circumstances known to or contemplated by the parties at any time before or at the conclusion of the contract;

(b) if a party does not have a place of business, reference is to be made to his habitual residence.

Article 11

A contract of sale need not be concluded in or evidenced by writing and is not subject to any other requirement as to form. It may be proved by any means, including witnesses.

Article 12

Any provision of article 11, article 29 or Part II of this Convention that allows a contract of sale or its modification or termination by agreement or any offer, acceptance or other indication of intention to be made in any form other than in writing does not apply where any party has his place of business in a Contracting State which has made a declaration under article 96 of this Convention. The parties may not derogate from or vary the effect of this article.

Article 13

For the purposes of this Convention "writing" includes telegram and telex.

PART II. FORMATION OF THE CONTRACT

Article 14

(1) A proposal for concluding a contract addressed to one or more specific persons constitutes an offer if it is sufficiently definite and indicates the intention of the offeror to be bound in case of acceptance. A proposal is sufficiently definite if it indicates the goods and expressly or implicitly fixes or makes provision for determining the quantity and the price.

(2) A proposal other than one addressed to one or more specific persons is to be considered merely as an invitation to make offers, unless the contrary is clearly indicated by the person making the proposal.

Article 15

(1) An offer becomes effective when it reaches the offeree.

(2) An offer, even if it is irrevocable, may be withdrawn if the withdrawal reaches the offeree before or at the same time as the offer.

Article 16

(1) Until a contract is concluded an offer may be revoked if the revocation reaches the offeree before he has dispatched an acceptance.

(2) However, an offer cannot be revoked:

(a) if it indicates, whether by stating a fixed time for acceptance or otherwise, that it is irrevocable; or

(b) if it was reasonable for the offeree to rely on the offer as being irrevocable and the offeree has acted in reliance on the offer.

Article 17

An offer, even if it is irrevocable, is terminated when a rejection reaches the offeror.

Article 18

(1) A statement made by or other conduct of the offeree indicating assent to an offer is an acceptance. Silence or inactivity does not in itself amount to acceptance.

(2) An acceptance of an offer becomes effective at the moment the indication of assent reaches the offeror. An acceptance is not effective if the indication of assent does not reach the offeror within the time he has fixed or, if no time is fixed, within a reasonable time, due account being taken of the circumstances of the transaction, including the rapidity of the means of communication employed by the offeror. An oral offer must be accepted immediately unless the circumstances indicate otherwise.

(3) However, if, by virtue of the offer or as a result of practices which the parties have established between themselves or of usage, the offeree may indicate assent by performing an act, such as one relating to the dispatch of the goods or payment of the price, without notice to the offeror, the acceptance is effective at the moment the act is performed, provided that the act is performed within the period of time laid down in the preceding paragraph.

Article 19

(1) A reply to an offer which purports to be an acceptance but contains additions, limitations or other modifications is a rejection of the offer and constitutes a counter-offer.

(2) However, a reply to an offer which purports to be an acceptance but contains additional or different terms which do not materially alter the terms of the offer constitutes an acceptance, unless the offeror, without undue delay, objects orally to the discrepancy or dispatches a notice to that effect. If he does not so object, the terms of the contract are the terms of the offer with the modifications contained in the acceptance.

(3) Additional or different terms relating, among other things, to the price, payment, quality and quantity of the goods, place and time of delivery, extent of one party's liability to the other or the settlement of disputes are considered to alter the terms of the offer materially.

Article 20

(1) A period of time for acceptance fixed by the offeror in a telegram or a letter begins to run from the moment the telegram is handed in for dispatch or from the date shown on the letter or, if no such date is shown, from the date shown on the envelope. A period of time for acceptance fixed by the offeror by telephone, telex or other means of instantaneous communication, begins to run from the moment that the offer reaches the offeree.

(2) Official holidays or non-business days occurring during the period for acceptance are included in calculating the period. However, if a notice of acceptance cannot be delivered at the address of the offeror on the last day of the period because that day falls on an official holiday or a non-business

Article 21

(1) A late acceptance is nevertheless effective as an acceptance if without delay the offeror orally so informs the offeree or dispatches a notice to that effect.

(2) If a letter or other writing containing a late acceptance shows that it has been sent in such circumstances that if its transmission had been normal it would have reached the offeror in due time, the late acceptance is effective as an acceptance unless, without delay, the offeror orally informs the offeree that he considers his offer as having lapsed or dispatches a notice to that effect.

Article 22

An acceptance may be withdrawn if the withdrawal reaches the offeror before or at the same time as the acceptance would have become effective.

Article 23

A contract is concluded at the moment when an acceptance of an offer becomes effective in accordance with the provisions of this Convention.

Article 24

For the purposes of this Part of the Convention, an offer, declaration of acceptance or any other indication of intention "reaches" the addressee when it is made orally to him or delivered by any other means to him personally, to his place of business or mailing address or, if he does not have a place of business or mailing address, to his habitual residence.

PART III. SALE OF GOODS

CHAPTER I. GENERAL PROVISIONS

Article 25

A breach of contract committed by one of the parties is fundamental if it results in such detriment to the other party as substantially to deprive him of what he is entitled to expect under the contract, unless the party in breach did not foresee and a reasonable person of the same kind in the same circumstances would not have foreseen such a result.

Article 26

A declaration of avoidance of the contract is effective only if made by notice to the other party.

Article 27

Unless otherwise expressly provided in this Part of the Convention, if any notice, request or other communication is given or made by a party in accordance with this Part and by means appropriate in the circumstances, a delay or error in the transmission of the communication or its failure to arrive does not deprive that party of the right to rely on the communication.

Article 28

If, in accordance with the provisions of this Convention, one party is entitled to require performance of any obligation by the other party, a court is not bound to enter a judgment for specific performance unless the court would do so under its own law in respect of similar contracts of sale not governed by this Convention.

Article 29

(1) A contract may be modified or terminated by the mere agreement of the parties.

(2) A contract in writing which contains a provision requiring any modification or termination by agreement to be in writing may not be otherwise modified or terminated by agreement. However, a party may be precluded by his conduct from asserting such a provision to the extent that the other party has relied on that conduct.

CHAPTER II. OBLIGATIONS OF THE SELLER

Article 30

The seller must deliver the goods, hand over any documents relating to them and transfer the property in the goods, as required by the contract and this Convention.

Section I.
Delivery of the Goods and Handing Over of Documents

Article 31

If the seller is not bound to deliver the goods at any other particular place, his obligation to deliver consists:

(a) if the contract of sale involves carriage of the goods—in handing the goods over to the first carrier for transmission to the buyer;

(b) if, in cases not within the preceding subparagraph, the contract relates to specific goods, or unidentified goods to be drawn from a specific stock or to be manufactured or produced, and at the time of the conclusion of the contract the parties knew that the goods were at, or were to be manufactured or produced at, a particular place—in placing the goods at the buyer's disposal at that place;

(c) in other cases—in placing the goods at the buyer's disposal at the place where the seller had his place of business at the time of the conclusion of the contract.

Article 32

(1) If the seller, in accordance with the contract or this Convention, hands the goods over to a carrier and if the goods are not clearly identified to the contract by markings on the goods, by shipping documents or otherwise, the seller must give the buyer notice of the consignment specifying the goods.

(2) If the seller is bound to arrange for carriage of the goods, he must make such contracts as are necessary for carriage to the place fixed by means of transportation appropriate in the circumstances and according to the usual terms for such transportation.

(3) If the seller is not bound to effect insurance in respect of the carriage of the goods, he must, at the buyer's request, provide him with all available information necessary to enable him to effect such insurance.

Article 33

The seller must deliver the goods:

(a) if a date is fixed by or determinable from the contract, on that date;

(b) if a period of time is fixed by or determinable from the contract, at any time within that period unless circumstances indicate that the buyer is to choose a date; or

(c) in any other case, within a reasonable time after the conclusion of the contract.

Article 34

If the seller is bound to hand over documents relating to the goods, he must hand them over at the time and place and in the form required by the contract. If the seller has handed over documents before that time, he may, up to that time, cure any lack of conformity in the documents, if the exercise of this right does not cause the buyer unreasonable inconvenience or unreasonable expense. However, the buyer retains any right to claim damages as provided for in this Convention.

Section II.
Conformity of the Goods and Third Party Claims

Article 35

(1) The seller must deliver goods which are of the quantity, quality and description required by the contract and which are contained or packaged in the manner required by the contract.

(2) Except where the parties have agreed otherwise, the goods do not conform with the contract unless they;

(a) are fit for the purposes for which goods of the same description would ordinarily be used;

(b) are fit for any particular purpose expressly or impliedly made known to the seller at the time of the conclusion of the contract, except where the circumstances show that the buyer did not rely, or that it was unreasonable for him to rely, on the seller's skill and judgement;

(c) possess the qualities of goods which the seller has held out to the buyer as a sample or model;

(d) are contained or packaged in the manner usual for such goods or, where there is no such manner, in a manner adequate to preserve and protect the goods.

(3) The seller is not liable under subparagraphs (a) to (d) of the preceding paragraph for any lack of conformity of the goods if at the time of the conclusion of the contract the buyer knew or could not have been unaware of such lack of conformity.

Article 36

(1) The seller is liable in accordance with the contract and this Convention for any lack of conformity which exists at the time when the risk passes to the buyer, even though the lack of conformity becomes apparent only after that time.

(2) The seller is also liable for any lack of conformity which occurs after the time indicated in the preceding paragraph and which is due to a breach of any of his obligations, including a breach of any guarantee that for a period of time the goods will remain fit for their ordinary purpose or for some particular purpose or will retain specified qualities or characteristics.

Article 37

If the seller has delivered goods before the date for delivery, he may, up to that date, deliver any missing part or make up any deficiency in the quantity of the goods delivered, or deliver goods in replacement of any non-conforming goods delivered or remedy any lack of conformity in the goods delivered, provided that the exercise of this right does not cause the buyer unreasonable inconvenience or unreasonable expense. However, the buyer retains any right to claim damages as provided for in this Convention.

Article 38

(1) The buyer must examine the goods, or cause them to be examined, within as short a period as is practicable in the circumstances.

(2) If the contract involves carriage of the goods, examination may be deferred until after the goods have arrived at their destination.

(3) If the goods are redirected in transit or redispatched by the buyer without a reasonable opportunity for examination by him and at the time of the conclusion of the contract the seller knew or ought to have known of the possibility of such redirection or redispatch, examination may be deferred until after the goods have arrived at the new destination.

Article 39

(1) The buyer loses the right to rely on a lack of conformity of the goods if he does not give notice to the seller specifying the nature of the lack of conformity within a reasonable time after he has discovered it or ought to have discovered it.

(2) In any event, the buyer loses the right to rely on a lack of conformity of the goods if he does not give the seller notice thereof at the latest within a period of two years from the date on which the goods were actually handed over to the buyer, unless this time-limit is inconsistent with a contractual period of guarantee.

Article 40

The seller is not entitled to rely on the provisions of articles 38 and 39 if the lack of conformity relates to facts of which he knew or could not have been unaware and which he did not disclose to the buyer.

Article 41

The seller must deliver goods which are free from any right or claim of a third party, unless the buyer agreed to take the goods subject to that right or claim. However, if such right or claim is based on industrial property or other intellectual property, the seller's obligation is governed by article 42.

Article 42

(1) The seller must deliver goods which are free from any right or claim of a third party based on industrial property or other intellectual property, of which at the time of the conclusion of the contract the seller knew or could not have been unaware, provided that the right or claim is based on industrial property or other intellectual property:

(a) under the law of the State where the goods will be resold or otherwise used, if it was contemplated by the parties at the time of the conclusion of the contract that the goods would be resold or otherwise used in that State; or

(b) in any other case, under the law of the State where the buyer has his place of business.

(2) The obligation of the seller under the preceding paragraph does not extend to cases where:

(a) at the time of the conclusion of the contract the buyer knew or could not have been unaware of the right or claim; or

(b) the right or claim results from the seller's compliance with technical drawings, designs, formulae or other such specifications furnished by the buyer.

CONVENTION ON CONTRACTS FOR THE INTERNATIONAL SALE OF GOODS

Article 43

(1) The buyer loses the right to rely on the provisions of article 41 or article 42 if he does not give notice to the seller specifying the nature of the right or claim of the third party within a reasonable time after he has become aware or ought to have become aware of the right or claim.

(2) The seller is not entitled to rely on the provisions of the preceding paragraph if he knew of the right or claim of the third party and the nature of it.

Article 44

Notwithstanding the provisions of paragraph (1) of article 39 and paragraph (1) of article 43, the buyer may reduce the price in accordance with article 50 or claim damages, except for loss of profit, if he has a reasonable excuse for his failure to give the required notice.

SECTION III.
REMEDIES FOR BREACH OF CONTRACT BY THE SELLER

Article 45

(1) If the seller fails to perform any of his obligations under the contract or this Convention, the buyer may:

(a) exercise the rights provided in articles 46 to 52;

(b) claim damages as provided in articles 74 to 77.

(2) The buyer is not deprived of any right he may have to claim damages by exercising his right to other remedies.

(3) No period of grace may be granted to the seller by a court or arbitral tribunal when the buyer resorts to a remedy for breach of contract.

Article 46

(1) The buyer may require performance by the seller of his obligations unless the buyer has resorted to a remedy which is inconsistent with this requirement.

(2) If the goods do not conform with the contract, the buyer may require delivery of substitute goods only if the lack of conformity constitutes a fundamental breach of contract and a request for substitute goods is made either in conjunction with notice given under article 39 or within a reasonable time thereafter.

(3) If the goods do not conform with the contract, the buyer may require the seller to remedy the lack of conformity by repair, unless this is unreasonable having regard to all the circumstances. A request for repair must be made either in conjunction with notice given under article 39 or within a reasonable time thereafter.

Article 47

(1) The buyer may fix an additional period of time of reasonable length for performance by the seller of his obligations.

(2) Unless the buyer has received notice from the seller that he will not perform within the period so fixed, the buyer may not, during that period, resort to any remedy for breach of contract. However, the buyer is not deprived thereby of any right he may have to claim damages for delay in performance.

Article 48

(1) Subject to article 49, the seller may, even after the date for delivery, remedy at his own expense any failure to perform his obligations, if he can do so without unreasonable delay and without causing the buyer unreasonable inconvenience or uncertainty of reimbursement by the seller of expenses advanced by the buyer. However, the buyer retains any right to claim damages as provided for in this Convention.

(2) If the seller requests the buyer to make known whether he will accept performance and the buyer does not comply with the request within a reasonable time, the seller may perform within the time indicated in his request. The buyer may not, during that period of time, resort to any remedy which is inconsistent with performance by the seller.

(3) A notice by the seller that he will perform within a specified period of time is assumed to include a request, under the preceding paragraph, that the buyer make known his decision.

(4) A request or notice by the seller under paragraph (2) or (3) of this article is not effective unless received by the buyer.

Article 49

(1) The buyer may declare the contract avoided:

(a) if the failure by the seller to perform any of his obligations under the contract or this Convention amounts to a fundamental breach of contract; or

(b) in case of non-delivery, if the seller does not deliver the goods within the additional period of time fixed by the buyer in accordance with paragraph (1) of article 47 or declares that he will not deliver within the period so fixed.

(2) However, in cases where the seller has delivered the goods, the buyer loses the right to declare the contract avoided unless he does so:

(a) in respect of late delivery, within a reasonable time after he has become aware that delivery has been made;

(b) in respect of any breach other than late delivery, within a reasonable time:

(i) after he knew or ought to have known of the breach;

(ii) after the expiration of any additional period of time fixed by the buyer in accordance with paragraph (1) of article 47, or after the seller has declared that he will not perform his obligations within such an additional period; or

(iii) after the expiration of any additional period of time indicated by the seller in accordance with paragraph (2) of article 48, or after the buyer has declared that he will not accept performance.

Article 50

If the goods do not conform with the contract and whether or not the price has already been paid, the buyer may reduce the price in the same proportion as the value that the goods actually delivered had at the time of the delivery bears to the value that conforming goods would have had at that time. However, if the seller remedies any failure to perform his obligations in accordance with article 37 or article 48 or if the buyer refuses to accept performance by the seller in accordance with those articles, the buyer may not reduce the price.

CONVENTION ON CONTRACTS FOR THE INTERNATIONAL SALE OF GOODS

Article 51

(1) If the seller delivers only a part of the goods or if only a part of the goods delivered is in conformity with the contract, articles 46 to 50 apply in respect of the part which is missing or which does not conform.

(2) The buyer may declare the contract avoided in its entirety only if the failure to make delivery completely or in conformity with the contract amounts to a fundamental breach of the contract.

Article 52

(1) If the seller delivers the goods before the date fixed, the buyer may take delivery or refuse to take delivery.

(2) If the seller delivers a quantity of goods greater than that provided for in the contract, the buyer may take delivery or refuse to take delivery of the excess quantity. If the buyer takes delivery of all or part of the excess quantity, he must pay for it at the contract rate.

CHAPTER III. OBLIGATIONS OF THE BUYER

Article 53

The buyer must pay the price for the goods and take delivery of them as required by the contract and this Convention.

SECTION I.

PAYMENT OF THE PRICE

Article 54

The buyer's obligation to pay the price includes taking such steps and complying with such formalities as may be required under the contract or any laws and regulations to enable payment to be made.

Article 55

Where a contract has been validly concluded but does not expressly or implicitly fix or make provision for determining the price, the parties are considered, in the absence of any indication to the contrary, to have impliedly made reference to the price generally charged at the time of the conclusion of the contract for such goods sold under comparable circumstances in the trade concerned.

Article 56

If the price if fixed according to the weight of the goods, in case of doubt it is to be determined by the net weight.

Article 57

(1) If the buyer is not bound to pay the price at any other particular place, he must pay it to the seller:

(a) at the seller's place of business; or

(b) if the payment is to be made against the handing over of the goods or of documents, at the place where the handing over takes place.

(2) The seller must bear any increase in the expenses incidental to payment which is caused by a change in his place of business subsequent to the conclusion of the contract.

Article 58

(1) If the buyer is not bound to pay the price at any other specific time, he must pay it when the seller places either the goods or documents controlling their disposition at the buyer's disposal in accordance with the contract and this Convention. The seller may make such payment a condition for handing over the goods or documents.

(2) If the contract involves carriage of the goods, the seller may dispatch the goods on terms whereby the goods, or documents controlling their disposition, will not be handed over to the buyer except against payment of the price.

(3) The buyer is not bound to pay the price until he has had an opportunity to examine the goods, unless the procedures for delivery or payment agreed upon by the parties are inconsistent with his having such an opportunity.

Article 59

The buyer must pay the price on the date fixed by or determinable from the contract and this Convention without the need for any request or compliance with any formality on the part of the seller.

Section II.

Taking delivery

Article 60

The buyer's obligation to take delivery consists:

(a) in doing all the acts which could reasonably be expected of him in order to enable the seller to make delivery; and

(b) in taking over the goods.

Section III.

Remedies for Breach of Contract by the Buyer

Article 61

(1) If the buyer fails to perform any of his obligations under the contract or this Convention, the seller may:

(a) exercise the rights provided in articles 62 to 65;

(b) claim damages as provided in articles 74 to 77.

(2) The seller is not deprived of any right he may have to claim damages by exercising his right to other remedies.

(3) No period of grace may be granted to the buyer by a court or arbitral tribunal when the seller resorts to a remedy for breach of contract.

Article 62

The seller may require the buyer to pay the price, take delivery or perform his other obligations, unless the seller has resorted to a remedy which is inconsistent with this requirement.

Article 63

(1) The seller may fix an additional period of time of reasonable length for performance by the buyer of his obligations.

(2) Unless the seller has received notice from the buyer that he will not perform within the period so fixed, the seller may not, during that period, resort to any remedy for breach of contract. However, the seller is not deprived thereby of any right he may have to claim damages for delay in performance.

Article 64

(1) The seller may declare the contract avoided:

(a) if the failure by the buyer to perform any of his obligations under the contract or this Convention amounts to a fundamental breach of contract; or

(b) if the buyer does not, within the additional period of time fixed by the seller in accordance with paragraph (1) of article 63, perform his obligation to pay the price or take delivery of the goods, or if he declares that he will not do so within the period so fixed.

(2) However, in cases where the buyer has paid the price, the seller loses the right to declare the contract avoided unless he does so:

(a) in respect of late performance by the buyer, before the seller has become aware that performance has been rendered; or

(b) in respect of any breach other than late performance by the buyer, within a reasonable time:

(i) after the seller knew or ought to have known of the breach; or

(ii) after the expiration of any additional period of time fixed by the seller in accordance with paragraph (1) of article 63, or after the buyer has declared that he will not perform his obligations within such an additional period.

Article 65

(1) If under the contract the buyer is to specify the form, measurement or other features of the goods and he fails to make such specification either on the date agreed upon or within a reasonable time after receipt of a request from the seller, the seller may, without prejudice to any other rights he may have, make the specification himself in accordance with the requirements of the buyer that may be known to him.

(2) If the seller makes the specification himself, he must inform the buyer of the details thereof and must fix a reasonable time within which the buyer may make a different specification. If, after receipt of such a communication, the buyer fails to do so within the time so fixed, the specification made by the seller is binding.

CHAPTER IV. PASSING OF RISK

Article 66

Loss of or damage to the goods after the risk has passed to the buyer does not discharge him from his obligation to pay the price, unless the loss or damage is due to an act or omission of the seller.

Article 67

(1) If the contract of sale involves carriage of the goods and the seller is not bound to hand them over at a particular place, the risk passes to the buyer when the goods are handed over to the first carrier for transmission to the buyer in accordance with the contract of sale. If the seller is bound to hand the goods over to a carrier at a particular place, the risk does not pass to the buyer until the goods are handed over to the carrier at that place. The fact that the seller is authorized to retain documents controlling the disposition of the goods does not affect the passage of the risk.

(2) Nevertheless, the risk does not pass to the buyer until the goods are clearly identified to the contract, whether by markings on the goods, by shipping documents, by notice given to the buyer or otherwise.

Article 68

The risk in respect of goods sold in transit passes to the buyer from the time of the conclusion of the contract. However, if the circumstances so indicate, the risk is assumed by the buyer from the time the goods were handed over to the carrier who issued the documents embodying the contract of carriage. Nevertheless, if at the time of the conclusion of the contract of sale the seller knew or ought to have known that the goods had been lost or damaged and did not disclose this to the buyer, the loss or damage is at the risk of the seller.

Article 69

(1) In cases not within articles 67 and 68, the risk passes to the buyer when he takes over the goods or, if he does not do so in due time, from the time when the goods are placed at his disposal and he commits a breach of contract by failing to take delivery.

(2) However, if the buyer is bound to take over the goods at a place other than a place of business of the seller, the risk passes when delivery is due and the buyer is aware of the fact that the goods are placed at his disposal at that place.

(3) If the contract relates to goods not then identified, the goods are considered not to be placed at the disposal of the buyer until they are clearly identified to the contract.

Article 70

If the seller had committed a fundamental breach of contract, articles 67, 68 and 69 do not impair the remedies available to the buyer on account of the breach.

CHAPTER V. PROVISIONS COMMON TO THE OBLIGATIONS OF THE SELLER AND OF THE BUYER

Section I.
Anticipatory Breach and Instalment Contracts

Article 71

(1) A party may suspend the performance of his obligations if, after the conclusion of the contract, it becomes apparent that the other party will not perform a substantial part of his obligations as a result of:

(a) a serious deficiency in his ability to perform or in his creditworthiness; or

(b) his conduct in preparing to perform or in performing the contract.

(2) If the seller has already dispatched the goods before the grounds described in the preceding paragraph become evident, he may prevent the handing over of the goods to the buyer even though the buyer holds a document which entitles him to obtain them. The present paragraph relates only to the rights in the goods as between the buyer and the seller.

(3) A party suspending performance, whether before or after dispatch of the goods, must immediately give notice of the suspension to the other party and must continue with performance if the other party provides adequate assurance of his performance.

CONVENTION ON CONTRACTS FOR THE INTERNATIONAL SALE OF GOODS

Article 72

(1) If prior to the date for performance of the contract it is clear that one of the parties will commit a fundamental breach of contract, the other party may declare the contract avoided.

(2) If time allows, the party intending to declare the contract avoided must give reasonable notice to the other party in order to permit him to provide adequate assurance of his performance.

(3) The requirements of the preceding paragraph do not apply if the other party has declared that he will not perform his obligations.

Article 73

(1) In the case of a contract for delivery of goods by instalments, if the failure of one party to perform any of his obligations in respect of any instalment constitutes a fundamental breach of contract with respect to that instalment, the other party may declare the contract avoided with respect to that instalment.

(2) If one party's failure to perform any of his obligations in respect of any instalment gives the other party good grounds to conclude that a fundamental breach of contract will occur with respect to future instalments, he may declare the contract avoided for the future, provided that he does so within a reasonable time.

(3) A buyer who declares the contract avoided in respect of any delivery may, at the same time, declare it avoided in respect of deliveries already made or of future deliveries if, by reason of their interdependence, those deliveries could not be used for the purpose contemplated by the parties at the time of the conclusion of the contract.

SECTION II.

DAMAGES

Article 74

Damages for breach of contract by one party consist of a sum equal to the loss, including loss of profit, suffered by the other party as a consequence of the breach. Such damages may not exceed the loss which the party in breach foresaw or ought to have foreseen at the time of the conclusion of the contract, in the light of the facts and matters of which he then knew or ought to have known, as a possible consequence of the breach of contract.

Article 75

If the contract is avoided and if, in a reasonable manner and within a reasonable time after avoidance, the buyer has bought goods in replacement or the seller has resold the goods, the party claiming damages may recover the difference between the contract price and the price in the substitute transaction as well as any further damages recoverable under article 74.

Article 76

(1) If the contract is avoided and there is a current price for the goods, the party claiming damages may, if he has not made a purchase or resale under article 75, recover the difference between the price fixed by the contract and the current price at the time of avoidance as well as any further damages recoverable under article 74. If, however, the party claiming damages has avoided the contract after taking over the goods, the current price at the time of such taking over shall be applied instead of the current price at the time of avoidance.

(2) For the purpose of the preceding paragraph, the current price is the price prevailing at the place where delivery of the goods should have been made or, if there is no current price at that place,

the price at such other place as serves as a reasonable substitute, making due allowance for differences in the cost of transporting the goods.

Article 77

A party who relies on a breach of contract must take such measures as are reasonable in the circumstances to mitigate the loss, including loss of profit, resulting from the breach. If he fails to take such measures, the party in breach may claim a reduction in the damages in the amount by which the loss should have been mitigated.

SECTION III.

INTEREST

Article 78

If a party fails to pay the price or any other sum that is in arrears, the other party is entitled to interest on it, without prejudice to any claim for damages recoverable under article 74.

SECTION IV.

EXEMPTIONS

Article 79

(1) A party is not liable for a failure to perform any of his obligations if he proves that the failure was due to an impediment beyond his control and that he could not reasonably be expected to have taken the impediment into account at the time of the conclusion of the contract or to have avoided or overcome it or its consequences.

(2) If the party's failure is due to the failure by a third person whom he has engaged to perform the whole or a part of the contract, that party is exempt from liability only if:

(a) he is exempt under the preceding paragraph; and

(b) the person whom he has so engaged would be so exempt if the provisions of that paragraph were applied to him.

(3) The exemption provided by this article has effect for the period during which the impediment exists.

(4) The party who fails to perform must give notice to the other party of the impediment and its effects on his ability to perform. If the notice is not received by the other party within a reasonable time after the party who fails to perform knew or ought to have known of the impediment, he is liable for damages resulting from such non-receipt.

(5) Nothing in this article prevents either party from exercising any right other than to claim damages under this Convention.

Article 80

A party may not rely on a failure of the other party to perform, to the extent that such failure was caused by the first party's act or omission.

SECTION V.

EFFECTS OF AVOIDANCE

Article 81

(1) Avoidance of the contract releases both parties from their obligations under it, subject to any damages which may be due. Avoidance does not affect any provision of the contract for the

settlement of disputes or any other provision of the contract governing the rights and obligations of the parties consequent upon the avoidance of the contract.

(2) A party who has performed the contract either wholly or in part may claim restitution from the other party of whatever the first party has supplied or paid under the contract. If both parties are bound to make restitution, they must do so concurrently.

Article 82

(1) The buyer loses the right to declare the contract avoided or to require the seller to deliver substitute goods if it is impossible for him to make restitution of the goods substantially in the condition in which he received them.

(2) The preceding paragraph does not apply:

(a) if the impossibility of making restitution of the goods or of making restitution of the goods substantially in the condition in which the buyer received them is not due to his act or omission;

(b) if the goods or part of the goods have perished or deteriorated as a result of the examination provided for in article 38; or

(c) if the goods or part of the goods have been sold in the normal course of business or have been consumed or transformed by the buyer in the course of normal use before he discovered or ought to have discovered the lack of conformity.

Article 83

A buyer who has lost the right to declare the contract avoided or to require the seller to deliver substitute goods in accordance with article 82 retains all other remedies under the contract and this Convention.

Article 84

(1) If the seller is bound to refund the price, he must also pay interest on it, from the date on which the price was paid.

(2) The buyer must account to the seller for all benefits which he has derived from the goods or part of them:

(a) if he must make restitution of the goods or part of them; or

(b) if it is impossible for him to make restitution of all or part of the goods or to make restitution of all or part of the goods substantially in the condition in which he received them, but he has nevertheless declared the contract avoided or required the seller to deliver substitute goods.

Section VI.

Preservation of the Goods

Article 85

If the buyer is in delay in taking delivery of the goods or, where payment of the price and delivery of the goods are to be made concurrently, if he fails to pay the price, and the seller is either in possession of the goods or otherwise able to control their disposition, the seller must take such steps as are reasonable in the circumstances to preserve them. He is entitled to retain them until he has been reimbursed his reasonable expenses by the buyer.

Article 86

(1) If the buyer has received the goods and intends to exercise any right under the contract or this Convention to reject them, he must take such steps to preserve them as are reasonable in the circumstances. He is entitled to retain them until he has been reimbursed his reasonable expenses by the seller.

(2) If goods dispatched to the buyer have been placed at his disposal at their destination and he exercises the right to reject them, he must take possession of them on behalf of the seller, provided that this can be done without payment of the price and without unreasonable inconvenience or unreasonable expense. This provision does not apply if the seller or a person authorized to take charge of the goods on his behalf is present at the destination. If the buyer takes possession of the goods under this paragraph, his rights and obligations are governed by the preceding paragraph.

Article 87

A party who is bound to take steps to preserve the goods may deposit them in a warehouse of a third person at the expense of the other party provided that the expense incurred is not unreasonable.

Article 88

(1) A party who is bound to preserve the goods in accordance with article 85 or 86 may sell them by any appropriate means if there has been an unreasonable delay by the other party in taking possession of the goods or in taking them back or in paying the price or the cost of preservation, provided that reasonable notice of the intention to sell has been given to the other party.

(2) If the goods are subject to rapid deterioration or their preservation would involve unreasonable expense, a party who is bound to preserve the goods in accordance with article 85 or 86 must take reasonable measures to sell them. To the extent possible he must give notice to the other party of his intention to sell.

(3) A party selling the goods has the right to retain out of the proceeds of sale an amount equal to the reasonable expenses of preserving the goods and of selling them. He must account to the other party for the balance.

PART IV. FINAL PROVISIONS

Article 89

The Secretary-General of the United Nations is hereby designated as the depositary for this Convention.

Article 90

This Convention does not prevail over any international agreement which has already been or may be entered into and which contains provisions concerning the matters governed by this Convention, provided that the parties have their places of business in States parties to such agreement.

Article 91

(1) This Convention is open for signature at the concluding meeting of the United Nations Conference on Contracts for the International Sale of Goods and will remain open for signature by all States at the Headquarters of the United Nations, New York until 30 September 1981.

(2) This Convention is subject to ratification, acceptance or approval by the signatory States.

(3) This Convention is open for accession by all States which are not signatory States as from the date it is open for signature.

(4) Instruments of ratification, acceptance, approval and accession are to be deposited with the Secretary-General of the United Nations.

Article 92

(1) A Contracting State may declare at the time of signature, ratification, acceptance, approval or accession that it will not be bound by Part II of this Convention or that it will not be bound by Part III of this Convention.

(2) A Contracting State which makes a declaration in accordance with the preceding paragraph in respect of Part II or Part III of this Convention is not to be considered a Contracting State within paragraph (1) of article 1 of this Convention in respect of matters governed by the Part to which the declaration applies.

Article 93

(1) If a Contracting State has two or more territorial units in which, according to its constitution, different systems of law are applicable in relation to the matters dealt with in this Convention, it may, at the time of signature, ratification, acceptance, approval or accession, declare that this Convention is to extend to all its territorial units or only to one or more of them, and may amend its declaration by submitting another declaration at any time.

(2) These declarations are to be notified to the depositary and are to state expressly the territorial units to which the Convention extends.

(3) If, by virtue of a declaration under this article, this Convention extends to one or more but not all of the territorial units of a Contracting State, and if the place of business of a party is located in that State, this place of business, for the purposes of this Convention, is considered not to be in a Contracting State, unless it is in a territorial unit to which the Convention extends.

(4) If a Contracting State makes no declaration under paragraph (1) of this article, the Convention is to extend to all territorial units of that State.

Article 94

(1) Two or more Contracting States which have the same or closely related legal rules on matters governed by this Convention may at any time declare that the Convention is not to apply to contracts of sale or to their formation where the parties have their places of business in those States. Such declarations may be made jointly or by reciprocal unilateral declarations.

(2) A Contracting State which has the same or closely related legal rules on matters governed by this Convention as one or more non-Contracting States may at any time declare that the Convention is not to apply to contracts of sale or to their formation where the parties have their places of business in those States.

(3) If a State which is the object of a declaration under the preceding paragraph subsequently becomes a Contracting State, the declaration made will, as from the date on which the Convention enters into force in respect of the new Contracting State, have the effect of a declaration made under paragraph (1), provided that the new Contracting State joins in such declaration or makes a reciprocal unilateral declaration.

Article 95

Any State may declare at the time of the deposit of its instrument of ratification, acceptance, approval or accession that it will not be bound by subparagraph (1)(b) of article 1 of this Convention.

[The United States has declared a reservation to CISG under Article 95].

Article 96

A Contracting State whose legislation requires contracts of sale to be concluded in or evidenced by writing may at any time make a declaration in accordance with article 12 that any provision of article 11, article 29, or Part II of this Convention, that allows a contract of sale or its modification or termination by agreement or any offer, acceptance, or other indication of intention to be made in any form other than in writing, does not apply where any party has his place of business in that State.

Article 97

(1) Declarations made under this Convention at the time of signature are subject to confirmation upon ratification, acceptance or approval.

(2) Declarations and confirmations of declarations are to be in writing and be formally notified to the depositary.

(3) A declaration takes effect simultaneously with the entry into force of this Convention in respect of the State concerned. However, a declaration of which the depositary receives formal notification after such entry into force takes effect on the first day of the month following the expiration of six months after the date of its receipt by the depositary. Reciprocal unilateral declarations under article 94 take effect on the first day of the month following the expiration of six months after the receipt of the latest declaration by the depositary.

(4) Any State which makes a declaration under this Convention may withdraw it at any time by a formal notification in writing addressed to the depositary. Such withdrawal is to take effect on the first day of the month following the expiration of six months after the date of the receipt of the notification by the depositary.

(5) A withdrawal of a declaration made under article 94 renders inoperative, as from the date on which the withdrawal takes effect, any reciprocal declaration made by another State under that article.

Article 98

No reservations are permitted except those expressly authorized in this Convention.

Article 99

(1) This Convention enters into force, subject to the provisions of paragraph (6) of this article, on the first day of the month following the expiration of twelve months after the date of deposit of the tenth instrument of ratification, acceptance, approval or accession, including an instrument which contains a declaration made under article 92.

(2) When a State ratifies, accepts, approves or accedes to this Convention after the deposit of the tenth instrument of ratification, acceptance, approval or accession, this Convention, with the exception of the Part excluded, enters into force in respect of that State, subject to the provisions of paragraph (6) of this article, on the first day of the month following the expiration of twelve months after the date of the deposit of its instrument of ratification, acceptance, approval or accession.

(3) A State which ratifies, accepts, approves or accedes to this Convention and is a party to either or both the Convention relating to a Uniform Law on the Formation of Contracts for the International Sale of Goods done at The Hague on 1 July 1964 (1964 Hague Formation Convention) and the Convention relating to a Uniform Law on the International Sale of Goods done at The Hague on 1 July 1964 (1964 Hague Sales Convention) shall at the same time denounce, as the case may be, either or both the 1964 Hague Sales Convention and the 1964 Hague Formation Convention by notifying the Government of the Netherlands to that effect.

(4) A State party to the 1964 Hague Sales Convention which ratifies, accepts, approves or accedes to the present Convention and declares or has declared under article 92 that it will not be

bound by Part II of this Convention shall at the time of ratification, acceptance, approval or accession denounce the 1964 Hague Sales Convention by notifying the Government of the Netherlands to that effect.

(5) A State party to the 1964 Hague Formation Convention which ratifies, accepts, approves or accedes to the present Convention and declares or has declared under article 92 that it will not be bound by Part III of this Convention shall at the time of ratification, acceptance, approval or accession denounce the 1964 Hague Formation Convention by notifying the Government of the Netherlands to that effect.

(6) For the purpose of this article, ratifications, acceptances, approvals and accessions in respect of this Convention by States parties to the 1964 Hague Formation Convention or to the 1964 Hague Sales Convention shall not be effective until such denunciations as may be required on the part of those States in respect of the latter two Conventions have themselves become effective. The depositary of this Convention shall consult with the Government of the Netherlands, as the depositary of the 1964 Convention, so as to ensure necessary co-ordination in this respect.

Article 100

(1) This Convention applies to the formation of a contract only when the proposal for concluding the contract is made on or after the date when the Convention enters into force in respect of the Contracting States referred to in subparagraph (1)(a) or the Contracting State referred to in subparagraph (1)(b) of article 1.

(2) This Convention applies only to contracts concluded on or after the date when the Convention enters into force in respect of the Contracting States referred to in subparagraph (1)(a) or the Contracting State referred to in subparagraph (1)(b) of article 1.

Article 101

(1) A Contracting State may denounce this Convention, or Part II or Part III of the Convention, by a formal notification in writing addressed to the depositary.

(2) The denunciation takes effect on the first day of the month following the expiration of twelve months after the notification is received by the depositary. Where a longer period for the denunciation to take effect is specified in the notification, the denunciation takes effect upon the expiration of such longer period after the notification is received by the depositary.

UNITED NATIONS CONVENTION ON THE USE OF ELECTRONIC COMMUNICATIONS IN INTERNATIONAL CONTRACTS

(2005)

(Excerpts)

[Like the U.S. Electronic Signatures in Global and National Commerce Act ("E-Sign") and the Uniform Electronic Transactions Act ("UETA"), both included in Part V of this pamphlet, the United Nations Convention on the Use of Electronic Communications in International Contracts ("CUECIC") aims to enhance legal certainty and commercial predictability. It applies when parties make international contracts using electronic means. Primarily, it prevents such a contract from being held invalid or unenforceable solely because the parties made it in electronic form. The CUECIC thereby displaces such laws as statutes of frauds. CUECIC, Arts. 8.1, 9. The CUECIC entered into force on March 1, 2013 when three States had ratified, accepted, approved, or acceded to it. As of May 1, 2018, only seven states had done so.]

Chapter I
Sphere of application

Article 1
Scope of application

1. This Convention applies to the use of electronic communications in connection with the formation or performance of a contract between parties whose places of business are in different States.

2. The fact that the parties have their places of business in different States is to be disregarded whenever this fact does not appear either from the contract or from any dealings between the parties or from information disclosed by the parties at any time before or at the conclusion of the contract.

3. Neither the nationality of the parties nor the civil or commercial character of the parties or of the contract is to be taken into consideration in determining the application of this Convention.

Article 2
Exclusions

1. This Convention does not apply to electronic communications relating to any of the following:

   (a) Contracts concluded for personal, family or household purposes;

   (b) (i) Transactions on a regulated exchange; (ii) foreign exchange transactions; (iii) inter-bank payment systems, inter-bank payment agreements or clearance and settlement systems relating to securities or other financial assets or instruments; (iv) the transfer of security rights in sale, loan or holding of or agreement to repurchase securities or other financial assets or instruments held with an intermediary.

2. This Convention does not apply to bills of exchange, promissory notes, consignment notes, bills of lading, warehouse receipts or any transferable document or instrument that entitles the bearer or beneficiary to claim the delivery of goods or the payment of a sum of money.

UNITED NATIONS CONVENTION ON THE USE OF ELECTRONIC COMMUNICATIONS

Article 3
Party autonomy

The parties may exclude the application of this Convention or derogate from or vary the effect of any of its provisions.

Chapter II
General provisions

Article 4
Definitions

For the purposes of this Convention:

(a) "Communication" means any statement, declaration, demand, notice or request, including an offer and the acceptance of an offer, that the parties are required to make or choose to make in connection with the formation or performance of a contract;

(b) "Electronic communication" means any communication that the parties make by means of data messages;

(c) "Data message" means information generated, sent, received or stored by electronic, magnetic, optical or similar means, including, but not limited to, electronic data interchange, electronic mail, telegram, telex or telecopy;

(d) "Originator" of an electronic communication means a party by whom, or on whose behalf, the electronic communication has been sent or generated prior to storage, if any, but it does not include a party acting as an intermediary with respect to that electronic communication;

(e) "Addressee" of an electronic communication means a party who is intended by the originator to receive the electronic communication, but does not include a party acting as an intermediary with respect to that electronic communication;

(f) "Information system" means a system for generating, sending, receiving, storing or otherwise processing data messages;

(g) "Automated message system" means a computer program or an electronic or other automated means used to initiate an action or respond to data messages or performances in whole or in part, without review or intervention by a natural person each time an action is initiated or a response is generated by the system;

(h) "Place of business" means any place where a party maintains a non-transitory establishment to pursue an economic activity other than the temporary provision of goods or services out of a specific location.

Article 5
Interpretation

1. In the interpretation of this Convention, regard is to be had to its international character and to the need to promote uniformity in its application and the observance of good faith in international trade.

2. Questions concerning matters governed by this Convention which are not expressly settled in it are to be settled in conformity with the general principles on which it is based or, in the absence of such principles, in conformity with the law applicable by virtue of the rules of private international law.

Article 6
Location of the parties

1. For the purposes of this Convention, a party's place of business is presumed to be the location indicated by that party, unless another party demonstrates that the party making the indication does not have a place of business at that location.

2. If a party has not indicated a place of business and has more than one place of business, then the place of business for the purposes of this Convention is that which has the closest relationship to the relevant contract, having regard to the circumstances known to or contemplated by the parties at any time before or at the conclusion of the contract.

3. If a natural person does not have a place of business, reference is to be made to the person's habitual residence.

4. A location is not a place of business merely because that is: (a) where equipment and technology supporting an information system used by a party in connection with the formation of a contract are located; or (b) where the information system may be accessed by other parties.

5. The sole fact that a party makes use of a domain name or electronic mail address connected to a specific country does not create a presumption that its place of business is located in that country.

Article 7
Information requirements

Nothing in this Convention affects the application of any rule of law that may require the parties to disclose their identities, places of business or other information, or relieves a party from the legal consequences of making inaccurate, incomplete or false statements in that regard.

Chapter III
Use of electronic communications in international contracts

Article 8
Legal recognition of electronic communications

1. A communication or a contract shall not be denied validity or enforceability on the sole ground that it is in the form of an electronic communication.

2. Nothing in this Convention requires a party to use or accept electronic communications, but a party's agreement to do so may be inferred from the party's conduct.

Article 9
Form requirements

1. Nothing in this Convention requires a communication or a contract to be made or evidenced in any particular form.

2. Where the law requires that a communication or a contract should be in writing, or provides consequences for the absence of a writing, that requirement is met by an electronic communication if the information contained therein is accessible so as to be useable for subsequent reference.

3. Where the law requires that a communication or a contract should be signed by a party, or provides consequences for the absence of a signature, that requirement is met in relation to an electronic communication if:

(a) A method is used to identify the party and to indicate that party's intention in respect of the information contained in the electronic communication; and

(b) The method used is either:

(i) As reliable as appropriate for the purpose for which the electronic communication was generated or communicated, in the light of all the circumstances, including any relevant agreement; or

(ii) Proven in fact to have fulfilled the functions described in subparagraph (a) above, by itself or together with further evidence.

4. Where the law requires that a communication or a contract should be made available or retained in its original form, or provides consequences for the absence of an original, that requirement is met in relation to an electronic communication if:

(a) There exists a reliable assurance as to the integrity of the information it contains from the time when it was first generated in its final form, as an electronic communication or otherwise; and

(b) Where it is required that the information it contains be made available, that information is capable of being displayed to the person to whom it is to be made available.

5. For the purposes of paragraph 4(a):

(a) The criteria for assessing integrity shall be whether the information has remained complete and unaltered, apart from the addition of any endorsement and any change that arises in the normal course of communication, storage and display; and

(b) The standard of reliability required shall be assessed in the light of the purpose for which the information was generated and in the light of all the relevant circumstances.

Article 10
Time and place of dispatch and receipt of electronic communications

1. The time of dispatch of an electronic communication is the time when it leaves an information system under the control of the originator or of the party who sent it on behalf of the originator or, if the electronic communication has not left an information system under the control of the originator or of the party who sent it on behalf of the originator, the time when the electronic communication is received.

2. The time of receipt of an electronic communication is the time when it becomes capable of being retrieved by the addressee at an electronic address designated by the addressee. The time of receipt of an electronic communication at another electronic address of the addressee is the time when it becomes capable of being retrieved by the addressee at that address and the addressee becomes aware that the electronic communication has been sent to that address. An electronic communication is presumed to be capable of being retrieved by the addressee when it reaches the addressee's electronic address.

3. An electronic communication is deemed to be dispatched at the place where the originator has its place of business and is deemed to be received at the place where the addressee has its place of business, as determined in accordance with article 6.

4. Paragraph 2 of this article applies notwithstanding that the place where the information system supporting an electronic address is located may be different from the place where the electronic communication is deemed to be received under paragraph 3 of this article.

Article 11
Invitations to make offers

A proposal to conclude a contract made through one or more electronic communications which is not addressed to one or more specific parties, but is generally accessible to parties making use of information systems, including proposals that make use of interactive applications for the placement of orders through such information systems, is to be considered as an invitation to make offers, unless it clearly indicates the intention of the party making the proposal to be bound in case of acceptance.

Article 12
Use of automated message systems for contract formation

A contract formed by the interaction of an automated message system and a natural person, or by the interaction of automated message systems, shall not be denied validity or enforceability on the sole ground that no natural person reviewed or intervened in each of the individual actions carried out by the automated message systems or the resulting contract.

Article 13
Availability of contract terms

Nothing in this Convention affects the application of any rule of law that may require a party that negotiates some or all of the terms of a contract through the exchange of electronic communications to make available to the other party those electronic communications which contain the contractual terms in a particular manner, or relieves a party from the legal consequences of its failure to do so.

Article 14
Error in electronic communications

1. Where a natural person makes an input error in an electronic communication exchanged with the automated message system of another party and the automated message system does not provide the person with an opportunity to correct the error, that person, or the party on whose behalf that person was acting, has the right to withdraw the portion of the electronic communication in which the input error was made if:

    (a) The person, or the party on whose behalf that person was acting, notifies the other party of the error as soon as possible after having learned of the error and indicates that he or she made an error in the electronic communication; and

    (b) The person, or the party on whose behalf that person was acting, has not used or received any material benefit or value from the goods or services, if any, received from the other party.

2. Nothing in this article affects the application of any rule of law that may govern the consequences of any error other than as provided for in paragraph 1. . . .

Pt. VI UNIDROIT PRINCIPLES

THE UNIDROIT PRINCIPLES OF INTERNATIONAL COMMERCIAL CONTRACTS*

(2016)

[The International Institute for the Unification of Private Law ("UNIDROIT") is an independent intergovernmental organization located in Rome. Sixty-three member States—from all regions of the world—support it. UNIDROIT's principal purposes include promoting the modernization, harmonization, and uniformity of commercial law internationally. It furthers these purposes by, among other things, developing and publishing collections of principles on private law topics. In 1971, the governing council of the Institute determined to include a codification of the law of contracts in its program. A Working Group consisting of academics, judges, and civil servants was created in 1980. The members of the Working Group were of different nationalities, but sat in their personal capacities, not to express the views of their governments. The result was the UNIDROIT Principles of International Commercial Contracts, which was first published in 1994 and has since been revised. The goal of the UNIDROIT Principles is to set forth general rules for international commercial contracts. The Principles are intended to enunciate communal principles and rules of existing legal systems, and to select the solutions that are best adapted to the special requirements of international commercial contracts. In preparing the Principles, particular attention was paid to recent codifications of contract and commercial law, including the UCC, the Restatement Second of Contracts, the Netherlands Civil Code, the 1985 Foreign Economic Contract law of the People's Republic of China, the Draft New Civil Code of Quebec, and the United Nations Convention on Contracts for the International Sale of Goods.

[As such, the UNIDROIT Principles, much like the American Law Institute's Restatements, offers general principles and rules that are not binding law in any State. The Preamble to the UNIDROIT Principles states that the general rules for international contracts stated therein *shall* be applied when the parties to an international commercial contract have agreed that these principles and rules shall govern their contract and *may* be applied (1) when the parties have not agreed on the governing law; (2) when the parties have agreed that general principles of law or the *lex mercatoria* shall govern; (3) to interpret or supplement international uniform-law instruments; and (4) to interpret or supplement domestic contract law when an international commercial contract is involved. Because the Principles stem from an internationally negotiated blend of common law, civil law, and other legal traditions, and are supportive of evolving international contracting practices, they have a distinctive international character.]

PREAMBLE**

(Purpose of the Principles)

These Principles set forth general rules for international commercial contracts.

They shall be applied when the parties have agreed that their contract be governed by them.

---

* Copyright UNIDROIT 2016—The complete version of the UNIDROIT Principles contains not only the black-letter rules reproduced herein, but also detailed comments on each article and, where appropriate, illustrations, which are to be seen as an integral part of the Principles. This complete version, which is published in English, French, German, Italian and Spanish, may be ordered directly from UNIDROIT, Via Panisperna, 28, 00184 Rome, Italy—Fax: +39 6/6994 1394.

** Parties wishing to provide that their agreement be governed by the Principles might use one of the *Model Clauses for the Use of the UNIDROIT Principles* (see http://www.unidroit.org/instruments/commercial-contracts/upicc-model-clauses).

They may be applied when the parties have agreed that their contract be governed by general principles of law, the *lex mercatoria* or the like.

They may be applied when the parties have not chosen any law to govern their contract.

They may be used to interpret or supplement international uniform law instruments.

They may be used to interpret or supplement domestic law.

They may serve as a model for national and international legislators.

CHAPTER 1—GENERAL PROVISIONS

ARTICLE 1.1

(Freedom of contract)

The parties are free to enter into a contract and to determine its content.

ARTICLE 1.2

(No form required)

Nothing in these Principles requires a contract, statement or any other act to be made in or evidenced by a particular form. It may be proved by any means, including witnesses.

ARTICLE 1.3

(Binding character of contract)

A contract validly entered into is binding upon the parties. It can only be modified or terminated in accordance with its terms or by agreement or as otherwise provided in these Principles.

ARTICLE 1.4

(Mandatory rules)

Nothing in these Principles shall restrict the application of mandatory rules, whether of national, international or supranational origin, which are applicable in accordance with the relevant rules of private international law.

ARTICLE 1.5

(Exclusion or modification by the parties)

The parties may exclude the application of these Principles or derogate from or vary the effect of any of their provisions, except as otherwise provided in the Principles.

ARTICLE 1.6

(Interpretation and supplementation of the Principles)

(1) In the interpretation of these Principles, regard is to be had to their international character and to their purposes including the need to promote uniformity in their application.

(2) Issues within the scope of these Principles but not expressly settled by them are as far as possible to be settled in accordance with their underlying general principles.

ARTICLE 1.7

(Good faith and fair dealing)

(1) Each party must act in accordance with good faith and fair dealing in international trade.

(2) The parties may not exclude or limit this duty.

ARTICLE 1.8

(Inconsistent Behaviour)

A party cannot act inconsistently with an understanding it has caused the other party to have and upon which that other party reasonably has acted in reliance to its detriment.

ARTICLE 1.9

(Usages and practices)

(1) The parties are bound by any usage to which they have agreed and by any practices which they have established between themselves.

(2) The parties are bound by a usage that is widely known to and regularly observed in international trade by parties in the particular trade concerned except where the application of such a usage would be unreasonable.

ARTICLE 1.10

(Notice)

(1) Where notice is required it may be given by any means appropriate to the circumstances.

(2) A notice is effective when it reaches the person to whom it is given.

(3) For the purpose of paragraph (2) a notice "reaches" a person when given to that person orally or delivered at that person's place of business or mailing address.

(4) For the purpose of this article "notice" includes a declaration, demand, request or any other communication of intention.

ARTICLE 1.11

(Definitions)

In these Principles

—"court" includes an arbitral tribunal;

—where a party has more than one place of business the relevant "place of business" is that which has the closest relationship to the contract and its performance, having regard to the circumstances known to or contemplated by the parties at any time before or at the conclusion of the contract;

—"long-term contract" refers to a contract which is to be performed over a period of time and which normally involves, to a varying degree, complexity of the transaction and an ongoing relationship between the parties;

—"obligor" refers to the party who is to perform an obligation and "obligee" refers to the party who is entitled to performance of that obligation.

—"writing" means any mode of communication that preserves a record of the information contained therein and is capable of being reproduced in tangible form. . . .

CHAPTER 2—FORMATION...

SECTION 1: FORMATION

ARTICLE 2.1.1

(Manner of formation)

A contract may be concluded either by the acceptance of an offer or by conduct of the parties that is sufficient to show agreement.

ARTICLE 2.1.2

(Definition of offer)

A proposal for concluding a contract constitutes an offer if it is sufficiently definite and indicates the intention of the offeror to be bound in case of acceptance.

ARTICLE 2.1.3

(Withdrawal of offer)

(1) An offer becomes effective when it reaches the offeree.

(2) An offer, even if it is irrevocable, may be withdrawn if the withdrawal reaches the offeree before or at the same time as the offer.

ARTICLE 2.1.4

(Revocation of offer)

(1) Until a contract is concluded an offer may be revoked if the revocation reaches the offeree before it has dispatched an acceptance.

(2) However, an offer cannot be revoked

(a) if it indicates, whether by stating a fixed time for acceptance or otherwise, that it is irrevocable; or

(b) if it was reasonable for the offeree to rely on the offer as being irrevocable and the offeree has acted in reliance on the offer.

ARTICLE 2.1.5

(Rejection of offer)

An offer is terminated when a rejection reaches the offeror.

ARTICLE 2.1.6

(Mode of acceptance)

(1) A statement made by or other conduct of the offeree indicating assent to an offer is an acceptance. Silence or inactivity does not in itself amount to acceptance.

(2) An acceptance of an offer becomes effective when the indication of assent reaches the offeror.

(3) However, if, by virtue of the offer or as a result of practices which the parties have established between themselves or of usage, the offeree may indicate assent by performing an act without notice to the offeror, the acceptance is effective when the act is performed.

ARTICLE 2.1.7

(Time of acceptance)

An offer must be accepted within the time the offeror has fixed or, if no time is fixed, within a reasonable time having regard to the circumstances, including the rapidity of the means of communication employed by the offeror. An oral offer must be accepted immediately unless the circumstances indicate otherwise.

ARTICLE 2.1.8

(Acceptance within a fixed period of time)

A period of acceptance fixed by the offeror begins to run from the time that the offer is dispatched. A time indicated in the offer is deemed to be the time of dispatch unless the circumstances indicate otherwise.

ARTICLE 2.1.9

(Late acceptance. Delay in transmission)

(1) A late acceptance is nevertheless effective as an acceptance if without undue delay the offeror so informs the offeree or gives notice to that effect.

(2) If a communication containing a late acceptance shows that it has been sent in such circumstances that if its transmission had been normal it would have reached the offeror in due time, the late acceptance is effective as an acceptance unless, without undue delay, the offeror informs the offeree that it considers the offer as having lapsed.

ARTICLE 2.1.10

(Withdrawal of acceptance)

An acceptance may be withdrawn if the withdrawal reaches the offeror before or at the same time as the acceptance would have become effective.

ARTICLE 2.1.11

(Modified acceptance)

(1) A reply to an offer which purports to be an acceptance but contains additions, limitations or other modifications is a rejection of the offer and constitutes a counter-offer.

(2) However, a reply to an offer which purports to be an acceptance but contains additional or different terms which do not materially alter the terms of the offer constitutes an acceptance, unless the offeror, without undue delay, objects to the discrepancy. If the offeror does not object, the terms of the contract are the terms of the offer with the modifications contained in the acceptance.

ARTICLE 2.1.12

(Writings in confirmation)

If a writing which is sent within a reasonable time after the conclusion of the contract and which purports to be a confirmation of the contract contains additional or different terms, such terms become part of the contract, unless they materially alter the contract or the recipient, without undue delay, objects to the discrepancy.

ARTICLE 2.1.13

(Conclusion of contract dependent on agreement on specific matters or in a particular form)

When in the course of negotiations one of the parties insists that the contract is not concluded until there is agreement on specific matters or in a particular form, no contract is concluded before agreement is reached on those matters or in that form.

ARTICLE 2.1.14

(Contract with terms deliberately left open)

(1) If the parties intend to conclude a contract, the fact that they intentionally leave a term to be agreed upon in further negotiations or to be determined by one of the parties or a third person does not prevent a contract from coming into existence.

(2) The existence of the contract is not affected by the fact that subsequently

   (a) the parties reach no agreement on the term;

   (b) the party who is to determine the term does not do so; or

   (c) the third person does not determine the term,

provided that there is an alternative means of rendering the term definite that is reasonable in the circumstances, having regard to the intention of the parties.

ARTICLE 2.1.15

(Negotiations in bad faith)

(1) A part is free to negotiate and is not liable for failure to reach an agreement.

(2) However, a party who negotiates or breaks off negotiations in bad faith is liable for the losses caused to the other party.

(3) It is bad faith, in particular, for a party to enter into or continue negotiations when intending not to reach an agreement with the other party.

ARTICLE 2.1.16

(Duty of confidentiality)

Where information is given as confidential by one party in the course of negotiations, the other party is under a duty not to disclose that information or to use it improperly for its own purposes, whether or not a contract is subsequently concluded. Where appropriate, the remedy for breach of that duty may include compensation based on the benefit received by the other party.

ARTICLE 2.1.17

(Merger clauses)

A contract in writing which contains a clause indicating that the writing completely embodies the terms on which the parties have agreed cannot be contradicted or supplemented by evidence of prior statements or agreements. However, such statements or agreements may be used to interpret the writing.

ARTICLE 2.1.18

(Modification in a particular form)

A contract in writing which contains a clause requiring any modification or termination by agreement to be in a particular form may not be otherwise modified or terminated. However, a party may be precluded by its conduct from asserting such a clause to the extent that the other party has reasonably acted in reliance on that conduct.

ARTICLE 2.1.19

(Contracting under standard terms)

(1) Where one party or both parties use standard terms in concluding a contract, the general rules on formation apply, subject to Articles 2.1.20–2.1.22.

(2) Standard terms are provisions which are prepared in advance for general and repeated use by one party and which are actually used without negotiation with the other party.

ARTICLE 2.1.20

(Surprising terms)

(1) No term contained in standard terms which is of such a character that the other party could not reasonably have expected it, is effective unless it has been expressly accepted by that party.

(2) In determining whether a term is of such a character regard shall be had to its content, language and presentation.

ARTICLE 2.1.21

(Conflict between standard terms and non-standard terms)

In case of conflict between a standard term and a term which is not a standard term the latter prevails.

ARTICLE 2.1.22

(Battle of forms)

Where both parties use standard terms and reach agreement except on those terms, a contract is concluded on the basis of the agreed terms and of any standard terms which are common in substance unless one party clearly indicates in advance, or later and without undue delay informs the other party, that it does not intend to be bound by such a contract. . . .

CHAPTER 3—VALIDITY

SECTION 1: GENERAL PROVISIONS

ARTICLE 3.1.1

(Matters not covered)

This Chapter does not deal with lack of capacity.

. . .

1. No need for consideration

In common law systems, "consideration" is traditionally seen as a prerequisite for the validity or enforceability of a contract, as well as for the modification or termination of a contract by the parties.

However, in commercial dealings this requirement is of minimal practical importance since in that context obligations are almost always undertaken by both parties. It is for this reason that Article 29(1) CISG dispenses with the requirement of consideration in relation to the modification and termination by the parties of contracts for the international sale of goods. The fact that this Article extends this approach to the conclusion, modification and termination by the parties of international commercial contracts in general can only bring about greater certainty and reduce litigation.

2. No need for *cause*

This Article also excludes the requirement of *"cause"* which exists in some civil law systems and is in certain respects functionally similar to the common law "consideration".

. . .

ARTICLE 3.1.3

(Initial impossibility)

(1) The mere fact that at the time of the conclusion of the contract the performance of the obligation assumed was impossible does not affect the validity of the contract.

(2) The mere fact that at the time of the conclusion of the contract a party was not entitled to dispose of the assets to which the contract relates does not affect the validity of the contract.

ARTICLE 3.1.4

(Mandatory character of the provisions)

The provisions on fraud, threat, gross disparity and illegality contained in this Chapter are mandatory.

SECTION 2: GROUNDS FOR AVOIDANCE

ARTICLE 3.2.1

(Definition of mistake)

Mistake is an erroneous assumption relating to facts or to law existing when the contract was concluded.

ARTICLE 3.2.2

(Relevant mistake)

(1) A party may only avoid the contract for mistake if, when the contract was concluded, the mistake was of such importance that a reasonable person in the same situation as the party in error would only have concluded the contract on materially different terms or would not have concluded it at all if the true state of affairs had been known, and

    (a) the other party made the same mistake, or caused the mistake, or knew or ought to have known of the mistake and it was contrary to reasonable commercial standards of fair dealing to leave the mistaken party in error; or

    (b) the other party had not at the time of avoidance reasonably acted in reliance on the contract.

(2) However, a party may not avoid the contract if

    (a) it was grossly negligent in committing the mistake; or

    (b) the mistake relates to a matter in regard to which the risk of mistake was assumed or, having regard to the circumstances, should be borne by the mistaken party.

ARTICLE 3.2.3

(Error in expression or transmission)

An error occurring in the expression or transmission of a declaration is considered to be a mistake of the person from whom the declaration emanated.

ARTICLE 3.2.4

(Remedies for non-performance)

A party is not entitled to avoid the contract on the ground of mistake if the circumstances on which that party relies afford, or could have afforded, a remedy for non-performance.

ARTICLE 3.2.5

(Fraud)

A party may avoid the contract when it has been led to conclude the contract by the other party's fraudulent representation, including language or practices, or fraudulent non-disclosure of circumstances which, according to reasonable commercial standards of fair dealing, the latter party should have disclosed.

ARTICLE 3.2.6

(Threat)

A party may avoid the contract when it has been led to conclude the contract by the other party's unjustified threat which, having regard to the circumstances, is so imminent and serious as to leave the first party no reasonable alternative. In particular, a threat is unjustified if the act or omission with which a party has been threatened is wrongful in itself, or it is wrongful to use it as a means to obtain the conclusion of the contract. . . .

ARTICLE 3.2.8

(Third persons)

(1) Where fraud, threat, gross disparity or a party's mistake is imputable to, or is known or ought to be known by, a third person for whose acts the other party is responsible, the contract may be avoided under the same conditions as if the behaviour or knowledge had been that of the party itself.

(2) Where fraud, threat or gross disparity is imputable to a third person for whose acts the other party is not responsible, the contract may be avoided if that party knew or ought to have known of the fraud, threat or disparity, or has not at the time of avoidance reasonably acted in reliance on the contract.

ARTICLE 3.2.9

(Confirmation)

If the party entitled to avoid the contract expressly or impliedly confirms the contract after the period of time for giving notice of avoidance has begun to run, avoidance of the contract is excluded.

ARTICLE 3.2.10

(Loss of right to avoid)

(1) If a party is entitled to avoid the contract for mistake but the other party declares itself willing to perform or performs the contract as it was understood by the party entitled to avoidance, the contract is considered to have been concluded as the latter party understood it. The other party

must make such a declaration or render such performance promptly after having been informed of the manner in which the party entitled to avoidance had understood the contract and before that party has reasonably acted in reliance on a notice of avoidance.

(2) After such a declaration or performance the right to avoidance is lost and any earlier notice of avoidance is ineffective.

ARTICLE 3.2.11

(Notice of avoidance)

The right of a party to avoid the contract is exercised by notice to the other party.

ARTICLE 3.2.12

(Time limits)

(1) Notice of avoidance shall be given within a reasonable time, having regard to the circumstances, after the avoiding party knew or could not have been unaware of the relevant facts or became capable of acting freely.

(2) Where an individual term of the contract may be avoided by a party under Article 3.2.7, the period of time for giving notice of avoidance begins to run when that term is asserted by the other party.

ARTICLE 3.2.13

(Partial avoidance)

Where a ground of avoidance affects only individual terms of the contract, the effect of avoidance is limited to those terms unless, having regard to the circumstances, it is unreasonable to uphold the remaining contract.

ARTICLE 3.2.14

(Retroactive effect of avoidance)

Avoidance takes effect retroactively.

ARTICLE 3.2.15

(Restitution)

(1) On avoidance either party may claim restitution of whatever it has supplied under the contract, or the part of it avoided, provided that such party concurrently makes restitution of whatever it has received under the contract, or the part of it avoided.

(2) If restitution in kind is not possible or appropriate, an allowance has to be made in money whenever reasonable.

(3) The recipient of the performance does not have to make an allowance in money if the impossibility to make restitution in kind is attributable to the other party.

(4) Compensation may be claimed for expenses reasonably required to preserve or maintain the performance received.

ARTICLE 3.2.16

(Damages)

Irrespective of whether or not the contract has been avoided, the party who knew or ought to have known of the ground for avoidance is liable for damages so as to put the other party in the same position in which it would have been if it had not concluded the contract.

ARTICLE 3.2.17

(Unilateral declarations)

The provisions of this Chapter apply with appropriate adaptations to any communication of intention addressed by one party to the other.

SECTION 3: ILLEGALITY

ARTICLE 3.3.1

(Contracts infringing mandatory rules)

(1) Where a contract infringes a mandatory rule, whether of national, international or supranational origin, applicable under Article 1.4 of these Principles, the effects of that infringement upon the contract are the effects, if any, expressly prescribed by that mandatory rule.

(2) Where the mandatory rule does not expressly prescribe the effects of an infringement upon a contract, the parties have the right to exercise such remedies under the contract as in the circumstances are reasonable.

(3) In determining what is reasonable regard is to be had in particular to:

   (a) the purpose of the rule which has been infringed;
   (b) the category of persons for whose protection the rule exists;
   (c) any sanction that may be imposed under the rule infringed;
   (d) the seriousness of the infringement;
   (e) whether one or both parties knew or ought to have known of the infringement;
   (f) whether the performance of the contract necessitates the infringement; and
   (g) the parties' reasonable expectations.

ARTICLE 3.3.2

(Restitution)

(1) Where there has been performance under a contract infringing a mandatory rule under Article 3.3.1, restitution may be granted where this would be reasonable in the circumstances.

(2) In determining what is reasonable, regard is to be had, with the appropriate adaptations, to the criteria referred to in Article 3.3.1(3).

(3) If restitution is granted, the rules set out in Article 3.2.15 apply with appropriate adaptations.

CHAPTER 4—INTERPRETATION

ARTICLE 4.1

(Intention of the parties)

(1) A contract shall be interpreted according to the common intention of the parties.

(2) If such an intention cannot be established, the contract shall be interpreted according to the meaning that reasonable persons of the same kind as the parties would give to it in the same circumstances.

ARTICLE 4.2

(Interpretation of statements and other conduct)

(1) The statements and other conduct of a party shall be interpreted according to that party's intention if the other party knew or could not have been unaware of that intention.

(2) If the preceding paragraph is not applicable, such statements and other conduct shall be interpreted according to the meaning that a reasonable person of the same kind as the other party would give to it in the same circumstances.

ARTICLE 4.3

(Relevant circumstances)

In applying Articles 4.1 and 4.2, regard shall be had to all the circumstances, including

(a) preliminary negotiations between the parties;

(b) practices which the parties have established between themselves;

(c) the conduct of the parties subsequent to the conclusion of the contract;

(d) the nature and purpose of the contract;

(e) the meaning commonly given to terms and expressions in the trade concerned;

(f) usages.

ARTICLE 4.4

(Reference to contract or statement as a whole)

Terms and expressions shall be interpreted in the light of the whole contract or statement in which they appear.

ARTICLE 4.5

(All terms to be given effect)

Contract terms shall be interpreted so as to give effect to all the terms rather than to deprive some of them of effect.

ARTICLE 4.6

(Contra proferentem rule)

If contract terms supplied by one party are unclear, an interpretation against that party is preferred.

ARTICLE 4.7

(Linguistic discrepancies)

Where a contract is drawn up in two or more language versions which are equally authoritative there is, in case of discrepancy between the versions, a preference for the interpretation according to a version in which the contract was originally drawn up.

ARTICLE 4.8

(Supplying an omitted term)

(1) Where the parties to a contract have not agreed with respect to a term which is important for a determination of their rights and duties, a term which is appropriate in the circumstances shall be supplied.

(2) In determining what is an appropriate term regard shall be had, among other factors, to

  (a) the intention of the parties;

  (b) the nature and purpose of the contract;

  (c) good faith and fair dealing;

  (d) reasonableness.

CHAPTER 5—CONTENT AND THIRD PARTY RIGHTS

SECTION 1: CONTENT

ARTICLE 5.1.1

(Express and implied obligations)

The contractual obligations of the parties may be express or implied.

ARTICLE 5.1.2

(Implied obligations)

Implied obligations stem from

  (a) the nature and purpose of the contract;

  (b) practices established between the parties and usages;

  (c) good faith and fair dealing;

  (d) reasonableness.

ARTICLE 5.1.3

(Co-operation between the parties)

Each party shall co-operate with the other party when such co-operation may reasonably be expected for the performance of that party's obligations.

ARTICLE 5.1.4

(Duty to achieve a specific result; Duty of best efforts)

(1) To the extent that an obligation of a party involves a duty to achieve a specific result, that party is bound to achieve that result.

(2) To the extent that an obligation of a party involves a duty of best efforts in the performance of an activity, that party is bound to make such efforts as would be made by a reasonable person of the same kind in the same circumstances.

ARTICLE 5.1.5

(Determination of kind of duty involved)

In determining the extent to which an obligation of a party involves a duty of best efforts in the performance of an activity or a duty to achieve a specific result, regard shall be had, among other factors, to

(a) the way in which the obligation is expressed in the contract;

(b) the contractual price and other terms of the contract;

(c) the degree of risk normally involved in achieving the expected result;

(d) the ability of the other party to influence the performance of the obligation.

ARTICLE 5.1.6

(Determination of quality of performance)

Where the quality of performance is neither fixed by, nor determinable from, the contract a party is bound to render a performance of a quality that is reasonable and not less than average in the circumstances.

ARTICLE 5.1.7

(Price determination)

(1) Where a contract does not fix or make provision for determining the price, the parties are considered, in the absence of any indication to the contrary, to have made reference to the price generally charged at the time of the conclusion of the contract for such performance in comparable circumstances in the trade concerned or, if no such price is available, to a reasonable price.

(2) Where the price is to be determined by one party and that determination is manifestly unreasonable, a reasonable price shall be substituted notwithstanding any contract term to the contrary.

(3) Where the price is to be fixed by one party or a third person, and that party or the third person cannot or will not do so, the price shall be a reasonable price.

(4) Where the price is to be fixed by reference to factors which do not exist or have ceased to exist or to be accessible, the nearest equivalent factor shall be treated as a substitute.

ARTICLE 5.1.8

(Termination of a contract for an indefinite period)

A contract for an indefinite period may be ended by either party by giving notice a reasonable time in advance. As to the effects of termination in general, and as to restitution, the provisions in Articles 7.3.5 and 7.3.7 apply.

ARTICLE 5.1.9

(Release by agreement)

(1) An obligee may release its right by agreement with the obligor.

(2) An offer to release a right gratuitously shall be deemed accepted if the obligor does not reject the offer without delay after having become aware of it.

UNIDROIT PRINCIPLES

SECTION 2: THIRD PARTY RIGHTS

ARTICLE 5.2.1

(Contracts in favour of third parties)

(1) The parties (the "promisor" and the "promisee") may confer by express or implied agreement a right on a third party (the "beneficiary").

(2) The existence and content of the beneficiary's right against the promisor are determined by the agreement of the parties and are subject to any conditions or other limitations under the agreement.

ARTICLE 5.2.2

(Third party identifiable)

The beneficiary must be identifiable with adequate certainty by the contract but need not be in existence at the time the contract is made.

ARTICLE 5.2.3

(Exclusion and limitation clauses)

The conferment of rights in the beneficiary includes the right to invoke a clause in the contract which excludes or limits the liability of the beneficiary.

ARTICLE 5.2.4

(Defences)

The promisor may assert against the beneficiary all defences which the promisor could assert against the promisee.

ARTICLE 5.2.5

(Revocation)

The parties may modify or revoke the rights conferred by the contract on the beneficiary until the beneficiary has accepted them or reasonably acted in reliance on them.

ARTICLE 5.2.6

(Renunciation)

The beneficiary may renounce a right conferred on it.

CHAPTER 6—PERFORMANCE

SECTION 1: PERFORMANCE IN GENERAL

ARTICLE 6.1.1

(Time of performance)

A party must perform its obligations:

    (a) if a time is fixed by or determinable from the contract, at that time;

    (b) if a period of time is fixed by or determinable from the contract, at any time within that period unless circumstances indicate that the other party is to choose a time;

(c) in any other case, within a reasonable time after the conclusion of the contract.

ARTICLE 6.1.2

(Performance at one time or in instalments)

In cases under Article 6.1.1(b) or (c), a party must perform its obligations at one time if that performance can be rendered at one time and the circumstances do not indicate otherwise.

ARTICLE 6.1.3

(Partial performance)

(1) The obligee may reject an offer to perform in part at the time performance is due, whether or not such offer is coupled with an assurance as to the balance of the performance, unless the obligee has no legitimate interest in so doing.

(2) Additional expenses caused to the obligee by partial performance are to be borne by the obligor without prejudice to any other remedy.

ARTICLE 6.1.4

(Order of performance)

(1) To the extent that the performances of the parties can be rendered simultaneously, the parties are bound to render them simultaneously unless the circumstances indicate otherwise.

(2) To the extent that the performance of only one party requires a period of time, that party is bound to render its performance first, unless the circumstances indicate otherwise.

ARTICLE 6.1.5

(Earlier performance)

(1) The obligee may reject an earlier performance unless it has no legitimate interest in so doing.

(2) Acceptance by a party of an earlier performance does not affect the time for the performance of its own obligations if that time has been fixed irrespective of the performance of the other party's obligations.

(3) Additional expenses caused to the obligee by earlier performance are to be borne by the obligor, without prejudice to any other remedy.

ARTICLE 6.1.6

(Place of performance)

(1) If the place of performance is neither fixed by, nor determinable from, the contract, a party is to perform:

(a) a monetary obligation, at the obligee's place of business;

(b) any other obligation, at its own place of business.

(2) A party must bear any increase in the expenses incidental to performance which is caused by a change in its place of business subsequent to the conclusion of the contract.

ARTICLE 6.1.7

(Payment by [check] or other instrument)

(1) Payment may be made in any form used in the ordinary course of business at the place for payment.

(2) However, an obligee who accepts, either by virtue of paragraph (1) or voluntarily, a [check], any other order to pay or a promise to pay, is presumed to do so only on condition that it will be [honored].

ARTICLE 6.1.8

(Payment by funds transfer)

(1) Unless the obligee has indicated a particular account, payment may be made by a transfer to any of the financial institutions in which the obligee has made it known that it has an account.

(2) In case of payment by a transfer the obligation of the obligor is discharged when the transfer to the obligee's financial institution becomes effective.

ARTICLE 6.1.9

(Currency of payment)

(1) If a monetary obligation is expressed in a currency other than that of the place for payment, it may be paid by the obligor in the currency of the place for payment unless

  (a) that currency is not freely convertible; or

  (b) the parties have agreed that payment should be made only in the currency in which the monetary obligation is expressed.

(2) If it is impossible for the obligor to make payment in the currency in which the monetary obligation is expressed, the obligee may require payment in the currency of the place for payment, even in the case referred to in paragraph (1)(b).

(3) Payment in the currency of the place for payment is to be made according to the applicable rate of exchange prevailing there when payment is due.

(4) However, if the obligor has not paid at the time when payment is due, the obligee may require payment according to the applicable rate of exchange prevailing either when payment is due or at the time of actual payment.

ARTICLE 6.1.10

(Currency not expressed)

Where a monetary obligation is not expressed in a particular currency, payment must be made in the currency of the place where payment is to be made.

ARTICLE 6.1.11

(Costs of performance)

Each party shall bear the costs of performance of its obligations.

ARTICLE 6.1.12

(Imputation of payments)

(1) An obligor owing several monetary obligations to the same obligee may specify at the time of payment the debt to which it intends the payment to be applied. However, the payment discharges first any expenses, then interest due and finally the principal.

(2) If the obligor makes no such specification, the obligee may, within a reasonable time after payment, declare to the obligor the obligation to which it imputes the payment, provided that the obligation is due and undisputed.

(3) In the absence of imputation under paragraphs (1) or (2), payment is imputed to that obligation which satisfies one of the following criteria and in the order indicated:

   (a) an obligation which is due or which is the first to fall due;

   (b) the obligation for which the obligee has least security;

   (c) the obligation which is the most burdensome for the obligor;

   (d) the obligation which has arisen first.

If none of the preceding criteria applies, payment is imputed to all the obligations proportionally.

ARTICLE 6.1.13

(Imputation of non-monetary obligations)

Article 6.1.12 applies with appropriate adaptations to the imputation of performance of non-monetary obligations.

ARTICLE 6.1.14

(Application for public permission)

Where the law of a State requires a public permission affecting the validity of the contract or its performance and neither that law nor the circumstances indicate otherwise

   (a) if only one party has its place of business in that State, that party shall take the measures necessary to obtain the permission;

   (b) in any other case the party whose performance requires permission shall take the necessary measures.

ARTICLE 6.1.15

(Procedure in applying for permission)

(1) The party required to take the measures necessary to obtain the permission shall do so without undue delay and shall bear any expenses incurred.

(2) That party shall whenever appropriate give the other party notice of the grant or refusal of such permission without undue delay.

ARTICLE 6.1.16

(Permission neither granted nor refused)

(1) If, notwithstanding the fact that the party responsible has taken all measures required, permission is neither granted nor refused within an agreed period or, where no period has been agreed, within a reasonable time from the conclusion of the contract, either party is entitled to terminate the contract.

(2) Where the permission affects some terms only, paragraph (1) does not apply if, having regard to the circumstances, it is reasonable to uphold the remaining contract even if the permission is refused.

ARTICLE 6.1.17

(Permission refused)

(1) The refusal of a permission affecting the validity of the contract renders the contract void. If the refusal affects the validity of some terms only, only such terms are void if, having regard to the circumstances, it is reasonable to uphold the remaining contract.

(2) Where the refusal of a permission renders the performance of the contract impossible in whole or in part, the rules on non-performance apply.

SECTION 2: HARDSHIP

ARTICLE 6.2.1

(Contract to be observed)

Where the performance of a contract becomes more onerous for one of the parties, that party is nevertheless bound to perform its obligations subject to the following provisions on hardship.

ARTICLE 6.2.2

(Definition of hardship)

There is hardship where the occurrence of events fundamentally alters the equilibrium of the contract either because the cost of a party's performance has increased or because the value of the performance a party receives has diminished, and

(a) the events occur or become known to the disadvantaged party after the conclusion of the contract;

(b) the events could not reasonably have been taken into account by the disadvantaged party at the time of the conclusion of the contract;

(c) the events are beyond the control of the disadvantaged party; and

(d) the risk of the events was not assumed by the disadvantaged party.

ARTICLE 6.2.3

(Effects of hardship)

(1) In case of hardship the disadvantaged party is entitled to request renegotiations. The request shall be made without undue delay and shall indicate the grounds on which it is based.

(2) The request for renegotiation does not in itself entitle the disadvantaged party to withhold performance.

(3) Upon failure to reach agreement within a reasonable time either party may resort to the court.

(4) If the court finds hardship it may, if reasonable,

(a) terminate the contract at a date and on terms to be fixed; or

(b) adapt the contract with a view to restoring its equilibrium.

CHAPTER 7—NON-PERFORMANCE

SECTION 1: NON-PERFORMANCE IN GENERAL

ARTICLE 7.1.1

(Non-performance defined)

Non-performance is failure by a party to perform any of its obligations under the contract, including defective performance or late performance.

ARTICLE 7.1.2

(Interference by the other party)

A party may not rely on the non-performance of the other party to the extent that such non-performance was caused by the first party's act or omission or by another event as to which the first party bears the risk.

ARTICLE 7.1.3

(Withholding performance)

(1) Where the parties are to perform simultaneously, either party may withhold performance until the other party tenders its performance.

(2) Where the parties are to perform consecutively, the party that is to perform later may withhold its performance until the first party has performed.

ARTICLE 7.1.4

(Cure by non-performing party)

(1) The non-performing party may, at its own expense, cure any non-performance, provided that

   (a) without undue delay, it gives notice indicating the proposed manner and timing of the cure;

   (b) cure is appropriate in the circumstances;

   (c) the aggrieved party has no legitimate interest in refusing cure; and

   (d) cure is effected promptly.

(2) The right to cure is not precluded by notice of termination.

(3) Upon effective notice of cure, rights of the aggrieved party that are inconsistent with the non-performing party's performance are suspended until the time for cure has expired.

(4) The aggrieved party may withhold performance pending cure.

(5) Notwithstanding cure, the aggrieved party retains the right to claim damages for delay as well as for any harm caused or not prevented by the cure.

ARTICLE 7.1.5

(Additional period for performance)

(1) In a case of non-performance the aggrieved party may by notice to the other party allow an additional period of time for performance.

(2) During the additional period the aggrieved party may withhold performance of its own reciprocal obligations and may claim damages but may not resort to any other remedy. If it receives notice from the other party that the latter will not perform within that period, or if upon expiry of that

period due performance has not been made, the aggrieved party may resort to any of the remedies that may be available under this Chapter.

(3) Where in a case of delay in performance which is not fundamental the aggrieved party has given notice allowing an additional period of time of reasonable length, it may terminate the contract at the end of that period. If the additional period allowed is not of reasonable length it shall be extended to a reasonable length. The aggrieved party may in its notice provide that if the other party fails to perform within the period allowed by the notice the contract shall automatically terminate.

(4) Paragraph (3) does not apply where the obligation which has not been performed is only a minor part of the contractual obligation of the non-performing party.

ARTICLE 7.1.6

(Exemption clauses)

A clause which limits or excludes one party's liability for non-performance or which permits one party to render performance substantially different from what the other party reasonably expected may not be invoked if it would be grossly unfair to do so, having regard to the purpose of the contract.

ARTICLE 7.1.7

(Force majeure)

(1) Non-performance by a party is excused if that party proves that the non-performance was due to an impediment beyond its control and that it could not reasonably be expected to have taken the impediment into account at the time of the conclusion of the contract or to have avoided or overcome it or its consequences.

(2) When the impediment is only temporary, the excuse shall have effect for such period as is reasonable having regard to the effect of the impediment on the performance of the contract.

(3) The party who fails to perform must give notice to the other party of the impediment and its effect on its ability to perform. If the notice is not received by the other party within a reasonable time after the party who fails to perform knew or ought to have known of the impediment, it is liable for damages resulting from such non-receipt.

(4) Nothing in this article prevents a party from exercising a right to terminate the contract or to withhold performance or request interest on money due.

SECTION 2: RIGHT TO PERFORMANCE

ARTICLE 7.2.1

(Performance of monetary obligation)

Where a party who is obliged to pay money does not do so, the other party may require payment.

ARTICLE 7.2.2

(Performance of non-monetary obligation)

Where a party who owes an obligation other than one to pay money does not perform, the other party may require performance, unless

    (a) performance is impossible in law or in fact;

    (b) performance or, where relevant, enforcement is unreasonably burdensome or expensive;

    (c) the party entitled to performance may reasonably obtain performance from another source;

(d) performance is of an exclusively personal character; or

(e) the party entitled to performance does not require performance within a reasonable time after it has, or ought to have, become aware of the non-performance.

ARTICLE 7.2.3

(Repair and replacement of defective performance)

The right to performance includes in appropriate cases the right to require repair, replacement, or other cure of defective performance. The provisions of Articles 7.2.1 and 7.2.2 apply accordingly.

ARTICLE 7.2.4

(Judicial penalty)

(1) Where the court orders a party to perform, it may also direct that this party pay a penalty if it does not comply with the order.

(2) The penalty shall be paid to the aggrieved party unless mandatory provisions of the law of the forum provide otherwise. Payment of the penalty to the aggrieved party does not exclude any claim for damages.

ARTICLE 7.2.5

(Change of remedy)

(1) An aggrieved party who has required performance of a non-monetary obligation and who has not received performance within a period fixed or otherwise within a reasonable period of time may invoke any other remedy.

(2) Where the decision of a court for performance of a non-monetary obligation cannot be enforced, the aggrieved party may invoke any other remedy.

SECTION 3: TERMINATION

ARTICLE 7.3.1

(Right to terminate the contract)

(1) A party may terminate the contract where the failure of the other party to perform an obligation under the contract amounts to a fundamental non-performance.

(2) In determining whether a failure to perform an obligation amounts to a fundamental non-performance regard shall be had, in particular, to whether

(a) the non-performance substantially deprives the aggrieved party of what it was entitled to expect under the contract unless the other party did not foresee and could not reasonably have foreseen such result;

(b) strict compliance with the obligation which has not been performed is of essence under the contract;

(c) the non-performance is intentional or reckless;

(d) the non-performance gives the aggrieved party reason to believe that it cannot rely on the other party's future performance;

(e) the non-performing party will suffer disproportionate loss as a result of the preparation or performance if the contract is terminated.

(3) In the case of delay the aggrieved party may also terminate the contract if the other party fails to perform before the time allowed it under Article 7.1.5 has expired.

ARTICLE 7.3.2

(Notice of termination)

(1) The right of a party to terminate the contract is exercised by notice to the other party.

(2) If performance has been offered late or otherwise does not conform to the contract the aggrieved party will lose its right to terminate the contract unless it gives notice to the other party within a reasonable time after it has or ought to have become aware of the offer or of the non-conforming performance.

ARTICLE 7.3.3

(Anticipatory non-performance)

Where prior to the date for performance by one of the parties it is clear that there will be a fundamental non-performance by that party, the other party may terminate the contract.

ARTICLE 7.3.4

(Adequate assurance of due performance)

A party who reasonably believes that there will be a fundamental non-performance by the other party may demand adequate assurance of due performance and may meanwhile withhold its own performance. Where this assurance is not provided within a reasonable time the party demanding it may terminate the contract.

ARTICLE 7.3.5

(Effects of termination in general)

(1) Termination of the contract releases both parties from their obligation to effect and to receive future performance.

(2) Termination does not preclude a claim for damages for non-performance.

(3) Termination does not affect any provision in the contract for the settlement of disputes or any other term of the contract which is to operate even after termination.

ARTICLE 7.3.6

(Restitution with respect to contracts to be performed at one time)

(1) On termination of a contract to be performed at one time either party may claim restitution of whatever it has supplied under the contract, provided that such party concurrently makes restitution of whatever it has received under the contract.

(2) If restitution in kind is not possible or appropriate, an allowance has to be made in money whenever reasonable.

(3) The recipient of the performance does not have to make an allowance in money if the impossibility to make restitution in kind is attributable to the other party.

(4) Compensation may be claimed for expenses reasonably required to preserve or maintain the performance received.

ARTICLE 7.3.7

(Restitution with respect to long-term contracts)

(1) On termination of a long-term contract restitution can only be claimed for the period after termination has taken effect, provided the contract is divisible.

(2) As far as restitution has to be made, the provisions of Article 7.3.6 apply.

SECTION 4: DAMAGES

ARTICLE 7.4.1

(Right to damages)

Any non-performance gives the aggrieved party a right to damages either exclusively or in conjunction with any other remedies except where the non-performance is excused under these Principles.

ARTICLE 7.4.2

(Full compensation)

(1) The aggrieved party is entitled to full compensation for harm sustained as a result of the non-performance. Such harm includes both any loss which it suffered and any gain of which it was deprived, taking into account any gain to the aggrieved party resulting from its avoidance of cost or harm.

(2) Such harm may be non-pecuniary and includes, for instance, physical suffering or emotional distress.

ARTICLE 7.4.3

(Certainty of harm)

(1) Compensation is due only for harm, including future harm, that is established with a reasonable degree of certainty.

(2) Compensation may be due for the loss of a chance in proportion to the probability of its occurrence.

(3) Where the amount of damages cannot be established with a sufficient degree of certainty, the assessment is at the discretion of the court.

ARTICLE 7.4.4

(Foreseeability of harm)

The non-performing party is liable only for harm which it foresaw or could reasonably have foreseen at the time of the conclusion of the contract as being likely to result from its non-performance.

ARTICLE 7.4.5

(Proof of harm in case of replacement transaction)

Where the aggrieved party has terminated the contract and has made a replacement transaction within a reasonable time and in a reasonable manner it may recover the difference between the contract price and the price of the replacement transaction as well as damages for any further harm.

ARTICLE 7.4.6

(Proof of harm by current price)

(1) Where the aggrieved party has terminated the contract and has not made a replacement transaction but there is a current price for the performance contracted for, it may recover the difference between the contract price and the price current at the time the contract is terminated as well as damages for any further harm.

(2) Current price is the price generally charged for goods delivered or services rendered in comparable circumstances at the place where the contract should have been performed or, if there is no current price at that place, the current price at such other place that appears reasonable to take as a reference.

ARTICLE 7.4.7

(Harm due in part to aggrieved party)

Where the harm is due in part to an act or omission of the aggrieved party or to another event as to which that party bears the risk, the amount of damages shall be reduced to the extent that these factors have contributed to the harm, having regard to the conduct of each of the parties.

ARTICLE 7.4.8

(Mitigation of harm)

(1) The non-performing party is not liable for harm suffered by the aggrieved party to the extent that the harm could have been reduced by the latter party's taking reasonable steps.

(2) The aggrieved party is entitled to recover any expenses reasonably incurred in attempting to reduce the harm.

ARTICLE 7.4.9

(Interest for failure to pay money)

(1) If a party does not pay a sum of money when it falls due the aggrieved party is entitled to interest upon that sum from the time when payment is due to the time of payment whether or not the non-payment is excused.

(2) The rate of interest shall be the average bank short-term lending rate to prime borrowers prevailing for the currency of payment at the place for payment, or where no such rate exists at that place, then the same rate in the State of the currency of payment. In the absence of such a rate at either place the rate of interest shall be the appropriate rate fixed by the law of the State of the currency of payment.

(3) The aggrieved party is entitled to additional damages if the non-payment caused it a greater harm.

ARTICLE 7.4.10

(Interest on damages)

Unless otherwise agreed, interest on damages for non-performance of non-monetary obligations accrues as from the time of non-performance.

ARTICLE 7.4.11

(Manner of monetary redress)

(1) Damages are to be paid in a lump sum. However, they may be payable in instalments where the nature of the harm makes this appropriate.

(2) Damages to be paid in instalments may be indexed.

ARTICLE 7.4.12

(Currency in which to assess damages)

Damages are to be assessed either in the currency in which the monetary obligation was expressed or in the currency in which the harm was suffered, whichever is more appropriate.

ARTICLE 7.4.13

(Agreed payment for non-performance)

(1) Where the contract provides that a party who does not perform is to pay a specified sum to the aggrieved party for such non-performance, the aggrieved party is entitled to that sum irrespective of its actual harm.

(2) However, notwithstanding any agreement to the contrary the specified sum may be reduced to a reasonable amount where it is grossly excessive in relation to the harm resulting from the non-performance and to the other circumstances. . . .

CHAPTER 9—ASSIGNMENT OF RIGHTS, TRANSFER OF OBLIGATIONS, ASSIGNMENT OF CONTRACTS

SECTION 1: ASSIGNMENT OF RIGHTS

ARTICLE 9.1.1

(Definitions)

"Assignment of a right" means the transfer by agreement from one person (the "assignor") to another person (the "assignee"), including transfer by way of security, of the assignor's right to payment of a monetary sum or other performance from a third person ("the obligor").

ARTICLE 9.1.2

(Exclusions)

This Section does not apply to transfers made under the special rules governing the transfers:

(a) of instruments such as negotiable instruments, documents of title or financial instruments, or

(b) of rights in the course of transferring a business.

ARTICLE 9.1.3

(Assignability of non-monetary rights)

A right to non-monetary performance may be assigned only if the assignment does not render the obligation significantly more burdensome.

ARTICLE 9.1.4

(Partial assignment)

(1) A right to the payment of a monetary sum may be assigned partially.

(2) A right to other performance may be assigned partially only if it is divisible, and the assignment does not render the obligation significantly more burdensome.

ARTICLE 9.1.5

(Future rights)

A future right is deemed to be transferred at the time of the agreement, provided the right, when it comes into existence, can be identified as the right to which the assignment relates.

ARTICLE 9.1.6

(Rights assigned without individual specification)

A number of rights may be assigned without individual specification, provided such rights can be identified as rights to which the assignment relates at the time of the assignment or when they come into existence.

ARTICLE 9.1.7

(Agreement between assignor and assignee sufficient)

(1) A right is assigned by mere agreement between the assignor and the assignee, without notice to the obligor.

(2) The consent of the obligor is not required unless the obligation in the circumstances is of an essentially personal character.

ARTICLE 9.1.8

(Obligor's additional costs)

The obligor has a right to be compensated by the assignor or the assignee for any additional costs caused by the assignment.

ARTICLE 9.1.9

(Non-assignment clauses)

(1) The assignment of a right to the payment of a monetary sum is effective notwithstanding an agreement between the assignor and the obligor limiting or prohibiting such an assignment. However, the assignor may be liable to the obligor for breach of contract.

(2) The assignment of a right to other performance is ineffective if it is contrary to an agreement between the assignor and the obligor limiting or prohibiting the assignment. Nevertheless, the assignment is effective if the assignee, at the time of the assignment, neither knew nor ought to have known of the agreement. The assignor may then be liable to the obligor for breach of contract.

ARTICLE 9.1.10

(Notice to the obligor)

(1) Until the obligor receives a notice of the assignment from either the assignor or the assignee, it is discharged by paying the assignor.

(2) After the obligor receives such a notice, it is discharged only by paying the assignee.

ARTICLE 9.1.11

(Successive assignments)

If the same right has been assigned by the same assignor to two or more successive assignees, the obligor is discharged by paying according to the order in which the notices were received.

ARTICLE 9.1.12

(Adequate proof of assignment)

(1) If notice of the assignment is given by the assignee, the obligor may request the assignee to provide within a reasonable time adequate proof that the assignment has been made.

(2) Until adequate proof is provided, the obligor may withhold payment.

(3) Unless adequate proof is provided, notice is not effective.

(4) Adequate proof includes, but is not limited to, any writing emanating from the assignor and indicating that the assignment has taken place.

ARTICLE 9.1.13

(Defences and rights of set-off)

(1) The obligor may assert against the assignee all defences that the obligor could assert against the assignor.

(2) The obligor may exercise against the assignee any right of set-off available to the obligor against the assignor up to the time notice of assignment was received.

ARTICLE 9.1.14

(Rights related to the right assigned)

The assignment of a right transfers to the assignee:

(a) all the assignor's rights to payment or other performance under the contract in respect of the right assigned, and

(b) all rights securing performance of the right assigned.

ARTICLE 9.1.15

(Undertakings of the assignor)

The assignor undertakes towards the assignee, except as otherwise disclosed to the assignee, that:

(a) the assigned right exists at the time of the assignment, unless the right is a future right;

(b) the assignor is entitled to assign the right;

(c) the right has not been previously assigned to another assignee, and it is free from any right or claim from a third party;

(d) the obligor does not have any defences;

(e) neither the obligor nor the assignor has given notice of set-off concerning the assigned right and will not give any such notice;

(f) the assignor will reimburse the assignee for any payment received from the obligor before notice of the assignment was given.

SECTION 2: TRANSFER OF OBLIGATIONS

ARTICLE 9.2.1

(Modes of transfer)

An obligation to pay money or render other performance may be transferred from one person (the "original obligor") to another person (the "new obligor") either

(a) by an agreement between the original obligor and the new obligor subject to Article 9.2.3, or

(b) by an agreement between the obligee and the new obligor, by which the new obligor assumes the obligation.

ARTICLE 9.2.2

(Exclusion)

This Section does not apply to transfers of obligations made under the special rules governing transfers of obligations in the course of transferring a business.

ARTICLE 9.2.3

(Requirement of obligee's consent to transfer)

The transfer of an obligation by an agreement between the original obligor and the new obligor requires the consent of the obligee.

ARTICLE 9.2.4

(Advance consent of obligee)

(1) The obligee may give its consent in advance.

(2) If the obligee has given its consent in advance, the transfer of the obligation becomes effective when a notice of the transfer is given to the obligee or when the obligee acknowledges it.

ARTICLE 9.2.5

(Discharge of original obligor)

(1) The obligee may discharge the original obligor.

(2) The obligee may also retain the original obligor as an obligor in case the new obligor does not perform properly.

(3) Otherwise the original obligor and the new obligor are jointly and severally liable.

ARTICLE 9.2.6

(Third party performance)

(1) Without the obligee's consent, the obligor may contract with another person that this person will perform the obligation in place of the obligor, unless the obligation in the circumstances has an essentially personal character.

(2) The obligee retains its claim against the obligor.

ARTICLE 9.2.7

(Defences and rights of set-off)

(1) The new obligor may assert against the obligee all defences which the original obligor could assert against the obligee.

(2) The new obligor may not exercise against the obligee any right of set-off available to the original obligor against the obligee.

ARTICLE 9.2.8

(Rights related to the obligation transferred)

(1) The obligee may assert against the new obligor all its rights to payment or other performance under the contract in respect of the obligation transferred.

(2) If the original obligor is discharged under Article 9.2.5(1), a security granted by any person other than the new obligor for the performance of the obligation is discharged, unless that other person agrees that it should continue to be available to the obligee.

(3) Discharge of the original obligor also extends to any security of the original obligor given to the obligee for the performance of the obligation, unless the security is over an asset which is transferred as part of a transaction between the original obligor and the new obligor.

SECTION 3: ASSIGNMENT OF CONTRACTS

ARTICLE 9.3.1

(Definitions)

"Assignment of a contract" means the transfer by agreement from one person (the "assignor") to another person (the "assignee") of the assignor's rights and obligations arising out of a contract with another person (the "other party").

ARTICLE 9.3.2

(Exclusion)

This Section does not apply to the assignment of contracts made under the special rules governing transfers of contracts in the course of transferring a business.

ARTICLE 9.3.3

(Requirement of consent of the other party)

The assignment of a contract requires the consent of the other party.

ARTICLE 9.3.4

(Advance consent of the other party)

(1) The other party may give its consent in advance.

(2) If the other party has given its consent in advance, the assignment of the contract becomes effective when a notice of the assignment is given to the other party or when the other party acknowledges it.

ARTICLE 9.3.5

(Discharge of the assignor)

(1) The other party may discharge the assignor.

(2) The other party may also retain the assignor as an obligor in case the assignee does not perform properly.

(3) Otherwise the assignor and the assignee are jointly and severally liable.

ARTICLE 9.3.6

(Defences and rights of set-off)

(1) To the extent that the assignment of a contract involves an assignment of rights, Article 9.1.13 applies accordingly.

(2) To the extent that the assignment of a contract involves a transfer of obligations, Article 9.2.7 applies accordingly.

ARTICLE 9.3.7

(Rights transferred with the contract)

(1) To the extent that the assignment of a contract involves an assignment of rights, Article 9.1.14 applies accordingly.

(2) To the extent that the assignment of a contract involves a transfer of obligations, Article 9.2.8 applies accordingly. . . .

INTERNATIONAL CONTRACT LAW   Pt. VI

THE PRINCIPLES OF EUROPEAN CONTRACT LAW

(2002)

(Excerpts)

[In 1982, the European Commission directed its Commission on European Contract Law ("CECL") to begin the process of creating a modern and uniform contract law among the member States of what is now the European Union ("EU"). The goal was to develop a common body of contract law that harmonizes the member States' often-inconsistent domestic laws, as required for the proper functioning of their common market. Without such a trans-European body of law, a contract made within the European common market would be governed by the law of one nation on the basis of choice-of-law principles and the contractual designation, if any, of that nation's law. With such a body of law, the European Commission hoped, the flow of goods and services within the European common market would be facilitated.

[Though progress was slow, a revised text of the Principles of European Contract Law ("PECL") was published in 2002. The PECL deals mainly with issues that affect international commercial contracts, but they are intended to apply to other contracts as well. When formulating them, the CECL drew on the contract laws of the EU member States, and non-EU sources such as the United Nations Convention on Contracts for the International Sale of Goods and the American Law Institute's Restatement (Second) of Contracts, both of which are included in this pamphlet above. The PECL is not binding on anyone; instead, the CECL hopes, it will serve as the first draft of part of an eventual European Civil Code, which would address contract law as well as many other topics.

[The EU has issued Directives (laws) on several specific topics within contract law. Two of them, which affect consumer contracts, are included in this pamphlet below.]

CHAPTER 1. GENERAL PROVISIONS

1. Scope of the Principles.
    - 1.101. Application of the Principles.
    - 1.102. Freedom of Contract.
    - 1.103. Mandatory Law.
    - 1.104. Application to Questions of Consent.
    - 1.105. Usages and Practices.
    - 1.106. Interpretation and Supplementation.
    - 1.107. Application of the Principles by Way of Analogy.
2. General Duties.
    - 1.201. Good Faith and Fair Dealing.
    - 1.202. Duty to Co-operate.
3. Terminology and Other Provisions.
    - 1.301. Meaning of Terms.
    - 1.302. Reasonableness.
    - 1.303. Notice.
    - 1.304. Computation of Time.
    - 1.305. Imputed Knowledge and Intention.

CHAPTER 2. FORMATION

1. General Provisions.
    - 2.101. Conditions for the Conclusion of a Contract.
    - 2.102. Intention.

Pt. VI   THE PRINCIPLES OF EUROPEAN CONTRACT LAW

       2.103.   Sufficient Agreement.
       2.104.   Terms Not Individually Negotiated.
       2.105.   Merger Clause.
       2.106.   Written Modification Only.
       2.107.   Promises Binding Without Acceptance.
2. Offer and Acceptance.
       2.201.   Offer.
       2.202.   Revocation of an Offer.
       2.203.   Rejection.
       2.204.   Acceptance.
       2.205.   Time of Conclusion of the Contract.
       2.206.   Time Limit for Acceptance.
       2.207.   Late Acceptance.
       2.208.   Modified Acceptance.
       2.209.   Conflicting General Conditions.
       2.210.   Professional's Written Confirmation.
       2.211.   Contracts Not Concluded Through Offer and Acceptance.
3. Liability for Negotiations.
       2.301.   Negotiations Contrary to Good Faith.
       2.302.   Breach of Confidentiality.

CHAPTER 3. AUTHORITY OF AGENTS

1. General Provisions.
       3.101.   Scope of the Chapter.
       3.102.   Categories of Representation.
2. Direct Representation.
       3.201.   Express, Implied and Apparent Authority.
       3.202.   Agent Acting in Exercise of Its Authority.
       3.203.   Unidentified Principal.
       3.204.   Agent Acting Without or Outside Its Authority.
       3.205.   Conflict of Interest.
       3.206.   Subagency.
       3.207.   Ratification by Principal.
       3.208.   Third Party's Right With Respect to Confirmation of Authority.
       3.209.   Duration of Authority.
3. Indirect Representation.
       3.301.   Intermediaries Not Acting in the Name of a Principal.
       3.302.   Intermediary's Insolvency or Fundamental Non-performance to Principal.
       3.303.   Intermediary's Insolvency or Fundamental Non-performance to Third Party.
       3.304.   Requirement of Notice.

CHAPTER 4. VALIDITY

       4.101.   Matters Not Covered.
       4.102.   Initial Impossibility.
       4.103.   Fundamental Mistake as to Facts or Law.
       4.104.   Inaccuracy in Communication.
       4.105.   Adaptation of Contract.
       4.106.   Incorrect Information.
       4.107.   Fraud.
       4.108.   Threats.
       4.109.   Excessive Benefit or Unfair Advantage.

4.110. Unfair Terms Not Individually Negotiated.
4.111. Third Persons.
4.112. Notice of Avoidance.
4.113. Time Limits.
4.114. Confirmation.
4.115. Effect of Avoidance.
4.116. Partial Avoidance.
4.117. Damages.
4.118. Exclusion or Restriction of Remedies.
4.119. Remedies for Non-performance.

CHAPTER 5. INTERPRETATION

5.101. General Rules of Interpretation.
5.102. Relevant Circumstances.
5.103. Contra Proferentem Rule.
5.104. Preference to Negotiated Terms.
5.105. Reference to Contract as a Whole.
5.106. Terms to Be Given Effect.
5.107. Linguistic Discrepancies.

CHAPTER 6. CONTENTS AND EFFECTS

6.101. Statements Giving Rise to Contractual Obligations.
6.102. Implied Terms.
6.103. Simulation.
6.104. Determination of Price.
6.105. Unilateral Determination by a Party.
6.106. Determination by a Third Person.
6.107. Reference to a Non-Existent Factor.
6.108. Quality of Performance.
6.109. Contract for an Indefinite Period.
6.110. Stipulation in Favor of a Third Party.
6.111. Change of Circumstances.

CHAPTER 7. PERFORMANCE

7.101. Place of Performance.
7.102. Time of Performance.
7.103. Early Performance.
7.104. Order of Performance.
7.105. Alternative Performance.
7.106. Performance by a Third Person.
7.107. Form of Payment.
7.108. Currency of Payment.
7.109. Appropriation of Performance.
7.110. Property Not Accepted.
7.111. Money Not Accepted.
7.112. Costs of Performance.

CHAPTER 8. NON-PERFORMANCE AND REMEDIES IN GENERAL

8.101. Remedies Available.
8.102. Cumulation of Remedies.
8.103. Fundamental Non-Performance.

Pt. VI THE PRINCIPLES OF EUROPEAN CONTRACT LAW

    8.104. Cure by Non-Performing Party.
    8.105. Assurance of Performance.
    8.106. Notice Fixing Additional Period for Performance.
    8.107. Performance Entrusted to Another.
    8.108. Excuse Due to an Impediment.
    8.109. Clause Excluding or Restricting Remedies.

CHAPTER 9. PARTICULAR REMEDIES FOR NON-PERFORMANCE

1. Right to Performance.
    - 9.101. Monetary Obligations.
    - 9.102. Non-Monetary Obligations.
    - 9.103. Damages Not Precluded.
2. Withholding Performance.
    - 9.201. Right to Withhold Performance.
3. Termination of the Contract.
    - 9.301. Right to Terminate the Contract.
    - 9.302. Contract to Be Performed in Parts.
    - 9.303. Notice of Termination.
    - 9.304. Anticipatory Non-Performance.
    - 9.305. Effects of Termination in General.
    - 9.306. Property Reduced in Value.
    - 9.307. Recovery of Money Paid.
    - 9.308. Recovery of Property.
    - 9.309. Recovery for Performance That Cannot Be Returned.
4. Price Reduction.
    - 9.401. Right to Reduce Price.
5. Damages and Interest.
    - 9.501. Right to Damages.
    - 9.502. General Measure of Damages.
    - 9.503. Foreseeability.
    - 9.504. Loss Attributable to Aggrieved Party.
    - 9.505. Reduction of Loss.
    - 9.506. Substitute Transaction.
    - 9.507. Current Price.
    - 9.508. Delay in Payment of Money.
    - 9.509. Agreed Payment for Non-Performance.
    - 9.510. Currency by Which Damages to Be Measured.

CHAPTER 10. PLURALITY OF PARTIES [Omitted]

CHAPTER 11. ASSIGNMENT OF CLAIMS

1. General Principles.
    - 11.101. Scope of Chapter.
    - 11.102. Contractual Claims Generally Assignable.
    - 11.103. Partial Assignment.
    - 11.104. Form of Assignment.
2. Effects of Assignment As Between Assignor and Assignee.
    - 11.201. Rights Transferred to Assignee.
    - 11.202. When Assignment Takes Effect.
    - 11.203. Preservation of Assignee's Rights Against Assignor.
    - 11.204. Undertakings by Assignor.

3. Effects of Assignment As Between Assignee and Debtor.
   - 11.301. Contractual Prohibition of Assignment.
   - 11.302. Other Ineffective Assignments.
   - 11.303. Effect on Debtor's Obligation.
   - 11.304. Protection of Debtor.
   - 11.305. Competing Demands.
   - 11.306. Place of Performance.
   - 11.307. Defences and Rights of Set-Off.
   - 11.308. Unauthorized Modification Not Binding on Assignee.
4. Order of Priority Between Assignee and Competing Claimants.
   - 11.401. Priorities.

CHAPTER 12. SUBSTITUTION OF NEW DEBTOR: TRANSFER OF CONTRACT

1. Substitution of New Debtor.
   - 12.101. Substitution; General Rules.
   - 12.102. Effects of Substitution on Defences and Securities.
2. Transfer of Contract.
   - 12.201. Transfer of Contract.

CHAPTER 13. SET-OFF [Omitted]

CHAPTER 14. PRESCRIPTION

1. General Provision.
   - 14.101. Claims Subject to Prescription.
2. Periods of Prescription and Their Commencement.
   - 14.201. General Period.
   - 14.202. Period for a Claim Established by Legal Proceedings.
4. Renewal of Periods.
   - 14.401. Renewal by Acknowledgement.
6. Modification by Agreement.
   - 14.601. Agreements Concerning Prescription.

CHAPTER 15. ILLEGALITY

- 15.101. Contracts Contrary to Fundamental Principles.
- 15.102. Contracts Infringing Mandatory Rules.
- 15.103. Partial Ineffectiveness.
- 15.104. Restitution.
- 15.105. Damages.

CHAPTER 16. CONDITIONS

- 16.101. Types of Condition.
- 16.102. Interference With Conditions.
- 16.103. Effect of Conditions.

CHAPTER 17. CAPITALISATION OF INTEREST [Omitted]

THE PRINCIPLES OF EUROPEAN CONTRACT LAW

CHAPTER 1—GENERAL PROVISIONS*

Section 1: Scope of the Principles

Article 1.101. Application of the Principles

(1) These Principles are intended to be applied as general rules of contract law in the European Union.

(2) These Principles will apply when the parties have agreed to incorporate them into their contract or that their contract is to be governed by them.

(3) These Principles may be applied when the parties:

(a) have agreed that their contract is to be governed by "general principles of law", the "lex mercatoria" or the like; or

(b) have not chosen any system or rules of law to govern their contract.

(4) These Principles may provide a solution to the issue raised where the system or rules of law applicable do not do so.

Article 1.102. Freedom of Contract

(1) Parties are free to enter into a contract and to determine its contents, subject to the requirements of good faith and fair dealing, and the mandatory rules established by these Principles.

(2) The parties may exclude the application of any of the Principles or derogate from or vary their effects, except as otherwise provided by these Principles.

Article 1.103. Mandatory Law

(1) Where the law otherwise applicable so allows, the parties may choose to have their contract governed by the Principles, with the effect that national mandatory rules are not applicable.

(2) Effect should nevertheless be given to those mandatory rules of national, supranational and international law which, according to the relevant rules of private international law, are applicable irrespective of the law governing the contract.

Article 1.104. Application to Questions of Consent

(1) The existence and validity of the agreement of the parties to adopt or incorporate these Principles shall be determined by these Principles.

(2) Nevertheless, a party may rely upon the law of the country in which it has its habitual residence to establish that it did not consent if it appears from the circumstances that it would not be reasonable to determine the effect of the party's conduct in accordance with these Principles.

Article 1.105. Usages and Practices

(1) The parties are bound by any usage to which they have agreed and by any practice they have established between themselves.

(2) The parties are bound by a usage which would be considered generally applicable by persons in the same situation as the parties, except where the application of such usage would be unreasonable.

---

* For ease of reading, where the English and American spelling of words used in the Principles of European Contract Law differ, American spellings have been substituted for the English spellings. For example, "favor" has been substituted for "favour" and "authorized" has been substituted for "authorised". (Footnote by ed.)

Article 1.106. Interpretation and Supplementation

(1) These Principles should be interpreted and developed in accordance with their purposes. In particular, regard should be had to the need to promote good faith and fair dealing, certainty in contractual relationships and uniformity of application.

(2) Issues within the scope of these Principles but not expressly settled by them are so far as possible to be settled in accordance with the ideas underlying the Principles. Failing this, the legal system applicable by virtue of the rules of private international law is to be applied.

Article 1.107. Application of the Principles by Way of Analogy

These Principles apply with appropriate modifications to agreements to modify or end a contract, to unilateral promises and to other statements and conduct indicating intention.

Section 2: General Duties

Article 1.201. Good Faith and Fair Dealing

(1) Each party must act in accordance with good faith and fair dealing.

(2) The parties may not exclude or limit this duty.

Article 1.202. Duty to Co-operate

Each party owes to the other a duty to co-operate in order to give full effect to the contract.

Section 3: Terminology and Other Provisions

Article 1.301. Meaning of Terms

In these Principles, except where the context otherwise requires:

(1) 'act' includes omission;

(2) 'court' includes arbitral tribunal;

(3) an 'intentional' act includes an act done recklessly;

(4) 'non-performance' denotes any failure to perform an obligation under the contract, whether or not excused, and includes delayed performance, defective performance and failure to co-operate in order to give full effect to the contract.

(5) a matter is 'material' if it is one which a reasonable person in the same situation as one party ought to have known would influence the other party in its decision whether to contract on the proposed terms or to contract at all;

(6) 'written' statements include communications made by telegram, telex, telefax and electronic mail and other means of communication capable of providing a readable record of the statement on both sides

Article 1.302. Reasonableness

Under these Principles reasonableness is to be judged by what persons acting in good faith and in the same situation as the parties would consider to be reasonable. In particular, in assessing what is reasonable the nature and purpose of the contract, the circumstances of the case and the usages and practices of the trades or professions involved should be taken into account.

Article 1.303. Notice

(1) Any notice may be given by any means, whether in writing or otherwise, appropriate to the circumstances.

(2) Subject to paragraphs (4) and (5), any notice becomes effective when it reaches the addressee.

(3) A notice reaches the addressee when it is delivered to it or to its place of business or mailing address, or, if it does not have a place of business or mailing address, to its habitual residence.

(4) If one party gives notice to the other because of the other's non-performance or because such non-performance is reasonably anticipated by the first party, and the notice is properly dispatched or given, a delay or inaccuracy in the transmission of the notice or its failure to arrive does not prevent it from having effect. The notice shall have effect from the time at which it would have arrived in normal circumstances.

(5) A notice has no effect if a withdrawal of it reaches the addressee before or at the same time as the notice.

(6) In this Article, 'notice' includes the communication of a promise, statement, offer, acceptance, demand, request or other declaration.

Article 1.304. Computation of Time

(1) A period of time set by a party in a written document for the addressee to reply or take other action begins to run from the date stated as the date of the document. If no date is shown, the period begins to run from the moment the document reaches the addressee.

(2) Official holidays and official non-working days occurring during the period are included in calculating the period. However, if the last day of the period is an official holiday or official non-working day at the address of the addressee, or at the place where a prescribed act is to be performed, the period is extended until the first following working day in that place.

(3) Periods of time expressed in days, weeks, months or years shall begin at 00.00 on the next day and shall end at 24.00 on the last day of the period; but any reply that has to reach the party which set the period must arrive, or other act which is to be done must be completed, by the normal close of business in the relevant place on the last day of the period.

Article 1.305. Imputed Knowledge and Intention

If any person who with a party's assent was involved in making a contract, or who was entrusted with performance by a party or performed with its assent:

    (a) knew or foresaw a fact, or ought to have known or foreseen it; or

    (b) acted intentionally or with gross negligence, or not in accordance with good faith and fair dealing, this knowledge, foresight or behaviour is imputed to the party itself.

CHAPTER 2—FORMATION

Section 1: General Provisions

Article 2.101. Conditions for the Conclusion of a Contract

(1) A contract is concluded if:

    (a) the parties intend to be legally bound, and

    (b) they reach a sufficient agreement without any further requirement.

(2) A contract need not be concluded or evidenced in writing nor is it subject to any other requirement as to form. The contract may be proved by any means, including witnesses.

Article 2.102. Intention

The intention of a party to be legally bound by contract is to be determined from the party's statements or conduct as they were reasonably understood by the other party.

Article 2.103. Sufficient Agreement

(1) There is sufficient agreement if the terms:

(a) have been sufficiently defined by the parties so that the contract can be enforced, or

(b) can be determined under these Principles.

(2) However, if one of the parties refuses to conclude a contract unless the parties have agreed on some specific matter, there is no contract unless agreement on that matter has been reached.

Article 2.104. Terms Not Individually Negotiated

(1) Contract terms which have not been individually negotiated may be invoked against a party which did not know of them only if the party invoking them took reasonable steps to bring them to the other party's attention before or when the contract was concluded.

(2) Terms are not brought appropriately to a party's attention by a mere reference to them in a contract document, even if that party signs the document.

Article 2.105. Merger Clause

(1) If a written contract contains an individually negotiated clause stating that the writing embodies all the terms of the contract (a merger clause), any prior statements, undertakings or agreements which are not embodied in the writing do not form part of the contract.

(2) If the merger clause is not individually negotiated it will only establish a presumption that the parties intended that their prior statements, undertakings or agreements were not to form part of the contract. This rule may not be excluded or restricted.

(3) The parties' prior statements may be used to interpret the contract. This rule may not be excluded or restricted except by an individually negotiated clause.

(4) A party may by its statements or conduct be precluded from asserting a merger clause to the extent that the other party has reasonably relied on them.

Article 2.106. Written Modification Only

(1) A clause in a written contract requiring any modification or ending by agreement to be made in writing establishes only a presumption that an agreement to modify or end the contract is not intended to be legally binding unless it is in writing.

(2) A party may by its statements or conduct be precluded from asserting such a clause to the extent that the other party has reasonably relied on them.

Article 2.107. Promises Binding Without Acceptance

A promise which is intended to be legally binding without acceptance is binding.

Section 2: Offer and Acceptance

Article 2.201. Offer

(1) A proposal amounts to an offer if:

(a) it is intended to result in a contract if the other party accepts it, and

(b) it contains sufficiently definite terms to form a contract.

(2) An offer may be made to one or more specific persons or to the public.

(3) A proposal to supply goods or services at stated prices made by a professional supplier in a public advertisement or a catalogue, or by a display of goods, is presumed to be an offer to sell or supply at that price until the stock of goods, or the supplier's capacity to supply the service, is exhausted.

Article 2.202. Revocation of an Offer

(1) An offer may be revoked if the revocation reaches the offeree before it has dispatched its acceptance or, in cases of acceptance by conduct, before the contract has been concluded under Article 2.205(2) or (3).

(2) An offer made to the public can be revoked by the same means as were used to make the offer.

(3) However, a revocation of an offer is ineffective if:

(a) the offer indicates that it is irrevocable; or

(b) it states a fixed time for its acceptance; or

(c) it was reasonable for the offeree to rely on the offer as being irrevocable and the offeree has acted in reliance on the offer.

Article 2.203. Rejection

When a rejection of an offer reaches the offeror, the offer lapses.

Article 2.204. Acceptance

(1) Any form of statement or conduct by the offeree is an acceptance if it indicates assent to the offer.

(2) Silence or inactivity does not in itself amount to acceptance.

Article 2.205. Time of Conclusion of the Contract

(1) If an acceptance has been dispatched by the offeree the contract is concluded when the acceptance reaches the offeror.

(2) In case of acceptance by conduct, the contract is concluded when notice of the conduct reaches the offeror.

(3) If by virtue of the offer, of practices which the parties have established between themselves, or of a usage, the offeree may accept the offer by performing an act without notice to the offeror, the contract is concluded when the performance of the act begins.

Article 2.206. Time Limit for Acceptance

In order to be effective, acceptance of an offer must reach the offeror within the time fixed by it.

(1) In order to be effective, acceptance of an offer must reach the offeror within the time fixed by it.

(2) If no time has been fixed by the offeror acceptance must reach it within a reasonable time.

(3) In the case of an acceptance by an act of performance under art. 2.205 (3), that act must be performed within the time for acceptance fixed by the offeror or, if no such time is fixed, within a reasonable time.

Article 2.207. Late Acceptance

(1) A late acceptance is nonetheless effective as an acceptance if without delay the offeror informs the offeree that he treats it as such.

(2) If a letter or other writing containing a late acceptance shows that it has been sent in such circumstances that if its transmission had been normal it would have reached the offeror in due time, the late acceptance is effective as an acceptance unless, without delay, the offeror informs the offeree that it considers its offer as having lapsed.

Article 2.208. Modified Acceptance

(1) A reply by the offeree which states or implies additional or different terms which would materially alter the terms of the offer is a rejection and a new offer.

(2) A reply which gives a definite assent to an offer operates as an acceptance even if it states or implies additional or different terms, provided these do not materially alter the terms of the offer. The additional or different terms then become part of the contract.

(3) However, such a reply will be treated as a rejection of the offer if:

(a) the offer expressly limits acceptance to the terms of the offer; or

(b) the offeror objects to the additional or different terms without delay; or

(c) the offeree makes its acceptance conditional upon the offeror's assent to the additional or different terms, and the assent does not reach the offeree within a reasonable time.

Article 2.209. Conflicting General Conditions

(1) If the parties have reached agreement except that the offer and acceptance refer to conflicting general conditions of contract, a contract is nonetheless formed. The general conditions form part of the contract to the extent that they are common in substance.

(2) However, no contract is formed if one party:

(a) has indicated in advance, explicitly, and not by way of general conditions, that it does not intend to be bound by a contract on the basis of paragraph (1); or

(b) without delay, informs the other party that it does not intend to be bound by such contract.

(3) General conditions of contract are terms which have been formulated in advance for an indefinite number of contracts of a certain nature, and which have not been individually negotiated between the parties.

Article 2.210. Professional's Written Confirmation

If professionals have concluded a contract but have not embodied it in a final document, and one without delay sends the other a writing which purports to be a confirmation of the contract but which contains additional or different terms, such terms will become part of the contract unless:

(a) the terms materially alter the terms of the contract, or

(b) the addressee objects to them without delay.

Article 2.211. Contracts Not Concluded Through Offer and Acceptance

The rules in this section apply with appropriate adaptations even though the process of conclusion of a contract cannot be analyzed into offer and acceptance.

Section 3: Liability for Negotiations

Article 2.301. Negotiations Contrary to Good Faith

(1) A party is free to negotiate and is not liable for failure to reach an agreement.

(2) However, a party who has negotiated or broken off negotiations contrary to good faith and fair dealing is liable for the losses caused to the other party.

(3) It is contrary to good faith and fair dealing, in particular, for a party to enter into or continue negotiations with no real intention of reaching an agreement with the other party.

Article 2.302. Breach of Confidentiality

If confidential information is given by one party in the course of negotiations, the other party is under a duty not to disclose that information or use it for its own purposes whether or not a contract is subsequently concluded. The remedy for breach of this duty may include compensation for loss suffered and restitution of the benefit received by the other party.

CHAPTER 3—AUTHORITY OF AGENTS

Section 1: General Provisions

Article 3.101. Scope of the Chapter

(1) This Chapter governs the authority of an agent or other intermediary to bind its principal in relation to a contract with a third party.

(2) This Chapter does not govern an agent's authority bestowed by law or the authority of an agent appointed by a public or judicial authority.

(3) This Chapter does not govern the internal relationship between the agent or intermediary and its principal.

Article 3.102. Categories of Representation

(1) Where an agent acts in the name of a principal, the rules on direct representation apply (Section 2). It is irrelevant whether the principal's identity is revealed at the time the agent acts or is to be revealed later.

(2) Where an intermediary acts on instructions and on behalf of, but not in the name of, a principal, or where the third party neither knows nor has reason to know that the intermediary acts as an agent, the rules on indirect representation apply (Section 3).

Section 2: Direct Representation

Article 3.201. Express, Implied and Apparent Authority

(1) The principal's grant of authority to an agent to act in its name may be express or may be implied from the circumstances.

(2) The agent has authority to perform all acts necessary in the circumstances to achieve the purposes for which the authority was granted.

(3) A person is to be treated as having granted authority to an apparent agent if the person's statements or conduct induce the third party reasonably and in good faith to believe that the apparent agent has been granted authority for the act performed by it.

Article 3.202. Agent Acting in Exercise of Its Authority

Where an agent is acting within its authority as defined by Article 3.201, its acts bind the principal and the third party directly to each other. The agent itself is not bound to the third party.

Article 3.203. Unidentified Principal

If an agent enters into a contract in the name of a principal whose identity is to be revealed later, but fails to reveal that identity within a reasonable time after a request by the third party, the agent itself is bound by the contract.

Article 3.204. Agent Acting Without or Outside Its Authority

(1) Where a person acting as an agent acts without authority or outside the scope of its authority, its acts are not binding upon the principal and the third party.

(2) Failing ratification by the principal according to Article 3.207, the agent is liable to pay the third party such damages as will place the third party in the same position as if the agent had acted with authority. This does not apply if the third party knew or could not have been unaware of the agent's lack of authority.

Article 3.205. Conflict of Interest

(1) If a contract concluded by an agent involves the agent in a conflict of interest of which the third party knew or could not have been unaware, the principal may avoid the contract according to the provisions of Articles 4.112 to 4.116.

(2) There is presumed to be a conflict of interest where:

   (a) the agent also acted as agent for the third party; or

   (b) the contract was with itself in its personal capacity.

(3) However, the principal may not avoid the contract:

   (a) if it had consented to, or could not have been unaware of, the agent's so acting; or

   (b) if the agent had disclosed the conflict of interest to it and it had not objected within a reasonable time.

Article 3.206. Subagency

An agent has implied authority to appoint a subagent to carry out tasks which are not of a personal character and which it is not reasonable to expect the agent to carry out itself. The rules of this Section apply to the subagency; acts of the subagent which are within its and the agent's authority bind the principal and the third party directly to each other.

Article 3.207. Ratification by Principal

(1) Where a person acting as an agent acts without authority or outside its authority, the principal may ratify the agent's acts.

(2) Upon ratification, the agent's acts are considered as having been authorized, without prejudice to the rights of other persons.

Article 3.208. Third Party's Right With Respect to Confirmation of Authority

Where the statements or conduct of the principal gave the third party reason to believe that an act performed by the agent was authorized, but the third party is in doubt about the authorization, it may send a written confirmation to the principal or request ratification from it. If the principal does not object or answer the request without delay, the agent's act is treated as having been authorized.

Article 3.209. Duration of Authority

(1) An agent's authority continues until the third party knows or ought to know that:

(a) the agent's authority has been brought to an end by the principal, the agent, or both; or

(b) the acts for which the authority had been granted have been completed, or the time for which it had been granted has expired; or

(c) the agent has become insolvent or, where a natural person, has died or become incapacitated; or

(d) the principal has become insolvent.

(2) The third party is considered to know that the agent's authority has been brought to an end under paragraph(1)(a) above if this has been communicated or publicized in the same manner in which the authority was originally communicated or publicized.

(3) However, the agent remains authorized for a reasonable time to perform those acts which are necessary to protect the interests of the principal or its successors.

Section 3: Indirect Representation

Article 3.301. Intermediaries Not Acting in the Name of a Principal

(1) Where an intermediary acts:

(a) on instructions and on behalf, but not in the name, of a principal, or

(b) on instructions from a principal but the third party does not know and has no reason to know this,

the intermediary and the third party are bound to each other.

(2) The principal and the third party are bound to each other only under the conditions set out in Articles 3.302 to 3.304.

Article 3.302. Intermediary's Insolvency or Fundamental Non-performance to Principal

If the intermediary becomes insolvent, or if it commits a fundamental non-performance towards the principal, or if prior to the time for performance it is clear that there will be a fundamental non-performance:

(a) on the principal's demand, the intermediary shall communicate the name and address of the third party to the principal; and

(b) the principal may exercise against the third party the rights acquired on the principal's behalf by the intermediary, subject to any defences which the third party may set up against the intermediary.

Article 3.303. Intermediary's Insolvency or Fundamental Non-performance to Third Party

If the intermediary becomes insolvent, or if it commits a fundamental non-performance towards the third party, or if prior to the time for performance it is clear that there will be a fundamental non-performance:

(a) on the third party's demand, the intermediary shall communicate the name and address of the principal to the third party; and

(b) the third party may exercise against the principal the rights which the third party has against the intermediary, subject to any defences which the intermediary may set up against the third party and those which the principal may set up against the intermediary.

Article 3.304. Requirement of Notice

The rights under Articles 3.302 and 3.303 may be exercised only if notice of intention to exercise them is given to the intermediary and to the third party or principal, respectively. Upon receipt of the notice, the third party or the principal is no longer entitled to render performance to the intermediary.

CHAPTER 4—VALIDITY

Article 4.101. Matters Not Covered

This chapter does not deal with invalidity arising from illegality, immorality or lack of capacity.

Article 4.102. Initial Impossibility

A contract is not invalid merely because at the time it was concluded performance of the obligation assumed was impossible, or because a party was not entitled to dispose of the assets to which the contract relates.

Article 4.103. Fundamental Mistake as to Facts or Law

(1) A party may avoid a contract for mistake of fact or law existing when the contract was concluded if:

(a) (i) the mistake was caused by information given by the other party; or

(ii) the other party knew or ought to have known of the mistake and it was contrary to good faith and fair dealing to leave the mistaken party in error; or

(iii) the other party made the same mistake,

and

(b) the other party knew or ought to have known that the mistaken party, had it known the truth, would not have entered the contract or would have done so only on fundamentally different terms.

(2) However a party may not avoid the contract if:

(a) in the circumstances its mistake was inexcusable, or

(b) the risk of the mistake was assumed, or in the circumstances should be borne, by it.

Article 4.104. Inaccuracy in Communication

An inaccuracy in the expression or transmission of a statement is to be treated as a mistake of the person who made or sent the statement and Article 4.103 applies.

Article 4.105. Adaptation of Contract

(1) If a party is entitled to avoid the contract for mistake but the other party indicates that it is willing to perform, or actually does perform, the contract as it was understood by the party entitled to avoid it, the contract is to be treated as if it had been concluded as that party understood it. The other party must indicate its willingness to perform, or render such performance, promptly after being informed of the manner in which the party entitled to avoid it understood the contract and before that party acts in reliance on any notice of avoidance.

(2) After such indication or performance the right to avoid is lost and any earlier notice of avoidance is ineffective.

(3) Where both parties have made the same mistake, the court may at the request of either party bring the contract into accordance with what might reasonably have been agreed had the mistake not occurred.

Article 4.106. Incorrect Information

A party who has concluded a contract relying on incorrect information given it by the other party may recover damages in accordance with Article 4.117(2) and (3) even if the information does not give rise to a fundamental mistake under Article 4.103, unless the party who gave the information had reason to believe that the information was correct.

Article 4.107. Fraud

(1) A party may avoid a contract when it has been led to conclude it by the other party's fraudulent representation, whether by words or conduct, or fraudulent non-disclosure of any information which in accordance with good faith and fair dealing it should have disclosed.

(2) A party's representation or non-disclosure is fraudulent if it was intended to deceive.

(3) In determining whether good faith and fair dealing required that a party disclose particular information, regard should be had to all the circumstances, including:

　　(a) whether the party had special expertise;

　　(b) the cost to it of acquiring the relevant information;

　　(c) whether the other party could reasonably acquire the information for itself; and

　　(d) the apparent importance of the information to the other party.

Article 4.108. Threats

A party may avoid a contract when it has been led to conclude it by the other party's imminent and serious threat of an act:

　　(a) which is wrongful in itself, or

　　(b) which it is wrongful to use as a means to obtain the conclusion of the contract,

unless in the circumstances the first party had a reasonable alternative.

Article 4.109. Excessive Benefit or Unfair Advantage

(1) A party may avoid a contract if, at the time of the conclusion of the contract:

　　(a) it was dependent on or had a relationship of trust with the other party, was in economic distress or had urgent needs, was improvident, ignorant, inexperienced or lacking in bargaining skill, and

(b) the other party knew or ought to have known of this and, given the circumstances and purpose of the contract, took advantage of the first party's situation in a way which was grossly unfair or took an excessive benefit.

(2) Upon the request of the party entitled to avoidance, a court may if it is appropriate adapt the contract in order to bring it into accordance with what might have been agreed had the requirements of good faith and fair dealing been followed.

(3) A court may similarly adapt the contract upon the request of a party receiving notice of avoidance for excessive benefit or unfair advantage, provided that this party informs the party which gave the notice promptly after receiving it and before that party has acted in reliance on it.

Article 4.110. Unfair Terms Not Individually Negotiated

(1) A party may avoid a term which has not been individually negotiated if, contrary to the requirements of good faith and fair dealing, it causes a significant imbalance in the parties' rights and obligations arising under the contract to the detriment of that party, taking into account the nature of the performance to be rendered under the contract, all the other terms of the contract and the circumstances at the time the contract was concluded.

(2) This Article does not apply to:

(a) a term which defines the main subject matter of the contract, provided the term is in plain and intelligible language; or to

(b) the adequacy in value of one party's obligations compared to the value of the obligations of the other party.

Article 4.111. Third Persons

(1) Where a third person for whose acts a party is responsible, or who with a party's assent is involved in the making of a contract:

(a) causes a mistake by giving information, or knows of or ought to have known of a mistake,

(b) gives incorrect information,

(c) commits fraud,

(d) makes a threat, or

(e) takes excessive benefit or unfair advantage,

remedies under this Chapter will be available under the same conditions as if the behavior or knowledge had been that of the party itself.

(2) Where any other third person:

(a) gives incorrect information,

(b) commits fraud,

(c) makes a threat, or

(d) takes excessive benefit or unfair advantage,

remedies under this Chapter will be available if the party knew or ought to have known of the relevant facts, or at the time of avoidance it has not acted in reliance on the contract.

Article 4.112. Notice of Avoidance

Avoidance must be by notice to the other party.

Article 4.113. Time Limits

(1) Notice of avoidance must be given within a reasonable time, with due regard to the circumstances, after the avoiding party knew or ought to have known of the relevant facts or became capable of acting freely.

(2) However, a party may avoid an individual term under Article 4.110 if it gives notice of avoidance within a reasonable time after the other party has invoked the term.

Article 4.114. Confirmation

If the party which is entitled to avoid a contract confirms it, expressly or impliedly, after it knows of the ground for avoidance, or becomes capable of acting freely, avoidance of the contract is excluded.

Article 4.115. Effect of Avoidance

On avoidance either party may claim restitution of whatever it has supplied under the contract, provided it makes concurrent restitution of whatever it has received. If restitution cannot be made in kind for any reason, a reasonable sum must be paid for what has been received.

Article 4.116. Partial Avoidance

If a ground of avoidance affects only particular terms of a contract, the effect of an avoidance is limited to those terms unless, giving due consideration to all the circumstances of the case, it is unreasonable to uphold the remaining contract.

Article 4.117. Damages

(1) A party which avoids a contract under this Chapter may recover from the other party damages so as to put the avoiding party as nearly as possible into the same position as if it had not concluded the contract, provided that the other party knew or ought to have known of the mistake, fraud, threat or taking of excessive benefit or unfair advantage.

(2) If a party has the right to avoid a contract under this Chapter, but does not exercise its right or has lost its right under the provisions of Articles 4.113 or 4.114, it may recover, subject to paragraph (1), damages limited to the loss caused to it by the mistake, fraud, threat or taking of excessive benefit or unfair advantage. The same measure of damages shall apply when the party was misled by incorrect information in the sense of Article 4.106.

(3) In other respects, the damages shall be in accordance with the relevant provisions of Chapter 9, Section 5, with appropriate adaptations.

Article 4.118. Exclusion or Restriction of Remedies

(1) Remedies for fraud, threats and excessive benefit or unfair advantage-taking, and the right to avoid an unfair term which has not been individually negotiated, cannot be excluded or restricted.

(2) Remedies for mistake and incorrect information may be excluded or restricted unless the exclusion or restriction is contrary to good faith and fair dealing.

Article 4.119. Remedies for Non-performance

A party which is entitled to a remedy under this Chapter in circumstances which afford that party a remedy for non-performance may pursue either remedy.

CHAPTER 5—INTERPRETATION

Article 5.101. General Rules of Interpretation

(1) A contract is to be interpreted according to the common intention of the parties even if this differs from the literal meaning of the words.

(2) If it is established that one party intended the contract to have a particular meaning, and at the time of the conclusion of the contract the other party could not have been unaware of the first party's intention, the contract is to be interpreted in the way intended by the first party.

(3) If an intention cannot be established according to (1) or (2), the contract is to be interpreted according to the meaning that reasonable persons of the same kind as the parties would give to it in the same circumstances.

Article 5.102. Relevant Circumstances

In interpreting the contract, regard shall be had, in particular, to:

(a) the circumstances in which it was concluded, including the preliminary negotiations;

(b) the conduct of the parties, even subsequent to the conclusion of the contract;

(c) the nature and purpose of the contract;

(d) the interpretation which has already been given to similar clauses by the parties and the practices they have established between themselves;

(e) the meaning commonly given to terms and expressions in the branch of activity concerned and the interpretation similar clauses may already have received;

(f) usages; and

(g) good faith and fair dealing

Article 5.103. Contra Proferentem Rule

Where there is doubt about the meaning of a contract term not individually negotiated, an interpretation of the term against the party who supplied it is to be preferred.

Article 5.104. Preference to Negotiated Terms

Terms which have been individually negotiated take preference over those which are not.

Article 5.105. Reference to Contract as a Whole

Terms are to be interpreted in the light of the whole contract in which they appear.

Article 5.106. Terms to Be Given Effect

An interpretation which renders the terms of the contract lawful, or effective, is to be preferred to one which would not.

Article 5.107. Linguistic Discrepancies

Where a contract is drawn up in two or more language versions none of which is stated to be authoritative, there is, in case of discrepancy between the versions, a preference for the interpretation according to the version in which the contract was originally drawn up.

THE PRINCIPLES OF EUROPEAN CONTRACT LAW

CHAPTER 6—CONTENTS AND EFFECTS

Article 6.101. Statements Giving Rise to Contractual Obligations

(1) A statement made by one party before or when the contract is concluded is to be treated as giving rise to a contractual obligation if that is how the other party reasonably understood it in the circumstances, taking into account:

    (a) the apparent importance of the statement to the other party;

    (b) whether the party was making the statement in the course of business; and

    (c) the relative expertise of the parties.

(2) If one of the parties is a professional supplier who gives information about the quality or use of services or goods or other property when marketing or advertising them or otherwise before the contract for them is concluded, the statement is to be treated as giving rise to a contractual obligation unless it is shown that the other party knew or could not have been unaware that the statement was incorrect.

(3) Such information and other undertakings given by a person advertising or marketing services, goods or other property for the professional supplier, or by a person in earlier links of the business chain, are to be treated as giving rise to a contractual obligation on the part of the professional supplier unless it did not know and had no reason to know of the information or undertaking.

Article 6.102. Implied Terms

In addition to the express terms, a contract may contain implied terms which stem from

    (a) the intention of the parties,

    (b) the nature and purpose of the contract, and

    (c) good faith and fair dealing.

Article 6.103. Simulation

When the parties have concluded an apparent contract which was not intended to reflect their true agreement, as between the parties the true agreement prevails.

Article 6.104. Determination of Price

Where the contract does not fix the price or the method of determining it, the parties are to be treated as having agreed on a reasonable price.

Article 6.105. Unilateral Determination by a Party

Where the price or any other contractual term is to be determined by one party whose determination is grossly unreasonable, then notwithstanding any provision to the contrary, a reasonable price or other term shall be substituted.

Article 6.106. Determination by a Third Person

(1) Where the price or any other contractual term is to be determined by a third person, and it cannot or will not do so, the parties are presumed to have empowered the court to appoint another person to determine it.

(2) If a price or other term fixed by a third person is grossly unreasonable, a reasonable price or term shall be substituted.

Article 6.107. Reference to a Non-Existent Factor

Where the price or any other contractual term is to be determined by reference to a factor which does not exist or has ceased to exist or to be accessible, the nearest equivalent factor shall be substituted.

Article 6.108. Quality of Performance

If the contract does not specify the quality, a party must tender performance of at least average quality.

Article 6.109. Contract for an Indefinite Period

A contract for an indefinite period may be ended by either party by giving notice of reasonable length.

Article 6.110. Stipulation in Favor of a Third Party

(1) A third party may require performance of a contractual obligation when its right to do so has been expressly agreed upon between the promisor and the promisee, or when such agreement is to be inferred from the purpose of the contract or the circumstances of the case. The third party need not be identified at the time the agreement is concluded.

(2) If the third party renounces the right to performance the right is treated as never having accrued to it.

(3) The promisee may by notice to the promisor deprive the third party of the right to performance unless:

(a) the third party has received notice from the promisee that the right has been made irrevocable, or

(b) the promisor or the promisee has received notice from the third party that the latter accepts the right.

Article 6.111. Change of Circumstances

(1) A party is bound to fulfil its obligations even if performance has become more onerous, whether because the cost of performance has increased or because the value of the performance it receives has diminished.

(2) If, however, performance of the contract becomes excessively onerous because of a change of circumstances, the parties are bound to enter into negotiations with a view to adapting the contract or terminating it, provided that:

(a) the change of circumstances occurred after the time of conclusion of the contract,

(b) the possibility of a change of circumstances was not one which could reasonably have been taken into account at the time of conclusion of the contract, and

(c) the risk of the change of circumstances is not one which, according to the contract, the party affected should be required to bear.

(3) If the parties fail to reach agreement within a reasonable period, the court may:

(a) end the contract at a date and on terms to be determined by the court; or

(b) adapt the contract in order to distribute between the parties in a just and equitable manner the losses and gains resulting from the change of circumstances.

In either case, the court may award damages for the loss suffered through a party refusing to negotiate or breaking off negotiations contrary to good faith and fair dealing.

THE PRINCIPLES OF EUROPEAN CONTRACT LAW

CHAPTER 7—PERFORMANCE

Article 7.101. Place of Performance

(1) If the place of performance of a contractual obligation is not fixed by or determinable from the contract it shall be:

    (a) in the case of an obligation to pay money, the creditor's place of business at the time of the conclusion of the contract;

    (b) in the case of an obligation other than to pay money, the debtor's place of business at the time of conclusion of the contract.

(2) If a party has more than one place of business, the place of business for the purpose of the preceding paragraph is that which has the closest relationship to the contract, having regard to the circumstances known to or contemplated by the parties at the time of conclusion of the contract.

(3) If a party does not have a place of business its habitual residence is to be treated as its place of business.

Article 7.102. Time of Performance

A party has to effect its performance:

    (1) if a time is fixed by or determinable from the contract, at that time;

    (2) if a period of time is fixed by or determinable from the contract, at any time within that period unless the circumstances of the case indicate that the other party is to choose the time;

    (3) in any other case, within a reasonable time after the conclusion of the contract.

Article 7.103. Early Performance

(1) A party may decline a tender of performance made before it is due except where acceptance of the tender would not unreasonably prejudice its interests.

(2) A party's acceptance of early performance does not affect the time fixed for the performance of its own obligation.

Article 7.104. Order of Performance

To the extent that the performances of the parties can be rendered simultaneously, the parties are bound to render them simultaneously unless the circumstances indicate otherwise.

Article 7.105. Alternative Performance

(1) Where an obligation may be discharged by one of alternative performances, the choice belongs to the party which is to perform, unless the circumstances indicate otherwise.

(2) If the party which is to make the choice fails to do so by the time required by the contract, then:

    (a) if the delay in choosing is fundamental, the right to choose passes to the other party;

    (b) if the delay is not fundamental, the other party may give a notice fixing an additional period of reasonable length in which the party to choose must do so. If the latter fails to do so, the right to choose passes to the other party.

Article 7.106. Performance by a Third Person

(1) Except where the contract requires personal performance the creditor cannot refuse performance by a third person if:

(a) the third person acts with the assent of the debtor; or

(b) the third person has a legitimate interest in performance and the debtor has failed to perform or it is clear that it will not perform at the time performance is due.

(2) Performance by the third person in accordance with paragraph (1) discharges the debtor.

Article 7.107. Form of Payment

(1) Payment of money due may be made in any form used in the ordinary course of business.

(2) A creditor which, pursuant to the contract or voluntarily, accepts a check or other order to pay or a promise to pay is presumed to do so only on condition that it will be honored. The creditor may not enforce the original obligation to pay unless the order or promise is not honored.

Article 7.108. Currency of Payment

(1) The parties may agree that payment shall be made only in a specified currency.

(2) In the absence of such agreement, a sum of money expressed in a currency other than that of the place where payment is due may be paid in the currency of that place according to the rate of exchange prevailing there at the time when payment is due.

(3) If, in a case falling within the preceding paragraph, the debtor has not paid at the time when payment is due, the creditor may require payment in the currency of the place where payment is due according to the rate of exchange prevailing there either at the time when payment is due or at the time of actual payment.

Article 7.109. Appropriation of Performance

(1) Where a party has to perform several obligations of the same nature and the performance tendered does not suffice to discharge all of the obligations, then subject to paragraph (4) the party may at the time of its performance declare to which obligation the performance is to be appropriated.

(2) If the performing party does not make such a declaration, the other party may within a reasonable time appropriate the performance to such obligation as it chooses. It shall inform the performing party of the choice. However, any such appropriation to an obligation which:

(a) is not yet due, or

(b) is illegal, or

(c) is disputed,

is invalid.

(3) In the absence of an appropriation by either party, and subject to paragraph (4), the performance is appropriated to that obligation which satisfies one of the following criteria in the sequence indicated:

(a) the obligation which is due or is the first to fall due;

(b) the obligation for which the creditor has the least security;

(c) the obligation which is the most burdensome for the debtor

(d) the obligation which has arisen first.

If none of the preceding criteria applies, the performance is appropriated proportionately to all obligations.

(4) In the case of a monetary obligation, a payment by the debtor is to be appropriated, first, to expenses, secondly, to interest, and thirdly, to principal, unless the creditor makes a different appropriation.

Article 7.110. Property Not Accepted

(1) A party who is left in possession of tangible property other than money because of the other party's failure to accept or retake the property must take reasonable steps to protect and preserve the property.

(2) The party left in possession may discharge its duty to deliver or return:

(a) by depositing the property on reasonable terms with a third person to be held to the order of the other party, and notifying the other party of this; or

(b) by selling the property on reasonable terms after notice to the other party, and paying the net proceeds to that party.

(3) Where, however, the property is liable to rapid deterioration or its preservation is unreasonably expensive, the party must take reasonable steps to dispose of it. It may discharge its duty to deliver or return by paying the net proceeds to the other party.

(4) The party left in possession is entitled to be reimbursed or to retain out of the proceeds of sale any expenses reasonably incurred.

Article 7.111. Money Not Accepted

Where a party fails to accept money properly tendered by the other party, that party may after notice to the first party discharge its obligation to pay by depositing the money to the order of the first party in accordance with the law of the place where payment is due.

Article 7.112. Costs of Performance

Each party shall bear the costs of performance of its obligations.

CHAPTER 8—NON-PERFORMANCE AND REMEDIES IN GENERAL

Article 8.101. Remedies Available

(1) Whenever a party does not perform an obligation under the contract and the non-performance is not excused under Article 8.108, the aggrieved party may resort to any of the remedies set out in Chapter 9.

(2) Where a party's non-performance is excused under Article 8.108, the aggrieved party may resort to any of the remedies set out in Chapter 9 except claiming performance and damages.

(3) A party may not resort to any of the remedies set out in Chapter 9 to the extent that its own act caused the other party's non-performance.

Article 8.102. Cumulation of Remedies

Remedies which are not incompatible may be cumulated. In particular, a party is not deprived of its right to damages by exercising its right to any other remedy.

Article 8.103. Fundamental Non-Performance

A non-performance of an obligation is fundamental to the contract if:

(a) strict compliance with the obligation is of the essence of the contract; or

(b) the non-performance substantially deprives the aggrieved party of what it was entitled to expect under the contract, unless the other party did not foresee and could not reasonably have foreseen that result; or

(c) the non-performance is intentional and gives the aggrieved party reason to believe that it cannot rely on the other party's future performance.

Article 8.104. Cure by Non-Performing Party

A party whose tender of performance is not accepted by the other party because it does not conform to the contract may make a new and conforming tender where the time for performance has not yet arrived or the delay would not be such as to constitute a fundamental non-performance.

Article 8.105. Assurance of Performance

(1) A party which reasonably believes that there will be a fundamental non-performance by the other party may demand adequate assurance of due performance and meanwhile may withhold performance of its own obligations so long as such reasonable belief continues.

(2) Where this assurance is not provided within a reasonable time, the party demanding it may terminate the contract if it still reasonably believes that there will be a fundamental non-performance by the other party and gives notice of termination without delay.

Article 8.106. Notice Fixing Additional Period for Performance

(1) In any case of non-performance the aggrieved party may by notice to the other party allow an additional period of time for performance.

(2) During the additional period the aggrieved party may withhold performance of its own reciprocal obligations and may claim damages, but it may not resort to any other remedy. If it receives notice from the other party that the latter will not perform within that period, or if upon expiry of that period due performance has not been made, the aggrieved party may resort to any of the remedies that may be available under chapter 9.

(3) If in a case of delay in performance which is not fundamental the aggrieved party has given a notice fixing an additional period of time of reasonable length, it may terminate the contract at the end of the period of notice. The aggrieved party may in its notice provide that if the other party does not perform within the period fixed by the notice the contract shall terminate automatically. If the period stated is too short, the aggrieved party may terminate, or, as the case may be, the contract shall terminate automatically, only after a reasonable period from the time of the notice.

Article 8.107. Performance Entrusted to Another

A party which entrusts performance of the contract to another person remains responsible for performance.

Article 8.108. Excuse Due to an Impediment

(1) A party's non-performance is excused if it proves that it is due to an impediment beyond its control and that it could not reasonably have been expected to take the impediment into account at the time of the conclusion of the contract, or to have avoided or overcome the impediment or its consequences.

(2) Where the impediment is only temporary the excuse provided by this Article has effect for the period during which the impediment exists. However, if the delay amounts to a fundamental non-performance, the creditor may treat it as such.

(3) The non-performing party must ensure that notice of the impediment and of its effect on its ability to perform is received by the other party within a reasonable time after the non-performing party knew or ought to have known of these circumstances. The other party is entitled to damages for any loss resulting from the non-receipt of such notice.

Article 8.109. Clause Excluding or Restricting Remedies

Remedies for non-performance may be excluded or restricted unless it would be contrary to good faith and fair dealing to invoke the exclusion or restriction.

CHAPTER 9—PARTICULAR REMEDIES FOR NON-PERFORMANCE

Section 1: Right to Performance

Article 9.101. Monetary Obligations

(1) The creditor is entitled to recover money which is due.

(2) Where the creditor has not yet performed its obligation and it is clear that the debtor will be unwilling to receive performance, the creditor may nonetheless proceed with its performance and may recover any sum due under the contract unless:

    (a) it could have made a reasonable substitute transaction without significant effort or expense; or

    (b) performance would be unreasonable in the circumstances.

Article 9.102. Non-Monetary Obligations

(1) The aggrieved party is entitled to specific performance of an obligation other than one to pay money, including the remedying of a defective performance.

(2) Specific performance cannot, however, be obtained where:

    (a) performance would be unlawful or impossible; or

    (b) performance would cause the debtor unreasonable effort or expense; or

    (c) the performance consists [of] the provision of services or work of a personal character or depends upon a personal relationship, or

    (d) the aggrieved party may reasonably obtain performance from another source.

(3) The aggrieved party will lose the right to specific performance if it fails to seek it within a reasonable time after it has or ought to have become aware of the non-performance.

Article 9.103. Damages Not Precluded

The fact that a right to performance is excluded under this Section does not preclude a claim for damages.

Section 2: Withholding Performance

Article 9.201. Right to Withhold Performance

(1) A party which is to perform simultaneously with or after the other party may withhold performance until the other has tendered performance or has performed. The first party may withhold the whole of its performance or a part of it as may be reasonable in the circumstances.

(2) A party may similarly withhold performance for as long as it is clear that there will be a non-performance by the other party when the other party's performance becomes due.

Section 3: Termination of the Contract

Article 9.301. Right to Terminate the Contract

(1) A party may terminate the contract if the other party's non-performance is fundamental.

(2) In the case of delay the aggrieved party may also terminate the contract under Article 8.106(3).

Article 9.302. Contract to be Performed in Parts

If the contract is to be performed in separate parts and in relation to a part to which a counter-performance can be apportioned, there is a fundamental non-performance, the aggrieved party may exercise its right to terminate under this Section in relation to the part concerned. It may terminate the contract as a whole only if the non-performance is fundamental to the contract as a whole.

Article 9.303. Notice of Termination

(1) A party's right to terminate the contract is to be exercised by notice to the other party.

(2) The aggrieved party loses its right to terminate the contract unless it gives notice within a reasonable time after it has or ought to have become aware of the non-performance.

(3) (a) When performance has not been tendered by the time it was due, the aggrieved party need not give notice of termination before a tender has been made. If a tender is later made it loses its right to terminate if it does not give such notice within a reasonable time after it has or ought to have become aware of the tender.

(b) If, however, the aggrieved party knows or has reason to know that the other party still intends to tender within a reasonable time, and the aggrieved party unreasonably fails to notify the other party that it will not accept performance, it loses its right to terminate if the other party in fact tenders within a reasonable time.

(4) If a party is excused under Article 8.108 through an impediment which is total and permanent, the contract is terminated automatically and without notice at the time the impediment arises.

Article 9.304. Anticipatory Non-Performance

Where prior to the time for performance by a party it is clear that there will be a fundamental non-performance by it, the other party may terminate the contract.

Article 9.305. Effects of Termination in General

(1) Termination of the contract releases both parties from their obligation to effect and to receive future performance, but, subject to Articles 9.306 to 9.308, does not affect the rights and liabilities that have accrued up to the time of termination.

(2) Termination does not affect any provision of the contract for the settlement of disputes or any other provision which is to operate even after termination.

Article 9.306. Property Reduced in Value

A party which terminates the contract may reject property previously received from the other party if its value to the first party has been fundamentally reduced as a result of the other party's non-performance.

Article 9.307. Recovery of Money Paid

On termination of the contract a party may recover money paid for a performance which it did not receive or which it properly rejected.

Article 9.308. Recovery of Property

On termination of the contract a party which has supplied property which can be returned and for which it has not received payment or other counter-performance may recover the property.

Article 9.309. Recovery for Performance That Cannot Be Returned

On termination of the contract a party which has rendered a performance which cannot be returned and for which it has not received payment or other counter-performance may recover a reasonable amount for the value of the performance to the other party.

Section 4: Price Reduction

Article 9.401. Right to Reduce Price

(1) A party which accepts a tender of performance not conforming to the contract may reduce the price. This reduction shall be proportionate to the decrease in the value of the performance at the time this was tendered compared to the value which a conforming tender would have had at that time.

(2) A party which is entitled to reduce the price under the preceding paragraph and which has already paid a sum exceeding the reduced price may recover the excess from the other party.

(3) A party which reduces the price cannot also recover damages for reduction in the value of the performance but remains entitled to damages for any further loss it has suffered so far as these are recoverable under Section 5 of this Chapter.

Section 5: Damages and Interest

Article 9.501. Right to Damages

(1) The aggrieved party is entitled to damages for loss caused by the other party's non-performance which is not excused under Article 8.108.

(2) The loss for which damages are recoverable includes:

    (a) non-pecuniary loss; and

    (b) future loss which is reasonably likely to occur.

Article 9.502. General Measure of Damages

The general measure of damages is such sum as will put the aggrieved party as nearly as possible into the position in which it would have been if the contract had been duly performed. Such damages cover the loss which the aggrieved party has suffered and the gain of which it has been deprived.

Article 9.503. Foreseeability

The non-performing party is liable only for loss which it foresaw or could reasonably have foreseen at the time of conclusion of the contract as a likely result of its non-performance, unless the non-performance was intentional or grossly negligent.

Article 9.504. Loss Attributable to Aggrieved Party

The non-performing party is not liable for loss suffered by the aggrieved party to the extent that the aggrieved party contributed to the non-performance or its effects.

Article 9.505. Reduction of Loss

(1) The non-performing party is not liable for loss suffered by the aggrieved party to the extent that the aggrieved party could have reduced the loss by taking reasonable steps.

(2) The aggrieved party is entitled to recover any expenses reasonably incurred in attempting to reduce the loss.

Article 9.506. Substitute Transaction

Where the aggrieved party has terminated the contract and has made a substitute transaction within a reasonable time and in a reasonable manner, it may recover the difference between the contract price and the price of the substitute transaction as well as damages for any further loss so far as these are recoverable under this Section.

Article 9.507. Current Price

Where the aggrieved party has terminated the contract and has not made a substitute transaction but there is a current price for the performance contracted for, it may recover the difference between the contract price and the price current at the time the contract is terminated as well as damages for any further loss so far as these are recoverable under this Section.

Article 9.508. Delay in Payment of Money

(1) If payment of a sum of money is delayed, the aggrieved party is entitled to interest on that sum from the time when payment is due to the time of payment at the average commercial bank short-term lending rate to prime borrowers prevailing for the contractual currency of payment at the place where payment is due.

(2) The aggrieved party may in addition recover damages for any further loss so far as these are recoverable under this Section.

Article 9.509. Agreed Payment for Non-Performance

(1) Where the contract provides that a party which fails to perform is to pay a specified sum to the aggrieved party for such non-performance, the aggrieved party shall be awarded that sum irrespective of its actual loss.

(2) However, despite any agreement to the contrary the specified sum may be reduced to a reasonable amount where it is grossly excessive in relation to the loss resulting from the non-performance and the other circumstances.

Article 9.510. Currency by Which Damages to be Measured

Damages are to be measured by the currency which most appropriately reflects the aggrieved party's loss.

CHAPTER 10—PLURALITY OF PARTIES*

---

* Omitted.

Pt. VI   THE PRINCIPLES OF EUROPEAN CONTRACT LAW

CHAPTER 11—ASSIGNMENT OF CLAIMS

Section 1: General Principles

Article 11.101. Scope of Chapter

(1) This Chapter applies to the assignment by agreement of a right to performance ("claim") under an existing or future contract.

(2) Except where otherwise stated or the context otherwise requires, this Chapter also applies to the assignment by agreement of other transferable claims.

(3) This Chapter does not apply:

    (a) to the transfer of a financial instrument or investment security where, under the law otherwise applicable, such transfer must be by entry in a register maintained by or for the issuer; or

    (b) to the transfer of a bill of exchange or other negotiable instrument or of a negotiable security or a document of title to goods where, under the law otherwise applicable, such transfer must be by delivery (with any necessary endorsement).

(4) In this Chapter "assignment" includes an assignment by way of security.

(5) This Chapter also applies, with appropriate adaptations, to the granting by agreement of a right in security over a claim otherwise than by assignment.

Article 11.102. Contractual Claims Generally Assignable

(1) Subject to Articles 11.301 and 11.302, a party to a contract may assign a claim under it.

(2) A future claim arising under an existing or future contract may be assigned if at the time when it comes into existence, or at such other time as the parties agree, it can be identified as the claim to which the assignment relates.

Article 11.103. Partial Assignment

A claim which is divisible may be assigned in part, but the assignor is liable to the debtor for any increased costs which the debtor thereby incurs.

Article 11.104. Form of Assignment

An assignment need not be in writing and is not subject to any other requirement as to form. It may be proved by any means, including witnesses.

Section 2: Effects of Assignment As Between Assignor and Assignee

Article 11.201. Rights Transferred to Assignee

(1) The assignment of a claim transfers to the assignee:

    (a) all the assignor's rights to performance in respect of the claim assigned; and

    (b) all accessory rights securing such performance.

(2) Where the assignment of a claim under a contract is associated with the substitution of the assignee as debtor in respect of any obligation owed by the assignor under the same contract, this Article takes effect subject to Article 12.201.

Article 11.202. When Assignment Takes Effect

(1) An assignment of an existing claim takes effect at the time of the agreement to assign or such later time as the assignor and assignee agree.

(2) An assignment of a future claim is dependent upon the assigned claim coming into existence but thereupon takes effect from the time of the agreement to assign or such later time as the assignor and assignee agree.

Article 11.203. Preservation of Assignee's Rights Against Assignor

An assignment is effective as between the assignor and assignee, and entitles the assignee to whatever the assignor receives from the debtor, even if it is ineffective against the debtor under Article 11.301 or 11.302.

Article 11.204. Undertakings by Assignor

By assigning or purporting to assign a claim the assignor undertakes to the assignee that:

(a) at the time when the assignment is to take effect the following conditions will be satisfied except as otherwise disclosed to the assignee:

(i) the assignor has the right to assign the claim;

(ii) the claim exists and the assignee's rights are not affected by any defences or rights (including any right of set-off) which the debtor might have against the assignor; and

(iii) the claim is not subject to any prior assignment or right in security in favor of any other party or to any other encumbrance;

(b) the claim and any contract under which it arises will not be modified without the consent of the assignee unless the modification is provided for in the assignment agreement or is one which is made in good faith and is of a nature to which the assignee could not reasonably object; and

(c) the assignor will transfer to the assignee all transferable rights intended to secure performance which are not accessory rights.

Section 3: Effects of Assignment As Between Assignee and Debtor

Article 11.301. Contractual Prohibition of Assignment

(1) An assignment which is prohibited by or is otherwise not in conformity with the contract under which the assigned claim arises is not effective against the debtor unless:

(a) the debtor has consented to it; or

(b) the assignee neither knew nor ought to have known of the non-conformity; or

(c) the assignment is made under a contract for the assignment of future rights to payment of money.

(2) Nothing in the preceding paragraph affects the assignor's liability for the non-conformity.

Article 11.302. Other Ineffective Assignments

An assignment to which the debtor has not consented is ineffective against the debtor so far as it relates to a performance which the debtor, by reason of the nature of the performance or the relationship of the debtor and the assignor, could not reasonably be required to render to anyone except the assignor.

Article 11.303. Effect on Debtor's Obligation

(1) Subject to Articles 11.301, 11.302, 11.307 and 11.308, the debtor is bound to perform in favor of the assignee if and only if the debtor has received a notice in writing from the assignor or the assignee which reasonably identifies the claim which has been assigned and requires the debtor to give performance to the assignee.

(2) However, if such notice is given by the assignee, the debtor may within a reasonable time request the assignee to provide reliable evidence of the assignment, pending which the debtor may withhold performance.

(3) Where the debtor has acquired knowledge of the assignment otherwise than by a notice conforming to paragraph (1), the debtor may either withhold performance from or give performance to the assignee.

(4) Where the debtor gives performance to the assignor, the debtor is discharged if and only if the performance is given without knowledge of the assignment.

Article 11.304. Protection of Debtor

A debtor who performs in favor of a person identified as assignee in a notice of assignment under Article 11.303 is discharged unless the debtor could not have been unaware that such person was not the person entitled to performance.

Article 11.305. Competing Demands

A debtor who has received notice of two or more competing demands for performance may discharge liability by conforming to the law of the due place of performance, or, if the performances are due in different places, the law applicable to the claim.

Article 11.306. Place of Performance

(1) Where the assigned claim relates to an obligation to pay money at a particular place, the assignee may require payment at any place within the same country or, if that country is a Member State of the European Union, at any place within the European Union, but the assignor is liable to the debtor for any increased costs which the debtor incurs by reason of any change in the place of performance.

(2) Where the assigned claim relates to a non-monetary obligation to be performed at a particular place, the assignee may not require performance at any other place.

Article 11.307. Defences and Rights of Set-Off

(1) The debtor may set up against the assignee all substantive and procedural defences to the assigned claim which the debtor could have used against the assignor.

(2) The debtor may also assert against the assignee all rights of set-off which would have been available against the assignor under Chapter 13 in respect of any claim against the assignor:

    (a) existing at the time when a notice of assignment, whether or not conforming to Article 11.303(1), reaches the debtor; or

    (b) closely connected with the assigned claim.

Article 11.308. Unauthorized Modification Not Binding on Assignee

A modification of the claim made by agreement between the assignor and the debtor, without the consent of the assignee, after a notice of assignment, whether or not conforming to Article 11.303(1), reaches the debtor does not affect the rights of the assignee against the debtor unless the modification is provided for in the assignment agreement or is one which is made in good faith and is of a nature to which the assignee could not reasonably object.

Section 4: Order of Priority between Assignee and Competing Claimants

Article 11.401. Priorities

(1) Where there are successive assignments of the same claim, the assignee whose assignment is first notified to the debtor has priority over any earlier assignee if at the time of the later assignment the assignee under that assignment neither knew nor ought to have known of the earlier assignment.

(2) Subject to paragraph (1), the priority of successive assignments, whether of existing or future claims, is determined by the order in which they are made.

(3) The assignee's interest in the assigned claim has priority over the interest of a creditor of the assignor who attaches that claim, whether by judicial process or otherwise, after the time the assignment has taken effect under Article 11.202.

(4) In the event of the assignor's bankruptcy, the assignee's interest in the assigned claim has priority over the interest of the assignor's insolvency administrator and creditors, subject to any rules of the law applicable to the bankruptcy relating to:

(a) publicity required as a condition of such priority;

(b) the ranking of claims; or

(c) the avoidance or ineffectiveness of transactions in the bankruptcy proceedings.

CHAPTER 12—SUBSTITUTION OF NEW DEBTOR: TRANSFER OF CONTRACT

Section 1: Substitution of New Debtor

Article 12.101. Substitution; General Rules

(1) A third person may undertake with the agreement of the debtor and the creditor to be substituted as debtor, with the effect that the original debtor is discharged.

(2) A creditor may agree in advance to a future substitution. In such a case the substitution takes effect only when the creditor is given notice by the new debtor of the agreement between the new and the original debtor.

Article 12.102. Effects of Substitution on Defences and Securities

(1) The new debtor cannot invoke against the creditor any rights or defences arising from the relationship between the new debtor and the original debtor.

(2) The discharge of the original debtor also extends to any security of the original debtor given to the creditor for the performance of the obligation, unless the security is over an asset which is transferred to the new debtor as part of a transaction between the original and the new debtor.

(3) Upon discharge of the original debtor, a security granted by any person other than the new debtor for the performance of the obligation is released, unless that other person agrees that it should continue to be available to the creditor.

(4) The new debtor may invoke against the creditor all defences which the original debtor could have invoked against the creditor.

Section 2: Transfer of Contract

Article 12.201. Transfer of Contract

(1) A party to a contract may agree with a third person that that person is to be substituted as the contracting party. In such a case the substitution takes effect only where, as a result of the other party's assent, the first party is discharged.

(2) To the extent that the substitution of the third person as a contracting party involves a transfer of rights to performance ("claims"), the provisions of Chapter 11 apply; to the extent that obligations are transferred, the provisions of Section 1 of this Chapter apply.

CHAPTER 13—SET-OFF*

CHAPTER 14—PRESCRIPTION

Section 1: General Provision

Article 14.101. Claims Subject to Prescription

A right to performance of an obligation ("claim") is subject to prescription by the expiry of a period of time in accordance with these Principles.

Section 2: Periods of Prescription and Their Commencement

Article 14.201. General Period

The general period of prescription is three years.

Article 14.202. Period for a Claim Established by Legal Proceedings

(1) The period of prescription for a claim established by judgment is ten years.

(2) The same applies to a claim established by an arbitral award or other instrument which is enforceable as if it were a judgment. . . .

Section 4: Renewal of Periods

Article 14.401. Renewal by Acknowledgement

(1) If the debtor acknowledges the claim, vis-à-vis the creditor, by part payment, payment of interest, giving of security, or in any other manner, a new period of prescription begins to run.

(2) The new period is the general period of prescription. . . .

Section 6: Modification by Agreement

Article 14.601. Agreements Concerning Prescription

(1) The requirements for prescription may be modified by agreement between the parties, in particular by either shortening or lengthening the periods of prescription.

(2) The period of prescription may not, however, be reduced to less than one year or extended to more than thirty years after the time of commencement set out in Article 14.203.

---

* Omitted.

CHAPTER 15—ILLEGALITY

Article 15.101. Contracts Contrary to Fundamental Principles

A contract is of no effect to the extent that it is contrary to principles recognized as fundamental in the laws of the Member States of the European Union.

Article 15.102. Contracts Infringing Mandatory Rules

(1) Where a contract infringes a mandatory rule of law applicable under Article 1.103 of these Principles, the effects of that infringement upon the contract are the effects, if any, expressly prescribed by that mandatory rule.

(2) Where the mandatory rule does not expressly prescribe the effects of an infringement upon a contract, the contract may be declared to have full effect, to have some effect, to have no effect, or to be subject to modification.

(3) A decision reached under paragraph (2) must be an appropriate and proportional response to the infringement, having regard to all relevant circumstances, including:

- (a) the purpose of the rule which has been infringed;
- (b) the category of persons for whose protection the rule exists;
- (c) any sanction that may be imposed under the rule infringed;
- (d) the seriousness of the infringement;
- (e) whether the infringement was intentional; and
- (f) the closeness of the relationship between the infringement and the contract.

Article 15.103. Partial Ineffectiveness

(1) If only part of a contract is rendered ineffective under Articles 15.101 or 15.102, the remaining part continues in effect unless, giving due consideration to all the circumstances of the case, it is unreasonable to uphold it.

(2) Articles 15.104 and 15.105 apply, with appropriate adaptations, to a case of partial ineffectiveness.

Article 15.104. Restitution

(1) When a contract is rendered ineffective under Articles 15.101 or 15.102, either party may claim restitution of whatever that party has supplied under the contract, provided that, where appropriate, concurrent restitution is made of whatever has been received.

(2) When considering whether to grant restitution under paragraph (1), and what concurrent restitution, if any, would be appropriate, regard must be had to the factors referred to in Article 15.102(3).

(3) An award of restitution may be refused to a party who knew or ought to have known of the reason for the ineffectiveness.

(4) If restitution cannot be made in kind for any reason, a reasonable sum must be paid for what has been received.

Article 15.105. Damages

(1) A party to a contract which is rendered ineffective under Articles 15.101 or 15.102 may recover from the other party damages putting the first party as nearly as possible into the same

position as if the contract had not been concluded, provided that the other party knew or ought to have known of the reason for the ineffectiveness.

(2) When considering whether to award damages under paragraph (1), regard must be had to the factors referred to in Article 15.102(3).

(3) An award of damages may be refused where the first party knew or ought to have known of the reason for the ineffectiveness.

CHAPTER 16—CONDITIONS

Article 16.101. Types of Condition

A contractual obligation may be made conditional upon the occurrence of an uncertain future event, so that the obligation takes effect only if the event occurs (suspensive condition) or comes to an end if the event occurs (resolutive condition).

Article 16.102. Interference With Conditions

(1) If fulfillment of a condition is prevented by a party, contrary to duties of good faith and fair dealing or co-operation, and if fulfillment would have operated to that party's disadvantage, the condition is deemed to be fulfilled.

(2) If fulfillment of a condition is brought about by a party, contrary to duties of good faith and fair dealing or co-operation, and if fulfillment operates to that party's advantage, the condition is deemed not to be fulfilled.

Article 16.103. Effect of Conditions

(1) Upon fulfillment of a suspensive condition, the relevant obligation takes effect unless the parties otherwise agree.

(2) Upon fulfillment of a resolutive condition, the relevant obligation comes to an end unless the parties otherwise agree.

. . .

CHAPTER 17—CAPITALISATION OF INTEREST*

---

* Omitted.

EUROPEAN COMMUNITY COUNCIL DIRECTIVE 93/13/EEC OF 5 APRIL 1993 ON UNFAIR TERMS IN CONSUMER CONTRACTS

[The Directive on Unfair Terms in Consumer Contracts ("DUTCC") is law within the European Union ("EU") (formerly called the "European Community"). Its general thrust is comparable to the part of U.S. contract law's unconscionability doctrine that is widely known as "substantive unconscionability." Prior to its adoption, the EU's member States each had domestic laws that protected consumers. These laws differed in many respects, including in their definitions of "unfairness" (or the equivalent) and in the consequences they prescribed when a contract or term was unfair. The European Commission believed that these differences made consumers in one member State wary of contracting with parties elsewhere in the EU. To facilitate contracting in the EU's common market, the Commission developed the DUTCC to harmonize the laws of the member States and thereby increase consumer confidence in the fairness of contracting with parties elsewhere in the EU. The DUTCC, however, also applies to contracts between a seller or supplier and a consumer when both are in one member State.

[In 2015, the European Parliament and the Council adopted a Consumer Rights Directive. It will be found below in this pamphlet. This Directive, 2011/83/EC, does not supersede 93/13/EEC. 93/13EEC was amended in 2019 by Directive (EU) 2019/2161. 92/13/EEC appears here as amended.]

Article 1

1. The purpose of this Directive is to approximate the laws, regulations and administrative provisions of the Member States relating to unfair terms in contracts concluded between a seller or supplier and a consumer.

2. The contractual terms which reflect mandatory statutory or regulatory provisions and the provisions or principles of international conventions to which the Member States or the Community are party, particularly in the transport area, shall not be subject to the provisions of this Directive.

Article 2

For the purposes of this Directive:

(a) "unfair terms" means the contractual terms defined in Article 3;

(b) "consumer" means any natural person who, in contracts covered by this Directive, is acting for purposes which are outside his trade, business or profession;

(c) "seller or supplier" means any natural or legal person who, in contracts covered by this Directive, is acting for purposes relating to his trade, business or profession, whether publicly owned or privately owned.

Article 3

1. A contractual term which has not been individually negotiated shall be regarded as unfair if, contrary to the requirement of good faith, it causes a significant imbalance in the parties' rights and obligations arising under the contract, to the detriment of the consumer.

2. A term shall always be regarded as not individually negotiated where it has been drafted in advance and the consumer has therefore not been able to influence the substance of the term, particularly in the context of a pre-formulated standard contract.

The fact that certain aspects of a term or one specific term have been individually negotiated shall not exclude the application of this Article to the rest of a contract if an overall assessment of the contract indicates that it is nevertheless a pre-formulated standard contract.

UNFAIR TERMS IN CONSUMER CONTRACTS

Where any seller or supplier claims that a standard term has been individually negotiated, the burden of proof in this respect shall be incumbent on him.

3. The Annex shall contain an indicative and non-exhaustive list of the terms which may be regarded as unfair.

Article 4

1. Without prejudice to Article 7, the unfairness of a contractual term shall be assessed, taking into account the nature of the goods or services for which the contract was concluded and by referring, at the time of conclusion of the contract, to all the circumstances attending the conclusion of the contract and to all the other terms of the contract or of another contract on which it is dependent.

2. Assessment of the unfair nature of the terms shall relate neither to the definition of the main subject matter of the contract nor to the adequacy of the price and remuneration, on the one hand, as against the services or goods supplied in exchange, on the other, in so far as these terms are in plain intelligible language.

Article 5

In the case of contracts where all or certain terms offered to the consumer are in writing, these terms must always be drafted in plain, intelligible language. Where there is doubt about the meaning of a term, the interpretation most favourable to the consumer shall prevail. This rule on interpretation shall not apply in the context of the procedures laid down in Article 7(2).

Article 6

1. Member States shall lay down that unfair terms used in a contract concluded with a consumer by a seller or supplier shall, as provided for under their national law, not be binding on the consumer and that the contract shall continue to bind the parties upon those terms if it is capable of continuing in existence without the unfair terms.

2. Member States shall take the necessary measures to ensure that the consumer does not lose the protection granted by this Directive by virtue of the choice of the law of a non-Member country as the law applicable to the contract if the latter has a close connection with the territory of the Member States.

Article 7

1. Member States shall ensure that, in the interests of consumers and of competitors, adequate and effective means exist to prevent the continued use of unfair terms in contracts concluded with consumers by sellers or suppliers.

2. The means referred to in paragraph 1 shall include provisions whereby persons or organizations, having a legitimate interest under national law in protecting consumers, may take action according to the national law concerned before the courts or before competent administrative bodies for a decision as to whether contractual terms drawn up for general use are unfair, so that they can apply appropriate and effective means to prevent the continued use of such terms.

3. With due regard for national laws, the legal remedies referred to in paragraph 2 may be directed separately or jointly against a number of sellers or suppliers from the same economic sector or their associations which use or recommend the use of the same general contractual terms or similar terms.

Article 8

Member States may adopt or retain the most stringent provisions compatible with the Treaty in the area covered by this Directive, to ensure a maximum degree of protection for the consumer. . . .

Article 8b

1. Member States shall lay down the rules on penalties applicable to infringements of national provisions adopted pursuant to this Directive and shall take all measures necessary to ensure that they are implemented. The penalties provided for shall be effective, proportionate and dissuasive.

2. Member States may restrict such penalties to situations where the contractual terms are expressly defined as unfair in all circumstances in national law or where a seller or supplier continues to use contractual terms that have been found to be unfair in a final decision taken in accordance with Article 7(2).

3. Member States shall ensure that the following non-exhaustive and indicative criteria are taken into account for the imposition of penalties, where appropriate:

(a) the nature, gravity, scale and duration of the infringement;

(b) any action taken by the seller or supplier to mitigate or remedy the damage suffered by consumers;

(c) any previous infringements by the seller or supplier;

(d) the financial benefits gained or losses avoided by the seller or supplier due to the infringement, if the relevant data are available;

(e) penalties imposed on the seller or supplier for the same infringement in other Member States in cross-border cases where information about such penalties is available through the mechanism established by Regulation (EU) 2017/2394 of the European Parliament and of the Council . . .;

(f) any other aggravating or mitigating factors applicable to the circumstances of the case.

4. Without prejudice to paragraph 2 of this Article, Member States shall ensure that, when penalties are to be imposed in accordance with Article 21 of Regulation (EU) 2017/2394, they include the possibility either to impose fines through administrative procedures or to initiate legal proceedings for the imposition of fines, or both, the maximum amount of such fines being at least 4 % of the seller's or supplier's annual turnover in the Member State or Member States concerned.

5. For cases where a fine is to be imposed in accordance with paragraph 4, but information on the seller's or supplier's annual turnover is not available, Member States shall introduce the possibility to impose fines, the maximum amount of which shall be at least EUR 2 million.

6. Member States shall, by 28 November 2021, notify the Commission of the rules and measures referred to in paragraph 1 and shall notify it, without delay, of any subsequent amendment affecting them.

Article 9

The Commission shall present a report to the European Parliament and to the Council concerning the application of this Directive five years at the latest after the date in Article 10(1).

Article 10

1. Member States shall bring into force the laws, regulations and administrative provisions necessary to comply with this Directive no later than 31 December 1994. They shall forthwith inform the Commission thereof.

These provisions shall be applicable to all contracts concluded after 31 December 1994.

2. When Member States adopt these measures, they shall contain a reference to this Directive or shall be accompanied by such reference on the occasion of their official publication. The methods of making such a reference shall be laid down by the Member States.

3. Member States shall communicate the main provisions of national law which they adopt in the field covered by this Directive to the Commission.

Pt. VI UNFAIR TERMS IN CONSUMER CONTRACTS

Article 11

This Directive is addressed to the Member States....

ANNEX

TERMS REFERRED TO IN ARTICLE 3(3)

1. Terms which have the object or effect of:

(a) excluding or limiting the legal liability of a seller or supplier in the event of the death of a consumer or personal injury to the latter resulting from an act or omission of that seller or supplier;

(b) inappropriately excluding or limiting the legal rights of the consumer vis-à-vis the seller or supplier or another party in the event of total or partial non-performance or inadequate performance by the seller or supplier of any of the contractual obligations, including the option of offsetting a debt owed to the seller or supplier against any claim which the consumer may have against him;

(c) making an agreement binding on the consumer whereas provision of services by the seller or supplier is subject to a condition whose realization depends on his own will alone;

(d) permitting the seller or supplier to retain sums paid by the consumer where the latter decides not to conclude or perform the contract, without providing for the consumer to receive compensation of an equivalent amount from the seller or supplier where the latter is the party cancelling the contract;

(e) requiring any consumer who fails to fulfil his obligation to pay a disproportionately high sum in compensation;

(f) authorizing the seller or supplier to dissolve the contract on a discretionary basis where the same facility is not granted to the consumer, or permitting the seller or supplier to retain the sums paid for services not yet supplied by him where it is the seller or supplier himself who dissolves the contract;

(g) enabling the seller or supplier to terminate a contract of indeterminate duration without reasonable notice except where there are serious grounds for doing so;

(h) automatically extending a contract of fixed duration where the consumer does not indicate otherwise, when the deadline fixed for the consumer to express this desire not to extend the contract is unreasonably early;

(i) irrevocably binding the consumer to terms with which he had no real opportunity of becoming acquainted before the conclusion of the contract;

(j) enabling the seller or supplier to alter the terms of the contract unilaterally without a valid reason which is specified in the contract;

(k) enabling the seller or supplier to alter unilaterally without a valid reason any characteristics of the product or service to be provided;

(*l*) providing for the price of goods to be determined at the time of delivery or allowing a seller of goods or supplier of services to increase their price without in both cases giving the consumer the corresponding right to cancel the contract if the final price is too high in relation to the price agreed when the contract was concluded;

(m) giving the seller or supplier the right to determine whether the goods or services supplied are in conformity with the contract, or giving him the exclusive right to interpret any term of the contract;

(n) limiting the seller's or supplier's obligation to respect commitments undertaken by his agents or making his commitments subject to compliance with a particular formality;

(o) obliging the consumer to fulfil all his obligations where the seller or supplier does not perform his;

(p) giving the seller or supplier the possibility of transferring his rights and obligations under the contract, where this may serve to reduce the guarantees for the consumer, without the latter's agreement;

(q) excluding or hindering the consumer's right to take legal action or exercise any other legal remedy, particularly by requiring the consumer to take disputes exclusively to arbitration not covered by legal provisions, unduly restricting the evidence available to him or imposing on him a burden of proof which, according to the applicable law, should lie with another party to the contract.

2. Scope of subparagraphs (g), (j), and (l)

(a) Subparagraph (g) is without hindrance to terms by which a supplier of financial services reserves the right to terminate unilaterally a contract of indeterminate duration without notice where there is a valid reason, provided that the supplier is required to inform the other contracting party or parties thereof immediately.

(b) Subparagraph (j) is without hindrance to terms under which a supplier of financial services reserves the right to alter the rate of interest payable by the consumer or due to the latter, or the amount of other charges for financial services without notice where there is a valid reason, provided that the supplier is required to inform the other contracting party or parties thereof at the earliest opportunity and that the latter are free to dissolve the contract immediately.

Subparagraph (j) is also without hindrance to terms under which a seller or supplier reserves the right to alter unilaterally the conditions of a contract of indeterminate duration, provided that he is required to inform the consumer with reasonable notice and that the consumer is free to dissolve the contract.

(c) Subparagraphs (g), (j) and (l) do not apply to:

— transactions in transferable securities, financial instruments and other products or services where the price is linked to fluctuations in a stock exchange quotation or index or a financial market rate that the seller or supplier does not control;

— contracts for the purchase or sale of foreign currency, traveller's cheques or international money orders denominated in foreign currency;

(d) Subparagraph (l) is without hindrance to price-indexation clauses, where lawful, provided that the method by which prices vary is explicitly described.

DIRECTIVE 2005/29/EC OF THE EUROPEAN PARLIAMENT AND OF THE COUNCIL OF 11 MAY 2005

[Known as the "Unfair Commercial Practices Directive" ("UCPD"), this Directive aims to harmonize the laws of the member States of the European Union ("EU") that police unfair commercial practices disadvantaging consumers. Like the EU's Directive on Unfair Terms in Consumer Contracts ("DUTCC"), included in this pamphlet above, the purpose of such harmonization is to facilitate contracting in the EU's common market by increasing consumer confidence in the fairness of contracts with parties in other member States. The UCPD differs from the DUTCC because the latter concerns a contract's terms whereas the former concerns contracting practices. So, for example, UCPD prohibits practices that mislead consumers or are so aggressive as to cause a consumer to make a contract he or she otherwise would not have made. UCPD, Arts. 6–9. The UCPD is comparable to the part of U.S. contract law's unconscionability doctrine that is widely known as "procedural unconscionability." Directive 2005/29/EC was amended in 2019 by Directive (EU) 2019/2161. 2005/29/EC appears here as amended.]

CHAPTER 1

GENERAL PROVISIONS

Article 1

Purpose

The purpose of this Directive is to contribute to the proper functioning of the internal market and achieve a high level of consumer protection by approximating the laws, regulations and administrative provisions of the Member States on unfair commercial practices harming consumers' economic interests.

Article 2

Definitions

For the purposes of this Directive:

(a) 'consumer' means any natural person who, in commercial practices covered by this Directive, is acting for purposes which are outside his trade, business, craft or profession;

(b) 'trader' means any natural or legal person who, in commercial practices covered by this Directive, is acting for purposes relating to his trade, business, craft or profession and anyone acting in the name of or on behalf of a trader;

(c) 'product' means any good or service including immovable property, digital service and digital content as well as rights and obligations;

(d) 'business-to-consumer commercial practices' (hereinafter also referred to as commercial practices) means any act, omission, course of conduct or representation, commercial communication including advertising and marketing, by a trader, directly connected with the promotion, sale or supply of a product to consumers;

(e) 'to materially distort the economic behaviour of consumers' means using a commercial practice to appreciably impair the consumer's ability to make an informed decision, thereby causing the consumer to take a transactional decision that he would not have taken otherwise;

(f) 'code of conduct' means an agreement or set of rules not imposed by law, regulation or administrative provision of a Member State which defines the behaviour of traders who undertake to be bound by the code in relation to one or more particular commercial practices or business sectors;

(g) 'code owner' means any entity, including a trader or group of traders, which is responsible for the formulation and revision of a code of conduct and/or for monitoring compliance with the code by those who have undertaken to be bound by it;

(h) 'professional diligence' means the standard of special skill and care which a trader may reasonably be expected to exercise towards consumers, commensurate with honest market practice and/or the general principle of good faith in the trader's field of activity;

(i) 'invitation to purchase' means a commercial communication which indicates characteristics of the product and the price in a way appropriate to the means of the commercial communication used and thereby enables the consumer to make a purchase;

(j) 'undue influence' means exploiting a position of power in relation to the consumer so as to apply pressure, even without using or threatening to use physical force, in a way which significantly limits the consumer's ability to make an informed decision;

(k) 'transactional decision' means any decision taken by a consumer concerning whether, how and on what terms to purchase, make payment in whole or in part for, retain or dispose of a product or to exercise a contractual right in relation to the product, whether the consumer decides to act or to refrain from acting;

(*l*) 'regulated profession' means a professional activity or a group of professional activities, access to which or the pursuit of which, or one of the modes of pursuing which, is conditional, directly or indirectly, upon possession of specific professional qualifications, pursuant to laws, regulations or administrative provisions.

(m) 'ranking' means relative prominence given to products, as presented, organized or communicated by the trader, irrespective of the technological means used for such presentation, organization or communication;

(n) 'online marketplace' means a service using software, including a website, part of a website or an application, operated by or on behalf of a trader which allows consumers to conclude distance contracts with other traders or consumers.

Article 3

Scope

1. This Directive shall apply to unfair business-to-consumer commercial practices, as laid down in Article 5, before, during and after a commercial transaction in relation to a product.

2. This Directive is without prejudice to contract law and, in particular, to the rules on the validity, formation or effect of a contract.

3. This Directive is without prejudice to Community or national rules relating to the health and safety aspects of products.

4. In the case of conflict between the provisions of this Directive and other Community rules regulating specific aspects of unfair commercial practices, the latter shall prevail and apply to those specific aspects.

5. This Directive does not prevent Member States from adopting provisions to protect the legitimate interests of consumers with regard to aggressive or misleading marketing or selling practices in the context of unsolicited visits by a trader to a consumer's home or excursions organised by a trader with the aim or effect of promoting or selling products to consumers. Such provisions shall be proportionate, non-discriminatory and justified on grounds of consumer protection.

6. Member States shall notify the Commission without delay of any national provisions adopted on the basis of paragraph 5 as well as of any subsequent changes. The Commission shall make this information easily accessible to consumers and traders on a dedicated website.

7. This Directive is without prejudice to the rules determining the jurisdiction of the courts.

8. This Directive is without prejudice to any conditions of establishment or of authorisation regimes, or to the deontological codes of conduct or other specific rules governing regulated professions in order to uphold high standards of integrity on the part of the professional, which Member States may, in conformity with Community law, impose on professionals.

9. In relation to 'financial services', as defined in Directive 2002/65/EC, and immovable property, Member States may impose requirements which are more restrictive or prescriptive than this Directive in the field which it approximates.

10. This Directive shall not apply to the application of the laws, regulations and administrative provisions of Member States relating to the certification and indication of the standard of fineness of articles of precious metal.

Article 4

Internal market

Member States shall neither restrict the freedom to provide services nor restrict the free movement of goods for reasons falling within the field approximated by this Directive.

CHAPTER 2

UNFAIR COMMERCIAL PRACTICES

Article 5

Prohibition of unfair commercial practices

1. Unfair commercial practices shall be prohibited.

2. A commercial practice shall be unfair if:

(a) it is contrary to the requirements of professional diligence, and

(b) it materially distorts or is likely to materially distort the economic behaviour with regard to the product of the average consumer whom it reaches or to whom it is addressed, or of the average member of the group when a commercial practice is directed to a particular group of consumers.

3. Commercial practices which are likely to materially distort the economic behaviour only of a clearly identifiable group of consumers who are particularly vulnerable to the practice or the underlying product because of their mental or physical infirmity, age or credulity in a way which the trader could reasonably be expected to foresee, shall be assessed from the perspective of the average member of that group. This is without prejudice to the common and legitimate advertising practice of making exaggerated statements or statements which are not meant to be taken literally.

4. In particular, commercial practices shall be unfair which:

(a) are misleading as set out in Articles 6 and 7, or

(b) are aggressive as set out in Articles 8 and 9.

5. Annex I contains the list of those commercial practices which shall in all circumstances be regarded as unfair. The same single list shall apply in all Member States and may only be modified by revision of this Directive.

Section 1

Misleading commercial practices

Article 6

Misleading actions

1. A commercial practice shall be regarded as misleading if it contains false information and is therefore untruthful or in any way, including overall presentation, deceives or is likely to deceive the average consumer, even if the information is factually correct, in relation to one or more of the following elements, and in either case causes or is likely to cause him to take a transactional decision that he would not have taken otherwise:

   (a) the existence or nature of the product;

   (b) the main characteristics of the product, such as its availability, benefits, risks, execution, composition, accessories, after-sale customer assistance and complaint handling, method and date of manufacture or provision, delivery, fitness for purpose, usage, quantity, specification, geographical or commercial origin or the results to be expected from its use, or the results and material features of tests or checks carried out on the product;

   (c) the extent of the trader's commitments, the motives for the commercial practice and the nature of the sales process, any statement or symbol in relation to direct or indirect sponsorship or approval of the trader or the product;

   (d) the price or the manner in which the price is calculated, or the existence of a specific price advantage;

   (e) the need for a service, part, replacement or repair;

   (f) the nature, attributes and rights of the trader or his agent, such as his identity and assets, his qualifications, status, approval, affiliation or connection and ownership of industrial, commercial or intellectual property rights or his awards and distinctions;

   (g) the consumer's rights, including the right to replacement or reimbursement under Directive 1999/44/EC of the European Parliament and of the Council of 25 May 1999 on certain aspects of the sale of consumer goods and associated guarantees, or the risks he may face.

2. A commercial practice shall also be regarded as misleading if, in its factual context, taking account of all its features and circumstances, it causes or is likely to cause the average consumer to take a transactional decision that he would not have taken otherwise, and it involves:

   (a) any marketing of a product, including comparative advertising, which creates confusion with any products, trade marks, trade names or other distinguishing marks of a competitor;

   (b) non-compliance by the trader with commitments contained in codes of conduct by which the trader has undertaken to be bound, where:

   (i) the commitment is not aspirational but is firm and is capable of being verified, and

   (ii) the trader indicates in a commercial practice that he is bound by the code.

   (c) any marketing of a good, in one Member State, as being identical to a good marketed in other Member States, while that good has significantly different composition or characteristics, unless justified by legitimate and objective factors.

DIRECTIVE 2005/29/EC OF THE EUROPEAN PARLIAMENT

Article 7

Misleading omissions

1. A commercial practice shall be regarded as misleading if, in its factual context, taking account of all its features and circumstances and the limitations of the communication medium, it omits material information that the average consumer needs, according to the context, to take an informed transactional decision and thereby causes or is likely to cause the average consumer to take a transactional decision that he would not have taken otherwise.

2. It shall also be regarded as a misleading omission when, taking account of the matters described in paragraph 1, a trader hides or provides in an unclear, unintelligible, ambiguous or untimely manner such material information as referred to in that paragraph or fails to identify the commercial intent of the commercial practice if not already apparent from the context, and where, in either case, this causes or is likely to cause the average consumer to take a transactional decision that he would not have taken otherwise.

3. Where the medium used to communicate the commercial practice imposes limitations of space or time, these limitations and any measures taken by the trader to make the information available to consumers by other means shall be taken into account in deciding whether information has been omitted.

4. In the case of an invitation to purchase, the following information shall be regarded as material, if not already apparent from the context:

(a) the main characteristics of the product, to an extent appropriate to the medium and the product;

(b) the geographical address and the identity of the trader, such as his trading name and, where applicable, the geographical address and the identity of the trader on whose behalf he is acting;

(c) the price inclusive of taxes, or where the nature of the product means that the price cannot reasonably be calculated in advance, the manner in which the price is calculated, as well as, where appropriate, all additional freight, delivery or postal charges or, where these charges cannot reasonably be calculated in advance, the fact that such additional charges may be payable;

(d) the arrangements for payment, delivery and performance, if they depart from the requirements of professional diligence;

(e) for products and transactions involving a right of withdrawal or cancellation, the existence of such a right;

(f) for products offered on online marketplaces, whether the third party offering the products is a trader or not, on the basis of the declaration of that third party to the provider of the online marketplace.

4a. When providing consumers with the possibility to search for products offered by different traders or by consumers on the basis of a query in the form of a keyword, phrase or other input, irrespective of where transactions are ultimately concluded, general information, made available in a specific section of the online interface that is directly and easily accessible from the page where the query results are presented, on the main parameters determining the ranking of products presented to the consumer as a result of the search query and the relative importance of those parameters, as opposed to other parameters, shall be regarded as material. This paragraph does not apply to providers of online search engines as defined in point (6) of Article 2 of Regulation (EU) 2019/1150 of the European Parliament and of the Council . . . .

5. Information requirements established by Community law in relation to commercial communication including advertising or marketing . . . shall be regarded as material.

6. Where a trader provides access to consumer reviews of products, information about whether and how the trader ensures that the published reviews originate from consumers who have actually used or purchased the product shall be regarded as material.

Section 2

Aggressive commercial practices

Article 8

Aggressive commercial practices

A commercial practice shall be regarded as aggressive if, in its factual context, taking account of all its features and circumstances, by harassment, coercion, including the use of physical force, or undue influence, it significantly impairs or is likely to significantly impair the average consumer's freedom of choice or conduct with regard to the product and thereby causes him or is likely to cause him to take a transactional decision that he would not have taken otherwise.

Article 9

Use of harassment, coercion and undue influence

In determining whether a commercial practice uses harassment, coercion, including the use of physical force, or undue influence, account shall be taken of:

(a) its timing, location, nature or persistence;

(b) the use of threatening or abusive language or behaviour;

(c) the exploitation by the trader of any specific misfortune or circumstance of such gravity as to impair the consumer's judgement, of which the trader is aware, to influence the consumer's decision with regard to the product;

(d) any onerous or disproportionate non-contractual barriers imposed by the trader where a consumer wishes to exercise rights under the contract, including rights to terminate a contract or to switch to another product or another trader;

(e) any threat to take any action that cannot legally be taken.

Article 11a

Redress

1. Consumers harmed by unfair commercial practices, shall have access to proportionate and effective remedies, including compensation for damage suffered by the consumer and, where relevant, a price reduction or the termination of the contract. Member States may determine the conditions for the application and effects of those remedies. Member States may take into account, where appropriate, the gravity and nature of the unfair commercial practice, the damage suffered by the consumer and other relevant circumstances.

2. Those remedies shall be without prejudice to the application of other remedies available to consumers under Union or national law. . . .

DIRECTIVE 2005/29/EC OF THE EUROPEAN PARLIAMENT

ANNEX I

COMMERCIAL PRACTICES WHICH ARE IN ALL CIRCUMSTANCES CONSIDERED UNFAIR

Misleading commercial practices

1. Claiming to be a signatory to a code of conduct when the trader is not.

2. Displaying a trust mark, quality mark or equivalent without having obtained the necessary authorisation.

3. Claiming that a code of conduct has an endorsement from a public or other body which it does not have.

4. Claiming that a trader (including his commercial practices) or a product has been approved, endorsed or authorised by a public or private body when he/it has not or making such a claim without complying with the terms of the approval, endorsement or authorisation.

5. Making an invitation to purchase products at a specified price without disclosing the existence of any reasonable grounds the trader may have for believing that he will not be able to offer for supply or to procure another trader to supply, those products or equivalent products at that price for a period that is, and in quantities that are, reasonable having regard to the product, the scale of advertising of the product and the price offered (bait advertising).

6. Making an invitation to purchase products at a specified price and then:

    (a) refusing to show the advertised item to consumers; or

    (b) refusing to take orders for it or deliver it within a reasonable time; or

    (c) demonstrating a defective sample of it, with the intention of promoting a different product (bait and switch)

7. Falsely stating that a product will only be available for a very limited time, or that it will only be available on particular terms for a very limited time, in order to elicit an immediate decision and deprive consumers of sufficient opportunity or time to make an informed choice.

8. Undertaking to provide after-sales service to consumers with whom the trader has communicated prior to a transaction in a language which is not an official language of the Member State where the trader is located and then making such service available only in another language without clearly disclosing this to the consumer before the consumer is committed to the transaction.

9. Stating or otherwise creating the impression that a product can legally be sold when it cannot.

10. Presenting rights given to consumers in law as a distinctive feature of the trader's offer.

11. Using editorial content in the media to promote a product where a trader has paid for the promotion without making that clear in the content or by images or sounds clearly identifiable by the consumer (advertorial). This is without prejudice to Council Directive 89/552/EEC.

11a. Providing search results in response to a consumer's online search query without clearly disclosing any paid advertisement or payment specifically for achieving higher ranking of products within the search results.

12. Making a materially inaccurate claim concerning the nature and extent of the risk to the personal security of the consumer or his family if the consumer does not purchase the product.

13. Promoting a product similar to a product made by a particular manufacturer in such a manner as deliberately to mislead the consumer into believing that the product is made by that same manufacturer when it is not.
14. Establishing, operating or promoting a pyramid promotional scheme where a consumer gives consideration for the opportunity to receive compensation that is derived primarily from the introduction of other consumers into the scheme rather than from the sale or consumption of products.
15. Claiming that the trader is about to cease trading or move premises when he is not.
16. Claiming that products are able to facilitate winning in games of chance.
17. Falsely claiming that a product is able to cure illnesses, dysfunction or malformations.
18. Passing on materially inaccurate information on market conditions or on the possibility of finding the product with the intention of inducing the consumer to acquire the product at conditions less favourable than normal market conditions.
19. Claiming in a commercial practice to offer a competition or prize promotion without awarding the prizes described or a reasonable equivalent.
20. Describing a product as 'gratis', 'free', 'without charge' or similar if the consumer has to pay anything other than the unavoidable cost of responding to the commercial practice and collecting or paying for delivery of the item.
21. Including in marketing material an invoice or similar document seeking payment which gives the consumer the impression that he has already ordered the marketed product when he has not.
22. Falsely claiming or creating the impression that the trader is not acting for purposes relating to his trade, business, craft or profession, or falsely representing oneself as a consumer.
23. Creating the false impression that after-sales service in relation to a product is available in a Member State other than the one in which the product is sold.
23a. Reselling events tickets to consumers if the trader acquired them by using automated means to circumvent any limit imposed on the number of tickets that a person can buy or any other rules applicable to the purchase of tickets.
23b. Stating that reviews of a product are submitted by consumers who have actually used or purchased the product without taking reasonable and proportionate steps to check that they originate from such consumers.
23c. Submitting or commissioning another legal or natural person to submit false consumer reviews or endorsements, or misrepresenting consumer reviews or social endorsements, in order to promote products.

Aggressive commercial practices

24. Creating the impression that the consumer cannot leave the premises until a contract is formed.
25. Conducting personal visits to the consumer's home ignoring the consumer's request to leave or not to return except in circumstances and to the extent justified, under national law, to enforce a contractual obligation.
26. Making persistent and unwanted solicitations by telephone, fax, e-mail or other remote media except in circumstances and to the extent justified under national law to enforce a contractual obligation. . . .
27. Requiring a consumer who wishes to claim on an insurance policy to produce documents which could not reasonably be considered relevant as to whether the claim was valid, or

failing systematically to respond to pertinent correspondence, in order to dissuade a consumer from exercising his contractual rights.

28. Including in an advertisement a direct exhortation to children to buy advertised products or persuade their parents or other adults to buy advertised products for them. This provision is without prejudice to Article 16 of Directive 89/552/EEC on television broadcasting.

29. Demanding immediate or deferred payment for or the return or safekeeping of products supplied by the trader, but not solicited by the consumer except where the product is a substitute supplied in conformity with Article 7(3) of Directive 97/7/EC (inertia selling).

30. Explicitly informing a consumer that if he does not buy the product or service, the trader's job or livelihood will be in jeopardy.

31. Creating the false impression that the consumer has already won, will win, or will on doing a particular act win, a prize or other equivalent benefit, when in fact either:

    — there is no prize or other equivalent benefit, or

    — taking any action in relation to claiming the prize or other equivalent benefit is subject to the consumer paying money or incurring a cost. . . .

DIRECTIVE 2011/83/EU OF THE EUROPEAN PARLIAMENT AND OF THE COUNCIL OF 25 OCTOBER 2011

[Directive 2011/83/EU, the "Consumer Rights Directive," was adopted by the European Parliament and the Council of the European Union and became effective on December 13, 2011. Its purpose is to implement a part of the Treaty on the Functioning of the European Union, which provides that the EU should contribute to a high level of consumer protection. This Directive applies to "distance" and "off-premises" contracts as defined in the Directive, Article 2, Sections (7) and (8), which would include contracts between traders and consumers made door-to-door or over the Internet. It is up to Member States of the EU to enforce the directive, as provided in Article 23 below.

[The excerpted provisions focus on a consumer's "right of withdrawal," which empowers a consumer to cancel a covered contract within two weeks from, for example, taking delivery of goods, without giving any reason. The closest counterpart in U.S. law is the Federal Trade Commission's regulation providing for a "cooling off" period of three days following the making of a contract between a buyer and a door-to-door salesman. It is included in this book below. Clearly, the EU Directive is more protective of consumers. 2011/83/EU was amended in 2019 by Directive (EU) 2019/2161. 2011/83/EU appears here as amended.]

CHAPTER 1

SUBJECT MATTER, DEFINITIONS AND SCOPE

Article 1

Subject matter

The purpose of this Directive is, through the achievement of a high level of consumer protection, to contribute to the proper functioning of the internal market by approximating certain aspects of the laws, regulations and administrative provisions of the Member States concerning contracts concluded between consumers and traders.

Article 2

Definitions

For the purpose of this Directive, the following definitions shall apply:

(1) 'consumer' means any natural person who, in contracts covered by this Directive, is acting for purposes which are outside his trade, business, craft or profession;

(2) 'trader' means any natural person or any legal person, irrespective of whether privately or publicly owned, who is acting, including through any other person acting in his name or on his behalf, for purposes relating to his trade, business, craft or profession in relation to contracts covered by this directive;

. . .

(7) 'distance contract' means any contract concluded between the trader and the consumer under an organized distance sales or service-provision scheme without the simultaneous physical presence of the trader and the consumer, with the exclusive use of one or more means of distance communication up to and including the time at which the contract is conducted;

(8) 'off-premises contract' means any contract between the trader and the consumer;

(a) concluded in the simultaneous physical presence of the trader and the consumer, in a place which is not the business premises of the trader;

(b) for which an offer was made by the consumer in the same circumstances as referred to in point (a);

(c) concluded on the business premises of the trader or through any means of distance communication immediately after the consumer was personally and individually addressed in a place which is not the business premises of the trader in the simultaneous physical presence of the trader and the consumer, or

(d) concluded during an excursion organized by the trader with the aim or effect of promoting and selling goods or services to the consumer;

(9) 'business premises' means:

(a) any immovable retail premises where the trader carries out his activity on a permanent basis; or

(b) any movable retail premises where the trader carries out his activity on a usual basis;

(10) 'durable medium' means any instrument which enables the consumer or the trader to store information addressed personally to him in a way accessible for future reference for a period of time adequate for the purposes of the information and which allows the unchanged reproduction of the information stored . . .;

Article 4

Level of harmonization

Member States shall not maintain or introduce, in their national law, provisions diverging from those laid down in this Directive, including more or less stringent provisions to ensure a different level of consumer protection, unless otherwise provided for in this Directive.

. . .

CHAPTER III

CONSUMER INFORMATION AND RIGHT OF WITHDRAWAL FOR DISTANCE AND OFF-PREMISES CONTRACTS

Article 6

Information requirements for distance and off-premises contracts

1. Before the consumer is bound by a distance or off-premises contract, or any corresponding offer, the trader shall provide the consumer with the following information in a clear and comprehensible manner;

(a) the main characteristics of the goods or services, to the extent appropriate to the medium and to the goods or services;

(b) the identity of the trader, such as his trading name;

(c) the geographical address at which the trader is established as well as the trader's telephone number and email address; in addition, where the trader provides other means of online communication which guarantee that the consumer can keep any written correspondence, including the date and time of such correspondence, with the trader on a durable medium, the information shall also include details of those other means; all those means of communication provided by the trader shall enable the consumer to contact the trader quickly and communicate with him efficiently; where applicable, the trader shall also provide the geographical address and identity of the trader on whose behalf he is acting;

(d) if different from the address provided in accordance with point (c), the geographical address of the place of business of the trader, and, where applicable, that of the trader on whose behalf he is acting, where the consumer can address any complaints;

(e) the total price of the goods or services inclusive of taxes, or where the nature of the goods or services is such that the price cannot reasonably be calculated in advance, the manner in which the price is to be calculated, as well as, where applicable, all additional freight, delivery or postal charges and any other costs or, where those charges cannot reasonably be calculated in advance, the fact that such additional charges may be payable. In the case of a contract of indeterminate duration or a contract containing a subscription, the total price shall include the total costs per billing period. Where such contracts are charged at a fixed rate, the total price shall also mean the total monthly costs. Where the total costs cannot be reasonably calculated in advance, the manner in which the price is to be calculated shall be provided; . . .

(f) the cost of using the means of distance communication for the conclusion of the contract where that cost is calculated other than at the basic rate;

(g) the arrangements for payment, delivery, performance, the time by which the trader undertakes to deliver the goods or to perform the services and, where applicable, the trader's complaint handling policy;

(h) where a right of withdrawal exists, the conditions, time limit and procedures for exercising that right in accordance with Article 11(1), as well as the model withdrawal form set out in Annex 1(B);

(i) where applicable, that the consumer will have to bear the cost of returning the goods in case of withdrawal and, for distance contracts, if the goods, by their nature, cannot normally be returned by post, the cost of returning the goods;

(j) that, if the consumer exercises the right of withdrawal after having made a request in accordance with Article 7(3) or Article 8(8), the consumer shall be liable to pay the trader reasonable costs in accordance with Article 14(3);

(k) where a right of withdrawal is not provided for in accordance with Article 16, the information that the consumer will not benefit from a right of withdrawal or, where applicable, the circumstances under which the consumer loses his right of withdrawal;

(l) a reminder of the existence of a legal guarantee of conformity for goods, digital content and digital services;

(m) where applicable, the existence and the conditions of [after-sale] customer assistance, after-sales services and commercial guarantees;

(n) the existence of relevant codes of conduct, . . . and how copies of them can be obtained, where applicable;

(o) the duration of the contract, where applicable, or, if the contract is of indeterminate duration or is to be extended automatically, the conditions for terminating the contract;

(p) where applicable, the minimum duration of the consumer's obligations under the contract;

(q) where applicable, the existence and the conditions of deposits or other financial guarantees to be paid or provided by the consumer at the request of the trader;

(r) where applicable, the functionality, including applicable technical protection measures, of goods with digital elements, digital content and digital services;

(s) where applicable, any relevant compatibility and interoperability of goods with digital elements, digital content and digital services that the trader is aware of or can reasonably be expected to have been aware of;

(t) where applicable, the possibility of having recourse to an out-of-court complaint and redress mechanism, to which the trader is subject, and the methods for having access to it.

. . .

5. The information referred to in paragraph 1 shall form an integral part of the distance or off-premises contract and shall not be altered unless the contracting parties expressly agree otherwise.

Article 6a

Additional specific information requirements for contracts concluded on online marketplaces

1. Before a consumer is bound by a distance contract, or any corresponding offer, on an online marketplace, the provider of the online marketplace shall, without prejudice to Directive 2005/29/EC, provide the consumer with the following information in a clear and comprehensible manner and in a way appropriate to the means of distance communication:

(a) general information, made available in a specific section of the online interface that is directly and easily accessible from the page where the offers are presented, on the main parameters determining ranking, as defined in point (m) of Article 2(1) of Directive 2005/29/EC, of offers presented to the consumer as a result of the search query and the relative importance of those parameters as opposed to other parameters;

(b) whether the third party offering the goods, services or digital content is a trader or not, on the basis of the declaration of that third party to the provider of the online marketplace;

(c) where the third party offering the goods, services or digital content is not a trader, that the consumer rights stemming from Union consumer protection law do not apply to the contract;

(d) where applicable, how the obligations related to the contract are shared between the third party offering the goods, services or digital content and the provider of the online marketplace, such information being without prejudice to any responsibility that the provider of the online marketplace or the third-party trader has in relation to the contract under other Union or national law. . . .

. . .

Article 7

Formal requirements for off-premises contracts

1. With respect to off-premises contracts, the trader shall give the information provided for in Article 6(1) to the consumer on paper or, if the consumer agrees, on another durable medium. That information shall be legible and in plain, intelligible language.

. . .

Article 8

Formal requirements for distance contracts

1. With respect to distance contracts, the trader shall give the information provided for in Article 6(1) or make that information available to the consumer in a way appropriate to the means of distance communication used in plain and intelligible language. In so far as that information is provided on a durable medium, it shall be legible.

2. If a distance contract to be concluded by electronic means places the consumer under an obligation to pay, the trader shall make the consumer aware in a clear and prominent manner, and directly before the consumer places his order, of the information provided for in points (a), (e), (o) and (p) of Article 6(1).

The trader shall ensure that the consumer, when placing his order, explicitly acknowledges that the order implies an obligation to pay. If placing an order entails activating a button or a similar function, the button or similar function shall be labelled in an easily legible manner only with the words 'order with obligation to pay' or a corresponding unambiguous formulation indicating that placing the order entails an obligation to pay the trader. If the trader has not complied with this subparagraph, the consumer shall not be bound by the contract or order.

3. Trading websites shall indicate clearly and legibly at the latest at the beginning of the ordering process whether any delivery restrictions apply and which means of payment are accepted.

4. If the contract is concluded through a means of distance communication which allows limited space or time to display the information, the trader shall provide, on or through that particular means prior to the conclusion of such a contract, at least the pre-contractual information regarding the main characteristics of the goods or services, the identity of the trader, the total price, the right of withdrawal, the duration of the contract and, if the contract is of indeterminate duration, the conditions for terminating the contract, as referred to, respectively, in points (a), (b), (e), (h) and (o) of Article 6(1) except the model withdrawal form set out in Annex I (B) referred to in point (h). The other information referred to in Article 6(1), including the model withdrawal form, shall be provided by the trader to the consumer in an appropriate way in accordance with paragraph 1 of this Article.

5. Without prejudice to paragraph 4, if the trader makes a telephone call to the consumer with a view to concluding a distance contract, he shall, at the beginning of the conversation with the consumer, disclose his identity and, where applicable, the identity of the person on whose behalf he makes that call, and the commercial purpose of the call.

6. Where a distance contract is to be concluded by telephone, Member States may provide that the trader has to confirm the offer to the consumer who is bound only once he has signed the offer or has sent his written consent. Member States may also provide that such confirmations have to be made on a durable medium.

7. The trader shall provide the consumer with the confirmation of the contract concluded, on a durable medium within a reasonable time after the conclusion of the distance contract, and at the latest at the time of the delivery of the goods or before the performance of the service begins. . . .

. . .

Article 9

Right of withdrawal

1. Save where the exceptions provided for in Article 16 apply, the consumer shall have a period of 14 days to withdraw from a distance or off-premises contract, without giving any reason, and without incurring any costs other than those provided for in Article 13(2) and Article 14.

1a. Member States may adopt rules in accordance with which the withdrawal period of 14 days referred to in paragraph 1 is extended to 30 days for contracts concluded in the context of unsolicited visits by a trader to a consumer's home or excursions organised by a trader with the aim or effect of promoting or selling products to consumers for the purpose of protecting legitimate interests of consumers with regard to aggressive or misleading marketing or selling practices. Such rules shall be proportionate, non-discriminatory and justified on grounds of consumer protection.

2. Without prejudice to Article 10, the withdrawal period referred to in paragraph 1 of this Article shall expire after 14 days . . . from:

. . .

(b) in the case of sales contracts, the day on which the consumer or a third party other than the carrier and indicated by the consumer acquires physical possession of the good or;

  (i) in the case of multiple goods ordered by the consumer in one order and delivered separately, the day on which the consumer or a third party other than the carrier and indicated by the consumer acquires physical possession of the last good;

  (ii) in the case of delivery of a good consisting of multiple lots or pieces, the day on which the consumer or a third party other than the carrier indicated by the consumer acquires physical possession of the last lot or piece;

  (iii) in the case of contracts for regular delivery of goods during defined period of time, the day on which the consumer or a third party other than the carrier and indicated by the consumer acquires physical possession of the first good. . . .

. . .

Article 10

Omission of information on the right of withdrawal

1. If the trader has not provided the consumer with the information on the right of withdrawal as required by point (h) of Article 6(1), the withdrawal period shall expire 12 months from the end of the initial withdrawal period, as determined in accordance with Article 9(2).

2. If the trader has provided the consumer with the information provided for in paragraph 1 of this Article within 12 months from the day referred to in Article 9(2), the withdrawal period shall expire 14 days or, in cases where Member States have adopted rules in accordance with Article 9(1a), 30 days after the day upon which the consumer receives that information.

Article 11

Exercise of the right of withdrawal

1. Before the expiry of the withdrawal period, the consumer shall inform the trader of his decision to withdraw from the contract. . . .

. . .

2. The consumer shall have exercised his right of withdrawal within the withdrawal period referred to in Article 9(2) and Article 10 if the communication concerning the exercise of the right of withdrawal is sent by the consumer before that period has expired.

3. The trader may, in addition to the possibilities referred to in paragraph 1, give the option to the consumer to electronically fill in and submit either the model withdrawal form set out in Annex 1(B) or any other unequivocal statement on the trader's website. In those cases the trader shall communicate to the consumer an acknowledgement of receipt of such a withdrawal on a durable medium without delay.

4. The burden of proof of exercising the right of withdrawal in accordance with this Article shall be on the consumer.

Article 12

Effects of withdrawal

The exercise of the right of withdrawal shall terminate the obligations of the parties:

(a) to perform the distance or off-premises contract; or

(b) to conclude the distance or off-premises contract, in cases where an offer was made by the consumer.

Article 13

Obligations of the trader in the event of withdrawal

1. The trader shall reimburse all payments received from the consumer, including, if applicable, the costs of delivery without undue delay and in any event not later than 14 days from the day on which he is informed of the consumer's decision to withdraw from the contract in accordance with Article 11.

The trader shall carry out the reimbursement referred to in the first subparagraph using the same means of payment as the consumer used for the initial transaction, unless the consumer has expressly agreed otherwise and provided that the consumer does not incur any fees as a result of such reimbursement.

2. Notwithstanding paragraph 1, the trader shall not be required to reimburse the supplementary costs, if the consumer has expressly opted for a type of delivery other than the least expensive type of standard delivery offered by the trader.

3. Unless the trader has offered to collect the goods himself, with regard to sales contracts, the trader may withhold the reimbursement until he has received the goods back, or until the consumer has supplied evidence of having sent back the goods, whichever is the earliest. . . .

Article 14

Obligations of the consumer in the event of withdrawal

1. Unless the trader has offered to collect the goods himself, the consumer shall send back the goods or hand them over to the trader or to a person authorized by the trader to receive the goods, without undue delay and in any event not later than 14 days from the day of which he has communicated his decision to withdraw from the contract to the trader in accordance with Article 11. The deadline shall be met if the consumer sends back the goods before the period of 14 days has expired.

The consumer shall only bear the direct cost of returning the goods unless the trader has agreed to bear them or the trader failed to inform the consumer that the consumer has to bear them.

In the case of off-premises contracts where the goods have been delivered to the consumer's home at the time of the conclusion of the contract, the trader shall at his own expense collect the goods if, by their nature, those goods cannot normally be returned by post.

2. The consumer shall only be liable for any diminished value of the goods resulting from the handling of the goods other than what is necessary to establish the nature, characteristics and functioning of the goods. The consumer shall in any event not be liable for diminished value of the goods where the trader has failed to provide notice of the right of withdrawal in accordance with point (h) of Article 6(1). . . .

3. Where a consumer exercises the right of withdrawal after having made a request in accordance with Article 7(3) or Article 8(8), the consumer shall pay to the trader an amount which is in proportion to what has been provided until the time the consumer has informed the trader of the exercise of the right of withdrawal, in comparison with the full coverage of the contract. The proportionate amount to be paid by the consumer to the trader shall be calculated on the basis of the total price agreed in the contract. If the total price is excessive, the proportionate amount shall be calculated on the basis of the market value of what has been provided.

4. The consumer shall bear no cost for:

(a) the performance of services or the supply of water, gas or electricity, where they are not put up for sale in a limited volume or set quantity, or of district heating, in full or in part, during the withdrawal period, where:

(i) the trader has failed to provide information in accordance with points (h) or (j) of Article 6(1); or

(ii) the consumer has not expressly requested performance to begin during the withdrawal period in accordance with Article 7(3) and Article 8(8); or

(b) the supply, in full or in part, of digital content which is not supplied on a tangible medium where:

(i) the consumer has not given prior express consent to the beginning of the performance before the end of the 14-day or 30-day period referred to in Article 9;

(ii) the consumer has not acknowledged that he loses his right of withdrawal when giving his consent; or

(iii) the trader has failed to provide confirmation in accordance with Article 7(2) or Article 8(7).

5. Except as provided for in Article 13(2) and in this Article the consumer shall not incur any liability as a consequence of the exercise of the right of withdrawal.

. . .

CHAPTER V

GENERAL PROVISIONS

Article 23

Enforcement

1. Member States shall ensure that adequate and effective means exist to ensure compliance with this Directive.

2. The means referred to in paragraph 1 shall include provisions whereby one or more of the following bodies, as determined by national law, may take action under national law before the courts or before the competent administrative bodies to ensure that the national provisions transposing this Directive are applied:

(a) public bodies or their representatives;

(b) consumer organizations having a legitimate interest in protecting consumers;

(c) professional organizations having a legitimate interest in acting.

Article 24

Penalties

1. Member States shall lay down the rules on penalties applicable to infringements of the national provisions adopted pursuant to this Directive and shall take all measures necessary to ensure that they are implemented. The penalties provided for must be effective, proportionate and dissuasive. . . .

STANDARD CONTRACTS LAW 5743–1982 (ISRAEL)

[The Israeli Standard Contracts Law was enacted in 1982 "to protect customers against prejudicial conditions in standard contracts." Standard Contracts Law § 1. It establishes a tribunal to review a consumer contract to determine whether it gives a supplier an unfair advantage. Suppliers may apply to the tribunal for a certification that their contracts pass muster. If a contract passes muster, it is protected from claims that it is unfairly advantageous to the supplier for a period of five years, whether proceedings are brought before the tribunal or a court. It does not preclude claims under other Israeli laws, such as a claim that a contract is unenforceable because it is against public policy. The following is an unofficial translation.]

CHAPTER ONE: BASIC PROVISIONS

Objective

1. The objective of this Law is to protect customers against prejudicial conditions in standard contracts.

Definitions

2. In this Law—

   "standard contract"—the text of a contract, in which all or some of the conditions were determined in advance by one party, to be used as conditions in many contracts between that party and an indefinite number of unidentified persons;

   "condition"—a stipulation in a standard contract, including a stipulation referred to in it and also every other stipulation that is part of the contract, but exclusive of any stipulation on which the supplier and the customer agreed specially for purposes of a specific contract;

   "supplier"—whoever proposes that a contract with him shall be according to a standard contract and it does not matter whether he is the one who gives or receives a certain thing;

   "customer"—a person to whom a supplier proposes that a contract between them shall be according to a standard contract and it does not matter whether he is the one who gives or receives a certain thing;

   "Tribunal"—the Standard Contracts Tribunal set up under this Law.

Prejudicial conditions and there [sic] annulment

3. A Court and the Tribunal shall, according to the provisions of this Law, annul or change any condition of a standard contract that—taking the totality of the contract's conditions and other circumstances into account—imposes a prejudicial condition on customers or gives the supplier an unfair advantage that is likely to result in harm to customers

Presumptions

4. The presumption is that the following conditions are prejudicial:

   (1) a condition that fully or partly relieves the supplier of a responsibility he would have to bear under any statute, if not for that condition, or that unreasonably restricts the responsibility he would have to bear by virtue of the contract, if not for that condition;

   (2) a condition that gives the supplier an unreasonable right to cancel, suspend or defer performance of the contract or to alter his substantive obligations under the contract;

   (3) a condition that gives the supplier the right to transfer his responsibility to a third party;

(4) a condition that gives the supplier the right to determine or to change—at his sole discretion and after the contract was concluded—a price or other substantive obligation imposed on the customer, except when the change arises out of factors that the supplier does not control;

(5) a condition that unreasonably requires the customer to resort to the supplier or to some other person or otherwise limits the customer's freedom to enter or not to enter into contracts with others;

(6) a condition that denies or limits a right or remedy statutorily available to the customer, unreasonably restricts a right or remedy available to him by virtue of the contract or makes it conditional on giving notice in an unreasonable form or within an unreasonable time or on any other unreasonable requirement;

(7) a condition that imposes on the customer a burden of proof that he would not have to bear, if not for that condition;

(8) a condition that denies or limits the customer's right to present certain arguments to judicial authorities or that determines that any controversy between the supplier and the customer be heard by arbitration;

(9) a condition that stipulates a statutory provision on the place of jurisdiction or gives the supplier the exclusive right to choose the place of jurisdiction or of arbitration where a dispute is to be heard;

(10) a condition that prescribes that a dispute be referred to arbitration when the supplier has greater influence than the customer on the conditions of the arbitration, including selection of the arbitrator, the place of arbitration, conditions under which the arbitration shall proceed; how the arbitration shall be conducted and law procedures at the arbitration, all even if the supplier proved that bringing the controversy to arbitration by itself, as said in paragraph (8), is not discriminatory;

(11) a condition that prescribes the linkage of a price or other payment under the contract to any index, so that its decrease or increase will not benefit the customer.

Void conditions in a standard contract

5. (a) A condition in a standard contract that denies or restricts the customer's right to apply to judicial authorities is void.

   (b) A condition in a standard contract that wholly or partly exempts the supplier from liability for bodily harm or for a malicious act that he bears under a statute is void.

CHAPTER TWO: STANDARD CONTRACTS TRIBUNAL

The Tribunal and its members

6. (a) A Standard Contracts Tribunal is hereby set up. . . .

CHAPTER FOUR: ANNULMENT OF A PREJUDICIAL CONDITION

Petition to a Tribunal to annul a prejudicial condition

16. (a) The Attorney General or his representative, the Consumer Protection and Fair Trade Commissioner under the Consumer Protection Law 5741–1981, any customers' organization and public authority designated in regulations, as well as a customers' organization approved by the Minister of Justice for a particular matter may apply to the Tribunal for the annulment of a prejudicial condition in a standard contract. . . .

Annulment and change of a condition by the Tribunal

17. (a) If the Tribunal concluded that a condition is prejudicial, it shall annul it or change it to the extent necessary in order to eliminate the prejudice involved. . . .

Annulment and change of conditions by Court

19. (a) If in a proceeding between a supplier and a customer the Court concluded that a condition is prejudicial, it shall annul the condition in the contract between them or change it to the extent necessary in order to eliminate the prejudice. . . .

PART VII
MISCELLANEOUS STATUTES, DIRECTIVES, AND ADMINISTRATIVE REGULATIONS

MAGNUSON-MOSS WARRANTY ACT

(1975, as amended)

(Excerpts)

[The Magnuson-Moss Warranty Act ("MMWA"), codified at 15 U.S.C. §§ 2301 *et seq.*, primarily regulates written warranties on consumer products sold to consumers, and authorizes the Federal Trade Commission to implement the Act by promulgating additional rules of law. (These rules are in this pamphlet, below.) The MMWA aims to protect consumers by, among other things, preventing deception and requiring warrantors to disclose a written warranty's terms and conditions "fully and conspicuously in simple and readily understood language." 15 U.S.C § 2302(a). The MMWA applies to transactions that affect interstate commerce. The MMWA, and the FTC's implementing rules, establish a floor for consumer protection insofar as they provide it; consequently, they neither displace other federal consumer protection laws nor pre-empt state laws providing greater protections to consumers. 15 U.S.C § 2311(b). Article 2 of the Uniform Commercial Code also governs warranties in contracts for the sale of goods to consumers, as well as those in contracts for the sale of goods to merchants. *See* UCC §§ 2–312—2–318.]

TITLE I. CONSUMER PRODUCT WARRANTIES

Table of Contents

Sec.
101. Definitions.
102. Warranty Provisions.
103. Designation of Warranties.
104. Federal Minimum Standards for Warranty.
105. Full and Limited Warranting of a Consumer Product.
106. Service Contracts.
107. Designation of Representatives.
108. Limitation on Disclaimer of Implied Warranties.
109. Commission Rules.
110. Remedies.
111. Effect on Other Laws.
112. Effective Date.

§ 101. Definitions. [15 U.S.C.A. § 2301]

For the purposes of this title:

(1) The term "consumer product" means any tangible personal property which is distributed in commerce and which is normally used for personal, family, or household purposes (including any such property intended to be attached to or installed in any real property without regard to whether it is so attached or installed).

(2) The term "Commission" means the Federal Trade Commission.

(3) The term "consumer" means a buyer (other than for purposes of resale) of any consumer product, any person to whom such product is transferred during the duration of an implied or written warranty (or service contract) applicable to the product, and any other person who is entitled by the terms of such warranty (or service contract) or under applicable State law to

enforce against the warrantor (or service contractor) the obligations of the warranty (or service contract).

(4) The term "supplier" means any person engaged in the business of making a consumer product directly or indirectly available to consumers.

(5) The term "warrantor" means any supplier or other person who gives or offers to give a written warranty or who is or may be obligated under an implied warranty.

(6) The term "written warranty" means—

(A) any written affirmation of fact or written promise made in connection with the sale of a consumer product by a supplier to a buyer which relates to the nature of the material or workmanship and affirms or promises that such material or workmanship is defect free or will meet a specified level of performance over a specified period of time, or

(B) any undertaking in writing in connection with the sale by a supplier of a consumer product to refund, repair, replace, or take other remedial action with respect to such product in the event that such product fails to meet the specifications set forth in the undertaking,

which written affirmation, promise, or undertaking becomes part of the basis of the bargain between a supplier and a buyer for purposes other than resale of such product.

(7) The term "implied warranty" means an implied warranty arising under State law (as modified by sections 108 and 104(a)) in connection with the sale by a supplier of a consumer product.

(8) The term "service contract" means a contract in writing to perform, over a fixed period of time or for a specified duration, services relating to the maintenance or repair (or both) of a consumer product.

(9) The term "reasonable and necessary maintenance" consists of those operations (A) which the consumer reasonably can be expected to perform or have performed and (B) which are necessary to keep any consumer product performing its intended function and operating at a reasonable level of performance.

(10) The term "remedy" means whichever of the following actions the warrantor elects:

(A) repair,

(B) replacement, or

(C) refund,

except that the warrantor may not elect refund unless (i) the warrantor is unable to provide replacement and repair is not commercially practicable or cannot be timely made, or (ii) the consumer is willing to accept such refund.

(11) The term "replacement" means furnishing a new consumer product which is identical or reasonably equivalent to the warranted consumer product.

(12) The term "refund" means refunding the actual purchase price (less reasonable depreciation based on actual use where permitted by rules of the Commission).

(13) The term "distributed in commerce" means sold in commerce, introduced or delivered for introduction into commerce, or held for sale or distribution after introduction into commerce.

(14) The term "commerce" means trade, traffic, commerce, or transportation—

(A) between a place in a State and any place outside thereof, or

(B) which affects trade, traffic, commerce, or transportation described in subparagraph (A).

(15) The term "State" means a State, the District of Columbia, the Commonwealth of Puerto Rico, the Virgin Islands, Guam, the Canal Zone, or American Samoa. The term "State law" includes a law of the United States applicable only to the District of Columbia or only to a territory or possession of the United States; and the term "Federal law" excludes any State law.

§ 102. Warranty Provisions. [15 U.S.C.A. § 2302]

(a) In order to improve the adequacy of information available to consumers, prevent deception, and improve competition in the marketing of consumer products, any warrantor warranting a consumer product to a consumer by means of a written warranty shall, to the extent required by rules of the Commission, fully and conspicuously disclose in simple and readily understood language the terms and conditions of such warranty. Such rules may require inclusion in the written warranty of any of the following items among others:

(1) The clear identification of the names and addresses of the warrantors.

(2) The identity of the party or parties to whom the warranty is extended.

(3) The products or parts covered.

(4) A statement of what the warrantor will do in the event of a defect, malfunction, or failure to conform with such written warranty—at whose expense—and for what period of time.

(5) A statement of what the consumer must do and expenses he must bear.

(6) Exceptions and exclusions from the terms of the warranty.

(7) The step-by-step procedure which the consumer should take in order to obtain performance of any obligation under the warranty, including the identification of any person or class of persons authorized to perform the obligations set forth in the warranty.

(8) Information respecting the availability of any informal dispute settlement procedure offered by the warrantor and a recital, where the warranty so provides, that the purchaser may be required to resort to such procedure before pursuing any legal remedies in the courts.

(9) A brief, general description of the legal remedies available to the consumer.

(10) The time at which the warrantor will perform any obligations under the warranty.

(11) The period of time within which, after notice of a defect, malfunction, or failure to conform with the warranty, the warrantor will perform any obligations under the warranty.

(12) The characteristics or properties of the products, or parts thereof, that are not covered by the warranty.

(13) The elements of the warranty in words or phrases which would not mislead a reasonable, average consumer as to the nature or scope of the warranty.

(b)(1)(A) The Commission shall prescribe rules requiring that the terms of any written warranty on a consumer product be made available to the consumer (or prospective consumer) prior to the sale of the product to him.

(B) The Commission may prescribe rules for determining the manner and form in which information with respect to any written warranty of a consumer product shall be clearly and conspicuously presented or displayed so as not to mislead the reasonable, average consumer, when such information is contained in advertising, labeling, point-of-sale material, or other representations in writing.

(2) Nothing in this title (other than paragraph (3) of this subsection) shall be deemed to authorize the Commission to prescribe the duration of written warranties given or to require that a consumer product or any of its components be warranted.

(3) The Commission may prescribe rules for extending the period of time a written warranty or service contract is in effect to correspond with any period of time in excess of a reasonable period (not less than 10 days) during which the consumer is deprived of the use of such consumer product by reason of failure of the product to conform with the written warranty or by reason of the failure of the warrantor (or service contractor) to carry out such warranty (or service contract) within the period specified in the warranty (or service contract).

(4)(A) Except as provided in subparagraph (B), the rules prescribed under this subsection shall allow for the satisfaction of all requirements concerning the availability of terms of a written warranty on a consumer product under this subsection by—

(i) making available such terms in an accessible digital format on the Internet website of the manufacturer of the consumer product in a clear and conspicuous manner; and

(ii) providing to the consumer (or prospective consumer) information with respect to how to obtain and review such terms by indicating on the product or product packaging or in the product manual—

(I) the Internet website of the manufacturer where such terms can be obtained and reviewed; and

(II) the phone number of the manufacturer, the postal mailing address of the manufacturer, or another reasonable non-Internet based means of contacting the manufacturer to obtain and review such terms.

(B) With respect to any requirement that the terms of any written warranty for a consumer product be made available to the consumer (or prospective consumer) prior to sale of the product, in a case in which a consumer product is offered for sale in a retail location, by catalog, or through door-to-door sales, subparagraph (A) shall only apply if the seller makes available, through electronic or other means, at the location of the sale to the consumer purchasing the consumer product the terms of the warranty for the consumer product before the purchase.

(c) No warrantor of a consumer product may condition his written or implied warranty of such product on the consumer's using, in connection with such product, any article or service (other than article or service provided without charge under the terms of the warranty) which is identified by brand, trade, or corporate name; except that the prohibition of this subsection may be waived by the Commission if—

(1) the warrantor satisfies the Commission that the warranted product will function properly only if the article or service so identified is used in connection with the warranted product, and

(2) the Commission finds that such a waiver is in the public interest.

The Commission shall identify in the Federal Register, and permit public comment on, all applications for waiver of the prohibition of this subsection, and shall publish in the Federal Register its disposition of any such application, including the reasons therefor.

(d) The Commission may by rule devise detailed substantive warranty provisions which warrantors may incorporate by reference in their warranties.

(e) The provisions of this section apply only to warranties which pertain to consumer products actually costing the consumer more than $5.

§ 103. Designation of Warranties. [15 U.S.C.A. § 2303]

(a) Any warrantor warranting a consumer product by means of a written warranty shall clearly and conspicuously designate such warranty in the following manner, unless exempted from doing so by the Commission pursuant to subsection (c) of this section:

(1) If the written warranty meets the Federal minimum standards for warranty set forth in section 104 of this Act, then it shall be conspicuously designated a "full (statement of duration) warranty".

(2) If the written warranty does not meet the Federal minimum standards for warranty set forth in section 104 of this Act, then it shall be conspicuously designated a "limited warranty".

(b) Sections 102, 103, and 104 shall not apply to statements or representations which are similar to expressions of general policy concerning customer satisfaction and which are not subject to any specific limitations.

(c) In addition to exercising the authority pertaining to disclosure granted in section 102 of this Act, the Commission may by rule determine when a written warranty does not have to be designated either "full (statement of duration)" or "limited" in accordance with this section.

(d) The provisions of subsections (a) and (c) of this section apply only to warranties which pertain to consumer products actually costing the consumer more than $10 and which are not designated "full (statement of duration) warranties".

§ 104. Federal Minimum Standards for Warranty. [15 U.S.C.A. § 2304]

(a) In order for a warrantor warranting a consumer product by means of a written warranty to meet the Federal minimum standards for warranty—

(1) such warrantor must as a minimum remedy such consumer product within a reasonable time and without charge, in the case of a defect, malfunction, or failure to conform with such written warranty;

(2) notwithstanding section 108(b), such warrantor may not impose any limitation on the duration of any implied warranty on the product;

(3) such warrantor may not exclude or limit consequential damages for breach of any written or implied warranty on such product, unless such exclusion or limitation conspicuously appears on the face of the warranty; and

(4) if the product (or a component part thereof) contains a defect or malfunction after a reasonable number of attempts by the warrantor to remedy defects or malfunctions in such product, such warrantor must permit the consumer to elect either a refund for, or replacement without charge of, such product or part (as the case may be). The Commission may by rule specify for purposes of this paragraph, what constitutes a reasonable number of attempts to remedy particular kinds of defects or malfunctions under different circumstances. If the warrantor replaces a component part of a consumer product, such replacement shall include installing the part in the product without charge.

(b)(1) In fulfilling the duties under subsection (a) respecting a written warranty, the warrantor shall not impose any duty other than notification upon any consumer as a condition of securing remedy of any consumer product which malfunctions, is defective, or does not conform to the written warranty, unless the warrantor has demonstrated in a rulemaking proceeding, or can demonstrate in an administrative or judicial enforcement proceeding (including private enforcement), or in an informal dispute settlement proceeding, that such a duty is reasonable.

(2) Notwithstanding paragraph (1), a warrantor may require, as a condition to replacement of, or refund for, any consumer product under subsection (a), that such consumer product shall be made available to the warrantor free and clear of liens and other encumbrances, except as otherwise provided by rule or order of the Commission in cases in which such a requirement would not be practicable.

(3) The Commission may, by rule define in detail the duties set forth in section 104(a) of this Act and the applicability of such duties to warrantors of different categories of consumer products with "full (statement of duration)" warranties.

(4) The duties under subsection (a) extend from the warrantor to each person who is a consumer with respect to the consumer product.

(c) The performance of the duties under subsection (a) of this section shall not be required of the warrantor if he can show that the defect, malfunction, or failure of any warranted consumer product to conform with a written warranty, was caused by damage (not resulting from defect or malfunction) while in the possession of the consumer, or unreasonable use (including failure to provide reasonable and necessary maintenance).

(d) For purposes of this section and of section 102(c), the term "without charge" means that the warrantor may not assess the consumer for any costs the warrantor or his representatives incur in connection with the required remedy of a warranted consumer product. An obligation under subsection (a)(1)(A) to remedy without charge does not necessarily require the warrantor to compensate the consumer for incidental expenses; however, if any incidental expenses are incurred because the remedy is not made within a reasonable time or because the warrantor imposed an unreasonable duty upon the consumer as a condition of securing remedy, then the consumer shall be entitled to recover reasonable incidental expenses which are so incurred in any action against the warrantor.

(e) If a supplier designates a warranty applicable to a consumer product as a "full (statement of duration)" warranty, then the warranty on such product shall, for purposes of any action under section 110(d) or under any State law, be deemed to incorporate at least the minimum requirements of this section and rules prescribed under this section.

§ 105. Full and Limited Warranting of a Consumer Product. [15 U.S.C.A. § 2305]

Nothing in this title shall prohibit the selling of a consumer product which has both full and limited warranties if such warranties are clearly and conspicuously differentiated.

§ 106. Service Contracts. [15 U.S.C.A. § 2306]

(a) The Commission may prescribe by rule the manner and form in which the terms and conditions of service contracts shall be fully, clearly, and conspicuously disclosed.

(b) Nothing in this title shall be construed to prevent a supplier or warrantor from entering into a service contract with the consumer in addition to or in lieu of a written warranty if such contract fully, clearly, and conspicuously discloses its terms and conditions in simple and readily understood language.

§ 107. Designation of Representatives. [15 U.S.C.A. § 2307]

Nothing in this title shall be construed to prevent any warrantor from designating representatives to perform duties under the written or implied warranty: *Provided*, That such warrantor shall make reasonable arrangements for compensation of such designated representatives, but no such designation shall relieve the warrantor of his direct responsibilities to the consumer or make the representative a cowarrantor.

§ 108. Limitation on Disclaimer of Implied Warranties. [15 U.S.C.A. § 2308]

(a) No supplier may disclaim or modify (except as provided in subsection (b)) any implied warranty to a consumer with respect to such consumer product if (1) such supplier makes any written warranty to the consumer with respect to such consumer product, or (2) at the time of sale, or within 90 days thereafter, such supplier enters into a service contract with the consumer which applies to such consumer product.

(b) For purposes of this title (other than section 104(a)(2)), implied warranties may be limited in duration to the duration of a written warranty of reasonable duration, if such limitation is conscionable and is set forth in clear and unmistakable language and prominently displayed on the face of the warranty.

(c) A disclaimer, modification, or limitation made in violation of this section shall be ineffective for purposes of this title and State law.

§ 109. Commission Rules. [15 U.S.C.A. § 2309]

(a) Any rule prescribed under this title shall be prescribed in accordance with section 553 of title 5, United States Code; except that the Commission shall give interested persons an opportunity for oral presentations of data, views, and arguments, in addition to written submissions. A transcript shall be kept of any oral presentation. Any such rule shall be subject to judicial review under section 18(e) of the Federal Trade Commission Act (as amended by section 202 of this Act) in the same manner as rules prescribed under section 18(a)(1)(B) of such Act, except that section 18(e)(3)(B) of such Act shall not apply.

(b) The Commission shall initiate within one year after the date of enactment of this Act a rulemaking proceeding dealing with warranties and warranty practices in connection with the sale of used motor vehicles; and, to the extent necessary to supplement the protections offered the consumer by this title, shall prescribe rules dealing with such warranties and practices. In prescribing rules under this subsection, the Commission may exercise any authority it may have under this title, or other law, and in addition it may require disclosure that a used motor vehicle is sold without any warranty and specify the form and content of such disclosure.

§ 110. Remedies. [15 U.S.C.A. § 2310]

(a)(1) Congress hereby declares it to be its policy to encourage warrantors to establish procedures whereby consumer disputes are fairly and expeditiously settled through informal dispute settlement mechanisms.

(2) The Commission shall prescribe rules setting forth minimum requirements for any informal dispute settlement procedure which is incorporated into the terms of a written warranty to which any provision of this title applies. Such rules shall provide for participation in such procedure by independent or governmental entities.

(3) One or more warrantors may establish an informal dispute settlement procedure which meets the requirements of the Commission's rules under paragraph (2). If—

(A) a warrantor establishes such a procedure,

(B) such procedure, and its implementation, meets the requirements of such rules, and

(C) he incorporates in a written warranty a requirement that the consumer resort to such procedure before pursuing any legal remedy under this section respecting such warranty,

then (i) the consumer may not commence a civil action (other than a class action) under subsection (d) of this section unless he initially resorts to such procedure; and (ii) a class of consumers may not proceed in a class action under subsection (d) except to the extent the court determines necessary to establish the representative capacity of the named plaintiffs, unless the named plaintiffs (upon notifying the defendant that they are named plaintiffs in a class action with respect to a warranty obligation) initially resort to such procedure. In the case of such a class action which is brought in a district court of the United States, the representative capacity of the named plaintiffs shall be established in the application of rule 23 of the Federal Rules of Civil Procedure. In any civil action arising out of a warranty obligation and relating to a matter considered in such a procedure, any decision in such procedure shall be admissible in evidence.

(4) The Commission on its own initiative may, or upon written complaint filed by any interested person shall, review the bona fide operation of any dispute settlement procedure resort to which is stated in a written warranty to be a prerequisite to pursuing a legal remedy under this section. If the

Commission finds that such procedure or its implementation fails to comply with the requirements of the rules under paragraph (2), the Commission may take appropriate remedial action under any authority it may have under this title or any other provision of law.

(5) Until rules under paragraph (2) take effect, this subsection shall not affect the validity of any informal dispute settlement procedure respecting consumer warranties, but in any action under subsection (d), the court may invalidate any such procedure if it finds that such procedure is unfair.

(b) It shall be a violation of section 5(a)(1) of the Federal Trade Commission Act (15 U.S.C. 45(a)(1)) for any person to fail to comply with any requirement imposed on such person by this title (or a rule thereunder) or to violate any prohibition contained in this title (or a rule thereunder).

(c)(1) The district courts of the United States shall have jurisdiction of any action brought by the Attorney General (in his capacity as such), or by the Commission by any of its attorneys designated by it for such purpose, to restrain (A) any warrantor from making a deceptive warranty with respect to a consumer product, or (B) any person from failing to comply with any requirement imposed on such person by or pursuant to this title or from violating any prohibition contained in this title. Upon proper showing that, weighing the equities and considering the Commission's or Attorney General's likelihood of ultimate success, such action would be in the public interest and after notice to the defendant, a temporary restraining order or preliminary injunction may be granted without bond. In the case of an action brought by the Commission, if a complaint under section 5 of the Federal Trade Commission Act is not filed within such period (not exceeding 10 days) as may be specified by the court after the issuance of the temporary restraining order or preliminary injunction, the order or injunction shall be dissolved by the court and be of no further force and effect. Any suit shall be brought in the district in which such person resides or transacts business. Whenever it appears to the court that the ends of justice require that other persons should be parties in the action, the court may cause them to be summoned whether or not they reside in the district in which the court is held, and to that end process may be served in any district.

(2) For the purposes of this subsection, the term "deceptive warranty" means (A) a written warranty which (i) contains an affirmation, promise, description, or representation which is either false or fraudulent, or which, in light of all of the circumstances, would mislead a reasonable individual exercising due care; or (ii) fails to contain information which is necessary in light of all of the circumstances, to make the warranty not misleading to a reasonable individual exercising due care; or (B) a written warranty created by the use of such terms as "guaranty" or "warranty", if the terms and conditions of such warranty so limit its scope and application as to deceive a reasonable individual.

(d)(1) Subject to subsections (a)(3) and (e), a consumer who is damaged by the failure of a supplier, warrantor, or service contractor to comply with any obligation under this title, or under a written warranty, implied warranty, or service contract, may bring suit for damages and other legal and equitable relief—

(A) in any court of competent jurisdiction in any State or the District of Columbia; or

(B) in an appropriate district court of the United States, subject to paragraph (3) of this subsection.

(2) If a consumer finally prevails in any action brought under paragraph (1) of this subsection, he may be allowed by the court to recover as part of the judgment a sum equal to the aggregate amount of cost and expenses (including attorneys' fees based on actual time expended) determined by the court to have been reasonably incurred by the plaintiff for or in connection with the commencement and prosecution of such action, unless the court in its discretion shall determine that such an award of attorneys' fees would be inappropriate.

(3) No claim shall be cognizable in a suit brought under paragraph (1)(B) of this subsection—

(A) if the amount in controversy of any individual claim is less than the sum or value of $25;

(B) if the amount in controversy is less than the sum or value of $50,000 (exclusive of interests and costs) computed on the basis of all claims to be determined in this suit; or

(C) if the action is brought as a class action, and the number of named plaintiffs is less than one hundred.

(e) No action (other than a class action or an action respecting a warranty to which subsection (a)(3) applies) may be brought under subsection (d) for failure to comply with any obligation under any written or implied warranty or service contract, and a class of consumers may not proceed in a class action under such subsection with respect to such a failure except to the extent the court determines necessary to establish the representative capacity of the named plaintiffs, unless the person obligated under the warranty or service contract is afforded a reasonable opportunity to cure such failure to comply. In the case of such a class action (other than a class action respecting a warranty to which subsection (a)(3) applies) brought under subsection (d) for breach of any written or implied warranty or service contract, such reasonable opportunity will be afforded by the named plaintiffs and they shall at that time notify the defendant that they are acting on behalf of the class. In the case of such a class action which is brought in a district court of the United States, the representative capacity of the named plaintiffs shall be established in the application of rule 23 of the Federal Rules of Civil Procedure.

(f) For purposes of this section, only the warrantor actually making a written affirmation of fact, promise, or undertaking shall be deemed to have created a written warranty, and any rights arising thereunder may be enforced under this section only against such warrantor and no other person.

§ 111. Effect on Other Laws. [15 U.S.C.A. § 2311]

(a)(1) Nothing contained in this title shall be construed to repeal, invalidate, or supersede the Federal Trade Commission Act (15 U.S.C. 41 et seq.) or any statute defined therein as an Antitrust Act.

(2) Nothing in this title shall be construed to repeal, invalidate, or supersede the Federal Seed Act (7 U.S.C. 1551–1611) and nothing in this title shall apply to seed for planting.

(b)(1) Nothing in this title shall invalidate or restrict any right or remedy of any consumer under State law or any other Federal law.

(2) Nothing in this title (other than sections 108 and 104(a)(2) and (4)) shall (A) affect the liability of, or impose liability on, any person for personal injury, or (B) supersede any provision of State law regarding consequential damages for injury to the person or other injury.

(c)(1) Except as provided in subsection (b) and in paragraph (2) of this subsection, a State requirement—

(A) which relates to labeling or disclosure with respect to written warranties or performance thereunder;

(B) which is within the scope of an applicable requirement of sections 102, 103, and 104 (and rules implementing such sections), and

(C) which is not identical to a requirement of section 102, 103, or 104 (or a rule thereunder), shall not be applicable to written warranties complying with such sections (or rules thereunder).

(2) If, upon application of an appropriate State agency, the Commission determines (pursuant to rules issued in accordance with section 109) that any requirement of such State covering any transaction to which this title applies (A) affords protection to consumers greater than the requirements of this title and (B) does not unduly burden interstate commerce, then such State requirement shall be applicable (notwithstanding the provisions of paragraph (1) of this subsection)

to the extent specified in such determination for so long as the State administers and enforces effectively any such greater requirement.

(d) This title (other than section 102(c)) shall be inapplicable to any written warranty the making or content of which is otherwise governed by Federal law. If only a portion of a written warranty is so governed by Federal law, the remaining portion shall be subject to this title.

§ 112. Effective Date. [15 U.S.C.A. § 2312]

(a) Except as provided in subsection (b) of this section, this title shall take effect 6 months after the date of its enactment but shall not apply to consumer products manufactured prior to such date.

(b) Section 102(a) shall take effect 6 months after the final publication of rules respecting such section; except that the Commission, for good cause shown, may postpone the applicability of such sections until one year after such final publication in order to permit any designated classes of suppliers to bring their written warranties into compliance with rules promulgated pursuant to this title.

(c) The Commission shall promulgate rules for initial implementation of this title as soon as possible after the date of enactment of this Act but in no event later than one year after such date.

FEDERAL TRADE COMMISSION, TRADE REGULATION RULES: RULE CONCERNING COOLING-OFF PERIOD FOR SALES MADE AT HOMES OR AT CERTAIN OTHER LOCATIONS

(1995)

[In 1972, the Federal Trade Commission ("FTC") promulgated rules to restrain the overly aggressive sales practices of some door-to-door salesmen. These rules became effective as law in 1974, and the FTC adopted a few amendments in 1995. *See* 16 C.F.R. Part 429. These rules generally allow a buyer to cancel a contract within three days after making it with a door-to-door salesman. They do not pre-empt state laws concerning door-to-door sales unless the state laws are inconsistent with, or provide less protection to buyers than, these rules.]

§ 429.1 The Rule.

In connection with any door-to-door sale, it constitutes an unfair and deceptive act or practice for any seller to:

(a) Fail to furnish the buyer with a fully completed receipt or copy of any contract pertaining to such sale at the time of its execution, which is in the same language, e.g., Spanish, as that principally used in the oral sales presentation and which shows the date of the transaction and contains the name and address of the seller, and in immediate proximity to the space reserved in the contract for the signature of the buyer or on the front page of the receipt if a contract is not used and in boldface type of a minimum size of 10 points, a statement in substantially the following form:

"YOU, THE BUYER, MAY CANCEL THIS TRANSACTION AT ANY TIME PRIOR TO MIDNIGHT OF THE THIRD BUSINESS DAY AFTER THE DATE OF THIS TRANSACTION. SEE THE ATTACHED NOTICE OF CANCELLATION FORM FOR AN EXPLANATION OF THIS RIGHT."

(b) Fail to furnish each buyer, at the time he signs the door-to-door sales contract or otherwise agrees to buy consumer goods or services from the seller, a completed form in duplicate, captioned "NOTICE OF CANCELLATION", which shall be attached to the contract or receipt and easily detachable, and which shall contain in ten point bold face type the following information and statements in the same language, e.g., Spanish, as that used in the contract:

NOTICE OF CANCELLATION

(enter DATE OF TRANSACTION)

_____

(Date)

YOU MAY CANCEL THIS TRANSACTION, WITHOUT ANY PENALTY OR OBLIGATION, WITHIN THREE BUSINESS DAYS FROM THE ABOVE DATE.

IF YOU CANCEL, ANY PROPERTY TRADED IN, ANY PAYMENTS MADE BY YOU UNDER THE CONTRACT OR SALE, AND ANY NEGOTIABLE INSTRUMENT EXECUTED BY YOU WILL BE RETURNED WITHIN 10 BUSINESS DAYS FOLLOWING RECEIPT BY THE SELLER OF YOUR CANCELLATION NOTICE, AND ANY SECURITY INTEREST ARISING OUT OF THE TRANSACTION WILL BE CANCELED.

IF YOU CANCEL, YOU MUST MAKE AVAILABLE TO THE SELLER AT YOUR RESIDENCE, IN SUBSTANTIALLY AS GOOD CONDITION AS WHEN RECEIVED, ANY GOODS DELIVERED

TO YOU UNDER THIS CONTRACT OR SALE; OR YOU MAY IF YOU WISH, COMPLY WITH THE INSTRUCTIONS OF THE SELLER REGARDING THE RETURN SHIPMENT OF THE GOODS AT THE SELLER'S EXPENSE AND RISK.

IF YOU DO MAKE THE GOODS AVAILABLE TO THE SELLER AND THE SELLER DOES NOT PICK THEM UP WITHIN 20 DAYS OF THE DATE OF YOUR NOTICE OF CANCELLATION, YOU MAY RETAIN OR DISPOSE OF THE GOODS WITHOUT ANY FURTHER OBLIGATION. IF YOU FAIL TO MAKE THE GOODS AVAILABLE TO THE SELLER, OR IF YOU AGREE TO RETURN THE GOODS TO THE SELLER AND FAIL TO DO SO, THEN YOU REMAIN LIABLE FOR PERFORMANCE OF ALL OBLIGATIONS UNDER THE CONTRACT.

TO CANCEL THIS TRANSACTION, MAIL OR DELIVER A SIGNED AND DATED COPY OF THIS CANCELLATION NOTICE OR ANY OTHER WRITTEN NOTICE, OR SEND A TELEGRAM, TO _____, AT _____ NOT LATER THAN

    [Name of seller]   [Address of seller's place of business]

MIDNIGHT OF _____.

    [Date]

I HEREBY CANCEL THIS TRANSACTION.

_____

  (Date)   (Buyer's Signature)

(c) Fail, before furnishing copies of the "Notice of Cancellation" to the buyer, to complete both copies by entering the name of the seller, the address of the seller's place of business, the date of the transaction, and the date, not earlier than the third business day following the date of the transaction, by which the buyer may give notice of cancellation.

(d) Include in any door-to-door contract or receipt any confession of judgment or any waiver of any of the rights to which the buyer is entitled under this section including specifically his right to cancel the sale in accordance with the provisions of this section.

(e) Fail to inform each buyer orally, at the time he signs the contract or purchases the goods or services, of his right to cancel.

(f) Misrepresent in any manner the buyer's right to cancel.

(g) Fail or refuse to honor any valid notice of cancellation by a buyer and within 10 business days after the receipt of such notice, to (i) refund all payments made under the contract or sale; (ii) return any goods or property traded in, in substantially as good condition as when received by the seller; (iii) cancel and return any negotiable instrument executed by the buyer in connection with the contract or sale and take any action necessary or appropriate to terminate promptly any security interest created in the transaction.

(h) Negotiate, transfer, sell, or assign any note or other evidence of indebtedness to a finance company or other third party prior to midnight of the fifth business day following the day the contract was signed or the goods or services were purchased.

(i) Fail, within 10 business days of receipt of the buyer's notice of cancellation, to notify him whether the seller intends to repossess or to abandon any shipped or delivered goods.

Note 1: *Definitions.* For the purposes of the section the following definitions shall apply:

(a) *Door-to-door sale.* A sale, lease, or rental of consumer goods or services with a purchase price of $25 or more, whether under single or multiple contracts, in which the seller or his representative personally solicits the sale, including those in response to or following an invitation by the buyer, and the buyer's agreement or offer to purchase is made at a place other than the place of business of the seller. The term "door-to-door sale" does not include a transaction:

(1) Made pursuant to prior negotiations in the course of a visit by the buyer to a retail business establishment having a fixed permanent location where the goods are exhibited or the services are offered for sale on a continuing basis; or

(2) In which the consumer is accorded the right of rescission by the provisions of the Consumer Credit Protection Act (15 U.S.C. 1635) or regulations issued pursuant thereto; or

(3) In which the buyer has initiated the contact and the goods or services are needed to meet a bona fide immediate personal emergency of the buyer, and the buyer furnishes the seller with a separate dated and signed personal statement in the buyer's handwriting describing the situation requiring immediate remedy and expressly acknowledging and waiving the right to cancel the sale within 3 business days; or

(4) Conducted and consummated entirely by mail or telephone; and without any other contact between the buyer and the seller or its representative prior to delivery of the goods or performance of the services; or

(5) In which the buyer has initiated the contact and specifically requested the seller to visit his home for the purpose of repairing or performing maintenance upon the buyer's personal property. If in the course of such a visit, the seller sells the buyer the right to receive additional services or goods other than replacement parts necessarily used in performing the maintenance or in making the repairs, the sale of those additional goods or services would not fall within this exclusion; or

(6) Pertaining to the sale or rental of real property, to the sale of insurance or to the sale of securities or commodities by a broker-dealer registered with the Securities and Exchange Commission.

(b) *Consumer goods or services.* Goods or services purchased, leased, or rented primarily for personal, family, or household purposes, including courses of instruction or training regardless of the purpose for which they are taken.

(c) *Seller.* Any person, partnership, corporation, or association engaged in the door-to-door sale of consumer goods or services.

(d) *Place of business.* The main or permanent branch office or local address of a seller.

(e) *Purchase price.* The total price paid or to be paid for the consumer goods or services, including all interest and service charges.

(f) *Business day.* Any calendar day except Sunday, or the following business holidays: New Year's Day, Washington's Birthday, Memorial Day, Independence Day, Labor Day, Columbus Day, Veterans' Day, Thanksgiving Day, and Christmas Day.

Note 2: *Effect on State laws and municipal ordinances.*

(a) The Commission is cognizant of the significant burden imposed upon door-to-door sellers by the various and often inconsistent State laws which provide the buyer with the right to cancel door-to-door sales transactions. However, it does not believe that this constitutes sufficient justification for preempting all of the provisions of such laws or of the ordinances of the political subdivisions of the various States. The record in the proceedings supports the view that the joint and coordinated efforts of both the Commission and State and local officials are required to insure that a consumer who has purchased from a door-to-door seller something he does not want, does not need, or cannot afford, is accorded a unilateral right to rescind, without penalty, his agreement to purchase the goods or services.

(b) This section will not be construed to annul, or exempt any seller from complying with the laws of any State, or with the ordinances of political subdivisions thereof, regulating door-to-door sales, except to the extent that such laws or ordinances, if they permit door-to-door selling, are directly inconsistent with the provisions of this section. Such laws or ordinances which do not accord the buyer, with respect to the particular transaction, a right to cancel a door-to-door sale which is substantially the same or greater than that provided in this section, or which permit the imposition of any fee or penalty on the buyer for the exercise of such right, or which do not provide for giving the buyer notice of his right to cancel the transaction in substantially the same form and manner provided for in this section, are among those which will be considered directly inconsistent.

FEDERAL TRADE COMMISSION, TRADE REGULATION RULES: RETAIL FOOD STORE ADVERTISING AND MARKETING PRACTICES

(1989)

(Excerpts)

[The Federal Trade Commission's ("FTC's") rules on Retail Food Store Advertising and Marketing Practices, first promulgated in 1971, were amended in 1989. 16 C.F.R. Part 424. Subject to specified exceptions, they require retail food stores to have adequate stock to meet reasonable demand for items advertised for sale at specified prices. These rules apply to acts or practices in or affecting interstate commerce. The FTC can enforce these rules by ordering violators to cease and desist, or by obtaining injunctions, civil money penalties, or restitution for the victim in the federal courts. 15 U.S.C. § 45. The Uniform Deceptive Trade Practices Act, in this pamphlet below, pursues similar goals with respect to a broader range of advertising practices.]

Sec.
424.1 Unfair or Deceptive Acts or Practices.
424.2 Defenses.

---

§ 424.1 Unfair or Deceptive Acts or Practices.

In connection with the sale or offering for sale by retail food stores of food, grocery products or other merchandise to consumers in or affecting commerce as "commerce" is defined in section 4 of the Federal Trade Commission Act, 15 U.S.C. 44, it is an unfair or deceptive act or practice in violation of section 5(a)(1) of the Federal Trade Commission Act, 15 U.S.C. 45(a)(1), to offer any such products for sale at a stated price, by means of an advertisement disseminated in an area served by any stores which are covered by the advertisement, if those stores do not have the advertised products in stock and readily available to customers during the effective period of the advertisement, unless the advertisement clearly and adequately discloses that supplies of the advertised products are limited or the advertised products are available only at some outlets.

§ 424.2 Defenses.

No violation of § 424.1 shall be found if:

(a) The advertised products were ordered in adequate time for delivery in quantities sufficient to meet reasonably anticipated demand;

(b) The food retailer offers a "raincheck" for the advertised products;

(c) The food retailer offers at the advertised price or at a comparable price reduction a similar product that is at least comparable in value to the advertised product; or

(d) The food retailer offers other compensation at least equal to the advertised value.

FEDERAL TRADE COMMISSION, TRADE REGULATION RULES: PRESERVATION OF CONSUMERS' CLAIMS AND DEFENSES

(1975)

(Excerpts)

[Generally speaking, a party with rights under a contract (the "creditor") may transfer ("assign") its rights to a third party (the "assignee"), who then may enforce the rights against the other party to the original contract (the "debtor"). Before the Federal Trade Commission promulgated its rules on the Preservation of Consumers' Claims and Defenses, 16 C.F.R. § 433 (1975), the assignee might take such rights free of any claims or defenses (such as breach of warranty) that the debtor had against the creditor. The FTC rules changed the law by requiring credit contracts and purchase-money loans involving consumers to contain standardized terms that preserve the debtor's claims and defenses when the creditor assigns its rights to a third party. These rules are law. They apply to acts or practices in or affecting interstate commerce.]

Sec.
433.1   Definitions . . .
433.2   Preservation of Consumers' Claims and Defenses, Unfair or Deceptive Acts or Practices.

---

§ 433.1   Definitions . . .

(c) *Creditor.* A person who, in the ordinary course of business, lends purchase money or finances the sale of goods or services to consumers on a deferred payment basis; *Provided,* such person is not acting, for the purposes of a particular transaction, in the capacity of a credit card issuer.

(d) *Purchase money loan.* A cash advance which is received by a consumer in return for a "Finance Charge" within the meaning of the Truth in Lending Act and Regulation Z, which is applied, in whole or substantial part, to a purchase of goods or services from a seller who (1) refers consumers to the creditor or (2) is affiliated with the creditor by common control, contract, or business arrangement.*

(e) *Financing a sale.* Extending credit to a consumer in connection with a "Credit Sale" within the meaning of the Truth in Lending Act and Regulation Z. . . .**

(i) *Consumer credit contract.* Any instrument which evidences or embodies a debt arising from a "Purchase Money Loan" transaction or a "financed sale" as defined in paragraphs (d) and (e) of this section. . . .

§ 433.2   Preservation of Consumers' Claims and Defenses, Unfair or Deceptive Acts or Practices.

In connection with any sale or lease of goods or services to consumers, in or affecting commerce as "commerce" is defined in the Federal Trade Commission Act, it is an unfair or deceptive act or practice within the meaning of Section 5 of that Act for a seller, directly or indirectly, to:

---

*   Regulation Z is set forth at 12 C.F.R. § 226.1 et seq. Section 226.4 of Reg. Z defines "finance charge" to mean "the cost of consumer credit as a dollar amount." (Footnote by ed.)

**   Regulation Z defines "credit sale" to mean "a sale in which the seller is a creditor."

(a) Take or receive a consumer credit contract which fails to contain the following provision in at least ten point, bold face, type:

NOTICE

ANY HOLDER OF THIS CONSUMER CREDIT CONTRACT IS SUBJECT TO ALL CLAIMS AND DEFENSES WHICH THE DEBTOR COULD ASSERT AGAINST THE SELLER OF GOODS OR SERVICES OBTAINED PURSUANT HERETO OR WITH THE PROCEEDS HEREOF. RECOVERY HEREUNDER BY THE DEBTOR SHALL NOT EXCEED AMOUNTS PAID BY THE DEBTOR HEREUNDER.

or,

(b) Accept, as full or partial payment for such sale or lease, the proceeds of any purchase money loan (as purchase money loan is defined herein), unless any consumer credit contract made in connection with such purchase money loan contains the following provision in at least ten point, bold face, type:

NOTICE

ANY HOLDER OF THIS CONSUMER CREDIT CONTRACT IS SUBJECT TO ALL CLAIMS AND DEFENSES WHICH THE DEBTOR COULD ASSERT AGAINST THE SELLER OF GOODS OR SERVICES OBTAINED WITH THE PROCEEDS HEREOF. RECOVERY HEREUNDER BY THE DEBTOR SHALL NOT EXCEED AMOUNTS PAID BY THE DEBTOR HEREUNDER. . . .

Pt. VII   CONSUMER REVIEW FAIRNESS ACT OF 2016

CONSUMER REVIEW FAIRNESS ACT OF 2016

[The Consumer Review Fairness Act of 2016, Public Law 114–258, 130 Stat. 1355, aims to protect consumers from non-disparagement clauses in form contracts for the sale of goods or services. Such clauses have interfered with some consumers' efforts to post reviews of good and services on the internet or elsewhere. To simplify, the Act renders non-disparagement clauses void from the inception of a form contract. Many consumers benefit from crowd-sourcing reviews of products or services. This Act seeks to curtail non-disparagement clauses to preserve the credibility and value of online consumer reviews.]

SECTION 1. SHORT TITLE.

This Act may be cited as the "Consumer Review Fairness Act of 2016".

SEC. 2. CONSUMER REVIEW PROTECTION.

(a) DEFINITIONS.—In this section:

(1) COMMISSION.—The term "Commission" means the Federal Trade Commission.

(2) COVERED COMMUNICATION.—The term "covered communication" means a written, oral, or pictorial review, performance assessment of, or other similar analysis of, including by electronic means, the goods, services, or conduct of a person by an individual who is party to a form contract with respect to which such person is also a party.

(3) FORM CONTRACT.—

(A) IN GENERAL.—Except as provided in subparagraph (B), the term "form contract" means a contract with standardized terms—

(i) used by a person in the course of selling or leasing the person's goods or services; and

(ii) imposed on an individual without a meaningful opportunity for such individual to negotiate the standardized terms.

(B) EXCEPTION.—The term "form contract" does not include an employer-employee or independent contractor contract.

(4) PICTORIAL.—The term "pictorial" includes pictures, photographs, video, illustrations, and symbols.

(b) INVALIDITY OF CONTRACTS THAT IMPEDE CONSUMER REVIEWS.—

(1) IN GENERAL.—Except as provided in paragraphs (2) and (3), a provision of a form contract is void from the inception of such contract if such provision—

(A) prohibits or restricts the ability of an individual who is a party to the form contract to engage in a covered communication;

(B) imposes a penalty or fee against an individual who is a party to the form contract for engaging in a covered communication; or

(C) transfers or requires an individual who is a party to the form contract to transfer to any person any intellectual property rights in review or feedback content, with the exception of a non-exclusive license to use the content, that the individual may have in any otherwise lawful covered communication about such person or the goods or services provided by such person.

(2) RULE OF CONSTRUCTION.—Nothing in paragraph (1) shall be construed to affect—

(A) any duty of confidentiality imposed by law (including agency guidance);

(B) any civil cause of action for defamation, libel, or slander, or any similar cause of action;

(C) any party's right to remove or refuse to display publicly on an Internet website or webpage owned, operated, or otherwise controlled by such party any content of a covered communication that—

(i) contains the personal information or likeness of another person, or is libelous, harassing, abusive, obscene, vulgar, sexually explicit, or is inappropriate with respect to race, gender, sexuality, ethnicity, or other intrinsic characteristic;

(ii) is unrelated to the goods or services offered by or available at such party's Internet website or webpage; or

(iii) is clearly false or misleading; or

(D) a party's right to establish terms and conditions with respect to the creation of photographs or video of such party's property when those photographs or video are created by an employee or independent contractor of a commercial entity and solely intended for commercial purposes by that entity.

(3) EXCEPTIONS.—Paragraph (1) shall not apply to the extent that a provision of a form contract prohibits disclosure or submission of, or reserves the right of a person or business that hosts online consumer reviews or comments to remove—

(A) trade secrets or commercial or financial information obtained from a person and considered privileged or confidential;

(B) personnel and medical files and similar information the disclosure of which would constitute a clearly unwarranted invasion of personal privacy;

(C) records or information compiled for law enforcement purposes, the disclosure of which would constitute a clearly unwarranted invasion of personal privacy;

(D) content that is unlawful or otherwise meets the requirements of paragraph (2)(C); or

(E) content that contains any computer viruses, worms, or other potentially damaging computer code, processes, programs, applications, or files.

(c) PROHIBITION.—It shall be unlawful for a person to offer a form contract containing a provision described as void in subsection (b).

(d) ENFORCEMENT BY COMMISSION.—

(1) UNFAIR OR DECEPTIVE ACTS OR PRACTICES.—A violation of subsection (c) by a person with respect to which the Commission is empowered under section 5(a)(2) of the Federal Trade Commission Act (15 U.S.C. 45(a)(2)) shall be treated as a violation of a rule defining an unfair or deceptive act or practice prescribed under section 18(a)(1)(B) of the Federal Trade Commission Act (15 U.S.C. 57a(a)(1)(B)).

(2) POWERS OF COMMISSION.—

(A) IN GENERAL.—The Commission shall enforce this section in the same manner, by the same means, and with the same jurisdiction, powers, and duties as though all applicable terms and provisions of the Federal Trade Commission Act (15 U.S.C. 41 et seq.) were incorporated into and made a part of this Act.

(B) PRIVILEGES AND IMMUNITIES.—Any person who violates this section shall be subject to the penalties and entitled to the privileges and immunities provided in the Federal Trade Commission Act (15 U.S.C. 41 et seq.).

(e) ENFORCEMENT BY STATES.—

(1) AUTHORIZATION.—Subject to paragraph (2), in any case in which the attorney general of a State has reason to believe that an interest of the residents of the State has been or is threatened or adversely affected by the engagement of any person subject to subsection (c) in a practice that violates such subsection, the attorney general of the State may, as parens patriae, bring a civil action on behalf of the residents of the State in an appropriate district court of the United States to obtain appropriate relief.

(2) RIGHTS OF FEDERAL TRADE COMMISSION.—

(A) NOTICE TO FEDERAL TRADE COMMISSION.—

(i) IN GENERAL.—Except as provided in clause (iii), the attorney general of a State shall notify the Commission in writing that the attorney general intends to bring a civil action under paragraph (1) before initiating the civil action against a person described in subsection (d)(1).

(ii) CONTENTS.—The notification required by clause (i) with respect to a civil action shall include a copy of the complaint to be filed to initiate the civil action.

(iii) EXCEPTION.—If it is not feasible for the attorney general of a State to provide the notification required by clause (i) before initiating a civil action under paragraph (1), the attorney general shall notify the Commission immediately upon instituting the civil action.

(B) INTERVENTION BY FEDERAL TRADE COMMISSION.—The Commission may—

(i) intervene in any civil action brought by the attorney general of a State under paragraph (1) against a person described in subsection (d)(1); and

(ii) upon intervening—

(I) be heard on all matters arising in the civil action; and

(II) file petitions for appeal of a decision in the civil action.

(3) INVESTIGATORY POWERS.—Nothing in this subsection may be construed to prevent the attorney general of a State from exercising the powers conferred on the attorney general by the laws of the State to conduct investigations, to administer oaths or affirmations, or to compel the attendance of witnesses or the production of documentary or other evidence.

(4) PREEMPTIVE ACTION BY FEDERAL TRADE COMMISSION.—If the Federal Trade Commission institutes a civil action or an administrative action with respect to a violation of subsection (c), the attorney general of a State may not, during the pendency of such action, bring a civil action under paragraph (1) against any defendant named in the complaint of the Commission for the violation with respect to which the Commission instituted such action.

(5) VENUE; SERVICE OF PROCESS.—

(A) VENUE.—Any action brought under paragraph (1) may be brought in—

(i) the district court of the United States that meets applicable requirements relating to venue under section 1391 of title 28, United States Code; or

(ii) another court of competent jurisdiction.

(B) SERVICE OF PROCESS.—In an action brought under paragraph (1), process may be served in any district in which the defendant—

(i) is an inhabitant; or

(ii) may be found.

(6) ACTIONS BY OTHER STATE OFFICIALS.—

(A) IN GENERAL.—In addition to civil actions brought by attorneys general under paragraph (1), any other consumer protection officer of a State who is authorized by the State to do so may bring a civil action under paragraph (1), subject to the same requirements and limitations that apply under this subsection to civil actions brought by attorneys general.

(B) SAVINGS PROVISION.—Nothing in this subsection may be construed to prohibit an authorized official of a State from initiating or continuing any proceeding in a court of the State for a violation of any civil or criminal law of the State.

(f) EDUCATION AND OUTREACH FOR BUSINESSES.—Not later than 60 days after the date of the enactment of this Act, the Commission shall commence conducting education and outreach that provides businesses with non-binding best practices for compliance with this Act.

(g) RELATION TO STATE CAUSES OF ACTION.—Nothing in this section shall be construed to affect any cause of action brought by a person that exists or may exist under State law.

(h) SAVINGS PROVISION.—Nothing in this section shall be construed to limit, impair, or supersede the operation of the Federal Trade Commission Act or any other provision of Federal law.

(i) EFFECTIVE DATES.—This section shall take effect on the date of the enactment of this Act, except that—

(1) subsections (b) and (c) shall apply with respect to contracts in effect on or after the date that is 90 days after the date of the enactment of this Act; and

(2) subsections (d) and (e) shall apply with respect to contracts in effect on or after the date that is 1 year after the date of the enactment of this Act.

POSTAL REORGANIZATION ACT: MAILING OF UNORDERED MERCHANDISE

(1971)

[Prior to enactment of this part of the Postal Reorganization Act ("PRA"), 39 U.S.C. § 3009, an offeror could mail unordered merchandise to an offeree on terms specified by the offeror, and if the offeree acted inconsistently with the offeror's continued ownership, as by using or keeping the merchandise, a contract was formed, requiring the offeree to pay for the merchandise. Restatement (Second) of Contracts § 69(2) (1981). The PRA changed this law by making the mailing of unordered merchandise an "unfair method of competition and an unfair trade practice." 39 U.S.C. § 3009(a). Consequently, the Federal Trade Commission Act, 15 U.S.C. § 45, empowered the Federal Trade Commission to enforce this statute by ordering violators to cease and desist, or by obtaining injunctions, civil money penalties, or restitution for the offeree in the federal courts. Moreover, the offeree may do anything with the goods, including using them, without liability to the offeror.]

§ 3009. Mailing of Unordered Merchandise.

(a) Except for (1) free samples clearly and conspicuously marked as such, and (2) merchandise mailed by a charitable organization soliciting contributions, the mailing of unordered merchandise or of communications prohibited by subsection (c) of this section constitutes an unfair method of competition and an unfair trade practice in violation of section 45(a)(1) of title 15.

(b) Any merchandise mailed in violation of subsection (a) of this section, or within the exceptions contained therein, may be treated as a gift by the recipient, who shall have the right to retain, use, discard, or dispose of it in any manner he sees fit without any obligation whatsoever to the sender. All such merchandise shall have attached to it a clear and conspicuous statement informing the recipient that he may treat the merchandise as a gift to him and has the right to retain, use, discard, or dispose of it in any manner he sees fit without any obligation whatsoever to the sender.

(c) No mailer of any merchandise mailed in violation of subsection (a) of this section, or within the exceptions contained therein, shall mail to any recipient of such merchandise a bill for such merchandise or any dunning communications.

(d) For the purposes of this section, "unordered merchandise" means merchandise mailed without the prior expressed request or consent of the recipient.

BANKRUPTCY CODE

(As amended, 2010)

[The core purpose of bankruptcy law is to allow a debtor to file for bankruptcy when its debts exceed its ability to repay them, and there is little prospect that the debtor will be able to emerge from this deficit. The bankrupt must turn over most of her assets to a court-appointed trustee for the benefit of her creditors. The bankruptcy proceeding results in a discharge of most of the debtor's obligations to pay its creditors, and the creditors get a percentage of the amounts of the debts, depending on the value of the debtor's remaining assets. The discharge, it is hoped, will give the debtor a "fresh start" so that he or she can become a productive member of society again, or can restructure or wind up a business.

[One provision of a complicated federal statute, the Bankruptcy Code, 11 U.S.C. § 524, modifies an exception to the common law requirement of consideration in contract law. The common law allowed a creditor to enforce a debtor's promise to pay a debt that had been discharged in bankruptcy even when no new consideration supported enforcement of the new promise. Restatement (Second) of Contracts § 83 (1981). Section 524 makes it more difficult for a creditor to enforce such a promise by protecting a debtor from further improvidence or a creditor's predatory conduct. This section does not, however, require new consideration supporting the post-discharge promise.]

§ 524. Effect of Discharge.

(a) A discharge in a case under this title—

(1) voids any judgment at any time obtained, to the extent that such judgment is a determination of the personal liability of the debtor with respect to any debt discharged under section 727, 944, 1141, 1228, or 1328 of this title, whether or not discharge of such debt is waived;

(2) operates as an injunction against the commencement or continuation of an action, the employment of process, or an act, to collect, recover or offset any such debt as a personal liability of the debtor, whether or not discharge of such debt is waived; and

(3) operates as an injunction against the commencement or continuation of an action, the employment of process, or an act, to collect or recover from, or offset against, property of the debtor of the kind specified in section 541(a)(2) of this title that is acquired after the commencement of the case, on account of any allowable community claim, except a community claim that is excepted from discharge under section 523, 1228(a)(1), or 1328(a)(1), or that would be so excepted, determined in accordance with the provisions of sections 523(c) and 523(d) of this title, in a case concerning the debtor's spouse commenced on the date of the filing of the petition in the case concerning the debtor, whether or not discharge of the debt based on such community claim is waived.

. . .

(c) An agreement between a holder of a claim and the debtor, the consideration for which, in whole or in part, is based on a debt that is dischargeable in a case under this title is enforceable only to any extent enforceable under applicable nonbankruptcy law, whether or not discharge of such debt is waived, only if—

(1) such agreement was made before the granting of the discharge . . .;

(2) the debtor received the disclosures described in subsection (k) [omitted] at or before the time at which the debtor signed the agreement;

(3) such agreement has been filed with the court and, if applicable, accompanied by a declaration or an affidavit of the attorney that represented the debtor during the course of negotiating an agreement under this subsection, which states that—

(A) such agreement represents a fully informed and voluntary agreement by the debtor;

(B) such agreement does not impose an undue hardship on the debtor or a dependent of the debtor; and

(C) the attorney fully advised the debtor of the legal effect and consequences of—

(i) an agreement of the kind specified in this subsection; and

(ii) any default under such an agreement;

(4) the debtor has not rescinded such agreement at any time prior to discharge or within sixty days after such agreement is filed with the court, whichever occurs later, by giving notice of rescission to the holder of such claim;

(5) the provisions of subsection (d) of this section have been complied with; and

(6)(A) in a case concerning an individual who was not represented by an attorney during the course of negotiating an agreement under this subsection, the court approves such agreement as—

(i) not imposing an undue hardship on the debtor or a dependent of the debtor; and

(ii) in the best interest of the debtor.

(B) Subparagraph (A) shall not apply to the extent that such debt is a consumer debt secured by real property.

(d) In a case concerning an individual, when the court has determined whether to grant or not to grant a discharge under section 727, 1141, 1228, or 1328 of this title, the court may hold a hearing at which the debtor shall appear in person. At any such hearing, the court shall inform the debtor that a discharge has been granted or the reason why a discharge has not been granted. If a discharge has been granted and if the debtor desires to make an agreement of the kind specified in subsection (c) of this section and was not represented by an attorney during the course of negotiating such agreement, then the court shall hold a hearing at which the debtor shall appear in person and at such hearing the court shall—

(1) inform the debtor—

(A) that such an agreement is not required under this title, under nonbankruptcy law, or under any agreement not made in accordance with the provisions of subsection (c) of this section; and

(B) of the legal effect and consequences of—

(i) an agreement of the kind specified in subsection (c) of this section; and

(ii) a default under such an agreement; and

(2) determine whether the agreement that the debtor desires to make complies with the requirements of subsection (c)(6) of this section, if the consideration for such agreement is based in whole or in part on a consumer debt that is not secured by real property of the debtor.

(e) Except as provided in subsection (a)(3) of this section, discharge of a debt of the debtor does not affect the liability of any other entity on, or the property of any other entity for, such debt.

(f) Nothing contained in subsection (c) or (d) of this section prevents a debtor from voluntarily repaying any debt. . . .

UNIFORM CONSUMER CREDIT CODE

(1974)

(Excerpts)

[The National Conference of Commissioners on Uniform State Laws (now the Uniform Law Commission) proposed the Uniform Consumer Credit Code ("U3C") in 1968, as a consumer protection law. In 1974, the Commission proposed substantial amendments, largely due to the emergence of bank credit cards distributed extensively on a nationwide basis. As of May 1, 2011, only 11 states had enacted the U3C, some in its 1968 version and others in its 1974 version. However, a federal statute, and the Federal Reserve Board's implementing rules, now regulate many aspects of consumer credit contracts. See the Truth in Lending Act, as amended by the Credit Card Accountability Responsibility and Disclosure Act of 2009 (also known as the "Credit CARD Act of 2009"), 15 U.S.C. § 1601 *et seq.*; 12 C.F.R. Part 226. The U3C's provision on unconscionability is still significant for contract law.]

Sec.
1.301   [General Definitions] . . .
5.108   [Unconscionability; Inducement by Unconscionable Conduct . . .]

---

§ 1.301   [General Definitions] . . .

. . .

(12) "Consumer credit sale":

(a) Except as provided in paragraph (b), "consumer credit sale" means a sale of goods, services, or an interest in land in which:

(i) credit is granted either pursuant to a seller credit card or by a seller who regularly engages as a seller in credit transactions of the same kind;

(ii) the buyer is a person other than an organization;

(iii) the goods, services, or interest in land are purchased primarily for a personal, family, household, or agricultural purpose;

(iv) the debt is payable in instalments or a finance charge is made; and

(v) with respect to a sale of goods or services, the amount financed does not exceed $25,000.

(b) A "consumer credit sale" does not include . . .

(ii) . . . a sale of an interest in land if the finance charge does not exceed 12 per cent. . . .

(13) "Consumer credit transaction" means a consumer credit sale or consumer loan. . . .

§ 5.108   [Unconscionability; Inducement by Unconscionable Conduct . . .]

(1) With respect to . . . a consumer credit transaction, if the court as a matter of law finds:

(a) the agreement or transaction to have been unconscionable at the time it was made, or to have been induced by unconscionable conduct, the court may refuse to enforce the agreement; or

(b) any term or part of the agreement or transaction to have been unconscionable at the time it was made, the court may refuse to enforce the agreement, enforce the remainder of the agreement without the unconscionable term or part, or so limit the application of any unconscionable term or part as to avoid any unconscionable result....

(4) In applying subsection (1), consideration shall be given to each of the following factors, among others, as applicable....

    (b) ... knowledge by the seller ... at the time of the sale ... of the inability of the consumer to receive substantial benefits from the property or services sold or leased;

    (c) ... gross disparity between the price of the property or services sold ... and the value of the property or services measured by the price at which similar property or services are readily obtainable in credit transactions by like consumers....

    (e) the fact that the seller, lessor, or lender has knowingly taken advantage of the inability of the consumer or debtor reasonably to protect his interests by reason of physical or mental infirmities, ignorance, illiteracy, inability to understand the language of the agreement, or similar factors....

Comment...

4. [Subsection (4) lists] a number of specific factors to be considered on the issue of unconscionability. It is impossible to anticipate all of the factors and considerations which may support a conclusion of unconscionability in a given instance so the listing is not exclusive. The following are illustrative of individual transactions which would entitle a consumer to relief under this section....

Under subsection (4)(b), a sale to a Spanish speaking laborer-bachelor of an English language encyclopedia set, or the sale of two expensive vacuum cleaners to two poor families sharing the same apartment and one rug;

Under subsection (4)(c), a home solicitation sale of a set of cookware or flatware to a housewife for $375 in an area where a set of comparable quality is readily available on credit in stores for $125 or less;

Under subsection (4)(e), a sale of goods on terms known by the seller to be disadvantageous to the consumer where the written agreement is in English, the consumer is literate only in Spanish, the transaction was negotiated orally in Spanish by the seller's salesman, and the written agreement was neither translated nor explained to the consumer, but the mere fact a consumer has little education and cannot read or write and must sign with an "X" is not itself determinative of unconscionability....

TRUTH IN LENDING: REGULATION Z

(2011)

(Excerpts)

["Regulation Z" implements the Federal Truth in Lending Act, which is contained in Title I of the Consumer Credit Protection Act, as amended (15 U.S.C. § 1601 *et seq.*), and other statutes not relevant here. It was promulgated by the federal Bureau of Consumer Financial Protection and became effective on December 31, 2011. As excerpted, it (1) requires an issuer of credit cards to consider a consumer's "independent ability to make the required minimum periodic payments" under the credit card agreement (12 C.F.R. § 1026.51(a)); (2) prohibits an issuer from opening a credit card account for consumers under the age of 21 unless the consumer has submitted a written application agreement (12 C.F.R. § 1026.51(b); (3) requires an issuer to make extensive and detailed disclosures of the contract terms to consumers (12 C.F.R. §§ 1026.60, 1026.6); and (4) regulates credit card issuers in other ways (12 C.F.R. §§ 1026.53, 1026.55)]

Sec.

1026.6	Account Opening Disclosures . . .
1026.51	Ability to Pay.
1026.53	Allocation of Payments.
1026.55	Limitations on Increasing Annual Percentage Rates, Fees, and Charges.
1026.57	Reporting and Marketing Rules for College Student Open-End Credit.
1026.60	Credit and Charge Card Applications and Solicitations.

---

§ 1026.6 Account Opening Disclosures . . .

(b) Rules affecting open-end (not home-secured) plans. The requirements of paragraph (b) of this section apply to plans other than home-equity plans subject to the requirements of § 1026.40.

(1) Form of disclosures; tabular format for open-end (not home-secured) plans. Creditors must provide the account-opening disclosures specified in paragraph (b) (2)(i) through (b)(2)(v) (except for (b)(2)(i)(D)(2)) and (b)(2)(vii) through (b)(2) (xiv) of this section in the form of a table with the headings, content, and format substantially similar to any of the applicable tables in G-17 in Appendix G.

(i) Highlighting. In the table, any annual percentage rate required to be disclosed pursuant to paragraph (b)(2)(i) of this section; any introductory rate permitted to be disclosed pursuant to paragraph (b)(2)(i)(B) or required to be disclosed under paragraph (b)(2)(i)(F) of this section, any rate that will apply after a premium initial rate expires permitted to be disclosed pursuant to paragraph (b)(2)(i)(C) or required to be disclosed pursuant to paragraph (b)(2)(i)(F), and any fee or percentage amounts or maximum limits on fee amounts disclosed pursuant to paragraphs (b)(2)(ii), (b)(2)(iv), (b)(2)(vii) through (b)(2)(xii) of this section must be disclosed in bold text. However, bold text shall not be used for: The amount of any periodic fee disclosed pursuant to paragraph (b)(2) of this section that is not an annualized amount; and other annual percentage rates or fee amounts disclosed in the table.

(ii) Location. Only the information required or permitted by paragraphs (b)(2)(i) through (v) (except for (b)(2)(i)(D)(2)) and (b)(2)(vii) through (xiv) of this section shall be in the table. Disclosures required by paragraphs (b)(2)(i)(D)(2), (b)(2)(i) (D)(3), (b)(2)(vi), and (b)(2)(xv) of this section shall be placed directly below the table. Disclosures required by paragraphs (b)(3) through (5) of this section that are not otherwise required to be in the table and other information may be presented with the account agreement or account-opening disclosure statement, provided such information appears outside the required table. . . .

(2) Required disclosures for account-opening table for open-end (not home-secured) plans. A creditor shall disclose the items in this section, to the extent applicable:

(i) Annual percentage rate. Each periodic rate that may be used to compute the finance charge on an outstanding balance for purchases, a cash advance, or a balance transfer, expressed as an annual percentage rate (as determined by § 1026.14(b)). When more man one rate applies for a category of transactions, the range of balances to which each rate is applicable shall also be disclosed. The annual percentage rate for purchases disclosed pursuant to this paragraph shall be in at least 16-point type, except for the following: A penalty rate that may apply upon the occurrence of one or more specific events.

(A) Variable-rate information. If a rate disclosed under paragraph (b)(2)(i) of this section is a variable rate, the creditor shall also disclose the fact that the rate may vary and how the rate is determined. In describing how the applicable rate will be determined, the creditor must identify the type of index or formula that is used in setting the rate. The value of the index and the amount of the margin that are used to calculate the variable rate shall not be disclosed in the table. A disclosure of any applicable limitations on rate increases or decreases shall not be included in the table.

(B) Discounted initial rates. If the initial rate is an introductory rate, as that term is defined in § 1026.16(g)(2)(ii), the creditor must disclose the rate that would otherwise apply to the account pursuant to paragraph (b)(2)(i) of this section. Where the rate is not tied to an index or formula, the creditor must disclose the rate that will apply after the introductory rate expires. In a variable-rate account, the creditor must disclose a rate based on the applicable index or formula in accordance with the accuracy requirements of paragraph (b)(4)(ii)(G) of this section. Except as provided in paragraph (b)(2)(i)(F) of this section, the creditor is not required to, but may disclose in the table the introductory rate along with the rate that would otherwise apply to the account if the creditor also discloses the time period during which the introductory rate will remain in effect, and uses the term "introductory" or "intro" in immediate proximity to the introductory rate.

(C) Premium initial rate. If the initial rate is temporary and is higher than the rate that will apply after the temporary rate expires, the creditor must disclose the premium initial rate pursuant to paragraph (b)(2)(i) of this section. Consistent with paragraph (b)(2)(i) of this section, the premium initial rate for purchases must be in at least 16-point type. Except as provided in paragraph (b)(2)(i)(F) of this section, the creditor is not required to, but may disclose in the table the rate that will apply after the premium initial rate expires if the creditor also discloses the time period during which the premium initial rate will remain in effect. If the creditor also discloses in the table the rate that will apply after the premium initial rate for purchases expires, that rate also must be in at least 16-point type.

(D) Penalty rates.

(1) In general. Except as provided in paragraph (b)(2)(i)(D)(2) and (b) (2)(i)(D)(3) of this section, if a rate may increase as a penalty for one or more events specified in the account agreement, such as a late payment or an extension of credit that exceeds the credit limit, the creditor must disclose pursuant to paragraph (b)(2)(i) of this section the increased rate that may apply, a brief description of the event or events that may result in the increased rate, and a brief description of how long the increased rate will remain in effect. If more than one penalty rate may apply, the creditor at its option may disclose the highest rate that could apply, instead of disclosing the specific rates or the range of rates that could apply.

(2) Introductory rates. If the creditor discloses in the table an introductory rate, as that term is defined in § 1026.16(g)(2)(ii), creditors must briefly disclose directly beneath the table the circumstances under which the introductory rate may be revoked, and the rate that will apply after the introductory rate is revoked.

(3) Employee preferential rates. If a creditor discloses in the table a preferential annual percentage rate for which only employees of the creditor, employees of a third party, or other individuals with similar affiliations with the creditor or third party, such as executive officers, directors, or principal shareholders are eligible, the creditor must briefly disclose directly beneath the table the circumstances under which such preferential rate may be revoked, and the rate that will apply after such preferential rate is revoked. . . .

(F) Credit card accounts under an open-end (not home-secured) consumer credit plan. Notwithstanding paragraphs (b)(2)(i)(B) and (b)(2)(i)(C) of this section, for credit card accounts under an open-end (not home-secured) plan, issuers must disclose in the table:

(1) Any introductory rate as that term is defined in § 1026,16(g)(2)(ii) that would apply to the account, consistent with the requirements of paragraph (b)(2)(i)(B) of this section, and

(2) Any rate that would apply upon the expiration of a premium initial rate, consistent with the requirements of paragraph (b)(2)(i)(C) of this section.

(ii) Fees for issuance or availability.

(A) Any annual or other periodic fee that may be imposed for the issuance or availability of an open-end plan, including any fee based on account activity or inactivity; how frequently it will be imposed; and the annualized amount of the fee.

(B) Any non-periodic fee that relates to opening the plan. A creditor must disclose that the fee is a one-time fee.

(iii) Fixed finance charge; minimum interest charge. Any fixed finance charge and a brief description of the charge. Any minimum interest charge if it exceeds $1.00 that could be imposed during a billing cycle, and a brief description of the charge. The $1.00 threshold amount shall be adjusted periodically by the Bureau to reflect changes in the Consumer Price Index. The Bureau shall calculate each year a price level adjusted minimum interest charge using the Consumer Price Index in effect on the June 1 of that year. When the cumulative change in the adjusted minimum value derived from applying the annual Consumer Price level to the current minimum interest charge threshold has risen by a whole dollar, the minimum interest charge will be increased by $1.00. The creditor may, at its option, disclose in the table minimum interest charges below this threshold.

(iv) Transaction charges. Any transaction charge imposed by the creditor for use of the open-end plan for purchases.

(v) Grace period. The date by which or the period within which any credit extended may be repaid without incurring a finance charge due to a periodic interest rate and any conditions on the availability of the grace period. If no grace period is provided, that fact must be disclosed. If the length of the grace period varies, the creditor may disclose the range of days, the minimum number of days, or the average number of the days in the grace period, if the disclosure is identified as a range, minimum, or average. In disclosing in the tabular format a grace period that applies to all features on the account, the phrase "How to Avoid Paying Interest" shall be used as the heading for the row describing the grace period. If a grace period is not offered on all features of the account, in disclosing this fact in the tabular format, the phrase "Paying Interest" shall be used as the heading for the row describing this fact.

(vi) Balance computation method. The name of the balance computation method listed in § 1026.60(g) that is used to determine the balance on which the finance charge is computed for each feature, or an explanation of the method used if it is not listed, along with a statement that an explanation of the method(s) required by paragraph (b)(4)(i)(D) of this section is provided with the account-opening disclosures. In determining which balance computation method to disclose, the creditor shall assume that credit extended will not be repaid within any grace period, if any.

(vii) Cash advance fee. Any fee imposed for an extension of credit in the form of cash or its equivalent.

(viii) Late payment fee. Any fee imposed for a late payment.

(ix) Over-the-limit fee. Any fee imposed for exceeding a credit limit.

(x) Balance transfer fee. Any fee imposed to transfer an outstanding balance.

(xi) Returned-payment fee. Any fee imposed by the creditor for a returned payment.

(xii) Required insurance, debt cancellation or debt suspension coverage.

(A) A fee for insurance described in § 1026.4(b)(7) or debt cancellation or suspension coverage described in § 1026.4(b)(10), if the insurance, or debt cancellation or suspension coverage is required as part of the plan; and

(B) A cross reference to any additional information provided about the insurance or coverage, as applicable.

(xiii) Available credit. If a creditor requires fees for the issuance or availability of credit described in paragraph (b)(2)(ii) of this section, or requires a security deposit for such credit, and the total amount of those required fees and/or security deposit that will be imposed and charged to the account when the account is opened is 15 percent or more of the minimum credit limit for the plan, a creditor must disclose the available credit remaining after these fees or security deposit are debited to the account The determination whether the 15 percent threshold is met must be based on the minimum credit limit for the plan. However, the disclosure provided under this paragraph must be based on the actual initial credit limit provided on the account. In determining whether the 15 percent threshold test is met, the creditor must only consider fees for issuance or availability of credit, or a security deposit, that are required. If fees for issuance or availability are optional, these fees should not be considered in determining whether the disclosure must be given. Nonetheless, if the 15 percent threshold test is met, the creditor in providing the disclosure must disclose the amount of available credit calculated by excluding those optional fees, and the available credit including those optional fees. The creditor shall also disclose that the consumer has the right to reject the plan and not be obligated to pay those fees or any other fee or charges until the consumer has used the account or made a payment on the account after receiving a periodic statement. This paragraph does not apply with respect to fees or security deposits that are not debited to the account. . . .

§ 1026.51 Ability to Pay.

(a) General rule.

(1)(i) Consideration of ability to pay. A card issuer must not open a credit card account for a consumer under an open-end (not home-secured) consumer credit plan, or increase any credit limit applicable to such account, unless the card issuer considers the consumer's independent ability to make the required minimum periodic payments under the terms of the account based on the consumer's income or assets and current obligations.

(ii) Reasonable policies and procedures. Card issuers must establish and maintain reasonable written policies and procedures to consider a consumer's independent income or assets and current obligations. Reasonable policies and procedures to consider a consumer's independent ability to make the required payments include the consideration of at least one of the following: The ratio of debt obligations to income; the ratio of debt obligations to assets; or the income the consumer will have after paying debt obligations. It would be unreasonable for a card issuer to not review any information about a consumer's income, assets, or current obligations, or to issue a credit card to a consumer who does not have any independent income or assets.

(2) Minimum periodic payments.

(i) Reasonable method. For purposes of paragraph (a)(1) of this section, a card issuer must use a reasonable method for estimating the minimum periodic payments the consumer would be required to pay under the terms of the account.

(ii) Safe harbor. A card issuer complies with paragraph (a)(2)(i) of this section if it estimates required minimum periodic payments using the following method:

(A) The card issuer assumes utilization, from the first day of the billing cycle, of the full credit line that the issuer is considering offering to the consumer; and

(B) The card issuer uses a minimum payment formula employed by the issuer for the product the issuer is considering offering to the consumer or, in the case of an existing account, the minimum payment formula that currently applies to that account, provided that;

(1) If the applicable minimum payment formula includes interest charges, the card issuer estimates those charges using an interest rate that the issuer is considering offering to the consumer for purchases or, in the case of an existing account, the interest rate that currently applies to purchases; and

(2) If the applicable minimum payment formula includes mandatory fees, the card issuer must assume that such fees have been charged to the account.

(b) Rules affecting young consumers.

(1) Applications from young consumers. A card issuer may not open a credit card account under an open-end (not home-secured) consumer credit plan for a consumer less than 21 years old, unless the consumer has submitted a written application and the card issuer has:

(i) Financial information indicating the consumer has an independent ability to make the required minimum periodic payments on the proposed extension of credit in connection with the account, consistent with paragraph (a) of this section; or

(ii)(A) A signed agreement of a cosigner, guarantor, or joint applicant who is at least 21 years old to be either secondarily liable for any debt on the account incurred by the consumer before the consumer has attained the age of 21 or jointly liable with the consumer for any debt on the account, and

(B) Financial information indicating such cosigner, guarantor, or joint applicant has the independent ability to make the required minimum periodic payments on such debts, consistent with paragraph (a) of this section.

(2) Credit line increases for young consumers. If a credit card account has been opened pursuant to paragraph (b)(*l*)(ii) of this section, no increase in the credit limit may be made on such account before the consumer attains the age of 21 unless the cosigner, guarantor, or joint accountholder who assumed liability at account opening agrees in writing to assume liability on the increase.

§ 1026.53 Allocation of Payments.

(a) General rule. Except as provided in paragraph (b) of this section, when a consumer makes a payment in excess of the required minimum periodic payment for a credit card account under an open-end (not home-secured) consumer credit plan, the card issuer must allocate the excess amount first to the balance with the highest annual percentage rate and any remaining portion to the other balances in descending order based on the applicable annual percentage rate. . . .

§ 1026.55 Limitations on Increasing Annual Percentage Rates, Fees, and Charges.

(a) General rule. Except as provided in paragraph (b) of this section, a card issuer must not increase an annual percentage rate or a fee or charge required to be disclosed under § 1026.6(b)(2)(ii), (b)(2)(iii), or (b)(2)(xii) on a credit card account under an open-end (not home-secured) consumer credit plan.

(b) Exceptions. A card issuer may increase an annual percentage rate or a fee or charge required to be disclosed under § 1026.6(b)(2)(H), (b)(2)(iii), or (b)(2)(xii) pursuant to an exception set forth in this paragraph even if that increase would not be permitted under a different exception.

(1) Temporary rate, fee, or charge exception. A card issuer may increase an annual percentage rate or a fee or charge required to be disclosed under § 1026.6(b)(2)(ii), (b)(2)(iii), or (b)(2)(xii) upon the expiration of a specified period of six months or longer, provided that:

(i) Prior to the commencement of that period, the card issuer disclosed in writing to the consumer, in a clear and conspicuous manner, the length of the period and the annual percentage rate, fee, or charge that would apply after expiration of the period; and

(ii) Upon expiration of the specified period:

(A) The card issuer must not apply an annual percentage rate, fee, or charge to transactions that occurred prior to the period that exceeds the annual percentage rate, fee, or charge that applied to those transactions prior to the period;

(B) If the disclosures required by paragraph (b)(*l*)(i) of this section are provided pursuant to § 1026.9(c), the card issuer must not apply an annual percentage rate, fee, or charge to transactions that occurred within 14 days after provision of the notice that exceeds the annual percentage rate, fee, or charge that applied to that category of transactions prior to provision of the notice; and

(C) The card issuer must not apply an annual percentage rate, fee, or charge to transactions that occurred during the period that exceeds the increased annual percentage rate, fee, or charge disclosed pursuant to paragraph (b)(*l*)(i) of this section.

(2) Variable rate exception. A card issuer may increase an annual percentage rate when:

(i) The annual percentage rate varies according to an index that is not under the card issuer's control and is available to the general public; and

(ii) The increase in the annual percentage rate is due to an increase in the index.

(3) *Advance notice exception.* A card issuer may increase an annual percentage rate or a fee or charge required to be disclosed under § 1026.6(b)(2)(ii), (b)(2)(iii), or (b)(2)(xii) after complying with the applicable notice requirements in § 1026.9(b), (c), or (g), provided that:

(i) If a card issuer discloses an increased annual percentage rate, fee, or charge pursuant to § 1026.9(b), the card issuer must not apply that rate, fee, or charge to transactions that occurred prior to provision of the notice;

(ii) If a card issuer discloses an increased annual percentage rate, fee, or charge pursuant to § 1026.9(c) or (g), the card issuer must not apply that rate, fee, or charge to transactions that occurred prior to or within 14 days after provision of the notice; and

(iii) This exception does not permit a card issuer to increase an annual percentage rate or a fee or charge required to be disclosed under § 1026.6(b)(2)(ii), (iii), or (xii) during the first year after the account is opened, while the account is closed, or while the card issuer does not permit the consumer to use the account for new transactions. For purposes of this paragraph, an account is considered open no earlier than the date on which the account may first be used by the consumer to engage in transactions.

(4) *Delinquency exception.* A card issuer may increase an annual percentage rate or a fee or charge required to be disclosed under § 1026.6(b)(2)(ii), (b)(2)(iii), or (b)(2)(xii) due to the card issuer not receiving the consumer's required minimum periodic payment within 60 days after the due date for that payment, provided that:

(i) The card issuer must disclose in a clear and conspicuous manner in the notice of the increase pursuant to § 1026.9(c) or (g):

(A) A statement of the reason for the increase; and

(B) That the increased annual percentage rate, fee, or charge will cease to apply if the card issuer receives six consecutive required minimum periodic payments on or before the payment due date beginning with the first payment due following the effective date of the increase; and

(ii) If the card issuer receives six consecutive required minimum periodic payments on or before the payment due date beginning with the first payment due following the effective date of the increase, the card issuer must reduce any annual percentage rate, fee, or charge increased pursuant to this exception to the annual percentage rate, fee, or charge that applied prior to the increase with respect to transactions that occurred prior to or within 14 days after provision of the § 1026.9(c) or (g) notice.

(5) *Workout and temporary hardship arrangement exception.* A card issuer may increase an annual percentage rate or a fee or charge required to be disclosed under § 1026.6(b)(2)(ii), (b)(2)(iii), or (b)(2)(xii) due to the consumer's completion of a workout or temporary hardship arrangement or the consumer's failure to comply with the terms of such an arrangement, provided that:

(i) Prior to commencement of the arrangement (except as provided in § 1026.9(c) (2)(v)(D)), the card issuer has provided the consumer with a clear and conspicuous written disclosure of the terms of the arrangement (including any increases due to the completion or failure of the arrangement); and

(ii) Upon the completion or failure of the arrangement, the card issuer must not apply to any transactions that occurred prior to commencement of the arrangement an annual percentage rate, fee, or charge that exceeds the annual percentage rate, fee, or charge that applied to those transactions prior to commencement of the arrangement. . . .

§ 1026.57 Reporting and Marketing Rules for College Student Open-End Credit.

(a) Definitions.

(1) *College student credit card.* The term "college student credit card" as used in this section means a credit card issued under a credit card account under an open-end (not home-secured) consumer credit plan to any college student.

(2) *College student.* The term "college student" as used in this section means a consumer who is a full-time or part-time student of an institution of higher education.

(3) *Institution of higher education.* The term "institution of higher education" as used in this section has the same meaning as in sections 101 and 102 of the Higher Education Act of 1965 (20 U.S.C. 1001 and 1002).

(4) *Affiliated organization.* The term "affiliated organization" as used in this section means an alumni organization or foundation affiliated with or related to an institution of higher education.

(5) College credit card agreement. The term "college credit card agreement" as used in this section means any business, marketing or promotional agreement between a card issuer and an institution of higher education or an affiliated organization in connection with which college student credit cards are issued to college students currently enrolled at that institution.

(b) Public disclosure of agreements. An institution of higher education shall publicly disclose any contract or other agreement made with a card issuer or creditor for the purpose of marketing a credit card.

(c) Prohibited inducements. No card issuer or creditor may offer a college student any tangible item to induce such student to apply for or open an open-end consumer credit plan offered by such card issuer or creditor, if such offer is made:

(1) On the campus of an institution of higher education;

(2) Near the campus of an institution of higher education; or

(3) At an event sponsored by or related to an institution of higher education.

. . .

§ 1026.60   Credit and Charge Card Applications and Solicitations.

(a) General rules. The card issuer shall provide the disclosures required under this section on or with a solicitation or an application to open a credit or charge card account.

(1) Definition of solicitation. For purposes of this section, the term solicitation means an offer by the card issuer to open a credit or charge card account that does not require the consumer to complete an application. A "firm offer of credit" as defined in section 603(1) of the Fair Credit Reporting Act (15 U.S.C. 1681a(1)) for a credit or charge card is a solicitation for purposes of this section.

(2) Form of disclosures; tabular format.

(i) The disclosures in paragraphs (b)(1) through (5) (except for (b)(*l*)(iv)(B)) and (b)(7) through (15) of this section made pursuant to paragraph (c), (d)(2), (e)(1) or (f) of this section generally shall be in the form of a table with headings, content, and format substantially similar to any of the applicable tables found in G-10 in Appendix G to this part.

(ii) The table described in paragraph (a)(2)(i) of this section shall contain only the information required or permitted by this section. Other information may be presented on or with an application or solicitation, provided such information appears outside the required table.

(iii) Disclosures required by paragraphs (b)(1)(iv)(B), (b)(*l*)(iv)(C) and (b)(6) of this section must be placed directly beneath the table.

(iv) When a tabular format is required, any annual percentage rate required to be disclosed pursuant to paragraph (b)(1) of this section, any introductory rate required to be disclosed pursuant to paragraph (b)(*l*)(ii) of this section, any rate that will apply after a premium initial rate expires required to be disclosed under paragraph (b)(*l*)(iii) of this section, and any fee or percentage amounts or maximum limits on fee amounts disclosed pursuant to paragraphs (b)(2), (b)(4), (b)(8) through (b)(13) of this section must be disclosed in bold text. However, bold text shall not be used for: The amount of any periodic fee disclosed pursuant to paragraph (b)(2) of this section that is not an annualized amount; and other annual percentage rates or fee amounts disclosed in the table.

(v) For an application or a solicitation that is accessed by the consumer in electronic form, the disclosures required under this section may be provided to the consumer in electronic form on or with the application or solicitation.

§ 1026.60   MISCELLANEOUS STATUTES   Pt. VII

(vi)(A)   Except as provided in paragraph (a)(2)(vi)(B) of this section, the table described in paragraph (a)(2)(i) of this section must be provided in a prominent location on or with an application or a solicitation.

(B) If the table described in paragraph (a)(2)(i) of this section is provided electronically, it must be provided in close proximity to the application or solicitation.

(3)   Fees based on a percentage. If the amount of any fee required to be disclosed under this section is determined on the basis of a percentage of another amount, the percentage used and the identification of the amount against which the percentage is applied may be disclosed instead of the amount of the fee.

(4)   Fees that vary by state. Card issuers that impose fees referred to in paragraphs (b)(8) through (12) of this section that vary by state may, at the issuer's option, disclose in the table required by paragraph (a)(2)(i) of this section: The specific fee applicable to the consumer's account; or the range of the fees, if the disclosure includes a statement that the amount of the fee varies by state and refers the consumer to a disclosure provided with the table where the amount of the fee applicable to the consumer's account is disclosed. A card issuer may not list fees for multiple states in the table.

(5)   Exceptions. This section does not apply to:

(i)   Home-equity plans accessible by a credit or charge card that are subject to the requirements of § 1026.40;

(ii)   Overdraft lines of credit tied to asset accounts accessed by check-guarantee cards or by debit cards;

(iii)   Lines of credit accessed by check-guarantee cards or by debit cards that can be used only at automated teller machines;

(iv)   Lines of credit accessed solely by account numbers;

(v)   Additions of a credit or charge card to an existing open-end plan;

(vi)   General purpose applications unless the application, or material accompanying it, indicates that it can be used to open a credit or charge card account; or

(vii)   Consumer-initiated requests for applications.

(b)   Required disclosures. The card issuer shall disclose the items in this paragraph on or with an application or a solicitation in accordance with the requirements of paragraphs (c), (d), (e)(1) or (f) of this section. A credit card issuer shall disclose all applicable items in this paragraph except for paragraph (b)(7) of this section. A charge card issuer shall disclose the applicable items in paragraphs (b)(2), (4), (7) through (12), and (15) of this section.

(1)   Annual percentage rate. Each periodic rate that may be used to compute the finance charge on an outstanding balance for purchases, a cash advance, or a balance transfer, expressed as an annual percentage rate (as determined by § 1026.14(b)). When more than one rate applies for a category of transactions, the range of balances to which each rate is applicable shall also be disclosed. The annual percentage rate for purchases disclosed pursuant to this paragraph shall be in at least 16-point type, except for the following: Oral disclosures of the annual percentage rate for purchases; or a penalty rate that may apply upon the occurrence of one or more specific events.

(i)   Variable rate information. If a rate disclosed under paragraph (b)(1) of this section is a variable rate, the card issuer shall also disclose the fact that the rate may vary and how the rate is determined. In describing how the applicable rate will be determined, the card issuer must identify the type of index or formula that is used in setting the rate. The value of the index and the amount of the margin that are used to calculate the variable rate shall not be disclosed in the table. A disclosure of any applicable limitations on rate increases shall not be included in the table.

(ii) Discounted initial rate. If the initial rate is an introductory rate, as that term is defined in § 1026.16(g)(2)(ii), the card issuer must disclose in the table the introductory rate, the time period during which the introductory rate will remain in effect, and must use the term "introductory" or "intro" in immediate proximity to the introductory rate. The card issuer also must disclose the rate that would otherwise apply to the account pursuant to paragraph (b)(1) of this section. Where the rate is not tied to an index or formula, the card issuer must disclose the rate that will apply after the introductory rate expires. In a variable-rate account, the card issuer must disclose a rate based on the applicable index or formula in accordance with the accuracy requirements set forth in paragraphs (c)(2), (d)(3), or (e)(4) of this section, as applicable.

(iii) Premium initial rate. If the initial rate is temporary and is higher than the rate that will apply after the temporary rate expires, the card issuer must disclose the premium initial rate pursuant to paragraph (b)(1) of this section and the time period during which the premium initial rate will remain in effect. Consistent with paragraph (b)(1) of this section, the premium initial rate for purchases must be in at least 16-point type. The issuer must also disclose in the table the rate that will apply after the premium initial rate expires, in at least 16-point type.

(iv) Penalty rates.

(A) In general. Except as provided in paragraph (b)(*l*)(iv)(B) and (C) of this section, if a rate may increase as a penalty for one or more events specified in the account agreement, such as a late payment or an extension of credit that exceeds the credit limit, the card issuer must disclose pursuant to this paragraph (b)(1) the increased rate that may apply, a brief description of the event or events that may result in the increased rate, and a brief description of how long the increased rate will remain in effect.

(B) Introductory rates. If the issuer discloses an introductory rate, as that term is defined in § 1026.16(g)(2)(ii), in the table or in any written or electronic promotional materials accompanying applications or solicitations subject to paragraph (c) or (e) of this section, the issuer must briefly disclose directly beneath the table the circumstances, if any, under which the introductory rate may be revoked, and the type of rate that will apply after the introductory rate is revoked.

(C) Employee preferential rates. If a card issuer discloses in the table a preferential annual percentage rate for which only employees of the card issuer, employees of a third party, or other individuals with similar affiliations with the card issuer or third party, such as executive officers, directors, or principal shareholders are eligible, the card issuer must briefly disclose directly beneath the table the circumstances under which such preferential rate may be revoked, and the rate that will apply after such preferential rate is revoked.

(v) Rates that depend on consumer's creditworthiness: If a rate cannot be determined at the time disclosures are given because the rate depends, at least in part, on a later determination of the consumer's creditworthiness, the card issuer must disclose the specific rates or the range of rates that could apply and a statement that the rate for which the consumer may qualify at account opening will depend on the consumer's creditworthiness, and other factors if applicable. If the rate that depends, at least in part, on a later determination of the consumer's creditworthiness is a penalty rate, as described in paragraph (b)(*l*)(iv) of this section, the card issuer at its option may disclose the highest rate that could apply, instead of disclosing the specific rates or the range of rates that could apply.

(vi) APRs that vary by state. Issuers imposing annual percentage rates that vary by state may, at the issuer's option, disclose in the table: the specific annual percentage rate applicable to the consumer's account; or the range of the annual percentage rates, if the disclosure includes a statement that the annual percentage rate varies by state and refers the consumer to a disclosure provided with the table where the annual percentage rate applicable to the consumer's account is disclosed, A card issuer may not list annual percentage rates for multiple states in the table.

(2) Fees for issuance or availability.

(i) Any annual or other periodic fee that may be imposed for the issuance or availability of a credit or charge card, including any fee based on account activity or inactivity; how frequently it will be imposed; and the annualized amount of the fee.

(ii) Any non-periodic fee that relates to opening an account. A card issuer must disclose that the fee is a one-time fee.

(3) Fixed finance charge; minimum interest charge. Any fixed finance charge and a brief description of the charge. Any minimum interest charge if it exceeds $1.00 that could be imposed during a billing cycle, and a brief description of the charge. The $ 1.00 threshold amount shall be adjusted periodically by the Bureau to reflect changes in the Consumer Price Index. The Bureau shall calculate each year a price level adjusted minimum interest charge using the Consumer Price Index in effect on June 1 of that year. When the cumulative change in the adjusted minimum value derived from applying the annual Consumer Price level to the current minimum interest charge threshold has risen by a whole dollar, the minimum interest charge will be increased by $1.00. The issuer may, at its option, disclose in the table minimum interest charges below this threshold.

(4) Transaction charges. Any transaction charge imposed by the card issuer for the use of the card for purchases.

(5) Grace period. The date by which or the period within which any credit extended for purchases may be repaid without incurring a finance charge due to a periodic interest rate and any conditions on the availability of the grace period. If no grace period is provided, that fact must be disclosed. If the length of the grace period varies, the card issuer may disclose the range of days, the minimum number of days, or the average number of days in the grace period, if the disclosure is identified as a range, minimum, or average. In disclosing in the tabular format a grace period that applies to all types of purchases, the phrase "How to Avoid Paying Interest on Purchases" shall be used as the heading for the row describing the grace period. If a grace period is not offered on all types of purchases, in disclosing this fact in the tabular format, the phrase "Paying Interest" shall be used as the heading for the row describing this fact.

(6) Balance computation method. The name of the balance computation method listed in paragraph (g) of this section that is used to determine the balance for purchases on which the finance charge is computed, or an explanation of the method used if it is not listed. In determining which balance computation method to disclose, the card issuer shall assume that credit extended for purchases will not be repaid within the grace period, if any.

(7) Statement on charge card payments. A statement that charges incurred by use of the charge card are due when the periodic statement is received.

(8) Cash advance fee. Any fee imposed for an extension of credit in the form of cash or its equivalent.

(9) Late payment fee. Any fee imposed for a late payment. . . .

(c) Direct mail and electronic applications and solicitations.

  (1) General. The card issuer shall disclose the applicable items in paragraph (b) of this section on or with an application or solicitation that is mailed to consumers or provided to consumers in electronic form.

  (2) Accuracy.

   (i) Disclosures in direct mail applications and solicitations must be accurate as of the time the disclosures are mailed. An accurate variable annual percentage rate is one in effect within 60 days before mailing.

   (ii) Disclosures provided in electronic form must be accurate as of the time they are sent, in the case of disclosures sent to a consumer's email address, or as of the time they are viewed by the public, in the case of disclosures made available at a location such as a card issuer's Web site. An accurate variable annual percentage rate provided in electronic form is one in effect within 30 days before it is sent to a consumer's email address, or viewed by the public, as applicable. . . .

(e) Applications and solicitations made available to general public. The card issuer shall provide disclosures, to the extent applicable, on or with an application or solicitation that is made available to the general public, including one contained in a catalog, magazine, or other generally available publication. The disclosures shall be provided in accordance with paragraph (e)(1) or (e)(2) of this section.

  (1) Disclosure of required credit information. The card issuer may disclose in a prominent location on the application or solicitation the following:

   (i) The applicable information in paragraph (b) of this section;

   (ii) The date the required information was printed, including a statement that the required information was accurate as of that date and is subject to change after that date; and

   (iii) A statement that the consumer should contact the card issuer for any change in the required information since it was printed, and a toll-free telephone number or a mailing address for that purpose.

  (2) No disclosure of credit information. If none of the items in paragraph (b) of this section is provided on or with the application or solicitation, the card issuer may state in a prominent location on the application or solicitation the following:

   (i) There are costs associated with the use of the card; and

   (ii) The consumer may contact the card issuer to request specific information about the costs, along with a toll-tree telephone number and a mailing address for that purpose.

  (3) Prompt response to requests for information. Upon receiving a request for any of the information referred to in this paragraph, the card issuer shall promptly and fully disclose the information requested.

  (4) Accuracy. The disclosures given pursuant to paragraph (e)(1) of this section must be accurate as of the date of printing. A variable annual percentage rate is accurate if it was in effect within 30 days before printing.

(f) In-person applications and solicitations. A card issuer shall disclose the information in paragraph (b) of this section, to the extent applicable, on or with an application or solicitation that is initiated by the card issuer and given to the consumer in person. A card issuer complies with the requirements of this paragraph if the issuer provides disclosures in accordance with paragraph (c)(1) or (e)(1) of this section. . . .

PART VIII
SAMPLE CONTRACTS

SAMPLE CONTRACTS — Pt. VIII

AMERICAN INSTITUTE OF ARCHITECTS
SAMPLE FORM CONTRACTS

Standard Form of Agreement Between Owner and Contractor where the basis of payment is a Stipulated Sum

AGREEMENT made as of the _____ day of _____ in the year _____
(In words, indicate day, month and year.)

BETWEEN the Owner:
(Name, legal status, address and other information)

and the Contractor:
(Name, legal status, address and other information)

for the following Project:
(Name, location and detailed description)

The Architect:
(Name, legal status, address and other information)

This document has important legal consequences. Consultation with an attorney is encouraged with respect to its completion or modification.

The parties should complete A101™–2017, Exhibit A, Insurance and Bonds, contemporaneously with this Agreement.

AIA Document A201™–2017, General Conditions of the Contract for Construction, is adopted in this document by reference. Do not use with other general conditions unless this document is modified.

The Owner and Contractor agree as follows.

Init.
/

AIA Document A101™ – 2017. Copyright © 1915, 1918, 1925, 1937, 1951, 1958, 1961, 1963, 1967, 1974, 1977, 1987, 1991, 1997, 2007 and 2017 by The American Institute of Architects. All rights reserved. WARNING: This AIA® Document is protected by U.S. Copyright Law and International Treaties. Unauthorized reproduction or distribution of this AIA® Document, or any portion of it, may result in severe civil and criminal penalties, and will be prosecuted to the maximum extent possible under the law. To report copyright violations of AIA Contract Documents, e-mail The American Institute of Architects' legal counsel, copyright@aia.org.

1

Pt. VIII   A.I.A. SAMPLE FORM CONTRACTS

TABLE OF ARTICLES

1. THE CONTRACT DOCUMENTS
2. THE WORK OF THIS CONTRACT
3. DATE OF COMMENCEMENT AND SUBSTANTIAL COMPLETION
4. CONTRACT SUM
5. PAYMENTS
6. DISPUTE RESOLUTION
7. TERMINATION OR SUSPENSION
8. MISCELLANEOUS PROVISIONS
9. ENUMERATION OF CONTRACT DOCUMENTS

EXHIBIT A   INSURANCE AND BONDS

ARTICLE 1   THE CONTRACT DOCUMENTS

The Contract Documents consist of this Agreement, Conditions of the Contract (General, Supplementary, and other Conditions), Drawings, Specifications, Addenda issued prior to execution of this Agreement, other documents listed in this Agreement, and Modifications issued after execution of this Agreement, all of which form the Contract, and are as fully a part of the Contract as if attached to this Agreement or repeated herein. The Contract represents the entire and integrated agreement between the parties hereto and supersedes prior negotiations, representations, or agreements, either written or oral. An enumeration of the Contract Documents, other than a Modification, appears in Article 9.

ARTICLE 2   THE WORK OF THIS CONTRACT

The Contractor shall fully execute the Work described in the Contract Documents, except as specifically indicated in the Contract Documents to be the responsibility of others.

ARTICLE 3   DATE OF COMMENCEMENT AND SUBSTANTIAL COMPLETION

§ 3.1 The date of commencement of the Work shall be:
(Check one of the following boxes.)

☐ The date of this Agreement.

☐ A date set forth in a notice to proceed issued by the Owner.

☐ Established as follows:
(Insert a date or a means to determine the date of commencement of the Work.)

If a date of commencement of the Work is not selected, then the date of commencement shall be the date of this Agreement.

§ 3.2 The Contract Time shall be measured from the date of commencement of the Work.

§ 3.3 Substantial Completion
§ 3.3.1 Subject to adjustments of the Contract Time as provided in the Contract Documents, the Contractor shall achieve Substantial Completion of the entire Work:
(Check one of the following boxes and complete the necessary information.)

☐ Not later than   ( ) calendar days from the date of commencement of the Work.

☐ By the following date:

§ 3.3.2 Subject to adjustments of the Contract Time as provided in the Contract Documents, if portions of the Work are to be completed prior to Substantial Completion of the entire Work, the Contractor shall achieve Substantial Completion of such portions by the following dates:

Portion of Work	Substantial Completion Date

§ 3.3.3 If the Contractor fails to achieve Substantial Completion as provided in this Section 3.3, liquidated damages, if any, shall be assessed as set forth in Section 4.5.

ARTICLE 4 CONTRACT SUM
§ 4.1 The Owner shall pay the Contractor the Contract Sum in current funds for the Contractor's performance of the Contract. The Contract Sum shall be ($), subject to additions and deductions as provided in the Contract Documents.

§ 4.2 Alternates
§ 4.2.1 Alternates, if any, included in the Contract Sum:

Item	Price

§ 4.2.2 Subject to the conditions noted below, the following alternates may be accepted by the Owner following execution of this Agreement. Upon acceptance, the Owner shall issue a Modification to this Agreement.
(Insert below each alternate and the conditions that must be met for the Owner to accept the alternate.)

Item	Price	Conditions for Acceptance

§ 4.3 Allowances, if any, included in the Contract Sum:
(Identify each allowance.)

Item	Price

§ 4.4 Unit prices, if any:
(Identify the item and state the unit price and quantity limitations, if any, to which the unit price will be applicable.)

Item	Units and Limitations	Price per Unit ($0.00)

§ 4.5 Liquidated damages, if any:
(Insert terms and conditions for liquidated damages, if any.)

§ 4.6 Other:
(Insert provisions for bonus or other incentives, if any, that might result in a change to the Contract Sum.)

ARTICLE 5 PAYMENTS
§ 5.1 Progress Payments
§ 5.1.1 Based upon Applications for Payment submitted to the Architect by the Contractor and Certificates for Payment issued by the Architect, the Owner shall make progress payments on account of the Contract Sum to the Contractor as provided below and elsewhere in the Contract Documents.

§ 5.1.2 The period covered by each Application for Payment shall be one calendar month ending on the last day of the month, or as follows:

§ 5.1.3 Provided that an Application for Payment is received by the Architect not later than the   day of a month, the Owner shall make payment of the amount certified to the Contractor not later than the   day of the month. If an Application for Payment is received by the Architect after the application date fixed above, payment of the amount certified shall be made by the Owner not later than   (   ) days after the Architect receives the Application for Payment.
(Federal, state or local laws may require payment within a certain period of time.)

§ 5.1.4 Each Application for Payment shall be based on the most recent schedule of values submitted by the Contractor in accordance with the Contract Documents. The schedule of values shall allocate the entire Contract Sum among the various portions of the Work. The schedule of values shall be prepared in such form, and supported by such data to substantiate its accuracy, as the Architect may require. This schedule of values shall be used as a basis for reviewing the Contractor's Applications for Payment.

§ 5.1.5 Applications for Payment shall show the percentage of completion of each portion of the Work as of the end of the period covered by the Application for Payment.

§ 5.1.6 In accordance with AIA Document A201™–2017, General Conditions of the Contract for Construction, and subject to other provisions of the Contract Documents, the amount of each progress payment shall be computed as follows:

§ 5.1.6.1 The amount of each progress payment shall first include:
.1 That portion of the Contract Sum properly allocable to completed Work;
.2 That portion of the Contract Sum properly allocable to materials and equipment delivered and suitably stored at the site for subsequent incorporation in the completed construction, or, if approved in advance by the Owner, suitably stored off the site at a location agreed upon in writing; and
.3 That portion of Construction Change Directives that the Architect determines, in the Architect's professional judgment, to be reasonably justified.

§ 5.1.6.2 The amount of each progress payment shall then be reduced by:
.1 The aggregate of any amounts previously paid by the Owner;
.2 The amount, if any, for Work that remains uncorrected and for which the Architect has previously withheld a Certificate for Payment as provided in Article 9 of AIA Document A201–2017;
.3 Any amount for which the Contractor does not intend to pay a Subcontractor or material supplier, unless the Work has been performed by others the Contractor intends to pay;
.4 For Work performed or defects discovered since the last payment application, any amount for which the Architect may withhold payment, or nullify a Certificate of Payment in whole or in part, as provided in Article 9 of AIA Document A201–2017; and
.5 Retainage withheld pursuant to Section 5.1.7.

§ 5.1.7 Retainage
§ 5.1.7.1 For each progress payment made prior to Substantial Completion of the Work, the Owner may withhold the following amount, as retainage, from the payment otherwise due:
(Insert a percentage or amount to be withheld as retainage from each Application for Payment. The amount of retainage may be limited by governing law.)

§ 5.1.7.1.1 The following items are not subject to retainage:
(Insert any items not subject to the withholding of retainage, such as general conditions, insurance, etc.)

§ 5.1.7.2 Reduction or limitation of retainage, if any, shall be as follows:
(If the retainage established in Section 5.1.7.1 is to be modified prior to Substantial Completion of the entire Work, including modifications for Substantial Completion of portions of the Work as provided in Section 3.3.2, insert provisions for such modifications.)

§ 5.1.7.3 Except as set forth in this Section 5.1.7.3, upon Substantial Completion of the Work, the Contractor may submit an Application for Payment that includes the retainage withheld from prior Applications for Payment pursuant to this Section 5.1.7. The Application for Payment submitted at Substantial Completion shall not include retainage as follows:
(Insert any other conditions for release of retainage upon Substantial Completion.)

§ 5.1.8 If final completion of the Work is materially delayed through no fault of the Contractor, the Owner shall pay the Contractor any additional amounts in accordance with Article 9 of AIA Document A201–2017.

§ 5.1.9 Except with the Owner's prior approval, the Contractor shall not make advance payments to suppliers for materials or equipment which have not been delivered and stored at the site.

§ 5.2 Final Payment
§ 5.2.1 Final payment, constituting the entire unpaid balance of the Contract Sum, shall be made by the Owner to the Contractor when
 .1 the Contractor has fully performed the Contract except for the Contractor's responsibility to correct Work as provided in Article 12 of AIA Document A201–2017, and to satisfy other requirements, if any, which extend beyond final payment; and
 .2 a final Certificate for Payment has been issued by the Architect.

§ 5.2.2 The Owner's final payment to the Contractor shall be made no later than 30 days after the issuance of the Architect's final Certificate for Payment, or as follows:

§ 5.3 Interest
Payments due and unpaid under the Contract shall bear interest from the date payment is due at the rate stated below, or in the absence thereof, at the legal rate prevailing from time to time at the place where the Project is located.
(Insert rate of interest agreed upon, if any.)

_____ %

ARTICLE 6 DISPUTE RESOLUTION
§ 6.1 Initial Decision Maker
The Architect will serve as the Initial Decision Maker pursuant to Article 15 of AIA Document A201–2017, unless the parties appoint below another individual, not a party to this Agreement, to serve as the Initial Decision Maker.
(If the parties mutually agree, insert the name, address and other contact information of the Initial Decision Maker, if other than the Architect.)

§ 6.2 Binding Dispute Resolution

For any Claim subject to, but not resolved by, mediation pursuant to Article 15 of AIA Document A201–2017, the method of binding dispute resolution shall be as follows:

(Check the appropriate box.)

☐ Arbitration pursuant to Section 15.4 of AIA Document A201–2017

☐ Litigation in a court of competent jurisdiction

☐ Other *(Specify)*

If the Owner and Contractor do not select a method of binding dispute resolution, or do not subsequently agree in writing to a binding dispute resolution method other than litigation, Claims will be resolved by litigation in a court of competent jurisdiction.

ARTICLE 7 TERMINATION OR SUSPENSION

§ 7.1 The Contract may be terminated by the Owner or the Contractor as provided in Article 14 of AIA Document A201–2017.

§ 7.1.1 If the Contract is terminated for the Owner's convenience in accordance with Article 14 of AIA Document A201–2017, then the Owner shall pay the Contractor a termination fee as follows:
(Insert the amount of, or method for determining, the fee, if any, payable to the Contractor following a termination for the Owner's convenience.)

§ 7.2 The Work may be suspended by the Owner as provided in Article 14 of AIA Document A201–2017.

ARTICLE 8 MISCELLANEOUS PROVISIONS

§ 8.1 Where reference is made in this Agreement to a provision of AIA Document A201–2017 or another Contract Document, the reference refers to that provision as amended or supplemented by other provisions of the Contract Documents.

§ 8.2 The Owner's representative:
(Name, address, email address, and other information)

§ 8.3 The Contractor's representative:
(Name, address, email address, and other information)

§ 8.4 Neither the Owner's nor the Contractor's representative shall be changed without ten days' prior notice to the other party.

§ 8.5 Insurance and Bonds

§ 8.5.1 The Owner and the Contractor shall purchase and maintain insurance as set forth in AIA Document A101™–2017, Standard Form of Agreement Between Owner and Contractor where the basis of payment is a Stipulated Sum, Exhibit A, Insurance and Bonds, and elsewhere in the Contract Documents.

§ 8.5.2 The Contractor shall provide bonds as set forth in AIA Document A101™–2017 Exhibit A, and elsewhere in the Contract Documents.

§ 8.6 Notice in electronic format, pursuant to Article 1 of AIA Document A201–2017, may be given in accordance with AIA Document E203™–2013, Building Information Modeling and Digital Data Exhibit, if completed, or as otherwise set forth below:
(If other than in accordance with AIA Document E203-2013, insert requirements for delivering notice in electronic format such as name, title, and email address of the recipient and whether and how the system will be required to generate a read receipt for the transmission.)

§ 8.7 Other provisions:

ARTICLE 9 ENUMERATION OF CONTRACT DOCUMENTS
§ 9.1 This Agreement is comprised of the following documents:
 .1 AIA Document A101™–2017, Standard Form of Agreement Between Owner and Contractor
 .2 AIA Document A101™–2017, Exhibit A, Insurance and Bonds
 .3 AIA Document A201™–2017, General Conditions of the Contract for Construction
 .4 AIA Document E203™–2013, Building Information Modeling and Digital Data Exhibit, dated as indicated below:
  (Insert the date of the E203-2013 incorporated into this Agreement.)

 .5 Drawings

Number	Title	Date

 .6 Specifications

Section	Title	Date	Pages

 .7 Addenda, if any:

Number	Date	Pages

Portions of Addenda relating to bidding or proposal requirements are not part of the Contract Documents unless the bidding or proposal requirements are also enumerated in this Article 9.

 .8 Other Exhibits:
  (Check all boxes that apply and include appropriate information identifying the exhibit where required.)

  ☐ AIA Document E204™–2017, Sustainable Projects Exhibit, dated as indicated below:
   (Insert the date of the E204-2017 incorporated into this Agreement.)

A.I.A. SAMPLE FORM CONTRACTS

☐ The Sustainability Plan:

Title   Date   Pages

☐ Supplementary and other Conditions of the Contract:

Document   Title   Date   Pages

.9 Other documents, if any, listed below:
(*List here any additional documents that are intended to form part of the Contract Documents. AIA Document A201™–2017 provides that the advertisement or invitation to bid, Instructions to Bidders, sample forms, the Contractor's bid or proposal, portions of Addenda relating to bidding or proposal requirements, and other information furnished by the Owner in anticipation of receiving bids or proposals, are not part of the Contract Documents unless enumerated in this Agreement. Any such documents should be listed here only if intended to be part of the Contract Documents.*)

This Agreement entered into as of the day and year first written above.

_____   _____
OWNER *(Signature)*   **CONTRACTOR** *(Signature)*

_____   _____
(Printed name and title)   *(Printed name and title)*

AIA Document A101™ – 2017 Exhibit A

Insurance and Bonds

This Insurance and Bonds Exhibit is part of the Agreement, between the Owner and the Contractor, dated the _____ day of _____ in the year _____
(In words, indicate day, month and year.)

for the following **PROJECT:**
(Name and location or address)

THE OWNER:
(Name, legal status and address)

THE CONTRACTOR:
(Name, legal status and address)

> This document has important legal consequences. Consultation with an attorney is encouraged with respect to its completion or modification.
>
> This document is intended to be used in conjunction with AIA Document A201™–2017, General Conditions of the Contract for Construction. Article 11 of A201™–2017 contains additional insurance provisions.

TABLE OF ARTICLES

A.1 GENERAL

A.2 OWNER'S INSURANCE

A.3 CONTRACTOR'S INSURANCE AND BONDS

A.4 SPECIAL TERMS AND CONDITIONS

ARTICLE A.1 GENERAL

The Owner and Contractor shall purchase and maintain insurance, and provide bonds, as set forth in this Exhibit. As used in this Exhibit, the term General Conditions refers to AIA Document A201™–2017, General Conditions of the Contract for Construction.

ARTICLE A.2 OWNER'S INSURANCE
§ A.2.1 General
Prior to commencement of the Work, the Owner shall secure the insurance, and provide evidence of the coverage, required under this Article A.2 and, upon the Contractor's request, provide a copy of the property insurance policy or policies required by Section A.2.3. The copy of the policy or policies provided shall contain all applicable conditions, definitions, exclusions, and endorsements.

§ A.2.2 Liability Insurance
The Owner shall be responsible for purchasing and maintaining the Owner's usual general liability insurance.

§ A.2.3 Required Property Insurance
§ A.2.3.1 Unless this obligation is placed on the Contractor pursuant to Section A.3.3.2.1, the Owner shall purchase and maintain, from an insurance company or insurance companies lawfully authorized to issue insurance in the jurisdiction where the Project is located, property insurance written on a builder's risk "all-risks" completed value or equivalent policy form and sufficient to cover the total value of the entire Project on a replacement cost basis. The Owner's

property insurance coverage shall be no less than the amount of the initial Contract Sum, plus the value of subsequent Modifications and labor performed and materials or equipment supplied by others. The property insurance shall be maintained until Substantial Completion and thereafter as provided in Section A.2.3.1.3, unless otherwise provided in the Contract Documents or otherwise agreed in writing by the parties to this Agreement. This insurance shall include the interests of the Owner, Contractor, Subcontractors, and Sub-subcontractors in the Project as insureds. This insurance shall include the interests of mortgagees as loss payees.

§ A.2.3.1.1 **Causes of Loss.** The insurance required by this Section A.2.3.1 shall provide coverage for direct physical loss or damage, and shall not exclude the risks of fire, explosion, theft, vandalism, malicious mischief, collapse, earthquake, flood, or windstorm. The insurance shall also provide coverage for ensuing loss or resulting damage from error, omission, or deficiency in construction methods, design, specifications, workmanship, or materials. Sub-limits, if any, are as follows:
(Indicate below the cause of loss and any applicable sub-limit.)

Cause of Loss	Sub-Limit

§ A.2.3.1.2 **Specific Required Coverages.** The insurance required by this Section A.2.3.1 shall provide coverage for loss or damage to falsework and other temporary structures, and to building systems from testing and startup. The insurance shall also cover debris removal, including demolition occasioned by enforcement of any applicable legal requirements, and reasonable compensation for the Architect's and Contractor's services and expenses required as a result of such insured loss, including claim preparation expenses. Sub-limits, if any, are as follows:
(Indicate below type of coverage and any applicable sub-limit for specific required coverages.)

Coverage	Sub-Limit

§ A.2.3.1.3 Unless the parties agree otherwise, upon Substantial Completion, the Owner shall continue the insurance required by Section A.2.3.1 or, if necessary, replace the insurance policy required under Section A.2.3.1 with property insurance written for the total value of the Project that shall remain in effect until expiration of the period for correction of the Work set forth in Section 12.2.2 of the General Conditions.

§ A.2.3.1.4 **Deductibles and Self-Insured Retentions.** If the insurance required by this Section A.2.3 is subject to deductibles or self-insured retentions, the Owner shall be responsible for all loss not covered because of such deductibles or retentions.

§ A.2.3.2 **Occupancy or Use Prior to Substantial Completion.** The Owner's occupancy or use of any completed or partially completed portion of the Work prior to Substantial Completion shall not commence until the insurance company or companies providing the insurance under Section A.2.3.1 have consented in writing to the continuance of coverage. The Owner and the Contractor shall take no action with respect to partial occupancy or use that would cause cancellation, lapse, or reduction of insurance, unless they agree otherwise in writing.

§ A.2.3.3 **Insurance for Existing Structures**
If the Work involves remodeling an existing structure or constructing an addition to an existing structure, the Owner shall purchase and maintain, until the expiration of the period for correction of Work as set forth in Section 12.2.2 of the General Conditions, "all-risks" property insurance, on a replacement cost basis, protecting the existing structure against direct physical loss or damage from the causes of loss identified in Section A.2.3.1, notwithstanding the undertaking of the Work. The Owner shall be responsible for all co-insurance penalties.

§ A.2.4 **Optional Extended Property Insurance.**
The Owner shall purchase and maintain the insurance selected and described below.
(Select the types of insurance the Owner is required to purchase and maintain by placing an X in the box(es) next to the description(s) of selected insurance. For each type of insurance selected, indicate applicable limits of coverage or other conditions in the fill point below the selected item.)

☐ **§ A.2.4.1 Loss of Use, Business Interruption, and Delay in Completion Insurance,** to reimburse the Owner for loss of use of the Owner's property, or the inability to conduct normal operations due to a covered cause of loss.

☐ **§ A.2.4.2 Ordinance or Law Insurance,** for the reasonable and necessary costs to satisfy the minimum requirements of the enforcement of any law or ordinance regulating the demolition, construction, repair, replacement or use of the Project.

☐ **§ A.2.4.3 Expediting Cost Insurance,** for the reasonable and necessary costs for the temporary repair of damage to insured property, and to expedite the permanent repair or replacement of the damaged property.

☐ **§ A.2.4.4 Extra Expense Insurance,** to provide reimbursement of the reasonable and necessary excess costs incurred during the period of restoration or repair of the damaged property that are over and above the total costs that would normally have been incurred during the same period of time had no loss or damage occurred.

☐ **§ A.2.4.5 Civil Authority Insurance,** for losses or costs arising from an order of a civil authority prohibiting access to the Project, provided such order is the direct result of physical damage covered under the required property insurance.

☐ **§ A.2.4.6 Ingress/Egress Insurance,** for loss due to the necessary interruption of the insured's business due to physical prevention of ingress to, or egress from, the Project as a direct result of physical damage.

☐ **§ A.2.4.7 Soft Costs Insurance,** to reimburse the Owner for costs due to the delay of completion of the Work, arising out of physical loss or damage covered by the required property insurance: including construction loan fees; leasing and marketing expenses; additional fees, including those of architects, engineers, consultants, attorneys and accountants, needed for the completion of the construction, repairs, or reconstruction; and carrying costs such as property taxes, building permits, additional interest on loans, realty taxes, and insurance premiums over and above normal expenses.

§ A.2.5 Other Optional Insurance.
The Owner shall purchase and maintain the insurance selected below.
(Select the types of insurance the Owner is required to purchase and maintain by placing an X in the box(es) next to the description(s) of selected insurance.)

☐ **§ A.2.5.1 Cyber Security Insurance** for loss to the Owner due to data security and privacy breach, including costs of investigating a potential or actual breach of confidential or private information.
(Indicate applicable limits of coverage or other conditions in the fill point below.)

☐ **§ A.2.5.2 Other Insurance**
(List below any other insurance coverage to be provided by the Owner and any applicable limits.)

Coverage   Limits

ARTICLE A.3   CONTRACTOR'S INSURANCE AND BONDS
§ A.3.1 General
§ A.3.1.1 Certificates of Insurance. The Contractor shall provide certificates of insurance acceptable to the Owner evidencing compliance with the requirements in this Article A.3 at the following times: (1) prior to commencement of the Work; (2) upon renewal or replacement of each required policy of insurance; and (3) upon the Owner's written request. An additional certificate evidencing continuation of commercial liability coverage, including coverage for completed operations, shall be submitted with the final Application for Payment and thereafter upon renewal or replacement of such coverage until the expiration of the periods required by Section A.3.2.1 and Section A.3.3.1. The certificates will show the Owner as an additional insured on the Contractor's Commercial General Liability and excess or umbrella liability policy or policies.

§ A.3.1.2 Deductibles and Self-Insured Retentions. The Contractor shall disclose to the Owner any deductible or self-insured retentions applicable to any insurance required to be provided by the Contractor.

§ A.3.1.3 Additional Insured Obligations. To the fullest extent permitted by law, the Contractor shall cause the commercial general liability coverage to include (1) the Owner, the Architect, and the Architect's consultants as additional insureds for claims caused in whole or in part by the Contractor's negligent acts or omissions during the Contractor's operations; and (2) the Owner as an additional insured for claims caused in whole or in part by the Contractor's negligent acts or omissions for which loss occurs during completed operations. The additional insured coverage shall be primary and non-contributory to any of the Owner's general liability insurance policies and shall apply to both ongoing and completed operations. To the extent commercially available, the additional insured coverage shall be no less than that provided by Insurance Services Office, Inc. (ISO) forms CG 20 10 07 04, CG 20 37 07 04, and, with respect to the Architect and the Architect's consultants, CG 20 32 07 04.

§ A.3.2 Contractor's Required Insurance Coverage
§ A.3.2.1 The Contractor shall purchase and maintain the following types and limits of insurance from an insurance company or insurance companies lawfully authorized to issue insurance in the jurisdiction where the Project is located. The Contractor shall maintain the required insurance until the expiration of the period for correction of Work as set forth in Section 12.2.2 of the General Conditions, unless a different duration is stated below:
(If the Contractor is required to maintain insurance for a duration other than the expiration of the period for correction of Work, state the duration.)

§ A.3.2.2 Commercial General Liability
§ A.3.2.2.1 Commercial General Liability insurance for the Project written on an occurrence form with policy limits of not less than _____ ($__) each occurrence, _____ ($__) general aggregate, and _____ ($__) aggregate for products-completed operations hazard, providing coverage for claims including
   .1   damages because of bodily injury, sickness or disease, including occupational sickness or disease, and death of any person;
   .2   personal injury and advertising injury;
   .3   damages because of physical damage to, or destruction of, tangible property, including the loss of use of such property;
   .4   bodily injury or property damage arising out of completed operations; and
   .5   the Contractor's indemnity obligations under Section 3.18 of the General Conditions.

§ A.3.2.2.2 The Contractor's Commercial General Liability policy under this Section A.3.2.2 shall not contain an exclusion or restriction of coverage for the following:

.1 Claims by one insured against another insured, if the exclusion or restriction is based solely on the fact that the claimant is an insured, and there would otherwise be coverage for the claim.
.2 Claims for property damage to the Contractor's Work arising out of the products-completed operations hazard where the damaged Work or the Work out of which the damage arises was performed by a Subcontractor.
.3 Claims for bodily injury other than to employees of the insured.
.4 Claims for indemnity under Section 3.18 of the General Conditions arising out of injury to employees of the insured
.5 Claims or loss excluded under a prior work endorsement or other similar exclusionary language.
.6 Claims or loss due to physical damage under a prior injury endorsement or similar exclusionary language.
.7 Claims related to residential, multi-family, or other habitational projects, if the Work is to be performed on such a project.
.8 Claims related to roofing, if the Work involves roofing.
.9 Claims related to exterior insulation finish systems (EIFS), synthetic stucco or similar exterior coatings or surfaces, if the Work involves such coatings or surfaces.
.10 Claims related to earth subsidence or movement, where the work involves such hazards.
.11 Claims related to explosion, collapse, and underground hazards, where the Work involves such hazards.

§ A.3.2.3 Automobile Liability covering vehicles owned, and non-owned vehicles used, by the Contractor, with policy limits of not less than _____ ($__) per accident, for bodily injury, death of any person, and property damage arising out of the ownership, maintenance and use of those motor vehicles along with any other statutorily required automobile coverage.

§ A.3.2.4 The Contractor may achieve the required limits and coverage for Commercial General Liability and Automobile Liability through a combination of primary and excess or umbrella liability insurance, provided such primary and excess or umbrella insurance policies result in the same or greater coverage as the coverages required under Section A.3.2.2 and A.3.2.3, and in no event shall any excess or umbrella liability insurance provide narrower coverage than the primary policy. The excess policy shall not require the exhaustion of the underlying limits only through the actual payment by the underlying insurers.

§ A.3.2.5 Workers' Compensation at statutory limits.

§ A.3.2.6 Employers' Liability with policy limits not less than _____ ($__) each accident, _____ ($__) each employee, and _____ ($__) policy limit.

§ A.3.2.7 Jones Act, and the Longshore & Harbor Workers' Compensation Act, as required, if the Work involves hazards arising from work on or near navigable waterways, including vessels and docks

§ A.3.2.8 If the Contractor is required to furnish professional services as part of the Work, the Contractor shall procure Professional Liability insurance covering performance of the professional services, with policy limits of not less than _____ ($__) per claim and _____ ($__) in the aggregate.

§ A.3.2.9 If the Work involves the transport, dissemination, use, or release of pollutants, the Contractor shall procure Pollution Liability insurance, with policy limits of not less than _____ ($__) per claim and _____ ($__) in the aggregate.

§ A.3.2.10 Coverage under Sections A.3.2.8 and A.3.2.9 may be procured through a Combined Professional Liability and Pollution Liability insurance policy, with combined policy limits of not less than _____ ($__) per claim and _____ ($__) in the aggregate.

§ A.3.2.11 Insurance for maritime liability risks associated with the operation of a vessel, if the Work requires such activities, with policy limits of not less than _____ ($__) per claim and _____ ($__) in the aggregate.

§ A.3.2.12 Insurance for the use or operation of manned or unmanned aircraft, if the Work requires such activities, with policy limits of not less than _____ ($__) per claim and _____ ($__) in the aggregate.

§ A.3.3 Contractor's Other Insurance Coverage

§ A.3.3.1 Insurance selected and described in this Section A.3.3 shall be purchased from an insurance company or insurance companies lawfully authorized to issue insurance in the jurisdiction where the Project is located. The Contractor shall maintain the required insurance until the expiration of the period for correction of Work as set forth in Section 12.2.2 of the General Conditions, unless a different duration is stated below:

(If the Contractor is required to maintain any of the types of insurance selected below for a duration other than the expiration of the period for correction of Work, state the duration.)

§ A.3.3.2 The Contractor shall purchase and maintain the following types and limits of insurance in accordance with Section A.3.3.1.

(Select the types of insurance the Contractor is required to purchase and maintain by placing an X in the box(es) next to the description(s) of selected insurance. Where policy limits are provided, include the policy limit in the appropriate fill point.)

☐ **§ A.3.3.2.1** Property insurance of the same type and scope satisfying the requirements identified in Section A.2.3, which, if selected in this section A.3.3.2.1, relieves the Owner of the responsibility to purchase and maintain such insurance except insurance required by Section A.2.3.1.3 and Section A.2.3.3. The Contractor shall comply with all obligations of the Owner under Section A.2.3 except to the extent provided below. The Contractor shall disclose to the Owner the amount of any deductible, and the Owner shall be responsible for losses within the deductible. Upon request, the Contractor shall provide the Owner with a copy of the property insurance policy or policies required. The Owner shall adjust and settle the loss with the insurer and be the trustee of the proceeds of the property insurance in accordance with Article 11 of the General Conditions unless otherwise set forth below.

(Where the Contractor's obligation to provide property insurance differs from the Owner's obligations as described under Section A.2.3, indicate such differences in the space below. Additionally, if a party other than the Owner will be responsible for adjusting and settling a loss with the insurer and acting as the trustee of the proceeds of property insurance in accordance with Article 11 of the General Conditions, indicate the responsible party below.)

☐ **§ A.3.3.2.2 Railroad Protective Liability Insurance,** with policy limits of not less than _____ ($__) per claim and _____ ($__) in the aggregate, for Work within fifty (50) feet of railroad property.

☐ **§ A.3.3.2.3 Asbestos Abatement Liability Insurance,** with policy limits of not less than _____ ($__) per claim and _____ ($__) in the aggregate, for liability arising from the encapsulation, removal, handling, storage, transportation, and disposal of asbestos-containing materials.

☐ **§ A.3.3.2.4** Insurance for physical damage to property while it is in storage and in transit to the construction site on an "all-risks" completed value form.

☐ **§ A.3.3.2.5** Property insurance on an "all-risks" completed value form, covering property owned by the Contractor and used on the Project, including scaffolding and other equipment.

☐ **§ A.3.3.2.6 Other Insurance**
(List below any other insurance coverage to be provided by the Contractor and any applicable limits.)

Coverage	Limits

§ A.3.4 Performance Bond and Payment Bond

The Contractor shall provide surety bonds, from a company or companies lawfully authorized to issue surety bonds in the jurisdiction where the Project is located, as follows:
(Specify type and penal sum of bonds.)

Type	Penal Sum ($0.00)
Payment Bond	
Performance Bond	

Payment and Performance Bonds shall be AIA Document A312™, Payment Bond and Performance Bond, or contain provisions identical to AIA Document A312™, current as of the date of this Agreement.

ARTICLE A.4 SPECIAL TERMS AND CONDITIONS

Special terms and conditions that modify this Insurance and Bonds Exhibit, if any, are as follows:

Pt. VIII A.I.A. SAMPLE FORM CONTRACTS

Document A312™ – 2010

Performance Bond

CONTRACTOR:
(Name, legal status and address)

SURETY:
(Name, legal status and principal place of business)

OWNER:
(Name, legal status and address)

This document has important legal consequences. Consultation with an attorney is encouraged with respect to its completion or modification.

Any singular reference to Contractor, Surety, Owner or other party shall be considered plural where applicable.

AIA Document A312–2010 combines two separate bonds, a Performance Bond and a Payment Bond, into one form. This is not a single combined Performance and Payment Bond.

CONSTRUCTION CONTRACT
Date:

Amount:

Description:
(Name and location)

BOND
Date:
(Not earlier than Construction Contract Date)

Amount:

Modifications to this Bond: ☐ None   ☐ See Section 16

CONTRACTOR AS PRINCIPAL
Company: *(Corporate Seal)*

SURETY
Company: *(Corporate Seal)*

Signature: _____
Name and Title:

Signature: _____
Name and Title:

(Any additional signatures appear on the last page of this Performance Bond.)

(FOR INFORMATION ONLY — Name, address and telephone)
AGENT or BROKER:

OWNER'S REPRESENTATIVE:
(Architect, Engineer or other party:)

§ 1 The Contractor and Surety, jointly and severally, bind themselves, their heirs, executors, administrators, successors and assigns to the Owner for the performance of the Construction Contract, which is incorporated herein by reference.

§ 2 If the Contractor performs the Construction Contract, the Surety and the Contractor shall have no obligation under this Bond, except when applicable to participate in a conference as provided in Section 3.

§ 3 If there is no Owner Default under the Construction Contract, the Surety's obligation under this Bond shall arise after

    .1   the Owner first provides notice to the Contractor and the Surety that the Owner is considering declaring a Contractor Default. Such notice shall indicate whether the Owner is requesting a conference among the Owner, Contractor and Surety to discuss the Contractor's performance. If the Owner does not request a conference, the Surety may, within five (5) business days after receipt of the Owner's notice, request such a conference. If the Surety timely requests a conference, the Owner shall attend. Unless the Owner agrees otherwise, any conference requested under this Section 3.1 shall be held within ten (10) business days of the Surety's receipt of the Owner's notice. If the Owner, the Contractor and the Surety agree, the Contractor shall be allowed a reasonable time to perform the Construction Contract, but such an agreement shall not waive the Owner's right, if any, subsequently to declare a Contractor Default;

    .2   the Owner declares a Contractor Default, terminates the Construction Contract and notifies the Surety; and

    .3   the Owner has agreed to pay the Balance of the Contract Price in accordance with the terms of the Construction Contract to the Surety or to a contractor selected to perform the Construction Contract.

§ 4 Failure on the part of the Owner to comply with the notice requirement in Section 3.1 shall not constitute a failure to comply with a condition precedent to the Surety's obligations, or release the Surety from its obligations, except to the extent the Surety demonstrates actual prejudice.

§ 5 When the Owner has satisfied the conditions of Section 3, the Surety shall promptly and at the Surety's expense take one of the following actions:

§ 5.1 Arrange for the Contractor, with the consent of the Owner, to perform and complete the Construction Contract;

§ 5.2 Undertake to perform and complete the Construction Contract itself, through its agents or independent contractors;

§ 5.3 Obtain bids or negotiated proposals from qualified contractors acceptable to the Owner for a contract for performance and completion of the Construction Contract, arrange for a contract to be prepared for execution by the Owner and a contractor selected with the Owner's concurrence, to be secured with performance and payment bonds executed by a qualified surety equivalent to the bonds issued on the Construction Contract, and pay to the Owner the amount of damages as described in Section 7 in excess of the Balance of the Contract Price incurred by the Owner as a result of the Contractor Default; or

§ 5.4 Waive its right to perform and complete, arrange for completion, or obtain a new contractor and with reasonable promptness under the circumstances:

    .1   After investigation, determine the amount for which it may be liable to the Owner and, as soon as practicable after the amount is determined, make payment to the Owner; or

    .2   Deny liability in whole or in part and notify the Owner, citing the reasons for denial.

§ 6 If the Surety does not proceed as provided in Section 5 with reasonable promptness, the Surety shall be deemed to be in default on this Bond seven days after receipt of an additional written notice from the Owner to the Surety demanding that the Surety perform its obligations under this Bond, and the Owner shall be entitled to enforce any remedy available to the Owner. If the Surety proceeds as provided in Section 5.4, and the Owner refuses the payment or the Surety has denied liability, in whole or in part, without further notice the Owner shall be entitled to enforce any remedy available to the Owner.

§ 7 If the Surety elects to act under Section 5.1, 5.2 or 5.3, then the responsibilities of the Surety to the Owner shall not be greater than those of the Contractor under the Construction Contract, and the responsibilities of the Owner to the Surety shall not be greater than those of the Owner under the Construction Contract. Subject to the commitment by the Owner to pay the Balance of the Contract Price, the Surety is obligated, without duplication, for

.1 the responsibilities of the Contractor for correction of defective work and completion of the Construction Contract;
.2 additional legal, design professional and delay costs resulting from the Contractor's Default, and resulting from the actions or failure to act of the Surety under Section 5; and
.3 liquidated damages, or if no liquidated damages are specified in the Construction Contract, actual damages caused by delayed performance or non-performance of the Contractor.

§ 8 If the Surety elects to act under Section 5.1, 5.3 or 5.4, the Surety's liability is limited to the amount of this Bond.

§ 9 The Surety shall not be liable to the Owner or others for obligations of the Contractor that are unrelated to the Construction Contract, and the Balance of the Contract Price shall not be reduced or set off on account of any such unrelated obligations. No right of action shall accrue on this Bond to any person or entity other than the Owner or its heirs, executors, administrators, successors and assigns.

§ 10 The Surety hereby waives notice of any change, including changes of time, to the Construction Contract or to related subcontracts, purchase orders and other obligations.

§ 11 Any proceeding, legal or equitable, under this Bond may be instituted in any court of competent jurisdiction in the location in which the work or part of the work is located and shall be instituted within two years after a declaration of Contractor Default or within two years after the Contractor ceased working or within two years after the Surety refuses or fails to perform its obligations under this Bond, whichever occurs first. If the provisions of this Paragraph are void or prohibited by law, the minimum period of limitation available to sureties as a defense in the jurisdiction of the suit shall be applicable.

§ 12 Notice to the Surety, the Owner or the Contractor shall be mailed or delivered to the address shown on the page on which their signature appears.

§ 13 When this Bond has been furnished to comply with a statutory or other legal requirement in the location where the construction was to be performed, any provision in this Bond conflicting with said statutory or legal requirement shall be deemed deleted herefrom and provisions conforming to such statutory or other legal requirement shall be deemed incorporated herein. When so furnished, the intent is that this Bond shall be construed as a statutory bond and not as a common law bond.

§ 14 Definitions
§ 14.1 Balance of the Contract Price. The total amount payable by the Owner to the Contractor under the Construction Contract after all proper adjustments have been made, including allowance to the Contractor of any amounts received or to be received by the Owner in settlement of insurance or other claims for damages to which the Contractor is entitled, reduced by all valid and proper payments made to or on behalf of the Contractor under the Construction Contract.

§ 14.2 Construction Contract. The agreement between the Owner and Contractor identified on the cover page, including all Contract Documents and changes made to the agreement and the Contract Documents.

§ 14.3 Contractor Default. Failure of the Contractor, which has not been remedied or waived, to perform or otherwise to comply with a material term of the Construction Contract.

§ 14.4 Owner Default. Failure of the Owner, which has not been remedied or waived, to pay the Contractor as required under the Construction Contract or to perform and complete or comply with the other material terms of the Construction Contract.

§ 14.5 Contract Documents. All the documents that comprise the agreement between the Owner and Contractor.

§ 15 If this Bond is issued for an agreement between a Contractor and subcontractor, the term Contractor in this Bond shall be deemed to be Subcontractor and the term Owner shall be deemed to be Contractor.

§ 16 Modifications to this bond are as follows:

(Space is provided below for additional signatures of added parties, other than those appearing on the cover page.)

CONTRACTOR AS PRINCIPAL		SURETY	
Company:	*(Corporate Seal)*	Company:	*(Corporate Seal)*
Signature:		Signature:	
Name and Title:		Name and Title:	
Address		Address	

CAUTION: You should sign an original AIA Contract Document, on which this text appears in RED. An original assures that changes will not be obscured.

Pt. VIII A.I.A. SAMPLE FORM CONTRACTS

AIA® Document A312™ – 2010

Payment Bond

CONTRACTOR:
(Name, legal status and address)

SURETY:
(Name, legal status and principal place of business)

OWNER:
(Name, legal status and address)

> This document has important legal consequences. Consultation with an attorney is encouraged with respect to its completion or modification.
>
> Any singular reference to Contractor, Surety, Owner or other party shall be considered plural where applicable.
>
> AIA Document A312–2010 combines two separate bonds, a Performance Bond and a Payment Bond, into one form. This is not a single combined Performance and Payment Bond.

CONSTRUCTION CONTRACT
Date:

Amount:

Description:
(Name and location)

BOND
Date:
(Not earlier than Construction Contract Date)

Amount:

Modifications to this Bond: ☐ None   ☐ See Section 18

CONTRACTOR AS PRINCIPAL	SURETY
Company: *(Corporate Seal)*	Company: *(Corporate Seal)*
Signature: _____	Signature: _____
Name and Title:	Name and Title:

(Any additional signatures appear on the last page of this Payment Bond.)

(FOR INFORMATION ONLY — Name, address and telephone)
AGENT or BROKER:

OWNER'S REPRESENTATIVE:
(Architect, Engineer or other party:)

AIA Document A312™ – 2010. The American Institute of Architects.

§ 1 The Contractor and Surety, jointly and severally, bind themselves, their heirs, executors, administrators, successors and assigns to the Owner to pay for labor, materials and equipment furnished for use in the performance of the Construction Contract, which is incorporated herein by reference, subject to the following terms.

§ 2 If the Contractor promptly makes payment of all sums due to Claimants, and defends, indemnifies and holds harmless the Owner from claims, demands, liens or suits by any person or entity seeking payment for labor, materials or equipment furnished for use in the performance of the Construction Contract, then the Surety and the Contractor shall have no obligation under this Bond.

§ 3 If there is no Owner Default under the Construction Contract, the Surety's obligation to the Owner under this Bond shall arise after the Owner has promptly notified the Contractor and the Surety (at the address described in Section 13) of claims, demands, liens or suits against the Owner or the Owner's property by any person or entity seeking payment for labor, materials or equipment furnished for use in the performance of the Construction Contract and tendered defense of such claims, demands, liens or suits to the Contractor and the Surety.

§ 4 When the Owner has satisfied the conditions in Section 3, the Surety shall promptly and at the Surety's expense defend, indemnify and hold harmless the Owner against a duly tendered claim, demand, lien or suit.

§ 5 The Surety's obligations to a Claimant under this Bond shall arise after the following:

§ 5.1 Claimants, who do not have a direct contract with the Contractor,
.1 have furnished a written notice of non-payment to the Contractor, stating with substantial accuracy the amount claimed and the name of the party to whom the materials were, or equipment was, furnished or supplied or for whom the labor was done or performed, within ninety (90) days after having last performed labor or last furnished materials or equipment included in the Claim; and
.2 have sent a Claim to the Surety (at the address described in Section 13).

§ 5.2 Claimants, who are employed by or have a direct contract with the Contractor, have sent a Claim to the Surety (at the address described in Section 13).

§ 6 If a notice of non-payment required by Section 5.1.1 is given by the Owner to the Contractor, that is sufficient to satisfy a Claimant's obligation to furnish a written notice of non-payment under Section 5.1.1.

§ 7 When a Claimant has satisfied the conditions of Sections 5.1 or 5.2, whichever is applicable, the Surety shall promptly and at the Surety's expense take the following actions:

§ 7.1 Send an answer to the Claimant, with a copy to the Owner, within sixty (60) days after receipt of the Claim, stating the amounts that are undisputed and the basis for challenging any amounts that are disputed; and

§ 7.2 Pay or arrange for payment of any undisputed amounts.

§ 7.3 The Surety's failure to discharge its obligations under Section 7.1 or Section 7.2 shall not be deemed to constitute a waiver of defenses the Surety or Contractor may have or acquire as to a Claim, except as to undisputed amounts for which the Surety and Claimant have reached agreement. If, however, the Surety fails to discharge its obligations under Section 7.1 or Section 7.2, the Surety shall indemnify the Claimant for the reasonable attorney's fees the Claimant incurs thereafter to recover any sums found to be due and owing to the Claimant.

§ 8 The Surety's total obligation shall not exceed the amount of this Bond, plus the amount of reasonable attorney's fees provided under Section 7.3, and the amount of this Bond shall be credited for any payments made in good faith by the Surety.

§ 9 Amounts owed by the Owner to the Contractor under the Construction Contract shall be used for the performance of the Construction Contract and to satisfy claims, if any, under any construction performance bond. By the Contractor furnishing and the Owner accepting this Bond, they agree that all funds earned by the Contractor in the performance of the Construction Contract are dedicated to satisfy obligations of the Contractor and Surety under this Bond, subject to the Owner's priority to use the funds for the completion of the work.

§ 10 The Surety shall not be liable to the Owner, Claimants or others for obligations of the Contractor that are unrelated to the Construction Contract. The Owner shall not be liable for the payment of any costs or expenses of any Claimant under this Bond, and shall have under this Bond no obligation to make payments to, or give notice on behalf of, Claimants or otherwise have any obligations to Claimants under this Bond.

§ 11 The Surety hereby waives notice of any change, including changes of time, to the Construction Contract or to related subcontracts, purchase orders and other obligations.

§ 12 No suit or action shall be commenced by a Claimant under this Bond other than in a court of competent jurisdiction in the state in which the project that is the subject of the Construction Contract is located or after the expiration of one year from the date (1) on which the Claimant sent a Claim to the Surety pursuant to Section 5.1.2 or 5.2, or (2) on which the last labor or service was performed by anyone or the last materials or equipment were furnished by anyone under the Construction Contract, whichever of (1) or (2) first occurs. If the provisions of this Paragraph are void or prohibited by law, the minimum period of limitation available to sureties as a defense in the jurisdiction of the suit shall be applicable.

§ 13 Notice and Claims to the Surety, the Owner or the Contractor shall be mailed or delivered to the address shown on the page on which their signature appears. Actual receipt of notice or Claims, however accomplished, shall be sufficient compliance as of the date received.

§ 14 When this Bond has been furnished to comply with a statutory or other legal requirement in the location where the construction was to be performed, any provision in this Bond conflicting with said statutory or legal requirement shall be deemed deleted herefrom and provisions conforming to such statutory or other legal requirement shall be deemed incorporated herein. When so furnished, the intent is that this Bond shall be construed as a statutory bond and not as a common law bond.

§ 15 Upon request by any person or entity appearing to be a potential beneficiary of this Bond, the Contractor and Owner shall promptly furnish a copy of this Bond or shall permit a copy to be made.

§ 16 Definitions
§ 16.1 Claim. A written statement by the Claimant including at a minimum:
 .1 the name of the Claimant;
 .2 the name of the person for whom the labor was done, or materials or equipment furnished;
 .3 a copy of the agreement or purchase order pursuant to which labor, materials or equipment was furnished for use in the performance of the Construction Contract;
 .4 a brief description of the labor, materials or equipment furnished;
 .5 the date on which the Claimant last performed labor or last furnished materials or equipment for use in the performance of the Construction Contract;
 .6 the total amount earned by the Claimant for labor, materials or equipment furnished as of the date of the Claim;
 .7 the total amount of previous payments received by the Claimant; and
 .8 the total amount due and unpaid to the Claimant for labor, materials or equipment furnished as of the date of the Claim.

§ 16.2 Claimant. An individual or entity having a direct contract with the Contractor or with a subcontractor of the Contractor to furnish labor, materials or equipment for use in the performance of the Construction Contract. The term Claimant also includes any individual or entity that has rightfully asserted a claim under an applicable mechanic's lien or similar statute against the real property upon which the Project is located. The intent of this Bond shall be to include without limitation in the terms "labor, materials or equipment" that part of water, gas, power, light, heat, oil, gasoline, telephone service or rental equipment used in the Construction Contract, architectural and engineering services required for performance of the work of the Contractor and the Contractor's subcontractors, and all other items for which a mechanic's lien may be asserted in the jurisdiction where the labor, materials or equipment were furnished.

§ 16.3 Construction Contract. The agreement between the Owner and Contractor identified on the cover page, including all Contract Documents and all changes made to the agreement and the Contract Documents.

§ 16.4 Owner Default. Failure of the Owner, which has not been remedied or waived, to pay the Contractor as required under the Construction Contract or to perform and complete or comply with the other material terms of the Construction Contract.

§ 16.5 Contract Documents. All the documents that comprise the agreement between the Owner and Contractor.

§ 17 If this Bond is issued for an agreement between a Contractor and subcontractor, the term Contractor in this Bond shall be deemed to be Subcontractor and the term Owner shall be deemed to be Contractor.

§ 18 Modifications to this bond are as follows:

(Space is provided below for additional signatures of added parties, other than those appearing on the cover page.)

CONTRACTOR AS PRINCIPAL		**SURETY**	
Company:	*(Corporate Seal)*	Company:	*(Corporate Seal)*
Signature:		Signature:	
Name and Title:		Name and Title:	
Address:		Address:	

CAUTION: You should sign an original AIA Contract Document, on which this text appears in RED. An original assures that changes will not be obscured.

AIA Document A312™ – 2010. The American Institute of Architects.